T0234679

Lecture Notes in Computer Science   14411

Founding Editors

Gerhard Goos
Juris Hartmanis

Editorial Board Members

Elisa Bertino, *Purdue University, West Lafayette, IN, USA*
Wen Gao, *Peking University, Beijing, China*
Bernhard Steffen ⓘ, *TU Dortmund University, Dortmund, Germany*
Moti Yung ⓘ, *Columbia University, New York, NY, USA*

The series Lecture Notes in Computer Science (LNCS), including its subseries Lecture Notes in Artificial Intelligence (LNAI) and Lecture Notes in Bioinformatics (LNBI), has established itself as a medium for the publication of new developments in computer science and information technology research, teaching, and education.

LNCS enjoys close cooperation with the computer science R & D community, the series counts many renowned academics among its volume editors and paper authors, and collaborates with prestigious societies. Its mission is to serve this international community by providing an invaluable service, mainly focused on the publication of conference and workshop proceedings and postproceedings. LNCS commenced publication in 1973.

Elias Athanasopoulos · Bart Mennink
Editors

Information Security

26th International Conference, ISC 2023
Groningen, The Netherlands, November 15–17, 2023
Proceedings

 Springer

Editors
Elias Athanasopoulos
University of Cyprus
Nicosia, Cyprus

Bart Mennink
Radboud University
Nijmegen, The Netherlands

ISSN 0302-9743   ISSN 1611-3349 (electronic)
Lecture Notes in Computer Science
ISBN 978-3-031-49186-3   ISBN 978-3-031-49187-0 (eBook)
https://doi.org/10.1007/978-3-031-49187-0

© The Editor(s) (if applicable) and The Author(s), under exclusive license
to Springer Nature Switzerland AG 2023

This work is subject to copyright. All rights are reserved by the Publisher, whether the whole or part of the material is concerned, specifically the rights of translation, reprinting, reuse of illustrations, recitation, broadcasting, reproduction on microfilms or in any other physical way, and transmission or information storage and retrieval, electronic adaptation, computer software, or by similar or dissimilar methodology now known or hereafter developed.
The use of general descriptive names, registered names, trademarks, service marks, etc. in this publication does not imply, even in the absence of a specific statement, that such names are exempt from the relevant protective laws and regulations and therefore free for general use.
The publisher, the authors, and the editors are safe to assume that the advice and information in this book are believed to be true and accurate at the date of publication. Neither the publisher nor the authors or the editors give a warranty, expressed or implied, with respect to the material contained herein or for any errors or omissions that may have been made. The publisher remains neutral with regard to jurisdictional claims in published maps and institutional affiliations.

This Springer imprint is published by the registered company Springer Nature Switzerland AG
The registered company address is: Gewerbestrasse 11, 6330 Cham, Switzerland

Paper in this product is recyclable.

Preface

Welcome to the 26th Information Security Conference (ISC).

We are delighted to present to you the proceedings of ISC 2023. They are the outcome of several weeks of work from a group of people, representing a cross-section of the research community in cryptography and systems security. As program co-chairs, we had the great honor to handle this process, and we are grateful to all reviewers, authors, and members of the organizing committee who made it possible.

First, we have been able to assemble a diverse program committee composed of both young and senior researchers. Writing good reviews is a hard task, and yet we found that many colleagues were eager to volunteer their time and serve on the ISC program committee. One of the primary aims we had for ISC was to recruit part of the next generation of PC members, therefore we tried to invite a significant fraction of junior faculty members and researchers.

Overall we invited 90 members and our invitation was accepted by 41 researchers distributed over 17 different countries. We also tried to balance the expertise between cryptography and systems security. During the hard and long review process, we were impressed by the quality of the reviews and the positivity we saw in the online discussions. We were pleasantly surprised by the many PC members who championed papers energetically and engaged in constructive debates with the other reviewers. At this point, we also want to recognize those who provided additional reviews at the last minute, in some cases with only a few hours' notice, namely Chitchanok Chuengsatiansup, Lilika-Evangelia Markatou, and Koen de Boer. Unfortunately, a few PC members were unable to complete all their reviews.

Additionally, the papers included in these proceedings reflect the high quality of research established through the years by ISC. We received 98 submissions, and the PC decided to accept 29 of them, resulting in an acceptance rate of around 30%, which is in line with previous ISC events. The final program of 29 papers includes advances in cryptography, and in particular in symmetric cryptography, key management, post-quantum cryptography, and multiparty computation, as well as works in systems security, and in particular in machine learning and privacy, web/mobile security, and intrusion detection systems.

Every organizer undertakes financial risks associated with the conference's organization and needs to overcome several issues with the conference logistics. We are grateful to our sponsors for making ISC 2023 possible and for ensuring that the registration fees remained sufficiently low for students to attend the event. In particular, we thank our sponsor Gemeente Groningen for their financial and logistical support in realizing the conference, and our publisher, Springer, for sponsoring the best paper award.

We further thank the rest of the organizing committee for their commitment and support in preparing the ISC 2023 proceedings: the publication chair, Olga Gadyatskaya, and the publicity chair, Kaitai Liang. Above all, we thank the general chair Fatih Turkmen for organizing ISC 2023 in Groningen, The Netherlands, and for ensuring the smooth operation of the conference, and Apostolis Zarras for initial discussions about the organizational matters.

As a final word, we would like to express our gratitude to the community of cryptographers and systems security researchers who made these proceedings possible with their great work. We believe that ISC is a unique event in the calendar circus of security conferences that offers such a balance between cryptography and systems security. We therefore would like to close by thanking the sponsors, organizers, reviewers, authors, and all attendees for making ISC such a lively conference!

October 2023

Elias Athanasopoulos
Bart Mennink
ISC 2023 PC Co-chairs

Organization

General Chairs

Fatih Turkmen   University of Groningen, The Netherlands
Apostolis Zarras   University of Piraeus, Greece

Program Committee Chairs

Elias Athanasopoulos   University of Cyprus, Cyprus
Bart Mennink   Radboud University Nijmegen, The Netherlands

Steering Committee

Zhiqiang Lin   Ohio State University, USA
Javier Lopez   University of Malaga, Spain
Masahiro Mambo   Kanazawa University, Japan
Eiji Okamoto   University of Tsukuba, Japan
Michalis Polychronakis   Stony Brook University, USA
Jianying Zhou   Singapore University of Technology and Design, Singapore
Willy Susilo   University of Wollongong, Australia

Program Committee

Cristina Alcaraz   University of Malaga, Spain
Tuomas Aura   Aalto University, Finland
Sébastien Bardin   CEA LIST, France
Christina Boura   University of Versailles, France
Michele Carminati   Politecnico di Milano, Italy
Liqun Chen   University of Surrey, UK
Xiaofeng Chen   Xidian University, China
Sherman S. M. Chow   Chinese University of Hong Kong, Hong Kong
Chitchanok Chuengsatiansup   University of Melbourne, Australia
Christoph Dobraunig   Intel Corporation, USA
Debiao He   Wuhan University, China

Akinori Hosoyamada	NTT Social Informatics Laboratories, Japan
Panagiotis Ilia	Technical University of Crete, Greece
Tibor Jager	University of Wuppertal, Germany
Kangkook Jee	University of Texas at Dallas, USA
Yuede Ji	University of North Texas, USA
Angelos Keromytis	Georgia Institute of Technology, USA
Doowon Kim	University of Tennessee, USA
Andrea Lanzi	University of Milan, Italy
Joseph Liu	Monash University, Australia
Evangelia Anna Markatou	Brown University, USA
Ange Martinelli	ANSSI, France
Tapti Palit	Purdue University, USA
Jiaxin Pan	NTNU, Norway
Mario Polino	Politecnico di Milano, Italy
Georgios Portokalidis	IMDEA Software Institute, Spain
Shahram Rasoolzadeh	Radboud University, The Netherlands
Kazuo Sakiyama	University of Electro-Communications, Japan
Mridula Singh	CISPA Helmholtz Center for Information Security, Germany
Daniel Slamanig	AIT Austrian Institute of Technology, Austria
Guillermo Suarez-Tangil	IMDEA Networks Institute, Spain
Aishwarya Thiruvengadam	IIT Madras, India
Monika Trimoska	Radboud University, The Netherlands
Giorgos Vasiliadis	Hellenic Mediterranean University and FORTH-ICS, Greece
Arkady Yerukhimovich	George Washington University, USA
Zuoxia Yu	University of Wollongong, Australia
Jianying Zhou	SUTD, Singapore
Albert Levi	Sabanci University, Turkey
Sevil Sen	Hacettepe University, Turkey
Sanjay Rawat	University of Bristol, UK

Additional Reviewers

Koen de Boer	Xuexuan Hao
Eyasu Getahun Chekole	Raphael Heitjohann
Thinh Dang	Alan Joel
Minxin Du	Junming Ke
Maryam Sheikhi Garjan	Kamil Kluczniak
Kai Gellert	Jodie Knapp
Tobias Handirk	Shangqi Lai

Yamin Li
Mingyu Liang
Linsheng Liu
Lea Nürnberger
Mahdi Mahdavi Oliaee
Ying-yu Pan
Jeongeun Park
Sebastian Ramacher
Lars Ran
Vishal Sharma

Yiwen Shi
Christoph Striecks
Yangguang Tian
Marloes Venema
Yalan Wang
Benedikt Wagner
Weiqiang Wen
Harry W. H. Wong
Yaxi Yang

Contents

Privacy

Exploring Privacy-Preserving Techniques on Synthetic Data as a Defense Against Model Inversion Attacks

Manel Slokom[1,2,3(✉)], Peter-Paul de Wolf[3], and Martha Larson[4]

[1] Delft University of Technology, Delft, The Netherlands
m.slokom@tudelft.nl
[2] Centrum Wiskunde & Informatica, Amsterdam, The Netherlands
[3] Statistics Netherlands, The Hague, The Netherlands
pp.dewolf@cbs.nl
[4] Radboud University, Nijmegen, The Netherlands
m.larson@cs.ru.nl

Abstract. In this work, we investigate privacy risks associated with model inversion attribute inference attacks. Specifically, we explore a case in which a governmental institute aims to release a trained machine learning model to the public (i.e., for collaboration or transparency reasons) without threatening privacy. The model predicts change of living place and is important for studying individuals' tendency to relocate. For this reason, it is called a *propensity-to-move model*. Our results first show that there is a potential leak of sensitive information when a propensity-to-move model is trained on the original data, in the form collected from the individuals. To address this privacy risk, we propose a data synthesis + privacy preservation approach: we replace the original training data with synthetic data on top of which we apply privacy preserving techniques. Our approach aims to maintain the prediction performance of the model, while controlling the privacy risk. Related work has studied a one-step synthesis of privacy preserving data. In contrast, here, we first synthesize data and then apply privacy preserving techniques. We carry out experiments involving attacks on individuals included in the training data ("inclusive individuals") as well as attacks on individuals not included in the training data ("exclusive individuals"). In this regard, our work goes beyond conventional model inversion attribute inference attacks, which focus on individuals contained in the training data. Our results show that a propensity-to-move model trained on synthetic training data protected with privacy-preserving techniques achieves performance comparable to a model trained on the original training data. At the same time, we observe a reduction in the efficacy of certain attacks.

Keywords: Synthetic data · privacy-preserving techniques · propensity-to-move · model inversion attack · attribute inference attack · machine learning

P.-P. de Wolf—The views expressed in this paper are those of the authors and do not necessarily reflect the policy of Statistics Netherlands.

© The Author(s), under exclusive license to Springer Nature Switzerland AG 2023
E. Athanasopoulos and B. Mennink (Eds.): ISC 2023, LNCS 14411, pp. 3–23, 2023.
https://doi.org/10.1007/978-3-031-49187-0_1

1   Introduction

A governmental institute that is responsible for providing reliable statistical information may use machine learning (ML) approaches to estimate values that are missing in their data or to infer attributes whose values are not possible to collect. Ideally, the machine learning model that is used to make the estimates can be made available outside of the institute in order to promote transparency and support collaboration with external parties. Currently, however, an important unsolved problem stands in the way of providing external access to machine learning models: the models may pose a privacy threat because they are susceptible to *model inversion attribute inference attacks*. In other words, they may leak information about sensitive characteristics of individuals whose data they were trained on ("inclusive individuals"). Further, going beyond the strict definition of model inversion, access to models may enable the inference of attributes of individuals whose data is not included in the original training set ("exclusive individuals").

In this paper, we investigate the potential leaks that could occur when external access is provided to machine learning models. We carry out a case study on a model that is trained to predict whether an individual is likely to move or to relocate within the next two years. Such models are helpful for understanding tendencies in the population to change their living location and are, for this reason, called *propensity-to-move models*. We study the case in which an institute would like to provide access to the model by allowing external parties to query the model and receive output predictions and by releasing the marginal distributions of the data the model is trained on. Additionally, the output might include confidence scores. Finally, access might include releasing a confusion matrix of the model calculated on the training data. Attackers wish to target a certain set of target individuals to obtain values of sensitive attributes for these individuals. We assume that for this set of target individuals, attackers possess a set of nonsensitive attributes that they have previously obtained, e.g., by scraping social media, including the correct value for the propensity-to-move attribute.

First, we show the effectiveness of our propensity-to-move prediction model. Then, we evaluate a number of existing model inversion attribute inference attacks [14,28] and demonstrate that, if access would be provided to the model, a privacy threat would occur. Next, we address this threat by proposing a synthesis + privacy preservation approach, which applies privacy preserving techniques designed to inhibit attribute inference attacks on top of synthetic data. This two-step approach is motivated by the fact that within our case study, training models on synthetic data is an already established practice and the goal is to address the threat posed by synthetic data. In our previous work [42], we demonstrated that training on synthetic data has the potential to provide a small measure of protection, and here we build on that result.

Our results show that a propensity-to-move model trained on data created with our synthesis + privacy preservation approach achieves performance comparable to a propensity-to-move model trained on original training data. We also observe that the data created by our synthesis + privacy preservation approach contributes to the reduced success of certain attacks over a certain group of target individuals. Last but not least, we use the Correct Attribution Probability (CAP) metric [27] from Statistical Disclosure Control as a disclosure risk measure to calculate the risk of attribute disclosure for individuals.

We summarize our contributions as follows:

- **Threat Model:** Our attacks consider both target individuals who are included in the data on which the model is trained ("inclusive individuals") and target individuals who are *not* ("exclusive individuals"). Studying exclusive individuals goes beyond the strict definition of model inversion and is not well-studied in the literature.
- **Data synthesis + privacy preservation:** We explore a two-step approach that applies privacy-preserving techniques on top of synthetic data. Our approach aims to maintain model utility, i.e., the prediction performance of the model, while at the same time inhibiting inference of the sensitive attributes of target individuals.
- **Disclosure Risk:** In contrast to measures that rely on machine learning metrics, which often average or aggregate scores, we employ the Correct Attribution Probability (CAP) to quantify the level of disclosure risk for individual cases.

2   Threat Model

We start characterizing the case we study in terms of a threat model [39], a theoretical formulation that describes: the adversary's objective, the resources at the adversary's disposal, the vulnerability that the adversary seeks to exploit, and the types of countermeasures that come into consideration. Table 1 presents our threat model. We cover each of the dimensions, in turn, explaining their specification for our case.

As objective, the attacker seeks to infer sensitive information about a set of target individuals. As resources, we assume that the attacker has collected a set of data for each target individual, i.e., from previous data releases or social media. The set contains non-sensitive attributes of the target individuals and that includes the individual's ID and the corresponding true label for propensity-to-move. The target individuals are either in the training data used to train the released model ("inclusive individuals") or not in the training data ("exclusive individuals"). The vulnerability is related to how the model is released, i.e., the access that has been provided to the model. The attacker can query the model and collect the output of the model, both predictions and confidence scores, for unlimited number of inputs. The attacker also has information about the marginal distribution for each attribute in the training data. The countermeasure that we study is a change in the model that is released, which is accomplished by modifying the training data.

Table 1. Model inversion attribute inference threat model, defined for our case.

Component	Description
Adversary: Objective	Specific sensitive attributes of the target individuals
Adversary: Resources	A set of non-sensitive attributes of the target individuals, including the correct value for the propensity-to-move attribute, for "inclusive individuals" (in the training set) or "exclusive individuals" (not in the training set)
Vulnerability:Opportunity	Ability to query the model to obtain output plus the marginal distributions of the data that the model was trained on. Additionally, the output might include confidence scores and a confusion matrix calculated on the training data might be available
Countermeasure	Modify the data on which the model is trained

3   Background and Related Work

In this section, we provide a brief overview of existing literature on data synthesis, privacy-preserving techniques, and model inversion attribute inference attacks.

3.1   Synthetic Data Generation

Synthetic data generation methods involve constructing a model of the data and generating synthetic data from this model. These methods are designed to preserve specific statistical properties and relationships between attributes in the original data [9,16,47]. Synthetic data generation techniques fall into two categories [20]: partially synthetic data and fully synthetic data. Partially synthetic data contain a mix of original and synthetic records [10]. Techniques to achieve partial synthesis replace only observed values for attributes that bear a high risk of disclosure (i.e., sensitive attributes) [11]. Fully synthetic data, which we use in our experiments, creates an entirely synthetic data set based on the original data [10,11]. Next, we discuss existing work on fully synthetic data generation from Statistical Disclosure Control [9,47] and deep learning [48,51].

Data Synthesis in Statistical Disclosure Control. Several approaches have been proposed in the literature for generating synthetic data, such as data distortion by probability distribution [23], synthetic data by multiple imputation [38], and synthetic data by Latin Hypercube Sampling [8]. In [12], the authors proposed an empirical evaluation of different machine learning algorithms, e.g., classification and regression trees (CART), bagging, random forests, and Support Vector Machines for generating synthetic data. The authors showed that data synthesis using CART results in synthetic data that provides reliable predictions and low disclosure risks. CART, being a non-parametric method, helps in handling mixed data types and effectively captures complex relationships between attributes [12].

Data Synthesis Using Generative Models. A lot of research has been carried out lately focusing on tabular data synthesis [7,31,51]. In [7], the authors proposed *MedGAN*, one of the earliest tabular GAN-based data synthesis used to generate synthetic Health Records. MedGAN transformed binary and categorical attributes into a continuous space by combining an auto-encoder with GAN. In [31], the authors proposed *TableGAN*, a GAN-based method to synthesize fake data that are statistically similar to the original data while protecting against information leakage, e.g., re-identification attack and membership attack. TableGAN uses a convolutional neural network that optimizes the label column's quality such that the generated data can be used to train classifiers. In [51], the authors pointed out different shortcomings that were not addressed in previous GAN models, e.g., a mixture of data types, non-Gaussian and multimodal distribution, learning from sparse one-hot encoded vectors and the problem of highly imbalanced categorical attributes. In [51], a new GAN model called *CTGAN* is introduced, which uses a conditional generator to properly model continuous and categorical columns.

3.2   Privacy-Preserving Techniques

In this section, we provide an overview of existing work on privacy-preserving techniques. Privacy-preserving techniques can be categorized as perturbative or non perturbative methods. Perturbative methods involve introducing slight modifications or noise to the original data to protect privacy, while non perturbative methods achieve privacy through data transformation techniques without altering the data itself [47]. These techniques, which have been studied for many years, include randomization, data shuffling, data swapping [29,33], obfuscation [4], post-randomization [50]. We discuss the privacy-preserving techniques that we use in our experiments in more depth:

Data swapping is a non-perturbative method that is based on randomly interchanging values of an attribute across records. Swapping maintains the marginal distributions in the shuffled data. By shuffling values of sensitive attributes, data swapping provides a high level of utility while minimizing risk of disclosure [29].

Post-randomization (PRAM) is a perturbative method. Applying PRAM to a specific attribute (or a number of attributes) means that the values of the record in the PRAMmed attribute will be changed according to a specific probability. Following notations used in [50], let ξ denote the categorical attribute in the original data to which PRAM will be applied. X denotes the same categorical attribute in the PRAMmed data. We suppose that ξ and X have K categories $1, \ldots, K$. $p_{kl} = \mathbb{P}(X = l | \xi = k)$ denotes the transition probabilities that define PRAM. This means the probability that an original value $\xi = k$ is changed to value $X = l$ for $k, l = 1, \ldots, K$. Using the transition probabilities as entries of a $K \times K$ matrix, we obtain $\boldsymbol{P}$ (called the PRAM-matrix).

Differential privacy has gained a lot of attention in recent years [1, 22]. Differential privacy (DP) uses a mathematical formulation to measure privacy. DP creates differentially private protected data by injecting noise expressed by ϵ into the original data. In [52] a differentially private Bayesian Network, PrivBayes is proposed to make possible the release of high-dimensional data. PrivBayes first constructs a Bayesian network that captures the correlations among the attributes and learns the distribution of data. After that, PrivBayes injects noise to ensure differential privacy and it uses the noisy marginals and the Bayesian network to construct an approximation of the data distribution. In [34], the authors introduced two methods for creating differentially private synthetic data. The first method adds noise to a cross-tabulation of all the attributes and creates synthetic data by a multinomial sampling from the resulting probabilities. The second method uses an iterative proportional fitting algorithm to obtain a fit to the probabilities computed from noisy marginals. Then, it generates synthetic data from the resulting probability distributions. A more recent work, Differentially Private CTGAN (DPCTGAN) [13] adds a differentially private noise to CTGAN. Specifically, DPCTGAN adds $\epsilon - \delta$ noise to the discriminator $\mathcal{D}$ and clips the norm to make it differentially private. We consider DPCTGAN to be a one-step synthesis approach, as it combines the application of noise and the synthesis process. Here, we test DPCTGAN, alongside our two-step synthesis + privacy preservation approaches.

3.3 Model Inversion Attribute Inference Attacks

Privacy attacks on data [25] include identification (or identity disclosure) attacks [2, 3, 51], membership inference attacks [41], and attribute inference attacks (or attribute disclosure) [3, 19, 44]. A lot of attention has been given to identification attacks on synthetic data [26, 40, 43]. However, less attention has been given to attribute inference attacks on synthetic data [40]. Attacks on data include attacks on models aimed at acquiring information about the training data. Here we investigate a model inversion attribute inference attack.

Model inversion attacks (MIA) aim to reconstruct the data a model is trained on or expose sensitive information inherent in the data [18, 49]. Attribute inference attacks use machine learning algorithms to predict, and perform attacks that infer sensitive attributes, i.e., gender, age, income. In a model inversion attribute inference attack, the attacker is interested in inferring sensitive information, e.g., demographic attributes, about an individual [14, 25, 28].

We distinguish between three categories of model inversion attribute inference attacks [18, 25]. An attack is black-box if the attacker only gets access to predictions generated by the model, i.e., can query the model with target individuals to receive the model's output. An attack is gray-box if the structure of the model and or some auxiliary information is further known, e.g., the attacker knows that the prediction is based on decision tree model, or attacker knows about the estimated weights of the model. An attack is white-box if an attacker has the full model, e.g., predictions, estimated weights or structure of model, and other information about training data.

In [14,15], the authors showed that it is possible to use black-box access to prediction models (access to commercial machine learning as a service APIs such as BigML) to learn genomic information about individuals. In [14], the authors developed an attack model that exploits adversarial access to a model to learn information about its training data. To perform the attack, the adversary uses the confidence scores included with the predictions as well as the confusion matrix of the target model and the marginal distributions of the sensitive attributes. In [28], the authors proposed two attack models: confidence score-based MIA (CSMIA) and label-only MIA (LOMIA). CSMIA exploits confidence scores returned by the target model. Different from Fredrikson et al. [14], in CSMIA an attacker is assumed to not have access to the marginal distributions or confusion matrix. LOMIA uses only the model's predicted labels. CSMIA, LOMIA, and Fredrikson et al., [14] are the attacks we study in our work. The three attacks aim to achieve the adversary's objective of inferring sensitive attributes about target individuals, while assuming different resources and opportunities available to the attacker. (Further details are in Sect. 4.4). Other model inversion attacks use variational inference [49] or imputation [21] to infer sensitive attributes.

3.4 Attribute Disclosure Risk

Previous work on identity and attribute disclosure risk has looked either at matching probability by comparing perceived, expected, and true match risk [36], or at a Bayesian estimation approach, assuming that an attacker seeks a Bayesian posterior distribution [37]. Similar to [36], other work [19,27,46] has looked at the concept of Correct Attribution Probability (CAP).

CAP assumes that the attacker knows the values of a set of key attributes for an individual in the original data set, and aims to learn the respective value of a target attribute. The key attributes encompass all attributes within the data, excluding the sensitive attribute that is the target attribute. Correct Attribution Probability (CAP) measures the disclosure risk of the individual's real value in the case where an adversary has access to protected data, and was originally proposed for synthetic data [19,46]. The basic idea of CAP is that an attacker is supposed to search for all records in the synthetic data that match records in the original data for given key attributes. The CAP score is the proportion of matches leading to correct attribution out of the total matches for a given individual [46]. In [46], the authors extended their previous preliminary work [27]. They proposed a new CAP measure called differential correct attribution probability (DCAP). DCAP captures the effect of multiple imputations on the disclosure risk of synthetic data. The authors of [46] stated that DCAP is well-suited for fully synthetic data. In [24], the authors introduced TCAP, for targeted correct attribution probability. TCAP calculates CAP value for targeted individuals that the attacker knows their existence in the original data. In our experiments, we use the CAP measure introduced in [27].

4   Experimental Setup

In this section, we describe our experimental setup. First, we provide an overview of our data set. Second, we describe how we synthesize data and the privacy protection techniques that we use. Next, we discuss target machine learning algorithms that we will use to predict propensity-to-move. Then, we describe the model inversion attribute inference attacks we study in our experiments.

4.1   Data Set

For our experiments, we use a data set from a governmental institute. The data set was previously collected and first used in [5]. It combines different registers from the System of Social Statistical Data sets (SSD). In our experiments, we use the same version of the data set used in [42]. Our data contains 150K individuals' records between 2013 and 2015. We have 40 attributes (categorical and numerical) containing information about individual demographic attributes such as gender and age, and time-dependent personal, household, and housing attributes. The target attribute "$y01$" is binary, indicating whether ($=1$) or not ($=0$) a person moved in year j where $j = 2013, 2015$. The target attribute is imbalanced with 129428 0 s (majority class) and 24971 1 s (minority class).

We have three distinct groups of individuals within the data. The difference between the three groups resides in the fact that there are some individuals who are in the data in the year 2013 (called Inclusive individuals 2013). The same individuals appear again in the year 2015 (called Inclusive individuals 2015), where they may have different values for the time-dependent attributes than they did in 2013. The last group (called Exclusive individuals 2015) contains individuals who are "new in the country". We have a total of: 76904 Inclusive individuals 2013, 74591 Inclusive individuals 2015, and 2904 Exclusive individuals 2015.

Our propensity-to-move classifier (i.e., the target model) is trained on all 2013 data (76904 records). The classifier is tested on the 2015 data (77495 records) as in [42]. For the target model trained on (privacy-preserving) synthetic data, we use $TSTR$ evaluation strategy such that we train classifiers on 2013 (privacy-preserving) synthetically generated data and we test on 2015 original data [17, 42].

As adversary resources, we assume that the attacker has access to a set of non-sensitive attributes of the target individuals (see our threat model in Sect. 2). As in [42], we consider three cases:

- Inclusive individuals (2013): the attacker has access to data from the year 2013, which aligns with the data used to train the target model.
- Inclusive individuals (2015): Here, the attacker possesses more recent data from 2015, but it corresponds to the same set of individuals used in training the target model. The data being more recent implies that some of the (time-sensitive) attributes for particular individuals may have changed somewhat.

– **Exclusive individuals (2015):** In this case, the attacker's data is from 2015, but it pertains to a distinct group of individuals who were not part of the training set for the target model.

We create data sets for each of the three cases. As in [42], for Exclusive individuals (2015) we use all 2904 individuals and for the other two cases we randomly sample to create data sets of the same size (2904 individuals each). The attributes of the target individuals that are in the possession of the attacker include the correct value of the propensity-to-move attribute but do not include the sensitive attributes gender, age, and income, which are targeted by the attack.

4.2   Privacy-Preserving Techniques on Synthetic Training Data

In this section, we describe how we synthesized data, and how we then applied privacy preserving approaches to it. The synthesis and privacy-preserving techniques are applied to the training data of the target model (the 76904 Inclusive individuals 2013), which is intended for release.

Our experiments with our two-step synthesis + privacy protection approach use a *classification and regression tree* (CART) model to synthesize data since it is shown to perform the best in the literature [12,35]. Recall that CART is a non-parametric method that can handle mixed data types and is able to capture complex and non-linear relationships between attributes. We apply CART to the training data of the target model, which includes individuals from 2013. We use the open public R package, Synthpop for our implementation of the CART model [30][1]. Within Synthpop, there are a number of parameters that can be optimized to achieve a good quality of synthesis [30]. *Visiting.sequence* parameter specifies the order in which attributes are synthesized. The order is determined institute-internally by a human expert. *Stopping rules* parameter dictates the number of observations that are assigned to a node in the tree. Stopping rules parameter helps to avoid over-fitting.

Following synthesis using CART, we apply privacy-preserving techniques, data swapping and PRAM (cf. Sect. 3.2), to the synthetic data. We use two data swapping approaches, referred to as *Swapping* and *Conditional swapping*. For Swapping, we perform data swapping separately for each sensitive attribute, which includes gender, age, and income. Specifically, for the age attribute, we interchange numerical age values among individuals and subsequently map these values to their respective age groups. For Conditional swapping, we perform simultaneous data swapping for gender, age, and income conditioned on the propensity-to-move target attribute. Conditional data swapping ensures that sensitive attributes are swapped while preserving the influence of the target attribute. Additionally, we apply Post-randomization (PRAM) independently to the attributes of gender, age, and income within the synthetic data generated using CART. Our transition matrices can be found in supplementary material.[2]

---

[1] http://www.synthpop.org.uk/.
[2] Supplemental material is at this link in Section.2: PRAM.

We use the sdcMicro toolkit.[3] It is important to note that our evaluation includes separate testing of PRAM and data-swapping techniques.

In addition to experiments with our two-step synthesis + privacy protection approach, we explore a GAN-based one-step approach for generating (privacy preserving) synthetic data generation. We use *CTGAN*, a popular and widely used GAN-based generative model [51]. The data synthesis procedure of CTGAN involves three key elements, namely: the conditional vector, the generator loss, and the training-by-sampling method. CTGAN uses a conditional generator to deal with the class imbalance problem. The conditional generator generates synthetic rows conditioned on one of the discrete columns. With training-by-sampling, the conditional and training data are sampled according to the log frequency of each category. We used open public toolkit Synthetic Data Vault (SDV)[4] implemented in Python [32]. In our implementation, hyperparameter tuning is applied to batch size, number of epochs, generator dimension, and discriminator dimension. We left other parameters set to default. We generate differentially private CTGAN data using DPCTGAN, which takes the state-of-the-art CTGAN and incorporates differential privacy. We chose to make a comparison with CTGAN and DPCTGAN because of the success of the two techniques reported in the literature [51].

4.3   Target Machine Learning Model

In this section, we discuss the target machine learning algorithm used to predict the propensity to move. We trained and tested a number of machine learning algorithms, including decision tree, random forest, naïve Bayes, and extra trees. We found that all classifiers outperform the majority-class classifier, with classifiers using trees generally being the best performers. For simplicity, in the rest of the paper, we will use random forest classifier as it is shown to perform the best on the original data and on the synthetic data. We report the results of random classifier using the most frequent (majority-class) strategy as a naïve baseline.

Recall that we must ensure that the prediction performance of the model is maintained when it is trained on synthetic + privacy-preservation data. To this end, we use the following metrics: F1-Macro, Matthews Correlation Coefficient (MCC), geometric mean (G-mean), True Negative (TN), False Positive (FP), False Negative (FN), and True Positive (TP). Our choice is motivated by the imbalance of the target attribute.

The macro-averaged F1 score (F1-Macro) is computed using the arithmetic mean (i.e., unweighted mean) of all the per-class F1 scores. This method treats all classes equally regardless of their support values.

The Geometric mean (G-mean) is the geometric mean of sensitivity and specificity [45]. G-mean takes all of the TP, TN, FP, and FN into account.

$$\text{G-mean} = \sqrt{\frac{TP}{TP+FN} * \frac{TN}{TN+FP}} \tag{1}$$

---

[3] https://cran.r-project.org/web/packages/sdcMicro/sdcMicro.pdf.
[4] https://github.com/sdv-dev/SDV.

Matthews Correlation Coefficient (MCC) metric is a balanced measure that can be used especially if the classes of the target attribute are of different sizes [6]. It returns a value between -1 and 1.

$$\text{MCC} = \frac{(TP * TN) - (FP * FN)}{\sqrt{(TP + FP) * (TP + FN) * (TN + FP) * (TN + FN)}} \tag{2}$$

4.4 Model Inversion Attribute Inference Attacks

In this section, we describe three model inversion attacks that we use in our paper: confidence-score MIA (CSMIA) [28], label-only MIA (LOMIA + Marginals), and the Fredrikson et al. MIA (FMIA) [14].

Confidence-Score MIA (CSMIA) [28] uses the output and confidence scores returned when the attacker queries the target propensity-to-move model. The attacker also has knowledge of the possible values for the sensitive attribute. For each target individual, the attacker creates different versions of the individual's records by substituting in for the missing sensitive attribute all values that would be possible for that attribute. The attacker then queries the model with each version and obtains the predicted class labels and the corresponding model confidence scores. Then, the attacker uses the predicted labels and confidence scores as follows [28]:

`Case (1)`: when the target model's prediction is *correct for only a single* sensitive attribute value, then, the attacker selects the sensitive attribute value to be the one for which the prediction is correct.

`Case (2)`: when target model's prediction is *correct for multiple* sensitive attribute values, then the attacker selects the sensitive value to be the one for which prediction confidence score is maximum.

`Case (3)`: when target model's prediction is *incorrect for all* sensitive attribute values, then the attacker selects the sensitive value to be the one for which prediction confidence score is minimum.

Label-Only MIA with Marginals (LOMIA + Marginals) is based on the LOMIA attack proposed by [28]. LOMIA + Marginals uses the output returned when the attacker queries the target propensity-to-move model and the marginal distributions of the training data (which includes the information about the possible values of sensitive attributes).

As with CSMIA, for each target individual, the attacker queries the target model multiple times, varying the value of the sensitive attribute. To determine the value of the sensitive attribute, the attacker follows `Case (1)` of CSMIA, as described in [28]. Specifically, if the target model's prediction is correct for a single sensitive attribute value, the attacker selects that value as the sensitive attribute. Differently from [28], for cases where the attacker cannot infer the sensitive attribute, we do not run an auxiliary machine learning model. Instead, the attacker uses the released marginal distribution to predict the most probable value of the sensitive attribute.

The Fredrikson et al. MIA (FMIA) [14] uses the output returned when the attacker queries the target propensity-to-move model and the marginal distributions of the training data. Following the threat model of [14], the attacker also has access to a confusion matrix of the target model's predictions on its training data. As with CSMIA and LOMIA + Marginals, the attacker queries the target model multiple times for each target individual, changing the sensitive attribute to take on all possible values and obtaining the predicted labels. Next, the attacker calculates the product of the probability that the target model's prediction aligns with the true label and the marginal distribution for each potential sensitive attribute value across all possibilities. Then, the attacker predicts the sensitive attribute value for which this product is maximized.

Measuring Success of Attribute Inference Attack. We use two ways to measure attribute inference attacks:

(1) From a machine learning perspective, we evaluate the success of the attack by measuring precision (also called the positive predicted value (PPV) [21]). The precision metric measures the ratio of true positive predictions considering all positive predictions. A precision score of 1 indicates that the positive predictions of the attack are always correct.

(2) From statistical disclosure control, we use CAP to measure the disclosure risk of the individuals. Following [46], we define D_{org} as the original data and K_{org} and T_{org} as vectors for the key and target sensitive attributes of the original data: $D_{org} = \{K_{org}, T_{org}\}$. Similarly, we denote by D_{syn} as the synthetic data and K_{syn} and T_{syn} as the vectors for the key and target sensitive attributes of the synthetic data: $D_{syn} = \{K_{syn}, T_{syn}\}$. Note that when we are calculating CAP, the synthetic data we use is the data reconstructed by the attacker by inferring the missing sensitive value and adding it to the previously-possessed non-sensitive attributes used for the attack. We consider gender, age, and income as target sensitive attributes, evaluating CAP for each sensitive attribute separately. Key attributes are all other attributes for an individual except for the sensitive attribute being measured by CAP. The CAP for a record j is the probability of its target attributes given its key attributes.

$$\text{CAP}_{org,j} = Pr(T_{org,j}|K_{org,j}) = \frac{\sum_{i=1}^{M}[T_{org,i}=T_{org,j}, K_{org,i}=K_{org,j}]}{\sum_{i=1}^{M}(K_{org,i}=K_{org,j})} \quad (3)$$

where M is the number of records. The CAP score for the original data is considered as an approximate upper bound. Then, the CAP for the record j based on a corresponding synthetic data D_{syn} is the same probability but derived from synthetic data D_{syn}.

$$\text{CAP}_{syn,j} = (Pr(T_{org,j}|K_{org,j}))_{syn} = \frac{\sum_{i=1}^{M}[T_{syn,i}=T_{org,j}, K_{syn,i}=K_{org,j}]}{\sum_{i=1}^{M}(K_{syn,i}=K_{org,j})} \quad (4)$$

CAP has a score between 0 and 1: a low score (close to 0) indicates that the synthetic data has a little risk of disclosure and a high score (close to 1) indicates a high risk of disclosure.

5 Performance of the Target Models

In this section, we compare the performance of the target propensity-to-move models. We evaluate whether a random forest classifier trained on protected synthetic data can attain performance comparable to a random forest classifier trained on the original data. Our results are reported in Table 2. Column "privacy-preservation" provides different privacy-preserving techniques that we applied to synthetic training data. "Privacy-preservation" with "None" means that there are no privacy-preserving techniques applied on top of the synthesis.

In Table 2, we see that random forest classifier trained on synthetic data using CART with *None* (i.e., no privacy-preserving technique applied) has quite close and comparable results to random forest classifier trained on original data. As a sanity check, we observe that both outperform the majority-class classifier.

Table 2. Classification performance of the target model. We generate synthetic data using CART and CTGAN. For privacy-preserving techniques, we used swapping, conditional swapping, PRAM, and differential privacy ($\epsilon = 3$). In each case, the test data is used in its original (unprotected) form.

Target MLs to be Released	Data sets	Privacy-preservation	F1-Macro	MCC	G-mean	TN	FP	FN	TP
Majority-class	Original data	None	0.4924	0.0012	0.4924	46452	9539	17818	3686
Random Forest	Original Data	None	0.5946	0.2407	0.5779	61907	2363	10677	2548
Random Forest	Synthetic data using CART	None	0.5946	0.2426	0.5793	61848	2422	10628	2597
		Swapping	0.5881	0.2389	0.5742	62174	2096	10831	2394
		Conditional swapping	0.4654	0.0216	0.5028	63704	566	13034	191
		PRAM	0.5941	0.2415	0.5789	61844	2426	10638	2587
	Synthetic data using CTGAN	None	0.4586	0.0392	0.5021	64207	63	13155	70
		Differential privacy	0.4534	0.000	0.5000	64270	0	13225	0

We observe that in two cases the model trained on our synthesis + privacy preservation data retains a level of performance comparable to a model trained on the original data: CART with *Swapping* and CART with *PRAM*. Surprisingly, we find that when the training data is created with CART synthesis and *Conditional swapping* or CTGAN (with or without *Differential privacy*) the performance is comparable to that of a majority-class classifier. This result suggests that the use of conditional swapping and differential privacy may not effectively preserve the utility of the propensity-to-move data. For the rest of the paper, we will assume that we intend to release machine learning models trained on synthetic data using CART with: *None*, *Swapping*, and *PRAM* as privacy-preserving techniques.

6 Results of Model Inversion Attribute Inference Attacks

In this section, we report the performance of different model inversion attribute inference attacks. We evaluate the performance of attacks on the model when it is trained on the original training data. Then, we investigate whether training the model on synthesis + privacy preservation data can protect against model inversion attribute inference attacks.

6.1   Attacks on the Model Trained on Original Data

First, we look at the performance of model inversion attribute inference attacks on the target model trained on original training data. The results are reported in Table 3.

Table 3. Results of model inversion attribute inference attacks measured using precision (positive predictive value) for three different target individual sets. The target propensity-to-move model is trained on **original training data**. Numbers in bold and italic represent the first and second best inference scores across conditions. A high precision indicates that the attack is good at correctly inferring the sensitive attribute values. We run experiments ten times and we report average scores. The standard deviation is below 0.01.

Adversary Resources	Inclusive individuals (2013)			Inclusive individuals (2015)			Exclusive individuals (2015)		
Attack models	Gender	Age	Income	Gender	Age	Income	Gender	Age	Income
Marginals Only	0.4977	0.1238	0.1982	0.5029	0.1244	0.1991	0.5012	0.1275	0.2001
CSMIA	0.3206	0.0105	0.0514	0.4660	0.0638	0.1581	0.4943	0.0721	0.1602
LOMIA + Marginals	*0.5157*	*0.1336*	*0.2105*	**0.5035**	**0.1291**	0.1983	*0.5014*	0.1234	**0.2005**
FMIA	**0.7563**	**0.6777**	**0.6898**	0.4647	0.0170	**0.2499**	**0.5205**	0.1091	0.1452

The attack models show varying performances compared to the Marginals Only Attack. We observe that attribute inference scores for the attack models "LOMIA + Marginals" and "FMIA" outperform the inference scores of the Marginals Only Attack. In particular, FMIA for Inclusive individuals (2013) achieves the highest precision for all three sensitive attributes gender, age, and income. It outperforms other attack models in terms of correctly predicting positive instances. LOMIA + Marginals shows moderate performance, obtaining precision values higher than Marginals Only Attack. The fact that the attack performance for Inclusive individuals (2013) is highest is not surprising since these individuals are in the training set of the target model. For Inclusive individuals (2015) and Exclusive individuals (2015), we see that the performance for all attack models is relatively low and comparable to the Marginals Only Attack, except for a few cases such as FMIA on age for Inclusive individuals (2015). Recall that for FMIA, the attacker is exploiting a larger opportunity for attack than for the other attacks. Specifically, the attacker can query the model but also possesses the marginal distributions of the training data and a confusion matrix (cf. Sect. 4.4. For this reason, it is not particularly surprising that FMIA is the strongest attack).

6.2   Attacks on the Model Trained on Protected Synthetic Data

Second, we investigate whether we can counter the attack by replacing original data used to train target model by a privacy-preserving synthetic data. The results of the model inversion attribute inference attacks are reported in Table 4.

Table 4. Results of model inversion attribute inference attacks measured using precision for three different target individual sets. The target propensity to move model is trained on *privacy-preserving (PP) + synthetic training* data. Numbers in bold and italic represent the first and second best inference scores across conditions. We run experiments ten times and we report average scores. The standard deviation is below 0.02.

PP+ Synthetic data	Attack Models	Inclusive individuals (2013)			Inclusive individuals (2015)			Exclusive individuals (2015)		
		Gender	Age	Income	Gender	Age	Income	Gender	Age	Income
Synthesis Only	Marginals Only	0.5036	0.1228	0.2021	0.4938	0.1225	0.2033	0.4979	**0.1233**	0.1980
	CSMIA	0.4901	0.0675	0.1423	0.4947	0.0775	0.1544	*0.5018*	0.1012	0.1826
	LOMIA + Marginals	0.4980	*0.1261*	0.1995	*0.5003*	**0.1282**	0.1972	*0.4989*	0.1252	0.1985
	FMIA	**0.5153**	0.0498	**0.3453**	**0.5007**	0.0588	**0.2772**	0.5069	0.1080	0.1452
Synthesis + Swapping	Marginals Only	0.4980	0.1238	0.1974	0.4979	0.1233	0.2060	0.4975	0.1248	**0.1973**
	CSMIA	0.4958	0.1198	**0.2032**	**0.4996**	0.1175	0.1848	*0.5093*	**0.1457**	*0.1986*
	LOMIA + Marginals	**0.5012**	**0.1280**	*0.1984*	0.4972	*0.1265*	0.1984	*0.5032*	0.1242	**0.1988**
	FMIA	0.4473	0.0901	0.0792	0.4320	**0.1362**	0.3098	**0.5351**	0.1020	0.1452
Synthesis + PRAM	Marginals Only	0.5002	0.1259	0.2010	0.5063	0.1239	0.2039	0.5002	0.1255	0.2000
	CSMIA	0.4967	0.1175	0.1701	0.4913	0.1059	0.1827	0.4895	**0.1371**	**0.2070**
	LOMIA + Marginals	**0.5038**	**0.1274**	0.1963	0.5004	0.1238	0.2002	0.5004	0.1247	*0.1987*
	FMIA	0.4827	0.0282	0.1635	**0.5286**	0.1129	0.1188	**0.5120**	0.1019	0.1452

Overall we see that the effectiveness of the synthesis + privacy-preserving techniques varies across different attributes, attack models, and adversary resources (target sets). While some attributes have an inference score higher than the inference score of the Marginals Only attack, others only have comparable performance to the Marginals Only attack. We notice a decrease in the performance of attack models specifically for Inclusive individuals (2013) compared to the performance of attack models for the same group of individuals in Table 3. For Inclusive individuals (2015) and Exclusive individuals (2015) which were not part of the training of the synthesis nor the training of the target model, we do not see a clear impact of privacy-preserving techniques on attack models. In most cases, the leak of sensitive information is low and comparable to the performance of the Marginals Only attack.

7   Correct Attribution Probability

Now, we shift our focus to calculate the risk of attribute disclosure for individual target subjects using CAP (Correct Attribution Probability). CAP captures how many specific individuals face a high risk of attribute disclosure and how many a lower risk. We measure CAP using Eq. 4, where D_{org} is the attacker's data with key attributes K_{org} and the original target sensitive attribute T_{org} (gender, age, income). D_{syn} represents the attacker's data where $K_{syn} = K_{org}$ are the key attributes and T_{syn} is the outcome of the model inversion attribute inference attacks.

Figure 1 and Fig. 2 show the frequency of CAP scores for sensitive attributes age and income, respectively. Due to space limitation, we specifically, focus on FMIA attack because it outperformed other attack models in Table 3. The top row of Fig. 1 and Fig. 2 shows the frequency of CAP scores on the original data

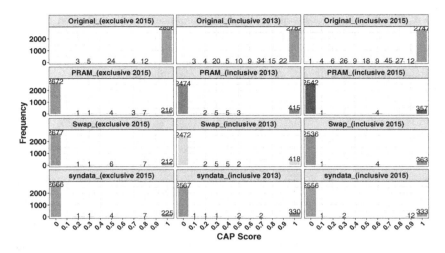

Fig. 1. Frequency of CAP scores for attribute *age*. The total number of queries is 2904. The numbers inside the bars represent the count of individuals with corresponding CAP scores.

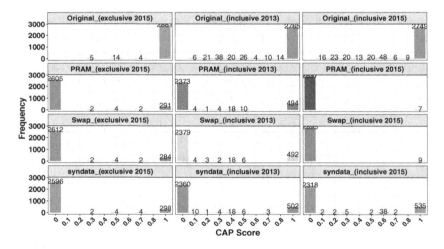

Fig. 2. Frequency of CAP scores for attribute *income*. The attack model is FMIA. The total number of queries is 2904. The numbers inside the bars represent the count of individuals with corresponding CAP scores.

(unprotected data). We see that across all three cases, Inclusive individuals (2013), Inclusive individuals (2015), and Exclusive individuals (2015), there is a high CAP score, signifying a high disclosure risk. However, when we calculate CAP scores based on the outcome of the model inversion attack, we observe that the risk of disclosure is relatively low, with approximately up to 92% of individuals considered protected. Only for the remaining individuals (8% individuals), we observe that an attacker can easily infer sensitive attributes age, and income with high CAP scores. Also, the number of disclosed individuals varies depending on the privacy-preserving technique applied. Comparing different resources, we see that for sensitive attribute age, Inclusive individuals (2013) have the highest number of disclosed individuals, next are Inclusive individuals (2015), and finally, Exclusive individuals (2015) have the lowest number of disclosed individuals. This aligns with the findings in Table 4. Notably, even though we generated privacy-preserving synthetic training data sets, the target model appears to retain some information about the original data, leading to a risk of disclosure for certain individuals.

8   Conclusion and Future Work

We have conducted an investigation aimed at protecting sensitive attributes against model inversion attacks, with a specific focus on a case study for a governmental institute. Our objective was to determine the feasibility of releasing a trained machine learning model predicting propensity-to-move to the public without causing privacy concerns. To accomplish this, we evaluated a number of existing privacy attacks, including CSMIA, LOMIA + Marginals, and FMIA, each distinguished by the resources available to the attacker. Our findings revealed that FMIA presented the highest degree of information leakage, followed by LOMIA + Marginals, while CSMIA exhibited the least leakage.

To mitigate these privacy risks, we employed privacy-preserving techniques on top of synthetic data utilized to train the machine learning model prior to its public release. Our results indicated that, in specific cases, such as with Inclusive individuals (2013), our privacy-preserving techniques successfully reduced information leakage. However, in other cases Inclusive individuals (2015) and Exclusive individuals (2015), the leakage remained comparable to that of a Marginals Only Attack, which uses the marginal distributions of the training data. We found a high disclosure risk, measured with CAP, when the target model is trained on original data. When the target model is trained on data protected with our two step synthesis + privacy preservation approach a lower percentage of individuals risk disclosure.

Furthermore, we think that the performance of the target machine learning model, as well as the correlation between the sensitive attribute and the target attribute, play a key role in the success of model inversion attacks. Future work should explore other case studies, in which this correlation might be different. Also, future work can look at other threat models such as white-box attacks, where the model predictions, model parameters, and explanation of the model's output are made public.

References

1. Abay, N.C., Zhou, Y., Kantarcioglu, M., Thuraisingham, B., Sweeney, L.: Privacy preserving synthetic data release using deep learning. In: Berlingerio, M., Bonchi, F., Gärtner, T., Hurley, N., Ifrim, G. (eds.) ECML PKDD 2018. LNCS (LNAI), vol. 11051, pp. 510–526. Springer, Cham (2019). https://doi.org/10.1007/978-3-030-10925-7_31
2. Agrawal, R., Srikant, R.: Privacy-preserving data mining. In: Proceedings of the ACM International Conference on Management of Data, vol. 29, pp. 439–450 (2000)
3. Andreou, A., Goga, O., Loiseau, P.: Identity vs. attribute disclosure risks for users with multiple social profiles. In: Proceedings of the IEEE/ACM International Conference on Advances in Social Networks Analysis and Mining, pp. 163–170 (2017)
4. Brunton, F., Nissenbaum, H.: Obfuscation: A User's Guide for Privacy and Protest. MIT Press, Cambridge (2015)
5. Burger, J., Buelens, B., de Jong, T., Gootzen, Y.: Replacing a survey question by predictive modeling using register data. In: ISI World Statistics Congress, pp. 1–6 (2019)
6. Chicco, D., Jurman, G.: The advantages of the Matthews Correlation Coefficient (MCC) over F1 score and accuracy in binary classification evaluation. BMC Genom. **21**(1), 1–13 (2020)
7. Choi, E., Biswal, S., Malin, B., Duke, J., Stewart, W.F., Sun, J.: Generating multi-label discrete patient records using generative adversarial networks. In: Doshi-Velez, F., Fackler, J., Kale, D., Ranganath, R., Wallace, B., Wiens, J. (eds.) Proceedings of the 2nd Machine Learning for Healthcare Conference, vol. 68, pp. 286–305 (2017)
8. Dandekar, R.A., Cohen, M., Kirkendall, N.: Sensitive micro data protection using Latin hypercube sampling technique. In: Domingo-Ferrer, J. (ed.) Inference Control in Statistical Databases. LNCS, vol. 2316, pp. 117–125. Springer, Heidelberg (2002). https://doi.org/10.1007/3-540-47804-3_9
9. Domingo-Ferrer, J.: A survey of inference control methods for privacy-preserving data mining. In: Aggarwal, C.C., Yu, P.S. (eds.) Privacy-Preserving Data Mining. Advances in Database Systems, vol. 34, pp. 53–80. Springer, Boston (2008). https://doi.org/10.1007/978-0-387-70992-5_3
10. Drechsler, J.: Synthetic Datasets for Statistical Disclosure Control: Theory and Implementation, vol. 201. Springer, New York (2011). https://doi.org/10.1007/978-1-4614-0326-5
11. Drechsler, J., Bender, S., Rässler, S.: Comparing fully and partially synthetic datasets for statistical disclosure control in the German IAB establishment panel. Trans. Data Priv. **1**(3), 105–130 (2008)
12. Drechsler, J., Reiter, J.P.: An empirical evaluation of easily implemented, non-parametric methods for generating synthetic datasets. Comput. Stat. Data Anal. **55**(12), 3232–3243 (2011)
13. Fang, M.L., Dhami, D.S., Kersting, K.: DP-CTGAN: differentially private medical data generation using CTGANs. In: Michalowski, M., Abidi, S.S.R., Abidi, S. (eds.) AIME 2022. LNCS, vol. 13263, pp. 178–188. Springer, Cham (2022). https://doi.org/10.1007/978-3-031-09342-5_17
14. Fredrikson, M., Jha, S., Ristenpart, T.: Model inversion attacks that exploit confidence information and basic countermeasures. In: Proceedings of the 22nd ACM Conference on Computer and Communications Security, pp. 1322–1333 (2015)

15. Fredrikson, M., Lantz, E., Jha, S., Lin, S., Page, D., Ristenpart, T.: Privacy in pharmacogenetics: an end-to-end case study of personalized warfarin dosing. In: 23rd USENIX Security Symposium, pp. 17–32. USENIX Association (2014)
16. Garofalo, G., Slokom, M., Preuveneers, D., Joosen, W., Larson, M.: Machine learning meets data modification. In: Batina, L., Bäck, T., Buhan, I., Picek, S. (eds.) Security and Artificial Intelligence. LNCS, vol. 13049, pp. 130–155. Springer, Cham (2022). https://doi.org/10.1007/978-3-030-98795-4_7
17. Heyburn, R., et al.: Machine learning using synthetic and real data: similarity of evaluation metrics for different healthcare datasets and for different algorithms. In: Data Science and Knowledge Engineering for Sensing Decision Support: Proceedings of the 13th International FLINS Conference, pp. 1281–1291. World Scientific (2018)
18. Hidano, S., Murakami, T., Katsumata, S., Kiyomoto, S., Hanaoka, G.: Exposing private user behaviors of collaborative filtering via model inversion techniques. In: Proceedings on Privacy Enhancing Technologies, no. 3, pp. 264–283 (2020)
19. Hittmeir, M., Mayer, R., Ekelhart, A.: A baseline for attribute disclosure risk in synthetic data. In: Proceedings of the 10th ACM Conference on Data and Application Security and Privacy, pp. 133–143 (2020)
20. Hundepool, A., et al.: Statistical Disclosure Control. Wiley, Hoboken (2012)
21. Jayaraman, B., Evans, D.: Are attribute inference attacks just imputation? In: Proceedings of the ACM Conference on Computer and Communications Security, pp. 1569–1582 (2022)
22. Li, H., Xiong, L., Zhang, L., Jiang, X.: DPSynthesizer: differentially private data synthesizer for privacy preserving data sharing. Proc. Very Large Data Bases (VLDB Endow.) 7(13), 1677–1680 (2014)
23. Liew, C.K., Choi, U.J., Liew, C.J.: A data distortion by probability distribution. ACM Trans. Database Syst. 10(3), 395–411 (1985)
24. Little, C., Elliot, M., Allmendinger, R.: Comparing the utility and disclosure risk of synthetic data with samples of microdata. In: Domingo-Ferrer, J., Laurent, M. (eds.) PSD 2022. LNCS, vol. 13463, pp. 234–249. Springer, Cham (2022). https://doi.org/10.1007/978-3-031-13945-1_17
25. Liu, B., Ding, M., Shaham, S., Rahayu, W., Farokhi, F., Lin, Z.: When machine learning meets privacy: a survey and outlook. ACM Comput. Surv. 54(2), 1–36 (2021)
26. Lu, P.H., Wang, P.C., Yu, C.M.: Empirical evaluation on synthetic data generation with generative adversarial network. In: Proceedings of the 9th International Conference on Web Intelligence, Mining and Semantics, pp. 1–6 (2019)
27. Elliot, M.: Final report on the disclosure risk associated with synthetic data produced by the SYLLS team (2014). http://hummedia.manchester.ac.uk/institutes/cmist/archive-publications/reports/. Accessed 13 Oct 2023
28. Mehnaz, S., Dibbo, S.V., Kabir, E., Li, N., Bertino, E.: Are your sensitive attributes private? novel model inversion attribute inference attacks on classification models. In: Proceedings of the 31st USENIX Security Symposium, pp. 4579–4596. USENIX Association (2022)
29. Muralidhar, K., Sarathy, R.: Data shuffling: a new masking approach for numerical data. Manage. Sci. 52(5), 658–670 (2006)
30. Nowok, B., Raab, G.M., Dibben, C.: Synthpop: bespoke creation of synthetic data in R. J. Stat. Softw. 74(11), 1–26 (2016)
31. Park, N., Mohammadi, M., Gorde, K., Jajodia, S., Park, H., Kim, Y.: Data synthesis based on Generative Adversarial Networks. In: Proceedings of the 44th

International Conference on Very Large Data Bases (VLDB Endowment), vol. 11, no. 10, pp. 1071–1083 (2018)

32. Patki, N., Wedge, R., Veeramachaneni, K.: The synthetic data vault. In: IEEE International Conference on Data Science and Advanced Analytics, pp. 399–410 (2016)

33. Polat, H., Du, W.: Privacy-preserving collaborative filtering using randomized perturbation techniques. In: Proceedings of the 3rd IEEE International Conference on Data Mining, pp. 625–628 (2003)

34. Raab, G.M.: Utility and disclosure risk for differentially private synthetic categorical data. In: Domingo-Ferrer, J., Laurent, M. (eds.) PSD 2022. LNCS, vol. 13463, pp. 250–265. Springer, Cham (2022). https://doi.org/10.1007/978-3-031-13945-1_18

35. Reiter, J.P.: Using CART to generate partially synthetic public use microdata. J. Off. Stat. **21**(3), 441 (2005)

36. Reiter, J.P., Mitra, R.: Estimating risks of identification disclosure in partially synthetic data. J. Priv. Confidentiality **1**(1) (2009)

37. Reiter, J.P., Wang, Q., Zhang, B.: Bayesian estimation of disclosure risks for multiply imputed, synthetic data. J. Priv. Confidentiality **6**(1) (2014)

38. Rubin, D.B.: Discussion statistical disclosure limitation. J. Off. Stat. **9**(2), 461–468 (1993)

39. Salter, C., Saydjari, O.S., Schneier, B., Wallner, J.: Toward a secure system engineering methodology. In: Proceedings of the Workshop on New Security Paradigms, pp. 2–10 (1998)

40. Shlomo, N.: How to measure disclosure risk in microdata? Surv. Stat. **86**(2), 13–21 (2022)

41. Shokri, R., Stronati, M., Song, C., Shmatikov, V.: Membership inference attacks against machine learning models. In: IEEE Symposium on Security and Privacy, pp. 3–18 (2017)

42. Slokom, M., de Wolf, P.P., Larson, M.: When machine learning models leak: an exploration of synthetic training data. In: Domingo-Ferrer, J., Laurent, M. (eds.) Proceedings of the International Conference on Privacy in Statistical Databases (2022). Corrected and updated version on arXiv at https://arxiv.org/abs/2310.08775

43. Stadler, T., Oprisanu, B., Troncoso, C.: Synthetic data-anonymisation groundhog day. In: Proceedings of the 29th USENIX Security Symposium. USENIX Association (2020)

44. Sun, M., Li, C., Zha, H.: Inferring private demographics of new users in recommender systems. In: Proceedings of the 20th ACM International Conference on Modelling, Analysis and Simulation of Wireless and Mobile Systems, pp. 237–244 (2017)

45. Sun, Y., Wong, A.K., Kamel, M.S.: Classification of imbalanced data: a review. Int. J. Pattern Recognit. Artif. Intell. **23**(04), 687–719 (2009)

46. Taub, J., Elliot, M., Pampaka, M., Smith, D.: Differential correct attribution probability for synthetic data: an exploration. In: Domingo-Ferrer, J., Montes, F. (eds.) PSD 2018. LNCS, vol. 11126, pp. 122–137. Springer, Cham (2018). https://doi.org/10.1007/978-3-319-99771-1_9

47. Torra, V.: Privacy in data mining. In: Maimon, O., Rokach, L. (eds.) Data Mining and Knowledge Discovery Handbook, pp. 687–716. Springer, Boston (2009). https://doi.org/10.1007/978-0-387-09823-4_35

48. Tripathy, A., Wang, Y., Ishwar, P.: Privacy-preserving adversarial networks. In: 57th IEEE Annual Allerton Conference on Communication, Control, and Computing, pp. 495–505 (2019)
49. Wang, K.C., Fu, Y., Li, K., Khisti, A.J., Zemel, R., Makhzani, A.: Variational model inversion attacks. In: Beygelzimer, A., Dauphin, Y., Liang, P., Vaughan, J.W. (eds.) Advances in Neural Information Processing Systems, vol. 34, pp. 9706–9719 (2021)
50. Wolf, P.-P.: Risk, utility and PRAM. In: Domingo-Ferrer, J., Franconi, L. (eds.) PSD 2006. LNCS, vol. 4302, pp. 189–204. Springer, Heidelberg (2006). https://doi.org/10.1007/11930242_17
51. Xu, L., Skoularidou, M., Cuesta-Infante, A., Veeramachaneni, K.: Modeling tabular data using conditional GAN. In: Wallach, H., Larochelle, H., Beygelzimer, A., d'Alche Buc, F., Fox, E., Garnett, R. (eds.) Advances in Neural Information Processing Systems, vol. 32, pp. 7335–7345 (2019)
52. Zhang, J., Cormode, G., Procopiuc, C.M., Srivastava, D., Xiao, X.: PrivBayes: private data release via Bayesian networks. ACM Trans. Database Syst. **42**(4), 1–41 (2017)

Privacy-Preserving Medical Data Generation Using Adversarial Learning

Pronaya Prosun Das[1]([✉]) [iD], Despina Tawadros[1] [iD], and Lena Wiese[1,2]([✉]) [iD]

[1] Fraunhofer Institute for Toxicology and Experimental Medicine,
Hannover, Germany
{pronaya.prosun.das,lena.wiese}@item.fraunhofer.de
[2] Institute of Computer Science, Goethe University Frankfurt,
Frankfurt am Main, Germany

Abstract. Outstanding performance has been observed in a number of real-world applications such as speech processing and image classification using deep learning models. However, developing these kinds of models in sensitive domains such as healthcare usually necessitates dealing with a specific level of privacy challenges which provide unique concerns. For managing such privacy concerns, a practical method might involve generating feasible synthetic data that not only provides acceptable data quality but also helps to improve the efficiency of the model. Synthetic Data Generation (SDG) innately includes Generative Adversarial Networks (GANs) that have drawn significant interest in this field as a result of their achievement in various other research areas. In the study, a framework safeguarding privacy, which employs Rényi Differential Privacy along with Generative Adversarial Networks and a Variational Autoencoder (RDP-VAEGAN), is introduced. This approach is evaluated and contrasted with other top-tier models having identical privacy constraints, utilizing both unsupervised and supervised methods on two medical datasets that are publicly accessible.

Keywords: Adversarial Learning · Rényi Differential Privacy · GAN · Variational Autoencoders · Synthetic Data Generation · Healthcare · Medical data

1 Introduction

Deep learning (DL) has shown remarkable achievements in various domains, including natural language processing, information retrieval, and computer vision, thanks to its immense capabilities. However, the effectiveness of deep learning heavily depends on having access to large volumes of training data. Consequently, incorporating deep learning models into industries that prioritize data privacy, such as healthcare, may face obstacles. In order to effectively utilize data-driven approaches in medical fields, it is crucial to address privacy concerns. Typically, personally identifiable information is anonymized to protect

© The Author(s), under exclusive license to Springer Nature Switzerland AG 2023
E. Athanasopoulos and B. Mennink (Eds.): ISC 2023, LNCS 14411, pp. 24–41, 2023.
https://doi.org/10.1007/978-3-031-49187-0_2

the sensitivity of the data. However, these methods can be vulnerable to de-anonymization attacks [22], leading researchers to explore alternative approaches like privacy-preserving machine learning (ML) [3] to further improve a system's resilience against such attacks. In addition to this primary privacy concern, handling noisy and intricate data further adds complexity to the process, as the data may include different types, such as categorical, discrete, and continuous variables.

Synthetic Data Generation (SDG) stands out as one of the most viable methods for maintaining privacy. By generating synthetic data, privacy concerns can be alleviated, opening up numerous collaborative research opportunities. This process is particularly advantageous in tasks such as pattern identification and predictive model creation. Generative Adversarial Networks (GANs) have drawn substantial interest in the realm of SDG due to their achievements in other areas [10]. Since SDG relies on a generative process, GANs are well-suited for this purpose. Utilizing GANs makes it challenging to differentiate between real samples and those that are generated, due to the underlying distribution of the actual data. Consequently, the results of GANs cannot be reversed using a deterministic function.

On the other hand, the utilization of GANs for SDG solely does not actually ensure the privacy of the system. Depending only on the irreversibility of GANs is not sufficient, as GANs have already been proven to be vulnerable [13]. Therefore, additional steps must be considered to assure the privacy of SDG systems. The usage of private patient data in medical applications increases concerns about the severe consequences of privacy breaches. Consequently, two fundamental questions must be considered: (1) What amount of information becomes revealed during the training stage? and (2) How strong are the system's security measures? Hence, evaluating the system's privacy level is crucial to ensure its commitment to safeguarding privacy.

Differential Privacy (DP) [9] is a mathematical framework that provides a means of ensuring and quantifying the privacy of a system. It has emerged as the standard approach for exploring databases containing sensitive information. DP's strength lies in its ability to provide precise mathematical representation to ensure privacy without limiting statistical reasoning. Additionally, DP allows for the measurement of the privacy level of a system. In the domains of ML and DL, where sensitive data is often employed to enhance predictive accuracy, the role of DP is crucial. The privacy of an ML model can be compromised by various attacks, therefore it's wise to anticipate the existence of a potent adversary with a thorough understanding of the system's entire pipeline, including the model and its training process [27]. In order to shield the privacy of the system, it's imperative to defend from this type of adversary, or at the minimum, quantify the greatest possible extent of privacy intrusion in that context. A system that is entirely differentially private guarantees that the training of the algorithm does not depend on the sensitive information of any individual.

Differentially Private Stochastic Gradient Descent (DP-SGD), introduced in [1], is a widely adopted technique that ensures differential privacy while maintaining model accuracy within a given privacy budget. DP-SGD serves as the foundation for numerous research studies [2,31]. In essence, the DP-SGD approach consists of three primary steps. Firstly, it limits the gradients to set the algorithm's sensitivity to individual data. Secondly, it introduces Gaussian noise into the data. Finally, it performs gradient descent optimization. Currently, the utilization of SGD within the DP-SGD framework is regarded as a very important technique for preserving privacy without sacrificing accuracy in ML models.

Generating synthetic data in the medical domain is faced with a number of challenges. The first challenge is ensuring privacy during the model training, which is often not directly addressed in current works, and instead, statistical or machine learning-based techniques are used. The second difficulty involves handling discrete data, a task with which GAN-based techniques often grapple, as these are designed for continuous data. The third challenge involves evaluating the quality of generated data within realistic, real-world contexts, which is particularly important in the healthcare sector. Here, inferior synthetic data can result in serious repercussions, potentially endangering human lives. The fourth challenge is the integration of local and temporal correlations among features, something that is frequently overlooked but is vital in the medical field. This is because patient histories and disease occurrences frequently display coherent patterns, and acknowledging these interdependencies can substantially enhance the reliability of synthetic data.

In this paper, we present our model that produces higher-quality synthetic data while working within similar privacy constraints. Additionally, our model provides not just high-quality synthetic data but also superior privacy safeguards.

The layout of the paper is arranged in the following manner: In Sect. 2, previous research on synthetic data generation, GAN, and their challenges are discussed. Section 3 presents the proposed algorithmic framework for privacy-preserving medical data generation. The experimental results are outlined in Sect. 4. Section 5 offers a conclusion of the research.

2   Background

2.1   Related Works

Many studies utilize Differential Privacy to generate synthetic data, often following a method described in [1]. This approach involves training a neural network while maintaining differential privacy by adding noise and using gradient clipping to restrict the norms of the gradients, in accordance with the standard procedure introduced in [9]. One of the major contributions of [1] is the introduction of the privacy accountant that monitors privacy loss. Inspired by the effectiveness of this method, we expand our privacy-preserving framework by adopting Rényi Differential Privacy (RDP) [20] as a novel notion of DP to estimate privacy loss.

Recent research has focused on tackling the challenges related to generating synthetic healthcare data [5,11]. MedGAN is an early system used to generate synthetic medical data, which only relies on GAN models and does not implement any privacy-preserving mechanism [8]. While the method exhibits strong performance in data generation, it lacks privacy assurance, as GANs can be susceptible to attacks. In contrast, MedGAN utilizes denoising autoencoders to produce discrete data [8]. Tools like Synthea, synthetic patient generator, are not widely utilized as they depend solely on conventional specifications and do not account for factors vital to predictive analysis [7,30]. Other research, such as CorGAN [19] and TableGAN [23], employs convolutional GANs for generating sequences of longitudinal events, while CTGAN [32] is specifically designed to handle tabular data comprising both continuous and discrete features. However, none of these approaches ensures any privacy during data generation. This lack of privacy protection makes these models vulnerable in practice and could compromise the privacy of original medical data. This paper will delve into different strategies for preserving privacy.

2.2 Differential Privacy

Differential Privacy ensures the safeguarding of individual privacy by quantifying the privacy loss that takes place when information is disclosed from a database, relying on a defined mathematical concept [9]. The most commonly used definition of Differential Privacy is (ϵ, δ)-differential privacy.

Definition 1 ((ϵ, δ)-DP). *If a randomized algorithm A that takes a dataset X as input and returns a query outcome Q satisfies the definition of (ϵ, δ)-differential privacy, then it ensures individuals' privacy for all possible query outcomes Q and all neighbouring datasets D and D'.*

$$\Pr[A(D) \in Q] \leq e^{\epsilon} \Pr[A(D') \in Q] + \delta \tag{1}$$

Datasets D and D', which differ only by one record, are referred to as neighbor datasets, highlighting the importance of maintaining individual privacy. The parameters (ϵ, δ) are used to represent the privacy budget, meaning that differentially private algorithms do not guarantee absolute privacy but only indicate the level of confidence in privacy preservation for the given (ϵ, δ) values. The smaller the values of (ϵ, δ), the more confident we are about the algorithm's privacy. The value of (ϵ, δ) with $\delta = 0$ is known as ϵ-DP, which is the original definition [9] and provides a stronger promise of privacy since even a small value of δ can lead to privacy violations due to the shift in the distribution. The use of (ϵ, δ)-DP is common because it allows for advanced composition theorem to be applied.

Theorem 1 (Advanced Composition [9]). *Suppose we apply an adaptive composition of a (ϵ, δ)-DP mechanism k times. Then, the resulting composite mechanism will be $(\epsilon', k\delta' + \delta) - DP$ with respect to δ', where the parameter ϵ' is defined as $\epsilon' = \sqrt{2k \ln\left(\frac{1}{\delta'}\right)}\epsilon + k\epsilon(e^{\epsilon} - 1)$.*

2.3   Rényi Differential Privacy

Compared to the basic composition theorem, Theorem 1, known as strong or advanced composition, establishes a more precise upper limit for the privacy loss in (ϵ, δ) − DP compositions. However, the strong composition theorem has the drawback of rapidly increasing privacy parameters as the theorem is used repeatedly, leading to a selection of possible $(\epsilon(\delta), \delta)$ values. A novel approach called Rényi Differential Privacy (RDP) was introduced in [20] to overcome some of the constraints associated with (ϵ, δ) − DP. This approach is grounded in the idea of Rényi divergence, as detailed in Eq. 2.

Definition 2 (*Rényi divergence of order* α [25]**).** *Rényi divergence of order α, which quantifies the difference between two probability distributions P and P', is specified as follows:*

$$D_\alpha(P||P') = \frac{1}{\alpha - 1} \log \left(\sum_{x \in X} \left(P(x)^\alpha P'(x)^{1-\alpha} \right) \right) \tag{2}$$

The Rényi divergence, which is a more general form of the Kullback-Leibler divergence, is equivalent to the Kullback-Leibler divergence when α is equal to 1. When α is equal to infinity, the special case is:

$$D_\infty(P||P') = \log \left(\sup_{x \in X} \frac{P(x)}{P'(x)} \right) \tag{3}$$

The value given by the logarithm of the highest ratio of probabilities for a given x over $P'(x)$ is used to calculate the Rényi divergence. The relationship between ϵ-DP and Rényi divergence is established when the value of $\alpha = \infty$. In case a randomized mechanism $\mathcal{A}$ demonstrates ϵ-differential privacy, then for a pair of datasets D and D', differing by a single record, the condition depicted in Eq. 4 has to be satisfied. Using the definitions discussed earlier, the work [20] unveiled a novel concept in differential privacy known as RDP.

Definition 3 (*RDP* rm [20]). *The (α, ϵ) − RDP is a randomized algorithm $\mathcal{A} : \mathcal{D} \to U$, and it is defined as satisfying the condition that for all neighbour datasets D and D', the following condition is satisfied:*

$$D_\alpha(\mathcal{A}(D)||\mathcal{A}(D')) \leq \epsilon \tag{4}$$

Two essential characteristics of the RDP definition (Definition 3) must be taken into account.

Proposition 1 (*Composition of RDP* [20]). *Assuming $\mathcal{A}$ is a randomized function that maps from a set $\mathcal{X}$ to a set U_1 and conforms to (α, ϵ_1) − RDP, and $\mathcal{B}$ is a randomized function that maps from $U_1 \times \mathcal{X}$ to a set U_2 and conforms to (α, ϵ_2) − RDP. Then, by applying $\mathcal{A}$ to $\mathcal{X}$, we obtain M_1, and by applying $\mathcal{B}$ to M_2 and $\mathcal{X}$, we obtain M_2. The resulting mechanism (M_1, M_2) meets the conditions of $(\alpha, \epsilon_1 + \epsilon_2)$-RDP.*

Proposition 2. *Assuming $\mathcal{A}$ is a randomized function that maps from a set $\mathcal{X}$ to a set $\mathcal{U}$ and adheres to $(\alpha,\ \epsilon) - RDP$, then it must also comply with $(\epsilon + \frac{\log(\frac{1}{\delta})}{(\alpha-1)},\ \delta) - DP$ for any value of δ that falls between 0 and 1.*

The two propositions mentioned above are fundamental to our privacy preservation approach. Proposition 1 deals with computing the privacy cost by combining the autoencoder and GAN structures. Proposition 2 is useful for evaluating the level of differential privacy in our system using the standard $(\epsilon,\ \delta)$ definition (as defined in Definition 1).

3   Algorithmic Framework

We have developed a GAN model that secures privacy through the implementation of Rényi differential privacy. GAN models have historically faced challenges when generating non-continuous data [15], prompting us to integrate autoencoders [18] to establish a continuous feature space representative of the input. This enables the GAN to produce high-quality synthetic data, simultaneously protecting privacy. No matter the type of input data, whether continuous, discrete, or a combination of both, the autoencoder can convert the input space into a continuous one. The autoencoder functions as a conduit between the non-continuous data and the GAN model which is often common in medical domains.

The framework we propose is depicted in Fig. 1. In this configuration, random noise $z \in \mathbb{R}^r$, which follows a normal distribution $\mathcal{N}(0, 1)$, is taken by the generator G and mapped to the generator's domain D_g^d. The discriminator D takes real data $x \in \mathbb{R}^n$ and maps it to the discriminator domain D_d, typically a set of binary values or values within the range $[-1, 1]$. In our RDPVAEGAN framework, the synthetic data undergoes decoding before being inputted into the discriminator, which deviates from the standard training process used in traditional GANs. This decoding step involves guiding the artificial data through a pre-trained variational autoencoder.

3.1   GAN

Most of the studies in synthetic data generation [8] overlook the local or temporal correlations of the features. Multilayer perceptrons are commonly used, though they don't correspond well with real-life situations such as the development of diseases. To overcome this limitation, we deploy one-dimensional convolutional neural networks (CNNs) in our variational autoencoder as well as in the generator and discriminator components of our GAN architecture. CNNs are capable of recognizing patterns in correlated input features as well as capturing temporal information [12].

The procedure for training the GAN is described in Algorithm 2, referred to as the GAN Training Step. Remarkably, differential privacy is exclusively applied to the discriminator, as it is the pivotal component with access to authentic data. To effectively thwart mode collapse during training, we harness

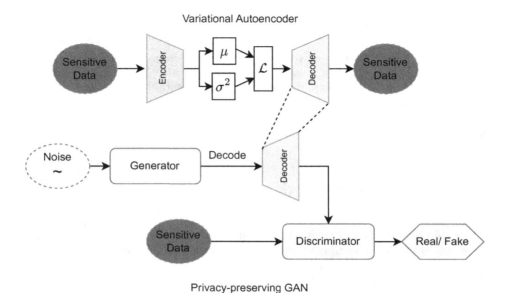

Fig. 1. The overall block diagram of GAN framework

the remarkable capabilities of the Wasserstein GAN [4], which adeptly approximates the Earth Mover's (EM) distance. The Wasserstein GAN has garnered acclaim for its unparalleled effectiveness in evading mode collapse. Distinguished as the Wasserstein-1 distance, the EM distance signifies the minimal expenditure required to seamlessly convert a synthesized data distribution $\mathbb{P}_g$ into an authentic data distribution $\mathbb{P}_x$.

$$W\left(\mathbb{P}_x,\ \mathbb{P}_g\right) = \inf_{v \in \prod \mathbb{P}_x,\ \mathbb{P}_g} E_{(x,y)\sim\ v}\left[\|x - y\|\right] \tag{5}$$

Here, $\prod \mathbb{P}_x,\ \mathbb{P}_g$ represents the collection of all joint distributions $\vartheta(x,\ y)$ with marginals given by $\mathbb{P}_x$ and $\mathbb{P}_g$, respectively. The function $\vartheta(x,\ y)$ measures the amount of "mass" that needs to be shifted from x to y to effectively transform $\mathbb{P}_x$ into $\mathbb{P}_g$.

To tackle the challenging infimum in Eq. 5, WGAN employs an optimization strategy outlined in Eq. 6, inspired by the Kantorovich-Rubinstein duality [29], reflecting the intrinsic difficulty of the issue.

$$W\left(\mathbb{P}_x,\ \mathbb{P}_g\right) = \sup_{\|f\|_L \leq 1} E_{x\sim\mathbb{P}_x}\left[f(x)\right] - E_{x\sim\mathbb{P}_g}\left[f(x)\right] \tag{6}$$

To offer a more simplified explanation, the terms "supremum" and "infimum" correspond to the smallest upper bound and the largest lower bound, respectively.

Definition 4 (1-Lipschitz functions). *If we have two metric spaces* (X, d_X) *and* (Y, d_Y) *where* $'d'$ *is the distance metric, the function* $f : X \rightarrow Y$ *is known as* $K - Lipschitz$ *when:*

$$\forall (x, x') \in \mathbb{X}, \exists K \in \mathbb{R} : d_Y (f(x), f(x')) \leq K d_X(x, x') \tag{7}$$

With $K = 1$ *and using the distance metric, Eq. 7 can be expressed as:*

$$\forall (x, x') \in \mathbb{X} : |f(x) - f(x')| \leq |x - x'| \tag{8}$$

In order to compute the Wasserstein distance, it becomes imperative to discover a function that adheres to the 1-Lipschitz constraint (as specified in Definition 4 and Eq. 8). To accomplish this, a neural model is constructed to acquire knowledge of the function. This entails the development of a discriminator D, which deviates from employing the Sigmoid function and instead produces a scalar output, rather than a probability of confidence.

When it comes to privacy issues, it should be highlighted that the generator is not granted direct access to the actual data, yet it is able to access the discriminator's gradients. Solely the discriminator is granted access to real data, and we propose training it while maintaining differential privacy. Fundamentally, this approach is rooted in the post-processing theorem of differential privacy, which presents the following recommended methodology.

Theorem 2 *(Post-processing* [9]*).* *Suppose we have an algorithm* **D** : $\mathbb{N}^{|\mathcal{X}|} \rightarrow \mathbb{D}$ *that satisfies* $(\epsilon, \delta)-differential privacy, and we have an arbitrary function* **G**: $\mathbb{D} \rightarrow \mathbb{O}$. *If we compose G with D, i.e.,* **G** $\circ$ **D** : $\mathbb{N}^{|\mathcal{X}|} \rightarrow \mathbb{O}$, *then the resulting algorithm also satisfies* (ϵ, δ)-differential privacy, as per the post-processing theorem* [9].

Drawing from the aforementioned rationale, we consider the generator and discriminator as G and D, respectively. By considering the generator as a random mapping that's layered over the discriminator, ensuring differential privacy solely on the discriminator ensures the entire system maintains differential privacy. This makes it unnecessary to train a generator that maintains privacy. During the generator's training process, as demonstrated in lines 17–20 of Algorithm 2, a private generator is unnecessary, and we can employ the conventional loss function for the generator within the WGAN framework [4].

3.2   Variational Autoencoders

The autoencoder is architected to realize multiple goals at the same time, such as detecting correlations among neighbouring features, creating a compressed feature space, converting discrete records into a continuous domain, and handling both discrete and continuous data. Autoencoders are a type of neural network design composed of an encoder and a decoder. The encoding function $Enc(\cdot)$: $\mathbb{R}^n \rightarrow \mathbb{R}^d$ is crafted to map the input $x \in \mathbb{R}^n$ into the latent space $\mathcal{L} \in \mathbb{R}^d$, equipped with weights and biases θ. Alternatively, the decoding function $Dec(\cdot)$:

Algorithm 1. Pre-Training of Variational Autoencoder

Require: Real dataset $X = \{x_i\}_{i=1}^N$, weights of the network θ, ϕ, learning rate η, number of epochs n_{vae} and standard deviation of the additive noise σ_{vae}.

2: **for** $k = 1 \ldots n_{\text{vae}}$ **do**
    Sample a mini − batch of n examples. $\mathcal{X} = \{x_i\}_{i=1}^n$
4:     Split X into $\mathcal{X}_1, \ldots, \mathcal{X}_r$ *where* $r = \lfloor \frac{n}{k} \rfloor$
    for $l = 1 \ldots r$ **do**
6:       *Calculate* $Loss(\theta, \phi, \mathcal{X}_l)$ *using Eq. 10.*
      $g_{\theta,\phi,l} \leftarrow \nabla_{\theta,\phi} Loss(\theta, \phi \; \mathcal{X}_l)$
8:     **end for**
    $\widehat{g_{\theta,\phi}} \leftarrow \frac{1}{r} \sum_{l=1}^r (g_{\theta,\phi,l} + \mathcal{N}(0, \; \sigma_{\text{vae}}^2))$
10:    $\widehat{\theta, \phi} = Update(\theta, \phi, \eta, \widehat{g_{\theta,\phi}})$
   end for

Algorithm 2. GAN Training

Require: Real dataset $X = \{x_i\}_{i=1}^N$, generator and discriminator weights ψ and ω, respectively, learning rate η, random noise z where each z_i follows a normal distribution $z_i \sim \mathcal{N}(0,1)$, number of epochs n_{gan}, number of training steps for discriminator per one step of generator training n_d, norm bound C and standard deviation of the additive noise σ_{gan}.

2: **for** $j = 1 \ldots n_{\text{gan}}$ **do**
    for $k = 1 \ldots n_d$ **do**
4:       *Take a mini − batch from real data* $\mathcal{X} = \{x_i\}_{i=1}^n$
      Sample a mini − batch $\mathcal{Z} = \{z_i\}_{i=1}^n$
6:       *Partition real data mini − batches into* $\mathcal{X}_1, \ldots, \mathcal{X}_r$
      Partition noise data mini − batches into $\mathcal{Z}_1, \ldots, \mathcal{Z}_r$
8:       **for** $l = 1 \ldots r$ **do**
         $x_i \in \mathcal{X}_l$ and $z_i \in \mathcal{Z}_l$
10:         $Loss = \frac{1}{k} \sum_{i=1}^k (D(x_i) - D(Dec(G(z_i))))$
         $g_{\omega,l} \leftarrow \nabla_\omega Loss(\omega, \; \mathcal{X}_l)$
12:         $\widehat{g_{\omega,l}} \leftarrow \dfrac{g_{\omega,l}}{max(1, \frac{\|g_{\omega,l}\|_2}{C})}$
      end for
14:      $\widehat{g_\omega} \leftarrow \frac{1}{r} \sum_{l=1}^r (\widehat{g_{\omega,l}} + \mathcal{N}(0, \; \sigma_{\text{gan}}^2 C^2 \mathbb{I}))$
      Update: $\widehat{\omega} = \omega - \eta \widehat{g_\omega}$
16:     **end for**
    Sample $\{z_i\}_{i=1}^n$ from noise prior
18:    $Loss = -\frac{1}{n} \sum_i^n (D(Dec(G(z_i))))$
    $g_\psi \leftarrow \nabla_\psi Loss(\psi, \; \mathcal{Z})$
20:    $Update: \widehat{\psi} \leftarrow \psi - \eta g_\psi$
   end for

$\mathbb{R}^d \to \mathbb{R}^n$ seeks to reconstruct $\hat{x} \in \mathbb{R}^n$ from the latent space, also with its own set of weights and biases ϕ. The end goal is to precisely recreate the initial input data, which means that $x = \hat{x}$. Autoencoders typically utilize Mean Square Error (MSE) for handling continuous inputs and Binary Cross Entropy (BCE) for managing binary inputs. However, in this research, we apply Variational Autoencoders (VAEs) which serve as a generative model offering a method to learn complex data distributions. Unlike conventional autoencoders which can encode and then reconstruct input data, VAEs also learn a model of the data distribution, enabling the generation of new instances. Training a VAE involves managing two main tasks:

- The aim of the Encoder is to approximate the posterior $P(\mathcal{L} \mid x)$ in such a manner that $P(\mathcal{L})$ conforms to a unit Gaussian distribution.
- The goal of the Decoder is to estimate $P(x \mid \mathcal{L})$ in such a manner that it permits a highly probable reconstruction of the original input x.

$$P(x) = \int P(x \mid \mathcal{L})P(\mathcal{L})d\mathcal{L} \tag{9}$$

The loss function for the VAE is the negative log-likelihood with a regularizer. Since there are no shared global representations for all data points, we can decompose the loss function into only terms that depend on a single datapoint l_i. The total loss is then given by $\sum_{i=1}^{N} l_i$ for N total data points. The loss function l_i for each datapoint x_i is given by:

$$\begin{aligned} l_i(\theta, \phi) = &-\mathbb{E}_{\mathcal{L} \sim Enc(\mathcal{L} \mid x_i, \theta)}[\log Dec(x_i \mid \mathcal{L}, \phi)] \\ &+ \mathcal{KL}(Enc(\mathcal{L} \mid x_i, \theta) \parallel Dec(\mathcal{L})) \end{aligned} \tag{10}$$

The initial part refers to the reconstruction loss, which is essentially the expected negative log-likelihood of the i-th data point. The subsequent component is a regularization term often referred to as the Kullback-Leibler divergence. This divergence measures the difference between the distribution produced by the encoder $Enc(\mathcal{L} \mid x_i)$ and the distribution generated by the decoder $Dec(\mathcal{L})$.

Algorithm 1 presents the step-by-step guide to the pre-training process of the autoencoder, encapsulating the following:

We pre-train the VAE for n_{vae} steps, where the number of steps is determined based on the desired level of privacy budget ϵ. To process a mini-batch, we split it into several micro-batches. We compute the loss (line 6) and determine the gradients (line 7) for each individual micro-batch with a size of 1. We then introduce Gaussian noise $\mathcal{N}(0, \sigma_{\text{vae}}^2)$ independently to the gradients which are calculated from micro-batch (line 9). Finally, the optimizer updates the parameters (line 10). Encoder mainly approximates mean μ and variance σ^2 from the input. Afterwards, latent space is sampled using μ and σ^2.

3.3 Model Architecture

To maximize effectiveness, we strategically employed four 1 dimensional (D) convolutional layers in both the GAN discriminator and generator, as well as in the encoder of the autoencoder. Notably, the final dense layer, pivotal for decision-making, possesses an output size of 1. Throughout the network, each layer employed the PReLU activation function [14], with the exception of the concluding layer, which operated without any activation. We employed 1-D fractionally-strided convolutions, usually referred to as transposed convolutions in the generator, following the approach described in [24]. Notably, the generator was fed with a noise of size 128 in the input, ultimately yielding an output size of 128 for optimal outcomes.

The encoder's architecture closely resembled that of the GAN discriminator, except for the omission of the last layer. In the decoder, we made use of 1-D transposed convolutional layers, arranging them in the reverse sequence of those utilized in the encoder, similar to the approach used in the generator. The encoder efficiently utilized PReLU activation functions, with the exception of the final layer, which employed Tanh activation to align with the generator's output. The decoder also adopted PReLU activation for all of its layers, with the exception of the final layer. The concluding layer used a Sigmoid activation function to restrict the output data range to be between [0, 1]. This strategic choice facilitated the reconstruction of discrete data that accurately corresponded to the input data. Importantly, the input size of the decoder was meticulously matched with the output dimension of the GAN generator.

To ensure versatility across diverse datasets, we adeptly tailored the input pipeline of both the GAN discriminator and autoencoder to seamlessly accommodate varying input sizes. Notably, these adjustments enabled smooth adaptability and compatibility. However, it is worth highlighting that no modifications were required for the GAN generator, as we consistently employed a fixed noise dimension throughout all experiments. This approach demonstrated the generator's robustness and autonomy, eliminating the need for additional adaptations.

3.4 Privacy Loss

For precise and efficient privacy loss calculations, we leveraged the advanced RDP privacy accountant [1], surpassing the computational accuracy of conventional DP methods. Proposition 2 proved instrumental in seamlessly converting RDP computations to DP, expanding the applicability of our approach. The technique of adding Gaussian noise, commonly known as the Sampled Gaussian Mechanism (SGM) [21], served as a reliable tool for introducing noise. To effectively monitor and track privacy loss, we relied upon the guidance of the following theorem, ensuring a comprehensive understanding of the privacy landscape.

Theorem 3 (Privacy loss of SGM [21]). *Assume that D and D' are two datasets that differ by only one entry, and let $\mathcal{G}$ be a Sampled Gaussian Mechanism applied to a function f with an l_2 sensitivity of one, then if we define the following:*

$$\mathcal{G}(D) \sim \varphi_1 \triangleq \mathcal{N}(0, \ \sigma^2) \tag{11}$$

$$G(D') \sim \varphi_2 \triangleq (1 \ - \ q)\mathcal{N}(0, \ \sigma^2) \ + \ q\mathcal{N}(1, \ \sigma^2) \tag{12}$$

Assuming φ_1 and φ_2 represent probability density functions, the $(\alpha, \epsilon)-RDP$ privacy requirement is met by G, if the following condition holds:

$$\epsilon \leq \frac{1}{\alpha - 1} log(max \; \{A_\alpha, \; B_\alpha\}) \tag{13}$$

where, $A_\alpha \triangleq \mathbb{E}_{x \sim \varphi_1}[(\frac{\varphi_2}{\varphi_1})^\alpha]$ and $B_\alpha \triangleq \mathbb{E}_{x \sim \varphi_2}[(\frac{\varphi_1}{\varphi_2})^\alpha]$.

Through careful analysis, it has been firmly established that A_α is consistently less than or equal to B_α, effectively simplifying the privacy computations utilizing the RDP framework. This simplified approach strategically focuses on upper bounding A_α, streamlining the privacy calculations. By employing a combination of closed-form bounds and numerical computations, we are able to accurately determine the value of A_α [21]. It should be noted, this method sets a limit on ϵ for each individual step. Nonetheless, to ascertain the cumulative bound of ϵ for the full training procedure, we need to multiply the number of steps by ϵ, in line with what Proposition 1 delineates. For a tighter upper bound assurance, we execute experiments across a range of α values and use the RDP privacy accountant to pinpoint the smallest (ϵ) and its associated α. Finally, Proposition 2 is employed to precisely compute the $(\epsilon, \delta) - DP$, providing a comprehensive measure of privacy.

When combining autoencoder and GAN training, it is important to determine how to calculate the $(\alpha, \epsilon) - RDP$. Proposition 1 examines the specific input and output domains, denoted by $\mathcal{X}$, U_1, and U_2, corresponding to the autoencoder and the discriminator in the given context. Here, the autoencoder is represented by the mechanism $\mathcal{A}$, and the discriminator is represented by the mechanism $\mathcal{B}$. U_1 becomes the output space after the decoder processes the fake samples. Subsequently, the discriminator observes U_1, while the real input space is represented by $\mathcal{X}$. With α held constant, Proposition 1 suggests that the entire system maintains $(\alpha, \epsilon_{vae} + \epsilon_{gan}) - RDP$. Nevertheless, it's not assured that there can be a constant value for α, since the RDP contains a budget constraint that is specified by this variable. To determine a fixed α, we use the following procedure: Consider two systems, S_1 one for the autoencoder with $(\alpha_1, \epsilon_1) - RDP$ and S_2 for the GAN with $(\alpha_2, \epsilon_2) - RDP$. Assuming $\epsilon_1 \leq \epsilon_2$ without any loss of generality, we can choose $\alpha_{total} = \alpha_2$. This results in S_2 having $(\alpha_{total}, \epsilon_2) - RDP$. For the system S_1, we choose $\alpha_{total} = \alpha_1$ and compute ϵ' in a way that ensures $\epsilon \leq \epsilon'$. The entire system, comprised of S_1 and S_2, subsequently meets the $(\alpha_{total}, \epsilon_2 + \epsilon') - RDP$ condition.

4   Experimental Evaluation

In this section, we outline the specifics of the experimental design, convey the results procured from multiple experiments, and perform a comparative analysis with multiple approaches documented in the existing research literature.

The dataset is partitioned into two segments.: D_{tr} for training and D_{te} for testing. We employ D_{tr} for model training, subsequently using these trained models to generate synthesized samples, denoted as D_{syn}. As elaborated in Sect. 3, although the structures may change depending on the size of the dataset, the dimensions of the latent space (also serving as the input space for the decoder) sampled from encoder's output (mean μ and variance σ^2) and the output space of the generator remain unchanged. Likewise, the dimensions of the input space for the encoder, the output space for the decoder, and the input space for the discriminator also remain the same. It's essential to highlight that all stated ϵ values correspond to the definition of $(\epsilon, \delta) - DP$ where $\delta = 10^{-5}$, except when explicitly stated otherwise.

We trained both the Convolutional GAN and the Convolutional Variational Autoencoder with a mini-batch size of 64, using the Adam optimizer [17], and applying a learning rate of 0.005. To enhance the training process, we employed Batch Normalization (BN) [16] for both the discriminator and the generator. A single GeForce RTX 3080 NVIDIA GPU was utilized for our experimental work.

4.1   Datasets

In our research, we utilized two datasets to assess the effectiveness of our model.

- **Early Prediction of Sepsis from Clinical Data (Sepsis)** [26]: The first dataset used in this study was obtained from the publicly available 2019 PhysioNet Challenge. In accordance with the Sepsis III guidelines, the diagnosis of sepsis relies on the identification of a two-point increase in the patient's Sequential Organ Failure Assessment (SOFA) score, along with the presence of clinical signs and symptoms indicating a potential infection. The dataset consists of approximately 40,000 electronic health records of patients admitted to the ICU with suspected or confirmed sepsis. The data was collected from Beth Israel Deaconess Medical Center and Emory University Hospital. Each patient record comprises a time series of clinical measurements taken at 1-hour intervals with a binary label indicating the presence or absence of sepsis at each time point, thereby represented by a single row. The clinical measurements are a set of 40 numerical and categorical attributes that encompass patient demographics, vital signs and laboratory values. Notably, the dataset contains a total of 2,932 septic and 37,404 non-septic patients.
- **Cardiovascular Diseases Dataset** [28]: The second dataset utilized in this study was retrieved from Kaggle. The dataset includes approximately 70,000 records of patients' data with 12 attributes encompassing both numerical and categorical types. The dataset is primarily composed of three types of input features, namely objective features representing patient demographics, results of medical examination conducted at that time and subjective information provided by the patients themselves. The target feature is denoted by a binary value that signifies the presence or absence of cardiovascular disease. Additionally, the dataset demonstrates a well-balanced distribution of male and female records. Similarly, the target feature exhibits a balanced spread of binary values, enhancing the dataset's reliability.

4.2   Comparison

Our model is juxtaposed with two benchmark methods for comparison. The choice of benchmark models hinges on the specific characteristics inherent to the experiments being performed.

DPGAN [31]: This model is capable of generating superior quality data points while maintaining adequate differential privacy safeguards. This is accomplished by injecting carefully engineered noise into the gradients during the learning phase. For this research, we employed an open-source edition of DPGAN.

MedGAN [8]: Structured to generate discrete entries, such as those required for unsupervised synthetic data creation, MedGAN's architecture incorporates an autoencoder and a traditional GAN. However, it does not ensure data privacy. For our experimentation, we used an open-source version of MedGAN.

4.3   Synthetic Data Generation

We opted for electronic health records, which were transformed into a high-dimensional dataset, to illustrate the privacy-protection abilities of our suggested model. In this situation, the data features are comprised of two types: numerical and multi-label. Multi-label features (such as gender categories) are encoded using one-hot encoding. Our aim is to harness the insight relating to a private dataset and utilize it to generate a synthetic dataset that have a comparable distribution while maintaining a commitment to privacy. At first, we aligned our method with various models that neither require labeled data nor rely on it, and are tailored for creating synthetic data in an unsupervised manner, all while continuing to adhere to the principles of privacy preservation. We employed Eq. 10 as the loss function for pretraining the variational autoencoder.

In order to gauge the quality of the artificially generated data in an unsupervised setting, we employed two evaluative metrics:

- Maximum Mean Discrepancy (MMD): This metric shows the magnitude to which the model replicates the statistical distribution acquired from the actual data. Recently, a work [33] underscored that MMD encapsulates many desirable characteristics of an evaluative metric, especially pertinent to GANs. MMD is typically employed in an unsupervised environment due to the absence of labelled data for statistical quantifications. To record MMD, we drew comparisons between two sample sets of real and synthetic data, each comprising 800 entries. Figure 2 shows the comparison of MMD scores obtain from generated and real data distributions from different datasets. A lower MMD score suggests a greater similarity between the synthetic and real data distributions, suggesting a more effective model.
- Dimension-wise Prediction: This evaluation method elucidates the interdependencies among features, in other words, it assesses the model's capability to predict absent features by using the features already present in the dataset. Let's suppose that from D_{tr}, we derive D_{syn}. We then randomly pick one specific dimension (denoted as k) from both D_{syn} and D_{tr}, labeling them

as $D_{syn,k}$ and $D_{tr,k}$ respectively. This chosen dimension is what we refer to as the testing dimension. All the remaining dimensions, namely $D_{syn,nk}$ and $D_{tr,nk}$, serve to train a classifier. The classifier's objective is to anticipate the test set's testing dimension value, represented by $D_{te,k}$. For prediction tasks, the Random Forests algorithm [6] was used. The efficiency of the holistic predictive models (those trained on synthetic data) and across all attributes are presented in terms of the F1-score in Table 1.

From Table 1, it's evident that our proposed model (RDPVAEGAN) has a superior performance in capturing correlated features compared to DPGAN and MedGAN across both datasets. The nearer the outcomes align with real data experiments, the superior the quality of the synthetic data, indicating a more effective model. However, it's worth noting that only RDPVAEGAN and DPGAN provide privacy guarantees as previously mentioned.

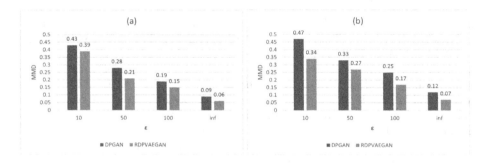

Fig. 2. The analysis of the differences and similarities between the real and the generated distributions. A lower MMD score means a greater similarity between the data distributions. (a) for the Sepsis dataset and (b) for the Cardiovascular Diseases dataset

Table 1. The table illustrates a comparison of different techniques utilizing the F-1 score within the dimension-wise prediction setting. Except for the column labelled "Real Data", classifiers are trained using synthetic data

Dataset	Real Data	DPGAN	MedGAN	RDPVAEGAN
Sepsis	0.53	0.39	0.43	0.45
Cardiovascular Disease	0.49	0.27	0.31	0.38

We've extended our approach to accommodate a supervised environment and create labelled synthetic data as well. All the experiments were carried out, with each one repeated ten times. To assess the models, we provide the average AUROC (Area Under the Receiver Operating Characteristic Curve) and AUPRC (Area Under the Precision-Recall Curve) scores. Table 2 provides the AUROC results, while Table 3 details the AUPRC outcomes. When $\epsilon = \infty$, privacy constraints are not applied. Based on the information in these tables, our model surpasses DPGAN in a supervised setting. Even though MedGAN displays superior results compared to both DPGAN and RDPVAEGAN in terms of AUROC and AUPRC, it does not ensure the privacy of the generated data.

Table 2. This table compares various models in terms of AUROC within the context of the $(1, 10^{-5}) - DP$ setting. For $\epsilon = \infty$, we implemented our RDPVAEGAN model without the privacy enforcement component. MedGAN does not have any privacy enforcement as well. All models were trained utilizing synthetic data

Dataset	$\epsilon = \infty$	DPGAN	MedGAN	RDPVAEGAN
Sepsis	0.86	0.69	0.81	0.75
Cardiovascular Disease	0.77	0.62	0.73	0.70

Table 3. This table compares various models in terms of AUPRC within the context of the $(1, 10^{-5}) - DP$ setting. For $\epsilon = \infty$, we implemented our RDPVAEGAN model without the privacy enforcement component. MedGAN does not have any privacy enforcement as well. All models were trained utilizing synthetic data.

Dataset	$\epsilon = \infty$	DPGAN	MedGAN	RDPVAEGAN
Sepsis	0.83	0.67	0.80	0.76
Cardiovascular Disease	0.76	0.60	0.72	0.68

This discussion outlines the performance of different methods within the framework of DP. The base model is anticipated to yield the highest accuracy. Thus, the primary investigation is: To what extent does the accuracy decrease across different models when keeping the privacy budget (ϵ, δ) at the same level? Tables 2 and 3 illustrate the results for this specific condition. In most experiments, the artificial data generated by our system demonstrates superior quality in classification tasks when contrasted with other models, all while operating under the equal privacy budget.

5   Conclusion

In this research, we formulated and implemented a method for generating synthetic data that maintains differential privacy, making use of Rényi Differential Privacy. The objective of our model was to extract temporal data and feature correlations through the use of convolutional neural networks. The empirical evidence showed that utilizing variational autoencoders allows for effective management of variables, whether they are discrete, continuous, or a blend of the two. We found that our model surpasses other models in performance while operating within the same privacy constraints. This superior performance can be partially attributed to the reporting of a tighter bound, the use of convolutional networks, and the variational autoencoder. We demonstrated the performance of several models in both supervised and unsupervised approaches, utilizing various metrics across two distinct datasets.

Acknowledgements. This project has been partially funded by the BMBF and the European Union (NextGenerationEU) under project number 16KISA001K (PrivacyUmbrella).

References

1. Abadi, M., et al.: Deep learning with differential privacy. In: Proceedings of the 2016 ACM SIGSAC Conference on Computer and Communications Security, pp. 308–318 (2016)
2. Acs, G., Melis, L., Castelluccia, C., De Cristofaro, E.: Differentially private mixture of generative neural networks. IEEE Trans. Knowl. Data Eng. **31**(6), 1109–1121 (2018)
3. Al-Rubaie, M., Chang, J.M.: Privacy-preserving machine learning: threats and solutions. IEEE Secur. Priv. **17**(2), 49–58 (2019)
4. Arjovsky, M., Chintala, S., Bottou, L.: Wasserstein generative adversarial networks. In: International Conference on Machine Learning, pp. 214–223. PMLR (2017)
5. Baowaly, M.K., Lin, C.C., Liu, C.L., Chen, K.T.: Synthesizing electronic health records using improved generative adversarial networks. J. Am. Med. Inform. Assoc. **26**(3), 228–241 (2019)
6. Breiman, L.: Random forests. Mach. Learn. **45**, 5–32 (2001)
7. Chen, J., Chun, D., Patel, M., Chiang, E., James, J.: The validity of synthetic clinical data: a validation study of a leading synthetic data generator (Synthea) using clinical quality measures. BMC Med. Inform. Decis. Mak. **19**(1), 1–9 (2019)
8. Choi, E., Biswal, S., Malin, B., Duke, J., Stewart, W.F., Sun, J.: Generating multi-label discrete patient records using generative adversarial networks. In: Machine Learning for Healthcare Conference, pp. 286–305. PMLR (2017)
9. Dwork, C., Roth, A., et al.: The algorithmic foundations of differential privacy. Found. Trends® Theor. Comput. Sci. **9**(3–4), 211–407 (2014)
10. Goodfellow, I., et al.: Generative adversarial networks. Commun. ACM **63**(11), 139–144 (2020)
11. Guan, J., Li, R., Yu, S., Zhang, X.: Generation of synthetic electronic medical record text. In: 2018 IEEE International Conference on Bioinformatics and Biomedicine (BIBM), pp. 374–380. IEEE (2018)
12. Han, H., Li, Y., Zhu, X.: Convolutional neural network learning for generic data classification. Inf. Sci. **477**, 448–465 (2019)
13. Hayes, J., Melis, L., Danezis, G., De Cristofaro, E.: LOGAN: membership inference attacks against generative models. arXiv preprint arXiv:1705.07663 (2017)

14. He, K., Zhang, X., Ren, S., Sun, J.: Delving deep into rectifiers: surpassing human-level performance on ImageNet classification. In: Proceedings of the IEEE International Conference on Computer Vision, pp. 1026–1034 (2015)
15. Hjelm, R.D., Jacob, A.P., Che, T., Trischler, A., Cho, K., Bengio, Y.: Boundary-seeking generative adversarial networks. arXiv preprint arXiv:1702.08431 (2017)
16. Ioffe, S., Szegedy, C.: Batch normalization: accelerating deep network training by reducing internal covariate shift. In: International Conference on Machine Learning, pp. 448–456. PMLR (2015)
17. Kingma, D.P., Ba, J.: Adam: a method for stochastic optimization. arXiv preprint arXiv:1412.6980 (2014)
18. Kingma, D.P., Welling, M.: Auto-encoding variational bayes. arXiv preprint arXiv:1312.6114 (2013)
19. Kroes, S., van Leeuwen, M., Groenwold, R.H.H., Janssen, M.P.: Generating synthetic mixed discrete-continuous health records with mixed sum-product networks, no. 1, pp. 16–25 (2022)
20. Mironov, I.: Rényi differential privacy. In: 2017 IEEE 30th Computer Security Foundations Symposium (CSF), pp. 263–275. IEEE (2017)
21. Mironov, I., Talwar, K., Zhang, L.: Rényi differential privacy of the sampled gaussian mechanism. arXiv preprint arXiv:1908.10530 (2019)
22. Narayanan, A., Shmatikov, V.: Robust de-anonymization of large sparse datasets. In: 2008 IEEE Symposium on Security and Privacy (SP 2008), pp. 111–125. IEEE (2008)
23. Park, N., Mohammadi, M., Gorde, K., Jajodia, S., Park, H., Kim, Y.: Data synthesis based on generative adversarial networks. arXiv preprint arXiv:1806.03384 (2018)
24. Radford, A., Metz, L., Chintala, S.: Unsupervised representation learning with deep convolutional generative adversarial networks. arXiv preprint arXiv:1511.06434 (2015)
25. Rényi, A.: On measures of entropy and information. In: Proceedings of the Fourth Berkeley Symposium on Mathematical Statistics and Probability, Volume 1: Contributions to the Theory of Statistics, vol. 4, pp. 547–562. University of California Press (1961)
26. Reyna, M.A., et al.: Early prediction of sepsis from clinical data: the PhysioNet/computing in cardiology challenge 2019. In: 2019 Computing in Cardiology (CinC), pp. Page-1. IEEE (2019)
27. Shokri, R., Shmatikov, V.: Privacy-preserving deep learning. In: Proceedings of the 22nd ACM SIGSAC Conference on Computer and Communications Security, pp. 1310–1321 (2015)
28. Ulianova, S.: Cardiovascular disease dataset (2019). https://www.kaggle.com/datasets/sulianova/cardiovascular-disease-dataset
29. Villani, C.: Grundlehren der mathematischen wissenschaften (2008)
30. Walonoski, J., et al.: Synthea: an approach, method, and software mechanism for generating synthetic patients and the synthetic electronic health care record. J. Am. Med. Inform. Assoc. 25(3), 230–238 (2018)
31. Xie, L., Lin, K., Wang, S., Wang, F., Zhou, J.: Differentially private generative adversarial network. arXiv preprint arXiv:1802.06739 (2018)
32. Xu, L., Skoularidou, M., Cuesta-Infante, A., Veeramachaneni, K.: Modeling tabular data using conditional GAN. In: Advances in Neural Information Processing Systems, vol. 32 (2019)
33. Xu, Q., et al.: An empirical study on evaluation metrics of generative adversarial networks. arXiv preprint arXiv:1806.07755 (2018)

Balanced Privacy Budget Allocation for Privacy-Preserving Machine Learning

Bingchang He[(✉)] [ID] and Atsuko Miyaji [ID]

Graduate School of Engineering, Osaka University, Suita, Japan
he@cy2sec.comm.eng.osaka-u.ac.jp, miyaji@comm.eng.osaka-u.ac.jp

Abstract. The preservation of privacy during the learning phase of machine learning is challenging. There are two methods to achieve privacy-preserving machine learning: adding noise to machine-learning model parameters, which is often selected for its higher accuracy; and executing learning using noisy data, which is preferred for privacy. Recently, a Scalable Unified Privacy-preserving Machine learning framework (SUPM) has been proposed, which controls the balance between privacy and accuracy by harmonizing the privacy mechanisms used in dimension reduction, training and testing phases. This paper proposes a novel method that allocates privacy budgets according to their effectiveness that improves the accuracy without sacrificing the number of available attributes. Our privacy budget allocation algorithm can be applied into SUPM and improve the accuracy while keeping the privacy. We evaluate its performance using logistic regression and support vector machines as machine learning algorithms. SUPM using our privacy budget allocation algorithm is effective in terms of accuracy and the number of available attributes. We also clarify the conditions under which our method is more effective for a given dataset.

Keywords: local differential privacy · dimension reduction · odds ratio

1 Introduction

Machine learning is a powerful technique that is used to extract useful insights from large and complex datasets. However, the application of machine learning to sensitive data, such as personal or medical information, poses serious privacy risks. One approach for preserving privacy is to de-identify data [2], safeguarding individuals' privacy by processing the data or data parameters. These studies focus on differential privacy, particularly to counteract complex attacks on machine learning models [3]. Differential privacy mechanisms can be centralized or localized. Centralized mechanisms build models using raw data, but with the addition of noise to parameters during the learning phase, as shown in Fig. 1.

Localized mechanisms enable each data owner to add noise to their own data, and use noisy data instead of raw data to build models, as shown in Fig. 2.

In many cases, the centralized method is chosen because achieving high accuracy with the localized method is difficult. However, the centralized method is

ⓒ The Author(s), under exclusive license to Springer Nature Switzerland AG 2023
E. Athanasopoulos and B. Mennink (Eds.): ISC 2023, LNCS 14411, pp. 42–56, 2023.
https://doi.org/10.1007/978-3-031-49187-0_3

① Each data owner sends raw privacy data to machine learning model trainer.

② Trainer trains the model using raw data and add noise to model parameters.

Fig. 1. Collect raw data and add noise when building models (centralized differential privacy mechanism)

① Each data owner add noise to their own privacy data and sends noise-added data to machine learning model trainer.

② Trainer trains the model using noisy data.

Fig. 2. Collect noise-added data and build models (local differential privacy mechanism)

inferior in terms of privacy because it sends all raw data to an entity that executes the learning phase. In contrast, the localized methods, those which execute learning using noisy data, can deal with privacy well, but controlling reasonable accuracy using multiple attributes while maintaining privacy is not easy. Local differential privacy (LDP) has been proposed and applied to the parameters of federated learning as a localized differential privacy mechanism in [10]. Although a privacy-preserving dimension reduction using PCA is based on LDP in [9], it cannot achieve a balance between privacy and performance in combination with the training and testing phases. Recently, a Scalable Unified Privacy-preserving Machine learning framework (SUPM) has been proposed, which controls both privacy and accuracy by dealing with the dimension reduction, training and testing phases separately [5,6]. SUPM harmonizes and controls privacy mechanisms used in the three phases to enhance not only privacy but also performance. They also proposed a unified, data-independent anonymization algorithm WALDP to control the performance and privacy of machine learning, where the data is first normalized and converted to discrete values (i.e. WA) and then randomized response noise is added. To effectively decide the attributes used for training and testing, three privacy-preserving dimension reduction algorithms have also been proposed: correlation coefficient with WA and WALDP [5], and odds ratio with WALDP [6].

In this study, we propose a novel method for allocating the privacy budget to each attribute in a more efficient manner when applying the LDP mechanism with dimension reduction based on odds ratio (OR). Since SUPM uses the same privacy budget for attributes selected for dimension reduction phase and executes training and testing phases, it may cause degradation of accuracy. Our purpose for the privacy budget allocation is to increase the number of available attributes as much as possible with the same overall privacy budget and improve performance. Our method, which is called balanced privacy budget allocation (BPBA), considers the effectiveness of each attribute with respect to the target attribute and assigns a higher privacy budget to the attributes that have a greater impact on the target attribute rather than treating each attribute equally. In this way, we can preserve more attributes of the data while keeping privacy budget small; moreover, it improves accuracy. We apply BPBA into the training and testing phases in SUPM and propose a new privacy-reserving machine learning workflow, BPP.ML. We evaluate its performance by conducting experiments on two datasets from the UCI Machine Learning Repository using logistic regression and support vector machine as machine learning algorithms from the point of view of accuracy, privacy budget, and the number of attributes. We have experimentally shown that our method can utilize more attributes and achieve better accuracy while keeping the same privacy budget. From our experimental results, we expect to be able to control privacy and accuracy more smoothly in datasets where more attributes are desired. We also analyzed the dependence of the BPP.ML performance on the characteristics of the datasets and the number of selected attributes.

The remainder of this paper is organized as follows. Section 2 introduces the preliminary concepts and notations. Section 3 reviews related works on privacy-preserving machine learning with LDP and dimension reduction. Section 4 presents the proposed method BPBA and workflow BPP.ML. Then, Sect. 5 presents the experimental results and analysis. Finally, Sect. 6 concludes the paper and discusses future work.

2   Preliminary

2.1   Notation

The notation used in this study is as follows:

- LDP(DP): local differential privacy (differential privacy)
- RR: randomized response mechanism
- Agg: aggregator
- n: total number of records
- m: total number of attributes for one data (i.e., dimension)

- K: number of explanatory attributes selected from $m - 1$ explanatory attributes
- L: number of setting classes of attributes
- TA: target attribute, which should be binary
- A_j: j-th (continuous/discrete) explanatory attributes ($j \in [1, m-1]$) (excluding TA). Assume that A_j has L classes of $\{A_j [1], \cdots , A_j[L]\}$ if it is discrete, or is normalized in $[-1, 1]$ if continuous.
- D, D_i: record, i-th record, $i = 1, \cdots , n$, which consists of m attributes, $D_i = [D_{i,1}, \cdots , D_{i,m-1}, TA_i]$
- $D_{i,j}$: j-th attribute of i-th record D_i ($j \in [1, m - 1]$)
- ta_i: target attribute of D_i
- ϵ_j: privacy budget for j-th explanatory attribute
- ϵ_{TA}: privacy budget for target attribute
- ϵ: privacy budget for one record, which has $\epsilon = \epsilon_{TA} + \sum \epsilon_j$
- $A_{j_1}, \cdots , A_{j_K}$: selected attributes
- $WA_j [1], \cdots , WA_j[L]$: WA-transformed A_j's data

2.2 Local Differential Privacy

Local differential privacy [1], where each data owner uses a random noise function $f(D_i)$, is defined in Definition 1.

Definition 1. *For every possible input combination x, x' of the function f, $\Pr[f(x) = y] \leq \exp(\epsilon) \cdot \Pr[f(x') = y]$, f satisfies ϵ-local differential privacy.*

The randomized response (RR) mechanism [4] is a random noise function that satisfies the local differential privacy for discrete values, and is given by Algorithm 1. The input x and output y take L kinds of values as well, and

---

Algorithm 1. Randomized response mechanism (RR) [4]

Require: discrete value x_j, number of classes L, privacy budget ϵ
Ensure: perturbed data y_j
 1: Sample x uniformly at random from $[0, 1]$
 2: **if** $x \leq \frac{\exp(\epsilon)}{L-1+\exp(\epsilon)}$ **then**
 3:     $y_j = x_j$
 4: **else**
 5:     Sample y_j uniformly at random from $\{1, \cdots , L\}$ except x_j
 6: **end if**
 7: **return** y_j

---

the output value is equal to or different from the original value with probability $\frac{\exp(\epsilon)}{n-1+\exp(\epsilon)}$ or $\frac{n}{n-1+\exp(\epsilon)}$, respectively. The RR mechanism adds noise as follows:

$$p(y \mid x) = \begin{cases} \frac{\exp(\epsilon)}{L-1+\exp(\epsilon)}, & \text{if } y = x, \\ \frac{1}{L-1+\exp(\epsilon)}, & \text{if } y \neq x. \end{cases}$$

2.3   Classification Methods Using Machine Learning

Logistic Regression is an algorithm that fits a logistic model, and takes explanatory variables $\mathbf{x}_{n \times m}$ and target variable $\mathbf{y}_{n \times 1}$ as inputs and outputs a weight vector, where n represents the number of records. Logistic models are used to statistically model the probability of the occurrence of an event. Logistic regression is used to estimate the parameters of the logistic model, which has the following form:

$$p(\mathbf{x}_{1 \times m}) = \frac{1}{1 + \exp\left(-\left(w_0 + \mathbf{w}_{1 \times m}\mathbf{x}_{1 \times m}^{\mathsf{T}}\right)\right)},$$

where m represents the number of attributes, $\mathbf{x}_{1 \times m}$ is a vector of explanatory variables, and $\mathbf{w}_{1 \times m}$ is a weight vector. In the logistic model, w_j is defined as the *log-odds* of attribute A_j; thus, $\mathbf{w}$ is also a vector of log-odds. A logistic model can be used to predict the target variable y (which must be binary) as follows:

$$y = \begin{cases} 1, & p(\mathbf{x}) \geq 0.5, \\ 0, & p(\mathbf{x}) < 0.5. \end{cases}$$

For reproducibility, all logistic regression algorithms in this study use the implementation by scikit-learn [7]. Let LR denote such logistic regression algorithm, which takes the data of explanatory attributes $\mathbf{x}_{n \times m}$ and the data of target attribute $\mathbf{y}_{n \times 1}$ as input, and outputs the weight vector $\mathbf{w} = \{w_1, \cdots, w_m\}$.

Support Vector Machine (SVM) is an algorithm that finds a hyperplane that separates the data into different classes such that the margin between the hyperplane and closest data points is maximized. The decision function for a binary classification problem is given by

$$f(\mathbf{x}) = \mathrm{sgn}\left(\sum_{i=1}^{n} \alpha_i y_i K(\mathbf{x}_i, \mathbf{x}) + b\right),$$

where $\mathbf{x}$ denotes the input vector, y_i the target attribute of the ith record, α_i the Lagrange multiplier associated with the ith record, $K(\mathbf{x}_i, \mathbf{x})$ the kernel function that maps the input vectors into a higher-dimensional space, b the bias term, and n the total number of records.

SVM can handle both linear and nonlinear classification problems using different kernel functions such as polynomials, radial basis functions (RBF), or sigmoids. In this study, we used RBF as the kernel function, and it is defined as

$$K(x_i, x) = \exp\left(-\gamma \left\|x_i - x\right\|^2\right),$$

where γ is a parameter that controls the shape of the kernel.

3   Related Work

In machine learning, models are constructed by establishing mappings between explanatory and target attributes. The private data of individuals maybe used for model training and testing. If the data owner does not want to provide their raw data to either entity who constructs a training model or tests the training model, it is necessary for the owner to generate LDP data by adding noise to the raw data.

Generally, data used in machine learning consists of multiple attributes. Some attributes are continuous values, while others are discrete values. In this section, we review the previous unified, data-independent anonymization algorithms WA and WALDP, and the privacy-preserving machine learning framework SUPM proposed in [5].

3.1   Unified LDP-Algorithm

WALDP can effectively control the privacy and accuracy of machine learning using two parameters, ϵ and WA-parameter (K, L), as shown in Algorithm 2.

Algorithm 2. Unified LDP-Mechanism (WALDP)

Require: data $D_{i,j}$ of attribute A_j, $\min(A_j)$, $\max(A_j)$, number of classes L, privacy budget ϵ

Ensure: noisy data $\mathcal{D}_{i,j}$

 1: $D_{std} \leftarrow (D_{i,j} - \min(A_j)/(\max(A_j) - \min(A_j))$
 2: $D_{scaled} \leftarrow 2D_{std} - 1$ ▷ scale data to $[-1, 1]$
 3: $class\_index \leftarrow$ None
 4: $class\_mid \leftarrow [\,]$
 5: **for** $i = 1$ **to** L **do**   ▷ find the class where D_{scaled} is located
 6:     $class\_min \leftarrow -1 + 2i/L$
 7:     $class\_max \leftarrow -1 + 2(i+1)/L$
 8:     $class\_mid[i] \leftarrow (class\_min + class\_max)/2$
 9:     **if** $class\_min \leq D_{scaled} \leq class\_max$ **then**
10:         $class\_index \leftarrow i$
11:     **end if**
12: **end for**
13: $noisy\_class\_index \leftarrow$ RR$(class\_index, L, \epsilon)$ ▷ add some randomized response
14: **return** $class\_mid[noisy\_class\_index]$

3.2   Scalable Unified Privacy-Preserving Machine Learning Framework (SUPM)

To control the privacy and accuracy of machine learning, where perturbed data is used for both training and testing phases, the most difficult issue is to deal with the number of attributes. From the perspective of privacy, given the privacy budget for each attribute ε and the total number of attributes m, the privacy budget for a single record becomes $m\varepsilon$. The larger the number of attributes, the more privacy is wasted. To deal with such an issue, SUPM executes privacy-preserving dimension reduction first, then execute training and testing using

---

Algorithm 3. Computation of odds ratio with missing values (LR.OR.MV)

Require: $\mathbf{x}$: data of explanatory attributes $\mathbf{x}_{n \times m}$ with missing values; $\mathbf{y}$: data of target attribute $\mathbf{y}_{n \times 1}$.

Ensure: odds ratio $\mathsf{OR}_1, \cdots, \mathsf{OR}_m$ between each attributes $A_1, \cdots, A_m$ and target attribute TA.

1: **for** $j = 1$ **to** m **do**
2:     $\mathbf{x}' \leftarrow [], \mathbf{y}' \leftarrow []$
3:     **for** $i = 1$ **to** n **do**
4:         **if** $D_{i,j} \neq \mathsf{null}$ **then**
5:             $\mathbf{x}'$.append($\{D_{i,j}\}$), $\mathbf{y}'$.append(ta_i)
6:         **end if**
7:     **end for**
8:     $\{w_j\} \leftarrow \mathsf{LR}(\mathbf{x}', \mathbf{y}')$.
9: **end for**
10: **return** $\{e^{w_1}, \cdots, e^{w_m}\}$

Algorithm 4. Dimension reduction using odds ratio (DR.OR)

Require: m-dimension raw data $\mathsf{D} = [D_{i,1}, \cdots, D_{i,m-1}, \mathsf{TA}_i]$, $\min(A_j)$, Range_j, number of setting classes of attribute L, number of used attribute K, privacy budget ϵ

Ensure: selected attributes $A_{j_1}, \cdots, A_{j_K}$

1: Sample K values of $(D_{i,j_1}, \cdots, D_{i,j_K})$ and target attribute $\mathsf{TA}_i \in \{-1, 1\}$ uniformly.
2: $\epsilon_{j_s} \leftarrow \epsilon/(K + 1)$ for $s = 1, \cdots, K$.
3: $\{y_{j_s}\} \leftarrow \{\mathsf{WALDP}(D_{i,j_s}, \min(A_{j_s}), \max(A_{j_s}), L, \epsilon_{j_s})\}$ for $s = 1, \cdots, K$.
4: $\{y_t\} \leftarrow \{y_{j_s}$ if $\exists j_s = t$ else $\mathsf{null}\}$ for $t = 1, \cdots, m$.
5: $y_{m+1} \leftarrow \mathsf{WALDP}(\mathsf{TA}_i, -1, 1, 2, \epsilon/(K + 1))$.
6: Send $\{y_1, \cdots, y_m, y_{m+1}\}$ to Agg.
7: Agg collects perturbed parts of data without seeing any raw data:
8: **if** received data $\{y_1, \cdots, y_m, y_{m+1}\}$ **then**
9:     $\mathbf{x}$.append($\{y_1, \cdots, y_m\}$).
10:     $\mathbf{y}$.append(y_{m+1}).
11: **end if**
12: $\{\mathsf{OR}_1, \cdots, \mathsf{OR}_m\} \leftarrow \mathsf{LR.OR.MV}(\mathbf{x}, \mathbf{y})$.
13: $\{w_1, \cdots, w_m\} \leftarrow \{\ln(\mathsf{OR}_1), \cdots, \ln(\mathsf{OR}_m)\}$.
14: $\{\ell_1, \cdots, \ell_K\} \leftarrow \mathrm{argmax}_K(|w_1|, \cdots, |w_m|)$
15: **return** K attribute $A_{\ell_1}, \cdots, A_{\ell_K}$

---

selected attributes. In Algorithm 3, we show LR.OR.MV for computing odds ratios with missing values and show DR.OR in Algorithm 4 for the dimension reduction [6]. Remark that SUPM considers the privacy also in the dimension reduction phase, so that WALDP is used as a subroutine in DR.OR.

WALDP is also used as a subroutine for the training and testing phases, which is denoted by PPTraining and PPTesting. Algorithms 5 and 6 respectively represent PPTraining and PPTesting when WALDP is used.

Algorithm 5. Privacy-preserving training (PPTraining)

Require: K data and target data $[D_{i,j_1}, \cdots, D_{i,j_K}, ta_i]$ for each training record D_i, number of setting classes of attribute L, privacy budget ϵ

Ensure: training model

1: **for each** training record D_i **do** ▷ locally executed by i-th data provider
2: $\epsilon_j \leftarrow \epsilon/(K+1)$ for $j = j_1, \cdots, j_K$.
3: $\epsilon_{\mathsf{TA}} \leftarrow \epsilon/(K+1)$.
4: $y_j \leftarrow \mathsf{WALDP}(D_{i,j}, \min(A_j), \max(A_j), L, \epsilon_j)$ for $j = j_1, \cdots, j_K$.
5: $y_{j_{K+1}} \leftarrow \mathsf{WALDP}(ta_i, -1, 1, 2, \epsilon_{\mathsf{TA}})$.
6: Send $(K+1)$-tuple perturbed data to Agg.
7: **end for**
8: Agg collects perturbed $K+1$ data and constructs training model.
9: **return** training model.

Algorithm 6. Privacy-preserving testing (PPTesting)

Require: K data and target data $[D_{i,j_1}, \cdots, D_{i,j_K}, ta_i]$ for each testing record D_i, number of setting classes of attribute L, privacy budget ϵ

Ensure: results.

1: **for each** testing record D_i **do** ▷ locally executed by i-th data provider
2: $\epsilon_j \leftarrow \epsilon/(K+1)$ for $j = j_1, \cdots, j_K$.
3: $\epsilon_{\mathsf{TA}} \leftarrow \epsilon/(K+1)$.
4: $y_j \leftarrow \mathsf{WALDP}(D_{i,s}, \min(A_s), \max(A_s), \epsilon_j)$ for $j = j_1, \cdots, j_K$.
5: $y_{j_{K+1}} \leftarrow \mathsf{WALDP}(ta_i, -1, 1, 2, \epsilon_{\mathsf{TA}})$.
6: Send $(K+1)$-tuple perturbed data to training model.
7: **end for**
8: Training model executes perturbed data and gets the results.
9: **return** results.

---

4 Contribution-Based Privacy-Budget Allocation

In this section, we demonstrate the privacy budget allocation to each attribute considering its contribution to the target attribute when adding noise to the data, and we propose a modified version of a privacy-preserving machine learning workflow called BPP.ML, which fully utilizes the overall privacy budget.

4.1 Contribution-Based Dimension Reduction Using Odds Ratio

The OR of the explanatory attribute A_j is defined in [6] as e^{w_j}, where w_j is the log-odds (defined in Sect. 2.3) of A_j in the logistic model; hence, $w_j = \ln(\mathsf{OR}_j)$. For clarity, we call the log-odds w_j the weight of the attribute, A_j. The dimension-reduction algorithm DR.OR determines the attributes used in machine learning by computing the odds ratio OR_j between each explanatory attribute A_j and target attribute TA, and by selecting K attributes with the largest absolute value of weight $|w_j|$, $j \in [1, m-1]$. Weights are used not only for dimension reduction but also when adding noise. Instead of assigning $\epsilon_j = \epsilon/(K+1)$ to each attribute, we add weights to the privacy budget assigned to each attribute, which is divided into explanatory and target attributes. We define a contribution-based privacy budget allocation in Definition 2:

Definition 2. *For the given data* $\{x_1, \cdots, x_K\}$ *of* K *explanatory attributes* $\{A_j\}$ *and data ta for the target attribute* TA*, let each weight* w_j *of the logistic regression* LR(x_j, ta)*. Then, for a given privacy budget* ϵ*, we define the balanced allocation of contribution-based privacy budgets for the explanatory and target attributes as follows:*

$$\epsilon_j = \frac{K}{K+1} \cdot \frac{w_j}{\sum_{\ell=1}^{K} w_\ell} \cdot \epsilon,$$

$$\epsilon_{\mathsf{TA}} = \frac{\epsilon}{K+1},$$

respectively.

Definition 2 implies that the attributes that are most associated with the target attributes will have the greatest allocation of the privacy budget so that the data will retain as many features as possible, even when there are many attributes.

In order to use weights in the training and testing phases, we need to additionally return the weights of each attribute in the dimension reduction phase. Here we extend Algorithm 4 as Algorithm 7 to output the weight of each selected attribute.

Algorithm 7. Contribution-based dimension reduction using odds ratio (C.DR.OR)

Require: m-dimension raw data D $= [D_{i,1}, \cdots, D_{i,m-1}, \mathsf{TA}_i]$, $\min(A_j)$, Range$_j$, number of setting classes of attribute L, number of used attribute K, privacy budget ϵ

Ensure: selected attributes and corresponding weights $(A_{j_1}, w_{j_1}), \cdots, (A_{j_K}, w_{j_K})$

1: Sample K values of $(D_{i,j_1}, \cdots, D_{i,j_K})$ and target attribute $\mathsf{TA}_i \in \{-1, 1\}$ uniformly.
2: $\epsilon_{j_s} \leftarrow \epsilon/(K+1)$ for $s = 1, \cdots, K$.
3: $\{y_{j_s}\} \leftarrow \{\mathsf{WALDP}(D_{i,j_s}, \min(A_{j_s}), \max(A_{j_s}), L, \epsilon_{j_s}\}$ for $s = 1, \cdots, K$.
4: $\{y_t\} \leftarrow \{y_{j_s}$ if $\exists j_s = t$ else null$\}$ for $t = 1, \cdots, m$.
5: $y_{m+1} \leftarrow \mathsf{WALDP}(\mathsf{TA}_i, -1, 1, 2, \epsilon/(K+1))$.
6: Send $\{y_1, \cdots, y_m, y_{m+1}\}$ to Agg.
7: Agg collects perturbed parts of data without seeing any raw data:
8: **if** received data $\{y_1, \cdots, y_m, y_{m+1}\}$ **then**
9:     x.append($\{y_1, \cdots, y_m\}$).
10:     y.append(y_{m+1}).
11: **end if**
12: $\{\mathsf{OR}_1, \cdots, \mathsf{OR}_m\} \leftarrow \mathsf{LR.OR.MV}(\mathbf{x}, \mathbf{y})$.
13: $\{w_1, \cdots, w_m\} \leftarrow \{\ln(\mathsf{OR}_1), \cdots, \ln(\mathsf{OR}_m)\}$.
14: $\{\ell_1, \cdots, \ell_K\} \leftarrow \mathrm{argmax}_K(|w_1|, \cdots, |w_m|)$
15: **return** K attribute and weight tuples $(A_{\ell_1}, w_{\ell_1}), \cdots, (A_{\ell_K}, w_{\ell_K})$

4.2   Privacy-Preserving Machine Learning with Balanced Privacy Budget Allocation

We defined a contribution-based privacy budget allocation in Definition 2. As it may not be the only method of allocation, we abstract the contribution-based privacy budget allocation to the AllocateEpsilon algorithm as defined in Algorithm 8, which will be invoked as a subroutine in privacy-preserving training and testing.

Algorithm 8. Contribution-based privacy budget allocation (AllocateEpsilon)

Require: number of selected attributes K, weights of K attributes $[w_{j_1}, \cdots, w_{j_K}]$, privacy budget ϵ
Ensure: privacy budget for each explanatory and target attribute $\epsilon_{j_1}, \cdots, \epsilon_{j_K}, \epsilon_{\mathsf{TA}}$
1: **for** $j = j_1, \cdots, j_K$ **do**
2:     $\epsilon_j = \frac{K}{K+1} \frac{w_j}{\sum_{\ell=1}^{K} w_\ell} \epsilon$
3: **end for**
4: $\epsilon_{\mathsf{TA}} \leftarrow \epsilon/(K+1)$
5: **return** $\epsilon_{j_1}, \cdots, \epsilon_{j_K}, \epsilon_{\mathsf{TA}}$

Based on the previous privacy-preserving training and testing algorithms PPTraining and PPTesting defined in Algorithms 5 and 6, we formally propose privacy-preserving training and testing algorithms with balanced privacy budget allocations BPPTraining and BPPTesting which use the output of C.DR.OR as input, as defined in Algorithms 9 and 10.

Algorithm 9. Balanced privacy-preserving training (BPPTraining)

Require: K data and target data $[D_{i,j_1}, \cdots, D_{i,j_K}, ta_i]$ for each training record D_i, weights of K attributes $[w_{j_1}, \cdots, w_{j_K}]$, number of setting classes of attribute L, privacy budget ϵ
Ensure: training model
1: $\epsilon_{j_1}, \cdots, \epsilon_{j_K}, \epsilon_{\mathsf{TA}} \leftarrow$ AllocateEpsilon$(K, [w_{j_1}, \cdots, w_{j_K}], \epsilon)$
2: **for each** training record D_i **do**   ▷ locally executed by i-th data provider
3:     **for** $j = j_1, \cdots, j_K$ **do**
4:         $y_j \leftarrow$ WALDP$(D_{i,j}, \min(A_j), \max(A_j), L, \epsilon_j)$
5:     **end for**
6:     $y_{j_{K+1}} \leftarrow$ WALDP$(ta_i, -1, 1, 2, \epsilon_{\mathsf{TA}})$.
7:     Send $(K+1)$-tuple perturbed data to Agg.
8: **end for**
9: Agg collects perturbed $K+1$ data and constructs training model.
10: **return** training model.

In Sect. 5, we will compare the performances of PP.ML and BPP.ML using noise-added dimension reduction based on the odds ratios DR.OR. This performance comparison reflects the usefulness of a balanced privacy budget allocation with a relatively small overall privacy budget ϵ and more explanatory attributes.

Algorithm 10. Balanced privacy-preserving testing (BPPTesting)

Require: K data and target data $[D_{i,j_1}, \cdots, D_{i,j_K}, ta_i]$ for each testing record D_i, weights of K attributes $[w_{j_1}, \cdots, w_{j_K}]$, number of setting classes of attribute L, privacy budget ϵ

Ensure: results.

1: $\epsilon_{j_1}, \cdots, \epsilon_{j_K}, \epsilon_{\mathsf{TA}} \leftarrow \mathsf{AllocateEpsilon}(K, [w_{j_1}, \cdots, w_{j_K}], \epsilon)$
2: **for each** testing record D_i **do**   ▷ locally executed by i-th data provider
3:      **for** $j = j_1, \cdots, j_K$ **do**
4:          $y_j \leftarrow \mathsf{WALDP}(x_{i,j}, \min(A_j), \max(A_j), L, \epsilon_j)$
5:      **end for**
6:      $y_{j_{K+1}} \leftarrow \mathsf{WALDP}(\mathsf{TA}_i, -1, 1, 2, \epsilon_{\mathsf{TA}})$,
7:      Send $(K+1)$-tuple perturbed data to training model.
8: **end for**
9: Training model executes perturbed data and gets the results.
10: **return** results.

5 Experiments Analysis

In this section, we experimentally confirm how the proposed BPP.ML can increase the number of attributes while keeping high accuracy. We also compare our BPP.ML to the previous PP.ML from the point of view of accuracy and the number of available attributes while keeping the privacy.

5.1 Experiment Settings

This study used two datasets from the UCI Machine Learning Repository: Breast Cancer Wisconsin (Diagnostic) (WDBC) [11] and Ionosphere (Ionosphere) [8]. The WDBC dataset contains 30 continuous features and one categorical target, whereas the Ionosphere dataset contains 34 continuous features and one categorical target.

We   used   logistic   regression   (LR)   and   support   vector machines (SVM) as machine learning algorithms in PPTraining/PPTesting and BPPTraining/BPPTesting. Both algorithms were implemented by invoking the classifier of the scikit-learn [7] machine learning library (version 1.2.1). We set some initial parameters as follows and left the others as defaults.

```
LogisticRegression(random_state=0, max_iter=10000,)    # LR
SVC(random_state=0, max_iter=10000,)                    # SVM
```

For each machine learning algorithm, we evaluated the accuracy of the two frameworks with a fixed ϵ and each $K \in [2,10] \cap \mathbb{Z}$ for WDBC and $[2,11] \cap \mathbb{Z}$ for Ionosphere. For each K_i, the accuracy is defined as the maximum score with (K_i, L), where the number of classes L takes each integer in $[2,5] \cap \mathbb{Z}$. To confirm the performance of the proposed BPP.ML with a relatively small overall privacy budget, we set $\epsilon = 5$ in the PPTraining and BPPTraining phases. To clearly confirm the performance of the trained model on data with and without noise, in both the PPTesting and BPPTesting phases, we also conducted experiments for $\epsilon = 10000$ in addition to $\epsilon = 5$ to simulate weak anonymization WA.

5.2 Logistic Regression

The results of the evaluation using logistic regression on WDBC and Ionosphere data sets are shown in Figs. 3 and 4, respectively.

The experimental results show that for a relatively small ϵ, the proposed BPP.ML performs better than PP.ML. Furthermore, with an increased K, the performance advantage of BPP.ML continues to increase. This enables privacy-preserving machine learning frameworks to achieve better performance when the dataset has more attributes without increasing the privacy budget.

In Figs. 3 and 4, the accuracy shows a different tendency as K increases. This indicates that although our method is better than PP.ML in general, it performs differently for different datasets. We collected the weights $w_1, \cdots, w_k$ that were output from C.DR.OR for the two datasets, and computed the variance of their absolute values $|w_1|, \cdots, |w_k|$ to learn their distributions. The results show that the attribute weights of the Ionosphere dataset have a variance of 0.397, which is significantly lower than that of the WDBC dataset, which has a

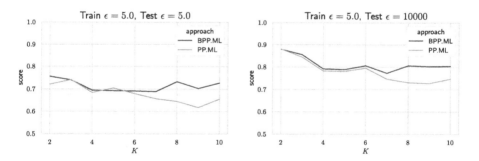

Fig. 3. Accuracy of model trained by LR in BPP.ML and PP.ML on WDBC dataset with different K

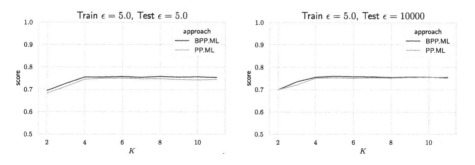

Fig. 4. Accuracy of model trained by LR in BPP.ML and PP.ML on Ionosphere dataset with different K

variance of 8.829. This indicates that the performance advantage of our proposed method is greater when the attribute weights are unevenly distributed, whereas the performance is slightly better than PP.ML when the attribute weights are more evenly distributed.

5.3 Support Vector Machine

The evaluation results obtained using SVM on WDBC and Ionosphere datasets are shown in Figs. 5 and 6.

The experimental results do not differ significantly from those in Sect. 5.2. For the same privacy budget, BPP.ML outperformed PP.ML. The performance advantage is more significant for more selected attributes (i.e., K) if the attribute weights are unevenly distributed. This indicates that our method also performs well without using LR as a machine learning algorithm.

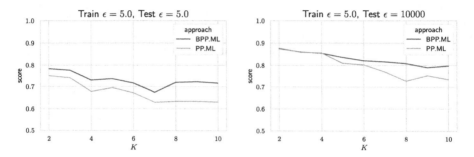

Fig. 5. Accuracy of model trained by SVM in BPP.ML and PP.ML on WDBC dataset with different K

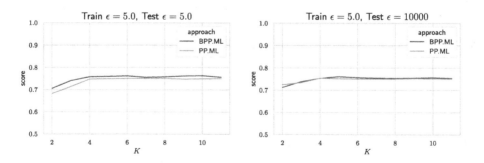

Fig. 6. Accuracy of model trained by SVM in BPP.ML and PP.ML on Ionosphere dataset with different K

6   Conclusion

This study proposed a new method for the allocation of the overall privacy budget to each attribute for privacy-preserving machine learning frameworks, and confirmed the effectiveness of the privacy-preserving machine learning framework for LR and SVM with this mechanism, BPP.ML, based on WALDP with DR.OR. The proposed mechanism allocates the privacy budget to each attribute considering its weight to the target; thus, the mechanism shows better performance with a small ϵ and large number of attributes. Our proposed allocation mechanism has been abstracted as AllocateEpsilon algorithm to facilitate future research to come up with better algorithms.

We further confirmed the performance advantage of learning models using WALDP-data in tests with both WALDP-data and weakly anonymized WA-data.

We also observe that the proposed BPP.ML almost certainly results in a performance improvement compared to PP.ML, but the degree of performance improvement depends on the characteristics of the dataset. When there is a significant difference in the weights of the individual attributes with respect to the target attribute, our method leads to a more substantial performance improvement. However, for small weight differences, the performance improvement is relatively modest.

Acknowledgements. This work is partially supported by JSPS KAKENHI Grant Number JP21H03443 and SECOM Science and Technology Foundation.

References

1. Duchi, J.C., Jordan, E.: Local privacy and statistical minimax rates. In: 54th Annual Symposium on Foundations of Computer Science, pp. 429–438. IEEE (2013)
2. Feng, J., Yang, L.T., Nie, X., Gati, N.J.: Edge-cloud-aided differentially private tucker decomposition for cyber-physical-social systems. IEEE Internet Things J. **9**(11), 8387–8396 (2020)
3. Hu, H., Salcic, Z., Sun, L., Dobbie, E.: Membership inference attacks on machine learning: a survey. ACM Comput. Surv. (CSUR) **54**, 1–37 (2021)
4. Kairouz, P., Oh, S., Viswanath, P.: Extremal mechanisms for local differential privacy. In: Ghahramani, Z., Welling, M., Cortes, C., Lawrence, N., Weinberger, K. (eds.) Advances in Neural Information Processing Systems, vol. 27. Curran Associates, Inc. (2014)
5. Miyaji, A., Takahashi, T., Wang, P., Yamatsuki, T., Mimoto, T.: Privacy-preserving data analysis without trusted third party. In: IEEE International Conference on Trust, Security and Privacy in Computing and Communications, TrustCom 2022, pp. 710–717. IEEE (2022)
6. Miyaji, A., Yamatsuki, T., He, B., Yamashita, S., Mimoto, T.: Re-visited privacy-preserving machine learning. In: International Conference on Privacy, Security & Trust, PST 2023. IEEE (2023)
7. Pedregosa, F., et al.: Scikit-learn: machine learning in python. J. Mach. Learn. Res. **12**(85), 2825–2830 (2011). http://jmlr.org/papers/v12/pedregosa11a.html

8. Sigillito, V., Wing, S., Hutton, L., Baker, K.: Ionosphere. UCI Machine Learning Repository (1989). https://doi.org/10.24432/C5W01B
9. Wang, D., Xu, J.: Principal component analysis in the local differential privacy model. In: Proceedings of the Twenty-Eighth International Joint Conference on Artificial Intelligence, IJCAI 2019, pp. 4795–4801. International Joint Conferences on Artificial Intelligence Organization (2019). https://doi.org/10.24963/ijcai.2019/666
10. Wei, K., et al.: Federated learning with differential privacy: algorithms and performance analysis. IEEE Trans. Inf. Forensics Secur. **15**, 3454–3469 (2020)
11. Wolberg, W., Mangasarian, O., Street, N., Street, W.: Breast Cancer Wisconsin (Diagnostic). UCI Machine Learning Repository (1995). https://doi.org/10.24432/C5DW2B

Intrusion Detection and Systems

SIFAST: An Efficient Unix Shell Embedding Framework for Malicious Detection

Songyue Chen[1,2,3], Rong Yang[1,2,3]($\boxtimes$), Hong Zhang[4], Hongwei Wu[1,2,3], Yanqin Zheng[5], Xingyu Fu[1,2,3], and Qingyun Liu[1,2,3]

[1] Institute of Information Engineering, Chinese Academy of Science, Beijing, China
yangrong@iie.ac.cn
[2] School of CyberSecurity, University of Chinese Academy of China, Beijing, China
[3] National Engineering Laboratory of Information Security Technologies, Beijing, China
[4] National Computer network Emergency Response technical Team/Coordination Center of China, Beijing, China
[5] Chinatelecom Cloud, Beijing, China

Abstract. Unix Shell is a powerful tool for system developers and engineers, but it poses serious security risks when used by cybercriminals to execute malicious scripts. These scripts can compromise servers, steal confidential data, or cause system crashes. Therefore, detecting and preventing malicious scripts is an important task for intrusion detection systems. In this paper, we propose a novel framework, called SIFAST, for embedding and detecting malicious Unix Shell scripts. Our framework consists of Smooth Inverse Frequency (SIF) and Abstract Syntax Tree (AST) techniques to rapidly convert Unix Shell commands and scripts into vectors and capture their semantic and syntactic features. These vectors can then be beneficial for various downstream machine learning models for classification or anomaly detection. Compared with other embedding methods with multiple downstream detection models, We have demonstrated that SIFAST can significantly improve the accuracy and efficiency on different downstream models. We also provide a supervised dataset of normal and abnormal Unix commands and scripts, which was collected from various open-source data. Hopefully, we can make a humble contribution to the field of intrusion detection systems by offering a solution to identifying malicious scripts in Unix Shell.

Keywords: Unix Shell · Malicious Detection · Sentence Embedding

1 Introduction

Developers, system engineers and DevOps engineers frequently use the command-line(CLI) as the operating system interface. And among all the CLIs, Unix Shell interface is the most widely used interface in web servers. Although

© The Author(s), under exclusive license to Springer Nature Switzerland AG 2023
E. Athanasopoulos and B. Mennink (Eds.): ISC 2023, LNCS 14411, pp. 59–78, 2023.
https://doi.org/10.1007/978-3-031-49187-0_4

the Graphic User Interface(GUI) seems like a more friendly choice, the Unix Shell interface is still the most convenient, accurate and efficient way for the programmers to connect to the Unix servers.

The Unix Shell is the core component of the Unix. It can receive user-input commands and Shell scripts, interpret them and send the results into the Unix kernel for execution [24]. With the sufficient user authority, Unix Shell has the ability to schedule nearly all the commands in the Unix according to the requirements. It is powerful, but it may cause some exceptions on Unix. Thus, the Unix Shell gradually becomes a favorite tool for many cybercriminals to execute attacks, like Living-off-the-Land attacks on Unix. In order to attack a certain server and steal confidential data, reverse shell or privilege escalation is used to obtain Unix Shell and write Shell scripts or directly run malicious commands to get access to the host server's confidential data [5].

Because of the various security problems that may be caused by the Unix Shell, empirical rules have been used by the security companies to detect malicious Unix scripts and commands, including setting regular expressions and detecting system indicators [2]. In addition, traditional machine learning methods have also been used [33]. However, due to the complexity and flexibility of the Unix commands and scripts, these types of methods will probably make false alarms, which lead to great deviations from the correct results in the real-world scenarios. In recent years, with the development of NLP techniques, it has been proved that NLP algorithms can solve part of the malicious command detection and script detection problems, and that using NLP methods to find specific patterns of high-risk scripts has been tried. Some malicious detection methods from other script languages have been widely used by collecting structural data from Abstract Syntax Trees(AST) and Control Flow Graphs(CFG). However, these pre-trained models require a large amount of data for training, and hardware resources to support their running which are not available in many Unix servers. Although these pre-trained models provide open APIs to support downstream detection models, it is not acceptable for companies to provide confidential shell scripts which contain file names, accessed URLs, OS information, user behaviors, etc. to external service providers. Therefore, it is urgent to have a detection tool that can directly detect malicious scripts in Unix servers with efficiency.

In this paper, we propose an efficient Unix Shell script embedding method based on SIF and AST, which embeds Unix Shell commands and scripts to support malicious detection. We call it SIFAST. This method extracts the AST in the Shell scripts to generate the AST depth vectors, then uses the pre-trained word embedding model to construct the token vectors of the Shell scripts tokenized by AShellTokenizer, and finally send these two vectors to the SIFAST model. SIFAST is based on the SIF embedding, a sentence embedding method, which makes the word vectors in a script weighted and averaged from the AST depth vector to jointly synthesize the embedding vector of the Shell scripts. It has proved through experiments that, compared with other embedding models, the SIFAST Embedding Framework can greatly improve the accuracy of almost all downstream machine learning models.

The contributions of our work are summarized as follows:

1. We propose an efficient Embedding framework for malicious Unix Shell detection. Our framework can convert the Unix Shell scripts and commands into vectors in the Unix servers to provide support to the downstream detection model.
2. We use word vector representations in Shell scripts to establish a Unix Shell script embedding model based on SIF, and use AST features to generate AST Depth vectors to anisotropically normalize SIF vectors which can greatly improve the detection ability of the downstream malicious detection models.
3. Likewise, we conducted experiments on several downstream machine learning models and deep learning models. The experiments showed that our model can greatly improve the accuracy. It can be demonstrated that our embedding framework is feasible to detect malicious Shell scripts.

2   Problem Definition and Background

2.1   Malicious Unix Shell Operations

Since the emergence of Unix Operating System in 1969, the Unix Shell has undertaken the work of parsing and executing user commands. As an important system tool, Unix Shell can connect to the system kernel and perform almost all Unix operations under the premise of sufficient user privileges.

In a Unix server, in order to disrupt or control the system, adversaries often need to use Unix Shell commands to elevate privileges, evade defenses, search information and control the system. To achieve these goals, adversaries often implant well-written malicious scripts by using the Unix Shell as a means of attack. Although there are already methods, like static regular expressions and Anti-Virus tools, to evade malicious scripts executing, adversaries often write scripts or directly execute commands to uninstall monitoring agents, disable firewalls, interrupt Unix security modules, modify ACLs, change attributes, and rename public utilities [1]. [2] introduces a malicious script, which can uninstall Cloud related monitoring agent, causing malfunction of security services.

It has been noticed that in recent years, Living-Off-the-Land(LOL) attacks have gradually been used by advanced adversaries [20]. LOL attacks mainly use the system tools to achieve the purpose of fileless attacks, which aim to erase their relevant traces after the attack. One commonly used tool for LOL attacks is CLI. PowerShell is the most commonly used CLI for LOL attacks, for Windows is one of the most popular system today. Unix Shell is also a CLI that cannot be ignored, because Unix is the most used system on web servers. For the convenience of using Unix Shell, some configured scripts are set which are used by Unix users almost every day and become an integral part of Unix, like "memfd_create". At the same time, developers will also write multiple scripts to quickly execute designated commands. Although this gives the developers freedom to have access to the Unix, it gives a chance for adversaries to make it as an execution tool for LOL attacks [7].

Aiming at the adversaries' attack methods, we have designed a framework that can quickly detect malicious Unix Shell commands and scripts called SIFAST. Through our detection framework, malicious scripts executed on Unix servers and related users who have executed malicious commands will be detected in a timely manner.

2.2   Threat Model

We consider a type of attack, where the adversaries can get access to Unix Shell through some means (external intervention or internal control) in a Unix server. The adversaries need to evade existing shell detection tools for further attacks to ensure the effect of covert attacks. The adversaries may interfere with the command detection tools by writing obfuscated Unix scripts, or by slightly modifying the malicious commands to evade static regular expression rules. The adversaries may need to remain undetected for a long time to maintain the attack chain for the ultimate goal may be to steal information to disrupt a system.

We assume that our shell detection framework cannot be disabled from adversaries because it will be part of the Unix kernel. Although the adversary may disable some common tools that can collect commands, such as "bash_history", "auditd", as part of a Unix kernel, has the ability to collects all the operations from users. We can collect the scripts and commands added by the system in memory at the first time through "auditd", transform them into confidential data through our framework, and quickly send the embedded result to cloud monitors for further classification and analysis.

3   Related Works

3.1   Command and Script Detection Using NLP Techniques

For Unix Shell commands and scripts, Elmasry et al. [15] proposed using Deep Neural Networks to detect masquerade detection. They used DNN, CNN and LSTM to detect masqueraders and reached 0.99 F1 score on SEA, Greenberg and Lane's dataset. Liu et al. [28] proposed a sequence-to-sequence model for masquerade detection on SEA. Zhai et al. [40] proposed using TCN to detect masqueraders on SEA dataset with the same accuracy but lower time cost. These models can greatly catch the relationship between user commands, however, because their ideas were to build the command detection models to detect user behaviors from command blocks which contain several commands, it is impossible for masquerade detection models to detect specific malicious Unix commands. In order to detect maliciousness of one command or script, Al-janabi et al. [8] proposed several machine learning models to detect malicious software, including malicious Shell scripts. Hussain et al. [23] proposed NLP techniques to calculate the command similarities by using Unix system manuals to get the descriptions and arguments of one command. At last, he used TF-IDF and cosine similarity to calculate. Trizna et al. [38] proposed a tokenizer called ShellTokenizer to tokenize all the Unix Shell scripts and commands for malicious detection. They also proposed a dataset containing different commands collected from NL2Bash [26] and GitHub. Andrew et al. [10] proposed a mapping method which used NLP techniques to map malicious Unix commands to MITRE ATT&CK. They evaluated different NLP embeddings including TF-IDF, BOW and pre-trained word embeddings. Boffa et al. [11] proposed using clustering methods to detect malicious Shell command actions on Honeypot. They used NLP embeddings to embed all the Unix Shell commands. These methods used different NLP techniques on different Unix command datasets, but they simply treat Unix commands or scripts as text, not considering their programming grammars.

Apart from Unix Shell commands and scripts, several malicious detection using NLP techniques on PowerShell scripts were proposed. Hendler et al. [21] proposed character-level CNN to detect malicious PowerShell scripts and reached high accuracy and recall. In the later research [22], they also proposed using contextual embeddings and information collected from AMSI, an Anti-Virus software created by Microsoft, to detect malicious PowerShell commands and scripts. Mimura et al. [30] proposed using Word Embedding techniques to split malicious PowerShell commands for static analysis. Ongun et al. [31] proposed a framework by using Active Learning and a novel embedding technique to detect Living-Off-the-Land(LOtL) PowerShell commands. Their framework can greatly lower the annotation cost and improve detection performance. Alahmadi et al. [9] proposed a stacked Denoising AutoEncoders(sDAs) to embed PowerShell scripts in character-level then use logistic classifier to detection maliciousness of one script. Except MPSAutodetect, other detection methods all require some external information in PowerShell language, including AMSI messages, expert annotation, which is much difficult to migrate them to Unix Shell.

3.2 Command and Script Detection Using Hybrid Features

Recently, inspired by Maxion et al., many researchers found that other features hidden in PowerShell or Unix Shell commands can greatly improve the accuracy of the detection models. Bohannon and Holmes [12] proposed Revoke-Obfuscation to detect obfuscated malicious PowerShell scripts. They used AST to extract thousands of features in PowerShell scripts and compared feature vector with pre-defined feature vector for classification. Rousseau [35] proposed "hijacking" .NET structure to defend against malicious PowerShell attacks which can evade the AMSI interface. Fang et al. [17] proposed using hybrid features, including AMSI information, Control Flow Graph(CFG) and other features to classify malicious PowerShell scripts. Song et al. [36] also proposed a deep learning framework by using AST to detect malicious PowerShell scripts. They split the token vectors into AST tree and used contextual embeddings to find the maliciousness of scripts. Chai et al. [14] proposed an AST-based method to deobfuscate possible malicious PowerShell scripts to readable scripts, which can improve the accuracy of downstream malicious detection models. Fang et al. [16] proposed an AST-based and CFG-based framework for detecting malicious JavaScript by using Graph Neural Network. Tsai et al. [39] proposed PowerDP framework to deobfuscate and detect malicious PowerShell scripts. These methods all used their detection target's unique features, including different AST, CFG, AMSI information, special tokens, etc. However, due to the unique AST structure in the Unix Shell, it is hard to simply use the Unix Shell AST Parser in the above methods to detect malicious Unix Shell commands and scripts. Bashlex's generated ASTs lack many node features compared to the PowerShell AST parser and JavaScript AST parser. It's also hard to obtain a full CFG or Anti-Virus software messages from Unix Shell commands and scripts.

4   Methodology

In this section, we will elaborate on the details of the overall framework. Given that our work focuses on the analysis of the Shell commands and scripts in the Unix, we propose an embedding framework for Unix scripts based on SIF and AST. An overview of SIFAST is shown in Fig. 1:

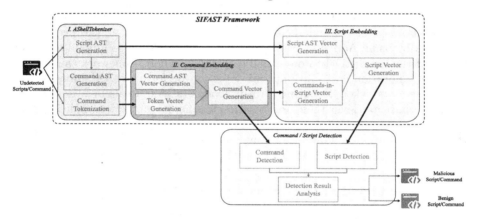

Fig. 1. An Overview of SIFAST Framework

The overall SIFAST can be divided into three parts:

1. **AShellTokenizer**. Inspired by Trizna et al. [38], we used the ShellTokenizer designed by them to tokenize Unix script text, but we have also made some change to fit our needs. First, we used the whole script to build script ASTs. Then we tokenized all the commands in the script and built command ASTs.
2. **Command Embedding**. This is the core of our architecture. We input the tokenized commands and ASTs built in the AShellTokenizer into the Word2Vec model and AST Depth Parser respectively to build the word vectors and AST depth vectors for each token, and then input the word vectors and AST depth vectors into the Command Embedding model to build command vectors. Here, we modified SIF to build command vectors, and our word frequency database and Word2Vec model are obtained through pre-acquisition and pre-training.

3. **Script Embedding**. When all the command vectors are collected, we can extract the features of these vectors to make a "commands-in-script vector" by Max-Pooling. Then we used the script AST to build an AST vector(Not AST Depth Vector) through AST-Node-Embedding. Then we concatenated these two vectors together to build a script vector. Here, The script AST is different from the command AST, which can be regarded as a subtree of the former.

After obtaining the script vector, we input the script vector into the detection model. Model selection is not one of our concerns. We will prove that our embedding can improve any machine learning model in the experiment section.

4.1   Data Preprocessing and AShellTokenizer

Data Preprocessing. We first collected numerous Unix Shell scripts from different repositories on GitHub, and read some of them in detail. We did the some measures to preprocess the scripts for better training.

Since malicious URLs that may be contained in scripts are not included in our analysis, we replaced all URLs with the same name to improve the Word2Vec model. Since the file distributions are different in different hosts, we replaced all relative file paths except .sh files with the same placeholder. Note that we have reserved some absolute file paths, because we believe that the absolute file paths may infer the intentions of scripts. For customized commands, we have partially reserved them, because we believe that customized commands and their corresponding command identifiers and command arguments often have some characteristics. We insert a script directly into another script that calls it to simulate script execution.

AShellTokenizer. Traditional NLP tokenizers have the following problems:

1. The traditional NLP tokenizer is oriented to natural language, and its rules are mainly for natural language, which cannot be applied to scripting language.
2. Traditional NLP tokenizers cannot build abstract syntax trees based on Unix Shell.

In response to the above problems, we adopted the method mentioned by Trizna et al. [38] and established a Tokenizer based on Bashlex as the backend to generate the AST of Unix Shell while performing word tokenization. Bashlex is a powerful tool for "Unix Shell command" syntax analyzing as it can simulate the Unix shell interpretation process for complicated command. However, it is difficult for Bashlex to effectively generate a script AST for loops, conditions, and functions, so we firstly used Tree-Sitter [4] to analyze complex Unix scripts and leave command node to Bashlex for command analysis. Tree-Sitter is a widely-used tool for generating AST of different programming languages. It has been used in multiple code analysis tools like CodeBERT [18]. However, Tree-Sitter is not well-performed in generating Unix Shell Command for it will take all

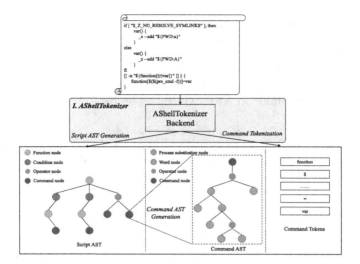

Fig. 2. The Structure of AShellTokenizer

the tokens after the command as "arguments", which is harmful for generating AST depth features. We extended Bashlex by setting command flags as the separated nodes directly connected to commands, not just one of the command arguments in AST. Command flags come from Unix Shell Manual gained from "man" command. It means that if one command has a "flag", the "flag node" will be connected to the command node and the argument nodes belonging to the flag will be connected to the flag node. This is to ensure the structural complexity of each AST so that the AST structural feature will contain more information which can better benefit for generating AST vector.

We call our tokenizer AShellTokenizer. Figure 2 shows the structure of AShell-Tokenizer. The script AST is generated by Tree-Sitter while the command AST is by Bashlex.

For the subsequent Command Embedding and AST-Embedding, our AShell-Tokenizer can simultaneously build the script AST and the command AST. We can think of the latter as distinct subtrees of the former. We do this to reduce the complexity of the AST in complex scripts to improve the speed of Embedding, and also to avoid the ambiguous command AST interfering total structure of the script AST.

4.2 Command Embedding

Command Embedding is the core component of our framework, which relies on SIF. SIF is an embedding method for generating sentence vectors by using weighted word vectors, which has been proved to be effective in many tasks. SIF uses Eq. 1 to generate sentence vectors:

$$f_w\left(\tilde{c}_s\right) = \log\left[\alpha p(w) + (1-\alpha)\frac{\exp\left(\langle v_w, \tilde{c}_s\rangle\right)}{Z}\right] \tag{1}$$

where $\tilde{c}_s$ represents the sentence vector, $\tilde{c}_s = \beta c_0 + (1 - \beta)c_s$, $c_0 \perp c_s$, α and β are scalar hyperparameters, and

$$Z_{(\tilde{c}_s)} = \sum_{w \in V} \exp\left(< \tilde{c}_s, v_w >\right)$$

is the normalizing constant.

When weighting the word vectors in a sentence, SIF believes that words with smaller word frequencies are more important for the expression of the entire sentence. Based on this, we are inspired to integrate the command AST in Unix commands into SIF. This will make the representation of the Unix commands more differentiated.

Because of the flexibility of Unix commands, the command identifiers and arguments can be adjusted almost arbitrarily, which makes the command AST unable to be unified. The overall structure of the AST can be easily broken due to changes in command identifiers or argument positions. But we found that no matter how the positions of command arguments and identifiers change, their depth in the entire AST does not change. So we can represent the command AST structure by the AST depth vector d_w. The definition of a token's d_w is:

$$\mathbf{d_w}\left(tree_w\right) = \begin{bmatrix} d_1 \\ d_2 \\ \vdots \\ d_n \end{bmatrix}, d_i \in \{0,1\}, \sum_{i=1}^{n} d_i = 1, i \in \{1, 2, \cdots, n\} \tag{2}$$

where n represents the AST depth. Since one token can have only one depth in the AST, we let $\sum_{i=1}^{n} d_i = 1$ to make a one-hot encoding.

After generating the AST depth vector, we pass it through a weight matrix to get the weighted AST depth vector. We then perform Hadamard product on the obtained weighted AST vector and the token's word vector to obtain the weighted AST word vector. The total algorithm is as follows:

$$\tilde{v}_w = v_w \circ f_{\mathbf{w}_\beta}\left(d_w\right) \tag{3}$$

where $\tilde{v}_w$ is the weighted AST word vector, $\mathbf{w}_\beta$ is the AST depth weight, and f_{w_β} is the AST weight function. $\mathbf{w}_\beta$ is from:

$$\mathbf{w}_\beta(\mathbf{d} \times \mathbf{m}) = \left(\text{softmax}\left(\mathbf{w_v}\left(\mathbf{w_d}\mathfrak{J} + \mathbf{b_d}\right)^T + \mathbf{b_v}\right)\right)^T \tag{4}$$

where

$$\mathfrak{J} = \begin{bmatrix} 1 & 1 & \cdots & 1 \\ 1 & \ddots & & 1 \\ \vdots & & \ddots & \vdots \\ 1 & 1 & \cdots & 1 \end{bmatrix}$$

$\mathbf{w_v}$, $\mathbf{b_v}$, $\mathbf{w_d}$, $\mathbf{b_d}$ are all neural network parameters for Pre-training AST depth weights. d is the max AST depth and m is the word vector size. We used

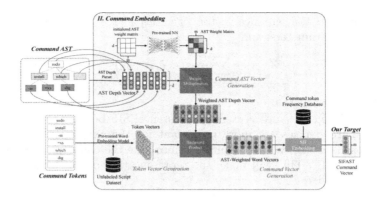

Fig. 3. SIFAST Algorithm for Command Vector

Command Embedding and MLP for pre-training to get a fine-tuned $\mathbf{w}_\beta$. Note that AST depth weights will be certain once after the pre-training. These neural networks which requires GPU will never be used again in malicious detection.

Recall the SIF equation. By computing the gradient of $\tilde{c}_s$ and by Taylor expansion on it, we have the maximum likelihood estimator for $\tilde{c}_s$ which is approximately:

$$\arg\max \sum_{w\in s} f_w\left(\tilde{c}_s\right) \propto \sum_{w\in s} \frac{a}{p(w)+a} v_w, \text{ where } a = \frac{1-\alpha}{\alpha Z}$$

Now we replace v_w with $\tilde{v_w}$, so that we get the SIF sentence vector weighted by the AST depth vector:

$$\arg\max \sum_{w\in s} f_w\left(\tilde{v}_c\right) \propto \sum_{w\in s} \frac{a}{p(w)+a} v_w \circ f_{w_\beta}\left(d_w\right) \tag{5}$$

where $\tilde{v}_c$ now represents the Shell command embeddings. Finally, in order to ensure the isotropy of the Shell command embedding vectors, we need to remove the principal component in all the Shell commands.

At last, while FastText can handle the out-of-vocabulary tokens while Word2Vec cannot, we set all the out-of-vocabulary tokens as nomarlized all-one vectors to attend the SIF vectorization.

Through the above algorithm, we combine word vectors and AST depth vectors to represent Shell command embedding vectors. In general, the Shell command vector embedding algorithm can be expressed in the pseudo codes Algorithm 1, and all the Algorithm procedure can be expressed in Fig. 3.

4.3   Script Embedding

After obtaining the command embedding vector, we also need to fuse the AST structure of each script, which is script AST, and finally obtain multiple script

Algorithm 1. Shell Command Vector Generation Algorithm based on Command Embedding

---

Input: Shell token embeddings $\{v_w : v_w \in \mathbb{V}\}$, token corpus $\{\mathcal{W}\}$ Shell commands $\{\mathcal{C}\}$, estimated probabilities $\{p(w) : w \in \mathbb{V}\}$, AST depth vectors $\{d_w : d \in \mathbb{D}\}$, AST depth weights $\{w_\beta\}$

Output: Command embeddings $\{\tilde{v}_c : c \in \mathcal{C}\}$

    while $c \in \mathcal{C}$ **do**
        if $w \in \mathcal{W}$ **then**
            $\tilde{v_w} \leftarrow v_w \circ f_{w_\beta}(d_w)$
        else
            $d_w \leftarrow$ assume $w \in$ AST's first layer
            $v_w \leftarrow$ normalized all-ones vector
            $\tilde{v_w} \leftarrow v_w \circ f_{w_\beta}(d_w)$
        end if
        $v_c \leftarrow \frac{1}{|c|} \sum_{w \in c} \frac{a}{p(w)+a} \tilde{v_w}$
    end while
    Calculate u as the first singular vector in $c \in \mathcal{C}$
    while $c \in \mathcal{C}$ **do**
        $v_c \leftarrow v_c - u u^T v_c$
    end while

---

vectors for each Unix Shell script. Note that Script Embedding is different from Command Embedding, because we do not have "command token frequency" for each command, so we cannot balance the AST depth vector by using $p(c)$. It should also be noticed that the script AST's structure is clearer than the command AST, so its structure contains much information. In order to ensure the speed of our overall SIFAST architecture, we use a lightweight method to perform Max-Pooling on multiple Shell command vectors from Command Embedding. Then we transformed AST into an AST structure vector based on the modified AST-Node-Encoding [32]. Equation 6 shows how an AST structure vector is built. Supposing vec(p) is the non-leaf node p's representation, then all the vec(c_i) are the vec(p)'s leaf node representations.

$$\text{vec}(p) \approx \tanh \left(\sum_{i=1}^{n} l_i W_i \cdot \text{vec}(c_i) + \boldsymbol{b} \right) \tag{6}$$

where $\text{vec}(\cdot) \in \mathbb{R}^{N_f}$, $l_i = \frac{\#\text{ leaves under } c_i}{\#\text{ leaves under } p}$ and

$$W_i = \frac{n-i}{n-1} W_l + \frac{i-1}{n-1} W_r$$

i is the ith leaf node of vec(p).

The reason why we don't use the AST-Node-Encoding in our SIFAST command embedding is the Unix Shell commmand's flexibility that the command ASTs are more ambiguous than script ASTs which makes the positions of parameters, flags, combinations in AST much more flexible than script ASTs. However, a proper AST-Node-Encoding deeply relies on the node positions of one AST which will make the command AST encoding over-fitting.

At last, we take the root node vector, which is the script node's vector as the AST vector and connect the obtained AST vector with the command vectors after Max-Pooling, and finally generate the script vector, as is shown in Fig. 4.

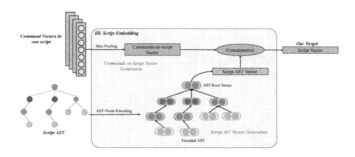

Fig. 4. Generating the script vector by Using Max-Pooling and AST-Node-Encoding

5   Experiment Settings and Results

In this section, we will elaborate on our experiment settings and evaluation results.

5.1   Experiment Settings

We will elaborate on three parts: dataset setting, embedding method selection and detection model selection.

Dataset Settings. In order to prove that the command embedding method and script embedding method of the SIFAST model have certain effects, we need to build a Unix command dataset and a Unix script dataset. At the same time, in order to train our Word2Vec model, we also need to collect numerous unlabeled Unix Shell scripts to support training. We explained our data sources and dataset generating methods below. The distribution of labeled and unlabeled dataset is shown in Table 1.

We used shell scripts from GitHub high-star repositories as the training data of our word embedding model. We conducted data pre-processing of these shell scripts according to the method described in Sect. 3 to ensure the training effectiveness. Furthermore, we use our AShellTokenizer to obtain accurate tokens. At the same time, we once again remove meaningless tokens, such as "#", "$" and other identifiers, but we retain pipelines and concatenation labels like "||"

Table 1. Distribution of Labeled and Unlabeled Dataset on Commands and Scripts

	Class	Labeled	Unlabeled
Command	Benign	5681607	Null
	Malicious	1564381	
Script	Benign	160000	1064509
	Malicious	160000	

and "&&". In the end, we got an unlabeled dataset containing 1064,509 scripts, including about 34,416,978 tokenized commands with about 650,000,000 token.

We used the following data sources to create our labeled Unix command dataset:

NL2Bash [26] A bash dataset collected from stackoverflow.com and other Q&A forums. The dataset contains Unix commands and their corresponding natural language explanations, which allows us to clearly understand that all the commands contained in the dataset are benign and do no harm to any servers

Reverse Shell Cheat Sheet [37] A reverse shell script command sheet from GitHub, which contains many commands for reverse shell in Unix Shell, and can automatically build reverse shell commands based on the tools it provides.

GTFOBins [6] This data set contains commands and scripts corresponding to various methods that might cause LOL attacks, such as reverse shell, file upload, file download, file read and write, and library loading. There is also a Windows PowerShell version of the LOL dataset called LOLBAS [3].

LinEnum [34] a repository containing multiple malicious scripts on GitHub. These scripts can be used to steal user data, disrupt system, etc.

Furthermore, we separated our malicious commands into multi classes by GTFOBins classification including Reverse Shell, Bind Shell, File Upload, File Download, File Write, File read, Library Load, SUID, Sudo, Capabilities, Limited SUID. This is to test our embedding method is useful to diversify malicious commands. We used data augmentation method [27] to expand our data size by changing variable names, move/remove identifiers, modifying positions of different arguments while remaining the functionality of these commands.

Embedding Method and Model Selection. In order to test the ability of our embedding method to improve the downstream model, we selected a variety of different embedding methods and downstream models to test the general ability of SIFAST. We chose some embedding methods for comparison, including TF-IDF, Doc2Vec, MPSAutodetect, SimCSE, etc.

We also selected two word embedding models in our SIFAST framework to support SIF algorithm: Word2Vec [29] and FastText [13], and we selected Random Forest, XGBoost, SVM and MLP as the downstream models for performance evaluation.

5.2   Evaluations

Evaluations on Unix Shell Command Dataset. We first tested on the command dataset with multiple labels. After detecting all the labels' classification accuracy and FPR, The average test results on different labels were collected altogether and shown in the table Tables 2 and 3. **Note that** we have tested all the averaged accuracy and FPR between different labels and benign commands. The results from different labels have all been averaged and shown in the table. We used this average multi-classification result as the result in the following experiments.

Table 2. Avg. F1 Score Results from Different Labels in Command Dataset. Results Averaged from Multiple Label Classification Results

	TF-IDF	Doc2Vec	MPSAutodetect	SimCSE	**SIFAST**
Random Forest	0.63	0.67	0.79	0.84	**0.96**
XGBoost	0.65	0.7	0.76	0.86	**0.99**
SVM	0.68	0.69	0.73	0.86	**0.95**
MLP	0.65	0.71	0.75	0.87	**0.98**
avg	0.63	0.69	0.73	0.86	**0.97**

Table 3. Avg. FPR Results on Command Dataset. Results Averaged from Multiple Label Classification Results

	TF-IDF	Doc2Vec	MPSAutodetect	SimCSE	**SIFAST**
Random Forest	0.397	0.229	0.191	0.073	**0.036**
XGBoost	0.368	0.225	0.192	0.044	**0.006**
SVM	0.300	0.293	0.194	0.088	**0.028**
MLP	0.312	0.227	0.190	0.166	**0.017**
avg	0.324	0.218	0.191	0.092	**0.021**

Before the experiment, we trained our AST depth weight neural network. As described in Sect. 3.2, after training, we only need to obtain AST depth weights and do not need to use the network in SIFAST again. According to the content of the table Tables 2 and 3, we found that our SIFAST embedding has been greatly improved compared to non-deep learning models. In Trizna's experiments, TF-IDF with XGBoost has reached 0.99 AUC and 0.03 FPR, but because we have increased the number of LOL attack commands compared to the dataset provided by Trizna [38], the diversity of data has been increased, causing AUC relatively reduced and FPR added. SIFAST with XGBoost model is the best combination as FPR has reached 0.006, and F1 score has reached 0.97. Compared to deep learning models, SIFAST is better than MPSAutodetect, and the detection speed is far faster than MPSAutodetect. The effect of SimCSE is not as good as imagined. The reason may be that the SimCSE itself is not a sentence vector model for Unix Shell script, but a model for natural language. According to our experimental results, we found that the F1 value and AUC of the SIFAST command embedding based on the Word2Vec model increased by 0.01 compared to FastText, which may be because we processed unregistered tokens in the Word2Vec model in the SIF algorithm. In the commands, the tokens not included in the Word2Vec model are often file names, path names, etc., and they express the same semantics in the commands. We uniformly represent this type of token with the same vector, which increases the versatility of the Word2Vec model.

Evaluations on Unix Shell Script Dataset. We also conducted related tests in the labeled Unix Shell script dataset, and the test results are in the table Tables 4 and 5:

Table 4. Avg. F1 Score Results in Script Dataset. Results Averaged from Multiple Label Classification Results

	TF-IDF	Doc2Vec	MPSAutodetect	SimCSE	**SIFAST**
Random Forest	0.68	0.8	0.81	0.84	**0.93**
XGBoost	0.65	0.79	0.82	0.86	**0.95**
SVM	0.7	0.81	0.76	0.86	**0.92**
MLP	0.71	0.8	0.84	0.87	**0.94**
avg	0.69	0.80	0.81	0.86	**0.94**

Table 5. Avg. FPR Results in Script Dataset. Results Averaged from Multiple Label Classification Results

	TF-IDF	Doc2Vec	MPSAutodetect	SimCSE	**SIFAST**
Random Forest	0.466	0.359	0.190	0.272	**0.144**
XGBoost	0.469	0.353	0.189	0.291	**0.139**
SVM	0.452	0.375	0.191	0.271	**0.146**
MLP	0.480	0.369	0.193	0.260	**0.142**
avg	0.470	0.361	0.190	0.274	**0.143**

The results show that compared with other machine learning models, SIFAST with XGBoost still achieves better results, with an average F1-score of 0.94 and FPR of 0.039.

We concurrently conducted several performance tests to ensure the detection efficiency of our embedding framework on general servers. Additionally, we conducted comparative experiments with several baseline models, the results of which are illustrated in the Fig. 5. The experimental outcomes indicate that our embedding framework achieves a high detection speed on general servers, with relatively low resource consumption. The primary memory resource consumption in our framework arises from the Word2Vec model, while the CPU resource consumption stems from the AST construction process. Furthermore, our model does not require GPU usage, enabling deployment on the majority of servers.

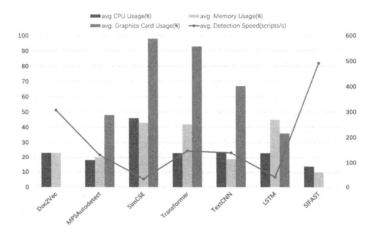

Fig. 5. Performance Test on Script Dataset

We also conducted ablation experiments for SIFAST and AST-Embedding module, and the experimental results are shown in the Table 6 and 7. We eliminated the Max-Pooling commands vector and AST-Node-Embedding vector before script vector generation to verify their impact on the overall architecture. Experiments show that the Max-Pooling commands vector is crucial to the generation of script vectors, and AST-Node-Embedding has relatively little effect on it, and may even interfere. However, AST-Node-Embedding also requires little computing resources. We can split out this module when an Unix server is facing short-text scripts or user commands. But when faced with long-text Unix scripts with complicated grammars, AST-Node-Embedding module can be added to the total framework.

Table 6. Ablation Experiment Results by using F1 score on Command Dataset

	SIF	SIFAST RDV	SIFAST RW	SIFAST
Random Forest	0.86	0.89	0.79	**0.92**
XGBoost	0.93	0.94	0.85	**0.98**
SVM	0.90	0.88	0.84	**0.91**
MLP	0.87	0.89	0.67	**0.94**
avg	0.89	0.90	0.79	**0.94**

Table 7. Ablation Experiment by using F1 Score on Script Dataset

	Max-Pooling SIFAST	AST-Node-Embedding	SIFAST
Random Forest	0.85	0.76	**0.88**
XGBoost	0.86	0.74	**0.9**
SVM	**0.88**	0.77	0.87
MLP	0.89	0.71	**0.89**
avg	0.87	0.75	**0.89**

6   Conclusion

We propose a Unix Shell Embedding Framework which leverages the SIF sentence embedding combined with the limited depth features and structural features of the Unix Shell AST to enhance the discrimination between benign and malicious commands and scripts. Our embedding model can be applied to a variety of detection models and can significantly enhance the detection capabilities of downstream detection models. Compared with various deep learning embedding models, our embedding model has better universality and faster speed, which can be applied in Unix servers. We collected multiple public data sources to create a command dataset and script dataset for training and testing. Through experiments, we found that our embedding method combined with the XGBoost downstream detection model can achieve the highest 0.98 F1-Score on the command dataset, which surpasses deep learning models. Besides, regarding the detection performance on the script dataset, our model rivals deep learning models. But more significantly, our model shows remarkably better performances in terms of detection accuracy and false alarm rate. We believe that with the continuous development of the Unix Shell detection model in the future, we can find more command and script's related features to enhance the detection capabilities of different types of Unix Shell malicious scripts and commands.

Acknowledgements. This work is supported by the Strategic Priority Research Program of the Chinese Academy of Sciences with No.XDC02030400, the Scaling Program of Institute of Information Engineering, CAS (Grant No. E3Z0041101), the Scaling Program of Institute of Information Engineering, CAS (Grant No. E3Z0191101).

Appendix

TF-IDF This is the most basic sentence vector generation method in the field of natural language, and it is also the sentence vector embedding method mentioned in Trizna et al. It first generates a TF-IDF representation of each word in a sentence, and then adds each word to form a TF-IDF representation of a sentence.

Doc2Vec [25] This is a method that trains the sentence vector and other words in the sentence to directly generate the sentence vector. Its method is similar to Word2Vec, but on the basis of Word2Vec, sentence vectors are added for joint training.

MPSAutodetect [9] This is a deep learning framework for detecting PowerShell malicious scripts, which uses a character-based embedding method and inputs it into a denoising AutoEncoder to extract features, and finally inputs the features into a classifier for classification.

SimCSE [19] An Advanced Pretrained Sentence Vector Embedding Model Based on Contrastive Learning. We employ the unsupervised learning part of SimCSE to learn code representations for shell scripts. Although SimCSE requires powerful hardware capabilities, making it impossible to be embedded in Unix, we still use it as one of our comparison objects to illustrate the gap between our model and conventional deep learning models.

References

1. Different linux Commands and Utilities Commonly Used by Attackers. https://www.uptycs.com/blog/linux-commands-and-utilities-commonly-used-by-attackers
2. Evasive techniques used by malicious shell scripts on different unix systems. https://www.uptycs.com/blog/evasive-techniques-used-by-malicious-linux-shell-scripts
3. LOLBAS. https://lolbas-project.github.io/
4. Tree-sitter Using Parsers. https://tree-sitter.github.io/tree-sitter/using-parsers
5. What Is a Reverse Shell | Examples & Prevention Techniques | Imperva
6. GTFOBins (2022). https://gtfobins.github.io/
7. Living Off the Land: How to Defend Against Malicious Use of Legitimate Utilities (2022). https://threatpost.com/living-off-the-land-malicious-use-legitimate-utilities/177762/
8. Al-Janabi, M., Altamimi, A.M.: A comparative analysis of machine learning techniques for classification and detection of Malware. In: 2020 21st International Arab Conference on Information Technology (ACIT), pp. 1–9 (2020). https://doi.org/10.1109/ACIT50332.2020.9300081
9. Alahmadi, A., Alkhraan, N., BinSaeedan, W.: MPSAutodetect: a malicious powershell script detection model based on stacked denoising auto-encoder. Comput. Secur. **116**, 102658 (2022). https://doi.org/10.1016/j.cose.2022.102658
10. Andrew, Y., Lim, C., Budiarto, E.: Mapping Linux shell commands to MITRE ATT&CK using NLP-based approach. In: 2022 International Conference on Electrical Engineering and Informatics (ICELTICs), pp. 37–42 (2022). https://doi.org/10.1109/ICELTICs56128.2022.9932097

11. Boffa, M., Milan, G., Vassio, L., Drago, I., Mellia, M., Ben Houidi, Z.: Towards NLP-based processing of honeypot logs. In: 2022 IEEE European Symposium on Security and Privacy Workshops (EuroS&PW), pp. 314–321 (2022). https://doi.org/10.1109/EuroSPW55150.2022.00038

12. Bohannon, D., Holmes, L.: Revoke-Obfuscation: PowerShell Obfuscation Detection Using Science (2017)

13. Bojanowski, P., Grave, E., Joulin, A., Mikolov, T.: Enriching Word Vectors with Subword Information (2017)

14. Chai, H., Ying, L., Duan, H., Zha, D.: Invoke-Deobfuscation: AST-based and semantics-preserving deobfuscation for powershell scripts. In: 2022 52nd Annual IEEE/IFIP International Conference on Dependable Systems and Networks (DSN), pp. 295–306 (2022). https://doi.org/10.1109/DSN53405.2022.00039

15. Elmasry, W., Akbulut, A., Zaim, A.H.: Deep learning approaches for predictive masquerade detection. Secur. Commun. Netw. **2018**, e9327215 (2018). https://doi.org/10.1155/2018/9327215

16. Fang, Y., Huang, C., Zeng, M., Zhao, Z., Huang, C.: JStrong: malicious JavaScript detection based on code semantic representation and graph neural network. Comput. Secur. **118**, 102715 (2022). https://doi.org/10.1016/j.cose.2022.102715

17. Fang, Y., Zhou, X., Huang, C.: Effective method for detecting malicious PowerShell scripts based on hybrid features. Neurocomputing **448**, 30–39 (2021). https://doi.org/10.1016/j.neucom.2021.03.117

18. Feng, Z., et al.: CodeBERT: a pre-trained model for programming and natural languages (2020). https://doi.org/10.48550/arXiv.2002.08155

19. Gao, T., Yao, X., Chen, D.: SimCSE: simple contrastive learning of sentence embeddings. In: Proceedings of the 2021 Conference on Empirical Methods in Natural Language Processing, pp. 6894–6910. Association for Computational Linguistics, Online and Punta Cana, Dominican Republic (2021). https://doi.org/10.18653/v1/2021.emnlp-main.552

20. Goudie, M.: The Rise of "Living off the Land" Attacks | CrowdStrike (2019). https://www.crowdstrike.com/blog/going-beyond-malware-the-rise-of-living-off-the-land-attacks/

21. Hendler, D., Kels, S., Rubin, A.: Detecting malicious powershell commands using deep neural networks. In: Proceedings of the 2018 on Asia Conference on Computer and Communications Security, pp. 187–197. ASIACCS '18, Association for Computing Machinery, New York, NY, USA (2018). https://doi.org/10.1145/3196494.3196511

22. Hendler, D., Kels, S., Rubin, A.: AMSI-based detection of malicious powershell code using contextual embeddings. In: Proceedings of the 15th ACM Asia Conference on Computer and Communications Security, pp. 679–693. ASIA CCS '20, Association for Computing Machinery, New York, NY, USA (2020). https://doi.org/10.1145/3320269.3384742

23. Hussain, Z., Nurminen, J., Mikkonen, T., Kowiel, M.: Command Similarity Measurement Using NLP (2021). https://doi.org/10.4230/OASIcs.SLATE.2021.13

24. Kidwai, A., et al.: A comparative study on shells in Linux: a review. Mater. Today Proc. **37**, 2612–2616 (2021). https://doi.org/10.1016/j.matpr.2020.08.508

25. Le, Q., Mikolov, T.: Distributed representations of sentences and documents. In: Proceedings of the 31st International Conference on International Conference on Machine Learning, vol. 32, pp. II-1188-II-1196. ICML'14, JMLR.org, Beijing, China (2014)

26. Lin, X.V., Wang, C., Zettlemoyer, L., Ernst, M.D.: NL2Bash: a corpus and semantic parser for natural language interface to the Linux operating system (2018). arXiv:1802.08979 [cs]
27. Liu, C., et al.: Code execution with pre-trained language models (2023). https://doi.org/10.48550/arXiv.2305.05383
28. Liu, W., Mao, Y., Ci, L., Zhang, F.: A new approach of user-level intrusion detection with command sequence-to-sequence model. J. Intell. Fuzzy Syst. **38**(5), 5707–5716 (2020). https://doi.org/10.3233/JIFS-179659
29. Mikolov, T., Chen, K., Corrado, G., Dean, J.: Efficient estimation of word representations in vector space (2013). arXiv:1301.3781 [cs]
30. Mimura, M., Tajiri, Y.: Static detection of malicious PowerShell based on word embeddings. Internet Things **15**, 100404 (2021). https://doi.org/10.1016/j.iot.2021.100404
31. Ongun, T., et al.: Living-off-the-land command detection using active learning. In: Proceedings of the 24th International Symposium on Research in Attacks, Intrusions and Defenses, pp. 442–455. RAID '21, Association for Computing Machinery, New York, NY, USA (2021). https://doi.org/10.1145/3471621.3471858
32. Peng, H., Mou, L., Li, G., Liu, Y., Zhang, L., Jin, Z.: Building program vector representations for deep learning. In: Zhang, S., Wirsing, M., Zhang, Z. (eds.) KSEM 2015. LNCS (LNAI), vol. 9403, pp. 547–553. Springer, Cham (2015). https://doi.org/10.1007/978-3-319-25159-2_49
33. Rathore, H., Agarwal, S., Sahay, S.K., Sewak, M.: Malware detection using machine learning and deep learning. In: Mondal, A., Gupta, H., Srivastava, J., Reddy, P.K., Somayajulu, D.V.L.N. (eds.) BDA 2018. LNCS, vol. 11297, pp. 402–411. Springer, Cham (2018). https://doi.org/10.1007/978-3-030-04780-1_28
34. Rebootuser: LinEnum (2023)
35. Rousseau, A.: Hijacking.NET to Defend PowerShell (2017). https://doi.org/10.48550/arXiv.1709.07508
36. Song, J., Kim, J., Choi, S., Kim, J., Kim, I.: Evaluations of AI-based malicious PowerShell detection with feature optimizations. ETRI J. **43**(3), 549–560 (2021). https://doi.org/10.4218/etrij.2020-0215
37. Swissky: Payloads All The Things (2023)
38. Trizna, D.: Shell language processing: Unix command parsing for machine learning (2021). arXiv:2107.02438 [cs]
39. Tsai, M.H., Lin, C.C., He, Z.G., Yang, W.C., Lei, C.L.: PowerDP: de-obfuscating and profiling malicious PowerShell commands with multi-label classifiers. IEEE Access **11**, 256–270 (2023). https://doi.org/10.1109/ACCESS.2022.3232505
40. Zhai, H., et al.: Masquerade detection based on temporal convolutional network. In: 2022 IEEE 25th International Conference on Computer Supported Cooperative Work in Design (CSCWD), pp. 305–310 (2022). https://doi.org/10.1109/CSCWD54268.2022.9776088

VNGuard: Intrusion Detection System for In-Vehicle Networks

Yan Lin Aung[1]([✉])[iD], Shanshan Wang[2][iD], Wang Cheng[1][iD],
Sudipta Chattopadhyay[1][iD], Jianying Zhou[1][iD], and Anyu Cheng[2][iD]

[1] Singapore University of Technology and Design, Singapore, Singapore
{linaung_yan,cheng_wang,sudipta_chattopadhyay,jianying_zhou}@sutd.edu.sg
[2] Chongqing University of Posts and Telecommunications, Chongqing, China
{s210332020,chengay}@cqupt.edu.cn

Abstract. Recently, autonomous and connected vehicles have gained popularity, revolutionizing consumer mobility. On the other hand, they are also becoming new targets exposing new attack vectors and vulnerabilities that may lead to critical consequences. In this paper, we propose VNGuard, an intrusion detection system for two critical in-vehicle networks (IVNs), namely, the Local Interconnect Network (LIN) and the Automotive Ethernet (AE). In the proposed system, LIN messages and AE network packets are converted into images, and then a state-of-the-art deep convolutional neural networks (DCNN) model is applied to not only detect anomalous traffic, but also to classify types of attacks. Our experimental results showed that the VNGuard achieves more than 96% detection accuracy for LIN and 99% attack classification accuracy for AE. In addition, the VNGuard is able to perform the intrusion detection within 3 ms for LIN and 4 ms for AE significantly within the latency constraint required by the autonomous and connected vehicles to achieve human-level safety.

Keywords: Intrusion Detection System · Local Interconnect Network · Automotive Ethernet · Deep Learning · Autonomous Vehicles

1 Introduction

The development of autonomous driving (AD) has the potential to revolutionize the way consumers experience mobility. AD systems could make driving safer, more convenient and enjoyable. Most vehicles today include basic advanced driver-assistance systems (ADAS) features. Technological advancement in Artificial Intelligence (AI), computer vision, Internet of Things (IoT), cloud technologies, smart robotics and mobility are fostering innovation in the connected and autonomous vehicles industry. It is anticipated that vehicles will ultimately achieve Society of Automotive Engineers (SAE) Level 4 (L4), or driverless control under certain conditions. McKinsey's report in 2023 indicated that consumers would like to have access to AD features [5]. While autonomous and connected

© The Author(s), under exclusive license to Springer Nature Switzerland AG 2023
E. Athanasopoulos and B. Mennink (Eds.): ISC 2023, LNCS 14411, pp. 79–98, 2023.
https://doi.org/10.1007/978-3-031-49187-0_5

vehicles improve traffic flow, safety and other benefits, they are also becoming a new target exposing new attack vectors and vulnerabilities according to Upstream's global automotive cybersecurity report 2023 [25]. A compromise of security may result in, among others, failure of the driving function, failure of the vehicle system, theft of the vehicle, data theft, collision, commercial loss, and other consequences.

Typically, autonomous and connected vehicles communicate with IVNs, with infrastructure (V2I), with devices (V2D), with each other (V2V) and with other networks (V2N). IVNs comprise a variety of communication networks within a vehicle designed to enable electronic components and systems to communicate with one another and exchange information. IVNs facilitate the transmission of data, commands, and signals among different modules, control units, sensors, and actuators. Commonly used IVNs in modern autonomous and connected vehicles include Controller Area Network (CAN), flexible data rate CAN (CAN-FD), LIN, FlexRay, AE and Media Oriented Systems Transport (MOST).

In this work, we propose VNGuard, an intrusion detection system for two critical IVNs, namely, LIN and AE. The VNGuard system transforms LIN messages and AE network packets into images and employs a state-of-the-art DCNN model to detect the anomalous traffic and perform attack type classification.

Our Contributions: (a) To the best of our knowledge, there is no publicly available dataset for the LIN bus. We are the first to develop comprehensive attack scenarios for the LIN bus and have created the labelled dataset collected using an autonomous vehicles security testbed which features actual vehicle components.

(b) We are also the first to propose a deep learning based intrusion detection system for the LIN bus. Using two data pre-processing techniques, we show that the proposed DCNN model is able to classify anomalous LIN messages against normal ones with more than 96% detection accuracy while meeting the real-time constraints required by autonomous and connected vehicles.

(c) A recent state-of-the-art intrusion detection system for AE achieved high detection accuracy to classify anomalous network traffic from normal traffic. In this paper, we show that we are able to perform not only a binary classification but also a multi-class classification of attack types. Again, we are not aware of any prior work on multi-class classification for attacks targeting AE.

(d) Last but not least, we evaluated the DCNN model on an embedded single-board computing platform reComputer 2021 powered by Nvidia Jetson Xavier NX GPU and assessed its potential use as an edge AI system within autonomous or connected vehicles.

Organization: The remainder of this paper is organised as follows. Section 2 provides a brief background on LIN and AE, and related work on intrusion detection systems for IVNs. Section 3 and 4 provides attack scenarios for LIN and AE respectively. We present our methods of intrusion detection based on deep convolutional networks in Sect. 5 followed by a detailed implementation of the proposed approach and its evaluation in Sect. 6. We provide conclusion for this work in Sect. 7.

2   Background and Related Work

This section begins with a brief introduction on LIN and AE, and reviews the existing start-of-the-art work on intrusion detection systems for IVNs.

2.1   Local Interconnect Network (LIN)

LIN bus technology has been widely used since its inception in the automotive industry. As compared with the more expensive CAN/CAN-FD networks, this is primarily due to its cost-effectiveness, particularly for components that do not require high bandwidth, such as doors, windows, sunroofs, mirrors, seat controls, and door locks. LIN networks serve as an invaluable complement to CAN/CAN-FD networks, minimizing resource requirements and reducing cost. LIN bus is a serial unidirectional messaging system where the slaves listen for message identifiers addressed by a master. A typical LIN network is limited to one master and 15 slave nodes. The bandwidth for LIN is limited to 20 kbps.

There are several distinct segments in a complete LIN frame, which include the frame interval, synchronization interval segment, synchronization segment, inter-byte interval, protected ID (PID) segment, answer interval, data segment, and checksum segment. The synchronization interval segment serves as the 'Start of the Frame' by maintaining a continuous 11-bit dominant level on the bus. The synchronization segment plays a crucial role in determining the baud rate of the master node. The PID serves the purpose of identifying the message class and length. Messages are carried by the data segment within the frame structure, which may contain 2, 4 or 8 bytes of data. The checksum segment ensures the validity and integrity of the LIN frame, and represents the end of the LIN frame.

2.2   Automotive Ethernet (AE)

Automotive Ethernet addresses the higher bandwidth requirements of ADAS and autonomous vehicle components, such as LIDAR, raw camera data, GPS, image data, high resolution displays, etc. AE typically consists of the following main protocols: Audio Video Transport Protocol (AVTP), (Precision Time Protocol) gPTP, and CAN protocol. The AVTP protocol is designed for the transmission of audio, video, and control information over a network that is capable of Time-Sensitive Networking. It consists of the Audio-Video Bridging (AVB) talker (i.e., a producer of an AVTP stream) and AVB listener (i.e., a consumer of an AVTP stream). AVTP is synchronized with one or more linked AVB listeners for transmitting streams from the AVB talker depending on gPTP. gPTP performs precision time synchronization of all endpoints included in the AVB network and provides the time information required for audio or video stream transmission. The CAN protocol is used in AE networks as the core method of communication between the various devices of a vehicle. This protocol transmits and receives CAN messages through Engine Control Unit (ECU) nodes parallel in the CAN bus.

2.3   Intrusion Detection Systems for In-Vehicle Networks

Threats targeting autonomous and connected vehicles have prompted a greater emphasis on the security of in-vehicle networks in recent years [26]. AI-based intrusion detection systems have been proposed as a complementary approach to access control and encryption algorithms due to their advantages in scalability, extensibility and effectiveness to enhance security [15]. They rely on observation of data in the context of in-vehicle networks, which primarily involves data exchange between ECUs. A typical CAN message, for example, includes a message ID, data content, and checksum, and represents a specific process or event. Features such as message timestamps and data ranges could be utilized to differentiate between normal and abnormal messages, enabling the intrusion detection.

Rajapaksha et al. [20] conducted a comprehensive study on AI-based intrusion detection systems (IDSs) for IVNs. Seo et al. [21] proposed an IDS for the CAN bus utilizing Generative Adversarial Networks that is capable of detecting multiple attack types, including Denial of Service (DoS), fuzzing, and remote packet manipulation. Furthermore, Cheng et al. [4] presented a temporal convolutional network intrusion detection system (TCAN-IDS) based on sequence features of CAN IDs. Song et al. [22] presented a DCNN based IDS that takes advantage of the sequential characteristics of CAN data. Qin et al. [19] and Ashraf et al. [2] have proposed an anomaly detection algorithm based on Long Short-Term Memory utilizing the CAN message payload.

In addition, Limbasiya et al. [13] provided a comprehensive review on attack detection and defense systems that target the CAN network in autonomous and connected vehicles. As indicated by our literature review, existing intrusion detection systems focus primarily on the security of the CAN bus. However, modern IVN incorporates hybrid architectures. A study conducted by Huang et al. [10] highlighted the vulnerabilities present in hybrid networks, so it is important to consider the security of other networks as well. Huang et al. [9] developed the attack traffic generation tool, while Yeo et al. [24] proposed the VitroBench testbed. Both works demonstrated the successful execution of spoofing, fuzzing, injection and flooding attacks, thereby affirming the significant risk they impose on the safety of vehicular operations.

The significance of addressing security issues with the LIN network has only recently gained attention. Ernst et al. [6] conducted a study on the security issues associated with the LIN bus. Their study highlighted that the physical layer of LIN is susceptible to compromise, making the encryption techniques employed in LIN insecure. Moreover, the study also compared LIN's vulnerability to attacks with that of other bus systems, such as CAN and FlexRay, emphasizing LIN's heightened vulnerability to attacks. Páez et al. [16] [17] [18] proposed a message authentication code that utilizes the BLAKE2s hash function and symmetric encryption algorithm Speck64 for LIN. Since LIN's maximum payload size is only 8 bytes, they utilized two consecutive response frames in order to authenticate and encrypt the payload. The authors mitigated replay attacks by utilizing the timestamp feature of LIN data packets. Takahashi et al. [23] looked at how the proposed attack scenarios for LIN might be countered through an experimental analysis. The LIN node detects the consistency of bus voltage level and sends an abnormal signal to notify others of the need to transition to a secure state. Additionally, the study also identified the absence of detailed error-handling mechanisms in the LIN protocol specification.

Regarding the AE network, despite its numerous advantages such as high bandwidth and low latency, the interconnected nature of vehicle leads to increasingly complex IVNs, thereby expanding the attack surface. The evolution of AE from traditional Ethernet also entails its advantages and security vulnerabilities. As a result, while harnessing the technical benefits of AE, it becomes imperative to address vulnerabilities caused by AE in the automotive context. As discussed in Sect. 2.2, AE consists of several protocols, such as AVTP, gPTP, and CAN, each with its own set of characteristics. However, existing intrusion detection systems are proposed mainly for use with individual protocols. For instance, Jeong et al. [11] have developed a feature generator and convolutional neural network-based intrusion detection model for the AVTP protocol. Buscemi et al. [3] introduced a machine learning-based intrusion detection system for gPTP. Koyama et al. [12] proposed a whitelist-based IDS for SOME/IP protocol whereas Alkhatib et al. [1] proposed an offline IDS based on a sequential deep learning model for detecting intrusions. In a recent paper, Han et al. [7] proposed TOW-IDS, a state-of-the-art intrusion detection system for AE that considers multiple protocols. Nevertheless, their work primarily focused on binary classification and they did not explore multi-class classification.

Our literature review indicates that future research on novel intrusion detection techniques for LIN and AE is essential. On the one hand, it is necessary to deal with the challenges posed by the use of cryptography and message authentication on the LIN bus, which could result in increased data processing and computation burdens, and, in turn, increased transmission delays. While on the other hand, it is imperative to address the limitations of most existing IDS that are focused only on a single AE protocol, while exploring the possibility of a multi-class classification approach.

3   Attack Scenarios for LIN

We consider four attack scenarios targeting the LIN bus: 1) collision between responses, 2) header bombing, 3) flooding attack, and 4) injection attack as illustrated in Fig. 1. We describe the details of each attack scenario as follows.

Collision Between Responses: The details of this attack scenario are described in [23], and illustrated in Fig. 1(a). Typically, the master node sends a frame header (PID : 0x2E), the slave node 1 (PID : 0x2E) receives the frame header and sends a corresponding response (Data : 0x0A). The slave node 2

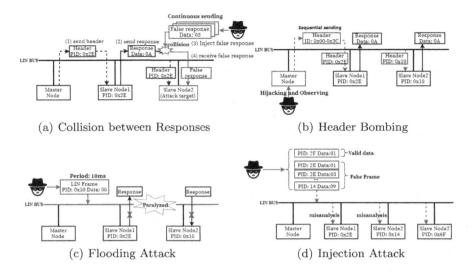

(a) Collision between Responses   (b) Header Bombing

(c) Flooding Attack   (d) Injection Attack

Fig. 1. Attack Scenarios for LIN

receives the response and executes the corresponding commands. Provided that the attacker has access to the LIN bus, then according to the scheduling table, the attacker sends a fake response (`Data : 0x05`) at the same time as the response from the slave node 1 leading to the response collision. At this time, the slave node 1 stops sending the response due to bit errors, and the attacker keeps sending the fake response, and the slave node 2 (attack target) receives and stores the fake response.

Header Bombing: A cluster with LIN devices, via LIN bus, is generally connected to the CAN bus in which the CAN node is acting as a master node. When the master node is subjected to a hijacking attack, the attacker is able to continuously send frame headers `ID : 0x00 − 0x3C`, known as header bombing as the master node, and corresponding LIN slaves send valid responses (see Fig. 1(b)). By exploiting this situation, the attacker gains access to all the transmitted content on the LIN bus, enabling further attacks such as spoofing, data tampering, and replay.

Flooding Attack: In a flooding attack, the attacker gains access to the LIN bus and employs a software tool to rapidly send a large number of invalid messages (refer to Fig. 1(c)), causing bandwidth and resource exhaustion impact on the LIN bus. A breakdown in LIN communication may prevent the engine control module from receiving and processing data from sensors in a timely manner, and the instrument panel module may not accurately display vehicle status information and posing serious risks.

Injection Attack: Injection attacks manifest in various forms, except for the flooding attack above, in this case, we mainly consider message replay injection and forged data injection, as shown in Fig. 1(d). An attacker controls one of the ECUs of the CAN serving as the master node for a LIN cluster. Through this compromised master node, the attacker transmits false or altered messages to the slave nodes, leading to erroneous data and status on these nodes. Replay attacks involve the attacker reinserting a valid message onto the bus, deceiving either the slave node or the system into executing a duplicate operation. The communication mechanism of LIN makes it relatively easy for attackers to carry out message injection attacks on LIN [6].

4   Attack Scenarios for AE

In this work, we rely on the AE intrusion dataset, which was published via the IEEE DataPort by Han et al [8]. The authors focus on the CAN, AVB, and gPTP protocols in Automotive Ethernet. These protocols generate and transmit network traffic, such as AVB stream data, gPTP sync, and encapsulated CAN messages. The IVN traffic data is extracted using port mirroring with the 100BASE-T1 switch while all linked nodes communicate each other. The dataset contains three kinds of IVN data, i.e., AVTP, gPTP, and UDP. In particular, the UDP traffic is converted from CAN messages. The collected data were divided into two separate datasets. One contains normal driving data without any attack. The other includes abnormal driving data that occurred when an attack is performed. The abnormal traffic is based on the defined five attack scenarios. A brief description of each attack scenario is provided below.

Frame Injection Attack: Frame injection attack refers to a form of attack that continuously injects back into the normal output stream after extracting an MPEG frame corresponding to a specific part of a typical video stream. The hexadecimal data in the header of the MPEG frame starts with '47 40', and this part can be extracted and inserted as video content for the attack into the middle of the MPEG frame. If this attack occurs in an autonomous driving environment where a driver's cognition is not required, the driving function will fail since the detection system of the IVN is not able to identify and detect external objects.

PTP Sync Attack: In order to provide audio or video services in real-time, all network devices on the data transmission path must be synchronized. Time synchronization between vehicle network devices is performed through PTP of the IEEE 1588 standard, which provides a protocol that enables networked devices to utilize the most precise and accurate clock synchronization. The PTP sync attack causes a time delay in the time synchronization process by modulating or flooding the time information of the sync message during the PTP synchronization. This attack makes the time synchronization between master and slaves impossible after injecting an incorrect sync message during the initial synchronization of the PTP.

Switch Attack (MAC Flooding): A network switch is often utilized to route various network packets in Automotive Ethernet. In general, a switch follows a fail-open-policy allowing specific elements in the event of a traffic, permission, or service failure. If there is a problem in the system itself, the switch operates as a type of hub. If an attacker sends a large amount of frame packets to the switch, all the Media Access Control (MAC) addresses coming into the switch are stored in the buffer of the MAC table. Eventually, this leads to overflow, the switch starts functioning as a hub. Alternatively, an environment is created in which other hosts are able to sniff all the frame packets being broadcasted and the Automotive network becomes overloaded. As such, the authors injected packets randomly composed of MAC and IP addresses for the source and destination into the Automotive Ethernet network to achieve the MAC flooding attack.

CAN DoS and CAN Replay Attacks: As a multi-master of all ECU nodes connected to the CAN bus, the method of message broadcasting in a CAN bus topology and the priority principle for CAN messages constitute the main characteristics of the CAN protocol. However, these characteristics can be the basis for DoS, replay, and fuzzing types of attacks. Firstly, the CAN DoS attack allows the highest priority arbitration ID transmitted from a malicious ECU node to occupy many of the resources allocated to the CAN bus. Subsequently, in the CAN replay attack, the series of dumped data extracted from the normal traffic of the CAN bus are injected into the CAN bus again. This attacks the CAN bus system without conducting the reversing engineering for the functional information assigned to the arbitration ID. The CAN replay attack is performed by changing only the data field values in the CAN message frame.

5   Methodology

This section presents VNGuard, an intrusion detection system for in-vehicle networks, particularly for LIN and AE. The VNGuard system comprises of three major components, namely, 1) data extraction, 2) data pre-processing and 3) intrusion detection with DCNN as shown in Fig. 2.

5.1   Data Extraction

LIN. According to our findings in the existing literature, there is no publicly available dataset for the LIN bus. As such, we rely on the VitroBench [24], an autonomous vehicle security testbed, to generate the LIN dataset. The testbed consists of real vehicle components, including a few devices interconnected via the LIN bus. The available LIN devices include mirror adjusting (top/bottom/left/right), fold-in and fold-out, left/right and auto curb monitor, power windows and safety switch. Additionally, the LIN bus analyzer hardware kit connects to the LIN bus, and the software running on the PC performs trace logging. By activating one function at a time, we collect various LIN messages, log them using the LIN Bus Analyzer, and obtain a dataset labelled as 'Normal' under normal conditions.

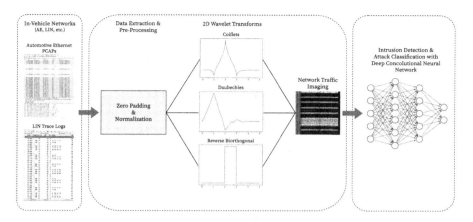

Fig. 2. VNGuard: Intrusion Detection System for In-Vehicle Networks

The attacks for LIN encompass the four previously mentioned attack scenarios in Sect. 3. 1) Response Collision: Though the response data from the slave node is supposed to be 0x00/0x0A, the data changes to 0x05 by means of this attack. 2) Flooding Attack: No attack is performed in the beginning for 20 s. After that, a large amount of invalid data (ID = 0x10, DLC = 0x4, Data = 0x00) is sent, which consequently overwhelms the LIN communication and prevents the devices from operating normally. 3) Header Bombing: This attack involves utilizing the LIN Bus Analyzer software to send frame headers with IDs ranging from 0x00–0x3C. The attacker waits for the response from the corresponding slave nodes and captures the transmitted content on the LIN bus. 4) Injection Attacks: One of these attacks involves sending forged LIN messages while the button is in normal operation. The bus transmits normal traffic, but at the same time, the attacker constantly injects forged messages with (PID = 0x6F, alter the third byte of data). The other is to replay valid messages, manually operate the right mirror button to send a message and use the LIN Bus Analyzer software to re-transmit valid messages to make the left mirror rotate at the same time, resulting in two mirrors rotating at the same time, forming an attack. Table 1 provides the distribution of LIN messages under normal operations and four attack scenarios. The dataset contains 121,926 LIN messages both normal and abnormal messages combined. It is noted that normal LIN messages are also captured before and after the attacks are undertaken since LIN devices are communicating periodically.

AE. The AE intrusion dataset released by Han et al. consists of two network traffic PCAP files; one used for training and another used for testing purpose. Furthermore, the dataset contains two CSV files that provide labels for all the packets in the two PCAP files. There are six distinct labels: 'Normal' for network packet without any attack, 'F_I' for the packets with Frame Injection attack, 'P_I' for PTP Sync attack, 'M_F' for Switch (MAC Flooding) attack, 'C_D' for CAN

Table 1. LIN Dataset

Data Type	# Packets	
	Normal	Abnormal
Normal	29,149	0
Collision between Responses	1,654	75
Header Bombing	3,600	324
Flooding Attack	6,551	3,286
Injection Attacks	73,326	3,961
Total	114,280	7,646

DoS attack and 'C_R' for CAN Replay attack according to the attack scenarios described in Sect. 4. The number of packets for each label in the training and test dataset is provided in Table 2. Overall, the training dataset contains 1,196,737 packets and the test dataset contains 791,611 packets.

Table 2. AE Dataset with Network Packets

Data Type	# Packets	
	Train Dataset	Test Dataset
Normal	947,912	660,777
Frame Injection	35,112	16,962
PTP Sync	64,635	26,013
Switch	33,765	16,809
CAN DoS	85,466	41,203
CAN Replay	29,847	29,847
Total	1,196,737	791,611

5.2 Data Pre-processing

LIN. The raw LIN traces contain various attributes such as timestamp, PID, data field length, and data field for each LIN message. As a result, it is necessary to perform data cleaning and feature selection in order to reduce the complexity of the neural network and trainable parameters. We first extracts and concatenates the PID, data field length, and data field content of each LIN message. We then convert each LIN message into an image utilizing (1) one-hot encoding and (2) 2D Discrete Wavelet Transform (DWT) techniques. Both methods are described in details below.

(1) One-Hot Encoding: As shown in Fig. 3, the processed LIN message consists of a string of hexadecimal numbers with a length equal to or less than 76 bits (PID: 1 byte, Data Length: a nibble, Data: 8 bytes). To ensure a uniform image size, LIN messages with a length less than n bits are appended with the '*' symbol. This feature vector representation is referred to as LIN_pac.

Considering that each bit of the n-bit LIN_pac takes 16 possible values (0x00 – 0x0F), with the '*' sign represented as 0, we encode each bit into a 16-dimensional one-hot vector. Therefore, a single LIN_pac is encoded into a $16 \times n = 16n$ dimension one-hot vector. For instance, if the LIN_pac is 0x8E43C003CC3 * * * * * * * *, the equivalent one-hot encoding is $[0 \ldots 10000000]$, $[0000 \ldots 0010]$, $[00001 \ldots 000]$, $[0001 \ldots 0000]$, $[0000 \ldots 1000]$, ..., $[0000 \ldots 0000]$, $[0000 \ldots 0000]$. Subsequently, 10 LIN_pacs are grouped to form a $16 \times n \times 10 = 160n$ dimension one-hot matrix, referred to as the 'LIN image'. The 'LIN image' is then converted into a feature image comprised of $16 \times 10n$ pixel values. This 10n-pixel valued feature image is labeled as 'Normal' or 'Abnormal', where the presence of any abnormal LIN message within the 10 messages classifies the feature image as abnormal. Following processing of the entire LIN dataset, a total of 8,561 feature images were generated, of which 5,175 represented normal images and 3,386 represented abnormal images.

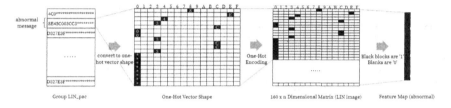

Fig. 3. One-Hot Encoding of LIN Messages

(2) 2D DWT: Wavelet transforms ensure efficient utilization of limited resources and faster model learning. Moreover, two dimensional discrete wavelet transform has the data compression capability while preserving the core information of the image. 2D DWT decomposes a given image into four sub-bands: low-low (LL), low-high (LH), high-low (HL), and high-high (HH). The LL subband is the approximate input image and the size is around 1/4 of the input image. LH, HL and HH sub-bands extract horizontal, vertical, and diagonal features respectively.

Similar to the one-hot encoding approach, we extract and concatenate the LIN PID, data field length, and data content to form a feature vector. However, LIN messages have varying lengths (0–8 bytes) depending on the data field length. In order to have a uniform feature vector, we fix the LIN message length to 32 bytes. If the LIN message length is less than 32, it is padded with zeros. Since the range of input values (i.e., 0–255) could affect the feature value's saturation and weight convergence in the deep learning step, we normalize them to be between 0 and 1. Considering 32 consecutive LIN messages, 32×32 images are obtained.

Subsequently, a 2D DWT is employed to compress the data. We use three wavelet filters (Coiflet 1, Daubechies 3, and Reverse Biorthogonal 1.3) each decomposing the LIN image into four sub-bands. The three low-low (LL) sub-bands, which are approximate of the input image, coefficients are stacked together to form a single RGB image. Labeling of the images is performed similarly to the one-hot encoding approach. A total of 3,809 RGB images were generated which comprise of 2,118 normal images and 1,691 abnormal images.

AE. The number of bytes in each packet varies for each AE protocol. For example, AVTP packets contain 434 bytes whereas gPTP packet ranges from 60–90 bytes. The UDP packets, which are converted from CAN messages, have 60 bytes. In order to train, validate and test the DCNN for intrusion detection, $N \times M$ images are generated from the network packets. In this case, N refers to the number of packets and M refers to the packet length. If M is less than a selected image width, zero padding is performed. On the other hand, if M is larger than the image width, the number of bytes that correspond to the image width are considered and the remaining bytes are discarded.

The value of each byte of the network packet ranges from 0 to 255. This wide range affects the feature value's saturation (no weight update) and weight convergence (fast gradient descent convergence) in the deep learning step. Hence, the pixel values are normalized between zero and one. Similar to generating RGB images from LIN messages, we use the same wavelet filters for the AE packets. The resulting LL sub-bands are stacked together to create RGB images from the network packets. These images are used as inputs to the DCNN in training, validation and testing to realize the intrusion detection system.

5.3   Model Structure

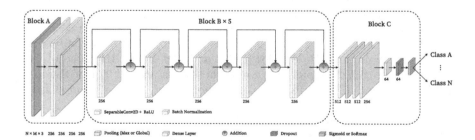

Fig. 4. Deep Convolutional Neural Network Model for Intrusion Detection

Our classification model to detect intrusion on LIN and AE is based on the ResNet deep learning model. As the authors proposed in [7], we performed the adjustment to the ResNet model to reduce the number of parameters. Our proposed DCNN model is shown in Fig. 4. The model consists of three main convolutional blocks, namely, Block A, Block B and Block C.

Block A: This first layer serves as the input layer with an expected input feature image dimension of (N, M, 3), taking (16, 190, 3) for example. The second and third layers consist of separable convolutional layers with 256 filters of size 3 × 3 and a stride of 2. The Rectified Linear Unit (ReLU) activation function is then applied, resulting in an image dimensionality of (4, 48, 256). The fourth layer corresponds to the batch mormalization layer, which ensures batch-wise normalization of the output from the convolutional layer, preserving the dimensionality. The final layer is the max-pooling layer, modifying the feature image dimension to (2, 24, 256) through the max-pooling operation.

Block B: The first and second layers are separable convolutional layers, similar to those in Block A, with identical filter sizes and numbers. However, the stride size is set to 1 in this case, and the ReLU activation function is used. The third layer corresponds to the batch normalization layer. Notably, a residual network architecture is employed, connecting the five instances of Block B by summing the features from previous layers with the output of the current layer. This approach addresses the challenge of vanishing gradients and enhances the network's ability to learn and optimize more effectively, thereby improving the detection accuracy of the model.

Block C: The first layer is also a separable convolutional layer, but with a doubled number of filters and a stride size of 3. The activation function used remains the same. After this layer, the image dimension becomes (1, 8, 512). The second layer is a global average pooling layer, which transforms the feature images into feature vectors with a length of 512. The third, fourth, and fifth layers are fully-connected layers with 512, 256, and 64 neurons, respectively, all employing the ReLU activation function. The sixth layer is the dropout layer, which randomly drops neurons during the training process with a probability of 0.3 to prevent overfitting of the model. Lastly, a Sigmoid is used as the output layer for binary classification. A Softmax is used in the case of multi-class classification, as it produces a probability distribution and exhibits better numerical stability.

The proposed intrusion detection model is trained, validated and tested using both normal and abnormal dataset. The dataset encompasses various attack scenarios targeting LIN and AE as described in Sect. 3 and 4.

6   Experimental Results

In this section, we present experimental results on intrusion detection for LIN and AE. We evaluate the detection performance of the proposed IDS model by analyzing the confusion matrix, accuracy, and F1 score. Moreover, we evaluate the system's response time to determine whether it meets the real-time requirements of autonomous vehicles (AVs).

6.1   IDS for LIN

The pre-processing of data and the generation of feature images have been discussed in Sect. 5.2. After one-hot encoding, 8,561 feature images of size 16 × 190 are generated whereas 3,809 feature images of size 32×32 are obtained following the 2D DWT processing. We divide both datasets into training, validation, and test sets maintaining a ratio of 65%, 15% and 20% respectively.

We use the Keras Python library for deep learning and build the DCNN model. Using the pre-processed dataset with one-hot encoding and 2D DWT, iterative training and learning take place in two separate workflows The gradient descent optimization algorithm is employed, along with the Adam optimizer and a Binary Cross-Entropy (BCE) loss function. During each iteration, 10 feature images are extracted for training and validation, with a learning rate of 0.0001. To prevent overfitting and enhance training efficiency, we use early stopping criteria where training is halted if the validation loss does not improve for three consecutive training epochs. Figure 5(a) shows the training and validation accuracy for the LIN IDS with 2D wavelet transform implementation.

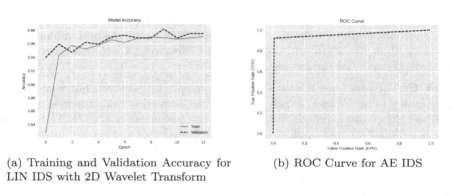

(a) Training and Validation Accuracy for   (b) ROC Curve for AE IDS
LIN IDS with 2D Wavelet Transform

Fig. 5. Training Accuracy for LIN IDS and ROC Curve for AE IDS

Testing is conducted after training, and the experimental results are shown in Table 3. The results obtained from both approaches achieve more than 95% for both the intrusion detection accuracy and the F1 score. This indicates that the DCNN model is capable to detect and classify normal and abnormal LIN messages. Comparing the two approaches, the 2D DWT approach slightly outperforms the one-hot encoding achieving 1% higher in detection accuracy and F1 score.

As provided in Table 1, the LIN dataset consists of a significantly smaller number of **Abnormal** LIN messages. This is mainly due to a very limited devices interconnected via the LIN bus with the VitroBench testbed. We anticipate a more comprehensive LIN dataset to perform a meaningful multi-class attack type classification and the detection accuracy evaluation for LIN IDS.

Table 3. Detection Accuracy, Performance and Response Time of LIN IDS

Method	Accuracy	TN*	FN*	FP*	TP*	F1 Score	Time
One-Hot (16 × 190)	95.43%	445	3	56	777	0.9638	2.1 ms
2D DWT (32 × 32)	96.86%	256	8	10	299	0.9708	3 ms

* True Negative (TN), False Negative (FN), False Positive (FP) and True Positive (TP).

6.2 IDS for AE

We use two network traffic PCAP files as provided by Han et al. in [8] to generate RGB color images. We also set the height N and width M of images to be the same. Since the packet size varies among different types of packets, five image resolutions (i.e., 32 × 32, 60 × 60, 116 × 116, 228 × 228 and 452 × 452) are considered in our experiments. For binary classification, Table 4 provides total number of images generated for **Normal** and **Abnormal** in the training and test dataset for each image resolution. For multi-class classification, Table 5 shows total number of images for **Normal** and five other attack types for each image resolution.

Table 4. AE Dataset with Pre-Processed Images

Image	Training		Test	
	Normal	Abnormal	Normal	Abnormal
32 × 32	17,753	19,863	13,958	10,779
60 × 60	9,209	10,853	7,316	5,877
116 × 116	4,501	5,876	3,660	3,164
228 × 228	2,141	3,138	1,796	1,675
452 × 452	1,075	1,589	903	848

Table 5. AE Dataset for Multi-Class Classification

Image	Normal	FI*	PI*	MF*	CD*	CR*	Total
32 × 32	31,711	2,684	8,423	4,847	8,296	6,394	62,353
60 × 60	16,525	1,812	4,495	2,587	4,424	3,412	33,255
116 × 116	8,161	1,317	2,329	1,340	2,289	1,765	17,201
228 × 228	3,987	877	1,186	684	1,166	900	8,750
452 × 452	1,977	446	601	346	589	455	4,414

* Frame Injection Attack (FI), PTP Sync Attack (PI), MAC Flooding Attack (MF), CAN DoS Attack (CD) and CAN Replay Attack (CR).

As described in Sect. 5.2, the image size becomes 1/4 of the input image after 2D wavelet transform. For example, 2D wavelet transform outputs 228 × 228 resolution LL sub-band images for 452 × 452 resolution input images. For binary classification, we consider an image as **Abnormal** whenever there are one or more attack packets in the image. For multi-class classification, we label an image accordingly if it contains at least one packet that corresponds to a specific attack type. We also noted that there is no overlap of attacks within an image for all image resolutions.

Subsequently, the DCNN model for intrusion detection is trained and validated with the training dataset using the Keras library in the Google Colab environment. Again, we use the BCE loss function, which measures the BCE between the target and the input probabilities. We also set the learning rate of the Adam optimizer to 0.0001 and the maximum number of iterations to 100. During the training and validation, early stopping criteria are also set to monitor the validation loss and to stop the training after no improvement is made between three consecutive epochs. The model checkpoint functionality is also configured to monitor the validation accuracy and to save the trained model with the best performance. After the training is completed, the model performance is evaluated with the test dataset using *evaluate()* method of the Keras library to obtain the testing loss as well as testing accuracy.

Binary Classification Results: Table 6 provides detection accuracy, performance and response time of AE IDS for binary classification. Based on the five different image resolutions considered, the 'Accuracy' column provides the testing accuracy of the intrusion detection system for AE. It is noted the detection accuracy for 32 × 32 resolution is a mere 76.67% while other resolutions achieve more than 95% accuracy. For 32 × 32 resolution, the image width (i.e., packet length) is 32 bytes and all AE packet types in the dataset have at least 60 bytes. The poor detection performance is due to the significant number of data bytes in the packet are discarded when the packet length is larger than 32 bytes as it occurs to all packet types in the dataset. The 116 × 116 resolution achieves the highest detection accuracy of 98.01%. To provide a deeper understanding of the detection performance of the intrusion detection model, we measure True Negative (TN), False Negative (FN), False Positive (FP), and True Positive (TP) as well as the F1 score for the test dataset. The results are also reported in Table 6. Receiver Operating Characteristics (ROC) curve measures the performance of the classification model at various threshold settings. ROC is a probability curve and area under the curve represents the degree of separability indicating how much the model is capable of distinguishing between classes. We plotted the ROC curve for 228 × 228 resolution as shown in Fig. 5(b).

Multi-class Classification Results: Table 7 provides detection accuracy, performance and response time of AE IDS for multi-class classification. Similar to the binary classification results, the 32 × 32 resolution exhibits poor detection accuracy. Meanwhile, all other resolutions except 452 × 452 achieve more than 98% accuracy, resulting in higher accuracy than the binary classification. In particular, the 116 × 116 resolution reports more than 99% detection accuracy with F1 score of 0.9913.

Table 6. Detection Accuracy, Performance and Response Time of AE IDS for Binary Classification

Image	Accuracy	TN*	FN*	FP*	TP*	F1 Score	Time*
32 × 32	76.67%	8,060	3,052	2,719	10,906	0.7364	4 ms
60 × 60	96.48%	5,764	352	113	6,964	0.9612	4 ms
116 × 116	98.01%	3,048	20	116	3,640	0.9782	4 ms
228 × 228	96.74%	1,593	31	82	1,765	0.9657	5 ms
452 × 452	97.43%	809	6	39	897	0.9729	5 ms

* True Negative (TN), False Negative (FN), False Positive (FP) and True Positive (TP).

Table 7. Detection Accuracy, Performance and Response Time of AE IDS for Multi-Class Classification

Image	Accuracy	TN*	FN*	FP*	TP*	F1 Score	Time
32 × 32	76.17%	45,436	2,720	1,604	6,688	0.7557	3 ms
60 × 60	98.68%	24,894	66	66	4,926	0.9868	3 ms
116 × 116	99.14%	13,417	24	23	2,664	0.9913	3 ms
228 × 228	98.74%	6,705	17	15	1,327	0.9881	3 ms
452 × 452	92.84%	3,786	55	54	713	0.9290	4 ms

6.3   Response Time Evaluation

We also evaluated the response time (i.e., the inference time required by the model to perform the classification) of the intrusion detection model for both LIN and AE in Google Colab using *predict()* method of the Keras library. The Google Colab runtime includes Intel Xeon CPU (2.30 GHz) with 2 virtual CPUs (vCPUs) and 13 GB of RAM, and Nvidia Tesla T4 GPU with 16 GB of RAM. For LIN, the one-hot encoding approach takes 2.1 ms whereas the 2D wavelet transform approach takes 3 ms. The response time difference in this case could be explained by the fact that the one-hot encoding approach has 10 LIN messages in one image while the 2D wavelet transform considers 32 LIN messages in one image.

Table 6 and 7 provides the response time of AE IDS for binary and multi-class classification respectively. For the binary classification, smaller image resolutions require 4 ms whereas 228 × 228 and 452 × 452 resolutions require 5 ms to perform the detection. On the other hand, the multi-class classifications requires 3 ms response time except 452 × 452 resolution which takes 4 ms.

To access the feasibility of using the proposed detection model as the edge AI system, the response time is also evaluated using an embedded single-board computing platform reComputer 2021 with Nvidia Jetson Xavier NX with 8 GB RAM. In this case, the trained model is ported to reComputer J2021 and response time is measured during the AI inference. The intrusion detection for

LIN with 2D wavelet transform and Automotive Ethernet with binary classification requires 14 ms whereas multi-class classification requires 12 ms.

According to [14], AV systems should normally complete the operations faster than human drivers, within the latency of 100 ms to offer better safety in autonomous driving environments. The response time of the DCNN is significantly less than 100 ms, which is the end-to-end processing latency constraint for AV systems to achieve human-level safety. Therefore, the proposed DCNN model for intrusion detection is well-suited for deployment on connected vehicles or AV that incorporates AI hardware accelerators/components.

7   Conclusion

Given the increasing security threats targeting autonomous and connected vehicles, intrusion detection systems are becoming essential to ensure in-vehicle network security. Addressing the existing challenges in anomaly detection within the in-vehicle LIN and AE networks, this work proposes VNGuard intrusion detection system based on deep learning model. Leveraging the one-hot encoding and 2D DWT techniques, the LIN messages are transformed into images capturing the characteristics of PIDs, data field length, and data content as feature vectors. This approach enhances model performance and computational efficiency while reducing data dimensionality. Using the dataset with 121,926 LIN messages from which 3,809 32×32 images are generated, our experimental results demonstrate that the proposed LIN IDS model achieves more than 96% detection accuracy with the 2D DWT method slightly outperforming the one-hot approach while meeting real-time latency constraint. Similarly, the experimental results evaluated with the AE dataset, which contains 1,988,348 packets from which 17,201 116×116 images are generated, the IDS for AE achieves more than 98% and 99% detection accuracy for binary and multi-class classification respectively thereby validating the effectiveness of the proposed deep learning model. In addition, the proposed IDS is able to achieve a response time of 3 ms and 4 ms for LIN and AE respectively meeting the real-time latency constraint for autonomous and connected vehicles.

Acknowledgements. This research/project is supported by the National Research Foundation, Singapore, and Land Transport Authority under Urban Mobility Grand Challenge (UMGC-L011). Any opinions, findings and conclusions or recommendations expressed in this material are those of the author(s) and do not reflect the views of National Research Foundation, Singapore and Land Transport Authority. The work is also supported by Singapore Ministry of Education (MOE) Tier 2 Award MOE-T2EP20122-0015. Any opinions, findings and conclusions or recommendations expressed in this material are those of the author(s) and do not reflect the views of MOE.

References

1. Alkhatib, N., Ghauch, H., Danger, J.L.: SOME/IP intrusion detection using deep learning-based sequential models in automotive ethernet networks. In: 2021 IEEE 12th Annual Information Technology, Electronics and Mobile Communication Conference (IEMCON), pp. 0954–0962. IEEE (2021)
2. Ashraf, J., Bakhshi, A.D., Moustafa, N., Khurshid, H., Javed, A., Beheshti, A.: Novel deep learning-enabled LSTM autoencoder architecture for discovering anomalous events from intelligent transportation systems. IEEE Trans. Intell. Transp. Syst. **22**(7), 4507–4518 (2020)
3. Buscemi, A., Ponaka, M., Fotouhi, M., Koebel, C., Jomrich, F., Engel, T.: An intrusion detection system against rogue master attacks on gPTP. In: IEEE Vehicular Technology Conference (VTC2023-Spring), Florence, 20–23 June 2023 (2023)
4. Cheng, P., Xu, K., Li, S., Han, M.: TCAN-IDS: intrusion detection system for internet of vehicle using temporal convolutional attention network. Symmetry **14**(2) (2022)
5. Deichmann, J., Ebel, E., Heineke, K., Heuss, R., Kellner, M., Steiner, F.: Autonomous driving's future: convenient and connected. https://www.mckinsey.com/industries/automotive-and-assembly/our-insights/autonomous-drivings-future-convenient-and-connected (Jan 2023)
6. Ernst, J.M., Michaels, A.J.: LIN bus security analysis. In: 44th Annual Conference of the IEEE Industrial Electronics Society, IECON 2018, pp. 2085–2090. IEEE (2018)
7. Han, M.L., Kwak, B.I., Kim, H.K.: TOW-IDS: intrusion detection system based on three overlapped wavelets for automotive ethernet. IEEE Trans. Inf. Forensics Secur. **18**, 411–422 (2023)
8. Han, M.L., Kwak, B., Kim, H.K.: TOW-IDS: automotive ethernet intrusion dataset (2022). https://doi.org/10.21227/bz0w-zc12
9. Huang, T., Zhou, J., Bytes, A.: ATG: an attack traffic generation tool for security testing of in-vehicle CAN bus. In: Proceedings of the 13th International Conference on Availability, Reliability and Security, ARES 2018. Association for Computing Machinery, New York (2018)
10. Huang, T., Zhou, J., Wang, Y., Cheng, A.: On the security of in-vehicle hybrid network: status and challenges. In: Liu, J.K., Samarati, P. (eds.) ISPEC 2017. LNCS, vol. 10701, pp. 621–637. Springer, Cham (2017). https://doi.org/10.1007/978-3-319-72359-4_38
11. Jeong, S., Jeon, B., Chung, B., Kim, H.K.: Convolutional neural network-based intrusion detection system for AVTP streams in automotive ethernet-based networks. Veh. Commun. **29**, 100338 (2021)
12. Koyama, T., Tanaka, M., Miyajima, A., Ukai, S., Sugashima, T., Egawa, M.: SOME/IP intrusion detection system using real-time and retroactive anomaly detection. In: 2022 IEEE 95th Vehicular Technology Conference: (VTC2022-Spring), pp. 1–7. IEEE (2022)
13. Limbasiya, T., Teng, K.Z., Chattopadhyay, S., Zhou, J.: A systematic survey of attack detection and prevention in connected and autonomous vehicles. Veh. Commun. 100515 (2022)
14. Lin, S.C., et al.: The architectural implications of autonomous driving: constraints and acceleration. In: Proceedings of the Twenty-Third International Conference on Architectural Support for Programming Languages and Operating Systems, pp. 751–766 (2018)

15. Man, D., Zeng, F., Lv, J., Xuan, S., Yang, W., Guizani, M.: AI-based intrusion detection for intelligence internet of vehicles. IEEE Consum. Electron. Mag. **12**(1), 109–116 (2023). https://doi.org/10.1109/MCE.2021.3137790
16. Páez, F., Kaschel, H.: A proposal for data authentication, data integrity and replay attack rejection for the LIN bus. In: 2021 IEEE CHILEAN Conference on Electrical, Electronics Engineering, Information and Communication Technologies (CHILECON), pp. 1–7. IEEE (2021)
17. Páez, F., Kaschel, H.: Towards a robust computer security layer for the LIN bus. In: 2021 IEEE International Conference on Automation/XXIV Congress of the Chilean Association of Automatic Control (ICA-ACCA), pp. 1–8. IEEE (2021)
18. Páez, F., Kaschel, H.: Design and testing of a computer security layer for the LIN bus. Sensors **22**(18), 6901 (2022)
19. Qin, H., Yan, M., Ji, H.: Application of controller area network (CAN) bus anomaly detection based on time series prediction. Veh. Commun. **27**, 100291 (2021)
20. Rajapaksha, S., Kalutarage, H., Al-Kadri, M.O., Petrovski, A., Madzudzo, G., Cheah, M.: AI-based intrusion detection systems for in-vehicle networks: a survey. ACM Comput. Surv. **55**(11), 1–40 (2023)
21. Seo, E., Song, H.M., Kim, H.K.: GIDS: GAN based intrusion detection system for in-vehicle network. In: 2018 16th Annual Conference on Privacy, Security and Trust (PST), pp. 1–6. IEEE (2018)
22. Song, H.M., Woo, J., Kim, H.K.: In-vehicle network intrusion detection using deep convolutional neural network. Veh. Commun. **21**, 100198 (2020)
23. Takahashi, J., et al.: Automotive attacks and countermeasures on LIN-bus. J. Inf. Process. **25**, 220–228 (2017)
24. Teck, A.Y.K., Garbelini, M.E., Chattopadhyay, S., Zhou, J.: VitroBench: manipulating in-vehicle networks and COTS ECUs on your bench: a comprehensive test platform for automotive cybersecurity research. Veh. Commun. 100649 (2023)
25. Upstream: 2023 global automotive cybersecurity report (2023). https://upstream.auto/reports/global-automotive-cybersecurity-report/
26. Zhang, Y., Liu, T., Zhao, H., Ma, C.: Risk analysis of CAN bus and ethernet communication security for intelligent connected vehicles. In: 2021 IEEE International Conference on Artificial Intelligence and Industrial Design (AIID), pp. 291–295. IEEE (2021)

RLTrace: Synthesizing High-Quality System Call Traces for OS Fuzz Testing

Wei Chen[1], Huaijin Wang[1], Weixi Gu[2(✉)], and Shuai Wang[1(✉)]

[1] Hong Kong University of Science and Technology, Hong Kong, China
{wchenbt,hwangdz,shuaiw}@cse.ust.hk
[2] China Academy of Industrial Internet, Beijing, China
guweixi@china-aii.com

Abstract. Securing operating system (OS) kernel is one central challenge in today's cyber security landscape. The cutting-edge testing technique of OS kernel is software fuzz testing. By mutating the program inputs with random variations for iterations, fuzz testing aims to trigger program crashes and hangs caused by potential bugs that can be abused by the inputs. To achieve high OS code coverage, the de facto OS fuzzer typically composes *system call traces* as the input seed to mutate and to interact with OS kernels. Hence, quality and diversity of the employed system call traces become the prominent factor to decide the effectiveness of OS fuzzing. However, these system call traces to date are generated with *hand-coded rules*, or by analyzing *system call logs* of OS utility programs. Our observation shows that such system call traces can only subsume common usage scenarios of OS system calls, and likely omit hidden bugs.

In this research, we propose a deep reinforcement learning-based solution, called RLTrace, to synthesize diverse and comprehensive system call traces as the seed to fuzz OS kernels. During model training, the deep learning model interacts with OS kernels and infers optimal system call traces w.r.t. our learning goal — maximizing kernel code coverage. Our evaluation shows that RLTrace outperforms other seed generators by producing more comprehensive system call traces, subsuming system call corner usage cases and subtle dependencies. By feeding the de facto OS fuzzer, SYZKALLER, with system call traces synthesized by RLTrace, we show that SYZKALLER can achieve higher code coverage for testing Linux kernels. Furthermore, RLTrace found one vulnerability in the Linux kernel (version 5.5-rc6), which is publicly unknown to the best of our knowledge by the time of writing. We conclude the paper with discussions on the limitations, tentative exploration of technical migration to other OS kernels, and future directions of our work. We believe the proposed RLTrace can be a promising solution to improve the reliability of OS fuzzing in various scenarios, over different OS kernels, and for different reliability purposes.

© The Author(s), under exclusive license to Springer Nature Switzerland AG 2023
E. Athanasopoulos and B. Mennink (Eds.): ISC 2023, LNCS 14411, pp. 99–118, 2023.
https://doi.org/10.1007/978-3-031-49187-0_6

1   Introduction

An operating system (OS) kernel usually contains millions lines of code, with complex program structures, deep call hierarchies, and also stateful execution models. Nowadays, OS-level vulnerabilities are gaining more and more attention, not only because it is usually much more challenging to be detected, but also because OS vulnerabilities, once being exploited, can lead to whole-system security breaches with much more severe damages. To date, real-world vulnerabilities has been constantly reported from OS kernels on various computing platforms, including the multi-purpose computers (e.g., Windows and Mac OS), mobile phones, and also embedded devices. Demonstrated by industrial hackers, such vulnerabilities can often lead to severe threats to the financial stability and public safety towards tremendous amounts of users in the real world [2,22].

Software fuzz testing performs vast mutation towards program inputs, exercises its underlying functionalities and reveals vulnerabilities residing within the target software that is difficult to find by traditional testing tools [25]. Despite its simplicity, fuzz testing outperforms many vulnerability detection techniques due to its efficiency and robustness. So far, fuzz testing has helped to detect tremendous amounts of defects from real-life applications, including PDF readers, web browsers, and commonly-used mobile apps [5–7].

To fuzz an OS kernel, the primary strategy is to extensively mutate inputs of the system-call interface, since the interface serves as the main points to interact between the OS kernel and user-level applications [1,9]. The state-of-the-art (SOTA) OS fuzzer takes OS system call traces as the fuzzing seed, and extensively mutates values of system call parameters to achieve high kernel code coverage [11,18]. This naturally solves the problem to generate valid inputs for a system call, for instance, a legitimate file descriptor for `write` can be created by first calling `open` and returning a file descriptor. More importantly, OS kernels are *stateful* software, meaning that the coverage of invoking each system call depends on the OS kernel state created by previously executed system calls. Therefore, de facto OS fuzzers often take traces of system calls as the starting point (i.e., fuzzing seeds) to bootstrap the campaign.

Existing research work mostly relies on ad-hoc approaches to generating valid system call traces as OS fuzzer seeds [1,9,11,18]. For instance, the de facto industry strength OS fuzzer, SYZKALLER, pre-defines thousands of hand-coded rules to encode dependencies among different system calls (see Sect. 2.1 on why "dependencies" are critical) and use them to generate system call traces. A recent work [18] extracts system call traces from the system call logs of OS utility programs. Despite the simplicity, our observation (see Sect. 3) shows that system call traces generated from logs or manually-written rules could only subsume some *commonly-seen cases*. Rarely-used system call traces may not be included, and even for the executed system calls, many of the corner usage scenarios may not be covered as well. Indeed, the performance of software fuzzing tools largely depends on the quality and diversity of their input seeds [19,26], and as shown in our study, the quality of system call traces undoubtedly limits the OS attack surface that can be tested, which further impedes OS fuzzers from identifying real-world security flaws to a great extent.

In this research, we propose a unified and systematic solution, called RLTRACE, to synthesize high quality seeds to promote OS kernel fuzzing. RLTRACE employs deep reinforcement learning (RL), particularly Deep Q-Network (DQN), to synthesize comprehensive sets of system call traces as the kernel fuzzing seeds. RLTRACE trains a DQN model to interact with the OS kernel and explore optimal combinations of system calls. The kernel code coverage is used as the reward for the learning process, and we feed our synthesized system call traces as the seed of the SOTA OS fuzzer, SYZKALLER, to fuzz Linux kernels. After training for 14.9 h, RLTRACE generates a set of 1,526 system call traces to test the Linux kernel (ver. 5.5-rc6). We compare our synthesized system call traces with the SOTA research in this field, MOONSHINE [18], which leverages heavyweight static analysis techniques to generate fuzzing seeds. Our evaluation shows promising findings: 42.0% of traces synthesized by RLTRACE overlap with outputs of MOONSHINE. Moreover, manual study from the non-overlapped traces (58.0%) shows that RLTRACE can find many corner cases where MOONSHINE is incapable of reasoning. Further inspection reveals that the seed generated by RLTRACE, without employing any pre-knowledge or static analysis techniques, can extensively capture subtle dependencies among system calls, outperforming seeds generated by MOONSHINE (for 300.0%) and the default seeds used by SYZKALLER (for 20.1%). By fuzzing with seeds produced by RLTRACEfor 24 h, we successfully found one 0-day kernel vulnerability. Moreover, we illustrate the high generalizability of RLTRACE by discussing the migration to other (embedded) OS kernels. We show that RLTRACE can be easily migrated to fuzz other OS kernels, and we expect that the synthesized seeds can achieve comparable performance as the seeds generated by MOONSHINE. This indicates the high potential of RLTRACE in promoting OS kernel fuzzing in various scenarios, over different OS kernels, and for different reliability purposes. We leave it as our future work to extend RLTRACE and demonstrate its high generalizability on other OS kernels. We also discuss the limitations and future directions of our work to paint a complete picture and the high potential of RLTRACE. In sum, we make the following contributions:

- We introduce a *new* focus to use a generative learning model to promote OS kernel fuzzing by synthesizing quality seeds — system call traces. Our technique is unified and systematic, without relying on any manual-written rules or heavy-weight static analysis techniques.
- We build a practical tool named RLTRACE in coordinating with the de facto industry OS fuzzer, SYZKALLER. Our throughout design and implementation enables the comprehensive testing of production Linux kernels.
- Our evaluation shows that RLTRACE can outperform the SOTA fuzzing seed generators by generating more comprehensive system call traces, achieving higher code coverage, and unveiling more vulnerabilities.
- We present a case study to demonstrate the high generalizability of RLTRACE by discussing the migration to other OS kernels. We show that RLTRACE can be easily migrated to fuzz other OS kernels, and we expect that by extending RLTRACE, we shall be able to achieve comparable performance and constantly

uncover security defects of various properties on other OS kernels or platforms. We accordingly discuss the limitations and future directions of our work.

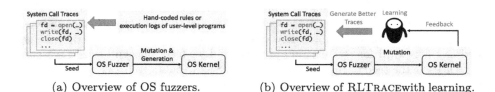

(a) Overview of OS fuzzers.   (b) Overview of RLTRACEwith learning.

Fig. 1. Overviews of OS fuzzers and RLTRACE.

2 Background

2.1 Testing OS Kernels

To secure OS kernels, the de facto technique is OS kernel *fuzz testing* [11,18]. The SOTA OS fuzzers, SYZKALLER [9] and Trinity [1], take a set of *system call traces* (each set is called a "corpus") as their seed inputs for fuzzing. Figure 1(a) presents an overview of OS fuzzing workflow. By feeding a corpus of system call traces into the OS fuzzer, the OS fuzzer will vastly perturb the corpus (including fuzzing parameter values and shuffling system calls on the trace) to interact with the OS kernel. Advanced OS fuzzer like SYZKALLER can also generate new traces during the fuzzing campaign (see Sect. 5.1 on how SYZKALLER mutates and generates new traces). Taking system call traces as the fuzzing inputs is intuitive. The execution of a system call depends on the validity of its input parameters (e.g., a legitimate file descriptor). In addition, internal kernel state created or changed by previous system calls can also influence the execution of succeeding system calls. Invoking a single system call without setting up the proper "context" would merely explore all the functional components of this system call.

Fig. 2. A sample system call trace used by the OS fuzzer, SYZKALLER. To achieve high coverage, both explicit and implicit dependencies need to be satisfied, which is quite challenging for existing rule-based or program analysis-based seed generators [9,18].

In fact, a common assumption shared by existing research and industry OS fuzzers [1,9,11,18] is that the quality of fuzzing seeds heavily depends on the number of explicit and implicit dependencies satisfied on each system call trace. Figure 2 presents a sample trace of five Linux system calls used as a high-quality seed. System call **read** and **close** *explicitly depend* on system call **open**, since the output of open creates a valid file descriptor which can be used as the input parameter of read and close. As a result, simultaneously fuzzing open, write, and close can effectively cover functional components of all these system calls [18], while merely fuzzing read or close along may be trapped in the exception handling routines for most of the time (since the inputs are usually invalid). More importantly, a system call may *implicitly depend* on another system call, if the execution of one system call affects the execution of the other system call via shared kernel data structures (i.e., OS *internal states*), for example the execution of accept4 and setsocketopt both affect and depend on the socket's private data, and by mutating the parameters of accept4, execution of setsocketopt will cover different paths in the kernel (see the third diagram in Fig. 2), although their parameters do not depend on each other explicitly.

While explicit dependencies can be summarized by analyzing the system call documents, obtaining implicit dependencies among system calls, however, is very difficult. Typical (closed-source) OS kernels are highly complex and conducting precise program analysis to pinpoint such dependencies are very challenging, if at all possible. Indeed, as shown in Fig. 1(a), existing OS fuzzers derive system call traces with manually-written rules, or by analyzing system call logs of OS utility programs to infer dependencies. However, our investigation (Sect. 3) shows that these ad-hoc approaches have limited comprehension and presumably miss hidden defects in the kernel. In contrast, our research takes a learning approach to synthesize diverse system call traces from scratch. Our evaluation shows RLTRACE successfully finds four times more implicitly dependent system calls, without any manual efforts (see evaluations reported in Table 2) (Table 1).

Table 1. Kernel data access dependencies of a Linux system call pwritev. We report that the state-of-the-art OS fuzzing seed generator (MOONSHINE [18]) only covers open.

Total Number	System Call Names
27	openat; mq_open; epoll_ctl; shmdt; epoll_create1; mmap_pgoff; fadvise64_64; swapoff; acct shmctl; msync; flock; open; uselib; accept4; dup; setns; socketpair; remap_file_pages; dup3 shmat; socket; open_by_handle_at; memfd_create; pipe2; eventfd2; perf_event_open

2.2 Deep Reinforcement Learning (DRL)

RLTRACE is built on top of a deep reinforcement learning (DRL) model to synthesize quality system call traces. RL is a framework that trains an agent's behavior by interacting with the surrounding environment. During the learning process, the agent observes the environment and performs actions accordingly. For each step of interaction, the agent earns some rewards from the environment, and usually the system goes through a state transition as well. During the overall time of learning, the agent gradually learns to maximize its cumulative reward (i.e., a long-term objective).

We formulate a typical RL process related to the presentation given in [24], where the action of the agent can be viewed as a stochastic process. In particular, the Markov decision procedure is a triple $\mathcal{M} = (\mathcal{X}, \mathcal{A}, \mathcal{P})$, where $\mathcal{X}$ denotes the set of states in the environment, $\mathcal{A}$ is the set of actions an agent can take, and $\mathcal{P}$ represents the *transition probability kernel*, which assigns a probabilistic value denoted as $\mathcal{P}(\cdot|x, a)$ for each state-action pair (x, a) $\in \mathcal{X} \times \mathcal{A}$. For each reward $U \in \mathbb{R}$, $\mathcal{P}(U|x, a)$ gives probability such that performing action a at state x engenders the system to transition from x into $y \in \mathcal{X}$ and returns reward value $U \in \mathbb{R}$. During the stochastic process $(x_{t+1}, r_{t+1}) \sim \mathcal{P}(\cdot|x_t, a_t)$, the goal of the agent is to choose a sequence of actions to maximizes the expected cumulative rewards $\mathcal{R} = \sum_{t=0}^{\infty} \gamma^t R_{t+1}$, where $\gamma \in (0, 1)$ is discount factor.

The deep Q-network (DQN) technique is a specific approach for training a model to select optimal sequences of actions. It has been broadly used in solving real-world challenges and achieved prominent success, including playing strategy board games [21] and video games [16]. In this research, we show that DQN can be leveraged to synthesize quality OS fuzzing seeds and outperform existing rule-based or log-based seed generators.

3   Limitation of De Facto OS Fuzzers

The de facto industry strength OS fuzzer, SYZKALLER, implements thousands of *manually-written* rules to summarize potential dependencies among system calls and generate system call traces (i.e., default seeds shipped with SYZKALLER). Nevertheless, it has been pointed out [18] (and also consistently reported in our evaluation; see Sect. 6) that such rule-based approach cannot achieve highly effective fuzz testing. The reason is that many of its generated traces are *lengthy and repetitive*. From a holistic view, while having a large number of system calls on each trace intuitively improve the "diversity" and coverage, an unforeseen drawback is that within a given amount of time, fuzzer would perform less throughout exploration for each individual system call (too many system calls on a trace), thus scaling down the coverage.

In contrast, the SOTA research, MOONSHINE [18], generates system call traces by analyzing system call logs of OS utility programs. By further performing OS kernel dependency analysis, this work detects dependencies across different system calls to "distills" system call logs; system call traces will primarily retain system calls that depend on each other. It is reported that MOONSHINE can largely promote the fuzzing efficiency compared to the vanilla seeds of SYZKALLER [18]. Intuitively, by *decreasing* the number of system calls present on a trace and only focusing on system calls dependent on each other, the fuzzer can allocate more time to mutate inputs of each system call, and likely increase the code coverage. Nevertheless, our preliminary study shows that system call traces simplified from program execution logs become *less comprehensive* and insufficient to cover the diverse set of Linux kernel system calls.

We collecte system call traces covered by MOONSHINE and compared them with the whole set of Linux system calls. Linux kernel (version 5.5-rc6) has 407 system calls, and the OS fuzzing tool, SYZKALLER, supports 331 system calls. We report that out of these 331 system calls, MOONSHINE can only cover 180 system calls (53.9%; see Table 2) since certain system calls are never used by selected OS utility programs or are trimmed off after its dependency analysis. Moreover, MOONSHINE can hardly consider all usage scenarios of a system call and rarely-used system calls may not be included since it depends on selected programs, which undoubtedly limits the OS attack surface that can be tested.

4 Design

Figure 1(b) depicts the overview of the proposed technique. Instead of pulling out system call traces from execution logs or some manually-written rules, we synthesize system call traces from scratch with the guidance of learning-based methods and with the learning goal of achieving high code coverage. The synthesized traces would form a diverse and comprehensive basis to explore OS kernels, by smoothly taking rarely-used system calls and different system call execution contexts into account, as long as they notably increase code coverage.

Inspired by recent advances in RL-based program analysis and testing [8, 10, 20], where an agent is trained to learn good policies by trial-and-error, we leverage RL models to synthesize system call traces and solve this demanding problem. RLTRACE is constructed as a DQN with two fully connected layer with non-linear activation function `relu`. Each hidden layer contains 512 hidden units. We encode system call traces as a practical learning representation (Sect. 4.1), and our agent is trained to continuously perturb system calls on a trace (Sect. 4.2). The code coverage will be used as the learning reward to train the agent (Sect. 4.3). For each episode, the model training forms an iterative process until our cumulative reward becomes higher than a predefined threshold T_1, or becomes lower than another threshold T_2. Parameters T_1 and T_2 can be configured by users. We harvest optimal traces and pack them into a seed file (i.e., named "corpus") for use.

Application Scope. RLTRACE is evaluated on widely-used Linux OS kernels. Although the source code is available, we treat the OS kernel as a "black-box" (no need for source code). Hence, the proposed techniques can be used during in-house development where source code is available, and also smoothly employed to test *closed-source* OS kernels (e.g., Windows or Mac OS). In contrast, one SOTA seed generator, MOONSHINE, performs heavy-weight static dependency analysis on the source code of the Linux kernel. One may question if RLTRACE, to some extent, is only applicable to mainstream OS kernerls (e.g., Linux) which are fully and clearly documented. We however anticipate that RLTRACE can be seamlessly integrated to test commercial, embedded OS kernels even if the APIs documents are not fully disclosed (e.g., due to commercial confidentiality or IP protection). We believe there is no major technical challenges with the enhancement of modern learning techniques like transfer learning or active learning. See our discussions on extension and future directions in Sect. 7.

4.1 State

State is a basic element in formulating a RL learning procedure. We define a state is a trace of OS system calls $(f_1, f_2, \ldots, f_L)$ where L is the length of the trace (see Sect. 5). We encode the system call with one-hot embedding. Then, a system call trace is treated as a set of system calls, which is encoded with the sum of all system call embeddings. The reason to not adopt sequential embedding methods (e.g., LSTM [4]) is that SYZKALLER indeed *shuffles* each system call trace during fuzzing. In other words, it is sufficient to only use the multi-hot embedding (no need to preserve the "order" with sequential embedding methods).

Typical RL process takes a considerable number of episodes to train an agent: each episode denotes a sequence of state changes starting from the initial state and ending at a terminal state (see Sect. 4.3 for terminal state definition). In this research, we randomly generate the initial state as the starting point of each episode. Also, note that the encoding is only fed to the agent for learning within each episode. We translate each numeric encoding in a state back to its corresponding OS system call before fuzzing the OS kernel.

Deciding an optimal and adaptive length of each trace is difficult. As discussed in Sect. 3, deciding optimal length forms a dilemma: by decreasing the number of system calls present on the trace, the fuzzer allocates more time to mutate inputs of each system call. However, succinct trace may only subsume limited system calls and prone to missing a large portion of OS interfaces, exposing negative effects on code coverage. Similarly, lengthy traces (e.g., the default seed of SYZKALLER) possess more system calls, but can allocate less time to mutate each individual call. Given the general challenge to infer an optimal length, we resort to launch empirical studies and find out that length $L = 5$ usually leads to favorable coverage (see Sect. 5.2).

4.2 Action

We now define all the actions that an agent can perform toward the state during the learning. Given a state $(f_1, f_2, \ldots, f_L)$ which consists of L system calls, we mimic how a human agent could take actions and perturb the trace. Overall, the agent first navigates within the trace, flags certain f_i where $i \in [1, L]$, and then updates the state by changing f_i to some other system call f_i'. While a "random" navigation could provide maximal flexibility by selecting one arbitrary element f_i within the state to perturb, the search space is indeed quite large: $L \times N$ where N is the total number of system calls that can be tested (331 for Linux kernel 5.5-rc6).

To practically reduce the search space, our agent starts from the first element f_1 to mutate, and each learning step only moves one element forward. When it reaches the end, it will re-start from the first element again. This way, our agent picks only one system call f_i each learning step and replaces it with a predicted f_i'. Note that our agent can also retain the current state, as long as f_i equals to f_i'. The search space of our agent is reduced into N. Evaluation shows that the model training is efficient in practice. Although there are still considerable states to explore (since N is still large), deep Q-networks have been shown to handle large state spaces efficiently, as we will show in Sect. 6.

4.3   Reward

The reward function is the key to RL frameworks. The central assumption behind the SOTA coverage-based fuzzer is that coverage increase indicates a higher possibility of detecting new vulnerabilities. Therefore, to construct the search witness, we take the coverage increase into account. The OS fuzzer employed in this research provides basic block coverage for each individual system call on the trace for use. Let $c_1c_2 \ldots c_i \ldots c_L$ be the code coverage of individual system calls on the trace $s = (f_1f_2 \ldots f_i \ldots f_L)$. Suppose by replacing f_i with f_i', the produced new system call trace is $s' = (f_1f_2 \ldots f_i' \ldots f_L)$. Then, the reward function w.r.t. this action $f_i \rightarrow f_{i'}$ is formulated as, $R = \frac{\sum_{i=1}^{L} \log \frac{c_i'}{c_i}}{L}$, where c_i' are the code coverage of individual system calls on our new trace. The learning reward is a positive number, in case a higher code coverage is achieved by the new trace. Nevertheless, we penalize coverage decrease by computing and assigning a negative reward to the agent.

Overall, the coverage feedback depends on the entire system call trace synthesized so far rather than on the very last system call being picked. In other words, our formulation indeed takes long-term rewards into consideration, which progressively infers the optimal system call traces.

Hyperparameters. For long-term reward harvesting, we use a discount rate of 0.9. Our learning rate is 0.01. We follow the common practice to adopt a ϵ-greedy policy with ϵ decayed from 0.95 to 0. ϵ will be fixed at 0 thereafter. The agent will select the predicted optimal action with the probability of $1 - \epsilon$, and explores random actions with the probability of ϵ. Hence, the training starts by focusing on random explorations and gradually converge to optimal decisions. Overall, while we follow common and standard practice to decide model hyperparameters and settings, evaluation results already report promising findings.

Terminal State. In the context of RL, "episode" defines a sequence of state transitions which ends with terminal state. A RL model training usually takes hundreds of episodes until saturation. We define the terminal state such that the cumulative reward is greater than a threshold T_1 (10.0 in our current implementation). The current episode will also be terminated, if the cumulative reward is lower than another threshold T_2 (–5.0 in our current implementation), indicating that there should be few chances we can find an optimal trace during this episode. Hence, we terminate the current episode. At the end of an episode, we archive the synthesized optimal trace for reuse. Archived traces will be packed into a corpus and fed to the OS fuzzer as its seed.

5   Implementation

The RL learning framework is built on top of Tensorflow (ver. 1.14.0), written in Python (about 500 lines of code). We also instrumented the OS fuzzer, SYZKALLER (see Sect. 5.1). This patch is written in Go, with approximate 300 lines of code.

5.1   Syzkaller Instrumentation

The de facto OS fuzzer used in this research, SYZKALLER, is widely used in testing real-world OS kernels and has been constantly finding (security-critical) bugs. Given a seed generated by packing system call traces, SYZKALLER performs four mutation strategies including 1) mutating system call parameters, 2) shuffling system calls on a trace, 3) removing system calls on a trace or adding extra calls, and 4) generating new system call traces from hand-written rules and templates. In general, the first three strategies primarily depend on the quality of seeds, while the last one implements a carefully crafted "generation" strategy to synthesize new inputs during the long run. Although the standard SYZKALLER mingles all four mutation strategies together, during model training, we instrument SYZKALLER and only enable the first three strategies to better reflect quality of synthesized seeds. Similarly for the fuzzing evaluation, we measure the seed quality by only using the first three strategies (Sect. 6.3). We also resort to the default setting of SYZKALLER with all strategies enabled to mimic the "real-world" usage in the evaluation (Sect. 6.3).

The standard workflow of SYZKALLER requires to re-boot the tested OS kernel (hosted in a virtual machine instance) every time before fuzzing. Hence for every learning step, we need to terminate and reboot the VM instance, exposing high cost to model training. To optimize the procedure, we instrument SYZKALLER by adding an agent module. After booting the VM instance for the first time, the agent listens for requests from RLTRACE and forwards synthesized traces to the fuzzer module of SYZKALLER. In this way, the VM instance will be booted for only once during the entire training. This instrumentation reduces the training time from 67.4 CPU hours to 14.9 CPU hours (see Sect. 6.1 for model training).

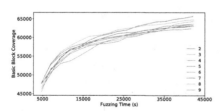

(a) Kernel code coverage w.r.t. different trace lengths.

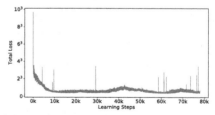

(b) Loss function decrease over episodes. We present overall 80k steps corresponding to 480 episodes trained in this evaluation.

Fig. 3. Kernal code coverage and loss function curves.

5.2   Decide the Length of System Call Trace

To decide the length of an optimal system call trace, we launch empirical studies to explore the change of length with respect to their corresponding coverage data. In general, our observation shows that too lengthy traces can notably slow down the fuzzer, and therefore are not desired. Hence, we empirically decide to vary the trace length from two to nine and record the corresponding basic block coverage.

Let N be the number of total system calls we decide to use in this study, we start by randomly constructing S_2 system call traces with a fixed length as two, such that $S_2 \times 2 \approx N$. We then feed SYZKALLER with this set of traces, fuzz the Linux kernel, and record the coverage increase. We then randomly construct S_3 traces of three system calls (to present a fair comparison, here $S_3 \times 3 \approx N$) and re-launch the whole experiments until we have tested S_9 traces of nine system calls (again, $S_9 \times 9 \approx N$). For this study, N is 7,679 which equals to the total number of system calls used in the seed generated by MOONSHINE (see relevant information in Sect. 6). Figure 3(a) reports the evaluation results in terms of basic block coverage increase. We report that traces with five system calls can outperform other settings with sufficient time of fuzzing (after about 27,000 s). Given this empirical observation, the implementation adopts five as the length of each synthesized system call traces. Indeed, we report that empirical results revealed at this step is essentially consistent with MOONSHINE: the average length of traces generated by MOONSHINE is 5.2.

6 Evaluation

We evaluate the proposed technique in terms of its ability to promote real-world OS fuzz testing. As aforementioned, we feed the synthesized system call traces into an industrial-strength OS fuzzer, SYZKALLER [9], to fuzz the Linux kernel. We use Linux kernel version 5.5-rc6 (released 12 January 2020) for the evaluation unless stated otherwise. To evaluate the effectiveness of RLTRACE, we compare the outputs of RLTRACE with the SOTA OS fuzzing input generator, MOONSHINE [18], and also the default seeds of SYZKALLER generated by hand-written rules. For the ease of presentation, we use S_{rl} and S_{moon} to represent seeds generated by RLTRACE and MOONSHINE, and S_{def} to represent the default seeds of SYZKALLER.

The empirical study in Sect. 5.2 decides the length of each system call trace as five. To provide a fair comparison, we first compute the total number of system calls from S_{moon} (S_{moon} is shared by the paper author): we report that from 525 traces in S_{moon}, 7,679 system calls are included. Hence, we decide to configure RLTRACE and generate 1,526 traces. Recall as introduced in Sect. 5.1, SYZKALLER implements mutation strategies to extend certain traces with extra system calls. We observe that when feeding these 1,526 traces into SYZKALLER, SYZKALLER indeed extends certain traces with in total 47 extra system calls (e.g., when detecting `timespec`, SYZKALLER will add `clock_gettime` ahead of `timespec`). In short, the total system call numbers in S_{rl} is 7,677 ($1526 \times 5 + 47$). Also, we confirm that *no* extra system calls need to be inserted into S_{moon} when fed to SYZKALLER; this is reasonable since S_{moon} is derived from system call logs, where real programs are generally required to "compensate" extra system calls.

SYZKALLER leverages hand-written rules to generate a large amount of lengthy and repetitive traces: we randomly select 1,027 traces from S_{def} that also include 7,679 system calls in total (no extra system calls are added as well). Overall, while S_{rl} and its two competitors have different number of traces, the total number of system calls are (almost) identical, qualifying a fair comparison.

A Fair Comparison. It is easy to see that RLTRACE can smoothly synthesize more traces with little cost, by simply taking more episodes. In contrast, MOONSHINE and SYZKALLER are bounded by the availability of quality OS test suites or expert efforts. We consider this actually highlights the conceptual-level *difference* and *advantage* of RLTRACE. Overall, we would like to emphasize that our evaluation in the rest of this section presents a fair comparison which indeed **undermines** the full potential of RLTRACE.

6.1   Model Training

We first report the model training results. The training was conducted on a server machine with an Intel Xeon E5-2680 v4 CPU at 2.40 GHz and 256 GB of memory. The machine runs Ubuntu 18.04. The training takes in total 14.9 CPU hours for 480 episodes. As reported in Fig. 3(b), the loss function keeps decreasing until reaching low total loss scores (after about 9.5K steps). We interpret the results as promising; the trained model can be progressively improved to a good extent and find optimal system call traces more rapidly along the training. We then randomly select 1,526 optimal traces and pack them into a seed (i.e., "corpus"). Further studies on the seed quality (Sect. 6.2) and code coverage (Sect. 6.3) will be conducted on this seed.

6.2   Exploring System Call Trace Quality

Cross Comparison. We now take a close look at S_{rl} and compare it with S_{moon} and S_{def}. To this end, we first count and compare the number of unique system calls that are included in these three seeds.

Table 2. System call coverage and explicit/implicit dependencies comparison.

Seed	#Covered Unique System Calls	Explicit Dependency	Implicit Dependency
S_{rl}	291	423	376
S_{moon}	180	247	94
S_{def}	115	775	313

Table 2 reports the comparison results which is encouraging. Out of in total 331 Linux system calls, 1,526 traces synthesized by RLTRACE cover 291 unique system calls. In contrast, S_{moon} has a low coverage: from in total 525 system call traces subsumed in S_{moon}, only 180 unique system calls are covered. S_{def} yields an even worse coverage: 115 unique system calls are included.

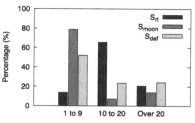 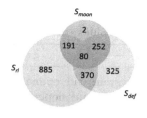

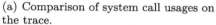

(a) Comparison of system call usages on the trace.

(b) Agreement among system call traces.

Fig. 4. Analysis of call trace quality.

Figure 4(a) reports and compares the usage of each system call in these three seeds. In particular, we count how many different traces a system call can be found from. As aforementioned, different traces intuitively denote various "execution contexts." We are anticipating to systematically explore a system call, if more contexts can be provided. As reported in Fig. 4(a), 78.9% of system calls are used for only less than ten times by S_{moon}. Similar trending can also be observed from S_{def}. In contrast, the output of RLTRACE domains the second range: majority system calls are used for over ten times. Overall, we interpret that Table 2 and Fig. 4(a) demonstrate promising and intuitive findings. Enabled by the systematic and in-depth exploration in RLTRACE, less commonly used system calls and diverse contexts can be taken into account as long as they reasonably contribute to code coverage.

We also measured the agreement of three seeds by counting the number of equivalent traces. We relax the notion of trace "equivalence" by entailing the partial order of two traces (note that traces are shuffled within SYZKALLER and therefore is reasonable to treat as "sets" without considering orders): $t \doteq t' \leftrightarrow t \subseteq t' \vee t' \subseteq t$.

Figure 4(b) reports the analysis results. S_{rl} and S_{moon} agree on 271 traces, while S_{rl} and S_{def} agree on 450. S_{moon} and S_{def} have 332 agreements (63.2% of all traces in S_{moon}; highest in terms of percentage). Overall, we interpret the results as promising: we show that considerable amount of system call traces (641; 42.0% of all traces in S_{rl}) can be synthesized without employing heavyweight program analysis or hand-coded rules. Moreover, the 58.0% disagreement, to some extent, shows that RLTRACE enables the construction of more diverse system call traces enable the coverage of corner cases. Accordingly, we now present case studies on system call traces generated by RLTRACE.

Case Study. Our study shows that `pwritev` implicitly depends on 27 system calls of the Linux kernel. S_{rl} consists of 10 traces containing `pwritev`, and these 10 traces cover three unique system calls that `pwritev` implicitly depends on. In contrast, as noted in Sect. 3, `pwritev` and only one of its implicitly dependent system call can be found from S_{moon}, and this particular case is subsumed by S_{rl} as well. Consider the system call trace below:

```
lseek  →  openat  →  getxattr  →  chmod  →  pwritev
```

where the system call openat and pwritev implicitly depend on each other (i.e., they access and depend on the same kernel data structure). We report that this system call trace can be found in S_{rl}, but is not included in S_{moon}. In other words, kernel code coverage derived from this implicit dependency will presumably not be revealed by MOONSHINE.

Similarly, we find another system call fchown implicitly depends on 97 system calls of the kernel. RLTRACE generates 32 traces containing this system calls, covering 15 unique system calls that fchown implicitly depends on. For instance:

```
pipe2  →  getresuid  →  fchown  →  getresuid  →  getpgrp
```

where the system call pipe2 and fchown implicitly depend on each other. In contrast, we report that MOONSHINE only identifies **one** implicitly dependent system call for fchown. Further quantitative data regarding explicit/implicit dependencies is given in Sect. 6.2.

Dependency Analysis. As discussed in Sect. 2.1, OS fuzz testing leverages system call traces of good quality, and therefore, aims at satisfying both explicit and implicit dependencies and achieving high code coverage. Nevertheless, directly analyzing dependencies could be challenging. We now measure the quality of system traces, in terms of how they subsume explicit and implicit dependencies.

Explicit Dependency. Explicit dependencies denote system call parameter and return value-level dependencies. To measure the performance, we collect all the explicit dependencies of each system call. SYZKALLER provides a data structure named target which can be parsed to acquire such information. The summarized explicit dependencies (i.e., pairs of system calls; in total 4,429) deem a "ground truth" dataset, and we measure three seeds w.r.t. this ground truth. The evaluation results are reported in the second column of Table 2.

Overall, enabled by thousands of manually-written rules which extensively encode system call dependencies among parameters and return values, S_{def} largely outperforms the other two seeds by recovering more explicitly dependent system calls. MOONSHINE analyzes execution logs of OS utility programs to gather system call traces. Real-world programs must satisfy these explicit dependencies to function properly. Nevertheless, RLTRACE still demonstrates encouraging results, by inferring considerable explicit dependencies *from scratch* and outperform S_{moon} (finding 176 more explicit dependencies). Envisioning the necessity and opportunity of improving RLTRACE at this step, we present discussions in Sect. 7.

Implicit Dependency. MOONSHINE releases a dataset to summarize implicit dependencies among system calls, which is gathered by performing static dependency analysis toward Linux kernel. Similarly, we reuse this dataset (in total

9,891 pairs of system calls) to measure three seeds. Performing static dependency analysis toward complex system software like Linux kernel is unlikely to yield accurate results. Nevertheless, by measuring dependency recovery regarding the same baseline, this is still an "apple-to-apple" comparison.

The third column of Table 2 reports *highly promising* results. S_{rl} notably outperforms its competitors, by finding more implicitly-dependent system calls without adopting any hand-coded rules or static analysis. S_{def} primarily encodes explicit dependencies: implicit dependencies are hard to be identified with only manual efforts. Careful readers may wonder about the performance of MOON-SHINE (since the "ground truth" dataset is even provided by MOONSHINE). To clarify potential confusions: MOONSHINE performs whole kernel static analysis to collect implicit dependencies. It also performs execution trace-based analysis to collect system call traces. In short, a system call trace will be kept if it matches certain implicit dependencies collected by the static analysis. Since not all "implicitly dependent" system calls will appear on execution traces, S_{moon} does not indeed perform well.

6.3   Fuzzing Evaluation

Fuzzing Without Runtime Trace Generation Enabled. We feed SYZKALLER with three seeds to fuzz the Linux kernel 5.5-rc6. To faithfully explore the quality of the generated seeds, we disable the "generation" strategy of SYZKALLER. Recall Sect. 5.1 introduces four mutation strategies implemented in SYZKALLER. At this step, SYZKALLER will only perform the first three mutation strategies to vastly perturb input seeds. Evaluation by enabling all mutation options will be given in Sect. 6.3. Since no "new traces" are generated, our observation shows that the fuzzing procedures rapidly reach to the saturation point after around 0.5 h for all three seeds. Still, we fuzz each seed for 3 h to explore their full potentials. Table 3 reports the basic block coverage after 3-h fuzzing. S_{rl} outperforms its competitors by achieving a higher code coverage, while S_{def} has the worst coverage (consistent with the MOONSHINE paper). We interpret the results as generally encouraging; the high quality fuzzing seed generated by RLTRACE enables a practical exploration of production Linux kernels, achieving higher coverage. We present more comprehensive evaluation in terms of coverage and crashes in the following section.

Table 3. Kernel coverage comparison using different seeds.

	S_{rl}	S_{moon}	S_{def}
coverage	25,252	24,932	14,902

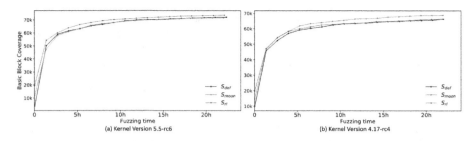

Fig. 5. Code coverage with runtime trace generation enabled during 24 h of fuzzing.

Fuzzing with Runtime Trace Generation Enabled. As aforementioned, SYZKALLER can be configured to continuously generate new traces with its thousands of hand-written rules. In this research, we enable this feature to mimic the "normal" way of using SYZKALLER and launch a 24-h fuzzing. To present a comprehensive comparison, besides the latest kernel (ver. 5.5-rc6), we also test another kernel (ver. 4.17-rc4) evaluated in the MOONSHINE paper. Figure 5 reports the coverage increase during 24 h of fuzzing. Again, to present a fair comparison with MOONSHINE, we only generate 1,526 traces in the evaluation. For practical usage, users can certainly generate more traces with RLTRACE. Within 24 h of fuzzing, the SYZKALLER generates a large amount of extra traces (close to 100K), and therefore, seeds produced by RLTRACE and MOONSHINE become "insignificant" to some extent. Nevertheless, RLTRACE still outperform its competitors, by achieving a higher coverage in kernel 5.5-rc6. In contrast, RLTRACE and SYZKALLER has less coverage compared to MOONSHINE while fuzzing the older kernel. Note that we synthesize S_{rl} w.r.t. kernel 5.5-rc6, and some system calls in S_{rl} are *not* supported by kernel 4.17-rc4. Hence, 254 traces in S_{rl} are directly rejected without contributing to any coverage, presumably undermining RLTRACE for kernel 4.17-rc4.

Table 4 reports the triggered kernel crashes during the 24-h campaign in kernel 5.5-rc6 and 4.17-rc4. We count crashes by analyzing the crash report provided by SYZKALLER and deduplicate if two crashes have identical call stacks. While these seeds find close number of crashes from kernel 5.5-rc6, cross comparison shows that each tool can find unique crashes that are *not* detected by others. Those cases are more interesting and are reported in the column #**UU** of Table 4. We further check whether those unique crashes have been reported before. We carefully searched the crash stack trace from the Linux Kernel Mailing List [3], Red Hat Bugzilla [12], Lore Kernel [15], and Google. We find three (1+2) crashes in total that cannot be found anywhere, and presumably deem *unknown bugs* in kernel 5.5-rc6. Regarding the old kernel (4.17-rc4) evaluated by MOONSHINE, RLTRACE finds considerable more crashes compared to the other seeds, and by checking each unique crash, ten crashes exposed by RLTRACE are not disclosed publicly to our best knowledge.

Table 4. Crashes found in kernel 5.5-rc6 and 4.17-rc4 using different seeds. To clarify potential confusions, "#Deduped Crashes" (**#D**) deduplicates repeated crashes and each reported crash has a different call stack. "#Unique Crashes" (**#U**) reports number of deduped crashes that are only found by this particular seed. **#UU** denotes unique and unknown crashes by the time of writing.

Seeds	5.5-rc6			4.17-rc4		
	#D	#U	#UU	#D	#U	#UU
S_{rl}	20	2	1	34	16	10
S_{moon}	19	2	0	25	5	4
S_{def}	20	4	2	20	2	1

7   Discussion and Future Direction to Industrial Scenarios

We believe this paper has revealed high potential of RLTRACE in promoting OS kernel fuzzing and reliability. As a starting point for future research and engineering efforts, we list future directions of our work from the following aspects.

Combining with Offline Analysis. RLTRACE trains the model from scratch to highlight the key contribution and novelty — synthesizing diverse system call traces from scratch with RL. To this end, RLTRACE takes code coverage to form learning reward. Nevertheless, our evaluation in Sect. 6.2 indicates the need of integrating dependencies into the reward. Overall, to enhance the fuzzing performance, we plan to combine RLTRACE with offline analysis. For instance, as an offline phase, we can leverage active learning techniques to gradually form dependencies among system calls, and then integrate the analysis results to enhance our online fuzzing and learning process. Moreover, we expect to leverage recent progress in AI, particularly large language models (LLMs), to extract the dependencies among system calls from OS kernel source code or documents. For instance, GPT-4 [17] is a recently proposed LLM that can generate high-quality text. We envision that GPT-4 can be leveraged to generate system call traces from scratch, and we plan to explore this direction in the future.

Feasibility Study of Fuzzing Industrial, Embedded OS Kernels. From a holistic perspective, RLTRACE can be easily migrated to fuzz other OS kernels since its technical pipeline is generic and systematic. We have tentatively explored the feasibility of migrating RLTRACE to fuzz other OS kernels, in particular, a commercial embedded OS kernel, *xxxOS*, that is being adopted in real-world, industrial sectors.[1] In short, we find that fuzzing those embedded OS kernels is not conceptually more challenging than fuzzing Linux kernels. They however impose new technical challenges that require further research efforts. In particular, we list the number of APIs of the two kernels in Table 5. We observe that the number of APIs of *xxxOS* is much smaller than that of Linux. This is reasonable, as typical embedded OS kernels are designed to be lightweight and resource-efficient. However, the small number of APIs makes it potentially more

---

[1] The OS kernel name is blinded for commercial reasons.

challenging to synthesize diverse system call traces. For instance, we find that the number of system calls that can be invoked by a single API is much larger than that of Linux. This indicates that the dependencies among system calls are less comprehensive, and presumably more subtle. To combat this challenge, we plan to leverage recent progress in AI, particularly large language models (LLMs), to extract the dependencies among system calls from OS kernel source code or documents. We also anticipate to use other static analysis or learning techniques, whose rational has been presented above.

Table 5. Comparison of APIs in the Linux version evaluated in this research and *xxxOS*.

	Linux	xxxOS
The number of APIs	331	112

Another major challenge is that *xxxOS* is an embedded OS kernel running on a specific hardware platform. To fuzz *xxxOS*, our tentative exploration shows that the underlying fuzzing framework, SYZKALLER, cannot be directly used. This is reasonable, as SYZKALLER is designed to fuzz general-purpose OS kernels and it largely relies on the full-system virtualization environment to monitor the kernel execution. However, *xxxOS* is an embedded OS kernel, and it is not designed to run in a full-system virtualization environment. Note that this could be a general and pervasive challenge when benchmarking industrial, commercial OS kernels. To address this challenge, we anticipate to investigate a high volume of engineering efforts to re-develop a proper fuzzing framework for *xxxOS*. We leave it as our future work.

Securing Industrial, Embedded OS Kernels. From a more general perspective, we believe that securing embedded OS kernels requires more than fuzzing. In short, software fuzz testing mainly focuses on more obvious security properties like memory safety, and during testing, its "testing oracle" is mainly derived from system crash, hang, or other obvious symptoms. However, it has been reported that embedded OS kernels are vulnerable to more subtle security properties like information leakage, functional (driver) bugs, side channel attacks, and so on. To this end, we believe it is of great importance to develop a more comprehensive and systematic solution to secure embedded OS kernels. Our effort and tentative exploration reported in this section is a starting point, and we plan to explore this direction in the future. In particular, we plan to leverage recent progress in AI, particularly LLMs, to explore potential privacy leakage issues in embedded OS kernels. Note that typical commercial embedded OS kernels may operate on various critical devices, such as medical devices, automobiles, and so on. Therefore, it is of great importance to secure them from the perspective of privacy leakage. The authors have accumulated rich experience in handling and detecting privacy leakage bugs using software testing, static analysis, and side channel analysis methods. We plan to explore this direction in the future.

8   Related Work

OS Fuzzers. Trinity [1] is another popular OS fuzzer. We choose SYZKALLER since it is the de facto OS fuzzing framework maintained by Google and MOON-SHINE only uses this tool for fuzzing and comparison. Note that Trinity [1] is generally not desired in our research: Trinity is not a coverage-guided fuzzer, and, therefore, "code coverage" cannot be obtained from Trinity for model training. Overall, RLTRACE does not rely on any particular OS fuzzer design, and all OS kernel fuzzers (including Trinity) can potentially benefit from high-quality inputs offered by RLTRACE.

Security Testing of OS Kernels. In addition to perform fuzz testing toward OS kernel system call interface and expose memory related vulnerabilities, existing research also aims to fine-tune the performance of fuzz testing with respect to certain *specific* OS kernel components and vulnerabilities. For instance, Razzer [13] performs fuzz testing to pinpoint race conditions within Linux kernels. Xu et al. [27] launches effective fuzz testing toward file systems by re-scoping the mutation target from large file image blobs into metadata blocks. Also, besides the system call interfaces, recent research works [14,23] also propose fuzz testing framework to probe and detect bugs from the device-driver interactions with OS kernels. Looking ahead, we leave it as one future work to integrate those critical and specific testing tasks into RLTRACE.

9   Conclusion

We have proposed a RL-based method to synthesize high-quality and diverse system call traces for fuzzing OS kernels. The propose technique generates high-quality traces without using software analysis or rule-based techniques. Our evaluation shows that the synthesized system call traces engender high OS code coverage and also reveal vulnerabilities overlooked by existing tools.

Acknowledgement. The authors would like to thank the anonymous reviewers for their valuable comments and suggestions. The authors also thank the engineers from the China Academy of Industrial Internet for their help in this research.

References

1. Trinity (2018). https://github.com/kernelslacker/trinity
2. The Top 10 Linux Kernel Vulnerabilities You Should Know (2019). https://resources.whitesourcesoftware.com/blog-whitesource/top-10-linux-kernel-vulnerabilities
3. Linux kernel mailing list (2023). https://lkml.org/
4. Gers, F.A., Schmidhuber, J., Cummins, F.: Learning to forget: continual prediction with LSTM (1999)
5. Godefroid, P., Kiezun, A., Levin, M.Y.: Grammar-based whitebox fuzzing. In: ACM Sigplan Notices, vol. 43, pp. 206–215. ACM (2008)

6. Godefroid, P., Levin, M.Y., Molnar, D.: Sage: whitebox fuzzing for security testing. Commun. ACM **55**(3), 40–44 (2012)
7. Godefroid, P., Levin, M.Y., Molnar, D.A., et al.: Automated whitebox fuzz testing. In: NDSS, vol. 8, pp. 151–166. Citeseer (2008)
8. Godefroid, P., Peleg, H., Singh, R.: Learn&fuzz: machine learning for input fuzzing. In: Proceedings of the 32nd IEEE/ACM International Conference on Automated Software Engineering, pp. 50–59. ASE 2017 (2017)
9. Google: Syzkaller (2018). https://github.com/google/syzkaller
10. Gupta, R., Kanade, A., Shevade, S.: Deep reinforcement learning for syntactic error repair in student programs. In: Proceedings of the Thirty-Third AAAI Conference on Artificial Intelligence. AAAI 2019 (2019)
11. Han, H., Cha, S.K.: IMF: inferred model-based fuzzer. In: Proceedings of the 2017 ACM SIGSAC Conference on Computer and Communications Security, pp. 2345–2358. CCS '17 (2017)
12. Hat, R.: Red hat Bugzilla (2023). https://bugzilla.redhat.com/
13. Jeong, D.R., Kim, K., Shivakumar, B., Lee, B., Shin, I.: Razzer: finding kernel race bugs through fuzzing. In: Razzer: Finding Kernel Race Bugs through Fuzzing. IEEE (2019)
14. Jiang, Z.M., Bai, J.J., Lawall, J., Hu, S.M.: Fuzzing error handling code in device drivers based on software fault injection (2019)
15. Kernel, L.: Lore kernel (2023). https://lore.kernel.org/lists.html
16. Mnih, V., et al.: Playing Atari with deep reinforcement learning. arXiv preprint arXiv:1312.5602 (2013)
17. OpenAI: Gpt-4 (2023). https://openai.com/research/gpt-4
18. Pailoor, S., Aday, A., Jana, S.: Moonshine: optimizing OS fuzzer seed selection with trace distillation. In: UNISEX Security (2018)
19. Rebert, A., et al.: Optimizing seed selection for fuzzing. In: Proceedings of the 23rd USENIX Conference on Security Symposium, pp. 861–875. SEC'14, USENIX Association, USA (2014)
20. Si, X., Dai, H., Raghothaman, M., Naik, M., Song, L.: Learning loop invariants for program verification. In: Advances in Neural Information Processing Systems (NeurIPS) (2018)
21. Silver, D., et al.: Mastering the game of go with deep neural networks and tree search. Nature **529**(7587), 484 (2016)
22. Skybox: 2019 Vulnerability and Threat Trends (2019). https://lp.skyboxsecurity. com/rs/440-MPQ-510/images/Skybox_Report_Vulnerability_and_Threat_Trends_2019.pdf
23. Song, D., et al.: PeriScope: an effective probing and fuzzing framework for the hardware-OS boundary. In: NDSS (2019)
24. Szepesvári, C.: Algorithms for Reinforcement Learning. In: Synthesis Lectures on Artificial Intelligence and Machine Learning, vol. 4, no. 1, pp. 1–103. Springer, Cham (2010). https://doi.org/10.1007/978-3-031-01551-9
25. Takanen, A., DeMott, J., Miller, C.: Fuzzing for Software Security Testing and Quality Assurance, 1st edn. Artech House Inc., USA (2008)
26. Wang, J., Chen, B., Wei, L., Liu, Y.: Skyfire: data-driven seed generation for fuzzing. In: 2017 IEEE Symposium on Security and Privacy (SP), pp. 579–594. IEEE (2017)
27. Xu, W., Moon, H., Kashyap, S., Tseng, P.N., Kim, T.: Fuzzing file systems via two-dimensional input space exploration. In: 2019 IEEE Symposium on Security and Privacy (SP), pp. 818–834. IEEE (2019)

Machine Learning

Loss and Likelihood Based Membership Inference of Diffusion Models

Hailong Hu[1]($\boxtimes$) and Jun Pang[1,2]

[1] SnT, University of Luxembourg, Esch-sur-Alzette, Luxembourg
`hailong.hu@uni.lu`
[2] FSTM, University of Luxembourg, Esch-sur-Alzette, Luxembourg
`jun.pang@uni.lu`

Abstract. Recent years have witnessed the tremendous success of diffusion models in data synthesis. However, when diffusion models are applied to sensitive data, they also give rise to severe privacy concerns. In this paper, we present a comprehensive study about membership inference attacks against diffusion models, which aims to infer whether a sample was used to train the model. Two attack methods are proposed, namely loss-based and likelihood-based attacks. Our attack methods are evaluated on several state-of-the-art diffusion models, over different datasets in relation to privacy-sensitive data. Extensive experimental evaluations reveal the relationship between membership leakages and generative mechanisms of diffusion models. Furthermore, we exhaustively investigate various factors which can affect membership inference. Finally, we evaluate the membership risks of diffusion models trained with differential privacy.

Keywords: Membership inference attacks · Diffusion models · Human face synthesis · Medical image generation · Privacy threats

1 Introduction

Diffusion models [34] have recently made remarkable progress in image synthesis [16,19,38], even being able to generate better-quality images than generative adversarial networks (GANs) [11] in some situations [8]. They have also been applied to sensitive personal data, such as the human face [19,37] or medical images [21,30], which might unwittingly lead to the leakage of training data. As a consequence, it is paramount to study privacy breaches in diffusion models.

Membership inference (MI) attacks aim to infer whether a given sample was used to train the model [33]. In practice, they are widely applied to analyze the privacy risks of a machine learning model [27,35]. To date, a growing number of studies concentrate on classification models [2,25,32,33,40], GANs [6,13], text-to-image generative models [39], and language models [4,5]. However, there is

---

Our code is available at: https://github.com/HailongHuPri/MIDM.

© The Author(s), under exclusive license to Springer Nature Switzerland AG 2023
E. Athanasopoulos and B. Mennink (Eds.): ISC 2023, LNCS 14411, pp. 121–141, 2023.
https://doi.org/10.1007/978-3-031-49187-0_7

still a lack of work on MI attacks against diffusion models. In addition, data protection regulations, such as GDPR [29], require that it is mandatory to assess privacy threats of technologies when they are involving sensitive data. Therefore, all of these drive us to investigate the membership vulnerability of diffusion models.

In this paper, we systematically study the problem of membership inference of diffusion models. Specifically, we consider two threat models: in threat model I, adversaries are allowed to obtain the target diffusion model, and adversaries also can calculate the loss values of a sample through the model. This scenario might occur when institutions share a generative model with their collaborators to avoid directly sharing original data [24, 28]. We emphasize that obtaining losses of a model is realistic because it is widely adopted in studying MI attacks on classification models [2, 25, 33, 40]. In threat model II, adversaries can obtain the likelihood value of a sample from a diffusion model. Providing the exact likelihood value of any sample is one of the advantages of diffusion models [38]. Thus, here we aim to study whether the likelihood value of a sample can be considered as a clue to infer membership. Based on both threat models, two types of attack methods are developed respectively: loss-based attack and likelihood-based attack. They are detailed in Sect. 3.

We evaluate our methods on four state-of-the-art diffusion models: DDPM [16], SMLD [37], VPSDE [38] and VESDE [38]. We use two privacy-sensitive datasets: a human face dataset FFHQ [20] and a diabetic retinopathy dataset DRD [18]. Extensive experimental evaluations show that our methods can achieve excellent attack performance, and provide novel insights into membership vulnerabilities in diffusion models (see Sect. 5). For instance, the loss-based attack demonstrates that different diffusion steps of a diffusion model have significantly different privacy risks, and there exist high-risk regions which lead to leakage of training samples. The likelihood-based attack shows that the likelihood values of samples from a diffusion model provide a strong indication to infer training samples. We also analyze attack performance with respect to various factors in Sect. 6. For example, we find that the high-risk regions still exist with the increase in the number of training samples (see Fig. 5). This indicates that it is urgent to redesign the current noise mechanisms used by almost all diffusion models. Finally, we evaluate our attack performance on a classical defense - differential privacy [10] (see Sect. 7). Specifically, we train target models using differentially-private stochastic gradient descent (DP-SGD) [1]. Extensive evaluations show that although the performance of both types of attack can be alleviated on models trained with DP-SGD, they sacrifice too much model utility, which also gives a new research direction for the future.

Our contributions in this paper are twofold. (1) We propose two types of attacks to infer the membership of diffusion models. Our attack methods reveal the relationship between the leakage of training samples and the generative mechanism of diffusion models. (2) We evaluate our attacks on one classical defense— diffusion models trained with DP-SGD, showing that it mitigates our attacks at the cost of the quality of synthetic samples.

In the end, we want to emphasize that although we study membership inference from the perspective of attackers, our proposed methods can directly be applied to audit the privacy risks of diffusion models when model providers need to evaluate the privacy risks of their models.

2   Background: Diffusion Models

Diffusion models [34] are a class of probabilistic generative models. They aim to learn the distribution of a training set, and the resulting model can be utilized to synthesize new data samples.

In general, a diffusion model includes two processes: a forward process and a reverse process [34]. In the forward process, i.e. the diffusion process, it aims to transform a complex data distribution p_{data} into a simple prior distribution, e.g. Gaussian distribution $\mathcal{N}(0, \sigma^2 I)$, by gradually adding different levels of noise $0 = \sigma_0 < \sigma_1 <, ..., < \sigma_T = \sigma_{max}$, into the data x. In the reverse process, it targets at synthesizing a new data sample $\tilde{x}_0$ through step by step denoising a data sample $\tilde{x}_T \sim \mathcal{N}(0, \sigma_{max}^2 I)$. Both processes are defined as Markov chains, and the transitions from one step to another step are described by transition kernels. In the following, we briefly introduce three typical diffusion models.

DDPM. A denoising diffusion probabilistic model (DDPM) proposed by Ho et al. [16] defines the forward process: $q(x_1, ..., x_T | x_0) = \prod_{t=1}^{T} q(x_t | x_{t-1})$, where T is the number of diffusion steps. The transition kernel uses a Gaussian transition kernel: $q(x_t | x_{t-1}) = \mathcal{N}(x_t; \sqrt{1 - \beta_t} x_{t-1}, \beta_t I)$, where the hyperparameter $\beta_t \in (0, 1)$ is a variance schedule. Based on the transition kernel, we can get a perturbed sample by: $x_t \leftarrow \sqrt{1 - \beta_t} x_{t-1} + \sqrt{\beta_t} \varepsilon$, where $\varepsilon \sim \mathcal{N}(0, I)$. The transition kernel from the initial step to any t step can be expressed as: $q(x_t | x_0) = \mathcal{N}(x_t; \sqrt{\bar{\alpha}_t} x_0, (1 - \bar{\alpha}_t) I)$, where $\bar{\alpha}_t = \prod_{i=0}^{t} \alpha_i$ and $\alpha_t := 1 - \beta_t$. Therefore, any perturbed sample can be obtained by: $x_t \leftarrow \sqrt{\bar{\alpha}_t} x_0 + \sqrt{1 - \bar{\alpha}_t} \varepsilon$. In the reverse process, DDPM generates a new sample by: $\tilde{x}_{t-1} \leftarrow \frac{1}{\sqrt{\alpha_t}} (\tilde{x}_t - \frac{\beta_t}{\sqrt{1 - \bar{\alpha}_t}} \varepsilon_\theta(\tilde{x}_t, t)) + \sigma_t \epsilon$, where $\epsilon_\theta(x_t, t)$ is a neural network predicting noise. In practice, DDPM is trained by minimizing the following loss:

$$L(\theta) = \mathbb{E}_{t \sim [1,T], x \sim p_{data}, \varepsilon \sim \mathcal{N}(0,I)} [||\varepsilon - \varepsilon_\theta(\sqrt{\bar{\alpha}_t} x + \sqrt{1 - \bar{\alpha}_t} \varepsilon, t)||^2]. \quad (1)$$

SMLD. Score matching with Langevin dynamics (SMLD) [37] first learns to estimate the *score*, then generates new samples by Langevin dynamics. The *score* refers to the gradient of the log probability density with respect to data, i.e. $\nabla_x log\, p(x)$. The transition kernel in the forward process is: $q(x_t | x_0) = \mathcal{N}(x_t; x_0, \sigma_t^2 I)$. Thus, a perturbed sample is obtained by: $x_t \leftarrow x_0 + \sigma_t \varepsilon$. In the reverse process, SMLD uses an annealed Langevin dynamics to generate a new sample by: $\tilde{x} \leftarrow \tilde{x}_{t-1} + \frac{\alpha_i}{2} s_\theta(\tilde{x}_{t-1}, \sigma_i) + \sqrt{\alpha_i} \epsilon$, where the hyperparameter σ_i controls the updating magnitudes and $s_\theta(x_t, \sigma_i)$ is a noise conditioned neural network predicting the *score*. Training of the SMLD is performed by minimizing the following loss:

$$L_\theta = \mathbb{E}_{t \sim [1,T], x \sim p_{data}, x_t \sim q(x_t | x)} [\lambda(\sigma_t) || s_\theta(x_t, \sigma_t) - \nabla_{x_t} \log q(x_t | x) ||^2], \quad (2)$$

where $\lambda(\sigma_t)$ is a coefficient function and $\nabla_{x_t} \log q(x_t|x) = -\frac{x_t - x}{\sigma_t^2}$.

SSDE. Unlike prior works DDPM or SMLD which utilize a finite number of noise distributions, i.e. t is discrete and usually at most T, Song et al. [38] propose a score-based generative framework through the lens of stochastic differential equations (SDEs), which can add an infinite number of noise distributions to further improve the performance of generative models. The forward process which adds an infinite number of noise distributions can be described as a continuous-time stochastic process. Specifically, the forward process of the score-based SDE (SSDE) is defined as:

$$dx = f(x,t)dt + g(t)dw, \tag{3}$$

where $f(x,t)$, $g(t)$ and dw are the drift coefficient, the diffusion coefficient and a standard Wiener process, respectively. The reverse process corresponds to a reverse-time SDE: $dx = [f(x,t) - g(t)^2 \nabla_x \log q_t(x)]dt + g(t)d\bar{w}$, where $\bar{w}$ is a standard Wiener process in the reverse time. Training of the SSDE is performed by minimizing the following loss:

$$L_\theta = \mathbb{E}_{t \in \mathcal{U}(0,T), x \sim p_{data}, x_t \sim q(x_t|x)}[\lambda(t)||s_\theta(x_t, t) - \nabla_{x_t} \log q(x_t|x)||^2]. \tag{4}$$

The SSDE is a general and unified framework. Based on different coefficients in Eq. 3, the variance preserving (VP) and variance exploding (VE) are instantiated. The VPSDE is defined as: $dx = -\frac{1}{2}\beta(t)xdt + \sqrt{\beta(t)}dw$. The VESDE is defined as: $dx = \sqrt{\frac{d[\sigma^2(t)]}{dt}}dw$. Furthermore, the SSDE also shows the noise perturbations of DDPM and SMLD are discretizations of VP and VE, respectively. Note that, diffusion steps usually used in diffusion models also refer to time steps that are used in SDEs. In this work, we study the privacy risks of four target models: DDPM, SMLD, VPSDE, and VESDE.

3 Methodology

The objective of MI attacks is to infer if a sample was used to train a model. This provides model providers with a method to evaluate the information leakage of a machine learning model. In this section, we first introduce threat models and then present our MI methods.

3.1 Threat Models

Threat Model I. In this setting, we assume adversaries can only obtain the target model, i.e. the victim diffusion model. This setting is realistic because institutions might share generative models with their collaborators instead of directly utilizing original data, considering privacy threats or data regulations [24,28]. We emphasize that adversaries do not gain any knowledge of the training set. Obtaining the target model indicates that adversaries can get the loss values through the model, and this is realistic because most MI attacks on classification models also assume adversaries can get loss values [2,25,33,40]. Under this threat model, we propose a loss-based MI attack.

Threat Model II. In this setting, we assume adversaries can have access to the likelihood values of samples from a diffusion model. Diffusion models have advantages in providing the exact likelihood value of any sample [38]. Here we aim to study whether the likelihood values of samples can be utilized as a signal to perform membership inference. Under this threat model, we propose a likelihood-based MI attack.

3.2 Intuition

We propose MI attacks based on the following two intuitions.

Intuition I. As introduced in Sect. 2, a diffusion model aims to minimize the loss values over the training set in the training phase. One intuition is that member samples, i.e. the training samples, should have smaller loss values, compared to nonmember samples. This is because training/member samples involve the training process and their loss values could be minimized.

Intuition II. A diffusion model is a generative model that learns the distribution of a training set. Therefore, the likelihood values of training/member samples should be higher than these of nonmember samples. This is because training/member samples are from the distribution of the training set.

3.3 Attack Methods

Problem Formulation. Given a target diffusion model G_{tar}, the objective of MI attacks is to infer whether a sample x from a target dataset X_{tar} is used to train the G_{tar}.

Loss-Based Attack. For threat model I and following intuition I, we develop a loss-based attack. As illustrated in Sect. 2, diffusion models can add an infinite or finite number of noise distributions, which are corresponding to continuous or discrete SDE, respectively. Therefore, we can calculate the loss value of a sample at each diffusion step t. Specifically, based on Eq. 1, the loss of a sample x at t diffusion step of DDPM is calculated by:

$$L = \frac{1}{m} \sum ||\varepsilon - \varepsilon_{\theta^*}(\sqrt{\bar{\alpha}_t}x + \sqrt{1 - \bar{\alpha}_t}\varepsilon, t)||^2, \tag{5}$$

where m is the dimension of x and $\varepsilon_{\theta^*}(.)$ is the trained network. By Eq. 2, the loss of a sample x at t diffusion step of SMLD is calculated by:

$$L = \frac{1}{m} \sum \lambda(\sigma_t)||s_{\theta^*}(x_t, \sigma_t) - \nabla_{x_t} \log q(x_t|x)||^2, \tag{6}$$

where $s_{\theta^*}(.)$ is the trained network. Based on Eq. 4, the loss of a sample x at t diffusion step of VPSDE and VESDE is:

$$L = \frac{1}{m} \sum \lambda(t) ||s_{\theta^*}(x_t, t) - \nabla_{x_t} \log q(x_t|x)||^2. \tag{7}$$

Then, we make a membership inference directly based on the loss value of a sample at one diffusion step. Namely, if a sample's loss value is less than certain thresholds, this sample is marked as a member sample. For one sample, we can get T or infinite losses, depending on continuous or discrete SDEs. In this work, in order to thoroughly demonstrate the performance of our attack, we compute losses of all diffusion steps T for the discrete case. We randomly select T diffusion steps for the continuous case although it has infinite steps.

Likelihood-Based Attack. For threat model II and following intuition II, we propose to utilize the likelihood value of a sample to infer membership. We compute the log-likelihood of a sample x based on the equation proposed by [38].

$$\log p(x) = \log p_T(x_T) - \int_0^T \nabla \cdot \tilde{f}_{\theta^*}(x_t, t) dt, \tag{8}$$

where $\nabla \cdot \tilde{f}_{\theta^*}(x, t)$ is estimated by the Skilling-Hutchinson trace estimator [12]. If the log-likelihood value of a sample is higher than certain thresholds, this sample is predicted as a member sample. As introduced in Sect. 2, the work SSDE [38] is a unified framework. In other words, DDPM, SMLD, VPSDE and VESDE can be described by Eq. 3. Therefore, Eq. 8 can be applied to these models to estimate the likelihood of one sample. In this work, we compute the likelihood values of all training samples.

4   Experiments

4.1   Datasets

We use two different datasets to evaluate our attack methods. They cover the human face and medical images, which are all considered privacy-sensitive data.

FFHQ. The Flickr-Faces-HQ dataset (FFHQ) [20] is a new dataset that contains $70,000$ high-quality human face images. In this work, we randomly choose $1,000$ images to train target models. We also explore the effect of the size of the training set in Sect. 6.1.

DRD. The Diabetic Retinopathy dataset (DRD) [18] contains $88,703$ retina images. In this work, we only consider images that have diabetic retinopathy, which is a total of $23,359$ images. Furthermore, we randomly choose $1,000$ images to train target models. Note that images in all datasets are resized to 64×64 just for the purpose of computation efficiency.

4.2 Metrics

Evaluation Metrics for Diffusion Models. We use the popular Fréchet Inception Distance (FID) metric to evaluate the performance of a diffusion model [14]. A lower FID score is better, which implies that the generated samples are more realistic and diverse. Considering the efficiency of sampling, in our work the FID score is computed with all training samples and 1,000 generated samples.

Evaluation Metrics for MI Attacks. We primarily use the full log-scale receiver operating characteristic (ROC) curve to evaluate the performance of our attack methods, because it can better characterize the worst-case privacy threats of a victim model [2]. We also report the true-positive rate (TPR) at the false-positive rate (FPR) as it can give a quick evaluation. We use average-case metrics—accuracy as a reference, although it cannot assess the worst-case privacy.

4.3 Experimental Setups

In terms of target models, we use open source codes [36] to train diffusion models, and their recommended hyperparameters about training and sampling are adopted. More specifically, the number of training steps for all models is fixed at 500,000. For discrete SDEs, T is fixed as 1,000 while T is set as 1 for continuous SDEs. In terms of our attack methods, we evaluate the attack performance using all training samples as member samples and equal numbers of nonmember samples.

5 Evaluation

5.1 Performance of Target Models

Considering their excellent performance in image generation, we choose DDPM [16], SMLD [37], VPSDE [38] and VESDE [38] as our target models. They are trained on the FFHQ dataset containing 1k samples. Target models with the best FID during the training progress are selected to be attacked. Table 1 shows the performance of the target models. Figure 9 in Appendix shows the qualitative results for these target models. Overall, all target models can synthesize high-quality and realistic images.

Table 1. The performance of target models on FFHQ.

Target Models	DDPM	SMLD	VPSDE	VESDE
FID	57.88	92.81	20.27	63.37

5.2   Performance of Loss-Based Attack

We present our attack performance from two aspects: TPRs at fixed FPRs for all diffusion steps and log-scale ROC curves at one diffusion step. The former aims to provide the holistic performance of our attacks in diffusion models. In contrast, the latter concentrates on one diffusion step and is able to exhaustively show TPR values at a wide range of FPR values, which is key to assessing the worst-case privacy risks of a model.

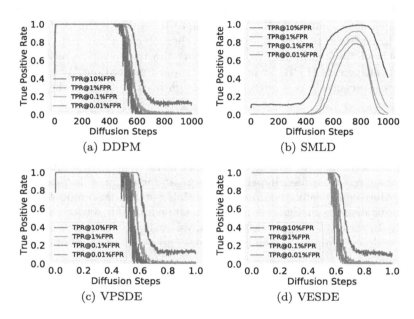

Fig. 1. Performance of the loss-based attack on all diffusion steps. Target models are trained on FFHQ.

TPRs at Fixed FPRs for all Diffusion Steps. Figure 1 shows the performance of our loss-based attack on four target models trained on FFHQ. We plot TPRs at different FPRs with regard to diffusion steps for each target model. Recall DDPM and SMLD models are discrete SDEs while VPSDE and VESDE models are continuous SDEs. Thus, the number of diffusion steps for DDPM and SMLD is finite and is fixed as 1,000, while for VPSDE and VESDE models, we uniformly generate 1,000 points within $[0, 1]$ and compute corresponding losses. Overall, all models are vulnerable to our attacks, even under the worst-case, i.e. TPR at 0.01% FPR, depicted by the purple line of Fig. 1.

We observe that *our attack presents different performances in different diffusion steps.* To be more specific, there exist high privacy risk regions for diffusion models in terms of diffusion steps. In these regions (i.e. diffusion steps), our attack can achieve as high as 100% TPR at 0.01% FPR. Even for the SMLD model, close to 80% TPR at 0.01% FPR can be achieved. Recall the training mechanisms of diffusion models, different levels of noise at different diffusion steps are added during the forward process. DDPM and VPSDE and VESDE are added growing levels of noise while SMLD starts with maximum levels of noise and gradually decreases the levels of noise. Thus, we can see that these models (DDPM and VPSDE, and VESDE) are more vulnerable to leak training samples in the first half part of the diffusion steps while the SMLD model shows membership vulnerability in the second half part of the diffusion steps.

In brief, all models are prone to suffer from membership leakage in low levels of noise while they become more resistant in high levels of noise. In fact, in these diffusion steps where high levels of noise are added to training data, perturbed data is almost close to pure Gaussian noise, which can enhance the privacy of training data to some degree. We also notice that at the starting diffusion step, our attack performance suffers from a decrease. This is because there is an instability issue at this step during the training process [38]. Despite this, these peak regions still show the effectiveness of our attack.

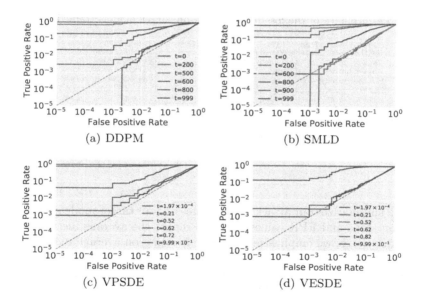

Fig. 2. Performance of the loss-based attacks at one diffusion step. Target models are trained on FFHQ.

Log-Scale ROC Curves at One Diffusion Step. Figure 2 plots full log-scale ROC curves of the loss-based attack on four target models. We choose six different diffusion steps for each target model. The rules of choosing diffusion steps for discrete SDEs (i.e. DDPM and SMLD) are: starting and ending diffusion step and the diffusion step that experiences significant changes in terms of attack performance. For continuous SDEs (i.e. VPSDE and VESDE), we first get $1,000$ points that are uniformly sampled from $[0, 1]$. Then, we choose diffusion steps from these points based on the same rule of discrete SDEs. Overall, our excellent attack performance is exhaustively shown through log-scale ROC curves.

We can observe that when the levels of noise are not too large, our method can achieve a perfect attack, such as at $t = 200$ for the DDPM model, $t = 800$ for the SMLD model, and $t = 0.21$ for the VPSDE and VESDE models. Again, we can clearly see that the ROC curves on all target models are more aligned with the grey diagonal line with the increase in the magnitudes of noise. The grey diagonal line means that the attack performance is equivalent to random guesses. For example, the ROC curves are almost close to the grey diagonal line when the maximal level of noise is added, such as the DDPM model at $t = 999$, the SMLD model at $t = 0$, and the VPSDE and VESDE models at $t = 9.99 \times 10^{-1}$. It is not surprising because at that time the input samples are perturbed as Gaussian noise data in theory and indeed do not have something with original training samples.

Table 2. Performance of the loss-based attack on target models trained on FFHQ.

Models	T	TPR@ 10%FPR	TPR@ 1%FPR	TPR@ 0.1%FPR	TPR@ 0.01%FPR	Accuracy	Models	T	TPR@ 10%FPR	TPR@ 1%FPR	TPR@ 0.1%FPR	TPR@ 0.01%FPR	Accuracy
DDPM	0	63.50%	36.40%	22.50%	21.10%	78.25%	SMLD	0	7.90%	0.80%	0.00%	0.00%	51.20%
	200	100.00%	100.00%	100.00%	100.00%	100.00%		200	11.20%	0.70%	0.10%	0.00%	52.30%
	500	100.00%	99.50%	80.80%	72.50%	99.30%		500	88.50%	64.40%	56.10%	35.70%	89.50%
	600	59.50%	18.80%	4.30%	2.30%	81.15%		800	99.10%	91.70%	78.60%	76.10%	96.40%
	800	13.90%	2.50%	0.60%	0.30%	52.80%		900	85.80%	52.00%	22.80%	15.30%	88.80%
	999	12.60%	1.70%	0.00%	0.00%	52.45%		999	41.50%	8.60%	1.90%	0.10%	70.55%
VPSDE	1.97×10^{-4}	93.00%	85.00%	81.60%	77.60%	93.15%	VESDE	1.97×10^{-4}	100.00%	100.00%	100.00%	100.00%	100.00%
	0.21	100.00%	100.00%	100.00%	100.00%	100.00%		0.21	100.00%	100.00%	100.00%	100.00%	100.00%
	0.52	100.00%	100.00%	99.50%	78.40%	99.90%		0.52	100.00%	100.00%	100.00%	99.90%	99.95%
	0.62	66.50%	14.50%	8.20%	4.30%	85.70%		0.62	96.00%	53.60%	18.60%	14.20%	93.25%
	0.72	17.90%	3.70%	1.20%	0.20%	57.30%		0.82	13.10%	1.90%	0.50%	0.30%	52.50%
	9.99×10^{-1}	13.00%	1.8%	0.40%	0.10%	52.20%		9.99×10^{-1}	11.60%	1.70%	0.30%	0.10%	51.50%

Table 2 summarizes our attack performance on four target models with regard to diffusion steps and FPR values. We also report the average metric accuracy for reference. Here, we emphasize that only focusing on average metrics cannot assess the worst-case privacy risks. For instance, for the DDPM model at $t = 800$, the attack accuracy is 52.80%, which indicates the model at this diffusion step almost does not lead to the leakage of training samples, because it is close to 50% (the accuracy of random guesses). In fact, the TPR is 0.3% at the false positive rate of 0.01%, which is 30 times more powerful than random guesses. It means that adversaries can infer confidently member samples under extremely low false positive rates.

Figure 3 shows perturbed data of four target models under different diffusion steps. The diffusion steps in Fig. 3 are corresponding to these in Fig. 2. We observe that even when some perturbed data that is almost not recognized by human beings is used to train the model, it seems not to prevent model memorization. For example, for the DDPM model at $t = 600$, the perturbed image is meaningless for humans. However, the attack accuracy is as high as 81.15%. At

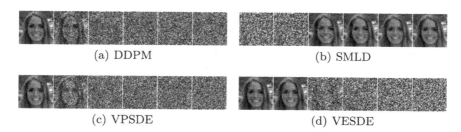

(a) DDPM   (b) SMLD

(c) VPSDE   (d) VESDE

Fig. 3. Perturbed data of four target models under different diffusion steps. The diffusion steps correspond to these in Fig. 2. Specifically, from left to right for each model: DDPM (0, 200, 500, 600, 800, 999); SMLD (0, 200, 600, 800, 900, 999); VPSDE (1.97×10^{-4}, 0.21, 0.52, 0.62, 0.72, 9.99×10^{-1}); VESDE (1.97×10^{-4}, 0.21, 0.52, 0.62, 0.82, 9.99×10^{-1}).

the same time, the TPR at 0.01% FPR is 2.30%, which is 230 times more powerful times than random guesses. It indicates that models trained on perturbed data, except for Gaussian noise data, can still leak training samples. *The noise mechanism of diffusion models does not provide privacy protection.*

5.3   Performance of Likelihood-Based Attack

Figure 4(a) demonstrates our likelihood-based attack performance on four target models. Overall, our attacks still perform well on all target models. For example, our attack on the SMLD and VPSDE models almost remains 100% true positive rates on all false positive rate regimes. For the VESDE model, attack results are slightly inferior to the SMLD model, yet still higher than the 10% true positive rate at an extremely low 0.001% false positive rate.

Table 3 shows our attack results at different FPR values for all target models. Once again, we can clearly see that even at the 0.01% FPR, the lowest TPR among all models is as high as 23.10%, which is 2, 310 times than random guesses. In addition, we also observe that the attack accuracy is above 98% for all target models. Our attack results also remind model providers that they should be careful when using likelihood values.

Table 3. Likelihood-based attack. Target models are trained on FFHQ.

Models	TPR@ 10%FPR	TPR@ 1%FPR	TPR@ 0.1%FPR	TPR@ 0.01%FPR	Accuracy
DDPM	98.00%	89.00%	79.70%	71.00%	95.75%
SMLD	100.00%	100.00%	100.00%	100.00%	100.00%
VPSDE	100.00%	99.60%	98.90%	98.20%	99.45%
VESDE	100.00%	93.80%	58.40%	23.10%	98.50%

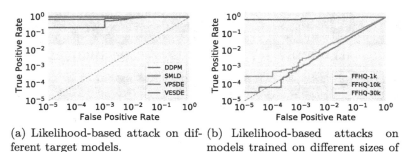

(a) Likelihood-based attack on different target models.

(b) Likelihood-based attacks on models trained on different sizes of datasets.

Fig. 4. Performance of the likelihood-based attack.

5.4 Takeaways

Our loss-based attack utilizes loss values to make a membership inference. Although the loss-based attack requires adversaries to choose a suitable diffusion step to mount the attack, our extensive experiments identify the high privacy risk region. More importantly, our loss-based attack reveals the relationship between membership risks and the generative mechanism of diffusion models. This provides a new angle to mitigate membership risks by designing novel noise mechanisms of diffusion models. Our likelihood-based attack does not need to choose a diffusion step and infers membership directly based on likelihood values. Both loss and likelihood information can lead to the leakage of training samples.

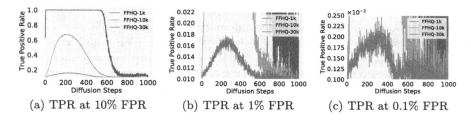

(a) TPR at 10% FPR   (b) TPR at 1% FPR   (c) TPR at 0.1% FPR

Fig. 5. Performance of loss-based attack with different sizes of datasets. The target model is DDPM trained on FFHQ. Each subfigure shows attack performance with different sizes of datasets on fixed FPRs.

6   Analysis

6.1   Effects of Size of a Training Dataset

We study attack performance with regard to different sizes of the training set of a target model. Here, we choose the DDPM models trained on FFHQ as target models. We use FFHQ-1k, FFHQ-10k, and FFHQ-30k to represent different sizes of a dataset, which refer to 1,000, 10,000, and 30,000 training samples in each dataset respectively. The FID of the target model DDPM trained on FFHQ-1k, FFHQ-10k, and FFHQ-30k are 57.88, 34.34, and 24.06, respectively. In the following, we present the performance of our both attacks.

Performance of Loss-Based Attack. Figure 5 depicts the performance of loss-based attacks on all diffusion steps under different sizes of a training set. Overall, we can observe that attack performance gradually becomes weak when the size of training sets increases. For example, at diffusion step $t = 200$, the TPR at 10% FPR decreases from 100% to about 15% when the training samples increase from 1k to 30k. Here, note that the starting points of the y-axis in Fig. 5 are not 0 and we set them as the probability of random guesses. Thus, as long as the lines can be shown in the figure, it indicates this is an effective attack.

However, *the peak regions still exist even if the number of training samples increases to 30k and the FPR value is as low as 0.1%.* For instance, as shown in Fig. 5(c), it shows our attack performance of 0.1% FPR on all models. Diffusion steps in the range of 0 to 400 are still vulnerable to our attack, compared to other steps. It indicates that these diffusion steps indeed lead a model to more easily leak training data. We further show the attack performance based on each dataset in Fig. 11 in Appendix.

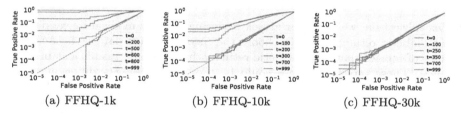

(a) FFHQ-1k   (b) FFHQ-10k   (c) FFHQ-30k

Fig. 6. Performance of loss-based attack with different sizes of datasets. The target model is DDPM. TPR-FPR Curves under different time steps.

Figure 6 shows ROC curves of our attack against target models trained on different sizes of training sets. Based on the same rules described in Sect. 5.2, we select several different diffusion steps and plot their ROC curves. On the one hand, we can see that indeed models become less vulnerable as the number of training samples increases. For instance, Fig. 6(c) shows the DDPM trained on FFHQ-30K is more resistant to MI attacks on the full log-scale TPR-FPR curve. On the other hand, when diffusion step t equals 250, our attack shows higher attack performance than random guesses at the low false positive rate, such as 10^{-4}. This is also corresponding to the peak steps in Fig. 5.

We also observe from Fig. 6 that TPR values in diffusion steps of high privacy risks do not further go down with the increase in FPR values, especially in extremely low FPR regimes. Take the DDPM trained on FFHQ-30K as an example (see Fig. 6(c)), the TPR value at diffusion step $t = 250$ are still about

10^{-4} at the FPR value of 10^{-5}, while at $t = 999$, the TPR value at 10^{-5} FPR value is 0. This indicates that at $t = 250$, there are some training samples whose loss values are always smaller than the minimal loss value of the nonmember sample. Otherwise, the green line ($t = 250$) will go down to zero, similar to the brown line ($t = 999$). In other words, there are partial training samples that can be inferred with 100% confidence at this diffusion step. Note that in reality, even if only one sample can be inferred as a member confidently, it still constitutes a severe privacy violation [2, 17, 22].

Performance of Likelihood-Based Attack. Figure 4(b) shows the performance of likelihood-based attacks in terms of different sizes of training sets. Similar to the loss-based attack, the performance of the likelihood-based attack decrease with an increase in the sizes of training sets. Specifically, the likelihood-based attack shows perfect performance on the target model trained on FFHQ-1k. When the size of a training set increases to 10K, there is a significant drop but still better than random guesses on the full log-scale ROC curve. In particular, in the extremely low false positive rate regime, such as 10^{-4}, the true positive rate is about 6×10^{-4}, which is 6 times more powerful than random guesses. In the model trained on FFHQ-30K, the ROC curve is almost close to the diagonal line, which indicates that adversaries are difficult to infer member samples through likelihood values.

6.2   Effects of Different Datasets

In this subsection, we show our attack performance on a medical image dataset about diabetic retinopathy. We choose the medical image dataset because the number of images that have diabetic retinopathy is usually insufficient in practice [21]. These types of images could be used for training a diffusion model and later the trained model is utilized to generate more novel images. We have described this dataset DRD in Sect. 4.1. We choose the SMLD as the target model and the number of training samples is 1, 000. Overall, the SMLD model can achieve excellent performance in image synthesis, with an FID of 33.20. Figure 10 in Appendix visualizes synthetic samples, which all show good quality.

Performance of Loss-Based Attack. Figure 7 shows the performance of loss-based attacks for the target model SMLD trained on DRD. Here, note that the levels of the noise of the SMLD model gradually become small with an increase in diffusion steps. Figure 7(a) shows the performance of our loss-based attack on all diffusion steps. Figure 7(b) depicts ROC curves for different diffusion steps on target model SMLD trained on DRD. We can again observe our attacks can still perform perfectly on DRD at diffusion steps of low levels of noise.

Performance of Likelihood-Based Attack. Figure 7(c) reports the performance of our likelihood-based attack on the SMLD model trained on DRD. As expected, our attack still shows excellent performance. We can clearly find that the attack achieves 100% TPR on all FPR values, which means that all member samples are inferred correctly. Table 4 in Appendix reports the quantitative results of both attacks.

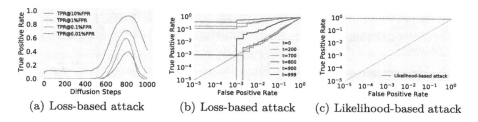

(a) Loss-based attack   (b) Loss-based attack   (c) Likelihood-based attack

Fig. 7. Attack performance on the DRD dataset.

7   Defenses

Differential privacy (DP) [1,10] is considered as a common defense measure for preventing the leakage of training samples of a machine learning model. In this section, we present our attack results on diffusion models using the DP defense.

We adopt Differentially-Private Stochastic Gradient Descent (DP-SGD) [1] to train diffusion models. DP-SGD is widely used for privately training a machine learning model. Generally, DP-SGD achieves differential privacy by adding noise into per-sample gradients. In our work, we implement DP diffusion models through the Opacus library [41] which allows us to set privacy budgets through hyperparameters. Here, we set the clip bound C and the failure probability δ as 1 and 5×10^{-4}. The batch size and the number of epochs are 64 and $1,800$. Thus, the final privacy budget ϵ is 19.62. Generally, a smaller privacy budget means a higher privacy setting and more severe model utility loss. The common choice of privacy budget is $\epsilon \leq 10$ [1,41], and in this work we choose a higher privacy budget because we consider the utility of a diffusion model. We choose the DDPM model as the target model. It is trained on FFHQ containing $1,000$ training samples, and the FID is 393.94.

Performance of Loss-Based Attack. Figure 8 shows the performance of both types of attacks on DDPM trained with DP-SGD on FFHQ. In Fig. 8(a), we present the performance of the loss-based attack on all diffusion steps. Clearly, we can see that although differentially training DDPM, i.e. DDPM with DP-SGD, indeed can significantly decrease the membership leakages, the peak regions can be still identified between 400 and 800 diffusion step. Figure 8(b) further shows ROC curves of our loss-based attack on different diffusion steps. Again, we can observe that in the low FPR regimes, some training samples are still inferred with a higher probability, such as 10^{-2} TPR at 10^{-4} FPR at $t = 500$. This is higher than 100 times than random guesses (TPR is 10^{-4} at 10^{-4} FPR).

Performance of Likelihood-Based Attack. Figure 8(c) shows the performance of the likelihood-based attack on DDPM training with DP-SGD on FFHQ. Again, we can see that differentially private training of a diffusion model indeed can mitigate our attack. At the same time, we also see at the low false positive rate regime, our attack still remains at 0.1% true positive rate, which illustrates the effectiveness of our attack even in the worst-case. Here, we also

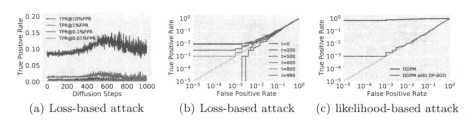

(a) Loss-based attack   (b) Loss-based attack   (c) likelihood-based attack

Fig. 8. Attack performance on DDPM with DP-SGD.

note that the FID of the target model is 393.94, which means that the utility of the target model suffers from a severe performance drop. We leave developing more usable techniques to train a diffusion model with DP-SGD as future work. Table 5 in Appendix summarizes the quantitative results of both attacks.

8   Related Work

Diffusion Models. Diffusion models have attracted increasing attention in the past years. Sohl-Dickstein et al. [34] first introduce nonequilibrium thermodynamics to build generative models. The key idea is to slowly add noise into data in the forward process and learn to generate data from noise through a reverse process. Ho et al. [16] further propose to use parameterization techniques in diffusion models, which enable diffusion models to generate high-quality images. Song et al. [37] present to train a generative model by estimating gradients of data distribution, i.e. score. Furthermore, Song et al. [38] propose a unified framework to describe these diffusion models through the lens of stochastic differential equations. However, in this work, we study diffusion models from the perspective of privacy.

Membership Inference Attacks. There are extensive works on membership inference (MI) attacks on classification models. Various attack methods under different threat models are proposed, such as using fewer shadow models [32], using loss values [2,25,33,40] and using labels of victim models [7,23]. In addition, there are several MI attacks on generative models [6,13,15]. Nevertheless, these attacks are more specific to GANs and heavily rely on the unique characteristics of GANs, such as discriminators or generators. They cannot be extended to diffusion models, because diffusion models have different training and sampling mechanisms. Therefore, our work on MI of diffusion models aims to fill this gap.

Membership Inference Attacks in Diffusion Models. In this paragraph, we discuss our work and its relation to several similar/concurrent works studying MI attacks in diffusion models. Wu et al. [39] study MI attacks against text-to-image generative models. One diffusion-based text-to-image generative model, LDM [31], is attacked by their methods based on query data pair, i.e. text and corresponding output image. Unlike text-to-image generative models, we focus on unconditional diffusion models. Furthermore, our MI attack methods, such as the loss-based attack, are totally different from their methods [39]. Subsequently, there are several concurrent works that investigate MI attacks against diffusion models based on the loss information [3,9,26,42]. However, they only consider discrete diffusion models where the number of noise distributions is finite. Our work systematically studies both discrete and continuous diffusion models. Although Carlini et al. [3] design more sophisticated and effective methods, they require extraordinarily huge computation resources, such as training hundreds of shadow diffusion models or millions of queries from diffusion models. In contrast, our method only utilizes loss values, which is much more computationally efficient. In addition, we also propose the likelihood-based method which is not considered in these works [3,9,26,42].

9   Conclusion

In this paper, we have developed two types of membership inference attack methods: loss-based attack and likelihood-based attack. Our methods have demonstrated the connection between membership inference risks and the generative mechanism of diffusion models. To be more specific, our loss-based attack reveals that in terms of diffusion steps, there exist high-risk regions where training samples can be inferred with high precision. Although membership inference becomes more challenging with the increase in the number of training samples, the high-risk regions still exist. Our experimental results on classic privacy protection mechanisms, i.e. diffusion models trained with DP-SGD, further show that DP-SGD alleviates our attacks at the expense of severe model utility.

Designing an effective differential privacy strategy to produce high-quality images for diffusion models is promising and challenging, which is part of our future work. In addition, it is an interesting direction to study MI attacks of diffusion models in stricter scenarios, such as only obtaining synthetic data.

Acknowledgments. This research was funded in whole by the Luxembourg National Research Fund (FNR), grant reference 13550291.

Appendix

In this section, we show additional results and introduce each result in its caption.

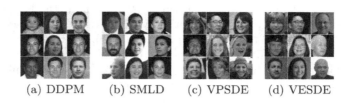

(a) DDPM   (b) SMLD   (c) VPSDE   (d) VESDE

Fig. 9. Generated images from different target models trained on FFHQ. It is corresponding to Sect. 5.1.

Fig. 10. Generated images from the target model SMLD trained on the DRD dataset. It is corresponding to Sect. 6.2.

Table 4. Quantitative results of our attacks on SMLD trained on DRD. It is corresponding to Sect. 6.2.

Attack	T	TPR@ 10%FPR	TPR@ 1%FPR	TPR@ 0.1%FPR	TPR@ 0.01%FPR	Accuracy
Loss-based	0	7.50%	1.10%	0.00%	0.00%	50.25%
	200	11.20%	0.70%	0.10%	0.00%	52.25%
	700	80.60%	50.50%	33.34%	18.80%	85.45%
	800	93.30%	72.20%	60.00%	40.10%	92.25%
	900	79.80%	42.40%	17.70%	12.30%	86.35%
	999	43.60%	9.70%	2.00%	0.10%	70.95%
Likelihood-based	–	100.00%	100.00%	100.00%	99.90%	99.95%

Table 5. Quantitative results of our attacks on DDPM trained with DP-SGD. It is corresponding to Sect. 7.

Attacks	T	TPR@ 10%FPR	TPR@ 1%FPR	TPR@ 0.1%FPR	TPR@ 0.01%FPR	Accuracy
Loss-based	0	8.80%	1.40%	0.00%	0.00%	52.25%
	200	8.60%	1.40%	0.40%	0.30%	53.20%
	500	**10.70%**	**1.60%**	**0.90%**	**0.90%**	**51.85%**
	600	**13.00%**	**2.30%**	**1.00%**	**1.00%**	**51.85%**
	800	11.60%	2.10%	0.30%	0.30%	51.75%
	999	10.40%	0.60%	0.00%	0.00%	53.90%
Likelihood-based	–	8.40%	1.10%	0.20%	0.10%	51.75%

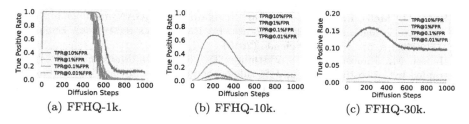

(a) FFHQ-1k.   (b) FFHQ-10k.   (c) FFHQ-30k.

Fig. 11. Performance of loss-based attacks with different sizes of datasets. The target model is DDPM trained on FFHQ. Each subfigure shows attack performance with different FPRs on fixed dataset sizes. It is corresponding to Sect. 6.1.

References

1. Abadi, M., et al.: Deep learning with differential privacy. In: ACM SIGSAC Conference on Computer and Communications Security (CCS), pp. 308–318. ACM (2016)
2. Carlini, N., Chien, S., Nasr, M., Song, S., Terzis, A., Tramer, F.: Membership inference attacks from first principles. In: IEEE Symposium on Security and Privacy (S&P), p. 1519. IEEE (2022)
3. Carlini, N., et al.: Extracting training data from diffusion models. arXiv preprint arXiv:2301.13188 (2023)
4. Carlini, N., Liu, C., Erlingsson, Ú., Kos, J., Song, D.: The secret sharer: evaluating and testing unintended memorization in neural networks. In: USENIX Security Symposium (USENIX Security), pp. 267–284. USENIX Association (2019)
5. Carlini, N., et al.: Extracting training data from large language models. In: USENIX Security Symposium (USENIX Security), pp. 2633–2650. USENIX Association (2021)
6. Chen, D., Yu, N., Zhang, Y., Fritz, M.: GAN-leaks: a taxonomy of membership inference attacks against generative models. In: ACM SIGSAC Conference on Computer and Communications Security (CCS), pp. 343–362. ACM (2020)
7. Choquette-Choo, C.A., Tramer, F., Carlini, N., Papernot, N.: Label-only membership inference attacks. In: International Conference on Machine Learning (ICML), pp. 1964–1974. PMLR (2021)
8. Dhariwal, P., Nichol, A.: Diffusion models beat GANs on image synthesis. In: Advances in Neural Information Processing Systems (NeurIPS), vol. 34, pp. 8780–8794. Curran Associates, Inc. (2021)
9. Duan, J., Kong, F., Wang, S., Shi, X., Xu, K.: Are diffusion models vulnerable to membership inference attacks? arXiv preprint arXiv:2302.01316 (2023)
10. Dwork, C.: Differential privacy: a survey of results. In: Agrawal, M., Du, D., Duan, Z., Li, A. (eds.) TAMC 2008. LNCS, vol. 4978, pp. 1–19. Springer, Heidelberg (2008). https://doi.org/10.1007/978-3-540-79228-4_1
11. Goodfellow, I., et al.: Generative adversarial nets. In: Advances in Neural Information Processing Systems (NeurIPS), pp. 2672–2680. Curran Associates, Inc. (2014)
12. Grathwohl, W., Chen, R.T., Bettencourt, J., Sutskever, I., Duvenaud, D.: FFJORD: free-form continuous dynamics for scalable reversible generative models. In: International Conference on Learning Representations (ICLR) (2018)

13. Hayes, J., Melis, L., Danezis, G., De Cristofaro, E.: LOGAN: membership inference attacks against generative models. In: Proceedings on Privacy Enhancing Technologies, pp. 133–152. Sciendo (2019)
14. Heusel, M., Ramsauer, H., Unterthiner, T., Nessler, B., Hochreiter, S.: GANs trained by a two time-scale update rule converge to a local Nash equilibrium. In: Advances in Neural Information Processing Systems (NeurIPS), pp. 6626–6637. Curran Associates, Inc. (2017)
15. Hilprecht, B., Härterich, M., Bernau, D.: Monte Carlo and reconstruction membership inference attacks against generative models. In: Proceedings on Privacy Enhancing Technologies, pp. 232–249. Sciendo (2019)
16. Ho, J., Jain, A., Abbeel, P.: Denoising diffusion probabilistic models. In: Advances in Neural Information Processing Systems (NeurIPS), vol. 33, pp. 6840–6851. Curran Associates, Inc. (2020)
17. Hu, H., Pang, J.: Membership inference attacks against GANs by leveraging overrepresentation regions. In: ACM SIGSAC Conference on Computer and Communications Security (CCS), pp. 2387–2389. ACM (2021)
18. Kaggle.com: Diabetic retinopathy detection (2015). https://www.kaggle.com/c/diabetic-retinopathy-detection/
19. Karras, T., Aittala, M., Aila, T., Laine, S.: Elucidating the design space of diffusion-based generative models. In: Advances in Neural Information Processing Systems (NeurIPS). Curran Associates, Inc. (2022)
20. Karras, T., Laine, S., Aila, T.: A style-based generator architecture for generative adversarial networks. In: IEEE/CVF Conference on Computer Vision and Pattern Recognition (CVPR), pp. 4401–4410. IEEE (2019)
21. Kazerouni, A., et al.: Diffusion models for medical image analysis: a comprehensive survey. arXiv preprint arXiv:2211.07804 (2022)
22. Leino, K., Fredrikson, M.: Stolen memories: leveraging model memorization for calibrated white-box membership inference. In: Proceedings of USENIX Security Symposium (USENIX Security), pp. 1605–1622. USENIX Association (2020)
23. Li, Z., Zhang, Y.: Membership leakage in label-only exposures. In: ACM SIGSAC Conference on Computer and Communications Security (CCS), pp. 880–895. ACM (2021)
24. Lin, Z., Jain, A., Wang, C., Fanti, G., Sekar, V.: Using GANs for sharing networked time series data: challenges, initial promise, and open questions. In: Proceedings of the ACM Internet Measurement Conference (IMC), pp. 464–483. ACM (2020)
25. Liu, Y., Zhao, Z., Backes, M., Zhang, Y.: Membership inference attacks by exploiting loss trajectory. In: ACM SIGSAC Conference on Computer and Communications Security (CCS), pp. 2085–2098 (2022)
26. Matsumoto, T., Miura, T., Yanai, N.: Membership inference attacks against diffusion models. arXiv preprint arXiv:2302.03262 (2023)
27. Murakonda, S.K., Shokri, R.: ML privacy meter: aiding regulatory compliance by quantifying the privacy risks of machine learning. arXiv preprint arXiv:2007.09339 (2020)
28. Park, N., Mohammadi, M., Gorde, K., Jajodia, S., Park, H., Kim, Y.: Data synthesis based on generative adversarial networks. Proc. VLDB Endow. 11(10), 1071–1083 (2018)
29. Parliament, E., of the European Union, C.: Art. 35 GDPR: Data protection impact assessment (2016). https://gdpr-info.eu/art-35-gdpr/
30. Pinaya, W.H.L., et al.: Brain imaging generation with latent diffusion models. In: Mukhopadhyay, A., Oksuz, I., Engelhardt, S., Zhu, D., Yuan, Y. (eds.)

DGM4MICCAI 2022. LNCS, vol. 13609, pp. 117–126. Springer, Cham (2022). https://doi.org/10.1007/978-3-031-18576-2_12

31. Rombach, R., Blattmann, A., Lorenz, D., Esser, P., Ommer, B.: High-resolution image synthesis with latent diffusion models. In: IEEE/CVF Conference on Computer Vision and Pattern Recognition (CVPR), pp. 10684–10695. IEEE (2022)

32. Salem, A., Zhang, Y., Humbert, M., Berrang, P., Fritz, M., Backes, M.: ML-leaks: model and data independent membership inference attacks and defenses on machine learning models. In: Network and Distributed Systems Security Symposium (NDSS). Internet Society (2019)

33. Shokri, R., Stronati, M., Song, C., Shmatikov, V.: Membership inference attacks against machine learning models. In: IEEE Symposium on Security and Privacy (S&P), pp. 3–18. IEEE (2017)

34. Sohl-Dickstein, J., Weiss, E., Maheswaranathan, N., Ganguli, S.: Deep unsupervised learning using nonequilibrium thermodynamics. In: International Conference on Machine Learning (ICML), pp. 2256–2265. PMLR (2015)

35. Song, S., Marn, D.: Introducing a new privacy testing library in tensorflow (2020). https://blog.tensorflow.org/2020/06/introducing-new-privacy-testing-library.html

36. Song, Y.: Score-based generative modeling through stochastic differential equations (2021). https://github.com/yang-song/score_sde_pytorch

37. Song, Y., Ermon, S.: Generative modeling by estimating gradients of the data distribution. In: Advances in Neural Information Processing Systems (NeurIPS), vol. 32. Curran Associates, Inc. (2019)

38. Song, Y., Sohl-Dickstein, J., Kingma, D.P., Kumar, A., Ermon, S., Poole, B.: Score-based generative modeling through stochastic differential equations. In: International Conference on Learning Representations (ICLR) (2021)

39. Wu, Y., Yu, N., Li, Z., Backes, M., Zhang, Y.: Membership inference attacks against text-to-image generation models. arXiv preprint arXiv:2210.00968 (2022)

40. Ye, J., Maddi, A., Murakonda, S.K., Shokri, R.: Enhanced membership inference attacks against machine learning models. In: ACM SIGSAC Conference on Computer and Communications Security (CCS), pp. 3093–3106 (2022)

41. Yousefpour, A., et al.: Opacus: user-friendly differential privacy library in PyTorch. arXiv preprint arXiv:2109.12298 (2021)

42. Zhu, D., Chen, D., Grossklags, J., Fritz, M.: Data forensics in diffusion models: a systematic analysis of membership privacy. arXiv preprint arXiv:2302.07801 (2023)

Symmetry Defense Against CNN Adversarial Perturbation Attacks

Blerta Lindqvist[(✉)] [ID]

Aalto University, Espoo, Finland
blerta.lindqvist@aalto.fi

Abstract. This paper uses symmetry to make Convolutional Neural Network classifiers (CNNs) robust against adversarial perturbation attacks. Such attacks add perturbation to original images to generate adversarial images that fool classifiers such as road sign classifiers of autonomous vehicles. Although symmetry is a pervasive aspect of the natural world, CNNs are unable to handle symmetry well. For example, a CNN can classify an image differently from its mirror image. For an adversarial image that misclassifies with a wrong label l_w, CNN inability to handle symmetry means that a symmetric adversarial image can classify differently from the wrong label l_w. Further than that, we find that the classification of a symmetric adversarial image reverts to the correct label. To classify an image when adversaries are unaware of the defense, we apply symmetry to the image and use the classification label of the symmetric image. To classify an image when adversaries are aware of the defense, we use mirror symmetry and pixel inversion symmetry to form a symmetry group. We apply all the group symmetries to the image and decide on the output label based on the agreement of any two of the classification labels of the symmetry images. Adaptive attacks fail because they need to rely on loss functions that use conflicting CNN output values for symmetric images. Without attack knowledge, the proposed symmetry defense succeeds against both gradient-based and random-search attacks, with up to near-default accuracies for ImageNet. The defense even improves the classification accuracy of original images.

Keywords: Adversarial perturbation defense · Symmetry · CNN adversarial robustness

1 Introduction

Despite achieving state-of-the-art status in computer vision [24, 29], Convolutional Neural Network classifiers (CNNs) lack adversarial robustness because they can classify imperceptibly perturbed images incorrectly [11, 23, 35, 46]. One of the first and still undefeated defenses against adversarial perturbation attacks is adversarial training (AT) [30, 35, 46], which uses adversarial images in training. However, AT reliance on attack knowledge during training [35] is a significant drawback since such knowledge might not be available in real-world attacks.

© The Author(s), under exclusive license to Springer Nature Switzerland AG 2023
E. Athanasopoulos and B. Mennink (Eds.): ISC 2023, LNCS 14411, pp. 142–160, 2023.
https://doi.org/10.1007/978-3-031-49187-0_8

Fig. 1. The flip symmetry defense against zero-knowledge adversaries reverts adversarial images to their correct classification by horizontally flipping the images before classification. The defense classifies non-adversarial images in the same way.

Although engineered to incorporate symmetries such as horizontal flipping, translations, and rotations, CNNs lack invariance with respect to these symmetries [19] in the classification of datasets such as ImageNet [15], CIFAR10 [28] and MNIST [33]. CNN lack of invariance means that CNNs can classify images differently after they have been horizontally flipped, or even slightly shifted or rotated [3,19]. Furthermore, CNNs only provide approximate translation invariance [3,4,19,26] and are unable to learn invariances with respect to symmetries such as rotation and horizontal flipping with data augmentation [3,4,19].

Against adversarial perturbation attacks causing misclassification, the inability of CNNs to handle symmetry well can be beneficial. While an adversarial image classifies with a wrong label, a symmetric adversarial image, obtained by applying a symmetry to an adversarial image, can classify with a label that is different from the wrong label of the adversarial image. Aiming to classify adversarial images correctly, we pose the question:

Can we achieve adversarial robustness by utilizing the inability of CNNs to handle symmetry correctly?

Addressing this question, we design a novel symmetry defense that only uses symmetry to counter adversarial perturbation attacks. The proposed symmetry defense makes the following main contributions:

- We show that the proposed symmetry defense succeeds against gradient-based attacks and a random search attack without using adversarial images or attack knowledge. In contrast, the current best defense needs attack knowledge to train the classifier with adversarial images.
- The symmetry defense counters zero-knowledge adversaries with near-default accuracies by using either the horizontal flip symmetry, shown in Fig. 1, or an artificial pixel inversion symmetry. Results are shown in Table 1 and in Table 2.
- The defense also counters perfect-knowledge adversaries with near-default accuracies, as shown in Table 4. Against such adversaries, the defense uses a symmetry subgroup that consists of the identity symmetry, the mirror symmetry (also called horizontal flip), the pixel inversion symmetry, and the symmetry that combines the mirror flip and the pixel inversion symmetry.
- The defense counters adaptive attacks that customize their loss with symmetric images. The optimization of such adaptive attacks relies on conflicting CNN outputs for symmetric images, causing non-optimal optimization of adaptive attacks.

- The usage of the pixel intensity inversion symmetry, discussed in Sect. 5.1 and in Sect. 5.2, that does not exist in natural images of the dataset means that the proposed defense could be applied even to datasets without inherent symmetries.
- The symmetry defense maintains and even exceeds the non-adversarial accuracy against perfect-knowledge adversaries, as shown in Table 4.

2 Related Work and Background

2.1 Symmetry, Equivariance and Invariance in CNNs

Symmetry of an object is a transformation that leaves that object invariant. Image symmetries include rotation, horizontal flipping, and inversion [37]. We provide definitions related to symmetry groups in Appendix 1. A function f is **equivariant** with respect to a transformation T if they commute with eachother [43]: $f \circ T = T \circ f$. **Invariance** is a special case of equivariance where the T transformation applied after the function is the identity transformation [43]: $f \circ T = f$.

CNNs stack equivariant convolution and pooling layers [22] followed by an invariant map in order to learn invariant functions [5] with respect to symmetries, following a standard blueprint used in machine learning [5,25]. Translation invariance for image classification means that the position of an object in an image should not impact its classification. To achieve translation invariance, CNN convolutional layers [29,31] compute feature maps over the translation symmetry group [21,45] using kernel sliding [21,32]. CNN pooling layers enable local translation invariance [5,16,22]. The pooling layers of CNNs positioned after convolutional layers enable local invariance to translation [16] because the output of the pooling operation does not change when the position of features changes within the pooling region. Cohen and Welling [12] show that convolutional layers, pooling, arbitrary pointwise nonlinearities, batch normalization, and residual blocks are equivariant to translation. CNNs learn invariance with respect to symmetries such as rotations, horizontal flipping, and scaling with data augmentation, which augments the training dataset with images obtained by applying symmetries to original images [29]. For ImageNet, data augmentation can consist of a random crop, horizontal flip, color jitter, and color transforms of original images [18].

CNN Lack of Translation Equivariance and Invariance. Studies suggest that CNNs are not equivariant to translation [3,4,19,26,48], not even to small translations or rotations [19]. Bouchacourt et al. [4] claim that the CNN translation invariance is approximate and that translation invariance is primarily learned from the data and data augmentation. The lack of translation invariance has been attributed to aliasing effects caused by the subsampling of the convolutional stride [3], by max pooling, average pooling, and strides [48], and by image boundary effects [26].

CNN Data Augmentation Marginally Effective. Studies show that data augmentation is only marginally effective at incorporating symmetries [3,4,12, 19,27] because CNNs cannot learn invariances with data augmentation [3,4,19]. Engstrom et al. [19] find that data augmentation only marginally improves invariance. Azulay and Weiss [3] find that data augmentation only enables invariance to symmetries of images that resemble dataset images. Bouchacourt et al. [4] claim that non-translation invariance is learned from the data independently of data augmentation.

Other Equivariance CNNs Approaches Have Dataset Limitation. CNN architectures that handle symmetry better have only been shown to work for simple MNIST [33], CIFAR10 [28] or synthetic datasets, not ImageNet [6,12,16, 20,21,36,41,43,44,49].

2.2 Adversarial Perturbation Attacks

Szegedy et al. [46] defined the problem of generating adversarial images as starting from original images and adding a small perturbation that results in misclassification. Szegedy et al. [46] formalized the generation of adversarial images as a minimization of the sum of perturbation and an adversarial loss function, as shown in Appendix 2. The loss function uses the distance between obtained function output values and desired function output values.

Most attacks use the classifier gradient to generate adversarial perturbation [11,35], but random search [1] is also used.

PGD Attack. PGD is an iterative white-box attack with a parameter that defines the magnitude of the perturbation of each step. PGD starts from an initial sample point x_0 and then iteratively finds the perturbation of each step and projects the perturbation on an L_p-ball.

Auto-PGD Attack. Auto-PGD (APGD) [14] is a variant of PGD that varies the step size and can use two different loss functions to achieve a stronger attack.

Square Attack. The Square Attack [1] is a score-based, black-box, random-search attack based on local randomized square-shaped updates.

Fast Adaptive Boundary. The white-box Fast Adaptive Boundary attack (FAB) [13] aims to find the minimum perturbation needed to change the classification of an original sample. However, FAB does not scale to ImageNet because of the large number of dataset classes.

AutoAttack. AutoAttack [14] is a parameter-free ensemble of attacks that includes: $APGD_{CE}$ and $APGD_{DLR}$, FAB [13] and Square Attack [1].

2.3 Adversarial Defenses

Adversarial Training. AT [30,35,46] trains classifiers with correctly-labeled adversarial images and is one of the first and few defenses that have not been defeated. The robust PGD AT defense [35] is formulated as a robust optimization problem and is considered one of the most successful adversarial defenses [34]. AT usage of adversarial images during training increases training time and makes AT reliant on attack knowledge, which is unrealistic for real-world attacks.

Failed Defenses. Many other defenses have been shown to fail against an adaptive adversary. For example, defensive distillation is not robust to adversarial attacks [8], many adversarial detection defenses have been bypassed [9, 10], and obfuscated gradient defenses [2] and other defenses have been circumvented [47].

2.4   Lack of Adversarial Robustness and Lack of Invariance Together

To the best of our knowledge, only one prior work [19] examines the lack of invariance and the lack of adversarial robustness together by analysing the interplay between rotations/translations and L_∞ adversarial perturbation. Engstrom et al. [19] apply first symmetries and then adversarial perturbation, finding rotation and translation symmetries orthogonal to adversarial perturbation in their experiments. In contrast, we examine symmetry transformations of adversarial samples, applying symmetry transformations after the adversarial perturbation.

2.5   Summary of Related Work

Relevant to the proposed defense, we derive the following key points from the related work:

- CNNs do not achieve full equivariance or full invariance with respect to symmetries such as translation, horizontal flipping, and rotation despite being designed and trained with data augmentation to incorporate these symmetries.
- Adversarial perturbation attacks are still an open problem as the best current AT defense requires advance knowledge of the attack, which is not available for real-world attacks.
- Approaches to better incorporate symmetries into CNNs have yet to succeed for big datasets such as ImageNet.

3   Threat Model

Based on recommendations for evaluating adversarial defenses [7], the examined threat model consists of three cases:

- **Zero-Knowledge Adversary.** The adversary is unaware of the symmetry defense.
- **Perfect-Knowledge Adversary.** The adversary is aware of the symmetry defense and adapts the attack to the defense.
- **Limited-Knowledge Adversary.** Based on [7], this threat only needs to be evaluated if the zero-knowledge attack fails and the perfect-knowledge attack succeeds. Since the defense succeeds against both zero-knowledge and perfect-knowledge adversaries, we do not evaluate this case.

4 The Proposed Symmetry Defense

Following, we note f as the CNN function that finds the classifier boundary and T as the pixel intensity inversion symmetry.

4.1 CNN Classifier Boundary Function f Lacks Equivariance with Respect to Symmetries

The inability of CNNs to handle symmetries well causes boundaries in symmetric settings to differ. As discussed in Sect. 2, CNNs can classify symmetric images differently. This lack of invariance of CNN classification with respect to symmetries [3,4,19,26] indicates that the CNN function f of finding the classification boundary lacks equivariance with respect to symmetries. That is, CNN classifier boundaries near symmetric images are not symmetric. Otherwise, if the CNN classifier boundaries were symmetric around symmetric images, then symmetric images would classify the same, and CNN classification would not lack invariance.

Formally, we base our reasoning on the definition of equivariance as $f \circ T = T \circ f$, where f is the function that finds the classifier boundary and T is the symmetry transformation. For the CNN function f that finds the classifier boundary, equivariance with respect to T would mean that the CNN classifier boundary would be the same whether we apply f or T first. However, the lack of invariance of CNN classification with respect to symmetries [3,4,19,26] indicates that $f \circ T \neq T \circ f$. Otherwise, if $f \circ T = T \circ f$, then the boundaries would be the same, and CNN classification would not lack invariance. Therefore, we conclude that function f is not equivariant with respect to symmetries. Taking pixel inversion as the example T symmetry, Fig. 2 shows that inverting all dataset images and finding the classifier boundary do not commute and would result in different class boundaries.

4.2 Adversarial Images Also Lack Equivariance

As a result of the lack of equivariance in finding classifier boundaries with respect to symmetries, finding adversarial also lacks equivariance with respect to symmetries. In other words, adversarial images generated from symmetric original images do not correspond. Conceptually, adversarial perturbation attacks [11,23,35,38,46] aim to change an original sample with a small perturbation in order to obtain an adversarial sample that is on the other side of the CNN classifier boundary and misclassifies as a result. Therefore, different class boundaries in symmetric settings would cause an adversarial perturbation attack to find adversarial images in symmetric settings that are different, as Fig. 2 shows.

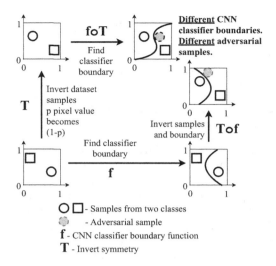

Fig. 2. We show in two-dimensional space the lack of equivariance of the CNN function f of finding the classifier boundary with respect to the pixel invert symmetry T. Applying first the inverse symmetry and then computing the classifier boundary (up and right) produces a different boundary from computing the classifier boundary first and then applying the inverse symmetry (right and up). Due to the different class boundaries, adversarial images are also different.

4.3   Adaptive Attacks Affected by CNN Inability to Handle Symmetry

The optimization of attacks adapting to the proposed symmetry defense is affected by CNN lack of invariance with respect to symmetries. Such adaptive attacks would need to incorporate symmetric images in their optimizations because the proposed symmetry defense makes no other changes. CNN inability to handle symmetry well means that the CNN output for a symmetric image can be different from the CNN output for the original image from which the symmetric image was obtained. Different CNN output values for symmetric images affect the loss function values that guide the optimization of adaptive attacks because loss functions depend on CNN output values. As a result, the attack optimization can become non-optimal and steered to obtain adversarial images that classify correctly.

5   Experimental Setting

We evaluate the proposed symmetry defense in the threat model cases identified in Sect. 3, based on [7]. Our implementation is based on the robustness AT package implementation [18] for ImageNet [42] with the same ResNet50 [24] architecture and parameters. ImageNet [42] is a 1000-class dataset of over $1.2M$

training images and $50K$ testing images. The ResNet50 [24] architecture model is trained with the stochastic gradient descent (SGD) optimizer with a momentum of 0.9, a learning rate decaying by a factor of 10 every 50 epochs, and a batch size of 256. The classifier takes as input images with $[0, 1]$ pixel value ranges. Based on [18], the evaluation is done on logits, non-softmax output.

Default Data Augmentation. We use the same data augmentation as in [18] in the models we train: random resized crops, random horizontal flips, color jitter, and Fancy Principal Component Analysis (Fancy PCA) [29]. The ColorJitter transform randomly changes the brightness, contrast, and saturation. Fancy PCA [29] is a form of data augmentation that changes the intensities of RGB channels in training images by performing PCA analysis on ImageNet [15] images and adding to every image multitudes of the principal components. The magnitudes are proportional to the eigenvalues and a random variable drawn from a Gaussian distribution with 0 mean and 0.05 standard deviation [18].

PGD Attacks. We evaluate the proposed defense against L_2 and L_∞ PGD [30] attacks parameterized according to [18] for ImageNet with ϵ values of 0.5, 1.0, 2.0, 3.0 for L_2 attacks, and ϵ values of $4/255$, $8/255$, $16/255$ for L_∞ attacks. All PGD [30] attacks have 100 steps, with a step perturbation value defined as the ratio of $2.5 \times \epsilon$ over the number of steps, following [18]. All PGD attacks are targeted according to [18], with the target label chosen uniformly at random among the labels other than the ground truth label.

AutoAttack Attacks. We evaluate against APGD, and SquareAttack attacks with $1,000$ random images for each experiment based on [14] experiments with ImageNet. We do not evaluate against FAB because it does not scale to ImageNet due to the large number of ImageNet classes [14]. All APGD attacks are targeted. Based on Square Attack [1] settings for ImageNet, Square Attack [1] is not targeted, has $10,000$ queries, $p = 0.02$ for L_2, and $p = 0.01$ for L_∞. APGD$_{CE}$ [14] and APGD$_{DLR}$ [14] settings were based on attack settings for ImageNet in [14].

Tools. The defense was written using PyTorch [40]. PGD attacks were generated with the Robustness (Python Library) [18], AutoAttack attacks were generated with the IBM Adversarial Robustness 360 Toolbox (ART) [39].

We assume that all adversaries know the model and its parameters.

5.1 Symmetry Defense Against Zero-Knowledge Adversaries

Here, we conduct experiments with the flip symmetry defense and the intensity inversion symmetry defense against zero-knowledge adversaries that are unaware of the symmetry defense.

Horizontal Flipping Symmetry Defense Against Zero-Knowledge Adversaries. Both the adversary and the defense use the same model trained with the default training dataset because horizontal flips are used in the default data augmentation. Figure 3 shows that the defense classifies an image by first horizontally flipping it and then classifying it with the same model used by the adversary to generate the adversarial images. Table 1 shows the experimental results of the defense using horizontal flip symmetry to counter zero-knowledge adversaries.

Table 1. Evaluation of the flip symmetry defense against zero-knowledge attacks.

Norm	Attack	No defense	Proposed defense
	$\epsilon = 0.0$	77.26%	77.15%
*L_2	PGD - $\epsilon = 0.5$	34.27%	76.13%
	PGD - $\epsilon = 1.0$	4.32%	75.21%
	PGD - $\epsilon = 2.0$	0.19%	74.25%
	PGD - $\epsilon = 3.0$	0.03%	73.74%
	*APGD$_{CE}$ - $\epsilon = 3.0$	0.0%	75.0%
	*APGD$_{DLR}$ - $\epsilon = 3.0$	37.9%	79.2%
	*Square Attack - $\epsilon = 5.0$	40.0%	71.9%
*L_∞	PGD - $\epsilon = 4/255$	0.00%	74.27%
	PGD - $\epsilon = 8/255$	0.00%	73.24%
	PGD - $\epsilon = 16/255$	0.00%	70.13%
	*APGD$_{CE}$ - $\epsilon = 4/255$	0.0%	71.8%
	*APGD$_{DLR}$ - $\epsilon = 4/255$	0.0%	78.7%
	*Square Attack - $\epsilon = 0.05$	4.9%	47.5%

*Evaluation based on $1,000$ random images.

The defense achieves close to the non-adversarial accuracy against most attacks, even exceeding it for APGD$_{DLR}$. Furthermore, the defense also exceeds the performance of the robust PGD AT defense [18] against PGD. The flip symmetry defense against a zero-knowledge adversary also maintains the default non-adversarial accuracy.

Inversion Symmetry Defense Against Zero-Knowledge Adversaries. The intensity inversion symmetry is a symmetry that is not present in natural images. This symmetry changes image pixel values from $p \in [0, 1]$ to $1 - p$. We train two models with the same preprocessing, parameters, and model architecture: M-Orig with original images and M-Invert with inverted images. The adversary generates adversarial images using the M-Orig model. The defense classifies a sample by inverting it and then classifying it with the M-Invert model. Figure 4 outlines the invert symmetry defense, and Table 2 shows that the inversion symmetry defense achieves near-default accuracies against most attacks and maintains non-adversarial accuracy.

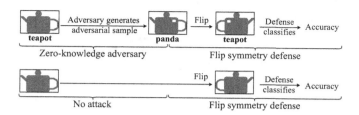

Fig. 3. The flip symmetry defense against zero-knowledge adversaries horizontally flips images before classifying them. The defense uses the same model that the adversary uses to generate adversarial images.

Table 2. Evaluation of the invert symmetry defense against zero-knowledge attacks.

Norm	Attack	No defense	Proposed defense
	$\epsilon = 0.0$	77.26%	76.88%
L_2	PGD - $\epsilon = 0.5$	34.27%	75.87%
	PGD - $\epsilon = 1.0$	4.32%	75.10%
	PGD - $\epsilon = 2.0$	0.19%	74.33%
	PGD - $\epsilon = 3.0$	0.03%	74.02%
	*APGD$_{CE}$ - $\epsilon = 3.0$	0.0%	73.8%
	*APGD$_{DLR}$ - $\epsilon = 3.0$	34.6%	76.0%
	*Square Attack - $\epsilon = 5.0$	40.4%	72.6%
L_∞	PGD - $\epsilon = 4/255$	0.00%	74.54%
	PGD - $\epsilon = 8/255$	0.00%	73.83%
	PGD - $\epsilon = 16/255$	0.00%	72.08%
	*APGD$_{CE}$ - $\epsilon = 4/255$	0.0%	69.8%
	*APGD$_{DLR}$ - $\epsilon = 4/255$	0.2%	71.2%
	*Square Attack - $\epsilon = 0.05$	4.0%	48.1%

*Evaluation based on $1,000$ random images.

Similarly to the flip symmetry defense, the invert symmetry defense achieves near-default accuracy against most attacks, exceeding the performance of the robust PGD AT defense [18] for PGD attacks. In addition, the invert symmetry defense accuracy maintains the accuracy for non-adversarial images.

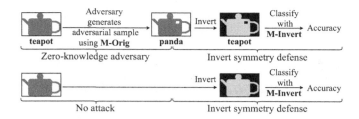

Fig. 4. Whether an image is original or an adversarial image generated with the M-Orig model by attacks, the defense first inverts the image and then classifies the inverted image with the M-Invert model.

5.2 Symmetry Defense Against Perfect-Knowledge Adversaries

Here, we assume that the adversary is aware of the proposed symmetry defense and can adapt the attack to the defense.

The Defense Needs more than One Symmetry. To counter a perfect-knowledge adversary, the defense must use more than one symmetry transformation. An adversary that is aware of the defense could apply the flip or invert symmetry after generating the adversarial sample, which would cancel out the symmetry transformation applied by the defense in Sect. 5.1 (flipping or inverting an image twice reverts it to the same image). In addition, the defense against a perfect-knowledge adversary would need to use such symmetry transformations that their possible combinations are reasonably limited in number to enable the defense to conduct experiments for all cases.

Definition of the Discrete Subgroup of Transformations. We define subgroup H with a discrete set of transformations $H = \{e, a, b, c\}$, where e, a, b, c denote the identity, horizontal flipping, intensity inversion, and the composition of flipping and inversion. The operation $*$ means that one transformation follows another. The Cayley table in Table 3 shows that the subgroup is closed since compositions of the elements also belong to the subgroup. The defined H subgroup is known as the **Klein four-group**. In this four-element group, each element is its own inverse, and composing any two non-identity elements results in the third non-identity element. Another way to define the Klein four-group H is: $H = \{a, b | a^2 = b^2 = (a * b)^2 = e\}$.

Theorem 1. $H = \{e, a, b, c\}$ *is a subgroup of the group of symmetry transformations of images.*

Proof. Based on the finite subgroup criterion in Sect. 2, a finite subset of a group should need only to be nonempty and closed under operation $*$ [17]. H is nonempty because it has four elements and is a subset of the symmetry transformations of images. Based on the definition of closure in Sect. 2, for H to be closed under the $*$ operation, we need to show that $\forall a, b \in H$, we get that $a * b^{-1} \in H$. Table 3 shows that $\forall a, b \in H$, we get that $a * b \in H$. Table 3 also shows that

Table 3. The Cayley table shows that the defined H subgroup is closed because all compositions of symmetries belong to the subgroup.

	*	e	a	b	c
identity - e		e	a	b	c
flip - a		a	e	c	b
invert - b		b	c	e	a
flip and invert - c		c	b	a	e

each element is its own inverse element because $\forall b \in H$, we get $b * b = e$, which means that $b = b^{-1}$. From $\forall a, b \in H$, $a * b \in H$ and $\forall b \in H$, $b = b^{-1}$, we derive that $\forall a, b \in H$, $a * b^{-1} \in H$.

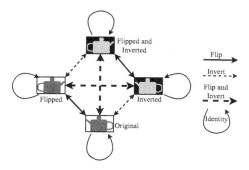

Fig. 5. No matter what sequence of H symmetries is performed, an image will be in one of the four states shown.

Figure 5 shows that the defined subgroup H confines the states that an image can be in after any consecutive combination of symmetries from H, which facilitates evaluating all the possible combinations of H transformations that an adversary can apply before or after the adversarial generation, as shown in Fig. 6.

Training. We impose the H subgroup shown in Fig. 5 on the CNN model by augmenting the original dataset with inverted images and using the default data augmentation, which includes horizontal flips.

Evaluation. The defense evaluates both original and adversarial images in the same way. To classify an image, the proposed defense applies all four H subgroup symmetries to the image and classifies all four images with the same model used by the attack to generate attacks. The defense assigns a class to the image if the classification labels of two of the four symmetric images agree. Experimental results are shown in Table 4. The defense achieves near-default accuracies for many attacks, surpassing the current best defense, robust PGD AT defense [18] against PGD attacks. The defense also exceeds the default accuracy.

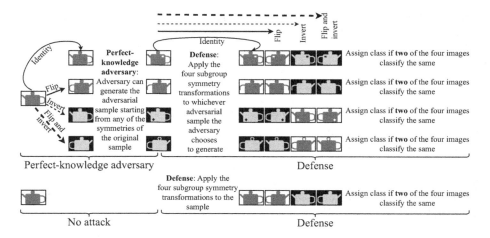

Fig. 6. The symmetry subgroup defense against adaptive perfect-knowledge adversaries considers that symmetries could be applied to images by adaptive adversaries both before and after adversarial generation. Moreover, even if adversaries applied consecutive subgroup symmetries to images, they would not result in any other cases due to the closure property of the symmetry subgroup.

Table 4. Accuracy evaluation of the proposed symmetry defense against an adaptive perfect-knowledge adversary.

Norm	Attack	No defense	**Proposed defense** Adversarial images generated from			
			Original images	Flipped images	Inverted images	Flip. & Inv. images
	$\epsilon = 0.0$	77.26%	78.30%	78.30%	78.30%	78.30%
	PGD - $\epsilon = 0.5$	34.27%	75.65%	75.80%	75.72%	75.69%
	PGD - $\epsilon = 1$	4.32%	73.16%	73.27%	73.46%	73.35%
	PGD - $\epsilon = 2$	0.19%	70.80%	70.81%	70.80%	70.77%
L_2	PGD - $\epsilon = 3$	0.03%	69.75%	69.82%	69.83%	69.89%
	*APGD$_{CE}$ - $\epsilon = 3.0$	0.0%	70.5%	70.4%	71.0%	70.7%
	*APGD$_{DLR}$ - $\epsilon = 3.0$	38.5%	77.7%	77.7%	78.0%	77.8%
	*SquareAttack - $\epsilon = 5.0$	43.0%	74.3%	74.5%	73.5%	73.1%
	PGD - $\epsilon = 4/255$	0.00%	70.68%	70.83%	70.77%	70.84%
	PGD - $\epsilon = 8/255$	0.00%	69.08%	69.12%	69.16%	69.21%
L_∞	PGD - $\epsilon = 16/255$	0.00%	65.26%	65.16%	65.32%	65.17%
	*APGD$_{CE}$ - $\epsilon = 4/255$	0.0%	66.5%	66.9%	68.1%	66.6%
	*APGD$_{DLR}$ - $\epsilon = 4/255$	0.6%	68.5%	68.1%	68.9%	69.4%
	*SquareAttack - $\epsilon = 0.05$	5.3%	49.0%	47.7%	48.7%	48.1%

*Evaluation based on $1,000$ random images.

The symmetry defense against perfect-knowledge adversaries exceeds the default accuracy and achieves near-default accuracies for many attacks. The defense also surpasses the robust PGD AT defense [18] against PGD attacks.

Adversary Adapts to the Defense. Here, we discuss how a perfect-knowledge adversary could adapt to the defense before, during, and after the generation of adversarial images.

1) **During the adversarial perturbation generation.** An adaptive adversarial attack must use symmetry in its adaptation because the symmetry defense makes no other changes. Both the gradient-based attacks and the random-search SquareAttack use loss functions that depend on CNN output values. Adaptive attacks using symmetry to counter the defense would need to update their optimization with loss functions that use CNN output values for symmetric images. However, these CNN output values are affected by CNNs' inability to handle symmetry correctly. Wrong function outputs for symmetric images will affect the loss function, making the optimizations of attacks non-optimal. We implement an adaptive PGD attack where the adversary attacks all four symmetries of the image by maximizing the sum of their losses, aiming to cause the misclassification of all symmetries of the image. We experiment with an L_∞ norm of $16/255$, the strongest PGD attack in [18]. The defense obtains an accuracy of **75.55%** against the adaptive attack, exceeding the 65.16% to 65.32% accuracies in Table 4 obtained against the default PGD attack for the same norm and perturbation. Therefore, **the adaptive attack against the proposed defense fails**. The adaptive adversary cannot make any other adaptations based on non-symmetry changes because the preprocessing, parameters, and model architecture do not change from [18].

2) **Before the adversarial generation.** An adversary can apply a subgroup H symmetry to the original image before the adversarial generation. Figure 5 shows that even if the adversary applies any sequence of subgroup H symmetries, the adversary can only construct an adversarial image starting from either an original, a flipped, an inverted, or a flipped and inverted image. We evaluate all four cases in Table 4.

3) **After the adversarial generation.** The adversary can apply any sequence of subgroup H symmetries to the adversarial image after generating it. However, this would be irrelevant because the defense applies all four symmetries and would obtain the same images regardless of any sequence of subgroup symmetries that the adversary applies, based on Fig. 5.

5.3 Discussion of the Proposed Defense

Why Adaptive Attacks Fail. We explain the failure of adaptive attacks from two different viewpoints:

– Custom-loss adaptive attacks fail because their optimization is also affected by CNN inability to handle symmetry well. Such attacks need to use symmetry because the symmetry defense makes no other changes. As a result, these attacks would need to update their loss functions to use CNN output values evaluated at symmetric images. However, CNN outputs for symmetric images can be different and incorrect due to CNN lack of invariance with respect to

symmetries. This leads to loss function values that steer attack optimization to non-optimal adversarial images.
- Adaptive attacks also fail because they are constrained in their optimizations by the perturbation value that attacks such as PGD, APGD, and SquareAttack take as input. These attacks search not in the entire space but for adversarial images with a given perturbation value. If the given perturbation value limits the attack search to where classifier boundaries are non-equivariant in symmetric settings, the attack will not be able to find an adversarial sample.

Computational Resources. The proposed method has negligible computational overhead for the flip symmetry defense and roughly doubles the computational resources for the invert symmetry defense and the symmetry subgroup defense. Detailed computational analysis is in Appendix 3.

Not a Detection Defense. The proposed defense is not a detection defense because it classifies original and adversarial images in the same way, as shown in Fig. 3, Fig. 4, and Fig. 6.

Not a Gradient Obfuscation Defense. The defense does not rely on obfuscation because it keeps the exact preprocessing, parameters, and model as in [18].

6   Conclusions

The proposed symmetry defense succeeds with near-default accuracies against different types of attacks that range from being unaware of the defense to being aware of it. Importantly, the symmetry defense also defeats attacks that are aware of the defense and adapt to it. Without using any attack knowledge, the defense exceeds the classification accuracies of the current best defense, which uses attack knowledge. The defense's non-reliance on attack knowledge or adversarial images makes the defense applicable to realistic attack scenarios where the attack is unknown in advance. The defense's preservation of classifier preprocessing, parameters, architecture, and training facilitates the deployment of the defense to existing classifiers. The defense maintains the non-adversarial classification accuracy and even exceeds it against attacks aware of the defense.

Acknowledgments. The author would like to thank Prof. Antti Ylä-Jääski, Prof. Tuomas Aura and Dr. Richard E. Howard for their support, feedback and discussions.

Appendix 1: Definitions Related to Symmetry Groups

According to [17], a group is an ordered pair $(G, *)$ where G is a set and $*$ is a binary operation on G that satisfies these axioms:

- *Associativity.* $*$ is associative: $\forall a, b, c \in G, (a * b) * c = a * (b * c)$.

- *Identity.* There exists an identity element $e \in G$, such that $a * e = e * a = a$, for $\forall a \in G$.
- *Inverse.* Every element in G has an inverse: $\forall a \in G$, there exists $a^{-1} \in G$ such that $a * a^{-1} = a^{-1} * a = e$.

Binary Operation. According to [17], a binary operation $*$ on a set G is a function $*\colon G \times G \mapsto G$. Instead of writing the binary operation $*$ on $a, b \in G$ as a function $*(a, b)$, we can write it as $a * b$.

Closure. Suppose that $*$ is a binary operation on the set G and H is a subset of G. If $*$ is a binary operation on H, that is, $\forall a, b \in H$, $a * b \in H$, then H is said to be closed under the $*$ binary operation [17].

Group. According to [17], a group is an ordered pair $(G, *)$ where G is a set and $*$ is a binary operation on G that satisfies the associativity, identity and inverse axioms.

Subgroup. According to [17], a subset H of G is a subgroup of G if H is nonempty and H is closed under products and inverses (that is, $x, y \in H$ implies that $x^{-1} \in H$ and $x * y \in H$). A subgroup H of group G is written as $H \leq G$. Informally, the subgroup of a group G is a subset of G, which is itself a group with respect to the binary operation defined in G.

The Subgroup Criterion. A subset H of a group G is a subgroup if and only if $H \neq \emptyset$ and $\forall x, y \in H$, $x * y^{-1} \in H$ [17].

The Finite Subgroup Criterion. A finite subset H is a subgroup if H is nonempty and closed under $*$ [17].

Appendix 2: The Minimization of Targeted Adversarial Perturbation Attacks

The minimization for adversarial perturbation attacks targeted at a specific adversarial label was first formulated by Szegedy et al. [46]:

$$\text{minimize} \qquad c \cdot \|\delta\| + L_f(x + \delta, l) \tag{1}$$
$$\text{such that} \qquad x + \delta \in [0, 1]^d,$$

where f is the classifier function, L_f is the classifier function loss, and l is an adversarial label, c is a constant, $\|\delta\|$ is the L_p norm of perturbation.

Appendix 3: Computational Resources

Here, we analyse the additional computational complexity of the proposed defense and the adversary.

Defense

Against a Zero-Knowledge Adversary. The flip symmetry defense uses the same computational complexity as a default classifier in training because it only trains one model with original images. The invert symmetry defense doubles the computational complexity of a default classifier in training because it trains two models with original and inverted images, respectively. In testing, there is $O(1)$ overhead per sample due to flipping or inverting the sample.

Against a Perfect-Knowledge Adversary. The symmetry subgroup defense doubles the computational complexity of a default classifier in training because it trains one model with both original and inverted images. In testing, there is $O(1)$ overhead per sample due to flipping, inverting, or flipping and inverting the sample.

Adversary

Zero-Knowledge Adversary. The zero-knowledge adversary is unaware of the defense and consumes the same resources as in the default case.

Perfect-Knowledge Adversary. The perfect-knowledge adversary can symmetrically transform the sample before and after generating the adversarial sample, using $O(1)$ additional computing resources per sample.

References

1. Andriushchenko, M., Croce, F., Flammarion, N., Hein, M.: Square attack: a query-efficient black-box adversarial attack via random search. In: Vedaldi, A., Bischof, H., Brox, T., Frahm, J.-M. (eds.) ECCV 2020. LNCS, vol. 12368, pp. 484–501. Springer, Cham (2020). https://doi.org/10.1007/978-3-030-58592-1_29
2. Athalye, A., Carlini, N., Wagner, D.: Obfuscated gradients give a false sense of security: circumventing defenses to adversarial examples. arXiv preprint arXiv:1802.00420 (2018)
3. Azulay, A., Weiss, Y.: Why do deep convolutional networks generalize so poorly to small image transformations? J. Mach. Learn. Res. **20**, 1–25 (2019)
4. Bouchacourt, D., Ibrahim, M., Morcos, A.: Grounding inductive biases in natural images: invariance stems from variations in data. Adv. Neural Inf. Process. Syst. **34**, 19566–19579 (2021)
5. Bronstein, M.M., Bruna, J., Cohen, T., Veličković, P.: Geometric deep learning: grids, groups, graphs, geodesics, and gauges. arXiv preprint arXiv:2104.13478 (2021)
6. Bruna, J., Mallat, S.: Invariant scattering convolution networks. IEEE Trans. Pattern Anal. Mach. Intell. **35**(8), 1872–1886 (2013)
7. Carlini, N., et al.: On evaluating adversarial robustness. arXiv preprint arXiv:1902.06705 (2019)
8. Carlini, N., Wagner, D.: Defensive distillation is not robust to adversarial examples. arXiv preprint arXiv:1607.04311 (2016)

9. Carlini, N., Wagner, D.: Adversarial examples are not easily detected: bypassing ten detection methods. In: Proceedings of the 10th ACM Workshop on Artificial Intelligence and Security, pp. 3–14. ACM (2017)
10. Carlini, N., Wagner, D.: Magnet and efficient defenses against adversarial attacks are not robust to adversarial examples. arXiv preprint arXiv:1711.08478 (2017)
11. Carlini, N., Wagner, D.: Towards evaluating the robustness of neural networks. In: 2017 IEEE Symposium on Security and Privacy (SP), pp. 39–57. IEEE (2017)
12. Cohen, T., Welling, M.: Group equivariant convolutional networks. In: International Conference on Machine Learning, pp. 2990–2999. PMLR (2016)
13. Croce, F., Hein, M.: Minimally distorted adversarial examples with a fast adaptive boundary attack. In: International Conference on Machine Learning, pp. 2196–2205. PMLR (2020)
14. Croce, F., Hein, M.: Reliable evaluation of adversarial robustness with an ensemble of diverse parameter-free attacks. In: International Conference on Machine Learning, pp. 2206–2216. PMLR (2020)
15. Deng, J., Dong, W., Socher, R., Li, L.J., Li, K., Fei-Fei, L.: Imagenet: a large-scale hierarchical image database. In: 2009 IEEE Conference on Computer Vision and Pattern Recognition, pp. 248–255. IEEE (2009)
16. Dieleman, S., De Fauw, J., Kavukcuoglu, K.: Exploiting cyclic symmetry in convolutional neural networks. In: International Conference on Machine Learning, pp. 1889–1898. PMLR (2016)
17. Dummit, D.S., Foote, R.M.: Abstract Algebra, vol. 3. Wiley, Hoboken (2004)
18. Engstrom, L., Ilyas, A., Salman, H., Santurkar, S., Tsipras, D.: Robustness (python library) (2019). https://github.com/MadryLab/robustness
19. Engstrom, L., Tran, B., Tsipras, D., Schmidt, L., Madry, A.: Exploring the landscape of spatial robustness. In: International Conference on Machine Learning, pp. 1802–1811. PMLR (2019)
20. Finzi, M., Stanton, S., Izmailov, P., Wilson, A.G.: Generalizing convolutional neural networks for equivariance to lie groups on arbitrary continuous data. In: International Conference on Machine Learning, pp. 3165–3176. PMLR (2020)
21. Gens, R., Domingos, P.M.: Deep symmetry networks. Adv. Neural Inf. Process. Syst. **27** (2014)
22. Goodfellow, I., Lee, H., Le, Q., Saxe, A., Ng, A.: Measuring invariances in deep networks. Adv. Neural Inf. Process. Syst. **22** (2009)
23. Goodfellow, I.J., Shlens, J., Szegedy, C.: Explaining and harnessing adversarial examples. arXiv preprint arXiv:1412.6572 (2014)
24. He, K., Zhang, X., Ren, S., Sun, J.: Deep residual learning for image recognition. In: Proceedings of the IEEE Conference on Computer Vision and Pattern Recognition, pp. 770–778 (2016)
25. Higgins, I., Racanière, S., Rezende, D.: Symmetry-based representations for artificial and biological general intelligence. Front. Comput. Neurosci. **16**, 836498 (2022)
26. Kayhan, O.S., Gemert, J.C.V.: On translation invariance in CNNs: convolutional layers can exploit absolute spatial location. In: Proceedings of the IEEE/CVF Conference on Computer Vision and Pattern Recognition, pp. 14274–14285 (2020)
27. Köhler, J., Klein, L., Noé, F.: Equivariant flows: exact likelihood generative learning for symmetric densities. In: International Conference on Machine Learning, pp. 5361–5370. PMLR (2020)
28. Krizhevsky, A., Hinton, G.: Learning multiple layers of features from tiny images. Master's thesis, University of Toronto (2009)
29. Krizhevsky, A., Sutskever, I., Hinton, G.E.: Imagenet classification with deep convolutional neural networks. Adv. Neural Inf. Process. Syst. **25** (2012)

30. Kurakin, A., Goodfellow, I., Bengio, S.: Adversarial machine learning at scale. arXiv preprint arXiv:1611.01236 (2016)
31. LeCun, Y., Bengio, Y., et al.: Convolutional networks for images, speech, and time series. Handb. Brain Theory Neural Netw. **3361**(10), 1995 (1995)
32. LeCun, Y., et al.: Backpropagation applied to handwritten zip code recognition. Neural Comput. **1**(4), 541–551 (1989)
33. LeCun, Y., Cortes, C., Burges, C.J.: The MNIST database of handwritten digits, 1998, vol. 10, p. 34. http://yann.lecun.com/exdb/mnist
34. Lindqvist, B.: A novel method for function smoothness in neural networks. IEEE Access **10**, 75354–75364 (2022)
35. Madry, A., Makelov, A., Schmidt, L., Tsipras, D., Vladu, A.: Towards deep learning models resistant to adversarial attacks. arXiv preprint arXiv:1706.06083 (2017)
36. Marcos, D., Volpi, M., Komodakis, N., Tuia, D.: Rotation equivariant vector field networks. In: Proceedings of the IEEE International Conference on Computer Vision, pp. 5048–5057 (2017)
37. Miller, W.: Symmetry Groups and Their Applications. Academic Press, Cambridge (1973)
38. Moosavi-Dezfooli, S.M., Fawzi, A., Frossard, P.: DeepFool: a simple and accurate method to fool deep neural networks. In: Proceedings of the IEEE Conference on Computer Vision and Pattern Recognition, pp. 2574–2582 (2016)
39. Nicolae, M.I., et al.: Adversarial robustness toolbox v1.0.1. CoRR 1807.01069 (2018). https://arxiv.org/pdf/1807.01069
40. Paszke, A., et al.: Pytorch: an imperative style, high-performance deep learning library. In: Wallach, H., Larochelle, H., Beygelzimer, A., d'Alché-Buc, F., Fox, E., Garnett, R. (eds.) Advances in Neural Information Processing Systems, vol. 32, pp. 8024–8035. Curran Associates, Inc. (2019). http://papers.neurips.cc/paper/9015-pytorch-an-imperative-style-high-performance-deep-learning-library.pdf
41. Romero, D.W., Cordonnier, J.B.: Group equivariant stand-alone self-attention for vision. In: International Conference on Learning Representations (2020)
42. Russakovsky, O., et al.: Imagenet large scale visual recognition challenge. Int. J. Comput. Vis. **115**(3), 211–252 (2015)
43. Schmidt, U., Roth, S.: Learning rotation-aware features: from invariant priors to equivariant descriptors. In: 2012 IEEE Conference on Computer Vision and Pattern Recognition, pp. 2050–2057. IEEE (2012)
44. Sifre, L., Mallat, S.: Rotation, scaling and deformation invariant scattering for texture discrimination. In: Proceedings of the IEEE Conference on Computer Vision and Pattern Recognition, pp. 1233–1240 (2013)
45. Sokolic, J., Giryes, R., Sapiro, G., Rodrigues, M.: Generalization error of invariant classifiers. In: Artificial Intelligence and Statistics, pp. 1094–1103. PMLR (2017)
46. Szegedy, C., et al.: Intriguing properties of neural networks. In: International Conference on Learning Representations (2013)
47. Tramer, F., Carlini, N., Brendel, W., Madry, A.: On adaptive attacks to adversarial example defenses. Adv. Neural Inf. Process. Syst. **33**, 1633–1645 (2020)
48. Zhang, R.: Making convolutional networks shift-invariant again. In: International Conference on Machine Learning, pp. 7324–7334. PMLR (2019)
49. Zhou, Y., Ye, Q., Qiu, Q., Jiao, J.: Oriented response networks. In: Proceedings of the IEEE Conference on Computer Vision and Pattern Recognition, pp. 519–528 (2017)

Web Security

LOAD-AND-ACT: Increasing Page Coverage of Web Applications

Nico Weidmann[1,2]($\boxtimes$), Thomas Barber[1] ⓘ, and Christian Wressnegger[2] ⓘ

[1] SAP Security Research, Karlsruhe, Germany
nicoweidmann@web.de, thomas.barber@sap.com
[2] KASTEL Security Research Labs, Karlsruhe Institute of Technology, Karlsruhe, Germany
christian.wressnegger@kit.edu

Abstract. Current solutions for automated vulnerability discovery increase coverage but typically do not interact with the web application. Thus, vulnerabilities in code for handling user interactions often remain undiscovered. This paper evaluates interactive strategies that simulate user interaction to increase client-side JavaScript code coverage. We exemplarily analyze 5 widely deployed, real-world web applications and find that simple random walks can double the number of covered branches compared to merely waiting for the page to be loaded ("load-and-wait"). Additionally, we propose novel approaches relying on state-independent models and demonstrate that these outperform the non-interactive baseline by 2.4× in terms of covered branches and 3.1× in terms of discovered data flows. Our interactive strategies have revealed a client-side data flow in SuiteCRM that is exploitable as a stored XSS and SSRF attack but cannot be found without user interaction.

Keywords: web security · crawling · tainting · client-side vulnerabilities

1 Introduction

Historically, web applications served static HTML pages [43], and tools for discovering vulnerabilities were focused on server-side code, e.g., reflected cross-site scripting (XSS) [19] and cross-site request forgery (CSRF) [18]. In recent years many complex web applications are now implemented with rich client-side components, utilizing browser APIs to dynamically modify the underlying "document object model" (DOM) [11] of the web page. As a result, new classes of vulnerabilities have emerged [43], including client-side XSS [20] and client-side CSRF [8]. Such vulnerabilities manifest themselves as insecure client-side data flows from attacker-controlled sources to security-sensitive sinks. As a simple example, Fig. 1 shows a website that parses a (potentially attacker-controlled) URL fragment and uses it to set the `innerHTML` property of a DOM element.

Due to JavaScript's highly dynamic and event-driven nature, statically analyzing it is challenging [32,36], and dynamic analysis such as taint-tracking

© The Author(s), under exclusive license to Springer Nature Switzerland AG 2023
E. Athanasopoulos and B. Mennink (Eds.): ISC 2023, LNCS 14411, pp. 163–182, 2023.
https://doi.org/10.1007/978-3-031-49187-0_9

```
1   <html>
2   <body>
3     <button onclick="clickHandler()">click me</button>
4       <div id="c"></div>
5       <script>
6         function clickHandler() {            // Only executed if a user clicks on the button
7           let hash = location.hash.slice(1);  // Attacker-controlled source
8           let view = decodeURIComponent(hash);
9           let c = document.getElementById('c');
10          c.innerHTML = view;                 // Security-sensitive sink leads to XSS!
11        }
12      </script>
13  </body>
14  </html>
```

Fig. 1. Example of interactive client-side XSS.

is preferable [3,22,25,31,40]. Recent advances in detecting client-side XSS are driven by techniques to more effectively track tainted inputs [22,31,40,41] or by automatically generating exploits [3,25]. However, these approaches often neglect interactive exploration of the target website, in stark conflict with the design principles of modern web applications.

The majority of client-side JavaScript code is responsible for handling events, e.g., for user interaction [34]. Since taint tracking can only discover data flows for executed code, large parts of the code may actually remain unexplored. The example in Fig. 1, for instance, shows such a vulnerability that becomes active only after the user clicks a button. It thus stands to reason that current approaches can only discover a subset of the client-side XSS vulnerabilities present in modern web applications.

In this work we explore various analysis strategies that simulate user interaction, aiming to maximize the client-side JavaScript code coverage and therefore increase the likelihood of client-side vulnerability discovery. We find that a simple strategy such as random walks in the web application's state space doubles the number of covered branches compared to merely waiting for the page to be loaded (load-and-wait). More evolved techniques that consider a state-independent model of the application even cover 140% more branches and discover 210% more taint flows than non-interactive approaches. Established related work [27] also improves on load-and-wait but falls behind random exploration. In summary, we make the following contributions:

– **Analysis Infrastructure.** We present an infrastructure for interactively analyzing web applications, transparently collecting client-side branch coverage information and dynamic taint flows (Sect. 3).
– **Interactive Strategies.** We define four interactive exploration strategies with the goal of maximizing client-side code coverage and improving vulnerability discovery (Sect. 4).
– **Comparative Evaluation.** We compare the proposed interactive strategies with non-interactive load-and-wait and established related work, Crawljax [27], finding that even the simplest strategies can significantly improve coverage. Additionally, we identify a previously unknown stored XSS and SSRF vulnerability in SuiteCRM 7.12.8 (Sect. 5).

2 Related Work

In this section, we review related work on (1) the discovery of client-side vulnerabilities (XSS and CSRF), and (2) on analyzing interactive web applications. For both, we highlight current limitations that our work attempts to eliminate.

2.1 Detection of Client-Side Vulnerabilities

A long line of research has used instrumented browsers to perform taint tracking for vulnerability discovery [e.g., 3,22,25,44]. For instance, by modifying the Chromium browser's JavaScript engine, Lekies et al. [22] show that 10% of the web pages in the Alexa Top 5,000 have at least one client-side XSS. Stock et al. [44] build upon this result and present a framework for detecting and preventing DOM-based XSS. Similarly, Bensalim et al. [3] obtain taint information using a fork of the Firefox browser that supports taint tracking in its JavaScript and rendering engine [39]. Melicher et al. [25] use an instrumented Chromium browser to show that 83% of client-side XSS originate from advertising and analytics domains. The same browser has been combined with a machine learning pre-filter for more efficient XSS detection [26], and also extended to detect other vulnerability classes such as prototype pollution [15]. Alternatively, FLAX [40] performs taint analysis on browser-generated execution traces in a simplified intermediate language called JASIL. Additionally, it relies on a sink-aware black-box fuzzer to validate its findings. To enable taint tracking without the high-maintenance cost of modifying a web browser, Parameshwaran et al. [31] instead opt for source-to-source rewriting of a web application's JavaScript code.

Khodayari and Pellegrino [16], in turn, focus on client-side CSRF [8]. Using a combination of static and dynamic analysis, they build a hybrid property graph that can be queried for insecure data flows. JAW contains a crawler that loads the target page and iteratively visits extracted URLs to collect runtime traces for HPG construction, but does not simulate user interaction with the target page. Similar techniques are deployed to detect other client-side vulnerabilities such as DOM clobbering [17].

Limitations. Most of the proposed methods for client-side XSS detection [3,22, 25,45] load the target page without any interaction and apply a fixed timeout during which taint flows are tracked. We refer to this non-interactive analysis strategy as `load-and-wait`. The FLAX tool [40] instead assumes an external test harness to be in place. Only DexterJS [31] includes elementary support for filling forms and triggering events. However, details on the exact operation are scarce as the authors focus on novel taint-tracking mechanisms. Since all studies that perform a large-scale analysis of client-side XSS in the wild [3,22,25,45] rely on `load-and-wait` they most likely underestimate the prevalence of client-side XSS.

2.2 Analyzing Interactive Web Applications

While previous work [2,6,24] has targeted increasing server-side code coverage, we focus on client-side JavaScript, which is heavily used by modern single-page applications. The research community has developed various analysis strategies that are suited to interactive web applications. Crawljax [27], for instance, has been extensively used in the past for regression [37], accessibility [9], and browser compatibility [28] testing. It uses the Selenium [46] browser automation framework to interact with the target page and extracts clickable elements to dispatch click events on them. jÄk [33], on the other hand, detects registered event listeners and dispatches synthetic events that should simulate user interaction. While this includes interaction beyond mere click events, the method might perform actions that are not possible for a real user. For instance, dispatching a click event on an element that is visually hidden. Both Crawljax and jÄk infer a state machine representing the analyzed application, where states represent DOM configurations and transitions correspond to actions performed by the analyzer. Different to Crawljax and jÄk, Black Widow [7] does not model DOM configurations explicitly, but infers a graph-based navigation model of the target application. It performs a breadth-first search on the navigation model to discover inter-page data dependencies that can be tested for injection vulnerabilities.

Limitations. Existing research mainly focuses on discovering as many distinct DOM states as possible. These approaches thus typically explore multiple subpages of the target web application. However, for discovering client-side vulnerabilities in JavaScript code, we need to increase client-side code coverage for individual sub-pages. Each sub-page can be considered a separate program (a navigation causes a new browsing context to be created). The Artemis framework [1] poses an exception: It uses various feedback-guided exploration strategies to maximize client-side code coverage. However, it requires control over the application's backend to reset it to a known state for each action the analyzer performs, hindering its general applicability.

3   Analysis Infrastructure

Figure 2 depicts an overview of our infrastructure for analyzing web applications. We load the URL of the target application in a remote-controlled browser and perform actions on the target according to a specific exploration strategy. The strategy uses information provided by the browser's instrumentation layer, including the page's DOM, the achieved code coverage, and observed taint flows. In the remainder of the section, we detail (1) the browser instrumentation and (2) the interactive analysis individually. We provide a description of the strategies themselves in Sect. 4.

3.1   Browser Instrumentation

Analysis based on standalone browser engines [33] or a JavaScript-based implementation of a browser environment [1] may cause side-effects [5]. We therefore build our infrastructure on the Foxhound browser [39], which extends Firefox

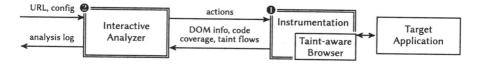

Fig. 2. Analysis infrastructure. Double line boxes denote novel contributions.

with taint-tracking capabilities. Similar to related work [7,27], we use the Selenium framework [46] to automate browser navigation and perform realistic user interaction. In the following, we elaborate on reliably gathering code coverage information and modifications to the browsing context.

Gathering Code Coverage Information. Measuring client-side JavaScript code coverage is essential to provide feedback for guiding our exploration strategies. Due to the lack of native support for determining code coverage in Firefox, we resort to source-to-source rewriting [12]. We create instrumented versions of a web application's HTML (necessary for inline scripts) and JavaScript resources by inserting monitoring statements at each control flow branch. For instrumenting loaded JavaScript code on-the-fly, we use the blocking `webRequest` API to intercept all script and document (HTML) requests as a "man-in-the-middle" between the browser tab and the web application's backend server.

Modifications to the Browsing Context. We also instrument the browser context in order to collect information about available actions and to block unwanted page navigations as follows. Information on registered event handlers (e.g., the `click` event) is crucial for determining which elements of a page to interact with. We follow the approach described by Pellegrino et al. [33] for hooking calls to the `addEventListener` function of the `Element`, `Document` and `Window` prototypes. When the hooked function registers a handler for event type e on object o, the hook increments a counter in a custom property of o to keep track of the listener registration for type e. In contrast to previous works [7, 27,33], the goal of our analyzer is to maximize the client-side code coverage for a single page. We therefore implement navigation blocking as part of our browser instrumentation by cancelling all document requests originating from the currently loaded top frame.

3.2 Interactive Analysis

All strategy-independent components of the analysis, namely extracting interesting elements from the DOM, identifying possible action candidates, or building and performing concrete actions are described in the following.

Extracting Interesting Elements. Similar to prior work [27,48], we extract interesting elements by their type (namely: `form`, `input`, `textarea`, `select`, and `anchor`) using XPath expressions on the DOM tree. Since we cannot assume that every element has an ID attribute, we recurse up the tree until we find an element with an ID, following the method used by the jÄk crawler [33]. For each extracted element, we determine whether it might be *pointer-interactable* by scrolling the element in question into view and applying the pointer-interactability algorithm defined in the W3C WebDriver standard [42, Sec. 12.1]. Finally, we verify that the analyzer can indeed interact with an element by checking whether the element is a *keyboard-focusable* area as defined by the HTML specification [47, Sec. 6.6.2].

Identifying Action Candidates. Based on the elements extracted from the DOM, the analyzer constructs action candidates by filtering out uninteresting elements. Action candidates represent abstract actions, and separate the challenge of finding potential interaction points from the task of generating suitable input values for actions requiring keyboard input. For extracted anchors, buttons, and inputs of type `checkbox` or `radio` the analyzer emits an action candidate if they are considered pointer-interactable. For anchor elements, the analyzer additionally checks whether the anchor has a click listener attached or points to a fragment on the same page. For elements that allow the user to enter data via the keyboard, the analyzer emits corresponding action candidates if they are keyboard-focusable.

Building Actions from Action Candidates. The analyzer builds actions from action candidates by choosing concrete values for candidates that require keyboard input. Our interactive analysis supports choosing inputs for `<textarea>` and `<select>` elements, as well as for `<input>` elements with one of the types `text`, `email`, `url`, `date`, `time`, and `number`. The input type `color` is not supported, while the types `datetime-local`, `month`, `tel`, `password`, `search`, and `week` fall back to `text` in the taint-aware browser [39]. For each of the supported input types, we can build random valid and invalid input values according to the client-side HTML-form validation attributes of the different elements. This includes the `pattern`, `minlength`, `maxlength`, `min`, `max`, and `step` attributes.

Running Actions on the Target Page. Because of JavaScript's asynchronous and event-driven execution model, the analyzer cannot determine whether an action is completed or whether the action has triggered asynchronous events that have yet to be processed. In line with related work [27,33], we hence make the analyzer wait for a fixed duration (0.5 s by default) after each action performed.

4   Exploration Strategies

In this section we define four distinct exploration strategies whose goal is to decide which actions the analyzer should take in order to maximize client-side code coverage. As motivated in the introduction, the aim is to increase the number of stimulated taint flows and aid vulnerability discovery.

4.1   Exploration with Random Walks

As a first step towards the development of more advanced interactive exploration strategies, we consider the `random-walk` strategy, similar to related work on GUI testing [10], that selects the next action randomly and independently of previously executed actions. This strategy does not use any feedback on the JavaScript code coverage or on observed taint flows nor does it depend on a model of the target application.

An analysis with `random-walk` is split into multiple episodes, each beginning by loading the target application. The strategy then enters a loop in which it interacts with the application by first extracting potentially interesting elements from the DOM and then analyzing them for available action candidates. The strategy samples a random action candidate, builds a concrete action from it, and executes the action on the application. An episode ends if the strategy cannot find any action candidates, a maximum number of actions has been executed during the episode, or the time budget for the analysis has been exhausted. We also introduce invalid HTML form values with a probability $p_{\text{invalid}} := 0.2$ in order to trigger multiple client-side code paths.

4.2 Random Walks with Model-Free Heuristics

In this section we introduce the `random-walk+heuristics` strategy, where the `random-walk` strategy is enhanced to increase the probability of executing previously unexplored code.

Heuristic Candidate Sampling. Given a set of action candidates, we sample each candidate c with a weight w_c, defined as:

$$w_c := w_c^{\text{unexplored}} \cdot w_c^{\text{errored}} \cdot w_c^{\text{pageload}} \cdot w_c^{\text{coverage}},$$

where

$$w_c^{\text{unexplored}} := \begin{cases} w^{\text{unexplored}}, & \text{if } c \text{ has not been executed before} \\ 1, & \text{otherwise} \end{cases}$$

$$w_c^{\text{coverage}} := \begin{cases} w^{\text{coverage}}, & \text{if the last execution of } c \text{ resulted in new coverage} \\ 1, & \text{otherwise} \end{cases}$$

$$w_c^{\text{errored}} := \begin{cases} w^{\text{errored}}, & \text{if executing } c \text{ caused an error} \\ 1, & \text{otherwise} \end{cases}$$

$$w_c^{\text{pageload}} := \begin{cases} w^{\text{pageload}}, & \text{if executing } c \text{ caused a page load} \\ 1, & \text{otherwise} \end{cases}$$

The parameters $w^{\text{unexplored}}$, w^{errored}, w^{pageload}, and w^{coverage} are configurable constants. Based on preliminary experiments described in Appendix A, we set $w^{\text{unexplored}} := 15$ and $w^{\text{coverage}} := 2$ to favor candidates that have not been executed before or achieved new coverage during the last execution, while $w^{\text{errored}} = w^{\text{pageload}} := 0.1$ to decrease the likelihood of executing candidates that led to an error or page load in the past.

Heuristic Detection of Dead Ends. If no new coverage has been observed during the last s_{stuck} actions and the number of distinct candidates in this window is below a configured threshold t_{stuck}, the strategy assumes the analyzer is stuck and ends the current episode (i.e., reloads the target application). For our experiments, we set $s_{\text{stuck}} := 5$ and $t_{\text{struck}} := 2$.

4.3   Model-Guided Random Walks

In this section we augment the `random-walk+heuristics` strategy with a model of the target application in order to guide the analyzer towards unexplored action candidates. To this end we define the `state-independent model` and `state machine model` strategies as follows.

State-Independent Model. The state-independent model is motivated by the assumption that many candidates are available in multiple states, and that their behavior with respect to code coverage is independent of the state in which they are executed. Intuitively, the model encodes relationships between action candidates of the form *"if you do A, then you can do B"*, for example, *"if you click the button that opens a menu, then you can enter text in the menu"*. This is assumed to be independent of the state in which the button for opening the menu is clicked. More formally, the *state-independent model* of a web application is defined as the tuple (Σ, λ), where Σ is the *set of all action candidates* observed during the analysis and for each executed candidate $c \in \Sigma$ and each successor candidate $c' \in \Sigma$, the partial *candidate probability function* $\lambda \colon \Sigma \times \Sigma \to [0,1]$ gives the probability $\lambda(c, c')$ that candidate c' is available after executing candidate c.

An example is shown in Fig. 3, where Σ consists of the action candidates $c_1, \ldots, c_9$. The candidate probability function λ is illustrated by an edge from the executed candidate c_i to the set of candidates c' for which $\lambda(c_i, c') > 0$.

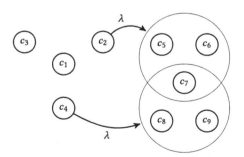

c'	$\lambda(c_2, c')$	$\lambda(c_4, c')$
c_5	0.3	0
c_6	0.8	0
c_7	0.9	0.4
c_8	0	0.5
c_9	0	0.7
others	0	0

Fig. 3. Example of a state-independent model.

Using the Model. The purpose of the state-independent model is to guide the analyzer towards candidates which not been have previously executed, even if they are not available in the current state. Referring to the previous example, this means assigning more weight to the action candidate that opens the menu if the menu contains action candidates that have not been explored before. In practice, the model is used to increase the weights of available candidates that have been executed before and have a large ratio of unexecuted successor candidates.

To formally define the assigned weight for an available candidate c, let s_c be the set of the successor candidates for c:

$$s_c := \{c' \mid c' \in \Sigma \land \lambda(c, c') > 0\}$$

We then define the ratio $r_c \in [0, 1]$ of non-executed successor candidates of c as follows:

$$r_c := \begin{cases} \dfrac{\sum_{c' \in s_c \land c' \text{ not executed}} \lambda(c, c')}{|s_c|}, & |s_c| > 0 \\ 0, & \text{otherwise} \end{cases}$$

To calculate the weight w_c assigned to candidate c, we multiply r_c with a constant weight parameter w^{model} and use it as an additional factor to the weight assigned by random-walk+heuristics:

$$w_c := w_c^{\text{random-walk+heuristics}} \cdot (1 + r_c \cdot w^{\text{model}}) \tag{1}$$

This allows balancing the weight assigned to previously executed candidates based on their unexplored successors with the weight assigned to unexplored candidates. For our evaluation, we set $w^{\text{model}} := 25$.

State Machine Model. The state-independent model assumes that the behavior of an action candidate does not depend on the state in which it is executed. In contrast, we define the state machine model as a non-deterministic finite state machine $(\Sigma, S, s_0, \delta, B, \omega, \lambda)$, where the *input alphabet* Σ is the set of all action candidates observed during the analysis; S is a set of *visible DOM states*; s_0 is the *initial state* before loading the target application; $\delta \colon S \times \Sigma \to \mathcal{P}(S)$ is the partial non-deterministic *state transition function*, such that $\delta(s, c)(s')$ is the probability that the target application will be in state s' when executing action candidate c in state s; B is the set of all *known code branches* of the target; the partial *transition output function* $\omega \colon S \times \Sigma \times S \to B^*$ assigns each transition (s, c, s') with $\delta(s, c)(s') > 0$ a set of branches covered when the transition occurs; the *state output function* $\lambda \colon S \times \Sigma \to [0, 1]$ maps each state $s \in S$ and action candidate $c \in \Sigma$ to the probability $\lambda(s, c)$ that c is available in s.

Intuitively, the states of the state machine represent different DOM states, while a transition encodes the change in the state caused by executing actions built from a given action candidate. Additionally, each transition is associated with a set of branches covered when executing the candidate belonging to the transition.

Figure 4 shows a simple state machine model, where transitions are labeled with the action candidate c_k that causes the transition, the probability

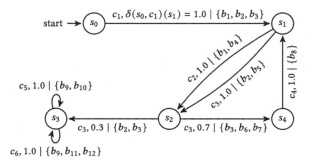

Fig. 4. A state machine model for a web application with 4 distinct DOM states.

$\delta(s_i, c_k)(s_j)$ that executing candidate c_k in state s_i results in state s_j, and the set of branches covered during the transition.

Identifying States. We define a state similarity measure Δ using Gestalt pattern matching [35] on the sequence of HTML tag names of elements extracted from the page's DOM. Two states s, s' are considered the same if their similarity $\Delta(s, s')$ is greater than a configured threshold $\Delta_{\min}$. This method of calculating state similarity is inspired by the method used by Zheng et al. [48], with the difference that we restrict the extracted token sequences to visible elements and do not consider the current URL in the similarity measure. For the evaluation of our strategies, we set $\Delta_{\min} := 0.9$ based on preliminary experiments (cf. Appendix B).

Using the Model. To guide the analyzer towards unexplored action candidates with the `state machine model` strategy, we first define a function that assigns each state s a score based on the number and likelihood of unexplored action candidates the analyzer can reach from state s. This includes candidates in s itself, but also in states reachable from s. We compute the score $\sigma(s)$ by applying a breadth-first search starting at state s. For each state s' visited during the search at depth d, we increment the score $\sigma(s)$ by

$$\gamma^d \cdot \sum_{c \in \Sigma^{s'}_{\text{unexpl}}} \lambda(s', c).$$

Here, γ is a constant, configurable discount factor and $\Sigma^{s'}_{\text{unexpl}} \subset \Sigma$ is the set of unexplored action candidates in state s'. For a state s' and each candidate c that has been executed in s' before, the search proceeds to the successor state $\arg\max_{s''} \delta(s', c, s'')$ for which the model predicts the highest probability when executing c in s'. The search terminates at a pre-configured maximum depth.

To incorporate the state scores into the analysis' decision when the application is in state s, we assign each available action candidate c executed before, a weight based on the score $\sigma(s_c)$ for the most likely successor state $s_c := \arg\max_{s'} \delta(s, c, s')$. The strategy then samples a candidate to execute according to the weights.

To find a trade-off between choosing an unexplored candidate from the currently available candidates and choosing a previously executed candidate with a high score, we allocate a large portion $r_{\text{unexpl}} \in [0,1]$ of the total weight to the available unexplored candidates C^s_{unexpl}. The remaining weight is distributed across the available previously executed candidates C^s_{expl} according to the scoring function. Each available candidate c is assigned the weight w_c as follows:

$$
w_c := \begin{cases} \dfrac{r_{\text{unexpl}}}{|C^s_{\text{unexpl}}|}, & c \in C^s_{\text{unexpl}} \\[2ex] \left(1 - \displaystyle\sum_{c' \in C^s_{\text{unexpl}}} w_{c'}\right) \cdot \dfrac{1 + \sigma(s_c)}{\sum_{c' \in C^s_{\text{expl}}}(1 + \sigma(s_{c'}))}, & c \in C^s_{\text{expl}} \end{cases} \tag{2}
$$

5 Evaluation

In this section, we evaluate the interactive exploration strategies presented above using five open-source, real-world web applications listed in Table 1, selected to offer rich user-interaction with varying degrees of client-side JavaScript usage. For each application, we provide application-specific login scripts where necessary, and fix the screen resolution of the virtual frame buffer for running the instrumented browser to 1920×1080 px. For each interactive strategy and application, we perform up to ten at most 30 min long analyses, excluding results which terminate early due to the application entering an error state. Strategy performance is evaluated using code-coverage and number of taint flows as metrics, with each metric scaled in relation to the non-interactive load-and-wait strategy used by previous works [3,22,25,45].

Table 1. List of web applications considered in our evaluation.

Application	Version	Description	Branches
code-server	[4] 4.3.0	in-browser IDE	114,629
diagrams.net	[13] 20.2.1	diagramming application	90,654
SuiteCRM	[38] 7.12.5	CRM platform	73,520
Odoo	[29] 15.0	CRM platform	62,354
ownCloud	[30] 10.10.0	file sharing application	34,071

5.1 Code Coverage

The mean percentage increase over load-and-wait in terms of distinct covered branches across all target applications for each strategy is shown in Fig. 5, with a detailed comparison shown in Table 2. All interactive exploration strategies achieve an increase in the number of covered branches on all target applications

Table 2. Mean distinct covered branches (**br**) and discovered taint flows (**t**). The maxima per target application are marked in bold.

Strategy	code-server br	t	diagrams.net br	t	SuiteCRM br	t	Odoo br	t	ownCloud br	t
load-and-wait	14,736	0.0	6,508	2.0	3,706	8.0	6,551	8.0	4,221	3.0
random-walk	36,028	2.1	13,743	**9.0**	7,820	14.3	18,575	17.3	6,531	7.6
random-walk+heur.	**38,399**	2.1	**14,040**	8.8	9,017	15.4	**18,998**	**17.6**	6,600	9.0
state-independent	38,262	**2.3**	13,864	**9.0**	**9,700**	**18.7**	18,767	17.2	**7,593**	**10.2**
state machine	35,912	1.9	13,770	**9.0**	8,520	14.6	18,420	17.2	7,036	9.3

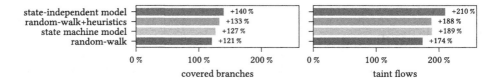

Fig. 5. Increase of covered branches and taint flows over load-and-wait.

compared to the non-interactive load-and-wait baseline, ranging from 54.7% for the random-walk strategy on ownCloud to 190.0% for random-walk+heuristics on Odoo. Figure 6 shows the ratio of distinct actions taken for each strategy and application, and can be interpreted as a measure of strategy efficiency.

Even the simple random-walk strategy allows a deep exploration of the target application with 121% more covered branches on average across all applications compared to load-and-wait. However, on some target applications, e.g., code-server, the strategy tends to get stuck in "dead ends" (i.e., a state where none of the available action candidates cause a change of the state) which it has no way of leaving until the end of the episode. Additionally, the random-walk strategy has no mechanism to prioritize action candidates it has not executed before, causing a low ratio of distinct executed action candidates and a decreased efficiency.

Extending the random-walk strategy with heuristics (random-walk+heuristics) increases the number of covered branches by an additional 5.5% on average. As can be seen in Fig. 6, the increased weight for previously unexecuted candidates leads to an increase in the ratio of distinct executed actions, which reflects the increased efficiency of the strategy.

Model-based approaches also help the analyzer find previously unexplored action candidates, especially during later stages of the analyses when unexplored candidates become more sparse: adding the state-independent model to the random-walk+heuristics strategy yields an additional increase of 4.0% on average compared to random-walk+heuristics. However, the state machine model strategy performs worse than the model-free random-walk+heuristics strategy. This may be founded in the different notion of action-candidate distinctness when using the state machine model: action candidate distinctness is determined per state when assigning weight based on the state machine model (cf. Eq. (2)). This leads to a lower ratio of globally distinct executed actions, as shown in Fig. 6. A global notion of candidate distinctness—as used with the `state-independent model` strategy—is thus preferable for maximizing code coverage.

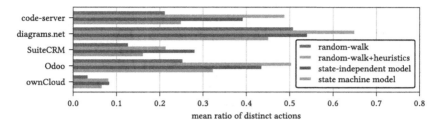

Fig. 6. Distinct actions vs total executed actions.

Detailed Example: SuiteCRM. Figure 7 shows the number of distinct covered branches over the number of actions executed by each strategy for Suite-CRM, showing the mean coverage. Shaded colors show the range between the pointwise minimum and maximum.

During the entire duration, the advanced strategies outperform the unguided `random-walk` strategy. Up until 1,200 actions, `random-walk+heuristics` achieves the most coverage on average. However, the model-based strategies catch up: Beyond 1,200 actions, the `state-independent model` outperforms all other strategies. This result illustrates the models' ability to assist the analyzer in locating previously unexplored candidates—in particular during later stages of the analysis where the ratio of unexplored candidates decreases. The large spread between minimum and maximum coverage on SuiteCRM is caused by individual actions that result in a large number of newly covered branches. These high-value actions lead to a sharp increase in coverage when they are executed.

Comparison to Crawljax. We compare our strategies to the established Crawljax [27] crawler by performing 14 crawls on the code-server [4] application. Each analysis is once again limited to 30 min, with no constraints on the number of states or depth, ensuring comparability with previous experiments. To discern states, we use the Levenshtein distance [23] with a threshold factor of 0.9. Additionally, we enable random form inputs, randomized action ordering, and repeated execution of actions in different states.

Overall, we find that Crawljax covers on average 31,656 branches in the code-server application. Referring the Table 2, while this is 2.4 times more than the non-interactive `load-and-wait` strategy, it falls behind the simple, unguided `random-walk` strategy by 13.8%. For our best strategy on code-server, `random-walk+heuristics`, the mean coverage is 21.3% higher than that of Crawljax. We attribute the superior performance of our interactive strategies to fundamental differences in the approach. Namely, Crawljax assumes that the target

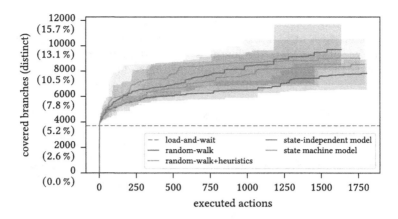

Fig. 7. Branches covered in SuiteCRM.

application is mostly deterministic, trying to follow shortest paths in its internal model of the application to reach states with unexplored actions. This strategy is inefficient if actions cannot reliably be replayed—either because of non-determinism or inaccuracies in the state-identification mechanism. In contrast, our strategies take a "best-effort" approach to exploiting models of the application, which degrades gracefully if the target is highly non-deterministic. Instead of using the model to calculate a path of actions to follow, our strategies make local, ad-hoc decisions based on the set of currently available actions.

5.2   Taint Flows

As a metric for the security relevance of executed code, we measure the number of distinct taint flows between potentially security-relevant sources and sinks that occur during analysis with the different exploration strategies. The results are shown in Table 2 and Fig. 5. All interactive strategies result in an increase in the number of observed taint flows compared to `load-and-wait` across all tested target applications. The improvement ranges from 78.1% for `random-walk` on SuiteCRM to 350% for `random-walk` and both model-based strategies on diagrams.net. The strategy based on the state-independent model performs better than or as well as all other strategies on all targets except Odoo, where `random-walk+heuristics` discovers the most flows. On average, it discovers 210% more taint flows than `load-and-wait`. In addition, we observed a strong positive correlation between the measured code coverage and the number of flows on all targets, with Pearson correlation coefficients ranging from 0.78 on code-server to 0.99 on diagrams.net and Odoo.

From Taint Flows to Vulnerabilities. We employ a semi-automated analysis of taint flows to answer the question of whether our interactive strategies can assist in the discovery of vulnerabilities. To identify the taint flows that warrant manual investigation, we apply several filters as follows. We first deduplicate the discovered flows according to their sources and sinks (F1). In a second step, only flows from an attacker-controlled or user-controlled source (the URL, the window name, the referrer, and values of form inputs) to sinks that are sensitive to client-side XSS or CSRF (HTML, JavaScript, XMLHttpRequest, and Web-Socket sinks) are retained (F2). The remaining taint flows are inspected manually by reviewing the relevant code to determine whether they correspond to an exploitable vulnerability (F3). As the taint flows contain the code location of sources, sinks and operations, only a moderate manual effort was required here.

We perform the analysis once for all flows found by all interactive strategies, and once for the flows discovered by `load-and-wait`. The number of flows after each filter is as follows:

$$\texttt{interactive:} \quad 2,069 \xrightarrow{\text{F1}} 88 \xrightarrow{\text{F2}} 18 \xrightarrow{\text{F3}} 2$$
$$\texttt{load-and-wait:} \quad 210 \xrightarrow{\text{F1}} 21 \xrightarrow{\text{F2}} 2 \xrightarrow{\text{F3}} 1$$

All exploration strategies (including `load-and-wait`) find a taint flow that corresponds to a known client-side CSRF vulnerability that has been reported by Khodayari and Pellegrino [16]. In addition, the interactive strategies also discover an additional flow that can be exploited in an SSRF and stored XSS attack, which cannot be found by the `load-and-wait` strategy. We have confirmed that the vulnerabilities exist in version 7.12.8 of SuiteCRM (the latest version at the time of writing) and have disclosed them to the maintainers.

6   Discussion

Our results show that even simple random walks cover more than twice as many branches and discover more than twice as many taint flows than the non-interactive `load-and-wait` strategy. The performance can be improved even more by using simple heuristics and automatically built models of the target application to guide the random walks. Our strategies are able to exercise security-relevant code that is not covered by `load-and-wait`, as illustrated by the vulnerabilities discovered in SuiteCRM.

Increasing the client-side code coverage through interaction is important for the completeness of dynamic client-side vulnerability analysis, as indicated by the strong correlation of the covered branches and the number of observed taint flows between security-relevant sources and sinks. Previous research [21] shows that accepting cookies by interacting with cookie banners increases the number of observed security-sensitive data flows by 63%. While these results were restricted to a specific type of user interaction, our results show that the same observation can be made for more general interactions with web applications.

One key insight from our study is that the common practice [7,27,33] of building stateful models of web applications to aid code discovery is extremely challenging due to hidden server-side states, non-deterministic application behavior, and model inaccuracies. This means that a model may determine the application is in a previously visited state, but the available actions may differ, leading to inefficient exploration or errors. This hypothesis is confirmed in Table 2, which shows that the `state machine model` strategy tends to underperform when compared to the `random-walk` strategies. This finding is reinforced by our comparison with Crawljax, where even the `random-walk` strategy performs better. On the other hand, the `state-independent model` strategy uses information about previously executed action candidates to decide which action to take next, *independently of the current state*. This technique outperforms the `state machine model` for all applications we tested. Overall, we have shown that guided random walks that perform on-the-fly decisions on the next action to execute are better suited to deal with these challenges that those which attempt to model an application's state.

Limitations and Threats to Validity. Our analysis infrastructure shares some limitations of existing approaches. Similar to Crawljax [27], the types of supported actions are restricted to mouse clicks and keyboard inputs. Some approaches [1,7,33] support the simulation of arbitrary events, but fail to ensure realistic interaction. We consider extending our approach to different types of events as engineering effort of future work. Additionally, our analyzer is currently restricted to random text inputs (while honoring HTML form validation attributes). By generating context-aware inputs the achievable code coverage could be increased even further. Also, in line with previous works [27,33], we considered automatically passing the log-in form of the target application to be an orthogonal line of research [14] and therefore out of scope.

Finally, our comparative evaluation against existing techniques is limited to Crawljax. Unfortunately, more recent approaches either lack an open source implementation [31], are no longer executable due to deprecated dependencies [33], or tightly couple the actual analyzer and the vulnerability scanner functionality [7] making it impossible to separate them.

7   Conclusion

Many existing approaches for discovering and measuring the prevalence of client-side XSS vulnerabilities use simple `load-and-wait` strategies for observing web pages. Our experiments show that loading the target application without any interaction leaves large parts of the client-side code uncovered. This strategy is thus insufficient for the automated discovery of client-side vulnerabilities. Our results highlight that even simple interaction strategies significantly increase the amount of code executed. Moreover, they discover additional vulnerable taint flows that would remain undetected without interaction.

By performing (guided) random walks we improve over the `load-and-wait` baseline by 140% (2.4×) in terms of covered branches and 210% (3.1×) regarding the number of discovered taint flows. Existing studies on the prevalence of client-side vulnerabilities relying on `load-and-wait` likely underestimate the number of actual vulnerabilities. Future research needs to ensure proper interaction with the web application during dynamic analysis to reliably assess a website's functionality.

A   Heuristic Candidate Weights

In this section we describe how we chose the parameterized weight values for the
`random-walk+heuristics` strategy (see Sect. 4.2) by performing experiments on
the code-server application. We vary each parameter individually while setting
the remaining parameters to 1.0, effectively disabling all but one heuristic. For
each configuration of the weight parameters we perform 6 runs of 10 min, with
the results shown in Fig. 8. For comparison, the dashed line shows the mean
number of branches covered by the `random-walk` strategy as a baseline.

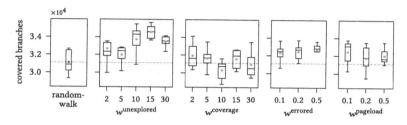

Fig. 8. Covered branches for the `random-walk+heuristics` strategy with different choices
for the heuristics' weights.

The parameter with the most significant effect on the coverage is $w^{\text{unexplored}}$.
For $w^{\text{unexplored}} = 15$ we see an improvement of the mean number of covered
branches by 9.6% compared to the baseline. For choices below and above 15 the
gain compared to the `random-walk` strategy with regard to covered branches and
number of unique candidates is smaller. We therefore set $w^{\text{unexplored}} := 15$ for our
experimental evaluation. For the parameter w^{coverage}, we choose $w^{\text{coverage}} := 2$
for the evaluation as it provides a small increase (3.9%) compared to the base-
line. For the parameters w^{errored} and w^{pageload} we observe a slight improvement
compared to the baseline for all parameter values. However, the significance of
these observations is limited since the number of actions that resulted in an
error or a page-load is very small: across the 6 baseline runs, only 5.7 actions
resulted in an error on average and only 2 actions led to a pageload in total.
Since actions resulting in an error or a pageload typically do not contribute any
new code coverage, we set $w^{\text{errored}} = w^{\text{pageload}} := 0.1$ in our experiments.

B   State Similarity Threshold

To choose an appropriate value for $\Delta_{\min}$ (see Sect. 4.3), we performed 3 runs
on the code-server application (15 min each) for different possible values. If
$\Sigma_s := \{c \in \Sigma \mid \lambda(s, c) > 0\}$ is the set of action candidates that are available in
state s, the mean candidate probability $\overline{\lambda}(s)$ of state s is defined as follows:

$$\overline{\lambda}(s) := \frac{\sum_{c \in \Sigma_s} \lambda(s, c)}{|\Sigma_s|}$$

Intuitively, $\overline{\lambda}(s)$ is a measure of the model's certainty about the action candidates that will be available in state s. If $\overline{\lambda}(s)$ is high, the model is good at predicting the candidates, while a low $\overline{\lambda}(s)$ indicates a high uncertainty of the model.

Figure 9 shows the mean candidate probability, the number of visits to each state and the number of states encountered during the analysis. While the mean candidate probability increases with $\Delta_{\min}$, a larger $\Delta_{\min}$ leads to fewer visits to each individual state and a larger mean number of distinct states per analysis. These results are intuitively expected: the higher $\Delta_{\min}$ is chosen, the more likely the model is to create a new state instead of considering a DOM token sequence to belong to a known state. This leads to a larger number of total states, while reducing the number of visits per state. Additionally, a higher similarity between DOM trees in the same state also increases the likelihood that the DOM trees contain the same action candidates, thus leading to a larger mean candidate probability. We therefore set $\Delta_{\min} := 0.9$ for the evaluation, which yields a good mean candidate probability of 0.8 and results in 4 visits to each state on average.

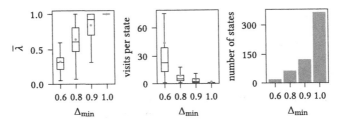

Fig. 9. Mean candidate probability $\overline{\lambda}$, visits per state and number of states vs. $\Delta_{\min}$.

References

1. Artzi, S., Dolby, J., Jensen, S.H., Møller, A., Tip, F.: A framework for automated testing of JavaScript web applications. In: Proceedings of the International Conference on Software Engineering (ICSE), pp. 571–580 (2011)
2. Bau, J., Bursztein, E., Gupta, D., Mitchell, J.: State of the art: automated black-box web application vulnerability testing. In: Proceedings of the IEEE Symposium on Security and Privacy (S&P), pp. 332–345 (2010)
3. Bensalim, S., Klein, D., Barber, T., Johns, M.: Talking about my generation: targeted DOM-based XSS exploit generation using dynamic data flow analysis. In: Proceedings of the European Workshop on System Security (EUROSEC) (2021)
4. coder/code-server. https://github.com/coder/code-server
5. Demir, N., Große-Kampmann, M., Urban, T., Wressnegger, C., Holz, T., Pohlmann, N.: Reproducibility and replicability of web measurement studies. In: Proceedings of the ACM Web Conference (WWW) (2022)
6. Doupé, A., Cavedon, L., Kruegel, C., Vigna, G.: Enemy of the state: a state-aware black-box web vulnerability scanner. In: Proceedings of the USENIX Security Symposium, pp. 523–538 (2012)
7. Eriksson, B., Pellegrino, G., Sabelfeld, A.: Black widow: blackbox data-driven web scanning. In: Proceedings of the IEEE Symposium on Security and Privacy (S&P), pp. 1125–1142 (2021)

8. Facebook: "client-side" CSRF (2018). https://web.archive.org/web/201805131847
14/https://www.facebook.com/notes/facebook-bug-bounty/client-side-csrf/20568
04174333798/
9. Ferruci, F., Sarro, F., Ronca, D., Abrahão, S.: A Crawljax based approach to
exploit traditional accessibility evaluation tools for AJAX applications. In: D'Atri,
A., Ferrara, M., George, J.F., Spagnoletti, P. (eds.) Information Technology and
Innovation Trends in Organizations. Physica, Heidelberg (2011)
10. Gross, F., Fraser, G., Zeller, A.: EXSYST: search-based GUI testing. In: Proceedings of the International Conference on Software Engineering (ICSE) (2012)
11. Ihm, S., Pai, V.S.: Towards understanding modern web traffic. In: Proceedings of
the Internet Measurement Conference (IMC), pp. 295–312 (2011)
12. Istanbul, a JavaScript test coverage tool. https://istanbul.js.org/
13. jgraph/docker-drawio. https://github.com/jgraph/docker-drawio
14. Jonker, H., Karsch, S., Krumnow, B., Sleegers, M.: Shepherd: a generic approach
to automating website login. In: MADWeb 2020 (2020)
15. Kang, Z., Song, D., Cao, Y.: Probe the proto: measuring client-side prototype
pollution vulnerabilities of one million real-world websites. In: Proceedings of the
Network and Distributed System Security Symposium (NDSS) (2022)
16. Khodayari, S., Pellegrino, G.: JAW: studying client-side CSRF with hybrid property graphs and declarative traversals. In: Proceedings of the USENIX Security
Symposium, pp. 2525–2542 (2021)
17. Khodayari, S., Pellegrino, G.: It's (DOM) clobbering time: attack techniques,
prevalence, and defenses. In: Proceedings of the IEEE Symposium on Security
and Privacy (S&P) (2023)
18. KirstenS: Cross site request forgery (CSRF). https://owasp.org/www-community/
attacks/csrf
19. KirstenS: Cross site scripting (XSS). https://owasp.org/www-community/attacks/
xss/
20. Klein, A.: DOM based cross site scripting or XSS of the third kind. Web Application
Security Consortium (2005)
21. Klein, D., Musch, M., Barber, T., Kopmann, M., Johns, M.: Accept all exploits:
exploring the security impact of cookie banners. In: Proceedings of the Annual
Computer Security Applications Conference (ACSAC), pp. 911–922 (2022)
22. Lekies, S., Stock, B., Johns, M.: 25 million flows later: large-scale detection of
DOM-based XSS. In: Proceedings of the ACM Conference on Computer and Communications Security (CCS), pp. 1193–1204 (2013)
23. Levenshtein, V.I.: Binary codes capable of correcting deletions, insertions, and
reversals. Doklady Phys. **10**, 707–710 (1966)
24. McAllister, S., Kirda, E., Kruegel, C.: Leveraging user interactions for in-depth
testing of web applications. In: Lippmann, R., Kirda, E., Trachtenberg, A. (eds.)
RAID 2008. LNCS, vol. 5230, pp. 191–210. Springer, Heidelberg (2008). https://
doi.org/10.1007/978-3-540-87403-4_11
25. Melicher, W., Das, A., Sharif, M., Bauer, L., Jia, L.: Riding out DOMsday: towards
detecting and preventing DOM cross-site scripting. In: Proceedings of the Network
and Distributed System Security Symposium (NDSS) (2018)
26. Melicher, W., Fung, C., Bauer, L., Jia, L.: Towards a lightweight, hybrid approach
for detecting DOM XSS vulnerabilities with machine learning. In: Proceedings of
the ACM Web Conference (WWW), pp. 2684–2695 (2021)
27. Mesbah, A., van Deursen, A., Lenselink, S.: Crawling Ajax-based web applications
through dynamic analysis of user interface state changes. ACM Trans. Web **6**(1),
1–30 (2012)

28. Mesbah, A., Prasad, M.R.: Automated cross-browser compatibility testing. In: Proceedings of the International Conference on Software Engineering (ICSE) (2011)
29. Odoo: Open source ERP and CRM. https://www.odoo.com
30. ownCloud GmbH: ownCloud. https://owncloud.com
31. Parameshwaran, I., Budianto, E., Shinde, S., Dang, H., Sadhu, A., Saxena, P.: DexterJS: robust testing platform for DOM-based XSS vulnerabilities. In: Proceedings of the Joint Meeting on Foundations of Software Engineering, pp. 946–949 (2015)
32. Park, J., Lim, I., Ryu, S.: Battles with false positives in static analysis of JavaScript web applications in the wild. In: Proceedings of the International Conference on Software Engineering (ICSE), pp. 61–70 (2016)
33. Pellegrino, G., Tschürtz, C., Bodden, E., Rossow, C.: jÄk: using dynamic analysis to crawl and test modern web applications. In: Bos, H., Monrose, F., Blanc, G. (eds.) RAID 2015. LNCS, vol. 9404, pp. 295–316. Springer, Cham (2015). https://doi.org/10.1007/978-3-319-26362-5_14
34. Ratanaworabhan, P., Livshits, B., Zorn, B.G.: JSMeter: comparing the behavior of JavaScript benchmarks with real web applications. In: USENIX Conference on Web Application Development (WebApps) (2010)
35. Ratcliff, J.W., Metzener, D.E.: Pattern-matching - the gestalt approach. Dr. Dobbs J. **13**(7), 46 (1988)
36. Richards, G., Lebresne, S., Burg, B., Vitek, J.: An analysis of the dynamic behavior of JavaScript programs. In: Proceedings of the ACM SIGPLAN International Conference on Programming Languages Design and Implementation (PLDI), pp. 1–12 (2010)
37. Roest, D., Mesbah, A., van Deursen, A.: Regression testing ajax applications: coping with dynamism. In: Proceedings of the International Conference on Software Testing, Verification and Validation (ICST), pp. 127–136 (2010)
38. SalesAgility: SuiteCRM. https://suitecrm.com
39. SAP/project-foxhound. https://github.com/SAP/project-foxhound
40. Saxena, P., Hanna, S., Poosankam, P., Song, D.: FLAX: systematic discovery of client-side validation vulnerabilities in rich web applications. In: Proceedings of the Network and Distributed System Security Symposium (NDSS) (2010)
41. Steffens, M., Rossow, C., Johns, M., Stock, B.: Don't trust the locals: investigating the prevalence of persistent client-side cross-site scripting in the wild. In: Proceedings of the Network and Distributed System Security Symposium (NDSS) (2019)
42. Stewart, S., Burns, D.: WebDriver. W3C working draft, W3C (2022)
43. Stock, B., Johns, M., Steffens, M., Backes, M.: How the web tangled itself: uncovering the history of client-side web (in)security. In: Proceedings of the USENIX Security Symposium, pp. 971–987 (2017)
44. Stock, B., Lekies, S., Mueller, T., Spiegel, P., Johns, M.: Precise client-side protection against DOM-based cross-site scripting. In: Proceedings of the USENIX Security Symposium, pp. 655–670 (2014)
45. Stock, B., Pfistner, S., Kaiser, B., Lekies, S., Johns, M.: From facepalm to brain bender: exploring client-side cross-site scripting. In: Proceedings of the ACM Conference on Computer and Communications Security (CCS), pp. 1419–1430 (2015)
46. The Selenium Project: Selenium (2022). https://www.selenium.dev/
47. WHATWG: HTML living standard (2022). https://html.spec.whatwg.org/
48. Zheng, Y., et al.: Automatic web testing using curiosity-driven reinforcement learning. In: Proceedings of the International Conference on Software Engineering (ICSE), pp. 423–435 (2021)

From Manifest V2 to V3: A Study on the Discoverability of Chrome Extensions

Valerio Bucci[✉][iD] and Wanpeng Li[iD]

Department of Computing Science, University of Aberdeen, Aberdeen AB24 3UE, UK
valerio.bucci@abdn.ac.uk, wanpeng.li@abdn.ac.uk

Abstract. Browser extensions allow users to customise and improve their web browsing experience. The Manifest protocol was introduced to mitigate the risk of accidental vulnerabilities in extensions, introduced by inexperienced developers. In Manifest V2, the introduction of web-accessible resources (WARs) limited the exposure of extension files to web pages, thereby reducing the potential for exploitation by malicious actors, which was a significant risk in the previous unrestricted access model. Building on this, Manifest V3 coupled WARs with match patterns, allowing extension developers to precisely define which websites can interact with their extensions, thereby limiting unintended exposures and reducing potential privacy risks associated with websites detecting user-installed extensions. In this paper, we investigate the impact of Manifest V3 on WAR-enabled extension discovery by providing an empirical study of the Chrome Web Store. We collected and analysed 108,416 extensions and found that Manifest V3 produces a relative reduction in WAR detectability ranging between 4% and 10%, with popular extensions exhibiting a higher impact. Additionally, our study revealed that 30.78% of extensions already transitioned to Manifest V3. Finally, we implemented *X-Probe*, a live demonstrator showcasing WAR-enabled discovery. Our evaluation shows that our demonstrator can detect 22.74% of Manifest V2 and 18.3% of Manifest V3 extensions. Moreover, within the 1000 most popular extensions, the detection rates rise to a substantial 58.07% and 47.61%, respectively. In conclusion, our research shows that developers commonly associate broad match patterns to their WARs either because of poor security practices, or due to the inherent functional requirements of their extensions.

Keywords: Browser extension fingerprinting · Web-accessible resources · Browser extension detection

1 Introduction

With the rapid proliferation of internet-based technologies and applications, web security has become a primary concern in the modern digital era. The emergence of browser extensions has played a significant role in enhancing the user experience by enabling users to customise and augment their browsing activities

© The Author(s), under exclusive license to Springer Nature Switzerland AG 2023
E. Athanasopoulos and B. Mennink (Eds.): ISC 2023, LNCS 14411, pp. 183–202, 2023.
https://doi.org/10.1007/978-3-031-49187-0_10

with a vast array of functionalities. However, the development and design of browser extensions often present a difficult trade-off between usability and security, necessitating careful consideration in order to achieve an optimal balance [2, 3, 6, 29, 39].

In particular, as most extensions are developed by non-professional programmers, they may exhibit unintentional vulnerabilities, exposing users to network attackers or malicious websites. To address this issue, Barth et al. [3] introduced in 2010 a browser architecture which implements the principles of least privilege, privilege separation, and process isolation. Their solution involves a protocol called *"Manifest"*, which requires extension developers to declare in advance a list of required and optional permissions. In the original Manifest protocol, however, websites could potentially access all resources within a browser extension. This posed a significant security risk because malicious websites could exploit this access to manipulate the extension's functionality or to exfiltrate sensitive information. Thus, in 2012, Manifest V2 introduced the concept of web-accessible resources (WARs), allowing developers to explicitly expose certain files to the web, thereby providing a more controlled and secure environment from potential misuse or unintentional vulnerabilities. Furthermore, WARs are accessed from a URL which embeds the associated extension's identifier, used by browsers to validate the integrity of its exposed files.

However, in 2017, Sjösten et al. [42] found that this measure allows the discovery of installed extensions by requesting large quantities of known URLs, associated to publicly-declared WARs. Consequently, by verifying the existence of a certain resource, adversarial websites can unequivocally conclude that the corresponding extension is installed on a visiting browser. Such exposure can lead to serious privacy infringements. For instance, it can reveal personal information about a user, such as the use of specific extensions like password managers, ad-blockers, or accessibility tools. Moreover, this exposure can enhance fingerprinting, as the combination of detected extensions may significantly boost the uniqueness of browser fingerprints, favouring stateless identification and cross-site tracking [12, 21, 23, 32, 48]. The uniqueness of these profiles may be further exacerbated when extensions are installed from different, interoperable web stores, such as those of Opera and Edge, as their WARs are reached via different URLs, thereby expanding the fingerprint complexity. Furthermore, this form of tracking can occur without knowledge or consent by users, further exacerbating the privacy concerns associated with browser extensions [16, 18].

As a mitigation to WAR-enabled extension discovery, in 2020, Manifest V3 introduced the concept of match patterns, allowing developers to further control the exposure of their WARs through predefined URL restrictions. Nevertheless, the efficacy of match patterns in thwarting WAR-enabled extension discovery is contingent upon their adoption by extension developers. Not only is the adoption rate of Manifest V3 yet to be reported on, but it is also unclear whether match patterns have produced a significant impact in curtailing extension discovery.

1.1   Our Contributions

In order to understand how match patterns are affecting WAR-enabled extension discovery, in this paper, we conduct an empirical study on the Chrome Web Store. With this focus, we compare the relative difference in discoverability between Manifest V2 and V3 extensions. Thus, our contributions are as follows:

1. We provide the first research effort of its kind to evaluate the impact of Manifest V3 on WAR-enabled discovery, by conducting an empirical study of the Chrome Web Store, and observe that 30% of extensions already transitioned to Manifest V3. However, most implemented match patterns do not preclude discovery. Overall, we measure discoverable Manifest V2 and V3 extensions to be 22.74% and 18.3%.
2. We introduce *X-Cavate*, a framework to construct a database of WARs, allowing to identify discoverable extensions. X-Cavate produces a database which can be updated regularly and yields a selection of WARs to be surveyed for conducting extension discovery.
3. We implement a live demonstrator, called *X-Probe*. Based on our evaluation, X-Probe can identify 21.34%, 38.16%, 54.9%, and 63% of Chrome Web Store extensions overall, and within the top 10,000, 1,000, and 100 most popular extensions, respectively. Additionally, we compare the performance of X-Probe against existing work on extension detection.
4. We propose additional measures for mitigating WAR-enabled discovery.

The remainder of our paper is structured as follows. Section 2 provides an overview of the Chrome Extension System. Section 3 describes how WARs can be exploited to detect installed extensions. Section 4 delineates the methodology of our study, illustrates the X-Cavate framework, and evaluates the X-Probe demonstrator. Section 5 showcases the results of our empirical study and provides a comparison of our results with previous literature. Section 6 discusses the implications of our results and drafts our conclusions. Section 7 identifies defensive measures to further limit WAR probing. Section 8 identifies the state of the art relatively to browser fingerprinting and extension detection. Section 9 summarises our contributions, highlights our key takeaways, and identifies potential avenues for future work.

2   The Chrome Extension System

Extensions are small programs which run in the browser, allowing user to customise their browsing experience. By interfacing with browser APIs, extensions may execute various functions such as manipulating web content, managing active tabs, accessing browsing history, and more. However, the use of extensions can introduce novel security risks, often as a consequence of their development by inexperienced programmers. This lack of expertise can lead to privilege escalation vulnerabilities, exposing users to exploitation by adversarial websites or network attackers. In 2009, Liverani and Freeman demonstrated such security risk in Firefox extensions [28]. Successively, Barth et al. identified that the Firefox architecture allowed full access to its powerful API [3], making most extensions over-privileged. Thus, they proposed a novel browser architecture, implementing the principles of *least-privilege*, *privilege separation*, and *process isolation*. Their architecture lays the foundation for the Chrome Extension System, and was also adopted by other popular browsers, including Firefox and Safari.

2.1   Architecture Overview

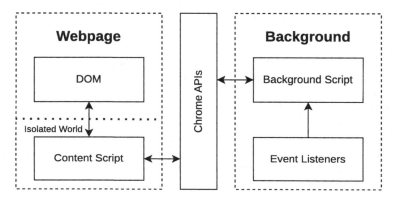

Fig. 1. A simplified representation of the Chrome Extension System.

The Chrome Extension System, illustrated in Fig. 1, aims to strike a balance between flexibility and security, ensuring that developers can create powerful extensions while minimizing the risks associated with accidental exposures. It mainly consists of two interdependent components implementing privilege separation and process isolation: the *content script* and the *background script*[1]. Furthermore, the *Manifest* protocol is aimed at standardising the development of extensions and enforcing least-privilege by providing developers with granular access to the Chrome APIs.

Chrome APIs. The Chrome APIs form the backbone of the Chrome Extension System, providing a set of JavaScript interfaces for accessing browser functionalities. APIs are grouped by category, each providing access to distinct capabilities. Namely, the `tabs` API allows to manipulate browser tabs, while the `storage` API provides methods for storing and retrieving data. Furthermore, the `runtime` API facilitates communication between extension components, such as the content script and background script. This granular approach allows extensions to

---

[1] For the sake of simplicity, we omitted various secondary components. Further information can be found on Google's official documentation at https://developer.chrome.com/docs/extensions/mv3/architecture-overview/.

carry out tasks while adhering to the principle of least-privilege, with developers declaring required permissions via the *Manifest* protocol.

Manifest. Manifests consist in JSON files, conveying metadata about extensions, including their name, version number, description, and required permissions. At the time of writing, Google is spearheading a shift from Manifest V2 to V3, with browser extensions gradually transitioning to the latest iteration. Such transition is equally significant and controversial, as it redefines the permissions and capabilities of background scripts [11].

Background Script. Background scripts, as the name suggests, run in the background of extensions. They access the Chrome and JavaScript APIs to perform tasks that do not require user interaction, such as listening for events, sending HTTP requests to the Web, running timers, storing data, and broadcasting messages to other components. In Manifest V2, background scripts could be either *persistent* or *non-persistent*. Persistent background scripts remain active for the whole duration of a browser session. Non-persistent background scripts, instead, are automatically unloaded when idle. In Manifest V3, "traditional" background scripts were deprecated in favour of *service workers*. In contrast, service workers are non-persistent, event-driven, and guarantee unique instance behaviour across all extension pages, windows, or tabs. However, the transition to fully-asynchronous service workers has sparked controversy due to its limitations on synchronous functionalities, namely, in the `webRequest` API [4,11,13]. Nevertheless, independently of the Manifest version, background scripts detain most operational capabilities, except for DOM manipulation, which is delegated to the content script via message passing.

Content Script. Content scripts are closely tied to webpages, with each tab or window initializing its own content script. While interacting with unsanitised webpages, content scripts face significant restrictions in accessing Chrome APIs. To circumvent these limitations, they delegate operations requiring broader access to the background script. Additionally, content scripts operate within a specialized, sandboxed environment known as *isolated world*. The isolated world is a distinct JavaScript runtime that provides a unique space for interacting with the DOM, preventing exposures to the host runtime environment. Consequently, their access to extension files is also limited to the Web-Accessible Resources (WARs) declared in the Manifest.

Web-Accessible Resources. Before Manifest V2 introduced WARs in 2012, websites could access all files within extensions installed on browsers. This design was insecure because it allowed for malicious websites to perform fingerprinting or detect exploitable vulnerabilities in installed extensions [19,20]. Additionally, it could lead to unintentional exposures of sensitive data by developers. In Manifest V2, the DOM is restrained from accessing extension filesystems. Instead, developers can optionally specify a list of WARs to be injected into the DOM, such as scripts, style sheets, or images. Each WAR can be defined as a specific path or as a wildcard encompassing a group of files. Consequently, WARs will

Listing 1. WARs declaration in Manifest V2 (left) and V3 (right).

```
{
    ...
    "manifest_version": 2,
    ...
    "web_accessible_resources": [
        "images/*.png",
        "extension.css"
    ],
    ...
}
```

```
{
    ...
    "manifest_version": 3,
    ...
    "web_accessible_resources": [{
        "resources": ["images/*.png"],
        "matches": [
            "https://*.google.com/*"
        ]
    }, {
        "resources": ["extension.css"],
        "matches": ["<all_urls>"]
    }],
    ...
}
```

be exposed to webpages at a specialised URL, embedding the extension identifier and the relative file path: `chrome-extension://[EXTENSION ID]/[PATH]`. The identifier is unique to each extension, and it allows browsers to validate the integrity of exposed files. Using Manifest V2, declared WARs are exposed to any arbitrary website. In contrast, as shown in Listing 1, Manifest V3 allows developers to implement further accessibility restrictions via match patterns.

Match Patterns. Match patterns specify which websites an extension can interact with. They are composed by a combination of URLs and wildcards. For example, a pattern such as `https://*.google.com/*` would match any URL within the Google domain. Since the inception of the Manifest protocol, match patterns have been used, namely, to grant host permissions, determining which websites an extension can access and modify. Additionally, they are also employed to dictate where content scripts should be injected, enhancing both performance and security. With the advent of Manifest V3, the role of match patterns has been expanded to compound WARs, allowing developers to restrict the exposure of WARs to specific websites, as shown in Listing 1. This measure provides developers with a more granular control over the accessibility of extension resources, mitigating potential misuse and reducing the risk of unexpected behaviour. However, extensions needing to inject their WARs in all websites require highly permissive match patterns. For instance, these include `https://*/*`, `*://*/*` and `<all_urls>`. Therefore, the effectiveness of match patterns is not only contingent on their thoughtful implementation by developers, but it can also be constrained by the functional necessities of extensions.

3   Probing WARs to Detect Extensions

As explained in Sect. 2.1, WARs are defined in the Manifest, and are accessed within the context of a webpage via extension-specific URLs. Such URLs embed unique extension identifiers, assigned by the publishing extension store. Consequently, as illustrated in Listing 2, a webpage could fetch a known WAR and observe whether the request is fulfilled. If so, the webpage can unequivocally determine that the corresponding extension is installed on the visiting browser. Furthermore, by collecting manifests from online stores, an adversarial website could survey a large dataset of known WARs to detect installed extensions. However, it is important to note that this technique has its limitations, as not all extensions employ WARs. Moreover, such exposure could be further mitigated in Manifest V3, provided developers employ stringent match patterns.

Listing 2. Working example to detect a password management extension.

```
fetch("chrome-extension://hdokiejnpimakedhajhdlcegeplioahd/overlay.html")
    .then(response => {
        if (response.ok) {
            console.log("LastPass is installed.");
        }
    }).catch(error => {
        console.log("LastPass is not installed.");
    });
```

4   Methodology

This section reports on the methodology employed in our study, conducted in March 2023, to evaluate the susceptibility of Chrome Web Store extensions to WAR-enabled discovery. To determine the popularity of each extension, we focused sequentially on the number of ratings, number of downloads, and star rating, all in descending order, to sort extensions from the most popular to the least popular. We prioritised the number of ratings as a metric due to observed inconsistencies and potential artificial inflation in download numbers, evidenced by some extensions having substantial downloads yet zero ratings.

In Sect. 4.1 we delineate the *X-Cavate* framework, employed to (a) collect identifiers and popularity metrics; (b) download extensions and extract their manifests; (c) construct a database of available extensions and associated features; and (d) produce a sample of WARs exposed to any arbitrary URL. Successively, in Sect. 4.2 we introduce our online demonstrator *X-Probe*, which implements extension discovery through the collected dataset.

4.1   X-Cavate Framework

For the purpose of this study, we developed a data collection utility following the *X-Cavate* framework, shown in Fig. 2. While in this study we focused our efforts on the Chrome Web Store, X-Cavate is aimed at automating the collection of extensions from any given online store. We present below the main modules constituting our proposed framework:

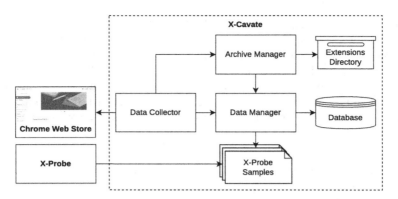

Fig. 2. Abstract structure of the X-Cavate Framework.

Data Collector. The Data Collector refers to a configuration file containing a URL to an online store and CSS selectors to the extension identifiers and associated metrics (e.g. downloads, ratings, and category) to be scraped from the DOM. After collecting an identifier, it downloads the corresponding extension. Finally, it provides the downloaded extensions and the scraped details to the Archive Manager and Data Manager, respectively.

Archive Manager. The Archive Manager handles downloaded extensions, which consist of CRX files – i.e. ZIP archives with additional headers. After an extension is downloaded, the Archive Manager stores it into a structured directory tree, strips the CRX headers, and extracts the `manifest.json` file. Successively, it redacts a list of exposed files, by matching the declared WARs (if any) with the files located in the archive. Therefore, if a WAR is not located in its specified path, it is not inserted in the list. Finally, the Archive Manager provides the extrapolated subset of WARs to the Data Manager.

Data Manager. The Data Manager processes online details scraped by the Data Collector and downloaded extensions' metadata, extrapolated by the Archive Manager. It maintains a normalised database by validating inserted records and ensuring relational consistency and integrity. The database architecture connects online information with data extrapolated from downloaded archives. Thus, it supports repeated insertions of various extension releases overtime, enabling researchers to perform long-term studies. Finally, based on popularity metrics, it compiles a series of datasets to be employed by the X-Probe demonstrator.

4.2   X-Probe Demonstrator

We introduce *X-Probe*, a practical implementation of WAR-enabled discovery, targeted at Chrome extensions[2]. X-Probe was evaluated against the four extensions shown in Table 1, each exposing their WARs with exclusively one vulnerable

---

[2] X-Probe can be tested on all Chromium-based browsers at: https://xprobe.dev.

match pattern. We repeated our evaluation on various Chromium-based browsers (i.e. Chrome, Brave, Opera, and Edge) and observed consistent results.

Table 1. Extensions used to validate discoverable patterns.

Extension	Release	Manifest	Pattern	Detected?
Speed Dial	81.3.1	V3	<all_urls>	yes
Custom Cursor	3.3.0	V3	*://*/*	yes
Talend API Tester	25.11.2	V3	https://*/*	yes
ShopQuangChauVN	5.1	V3	http://*/*	yes
Hola VPN	1.208.689	V2	N/A	yes

X-Probe relies on four JSON-formatted datasets produced with the X-Cavate framework, containing extension identifiers, each paired with one exposed WAR. Each dataset represents either the top 100, 1000, and 10,000 most popular extensions on the Chrome Web Store. Additionally, a dataset containing all discoverable extensions was included in the demonstration. While the comprehensive dataset provides a thorough but resource-intensive scan, smaller datasets offer a quicker analysis, albeit limited. Based on our evaluation, X-Probe can identify in the varying datasets 21.34%, 38.16%, 54.9%, and 63% of extensions, overall and within the 10,000, 1,000, and 100 most popular extensions, respectively.

5   Results

In March 2023 we scraped details for 111,467 extensions, of which 108,416 were successfully downloaded and analysed. Of the 3051 failures, 105 were due to corrupted archives, while 2946 were visible on the Chrome Web Store, but no longer available for downloading. We ranked extensions by their rating count, download count, and average rating. We prioritised the rating count as it is a continuous metric, and because reviews can only be provided by authenticated Google users. Finally, we grouped extensions in the *Top 100*, *Top 1000*, and *Top 10,000* popularity groups, shown in Fig. 3.

5.1   Susceptibility to WAR-Enabled Discovery

In total, 23,132 extensions are detectable via WAR-enabled discovery, accounting for 21.35% of the analysed set. Figure 4 shows a positive correlation between popularity and discoverable proportions, with a detection rate of 64%, 59.4%, and 38.14% in Top 100, Top 1000, and Top 10,000 groups, respectively. Additionally, we observe that some categories are more susceptible to WAR-enabled discovery. Namely, "Shopping" extensions consistently exhibit higher detection rates than other categories. We performed a one-sided Mann-Whitney U test

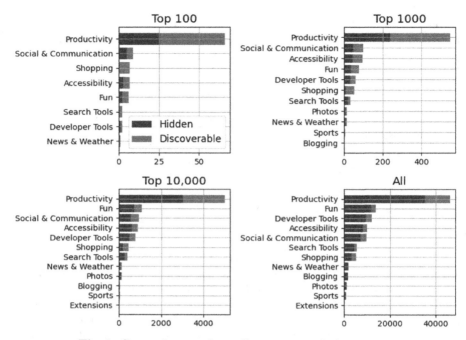

Fig. 3. Categories overview split across popularity groups.

to determine if there was a significant difference in the distribution of rating counts between discoverable and hidden extensions. A statistic of approximately 1.33×10^{12} and p-value < 0.05, rejected the null-hypothesis. Therefore, we conclude that discoverable extensions have a higher rating count than hidden ones.

5.2 Manifest V3 Adoption Rate

In total, 75,048 extensions use Manifest V2, while 33,368 transitioned to V3, corresponding to 30.78%. As shown in Fig. 5, Manifest V3 extensions account for 33%, 29.4%, and 28.89% of the Top 100, Top 1000, and Top 10,000 groups, respectively. Notably, none of the "Developer Tools" and "News & Weather" extensions in the Top 100 group transitioned to V3. Furthermore, "Blogging" extensions consistently exhibit lower adoption rates than other categories. This might be due to the requirements of extensions which extensively use background scripts and broad permissions to capture, modify, and deliver information: tasks that could become increasingly challenging to perform under the more restrictive and event-driven environment of Manifest V3.

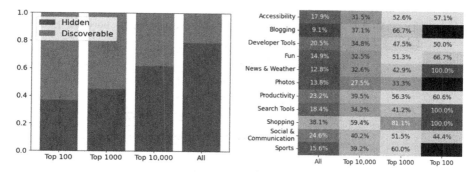

Fig. 4. WAR-enabled discovery rates.

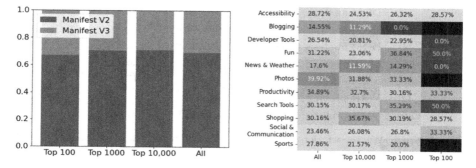

Fig. 5. Manifest V3 rate of adoption.

5.3   Manifest V3 Impact on WAR-Enabled Discovery

We employed Manifest V2 extensions to establish a baseline for evaluating the impact of Manifest V3 in mitigating WAR-enabled discovery. Successively, we compared the relative proportions of discoverable extensions to assess whether there was a difference between each Manifest iteration across popularity groups. Table 2 shows a consistent positive correlation between popularity and detectable rates in both Manifest iterations. However, we also observe an increasing mitigatory effect of Manifest V3, with a relative reduction ranging between 4% and 10%. In contrast, Manifest V2 extensions in the Top 100 group are less likely to be detectable than V3 extensions.

5.4   Comparative Evaluation

Table 3 provides a comparison between our work and the existing literature in the field of extension discovery. Despite DOM analysis being a popular method, its effectiveness is limited, with detection percentages below 10%. A substantial leap in detectability was observed with the advent of WAR probing, as demonstrated by [42]. In the work of [16], a multi-class strategy was employed,

Table 2. Discoverable rates across popularity groups, measured between Manifest iterations ($\Delta = V2 - V3$).

Group	Overall	V2	V3	Δ
All	21.35%	22.74%	18.3%	4.44%
Top 10,000	38.14%	40.47%	32.39%	8.08%
Top 1000	55%	58.07%	47.61%	10.46%
Top 100	65%	62.68%	66.67%	−3.99%

Table 3. Comparison with previous work.

Paper	Attack Class	# Extensions	% Detectable
[48]	DOM analysis	10,000	9.2%
[24]	DOM analysis (CSS rules)	116,485	3.8%
[44]	DOM analysis (user actions)	102,482	2.87%
[16]	Multi-class	102,482	28.72%*
[30]	Multi-class	91,147	17.68%*
[42]	WAR probing	43,429	28%*
Ours	WAR probing	108,416	21.34%

Note: We report percentages over the complete set of analysed extensions when the original work reports absolute numbers. *Evaluated on WARs prior to Manifest V3.

merging WAR probing with DOM analysis and interception broadcast communication by extension components, achieving even higher detection rates. Notably, within their approach, WAR probing alone was able to detect 25.24% of extensions, underscoring its superior efficacy in extension discovery. Similarly, [30] implemented a strategy combining WAR probing with DOM analysis, although, their results were significantly lower than [16], with 11.37% of extensions being detected through WAR probing alone. However, these studies were conducted with WARs under the Manifest V2 framework. With the transition to the more restrictive Manifest V3, a new set of challenges emerges, leaving the effectiveness of these previous methods in the updated constraints uncertain. Our research addresses this challenge by adapting WAR probing to the Manifest V3 environment, providing an up-to-date study on the effectiveness of this strategy.

6   Discussion

6.1   Popular Extensions are More Discoverable

The results from our analysis highlight a paradoxical correlation: as an extension's popularity increases, so too does their susceptibility to WAR-enabled discovery. In all analysed groups, there is a consistent trend of increased discoverability with increased popularity – as determined by rating count, download count, and average rating. However, this pattern has significant implications for user security and privacy. A particular concern lies in browser fingerprinting, as the set of detected extensions on a browser can greatly enhance the complexity of fingerprints, especially when coupled with other identifiable attributes. Thus, detectable extensions provide adversarial entities with an expanded toolset to uniquely identify and track users across the web in a stateless manner. This raises several questions regarding the security implications for the most used extensions, as they appear to be more visible and hence potentially more exposed to attacks. Extensions' popularity, in this context, might inadvertently serve as a double-edged sword. On the one hand, it makes these extensions more accessible to users, thereby contributing to their popularity. On the other hand, it simultaneously exposes them to potential malicious entities, aiming to carry out targeted attacks and cross-site tracking.

6.2   Developers Employ Broad Match Patterns

Manifest V3 allows developers to enforce least-privilege in their WARs through match patterns. Although Manifest V3 produces a quantifiable impact, its limitations lay in the assumption that developers will enact appropriate restrictions. Furthermore, many extensions provide functionalities which require exposing WARs to all websites. For example, extensions that modify the appearance of webpages, such as themes or custom cursors, need to inject their resources across all domains. Similarly, extensions that provide web development tools, like colour pickers or CSS inspectors, also require broad access to function effectively. In these cases, the use of highly permissive match patterns becomes a necessity rather than a choice. This implies that even with the best intentions, developers may be forced to compromise on least-privilege due to the inherent requirements of their extensions. Consequently, while Manifest V3's approach to WARs is a step in the right direction, it may not fully eliminate the risk of WAR-enabled discovery, especially for extensions that inherently require broad access.

7   Recommended Mitigation Measures

Based on our findings and expertise acquired while developing this project, we propose the following countermeasures for mitigating WAR-enabled discovery.

Limiting Failed Requests. WAR-enabled discovery involves probing a large sample of WARs. For instance, our demonstrator X-Probe employs a sample of 23,132 discoverable extensions. Consequently, the vast majority of surveyed WARs is expected to return an error from the browser API. Therefore, since this unreasonable amount of requests is unlikely to be performed for legitimate purposes, we propose the introduction of a failed-request cap in the browser API. Such cap could be enforced on the offending webpage by preventing its JavaScript environment from requesting further resources.

Limiting Accessibility. Content scripts use the Chrome API method `getUrl` to obtain a resource's URL given its relative path in the extension repository.

The process-isolation pattern allows browsers to determine whether `getUrl` was called from a content script or a webpage. Therefore, we propose a *"gate"* system, which only exposes WARs to a webpage after they are requested by the content script. While this measure would not prevent access to WARs of highly-active extensions (e.g. password managers), it may severely limit extension fingerprinting capabilities. Furthermore, as Manifest V3 introduces background service workers, webpages could be blocked from accessing the WARs of idle extensions.

User-Enforced Least-Privilege. Manifest V3 empowered extension distributors to arbitrarily restrict WAR exposure. However, users intending to replicate such restriction have to disable extensions from their browser settings, or open an "incognito" session. Realistically, the average user is unlikely to perform this procedure each time they visit a new website. Therefore, we recommend that browsers introduce functionalities allowing users to enact such restrictions on demand. This would involve blocking all WAR requests originating from untrusted websites, and informing the user about request attempts. Finally, the user could either deny or authorise all requests. Alternatively, they could decide to expose specific extensions. Naturally, users should be also allowed to tailor default settings based on their privacy needs to avoid hindering usability.

8 Related Work

8.1 Extension Detection

Over the past decade, extensions have begun to emerge as a new area of study, with researchers exploring its potential uses and challenges in the context of online privacy and security [4–6,8,10,16,18,33–36,39–41,46]. In this emerging field, different strategies have been developed for detecting extensions, mostly focused on analysing changes to the DOM and probing WARs.

DOM Analysis. Starov and Nikiforakis [48] examined the top 10,000 Chrome Web Store extensions, and showed that at least 9.2% introduced detectable DOM changes on any arbitrary URL. Additionally, they developed a proof-of-concept script, able to identify 90% of the analysed 1,656 identifiable extensions. Extending this research, Starov et al. [47] revealed that 5.7% of the 58,034 analysed extensions were detectable due to unnecessary DOM changes. Consequently, Laperdix et al. [24] investigated how CSS rules injected by content scripts can be used to detect installed extensions, revealing that 3.8% of the 116,485 analysed extensions could be uniquely identified with this method. Building on this existing body of knowledge, Solomos et al. [44] highlighted that user-triggered DOM changes had been overlooked by previous research. Thus, they identified 4,971 extensions, including over a thousand that were undetectable by previous methods. Additionally, they revealed that about 67% of extensions triggered by mouse or keyboard events could be detected through artificial user actions. Additionally, Solomos et al. [45] proposed continuous fingerprinting, a technique capable of capturing transient modifications made by extensions, previously undetectable due to their ephemeral nature. This technique substantially increases the coverage of extensions detectable through their DOM modifications.

WAR Probing. Before the introduction of Manifest V3, Sjösten et al. [42] conducted the first comprehensive study of non-behavioral extension discovery, focusing on the detection of WARs in both Chrome and Firefox. Their empirical study, found that over 28% of the 43,429 analysed Chrome extensions could be detected. Building on their work, Gulyas et al. [12] conducted a study on 16,393 participants for evaluating how browser extensions detected with WARs contributed to the uniqueness of users. They found that 54.86% of users which installed at least one extension were uniquely identifiable. Additionally, they found that testing 485 carefully selected extensions produced the same level of uniqueness. Subsequently, Sjösten et al. [43] further examined the issue of detecting browser extensions by web pages, particularly focusing on the recent introduction of randomised WAR URLs by Mozilla Firefox, which they found could potentially compromise user privacy rather than protect it. They introduced "revelation attacks", to detect these randomised URLs in the code injected by content scripts, thereby enabling enhanced user tracking.

Combined Techniques. Karami et al. [16] implemented a multi-class approach which involves DOM analysis, WAR probing, and interception of broadcast messages by extension components. Their technique detected 29,428 out of 102,482 extensions, demonstrating resilience against countermeasures to DOM analysis proposed by [50]. Although their results are best-performing among present literature, their evaluation dates before the diffusion of Manifest V3 on the Chrome Web Store. On the other hand, Lyu et al. [30] presented their approach comprising of DOM analysis and WAR probing, detecting 16,166 extensions out of 91,947, with 11,856 being detectable by their WAR probing approach. However, there is no mention of WAR match patterns or Manifest V3 throughout their paper. Furthermore, it is unclear why their WAR discovery rate (i.e. 13.01%) is comparatively lower than in previous literature and our results.

8.2   Browser Fingerprinting

There is a growing body of work exploring browser fingerprinting [51] and the ways it can be augmented by the virtually-unlimited combinations of potentially installed extensions [12,17,50]. Additionally, much work has been conducted on devising defensive and mitigatory measures [7,9,14,15,22,25,31,49]. Finally, literature has focused on the utilisation of fingerprinting as a tool for streamlining user authentication [1,37,38], although, some have highlighted the security limitations of such methods [26,27].

9   Conclusion

Manifest V3 coupled WARs with match patterns to further mitigate the exposure of extensions to webpages. We presented an empirical study on 108,416

Chrome Web Store extensions, with focus on WAR-enabled discovery. To the best of our knowledge, we are the first to evaluate the impact of Manifest V3 match patterns applied to WARs. Our results show that Manifest V3 produces a relative reduction in detectability, growing from 4% to 10% as extensions become more popular. In contrast, Manifest V3 extensions among the 100 most popular, exhibit a relative increase of 4% in detectability, when compared to V2. Furthermore, independently of the adopted Manifest iteration, popular extensions are more likely to be discoverable. We argue that match patterns do not fully eliminate the risk of WAR-enabled discovery, both because some developers neglect least-privilege practices, and due to inherent extension functionalities which require universal exposure of resources. Therefore, we proposed a range of defensive measures to be implemented on the browser side. Through a combination of these measures, we anticipate a significant improvement in preventing unwarranted probing of WARs.

In addition, we devise the *X-Cavate* framework to repetitively collect extensions from online stores and extract their Manifests to maintain a structured database overtime. Alongside X-Cavate, we developed a live demonstrator called *X-Probe* to emphasize the efficacy of WAR-enabled discovery. Based on our evaluation, X-Probe has proven its capability in detecting 22.74% of Manifest V2 and 18.3% of Manifest V3 extensions, overall. Moreover, relatively to the 1000 most popular extensions, the detection rates rise to a substantial 58.07% and 47.61%, respectively, further highlighting the severity of this exposure.

Future work could involve the integration of a diverse array of extension discovery techniques, alongside the development of a demonstrator that can function across various browser architectures. In addition, once the transition to Manifest V3 is fully completed, it could be especially insightful to conduct an updated user study. This would allow for an examination of the uniqueness of extension fingerprints, presenting a valuable opportunity to better understand and further contribute to this evolving field.

References

1. Andriamilanto, N., Allard, T., Le Guelvouit, G., Garel, A.: A large-scale empirical analysis of browser fingerprints properties for web authentication. ACM Trans. Web **16**(1), 4:1–4:62 (2021). https://doi.org/10.1145/3478026
2. Bandhakavi, S., Tiku, N., Pittman, W., King, S.T., Madhusudan, P., Winslett, M.: Vetting browser extensions for security vulnerabilities with Vex. Commun. ACM **54**(9), 91–99 (2011). https://doi.org/10.1145/1995376.1995398
3. Barth, A., Felt, A.P., Saxena, P., Boodman, A.: Protecting browsers from extension vulnerabilities. In: Network and Distributed System Security Symposium (2010)
4. Borgolte, K., Feamster, N.: Understanding the performance costs and benefits of privacy-focused browser extensions. In: Proceedings of The Web Conference 2020, pp. 2275–2286. ACM, Taipei Taiwan (2020). https://doi.org/10.1145/3366423.3380292
5. Bui, D., Tang, B., Shin, K.G.: Detection of inconsistencies in privacy practices of browser extensions. In: 2023 IEEE Symposium on Security and Privacy (SP), pp. 2780–2798 (2023). https://doi.org/10.1109/SP46215.2023.10179338

6. Calzavara, S., Bugliesi, M., Crafa, S., Steffinlongo, E.: Fine-grained detection of privilege escalation attacks on browser extensions. In: Vitek, J. (ed.) ESOP 2015. LNCS, vol. 9032, pp. 510–534. Springer, Heidelberg (2015). https://doi.org/10. 1007/978-3-662-46669-8_21
7. Datta, A., Lu, J., Tschantz, M.C.: Evaluating anti-fingerprinting privacy enhancing technologies. In: The World Wide Web Conference, pp. 351–362. WWW 2019, Association for Computing Machinery, New York, NY, USA (2019). https://doi. org/10.1145/3308558.3313703
8. Eriksson, B., Picazo-Sanchez, P., Sabelfeld, A.: Hardening the security analysis of browser extensions. In: Proceedings of the 37th ACM/SIGAPP Symposium on Applied Computing, pp. 1694–1703. SAC 2022, Association for Computing Machinery, New York, NY, USA (2022). https://doi.org/10.1145/3477314.3507098
9. FaizKhademi, A., Zulkernine, M., Weldemariam, K.: FPGuard: detection and prevention of browser fingerprinting. In: Samarati, P. (ed.) DBSec 2015. LNCS, vol. 9149, pp. 293–308. Springer, Cham (2015). https://doi.org/10.1007/978-3-319-20810-7_21
10. Fass, A., Somé, D.F., Backes, M., Stock, B.: DoubleX: statically detecting vulnerable data flows in browser extensions at scale. In: Proceedings of the 2021 ACM SIGSAC Conference on Computer and Communications Security, pp. 1789–1804. CCS 2021, Association for Computing Machinery, New York, NY, USA (2021). https://doi.org/10.1145/3460120.3484745
11. Frisbie, M.: Understanding the implications of manifest V3. In: Frisbie, M. (ed.) Building Browser Extensions: Create Modern Extensions for Chrome, Safari, Firefox, and Edge, pp. 167–185. Apress, Berkeley, CA (2023). https://doi.org/10.1007/978-1-4842-8725-5_6
12. Gulyas, G.G., Some, D.F., Bielova, N., Castelluccia, C.: To extend or not to extend: on the uniqueness of browser extensions and web logins. In: Proceedings of the 2018 Workshop on Privacy in the Electronic Society, pp. 14–27. WPES 2018, Association for Computing Machinery, New York, NY, USA (2018). https://doi.org/10.1145/3267323.3268959
13. Gunnarsson, P., Jakobsson, A., Carlsson, N.: On the impact of internal webpage selection when evaluating ad blocker performance. In: 2022 30th International Symposium on Modeling, Analysis, and Simulation of Computer and Telecommunication Systems (MASCOTS), pp. 41–48 (2022). https://doi.org/10.1109/MASCOTS56607.2022.00014
14. Hiremath, P.N., Armentrout, J., Vu, S., Nguyen, T.N., Minh, Q.T., Phung, P.H.: MyWebGuard: toward a user-oriented tool for security and privacy protection on the web. In: Dang, T.K., Küng, J., Takizawa, M., Bui, S.H. (eds.) FDSE 2019. LNCS, vol. 11814, pp. 506–525. Springer, Cham (2019). https://doi.org/10.1007/978-3-030-35653-8_33
15. Iqbal, U., Englehardt, S., Shafiq, Z.: Fingerprinting the fingerprinters: learning to detect browser fingerprinting behaviors. In: 2021 IEEE Symposium on Security and Privacy (SP), pp. 1143–1161. IEEE Computer Society (2021). https://doi.org/10. 1109/SP40001.2021.00017
16. Karami, S., Ilia, P., Solomos, K., Polakis, J.: Carnus: exploring the privacy threats of browser extension fingerprinting. In: Proceedings 2020 Network and Distributed System Security Symposium. Internet Society, San Diego, CA (2020). https://doi. org/10.14722/ndss.2020.24383
17. Karami, S., et al.: Unleash the simulacrum: shifting browser realities for robust {Extension-Fingerprinting} prevention. In: 31st USENIX Security Symposium (USENIX Security 22), pp. 735–752 (2022)

18. Kariryaa, A., Savino, G.L., Stellmacher, C., Schöning, J.: Understanding users' knowledge about the privacy and security of browser extensions. in: seventeenth symposium on usable privacy and security (SOUPS 2021), pp. 99–118 (2021)
19. Kettle, J.: Skeleton Scribe: Sparse Bruteforce Addon Detection. https://www.skeletonscribe.net/2011/07/sparse-bruteforce-addon-scanner.html
20. Krzysztof Kotowicz: Intro to Chrome addons hacking: Fingerprinting. http://blog.kotowicz.net/2012/02/intro-to-chrome-addons-hacking.html
21. Laperdrix, P., Bielova, N., Baudry, B., Avoine, G.: Browser fingerprinting: a survey. ACM Trans. Web **14**(2), 8:1–8:33 (2020). https://doi.org/10.1145/3386040
22. Laperdrix, P., Rudametkin, W., Baudry, B.: Mitigating browser fingerprint tracking: multi-level reconfiguration and diversification. In: 2015 IEEE/ACM 10th International Symposium on Software Engineering for Adaptive and Self-Managing Systems, pp. 98–108 (2015). https://doi.org/10.1109/SEAMS.2015.18
23. Laperdrix, P., Rudametkin, W., Baudry, B.: Beauty and the beast: diverting modern web browsers to build unique browser fingerprints. In: 2016 IEEE Symposium on Security and Privacy (SP), pp. 878–894 (2016). https://doi.org/10.1109/SP.2016.57
24. Laperdrix, P., Starov, O., Chen, Q., Kapravelos, A., Nikiforakis, N.: Fingerprinting in style: detecting browser extensions via injected style sheets. In: 30th USENIX Security Symposium (USENIX Security 21), pp. 2507–2524 (2021)
25. Li, T., Zheng, X., Shen, K., Han, X.: FPFlow: detect and prevent browser fingerprinting with dynamic taint analysis. In: Lu, W., Zhang, Y., Wen, W., Yan, H., Li, C. (eds.) CNCERT 2021. CCIS, vol. 1506, pp. 51–67. Springer, Singapore (2022). https://doi.org/10.1007/978-981-16-9229-1_4
26. Lin, X., Ilia, P., Solanki, S., Polakis, J.: Phish in sheep's clothing: exploring the authentication pitfalls of browser fingerprinting. In: 31st USENIX Security Symposium (USENIX Security 22), pp. 1651–1668 (2022)
27. Liu, Z., Shrestha, P., Saxena, N.: Gummy Browsers: Targeted Browser Spoofing Against State-of-the-Art Fingerprinting Techniques. In: Ateniese, G., Venturi, D. (eds.) Applied Cryptography and Network Security. Lecture Notes in Computer Science, vol. 13269, pp. 147–169. Springer, Cham (2022). https://doi.org/10.1007/978-3-031-09234-3_8
28. Liverani, R.S., Freeman, N.: Abusing Firefox extensions. Defcon17 (2009)
29. Ter Louw, M., Lim, J.S., Venkatakrishnan, V.N.: Extensible web browser security. In: M. Hämmerli, B., Sommer, R. (eds.) DIMVA 2007. LNCS, vol. 4579, pp. 1–19. Springer, Heidelberg (2007). https://doi.org/10.1007/978-3-540-73614-1_1
30. Lyu, T., Liu, L., Zhu, F., Hu, S., Ye, R.: BEFP: an extension recognition system based on behavioral and environmental fingerprinting. Secur. Commun. Netw. **2022**, e7896571 (2022). https://doi.org/10.1155/2022/7896571
31. Moad, D., Sihag, V., Choudhary, G., Duguma, D.G., You, I.: Fingerprint defender: defense against browser-based user tracking. In: You, I., Kim, H., Youn, T.-Y., Palmieri, F., Kotenko, I. (eds.) MobiSec 2021. CCIS, vol. 1544, pp. 236–247. Springer, Singapore (2022). https://doi.org/10.1007/978-981-16-9576-6_17
32. Nikiforakis, N., Kapravelos, A., Joosen, W., Kruegel, C., Piessens, F., Vigna, G.: Cookieless monster: exploring the ecosystem of web-based device fingerprinting. In: 2013 IEEE Symposium on Security and Privacy, pp. 541–555 (2013). https://doi.org/10.1109/SP.2013.43
33. Pantelaios, N., Nikiforakis, N., Kapravelos, A.: You've changed: detecting malicious browser extensions through their update deltas. In: Proceedings of the 2020 ACM SIGSAC Conference on Computer and Communications Security, pp. 477–491. ACM, Virtual Event USA (2020). https://doi.org/10.1145/3372297.3423343

34. Perrotta, R., Hao, F.: Botnet in the browser: understanding threats caused by malicious browser extensions. IEEE Secur. Priv. **16**(4), 66–81 (2018). https://doi.org/10.1109/msp.2018.3111249

35. Picazo-Sanchez, P., Eriksson, B., Sabelfeld, A.: No signal left to chance: driving browser extension analysis by download patterns. In: Proceedings of the 38th Annual Computer Security Applications Conference, pp. 896–910. ACSAC 2022, Association for Computing Machinery, New York, NY, USA (2022). https://doi.org/10.1145/3564625.3567988

36. Picazo-Sanchez, P., Ortiz-Martin, L., Schneider, G., Sabelfeld, A.: Are chrome extensions compliant with the spirit of least privilege? Int. J. Inf. Secur. **21**(6), 1283–1297 (2022). https://doi.org/10.1007/s10207-022-00610-w

37. Preuveneers, D., Joosen, W.: SmartAuth: dynamic context fingerprinting for continuous user authentication. In: Proceedings of the 30th Annual ACM Symposium on Applied Computing, pp. 2185–2191. SAC 2015, Association for Computing Machinery, New York, NY, USA (2015). https://doi.org/10.1145/2695664.2695908

38. Rochet, F., Efthymiadis, K., Koeune, F., Pereira, O.: SWAT: seamless web authentication technology. In: The World Wide Web Conference, pp. 1579–1589. WWW 2019, Association for Computing Machinery, New York, NY, USA (2019). https://doi.org/10.1145/3308558.3313637

39. Sam, J., Ancy Jenifer., J.: Mitigating the security risks of browser extensions. In: 2023 International Conference on Sustainable Computing and Smart Systems (ICSCSS), pp. 1460–1465 (2023). https://doi.org/10.1109/ICSCSS57650.2023.10169483

40. Sanchez-Rola, I., Santos, I., Balzarotti, D.: Extension breakdown: security analysis of browsers extension resources control policies. In: 26th USENIX Security Symposium (USENIX Security 17), pp. 679–694 (2017)

41. Schaub, F., et al.: Watching them watching me: browser extensions impact on user privacy awareness and concern. In: Proceedings 2016 Workshop on Usable Security. Internet Society, San Diego, CA (2016). https://doi.org/10.14722/usec.2016.23017

42. Sjösten, A., Acker, S.V., Sabelfeld, A.: Discovering browser extensions via web accessible resources. In: CODASPY 2017 - Proceedings of the 7th ACM Conference on Data and Application Security and Privacy, pp. 329–336 (2017). https://doi.org/10.1145/3029806.3029820

43. Sjosten, A., Van Acker, S., Picazo-Sanchez, P., Sabelfeld, A.: Latex gloves: protecting browser extensions from probing and revelation attacks. In: Proceedings 2019 Network and Distributed System Security Symposium. Internet Society, San Diego, CA (2019). https://doi.org/10.14722/ndss.2019.23309

44. Solomos, K., Ilia, P., Karami, S., Nikiforakis, N., Polakis, J.: The dangers of human touch: fingerprinting browser extensions through user actions. In: 31st USENIX Security Symposium (USENIX Security 22), pp. 717–733 (2022)

45. Solomos, K., Ilia, P., Nikiforakis, N., Polakis, J.: Escaping the confines of time: continuous browser extension fingerprinting through ephemeral modifications. In: Proceedings of the 2022 ACM SIGSAC Conference on Computer and Communications Security, pp. 2675–2688. CCS 2022, Association for Computing Machinery, New York, NY, USA (2022). https://doi.org/10.1145/3548606.3560576

46. Somé, D.F.: EmPoWeb: empowering web applications with browser extensions. In: 2019 IEEE Symposium on Security and Privacy (SP), pp. 227–245 (2019). https://doi.org/10.1109/SP.2019.00058

47. Starov, O., Laperdrix, P., Kapravelos, A., Nikiforakis, N.: Unnecessarily identifiable: quantifying the fingerprintability of browser extensions due to bloat. In: The

World Wide Web Conference, pp. 3244–3250. WWW '19, Association for Computing Machinery, New York, NY, USA (2019). https://doi.org/10.1145/3308558.3313458

48. Starov, O., Nikiforakis, N.: XHOUND: quantifying the fingerprintability of browser extensions. In: 2017 IEEE Symposium on Security and Privacy (SP), pp. 941–956 (2017). https://doi.org/10.1109/SP.2017.18

49. Torres, C.F., Jonker, H., Mauw, S.: FP-Block: usable web privacy by controlling browser fingerprinting. In: Pernul, G., Ryan, P.Y.A., Weippl, E. (eds.) ESORICS 2015. LNCS, vol. 9327, pp. 3–19. Springer, Cham (2015). https://doi.org/10.1007/978-3-319-24177-7_1

50. Trickel, E., Starov, O., Kapravelos, A., Nikiforakis, N., Doupé, A.: Everyone is different: client-side diversification for defending against extension fingerprinting. In: 28th USENIX Security Symposium (USENIX Security 19), pp. 1679–1696 (2019)

51. Zhang, D., Zhang, J., Bu, Y., Chen, B., Sun, C., Wang, T.: A survey of browser fingerprint research and application. Wirel. Commun. Mob. Comput. **2022**, 3363335 (2022). https://doi.org/10.1155/2022/3363335

Mobile Security and Trusted Execution

Libra: Library Identification in Obfuscated Android Apps

David A. Tomassi[1]([✉])(iD), Kenechukwu Nwodo[2](iD), and Mohamed Elsabagh[1](iD)

[1] Quokka, McLean, VA, USA
{dtomassi,melsabagh}@quokka.io
[2] Virginia Tech, Arlington, VA, USA
nwodok@vt.edu

Abstract. In the Android apps ecosystem, third-party libraries play a crucial role in providing common services and features. However, these libraries introduce complex dependencies that can impact stability, performance, and security. Therefore, detecting libraries used in Android apps is critical for understanding functionality, compliance, and security risks. Existing library identification approaches face challenges when obfuscation is applied to apps, leading to performance degradation. In this study, we propose *Libra*, a novel solution for library identification in obfuscated Android apps. *Libra* leverages method headers and bodies, encodes instructions compactly, and employs piecewise fuzzy hashing for effective detection of libraries in obfuscated apps. Our two-phase approach achieves high F1 scores of 88% for non-obfuscated and 50–87% for obfuscated apps, surpassing previous works by significant margins. Extensive evaluations demonstrate *Libra*'s effectiveness and robustness against various obfuscation techniques.

Keywords: Library Identification · Obfuscation · SBOM · Android

1 Introduction

With three billion active devices, Android has become the dominant mobile platform with over three and a half million apps on the Google Play Store alone [10,11]. These apps cater to the needs of billions of users in an ever-evolving landscape. To accelerate development and enhance user experience, apps often incorporate various third-party libraries to leverage their prebuilt functionalities [35,44]. While these third-party libraries offer considerable development advantages, they introduce complex dependencies into the apps that can significantly impact stability, performance, and security.

Detecting libraries used in Android apps has become a critical pursuit for developers, security analysts, and researchers alike [28]. Identifying the libraries that make up an app allows for a deeper understanding of the app's functionality, licensing compliance, and potential security risks. Moreover, tracking these

---

K. Nwodo—This work was done as part of an internship at Quokka.

© The Author(s), under exclusive license to Springer Nature Switzerland AG 2023
E. Athanasopoulos and B. Mennink (Eds.): ISC 2023, LNCS 14411, pp. 205–225, 2023.
https://doi.org/10.1007/978-3-031-49187-0_11

dependencies aids in the timely integration of updates, ensuring the apps stay current with the latest feature enhancements and security patches[1].

Various library identification approaches were introduced in the recent years, including clustering techniques [24,26,29,42], learning-based techniques [25,27], and similarity-based techniques [15,19–21,31,34,36,37,41,43]. A variety of different app and library features are used by these approaches, ranging from package and class hierarchies to GUI resources and layout files. These techniques operate with the same end goal, that is to identify the libraries (names and versions) used by an app given the app published binary package.

Most of these tools have been developed with obfuscation in mind and select features that have resiliency to obfuscation techniques. Yet, it has been shown [38,39,42] that when obfuscation is applied to apps the performance of the state-of-the-art tools degrades significantly. Obfuscation is not a new reality for software and has been used to hide malicious software such as the SolarWinds attack [8] where the attackers used multiple obfuscation layers to hide the malicious software from detection. This exemplifies the need for identification techniques with increased resilience to the various obfuscation techniques that can be applied to Android apps, including identifier renaming, code shrinking and removal, control-flow randomization, package flattening, among others.

To this end, we propose *Libra* in this study as a novel solution to identify library names and versions in an Android app package with higher resilience to obfuscation than the state of the art. By examining the current state-of-the-art techniques, we shed light on some of the overlooked challenges that arise when analyzing obfuscated apps and discuss how *Libra* tackles these challenges to achieve higher detection power than the state of the art.

Libra is designed around three novel ideas: (1) leveraging both method headers and bodies to enhance robustness to obfuscation, (2) encoding method instructions into a compact representation to mitigate learning bias of instruction sequences, and (3) employing piecewise fuzzy hashing for effective adaptation to changes introduced by obfuscators. *Libra* employs a two-phase approach for library identification. In the learning phase, it extracts packages, encodes methods, and generates signatures. In the detection phase, it extracts library candidates, follows the same procedure in learning for method encoding and signature generation, pairs library candidates and actual libraries to shrink the search space, then applies a two-component weighted similarity computation to arrive at a final similarity score between a library candidate and a library.

We performed an extensive evaluation using multiple state-of-the-art Android library identification tools on various obfuscated benchmarks. For each tool we look at its capabilities and its resilience to different obfuscation techniques and highlight how it compares to *Libra*. Our experiments reveal that *Libra* achieves a high F1 score of 88% for non-obfuscated apps, surpassing prior works by a margin ranging from 7% to 540%. For obfuscated apps, *Libra* achieves F1 scores

---

[1] The process of identifying components used in a software is generally known as creating a Software Bill of Materials (SBOM). See https://www.cisa.gov/sbom for more information about the SBOM concept and standards.

ranging from 50% to 87%, achieving a substantial improvement over previous approaches from 7% and up to 1386% in certain cases.

To summarize, the contributions of this work are:

- We introduce *Libra*, a novel approach to library identification using fuzzy method signatures of hashed instructions.
- We provide a characterization of the state-of-the-art tools and highlight challenges unique to identifying libraries in obfuscated apps.
- We demonstrate the effectiveness of *Libra* by extensively evaluating it against recent Android library identification tools on multiple datasets with various degrees of obfuscation.

2 Background

2.1 Android Third Party Libraries

An Android app is packaged into an Android Package file (APK) which contains the app's Dalvik Executable (DEX) bytecode files, resource files, and assets. The bytecode is organized into package hierarchies, e.g. `com/example`, where each package in the hierarchy may contain one or more implementation units (a class file) and other subpackages. The APK contains both the app's own bytecode as well as the bytecode for all the third-party libraries (and their transitive dependencies) on which the app depends.

Several recent studies have shown that almost all Android apps use third-party libraries [9,35,39,44]. These libraries are used to leverage existing functionalities and enable various services, such as advertisements, maps, and social networks [35,44]. However, despite the widespread usage of libraries in Android apps, concerns have been raised about the security impact of depending on third-party libraries. Multiple studies revealed that apps often use outdated libraries [14,16,35,44]. A recent study [9] of apps on Google Play has shown that 98% used libraries, with an average of 20 libraries per app. Alarmingly, nearly half of the apps used a library that suffered from a high-risk vulnerability.

These vulnerable libraries pose significant challenges for developers and end users. The scope of a vulnerability in a library does not only impact the library, but also extends to its dependencies and other apps and libraries depending on it. Therefore, it is paramount that libraries packaged with an app are identified in order to allow for quick remediation and confinement of potential vulnerabilities.

2.2 Library Detection and Obfuscated Apps

Android app developers use obfuscation techniques to mask the structure, data, and resources of their apps to hinder reverse engineering attempts. Bad actors also use obfuscation to hide malicious code. Obfuscation typically takes place during the build or post-build processes where the obfuscators operate on the bytecode in an APK. Given an obfuscated app APK, the line between what

bytecode is app code vs. library code is often blurred due to the various transformations that occur during the obfuscation process.

Android obfuscators such as ProGuard [6], DashO [2], and Allatori [1] are
among the most popular and studied obfuscators in the literature. Several studies [15,28,33] have analyzed the configurations of these obfuscators and summarized their distinct obfuscation techniques. Pertinent to this study are techniques
that apply transformations to the bytecode of an app, such as identifier renaming (transforming package/class/method names into random non-meaningful
strings), code addition (adding redundant or bloating code to increase analysis
cost), code removal (eliminating unused classes and methods while retaining the
functionality of the app), package flattening/repackaging (consolidating multiple
packages into one), control flow randomization (shuffling the app's basic blocks
while maintaining functionality), among others. Some of these techniques overlap
and may be categorized as optimization or code shrinking techniques.

To detect libraries integrated in an app APK, researchers have gone through
a number of techniques. Initial efforts to library detection involved utilizing a
whitelist of common library package names [29]. However, whitelisting disallows
the identification of library versions and does not perform well when obfuscation
techniques such as package renaming are applied, leading to low precision and
recall. This has led to the development of other detection techniques, such as
clustering and similarity comparisons. Clustering techniques [24,26,32,42] pack
app packages and library packages together and use a threshold for the cluster
size to determine if a cluster of packages can be identified as a library. Clustering can be an exhaustive process, especially given the overwhelming number
of library artifacts on the market[2]. To strike a better balance between performance and detection power, techniques based on similarity comparisons were
introduced [15,38] where they identify and compare certain features of library
candidates from an app against a prebuilt library features database. *Libra* falls
under this category. We discuss related work in more depth in Sect. 7.

3   Overview and Key Challenges

3.1   Motivating Example

By examining the state-of-the-art techniques, we observed that obfuscators
that perform code shrinking are particularly difficult to handle. Code shrinking removes unused classes, fields, methods, and instructions that do not have
an impact on the functionality of an app. This shrinks the size of libraries in the
app and leaves less bytecode to operate on to calculate similarity.

We
encountered an instance of this with a library called `com.github.gabriele`
`-mariotti.changeloglib:changelog:2.1.0`   within   the   SensorsSandbox
app [13]. A comparison of the package structures between the unobfuscated

---

[2] At the time of this writing, the Maven Central repository [5] had over 11 million
indexed library packages.

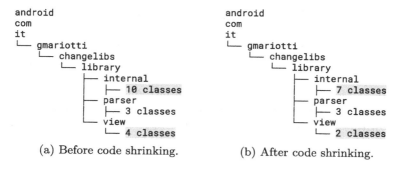

(a) Before code shrinking.   (b) After code shrinking.

Fig. 1. Library package structure for the SensorsSandbox app without (left) and with code shrinking (right). The removal of a few classes causes the library to be missed by all prior solutions examined in this work.

and obfuscated versions of the library is depicted in Fig. 1. Three classes from the library's `internal` subpackage and two classes from the `view` subpackage were removed due to code shrinkage during compilation process. Overall, code shrinking resulted in a decrease of 36.9% in the number of instructions within the library.

Despite the small size of the app, the fact it had only this third-party library dependency, and the low degree of shrinking, all recent tools failed at identifying the library in the app APK when code shrinking was applied. Specifically, Lib-Scout [15], ATVHunter [37], and Libloom [21], were able to detect the library *without* code shrinking, but not once it was applied, despite being obfuscation aware. On the other hand, LibScout [15], ATVHunter [37], Orlis [34], and others, do not have any mechanism to account for this common obfuscation.

Code shrinking is one example of the challenges encountered when identifying libraries in obfuscated apps. In the following, we highlight multiple key challenges to library identification in obfuscated apps and how *Libra* tackles them.

3.2   Challenges to Library Identification

C1: Multiple Root Packages. In some cases, a library may have multiple root packages, e.g., `com/foo` and `com/bar`, which presents a challenge for library identification techniques since they need to be able to accurately associate both packages with the same library. However, if there are no interactions between these packages, traditional approaches using method calls, inheritance, and field access/writes to create class and library relations may struggle.

To address this, *Libra* identifies all root packages in a library by looking for first-level code units, and ensuring that a root package subsumes all its sub packages. This is done with a bottom-up approach to ensure the root package has first-level code units. This allows *Libra* to independently evaluate each package in an app against all root packages of a library to accurately identify the library. This also allows *Libra* to effectively manage transitive dependencies by treating them as multiple root packages.

C2: Shared Root Packages. Libraries may have a common root package, either intentionally or due to obfuscation techniques such as package flattening. This causes an enlarged pool of classes, making it difficult to distinguish between the libraries under this shared root package as their classes in the APK, despite being under the same root package, belong to different libraries.

In order to address this challenge, *Libra* introduces a two-component similarity measure where the first component represents the number of matched methods within the library candidate in the app, and the second component represents the number of matched methods in the actual library. When multiple libraries are present under the same root package, the library-candidate component naturally yields a lower value. Conversely, the library ratio component remains unaffected by the number of libraries within the library candidate. Incorporating these two components together allows *Libra* to accurately detect libraries sharing a root package as the similarity measure adjusts per each candidate under the shared root package.

C3: Code Shrinking. A standard step in the building of an app APK is Code Shrinking, where the compiler or obfuscator removes code deemed not required at runtime, such as unused classes, fields, methods, and instructions, from the app [12]. This process permanently removes code artifacts from the app, potentially diminishing the identity of a library in an irreversible manner. Tools have made the observation that a substantial difference (e.g., three times or more) in the size of a candidate library in an APK and an actual library package indicates that they are likely different libraries [37,40]. As shown in Sect. 3.1, this causes problems for library identification as the overall similarity between a shrunk library bytecode in an app APK and its corresponding actual library package decreases significantly.

To address this, *Libra* utilizes a resilient two-component weighted similarity calculation. By incorporating weights, *Libra* effectively addresses the impact of missing methods, reducing its influence on the overall similarity score. Specifically, by assigning less weight to the in-app ratio, *Libra* maintains its effectiveness in scenarios involving Code Shrinking.

C4: Instruction Bias. The Dalvik bytecode Instruction Set encompasses a wide range of instructions, which may initially appear beneficial for improving discrimination power when used for learning the identity of a library. However, in reality, this complexity presents a challenge as app compilation and obfuscation can introduce alterations to the bytecode, resulting in discrepancies compared to the libraries' bytecode used to build the models. These alterations include instruction reordering, arithmetic operation splitting, condition flipping, call resolution changes, and more. If a detection approach learns too much about the instructions, it becomes overly sensitive to obfuscation techniques that modify instructions and opcodes. Conversely, learning too little about the instructions leads to a loss of precision, causing different methods to appear too similar.

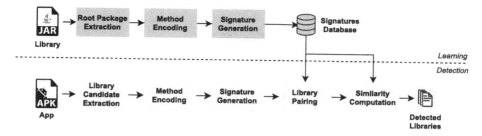

Fig. 2. Workflow of *Libra* with an offline learning phase and an online detection phase.

To overcome this, *Libra* encodes the instructions into a compact representation by mapping multiple opcodes to the same symbol. Moreover, it solely focuses on the mnemonic of the instructions, disregarding the operands as they are often subject to change by obfuscators. This approach enables *Libra* to strike a good balance between overlearning and underlearning the instructions, providing a more effective detection capability.

4   Detailed Design of *Libra*

Figure 2 shows the workflow of *Libra*. We formulate the problem of Android third-party library identification as a pair-wise similarity problem. The problem takes in a set of library artifacts (JAR or AAR files) and an input app (APK file) where both consist of a set of classes which need to be compared with particular data and a similarity operator. *Libra* uses a two phase approach: An offline learning phase in which it builds a database of library signatures by processing the library artifacts and extracting pertinent information; and an online detection phase in which it identifies library candidates in an app, extracts their signatures and performs a pair-wise similarity computation with the offline database to identify the names and versions of the library candidates used in the app.

4.1   Learning Library Identities

In the learning phase, *Libra* first takes in an input library file, disassembles it, then extracts the root package name(s) of the library and groups the associated classes for signature extraction. *Libra* processes the classes under each identified package and computes a signature composed of a header and a body for each method defined in a class. Finally, it stores the library metadata (e.g., name, version) and signature into a database for later retrieval during the online detection phase. The following learning phases of *Libra* will be elucidated: (1) Root Package Extraction and (2) Signature Extraction.

Root Package Extraction. *Libra* traverses the package hierarchy of the library in breadth-first order looking for the first non-empty package, i.e., a root package that contains at least one class definition. Note that there may be multiple

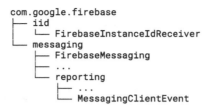

(a) Package structure for the library `com.google.firebase`:
`firebase-messaging:23.0.0`.

```
com.google.firebase.iid
└── FirebaseInstanceIdReceiver
```

(b) Root packages extracted and flattened for package `iid`

```
com.google.firebase.messaging
├── ...
├── FirebaseMessaging
└── MessagingClientEvent
```

(c) Root packages extracted and flattened for package `messaging`.

Fig. 3. An example of a library having multiple root packages and the resulting root packages extracted along with the classes.

packages associated with a single library if there are more than one package containing code units at the same level in the hierarchy. This allows *Libra* to handle the case of multiple root packages (C1). An example of this is shown in Fig. 3. Each package has the associated classes grouped with it for signature extraction. The extracted root package is flattened where each class under the package, including in subpackages, become associated with the root package.

Method Encoding. For each method in a class group, *Libra* encodes the Smali disassembly of the method body into a compact representation by mapping multiple instruction opcodes to the same symbol and discarding instruction operands. Figures 4a and 4b show a sample method and its encoded body. The full encoding map between is shown in Table 10. This encoding step allows *Libra* to avoid instruction bias during learning (C4) by creating a lower-resolution method body (counters overlearning) without destroying the information contained in the instructions order (counters underlearning).

Signature Generation. For each method in a class group, *Libra* extracts the method's parameter types, return type, and encoded body[3]. With these data points *Libra* constructs a fuzzy signature which includes a header and a body as explained in the following.

---

[3] We exclude the instance initializer method (`<init>`), the class initializer method (`<clinit>`), and the resources class (`R`) since these tend to be highly similar amongst apps and libraries which may lead to spurious matches.

```
.method newRealCall(Lokhttp3/OkHttpClient;Lokhttp3/Request;Z)Lokhttp3/RealCall;
    .locals 2
    .param p0, "client"     # Lokhttp3/OkHttpClient;
    .param p1, "originalRequest"   # Lokhttp3/Request;
    .param p2, "forWebSocket"    # Z
    new-instance v0, Lokhttp3/RealCall;
    invoke-direct {v0, p0, p1, p2},
Lokhttp3/RealCall;-><init>(Lokhttp3/OkHttpClient;Lokhttp3/Request;Z)V
    ...
    return-object v0
.end method
```

(a) Bytecode method in Smali.

```
header: (Lokhttp3/OkHttpClient;Lokhttp3/Request;Z)Lokhttp3/RealCall
body: call move call ... return
```

(b) Encoded method.

```
header: (XXZ)X
body: 3:yaGRLBMTdLBMTdLBMTdGEMGgCdGEMGgdMIKTyV:yaI6TJ6TJ6TBHgCBHgdJKTyV
```

(c) Signature with header and body.

Fig. 4. Encoding and signature generation process. The signature header has the method parameter and return types where non-primitives changed to X. The body has the computed fuzzy hash of method mnemonics.

To compute the signature header, *Libra* constructs a fuzzy method descriptor using the following transformation: The types are kept if they are primitives in Java, such as int, boolean, but are changed to X if they are non-primitive, such as java.lang.Object, java.lang.String (C4). Masking the types is essential in cases where identifier renaming obfuscation has been applied. If non-primitive types were utilized, and renaming has occurred, a mismatch would arise between the signature headers of the method signatures being compared (C4). For example, if the parameter types okhttp3/OkHttpClient, okhttp3/Request, and okhttp/RealCall, from Fig. 4, were used for the signature header instead of replacing each with X, and identifier renaming was applied renaming them to A, B, and C, respectively, the two signature headers, (okhttp3/OkHttpClientokhttp3/RequestZ)okhttp3/RealCall and (ABZ)C, would then never match.

To compute the signature body, *Libra* applies context-triggered piecewise hashing (CTPH) [22] on the encoded opcodes sequence, producing a hash in the format shown in Fig. 4c[4]. The first part of the hash is the size of the rolling window used to calculate each piece of the hash, the second part is a hash

---

[4] CTPH offers advantages over other hashing methods in this setup as it employs a recursive rolling hash where each piece of the hash is computed based on parts of the data and is not influenced by previously processed data. Consequently, if there are changes to the sequences being hashed, only a small portion of the hash is affected. This is a desirable property for library identification in obfuscated apps since changes to the library bytecode packed in the app are expected.

computed with the chunk size, and the third part is the hash with the chunk size doubled. This approach enhances the ability to handle both coarse- and fine-grained changes within a sequence due to obfuscation (C4).

Finally, and due to the nature of offline learning, it is necessary to store the results for lookup during the online detection phase. *Libra* stores each library identity (name and version), root package names, fuzzy signature (header and body), and metadata associated with the library in a database.

4.2 Detection and Similarity Computation

In the online detection phase, *Libra* identifies the library names and versions used by an incoming Android app (typically an APK file). The detection phase consists of the following stages: (1) Library Candidate Extraction, (2) Signature Extraction, (3) Library Pairing, (4) Similarity Computation. Each stage depends on the previous as pertinent information and data is extracted and propagated.

Library Candidate Extraction. Similar to the root package extraction step in the learning phase, *Libra* traverses the package hierarchy of the app and identifies all the app root packages. It then parses the `AndroidManifest.xml` file of the app and identifies the main components and their packages, and discards root packages that belong to the app main components since these belong the app's own code and therefore not libraries. It then considers each of the remaining root packages a library *candidate* and groups its classes in the same manner as in the learning phase for usage by the subsequent stages of the analysis.

Method Encoding and Signature Generation. For each library candidate, *Libra* encodes methods and constructs their signatures following the same approach in Sect. 4.1.

Library Pairing. To reduce detection time complexity, *Libra* attempts to avoid unnecessary similarity comparisons by first trying to pair each library candidate with libraries learned in the offline phase grouped by name, i.e., a group of different versions of the same library. *Libra* pairs a library candidate with a member of a library group if both of the following conditions are met: (1) The library candidate package name matches with one or more of the root package names of the library in the database. (2) The difference between the number of classes of the library candidate and the library in question is less than a predefined threshold τ (defaults to 0.4). A formulation of the reduction in search space is provided in Appendix B. The first condition states that *Libra* is aware of the root package linked with the library candidate and exclusively compares it with other libraries that have the same package association. The second condition originates from a heuristic, suggesting that a substantial discrepancy in the number of classes between the library candidate and another library indicates a lower probability of them being the same [37,40].

Similarity Computation. For each library candidate C and learned library L pair $\langle C, L \rangle$, *Libra* computes a pair-wise similarity score between the methods M_C of the library candidate and the methods M_L of the learned library by, first, computing the set M of pair-wise mutually-similar methods:

$$M = \{\langle m_C, m_L \rangle \mid m_C \in M_C, m_L \in M_L, \\ S(m_C) = S(m_L), \Delta(H(m_C), H(m_L)) \leq \delta\} \quad (1)$$

where S is the fuzzy method signature function, H is the fuzzy method hash function, Δ is the Levenshtein distance [23] which represents how similar the two method hashes are to each other, and δ is a predefined threshold (defaults to 0.85). The threshold δ is used to handle changes in the method instructions due to obfuscation (C3, C4) and was chosen from prior work [37].

Given M, *Libra* computes the final similarity score as the weighted sum of the ratios of matched methods in the library and the app, given by:

$$sim(C, L) = \alpha \cdot \frac{\min(|M_L|, |M|)}{|M_L|} + \beta \cdot \frac{\min(|M_C|, |M|)}{|M_C|} \quad (2)$$

where α, β are weighting parameters such that $\alpha + \beta = 1$. The similarity score ranges from 0 (lowest) to 1.0 (highest).

The purpose of these weighting parameters is to adapt to different degrees of code shrinkage by dampening the impact of code removal on the overall similarity score. In our experiments, we observed that α and β values of 0.8 and 0.2, respectively, yielded satisfactory overall results when code shrinking has been applied (C2), or there exists a shared root package between libraries (C3). The latter scenario arises when multiple libraries are associated with the same root package, potentially resulting in a low match ratio for the library candidate. However, through appropriate weighting, this challenge is overcome, enabling the determination that the library candidate and library are indeed similar.

Finally, *Libra* ranks the results based on the final similarity score, serving as a confidence indicator for the likelihood of the library's presence in the app, and reports the top k matches (defaults to 1).

5 Evaluation

We implemented *Libra* in Python in 2.4k SLOC. For fuzzy hashing, *Libra* relies on ssdeep [22]. Our experiments were conducted on an Ubuntu 20.04 server with Intel(R) Xeon(R) CPU E5-2630 v4 @ 2.20 GHz and 252 GiB of RAM.

We conducted several experiments to determine the effectiveness of *Libra* against state-of-the-art tools, including LibScout [15], LibPecker [43], Orlis [34], LibID-S [41], and Libloom [21][5].

---

[5] Note that the Android SDK Support Library [7] was excluded from the counts for consistency with all evaluated tools.

We used the default settings for all the tools. For LibID [41], we used the LibID-S variant since it performs the best [41] and set a 0.8 threshold for Lib-Scout to maintain consistency with LibID.

We used two public benchmarks in our experiments: the ATVHunter [37] and Orlis [4,34] datasets. These two datasets were selected due to their widespread usage by prior work and their inclusion of diverse obfuscation techniques. The ATVHunter dataset consists of 88 non-obfuscated apps, and three sets of 88 (3×88) apps obfuscated with control flow randomization, package flattening and renaming, and code shrinking using Dasho [2]. In contrast, the Orlis dataset is organized based on the obfuscator used, encompassing the obfuscation techniques used in the ATVHunter dataset along with string encryption. The dataset consists of 162 non-obfuscated apps, and three sets of 162 (3×162) apps obfuscated with the obfuscators Allatori [1], Dasho [2], and Proguard [6].

For each experiment, we measured Precision, Recall, and F1 score for detection effectiveness, and the average detection time for the runtime overhead. The identify of a library in all experiments consists of both a name and a version number. A *true positive* (TP) is identified when a tool reports a library and the app contains that library. A *false positive* (FP) is identified when a tool reports some library that is not contained in the app. A *false negative* (FN) is counted when a tool does not report a library even though it is contained in the app.

5.1 Effectiveness Results

Table 1 shows detection results on the non-obfuscated ATVHunter dataset. The effectiveness of *Libra* is evident where it successfully identifies all non-obfuscated libraries contained in the apps. Here, *Libra* outperforms prior studies achieving an overall 88% F1 score, showcasing an improvement from prior work ranging from 7% up to 484%. Other tools show lower precision values resulting from higher numbers of falsely identified libraries.

With obfuscation enabled, *Libra*'s TP rate consistently outperforms all prior work with its recall ranging from 43% to 90% across all techniques. Table 2 shows *Libra* and Libbloom both displaying effectiveness against control flow randomization with low FNs for the two, while others prove unsuccessful. Interestingly, Libbloom scores a higher F1 score with this technique. This is due to Libbloom discarding the order of instructions within a method, making it more resilient to techniques that also disrupt instructions order, at a cost of reduced precision as more methods appear similar (C4). Nevertheless, *Libra* still outperforms it across all the remaining obfuscation techniques.

With package flattening in Table 3, there is a general decrease in detection power for all tools as most utilize package hierarchy structures as features however, *Libra* maintains the best TP rate while achieving an F1 score performance increase from 67% up to 1386% across all tools. *Libra*'s robust weighted similarity calculation proves resilient against code shrinking in Table 4, correctly identifying 90% of libraries, and outperforming the remaining tools in F1 score by a range of 24% to 755%.

Table 1. Detection results on ATVHunter non-obfuscated apps.

Tool	TP	FP	FN	Precision	Recall	F1 score
LibScout	57	84	1	0.4043	0.9828	0.5729
LibPecker	50	43	8	0.5341	0.8621	0.6596
Orlis	5	3	53	0.5889	0.0862	0.1504
LibID-S	57	112	1	0.3373	0.9828	0.5022
Libbloom	58	25	0	0.6988	1.0000	0.8227
Libra	58	16	0	0.7838	1.0000	0.8788

Table 2. Detection results on ATVHunter control-flow-randomization-obfuscated apps.

Tool	TP	FP	FN	Precision	Recall	F1 score
LibScout	5	0	53	1.0000	0.0862	0.1587
LibPecker	23	15	35	0.6012	0.3966	0.4779
Orlis	5	4	53	0.5484	0.0862	0.1490
LibID-S	0	12	58	0.0000	0.0000	–
Libbloom	58	25	0	0.6988	1.0000	0.8227
Libra	48	40	10	0.5455	0.8276	0.6575

Table 3. Detection results on ATVHunter pkg-flattening-obfuscated apps.

Tool	TP	FP	FN	Precision	Recall	F1 score
LibScout	0	0	58	–	0.0000	–
LibPecker	2	1	56	0.5740	0.0345	0.0651
Orlis	5	3	53	0.5889	0.0862	0.1504
LibID-S	1	1	57	0.5000	0.0172	0.0333
Libbloom	12	11	46	0.5217	0.2069	0.2963
Libra	25	18	33	0.5814	0.4310	0.4950

Table 4. Detection results on ATVHunter code-shrinking-obfuscated apps.

Tool	TP	FP	FN	Precision	Recall	F1 score
LibScout	0	1	58	0.0000	0.0000	–
LibPecker	3	2	55	0.5735	0.0517	0.0949
Orlis	4	2	54	0.5904	0.0690	0.1235
LibID-S	3	11	55	0.2143	0.0517	0.0833
Libbloom	33	24	25	0.5789	0.5690	0.5739
Libra	52	36	6	0.5909	0.8966	0.7123

Table 5. Detection results on Orlis non-obfuscated apps.

Tool	TP	FP	FN	Precision	Recall	F1 score
LibScout	102	144	1	0.4146	0.9903	0.5845
LibPecker	99	87	4	0.5309	0.9612	0.6840
Orlis	8	5	95	0.6116	0.0777	0.1378
LibID-S	101	216	2	0.3186	0.9806	0.4810
Libloom	103	53	0	0.6603	1.0000	0.7954
Libra	101	25	2	0.8016	0.9806	0.8821

Table 6. Detection results on Orlis Allatori-obfuscated apps.

Tool	TP	FP	FN	Precision	Recall	F1 score
LibScout	7	0	96	1.0000	0.0680	0.1273
LibPecker	71	40	32	0.6357	0.6893	0.6614
Orlis	6	3	97	0.6169	0.0583	0.1065
LibID-S	72	166	31	0.3025	0.6990	0.4223
Libloom	89	61	14	0.5933	0.8641	0.7036
Libra	92	50	11	0.6479	0.8932	0.7510

Table 7. Detection results on Orlis Dasho-obfuscated apps.

Tool	TP	FP	FN	Precision	Recall	F1 score
LibScout	37	52	66	0.4157	0.3592	0.3854
LibPecker	6	11	97	0.3481	0.0583	0.0998
Orlis	8	11	95	0.4039	0.0777	0.1303
LibID-S	37	97	66	0.2761	0.3592	0.3122
Libloom	96	201	7	0.3232	0.9320	0.4800
Libra	51	30	52	0.6296	0.4951	0.5543

Table 8. Detection results on Orlis Proguard-obfuscated apps.

Tool	TP	FP	FN	Precision	Recall	F1 score
LibScout	102	144	1	0.4146	0.9903	0.5845
LibPecker	99	87	4	0.5309	0.9612	0.6840
Orlis	8	5	95	0.6116	0.0777	0.1378
LibID-S	101	216	2	0.3186	0.9806	0.4810
Libloom	103	53	0	0.6603	1.0000	0.7954
Libra	101	27	2	0.7891	0.9806	0.8745

Table 9. Average runtime of all experiments.

Tools	Library Learning (seconds per library)	App Learning (seconds per app)	Library Detection (seconds per app)
LibScout	1.66	–	5.04
LibPecker	–	–	509.40
Orlis	5.18	–	850.30
LibID-S	0.23	2.07	0.60
Libloom	0.25	0.42	1.26
Libra	4.39	–	9.20

With the non-obfuscated Orlis dataset in Table 5, *Libra* outperforms all compared tools by 11% to 540%, maintaining the same F1 score observed in the previous section and retaining the highest precision. This trend persists across all obfuscated apps, where *Libra* consistently achieves the highest F1 score.

Tables 6 and 7 show detection results for apps obfuscated by Allatori and Dasho. Overall, even though the results show a decline in F1 score performances by all tools, *Libra* demonstrates the most resilience towards these techniques with an improvement ranging from 7% to 605% and 15% to 455% for the F1 score on Allatori and Dasho-obfucated apps respectively. *Libra* correctly identifies the most libraries with the apps obfuscated by Allatori, and achieves the highest precision against both obfuscators. In contrast, the detection rates of LibScout, LibPecker, and LibID-S decline due to the effects of package flattening and control flow randomization on their package hierarchy structure features.

Finally, for Proguard in Table 8 where only identifier renaming and package flattening are enabled, the metrics across all tools remain unchanged from the non-obfuscated results. The results show that *Libra* outperforms other tools by 10% to 535%, displaying its resilience to the techniques applied by Proguard.

Overall, the results demonstrate *Libra*'s greater detection effectiveness than the state of the art, surpassing prior works by a margin ranging from 7% to 540% for non-obfuscated apps, and from 7% and to 1,386% for obfuscated ones.

5.2   Runtime Overhead

Table 9 shows the aggregate average learning and detection time per library and app for experimented tools. Time is divided into Library Learning, App Learning, and Library Detection, as tools perform different operations. *Libra* exhibits slightly longer learning and detection times (4.39 s learning per library, 9.20 s detection per app) than three of the five tools, although still within the same order of a few seconds. This is partially attributed to its relatively costly method-level granularity for computing fuzzy hashes. LibScout's fuzzy hashing similarly contributed to a higher detection time. LibPecker and Orlis were the least efficient, with longer runtimes due to class matching and code analysis.

Both LibID-S and Libloom demonstrated fast learning and detection, although this comes at the expense of precision.

Overall, the performance of *Libra* meets the practical requirements and expectations for its intended use.

6   Discussion and Limitations

6.1   Threats to Validity

The obfuscation techniques used to evaluate the effectiveness of *Libra* and the state of the art were chosen from readily available, established benchmarks in the field. There may exist other obfuscation techniques in the literature that are not captured by these obfuscators. The used obfuscation tools are what developers commercially use for their apps which gives an accurate representation of how the different detection tools perform on apps in the wild.

The default values for the thresholds in Sect. 4 were chosen to offer good trade-offs for library detection in general cases out of the box. However, these thresholds may prove to be too high when dealing with specific obfuscation techniques that involve the insertion or removal of significant amount of code. To address this, the thresholds could be parameterized based on the detection of certain obfuscation techniques, allowing for better adaptability and accuracy in different scenarios. Parameter tuning against different obfuscation techniques could also be performed to further refine the thresholds and the detection power of *Libra*.

6.2   Performance Optimization

Certain aspects of the approach and its implementation can be optimized to achieve higher runtime performance. First, libraries can be processed in parallel during the learning process to cut down on the overall effective learning time. Second, early cutoffs can be employed during the detection phase if it is unlikely that the number of matched methods would exceed what is need to produce a high-enough final similarity score. This can be a check that is calculated on-the-fly while comparisons are being made. Finally, the comparisons performed during the library pairing step are all independent and can be parallelized to reduce the overall detection time per app.

6.3   Native Libraries

Libra currently only supports identifying bytecode libraries within Android apps. Apps could also utilize native libraries, written in C/C++, via the Java Native Interface (JNI) [3]. Identifying (obfuscated) native libraries in an app comes with its own challenges that extend beyond the scope of this work [14, 17, 30]. As such, we defer the identification of native libraries to future work.

7   Related Work

Prior studies on bytecode library identification have explored diverse approaches with varying degrees of effectiveness against obfuscation. Earlier techniques relied on package and class hierarchies to measure similarity between app packages and libraries. For example, LibScout [15] used package-flattened Merkle trees to obtain fuzzy method signature hashes. LibPecker [43] constructed class signatures from class dependencies and employed fuzzy class matching at the package level for similarity comparisons. LibRadar [26] built clusters of apps and libraries and generated fuzzy hashing features from the clusters based on the frequency of Android API calls. Techniques dependent on class and package hierarchies showed limited resilience to obfuscation techniques [28,39], particularly package renaming and flattening, since obfuscators could easily manipulate class connectivity by merging or splitting classes and packages.

In more recent approaches, method instructions were used to enhance resilience to obfuscation. For instance, LibD [24] constructed library instances using homogeny graphs and utilized opcode hashes in each block of a method's Control-Flow Graph (CFG) for feature extraction. Orlis [34] constructed a textual call graph for methods and employed fuzzy method signatures to compute similarity. LibID [41] constructed CFGs from library binaries for feature extraction and utilized Locality-Sensitive Hashing for similarity. ATVHunter [37] used class dependency graphs to split library candidates and utilized both method CFGs and basic-block opcodes features for similarity measurement. Libbloom [21] encoded signature sets from package and classes in a Bloom Filter and computed similarity with a membership threshold. While these tools offered some resilience to obfuscation techniques, their detection power degraded with package flattening and code shrinking as demonstrated in our experiments.

8   Conclusion

We introduced *Libra*, an Android library identification tool designed to tackle the challenges of detecting libraries within Android apps, particularly in the presence of obfuscation. *Libra* effectively addresses issues such as multiple and shared root packages, code shrinking, and instruction bias. Employing a two-phase learning and detection approach, *Libra* utilizes novel techniques to handle obfuscation and code shrinkage. These techniques involve leveraging data from method descriptors and instructions, encoding method instructions, employing fuzzy algorithms, and utilizing a two-component weighted similarity calculation. Our benchmarking results on multiple datasets showcase the effectiveness of *Libra*, demonstrating its ability to accurately identify library names and versions across various degrees of obfuscation.

Acknowledgment. We thank the anonymous reviewers for their insightful feedback. Opinions expressed in this article are those of the authors and do not necessarily reflect the official policy or position of their respective institutions.

A   Method Encoding Codebook

Table 10 shows the codebook used by *Libra* to encode method instructions. We conducted feature selection to determine the best mapping using Fisher's score [18] to gain insights into the most discriminatory instructions. Our analysis revealed that field getters, setters, and arithmetic operators exhibited low variance, making them less useful for discrimination. Consequently, we decided to combine these arithmetic instructions into a single move instruction.

B   Search Space Reduction from Library Pairing

The pairing size complexity for pairs that satisfy condition one is $O(k)$, where n is the number of libraries in the database, and $k \ll n$ represents the group size. On the other hand, the pairing size complexity for condition two is $O(|P_{C2}|)$, where P_{C2} is defined as:

$$P_{C2} = \left\{ \langle C, L \rangle \mid C \in A, L \in D, \frac{\text{abs}(|A| - |D|)}{\max(|A|, |D|)} < \tau \right\}$$

Table 10. Bytecode encoding codebook used by *Libra*.

Smali Instruction	Encoded Representation
nop	–
move* v0, v1	move
move-result* v0	move
return*	return
const* v0, lit	move
monitor-* v0	monitor
check-cast v0, type	call
instance-of v0, v1, type	call; move
array-length v0, v1	call; move
new-* v0..vn, type	call; move
goto* ref	jump
cmp* v0, v1, v2	if; move
if-* v0, v1, ref	if
get v0, v1, v2	move
put v0, v1, v2	move
invoke-* v0..vn ref	call
neg-* v0, v1	move
not-* v0, v1	move
*-to-<type> v0, v1	call; move
arith./log.-* v0, v1, v2	move

where C is the library candidate, L is the library, A is the app, and D is the database. If no conditions are met, the library candidate is paired with the entire database, resulting in a pairing size complexity of $O(n)$. Note that this is unlikely as there are a wide range of library sizes from the order of 10^0 to 10^3 and condition two is likely to be met.

References

1. Allatori. https://allatori.com/
2. Dasho. https://www.preemptive.com/products/dasho/
3. Get started with the NDK. https://developer.android.com/ndk/guides
4. Libdetect dataset. https://sites.google.com/view/libdetect/home/dataset
5. Maven repository: Central. https://mvnrepository.com/repos/central
6. Proguard. https://www.guardsquare.com/proguard
7. Support Library | Android Developers. https://developer.android.com/topic/libraries/support-library
8. SolarWinds attack explained: And why it was so hard to detect (2020). https://www.csoonline.com/article/3601508/solarwinds-supply-chain-attack-explained-why-organizations-were-not-prepared.html
9. Synopsys research reveals significant security concerns in popular mobile apps amid pandemic (2021). https://news.synopsys.com/2021-03-25-Synopsys-Research-Reveals-Significant-Security-Concerns-in-Popular-Mobile-Apps-Amid-Pandemic
10. Number of apps available in leading app stores as of 3rd quarter 2022 (2021). https://www.statista.com/statistics/276623/number-of-apps-available-in-leading-app-stores/
11. Numbers from Google I/O: 3 billion active Android devices (2022). https://9to5google.com/2022/05/11/google-io-2022-numbers/
12. Shrink, obfuscate, and optimize your app (2023). https://developer.android.com/studio/build/shrink-code.html
13. Ali, M.: Sensors Sandbox. https://github.com/mustafa01ali/SensorsSandbox
14. Almanee, S., Ünal, A., Payer, M., Garcia, J.: Too quiet in the library: an empirical study of security updates in Android apps' native code. In: 2021 IEEE/ACM 43rd International Conference on Software Engineering (ICSE). IEEE (2021)
15. Backes, M., Bugiel, S., Derr, E.: Reliable third-party library detection in Android and its security applications. In: Proceedings of the 2016 ACM SIGSAC Conference on Computer and Communications Security (2016)
16. Derr, E., Bugiel, S., Fahl, S., Acar, Y., Backes, M.: Keep me updated: an empirical study of third-party library updatability on Android. In: Proceedings of the 2017 ACM SIGSAC Conference on Computer and Communications Security (2017)
17. Duan, R., Bijlani, A., Xu, M., Kim, T., Lee, W.: Identifying open-source license violation and 1-day security risk at large scale. In: Proceedings of the 2017 ACM SIGSAC Conference on Computer and Communications Security (2017)
18. Fisher, R.A.: The use of multiple measurements in taxonomic problems. Ann. Eugen. **7**(2), 179–188 (1936)
19. Glanz, L., et al.: CodeMatch: obfuscation won't conceal your repackaged app. In: Proceedings of the 2017 11th Joint Meeting on Foundations of Software Engineering (2017)
20. Han, H., Li, R., Tang, J.: Identify and inspect libraries in Android applications. Wirel. Pers. Commun. **103**(1), 491–503 (2018)

21. Huang, J., et al.: Scalably detecting third-party Android libraries with two-stage bloom filtering. IEEE Trans. Softw. Eng. (2022)
22. Kornblum, J.: Identifying almost identical files using context triggered piecewise hashing. Digit. Investig. **3**, 91–97 (2006)
23. Levenshtein, V.I., et al.: Binary codes capable of correcting deletions, insertions, and reversals. In: Soviet Physics Doklady (1966)
24. Li, M., et al.: LIBD: scalable and precise third-party library detection in Android markets. In: 2017 IEEE/ACM 39th International Conference on Software Engineering (ICSE) (2017)
25. Liu, B., Liu, B., Jin, H., Govindan, R.: Efficient privilege de-escalation for ad libraries in mobile apps. In: Proceedings of the 13th Annual International Conference on Mobile Systems, Applications, and Services, pp. 89–103 (2015)
26. Ma, Z., Wang, H., Guo, Y., Chen, X.: LibRadar: fast and accurate detection of third-party libraries in Android apps. In: Proceedings of the 38th International Conference on Software Engineering Companion (2016)
27. Narayanan, A., Chen, L., Chan, C.K.: AdDetect: automated detection of Android ad libraries using semantic analysis. In: 2014 IEEE Conference on Intelligent Sensors, Sensor Networks and Information Processing (ISSNIP) (2014)
28. Sihag, V., Vardhan, M., Singh, P.: A survey of Android application and malware hardening. Comput. Sci. Rev. **39**, 100365 (2021)
29. Soh, C., Tan, H.B.K., Arnatovich, Y.L., Narayanan, A., Wang, L.: LibSift: automated detection of third-party libraries in Android applications. In: 2016 23rd Asia-Pacific Software Engineering Conference (APSEC) (2016)
30. Tang, W., Luo, P., Fu, J., Zhang, D.: LibDX: a cross-platform and accurate system to detect third-party libraries in binary code. In: 2020 IEEE 27th International Conference on Software Analysis, Evolution and Reengineering (SANER) (2020)
31. Tang, Z., et al.: Securing Android applications via edge assistant third-party library detection. Comput. Secur. **80** (2019)
32. Wang, H., Guo, Y., Ma, Z., Chen, X.: Wukong: a scalable and accurate two-phase approach to Android app clone detection. In: Proceedings of the 2015 International Symposium on Software Testing and Analysis (2015)
33. Wang, Y., Rountev, A.: Who changed you? Obfuscator identification for Android. In: 2017 IEEE/ACM 4th International Conference on Mobile Software Engineering and Systems (MOBILESoft), pp. 154–164. IEEE (2017)
34. Wang, Y., Wu, H., Zhang, H., Rountev, A.: ORLIS: obfuscation-resilient library detection for Android. In: 2018 IEEE/ACM 5th International Conference on Mobile Software Engineering and Systems (MOBILESoft) (2018)
35. Wang, Y., et al.: An empirical study of usages, updates and risks of third-party libraries in Java projects. In: 2020 IEEE International Conference on Software Maintenance and Evolution (ICSME), pp. 35–45. IEEE (2020)
36. Xu, J., Yuan, Q.: LibRoad: rapid, online, and accurate detection of TPLs on Android. IEEE Trans. Mob. Comput. **21**(1) (2020)
37. Zhan, X., et al.: ATVHunter: reliable version detection of third-party libraries for vulnerability identification in Android applications. In: 43rd International Conference on Software Engineering (2021)
38. Zhan, X., et al.: Automated third-party library detection for Android applications: are we there yet? In: 2020 35th IEEE/ACM International Conference on Automated Software Engineering (ASE), pp. 919–930. IEEE (2020)
39. Zhan, X., et al.: Research on third-party libraries in Android apps: a taxonomy and systematic literature review. IEEE Trans. Softw. Eng. **48**(10) (2022)

40. Zhang, F., Huang, H., Zhu, S., Wu, D., Liu, P.: ViewDroid: towards obfuscation-resilient mobile application repackaging detection. In: Proceedings of the 2014 ACM Conference on Security and Privacy in Wireless & Mobile Networks (2014)
41. Zhang, J., Beresford, A.R., Kollmann, S.A.: LibID: reliable identification of obfuscated third-party Android libraries. In: Proceedings of the 28th ACM SIGSOFT International Symposium on Software Testing and Analysis, pp. 55–65 (2019)
42. Zhang, Y., Wang, J., Huang, H., Zhang, Y., Liu, P.: Understanding and conquering the difficulties in identifying third-party librariesfrom millions of Android apps. IEEE Trans. Big Data (2021)
43. Zhang, Y., et al.: Detecting third-party libraries in Android applications with high precision and recall. In: IEEE 25th Conference on Software Analysis, Evolution and Reengineering (2018)
44. Zhang, Z., Diao, W., Hu, C., Guo, S., Zuo, C., Li, L.: An empirical study of potentially malicious third-party libraries in Android apps. In: 13th ACM Conference on Security and Privacy in Wireless and Mobile Networks (2020)

Certificate Reuse in Android Applications

Fatemeh Nezhadian$^{(\boxtimes)}$ (ID), Enrico Branca (ID), and Natalia Stakhanova (ID)

University of Saskatchewan, Saskatoon, Canada
{flor.nezhadian,enb733}@usask.ca, natalia@cs.usask.ca

Abstract. The widespread adoption of Android apps has led to increasing concerns about the concept of "recycled trust" derived from the reuse of digital certificates. Android app developers frequently depend on digital certificates to sign their applications, and users place their trust in an app when they recognize the owner provided by the same certificate. Although the presence of cryptographic misuse has been acknowledged by several studies, its extent and characteristics are not well understood. In this work, we perform a large-scale analysis of certificate reuse across the Android ecosystem and malware binaries on a collection of over 19 million certificates and over 9 million keys extracted from PE files and Android applications collected over several years. Our results reveal that despite the growing nature of the Android ecosystem, the misuse of cryptographic elements is common and persistent. Our findings uncover several issues and enable us to provide a series of applicable solutions to the seen security flaws.

Keywords: Cryptography · Android · Malware · Digital Certificates

1 Introduction

Cryptography plays a crucial role in the Android ecosystem. Cryptographic operations are used to enable secure storage of sensitive information, verify the authenticity of the applications, and protect communication. The underlying system that enables this functionality is Public Key Infrastructure (PKI). PKI is a system that manages digital certificates and cryptographic keys and establishes trust between participating parties by associating a public key with an entity and enabling the verification of their identity. The trusted Certificate Authority (CA) plays a vital role in this infrastructure issuing certificates to software vendors and attesting to their identity.

Digital certificates and keys are essential components that enable secure communication, code signing, authentication, and other security-related features within apps. They play a vital role in establishing trust and ensuring the integrity of the Android ecosystem. However, the improper use or mishandling of these certificates and keys poses a substantial risk to the overall security of the ecosystem.

Instances of compromised certificates and keys within the PKI ecosystem are not uncommon. The infamous Stuxnet worm and Diqu malware were signed with

© The Author(s), under exclusive license to Springer Nature Switzerland AG 2023
E. Athanasopoulos and B. Mennink (Eds.): ISC 2023, LNCS 14411, pp. 226–245, 2023.
https://doi.org/10.1007/978-3-031-49187-0_12

legitimate digital certificates [6,15]. The study by Kim et al. [9] demonstrated that malware uses valid certificates to evade anti-virus programs and bypass system protection mechanisms. Kang et al. [8] showed that analyzing the serial numbers of certificates can potentially reveal indicators of Android malware. While these examples provide evidence of valid digital certificates being misused, it remains unclear whether this phenomenon is limited to a specific domain and what the broader security implications are.

In this work, we conduct a systematic study to measure and characterize the use of compromised digital certificates across two domains. We focus on Android applications (apps) and Windows executable files.

One of the challenges in this context is to collect compromised certificates and keys, as there is no official service that provides a list of all compromised certificates. To overcome this problem, we collect malicious binaries and Android apps to extract their corresponding digital certificates. We analyze the reuse of these deemed to be compromised certificates among the apps.

Our findings show that certificate reuse is more pervasive and widespread than previously observed, 48% of our collected certificates (over 9 million) are reused across the collected sets of APK and malicious binary files. Among them, 40% of the certificates used to sign malware binaries are also reused in Android malicious apps for various purposes. In other words, these certificates are extensively reused in malware across domains.

Although using the same certificate for signing multiple Android applications is generally discouraged by Google, we found this practice commonly ignored by both benign and malicious apps. For example, 59% benign apps in our collections were signed with duplicate certificates. At the same time, we discovered 9,931 unique certificates employed to sign 142,579 malicious and 84,922 benign apps.

To summarize, this study makes the following contributions:

- We conduct the most comprehensive and the largest analysis of cryptographic elements across Android applications.
- We measure and characterize the extent of certificates and RSA public keys sharing across APKs and malware binaries on a diverse set of over 19 million valid certificates and over 9 million reused keys collected from multiple sources over a period of several years (up to eleven years in some cases).
- Based on our analysis, we provide a set of recommendations to help security practitioners improve overall cryptographic security.
- To facilitate analysis of cryptographic reuse, we make the set of reused certificates publicly available[1,2].

2   Background

APK (Android Package Kit) file acts as a bundle containing all the necessary components and resources of an Android application, including the compiled

---

[1] https://key-explorer.com/.
[2] https://github.com/thecyberlab/RSA-keys-analysis.

code, assets, resources, cryptographic files (e.g., digital certificates, keys), etc. In Android applications, digital certificates and keys are used for various purposes:

Integrity and authenticity of the APK: The Android apps have to be signed, using unique digital certificates, before distribution. This mechanism not only ensures the integrity of the application but also provides Google, as the official market, with confidence that the owner's identity has been verified. However, Android apps can be self-signed by the owner, or signed with a verified third-party certificate.

There are two ways to create a key pair for signing apps[3]. The first involves using embedded manager tools in the development environment, such as Android Studio (apksigner, jarsigner) or Microsoft Visual Studio (archive manager), to automatically generate a keystore (a secure storage container where applications store and manage cryptographic keys and certificates) and a certificate with the identity information of the app's owner. Alternatively, developers can configure a personalized cryptographic key pair to create a custom key, allowing them to define their preferred signature and digest algorithms and key size. While this approach provides greater flexibility, it may also allow for weaker configurations. In the end, the cryptographic key pair, along with the owner's identity information, forms a signing certificate used to sign the APK file and consequently perform APK validation during installation.

Data protection and privacy: Cryptographic keys are employed to encrypt sensitive data within Android apps, safeguarding user information, passwords, and app-specific data from unauthorized access.

Authentication: Android applications that integrate with external services or APIs may use authentication and authorization services, e.g., OAuth. These credentials are used to authenticate the app and obtain access tokens for accessing protected resources.

Portable Executable (PE). Like APKs, other software applications, including executable files, utilize digital certificates and cryptographic keys for ensuring data integrity and authentication. PE serves as the standard format for Windows executables (.exe) and dynamic link libraries (.dll). Microsoft code-signing technologies, Authenticode and SignTool, are widely used for code signing and digital signature verification of Windows executable files, including PE (.exe), dynamic link libraries (.dll), installers (.msi), and other file types.

Cryptographic Infrastructure. *Digital certificates:* serve as an attestation of the identity of a certificate's owner (e.g., hostname, organization) bound to its public key. The X.509 format is one of the most widely used standards for digital certificates that, in addition to the public key and owner's identity, contains a period during which the certificate is considered valid, and a digital signature of the issuing certificate authority (CA). Generally, CA is a trusted third party that can vouch for the identity of a server/certificate's owner by signing the leaf certificate with its private key.

---

[3] https://developer.android.com/studio/publish/app-signing.

Pretty Good Privacy (PGP) and GNU Privacy Guard (GPG): PGP is crypto-graphic technology for secure communication. GPG, often seen as an alternative to PGP, is an open-source implementation of the OpenPGP standard. Both are widely used for securing email and data encryption. The standard extensions for such files include pgp, asc, sig, gpg, pubkey_pgp, seckey_pgp, and secring_pgp.

3 Related Work

Over the past decade, several studies explored the misuse of cryptographic APIs in Android applications. The vast majority of the approaches use verification-based analysis that offers assurances for the correct implementation of crypto-graphic primitives. For example, the static analysis frameworks CryptoLint [4] and BinSight [12] perform analysis of cryptographic misuse at scale. Cryp-toLint [4] discovered that 88% of 11,748 Android applications had at least one mistake in API use. BinSight [12] in its follow-up analysis showed that crypto-graphic API misuse originated in third-party libraries. Specifically, they observed that 90% of 132,000 Android apps violated cryptographic API guidelines. Sim-ilarly, Gao et al. [7] found that 96% of the analyzed 8 million APKs from the AndroZoo [1] dataset exhibited some crypto-API misuses.

CRYLOGGER [13] employed dynamic analysis for the detection of crypto-graphic misuse in Android apps. Similar to CryptoLint and BinSight, CRYLOG-GER explored the correctness of cryptographic API calls based on the defined rules (e.g., constant keys, weak passwords).

Zhang et al. [18] proposed LibExtractor to detect potentially malicious libraries and identify malware families based on their digital certificates.

Wickert et al. [16] focused on the crypto misuses of two Java libraries, the Java Cryptography Architecture (JCA) and Bouncy Castle (BC). Their study of 936 open-source Android apps showed that 88% of their collected apps failed to use cryptographic APIs securely.

Numerous studies explored more generic detection of cryptographic mis-uses. Li et al. [11] conducted a large-scale analysis of API misuse in GitHub projects. K-Hunt focused on weak cryptographic keys through analysis of bina-ries [10]. CryptoGuard [14] detected cryptographic misuse in Java programs including 6,181 Android apps. Similar to other studies, CryptoGuard discovered that around 95% of discovered vulnerabilities originate from libraries that are packaged with the application code.

Zhang et al. [17] have proposed CryptoREX, a framework to identify cryp-tographic misuse of IoT devices. Analyzing 521 firmware images with 165 pre-defined cryptographic APIs, CryptoREX showed that 24.2% of firmware images violate at least one misuse rule.

All these approaches focus on whether cryptographic functionality is imple-mented by the cryptographic libraries embedded in Android correctly. Hence, their primary focus is on benign applications. We, on the other hand, investi-gate the reuse of certificates. Kim et al. [9] was the first study to explore the presence of PE files signed by malicious certificates. We take this further and investigate the extent and characteristics of malicious certificates across domains of Windows binaries and Android apps including malicious and benign apps.

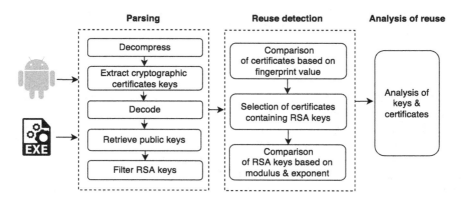

Fig. 1. The flow of the analysis

4   Methodology

The goal of our study is to measure and characterize the extent of compromised certificates and key reuse across Android apps. The flow of the analysis, illustrated in Fig. 1, includes 3 main steps.

In this study, we analyzed a large collection of Android apps and Windows executable files. For each of the files, we extracted all cryptographic elements such as digital certificates, and public and private keys that were included in the Android application packages and PE files.

The Android apps were unpacked and analyzed for the presence of cryptographic keys, i.e., files with standard extensions indicating the presence of cryptographic materials such as rsa, pem, crt, and cer. During this process, we observed the presence of files that did not match any of the standard extensions, yet appeared to contain digital certificates and keys. We thus parsed the remaining files using the Linux *file* command to identify hidden files that previously had standard cryptographic extensions that were later changed.

Malware binaries were parsed using GoLang's sigtool[4], which is a PE package designed to extract information from PE files. The certificates used for signing code are contained in the "Attribute certificate" section of PE files in DER format. For consistency, the extracted certificates were converted to the PEM format, which was then parsed to extract the certificate and key information.

In the next step, we obtained and verified signature schemes, package integrity, and package manifest using "apksigner" and AAPT2 (Android Asset

---

[4] https://github.com/doowon/sigtool.

Table 1. The summary of collected Android apks

Source	Collection Period	#apks	Valid apks	#apks with crypto
AndroGalaxy	2017–2019	7,462	6,845	6,839
AndroidAPKsFree	2020	1,333	1,316	1,312
Anzhi Market	2017, 2020	5,894	5,842	5,840
APKGOD	2020	4,690	4,046	4,044
Apkmaza	2020	111	109	109
APKPure	2020, 2021, 2023	109,216	109,048	108,512
AppsApk	2020	6,146	5,848	5,845
Appvn	2020	33,986	33,311	33,304
CracksHash	2021, 2022	3,486	3,469	3,461
F-Droid	2020	7,073	7,065	7,065
Google Play Store	2020, 2023	5,468	5,283	5,222
1Mobile Market	2020	1,370	1,370	1,370
Mob.org	2020	1,147	1,141	1,141
SlideME	2020	18,052	18,049	18,049
Uptodown	2020	59,717	56,819	56,686
VirusShare	2012–2023	440,106	411,629	411,214
VirusTotal	2020, 2021	8,160	98	85
Xiaomi	2020	1,199	1,175	1,175
Total	–	714,616	672,463	671,273

Packaging Tool) included in Android Studio SDK build tools and APK parser3[5]. At this stage, we discarded a set of 32,003 APKs that were not successfully compiled or verified.

Several cryptographic libraries were used to parse the files collected from the APKs and the PE files for certificates and keys. These libraries include the Java library keytool[6], and the Python libraries: CERT Keyfinder[7], PyOpenSSL, Cryptography, and PyJKS. However, not all the certificates and keys are parsable due to corrupted formats, password protections, or outdated (no longer supported by libraries) standards.

In order to assess the reuse within the collected data, we conducted a pairwise analysis of the collected certificates using their fingerprints, i.e., the SHA-1 hash of the certificates. Along with matching certificates, we also compared valid RSA keys.

---

[5] https://github.com/itomsu/apk_parse3.
[6] https://docs.oracle.com/javase/8/docs/technotes/tools/unix/keytool.html.
[7] https://github.com/CERTCC/keyfinder.

5   Data

To ensure a robust dataset, we collected Android apk files from several Android app distribution platforms, including Google's official market called Google Play Store, and Chinese app stores, which cater primarily to Chinese users, such as Xiaomi and Anzhi; free open-source repositories for Android apps such as F-Droid and AndroidAPKsFree; markets focused on game apps such as Mob.org; several unofficial repositories such as APKPure, Appvn, AppsApk, SlideME, Uptodown, APKGOD, Apkmaza, and CracksHash; and stores allowing a direct download of apps such as AndroGalaxy, and 1Mobile Market.

We also collected 448,266 apps from malware repositories VirusShare and VirusTotal.

By utilizing a combination of these sources, we aimed to gather a representative sample of Android apk files, encompassing benign used by different categories of users and malicious apps. Our set included benign applications collected between 2017 and 2023 thus presumably following the most recent standards and malicious apps from 2012 to 2022. Our final set consists of 714,616 of apk files summarized in Table 1.

From this set, 672,463 were found to be valid, i.e., parsable by the official Android tool, AAPT2, which verifies package correctness and integrity. Surprisingly, 1,190 apps did not contain any cryptographic components, which was unexpected. Although Google installation requirements require apps to be signed for distribution through the official Google Play application[8], we expected all Android developers to follow this security practice.

Overall, we were left with 671,273 applications containing cryptographic elements for our analysis. Although benign apps were collected from legitimate sources, we verified them using VirusTotal service and Malshare and VirusShare hashes. We gathered 3,266,932 hash values of malicious binaries from the Malshare Daily Digest[9] (covering the period from September 2017 to July 2023) along with 40,894,458 hash values of the malware samples provided by VirusShare[10]. We further matched our benign set against these hashes. As a result, 247 apk files from benign sources were detected as malicious. The rest of our analysis was conducted on a set of 259,677 benign apps (38.7%) and 411,596 malicious apk files (61.3%).

In addition to Android apps, we collected a set of 40,270,387 files in PE format reported as malicious from VX underground's APT collection[11] and VirusShare repository[12] ranging from 2012 to 2021.

---

[8] https://developer.android.com/google/play/requirements/target-sdk.
[9] https://malshare.com/daily/.
[10] https://virusshare.com/hashes.
[11] https://vx-underground.org/apts.html.
[12] https://virusshare.com.

Table 2. Summary of RSA certificates and public keys from APK files

Source	Certificate			Public key		
	Total	In files	In signature block	Total	From certificates	In files
Malicious APK	789,117	789,117	0	802,117	789,117	13,000
Benign APK	778,260	778,044	216	793,980	778,260	15,720
Total*	1,567,377	1,567,161	216	1,596,097	1,567,377	28,720

*duplicates within sets are removed, across sets retained

6 Analysis

In our study, the collected cryptographic files were parsed to identify the presence of certificates and keys. In cases where APK files included the signing certificate within the signature block rather than a distinct cryptographic file, we also extracted those certificates.

After filtering only RSA certificates and keys, we obtained 789,117 certificates and 802,117 public keys distributed across 411,596 malicious Android apps and 778,260 certificates and 793,980 public keys extracted from 259,677 benign apps (Table 2). Parsing 40,270,387 malware binary files, we identified 18,081,489 RSA certificates and their corresponding public keys. Overall, we derived 19,648,866 certificates for our analysis (Tables 5).

In the absence of an official repository providing a comprehensive list of compromised certificates, we focused on the certificates associated with instances of PE files and APKs that were officially reported as malicious. We consider these certificates to be compromised (as the adversary likely has access to the corresponding private key), and in short, we refer to them as *malicious certificates*.

6.1 Cryptographic File Formats

Out of 671,273 APKs analyzed, we discovered 2,376,721 files that may contain cryptographic components indicating digital certificates and keys (Table 3).

APKs typically incorporate a range of cryptographic components, utilizing diverse encryption algorithms, each serving specific purposes. Cryptographic file formats can exhibit varying configurations of cryptographic elements. As our analysis showed, cryptographic components may appear in file formats not related to cryptographic extensions, hence we parsed all collected files.

We discovered that not all of the initially identified file extensions within our collected APKs reflected the actual content of the file, i.e., many appeared to be renamed. This phenomenon typically happens when the original file extensions are changed, potentially to disguise or obfuscate the file content. Overall, out of 2,376,721 crypto-related files, 1,433,458 (60.3%) have been found renamed. The summary of renaming instances is presented in Table 4, where we can clearly observe two major recurring patterns.

Files containing certificates and keys (i.e., with file extensions appkey, pubkey_pgp, and seckey_pgp, along with others like pem, jks, exe, key, der, and csr) are commonly stripped of their original extensions (showed as <None>) or changed to pose as innocuous extensions. For example, a large number of files containing pgp keys were renamed to appear as image files, i.e., with png and jpg extensions.

Among the 104,044 files without extensions, 87,072 (83.7%) were identified as being in the "appkey" format. While the remaining formats were distributed randomly throughout the apps' file structures, the "appkey" files were specifically located either in the "assets" or the "assets/res" folders. Generally, the application key is the signature of the public key certificate of the private key, that is used to sign the APK, stored in a text format. Devices should only accept updates from an app when its signature matches the installed app's signature as a secure process. Another visible pattern is the renaming of Windows executables from exe extension to dll extension. This practice can help evade security measures and mislead users or analysts by disguising standalone executables.

Malicious apps appear to have fewer certificates in general, 817,479 in 411,596 apps, compared to benign apps, 820,997 in 259,677 apps (see Table 9). Having fewer certificates can help malicious apps avoid detection and maintain a low profile in their malicious activities. Similar behavior has been observed with public keys.

On the other hand, more private keys have been seen in malicious apps, (1,174 compared to 423) (see Table 9) which may be necessary to facilitate the decryption of encrypted malware data (e.g., in ransomware cases).

Table 3. Summary of parsable cryptographic files in apps

Category	Unique	Total	Benign apps	Malicious apps
All files	1,216,354	2,376,721	1,246,846 (52.46%)	1,129,875 (47.54%)
Files containing certificate(s)	646,176	826,674	294,323 (35.60%)	532,351 (64.40%)
Files containing public key(s)	2,150	28,872	15,764 (54.60%)	13,108 (45.40%)
Files containing private key(s)	500	1,604	425 (26.50%)	1,179 (73.50%)

6.2 Reused Certificates

Out of 19,648,866 RSA certificates, 9,412,099 (48%) are reused across the collected sets of APK and malicious PE files, with 11,251 (0.12%) of them being unique instances. As the results in Table 5 show, there is significant duplication of certificates within and across sets. Even more interesting is the presence of significant overlap between sets, which highlights the extensive reuse of certificates between benign apps and malware, including malicious apps and binaries. We will explore each of these aspects further.

Table 4. The summary of renamed file extensions

Renamed extensions	Total files	Unique	Malicious APK		Benign APK		Most frequent original extensions
			Total	Unique	Total	Unique	
exe	979,127	240,857	272,002	78,253	707,125	178,900	.dll, .temp, .binary, <None>, .so
seckey_pgp	217,462	145,336	110,759	74,191	106,703	68,564	.enc, .bin, .png, .html, .lhs
pubkey_pgp	139,184	89,700	84,809	55,307	83,998	55,969	.enc, .html, .png, <None>, .jpg
appkey	87,072	56,615	55,186	35,092	5,253	2,170	<None>
pem	10,116	1,244	4,863	562	2,263	911	<None>, .0, .jpg, .cer, .txt
jks	389	138	250	88	139	60	<None>, .jilin, .pro, .ts, .keystore
key	56	31	27	12	29	20	<None>, .txt, .mqtt, .dat
der	16	5	10	1	6	4	<None>, .pk, .ab, .split4
bks	13	1	9	1	4	1	<None>
cer	7	1	0	0	7	1	<None>
pfx	7	2	3	1	4	1	<None>
crt	6	2	4	1	2	1	<None>
keystore	2	1	2	1	0	0	<None>
csr	1	1	1	1	0	0	<None>
Total	1,433,458	533,934	527,925	243,511	905,533	306,602	.dll, .enc, <None>, .png, .bin

Table 5. Shared Certificates

Source	Total Certificates	Unique Certificates	Unique shared per set**	Shared across			
				Total	Malware binaries	Malicious APKs	Benign APKs
Malware binaries	18,081,489	41,282 (0.23%)	194	421,175	*	166,844	254,331
Malicious APKs	789,117	146,329 (18.54%)	11,234	5,224,399	4,629,047	*	595,352
Benign APKs	778,260	135,895 (17.46%)	11,213	3,766,525	3,256,951	509,574	*
Total	19,648,866	323,506	22,641	9,412,099 (48%)	11,251 (0.12%) are distinct across sets		

**duplicates within a set are removed, across sets retained

Reuse of Signing Certificates from Malware Binaries. As shown in Table 5, out of a total of 18,081,489 signing certificates extracted from malware binaries, 2% (421,175) were found to be reused in our collected set of APKs. To our surprise, only 3 of these certificates have been used for signing malicious apps, the rest were widely used for other purposes.

Around 60% (254,331) of these compromised certificates were reused in benign apps and as we saw in other instances of reuses, these certificates were heavily duplicated, where only 156 were unique. These apps are present in our Google Play Store and alternative market collections indicating that this reuse practice has been continuing over time.

In our analysis, we found that 40% (166,844) of the certificates found in malware binaries are also reused in Android malicious apps. The use of signed malware is not a new phenomenon, numerous sources reported that legitimate certificates are readily available for purchase in underground markets[13]. The previous study by Kim et al. [9] showed the use of legitimate certificates to sign malicious Windows binaries. However, our latest findings demonstrate that this practice is even more pervasive and widespread than previously observed.

---

[13] https://cyware.com/news/certificate-authorities-duped-to-sell-legitimate-digital-certificates-that-can-spread-malware-bcf63b15.

These certificates are being employed in malware across various domains and are extensively used.

During our investigation, we found 45 benign apps that were reported by Malshare and VirusShare as malware samples due to the contained cryptographic content. These benign apps appeared in both the official Google Play Store and alternative markets over several years (2019 to 2023). Further investigation revealed a total of 11 unique certificates were embedded in these apps. These files were flagged as malicious by multiple vendors and reported by VirusTotal. A pairwise match of certificates disclosed the usage of such certificates for signing 1,993 apps including 1,920 malicious apps and 73 benign apps.

Reuse of APK Signing Certificates. APKs are structured files that can include a signing digital certificate as a cryptographic file introduced in either a stand-alone META-INF file or included inside a signature block, depending on the version of the signature scheme. We parsed each APK to identify the presence of all signing certificates. As a result, out of 671,273 valid APKs, the majority (668,392) were digitally signed, while $< 1\%$ (2,881) lacked signing certificates, including 2,134 malicious apps, and 747 benign apps.

During this process, we discovered that the "jarsigner" tool treats a significant number of 594,971 (89%) signed apps as unsigned, issuing warnings due to deprecated signature algorithms and weak key sizes included in the signing certificate.

Out of 258,930 digitally signed benign apps, 59% (153,294) apps were signed with 25,135 certificates indicating significant reuse of certificates among benign apps. Using the same certificate for multiple Android applications is generally discouraged. Reusing certificate makes it challenging to determine the true source and verify the integrity of the application. If one app signed with a shared certificate becomes compromised, it can have significant implications for the security of all other apps that utilize the same signing certificate.

However, there are instances where a developer might reuse a certificate, for example, for different versions of their application or to facilitate communication between apps that belong to the same organization. A closer manual analysis of reused benign certificates showed that these legitimate cases are only responsible for a small portion of reuse. For example, one certificate has been used 6 times to sign apps belonging to Amazon Mobile LLC (Amazon Prime Video, Amazon Shopping, and Amazon Music). Similarly, another certificate has been used 4 times to sign apps published by Microsoft Corporation (Microsoft 365 and Microsoft Teams). Yet, our findings show that not all signing certificate reuse cases are related to developers following these legitimate practices.

Surprisingly, 9,931 unique certificates have been employed to sign 142,579 malicious apps, 34% of total 411,596 apps, while at the same time, these certificates have been also used to sign 84,922 benign apps, 32% of 259,677 apps. These benign apps were collected from all sets, excluding the SlideMe market which appeared to repackage and sign all posted apps with its market's certificate.

In November 2022, several platform certificates have been discovered to be used for signing malware[14]. The so-called platform certificates are used to sign the system Android apps, and thus give elevated privileges to apps signed with these certificates. Hence, if a malicious application is signed with such platform certificate, the Android OS will treat the malicious app with the same elevated access as a legitimate system app. Surprisingly, we found 332 apps in our collected set signed with 5 of the reported leaked platform certificates, within both our benign and malicious set of APKs, corresponding to apps released in 2023 and present in Google Play Store, and in sets dating as back as 2014.

The most shared default signing certificates are shown in Table 6. The top most widely used certificate is the default certificate of Android Studio, used in 12,639 benign and 34,291 malicious apps. This certificate, also known as "testkey", is one of the four key pairs that are generated by the Android team in the Android Open Source Project (AOSP) and are located in the "release-keys" folder. The other three pairs ("platform", "shared", and "media") are used to sign 911 benign apps and 1,482 malicious apps in total. However, it is crucial for developers to avoid using these default keys since they are publicly known. When multiple apps are signed with such certificates, they often gain a privileged position, granting them special access to those apps. As a result, if a malicious app is signed with the same certificate, it may gain elevated access to sensitive resources that would otherwise be inaccessible.

We also discovered 18,049 apps signed with a certificate associated with the SlideMe market. It appears that this certificate has been used to replace the original signing certificate in order to publish apps in the market. Another case of certificate reuse involves a service provider named "Qbiki Networks". The provider enables customers to create mobile apps with minimal coding and signs these apps on their behalf. This case was initially reported by Fahl et al. [5] back in 2014. Interestingly, after several years we still observe a similar situation in 1,590 apps in our benign and malicious sets containing apps from 2014 to 2022. The practice of certificate reuse by Qbiki Networks' customers seems to persist over time.

We were able to detect the presence of a total of 68,962 (10.27%) apps signed with these known key pairs (Table 6).

Reuse Beyond Signing Certificate. Another concern in this context is the reuse of signing certificates for other purposes beyond their intended use. Signing certificates are meant to verify the authenticity and integrity of specific software applications or digital documents.

We further examined the reuse of signing certificates for other operations. As a result, we found 297 unique signing certificates reused within 70,077 apps, including 20,758 benign and 49,319 malicious apps.

The CAs (Certificate Authorities) define the purpose of the keys when issuing digital certificates through designated fields known as *Key Usage, Extended Key Usage*, and *Basic Constraints*. These extensions provide additional insights into

---

[14] https://bugs.chromium.org/p/apvi/issues/detail?id=100.

Table 6. Use of known and default certificates in apps

SHA-1	Name	Total APKs	Benign APKs	Malicious APKs	Apps' Sources
61ED377E85D386A8D FEE6B864BD85B0B FAA5AF81	testkey	46,930	12,639	34,291	AndroGalaxy, AndroidAPKsFree, Anzhi Market, APKGOD, Apkmaza,APKPure, AppsApk, Appvn, CracksHash,Uptodown, VirusShare, VirusTotal, Xiaomi
27196E386B875E76 ADF700E7EA84E4C6 EEE33DFA	platform	1,230	9	1,221	APKPure, Appvn, Uptodown, VirusShare
5B368CFF2DA2686 996BC95EAC190EAA 4F5630FE5	shared	927	781	146	AndroGalaxy, Anzhi Market, APKPure, Appvn, Uptodown, VirusShare
B79DF4A82E90B57 EA76525AB7037AB2 38A42F5D3	media	236	121	115	AndroGalaxy, APKGOD, Appvn,Uptodown, VirusShare
C0DE76E80C8F1BF EDAC64231B9582DF 0EBC4F19E	SlideME	18,049	18,049	0	SlideME
9EDF7FE12ED2A247 2FB07DF1E398D1 039B9D2F5D	Qbiki Networks	1,590	1,441	149	AndroidAPKsFree, APKPure, Appvn, Google Play Store, 1Mobile Market, Mob.org, Uptodown, VirusShare
Total	–	68,962	33,040	35,922	–

permitted cryptographic operations and the intended purposes of the associated public key such as digital signature, key encipherment, client authentication, or code signing. These extensions enable certificate verifiers to assess the suitability of cryptographic operations and enforce robust security measures.

In other words, keys designated for signing code cannot be reused for other purposes. Yet, as our results show the key purpose does not appear to be properly verified.

Out of 9,412,099 reused certificates, 202,997 (2.2%) certificates were found to be lacking any extensions, i.e., theoretically should not have been signed by CAs. Out of the remaining certificates, 5,605,334 certificates have at least one of the extensions which means at least some constraints have been declared regarding their usage.

The extension characteristics of all reused certificates are summarized in Table 7. The results indicate that the absence of proper configurations and clear constraints for a signing certificate can result in the same certificate being reused across multiple domains.

Surprisingly, 5,179,277 (55%) certificates were labeled with "Certificate Sign" in their extensions, allowing them to sign other certificates and create a certificate hierarchy. Such certificates enable the certificate holders to act as trusted entities, issuing and signing certificates for subordinate authorities or entities. These certificates typically belong to CAs, and the presence of these 4,503,150 certificates in malware binaries raises concerns. We have only extracted code-signing certificates from malicious binary files, hence, the presence of these privileged certificates in signing malicious apps suggests potential unauthorized certificate use.

Table 7. Indented purposes of reused certificates

Characteristic	Unique	Total	APK signing certificate	Across sources		
				Benign APKs	Malicious APKs	Malware binaries
Key Usage	940	5,188,368	1,731	393,917	291,290	4,503,161
Digital Signature	524	852,104	1,731	98,494	73,862	679,748
Certificate Sign	568	5,179,277	0	390,262	285,865	4,503,150
Key Encipherment	342	22,210	10	9,938	6,143	6,129
Data Encipherment	31	1,774	0	832	942	0
Key Agreement	24	14,766	0	6,462	2,182	6,122
Extended Key Usage	492	810,480	1,954	16,205	15,983	778,292
Code Signing	116	764,571	1,834	1,672	2,777	760,122
TLS Web Client Authentication	373	43,911	55	4,322	11,263	28,326
TLS Web Server Authentication	374	56,568	0	14,851	13,389	28,328
Time Stamping	21	99,501	0	1,218	854	97,429
E-mail Protection	22	12,535	0	1,346	1,025	10,164
Microsoft Commercial Code Signing	12	168	0	42	126	0
Basic Constraints	1,322	5,591,123	63,589	458,363	376,025	4,756,735
CA: True	962	5,587,165	63,285	458,363	372,079	4,756,723
CA: False	360	7,384	304	3,426	3,946	12

Starting from 2008, certificate extensions have been categorized as either critical or non-critical. If a certificate-using system encounters critical extensions or information it cannot handle, it must reject the certificate. On the other hand, non-critical extensions can be disregarded if they are unrecognized, but they should be processed if they are recognized [3]. To ensure backward compatibility between applications and older versions of Android, applications may decide to implement a custom SDK overwrite that forcefully disables the verification of certificate extensions flagged as critical. Our analysis showed that malicious apps tend to use key extensions flagged as critical more often than benign apps. Out of 4,730,060 (50.2%) certificates set as critical, the vast majority (4,160,892) belongs to malware binaries, 245,592 to malicious apps, and 323,576 to benign apps.

Thus it appears that malware not only uses privileged certificates (i.e., the certificates issued to allow the signing of other certificates) but also commonly requests certificate verification to fit the target profile.

In the context of APKs and PE files, the presence of the CA flag set to True in the *Basic Constraints* extension indicates that the certificate is associated with a CA, signifying it as a trusted organization that has verified and signed the application or software from the vendor or developer. On the other hand, Android does not mandate apps to be signed by a CA and does not currently perform CA verification. It also provides code signing using self-signed certificates that developers can generate without external assistance or permission. However, a self-signed CA certificate implies that the owner of an apk file assumes the role of a certificate authority and has the authority to issue, validate, and sign other certificates for various purposes.

Out of 5,587,165 reused certificates found to be flagged as CA, we discovered 2,869,140 (51.35%) are self-signed distributed as 2,106,072 in malware binaries, 450,346 in benign apps, and 312,722 in malicious apps.

These findings highlight the significant reuse of signing certificates in the ecosystem of Android applications.

Public Keys Present in Reused Certificates. We conducted a deeper analysis of the key strength of the reused cryptographic elements found in our set to gain insights into the level of protection they offered. Table 8 presents the distribution of key size ranges for the public keys extracted from the reused certificates.

Table 8. Public key size of reused certificates

Key Size	Unique Keys	Total Keys	Benign APK	Malicious APK	Malware binaries
0–1023	9	728	649	47	32
1024–2047	4,540	731,740	306,780	325,600	99,360
2048–4095	6,294	8,208,281	3,256,459	4,665,343	286,479
4096–8191	287	471,348	202,636	233,408	35304
8192–up	1	2	1	1	0
Total	11,131	9,412,099	3,766,525	5,224,399	421,175

Among the reused keys, 732,468 (8%) are less than 2048 bits in length. They are considered cryptographically weak and should not be used for cryptographic protections. For example, NIST-compliant RSA keys are required to have a length greater or equal to 2048 bits [2]. NIST also recommended deprecating signing certificates that contained RSA keys of 1024 bits by the end of 2013. However, across all our scans, 528 signing certificates were found using a deprecated public key with a length of less than 1024 bits.

During our analysis, we encountered 1,597 private keys, out of which only 418 are unique. The presence of unencrypted and reused private keys in apps is concerning. Depending on the intended usage, the presence of these shared private keys opens up the possibility for misuse, allowing to decrypt protected data or hijack another app identity.

Out of these 418 unique private keys, we successfully reconstructed 251 RSA public keys, and by pairwise comparison with our existing collections, 34 shared public keys and 29 shared certificates were found to be matched to these private keys. Overall, 563 certificates and 1,108 public keys were found in 819 apps, distributed as 617 malicious apps and 202 benign apps, dated from 2012 to 2023.

7   Observations and Recommendations

The prevalence of compromised certificates being reused across Android apps and malicious binaries is substantial. Yet, our analysis highlights several observations that underline the existing problems and enable us to propose the following potential countermeasures:

Adequate Context-Relevant Extensions: We suggest defining context-relevant extensions with careful use of CA and *critical* flags to diminish the likelihood of potential certificate reuse for various purposes and in multiple domains. More specifically,

– *Specified/non-generic certificates:* Our analysis shows that only 5,605,334 certificates (59.5%) in our large-scale collection are well-defined. Without well-defined certificate extensions, relying parties have limited insight into the intended or recommended use of the certificate. This makes it challenging to enforce appropriate security measures and determine whether the certificate is suitable for specific operations or applications.
– *Non-CA signing certificates:* 4,756,723 certificates of malware binaries along with 63,285 signing certificates in APKs are set to be CA. If a signing certificate is designated in this way, it inherits the elevated and arguably unnecessary authority to issue new certificates.
– *Mandated purpose-related extensions:* Only 4,730,060 certificates (50.25%) mandate verifiers to process the purpose-related components of certificates. If a verifier lacks support for a critical extension, it can safely ignore such extension without affecting the overall validation process. Properly setting critical flags enhances the certificate's reliability while allowing for graceful handling of unsupported extensions by verifiers.

Use of prevention mechanisms may serve as a simple solution to vet apps, such as

– *Avoiding the use of default or publicly known certificates:* 49,323 apps (7.3%) in our set were signed with Android's default certificate and 19,639 apps (2.9%) were signed with publicly known certificates.
– *Use of reported malicious and compromised samples:* 1,993 benign apps in our set contain malicious files, and 332 apps were affected by the use of compromised platform certificates. Our analysis relied on publicly available information that is readily available to any developer.
– *Avoid using not-protected private keys:* We were able to extract 1,597 private keys from malicious and benign apps, and consequently 1,108 public keys and 563 certificates. In Android application development, it is advised not to package unencrypted private keys in APK files and refrain from including the signer certificate's private key within the APK. Securely storing private keys in trusted environments, such as servers or hardware security modules, with limited access during the signing process is essential to enhance app security and safeguard cryptographic assets.

Algorithm 1. An algorithm for verifying signing certificate

1: Step 1:   ▷ Save hash value while creating the signing certificate
2: *ExpectedAppKey* ← *signature of signing key pair*
3: Step 2:   ▷ Hard-coded validation procedure
4: **procedure** ONSTART
5:     *package_manager* ← *AndroidPackageManager*
6:     *package_info* ← *package_manager.GetPackageInfo()*
7:     *received_app_key* ← *package_info.GetSignature()*
8:     **if** *ExpectedAppKey* <> *received_app_key* **then return** false
9:     **end if**
10:     **Signature verified. return** true
11: **end procedure**

Validate Expectations

– *Embedded validation procedures:* Apart from considering all the settings and configurations of keys and certificates, an APK certificate should be further verified. We propose to use a set of steps in Algorithm 1 to guide app certificate validation. This process serves as a strong protection, ensuring that the APK's integrity remains intact and aligns with the expected attributes.
– *Use of tools:* The "jarsigner" tool used to verify signing certificates can give the "security risk" warning due to the use of deprecated signature algorithms, weak key sizes, and self-signed entries. This tool also informs if the *Extended Key Usage* extension allows the certificate to be used for code signing. Using such tools is encouraged to evaluate the signing certificate in order to reduce the risk of malicious modifications during distribution.

8   Conclusion

Digital certificates play a crucial role in Android app security, but many developers prioritize convenience over security. While there are cases where it may be justified - the app may not contain any important or identifying information - in numerous instances, it poses substantial risks to users and app owners. Our study reveals the extent of certificate reuse in Android apps and the widespread presence of compromised certificates. While reusing signing certificates in Android apps can simplify the app management process and maintain user trust, it also comes with significant security considerations. We hope that this research will urge developers to reassess the current security practices. Prioritizing certificate security is crucial for safeguarding both users and apps.

A   Appendix

Table 9. File formats containing cryptographic elements

Identified extensions	Total	Unique	Parsable	Benign APK			Malicious APK		
				Certificates	Public Keys	Private Keys	Certificates	Public Keys	Private Keys
aes	19,671	5,439	0	0	0	0	0	0	0
appkey	87,073	56,616	0	0	0	0	0	0	0
asc	6,008	5,169	1	0	0	1	0	0	0
bks	24,399	2,296	2,082	43,421	0	0	185,912	0	0
ca-bundle	3	2	2	6	0	0	0	0	0
cer	80,199	3,563	3,357	8,183	3	2	76,250	32	12
cert	2,338	150	87	78	0	0	95	0	0
crt	14,711	2,842	2,655	52,713	3	2	22,066	21	7
csr	431	274	0	0	0	0	0	0	0
der	18,137	763	715	1,654	603	27	9,079	282	47
dsa	6,076	6,040	0	0	0	0	0	0	0
ec	2	2	0	0	0	0	0	0	0
exe	980,685	241,893	0	0	0	0	0	0	0
gpg	91	89	0	0	0	0	0	0	0
jks	6,615	347	63	325,104	0	0	53,310	0	0
kdb	58	16	0	0	0	0	0	0	0
kdbx	57	20	0	0	0	0	0	0	0
key	9,912	827	206	7	158	95	6	253	227
keystore	1,102	385	17	0	3	0	0	37	0
ovpn	3,417	3,274	3,211	2,369	2	60	1,034	0	32
p12	2,310	717	4	0	0	0	0	1	4
p7b	89	22	14	244	0	0	104	0	0
p7m	13	10	0	0	0	0	0	0	0
p7s	1	1	0	0	0	0	0	0	0
pem	52,447	5,045	4,807	130,326	14,898	236	59,774	12,361	842
pfx	6,340	1,330	1	0	0	0	4	0	0
pgp	5	3	0	0	0	0	0	0	0
pkcs11	1	1	0	0	0	0	0	0	0
pkcs12	34	10	0	0	0	0	0	0	0
ppk	55	40	0	0	0	0	0	0	0
priv	3	1	1	0	0	0	0	0	3
private	34	4	0	0	0	0	0	0	0
pub	6,716	5,468	35	0	64	0	2	24	0
pubkey_pgp	139,184	89,700	0	0	0	0	0	0	0
public	52	8	4	18	2	0	5	0	0
rsa	666,428	632,089	631,852	256,874	1	0	409,837	0	0
sec	582	291	0	0	0	0	0	0	0
seckey_pgp	217,462	145,336	0	0	0	0	0	0	0
sig	23,395	6,416	3	0	5	0	1	0	0
sign	290	166	0	0	0	0	0	0	0
signature	281	68	0	0	0	0	0	0	0
spc	14	10	0	0	0	0	0	0	0
Total	2,376,721	1,216,354	649,117	820,997	15,742	423	817,479	13,011	1,174

References

1. Allix, K., Bissyandé, T.F., Klein, J., Traon, Y.L.: AndroZoo: collecting millions of Android apps for the research community. In: 2016 IEEE/ACM 13th Working Conference on Mining Software Repositories (MSR), pp. 468–471 (2016)
2. Barker, E., Chen, L., Roginsky, A., Vassilev, A., Davis, R., Simon, S.: Recommendation for pair-wise key establishment using integer factorization cryptography. Technical report, National Institute of Standards and Technology, Gaithersburg, MD (2019). https://nvlpubs.nist.gov/nistpubs/SpecialPublications/NIST.SP.800-56Br2.pdf
3. Boeyen, S., Santesson, S., Polk, T., Housley, R., Farrell, S., Cooper, D.: Internet X.509 public key infrastructure certificate and certificate revocation list (CRL) profile. RFC 5280 (2008). https://doi.org/10.17487/RFC5280. https://www.rfc-editor.org/info/rfc5280
4. Egele, M., Brumley, D., Fratantonio, Y., Kruegel, C.: An empirical study of cryptographic misuse in Android applications. In: Proceedings of the 2013 ACM SIGSAC Conference on Computer & Communications Security, CCS 2013, pp. 73–84. Association for Computing Machinery, New York (2013)
5. Fahl, S., Dechand, S., Perl, H., Fischer, F., Smrcek, J., Smith, M.: Hey, NSA: stay away from my market! Future proofing app markets against powerful attackers. In: Proceedings of the 2014 ACM SIGSAC Conference on Computer and Communications Security, CCS 2014, pp. 1143–1155. Association for Computing Machinery (2014)
6. Falliere, N., Murchu, L., Chien, E.: W32.Stuxnet Dossier (2010). https://www.wired.com/images_blogs/threatlevel/2010/11/w32_stuxnet_dossier.pdf
7. Gao, J., Kong, P., Li, L., Bissyandé, T.F., Klein, J.: Negative results on mining crypto-API usage rules in Android apps. In: 2019 IEEE/ACM 16th International Conference on Mining Software Repositories (MSR), pp. 388–398 (2019)
8. Kang, H., Jang, J.W., Mohaisen, A., Kim, H.K.: AndroTracker: creator information based Android malware classification system (2014)
9. Kim, D., Kwon, B.J., Dumitraş, T.: Certified malware: measuring breaches of trust in the windows code-signing PKI. In: Proceedings of the 2017 ACM SIGSAC Conference on Computer and Communications Security, CCS 2017, pp. 1435–1448. Association for Computing Machinery, New York (2017)
10. Li, J., Lin, Z., Caballero, J., Zhang, Y., Gu, D.: K-Hunt: pinpointing insecure cryptographic keys from execution traces. In: Proceedings of the 2018 ACM SIGSAC Conference on Computer and Communications Security, CCS 2018, pp. 412–425. ACM, New York (2018)
11. Li, X., Jiang, J., Benton, S., Xiong, Y., Zhang, L.: A large-scale study on API misuses in the wild. In: 2021 14th IEEE Conference on Software Testing, Verification and Validation (ICST), Los Alamitos, CA, USA, pp. 241–252. IEEE Computer Society (2021)
12. Muslukhov, I., Boshmaf, Y., Beznosov, K.: Source attribution of cryptographic API misuse in Android applications. In: Proceedings of the 2018 on Asia Conference on Computer and Communications Security, ASIACCS 2018, pp. 133–146. Association for Computing Machinery, New York (2018)
13. Piccolboni, L., Guglielmo, G.D., Carloni, L.P., Sethumadhavan, S.: CRYLOGGER: detecting crypto misuses dynamically. In: 2021 IEEE Symposium on Security and Privacy (SP). IEEE (2021)

14. Rahaman, S., et al.: CryptoGuard: high precision detection of cryptographic vulnerabilities in massive-sized Java projects. In: Proceedings of the 2019 ACM SIGSAC Conference on Computer and Communications Security, CCS 2019, pp. 2455–2472. Association for Computing Machinery, New York (2019)
15. Research, K.L.G., Team, A.: The Duqu 2.0 persistence module (2015). https://securelist.com/blog/research/70641/the-duqu-2-0-persistence-module/
16. Wickert, A.K., Baumgärtner, L., Schlichtig, M., Narasimhan, K., Mezini, M.: To fix or not to fix: a critical study of crypto-misuses in the wild. In: 2022 IEEE International Conference on Trust, Security and Privacy in Computing and Communications (TrustCom), Los Alamitos, CA, USA, pp. 315–322. IEEE Computer Society (2022)
17. Zhang, L., Chen, J., Diao, W., Guo, S., Weng, J., Zhang, K.: CryptoREX: large-scale analysis of cryptographic misuse in IoT devices. In: 22nd International Symposium on Research in Attacks, Intrusions and Defenses (RAID 2019), Chaoyang District, Beijing, pp. 151–164. USENIX Association (2019)
18. Zhang, Z., Diao, W., Hu, C., Guo, S., Zuo, C., Li, L.: An empirical study of potentially malicious third-party libraries in Android apps. In: Proceedings of the 13th ACM Conference on Security and Privacy in Wireless and Mobile Networks, WiSec 2020, pp. 144–154. Association for Computing Machinery, New York (2020)

TC4SE: A High-Performance Trusted Channel Mechanism for Secure Enclave-Based Trusted Execution Environments

Gilang Mentari Hamidy[1]([✉])[iD], Sri Yulianti[2][iD], Pieter Philippaerts[1][iD], and Wouter Joosen[1][iD]

[1] imec-DistriNet, KU Leuven, Leuven, Belgium
{gilang.hamidy,pieter.philippaerts,wouter.joosen}@kuleuven.be
[2] Jakarta, Indonesia
sriyulianti079@gmail.com

Abstract. We present TC4SE, a trusted channel mechanism suitable for secure enclave-based trusted execution environments, such as Intel SGX, that leverages the existing security properties provided by the TEE remote attestation scheme and Transport Layer Security (TLS) protocol. Unlike previous works that integrate attestation into the TLS handshake, TC4SE separates these two processes and binds the trust to the authentication primitives used by the TLS protocol. TC4SE avoids modifying the TLS protocol itself, thereby avoiding extra overhead, dependencies, and inadvertent introduction of security vulnerabilities. We argue that TC4SE provides the same level of security assurance as related works, while offering superior performance and implementation advantages, comparable to the regular TLS protocol.

Keywords: Intel SGX · attestation · trusted channel · Transport Layer Security · Trusted Execution Environment

1   Introduction

Having a secure communication channel is a common requirement in communication systems. The Transport Layer Security (TLS) protocol has been the de facto standard for constructing a secure channel between two entities. While the TLS protocol assures the integrity and confidentiality of the communication, it does not necessarily reflect its endpoint's integrity. To address this, Gasmi et al. proposed the term *trusted channel*, a secure channel where the trustworthiness is bound to the configuration of the endpoints [4].

The TLS protocol establishes trust by relying on a public key infrastructure, allowing endpoints to use certificates signed by a trusted Certificate Authority (CA). However, simply possessing a private key of a certificate does not directly

---

S. Yulianti—Independent.

© The Author(s), under exclusive license to Springer Nature Switzerland AG 2023
E. Athanasopoulos and B. Mennink (Eds.): ISC 2023, LNCS 14411, pp. 246–264, 2023.
https://doi.org/10.1007/978-3-031-49187-0_13

reflect the integrity of the software behind the endpoint claiming the identity. Any software that possesses the private key can claim the identity, rendering it inadequate in the context of a Trusted Execution Environment (TEE). TEE platforms address this issue by binding the authenticity of an entity to a combination of hardware and software state, which external parties can verify [2].

A TEE typically does not provide an out-of-the-box communication protocol between softwares running on the platform. However, a trusted channel protocol can be built by combining the attestation mechanism, which is present in every TEE platform, with an existing secure channel protocol [4,9,12,13]. Among known alternatives, most solutions are built for a TEE platform whose architecture is similar to the one in Trusted Platform Module (TPM). Secure enclave-based TEEs are a more recent development that differs considerably from the TPM architecture. As a result, it has unique security properties and capabilities to leverage when designing a trusted channel protocol.

In this paper, we propose to simplify the complex designs of trusted channel mechanisms in previous works, making it more suitable for secure enclave TEEs. We introduce TC4SE: Trusted Channel for Secure Enclaves, a novel trusted channel mechanism suitable for inter-enclave communication use cases. Leveraging on the security properties provided by the secure enclave and the TLS secure channel protocol, TC4SE is built on top of the underlying TLS protocol without any modification to the TLS protocol itself or its specific components, e.g., X.509 certificate. In addition, we evaluate the trust model of related proposals in [8,9] and contrast it against our design. We also analyze the performance of each approach and compare the results to TC4SE. We argue that TC4SE offers superior performance, comparable to the regular TLS protocol.

2   Background

This section introduces the fundamental concepts of a TEE, focusing on Intel's TEE implementation called *SGX*. Additionally, we provide an overview of the Intel SGX remote attestation scheme, which is relevant to the design presented in this paper.

2.1   Trusted Execution Environments and Intel SGX

A Trusted Execution Environment (TEE) defines a specification for the execution of a software that allows it to be trusted by external parties [1]. TEEs play a significant role in confidential computing technology, providing verifiable trust between different parties. Typically, a TEE guarantees confidentiality, integrity, and authenticity through hardware-based protection [11]. Intel Software Guard eXtension (SGX) is one of several implementations of a TEE. It is a set of processor extensions that enables a user program to establish a separate trusted execution domain called a *secure enclave* [3], which becomes an important component in building a trusted application.

Unlike the traditional operating system model, where a program runs on top of the operating system layer, a secure enclave allows a program to isolate a part of its execution context from the operating system through hardware support, effectively protecting its confidentiality against a higher-privilege adversary. Moreover, the processor cryptographically protects the integrity and authenticity of the enclave, and provides a measurement mechanism that can be used to verify the enclave's state to external parties. At the core of the TEE platform lies the Trusted Computing Base (TCB).

Intel SGX provides a sealing mechanism that allows enclave secrets to be encrypted and stored in untrusted memory [3]. The secrets are encrypted using a private sealing key that is derived from a unique key embedded into the processor during the manufacturing process. This key is not known by Intel, and it is unique for each processor. Sealing prevents an adversary from moving the encrypted secrets to another machine and decrypting the secrets by using another machine's key.

2.2 Remote Attestation (RA) Within Intel SGX Context

Attestation is an integral part of TEE technology. It allows a trusted application to make a claim and provide verifiable evidence to support the claim [2]. Attestation in a TEE relies on a hardware root of trust, which can perform reliable *measurements* of the system state and prepare the report as evidence. The TEE hardware digitally signs the report, ensuring that an external entity can verify its authenticity.

SGX uses a common static measurement technique, where it relies on a secure hash algorithm to measure the enclave image during enclave initialization. Along with this measurement, called *MRENCLAVE*, the enclave image also provides its author's signature, referred to as *MRSIGNER*. These two components form the *enclave identity*, indicating a specific enclave from a specific author.

SGX employs an embedded cryptographic *SGX hardware key* to authenticate itself to others. This cryptographic key is retained throughout the lifetime of the processor and cannot be changed in any way. However, unlike other TEE implementations, such as Trusted Platform Modules[1], SGX does not provide an embedded certificate to certify the key's authenticity. Instead, Intel provides a centralized system known as the *Intel Attestation Service* (IAS) to verify and confirm the authenticity of the private key. Developers can also use attestation functionality provided by the *Data Center Attestation Primitives* (DCAP). This paper focuses on DCAP attestation as it enables delegating the verification to the client enclave rather than using the fully centralized IAS model.

Figure 1 presents an overview of the DCAP components. DCAP features two special enclaves that facilitate the attestation process. The *Quoting Enclave* (QE) generates the quote, which is evidence of an SGX enclave's authenticity

---

[1] Some TPM devices are typically provisioned with an *endorsement key* certificate directly in the hardware, which can be retrieved from its API. However, this is not a strict requirement.

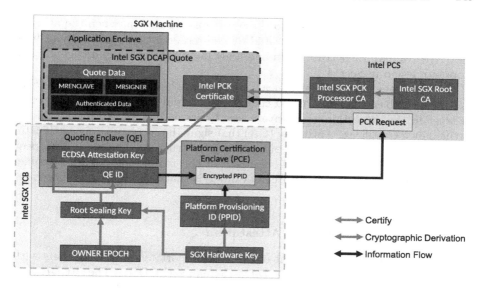

Fig. 1. The Intel SGX DCAP attestation trust chain

and integrity. The QE generates the *attestation key* from the *root sealing key*, which is in turn derived from the *owner epoch* and the SGX hardware key. The owner epoch is set by the owner of the platform during the provisioning process. It allows the platform owner to control the lifetime of the attestation certificate validity and sealed information. The SGX hardware key serves as a root of trust for cryptographic operations, ensuring the authenticity and integrity of attestation-related data.

The *Platform Certification Enclave* (PCE) generates a certificate that provides proof of the platform's integrity and security configuration. By verifying the platform certification, remote parties can verify the results of the attestation process and establish trust with the SGX enclaves on that platform.

The platform certification enclave relies on Intel's cloud-based *Provisioning Certification Service* (PCS) for certifying SGX platforms. To reduce the communication between the enclaves and the PCS server, Intel provides a proxy, called *Provisioning Certificate Caching Services* (PCCS), that can be run locally and caches certain cryptographic elements to accelerate the attestation process.

For more details about DCAP, we refer the reader to Intel's developer documentation [5].

3   Related Work

Other researchers have published work on securing communication between separated trusted systems. Walsh et al. [13] evaluated several mutually attested TLS mechanisms for microservice communication, relying on a TPM-based system as their trust anchor. Niemi et al. [9] also surveyed several attested TLS mechanisms and divided them into three categories based on when the attestation is done. In this section, we curated related research that specifically utilizes SGX. We evaluate their trust chain and trust boundary, to compare against our proposed design in Sect. 4.

Similar to the work of Walsh et al., we present the design of *mutual TLS* in Fig. 2a as the baseline of a trusted channel. A mutual TLS connection depends on trust in the ownership of a private key by its endpoints. The ownership is certified by a Certificate Authority (CA) that signs the corresponding certificate, which a peer can verify using the public key infrastructure. Therefore, each peer must trust the CA, as well as the entirety of the remote endpoint's machine. The only security property a peer can evaluate is that the remote peer possesses the private key.

3.1   Intel SGX ECDH with Attestation

The Intel SGX SDK provides out-of-the-box support for secure channels with attestation using Elliptic Curve Diffie-Helmann (ECDH). The ECDH key exchange payload is wrapped in an attestation payload, which the receiving party can verify to establish trust. According to the Intel SGX Developer Reference [6], SGX's ECDH protocol is designed to only be used within local attestation scenarios. This is reflected in the protocol steps, which are tightly coupled with the SGX local attestation mechanism, where an SGX-supporting processor mediates the attestation steps. However, developers can implement a similar ECDH key exchange protocol with another attestation mechanism to build a trusted channel.

Intel shipped a sample implementation of local attestation using this mechanism alongside the SGX SDK source code for Linux [7]. The sample demonstrates the SDK function that wraps the protocol into several function calls, which the enclave can call to establish the secure channel. The secure channel uses a 128-bit AES key which is derived from the ECDH shared key.

Figure 2b illustrates the trust model of the Intel ECDH trusted channel. The SGX TCB certifies the ECDH key material, enabling each peer to verify the authenticity of the remote endpoint. The trust boundary is limited to only the SGX TCB, and the participating enclaves, aligning with the SGX trust model that considers the non-enclave domain as untrusted. Because the private part of the ECDH key remains within the enclave, every participant can ensure that their peer is authentic throughout the trusted channel session.

3.2   Intel SGX Attested TLS (RA-TLS)

Knauth et al. [8] proposed integrating remote attestation with TLS, referred to as RA-TLS, to establish a secure channel to an enclave. This technique binds the SGX root of trust into the TLS protocol, extending the trust model of the TLS protocol. Therefore, it allows reusing an existing protocol to build a trusted channel that fits the SGX trust model and requirements.

(a) Regular mutual TLS with client and server authentication.

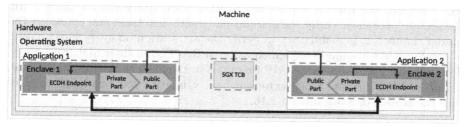

(b) Intel SGX ECDH [6]

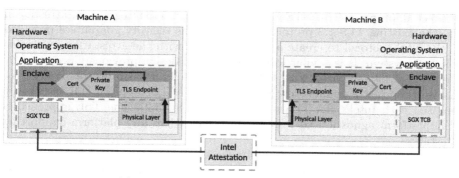

(c) Intel SGX Attested TLS (RA-TLS) [8]

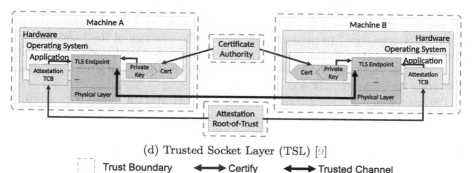

(d) Trusted Socket Layer (TSL) [9]

Fig. 2. Trust chains of several trusted channel designs

RA-TLS attaches the remote attestation quote to the X.509 certificate used within the TLS handshake. The attestation quote certifies the public key used in the certificate. As such, it provides additional security properties, which the remote peer can validate through attestation verification. The quote is generated only once during the certificate's creation. The verification occurs during the TLS handshake, where RA-TLS adds additional verification logic that invokes the quote verification API.

Figure 2c depicts the trust design of the RA-TLS protocol. Because the certificates used by the peers are self-signed, the PKI cannot be used to establish trust. Instead, the trust is rooted in the Intel SGX attestation infrastructure. The remote peer must verify the attestation to establish trust and construct the trusted channel. It is mandatory to verify the attestation on every handshake.

Intel provides a sample implementation of RA-TLS in their SDK repository. Moreover, Intel added relevant API functions in the SDK that simplify the integration of their custom X.509 extension and validation logic to SGX enclaves since the release of SDK version 2.16.

3.3 Trusted Socket Layer

Niemi et al. proposed Trusted Socket Layer (TSL, [9]) to integrate the attestation into the existing TLS 1.3 protocol. It extends the security guarantees provided by the TLS protocol to create a secure channel with the attestation guarantee of a TEE system. It is similar to the generalized design previously proposed by Gasmi et al. [4], updated with the more recent TLS 1.3 protocol. Walther et al. also proposed a similar design with their RATLS proposal [14] (not to be confused with Intel's RA-TLS proposal from Sect. 3.2). The TSL approach is TEE platform agnostic and may be implemented in any platform supporting attestation.

In principle, TSL is based on a similar approach as Intel's RA-TLS design, where the attestation evidence is attached to a custom X.509 extension. The attestation evidence is also verified during the handshaking steps, where a custom attestation verification function is added to the TLS verification function. Unlike RA-TLS, however, the evidence is created on every handshake attempt, as the TCB is required to measure the ClientHello message of the handshake as part of the attestation evidence that needs to be attached to the certificate. Consequently, the endpoint must regenerate a fresh certificate on each handshake right after the server receives the ClientHello message.

TSL provides a strong guarantee that every attestation quote is tied into a specific handshake, which makes replay and relay attacks impossible. It acknowledges that a powerful adversary with access to the system is able to obtain the active TLS session key. To partially mitigate this problem, the protocol disables TLS 1.3 session resumption to prevent the leaked session key from being used elsewhere without proper re-attestation. If TSL is implemented in a secure enclave, the problem can also be addressed by encapsulating the endpoint within this protected environment. Figure 2d depicts the trust chain of this approach, assuming that the TLS connection terminates in the untrusted domain.

3.4   Limitations

We identified several shortcomings of the designs proposed in related work that can affect the effectiveness to achieve their goal to build a trusted channel for a secure enclave. This section identifies three different areas of limitations.

Dependency on the Attestation Infrastructure. The designs we evaluated require a strong availability of the attestation infrastructure in order to establish a trusted channel. This is due to the trusted channel session primitives (e.g., shared key, session identification, etc.) being bound directly to the attestation primitives. In these scenarios, a secure enclave must repeatedly contact a central attestation provider to validate the attestation quotes. In the case of the DCAP infrastructure, the attestation provider is Intel's cloud-based Provisioning Cerfication Service.

As previously discussed in Sect. 2.2, Intel PCS holds the central authority to establish trust in an SGX enclave. The enclave needs data obtained from the PCS or cached by PCCS to validate the attestation quote correctly. If this data cannot be acquired from the PCS service, an enclave will not be able to establish a trusted channel to a remote enclave. A malicious actor can choose to sever the connection between an enclave and the PCS/PCCS infrastructure, resulting in a denial-of-service (DoS) to the enclave's trusted channel altogether.

The connection to the PCS server during the handshake also introduces an observable behavior where external adversaries can distinguish between trusted channel handshakes and regular handshakes. It may act as a side channel for an external adversary with access to the communication channel between secure enclaves.

Performance and Implementation Complexity. The reliance on the attestation infrastructure for the handshaking process results in a performance penalty during the initiation of the trusted channel. The attestation verification process adds additional complexity to the handshaking process, taking extra time to complete. Moreover, by involving the original PCS infrastructure setup, the verification step requires the enclave to contact the PCS server or the PCCS proxy, which can generate substantial latency.

Attaching attestation logic within the handshaking steps also increases the complexity of the implementation. While major TLS libraries, such as OpenSSL, support extending verification logic within the certificate verification step, the TSL design presented in this section adds additional processing right after the ClientHello message to obtain session parameters and to generate the attestation quote for the specific handshake session. OpenSSL does not provide an easy interface for developers to manipulate its handshake sequence, increasing the burden on the developers during implementation and maintenance.

Trust Chain and Boundary. The main principle of a trusted system is to minimize the size of the TCB and the size of the trusted domain, collectively forming a trust boundary. The regular mutual authentication in the TLS protocol requires all participants to trust the CA and the entire system possessing the authorized private key certified by the CA. The TSL design enhances trust by incorporating the TEE attestation, adding extra security derived from the TEE root of trust. However, the attestation and the CA trust chain remain separated, requiring the participant to verify the trust chain separately.

Meanwhile, the Intel RA-TLS design places trust solely in the SGX attestation scheme. The certificate used in the TLS protocol only serves as a container for the attestation quote. Consequently, this design may not be compatible with a traditional PKI architecture where the certificate is signed and rooted by a trusted CA.

4 Design

We propose TC4SE, a trusted channel design for secure enclaves that only requires performing attestation once and where trust is transferred between enclaves through hardware-enforced security guarantees and mutually authenticated TLS (mTLS). We show that our design is more performant than other designs, resilient to external dependency availability, and easy to implement.

TC4SE leverages the guarantees provided by the secure enclave where the information generated inside the enclave can maintain its confidentiality unless it is explicitly leaked outside the enclave. In this way, we can consider every secret generated in the enclave as a trust anchor, similar to a hardware-bound secret. This section presents the trust model and the high-level design of our approach.

4.1 Trust Model

The TC4SE design simplifies the creation of a trusted channel by delegating the trust to a private key within the secure enclave boundary. Like the Intel RA-TLS design, the private key involved in the channel creation is generated and sealed within the enclave. In this way, we can rely on the enclave security guarantees to retain the confidentiality of the key and to preserve the underlying trust in it, assuming that the enclave never leaks the private key. The main difference with Intel's proposal is the attestation procedure, wherein our design performs the attestation steps outside of the TLS handshake.

Figure 3 presents the trust model of TC4SE. Similar to several related works previously discussed in Sect. 3, TC4SE is built on top of the TLS secure channel protocol. However, in contrast to those designs, TC4SE does not use the X.509 certificate as an attestation quote container only. Instead, the private key in the certificate is directly linked to the attestation procedure. The client and server go through the attestation and verification procedure once, after which they use their respective private keys to convey trust between each other.

The TLS protocol uses a client/server paradigm and this is reflected in TC4SE as well. The enclave that acts as a server authenticates with a private key that is generated inside the enclave. The certificate for its public key can

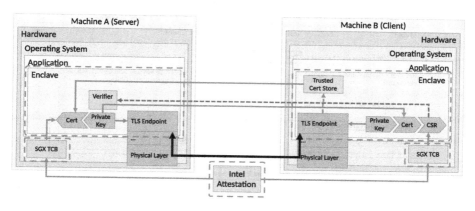

Fig. 3. The trust chain of TC4SE.

be self-signed. The server proves its authenticity to the client by quoting its certificate and sending the attestation quote to the client. The client can verify the attestation quote. If the verification is successful, the certificate is added to its trusted certificate store, which is also contained inside the secure enclave domain. From then on, any TLS connection where the certificate is used can be linked directly to the successfully attested identity of the server enclave.

The client's endpoint is similarly authenticated by a private key that is generated inside the client's enclave. To certify the client's private key, the server enclave acts as trust anchor for the trusted channel and offers functionality similar to a Certificate Authority (CA). For the server enclave to sign the client certificate, the client must present a Certificate Signing Request (CSR) that is authenticated by an attestation quote. Effectively, the CSR is cryptographically bound to the client enclave machine, as the attestation quote proves the authenticity of the CSR to originate from a legitimate enclave running in a secure-enclave-enabled machine. Upon successful verification of the attestation, the server enclave generates the client certificate, signs it, and transfers it to the client. The client can then use this certificate to establish trust with the other enclave in subsequent mTLS connections.

When an enclave is shut down, it must seal its internal state and store it in the untrusted domain, for it to be reloaded after an enclave restart. The internal state includes the CA and client certificates as well as their respective keys. Because the sealed data is bound to a specific enclave and hardware, it is impossible to transfer the sealed state elsewhere, except if the trusted software is programmed to do so. By preserving all secrets within the secure enclave boundary, the trust between every participant can be preserved and guaranteed through private key possession.

Because the cryptographic key is sealed to the SGX hardware, the key may be lost permanently in case of processor malfunction or root-of-trust reset (i.e., resetting the SGX's owner epoch parameter). To mitigate this risk, a backup strategy for cryptographic keys can be established, with particular emphasis on

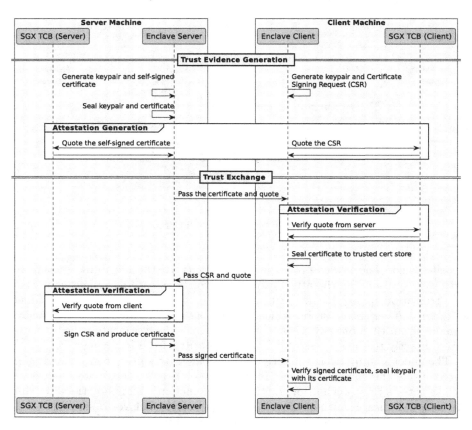

Fig. 4. The TC4SE trust establishment procedure between enclaves

safeguarding the CA key, the foundational root of trust in the TC4SE system. For example, a failover mechanism can be put into place by creating a replica of the CA server, using the same cryptographic key, which can be activated in the event of a system breakdown. If the backup needs to be stored outside of the SGX environment, the backup process must involve an external root-of-trust; for example, an alternative TEE device such as a TPM or smartcard. These backup systems are out-of-scope of the TC4SE design but can be implemented independently to increase the system's availability.

The TC4SE design allows for extending the chain of trust to a full-fledged external PKI infrastructure, where a recognized external CA authority signs the CA certificate of the TC4SE server. The TC4SE server can generate a CSR and send it to an external CA for signing. This signed certificate offers an added advantage if TC4SE is used within a system that requires additional identity verification other than the enclave identity, such as a domain name or IP address. It is particularly relevant in specialized scenarios where multiple parties may deploy the compiled enclave and interact with one another.

4.2   Establishing the Trust

As briefly mentioned in the previous section, TC4SE performs attestation outside of the secure channel protocol (i.e., the TLS handshake). Figure 4 describes the sequence to establish and transfer the trust from the secure enclave TCB (i.e., through attestation) into the PKI primitives (i.e., a certificate and its associated private key) between two enclaves. We divide the sequence into two parts: *trust evidence generation* and *trust exchange*.

Trust Evidence Generation. Both enclaves must generate their authenticity evidence and trust anchor. This is done by generating their own keypair within their enclave boundary. The server enclave then generates a self-signed certificate, which will act as its identity, and a CA to authenticate the client's identity. The client enclave generates a CSR to obtain a client certificate for its authentication to the server. The CA/server certificate and the CSR are quoted by the TEE's TCB and become the attestation evidence to establish the trust.

Trust Exchange. The generated authenticity evidence must be exchanged between the participants to establish mutual trust. The server hands its certificate and its attestation quote to the client, where the client can verify the attestation quote. Upon successful verification, the client can add and seal the server certificate to its trusted certificate store. The client can continue the process by sending its CSR and the respective quote. The server verifies the quote and signs the CSR on successful verification of the quote. It then hands back the signed certificate to the client. Finally, the client can store the keypair with its certificate.

The trust exchange process uses the TLS protocol in one-way mode (i.e., the client does not authenticate itself during the handshake) to secure the transaction. The attestation quote is included in the server's certificate as an X.509 extension. The client can verify the authenticity of the attestation and check that the TLS handshake uses the hash of the server's public key that is included in the attestation quote. The remainder of the trust exchange process continues over the channel that has been set up after the TLS handshake.

4.3   Constructing the Trusted Channel

The TC4SE design constructs the trusted channel on top of the existing TLS secure channel protocol. TC4SE specifically uses TLS 1.3 which provides stronger security properties compared to previous TLS protocols. In order to leverage the secure enclave protection for the TLS connection, the TLS endpoint must terminate inside the secure enclave. This approach has been demonstrated in several previous works, such as TaLoS [10] and Intel's sample code in the SDK repository.

The attestation procedure to establish trust between two parties, as described in Sect. 4.2, happens once before a TLS connection can be set up between the parties. TC4SE uses mutual authentication, which requires both participants to authenticate using X.509 certificates. As the certificates in TC4SE are directly linked to the attestation of an enclave, the use of the certificates implies that the peer is a trusted party according to the trusted software requirements.

The trust between the parties is pre-established before the TLS connection is initiated. A participant in the TLS connection is not required to perform reatesstation and reverification on every handshake. Performing attestation on every handshake does not yield additional security benefits, given that the attestation quote only changes infrequently (e.g., when the SGX firmware is updated).

5   Security Considerations

The trusted channel protocol should not undermine the security properties of the underlying protocol it is built on. TC4SE is built by combining TLS 1.3 and secure enclave security properties as a whole. It does not modify the existing TLS protocol and architecture, nor does it introduce additional logic in the protocol to achieve its security goal. Instead, TC4SE integrates the trust chain of both protocols that unifies the security guarantee to be suitable for the trusted channel use cases. This section presents a qualitative analysis of the security requirements and the protection domain offered by the TC4SE design.

5.1   Security Requirements

The TC4SE design should make sure it meets the essential security requirements of a trusted channel. We have summarized these requirements below, and evaluate them in the context of TC4SE.

R1 - End-to-End. The trusted channel must provide end-to-end encryption between two enclaves in different machines. The TC4SE design is built on top of the existing TLS 1.3 protocol, providing a solid end-to-end guarantee between endpoints. The TLS secure channel confidentiality is guaranteed as long as the session key used in the communication is not exposed to an adversary. Since the key exchange occurs inside the enclave boundary, this requirement is effectively fulfilled by leveraging the enclave's security properties.

R2 - Authenticated. The parties involved in the trusted channel must be able to identify themselves and verify the authenticity of their peers in relation to their enclave identities. The TC4SE design uses the mutually authenticated TLS (mTLS) protocol which requires both participants to present their certificate to prove their identity. The certificates in TC4SE are cryptographically bound to an enclave using the attestation mechanism, as described in Sect. 4.2. Accordingly, the mTLS protocol also authenticates every participant's enclave identity.

R3 - Indistinguishable. A man-in-the-middle (MITM) adversary that inspects the communication between two endpoints cannot distinguish the TC4SE TLS handshake and other regular TLS handshakes. In TLS 1.3, every handshake step after ServerHello is encrypted, which includes the server and client certificate. No other observable behavior from the handshake process can pinpoint the connection that belongs to secure enclaves trusted channel.

5.2 Trust Domain Evaluation

TC4SE guarantees the trustworthiness of the trusted channel through the cryptographic link between the TLS certificates and the enclave identities. The trust is verified through successful server and client certificate validation during the TLS handshake. Each certificate is linked to a keypair, and the private key never leaves the enclave boundary. Therefore, the certificate represents the guarantee that one is communicating with a secure enclave. TC4SE considers side-channel attacks where the secure enclave leaks private information as out-of-scope.

The remote attestation procedure establishes the trust between two remote enclaves. The server enclave that acts as the CA proves its trustworthiness by linking its certificate to the attestation quote from the enclave by attaching the certificate's hash in the quote's authenticated data. The resulting quote reports the link between the key pair, the enclave, and the enclave's author. Upon successful verification in the client enclave, the client registers the certificate into its internal trusted certificate store. The certificate store is also sealed to the enclave, preserving the trust within the enclave protection as well.

Like the server enclave, the client enclave also proves the link between the private key and the enclave using an attestation quote. However, the client uses a CSR, which the server signs if it can successfully verify the quote. This results in the creation of a client certificate that is signed with the server's private key. The signed client certificate serves as the server's acknowledgment of the client's attestation result. The client seals the signed certificate within its enclave and uses it to authenticate itself and establish a trusted channel.

In the case of Intel SGX, repeated attestation and the corresponding verification during the TLS handshake steps is unnecessary because the quote typically remains static for the lifetime of the enclave. The quote can change if the enclave is changed or if the Intel SGX TCB is updated.

Enclave updates can be anticipated by the enclave's author, allowing them to specify an update mechanism. Moreover, the enclave version information can also be attached to the certificate data, preserving the information in the trust chain.

Updates to the Intel SGX TCB occur relatively infrequent. The Intel SGX attestation scheme does not have a hard requirement to distrust a quote from an outdated SGX TCB. Instead, it is up to the enclave author to appropriately handle to an outdated TCB. Intel updates the SGX TCB when a potential vulnerability in SGX is fixed. Typically, this event also requires the enclave to be updated to apply the mitigation. Hence, the procedure is similar to a normal enclave update.

Apart from the TCB update, Intel also maintains a revocation list of the issued PCK certificates that sign the quotes. A PCK certificate can be revoked when the key is compromised. Since the key resides within the SGX enclave hardware, a compromised PCK key represents a larger problem where we can no longer trust the SGX confidentiality guarantee. Considering this fact, we deemed validating the CRL on every trusted channel handshake to be excessive for an improbable event.

6   Performance Evaluation

In this section, we evaluate the performance of TC4SE and compare the result with the related works described in Sect. 3. We analyze the results and argue why TC4SE can outperform other similar proposals.

6.1   Implementation and System Environment

We conducted our experiment in a Linux environment that runs on Fedora 38 with Linux kernel 6.2.12, running on an Intel Core i7-10700 CPU @ 2.90GHz and 32 GB RAM. The code is compiled using the Intel SGX SDK for Linux version 2.19 and Intel's SGX OpenSSL library. The source code[2] is implemented in C++ and built on top of the OpenSSL TLS library.

We also implemented TSL [9] and Intel's RA-TLS [8] for our evaluation. The RA-TLS implementation uses sample code from the SGX SDK repository. To the best of our knowledge, an implementation of TSL is not readily available. Therefore, we implemented the TSL approach according to the description in [9].

6.2   Performance Analysis

We divided our analysis into two phases: the one-time *initial setup* procedure and the *channel initiation* procedure that is executed whenever a trusted channel is needed. The measurements are conducted independently to avoid propagating the overhead between the processes. We identified four actions that are performed by the trusted channel schemes in our evaluation: *key generation*, (attestation) *quote generation*, *quote verification*, and *TLS handshake*. Table 1 highlights the differences between TC4SE and the related approaches. It already provides a first indication of why TC4SE outperforms competing designs. TC4SE is designed to do as much work as possible in the one-time initial setup phase, and as little work as possible in the channel initiation phase, which is executed whenever a new trusted channel is created.

Figure 5 illustrates the timing overhead of TC4SE and related approaches, computed by measuring the overhead for each protocol across 100 repetitions. Among the evaluated protocols, TC4SE has the largest overhead during the *initial setup* phase, with its average overhead being three times larger than that of

---

[2] https://github.com/DistriNet/TC4SE.

Table 1. Overview of the actions that are performed during the setup and initiation of a trusted channel, as implemented by TC4SE and related approaches

Actions	RA-TLS		TSL		TC4SE	
	Initial	Channel	Initial	Channel	Initial	Channel
	Setup	Initiation	Setup	Initiation	Setup	Initiation
Key Generation	•	-	•	-	•	-
Quote Generation	•	-	-	•	•	-
Quote Verification	-	•	-	•	•	-
TLS Handshake	-	•	-	•	•	•

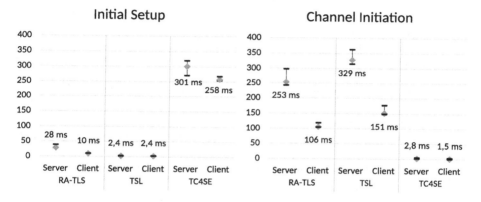

Fig. 5. Comparison of time overhead for trusted channel schemes during *initial setup* and *channel initiation* (in milliseconds)

Table 2. Comparison of network data overhead for trusted channel schemes during *initial setup* and *channel initiation*

Direction	RA-TLS		TSL		TC4SE	
	Initial	Channel	Initial	Channel	Initial	Channel
	Setup	Initiation	Setup	Initiation	Setup	Initiation
Client to Server	-	5.80 KB	-	5.81 KB	5.33 KB	1.89 KB
Server to Client	-	16.59 KB	-	17.01 KB	7.71 KB	3.14 KB
Combined	-	22.39 KB	-	22.82 KB	13.04 KB	5.02 KB

RA-TLS. However, the advantage of TC4SE becomes evident during the *channel initiation* phase, which is executed whenever a trusted channel is established. For the server endpoint, TC4SE achieves up to 90× and 116× lower overhead compared to RA-TLS and TSL, respectively. Similarly, for the client endpoint, TC4SE outperforms RA-TLS and TSL by up to 69× and 98×, respectively.

Table 2 shows the network load of the evaluated approaches. The table presents the total number of bytes exchanged until a trusted channel is established. For Intel RA-TLS and TSL, no network communication takes place during the initial setup phase. TC4SE shows a significant reduction in data transmitted during the channel initiation phase, thanks to its design that avoids the need to transmit quote data whenever a trusted channel is established.

7   Conclusions

We presented TC4SE, a novel approach that simplifies the creation of a trusted channel between secure enclaves. TC4SE leverages the standard TLS 1.3 secure channel protocol with mutual authentication (mTLS) and integrates it with the security properties of a secure enclave. Unlike related work, TC4SE's design eliminates the need for attestation verification during the TLS handshake, eliminating the performance overhead and potential attack surface that may cause a denial-of-service.

TC4SE relies on secure enclave guarantees to protect confidential information within the enclave boundary. This protection ensures that the authentication primitives used in trusted channel creation retain the trust established during the attestation procedure. We demonstrated that TC4SE performs on par with regular mTLS handshakes and much better compared to previous works, making it more suitable for performance-sensitive secure enclave use cases.

Acknowledgements. This research is partially funded by the Research Fund KU Leuven, and by the Flemish Research Program Cybersecurity.

A   Implementation Notes

We are dedicated to supporting others who wish to replicate the TC4SE implementation. This section contains notes on the implementation process, intended to assist developers who wish to adopt TC4SE in their own projects. The TC4SE design can be replicated with any TLS library that is compatible with the Intel SGX platform.

Our implementation is open source[3] and can be used as a starting point for custom implementations. It uses the OpenSSL library, which is officially supported by Intel to be used in the SGX secure enclave environment.

A.1   Remote Attestation Setup

To enable remote attestation for the enclave, the attestation infrastructure as described in Sect. 2 must be set up in the host machine. Intel provides the DCAP library, which includes the QE and PCE enclaves to allow the user enclave to create an attestation quote. According to Intel's reference design for DCAP, the

---

[3] https://github.com/DistriNet/TC4SE.

PCCS server must also be installed either in the same machine that hosts the enclave or in a separate machine within the same network as the host machine.

The enclave can verify the quote internally or use the DCAP-provided Quote Verification (QV) enclave. The QV enclave integrates directly with the DCAP infrastructure, including the PCCS server, from which it procures the attestation collateral. The DCAP repository also provides a reference implementation for developers who wish to implement attestation verification within the enclave, eliminating the additional communication with the QV enclave, which may introduce overhead.

A.2   OpenSSL API

Our TC4SE implementation uses the OpenSSL infrastructure to establish the trusted channel. This includes the **EVP_PKEY** interface to generate and represent public and private keys, the X509 certificate APIs, and the SSL APIs that implement the TLS protocol. The OpenSSL module is entirely encapsulated within the enclave boundary, preserving its internal data structure to protect its confidentiality from untrusted domains.

The enclave must also implement OCALLs (i.e., calling functions outside the enclave) to socket functions to allow the SSL API to communicate with the network socket in the untrusted domain. The Intel SGX OpenSSL implementation[4] provides the required OCALL to utilize the SSL API properly from inside the enclave. Developers can use the **support_tls** branch to make this option available when compiling the library.

References

1. Trusted Execution Environment Provisioning (TEEP) Architecture. https://www.ietf.org/archive/id/draft-ietf-teep-architecture-13.txt
2. Coker, G., et al.: Principles of remote attestation. Int. J. Inf. Secur. **10**, 63–81 (2011). https://doi.org/10.1007/s10207-011-0124-7
3. Costan, V., Devadas, S.: Intel SGX Explained. IACR Cryptology ePrint Archive, vol. 2016, no. 86, pp. 1–118 (2016)
4. Gasmi, Y., Sadeghi, A.R., Stewin, P., Unger, M., Asokan, N.: Beyond secure channels. In: Proceedings of the 2007 ACM Workshop on Scalable Trusted Computing, STC 2007, pp. 30–40. Association for Computing Machinery, New York (2007). https://doi.org/10.1145/1314354.1314363
5. Intel: Intel®SGX Data Center Attestation Primitives. https://download.01.org/intel-sgx/latest/dcap-latest/linux/docs/DCAP_ECDSA_Orientation.pdf
6. Intel: Intel® Software Guard Extensions Developer Guide (2023). https://download.01.org/intel-sgx/linux-1.7/docs/Intel_SGX_Developer_Guide.pdf
7. Intel: Intel® Software Guard Extensions (Intel® SGX) SDK for Linux* OS (2023). https://download.01.org/intel-sgx/linux-2.1.1/docs/Intel_SGX_Developer_Reference_Linux_2.1.1_Open_Source.pdf

---

[4] https://github.com/intel/intel-sgx-ssl.

8. Knauth, T., Steiner, M., Chakrabarti, S., Lei, L., Xing, C., Vij, M.: Integrating remote attestation with transport layer security (2019)
9. Niemi, A., Sovio, S., Ekberg, J.E.: Towards interoperable enclave attestation: learnings from decades of academic work. In: 2022 31st Conference of Open Innovations Association (FRUCT), pp. 189–200 (2022). https://doi.org/10.23919/FRUCT54823.2022.9770907
10. O'Keffe, D.: Talos: secure and transparent TLS termination inside SGX enclaves. https://doi.org/10.25561/94936
11. Sabt, M., Achemlal, M., Bouabdallah, A.: Trusted execution environment: what it is, and what it is not. In: 2015 IEEE Trustcom/BigDataSE/ISPA, vol. 1, pp. 57–64 (2015)
12. Wagner, P.G., Birnstill, P., Beyerer, J.: Establishing secure communication channels using remote attestation with TPM 2.0. In: Markantonakis, K., Petrocchi, M. (eds.) STM 2020. LNCS, vol. 12386, pp. 73–89. Springer, Cham (2020). https://doi.org/10.1007/978-3-030-59817-4_5
13. Walsh, K., Manferdelli, J.: Mechanisms for mutual attested microservice communication. In: Companion Proceedings of The10th International Conference on Utility and Cloud Computing, UCC 2017 Companion, pp. 59–64. Association for Computing Machinery, New York (2017). https://doi.org/10.1145/3147234.3148102
14. Walther, R., Weinhold, C., Roitzsch, M.: RATLS: integrating transport layer security with remote attestation. In: Zhou, J., et al. (eds.) ACNS 2022. LNCS, vol. 13285, pp. 361–379. Springer, Cham (2022). https://doi.org/10.1007/978-3-031-16815-4_20

Post-Quantum Cryptography

Performance Impact of PQC KEMs on TLS 1.3 Under Varying Network Characteristics

Johanna Henrich[1,2]($\boxtimes$) (ID), Andreas Heinemann[1,2] (ID), Alex Wiesmaier[1,2] (ID), and Nicolai Schmitt[1,2] (ID)

[1] Darmstadt University of Applied Sciences, Darmstadt, Germany
{johanna.henrich,andreas.heinemann,alex.wiesmaier,
nicolai.schmitt}@h-da.de
[2] National Research Center for Applied Cybersecurity ATHENE, Darmstadt, Germany

Abstract. Widely used asymmetric primitives such as RSA or Elliptic Curve Diffie Hellman (ECDH), which enable authentication and key exchange, could be broken by Quantum Computers (QCs) in the coming years. Quantum-safe alternatives are urgently needed. However, a thorough investigation of these schemes is crucial to achieve sufficient levels of security, performance, and integrability in different application contexts. The integration into Transport Layer Security (TLS) plays an important role, as this security protocol is used in about 90% of today's Internet connections and relies heavily on asymmetric cryptography. In this work, we evaluate different Post Quantum Cryptography (PQC) key establishment schemes in TLS 1.3 by extending the framework of Paquin et al.. We analyze the TLS handshake performance under variation of network parameters such as packet loss. This allows us to investigate the suitability of PQC KEMs in specific application contexts. We observe that Kyber and other structured lattice-based algorithms achieve very good overall performance and partially beat classical schemes. Other approaches such as FrodoKEM, HQC and BIKE show individual disadvantages. For these algorithms, there is a clear performance decrease when increasing the security level or using a hybrid implementation, e.g., a combination with ECDH. This is especially true for FrodoKEM, which, however, meets high security requirements in general. It becomes clear that performance is strongly influenced by the underlying network processes, which must be taken into account when selecting PQC algorithms.

Keywords: Public Key Cryptography · Post-Quantum Cryptography (PQC) · Key Encapsulation Mechanism (KEM) · Transport Layer Security (TLS) 1.3 · Network Performance · Crypto-Agility

1 Introduction

Cryptographic algorithms are permanently used to secure our daily digital communication, e.g., when sending instant messages or paying by credit card.

© The Author(s), under exclusive license to Springer Nature Switzerland AG 2023
E. Athanasopoulos and B. Mennink (Eds.): ISC 2023, LNCS 14411, pp. 267–287, 2023.
https://doi.org/10.1007/978-3-031-49187-0_14

Public-key cryptography is especially used for authentication and asymmetric encryption, to perform an authenticated key exchange (AKE) [8]. The algorithms rely on different mathematical problems, and it is currently assumed that these cannot be solved in a reasonable amount of time. However, Shor [53] found an algorithm that will allow a solution in polynomial time as soon as sufficiently powerful quantum computers (QC) are available. To counteract the resulting threat, new, quantum-safe technologies, e.g., Post Quantum Cryptography (PQC), need to be identified and migrated. Furthermore, encrypted messages could be stored now and decrypted later [50], so that schemes for key exchange should be adjusted as soon as possible. Unfortunately, due to the individual characteristics, a simple replacement of classical algorithms with PQC algorithms is not possible. Some schemes have larger keys or ciphertexts and the computational efficiency differs. The most important project concerning the PQC standardization is owned by the National Institute of Standards and Technology (NIST). While Kyber has already been selected as future standard, there remain some KEMs as potential alternatives. Looking at the infrastructure involved, TLS is one of the most affected protocols. It provides a secure channel between communication partners and it was used in more than 90% of all Internet connections in 2020 [37]. TLS uses asymmetric encryption for key agreement and authentication while executing handshakes for connection establishment. This raises the question of which NIST candidates could be used without significantly compromising security, performance, and usability. A performant execution plays a major role with respect to functionality, user satisfaction [30], and applications with real-time requirements [47]. When evaluating performance for PQC in TLS, the application context and varying network characteristics such as transmission rate, packet loss or latency are often neglected. In addition, there is a lack of comprehensive analysis that takes into account the multitude of algorithms as well as the parameterization and hybrid execution.

Contributions. This work focuses on the TLS handshake under varying network characteristics. We aim to identify suitable quantum-safe algorithms within TLS 1.3. The main contributions are as follows. (1) First, we extend the framework of Paquin et al. [44] to record the time required to establish a connection. We consider various (a) PQC KEMs and (b) KEM parameters. We evaluate (c) PQ-only and hybrid variants and we vary the (d) prevailing network conditions (e.g., packet loss). (2) Second, we investigate the correlations or contradictions between the measured performance of the handshake and the characteristics of the respective algorithm. (3) Furthermore, we provide recommendations regarding the use of algorithms and configurations given the prevailing network quality. (4) Finally, we analyze the impact of the network technology and configuration on handshake performance.

Outline. Section 2 gives a short introduction to cryptography, TLS and network emulation. Section 3 presents related work. Section 4 and 5 describes the experimental setup and results. Section 6 and 7 include discussion and outlook.

2   Background

2.1   Classical Cryptography

The Internet offers not only great benefits but also great potential for threats. Cryptography includes mathematical functions as well as associated procedures and protocols ensuring security goals like confidentiality, integrity and authenticity of data. In asymmetric cryptography, different keys are used for encryption and decryption. When ensuring confidentiality, a public key is used to encrypt a message, while the resulting ciphertext can be decrypted with a corresponding private key. The methods rely on various mathematical problems, mostly from the areas of factorization and discrete logarithms, which are described as practically unsolvable. That means that for every computing capacity available to date a solution is not possible in a reasonable amount of time. According to Easttom et al. [22], RSA is the most widely used asymmetric scheme enabling encryption as well as signing. Another scheme is Diffie-Hellmann key exchange, where NIST recommends Elliptic Curves for Diffie Hellman (ECDH) [28].

A so-called Key Encapsulation Mechanism (KEM) uses asymmetric encryption and enables a shared secret establishment by following a predefined scheme. It is independent of the underlying mathematical method and therefore promotes agility of the executing system. NIST requires that future key exchange standards be implemented in this way [57]. A KEM consists of three subalgorithms. (1) *KeyGen* generates a key pair (pk, sk). (2) *Encaps* takes the pk to compute a ciphertext c and a shared secret s. (3) *Decaps* uses sk and c to compute corresponding s. Figure 1 shows an example key agreement between two communication partners Alice and Bob. For more details see [11].

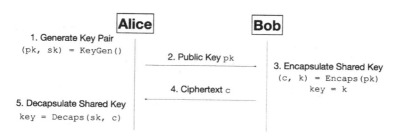

Fig. 1. Generic sequence of KEM with two communication parties

2.2   Post Quantum Cryptography and NIST Standardization

New technologies such as QCs pose a major threat to existing asymmetric schemes [53,62]. PQC deals with the development and application of quantum resistant cryptography. The topic has been discussed for several years by different organizations [18,42]. Ultimately, in 2016 NIST initiated an official process to develop new, quantum-safe cryptographic standards. It focuses on key exchange and digital signatures. The selection process went through several rounds and gains worldwide acceptance. In Round 1 and 2, basic aspects were reviewed and some algorithms were sorted out [18]. Round 3 began in 2020 with a total of seven candidates, four KEMs and three signature schemes. In addition, five KEMs and three signature schemes were selected as alternatives. NIST sees structured lattice-based methods as most promising [2]. Currently, the process is in Round 4 and Kyber (KEM) [15] has already been selected. Nevertheless, BIKE [3], Classic McEliece [39] and HQC [41] are still going to compete. In this work, we also consider KEMs that were eliminated, as they may still be of interest in certain use cases. However, due to TLS 1.3 size limitations, see Sect. 2.3, Classic McEliece is not included. Furthermore, the isogeny-based KEM SIKE [31] was provably broken in 2022 [17,38]. The investigated KEM algorithms are briefly described below. **NTRU** [29], **Kyber** and **Saber** [21] are structured lattice-based KEMs. They offer a comparatively efficient trade-off between security and performance [2]. NTRU is the best understood of these algorithms [23]. Nevertheless, Kyber and Saber are even more performant. The mathematical basis, in contrast, is comparatively young and little tested [2]. Saber's public keys and ciphers are a bit smaller than Kyber's, but it is even less explored. **NTRU Prime** [9] was developed to close potential security gaps of NTRU. That comes at the expense of performance. **FrodoKEM** is an unstructured lattice-based KEM. It is considered to be very well researched [1,2,26], but that also comes at the expense of performance. **BIKE** and **HQC** are code-based KEMS. BIKE offers a balanced performance, but with limitations [2]: encapsulation and decryption are slower and private keys are larger. HQC has larger public keys and ciphers, but key generation and decapsulation are significantly faster.

The security a particular algorithm can guarantee according to its choice of parameters is classified by NIST into 5 security levels, see [49]. Level 4 and 5 provide extended security to counteract future threats from technological breakthroughs [57]. Table 2 (Appendix) describes the data that needs to be sent while performing a key exchange depending on the chosen KEM algorithm and its security parameter set. Especially Classic McEliece and FrodoKEM, but also HQC and BIKE take larger values than comparable structured lattice-based KEMs like Kyber. It can be seen that a higher security level always results in a larger amount of data. However, the differences for each algorithm vary widely. While the difference between level 1 and 3 in terms of the public key is only about 400 bytes for Kyber, it is about 6000 bytes for FrodoKEM.

2.3   Transport Layer Security Protocol

TLS allows a secure communication channel to be established. The latest version was standardized in 2018 [48]. The protocol sits between the transport layer and application layer. The handshake is the central functional block for performing an AKE. It is the only part of the protocol that relies on asymmetric cryptography. Since TLS 1.3, only ECDH variants are used for key exchange. The client first sends a "ClientHello" to the server. In the *supported_groups* field it tells the server which ECDH groups are supported. In the "ServerHello", the server can, in turn, indicate which one it prefers and send its public key. In addition, the client guesses which decision the server will make and already sends a matching key in the *KeyShare* field of the "ClientHello". Optimally, the server can use this information directly and compute a shared secret to encrypt all subsequent messages. Authentication can be done using various signature schemes such as RSA or ECDSA. See also [48]. OpenSSL is one of the most widely used implementations [24].

Initially, integration of (PQC) KEMs and hybrid approaches were not provided in TLS 1.3. However, in recent years several methods have been presented [16,20,52] and standard designs have been published [51,55,59]. The currently most popular design is from Stebila et al. [55]. New *group* values are defined within *supported_groups* for the selection of algorithms and parameters. For hybrid variants, a new entry is created for each of the available combinations, and the number of algorithms for hybrid combinations has been limited to two. Linking two public keys is done by concatenation and the value is transmitted within the "ClientHello" *key_share*-extension or "ServerHello" *key_share*-extension. Similarly, the values for the *shared_secret* can also be concatenated so that the result can subsequently be used within the *key_schedule*. It should be noted that *key_exchange* values within the *key_share* are restricted to $2^{16} - 1$ Bytes. Figure 2 illustrates the message flow between client and server while performing a handshake using a hybrid KEM variant, as described above. Aspects affecting the key agreement are highlighted in blue. The required changes are marked with a "+".

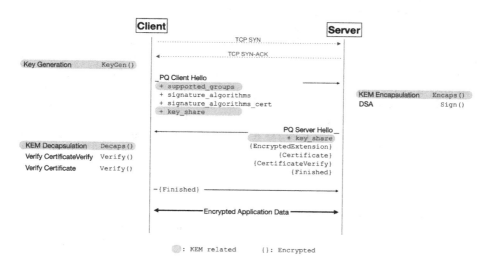

Fig. 2. Sketched flow of TLS 1.3 Handshake using hybrid KEM procedure according to the design of Stebila et al. [55] (Adapted from Fig. 1 from [45])

The public project Open Quantum Safe (OQS) [56] provides a TLS implementation with PQC integration. OQS OpenSSL implements the design of Stebila et al. [55] and includes all KEM schemes selected by NIST (Round 3). Only Classic McEliece is not considered. Its public key size exceeds the limit of the *key_share* entry. That would require a change to the TLS 1.3 standard.

2.4   Emulating Network Communication

A comprehensive performance evaluation should not be performed in isolation from application context. For this purpose we use various Linux Kernel tools. (1) **ip-netns** [10] enables emulating different connections or participants. *netns* creates isolated *namespaces* to which custom routing tables, network addresses and configurations can be assigned. (2) **veths** (Virtual Ethernets) [35] is used to assign virtual interfaces which allows to link the emulated networks. (3) **tc-netem** [34] is used to control outgoing data traffic. Latency, packet loss, transmission rates, jitter, packet duplicates, corrupt packets and packet reordering can be emulated. (4) NetEm builds on **tc** [33], which is generally used to control message traffic. The essential element of tc is QDISC, a kind of queue which is assigned to each interface and into which the packets are queued before processing.

3   Related Work

The related work can be roughly divided into (A) Architectural concepts and Internet drafts concerning the integration of PQC in TLS and (B) Implementation and evaluation of these concepts.

(**A**) There are a number of IETF Internet Drafts to implement TLS 1.3 in a quantum-safe manner. Currently most implementations (see (B)) focus on Stebila et al. [55], as described in Sect. 2.3. [59] describes a similar approach, although it allows combining up to ten mechanisms and tries to avoid redundancy for shared keys within a "ClientHello" message. On the other hand, [51] allows to combine two key exchange mechanisms by introducing an additional *supported_groups* extension. It offers a second list of algorithms and replicates the functionality of the *key_share*. [20] gives a short overview and summarizes the different Internet drafts. [16,43] discuss ways to combine multiple values for hybrid procedures with the help of Key Derivation Functions (KDFs). [43] argue that the appropriate combination is an important factor in terms of security and performance, which is still under research.

(**B**) Regarding evaluation, researchers from Google, Cloudflare and Amazon started to analyze hybrid KEMs like NTRU-HRSS, SIKE and BIKE in combination with ECDH in 2016 [44]. They used the TLS implementation BoringSSL and integrated PQC algorithms according to [55]. [36] take the same approach and evaluates SIKE and NTRU-HRSS in a realistic network environment. [45] investigates Kyber in combination with various signature schemes in WolfSSL. In addition, [61] evaluates Kyber and [7] evaluates Kyber, FrodoKEM, Saber,

NewHope, NTRU, BIKE, and SIKE. Both in local, compartmentalized networks. All of these approaches conclude that structured lattice-based KEMs perform particularly well. Even in a hybrid design. [54] analyzes the performance of TLS 1.3 and SSH by using Kyber, NewHope-512-CCA and NTRU for security level 1 and 3. To ensure realistic network conditions they use servers in three locations with average delays of 37, 67 and 163 ms. They also consider RSA-2048 and ECDH with P-256 as a control group and for hybrid runs. The experiments show that using the specified KEM algorithms, an error-free and high-performance handshake execution is generally possible. The same applies to hybrid runs. On the other hand, the authors note that the number of Round Trips (RTs) depends, among other things, on the initial size of the TCP congestion window. The duration can be reduced by increasing it within TCP configurations. [5] investigates the impact for resource-constrained networks. OQS OpenSSL is used to evaluate all NIST Round 3 KEM candidates at security level 1. Furthermore various transmission rates are considered via *tc*. For high bandwidths, the results are very similar to the experiments described previously, but it also becomes clear that an algorithm that performs well in ideal may suffer on sub-optimal connections and constrained resources. In [44] the authors introduce a framework based on OQS and Linux Kernel Tools. It allows to evaluate PQC KEMs as well as signature algorithms within TLS 1.3 under realistic network conditions. The authors run experiments for hybrid key exchange by combining Kyber, Sike and FrodoKEM with ECDH. To create realistic network scenarios they emulate packet loss between 0% and 20% as well as a delay of 5.5, 31.1, 78.6 and 195.6 ms. They also run their experiments on real servers in different locations to compare the results. They find that the *HandshakeCompletionTime* for fast to medium network connections is significantly affected by the performance of the algorithm operations. However, at packet loss rates above 3% a larger amount of data, e.g., when using FrodoKEM, has a noticable effect. This is due to the fragmentation of large messages and the resulting increase in the number of packets sent.

To summarize, Table 1 shows that there is still a lack of comprehensive comparison between the NIST candidates and alternatives. Often, only individual algorithms or specific security levels are considered. In addition, the investigations are often limited to either only hybrid or PQ-only variants only, and the authors usually have limited influence on the network conditions.

Table 1. Related work concerning evaluation of PQC KEMs within TLS 1.3

	[5]	[7]	[36]	[44]	[45]	[54]	[61]	our work
Considering network characteristics	✓		✓	✓	✓			✓
Dedicated investigation of network parameters	✓			✓				✓
PQ-only and hybrid						✓	✓	✓
Broader range of algorithms		✓						✓
Security levels 1,3, and 5		✓						✓

4   Experiment

The experiments can be roughly described as follows. Realistic client-server connections are emulated according to the network conditions described below and an automated execution of TLS handshakes is performed. The main goal is to measure the time required for a handshake when using different algorithms and varying network conditions. For this purpose, a script emulates network connections between some clients and servers and repeatedly initiates handshakes. A connection is terminated once the handshake is complete, and the time taken per handshake is measured within the client using a modified version of the OpenSSL function s_time. Authentication is performed via ECDSA. The process is outlined in Fig. 3. To emulate the physical client-server connection, virtual namespaces strictly separate the two areas. While the processing of the TLS records up to the virtual Ethernet interfaces takes place, the underlying network connection is emulated using Linux QDISC. Packets to be sent via the kernel are queued in the appropriate QDISC at the relevant interface and processed in order. Using NetEm, packet processing can be manipulated in different ways, such as adding delays or dropping packets. The following network parameter values are chosen for the study. In general, **packet delay** values between 2 and 200 ms are used for realistic simulations, depending on geographical distance and infrastructure [12,19,44,58,60]. However, values greater than 120 ms are considered exceptionally high and are rarely used [12,40]. We choose 16 values between 0 and 120 ms. Regarding **Jitter**, Shehza et al. [4] give the example that a dispersion of about 500 ns can hardly be avoided with largely error-free radio links. In contrast, delays of several milliseconds could result from the occurrence of punctual interference. Therefore, a usual latency of 20 ms is chosen for the test and the jitter is increased stepwise in the range from 0 to 20 ms. This results in the interval [0,40] for the actual latency of the data packets. For **transmission rate**, we choose values between 0.1 and 2000 Mbps. The selection is based on different works that consider values between 0.17 and 2000 Mbps [12,40,60]. We vary the transmission rates for servers and clients individually because Upstream and Downstream rates differ significantly in many use cases. For **packet loss** related works usually assume values up to 5% [12,44,58,60]. Values above 10% seems to be anomalously high [19,58]. Nevertheless, 12% [6] and 15% [27] could be measured when analyzing WLAN and mobile networks. In order to cover also rare edge cases and to be able to draw a direct comparison to [44], we evaluate the TLS handshakes for packet losses between 0% and 20%. Based on [12,58,60], we choose similar values for **reordering**, **duplicates** and **corrupt packets**. The servers are implemented using a freely available NGINX implementation. We establish 4 NGINX instances and a thread pool of 7 clients to emulate parallel transactions. 200 measurements are performed for each network configuration and KEM algorithm. The source code is freely available[1].

---

[1] https://code.fbi.h-da.de/pqc-benchmarking/benchmarking-pqc-in-tls.

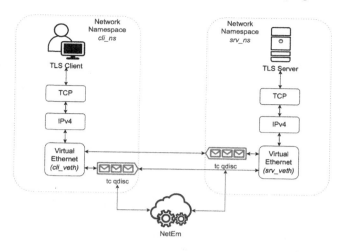

Fig. 3. Emulation setup using NetEm while performing TLS handshakes

5 Results

In this Section, the measured results are briefly described before a discussion follows. We focus on the median, which is not influenced by outliers at the edges. Furthermore 0.75- and 0.95-quantiles give an estimation regarding the upper 25% and 5%, respectively. In the figures, the different KEM algorithms are made clear by appropriate color coding. The color assignment is listed in the upper section of each figure. The KEMs are defined by their identifiers from OQS. Identifiers with corresponding key and ciphertext lengths for PQC algorithms can also be found in Table 2. For the classical ECDH variants, the identifiers are based on the curves used for security levels 1, 3 and 5 (*prime256v1*, *secp384r1*, *secp512r1*).The corresponding classic ECDH variant is always included in the presentation of the measurement results. This allows a comparison with the current status and a meaningful classification of the results.

Initially, the transmission rate was set to 500 Mbps on both sides, a constant delay of 2.648 ms per packet was added and all other parameters were set to zero. We started by investigating the basic behaviour of the algorithms by emulating constant (good) conditions. Figure 4 shows the handshake duration for 20 sets of measurements, focusing on security level 1. The measured times per KEM vary only within a range of about 2.5 ms. It is noticeable that algorithms with longer computation times, such as FrodoKEM or BIKE, show a larger variance. On the other hand, the Round 3 *candidates* as well as NTRU Prime (all structured lattice-based) show very good performance. They mostly undercut the ECDH method. The comparison of hybrid and PQ-only variants at security level 1 shows that hybrid execution has little effect on the time required. Only from security level 3 on there is a significant difference noticeable between FrodoKEM and FrodoKEM combined with ECDH. It is between 4 and 10 ms.

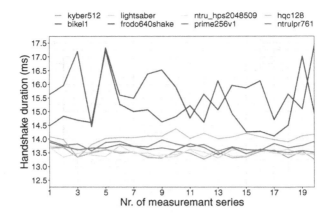

Fig. 4. Median handshake duration with constant network parameters (rate 500 Mbps, delay 2.648 ms) (PQ-only and security level 1)

As latency increases and the security level is low, the delay of the handshake is linear and strictly monotonic for all schemes. As the security level increases, the slope also increases significantly for algorithms with larger amounts of transmitted data. The same is true for hybrid variants. The evolution of the handshake duration for all the PQ-only variants investigated is shown in Fig. 5 for security levels 1 (Fig. 5a), 3 (Fig. 5c) and 5 (Fig. 5e). Figures 5b, 5d and 5f show a detailed view for the range between 0 and 2 ms. For security level 1 (Fig. 5b), it can be seen that the differences between the algorithms for a given delay roughly correspond to the values for constant network conditions. (See also Fig. 4.) However, this is not the case for security levels 3 and 5 (Figs. 5d and 5f). In all three views (Fig. 5a, Fig. 5c, Fig. 5e) it can be seen that the graphs become steeper from a delay of 150 ms.

When emulating transmission rates (Fig. 6), NetEm adds a delay to each packet that depends on the packet size. Accordingly, larger packets will have an immediate effect on the duration of the handshake (Fig. 6e). For sufficiently small rates, the times are delayed enormously. For FrodoKEM from about 20 Mbps, for the others between 4 and 8 Mbps. Figure 6f shows the critical range between 0 Mbps and 2 Mbps. Many of the algorithms considered have similar key and ciphertext sizes and perform similarly well, with HQC performing slightly worse and FrodoKEM far behind. For rates from 55 to 2000 Mbps, the converging behaviour continues as expected. If the rate is changed unilaterally, either on the client-side (Fig. 6a and 6b) or the server-side (Fig. 6c and 6d), the graphs have a similar shape. However, between about 0 and 2 Mbps, the handshake times increase as the server-side rate is reduced. At 0.5 Mbps, the measured times increase by between 30% to 90%, particularly for HQC.

Regarding packet loss, the authors in [44] have already noted, with very low packet loss below about 3% to 4% as well as low latency, the median measured times for all algorithms differ solely based on the speed of the particular algorithm. Only the handshake time of FrodoKEM is delayed at an early stage due to

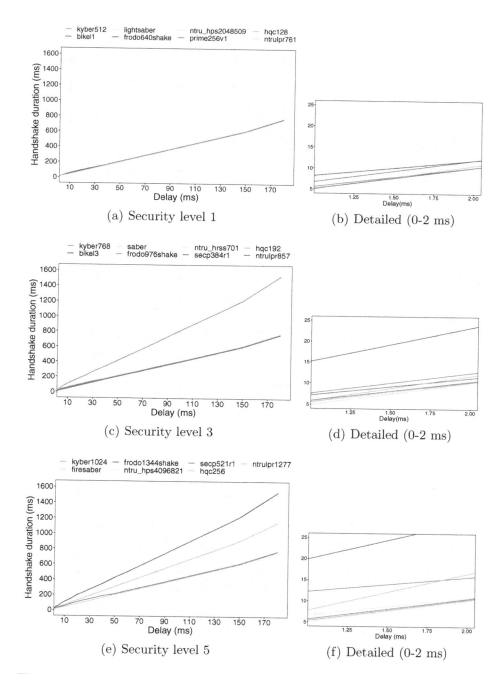

Fig. 5. Median handshake duration for all PQ-only-variants while latency increases. Classification according to the respective security level.

278   J. Henrich et al.

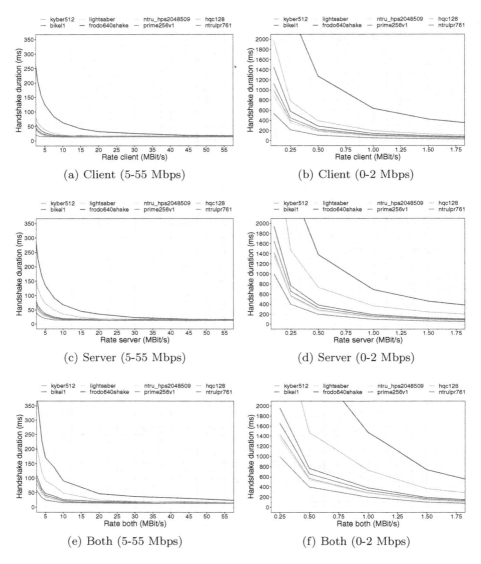

Fig. 6. Median handshake duration while transmission rate decreases for client, server and both. Investigation of PQ-only variants and security level 1.

the large amount of data. This could be confirmed in the conducted experiments for all candidates and alternatives, see Fig. 7a. Only the handshake duration of FrodoKEM is delayed from about 1.5% (Fig. 7b). In the further course, the values are initially largely constant and only from about 8% to 10% a strong increase is recognizable. Especially with FrodoKEM, which stands out with 12% to 15%. HQC, which also has a larger amount of data, likewise increases faster in the overall comparison. The high overall performance of the candidates Kyber,

Saber and NTRU ascribed by NIST, which has already been verified for Kyber (security level 1) [44], can be confirmed here for all security levels. In general, the algorithms only show a significant delay in handshake time at around 14% to 16%. However, in the range between 0 and 10, which is relevant for practical applications, a very good result is obtained with respect to the median. Hybrid schemes for security level 1 show no significant differences compared to PQ-only schemes. Up to 12% packet loss, a comparable speed of all schemes can be expected. Especially with respect to the candidates, a hybrid approach can therefore be chosen without hesitation in terms of handshaking time. At security level 3, however, there is a clear difference. Even with no or little loss, the times differ with respect to the corresponding associated PQ-only variant. The initial difference is justified by the additional use of the slightly less efficient ECDH. This intensifies for security level 5.

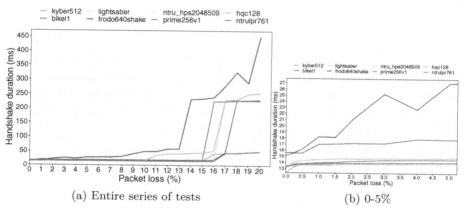

(a) Entire series of tests   (b) 0-5%

Fig. 7. Median handshake duration packet loss (PQ-only and security level 1)

6 Discussion

Under consistently good network conditions, the average handshake duration per KEM is relatively uniform, see Fig. 4. The differences between the algorithms can be attributed to the efficiency of the computational operations [44]. Looking at the results for the change in latency for security level 1 (Fig. 5a), it may be surprising that the slope of the measured times initially behaves the same for all algorithms. The differences between the KEMs mainly result from the different efficiency of the KEM operations. Only at security levels 3 (Fig. 5c) and 5 (Fig. 5e) do FrodoKEM and HQC show an increased slope of the handshake time. Due to the different amounts of data to be sent, it would be expected that the number of packets sent would increase due to the limited size. As each packet is given an additional delay by NetEm, a correspondingly greater increase in handshake duration should be expected for sequential processing across all security levels. The uniform increase at security level 1 implies that for all algorithms, the configured delay is added to the simple handshake duration by the same factor. In other words, the number of RTs is the same, even though the amount of data differs. In principle, the following factors are involved: **(1.) All TLS 1.3**

handshake messages can each fit into one IP packet. This means that the data is not split on any of the network layers considered. **TLS records** themself are usually fragmented, if the data exceeds 2^{14} bytes in size [48]. At the same time, however, a key change must not span multiple records. This means that handshake messages immediately preceding a key change ("ClientHello", "EndOfEarlyData", "ServerHello", "Finished" and "KeyUpdate") must fit into one record. Symmetric encryption has no effect on the results of the different KEMs. As shown in Fig. 2, only the TLS records following the *key_share* are symmetrically encrypted. At this point, the KEM process is complete. At the transport layer, the maximum size of a **TCP segment** body is communicated to each other within the TCP handshake [25]. This is called Maximum Segment Size (MSS) and is often derived from the local Maximum Transmission Unit (MTU). The MTU is the maximum packet size for a Layer 3 protocol to fit into the frame of the corresponding Layer 2 protocol without fragmentation [25,46]. A main objective of the MSS is to avoid IP-level fragmentation of TCP segments [14]. There are several mechanisms for finding the minimum MTU for a multi-hop path, e.g. [25]. At the network layer, **IP packets** are fragmented if their size exceeds the MTU defined on the interface, but this is expected in less than 1% [32]. The structure of a resulting packet is shown in Fig. 8. It is clear that MTU and MSS play a crucial role in the number of packets to be sent. **(2.) Multiple segments can be sent at once.** This is due to the control mechanisms of the intermediate network protocol TCP. It estimates the maximum capacity of the link and then bundles the segments. The number of segments that can be transmitted simultaneously is determined by the size of the *Receiving Window* and the *Congestion Window* (*cwnd*). Provided the window size is sufficiently large, larger keys and ciphertexts do not necessarily require additional TCP RTs. The gap between the PQC schemes is eliminated. Only if the number of additional segments exceeds the window size, the total time will be significantly delayed. During a TCP connection, *cwnd* is constantly updated. Initially, the value is based on the preconfigured (*init_cwnd*) and is gradually increased over time. This is done until segments are lost or a threshold value is reached. In the event of a loss, the window is drastically reduced and then gradually increased again. For further information see [13]. The key parameters in terms of performance are (*init_cwnd*), the slow-start threshold (*ssthresh*), as well as the maximum window size (*max_cwnd*). Our measurements show that (1) and (2) do not apply when using security levels 3 (Fig. 5c) and 5 (Fig. 5e) for FrodoKEM and HQC. This means that up to a certain threshold, increasing the amount of data to be transferred has little effect on overall performance. However, exceeding this value can lead to significant performance degradation. The increased slope from 150ms delay applies to all algorithms and security levels. It therefore appears to be a TCP-specific mechanism that does not need to be taken into account for PQC variants.

Looking at reduced transmission rates shows that the results for server-side (Fig. 6c and 6d) and client-side reduction (Fig. 6a and 6b) differ. These trends can be attributed to the different message content in the KEMs. The client-side reduction is affected by the key size and the server-side reduction is affected by the ciphertext size. For most algorithms, there is a relatively balanced relationship between keys and ciphertexts. For HQC, however, the ciphertext size clearly

IP Packet

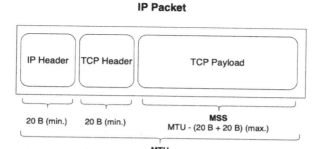

Fig. 8. IPv4 packet dimensions as specified in [14, 25]. Sizes in bytes (B).

dominates. For connections with limited transmission rates on server side, it is therefore not advisable to use HQC. The hybrid methods of the candidates and alternatives are clearly different from their corresponding PQ-only variants.

Packet loss and erroneous packets show outliers. Specifically, the mean handshake duration decreases at several points even though the ratio of missing or corrupt packets increases, see FrodoKEM in Fig. 7a. The following factors play an important part. **(1.) The probability configured in NetEm** is applied to each incoming packet individually. Due to the randomness, anomalies may occur. Increasing the number of handshakes could reduce the outliners, but not eliminate them. **(2.) Unwanted scheduling of operating system processes** may have affected performance, although the machine in use was disconnected from the network and unnecessary processes were stopped. In addition, as mentioned above, handshake performance is heavily influenced by **(3.) TCP control mechanisms**. Segmentation, flow control and error handling could all lead to variations in transmission times. Sikeridis et al. [54] integrate PQC candidates into TLS 1.3 and report a correlation between handshake duration and the size of the TCP $cwnd$. If the initial size $init\_cwnd$ is small, it is necessary to wait several times for an acknowledgment of receipt first, especially when large amounts of data are being sent. The authors show that a significant reduction in handshake time can be achieved by increasing $init\_cwnd$. Since $cwnd$ is variable during communication, and in particular depends on the proportion of unacknowledged (lost) TCP segments, an automatic change of $cwnd$ can be considered as the cause of the outliers. The behaviour is defined in RFC 5681 [13]. Finally, in rare cases, **(4.) decapsulation errors** may result in an incorrect key despite a correct ciphertext transmission. The maximum percentage of incorrect decapsulation operations is defined by the respective KEM.

7   Conclusion and Future Work

Firstly, our work confirms the results of Paquin et al. [44]. The handshake duration increases with poor network connections, while data-intensive PQC schemes are more affected. Furthermore, it becomes clear that many candidates and alternatives can stand up to comparison with the classic variants under normal conditions. This is especially true for the evaluated structured lattice-based candidates Kyber, Saber and NTRU. At transmission rates above 2 Mbps as well as with less than 10% lost or erroneous packets, they even outperform the comparable ECDH variant. This confirms NIST's assessment of the high overall performance of the *candidates* Kyber, Saber, and NTRU. In addition, the *alternative* NTRU Prime also scores almost consistently. Greater variance is observed for other *alternatives*. FrodoKEM shows a noticeable but acceptable difference for very good connections. However, due to the huge amount of data concerning public keys and ciphertexts, there is an increase in the time required, e.g., at around 2% packet loss or 4% erroneous packets. The behaviour can also be observed at higher security levels. There is no consistent pattern in the differences between security levels and hybrid variants. For the candidates as well as for NTRU Prime, the timing differences between PQ-only and hybrid execution are very small. Therefore, even with higher packet loss rates, increasing latency, or low transmission rates, a hybrid variant or higher security levels can be chosen. In contrast, for alternatives such as HQC and FrodoKEM, a significant increase in handshake time can be observed at higher security levels or for hybrid variants. The increase is already noticeable at security level 3 and expands at level 5. Especially at low transmission rates or increasing latency. The desired security level should be taken into account when selecting these algorithms. When changing transmission rates, a server-side reduction has a greater impact on the overall performance than a client-side reduction. This is due to the ratio of key to ciphertext size per algorithm. KEM algorithms with larger ciphertexts have a particularly large negative impact at low server-side transmission rates. It is noticeable that the trend is not consistent, especially as packet loss increases. Furthermore, PQC algorithms sometimes show similar performance trends despite significant differences in the amount of data being transmitted. E.g., while changing latency. On the other hand, when certain thresholds are exceeded, there are suddenly significant differences. In particular, MTU, MSS and the TCP congestion control configuration should be taken into account. This is especially true for algorithms with larger key and ciphertext sizes in combination with higher security levels.

As for future work, we are currently experimenting with real server connections and different hop distances. The performance impact of the prevailing network conditions, MSS, MTU and TCP congestion control are analysed. Changing from IPv4 to IPv6 or replacing the transport protocol involved could also have a significant impact. For TLS, a variation of the handshake flow would be useful. E.g., transmitting multiple *key_share* entries and "ServerHelloRetry". Authentication using quantum-safe digital signatures and alternative approaches such as pre-shared keys in TLS 1.3 and KEMTLS [52] should also be considered.

Acknowledgment. Funded by the German Federal Ministry of Education and Research and the Hessian Ministry of Higher Education, Research, Science and the Arts as part of the National Research Center for Applied Cybersecurity ATHENE and the Project DemoQuanDT (Reference 16KISQ072).

A Appendix

Table 2. KEM candidates and alternatives of NIST PQC standardization process as specified by Open Quantum Safe *liboqs* [56]. *pk* is public key, *sk* is secret key and *c* is ciphertext as described in Fig. 1. Sizes in bytes.

algorithm	identifier	security	pk size	sk size	c size
Classic McEliece	*Classic-McEliece-348864(f)*	level 1	261120	6492	128
	Classic-McEliece-460896(f)	level 3	524160	13608	188
	Classic-McEliece-6688128(f)	level 5	1044992	13932	240
	Classic-McEliece-6960119(f)	level 5	1047319	13948	226
	Classic-McEliece-8192128(f)	level 5	1357824	14120	240
KYBER	*Kyber512(-90 s)*	level 1	800	1632	768
	Kyber768(-90 s)	level 3	1184	2400	1088
	Kyber1024(-90 s)	level 5	1568	3168	1568
NTRU	*NTRU-HPS-2048-509*	level 1	699	935	699
	NTRU-HPS-2048-677	level 3	930	1234	930
	NTRU-HRSS-701	level 3	1138	1452	1138
	NTRU-HPS-4096-821	level 5	1230	1592	1230
	NTRU-HPS-4096-1229	level 5	1842	2366	1842
	NTRU-HRSS-1373	level 5	2401	2983	2401
SABER	*LightSaber*	level 1	672	1568	736
	Saber	level 3	992	2304	1088
	FireSaber	level 5	1312	3040	1472
BIKE	*BIKE-L1*	level 1	1541	5223	1573
	BIKE-L3	level 3	3083	10105	3115
	BIKE-L5	level 5	5122	16494	5154
FrodoKEM	*FrodoKEM-640*	level 1	9616	19888	9720
	FrodoKEM-976	level 3	15632	31296	15744
	FrodoKEM-1344	level 5	21520	43088	21632
HQC	*HQC-128*	level 1	2249	2289	4481
	HQC-192	level 3	4522	4562	9026
	HQC-256	level 5	7245	7285	14469
NTRU PRIME	*sntrup653*	level 1	994	1518	897
	sntrup857	level 3	1322	1999	1184
	sntrup1277	level 5	2067	3059	1847
	ntrulpr653	level 1	897	1125	1025
	ntrulpr857	level 3	1184	1463	1312
	ntrulpr1277	level 5	1847	2231	1975

References

1. Agence nationale de la sécurité des systèmes d'information (ANSSI): ANSSI views on the Post-Quantum Cryptography transition. Technical report (2022). Accessed 09 July 2023
2. Alagic, G., et al.: Status report on the second round of the nist post-quantum cryptography standardization process. Technical report, National Institute of Standards and Technology, Gaithersburg, Maryland, United States of America (2020)
3. Aragon, N.: Bike - bit flipping key encapsulation (2021). https://bikesuite.org
4. Ashraf, S.A., et al.: Ultra-reliable and low-latency communication for wireless factory automation: from LTE to 5G. In: 2016 IEEE 21st International Conference on Emerging Technologies and Factory Automation (ETFA)
5. Auten, D., et al.: Impact of resource-constrained networks on the performance of NIST round-3 PQC candidates. In: 2021 IEEE 45th Annual Computers, Software, and Applications Conference (COMPSAC)
6. Balasubramanian, A., et al.: Augmenting mobile 3G using WiFi. In: 8th International Conference on Mobile Systems, Applications, and Services. MobiSys '10, ACM (2010)
7. Barton, J., Buchanan, W.J., Abramson, W., Pitropakis, N.: Performance analysis of TLS for quantum robust cryptography on a constrained device (2019). https://doi.org/10.48550/arXiv.1912.12257. Accessed 01 Oct 2023
8. Bellare, M., et al.: A modular approach to the design and analysis of authentication and key exchange protocols. In: ACM Symposium on Theory of Computing (1998)
9. Bernstein, D.J., et al.: NTRU Prime (2020). https://ntruprime.cr.yp.to. Accessed 25 July 2022
10. Biederman, E.W., Nicolas, D.: ip-netns(8). Linux manual page (2021). https://man7.org/linux/man-pages/man8/ip-netns.8.html. Accessed 25 July 2022
11. Bindel, N., Brendel, J., Fischlin, M., Goncalves, B., Stebila, D.: Hybrid key encapsulation mechanisms and authenticated key exchange. In: Ding, J., Steinwandt, R. (eds.) PQCrypto 2019. LNCS, vol. 11505, pp. 206–226. Springer, Cham (2019). https://doi.org/10.1007/978-3-030-25510-7_12
12. Biswal, P., Gnawali, O.: Does QUIC make the web faster? In: 2016 IEEE Global Communications Conference (GLOBECOM), pp. 1–6. IEEE Press, Washington, DC, USA (2016). https://doi.org/10.1109/GLOCOM.2016.7841749
13. Blanton, E., Paxson, D.V., Allman, M.: TCP Congestion Control. RFC 5681, September 2009. https://doi.org/10.17487/RFC5681
14. Borman, D.: RFC 6691: TCP Options and Maximum Segment Size (MSS). Informational RFC6691, Internet Engineering Task Force (IETF), July 2012. https://doi.org/10.17487/rfc6691
15. Bos, J., et al.: CRYSTALS-Kyber: a CCA-secure module-lattice-based KEM. In: 2018 IEEE European Symposium on Security and Privacy (EuroS&P) (2018)
16. Campagna, M., Petcher, A.: Security of hybrid key encapsulation. IACR Cryptol. ePrint Arch. **2020**, 1364 (2020)
17. Castryck, W., Decru, T.: An efficient key recovery attack on SIDH. Cryptology ePrint Archive, August 2022. https://ia.cr/2022/975. Accessed 19 Jan 2023
18. Chen, L., et al.: Report on post-quantum cryptography, vol. 12. US Department of Commerce, National Institute of Standards and Technology, USA (2016)
19. Cook, S., Mathieu, B., Truong, P., Hamchaoui, I.: QUIC: better for what and for whom? In: 2017 IEEE International Conference on Communications (ICC) (2017)

20. Crockett, E., et al.: Prototyping post-quantum and hybrid key exchange and authentication in TLS and SSH. IACR Cryptol. ePrint Arch. **2019**, 858 (2019)
21. D'Anvers, J.P., et al.: Saber: MLWR-based KEM (2022). www.esat.kuleuven.be/cosic/pqcrypto/saber/. Accessed 25 July 2022
22. Easttom, W.: Modern Cryptography: Applied Mathematics for Encryption and Information Security. Springer, Cham (2021). https://doi.org/10.1007/978-3-030-63115-4
23. Easttom, W.: Quantum Computing and Cryptography, pp. 385–390. Springer, Cham (2021). https://doi.org/10.1007/978-3-030-63115-4_19
24. Easttom, W.: SSL/TLS. In: Modern Cryptography, pp. 277–298. Springer, Cham (2021). https://doi.org/10.1007/978-3-030-63115-4_13
25. Eddy, W.: Transmission Control Protocol (TCP). Internet Standard RFC9293, (IETF), USA, August 2022. https://doi.org/10.17487/RFC9293
26. Ehlen, S., et al.: Kryptografie quantensicher gestalten. Grundlagen, Entwicklungen, Empfehlungen. Technical report. BSI-Bro21/01, Bundesamt für Sicherheit in der Informationstechnik (BSI), October 2021. www.bsi.bund.de/SharedDocs/Downloads/DE/BSI/Publikationen/Broschueren/Kryptografie-quantensicher-gestalten.pdf
27. Goel, U., et al.: HTTP/2 performance in cellular networks: poster. In: 22nd Annual International Conference on Mobile Computing and Networking. ACM (2016)
28. Hall, T.A., Keller, S.S.: The fips 186–4 elliptic curve digital signature algorithm validation system (ecdsa2vs). Technical report, National Institute of Standards and Technology. Information Technology Laboratory, May 2010
29. Hoffstein, J., Pipher, J., Silverman, J.H.: NTRU: a ring-based public key cryptosystem. In: Buhler, J.P. (ed.) ANTS 1998. LNCS, vol. 1423, pp. 267–288. Springer, Heidelberg (1998). https://doi.org/10.1007/BFb0054868
30. Ihm, S., Pai, V.S.: Towards understanding modern web traffic. In: Proceedings of the 2011 ACM SIGCOMM Conference on Internet Measurement Conference (2011). https://doi.org/10.1145/2068816.2068845
31. Jao, D., et al.: SIKE - Supersingular Isogeny Key Encapsulation (2022). https://sike.org. Accessed 25 July 2022
32. John, W., Tafvelin, S.: Analysis of internet backbone traffic and header anomalies observed. In: Proceedings of the 7th ACM SIGCOMM Conference on Internet Measurement, October 2007. https://doi.org/10.1145/1298306.1298321
33. Kerrisk, M., et al.: tc(8). Linux manual page (2001). https://man7.org/linux/man-pages/man8/tc.8.html. Accessed 25 July 2022
34. Kerrisk, M., et al.: tc-netem(8). Linux manual page (2011). https://man7.org/linux/man-pages/man8/tc-netem.8.html. Accessed 25 July 2022
35. Kerrisk, M., et al.: veth(4). Linux manual page (2021). https://man7.org/linux/man-pages/man4/veth.4.html. Accessed 25 July 2022
36. Kwiatkowski, K., et al.: Measuring TLS key exchange with post-quantum KEM. record of second PQC standardization conference (2019). https://csrc.nist.gov/CSRC/media/Events/Second-PQC-Standardization-Conference/documents/accepted-papers/kwiatkowski-measuring-tls.pdf. Accessed 01 Dec 2021
37. Lee, H., Kim, D., Kwon, Y.: TLS 1.3 in practice: how TLS 1.3 contributes to the internet. In: Web Conference 2021, pp. 70–79. ACM (2021)
38. Maino, L., et al.: An attack on sidh with arbitrary starting curve. Cryptology ePrint Archive (2022). https://eprint.iacr.org/2022/1026.pdf. Accessed 19 Jan 2023
39. McEliece, R.J.: A public-key cryptosystem based on algebraic. Coding Thv **4244**, 114–116 (1978)

40. Megyesi, P., et al.: How quick is QUIC? In: IEEE International Conference on Communications. Springer (2016). https://doi.org/10.1109/ICC.2016.7510788
41. Melchor, C.A., et al.: HQC (2021). https://pqc-hqc.org. Accessed 25 July 2022
42. O. Saarinen, M.J.: Mobile energy requirements of the upcoming NIST post-quantum cryptography standards. In: 2020 8th IEEE International Conference on Mobile Cloud Computing, Services, and Engineering (MobileCloud) (2020)
43. Ott, D., Peikert, C., et al.: Identifying research challenges in post quantum cryptography migration and cryptographic agility. arXiv preprint arXiv:1909.07353 (2019)
44. Paquin, C., Stebila, D., Tamvada, G.: Benchmarking post-quantum cryptography in TLS. In: Ding, J., Tillich, J.-P. (eds.) PQCrypto 2020. LNCS, vol. 12100, pp. 72–91. Springer, Cham (2020). https://doi.org/10.1007/978-3-030-44223-1_5
45. Paul, S., et al.: Mixed certificate chains for the transition to post-quantum authentication in TLS 1.3. In: ASIA CCS '22: ACM Asia Conference on Computer and Communications Security
46. Postel, J.: RFC 791: Internet Protocol. Internet Standard RFC0791, University of Southern California, USA, September 1981. https://doi.org/10.17487/rfc0791
47. Prantl, T., Iffländer, L., Herrnleben, S., Engel, S., Kounev, S., Krupitzer, C.: Performance impact analysis of securing MQTT using TLS. In: ACM/SPEC International Conference on Performance Engineering. ACM (2021)
48. Rescorla, E.: The Transport Layer Security (TLS) Protocol Version 1.3. RFC 8446, August 2018. https://doi.org/10.17487/RFC8446
49. Romine, C.E.A.: Security requirements for cryptographic modules. Technical report. FIPS PUB 140–3, National Institute of Standards and Technology (2019). https://nvlpubs.nist.gov/nistpubs/FIPS/NIST.FIPS.140-3.pdf
50. Schanck, J.M., et al.: Criteria for selection of public-key cryptographic algorithms for quantum-safe hybrid cryptography. Internet-draft, IETF (2016). https://datatracker.ietf.org/doc/html/draft-whyte-select-pkc-qsh-02
51. Schanck, J.M., et al.: A Transport Layer Security (TLS) Extension For Establishing An Additional Shared Secret. Internet-Draft draft-schanck-tls-additional-keyshare-00, Internet Engineering Task Force (2017). https://datatracker.ietf.org/doc/html/draft-schanck-tls-additional-keyshare-00, work in Progress
52. Schwabe, P., Stebila, D., Wiggers, T.: Post-quantum TLS without handshake signatures. In: Proceedings of the 2020 ACM SIGSAC Conference on Computer and Communications Security (2020). https://doi.org/10.1145/3372297.3423350
53. Shor, P.W.: Algorithms for quantum computation: discrete logarithms and factoring. In: Proceedings 35th Annual Symposium on Foundations of Computer Science. IEEE, Santa Fe, NM, USA (1994). https://doi.org/10.1109/SFCS.1994.365700
54. Sikeridis, D., Kampanakis, P., Devetsikiotis, M.: Assessing the Overhead of Post-Quantum Cryptography in TLS 1.3 and SSH. Association for Computing Machinery, New York, NY, USA (2020). https://doi.org/10.1145/3386367.3431305
55. Stebila, D., Fluhrer, S., Gueron, S.: Hybrid key exchange in TLS 1.3. Internet-Draft draft-ietf-tls-hybrid-design-04, Internet Engineering Task Force, January 2022. https://datatracker.ietf.org/doc/html/draft-ietf-tls-hybrid-design-04
56. Stebila, D., Mosca, M.: Post-quantum key exchange for the internet and the open quantum safe project. In: Avanzi, R., Heys, H. (eds.) SAC 2016. LNCS, vol. 10532, pp. 14–37. Springer, Cham (2017). https://doi.org/10.1007/978-3-319-69453-5_2
57. US Department of Commerce, National Institute of Standards and Technology: Submission Requirements and Evaluation Criteria for the Post-Quantum Cryptography Standardization Process (2016)

58. Wang, P., Bianco, C., Riihijärvi, J., Petrova, M.: Implementation and performance evaluation of the QUIC protocol in Linux kernel. In: 21st ACM International Conference on Modeling, Analysis and Simulation of Wireless and Mobile Systems. ACM (2018)
59. Whyte, W., et al.: Quantum-Safe Hybrid (QSH) Key Exchange for Transport Layer Security (TLS) version 1.3. Internet-Draft draft-whyte-qsh-tls13-06, Internet Engineering Task Force, October 2017. https://datatracker.ietf.org/doc/html/draft-whyte-qsh-tls13-06, work in Progress
60. Yu, Y., et al.: When QUIC meets TCP: an experimental study. In: IEEE 36th International Performance Computing and Communications Conference (IPCCC) (2017). https://doi.org/10.1109/PCCC.2017.8280429
61. Zhang, L., Miranskyy, A.V., Rjaibi, W., Stager, G., Gray, M., Peck, J.: Making existing software quantum safe: lessons learned. preprint arXiv:2110.08661 (2021)
62. Zhu, Q., et al.: Applications of distributed ledger technologies to the internet of things: a survey. ACM Comput. Surv. (2019). https://doi.org/10.1145/3359982

Protecting Private Keys of Dilithium Using Hardware Transactional Memory

Lingjia Meng[1,2], Yu Fu[3], Fangyu Zheng[4(✉)], Ziqiang Ma[5], Mingyu Wang[1,2], Dingfeng Ye[1,2], and Jingqiang Lin[3]

[1] State Key Laboratory of Information Security, Institute of Information Engineering, Chinese Academy of Sciences, Beijing 100085, China
[2] School of Cyber Security, University of Chinese Academy of Sciences, Beijing 100049, China
[3] School of Cyber Security, University of Science and Technology of China, Hefei 230027, Anhui, China
[4] School of Cryptology, University of Chinese Academy of Sciences, Beijing 100049, China
zhengfy1028@hotmail.com
[5] School of Information Engineering, Ningxia University, Yinchuan 750021, Ningxia, China

Abstract. The confidentiality of cryptography keys is necessary in cryptographic implementations. In order to resist memory disclosure attacks that steal sensitive variables such as private keys, various schemes are proposed to implement RSA and ECDSA. Meanwhile, with the migration towards post-quantum cryptography, Dilithium has been considered as the most potential signature algorithm. It involves more and larger sensitive variables, so that existing solutions for traditional cryptographic primitives are unapplicable. In this paper, we employ hardware transactional memory (HTM) to construct the secure environment for Dilithium signing operations, protecting private keys and all other sensitive variables against memory disclosure attacks. Based on the comprehensive sensitivity analysis of variables in the Dilithium algorithm, we restrict the whole sensitive operations in transactional execution regions and adopt the transaction-splitting technology for efficiency. We implemented the prototype using Intel TSX, demonstrating its security against memory disclosure attacks and acceptable performance overheads. For example, the security-enhancement implementation of Dilithium3, which is recommended by NIST, achieves a factor of 0.75 compared to the throughput of reference implementations.

Keywords: Dilithium · Protection · Hardware transactional memory · Memory disclosure attacks

1 Introduction

Cryptography builds the foundation of cyberspace security. It requires the confidentiality of cryptographic keys to protect sensitive data. However, in conventional cryptographic software implementations, private keys appear in the main

© The Author(s), under exclusive license to Springer Nature Switzerland AG 2023
E. Athanasopoulos and B. Mennink (Eds.): ISC 2023, LNCS 14411, pp. 288–306, 2023.
https://doi.org/10.1007/978-3-031-49187-0_15

memory as ordinary variables. Therefore, they are vulnerable to different kinds of memory disclosure attacks, including software memory attacks which exploit vulnerabilities (e.g., the OpenSSL HeartBleed attack [7]) and physical memory attacks that directly access the RAM to obtain private keys (e.g., cold-boot attacks [14]).

In recent years, researchers have already proposed a variety of cryptographic key protection solutions [8–10,12,13,18,23,29] to resist cold-boot attacks and other memory disclosure attacks. These schemes make use of registers, cache, or advanced hardware features in processors to carefully manipulate sensitive values such as private keys. Therefore, the sensitive values will not appear in the main memory or RAM chips in the form of plain text, thereby providing secure cryptographic computing services against memory disclosure attacks. Among them, the most general and practical schemes are the register-based solutions [8–10,23,29] and protections [13,18] based on the hardware transactional memory (HTM), which have been successfully applied in popular signature primitives such as RSA and ECDSA.

However, with the development of the quantum computer, RSA and ECDSA will provide the required security no longer. Currently, NIST has announced three Post-Quantum Cryptography signature schemes for standardization. Among them, Dilithium stands out because of its strong security and excellent performance with the same security level, thus recommended by NIST as the mainstream signature scheme [24]. Compared to traditional signature algorithms such as RSA and ECDSA, the lattice-based Dilithium signature scheme has a larger private key size and a more complex signing process, therefore it faces more severe challenges in ensuring the security and efficiency of the Dilithium's implementation.

In this paper, we adopt hardware transactional memory to protect private keys and all other sensitive values that exist in Dilithium signing procedure against memory disclosure attacks. Meanwhile, we utilize transaction splitting to ensure that our proposed HTM-based solution is efficient and practical. The main contributions of this work are as follows:

(1) We perform a comprehensive variable sensitivity analysis about Dilithium, systematically analyzing the sensitive parameters and determining the protection boundary of sensitive operations. Based on the results, we found that the register-based schemes cannot meet the storage requirements of the sensitive variables in Dilithium, while the HTM-based protection is effective.

(2) We propose a solution to protect sensitive variables and operations in the Dilithium scheme based on the hardware transactional memory. Furthermore, we also divide the sensitive operations of Dilithium and employ the transaction splitting technology to "break the whole into parts" to improve the overall performance.

(3) We construct the prototype, demonstrating its security against memory disclosure attacks through confirmatory experiments. Performance evaluation shows that, for different security levels 2, 3, and 5, our solution achieves

a factor of 0.80, 0.75, and 0.66 compared to the throughput of Dilithium's reference signature implementation.

The remainder of this paper is organized as follows. Section 2 introduces the background about Dilithium and related cryptographic key protection solutions. We describe the design and implementation of the HTM-based protection for Dilithium in Sects. 3 and 4. Section 5 evaluates the security and performance. Finally, we draw the conclusion in Sect. 6.

2   Background and Related Works

In this section, we first give a brief overview of the Dilithium signature algorithm. This is followed by an introduction of typical cryptography key protection solutions based on register and hardware transactional memory respectively.

2.1   Dilithium

Dilithium is a digital signature algorithm that has been selected by the NIST Post-Quantum Cryptography standardization organization as the primary signature scheme for standardization. Its security is based on two hard problems over module lattices, namely, the MLWE (Module Learning With Errors) problem and the SelfTargetMSIS (Module Short Integer Solution) problem [17]. The design of Dilithium is mainly based on Bai-Galbraith scheme [2] proposed by Bai and Galbraith in 2014, which improves the "Fiat-Shamir with Aborts" approach [20,21]. It is worth noting that the pseudocode presented in this paper is the implementation version of Dilithium, which provides an alternative way of decomposing and computing the hints compared to the reference signature scheme. Dilithium offers three different parameter sets, namely Dilithium2, Dilithium3, and Dilithium5, correspond to three NIST security levels 2, 3, and 5 respectively. Table 1 details the Dilithium parameter sets for different security levels. We shall just simply describe the key generation and signing algorithms in the following paragraphs. For a comprehensive specification of the scheme, we refer the reader to the original proposal [6].

Key Generation. The key generation procedure is listed in Algorithm 1. Firstly, a bit string ζ is randomly generated, and placed into the hash function H to derive three seeds, namely ρ, ς, and K. Next, a $k*l$ polynomial matrix $\mathbf{A}$ is generated from seed ρ. Two secret vectors $\mathbf{s_1}$ and $\mathbf{s_2}$ of lengths l and k are sampled uniformly from ς. Then, the vector $\mathbf{t} = \mathbf{As_1} + \mathbf{s_2}$ is calculated, which is also the instance of the LWE problem on which Dilithium relies, i.e. $\mathbf{s_1}$ and $\mathbf{s_2}$ are hard to calculate given $\mathbf{A}$ and $\mathbf{t}$. Aiming at reducing the size of the public key, $\mathbf{t}$ is split into two parts: high order bits as $\mathbf{t_1}$ which is made public, and low order bits as $\mathbf{t_0}$ which is kept secret. Similarly, matrix $\mathbf{A}$ is also replaced by the small seed ρ, which forms the public key with $\mathbf{t_1}$. Finally, tr is computed by hashing $\rho \parallel \mathbf{t_1}$. Therefore, the output of key generation is the public key $pk = (\rho, \mathbf{t_1})$ and the secret key $sk = (\rho, K, tr, \mathbf{s_1}, \mathbf{s_2}, \mathbf{t_0})$.

Table 1. Overview of the Dilithium parameter sets.

NIST Security Level	2	3	5
q [modulus]	$2^{23} - 2^{13} + 1$	$2^{23} - 2^{13} + 1$	$2^{23} - 2^{13} + 1$
(k, l) [dimensions of $\mathbf{A}$]	$(4, 4)$	$(6, 5)$	$(8, 7)$
d [dropped bits from $\mathbf{t}$]	13	13	13
γ_1 [$\mathbf{y}$ coefficient range]	2^{17}	2^{19}	2^{19}
γ_2 [low-order rounding range]	$(q-1)/88$	$(q-1)/32$	$(q-1)/32$
τ [hamming weight of c]	39	49	60
β [range of $c\mathbf{s_1}$ and $c\mathbf{s_2}$]	78	196	120
Repetitions	4.25	5.1	3.85
public key size (in bytes)	1312	1952	2592
secret key size (in bytes)	2528	4000	4864
signature size (in bytes)	2420	3293	4595

Algorithm 1: Dilithium Key Generation(taken from [6]).

Output: A public/secret key pair (pk, sk).

1   $\zeta \leftarrow \{0, 1\}^{256}$
2   $(\rho, \varsigma, K) = H(\zeta)$
3   $\mathbf{A} = \text{ExpandA}(\rho)$
4   $(\mathbf{s_1}, \mathbf{s_2}) = \text{ExpandS}(\varsigma)$
5   $\mathbf{t} = \mathbf{As_1} + \mathbf{s_2}$
6   $(\mathbf{t_1}, \mathbf{t_0}) = \text{Power2Round}(\mathbf{t}, d)$
7   $tr = H(\rho \parallel \mathbf{t_1})$
8   **return** $pk = (\rho, \mathbf{t_1})$, $sk = (\rho, K, tr, \mathbf{s_1}, \mathbf{s_2}, \mathbf{t_0})$

Signature Generation. Algorithm 2 depicts Dilithium's signing procedure. The algorithm takes the secret key sk and the message M as the input. Initially, the matrix $\mathbf{A}$ is reconstructed by seed ρ, and M and tr are hashed to generate a fixed-length bit string μ. Dilithium signing has two options, the default deterministic signing and the other randomized signing admired in situations where the side-channel attacks [25,26] are taken seriously or the signer does not want to expose the message. The implementational difference between the two versions occurs on Line 4 where the seed ρ' is either produced using μ together with K (for deterministic signing) or generated completely at random (in randomized signing). Next, the masking vector $\mathbf{y}$ is sampled using the seed ρ' and a rejection counter κ whose initial value is set to 0. The vector $\mathbf{w} = \mathbf{Ay}$ is then decomposed into $\mathbf{w_1}$ and $\mathbf{w_0}$, where the high order bits $\mathbf{w_1}$ is used to compute the challenge $\tilde{c}$. Meanwhile, $\tilde{c}$ is also converted into a polynomial c, which participates in the calculation of $\mathbf{z}$ and $\mathbf{r_0}$ together with secret vectors $\mathbf{s_1}$ and $\mathbf{s_2}$. In order to guarantee the security and correctness of the signature, a boundary check on $\mathbf{z}$ and $\mathbf{r_0}$ is necessary. After the check passes, the hint $\mathbf{h}$ to make up

---

Algorithm 2: Dilithium Signature Generation(taken from [6]).

Input: Secret key sk and message M.
Output: Signature $\sigma = \text{Sign}(sk, M)$.

1   $\mathbf{A} = \text{ExpandA}(\rho)$
2   $\mu = \text{H}(tr \parallel M)$
3   $\kappa = 0$, $(\mathbf{z}, \mathbf{h}) = \perp$
4   $\rho' = \text{H}(K \parallel \mu)$ (or $\rho' \leftarrow \{0,1\}^{384}$ for randomized signing)
5   **while** $(\mathbf{z}, \mathbf{h}) = \perp$ **do**
6     $\mathbf{y} = \text{ExpandMask}(\rho', \kappa)$
7     $\mathbf{w} = \mathbf{A}\mathbf{y}$
8     $(\mathbf{w_1}, \mathbf{w_0}) = \text{Decompose}(\mathbf{w}, 2\gamma_2)$
9     $\tilde{c} = \text{H}(\mu \parallel \mathbf{w_1})$
10     $c = \text{SampleInBall}(\tilde{c})$
11     $\mathbf{z} = \mathbf{y} + c\mathbf{s_1}$
12     $\mathbf{r_0} = \mathbf{w_0} - c\mathbf{s_2}$
13   **if** $\|\mathbf{z}\|_\infty \geq \gamma_1 - \beta$ *or* $\|\mathbf{r_0}\|_\infty \geq \gamma_2 - \beta$ **then**
14 | $(\mathbf{z}, \mathbf{h}) = \perp$
15   **else**
16       $\mathbf{h} = \text{MakeHint}(\mathbf{r_0}, c, \mathbf{t_0}, \mathbf{w_1}, \gamma_2)$
17   **if** $\|c\mathbf{t_0}\|_\infty \geq \gamma_2$ *or the # of 1's in* $\mathbf{h} > \omega$ **then**
18 | $(\mathbf{z}, \mathbf{h}) = \perp$
19   **end**
20   **end**
21     $\kappa = \kappa + l$
22 **end**
23 **return** $\sigma = (\tilde{c}, \mathbf{z}, \mathbf{h})$

---

the lost information of $\mathbf{t_0}$ in the verification phase is calculated as described in Algorithm 2. Similarly, there are two additional checks about $c\mathbf{t_0}$ and $\mathbf{h}$ to be done here. If all conditions are met, the signature $\sigma = (\tilde{c}, \mathbf{z}, \mathbf{h})$ is generated successfully. Otherwise, the signing process needs to be repeated and a new nonce $\mathbf{y}$ will be generated.

2.2 Cryptographic Key Protection Solutions

Register-Based Solutions. Memory disclosure attacks can directly obtain the cryptographic key from the main memory or memory chips. A natural idea is to perform the sensitive cryptographic operations only inside the processor, without using memory. Therefore, register-based solutions [8–10,23,29] have been proposed.

TRESOR [23] selects the privileged debug registers for long-term storage of the symmetric key, and completes the AES encryption and decryption only with the participation of the registers. Compared with symmetric schemes, asymmetric schemes require more space to store the private key and intermediate states. But the privileged registers cannot meet the corresponding space requirements. Therefore, register-based public-key solutions implement the structure of

"Key Encryption Key (KEK)", the private key and other sensitive variables are encrypted with the AES master key and stored in the memory. Only when participating in sensitive operations, these values are decrypted in registers temporarily. Based on this creative idea, PRIME [10], RegRSA [29], and VIRSA [9] have completed the secure and efficient RSA solutions; while RegKey [8] is a register-based ECC enhanced implementation.

HTM-Based Solutions. Hardware transactional memory (HTM) [5,15] is originally proposed to eliminate expensive software synchronization mechanisms, thereby improving the performance of parallel computing. Intel TSX [16] adds hardware transactional memory support based on the caches. Only when a transaction succeeds, the operation results are submitted to the main memory; otherwise, all the performed operations are rolled back. In detail, transactional memory is typically divided into a write-set and a read-set [11], which are deployed in the L1 cache and L3 cache respectively. For a read-set of the transactional execution, the read operation from other threads or processes is allowed while the write operation will make the transaction abort. For a write-set of the transactional execution, both the read and write operations from others make the transaction abort.

Cryptographic key protection schemes can be constructed based on HTM. Mimosa [13,18] utilizes Intel TSX to achieve a secure RSA cryptosystem, which ensures that sensitive values such as private key only exist as cleartext in the exclusive cache at the core of the process (i.e. the L1D Cache). When the RSA private key does not participate in cryptographic operations, it is encrypted with the master key and stored in memory; while the master key is located in the privilege registers. In the computing phase, Mimosa creates a transaction for RSA private key operation, in which the private key is decrypted and the RSA operation is performed. In addition, Mimosa also proposes a transaction splitting mechanism to reduce the time-consuming cryptographic operation within a single transaction, thereby reducing the overhead caused by transaction rollback. This allows Mimosa to mitigate DoS attacks caused by cache contention while maintaining good performance. Some other schemes [4,11,28] leverage HTM to defend against cache side-channel attacks, which also enhances the robustness of the private key.

Comparison Between Two Solutions. The register-based scheme has a smaller security boundary, but due to the limited register space, it may not be suitable for more complex algorithms. Moreover, the register-based scheme has poor scalability, and the implementation based on assembly language has higher requirements for developers. In contrast, the HTM-based scheme has higher practicability, it can be easily migrated to the realization of complex algorithms due to the larger space provided by the cache.

3 Key Protection for Dilithium

In this section, we briefly discuss the challenges faced by key protection for Dilithium, prove the infeasibility of the register-based solution through quantitative variable sensitivity analysis, and then give an overview of our HTM-based protection scheme.

3.1 Technical Challenges

Compared with traditional asymmetric primitives such as RSA and ECDSA, Dilithium has a more complicated cryptographic key structure and signature logic. Therefore, when considering register-based or HTM-based protection of sensitive values such as private keys in the Dilithium algorithm to achieve secure and efficient signature operations, the following challenges need to be addressed.

(1) More sensitive variables need to be considered and protected. In RSA and ECDSA, there are limited variables related to the private key. Therefore, they do not need too much space to store these variables. Obviously, more and larger sensitive variables are involved in the Dilithium scheme. Once the values are leaked, the adversary could deduce the long-term secret key. Therefore, all sensitive variables must be protected against memory disclosure attacks.

(2) Hardening more complex sensitive operations will result in greater performance overhead. If we place the Dilithium signature operations in an atomic transaction for protection, it will waste lots of clock cycles and lead to a performance bottleneck. Because the long execution time and huge memory usage requirements will lead to lots of transaction aborts, the transactions cannot be successfully committed. Therefore, how to improve efficiency is also an important challenge.

3.2 Variable Sensitivity Analysis for Dilithium

We first discuss the public and secret key fields in Dilithium. Obviously, the public key $pk = (\rho, \mathbf{t_1})$ is non-sensitive in the whole scheme, and any participant or even the adversary can obtain it publicly. Similarly, the matrix $\mathbf{A}$ is also public, which is derived from the seed ρ and needs to be regenerated during both signing and verification. The secret key $sk = (\rho, K, tr, \mathbf{s_1}, \mathbf{s_2}, \mathbf{t_0})$ contains six entries. Among them, the seed ρ which appears at the intersection of the public and secret key need not be protected. tr is also non-sensitive since it is a hash of the public key, which does not contain any secret information. Moreover, the vector $\mathbf{t_0}$ in sk is also judged as the public variable, which can be leaked. Actually, the entire LWE vector $\mathbf{t}$ is publicly available in Dilithium's basic scheme [2]; the purpose of decomposing $\mathbf{t}$ into $\mathbf{t_1}$ and $\mathbf{t_0}$ is only to reduce the size of the public key, not involving security. The rest of the variables in the secret key (i.e., K, $\mathbf{s_1}$, $\mathbf{s_2}$) must be considered as sensitive, which must be protected against the memory disclosure that if leaked, an adversary can use them to forge signatures. Next, we conduct a detailed analysis of sensitive variables involved in the key generation

Table 2. Variable sensitivity analysis for Dilithium.

Item/Procedure	Sensitive	Non-Sensitive
Public key pk	–	$\rho, \mathbf{t}_1$
Secret key sk	$K, \mathbf{s}_1, \mathbf{s}_2$	$\rho, tr, \mathbf{t}_0$
KeyGen	$\zeta, \varsigma, K, \mathbf{s}_1, \mathbf{s}_2$	$\rho, tr, \mathbf{A}, \mathbf{t}, \mathbf{t}_1, \mathbf{t}_0$
Sign	$\rho', \mathbf{y}, \mathbf{w}, \mathbf{w}_0, \mathbf{z}, \mathbf{r}_0, K, \mathbf{s}_1, \mathbf{s}_2$	$\rho, tr, \mathbf{A}, \mu, \mathbf{w}_1, \tilde{c}, c, \mathbf{h}$

and signing process, which may cause the leakage of long-term secrets. Table 2 lists the sensitive and non-sensitive variables in the whole Dilithium scheme.

In the key generation process, the seed ς must be regarded as a sensitive variable, since it will derive the long-term secrets $\mathbf{s}_1$ and $\mathbf{s}_2$ directly. Similarly, the variable ζ also needs to be protected, because it can act as an initial seed to generate subsequent secret values, including ς and K. Other values (e.g., $\mathbf{A}$ and $\mathbf{t}$) that appear during the key generation are considered as non-sensitive variables, and thus can be made public and do not need to be protected against memory disclosure.

The signing procedure's sensitivity analysis is more complex than the key generation's sensitivity analysis. At first, μ is a non-sensitive variable, since it is the hash of the public value tr and the message M. The masking vector $\mathbf{y}$ is sensitive. The reason is that the secret vector $\mathbf{s}_1$ can be computed by the formula $\mathbf{z} = \mathbf{y} + c\mathbf{s}_1$ (Line 11 in Algorithm 2) when $\mathbf{y}$ is leaked [22], given a valid signature $\sigma = (\tilde{c}, \mathbf{z}, \mathbf{h})$. Therefore, the vector $\mathbf{w}$ must also be protected to prevent the adversary from recovering $\mathbf{y}$ through solving the system of equations: $\mathbf{w} = \mathbf{Ay}$. Considering backward the seed ρ' to obtain the sensitive vector $\mathbf{y}$, it must be identified as the protected variable, whether it is generated deterministically or randomly. Next, we analysis two composing parts of $\mathbf{w}$ (i.e., $\mathbf{w}_1$ and $\mathbf{w}_0$). The vector $\mathbf{w}_1$ does not contain more information than the signature itself when the signature is generated successfully. In fact, the verifier needs to recalculate $\mathbf{w}_1$ from the signature σ. Therefore, $\mathbf{w}_1$ does not require additional protection. The sensitivity determination about $\mathbf{w}_0$ is similar to $\mathbf{y}$. we directly draw on the theoretical achievements from [3] here, which demonstrates a practical attack leveraging $\mathbf{w}_0$'s leakage to recovery the secret vector $\mathbf{s}_2$. At last, there is a discussion of the signature output and bound checks. The challenge $\tilde{c}$, c and the hint $\mathbf{h}$ are all non-sensitive. The condition judgments about them are for correctness only. However, $\mathbf{z}$ and $\mathbf{r}_0$ must remain protected until the bound checks about them have passed. After that, they do not leak any valid information.[1]

Infeasibility of Register-Based Solution. As analyzed above, Dilithium contains a large number of sensitive variables that need to be protected, in addition to the original private key members. Once these variables are leaked, the secret information could be deduced by the adversary. Table 3 shows the sizes

---

[1] Refer to Literature [1] for more detailed explanation.

Table 3. The sizes of sensitive parameters in Dilithium's signing.

Sensitive variable's size (in bytes)	Dilithium2	Dilithium3	Dilithium5
K	32	32	32
s_1	4096	5120	7168
s_2	4096	6144	8192
ρ'	48	48	48
y	4096	5120	7168
w	4096	6144	8192
w_0	4096	6144	8192
z	4096	5120	7168
r_0	4096	6144	8192
Total	28752	40016	54352

of sensitive variables[2] involved in the Dilithium signature generation procedure under different NIST security levels. When the security levels are 2, 3, and 5, the maximum size of a single sensitive variable reaches 4096, 6144, and 8192 bytes, respectively. In detail, these variables refer to sensitive vectors s_2, w, w_0, and $\tilde{r}$, each of which stores a polynomial vector of length k, and the single polynomial occupies 1024 bytes. Moreover, the total sizes of all sensitive values included in the Dilithium signing phase have reached 28752, 40016, and 54352 bytes respectively. Therefore, these sensitive variables need to take up a large amount of storage space actually.

The register-based asymmetric solutions rely on user-accessible registers that exist in the system as secure data buffers for storing secret values, and carefully implement the RSA and ECC instances. It should be noted that these registers contain general-purpose registers and vector registers. RegRSA [29] has investigated the registers available in commodity processors, which have a total size of 704 bytes on an Intel Haswell CPU. The latest processors support the AVX-512 extension, thus providing thirty-two registers with a bandwidth of 512-bit, represented as ZMM0 - ZMM31. Overall, the latest available register space includes sixteen 64-bit general-purpose registers, eight 64-bit MM registers, and thirty-two 512-bit ZMM registers, and the total space reaches 2240 bytes.

According to our statistics of Dilithium's sensitive parameters and effective register space, we can confirm the following facts: the entire available register space in the system is not even enough to accommodate the single secret vector (e.g., the s_1 or s_2), let alone places all of the sensitive variables securely. Therefore, we cannot complete the protection of private keys and other sensitive variables in the Dilithium scheme based on the pure register's implementation. However, in the HTM-based solution, the transactional memory uses L1D Cache

---

[2] The sizes of sensitive variables s_1 and s_2 listed here refer to the space occupied by the form of the polynomial vector when participating in multiplication calculations, while s_1 and s_2 in the private key are actually in compressed byte form.

as the secure storage area, the size of which is generally 32KB. The space is sufficient since it can store several values, and sensitive variables do not appear in the transaction's write set simultaneously. Therefore, we will build key protection for Dilithium based on the HTM in our solution.

3.3 HTM-Based Key Protection

The target of this work is to achieve complete sensitive data protection for Dilithium's signing operations with the help of transactional memory mechanism, while maintaining efficiency as much as possible.

Goal. To prevent software memory attacks and cold-boot attacks, all of the sensitive information appearing in the entire crypto-system (including the AES master key, Dilithium's secret key, and intermediate sensitive variables that exist in the signing operations) needs to be strictly limited to the scope of the write set of the transaction (that is, the L1D Cache), and must not appear in the main memory or RAM chips in the form of plaintext.

Threat Model and Assumptions. First, the adversaries have the ability to launch different forms of memory disclosure attacks. Specifically, the attacker can exploit software vulnerabilities to read memory data or launch cold-boot attacks through physical access. Second, we assume that HTM can be implemented correctly to provide its claimed security capabilities. We also assume that the OS kernel is trustworthy, thus users can derive the AES master key securely during the initialization. Finally, since our solution borrows from TRESOR [23] to protect the master key, it also needs to follow the assumptions made by TRESOR, such as prohibiting system calls from accessing debug registers.

System Architecture. Similar to all previous register-based or HTM-based schemes, our solution adopts the KEK structure, which contains the two-level key structure of "master key - Dilithium secret key". The AES master key is generated when the system boots and then stored in the debug registers securely. Sensitive Dilithium private key members are symmetrically encrypted offline by using the AES master key. When participating in the signature operation, the private key is decrypted. Then, the decrypted private key is utilized to build the signing context and complete the final signature generation during the transaction execution. After that, the system cleans up all sensitive intermediate variables and returns the signature result.

The architecture of the system is shown in Fig. 1, along with the workflow. Our solution's operation can be divided into two phases, namely the **initialization phase** and the **protection computing phase**. The initialization phase is performed only once during the system initialization, responsible for initializing the AES master key and preparing computing resources. The protection computing phase is invoked on each Dilithium signing request and used to execute Dilithium's signature generation task. All sensitive operations during the protection computing phase are protected by transaction memory and do not reveal any secret values.

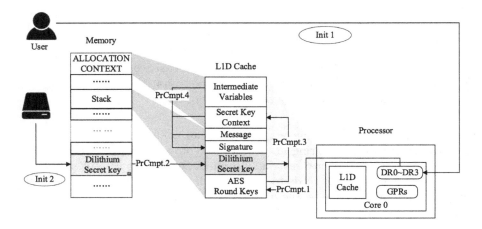

Fig. 1. The system architecture of key protection for Dilithium.

(1) Initialization Phase. This phase consists of two steps.

1) Init.1: During the system boot, the user enters a password to derive the AES master key, which is then stored in each CPU core's privileged debug registers. All intermediate variables need to be erased.
2) Init.2: The file containing the encrypted Dilithium's private key is loading from the hard disks into the main memory. The private key is generated in a secure offline environment and then symmetrically encrypted with the AES master key.

(2) Protection Computing Phase. In the protection computing phase, our solution creates the transaction execution environment for Dilithium's signing operations, in which the Dilithium secret key is decrypted. And then the decrypted key participates in the signing process. Our solution will perform the following steps:

1) Prepare: HTM starts tracking memory accesses in the cache (maintaining the read/write sets).
2) PrCmpt.1: Loading the AES master key to the cache from the debug registers, the round keys are then derived in the L1D cache.
3) PrCmpt.2: Loading the ciphertext Dilithium secret key to the L1D cache from the memory
4) PrCmpt.3: Using the master key to decrypt the secret key and generate the private key context.
5) PrCmpt.4: Using the private key context for requesting signing operations. The details will be covered in the following part.

6) PrCmpt.5: Clearing all sensitive variables that exist in registers and cache.
7) Commit: Completing the signing process and returning the signature results.

Transaction Splitting. Next, we focus on the transactional execution for Dilithium signing (i.e., PrCmpt.4 in the protection computing phase). Empirically, putting the entire signature generation procedure into a single transaction is almost impossible to realize. Since it involves plenty of time-consuming and memory-intensive operations such as polynomial multiplication, number theoretic transform (NTT) operations, and so on. In fact, we have also tried to implement this situation, and the result is unsurprisingly failed.

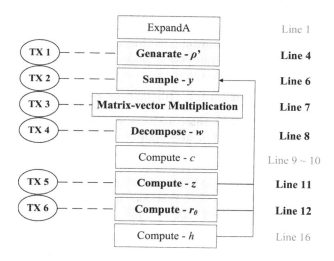

Fig. 2. Transaction splitting for Dilithium signing. The rectangles in the figure represent the basic operations in the Dilithium signature scheme. The shaded ones represent sensitive operations that need to be placed in the transaction. The mark (e.g., Line 4) on the right side of the figure indicates the specific line number in Algorithm 2 corresponding to the operation.

In order to provide an effective signature service with HTM, we must consider breaking the Dilithium signing procedure into several independent sensitive operations and placing them in different small transactions. Non-sensitive operations simply run in a normal manner. Based on the variable sensitivity analysis for Dilithium mentioned above, we determined the six sensitive operations in Dilithium signing logic (that is, the operations that take sensitive variables as operation objects or operation results). For each of these sensitive operations, we need to build an atomic transaction. Figure 2 shows the transaction splitting for Dilithium signing. Therefore, Dilithium signing is split into six transactions as follows.

TX1: Generation of the seed ρ'.
TX2: Sampling of temporary secret vector $\mathbf{y}$.
TX3: The matrix-vector multiplication $\mathbf{w} = \mathbf{Ay}$.
TX4: Decomposing operation against the vector $\mathbf{w}$.
TX5: Computation of $\mathbf{z}$, which involves the private $\mathbf{s_1}$ and secret vector $\mathbf{y}$.
TX6: Computation of $\mathbf{r_0}$ using the private $\mathbf{s_2}$ and secret vector $\mathbf{w_0}$.

4   Implementation

In order to complete the comprehensive protection of Dilithium's private key and sensitive variables in our design, and realize secure and efficient signing operations, we implement our HTM-based solution as a Linux kernel module. In this section, we introduce the implementation details of our solution, mainly including transactional execution for Dilithium's signature generation, the integration into Linux kernel space, and the protection of the AES master key.

4.1   Transactional Execution for Dilithium's Signing

HTM Primitive. We propose Intel TSX as an instance of HTM to build a transactional execution environment for Dilithium's signing against memory disclosure attacks. Specifically, we choose the Restricted Transaction Memory primitive as the programming interface of HTM, where the _xbegin function is called to start a transaction, and the _xend function is used to commit the transaction. The area between the two functions is the atomic region of transactional execution. Of course, our solution is applicable to HTM features on other platforms.

Listing 1.1. Pseudo code for the transactional execution.

```
while(1) {
  if(_xbegin() == _XBEGIN_STARTED)
    break;
  retry++;
  if(retry == THRESHOLD)
    goto fail;
}
  // sensitive operations in here;
  _xend();
fail:
  failure handler;
```

Transactional Execution and Splitting. Using Dilithium's reference implementation[3] as a basis, we provide security enhancements for Dilithium's signing,

---
[3] https://github.com/pq-crystals/dilithium.

where the key protection techniques described in Sect. 3 are applied. Our prototype implements the default deterministic signing version. We cannot place the entire signature logic in a single transaction. Therefore, we will divide the signing operation into several sub-processes based on the previous analysis of sensitive operations and place them in atomic transactions respectively. Since the abort may still occur, we will repeatedly call _xbegin in a loop to start the transaction, and only when the transaction is successfully committed or the number of failures reaches the threshold, the loop will exit. The logic for a single transaction is shown in Listing 1.1. In addition, intermediate sensitive variables need to be encrypted using the master key with the help of AES-NI hardware instructions before the small transaction commits. In the specific implementation, we also made a slight adjustment to the original code to fit into the transaction, avoiding calling non-sensitive functions (such as the generation of public matrix **A**) in the transactional region.

4.2   Integration into Linux Kernel

Kernel Module. We implement the transactional Dilithium signing as a char module and integrate it into the Linux kernel. This kernel module provides secure Dilithium signing services to user space. It depends on the `ioctl` system call to receive the messages to be signed and the private key in the form of ciphertext from the user-space invoker, complete the signing operation, and then return the signature to the user application.

Heap Allocation for Matrixes and Vectors. In the reference implementation, the public matrix **A** and all vectors (e.g., **y** and **w**) are defined in the form of local variables, which are stored in the stack. However, the size of the kernel stack is only 16KB, which cannot accommodate all of the parameters. Once the variables exceed the size of the kernel stack, a segmentation fault will be triggered. Therefore, these variables cannot be defined as local variables in the kernel module. It is necessary to allocate the memory space on the heap through the `vmalloc` function.

Disabling Interrupts and Kernel Preemption. Intel TSX provides atomicity guarantees for sensitive operations. However, Dilithium's signing procedure is time-consuming, and it will be interrupted by frequent context switches, which causes the transaction aborts. Therefore, it is necessary to disable interrupts and kernel preemption by calling `local_irq_save` and `preempt_disable` in the transactional region to improve the success rate of transaction commit. Correspondingly, when the transactional execution ends, the interrupts and kernel preemption need to be re-enabled by calling `local_irq_restore` and `preempt_enable`.

4.3   Protection for AES Master Key

We refer to the general method in TRESOR [23] to derive and protect the master key. During the system initialization, the user inputs the password to produce the

AES key and places it in the debug register on each CPU core. Since debug registers are used as the long-term storage unit of the master key, it needs to be guaranteed that other processes will not access them except the transactional signing tasks. We modified the relevant functions to ensure that neither user-mode nor normal kernel-mode processes can directly access the privileged debug registers. The functions include: `ptrace_set_debugreg` and `ptrace_get_debugreg` (blocking the `ptrace` system call), `native_set_debugreg` and `native_get_debugreg` (disabling the access from the kernel).

5   Evaluation

In this section, we conduct a security evaluation on our HTM-based solution for Dilithium signing and then evaluate the performance of the prototype. The experimental platform is Intel Core i7-6700 CPU with 3.4 GHz, 16 GB memory, and the operating system is Ubuntu 16.04 64-bit.

5.1   Security

Resistance to Memory Disclosure Attacks. Our solution relies on hardware transactional memory to provide security enhancements. First, all sensitive operations in the Dilithium signature process are running in atomic transactions, and the whole sensitive variables are encrypted outside the transactions. During cryptographic operations (i.e., transactional execution), other threads cannot obtain the private key or intermediate sensitive variables in plaintext except Dilithium's signature computing thread. Therefore, it can defend against software memory attacks. Second, due to the implementation characteristics of HTM, the entire signature operation is limited to the write set of the transaction. Sensitive values such as the private key only exist in the L1D Cache and will not appear in the RAM chips, thus cold-boot attacks can also be resisted.

We also introduce experimental validations to verify that our solution can resist memory disclosure. We perform Dilithium's signing in a loop and use the `lime` tool to dump the memory image. We used `hexdump` to look for known private key fragments in the memory image and can not obtain a binary string that overlaps for more than 4 bytes with the private key.

Resistance to Timing Attacks and Cache Side-Channel Attacks. We first consider the timing attacks. Dilithium adopts the design of uniform sampling, and all other basic operations such as polynomial multiplication and rounding are implemented in constant time in our reference implementation. In addition, the encryption and decryption of private keys and other sensitive variables are implemented using AES-NI, while AES-NI is resistant to timing attacks [23]. Therefore, timing attacks can be effectively prevented. Moreover, our solution performs the Dilithium signing calculations in HTM-backed transactions and ensures that all sensitive data resides in the L1D Cache during the execution. This prevents the attackers from distinguishing the timing differences between cache hits and misses accurately, thereby mitigating cache side-channel attacks [19,27].

5.2 Performance

We use the number of clock cycles consumed by a single signing procedure as the performance indicator according to the method officially demonstrated by Dilithium. The signing operation was repeated 1000 times and we chose the average value as the result. The specific results are shown in Table 4, which shows the cycles of the reference implementation of Dilithium and the implementation protected by Intel TSX under three different security levels. Although we try to reduce the abort rate as much as possible, transactional execution still has a certain probability of failure. Once any of these transactions abort, Dilithium's signing will fail. We considered the success rate of signing when comparing performance between two implementations. Therefore, the actual results in our solution should be the ratio of the original cycles to the success rate of signing. For different security levels Dilithium2, Dilithium3, and Dilithium5, our solution achieves a factor of 0.80, 0.75, and 0.66 compared to the throughout of Dilithium's reference implementation respectively.

Table 4. Performance comparison between reference implementation (denoted as ref) and our solution (denoted as htm).

Security Level	Cycles (ref)	Cycles (htm)	Success Rate (htm)	Ratio^a (ref/htm)
Dilithium2	1180137	1455316	98.7%	0.80
Dilithium3	1867274	2400121	96.9%	0.75
Dilithium5	2252741	3058802	90.1%	0.66

^{a} The calculation of Ratio is as follows: Ratio = Cycles(ref)/(Cycles(htm)/Success Rate(htm)).

We briefly analyze the experimental results. The operations that can introduce performance overhead in our solution include: 1) the transmission of messages, encrypted private keys, and signature results between the user space and the kernel space; 2) the encryption and decryption operations performed on sensitive variables in the single transaction; and 3) the transaction's rollback operation. Meanwhile, disabling interrupts and kernel preemption in kernel space and the transaction's atomic execution will also reduce the frequency of context switching during the signing process and improve performance to a certain extent. When the security level is 2 or 3, every small transactions will be submitted with a higher success rate without too many retries. Therefore, the performance overhead introduced by our solution is lower compared to the reference implementation. When the security level reaches 5, the sensitive values will occupy more space, thereby increasing the probability of transaction abort. Plenty of clock cycles are consumed in the transaction's rollback operation, therefore, greater performance overhead will be introduced.

6   Conclusion

The Post-Quantum Cryptography software implementation represented by the Dilithium scheme will be widely used in the future, but its private keys are vulnerable to various forms of memory disclosure attacks. In this paper, we thoroughly analyze all the sensitive variables involved in Dilithium's signing process and prove that the register-based solution cannot provide effective protection. Then, we propose the HTM-based key protection solution to execute the Dilithium signing operation transactionally and reduce the performance overhead by transaction splitting. We implemented the prototype with Intel TSX, and the evaluation results show that it has comparable efficiency to Dilithium's reference implementation.

Acknowledgments. We would like to thank the anonymous reviewers for their valuable comments and suggestions. This work is supported by the National Key R&D Program of China (No. 2020YFB1005800) and the National Natural Science Foundation of China (No. 61902392).

References

1. Azouaoui, M., et al.: Protecting Dilithium against leakage: revisited sensitivity analysis and improved implementations. IACR Trans. Cryptogr. Hardw. Embed. Syst. **2023**(4), 58–79 (2023)
2. Bai, S., Galbraith, S.D.: An improved compression technique for signatures based on learning with errors. In: Benaloh, J. (ed.) CT-RSA 2014. LNCS, vol. 8366, pp. 28–47. Springer, Cham (2014). https://doi.org/10.1007/978-3-319-04852-9_2
3. Berzati, A., Viera, A.C., Chartouni, M., Madec, S., Vergnaud, D., Vigilant, D.: A practical template attack on CRYSTALS-Dilithium. Cryptology ePrint Archive (2023)
4. Chen, S., et al.: Leveraging hardware transactional memory for cache side-channel defenses. In: Proceedings of the 2018 on Asia Conference on Computer and Communications Security, pp. 601–608 (2018)
5. Dice, D., Lev, Y., Moir, M., Nussbaum, D.: Early experience with a commercial hardware transactional memory implementation. In: Proceedings of the 14th International Conference on Architectural Support for Programming Languages and Operating Systems, pp. 157–168 (2009)
6. Ducas, L., et al.: CRYSTALS-Dilithium: a lattice-based digital signature scheme. IACR Trans. Cryptogr. Hardw. Embed. Syst. **2018**(1), 238–268 (2018)
7. Durumeric, Z., et al.: The matter of heartbleed. In: Proceedings of the 2014 Conference on Internet Measurement Conference, pp. 475–488 (2014)
8. Fu, Y., et al.: RegKey: a register-based implementation of ECC signature algorithms against one-shot memory disclosure. ACM Trans. Embed. Comput. Syst. **22**, 1–22 (2023)
9. Fu, Yu., Wang, W., Meng, L., Wang, Q., Zhao, Y., Lin, J.: VIRSA: vectorized in-register RSA computation with memory disclosure resistance. In: Gao, D., Li, Q., Guan, X., Liao, X. (eds.) ICICS 2021. LNCS, vol. 12918, pp. 293–309. Springer, Cham (2021). https://doi.org/10.1007/978-3-030-86890-1_17

10. Garmany, B., Müller, T.: PRIME: private RSA infrastructure for memory-less encryption. In: Proceedings of the 29th Annual Computer Security Applications Conference, pp. 149–158 (2013)
11. Gruss, D., Lettner, J., Schuster, F., Ohrimenko, O., Haller, I., Costa, M.: Strong and efficient cache side-channel protection using hardware transactional memory. In: 26th USENIX Security Symposium (USENIX Security 17), pp. 217–233 (2017)
12. Guan, L., Lin, J., Luo, B., Jing, J.: Copker: computing with private keys without ram. In: NDSS, pp. 23–26 (2014)
13. Guan, L., Lin, J., Luo, B., Jing, J., Wang, J.: Protecting private keys against memory disclosure attacks using hardware transactional memory. In: 2015 IEEE Symposium on Security and Privacy, pp. 3–19. IEEE (2015)
14. Halderman, J.A., et al.: Lest we remember: cold-boot attacks on encryption keys. Commun. ACM **52**(5), 91–98 (2009)
15. Herlihy, M., Moss, J.E.B.: Transactional memory: architectural support for lock-free data structures. In: Proceedings of the 20th Annual International Symposium on Computer Architecture, pp. 289–300 (1993)
16. Intel: Intel architecture instruction set extensions programming reference. Intel Corp., Mountain View, CA, USA, Technical Report (2016)
17. Langlois, A., Stehlé, D.: Worst-case to average-case reductions for module lattices. Des. Codes Crypt. **75**(3), 565–599 (2015)
18. Li, C., et al.: Mimosa: protecting private keys against memory disclosure attacks using hardware transactional memory. IEEE Trans. Depend. Secure Comput. **18**(3), 1196–1213 (2019)
19. Liu, F., Yarom, Y., Ge, Q., Heiser, G., Lee, R.B.: Last-level cache side-channel attacks are practical. In: 2015 IEEE Symposium on Security and Privacy, pp. 605–622. IEEE (2015)
20. Lyubashevsky, V.: Fiat-Shamir with aborts: applications to lattice and factoring-based signatures. In: Matsui, M. (ed.) ASIACRYPT 2009. LNCS, vol. 5912, pp. 598–616. Springer, Heidelberg (2009). https://doi.org/10.1007/978-3-642-10366-7_35
21. Lyubashevsky, V.: Lattice signatures without trapdoors. In: Pointcheval, D., Johansson, T. (eds.) EUROCRYPT 2012. LNCS, vol. 7237, pp. 738–755. Springer, Heidelberg (2012). https://doi.org/10.1007/978-3-642-29011-4_43
22. Marzougui, S., Ulitzsch, V., Tibouchi, M., Seifert, J.P.: Profiling side-channel attacks on Dilithium: a small bit-fiddling leak breaks it all. Cryptology ePrint Archive (2022)
23. Müller, T., Freiling, F.C., Dewald, A.: TRESOR runs encryption securely outside RAM. In: 20th USENIX Security Symposium (USENIX Security 11) (2011)
24. NIST: PQC standardization process: Announcing four candidates to be standardized, plus fourth round candidates. https://www.nist.gov/news-events/news/2022/07/pqc-standardization-process-announcing-four-candidates-be-standardized-plus
25. Poddebniak, D., Somorovsky, J., Schinzel, S., Lochter, M., Rösler, P.: Attacking deterministic signature schemes using fault attacks. In: 2018 IEEE European Symposium on Security and Privacy (EuroS&P), pp. 338–352. IEEE (2018)
26. Samwel, N., Batina, L., Bertoni, G., Daemen, J., Susella, R.: Breaking Ed25519 in WolfSSL. In: Smart, N.P. (ed.) CT-RSA 2018. LNCS, vol. 10808, pp. 1–20. Springer, Cham (2018). https://doi.org/10.1007/978-3-319-76953-0_1
27. Yarom, Y., Falkner, K.: FLUSH+RELOAD: a high resolution, low noise, L3 cache side-channel attack. In: 23rd USENIX security symposium (USENIX Security 14), pp. 719–732 (2014)

28. Zhang, R., Bond, M.D., Zhang, Y.: Cape: compiler-aided program transformation for htm-based cache side-channel defense. In: Proceedings of the 31st ACM SIG-PLAN International Conference on Compiler Construction, pp. 181–193 (2022)
29. Zhao, Y., Lin, J., Pan, W., Xue, C., Zheng, F., Ma, Z.: RegRSA: using registers as buffers to resist memory disclosure attacks. In: Hoepman, J.-H., Katzenbeisser, S. (eds.) SEC 2016. IAICT, vol. 471, pp. 293–307. Springer, Cham (2016). https://doi.org/10.1007/978-3-319-33630-5_20

Multiparty Computation

Mercury: Constant-Round Protocols for Multi-Party Computation with Rationals

Luke Harmon[iD] and Gaetan Delavignette[✉][iD]

Algemetric Inc., Colorado Springs, USA
{lharmon,gdelavignette}@algemetric.com

Abstract. Most protocols for secure multi-party computation (MPC) work over fields or rings, which means that encoding techniques are needed to map rational-valued data into the algebraic structure being used. Leveraging an encoding technique introduced in recent work of Harmon et al. that is compatible with any MPC protocol over a prime-order field, we present Mercury—a family of protocols for addition, multiplication, subtraction, and division of rational numbers. Notably, the output of our division protocol is exact (i.e., it does not use iterative methods). Our protocols offer improvements in both round complexity and communication complexity when compared with prior art, and are secure for a dishonest minority of semi-honest parties.

Keywords: secure multi-party computation · secret sharing · rational numbers · rational division

1 Introduction

Secure computation is a tool which allows functions of private data to be evaluated without revealing those data. A well-studied form of secure computation, and the focus of this work, is Multi-party Computation (MPC). In the classic setting, n mutually distrusting parties P_i possess private data d_i and wish to jointly compute a function $F(d_1, \ldots, d_n)$ without revealing any information about honest parties' inputs to any coalition of corrupted parties. This problem was first studied in detail by Yao [23]. Since then, much work has been done extending Yao's results, developing new tools for MPC, and implementing these tools in the real world (e.g., [6,13,14,16,18,19]). Many of these protocols rely on *secret sharing*. In secret sharing, each P_i is provided masked pieces (called *shares*) of private data (henceforth, *secrets*). These shares are chosen such that only authorized sets of parties can determine a secret if they pool their shares. The parties use their shares to perform computations on the secrets by communicating (e.g., sending/receiving shares, creating and sending new shares, etc.) with one another as needed. A common primitive for secret sharing is Shamir's scheme [20] based on polynomial interpolation over a finite field. An advantage of that scheme is that it is *additively homomorphic* so that shares of two secrets can be added locally to give a sharing of the sum of those secrets. Additively

© The Author(s), under exclusive license to Springer Nature Switzerland AG 2023
E. Athanasopoulos and B. Mennink (Eds.): ISC 2023, LNCS 14411, pp. 309–326, 2023.
https://doi.org/10.1007/978-3-031-49187-0_16

homomorphic secret sharing is also used by the well-known MP-SPDZ framework [18].

Most MPC protocols are defined over finite rings or fields such as $\mathbb{Z}/m\mathbb{Z}$ or $GF(2^\ell)$, and as such require real data (often in the form of fixed-point or floating-point numbers) to be encoded as elements of the ring (field). Further, since the goal is to evaluate certain functions (e.g., polynomials) over secret shared values, the encoding method must be homomorphic with respect to the operations that compose the function (e.g., addition and multiplication). Several works [9,11,22] encode a fixed-point or floating-point number a with f digits after the radix point as the integer $a \cdot 2^f$. Other approaches [1,10] work with floating-point numbers by separately encoding the sign, exponent, and significand, along with an extra bit that is set to 0 iff the number is 0.

Our approach differs significantly from all of these. Instead of choosing a set of fixed-point numbers and designing our protocols around that set, we start with a set of rationals (with bounded numerators and denominators) that contains some set of fixed-point numbers. This set of rationals, paired with an encoding of those rationals as elements of a ring/field that is homomorphic with respect to both addition and multiplication, forms the basis of our protocols. The range of the encoding can be any ring/field of the form $\mathbb{Z}/m\mathbb{Z}$, however we focus on the case of m prime. This means that, for the most part, our protocols are obtained by simply composing the encoder with existing protocols. An exception is the way we handle division, which relies heavily on the structure of the aforementioned set of rationals.

All our protocols for the basic arithmetic operations require only a constant number of rounds and have communication complexity at most $O(tn)$ field elements, where n is the number of parties and t is a bound on the number of corrupted parties.[1] Our protocols are also generic, by which we mean that they do not depend on the underlying primitives being used, whether the majority of parties are honest, or even whether adversaries are malicious. For example, even though we use Shamir's scheme as the foundation, our protocols for rational arithmetic could easily be translated to use additive secret sharing (e.g., as used in MP-SPDZ to tolerate all-but-one corrupted party).

The paper is organized as follows:

* Section 2 discusses notation and provides an overview of Shamir's scheme, and some "building block" protocols.
* Section 3 introduces the rational-to-ring-element encoder, and Mercury: our protocols for rational addition, multiplication, subtraction, and division. We close by discussing the security and correctness of our protocols.
* Section 4 contains a brief discussion of our (partial) compatibility with fixed-point numbers, and then investigates how to choose a subset of the domain of the encoder that allows for evaluation of (arithmetic) circuits up to a certain multiplicative depth. We end with an example of securely computing the kurtosis of a dataset held distributively by n parties.

---

[1] After optimizations, the *online* communication complexity of our protocols is at most $O(t + n)$ field elements.

* Section 5 discusses how the round complexity and communication complexity of Mercury can be reduced by using well-known optimizations.
* Section 6 compares Mercury with prior work [9,11,21,22].
* Section 7 summarizes our results and discusses additional protocols which we hope to include in Mercury in the future.

2   Preliminaries

2.1   Notation

For a positive integer m, $\mathbb{Z}/m\mathbb{Z}$ denotes the ring of integers modulo m. In case m is prime, we write $\mathbb{F}_m$. The elements of $\mathbb{Z}/m\mathbb{Z}$ will be represented by integers $0, 1, \ldots, m-1$. For a ring R, $R[x_1, x_2, \ldots]$ will denote the ring of polynomials in the variables $x_1, x_2, \ldots$ with coefficients in R. For $\mathsf{p} \in \mathbb{Q}[x_1, x_2, \ldots]$, $\|\mathsf{p}\|_1$ denotes the ℓ_1 norm of p, i.e., the sum of the absolute values of the coefficients of p. We use $y \leftarrow A(x)$ to denote that a randomized algorithm A on input x outputs y. If A is deterministic, we simply write $y = A(x)$. All circuits we consider are arithmetic over a field $\mathbb{F}_p$, and have gates with fan-in 2.

2.2   Shamir's Scheme

We pause here to provide a brief overview of Shamir secret sharing (SSS), and the notation used therein. Suppose we have n parties and wish for any set of $t + 1 \leq n$ parties to be able to reconstruct a secret by pooling their shares. This is called a $(t + 1)$-out-of-n threshold scheme. One creates *Shamir shares* of a secret $s \in \mathbb{F}_p$, where $|\mathbb{F}_p| \geq n$, by generating a random polynomial $f(x) \in \mathbb{F}_p[x]$ of degree at most t whose constant term is s (i.e., $f(0) = s$) and whose remaining coefficients are chosen uniformly from $\mathbb{F}_p$. Shares of s are the field elements $f(i)$, $i \in \mathbb{F}_p \backslash \{0\}$. We assume the ith party receives the share $f(i)$. We use $[x]_i$ to denote the ith party's share of $x \in \mathbb{F}_p$, and $[x]$ to denote a sharing of x among all parties. Then, for example, $[x] + [y]$ will mean "each party adds their share of x to their share of y," and $c[x]$ will mean "each party multiplies their share of x by c." Any collection of $t+1$ parties can pool their shares $[s]$ and reconstruct the polynomial f using Lagrange interpolation, thereby obtaining the secret $s = f(0)$.

2.3   Framework

We use $(t+1)$-out-of-n SSS over $\mathbb{F}_p$ for all protocols, and assume that all parties are connected by pair-wise secure channels which they use to send and receive shares when necessary. The communication complexity of a protocol is measured by the number of field elements sent by all parties in the protocol. When comparing our work with existing protocols that measure communication complexity in bits, we simply multiply our communication complexities by $\log_2(p)$. All adversaries are assumed to be semi-honest (honest-but-curious), and we tolerate at most t of them. As previously mentioned, given sharings $[x]$ and $[y]$, the parties can compute a sharing $[x + y]$ of their sum without interaction by computing $[x] + [y]$. For multiplication of shared values we use the protocol of Gennaro et al. [15], which is itself an optimization of the multiplication subroutine in the BGW protocol [5]. To ensure the multiplication protocol works, we require $t < n/2$. We present the details of the relevant building block protocols in the next section.

2.4   Building Blocks

SSS primitives will be the algorithms/protocols Share, Add, ScalarMult, and Mult. Respectively, these create shares of a secret value $s \in \mathbb{F}_p$, compute the shares of the sum of two secrets without revealing either, compute shares of the product of a secret value and a known value without revealing the secret value, and compute shares of the product of two secrets without revealing either. Add and ScalarMult are non-interactive. Borrowing from [1], we use $s \leftarrow \text{Output}([s])$ to mean that each of a set of t parties send their share of s to another party, which subsequently reconstructs s from the shares $[s]$ and sends s to the other $n - 1$ parties. We pause briefly to describe the multplication protocol from [15] (Fig. 1).

$$[xy] \leftarrow \text{Mult}([x], [y])$$

1. For $i = 1, \ldots, n$, the ith party P_i computes $z_i = [x]_i \cdot [y]_i$;
2. For $i = 1, \ldots, 2t + 1$, P_i computes $[z_i] \leftarrow \text{Share}(z_i)$, and sends the jth share to P_j;
3. once each party $P_1, \ldots, P_n$ has received $2t + 1$ shares, each party P_i locally computes $[xy]_i$ using Lagrange interpolation on the received shares;
4. output $[xy]$.

Fig. 1. Multiplying shared secrets without revealing.

Two additional protocols, RandInt and Inv ([2], Lemma 6), are required for our rational division protocol. These protocols allow all parties to obtain shares of a random field element (Fig. 2) and compute shares of the multiplicative inverse of a field element (Fig. 3), respectively (Table 1).

3   Protocols for Rational Numbers

We propose a family of efficient MPC protocols for performing computations with rational numbers. These protocols are obtained by pairing an encoder mapping certain rational numbers to field elements with compositions of the building block protocols described in Sect. 2.4. The protocols for computing the sum and

---

$$[r] \leftarrow \mathsf{RandInt}()$$

---

1. Each of a set of $t + 1$ parties select a uniform $r_i \in \mathbb{F}_p$, $i = 1, \ldots, t + 1$;
2. each of the $t + 1$ parties computes $[r_i] \leftarrow \mathsf{Share}(r_i)$, and sends the jth share to P_j;
3. $[r] = [r_1] + \cdots + [r_{t+1}]$;
4. return $[r]$.

Fig. 2. Generating shares of a random element of $\mathbb{F}_p$.

$$[x^{-1}] \leftarrow \mathsf{Inv}([x])$$

---

1. $[r] \leftarrow \mathsf{RandInt}()$;
2. $[rx] \leftarrow \mathsf{Mult}([r], [x])$;
3. $rx = \mathsf{Output}([rx])$;
4. abort and restart if $rx = 0$, otherwise continue;
5. each party locally computes $(rx)^{-1} = x^{-1}r^{-1} \bmod p$;
6. each party does $[x^{-1}] = \mathsf{ScalarMult}(x^{-1}r^{-1}, [r])$;
7. return $[x^{-1}]$.

Fig. 3. Calculating shares of a multiplicative inverse in $\mathbb{F}_p$.

Table 1. Total communication complexity (measured in field elements) of SSS building block protocols.

Protocol	Rounds	Comm. Complexity
Share	1	$n - 1$
Output	2	$t + (n - 1)$
Add	0	0
Mult	1	$(2t + 1)(n - 1)$
ScalarMult	0	0
RandInt	1	$(t + 1)(n - 1)$
Inv	4	$(t + 1)(3n - 2) - 1$

product of shared fractions remain unchanged from the analogous SSS primitives, except that rational operands are encoded to field elements before those protocols are executed. Subtraction and Division are an amalgam of the building blocks. Division, in particular, relies on the fact that our mapping for encoding rational numbers to integers is induced by a ring homomorphism, and therefore preserves inverses; likewise for the decode mapping. We elaborate below.

3.1   Encoding Rationals

We use the encoding map introduced in [17] which maps a subset of rationals, whose denominators are co-prime with a prime p, into $\mathbb{F}_p$. This map is defined by $\mathsf{encode}(x/y) = xy^{-1} \bmod p$, with domain the *Farey rationals*

$$\mathcal{F}_N := \{x/y \, : \, |x| \leq N, \, 0 < y \leq N, \, \gcd(x,y) = 1, \gcd(p,y) = 1\},$$

where $N = N(p) := \lfloor \sqrt{(p-1)/2} \rfloor$. Notice that $\mathcal{F}_N$ is *not* closed under addition and multiplication.

The map encode is induced by a ring isomorphism, so both it and its inverse decode are additively and multiplicatively homomorphic as long as the composition of operands in $\mathcal{F}_N$ remains in $\mathcal{F}_N$.[2] The inverse operations decode can be computed efficiently using a slight modification of the Extended Euclidean Algorithm. We summarize important properties of encode, decode, and $\mathcal{F}_N$ in the following lemma.

Lemma 1. *Let p be a prime, $N = N(p)$, and* encode, decode *be the encode and decode maps, respectively.*

(i) If $x/y \in \mathcal{F}_N$, then $-x/y \in \mathcal{F}_N$.
(ii) If $x/y \in \mathcal{F}_N$ is nonzero, then $y/x \in \mathcal{F}_N$.
(iii) $[-N, N] \cap \mathbb{Z} \subseteq \mathcal{F}_N$. Moreover, if $z \in [0, N] \cap \mathbb{Z}$, then $\mathsf{encode}(z) = z$.
(iv) encode *and* decode *are homomorphic w.r.t. addition and multiplication*

    as long as the composition of operands in $\mathcal{F}_N$ remains in $\mathcal{F}_N$.

Proof. (i)-(iii) are obvious. (iv) is proved in [17, Proposition 2]. ▢

3.2   Rational Addition, Multiplication, Subtraction, and Division

To represent shares of the encoding of $x/y \in \mathcal{F}_N$, we write $\big[\mathsf{encode}(x/y)\big]$. We first present the four protocols, and then list their complexities in Table 2. For all protocols, we use the field $\mathbb{F}_p$, and assume $x_0/y_0, x_1/y_1 \in \mathcal{F}_N$. Our addition and multiplication protocols HgAdd and HgMult are obtained by simply pairing the encoder with Add and Mult, respectively. As such, we omit the descriptions of both protocols. The remaining two protocols, HgSubtr and HgDiv are introduced below (Fig. 4).

Remark 1. We use the prefix "Hg" for our protocols because it is the chemical symbol for the element Mercury.

Let $\mathsf{enc}_0 = \mathsf{encode}(x_0/y_0)$ and $\mathsf{enc}_1 = \mathsf{encode}(x_1/y_1)$ (Figs. 5, 6 and 7). Observe that the output of HgDiv is exact – the output is $x_0 y_1/y_0 x_1$ on inputs dividend $= x_0/y_0$ and divisor $= x_1/y_1$.

Remark 2. ScalarMult can be turned into HgScalarMult by simply encoding a public element $\alpha \in \mathcal{F}_N$, and then computing $\big[\mathsf{encode}(\alpha)s\big] = $ ScalarMult$(\mathsf{encode}(\alpha), [s])$. Note that HgScalarMult also serves as a *division by public divisor* protocol - simply replace $\alpha \neq 0$ by $1/\alpha$.

---

[2] E.g., $\mathsf{encode}\left(\frac{x_0}{y_0} + \frac{x_1}{y_1}\right) = \mathsf{encode}\left(\frac{x_0}{y_0}\right) + \mathsf{encode}\left(\frac{x_1}{y_1}\right)$ if $\frac{x_0}{y_0}, \frac{x_1}{y_1}, \frac{x_0}{y_0} + \frac{x_1}{y_1} \in \mathcal{F}_N$.

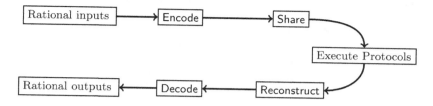

Fig. 4. Overview of Mercury protocols.

$$[\text{encode}(x_0/y_0 - x_1/y_1)] = \text{HgSubtr}([\text{encode}(x_0/y_0)], [\text{encode}(x_1/y_1)])$$

1. All parties compute $\text{encode}(-1) = -1_{\text{field}} \in \mathbb{F}_p$;
2. all parties compute $[-\text{enc}_1] = \text{ScalarMult}(-1_{\text{field}}, [\text{enc}_1])$;
3. $[\text{enc}_0 - \text{enc}_1] = \text{HgAdd}([\text{enc}_0], [-\text{enc}_1])$;
4. return $[\text{enc}_0 - \text{enc}_1] = [\text{encode}(x_0/y_0 - x_1/y_1)]$.

Fig. 5. Mercury subtraction protocol.

$$[\text{encode}(x_0 y_1/y_0 x_1)] = \text{HgDiv}([\text{encode}(x_0/y_0)], [\text{encode}(x_1/y_1)])$$

1. $[\text{enc}_1^{-1}] \leftarrow \text{Inv}([\text{enc}_1])$;
2. $[\text{enc}_0 \cdot \text{enc}_1^{-1}] \leftarrow \text{HgMult}([\text{enc}_0], [\text{enc}_1^{-1}])$;
3. return $[\text{enc}_0 \cdot \text{enc}_1^{-1}] = [\text{encode}(x_0 y_1/y_0 x_1)]$.

Fig. 6. Mercury division protocol.

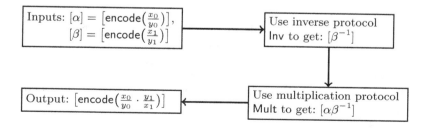

Fig. 7. Overview of HgDiv.

Table 2. Communication complexity (in field elements) of Mercury protocols.

Mercury		
Protocol	Rounds	Comm. Complexity
HgAdd	0	0
HgMult	1	$(2t+1)(n-1)$
HgSubtr	0	0
HgDiv	5	$(t+1)(5n-4)-n$

3.3 Security and Correctness

It is well-known (see, e.g., [4]) that SSS is perfectly secure in the sense that possession of fewer than the threshold number of shares does not reveal any information about the secret. It is also easy to see that the building block protocols Share, Output, Add, ScalarMult, and Mult do not reveal any information, as the only information received by the parties are shares and no party ever receives enough shares to reconstruct. By invoking Canetti's composition theorem [8], which roughly states that a composition of secure protocols yields a secure protocol, we see that both RandInt and Inv are also secure.

The authors of [17] remark that for p an odd prime and $N = N(p)$, $\mathcal{F}_N$ is not in bijective correspondence with $\mathbb{F}_p$. In fact, $|\mathcal{F}_N| \approx 0.6p$. A consequence of this is that an attacker can reduce the set of possible secret encodings in $\mathbb{F}_p$ to $\mathsf{encode}(\mathcal{F}_N) \subsetneq \mathbb{F}_p$. This is not problematic, however, as each value in $\mathsf{encode}(\mathcal{F}_N)$ is equally likely to be the secret.

The following theorem provides necessary conditions for correctness of the Mercury protocols.

Theorem 1 (Correctness of Mercury protocols). *Let p be an odd prime and $N = N(p)$. Suppose $x_i/y_i \in \mathcal{F}_N$ with $\alpha_i = \mathsf{encode}(x_i/y_i)$, for $i = 0, 1$.*

(i) $\mathsf{decode}\big(\mathsf{HgAdd}(\alpha_0, \alpha_1)\big) = x_0/y_0 + x_1/y_1$ *as long as* $x_0/y_0 + x_1/y_1 \in \mathcal{F}_N$.
(ii) $\mathsf{decode}\big(\mathsf{HgMult}(\alpha_0, \alpha_1)\big) = x_0/y_0 \cdot x_1/y_1$ *as long as* $x_0/y_0 \cdot x_1/y_1 \in \mathcal{F}_N$.
(iii) $\mathsf{decode}\big(\mathsf{HgSubtr}(\alpha_0, \alpha_1)\big) = x_0/y_0 - x_1/y_1$ *as long as* $x_0/y_0 - x_1/y_1 \in \mathcal{F}_N$.
(iv) $\mathsf{decode}\big(\mathsf{HgDiv}(\alpha_0, \alpha_1)\big) = x_0/y_0 \div x_1/y_1$ *as long as* $x_0/y_0 \div x_1/y_1 \in \mathcal{F}_N$.

Proof. HgAdd is trivially correct if we ignore the encoded fractions and only consider field elements. That is, $\mathsf{HgAdd}(\alpha_0, \alpha_1) = \alpha_0 + \alpha_1$. So correctness is guaranteed as long as $\mathsf{decode}(\alpha_0 + \alpha_1) = x_0/y_0 + x_1/y_1$.

Now, suppose $x_0/y_0 + x_1/y_1 \in \mathcal{F}_N$. Since decode is additively homomorphic when the sum remains in $\mathcal{F}_N$, $\mathsf{decode}(\alpha_0 + \alpha_1) = \mathsf{decode}(\alpha_0) + \mathsf{decode}(\alpha_1) = x_0/y_0 + x_1/y_1$, as desired. The correctness of the remaining Mercury protocols follows *mutatis mutandis*.

4   Which Rational Numbers Can We Use?

All our protocols use the aforementioned Farey rationals. As mentioned in Lemma 1, $\mathcal{F}_N$ is closed under additive inverses and multiplicative inverses, but is not closed under addition and multiplication. This means that for applications to MPC a suitable subset of $\mathcal{F}_N$ must be chosen as the set of rational inputs. In particular, we must include fractions with "small" numerators and denominators so that adding/multiplying those fractions yields fractions that remain in $\mathcal{F}_N$. Following closely the analysis of [17], this set will be chosen as

$$\mathcal{G}_{X,Y} := \left\{ x/y \in \mathcal{F}_N \mid X, Y \in [0, N], |x| \leq X, 0 < y \leq Y \right\},$$

for some X, Y to be specified.

4.1   Fixed-Point Numbers

Many previous works designed their protocols with fixed-point arithmetic in mind. So, to facilitate comparison with prior art, we briefly discuss conditions under which $\mathcal{F}_N$ contains a given set of fixed-point numbers.

Fixed-point numbers are rational numbers represented as a list of digits split by a radix point, and are defined by an integer (represented in a particular base b) in a given range along with a fixed scaling factor f (called the *precision*). For example, we can represent decimal numbers with integral part in the range $(-10^{\ell+1}, 10^{\ell+1})$ and up to f decimal places after the radix point as $a \cdot 10^{-f} = a/10^f$, $a \in (-10^{\ell+f+1}, 10^{\ell+f+1})$. We will represent a set of fixed point numbers with a tuple of the form (b, ℓ, f), where b is the base, $(-b^{\ell+1}, b^{\ell+1})$ is range of the integer part, and up to f base-b digits are allowed after the radix point. The set of Farey rationals $\mathcal{F}_N$ contains the fixed-point numbers given by (b, ℓ, f) as long as

$$N \geq \max\{b^{\ell+f+1} - 1, b^f - 1\} = b^{\ell+f+1} - 1. \tag{1}$$

Of course, N should be sufficiently large to ensure that adding/multiplying the fixed-point numbers does not cause overflow. While $\mathcal{F}_N$ can be made to contain a set of fixed-point numbers with precision f, addition and multiplication of Farey rationals does not coincide with addition and multiplication of fixed-point numbers. This is because the fixed-point representation requires the precision to remain f after each operation (this necessitates truncation), while $\mathcal{F}_N$ allows the precision to increase until overflow occurs and the output of a computation is no longer correct. We will use the fact that $\mathcal{F}_N$ contains certain fixed-point numbers in Sect. 6 when we compare our protocols with prior work.

4.2   Compatible Circuits

Again borrowing from [17], for positive integers d, τ we define the class of (arithmetic) (d, τ)-*circuits* over $\mathbb{Q}$ to be those that compute a polynomial $\mathsf{p} \in \mathbb{Q}[x_1, x_2, \ldots]$ such that p satisfying: (i) ℓ_1 norm is at most τ, (ii) total degree is at most d, and (iii) all nonzero coefficients have absolute value greater than or equal to 1. Note that nonzero polynomials $\mathsf{p} \in \mathbb{Z}[x_1, x_2, \ldots]$ with $\|\mathsf{p}\|_1 \leq \tau$ and $\deg(\mathsf{p}) \leq d$ satisfy (iii). Let $\mathcal{C}_{d,\tau}$ be the set of (d, τ)-circuits, and $\mathcal{P}_{d,\tau}$ be the set of polynomials those circuits compute. We obtain the following by slight modification of the proof of [17, Proposition 7], which allow us to determine d, τ so that evaluating any (d, τ)-circuit on inputs from $\mathcal{G}_{X,Y}$ will have output in $\mathcal{F}_N$.

Proposition 1. *Let $d, \tau \geq 1$. If x/y is the output of $C \in \mathcal{C}_{d,\tau}$ evaluated on inputs from $\mathcal{G}_{X,Y} \subseteq \mathcal{F}_N$, then $|x| \leq \tau X^d Y^{d(\tau-1)}$ and $|y| \leq Y^{d\tau}$.*

Proof. See Appendix A.

Intuitively, the bound on x is larger than the bound on y because the numerator grows faster than the denominator when fractions are summed (since $a/b+c/d = (ad + bc)/bd$), whereas they grow at the same rate when multiplied.

Table 3 shows some possible choices for d and τ if we use $\mathcal{G}_{2^{32},2^{14}} \subsetneq \mathcal{F}_{2^{1024}}$. Note that in this case, $p \approx 2^{2048}$.

Table 3. Possible values of d (total degree of polynomial computed by circuit) and τ (ℓ_1 norm of polynomial computed by (d, τ)-circuit) for fractions with numerators bounded in absolute value by 2^{32} and denominators bounded by 2^{14}.

$|\text{num}| \leq 2^{32}$, denom $\leq 2^{14}$					
d	1	2	3	4	5	10
τ	71	35	22	16	13	6

These numbers are not particularly useful, as many applications require thousands or even millions of additions to be performed on shared values. However, for many applications one is likely to work with decimal numbers with a small number of significant digits. In such cases, we can significantly improve the bounds on d and τ. In general, if the fractional data all have the same denominator, then Proposition 1 yields the following corollary.

Corollary 1. *Let $C \in \mathcal{C}_{d,\tau}$ with inputs from $\mathcal{F}_N$ whose denominators are all some fixed power e of an integer base b, $0 < b^e \leq N$, and whose numerators are bounded in absolute value by $X \leq N$. If x/y is the output of C, then $|x| \leq \tau(Xb^e)^d$ and $y \leq b^{ed}$.*

Proof. Note that $\mathsf{p} \in \mathcal{P}_{d,\tau}$ can be written as $\mathsf{p} = \sum_i c_i p_i$, where $\sum_i |c_i| \leq \tau$, each $|c_i| \geq 1$, and each p_i is a monomial of degree at most d. Let $\mathsf{p} = \sum_{i=1}^I c_i p_i$, and suppose we have k inputs x_i/b^e.
Since $\deg(p_i) \leq d$,

$$p_i(x_1/b^e, \ldots, x_k/b^e) = \frac{x_{i_1} x_{i_2} \cdots x_{i_\ell}}{b^{e\ell}}, \text{ for some } \ell \leq d \text{ and } \{i_1, \ldots, i_\ell\} \subseteq \{1, \ldots, k\}.$$

As each $|x_i| \leq X$, we have $|x_{i_1} x_{i_2} \cdots x_{i_\ell}| \leq X^\ell \leq X^d$.
Now, if $x/y = \sum_{i=1}^{I} c_i \cdot p_i(x_1/b^e, \ldots, x_k/b^e)$, then

$$x = (c_1 a_1) b^{e(I-1)} + (c_2 a_2) b^{e(I-1)} + \cdots + (c_I a_I) b^{e(I-1)} \text{ and } y = b^{eI}.$$

It follows that $|x| \leq \sum_{i=1}^{I} |c_i| (X b^e)^I \leq \tau \cdot (X b^e)^I$ and $|y| \leq b^{eI}$. The proof is completed by observing that $|c_\alpha| \geq 1$, for all α, implies $I \leq \tau$.

Rehashing the above example ($X = 2^{32}$ and $N \approx 2^{1024}$) with $b^e = 2^{14}$ we get $\tau (2^{32} 2^{14})^d \leq 2^{1024} \implies \log_2(\tau) \leq 1024 - 46d$ and $(2^{14})^d \leq 2^{1024} \implies d \leq 73$. The bound on d is in fact even smaller: since the ℓ_1 norm of a polynomial in $\mathcal{P}_{d,\tau}$ is at least 1, $\log_2(\tau) \geq 0 \implies 1024 - 46d \geq 0 \implies 22 \geq d$.

Table 4. Possible values of d (total degree of polynomial computed by a (d, τ)-circuit) and τ (ℓ_1 norm of polynomial computed by (d, τ)-circuit) for fractions with numerators bounded in absolute value by 2^{32} and denominators all equal to 2^{14}

$|\text{num}| \leq 2^{32}$, denom $= 2^{14}$					
d	1	2	10	15	20	22
τ	2^{978}	2^{932}	2^{564}	2^{334}	2^{104}	2^{12}

Table 4 shows that if we restrict inputs to have the same denominators, we can perform an enourmous number of additions and a reasonable number of multiplications before the output lands outside of $\mathcal{F}_N$. We can do even better though.

Degree-constant Circuits. Each gate of an arithmetic circuit computes a polynomial over (some of) the inputs. We define a *degree-constant (arithmetic) circuit* to be one in which every gate computes a polynomial whose monomial summands all have the same degree; e.g., a dot product. The goal of introducing these circuits is to ensure that whenever two fractions are summed, they already have a common denominator.

Corollary 2. *Let $C \in \mathcal{C}_{d,\tau}$ be degree-constant with inputs from $\mathcal{F}_N$ whose denominators are all b^e and whose numerators are bounded in absolute value by $X > 0$. If x/y is the output of C, then $|x| \leq \tau X^d$ and $y \leq b^{ed}$.*

Proof. This follows easily from the fact that whenever two terms are added during the evaluation of a degree-constant circuit, they already have a common denominator which is a power of b^e.

Again, using a 1024-bit N, $X = 2^{32}$, and $b^e = 2^{14}$, we get the inequalities $\log_2(\tau) \leq 1024 - 32d$ and $d \leq 32$, yielding the following table.

Table 5. Possible values of d (total degree of polynomial computed by a (d, τ)-circuit) and τ (ℓ_1 norm of polynomial computed by (d, τ)-circuit) for degree-constant $C \in \mathcal{C}_{d,\tau}$ taking inputs from $\mathcal{F}_N$ with numerators bounded in absolute value by 2^{32} and denominators all equal to 2^{14}

$|\text{num}| \leq 2^{32}$, denom $= 2^{14}$					
d	1	2	10	15	25	31
τ	2^{992}	2^{960}	2^{704}	2^{544}	2^{384}	2^{32}

Incorporating Division. Once divisions are allowed, the bounds given in Corollary 1 and Corollary 2 no longer apply, since the numerator of the divisor becomes a factor of denominator of the quotient. This means any necessary divisions should be performed as late as possible relative to other operations.

4.3   An Application: Computing Excess Kurtosis

The *excess kurtosis* of a distribution is a measure of its "tailedness" relative to a normal distribution: low excess kurtosis (<0) means the distribution has thin tails while high excess kurtosis (>0) means the distribution has thick tails. This measure is frequently-used in descriptive analytics and rather involved to calculate, which makes it a good candidate computation for Mercury. We derive below the parameters necessary to guarantee that the excess kurtosis of a sample of size k remains in $\mathcal{F}_N$. The excess kurtosis EK_s is defined as

$$EK_s = \frac{k(k+1)\sum_{i=1}^{k}\left(x_i - \bar{x}\right)^4}{(k-1)(k-2)(k-3)s^4} - \frac{3(k-1)^2}{(k-2)(k-3)} \text{ for } k \geq 4$$

where k is the size of the sample, s^2 the variance, and $\bar{x}$ is the mean of the sample. For simplicity, and to avoid calculating s^2 and $\bar{x}$ separately, the formula can be rewritten as

$$EK_s = \frac{k(k+1)(k-1)\sum_{i-1}^{k}\left(kx_i - \sum_{i=1}^{k} x_i\right)^4 - 3(k-1)^2\left(\sum_{i=1}^{k}\left(kx_i - \sum_{i=1}^{k} x_i\right)^2\right)^2}{(k-2)(k-3)\left(\sum_{i=1}^{k}\left(kx_i - \sum_{i=1}^{k} x_i\right)^2\right)^2}$$

Assuming that we need to compute the excess kurtosis of a sample of about one billion ($\approx 2^{30}$), and using data with denominators 2^{14} and numerators less than 2^{32}, as in Table 5. We determine that the numerator of EK_s is bounded by $k^8 2^{134}$ and the denominator is bounded by $k^6 2^{132}$. Therefore, to guarantee $EK_s \in \mathcal{F}_N$, it suffices to take $N \geq k^8 2^{134}$. Using $N \geq \left(2^{30}\right)^8 2^{134}$, we get $N \geq 2^{374}$, or a p on the order of 2^{749}.

5   Optimizations

The complexity of HgMult and HgDiv can be reduced by executing parts of the protocols asynchronously in an *offline phase*. This allows certain parts of the protocols to be executed before the desired computation, thereby reducing the *online* complexity. The complexity of the offline phase depends on chosen primitives, existence of a trusted dealer, etc. Henceforth, we emphasize the online round complexity and the online communication complexity.

We utilize two ubiquitous tools for optimization: Beaver triples (introduced in [3]) for more efficient multiplication, and Pseudo-Random Secret Sharing (PRSS, [12]) to generate random field elements without interaction.

In PRSS, the parties agree on a pseudo-random function (PRF) $\psi.(\cdot)$ and a common input a. They then use pre-distributed keys r_A (one for each set A of $n - (t + 1)$ parties) to locally compute shares of a random field element s using Replicated Secret Sharing (see [12] for details). The use of PRSS reduces the online round and communication complexity of RandInt from 1 and $(t+1)(n-1)$ to 0 and 0, respectively. Further, we assume that the PRF, common input, and keys are agreed upon and distributed during a *set-up phase*, whence using PRSS makes the offline round and communication complexity of RandInt both 0.

Beaver triples are 3-tuples of shares $([a], [b], [c])$ satisfying $ab = c$, and can be generated asynchronously in the offline phase using PRSS and Mult. These triples can be used to multiply secrets with only two online rounds of interaction. In particular, shares $[xy]$ can be obtained from $[x]$ and $[y]$ using only Add, ScalarMult, Output, and one Beaver triple $([a], [b], [c])$:

$$[xy] = (x + a)[y] - (y + b)[a] + [c].$$

Used triples must be discarded, else information is leaked. This means that a sufficiently-large reservoir of Beaver triples should be maintained to allow the desired functions to be computed.

These optimizations reduce the online complexities of HgMult and HgDiv, and leave the complexities of HgSubtr and HgAdd the same. Table 6 below summarizes the improvements.

The reader may notice that optimizing Mult actually *increases* the round complexity in the online phase from 1 to 2. This results from invocations of Output (executed in parallel) which requires 2 rounds per invocation, and is the cost of reducing the online communication from $O(tn)$ to $O(t + n)$. A user preferring instead to minimize the round complexity can do so by not using Beaver triples. Table 6 lists the optimized complexities of the Mercury protocols, along with the complexities of HgMult and HgDiv obtained by using PRSS but not Beaver triples.

We use the complexities listed in Table 6 for the comparisons in Sect. 6. Henceforth, "rounds" will mean "online rounds + offline rounds", and "total communication" will mean "online communication + offline communication".

Table 6. Optimized round and communication complexities for our protocols.

Optimizations	Protocol	Online Rounds	Offline Rounds	Online Comm.	Offline Comm.
PRSS and Beaver triples	HgAdd	0	0	0	0
•	HgSubtr	0	0	0	0
	HgMult	2	1	$t + (n-1)$	$(2t+1)(n-1)$
	HgDiv	6	2	$3t + 3(n-1)$	$2(2t+1)(n-1)$
PRSS	HgMult	1	0	$(2t+1)(n-1)$	0
	HgDiv	4	0	$(4t+3)(n-1)$	0

6 Comparison with Prior Work

In [11], Catrina and Saxena introduced semi-honest secure protocols for fixed-point multiplication and division - their division is based on (the iterative) Goldschmidt's method. A variant of their protocol is used by MP-SPDZ for fixed-point division. Catrina subsequently improved the round and communication complexities in [9]. To measure the complexities of their protocols, they use the set of fixed-point numbers given by $(2, 2f, f)$; i.e., the set of rationals $a \cdot 2^{-f}$ with $a \in [-2^{-2f}, 2^{2f}) \cap \mathbb{Z}$. Their fixed-point encoding technique requires a field $\mathbb{F}_q$ with $q > 2^{2f+\kappa}$, κ a statistical security parameter. For our protocols, we use the same field $\mathbb{F}_q$, whence our set of rationals is $\mathcal{F}_N$ with $N = N(q)$; specifically $\log_2(N) \geq f + \kappa/2$. Table 7 shows that for reasonable values of n and t (e.g. $n = 3$, $t = 1$), our protocols far outperform those of [9].

Table 7. Complexity comparison between our work (optimized with PRSS and Beaver triples) and that of [9]. Both the online and offline communication complexity are measured in elements of $\mathbb{F}_q$ sent among **all** parties throughout a protocol. n and t are the number of parties and the threshold, resp., θ is the number of iterations of Goldschmidt's method, and f is the fixed-point precision.

	Protocol	Rounds	Online Comm.	Offline Comm.
Mercury	Multiplication	3	$t + (n-1)$	$(2t+1)(n-1)$
	Division	8	$3t + 3(n-1)$	$2(2t+1)(n-1)$
[9]	Multiplication	1	n	nf
	Division	$9 + \theta$	$n(10f + 2\theta)$	$n(16f + 4\theta f)$

Let $n = 3$ and $t = 1$, so two parties can reconstruct. In an example, the authors choose $f \in [32, 56]$ and $\theta = 5$, which results in a 14 round division with online communication complexity $330n = 990$ field elements. In contrast, our division requires 8 rounds, and has online communication complexity 9 field elements. There is, however, a bit more subtlety to this comparison. As mentioned in Sect. 4.1, operations on fixed-point numbers require a truncation, and the protocols of Catrina et al. use truncation. Consequently, there is no limit to how many times they can multiply/divide two fixed-point numbers. However, there is a number of multiplications, say, that will render their outputs of little use because so many bits have been truncated. Our limitation, on the other hand, is overflow – computations over $\mathcal{F}_N$ are only meaningful if all intermediate outputs and the final output are in $\mathcal{F}_N$. We can address this in two ways: (i) only take inputs from the subset $\mathcal{G}_{X,Y} \subseteq \mathcal{F}_N$ defined in the beginning of Sect. 4, for X, Y sufficiently smaller than N, or (ii) use a larger field than [9]. As long as we don't choose too large a field, (ii) will preserve our complexity advantage.

Another interesting solution, albeit only for integer division, was proposed by Veugen and Abspoel in [21]. They present three division variations: public divisor, private divisor (only one party knows the divisor), and secret divisor (hidden from all parties). Their protocols are implemented using MP-SPDZ with three parties, and runtimes along with communication complexities (in MB) for dividing a k-bit integer by a $k/2$-bit integer are provided. Even though our division protocol uses rationals in general, comparison makes sense because $\mathcal{F}_N$ contains the integers $[-N, N] \cap \mathbb{Z}$ (see Lemma 1). For comparison, we use $n = 3$ and $t = 1$, and use the smallest prime field $\mathbb{F}_p$ allowed by [21]:

$$\log_2(p) \approx 4 \max \left\{ \log_2(\text{dividend}), \log_2(\text{divisor}) \right\} + 40$$

E.g., this means that for a 64 bit dividend and 32 bit divisor, we have $\log_2(p) = 296$ and $N = N(p) \approx 148$ bits (Table 8).

Table 8. Total communication complexity in megabytes (MB) of our division protocol (applied to integers) vs. the (secret divisor) integer division protocol of [21]. The communication complexity for (fully optimized) HgDiv was estimated using Table 6.

dividend bits	8	16	32	64
divisor bits	4	8	16	32
Mercury	0.00018MB	0.00026MB	0.00042MB	0.00074MB
[21] (semi-honest security)	8.6MB	32.6MB	121.0MB	492.7MB

The last comparison we shall show is against Pika [22]. Pika uses Function Secret Sharing [7] to construct a three-party protocol (one party is used only to generate correlated randomness) for computing functions such as reciprocal, sigmoid, and square root. Their protocol Pika takes as inputs (binary) fixed-point numbers x with precision f, such that $x \cdot 2^f \in (-2^{k-1}, 2^{k-1}]$, and creates shares in the ring $\mathbb{Z}_{2^\ell}$, where $\ell \geq 2k$. For comparison, we choose $N = N(p) = 2^{k-1}$ (meaning we share secrets over $\mathbb{F}_p$ with $p \approx 2^{2k}$). This guarantees that $\mathcal{F}_N$ contains the fixed-point numbers used by Pika regardless of the chosen precision f. As with the preceding comparisons, we take $n = 3$ and $t = 1$.

Using the same parameter values for (semi-honest secure) Pika as the author, we found that total communication complexity for securely computing the reciprocal with $k = 16$ and $\ell = 32$ was 8524 bits over three rounds (one offline). In contrast, we can compute the reciprocal of an element of $\mathcal{F}_{2^{15}}$ in 6 rounds (one offline) with communication complexity $21 \log_2(p) \approx 21 \cdot 2k = 672$ bits.

7   Conclusions and Future Work

Conclusion. This work uses Shamir Secret Sharing with a minority of semi-honest adversaries, but Mercury is flexible in the sense that it can be easily realized over other primitives with better security assumptions; e.g. additive secret sharing *à la* MP-SPDZ along with a majority of malicious adversaries. Mercury provides an efficient low round and communication complexity solution to exact computation over rational numbers using MPC. A cost of exactness, though, is that our protocols are not intrinsically compatible with fixed-point arithmetic. Instead of truncating after every operation to not exceed the chosen fixed-point precision, we allow the precision to grow until overflow occurs. This means that we may need to work over a larger field $\mathbb{F}_p$ than prior art ([9, 21, 22]), but our communication and round complexity are sufficiently low as to make using a slightly larger field not problematic.

Future Work. A sequel which introduces a novel truncation protocol and a private comparison protocol is currently in preparation. These new protocols will allow Mercury to perform fixed-point arithmetic in any base and make Mercury a more complete and versatile family of protocols for secure computation with rational numbers.
Our next step is to implement Mercury to facilitate more comprehensive comparison with existing protocols. As mentioned in the introduction, even though Mercury is built on SSS, its protocols could easily be adapted to use additive secret sharing, meaning we can implement Mercury using MP-SPDZ.

Acknowlegment. The authors warmly thank Professor Jonathan Katz for reading early drafts of this paper, and providing helpful insights and suggestions. This work is fully supported by Algemetric Inc.

A   Proofs

Proof (of Proposition 1). Note that $\mathsf{p} \in \mathcal{P}_{d,\tau}$ can be written as $\mathsf{p} = \sum_i c_i p_i$, where $\sum_i |c_i| \le \tau$, each $|c_i| \ge 1$, and each p_i is a monomial of degree at most d.

Let $\mathsf{p} = \sum_{i=1}^{I} c_i p_i$. Since $\deg(p_i) \le d$, the output $p_i(x_1/y_1, \ldots, x_k/y_k)$ is a fraction of the form

$$\frac{a_i}{b_i} = \frac{x_{i_1} x_{i_2} \cdots x_{i_\ell}}{y_{i_1} y_{i_2} \cdots y_{i_\ell}}, \quad \text{for some } \ell \le d \text{ and } \{i_1, \ldots, i_\ell\} \subseteq \{1, \ldots, k\}.$$

As each $x_i/y_i \in \mathcal{G}_M$, we have $|a_i| \leq X^\ell \leq X^d$ and $|b_i| \leq Y^\ell \leq Y^d$. Since $x/y = \sum_{i=1}^{I} c_i \cdot a_i/b_i$,

$$x = (c_1 a_1)b_2 b_3 \cdots b_I + b_1(c_2 a_2)b_3 \cdots b_I + b_1 b_2 \cdots b_{I-1}(c_I a_I) \text{ and}$$
$$y = b_1 b_2 \cdots b_I.$$

It follows from $\sum |c_i| \leq \tau$ and the above bound on $|a_i|, |b_i|$ that

$$|x| \leq \sum_{i=1}^{I} |c_i|(X^d)(Y^d)^{I-1} \leq \tau \cdot X^d Y^{d(I-1)} \text{ and } |y| \leq Y^{d(I-1)}.$$

The proof is completed by observing that $|c_\alpha| \geq 1$, for all α, implies $I \leq \tau$.

References

1. Aliasgari, M., Blanton, M., Zhang, Y., Steele, A.: Secure computation on floating point numbers. In: NDSS 2013. The Internet Society, February 2013
2. Bar-Ilan, J., Beaver, D.: Non-cryptographic fault-tolerant computing in constant number of rounds of interaction. In: Rudnicki, P. (ed.) 8th ACM PODC, pp. 201–209. ACM, August 1989. https://doi.org/10.1145/72981.72995
3. Beaver, D.: Efficient multiparty protocols using circuit randomization. In: Feigenbaum, J. (ed.) CRYPTO 1991. LNCS, vol. 576, pp. 420–432. Springer, Heidelberg (1992). https://doi.org/10.1007/3-540-46766-1_34
4. Beimel, A.: Secret-sharing schemes: a survey, pp. 11–46, May 2011. https://doi.org/10.1007/978-3-642-20901-7_2
5. Ben-Or, M., Goldwasser, S., Wigderson, A.: Completeness theorems for non-cryptographic fault-tolerant distributed computation (extended abstract). In: 20th ACM STOC, pp. 1–10. ACM Press, May 1988. https://doi.org/10.1145/62212.62213
6. Bogetoft, P., et al.: Multiparty computation goes live. Cryptology ePrint Archive, Report 2008/068 (2008). https://eprint.iacr.org/2008/068
7. Boyle, E., Gilboa, N., Ishai, Y.: Function secret sharing. In: Oswald, E., Fischlin, M. (eds.) EUROCRYPT 2015. LNCS, vol. 9057, pp. 337–367. Springer, Heidelberg (2015). https://doi.org/10.1007/978-3-662-46803-6_12
8. Canetti, R.: Security and composition of multiparty cryptographic protocols. J. Cryptol. 13(1), 143–202 (2000). https://doi.org/10.1007/s001459910006
9. Catrina, O.: Round-efficient protocols for secure multiparty fixed-point arithmetic. In: 2018 International Conference on Communications (COMM), pp. 431–436 (2018). https://doi.org/10.1109/ICComm.2018.8484794
10. Catrina, O.: Efficient secure floating-point arithmetic using Shamir secret sharing. In: International Conference on E-Business and Telecommunication Networks (2019)
11. Catrina, O., Saxena, A.: Secure computation with fixed-point numbers. In: Sion, R. (ed.) FC 2010. LNCS, vol. 6052, pp. 35–50. Springer, Heidelberg (2010). https://doi.org/10.1007/978-3-642-14577-3_6

12. Cramer, R., Damgård, I., Ishai, Y.: Share conversion, pseudorandom secret-sharing and applications to secure computation. In: Kilian, J. (ed.) TCC 2005. LNCS, vol. 3378, pp. 342–362. Springer, Heidelberg (2005). https://doi.org/10.1007/978-3-540-30576-7_19

13. Cramer, R., Damgård, I.B., et al.: Secure Multiparty Computation. Cambridge University Press, Cambridge (2015)

14. Damgård, I., Ishai, Y.: Scalable secure multiparty computation. In: Dwork, C. (ed.) CRYPTO 2006. LNCS, vol. 4117, pp. 501–520. Springer, Heidelberg (2006). https://doi.org/10.1007/11818175_30

15. Gennaro, R., Rabin, M.O., Rabin, T.: Simplified VSS and fast-track multiparty computations with applications to threshold cryptography. In: Coan, B.A., Afek, Y. (eds.) 17th ACM PODC, pp. 101–111. ACM, June/July 1998. https://doi.org/10.1145/277697.277716

16. Goldreich, O., Micali, S., Wigderson, A.: How to play any mental game or a completeness theorem for protocols with honest majority. In: Aho, A. (ed.) 19th ACM STOC, pp. 218–229. ACM Press, May 1987. https://doi.org/10.1145/28395.28420

17. Harmon, L., Delavignette, G., Roy, A., Silva, D.: Pie: p-adic encoding for high-precision arithmetic in homomorphic encryption. In: Tibouchi, M., Wang, X. (eds.) Applied Cryptography and Network Security. ACNS 2023. LNCS, vol. 13905, pp. 425–450. Springer, Cham (2023). https://doi.org/10.1007/978-3-031-33488-7_16

18. Keller, M.: MP-SPDZ: a versatile framework for multi-party computation. In: Ligatti, J., Ou, X., Katz, J., Vigna, G. (eds.) ACM CCS 2020, pp. 1575–1590. ACM Press, November 2020. https://doi.org/10.1145/3372297.3417872

19. Lindell, Y.: Secure multiparty computation (MPC). Cryptology ePrint Archive, Report 2020/300 (2020). https://eprint.iacr.org/2020/300

20. Shamir, A.: How to share a secret. Commun. Assoc. Comput. Mach. **22**(11), 612–613 (1979)

21. Veugen, T., Abspoel, M.: Secure integer division with a private divisor. PoPETs **2021**(4), 339–349 (2021). https://doi.org/10.2478/popets-2021-0073

22. Wagh, S.: Pika: secure computation using function secret sharing over rings. Cryptology ePrint Archive, Report 2022/826 (2022). https://eprint.iacr.org/2022/826

23. Yao, A.C.C.: How to generate and exchange secrets (extended abstract). In: 27th FOCS, pp. 162–167. IEEE Computer Society Press, October 1986. https://doi.org/10.1109/SFCS.1986.25

Evolving Conditional Disclosure of Secrets

Naty Peter[✉]

Georgetown University, Washington, DC, USA
np594@georgetown.edu

Abstract. In this work, we define and study the notion of *evolving conditional disclosure of secrets (CDS)* protocols. In this model, parties arrive infinitely in sequential order. Each party holds a private input, and when arrives, it sends a random message to a referee. In turn, at any stage of the protocol, the referee should be able to reconstruct a secret string, held by all the parties, from the messages it gets, if and only if the inputs of the parties that arrived satisfy some condition.

A similar notion was previously presented for *secret sharing*, a closely related cryptographic primitive used in many secure protocols. In a secret sharing scheme, a dealer holds a secret string. It randomly generates shares and distributes them to a set of parties, one share for each party, such that only some predefined subsets of the parties would be able to reconstruct the secret from their shares.

In addition to the initiation of evolving CDS, we present a few constructions of evolving CDS protocols, for different classes of conditions that should be satisfied by the inputs of the parties. We believe that our new notion can be used to better understand evolving secret sharing and other related cryptographic primitives, and that further applications and constructions of it will be found in the future.

Keywords: Evolving secret sharing · conditional disclosure of secrets · information-theoretic cryptography

1 Introduction

Secret sharing is a fundamental cryptographic primitive, first presented by Blakley [Bla79] and Shamir [Sha79] for the threshold setting, and later by Ito, Saito, and Nishizeki [ISN87, ISN93] for the general setting. In a secret sharing scheme, a dealer holds a *secret* string, and distributes random string *shares* to a set of n parties, such that only some *authorized subsets* of the parties can reconstruct the secret from their shares. Other *unauthorized subsets* should not learn information on the secret. The collection of authorized subsets of parties is referred to as the *access structure*. Secret sharing schemes have been used in many cryptographic

Work supported in part by the Massive Data Institute at Georgetown University.

© The Author(s), under exclusive license to Springer Nature Switzerland AG 2023
E. Athanasopoulos and B. Mennink (Eds.): ISC 2023, LNCS 14411, pp. 327–347, 2023.
https://doi.org/10.1007/978-3-031-49187-0_17

applications, such as attribute-based encryption (ABE), secure multi-party computation (MPC) protocols, access control, and threshold cryptography.

A main problem in the secret sharing regime is to determine the *share size* (i.e., the size of the share of each party) required in a secret sharing scheme for a given access structure. The first constructions for the threshold setting [Bla79, Sha79] are for *threshold access structures*, in which the authorized subsets are all the subsets of parties whose size is greater than some threshold. These constructions are very efficient in terms of the share size, i.e., the size of each share is logarithmic in the number of parties n. For general access structures, following the secret sharing scheme of [ISN87, ISN93], new constructions of secret sharing schemes were presented [BL88, BD91, BI92, KW93, LV18, ABF+19, ABNP20, AN21, BOP21, BOP23]. However, all these constructions require exponential (in the number of parties n) share size, while the best known lower bound on the share size of secret sharing schemes for general access structures is linear in n (up to a logarithmic factor) [Csi94, Csi96, Csi97].

Additionally, many variants of secret sharing were introduced, e.g., verifiable secret sharing [CGMA85, Fel87], proactive secret sharing [HJKY95, SW99], quantum secret sharing [HBB99, KKI99], leakage-resilient secret sharing [DP07, DDV10], function secret sharing [BGI15, BGI16b], homomorphic secret sharing [BGI16a, BCG+17], and non-malleable secret sharing [GK18a, GK18b].

Evolving secret sharing is another variant of secret sharing, presented by Komargodski, Naor, and Yogev [KNY16]. In contrast to classical secret sharing, in evolving secret sharing the number of parties is unbounded.

The parties arrive infinitely in sequential order, while when a new party arrives, the dealer provides it its share. After a share was given to a party from the dealer, this share cannot be updated later, when more parties arrive. However, in order to generate the random share of some party, the dealer can use the randomness used for the shares of previous parties that arrived before. As a consequence, the (possibly infinite) *evolving access structure* is constantly updated when each party arrives. That is, when a new party arrives, all authorized sets that contain this new party are added to the evolving access structure.

One of the motivations for considering and studying the evolving setting is that in the real world, updates could be very costly. In addition, the evolving setting supports infinitely many parties, and even for an unknown finite number of parties, the dealer does not need to assume it (or even the evolving access structure) beforehand.[1] If the dealer is required to do so and it overestimates the number of arriving parties, then it will distribute to the parties shares that are too large, resulting in inefficient scheme. Otherwise, if the dealer underestimates the number of arriving parties, then it will have to update the shares of the parties, and maybe even generate new shares to some parties that arrived first.

While in classical secret sharing the share size of each party is measured as a function of the foretold number of parties n, in evolving secret sharing the share size of the tth party is measured as a function of t. In [KNY16], they con-

---

[1] The dealer may learn the new authorized sets added to the evolving access structure when a new party arrives only at that stage, just before distributing the new share.

structed evolving secret sharing scheme for general evolving access structures, in which the share size of the tth party is exponential in t. The best known lower bound on the share size of evolving secret sharing schemes for general evolving access structure is almost tight [Maz23]. Evolving secret sharing schemes have been extensively studied for *evolving threshold access structures* [KP17, DPS+18, DDM19, PA20, OK20, CDS20, Cha20, XY21, PA21, YLH23]. In particular, these works showed constructions of evolving schemes for several different evolving variants of threshold access structures. Additionally, constructions of evolving secret sharing schemes for other evolving access structures were presented [BO18, DRF+19, BO20, PSAM21, Cha22], and other models closely related to evolving secret sharing were also studied [Cac95, CT12, CDS21].

Another cryptographic primitive related to secret sharing is *conditional disclosure of secrets (CDS)*, first presented by Gertner, Ishai, Kushilevitz, and Malkin [GIKM00]. In a CDS protocol, n parties holds a secret, and in addition each of them holds a private input. Each party sends a random message to a referee, that depends on its input, the secret, and a common randomness held by all the parties. The referee can reconstruct the secret from the messages it gets if and only if the inputs of the parties satisfy some condition, specified by a predicate. That is, the secret can be reconstructed by the referee only when some predicate holds on the inputs of the parties. Otherwise, the referee should not learn information about the secret.

CDS protocols are used in several applications, such as oblivious transfer (OT) protocols, attribute-based encryption (ABE), symmetrically private information retrieval (SPIR) protocols, and secret sharing schemes. One of the main goals when developing CDS protocols is to minimize the *message size*, that is, the size of the message sent by each party. Constructions of CDS protocols for general predicates have been developed in a few works [LVW18, AA18, BP18, BOP21, BOP23]. In the former, an efficient construction of CDS protocol with sub-exponential (in the number of parties n and the input domain size of each party) message size was presented. In particular, the CDS protocols of [LVW18, BP18, BOP21, BOP23] were used to construct the best known secret sharing schemes for general access structures [LV18, ABF+19, ABNP20, AN21, BOP21, BOP23].[2]

Our Contribution. As our conceptual contribution, we introduce the notion of *evolving conditional disclosure of secrets*, as described below. Besides its pedagogical and theoretical interest, this notion is motivated by the advantages of the evolving setting and the applications of CDS protocols. As in evolving secret sharing, the number of parties is unbounded also in evolving CDS, where the

---

[2] In [ABNP20, AN21], they used a robust version of the CDS protocols of [LVW18, BP18], in which the referee should learn no information on the secret, even when some parties deviated from the protocol by sending more than one message. In [BOP21, BOP23], they developed a new CDS protocol and used the robust version of it to construct a new secret sharing scheme.

parties arrive infinitely in sequential order. Each party, when arrives, sends one random message to a referee, that depends on its input, the secret, and a common randomness. It can use the randomness used by all the parties arrived before, and in addition another new fresh randomness. In evolving CDS protocols, the *evolving predicate* used to determine whether the secret can be reconstructed by the referee consists of an infinite sequence of multi-input predicates, one predicate for every possible number of inputs (of the parties), which is constantly updated when a new party arrives. This sequence of predicates is monotone, is a sense that if a predicate holds on some sequence of inputs, then the following predicate will also holds on the same sequence of inputs, while adding to it any new possible input, which is the one held by the new party.

Our technical contribution contains several constructions of evolving CDS protocols, with perfect information-theoretic security, described as follow.

- We first present an evolving CDS protocol for general evolving predicates, that is, a construction for any possible evolving predicate. In order to get the desired protocol, we show an evolving secret sharing scheme for *evolving hypergraph access structures*, obtained by optimizing the general evolving secret sharing scheme of [KNY16], and reduce evolving CDS protocols for general predicates to evolving secret sharing schemes for such evolving hypergraph access structures.
- In addition, we show an evolving CDS protocol for *evolving min-sum predicates*, which hold if and only if the sum of the inputs is larger than some minimal value.[3] This construction is obtained by reducing evolving CDS protocols for evolving min-sum predicates to evolving secret sharing schemes for evolving threshold access structures.
- Finally, we construct an evolving CDS protocol for *evolving constrained predicates*, which hold if and only if enough individual inputs satisfy some attributes. As the protocol for evolving min-sum predicates, we get it by a reduction to evolving threshold secret sharing schemes.

We believe that the notion of evolving CDS can be used to better understand evolving secret sharing, classical CDS, and other related cryptographic primitives, and that further applications and constructions of evolving CDS protocols will be found in the future.

2   Preliminaries

Notations. We denote the logarithmic function with base 2 by log. For $n \in \mathbb{N}$, we denote by $[n]$ the set $\{1, \ldots, n\}$. For a set $\mathcal{X}$, we denote $x \leftarrow \mathcal{X}$ as a uniformly random sample x from $\mathcal{X}$. We also denote $2^{\mathcal{X}}$ as the collection of all subsets of $\mathcal{X}$. For two probability distributions X and Y, we denote $X \equiv Y$ when the random variables X and Y are identically distributed.

---

[3] The minimal value can be different for any number of inputs. However, the sequence of minimal values should be non-decreasing.

Secret Sharing. In a secret sharing scheme, a dealer, which holds a secret s, samples a random string r, and uses the secret s and the random string r to generate n shares according to some access structures over a set of n parties $P_1, \ldots, P_n$. Then, it privately distributes the ith share to party P_i. Any authorized subset of parties in the access structure should be able to reconstruct the secret from its share, while subsets not in the access structure should learn no information on the secret. We now present the formal definition of secret sharing schemes.

Definition 1 (Access Structures). *Let $\mathcal{P} = \{P_1, \ldots, P_n\}$ be a set of parties. A collection $\mathcal{A} \subseteq 2^{\mathcal{P}}$ is* monotone *if $A \in \mathcal{A}$ and $A \subseteq B$ imply that $B \in \mathcal{A}$. An* access structure *is a monotone collection $\mathcal{A} \subseteq 2^{\mathcal{P}}$ of non-empty subsets of $\mathcal{P}$. Sets in $\mathcal{A}$ are called* authorized, *and sets not in $\mathcal{A}$ are called* unauthorized. *We say that $A \in \mathcal{A}$ is* minimal authorized set *if $B \notin \mathcal{A}$ for every $B \subset A$. The collection of minimal authorized sets of $\mathcal{A}$ is denoted by $\min \mathcal{A}$.*

Definition 2 (Secret Sharing Schemes). *Let $\mathcal{A} \subseteq 2^{\mathcal{P}}$ be an access structure. A secret sharing scheme Σ with domain of secrets $\mathcal{S}$, domain of random strings $\mathcal{R}$, and share domains $\mathcal{S}_1, \ldots, \mathcal{S}_n$, consists of deterministic sharing algorithm $\mathsf{Sh} : \mathcal{S} \times \mathcal{R} \to \mathcal{S}_1 \times \cdots \times \mathcal{S}_n$, that takes a secret and a random string, and outputs n shares for the n parties, and $|\mathcal{A}|$ deterministic reconstruction algorithms $\mathsf{Rec}_A : \mathcal{S}_{i_1} \times \cdots \times \mathcal{S}_{i_{|A|}} \to \mathcal{S}$, for every authorized set $A = \{P_{i_1}, \ldots, P_{i_{|A|}}\} \in \mathcal{A},^4$ that takes $|A|$ shares from the parties of A, and outputs a secret. For every set $A \subseteq \mathcal{P}$, denote $\mathsf{Sh}_A(s, r)$ as the restriction of $\mathsf{Sh}(s, r)$ to its A-entries (i.e., the shares of the parties in A). We say that Σ is a secret sharing scheme realizing the access structure $\mathcal{A}$ if it satisfies the following requirements.*

Correctness. The secret can be reconstructed by any authorized set of parties from $\mathcal{A}$. That is, for every set $A \in \mathcal{A}$, every secret $s \in \mathcal{S}$, and every random string $r \in \mathcal{R}$, it holds that

$$\mathsf{Rec}_A(\mathsf{Sh}_A(s, r)) = s.$$

Security. Any unauthorized set cannot learn any information about the secret from its shares. That is, for every set $A \notin \mathcal{A}$ and every two secrets $s, s' \in S$,

$$\mathsf{Sh}_A(s, r) \equiv \mathsf{Sh}_A(s', r),$$

where $r \leftarrow \mathcal{R}$.

---

4 Observe that the secret sharing scheme can contain reconstruction algorithms Rec_A only for every *minimal authorized set $A \in \min \mathcal{A}$*. In that case, a *non-minimal* authorized set can apply the reconstruction algorithm of some minimal authorized set that contained in it.

Complexity. The secret size *is defined as* $\log |\mathcal{S}|$, *the* share size of party P_i *is defined as* $\log |\mathcal{S}_i|$, *and the* total share size *is defined as* $\sum_{i=1}^{n} \log |\mathcal{S}_i|$.

Evolving Secret Sharing. In an evolving secret sharing scheme, the number of parties is unbounded, and the parties arrive infinitely in sequential order. When party P_t arrives, the dealer generates its share by first sampling a new fresh random string r_t, and then uses the secret s and all the random strings $r_1, \ldots, r_t$ sampled until party P_t arrived, to generate the tth share and send it to party P_t. The evolving access structure is therefore constantly updated when a new party arrives, by determining the authorized sets that contain the new party. Below we provide the formal definition of evolving secret sharing schemes.

Definition 3 (Evolving Access Structures). *Let* $\mathcal{P} = \{\mathsf{P}_t\}_{t \in \mathbb{N}}$ *be an* infinite *set of parties. An* evolving access structure *is a collection* $\mathcal{A} \subseteq 2^{\mathcal{P}}$, *where each set of* $\mathcal{A}$ *is* finite, *and for every* $t \in \mathbb{N}$, *the collection* $\mathcal{A}_t := \mathcal{A} \cap 2^{\{\mathsf{P}_1, \ldots, \mathsf{P}_t\}}$ *is an access structure, as in Definition 1. The collection of minimal authorized sets of* $\mathcal{A}$ *is denoted by* $\min \mathcal{A}$, *again as in Definition 1.*

Definition 4 (Evolving Secret Sharing Schemes). *Let* $\mathcal{A} \subseteq 2^{\mathcal{P}}$ *be an evolving access structure. An* evolving secret sharing scheme Σ *with domain of secrets* $\mathcal{S}$, *sequence of domains of random strings* $\{\mathcal{R}_t\}_{t \in \mathbb{N}}$, *and sequence of share domains* $\{\mathcal{S}_t\}_{t \in \mathbb{N}}$, *consists of a sequence of deterministic sharing algorithms* $\{\mathsf{Sh}_t : \mathcal{S} \times \mathcal{R}_1 \times \cdots \times \mathcal{R}_t \to \mathcal{S}_t\}_{t \in \mathbb{N}}$, *that takes a secret and* t *random strings, and outputs a share for party* P_t, *and (possibly infinite number of) deterministic reconstruction algorithms* $\mathsf{Rec}_A : \mathcal{S}_{t_1} \times \cdots \times \mathcal{S}_{t_{|A|}} \to \mathcal{S}$, *for every authorized set* $A = \{\mathsf{P}_{t_1}, \ldots, \mathsf{P}_{t_{|A|}}\} \in \mathcal{A}$, *that takes* $|A|$ *shares from the parties of* A, *and outputs a secret. We say that* Σ *is an evolving secret sharing scheme realizing the evolving access structure* $\mathcal{A}$ *if for every* $t \in \mathbb{N}$, *the secret sharing scheme* Σ_t, *with the sharing algorithm* $\mathsf{Sh}^t : \mathcal{S} \times \mathcal{R}_1 \times \cdots \times \mathcal{R}_t \to \mathcal{S}_1 \times \cdots \times \mathcal{S}_t$, *where* $\mathsf{Sh}^t(s, r_1, \ldots, r_n) = (\mathsf{Sh}_1(s, r_1), \ldots, \mathsf{Sh}_t(s, r_1, \ldots, r_n))$, *and the reconstruction algorithms* Rec_A *for every* $A \in \mathcal{A}_t$, *is a secret sharing scheme realizing the access structure* $\mathcal{A}_t$ *(defined in Definition 3), as in Definition 2.*

The following definition of evolving threshold access structures was presented in [KNY16, KP17].[5]

Definition 5 (Evolving Threshold Access Structures). *Let* $\mathcal{P} = \{\mathsf{P}_t\}_{t \in \mathbb{N}}$ *be an infinite set of parties, and let* $\mathcal{K} = \{k_t\}_{t \in \mathbb{N}}$ *be a sequence of non-decreasing integers, where* $k_t \leq t$ *for every* $t \in \mathbb{N}$. *The* evolving $\mathcal{K}$-threshold access structure $\mathcal{A}^{\mathcal{K}}$ *is the evolving access structure in which for every* $t \in \mathbb{N}$, *contain as minimal authorized sets all the subsets of size exactly* k_t, *such that* P_t *is the party with the larger index in the set.[6] I.e.,* $\mathcal{A}^k$ *is the infinite union, for every* $t \in \mathbb{N}$, *of the*

---

[5] In [KP17], they refer to it as *dynamic threshold access structures*. In this work, we also focus on the special case in which all the thresholds are the same constant value.

[6] In particular, if for a (possibly infinite) set of consecutive natural numbers $T \subseteq \mathbb{N}$, the integers k_t, for every $t \in T$, are equal to the same value k, then all subsets of size k that contain P_t as their larger party, are minimal authorized sets.

k_t-*out-of-t threshold access structure over the parties* $\mathsf{P}_1, \ldots, \mathsf{P}_t$. *If* $k_t = k$ *for every* $t \in \mathbb{N}$, *we say that* $\mathcal{A}^k := \mathcal{A}^\mathcal{K}$ *is the* evolving k-threshold access structure.

Example 1. Consider the evolving access structure $\mathcal{A}^2$ with the minimal authorized sets $\min \mathcal{A}^2 := \{\{\mathsf{P}_t, \mathsf{P}_{t'}\} : t \neq t' \in \mathbb{N}\}$, that is, any subset of 2 parties can reconstruct the secret, while single parties cannot learn information on the secret. Then, for example, after 3 parties have been arrived, the collection of minimal authorized sets is $\min \mathcal{A}_3^2 := \{\{\mathsf{P}_1, \mathsf{P}_2\}, \{\mathsf{P}_1, \mathsf{P}_3\}, \{\mathsf{P}_2, \mathsf{P}_3\}\}$.

Additionally, for $\mathcal{K} = \{t - 2\}_{t \in \mathbb{N}}$ (i.e., $k_t = t - 2$ for every $t \in \mathbb{N}$), we have

$$\min \mathcal{A}^\mathcal{K} := \{\{\mathsf{P}_{i_1}, \ldots, \mathsf{P}_{i_{t-3}}, \mathsf{P}_t\} : t \in \mathbb{N}, \{i_1, \ldots, i_{t-3}\} \subset [t-1]\}.$$

Then, after 4 parties have been arrived, the collection of minimal authorized sets is $\min \mathcal{A}_4^\mathcal{K} := \{\{\mathsf{P}_3\}, \{\mathsf{P}_1, \mathsf{P}_4\}, \{\mathsf{P}_2, \mathsf{P}_4\}, \{\mathsf{P}_3, \mathsf{P}_4\}\}$.

Conditional Disclosure of Secrets. In a conditional disclosure of secrets (CDS) protocol, n parties $\mathsf{Q}_1, \ldots, \mathsf{Q}_n$ hold a secret s and a common random string r,[7] and each of them holds a private input x_i for some n-input predicate f. Then, each of the parties Q_i sends one message to a referee, which is based on its private input x_i, the secret s, and the common random string r. The referee, knowing the inputs $x_1, \ldots, x_n$ of the parties, should learn the secret if and only if the inputs of the parties satisfy the predicate, that is, $f(x_1, \ldots, x_n) = 1$. We next show the formal definition of CDS protocols.

Definition 6 (Conditional Disclosure of Secrets Protocols). *Let* $\mathcal{X} := \mathcal{X}_1 \times \cdots \times \mathcal{X}_n$ *be an n-input domain and let* $f : \mathcal{X} \to \{0, 1\}$ *be an n-input predicate. A* conditional disclosure of secrets (CDS) protocol Π *with domain of secrets* $\mathcal{S}$, *domain of common random strings* $\mathcal{R}$, *and message domains* $\mathcal{M}_1, \ldots, \mathcal{M}_n$, *consists of n deterministic message computation algorithms* $\mathsf{Enc}_i : \mathcal{X}_i \times \mathcal{S} \times \mathcal{R} \to \mathcal{M}_i$, *for every* $i \in [n]$, *that takes an input, a secret, and a random string, and outputs a message for party* Q_i, *and deterministic reconstruction algorithm* $\mathsf{Dec} : \mathcal{X}_1 \times \cdots \times \mathcal{X}_n \times \mathcal{M}_1 \times \cdots \times \mathcal{M}_n \to \mathcal{S}$ *that takes n inputs and n messages, and (possibly) outputs a secret. For every input* $x = (x_1, \ldots, x_n) \in \mathcal{X}$, *denote* $\mathsf{Enc}(x, s, r) := (\mathsf{Enc}_1(x_1, s, r), \ldots, \mathsf{Enc}_n(x_n, s, r))$. *We say that* Π *is a CDS protocol for the predicate* f *if it satisfies the following requirements.*

Correctness. The secret can be reconstructed by the messages on any 1-input of f. *That is, for every input* $x \in \mathcal{X}$ *for which* $f(x) = 1$, *every secret* $s \in \mathcal{S}$, *and every common random string* $r \in \mathcal{R}$, *it holds that*

$$\mathsf{Dec}(x, \mathsf{Enc}(x, s, r)) = s.$$

---

[7] In order to distinguish from the parties in the secret sharing model, we denote the parties in the CDS model by $\mathsf{Q}_1, \ldots, \mathsf{Q}_n$.

Security. Any information about the secret cannot be learned from the messages on any 0-input of f. That is, for every input $x \in \mathcal{X}$ for which $f(x) = 0$ and every two secrets $s, s' \in \mathcal{S}$, it holds that

$$(x, \mathsf{Enc}(x, s, r)) \equiv (x, \mathsf{Enc}(x, s', r)),$$

where $r \leftarrow \mathcal{R}$.

Complexity. The secret size is defined as $\log |\mathcal{S}|$, the message size of party Q_i is defined as $\log |\mathcal{M}_i|$, and the total message size is defined as $\sum_{i=1}^{n} \log |\mathcal{M}_i|$.

3   Definition of Evolving Conditional Disclosure of Secrets

In this section, we present our definition of evolving conditional disclosure of secrets protocols. As in evolving secret sharing schemes, in an evolving CDS protocol, the number of parties is unbounded, and parties arrive infinitely in sequential order. The common random string is consists of infinite sequence of finite common random strings $r_1, r_2, r_3, \ldots$, where the random string r_t is associated with party Q_t. When party Q_t arrives, it sends one message to the referee, which is based on its private input x_t, the secret s, and the common random strings $r_1, \ldots, r_t$. The evolving predicate, through which it is determined whether the referee can reconstruct the secret or not, is constantly extended to be defined on one additional input, every time a new party arrives. We are now ready to introduce the formal definition of evolving CDS protocols.

Definition 7 (Evolving Predicates). *Let $\{\mathcal{X}_t\}_{t \in \mathbb{N}}$ be a sequence of input domains. An evolving predicate is a sequence of predicates $\mathcal{F} = \{f_t : \mathcal{X}_1 \times \cdots \times \mathcal{X}_t \to \{0, 1\}\}_{t \in \mathbb{N}}$, such that for every $t \in \mathbb{N}$ and every $(x_1, \ldots, x_{t+1}) \in \mathcal{X}_1 \times \cdots \times \mathcal{X}_{t+1}$, it holds that*

$$f_{t+1}(x_1, \ldots, x_{t+1}) \geq f_t(x_1, \ldots, x_t).$$

Note that Definition 7 implies that if f_t holds on the input $(x_1, \ldots, x_t) \in \mathcal{X}_1 \times \cdots \times \mathcal{X}_t$, then f_i also holds on $(x_1, \ldots, x_t, x_{t+1}, \ldots, x_i)$ for every $(x_{t+1}, \ldots, x_i) \in \mathcal{X}_{t+1} \times \cdots \times \mathcal{X}_i$, and if f_t does not hold on the input $(x_1, \ldots, x_t) \in \mathcal{X}_1 \times \cdots \times \mathcal{X}_t$, then f_i also does not hold on $(x_1, \ldots, x_i)$ for every $i \in [t-1]$.

Definition 8 (Evolving Conditional Disclosure of Secrets Protocols). *Let $\{\mathcal{X}_t\}_{t \in \mathbb{N}}$ be a sequence of input domains, and let $\mathcal{F} = \{f_t : \mathcal{X}_1 \times \cdots \times \mathcal{X}_t \to \{0, 1\}\}_{t \in \mathbb{N}}$ be an evolving predicate. An evolving conditional disclosure of secrets protocol Π with domain of secrets $\mathcal{S}$, sequence of domains of random strings $\{\mathcal{R}_t\}_{t \in \mathbb{N}}$, and sequence of message domains $\{\mathcal{M}_t\}_{t \in \mathbb{N}}$, consists of a sequence of deterministic message computation algorithms $\{\mathsf{Enc}_t : \mathcal{X}_t \times \mathcal{S} \times \mathcal{R}_1 \times \cdots \times \mathcal{R}_t \to \mathcal{M}_t\}_{t \in \mathbb{N}}$, that takes an input, a secret, and t random strings, and outputs a message for party Q_t, and an infinite number of deterministic reconstruction* *algorithms* $\mathsf{Dec}_t : \mathcal{X}_1 \times \cdots \times \mathcal{X}_t \times \mathcal{M}_1 \times \cdots \times \mathcal{M}_t \to \mathcal{S}$, *for every* $t \in \mathbb{N}$, *that takes t inputs and t messages, and (possibly) outputs a secret. We say that Π is an evolving CDS protocol for the evolving predicate $\mathcal{F}$ if for every $t \in \mathbb{N}$, the CDS protocol Π_t, with the message computation algorithms* $\mathsf{Enc}_i^t : \mathcal{X}_i \times \mathcal{S} \times \mathcal{R}_1 \times \cdots \times \mathcal{R}_t \to \mathcal{M}_i$, *for every* $i \in [t]$, *where* $\mathsf{Enc}_i^t(x_i, s, r_1, \ldots, r_t) := \mathsf{Enc}_i(x_i, s, r_1, \ldots, r_i)$,[8] *and the reconstruction algorithm* Dec_t, *is a CDS protocol for the predicate f_t, as in Definition 6.*

4 Evolving CDS for General Predicates

In this section, we consider the class of all possible evolving predicates, in which the input domain size of each party is N, that is, evolving predicates of the form $\mathcal{F}_N = \{f_t : [N]^t \to \{0,1\}\}_{t \in \mathbb{N}}$.

We show how to construct evolving CDS protocols for the every evolving predicate $\mathcal{F}_N$ using evolving secret sharing schemes for evolving hypergraph access structures, as defined below.

Definition 9 (Evolving Hypergraph Access Structures). *Let $N \in \mathbb{N}$. An* evolving hypergraph access structure $\mathcal{A}^N$ *is the evolving access structure in which for every* $t \in \mathbb{N}$, *the minimal authorized sets of size exactly t are some of the subsets of the form* $\{\mathsf{P}_{i_1}, \mathsf{P}_{N+i_2}, \ldots, \mathsf{P}_{(t-1)N+i_t}\}$, *for some* $i_1, i_2, \ldots, i_t \in [N]$. *That is, the minimal authorized sets of size t are some of the subsets that for every $i \in [t]$, contain exactly one party among the N parties* $\mathsf{P}_{(i-1)N+1}, \mathsf{P}_{(i-1)N+2}, \ldots, \mathsf{P}_{iN}$.

Remark 1. An evolving hypergraph access structure $\mathcal{A}^N$ can be represented by an infinite multi-partite hypergraph $\mathcal{H} = (\mathcal{V}, \mathcal{E})$, where the (infinite) set of vertices is $\mathcal{V} = (\mathcal{V}_1, \mathcal{V}_2, \mathcal{V}_3, \ldots)$, such that $|\mathcal{V}_t| = N$ for every $t \in \mathbb{N}$, and the set of hyperedges is $\mathcal{E} = (\mathcal{E}_1, \mathcal{E}_2, \mathcal{E}_3, \ldots)$, where $\mathcal{E}_t$ is a set of t-hyperedges (i.e., for every $e_t \in \mathcal{E}_t$ we have $|e_t| = t$), such that for every $e_t \in \mathcal{E}_t$, it holds that $|e_t \cap \mathcal{V}_i| = 1$ for every $i \in [t]$. That is, the vertices are partitioned into infinite number of subsets of size N, and every t-hyperedge contains exactly one vertex from each of the first t subsets of the partition.

Observe that in evolving secret sharing schemes realizing evolving hypergraph access structures, we require that every unauthorized set (i.e., an independent set not containing an hyperedge, in the hypergraph representation) should not learn any information about the secret, while in evolving CDS protocols, we require security only for inputs for which the predicate does not hold.

In particular, in evolving CDS, we do not require security for the case that the referee gets two messages (or more) from the same party on different inputs (unless the predicate holds on some combination of the inputs), while for evolving secret sharing schemes realizing evolving hypergraph access structures, we

---

[8] We define Enc_i^t, for every $i \in [t]$, only for syntactic reasons; the algorithm Enc_i^t just ignores the last $t - i$ random strings and simply applies Enc_i.

require security for unauthorized sets that may have two parties (or more) from the same part. One possible direction to obtain better evolving secret sharing schemes (in terms of the share size) may be to relax the definition of evolving hypergraph access structures, by adding to the access structure subsets with more than one party from the same part.

Theorem 1. *Let $\ell, N \in \mathbb{N}$, and let $\mathcal{F}_N = \{f_t : [N]^t \to \{0,1\}\}_{t \in \mathbb{N}}$ be an evolving predicate. Assume that for every evolving hypergraph access structure $\mathcal{A}^N$ there is an evolving secret sharing scheme realizing $\mathcal{A}^N$, in which the secret size is ℓ and the share size of party P_t is $c(t, N, \ell)$. Then, there is an evolving CDS protocol for $\mathcal{F}_N$, in which the secret size is ℓ and the message size of party Q_t is $c((t-1)N + x_t, N, \ell)$, where $x_t \in [N]$ is the input of party Q_t.*

- **Inputs:** Party Q_t holds $x_t \in [N]$ for every $t \in \mathbb{N}$.
- **The secret:** A string $s \in \{0,1\}^\ell$.
- **Common randomness:** A sequence of random strings $\{r_t\}_{t \in \mathbb{N}}$, where $r_t \leftarrow \mathcal{R}_t$ for every $t \in \mathbb{N}$. Also, define $q_t := (r_{(t-1)N+1}, r_{(t-1)N+2}, \ldots, r_{tN})$ for every $t \in \mathbb{N}$.
- **The oracle:** An evolving secret sharing scheme Σ_N realizing the evolving hypergraph access structure $\mathcal{A}^N$, where

$$\min \mathcal{A}^N := \left\{ \{\mathsf{P}_{x_1'}, \mathsf{P}_{N+x_2'}, \ldots, \mathsf{P}_{(t-1)N+x_t'}\} : t \in \mathbb{N}, f_t(x_1', x_2', \ldots, x_t') = 1 \right\},$$

  consists of a sequence of sharing algorithms $\{\mathsf{Sh}_t : \{0,1\}^\ell \times \mathcal{R}_1 \times \cdots \times \mathcal{R}_t \to \mathcal{S}_t\}_{t \in \mathbb{N}}$ and reconstruction algorithms $\mathsf{Rec}_A : \mathcal{S}_{t_1} \times \cdots \times \mathcal{S}_{t_{|A|}} \to \{0,1\}^\ell$, for every $A = \{\mathsf{P}_{t_1}, \ldots, \mathsf{P}_{t_{|A|}}\} \in \mathcal{A}^N$, in which the share size of party P_t is $c(t, N, \ell)$.
- **The protocol:**
  - For every $t \in \mathbb{N}$, party Q_t, when holding the input $x_t \in [N]$, computes and sends the message

  $$\mathsf{Enc}_t(x_t, s, q_1, \ldots, q_t) := \mathsf{Sh}_{g(t,x_t)}(s, r_1, \ldots, r_{g(t,x_t)}),$$

  where $g(t, x_t) := (t-1)N + x_t$.
  - For every $t \in \mathbb{N}$, denote $x^t := (x_1, \ldots, x_t)$ and $q^t := (q_1, \ldots, q_t)$. If $f_t(x^t) = 1$, the referee computes and returns

  $$\mathsf{Dec}(x^t, \mathsf{Enc}(x^t, s, q^t)) := \mathsf{Rec}_{A_t}(\mathsf{Enc}(x^t, s, q^t)),$$

  where $A_t := \{\mathsf{P}_{g(i,x_i)}\}_{i \in [t]}$ and

  $$\mathsf{Enc}(x^t, s, q^t) := (\mathsf{Enc}_1(x_1, s, q_1), \ldots, \mathsf{Enc}_t(x_t, s, q_1, \ldots, q_t)).$$

Fig. 1. An evolving CDS protocol for $\mathcal{F}_N = \{f_t : [N]^t \to \{0,1\}\}_{t \in \mathbb{N}}$.

Proof. Given an evolving secret sharing scheme realizing the evolving hypergraph access structure $\mathcal{A}^N$ (as defined in Fig. 1), we show how to construct an evolving CDS protocol for the evolving predicate $\mathcal{F}_N$. The construction is described in Fig. 1.

Correctness. To prove the correctness of the evolving CDS protocol, we need to show that for every $t \in \mathbb{N}$, the referee can compute the secret from any t messages on any t inputs for which the predicate f_t on the t inputs holds.

Let $(x_1, \ldots, x_t) \in [N]^t$ such that $f_t(x_1, \ldots, x_t) = 1$. Hence, by the definition of $\mathcal{A}^N$, we have that $A_t = \{P_{x_1}, P_{N+x_2}, \ldots, P_{(t-1)N+x_t}\} \in \mathcal{A}^N$. Moreover, for every $i \in [t]$, party Q_i sends to the referee the share $\mathsf{Sh}_{g(i,x_i)}(s, r_1, \ldots, r_{g(i,x_i)})$; also, since $g(i, x_i) = (i-1)N + x_i$, we get that it is the share of party $P_{g(i,x_i)} \in A_t$. Thus, the referee applies the reconstruction algorithm of the authorized set A_t on the shares of the parties in A_t, so by the correctness of the evolving secret sharing scheme Σ_N, it reconstructs the secret, that is, it computes and returns $\mathsf{Dec}(x^t, \mathsf{Enc}(x^t, s, q^t)) = \mathsf{Rec}_{A_t}(\{\mathsf{Sh}_i(s, r_1, \ldots, r_i)\}_{P_i \in A_t}) = s$.

Security. To prove the security of the evolving CDS protocol, we need to show that for every $t \in \mathbb{N}$, the referee cannot learn any information about the secret when receiving any t messages on any t inputs for which the predicate f_t on the t inputs does not hold.

Let $(x_1, \ldots, x_t) \in [N]^t$ such that $f_t(x_1, \ldots, x_t) = 0$. Hence, by the definition of $\mathcal{A}^N$, it holds that $A_t = \{P_{g(1,x_1)}, \ldots, P_{g(t,x_t)}\} \notin \mathcal{A}^N.$[9] Observe that the referee gets only the shares $\mathsf{Sh}_{g(1,x_1)}(s, r_1, \ldots, r_{g(1,x_1)}), \ldots, \mathsf{Sh}_{g(t,x_t)}(s, r_1, \ldots, r_{g(t,x_t)})$ from the parties $Q_1, \ldots, Q_t$, respectively. Therefore, since the referee gets the shares of the unauthorized set A_t, then by the security of the evolving secret sharing scheme Σ_N, the referee cannot learn any information on the secret s.

Complexity. The message size of party Q_t in the resulting evolving CDS protocol is equal to share size of party $P_{g(t,x_t)} = P_{(t-1)N+x_t}$ in the underlined evolving secret sharing scheme Σ_N, which is $c((t-1)N + x_t, N, \ell)$. □

In [KNY16], an evolving secret sharing scheme for every evolving access structure was presented. However, for the worst evolving access structures, the share size of party P_t in this scheme is 2^{t-1} (times the size of the secret). Next, we show that the share size in an optimized version of the scheme of [KNY16] is much smaller for evolving hypergraph access structures.

Theorem 2. *Let $\ell, N \in \mathbb{N}$, and let $\mathcal{A}^N$ be an evolving hypergraph access structure. Then, there is an evolving secret sharing scheme for $\mathcal{A}^N$, in which the secret size is ℓ and the share size of party P_t is at most $2N^{\frac{t-(t \bmod N)}{N}} \cdot \ell$.*

---

[9] By Definition 7, we have that $f_i(x_1, \ldots, x_i) = 0$ for every $i \in [t]$, so every subset of $A_t = \{P_{g(1,x_1)}, \ldots, P_{g(t,x_t)}\}$ is also unauthorized. Thus, the evolving access structure $\mathcal{A}^N$ is well defined.

Proof. First, let us present an optimized version of the evolving secret sharing scheme of [KNY16] for a secret $s \in \{0,1\}$,[10] realizing an arbitrary evolving access structure $\mathcal{A}$. For every $t \in \mathbb{N}$, the share of party P_t consists of two sets of bits:

- For every subset of parties $A = \{\mathsf{P}_{i_1}, \ldots, \mathsf{P}_{i_{|A|-1}}, \mathsf{P}_t\} \notin \mathcal{A}$ such that $A \subseteq \{\mathsf{P}_1, \ldots, \mathsf{P}_t\}$ and *there exists a subset* $A' \in \min \mathcal{A}$ *such that* $A \subset A'$,[11] the share of party P_t contains a random bit $r_A \leftarrow \{0,1\}$.
- For every subset of parties $A = \{\mathsf{P}_{i_1}, \ldots, \mathsf{P}_{i_{|A|-1}}, \mathsf{P}_t\} \in \min \mathcal{A}$ such that $A \subseteq \{\mathsf{P}_1, \ldots, \mathsf{P}_t\}$ and $A \setminus \{\mathsf{P}_t\} \notin \mathcal{A}$,[12] the share of party P_t contains the bit $s \oplus \bigoplus_{j=1}^{|A|-1} r_{A_j}$, where $A_j = \{\mathsf{P}_{i_1}, \ldots, \mathsf{P}_{i_j}\}$.

Observe that the bits $\{r_{A_j}\}_{j \in [|A|-1]}$, in the exclusive-or of the bit $s \oplus \bigoplus_{j=1}^{|A|-1} r_{A_j}$ of party P_t, are the random bits that were given to the parties of $\{\mathsf{P}_{i_j}\}_{j \in [|A|-1]}$ for the subsets $\{A_j\}_{j \in [|A|-1]}$, before party P_t received its share.

The correctness and the security of the scheme follow from similar arguments as detailed in [KNY16]. The share of party P_t contains at most one bit for every subset $A = \{\mathsf{P}_{i_1}, \ldots, \mathsf{P}_{i_{|A|-1}}, \mathsf{P}_t\}$ such that $A \subset \{\mathsf{P}_1, \ldots, \mathsf{P}_t\}$; since there are at most 2^{t-1} such sets, the share size of party P_t is at most 2^{t-1}.

Now, assume that $\mathcal{A} = \mathcal{A}^N$ is an evolving hypergraph access structure, and consider the party P_t, where $t = aN + b$ for some $a \in \mathbb{N}$ and $b \in \{0, \ldots, N-1\}$. In that case, by Definition 9, the unauthorized subsets $A \notin \mathcal{A}$ from the first item of the scheme must contain exactly $a+1$ parties (including P_t), where we have $\mathsf{P}_{i_j} \in \{\mathsf{P}_{(j-1)N+1}, \ldots, \mathsf{P}_{jN}\}$ for every $j \in [a]$ (otherwise, there is no $A' \in \min \mathcal{A}$ such that $A \subset A'$). The number of such sets is at most N^a. Additionally, again by Definition 9, the authorized subsets $A \in \min \mathcal{A}$ from the second item of the scheme must also satisfy exactly the same condition. Therefore, the number of such sets is also at most N^a.

Overall, for ℓ-bit secrets, we apply the above scheme independently for each bit of the secret. Thus, the share size of party P_t, when $t = aN + b$, is

$$c(t, N, \ell) \leq 2\, N^a \ell = 2\, N^{\frac{t-(t \bmod N)}{N}} \cdot \ell.$$

$\square$

Remark 2. The share size of the above evolving secret sharing scheme for evolving hypergraph access structures $\mathcal{A}^N$ is better than the non-optimized evolving secret sharing scheme of [KNY16], for every value of N. For example, the share size of P_t is less than $2^{t/2}$ for $N = 5$, and less than $2^{0.01t}$ for $N = 1000$, compared to 2^{t-1} as in [KNY16] (for one-bit secrets).

---

[10] Here and in [KNY16], the scheme is described for one-bit secrets; for larger secrets, we share each bit independently. Thus, we get a share size that is equal to the share size for one-bit secrets multiplied by the secret size.

[11] This condition was not appeared in the scheme of [KNY16]; we add it in order to reduce the share size. However, it is easy to verify that the correctness and the security of the scheme are still preserved.

[12] Here, we only consider subsets $A \in \min \mathcal{A}$, in contrast to [KNY16] that consider subsets $A \in \mathcal{A}$. Also, assume without loss of generality that $i_1 < \cdots < i_{|A|-1} < t$.

Finally, we use the evolving scheme of Theorem 2 and the construction of Theorem 1 to get an evolving CDS protocol for every evolving predicate.

Corollary 1. *Let $\ell, N \in \mathbb{N}$, and let $\mathcal{F}_N = \{f_t : [N]^t \to \{0,1\}\}_{t \in \mathbb{N}}$ be an evolving predicate. Then, there is an evolving CDS protocol for $\mathcal{F}_N$, in which the secret size is ℓ and the message size of party Q_t is at most $2N^{t-1}\ell$.*

Proof. By using Theorem 1 with the evolving secret sharing scheme of Theorem 2 as an oracle, we get an evolving CDS protocol for the evolving predicate $\mathcal{F}_N$, in which the message size of party Q_t is

$$c((t-1)N + x_t, N, \ell) \leq 2\,N^{\frac{(t-1)N+x_t-x_t}{N}} \cdot \ell = 2\,N^{t-1}\ell.$$

□

5   Evolving CDS for Min-Sum Predicates

We start by defining evolving min-sum predicates, which hold only when the sum of the inputs is at least some minimal value determined by the predicates. The formal definition of min-sum evolving predicates is given below.

Definition 10 (Evolving Min-Sum Predicates). *Let $N \in \mathbb{N}$ and let $\mathcal{W} = \{w_t\}_{t \in \mathbb{N}}$ be a non-decreasing sequence of integers, where $w_t \leq tN$ for every $t \in \mathbb{N}$. The evolving $\mathcal{W}$-min-sum predicate $\mathcal{F}_{\mathcal{W}} = \{f_t : \{0,1,\dots,N\}^t \to \{0,1\}\}_{t \in \mathbb{N}}$ is the evolving predicate in which for every $t \in \mathbb{N}$, we have that $f_t(x_1,\dots,x_t) = 1$ if and only if $\sum_{j=1}^{i} x_j \geq w_i$ for some $i \in [t]$. That is, the predicate f_t holds on the input $(x_1,\dots,x_t)$ if and only if for some $i \in [t]$, the sum of the first i inputs $x_1,\dots,x_i \in \{0,1,\dots,N\}$ is at least w_i. If $w_t = w$ for every $t \in \mathbb{N}$, we say that $\mathcal{F}_w := \mathcal{F}_{\mathcal{W}}$ is the evolving w-min-sum predicate.*

Example 2. Consider the evolving $\mathcal{W}$-min-sum predicate $\mathcal{F}_{\mathcal{W}} = \{f_t : \{0,1,\dots,10\}^t \to \{0,1\}\}_{t \in \mathbb{N}}$ with $\mathcal{W} = \{5t\}_{t \in \mathbb{N}}$ (i.e., $w_t = 5t$ for every $t \in \mathbb{N}$). Then, for every $t \in \mathbb{N}$, the predicate f_t holds on inputs $(x_1,\dots,x_t) \in \{0,1,\dots,10\}^t$, for which there exists some $i \in [t]$ such that $\sum_{j=1}^{i} x_j \geq 5i$. That is, f_t holds on $(x_1,\dots,x_t)$ only when the *average input* among *some prefix* of the inputs $x_1,\dots,x_t \in \{0,1,\dots,10\}$ is at least 5.

In the following, we show how to construct evolving CDS protocols for min-sum predicates.

Theorem 3. *Let $\ell, N \in \mathbb{N}$, let $\mathcal{W} = \{w_t\}_{t \in \mathbb{N}}$ be a non-decreasing sequence of integers such that $w_t \leq tN$ for every $t \in \mathbb{N}$, and let $\mathcal{F}_{\mathcal{W}} = \{f_t : \{0,1,\dots,N\}^t \to \{0,1\}\}_{t \in \mathbb{N}}$ be the evolving $\mathcal{W}$-min-sum predicate. Define $\mathcal{K} = \{k_t\}_{t \in \mathbb{N}}$, where $k_{(t-1)N+1} = k_{(t-1)N+2} = \dots = k_{tN} = w_t$ for every $t \in \mathbb{N}$, and assume that there is an evolving secret sharing scheme realizing the evolving $\mathcal{K}$-threshold access structure $\mathcal{A}^{\mathcal{K}}$, in which the secret size is ℓ and the share size of party P_t is $c(t, k_t, N, \ell)$. Then, there is an evolving CDS protocol for $\mathcal{F}_{\mathcal{W}}$, in which the secret* *size is ℓ and the message size of party Q_t is $\sum_{j=1}^{x_t} c((t-1)N+j, w_t, N, \ell)$, where $x_t \in \{0, 1, \ldots, N\}$ is the input of party Q_t.*[13]

Proof. Given an evolving secret sharing scheme realizing the evolving $\mathcal{K}$-threshold access structure $\mathcal{A}^{\mathcal{K}}$, we construct an evolving CDS protocol for the evolving min-sum predicate $\mathcal{F}_{\mathcal{W}}$. The construction is described in Fig. 2.

- **Inputs:** Party Q_t holds $x_t \in \{0, 1, \ldots, N\}$ for every $t \in \mathbb{N}$.
- **The secret:** A string $s \in \{0, 1\}^{\ell}$.
- **Common randomness:** A sequence of random strings $\{r_t\}_{t \in \mathbb{N}}$, where $r_t \leftarrow \mathcal{R}_t$ for every $t \in \mathbb{N}$. Also, define $q_t := (r_{(t-1)N+1}, r_{(t-1)N+2}, \ldots, r_{tN})$ for every $t \in \mathbb{N}$.
- **The oracle:** An evolving secret sharing scheme $\Sigma_{\mathcal{K}}$ realizing the evolving $\mathcal{K}$-threshold access structure $A^{\mathcal{K}}$, as defined in Definition 5, consists of a sequence of sharing algorithms $\{\mathsf{Sh}_t : \{0,1\}^{\ell} \times \mathcal{R}_1 \times \cdots \times \mathcal{R}_t \to \mathcal{S}_t\}_{t \in \mathbb{N}}$ and reconstruction algorithms $\mathsf{Rec}_A : \mathcal{S}_{t_1} \times \cdots \times \mathcal{S}_{t_{|A|}} \to \{0,1\}^{\ell}$, for every $A = \{P_{t_1}, \ldots, P_{t_{|A|}}\} \in \mathcal{A}^{\mathcal{K}}$, in which the share size of party P_t is $c(t, k_t, N, \ell)$.
- **The protocol:**
  - For every $t \in \mathbb{N}$, party Q_t, when holding the input $x_t \in \{0, 1, \ldots, N\}$, computes and sends the message

    $$\mathsf{Enc}_t(x_t, s, q_1, \ldots, q_t) := \{\mathsf{Sh}_{g(t,j)}(s, r_1, \ldots, r_{g(t,j)})\}_{j \in [x_t]}, \quad {}^{a}$$

    where $g(t, j) := (t-1)N + j$.
  - For every $t \in \mathbb{N}$, if $f_t(x^t) = 1$,[b] the referee computes and returns

    $$\mathsf{Dec}(x^t, \mathsf{Enc}(x^t, s, q^t)) := \mathsf{Rec}_{B_t}(\mathsf{Enc}(x^t, s, q^t)),$$

    where $B_t := \bigcup_{i=1}^{t} \{P_{g(i,j)}\}_{j \in [x_i]}$.

---

[a] If $x_t = 0$, then $\mathsf{Enc}_t(x_t, s, q_1, \ldots, q_t)$ is the empty message.
[b] As the notations in Figure 1, $x^t := (x_1, \ldots, x_t)$, $q^t := (q_1, \ldots, q_t)$, and $\mathsf{Enc}(x^t, s, q^t) := (\mathsf{Enc}_1(x_1, s, q_1), \ldots, \mathsf{Enc}_t(x_t, s, q_1, \ldots, q_t))$.

Fig. 2. An evolving CDS protocol for $\mathcal{F}_{\mathcal{W}} = \{f_t : \{0, 1, \ldots, N\}^t \to \{0, 1\}\}_{t \in \mathbb{N}}$.

Correctness. Let $(x_1, \ldots, x_t) \in \{0, 1, \ldots, N\}^t$ such that $f_t(x_1, \ldots, x_t) = 1$, and assume without loss of generality that $f_{t-1}(x_1, \ldots, x_{t-1}) = 0$ (otherwise, we look at the minimal $t \in \mathbb{N}$ that satisfies that). As described in the protocol, the referee gets x_i distinct shares from party Q_i, for every $i \in [t]$.

---

[13] However, for the special case $x_t = 0$, the message size of party Q_t is zero.

Therefore, the referee gets distinct $\sum_{i=1}^{t} x_i \geq w_t$ shares, where the inequality follows from Definition 10. In addition, the last share that referee gets (from party Q_t) is $\mathsf{Sh}_{g(t,x_t)}(s, r_1, \ldots, r_{g(t,x_t)})$ (since our assumption implies that $x_t \neq 0$), and by the definition of $\mathcal{K}$, we get that $k_{g(t,x_t)} = w_t$, regardless of $x_t \in [N]$ (recall that $g(t, x_t) = (t-1)N + x_t$). Thus, by the correctness of the scheme $\Sigma_{\mathcal{K}}$, the referee can reconstruct the secret using the reconstruction algorithm of the authorized subset $B_t = \bigcup_{i=1}^{t} \{\mathsf{P}_{g(i,j)}\}_{j \in [x_i]}$, that is, $\mathsf{Dec}(x^t, \mathsf{Enc}(x^t, s, r^t)) = \mathsf{Rec}_{B_t}(\{\mathsf{Sh}_i(s, r_1, \ldots, r_i)\}_{\mathsf{P}_i \in B_t}) = s$.

Security. Let $(x_1, \ldots, x_t) \in \{0, 1, \ldots, N\}^t$ such that $f_t(x_1, \ldots, x_t) = 0$. That is, for every $i \in [t]$, we have that $\sum_{j=1}^{i} x_j < w_i$. Moreover, as mention above, the referee gets x_i distinct shares from party Q_i, for every $i \in [t]$. Thus, by the definition of $\mathcal{K}$ and the security of the scheme $\Sigma_{\mathcal{K}}$, the referee cannot learn any information on the secret s from the messages it gets.

Complexity. The message size of party Q_t in the resulting evolving CDS protocol is equal to the sum of the sizes of the shares $\mathsf{Sh}_{g(t,j)}$, for every $j \in [x_t]$, in the evolving secret sharing scheme $\Sigma_{\mathcal{K}}$, which is $\sum_{j=1}^{x_t} c((t-1)N + j, w_t, N, \ell)$.[14] □

Theorem 3 together with the *evolving k-threshold secret sharing scheme* of [KNY16], in which the share size of party P_t is $(k-1)\log t + k^4 \ell \cdot o(\log t)$,[15] imply the following corollary.

Corollary 2. *Let* $\ell, N, w \in \mathbb{N}$, *and let* $\mathcal{F}_w = \{f_t : \{0, 1, \ldots, N\}^t \to \{0, 1\}\}_{t \in \mathbb{N}}$ *be the evolving w-min-sum predicate. Then, there is an evolving CDS protocol for* $\mathcal{F}_w$, *in which the secret size is* ℓ, *and the message size of party* Q_t *is at most*

$$x_t(w-1)\log(tN) + x_t \cdot w^4 \ell \cdot o(\log(tN)),$$

where $x_t \in \{0, 1, \ldots, N\}$ *is the input of party* Q_t. *Moreover, if* $w = 2$, *then for any constant* $\varepsilon > 0$ *and any large enough* t, *the message size of party* Q_t *is at most* $x_t(1+\varepsilon)\log(tN) \cdot \ell$.[16]

Theorem 3 together with the *evolving $\mathcal{K}$-threshold secret sharing scheme* of [XY21], in which the share size of party P_t is at most t^4 (times the secret size),[17] imply the following corollary.

---

[14] Note that as defined in the theorem, for every $t \in \mathbb{N}$ and every $j \in [x_t]$, the threshold $k_{g(t,j)}$ for the party $P_{g(t,j)}$, receiving the share $\mathsf{Sh}_{g(t,j)}$, is equal to w_t.

[15] We denote $f(n) = o(g(n))$ if and only if for every constant $c > 0$ there exists $n_0 \in \mathbb{N}$ such that $f(n) < c \cdot g(n)$ for every $n > n_0$.

[16] For $k = 2$, [KNY16] showed an evolving 2-threshold secret sharing scheme for one-bit secrets, in which the share size of party P_t is less than $(1 + \varepsilon)\log t$, for any constant $\varepsilon > 0$ and any large enough values of t (that depend on ε).

[17] Observe that the share size in the evolving $\mathcal{K}$-threshold secret sharing scheme of [XY21] is independent of $\mathcal{K}$.

Corollary 3. *Let $\ell, N \in \mathbb{N}$, let $\mathcal{W} = \{w_t\}_{t \in \mathbb{N}}$ be a non-decreasing sequence of integers such that $w_t \leq tN$ for every $t \in \mathbb{N}$, and let $\mathcal{F}_{\mathcal{W}} = \{f_t : \{0, 1, \ldots, N\}^t \to \{0, 1\}\}_{t \in \mathbb{N}}$ be the evolving $\mathcal{W}$-min-sum predicate. Then, there is an evolving CDS protocol for $\mathcal{F}_{\mathcal{W}}$, in which the secret size is ℓ and the message size of party Q_t is at most $x_t \cdot t^4 N^4 \ell$, where $x_t \in \{0, 1, \ldots, N\}$ is the input of party Q_t.*

6   Evolving CDS for Constrained Predicates

Finally, we discuss the class of evolving constrained predicates. Evolving predicates from this class hold if and only if there are enough individual inputs that satisfy some attributes; such evolving constrained predicates can be viewed as some (distant) threshold version of key-policy attribute-based encryption (KP-ABE). We specify the attributes that an individual input should satisfy as a subset of "non-valid" inputs, for which the input *should not belong* in order to be considered "valid".

In our construction, a party with an input that does not satisfy the attributes is not allowed to send a message to the referee, because the secret is disclosed to the referee only when enough parties with "valid" inputs have been arrived.

Definition 11 (Evolving Constrained Predicates). *Let $\mathcal{K} = \{k_t\}_{t \in \mathbb{N}}$ be a non-decreasing sequence of integers, where $k_t \leq t$ for every $t \in \mathbb{N}$. An evolving $\mathcal{K}$-constrained predicate $\mathcal{F}_{\mathcal{K}} = \{f_t : \mathcal{X}_1 \times \cdots \times \mathcal{X}_t \to \{0, 1\}\}_{t \in \mathbb{N}}$ is an evolving predicate, in which there exist a sequence of constrained subsets $\{S_t\}_{t \in \mathbb{N}}$ such that $S_t \subseteq \mathcal{X}_t$ for every $t \in \mathbb{N}$, where for every $t \in \mathbb{N}$, we have that $f_t(x_1, \ldots, x_t) = 1$ if and only if there exists some $i \in [t]$ and a set of indices $J \subseteq [i]$, such that $|J| \geq k_i$ and $x_j \notin S_j$ for every $j \in J$. That is, the predicate f_t holds on the input $(x_1, \ldots, x_t)$ if and only if for some $i \in [t]$, there are at least k_i "valid" inputs that are not in the constrained subsets (i.e., inputs $x_j \notin S_j$). If $k_t = k$ for every $t \in \mathbb{N}$, we say that $\mathcal{F}_k := \mathcal{F}_{\mathcal{K}}$ is an evolving k-constrained predicate.*

Example 3. Consider the evolving k-constrained predicate $\mathcal{F}_k = \{f_t : [N]^t \to \{0, 1\}\}_{t \in \mathbb{N}}$ with the constrained subsets $S_t = \{N/4, \ldots, 3N/4\}$ for every $t \in \mathbb{N}$. Then, for every $t \in \mathbb{N}$, the predicate f_t holds on inputs $(x_1, \ldots, x_t) \in [N]^t$, such that there are at least k inputs among $x_1, \ldots, x_t \in [N]$ that are *not* in the constrained range $[N/4, \ldots, 3N/4]$.

Given an evolving secret sharing scheme realizing $\mathcal{A}^{\mathcal{K}}$, we construct an evolving CDS protocol for $\mathcal{F}_{\mathcal{K}}$. The construction is described in Fig. 3; the proof of its correctness and security is similar to the proof of Theorem 3.

Theorem 4. *Let $\ell \in \mathbb{N}$, let $\mathcal{K} = \{k_t\}_{t \in \mathbb{N}}$ be a non-decreasing sequence of integers, where $k_t \leq t$ for every $t \in \mathbb{N}$, and let $\mathcal{F}_{\mathcal{K}} = \{f_t : \mathcal{X}_1 \times \cdots \times \mathcal{X}_t \to \{0, 1\}\}_{t \in \mathbb{N}}$ be an evolving $\mathcal{K}$-constrained predicate for a sequence of constrained subsets $\{S_t\}_{t \in \mathbb{N}}$. Assume that there is an evolving secret sharing scheme realizing the evolving $\mathcal{K}$-threshold access structure $\mathcal{A}^{\mathcal{K}}$, in which the secret size is ℓ and the share size of party Q_t is $c(t, k_t, \ell)$. Then, there is an evolving CDS protocol for $\mathcal{F}_{\mathcal{K}}$, in which the secret size is ℓ and the message size of party Q_t is $c(t, k_t, \ell)$.[18]*

---

[18] If $x_t \in S_t$, then the message size of party Q_t is zero.

- **Inputs:** Party Q_t holds $x_t \in \mathcal{X}_t$ for every $t \in \mathbb{N}$.
- **The secret:** A string $s \in \{0,1\}^\ell$.
- **Common randomness:** A sequence of random strings $\{r_t\}_{t \in \mathbb{N}}$, where $r_t \leftarrow \mathcal{R}_t$ for every $t \in \mathbb{N}$.
- **The oracle:** An evolving secret sharing scheme $\Sigma_\mathcal{K}$ realizing the evolving $\mathcal{K}$-threshold access structure $A^\mathcal{K}$, as described in Figure 2.
- **The protocol:**
  - For every $t \in \mathbb{N}$, party Q_t, when holding the input $x_t \in \mathcal{X}_t$, checks if $x_t \in S_t$. If so, it sends the empty message. Otherwise, it computes and sends the message

    $$\mathsf{Enc}_t(x_t, s, r_1, \ldots, r_t) := \mathsf{Sh}_t(s, r_1, \ldots, r_t).$$

  - For every $t \in \mathbb{N}$, if $f_t(x^t) = 1,$[a] the referee computes and returns

    $$\mathsf{Dec}(x^t, \mathsf{Enc}(x^t, s, r^t)) := \mathsf{Rec}_{C_t}(\mathsf{Enc}(x^t, s, r^t)),$$

    where $C_t := \{P_i\}_{i \in [t], x_i \notin S_i}$.

  ---

  [a] Similarly to the notations in Figure 1, $x^t := (x_1, \ldots, x_t)$, $r^t := (r_1, \ldots, r_t)$, and $\mathsf{Enc}(x^t, s, r^t) := (\mathsf{Enc}_1(x_1, s, r_1), \ldots, \mathsf{Enc}_t(x_t, s, r_1, \ldots, r_t))$.

Fig. 3. An evolving CDS protocol for $\mathcal{F}_\mathcal{K} = \{f_t : \mathcal{X}_1 \times \cdots \times \mathcal{X}_t \to \{0,1\}\}_{t \in \mathbb{N}}$.

Theorem 4 together with the evolving k-threshold secret sharing scheme of [KNY16] imply the following corollary.

Corollary 4. *Let $\ell, k \in \mathbb{N}$, and let $\mathcal{F}_k = \{f_t : \mathcal{X}_1 \times \cdots \times \mathcal{X}_t \to \{0,1\}\}_{t \in \mathbb{N}}$ be an evolving k-constrained predicate. Then, there is an evolving CDS protocol for $\mathcal{F}_k$, in which the secret size is ℓ and the message size of party Q_t is at most $(k-1) \log t + k^4 \ell \cdot o(\log t)$. Moreover, if $k = 2$, then for any constant $\varepsilon > 0$ and any large enough t, the message size of party Q_t is at most $(1 + \varepsilon) \log t \cdot \ell$.*

Theorem 4 together with the evolving $\mathcal{K}$-threshold secret sharing scheme of [XY21] imply the following corollary.

Corollary 5. *Let $\ell \in \mathbb{N}$, let $\mathcal{K} = \{k_t\}_{t \in \mathbb{N}}$ be a non-decreasing sequence of integers such that $k_t \leq t$ for every $t \in \mathbb{N}$, and let $\mathcal{F}_\mathcal{K} = \{f_t : \mathcal{X}_1 \times \cdots \times \mathcal{X}_t \to \{0,1\}\}_{t \in \mathbb{N}}$ be an evolving $\mathcal{K}$-constrained predicate. Then, there is an evolving CDS protocol for $\mathcal{F}_\mathcal{K}$, in which the secret size is ℓ and the message size of party Q_t is at most $t^4 \cdot \ell$.*

7   Conclusions and Open Problems

Motivated by evolving secret sharing, in this work we initiate the notion of evolving CDS. We formally present the definition of evolving CDS, and provide several constructions of evolving CDS protocols, for general evolving predicated, evolving min-sum predicated, and evolving constrained predicates. As CDS protocols were used to construct the best known secret sharing schemes, an interesting direction for future research is trying to find an efficient construction of evolving secret sharing schemes by using evolving CDS protocols. Another open problem is developing efficient evolving CDS protocols for more classes of evolving predicates. Furthermore, the model of evolving CDS (or the ideas behind it) may be used to show more notions of secure evolving protocols, in which the number of parties is not known in advance and could be unbounded. Additionally, other variants of evolving CDS protocols can be studied, e.g., where some of the parties do not know the evolving predicate or the secret.

References

[AA18]   Applebaum, B., Arkis, B.: On the power of amortization in secret sharing: d-uniform secret sharing and CDS with constant information rate. In: Beimel, A., Dziembowski, S. (eds.) TCC 2018. LNCS, vol. 11239, pp. 317–344. Springer, Cham (2018). https://doi.org/10.1007/978-3-030-03807-6_12

[ABF+19]   Applebaum, B., Beimel, A., Farràs, O., Nir, O., Peter, N.: Secret-sharing schemes for general and uniform access structures. In: Ishai, Y., Rijmen, V. (eds.) EUROCRYPT 2019. LNCS, vol. 11478, pp. 441–471. Springer, Cham (2019). https://doi.org/10.1007/978-3-030-17659-4_15

[ABNP20] Applebaum, B., Beimel, A., Nir, O., Peter, N.: Better secret sharing via robust conditional disclosure of secrets. In: STOC 2020, pp. 280–293. ACM (2020)

[AN21]   Applebaum, B., Nir, O.: Upslices, downslices, and secret-sharing with complexity of 1.5^n. In: Malkin, T., Peikert, C. (eds.) CRYPTO 2021. LNCS, vol. 12827, pp. 627–655. Springer, Cham (2021). https://doi.org/10.1007/978-3-030-84252-9_21

[BCG+17] Boyle, E., Couteau, G., Gilboa, N., Ishai, Y., Orrù, M.: Homomorphic secret sharing: optimizations and applications. In: CCS 2017, pp. 2105–2122. ACM (2017)

[BD91]   Brickell, E.F., Davenport, D.M.: On the classification of ideal secret sharing schemes. J. Cryptol. 4(2), 123–134 (1991)

[BGI15]   Boyle, E., Gilboa, N., Ishai, Y.: Function secret sharing. In: Oswald, E., Fischlin, M. (eds.) EUROCRYPT 2015. LNCS, vol. 9057, pp. 337–367. Springer, Heidelberg (2015). https://doi.org/10.1007/978-3-662-46803-6_12

[BGI16a] Boyle, E., Gilboa, N., Ishai, Y.: Breaking the circuit size barrier for secure computation under DDH. In: Robshaw, M., Katz, J. (eds.) CRYPTO 2016. LNCS, vol. 9814, pp. 509–539. Springer, Heidelberg (2016). https://doi.org/10.1007/978-3-662-53018-4_19

[BGI16b] Boyle, E., Gilboa, N., Ishai, Y.: Function secret sharing: improvements and extensions. In: CCS 2016, pp. 1292–1303. ACM (2016)

[BI92]   Bertilsson, M., Ingemarsson, I.: A construction of practical secret sharing schemes using linear block codes. In: Seberry, J., Zheng, Y. (eds.) AUSCRYPT 1992. LNCS, vol. 718, pp. 67–79. Springer, Heidelberg (1993). https://doi.org/10.1007/3-540-57220-1_53

[BL88]   Benaloh, J., Leichter, J.: Generalized secret sharing and monotone functions. In: Goldwasser, S. (ed.) CRYPTO 1988. LNCS, vol. 403, pp. 27–35. Springer, New York (1990). https://doi.org/10.1007/0-387-34799-2_3

[Bla79]   Blakley, G.R.: Safeguarding cryptographic keys. In: AFIPS NCC 1979, volume 48 of AFIPS Conference proceedings, pp. 313–317. AFIPS Press (1979)

[BO18]   Beimel, A., Othman, H.: Evolving ramp secret-sharing schemes. In: Catalano, D., De Prisco, R. (eds.) SCN 2018. LNCS, vol. 11035, pp. 313–332. Springer, Cham (2018). https://doi.org/10.1007/978-3-319-98113-0_17

[BO20]   Beimel, A., Othman, H.: Evolving ramp secret sharing with a small gap. In: Canteaut, A., Ishai, Y. (eds.) EUROCRYPT 2020. LNCS, vol. 12105, pp. 529–555. Springer, Cham (2020). https://doi.org/10.1007/978-3-030-45721-1_19

[BOP21]   Beimel, A., Othman, H., Peter, N.: Quadratic secret sharing and conditional disclosure of secrets. In: Malkin, T., Peikert, C. (eds.) CRYPTO 2021. LNCS, vol. 12827, pp. 748–778. Springer, Cham (2021). https://doi.org/10.1007/978-3-030-84252-9_25

[BOP23]   Beimel, A., Othman, H., Peter, N.: Quadratic secret sharing and conditional disclosure of secrets. IEEE Trans. Inf. Theory (2023)

[BP18]   Beimel, A., Peter, N.: Optimal linear multiparty conditional disclosure of secrets protocols. In: Peyrin, T., Galbraith, S. (eds.) ASIACRYPT 2018. LNCS, vol. 11274, pp. 332–362. Springer, Cham (2018). https://doi.org/10.1007/978-3-030-03332-3_13

[Cac95]   Cachin, C.: On-line secret sharing. In: Boyd, C. (ed.) Cryptography and Coding 1995. LNCS, vol. 1025, pp. 190–198. Springer, Heidelberg (1995). https://doi.org/10.1007/3-540-60693-9_22

[CDS20]   Chaudhury, S.S., Dutta, S., Sakurai, K.: AC^0 constructions of secret sharing schemes - accommodating new parties. In: Kutylowski, M., Zhang, J., Chen, C. (eds.) Network and System Security, NSS 2020. LNCS, vol. 12570, pp. 292–308. Springer, Cham (2020). https://doi.org/10.1007/978-3-030-65745-1_17

[CDS21]   Chaudhury, S.S., Dutta, S., Sakurai, K.: Perpetual secret sharing from dynamic data structures. In: DSC 2021, pp. 1–8. IEEE (2021)

[CGMA85] Chor, B., Goldwasser, S., Micali, S., Awerbuch, B.: Verifiable secret sharing and achieving simultaneity in the presence of faults (extended abstract). In: FOCS 1985, pp. 383–395. IEEE Computer Society (1985)

[Cha20]   Chaudhury, S.S.: A quantum evolving secret sharing scheme. Int. J. Theor. Phys. **59**(12), 3936–3950 (2020)

[Cha22]   Chaudhury, S.S.: On quantum evolving secret sharing schemes - further studies and improvements. Quantum Inf. Comput. **21**(5 & 6), 0385–0407 (2022)

[Csi94]   Csirmaz, L.: The size of a share must be large. In: De Santis, A. (ed.) EUROCRYPT 1994. LNCS, vol. 950, pp. 13–22. Springer, Heidelberg (1995). https://doi.org/10.1007/BFb0053420

[Csi96]   Csirmaz, L.: The dealer's random bits in perfect secret sharing schemes. Stud. Sci. Math. Hung. **32**(3), 429–438 (1996)

[Csi97]   Csirmaz, L.: The size of a share must be large. J. Cryptol. **10**(4), 223–231 (1997)

[CT12]   Csirmaz, L., Tardos, G.: On-line secret sharing. Des. Codes Cryptogr. **63**(1), 127–147 (2012)

[DDM19] Desmedt, Y., Dutta, S., Morozov, K.: Evolving perfect hash families: a combinatorial viewpoint of evolving secret sharing. In: Mu, Y., Deng, R.H., Huang, X. (eds.) CANS 2019. LNCS, vol. 11829, pp. 291–307. Springer, Cham (2019). https://doi.org/10.1007/978-3-030-31578-8_16

[DDV10] Davì, F., Dziembowski, S., Venturi, D.: Leakage-resilient storage. In: Garay, J.A., De Prisco, R. (eds.) SCN 2010. LNCS, vol. 6280, pp. 121–137. Springer, Heidelberg (2010). https://doi.org/10.1007/978-3-642-15317-4_9

[DP07] Dziembowski, S., Pietrzak,K.: Intrusion-resilient secret sharing. In: FOCS 2007, pp. 227–237. IEEE Computer Society (2007)

[DPS+18] D'Arco, P., De Prisco, R., De Santis, A., Pérez del Pozo, A.L., Vaccaro, U.: Probabilistic secret sharing. In: MFCS 2018, volume 117 of LIPIcs, pp. 64:1–64:16. Schloss Dagstuhl - Leibniz-Zentrum für Informatik (2018)

[DRF+19] Dutta, S., Roy, P.S., Fukushima, K., Kiyomoto, S., Sakurai, K.: Secret sharing on evolving multi-level access structure. In: You, I. (ed.) WISA 2019. LNCS, vol. 11897, pp. 180–191. Springer, Cham (2020). https://doi.org/10.1007/978-3-030-39303-8_14

[Fel87] Feldman, P.: A practical scheme for non-interactive verifiable secret sharing. In: FOCS 1987, pp. 427–437. IEEE Computer Society (1987)

[GIKM00] Gertner, Y., Ishai, Y., Kushilevitz, E., Malkin, T.: Protecting data privacy in private information retrieval schemes. J. Comput. Syst. Sci. 60(3), 592–629 (2000)

[GK18a] Goyal, V., Kumar, A.: Non-malleable secret sharing. In: STOC 2018, pp. 685–698. ACM (2018)

[GK18b] Goyal, V., Kumar, A.: Non-malleable secret sharing for general access structures. In: Shacham, H., Boldyreva, A. (eds.) CRYPTO 2018. LNCS, vol. 10991, pp. 501–530. Springer, Cham (2018). https://doi.org/10.1007/978-3-319-96884-1_17

[HBB99] Hillery, M., Bužek, V., Berthiaume, A.: Quantum secret sharing. Phys. Rev. A 59, 1829–1834 (1999)

[HJKY95] Herzberg, A., Jarecki, S., Krawczyk, H., Yung, M.: Proactive secret sharing or: how to cope with perpetual leakage. In: Coppersmith, D. (ed.) CRYPTO 1995. LNCS, vol. 963, pp. 339–352. Springer, Heidelberg (1995). https://doi.org/10.1007/3-540-44750-4_27

[ISN87] Ito, M., Saito, A., Nishizeki, T.: Secret sharing scheme realizing general access structure, pp. 99–102 (1987)

[ISN93] Ito, M., Saio, A., Nishizeki, T.: Multiple assignment scheme for sharing secret. J. Cryptol. 6(1), 15–20 (1993)

[KKI99] Karlsson, A., Koashi, M., Imoto, N.: Quantum entanglement for secret sharing and secret splitting. Phys. Rev. A 59, 162–168 (1999)

[KNY16] Komargodski, I., Naor, M., Yogev, E.: How to share a secret, infinitely. In: Hirt, M., Smith, A. (eds.) TCC 2016. LNCS, vol. 9986, pp. 485–514. Springer, Heidelberg (2016). https://doi.org/10.1007/978-3-662-53644-5_19

[KP17] Komargodski, I., Paskin-Cherniavsky, A.: Evolving secret sharing: dynamic thresholds and robustness. In: Kalai, Y., Reyzin, L. (eds.) TCC 2017. LNCS, vol. 10678, pp. 379–393. Springer, Cham (2017). https://doi.org/10.1007/978-3-319-70503-3_12

[KW93] Karchmer, M., Wigderson, A.: On span programs. In: SCT 1993, pp. 102–111. IEEE Computer Society (1993)

[LV18] Liu, T., Vaikuntanathan, V.: Breaking the circuit-size barrier in secret sharing. In: STOC 2018, pp. 699–708. ACM (2018)

[LVW18] Liu, T., Vaikuntanathan, V., Wee, H.: Towards breaking the exponential barrier for general secret sharing. In: Nielsen, J.B., Rijmen, V. (eds.) EUROCRYPT 2018. LNCS, vol. 10820, pp. 567–596. Springer, Cham (2018). https://doi.org/10.1007/978-3-319-78381-9_21

[Maz23] Mazor, N.: A lower bound on the share size in evolving secret sharing. In: ITC 2023, volume 267 of LIPIcs, pp. 2:1–2:9. Schloss Dagstuhl - Leibniz-Zentrum für Informatik (2023)

[OK20] Okamura, R., Koga, H.: New constructions of an evolving 2-threshold scheme based on binary or D-ary prefix codes. In: ISITA 2020, pp. 432–436. IEEE (2020)

[PA20] Pramanik, J., Adhikari, A.: Evolving secret sharing with essential participants. IACR Cryptol. ePrint Arch., 1035 (2020)

[PA21] Pramanik, J., Adhikari, A.: Evolving secret sharing in almost semi-honest model. IACR Cryptol. ePrint Arch., 1156 (2021)

[PSAM21] Phalakarn, K., Suppakitpaisarn, V., Attrapadung, N., Matsuura, K.: Evolving homomorphic secret sharing for hierarchical access structures. In: Nakanishi, T., Nojima, R. (eds.) IWSEC 2021. LNCS, vol. 12835, pp. 77–96. Springer, Cham (2021). https://doi.org/10.1007/978-3-030-85987-9_5

[Sha79] Shamir, A.: How to share a secret. Commun. ACM **22**(11), 612–613 (1979)

[SW99] Stinson, D.R., Wei, R.: Unconditionally secure proactive secret sharing scheme with combinatorial structures. In: Heys, H., Adams, C. (eds.) SAC 1999. LNCS, vol. 1758, pp. 200–214. Springer, Heidelberg (2000). https://doi.org/10.1007/3-540-46513-8_15

[XY21] Xing, C., Yuan, C.: Evolving secret sharing schemes based on polynomial evaluations and algebraic geometry codes. IACR Cryptol. ePrint Arch., 1115 (2021)

[YLH23] Yan, W., Lin, S.-J., Han, Y.S.: A new metric and the construction for evolving 2-threshold secret sharing schemes based on prefix coding of integers. IEEE Trans. Commun. **71**(5), 2906–2915 (2023)

Symmetric Cryptography

Permutation-Based Deterministic Authenticated Encryption with Minimum Memory Size

Yukihito Hiraga[1]([envelope]), Yusuke Naito[2], Yu Sasaki[3], and Takeshi Sugawara[1]

[1] The University of Electro-Communications, Tokyo, Japan
yukihito.hiraga@uec.ac.jp, sugawara@uec.ac.jp
[2] Mitsubishi Electric Corporation, Kanagawa, Japan
Naito.Yusuke@ce.MitsubishiElectric.co.jp
[3] NTT Social Informatics Laboratories, Tokyo, Japan
yusk.sasaki@ntt.com

Abstract. Deterministic authenticated encryption (DAE) provides data integrity and authenticity with certain robustness. Previous DAE schemes for low memory are based on block ciphers (BCs) or tweakable block ciphers (TBCs), which can be implemented with $3s$ bits of memory for s-bit security. On the other hand, schemes based on cryptographic permutations have attracted many researchers and standardization bodies. However, existing permutation-based DAEs require at least $4s$ bits, or even $5s$ bits of memory. In this paper, PALM, a new permutation-based DAE mode that can be implemented only with $3s$ bits of memory is proposed, implying that permutation-based DAEs achieve a competitive memory size with BC- and TBC-based DAEs. Our hardware implementation of PALM, instantiated with PHOTON$_{256}$ for 128-bit security, achieves 3,585 GE, comparable with the state-of-the-art TBC-based DAE. Finally, optimality of $3s$ bits of memory of PALM is shown.

Keywords: Deterministic Authenticated Encryption · Permutation · Low Memory · Mode · SIV · Security Proof · Hardware · PHOTON$_{256}$

1 Introduction

Authenticated encryption with associated data (AE) is fundamental symmetric-key cryptographic schemes, providing both integrity and authenticity of a message. Traditionally they were provided independently by encryption schemes and message authentication codes (MACs), while AE schemes generate both simultaneously. This simplifies complex security issues that arise when independently developed encryption schemes and MACs are combined, and enables more efficient computations by sharing computing resources between the two.

Some AE schemes use nonce, a value that must not be repeated more than once under the same key (nonce-based AEs). Those achieve elegant performance thanks to the nonce property. However, ensuring the uniqueness of nonce is

© The Author(s), under exclusive license to Springer Nature Switzerland AG 2023
E. Athanasopoulos and B. Mennink (Eds.): ISC 2023, LNCS 14411, pp. 351–371, 2023.
https://doi.org/10.1007/978-3-031-49187-0_18

not easy when implementing AE schemes, and in fact many security incidents occurred due to improper handling of nonce, e.g., a low-quality random number, a tiny nonce space, and even a constant nonce [12]. Even if implementers are careful enough, proper nonce management is impossible in resource-constrained platforms; stateful nonce management is necessary to ensure the uniqueness, but some devices may not have nonvolatile memory, and even if they have, wireless power supply may not provide enough power to write to it [4, 21].

For communicating sensitive data, more robust schemes that do not rely on nonce are required. Key wrap schemes used for sending keys is one example; National Institute of Standards and Technology (NIST) standardized a nonce-independent AE scheme for key wrap [17]. Rogaway and Shrimpton called such schemes deterministic AE (DAE) and formalized its definition and security [28].

Lightweight cryptography is a technology intended for use in extremely resource-constrained environments such as sensor networks and RFID tags. In particular, designs of lightweight schemes have been actively studied in recent years due to the NIST lightweight cryptography standardization process [26]. Because nonce support was a design requirement in NIST's standardization project, DAE is less discussed than nonce-based AE in the context of lightweight cryptography. For resource-constrained devices, DAE is a useful option, not only because of its security robustness, but also because it does not require a random number generator or non-volatile memory. Although DAE needs a buffer for scanning the entire message twice, numerous IoT protocols limit the message length to several dozen bytes (e.g., 64 bytes for CAN FD) [3] that fit within a cheap non-volatile memory, which makes DAE a practical option. As a result, there are several existing studies that propose low memory DAE, which includes SUNDAE [5], ANYDAE [14], ESTATE [13], and SIV-TEM-PHOTON [6].

The above lightweight DAEs use a block cipher (BC) or a tweakable block cipher (TBC) as an underlying primitive. On the other hand, cryptographic-permutation-based designs such as the sponge and duplex constructions [8–10] have been actively discussed recently. Permutation-based schemes do not require designing a key schedule and tweak schedule compared to BC- and TBC-based schemes, and have a clear advantage in terms of minimizing design and implementation. Also, various functions such as AEs, hash functions, stream ciphers, and extendable-output functions (XOFs) can be realized by making only minor changes to a single permutation design. Furthermore, it allows flexible support for different platforms by simply changing the parameters called rate and capacity. These properties make permutation-based design a very attractive option, and the goal of this paper is to propose a permutation-based DAE.

1.1   Memory Usage in DAE

There are several ways to count the memory size based on different philosophies. For example, some count the memory to store the key as the memory required to implement the scheme, while others do not include it assuming that it is supplied externally. Before summarizing the memory size for existing DAE schemes, We discuss what should be counted as a key performance indicator (KPI) for the memory amount of a hardware implementations in DAE.

Message Buffer (Uncounted). In the encryption of DAE, by security definition, the output (ciphertext C and tag T) must change randomly when the input (associated data A and message M) changes by even a single bit. Therefore, it is necessary to first compute a value using all bits of A, M, and then access M again for generating ciphertext based on the computed value. That is, encryption of DAE must be 2-passes, and DAE needs a message buffer for storing the entire message for two-pass scanning. We can safely exclude a message buffer in comparing DAE schemes because it is necessary for any DAE. Also, the memory size is not homogeneous because the message buffer can be implemented with an efficient SRAM, while implementing cryptographic algorithms requires expensive registers. The register size determines the cost of coprocessor, and the buffer size is not a KPI of hardware implementations.

Tweak Register Without Schedule (Counted). TBC-based schemes require a tweak value to compute the primitive. When a tweak schedule is not needed, some existing works e.g. [6] evaluate the tweak register as unnecessary, assuming that an external provider will send the tweak multiple times when it is needed. We argue that if the value is accessed multiple times, the tweak requires a memory even if a tweak schedule is not needed. Coprocessors receive data in a streaming manner and returns data also in a streaming manner, hence cannot read the data multiple times. Hence, the tweak must be stored in a memory.

Key Register (Counted). Similar to tweak, some existing works evaluate the key register as unnecessary when the scheme does not need the key schedule. We argue that the key register must be counted regardless of the presence or absence of a schedule. This is because DAE schemes needs K for both the first and second passes, so it is inevitable to access K multiple times.

Tag in Decryption of SIV-like DAE (Uncounted). In a popular DAE mode SIV [28], T is first generated from (A, M), and then C is generated using T as an initial value IV. In the decryption of SIV, M is first decrypted from C using T, then the tag is generated from (A, M) and verified if it matches T received at the beginning. Hence, it is necessary to keep T from the beginning to the end. We argue that T during the decryption of SIV-like DAEs does not count as memory required for implementing it by the following reasons. 1) Computations performed by a hardware is up to the tag generation and the cost of comparing tags should not be counted as a hardware cost for a DAE scheme. 2) Hardware implementations consider sharing the components used for encryption and decryption, thus tag comparison, performed only in decryption, should be done by an upper layer. 3) One of the purposes of hardware implementations is to accelerate the performance. Since it does not impact the performance, the tag comparison is naturally performed by an upper layer. In fact, previous schemes also do not count T as required memory.[1]

1.2   Related Works and Research Challenges

Using the above counting method, we discuss the memory size of existing BC- and TBC-based lightweight DAEs and permutation-based DAEs (Table 1).

BC- and TBC-Based Lightweight DAEs. SUNDAE [5] is a BC-based DAE mode, which updates a b-bit state by using a BC with b-bit block and a k-bit key to ensure $b/2$-bit security. When the target bit security level is s bits, $b = 2s$ and $k = s$. Hence, it requires total $3s$ bits of state. ESTATE [13] is a slight optimization of SUNDAE and the memory evaluation is the same. LM-DAE is a TBC-based DAE mode [24]. It uses a TBC with b-bit block, a t-bit tweak, and a k-bit key, to ensure b-bit security. A $b + t$-bit state is iteratively updated by the TBC. For s-bit security, it requires $b = t = k = s$. Hence, the total memory size is $3s$ bits. SIV-TEM-PHOTON [6] is a dedicated TBC-based DAE scheme. A b-bit state is updated with a TBC having b-bit block, a $b/2$-bit tweak, and a k-bit key to ensure $b/2$-bit security. For s-bit security, $b = 2s$ and $k = s$. Hence the total memory size is $4s$ bits.[2]

Permutation-Based DAEs. Bertoni et al. presented a permutation-based DAE called HADDOC [11], which is a permutation-based SIV using a $(r + c)$-bit permutation to ensure $c/2$-bit security. It first generates a t-bit tag T using a k-bit key K, then C is generated with a CTR-like mode; $K \| T \| i$, where i is the counter value, is processed by a sponge construction to provide a key stream for block i. Hence, besides the $r + c$-bit state, it needs a memory for K, T and $\tilde{i}$-bit memory for the counter value, where $\tilde{i}$ is the maximum counter size. For s-bit security, $c = t = 2s$ and $k = s$. Hence, the total memory size is $5s + r + \tilde{i}$. Bertoni et al. presented a parallel permutation-based mode Farfalle and specified its SIV variant Farfalle-SIV [7]. Owing to its parallel construction, it uses a $2s$-bit accumulator as well as a $2s$-bit state to compute a tag. Hence, together with an s-bit key, a total of $5s$ bits of memory is required. Another way to achieve DAE

---

[1] There may be a case that the tag comparison is included in hardware by using additional memory. As long as the comparison targets are all SIV-like schemes with the same tag size, as in this paper, there is no impact on the fairness of the comparison by whether or not T is counted during decryption. The situation changes when side-channel attack (SCA) is a concern. In such a case, tag comparison needs an SCA protection [16] and should be included in the hardware implementation. This increases the memory requirement in Table 1 in all the schemes but HADDOC that anyway stores the tag during encryption and decryption.

[2] The designers claim that "since key bits and tweak bits are used without schedule in TEM-PHOTON, in the case where they can be sent multiple times by the external provider, local storage can be saved." They also claim that "When key and tweak has to be stored locally, they can be stored using 256 regular 1-bit flip-flops." As discussed above, we argue that the latter is the most natural implementation.

with a permutation is to replace a BC of SUNDAE or ESTATE with the Even-Monsour construction [18], where an encryption is computed by $\pi((\cdot) \oplus K) \oplus K$ using a permutation π. To ensure s-bit security, both the permutation size and the key size must be $2s$ bits. Hence, the memory size is $4s$ bits.

Research Challenges. Both BC-based and TBC-based DAEs are realized with $3s$ bits of memory while existing permutation-based DAEs require a larger memory. Designing permutation-based DAEs with $3\,s$ bits of memory or even smaller DAEs is an important research challenge.

Table 1. Memory size comparison of DAE schemes with s-bit security.

Scheme	Primitive	Memory				Rate	Ref.	Remarks
		state	key	tweak	total	[bit/call]		
SUNDAE	BC	$2s$	s	–	$3s$	s	[5]	
ESTATE	BC	$2s$	s	–	$3s$	s	[13]	
LM-DAE	TBC	s	s	s	$3s$	$s/2$	[24]	
SIV-TEM-PHOTON	TBC	$2s$	s	s	$4s$	$6s/5$	[6]	high rate
HADDOC	perm.	$4s + r + \tilde{\imath}$	s	–	$5s + r + \tilde{\imath}$	$(r + 2s)/2$	[11]	high rate
Farfalle-SIV	perm.	$4s$	s	–	$5s$	$s/2$	[7]	parallel
EM + SUNDAE	perm.	$2s$	$2s$	–	$4s$	s	[5,18]	
PALM	perm.	$2s$	s	–	$3s$	s	Ours	

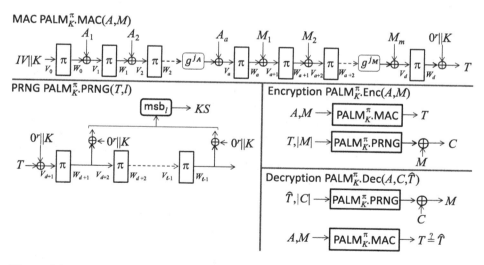

Fig. 1. PALM. If $A \neq \varepsilon \wedge M \neq \varepsilon$ then $IV = 0^{b-k}$; if $A = \varepsilon \wedge M \neq \varepsilon$ then $IV = 0^{b-k-2}10$; if $A \neq \varepsilon \wedge M = \varepsilon$ then $IV = 0^{b-k-1}1$; if $A \neq \varepsilon = M = \varepsilon$ then $IV = 0^{b-k-2}11$. g is an LFSR. $g^1(S) := g(S)$ and $g^2(S) := g(g(S))$. If $|A| \bmod b \neq 0$ then $j_A = 1$; else $j_A = 2$. If $|M| \bmod b \neq 0$ **then** $j_M = 1$; else $j_M = 2$.

356 Y. Hiraga et al.

1.3 Our Contribution

In this paper, we propose a permutation-based DAE mode PALM that can be implemented with $3s$ bits of memory. This shows that permutation-based DAEs can be implemented with a competitive memory size compared to existing BC- and TBC-based DAEs. Given the flexible functionality of permutation-based cryptography, this is a very useful result.

Design Overview. The structure of PALM is given in Fig. 1. We design PALM by following the SIV design paradigm [28], so PALM has the MAC-then-Encrypt structure. To minimize the state size, PALM has an iterated structure of a b-bit permutation π and does not require additional state except for a key K. Hence, the state size is $b + k$ bits, and $b = 2s$ and $k = s$ for s-bit security. The key masking is introduced to prevent internal state values being recovered.

In the MAC part, b-bit associated data (AD) blocks $A_1, \ldots, A_a$ are processed, and then b-bit plaintext blocks $M_1, \ldots, M_m$ are processed, where a one-zero padding is applied to the last AD and plaintext blocks if the length is less than b. After processing these blocks, a tag is defined. To avoid a length extension attack and an attack using the padding rule, a b-bit LFSR g is applied to the internal states with the last AD and plaintext blocks. j_A (resp. j_M) is the number of the LFSR calls and is defined according to the length $|A_a|$ (resp. $|M_m|$). In the PRNG part, each key stream block is defined by XORing an output of π with K. A plaintext block is encrypted by being XORed with a key stream block. The full description of PALM will be given in Sect. 3.

Note that the design of iterating a permutation has been employed by Chaskey [23] and Even-Mansour-based DAEs. These schemes require a key of length $k = b$, whereas PALM allows $k < b$.

Security. We prove that PALM achieves $\min\left\{k, \frac{b}{2}\right\}$-bit security[3] assuming that π is a random permutation (RP). Let σ be the number of π calls in online queries and p be the number of π calls in offline ones (direct access to π by an adversary). We give an intuition of obtaining the security bound below.

We first consider an event that some internal state value of PALM is recovered, that is, a collision event between π's values of PALM and of offline queries. By the masking with K, the k-bit part of the internal state becomes secret but the remaining r bits, where $r = b - k$, is public. If the Even-Mansour-style proof [2,23] is used, the probability for the state recovery event relies on only the length of the secret k-bit state, yielding the birthday bound $O\left(\frac{p\sigma}{2^k}\right)$ which is a $\frac{k}{2}$-bit security bound. We thus use the technique for sponge-based AE schemes [22] that uses a multi-collision on the r-bit public part. Using this technique, we can prove a $\min\left\{k, \frac{b}{2}\right\}$-bit bound regarding the collision event.

We next assume that the collision event does not occur. Then, the permutation π in PALM can be seen as a secret permutation. In this setting, similarly to the existing secret random permutation-based proofs such as [5,14], one can prove the $\frac{b}{2}$-bit security bound.

---

[3] Specifically, our security bound is $\min\left\{k - \log_2(b - k), \frac{b}{2}\right\}$ bits. Since $\log_2(b - k)$ is small, we omit the term in this paper.

By these bounds, we obtain the min $\left\{k, \frac{b}{2}\right\}$-bit security bound of PALM. More detailed analysis will be given in Sect. 4.

HW Implementation. Next, we instantiate PALM for 128-bit security using PHOTON$_{256}$ [20] and make hardware performance evaluation in Sect. 5. Our PALM implementation achieves 3,585 GE, which is smaller than 3,717 GE of the conventional LM-DAE implementation [24]. The overhead for extending PHOTON$_{256}$ to PALM is 1,059 GE, mostly occupied by the 128-bit key register. Moreover, the PALM implementation achieves the processing speed of 107.2 cycles/byte, outperforming 127.3 cycles/byte of LM-DAE.

Memory Optimality of PALM. Finally, we show that $3s$-bits of memory achieved by PALM is optimal as long as an SIV-like structure is used to achieve s-bit security. Specifically, in Sect. 6, we show an attack that breaks integrity with a complexity smaller than s bits when the memory size is less than $3s$ bits.

2   Preliminaries

Notation. Let ε be an empty string and $\{0,1\}^*$ be the set of all bit strings. For an integer $i \geq 0$, let $\{0,1\}^i$ be the set of all i-bit strings, $\{0,1\}^0 := \{\varepsilon\}$, and $\{0,1\}^{\leq i} := \{0,1\}^1 \cup \{0,1\}^2 \cup \cdots \cup \{0,1\}^i$ be the set of all bit strings of length at most i, except for ε. Let 0^i be the bit string of i-bit zeros. For integers $0 \leq i \leq j$, let $[i,j] := \{i, i+1, \ldots, j\}$ and $[j] := [1,j]$. For a non-empty set T, $T \xleftarrow{\$} T$ means that an element is chosen uniformly at random from T and is assigned to T. For sets T_1 and T_2, $T_1 \xleftarrow{\cup} T_2$ means $T_1 \leftarrow T_1 \cup T_2$. The concatenation of two bit strings X and Y is written as $X\|Y$ or XY when no confusion is possible. For integers $0 \leq i \leq j$ and $X \in \{0,1\}^j$, let $\mathsf{msb}_i(X)$ (resp. $\mathsf{lsb}_i(X)$) be the most (resp. least) significant i bits of X, and $|X|$ be the bit length of X, i.e., $|X| = j$. For an integer $b \geq 0$ and a bit string X, we denote the parsing into fixed-length b-bit strings as $(X_1, \ldots, X_\ell) \xleftarrow{b} X$, where if $X \neq \varepsilon$ then $X = X_1\| \cdots \|X_\ell$, $|X_i| = b$ for $i \in [\ell - 1]$, and $0 < |X_\ell| \leq b$; if $X = \varepsilon$ then $\ell = 1$ and $X_1 = \varepsilon$. For an integer $b > 0$, let $\mathsf{ozp} : \{0,1\}^{\leq b} \to \{0,1\}^b$ be a one-zero padding function: for $X \in \{0,1\}^{\leq b}$, $\mathsf{ozp}(X) = X$ if $|X| = b$; $\mathsf{ozp}(X) = X\|10^{b-1-|X|}$ if $|X| < b$.

Throughout this paper, the permutation size is denoted by b. Let Perm be the set of all b-bit permutations. For $\pi \in$ Perm, let π^{-1} be the inverse permutation.

TBC-Based DAE. Let $\mathcal{K}, \mathcal{M}, \mathcal{C}, \mathcal{A}$, and T be sets of keys, plaintexts, ciphertexts, associated data (AD), and tags, respectively. A DAE scheme Π using $\pi \in$ Perm and having a key $K \in \mathcal{K}$, denoted by Π_K^π, is a pair of encryption and decryption algorithms $(\Pi_K^\pi.\mathsf{Enc}, \Pi_K^\pi.\mathsf{Dec})$. The encryption algorithm $\Pi_K^\pi.\mathsf{Enc}$ takes AD $A \in \mathcal{A}$, and a plaintext $M \in \mathcal{M}$, and returns, deterministically, a pair of a ciphertext $C \in \mathcal{C}$ and a tag $T \in T$. The decryption algorithm $\Pi_K^\pi.\mathsf{Dec}$ takes a tuple $(A, C, \hat{T}) \in \mathcal{A} \times \mathcal{C} \times T$, and deterministically returns either the distinguished invalid symbol **reject** $\notin \mathcal{M}$ or a plaintext $M \in \mathcal{M}$. We require $|\Pi_K^\pi.\mathsf{Enc}(A, M)| = |\Pi_K^\pi.\mathsf{Enc}(A, M')|$ when $|M| = |M'|$.

Y. Hiraga et al.
We define an advantage function of permutation-based DAE. We consider dae-security which is indistinguishability between Π_K^π and an ideal DAE. An ideal DAE consists of two oracles $(\$, \perp)$. $\$$ is a random-bits oracle that has the same interface as Π_K^π.Enc and for a query (A, M) returns a random bit string of length $|\Pi_K^\pi.\mathsf{Enc}(A, M)|$. $\perp$ is a reject oracle that returns **reject** for any query. In the DAE-security game, firstly an adversary $\mathbf{A}$ interacts with either $(\Pi_K^\pi.\mathsf{Enc}, \Pi_K^\pi.\mathsf{Dec}, \pi, \pi^{-1})$ or $(\$, \perp, \pi, \pi^{-1})$ where $K \xleftarrow{\$} \mathcal{K}$ and $\pi \xleftarrow{\$} \mathsf{Perm}$. After finishing the interaction, $\mathbf{A}$ returns a decision bit. For a set of oracles $\mathcal{O}$, let $\mathbf{A}^{\mathcal{O}} \in \{0, 1\}$ be an $\mathbf{A}$'s output after interacting with $\mathcal{O}$. Then the DAE-security advantage function is defined as

$$\mathbf{Adv}_{\Pi}^{\mathsf{dae}}(\mathbf{A}) = \Pr[\mathbf{A}^{\Pi_K^\pi.\mathsf{Enc}, \Pi_K^\pi.\mathsf{Dec}, \pi, \pi^{-1}} = 1] - \Pr[\mathbf{A}^{\$, \perp, \pi, \pi^{-1}} = 1],$$

where the probabilities are taken over $\pi, K, \$$, and $\mathbf{A}$. Throughout this paper, we call queries to an encryption oracle, a decryption oracle, π, and π^{-1} "encryption queries," "decryption queries," "forward queries," and "inverse queries," respectively. We call queries to encryption or decryption queries "online queries," and forward or inverse queries "offline queries," respectively. We demand that $\mathbf{A}$ never asks a trivial decryption query (A, C, T), i.e., there is a prior encryption query (A, M) with $(C, T) = \Pi.\mathsf{Enc}[\pi](A, M)$, and that $\mathbf{A}$ never repeats a query.

3 PALM: Specification and Security Bound

Specification. The specification of PALM is given in Algorithm 1 and in Fig. 1. $\mathsf{PALM}_K^\pi.\mathsf{Enc}$ (resp. $\mathsf{PALM}_K^\pi.\mathsf{Dec}$) is an encryption (resp. a decryption) function of PALM. $\mathsf{PALM}_K^\pi.\mathsf{MAC}$ is a tag-generation function, and $\mathsf{PALM}_K^\pi.\mathsf{PRNG}$ is a pseudorandom generator that is used to encrypt/decrypt a plaintext/ciphertext. These functions are subroutines of $\mathsf{PALM}_K^\pi.\mathsf{Enc}$ and $\mathsf{PALM}_K^\pi.\mathsf{Dec}$. π is the underlying permutation and the permutation size is b bits.

In PALM, the sizes of AD block, plaintext/ciphertext block, and tag are equal to b. Let k be the key size of PALM and $r = b - k$.

Let g be a b-bit LFSR. For a b-bit value S, let $g^0(S) := S$, $g^1(S) := g(S)$ and $g^2(S) := g(g(S))$. We require the following properties: for b-bit variables S_1 and S_2, and two distinct values $i, j \in (2]$, if S_2 is fixed, then the equation $g^i(S_1) \oplus g^j(S_1) = S_2$ offers a unique solution for S_1. For a chunk size $n \le b$, the following LFSR satisfies the condition and is efficient both in software and hardware implementations.

$$g(S) = (S_2 \oplus S_3)\|S_3\|S_4\| \cdots \|S_{b/n}\|S_1, \text{ where } (S_1, S_2, \ldots, S_{b/n}) \xleftarrow{n} S. \quad (1)$$

Security of PALM. The following theorem gives PALM's DAE-security bound.

Theorem 1. *For any positive integer μ and adversary $\mathbf{A}$ making p offline queries and q online queries such that the total number of permutation calls in online queries is σ, we have* $\mathbf{Adv}_{\mathsf{PALM}}^{\mathsf{dae}}(\mathbf{A}) \le \frac{2\sigma}{2^k} + \frac{4.5\sigma^2}{2^b} + \frac{4p\sigma}{2^b} + \frac{2\mu p}{2^k} + 2^r \cdot \left(\frac{e\sigma}{\mu 2^r}\right)^\mu.$

Algorithm 1. PALM

Encryption $\mathsf{PALM}_K^\pi.\mathsf{Enc}(A, M)$

1: $T \leftarrow \mathsf{PALM}_K^\pi.\mathsf{MAC}(A, M); \; C \leftarrow M \oplus \mathsf{PALM}_K^\pi.\mathsf{PRNG}(T, |M|); \; \textbf{return } (C, T)$

Decryption $\mathsf{PALM}_K^\pi.\mathsf{Dec}(A, C, \hat{T})$

1: $M \leftarrow C \oplus \mathsf{PALM}_K^\pi.\mathsf{PRNG}(\hat{T}, |C|); \; T \leftarrow \mathsf{PALM}_K^\pi.\mathsf{MAC}(A, M)$
2: **if** $T = \hat{T}$ **then return** M **else return reject end if**

MAC $\mathsf{PALM}_K^\pi.\mathsf{MAC}(A, M)$

1: **if** $A \neq \varepsilon$ **then** $x_0 \leftarrow 0$ **else** $x_0 \leftarrow 1$ **end if**
2: **if** $M \neq \varepsilon$ **then** $x_1 \leftarrow 0$ **else** $x_1 \leftarrow 1$ **end if**
3: $IV \leftarrow 0^{b-k-2}\|x_1\|x_0; \; S \leftarrow \pi(IV\|K)$
4: $(A_1, \ldots, A_a) \xleftarrow{b} \mathsf{ozp}(A); \; (M_1, \ldots, M_m) \xleftarrow{b} \mathsf{ozp}(M)$
5: **if** $|A| \bmod b \neq 0$ **then** $j_A = 1$ **else** $j_A = 2$ **end if**
6: **if** $|M| \bmod b \neq 0$ **then** $j_M = 1$ **else** $j_M = 2$ **end if**
7: **if** $A = \varepsilon$ **then goto step 9 end if**
8: **for** $i = 1, \ldots, a$ **do if** $i = a$ **then** $S \leftarrow g^{j_A}(S)$ **end if**
$\qquad\qquad\qquad\qquad\qquad\qquad S \leftarrow S \oplus A_i; \; S \leftarrow \pi(S)$ **end for**
9: **if** $M = \varepsilon$ **then goto step 11 end if**
10: **for** $i = 1, \ldots, m$ **do if** $i = m$ **then** $S \leftarrow g^{j_M}(S)$ **end if**
$\qquad\qquad\qquad\qquad\qquad\qquad S \leftarrow S \oplus M_i; \; S \leftarrow \pi(S)$ **end for**
11: $T \leftarrow S \oplus 0^r\|K; \; \textbf{return } T$

PRNG $\mathsf{PALM}_K^\pi.\mathsf{PRNG}(T, l)$

1: $KS \leftarrow \varepsilon; \; S \leftarrow T \oplus (0^r\|K); \; m \leftarrow \lceil l/b \rceil$
2: **for** $i = 1, \ldots, m$ **do** $S \leftarrow \pi(S); \; KS \leftarrow KS\| \, (S \oplus (0^r\|K))$ **end for**
3: $KS \leftarrow \mathsf{msb}_l(KS); \; \textbf{return } KS$

Putting two concrete values for μ to the bound, we obtain the following bounds.

Corollary 1. *For any positive integer μ and adversary* **A** *making p offline queries and q online queries such that the total number of permutation calls in online queries is σ, if $r = k = b/2$ and $\mu = \frac{k}{\log_2 k}$, then we have*

$$\mathbf{Adv}_{\mathsf{PALM}}^{\mathsf{dae}}(\mathbf{A}) \leq \frac{2\sigma}{2^k} + \frac{4.5\sigma^2}{2^b} + \frac{4p\sigma}{2^b} + \frac{\frac{2k}{\log_2 k} \cdot p}{2^k} + \left(\frac{(e\log_2 k)\sigma}{2^k}\right)^{\frac{k}{\log_2 k}},$$

and if $\mu = \max\left\{r, \left(\frac{2e \cdot 2^k \sigma}{2^r p}\right)^{\frac{1}{2}}\right\}$, then we have

$$\mathbf{Adv}_{\mathsf{PALM}}^{\mathsf{dae}}(\mathbf{A}) \leq \frac{2\sigma}{2^k} + \frac{4.5\sigma^2}{2^b} + \frac{4p\sigma}{2^b} + \frac{2rp}{2^k} + \left(\frac{8ep\sigma}{2^b}\right)^{\frac{1}{2}}.$$

We study the above bounds. The above bounds show that PALM is DAE-secure as long as $\sigma \ll 2^{b/2}$, $p\sigma \ll 2^b$, $p \ll 2^k$, and $\sigma \ll 2^k$, that is, PALM achieves $\min\left\{k, \frac{b}{2}\right\}$-bit DAE-security. Note that both bounds show the same level of security but the first bound which does not have the term with the exponent $1/2$ is sharper than the second one.

4   Proof of Theorem 1

Without loss of generality, we assume that an adversary is deterministic. We also assume that $p + \sigma \leq 2^{b-1}$. In this proof, a random permutation π is realized by lazy sampling. Let $\mathcal{L}_\pi$ be a table that is initially empty and keeps query-response tuples of π or π^{-1}. Let $\mathcal{L}_\pi^1 := \{X \mid (X,Y) \in \mathcal{L}_\pi\}$ and $\mathcal{L}_\pi^2 := \{Y \mid (X,Y) \in \mathcal{L}_\pi\}$.[4]

4.1   Deriving the Upper-Bound Using Coefficient H Technique

Our proof uses the coefficient H technique [27]. Let T_R be a transcript in the real world obtained by random samples of a user's key and an RP. Let T_I be a transcript in the ideal world obtained by random samples of a random-bit oracle, an RP, and additional values defined later. For a transcript τ, an adversary's view (or information obtained) in the security game, we call τ a valid transcript if $\Pr[\mathsf{T}_I = \tau] > 0$. Let $\mathbf{T}$ be the set of all valid transcripts such that $\forall \tau \in \mathbf{T} : \Pr[\mathsf{T}_R = \tau] \leq \Pr[\mathsf{T}_I = \tau]$. Then, the advantage function $\mathbf{Adv}_{\mathsf{PALM}}^{\mathsf{dae}}(\mathbf{A})$ is upper-bounded by the statistical distance, i.e., $\mathbf{Adv}_{\mathsf{PALM}}^{\mathsf{dae}}(\mathbf{A}) \leq \mathsf{SD}(\mathsf{T}_R, \mathsf{T}_I) := \sum_{\tau \in \mathbf{T}}(\Pr[\mathsf{T}_I = \tau] - \Pr[\mathsf{T}_R = \tau])$. Using the following lemma, we can derive the upper-bound of $\mathbf{Adv}_{\mathsf{PALM}}^{\mathsf{dae}}(\mathbf{A})$.

Lemma 1. *Let $\mathbf{T}_{\mathsf{good}}$ and $\mathbf{T}_{\mathsf{bad}}$ be respectively the sets of good transcripts and of bad ones into which $\mathbf{T}$ is partitioned. For good transcripts $\mathbf{T}_{\mathsf{good}}$ and bad transcripts $\mathbf{T}_{\mathsf{bad}}$, if $\forall \tau \in \mathbf{T}_{\mathsf{good}} : \frac{\Pr[\mathsf{T}_R = \tau]}{\Pr[\mathsf{T}_I = \tau]} \geq 1 - \varepsilon$ s.t. $0 \leq \varepsilon \leq 1$, then $\mathsf{SD}(\mathsf{T}_R, \mathsf{T}_I) \leq \Pr[\mathsf{T}_I \in \mathbf{T}_{\mathsf{bad}}] + \varepsilon$.*

In the following proof, we (1) partition $\mathbf{T}$ into $\mathbf{T}_{\mathsf{good}}$ and $\mathbf{T}_{\mathsf{bad}}$ (Sect. 4.5); (2) upper-bound $\Pr[\mathsf{T}_I \in \mathbf{T}_{\mathsf{bad}}]$ (the bound is given in Eq. (2) in Sect. 4.6); and (3) lower-bound $\frac{\Pr[\mathsf{T}_R = \tau]}{\Pr[\mathsf{T}_I = \tau]}$ for any $\tau \in \mathbf{T}_{\mathsf{good}}$ (the bound is given in Eq. (3) in Sect. 4.7). We finally obtain the DAE-security bound in Theorem 1 by combining these bounds.

4.2   Definition

Let q, $q_{\mathcal{E}}$, and $q_{\mathcal{D}}$ be the number of online, forward, and inverse queries, respectively. Let $\sigma_{\mathcal{E}}$ (resp. $\sigma_{\mathcal{D}}$) be the number of π calls in encryption (resp. decryption) queries. The 1st through $q_{\mathcal{E}}$-th (resp. $(q_{\mathcal{E}} + 1)$-th through q-th) online queries are assigned to encryption (resp. decryption). Hence, α-th encryption (resp. decryption) query is said to be the α-th (resp. $(q_{\mathcal{E}} + \alpha)$-th) online query. Note that this assignment defines just online-query numbers, and does not restrict the order of adversary's queries.

For $\alpha \in [q]$, values defined at the α-th online query are denoted by using the superscript of (α), and the lengths a and m at the α-th online

---

[4] For a forward query X to π (resp. inverse query Y to π^{-1}), the response Y (resp. X) is defined as $Y \xleftarrow{\$} \{0,1\}^b \backslash \mathcal{L}_\pi^2$ (resp. $X \xleftarrow{\$} \{0,1\}^b \backslash \mathcal{L}_\pi^1$), and the query-response pair (X,Y) is added to $\mathcal{L}_\pi$: $\mathcal{L}_\pi \xleftarrow{\cup} \mathcal{L}_\pi \cup \{(X,Y)\}$.

Algorithm 2. Dummy Internal Values in the Ideal World

1: $K \xleftarrow{\$} \{0,1\}^k$ ▷ Dummy key
2: **for** $\alpha \in [q_{\mathcal{E}}]$ **do**   ▷ Dummy internal values of $\mathsf{PALM}_K^\pi.\mathsf{Enc}$
3:     **for** $i \in [d_\alpha]$ **do** $(V_{i-1}^{(\alpha)}, W_{i-1}^{(\alpha)}) \leftarrow \mathsf{PALM}_K^\pi.\mathsf{MAC}(A^{(\alpha)}, M^{(\alpha)})[i]$ **end for**
4:     $V_{d_\alpha}^{(\alpha)} \leftarrow g^{j_M^{(\alpha)}}(W_{d_\alpha-1}^{(\alpha)}) \oplus \mathsf{ozp}(M_{m_\alpha}^{(\alpha)}); \; W_{d_\alpha}^{(\alpha)} \leftarrow T^{(\alpha)} \oplus 0^r \| K; \; \mathcal{L}_\pi \xleftarrow{\cup} (V_{d_\alpha}^{(\alpha)}, W_{d_\alpha}^{(\alpha)})$
5:     **for** $i \in [d_\alpha + 1, \ell_\alpha - 1]$ **do** $R \leftarrow \{0,1\}^{b - |M_{i-d_\alpha}^{(\alpha)}|}; \; V_i^{(\alpha)} \leftarrow W_{i-1}^{(\alpha)};$
           $W_i^{(\alpha)} \leftarrow \left(\left(C_{i-d_\alpha}^{(\alpha)} \oplus M_{i-d_\alpha}^{(\alpha)} \right) \| R \right) \oplus (0^r \| K); \; \mathcal{L}_\pi \xleftarrow{\cup} (V_i^{(\alpha)}, W_i^{(\alpha)})$ **end for**
6: **end for**
7: **for** $\alpha \in [q_{\mathcal{E}} + 1, q]$ **do**   ▷ Dummy internal values of $\mathsf{PALM}_K^\pi.\mathsf{Dec}$
8:     $M^{(\alpha)} \leftarrow C^{(\alpha)} \oplus \mathsf{PALM}_K^\pi.\mathsf{PRNG}(\hat{T}^{(\alpha)}, |C^{(\alpha)}|)$
9:     **for** $i \in [d_\alpha + 1]$ **do** $(V_{i-1}^{(\alpha)}, W_{i-1}^{(\alpha)}) \leftarrow \mathsf{PALM}_K^\pi.\mathsf{MAC}(A^{(\alpha)}, M^{(\alpha)})[i]$ **end for**
10:    **for** $i \in [m_\alpha]$ **do**
           $(V_{d_\alpha+i}^{(\alpha)}, W_{d_\alpha+i}^{(\alpha)}) \leftarrow \mathsf{PALM}_K^\pi.\mathsf{PRNG}(\hat{T}^{(\alpha)}, |C^{(\alpha)}|)[i]$ **end for**
11: **end for**

query are denoted by a_α and m_α. Let $d_\alpha := a_\alpha + m_\alpha$ be the number of data blocks in the α-th online query. Let $\ell_\alpha := a_\alpha + 2m_\alpha + 1$ be the number of π calls in the α-th online query. Let $\mathsf{PALM}_K^\pi.\mathsf{MAC}(A^{(\alpha)}, M^{(\alpha)})[i]$ be an input-output pair of the i-th π call in $\mathsf{PALM}_K^\pi.\mathsf{MAC}(A^{(\alpha)}, M^{(\alpha)})$. Let $\mathsf{PALM}_K^\pi.\mathsf{PRNG}(T^{(\alpha)}, |M^{(\alpha)}|)[i]$ be an input-output pair of the i-th π call in $\mathsf{PALM}_K^\pi.\mathsf{PRNG}(T^{(\alpha)}, |M^{(\alpha)}|)$. In the real world, for $\alpha \in [q]$, $i \in [d_\alpha + 1]$, and $j \in [m_\alpha]$, let $(V_{i-1}^{(\alpha)}, W_{i-1}^{(\alpha)}) := \mathsf{PALM}_K^\pi.\mathsf{MAC}(A^{(\alpha)}, M^{(\alpha)})[i]$ and $(V_{d_\alpha+j}^{(\alpha)}, W_{d_\alpha+j}^{(\alpha)}) := \mathsf{PALM}_K^\pi.\mathsf{PRNG}(T^{(\alpha)}, |M^{(\alpha)}|)[j]$. See Fig. 1 for these values. In the ideal world, these values are defined in Sect. 4.3.

The β-th offline query-response pair is denoted by $(X^{(\beta)}, Y^{(\beta)})$, where $Y^{(\beta)} = \pi(X^{(\beta)})$ for a forward query and $X^{(\beta)} = \pi^{-1}(Y^{(\beta)})$ for an inverse query.

Hereafter, We call a period from the start of the game to the end of **A**'s queries "query phase", and a phase after finishing **A**'s queries "decision phase". In the decision phase, dummy internal values are defined in the ideal world (defined below).

4.3 Dummy Values in the Ideal World

In the decision stage of the ideal world, a dummy key K and dummy internal values $(V_i^{(\alpha)}, W_i^{(\alpha)})$ are defined by Algorithm 2. In this algorithm, first K is defined (Step 1). Then, for each encryption query, the dummy internal values are defined (Steps 2-6): For the MAC part, the internal values are defined by using π and by following the structure of the MAC part. The last output in the MAC part, in order to ensure consistency with the encryption query, is defined by using the tag and the key in Step 4, which does not perform π. The input-output pair is stored in the RP table $\mathcal{L}_\pi$. For the PRNG part, the internal values are defined by using plaintext blocks, ciphertext blocks, and the key according to the structure of this part. Finally, for each decryption query, the dummy internal values are defined by using π and by following the structure of $\mathsf{PALM}_K^\tau.\mathsf{Dec}$ (Steps 7–11). Note that since decryption queries are all **reject**, we define the dummy internal values without taking into account consistency with the queries.

4.4 Adversary's View

In the decision phase, the proof permits **A** to obtain a key and all internal values for online queries. Hence, a transcript τ (or an adversary's view) consists of a key K; online query-response tuples $(A^{(\alpha)}, M^{(\alpha)}, C^{(\alpha)}, T^{(\alpha)})$ where $\alpha \in [q_\mathcal{E}]$; online query-response tuples $(A^{(\alpha)}, C^{(\alpha)}, T'^{(\alpha)}, RV^{(\alpha)})$ where $\alpha \in [q_\mathcal{E} + 1, q]$ and $RV^{(\alpha)} \in \{\mathbf{reject}, M^{(\alpha)}\}$ is the response to the α-th online query; input-output pairs $(V_i^{(\alpha)}, W_i^{(\alpha)})$ where $\alpha \in [q]$ and $i \in [0, d_\alpha - 1]$; and offline query-response pairs $(X^{(\beta)}, Y^{(\beta)})$ where $\beta \in [p]$.

4.5 Good and Bad Transcripts

We define $\mathbf{T}_{\mathsf{bad}}$ such that at least one of the following conditions is satisfied, and $\mathbf{T}_{\mathsf{good}} := \mathbf{T} \backslash \mathbf{T}_{\mathsf{bad}}$.

The event bad_1 considers a collision between initial inputs in the MAC part and other inputs to π. The event bad_2 considers a collision in the MAC part. The event bad_3 considers a collision between the PRNG part of the encryption and the MAC part. The event bad_4 considers a collision in the PRNG part of the encryption. The event bad_5 considers a collision between online and offline queries. The event bad_6 considers a forgery event. Note that a collision event between the PRNG part of the decryption and other parts in online queries is not considered as a bad event, since the event does not trigger an attack.[5]

The formal definitions of these bad events are given below.

- bad_1: $\left(\exists \alpha \in [p] \text{ s.t. } \mathsf{lsb}_k(X^{(\alpha)}) = K \right) \vee \left(\exists \alpha \in [q_\mathcal{E}], i \in [\ell_\alpha] \text{ s.t. } \mathsf{lsb}_k(V_i^{(\alpha)}) = K \right) \vee \left(\exists \alpha \in [q_\mathcal{E} + 1, q], i \in [d_\alpha] \text{ s.t. } \mathsf{lsb}_k(V_i^{(\alpha)}) = K \right)$.

- bad_2: $\exists (\alpha, i) \in [q] \times [d_\alpha], (\beta, j) \in [q] \times [d_\beta] \text{ s.t. } V_{i-1}^{(\alpha)} \neq V_{j-1}^{(\beta)} \wedge V_i^{(\alpha)} = V_j^{(\beta)}$.

- bad_3: $\exists (\alpha, i) \in [q_\mathcal{E}] \times [d_\alpha + 1, \ell_\alpha], (\beta, j) \in [q] \times [d_\beta] \text{ s.t.}$
$$V_i^{(\alpha)} = V_j^{(\beta)} \vee \left(W_i^{(\alpha)} = W_j^{(\beta)} \wedge j \neq d_\beta \right).^6$$

- bad_4: $\exists (\alpha, i) \in [q_\mathcal{E}] \times [d_\alpha, \ell_\alpha], (\beta, j) \in [q_\mathcal{E}] \times [d_\beta, \ell_\beta] \text{ s.t.}$
$$(\alpha, i) \neq (\beta, j) \wedge W_i^{(\alpha)} = W_j^{(\beta)}.^7$$

- bad_5: $\exists (\alpha, i) \in [q] \times [\ell_\alpha], \beta \in [p] \text{ s.t. } V_i^{(\alpha)} = X^{(\beta)} \vee W_i^{(\alpha)} = Y^{(\beta)}$.

- bad_6: $\exists \alpha \in [q_\mathcal{E} + 1, q] \text{ s.t. } T^{(\alpha)} = \hat{T}^{(\alpha)}$.

---

[5] Specifically, internal values of the PRNG part of the decryption are not revealed as long as no forgery occurs (bad_6). Hence, the collision event does not yield an attack.

[6] Note that a collision for the last output block $W_{d_\beta}^{(\beta)}$, which is defined by using a tag, is not considered in this event, and instead considered in bad_4.

[7] Since $V_{i+1}^{(\alpha)} = W_i^{(\alpha)}$ and $V_{j+1}^{(\beta)} = W_j^{(\beta)}$, bad_4 covers collisions with the input blocks.

4.6 Analysis for Bad Transcripts

In this analysis, we use the following multi-collision event regarding r-bit state values in the PRNG part.

- bad_7: $\exists (\alpha_1, i_1) \in [q_{\mathcal{E}}] \times [d_{\alpha_1}, \ell_{\alpha_1}], \ldots, (\alpha_\mu, i_\mu) \in [q_{\mathcal{E}}] \times [d_{\alpha_\mu}, \ell_{\alpha_\mu}]$ s.t.
  $\left(j \neq j' \Rightarrow (\alpha_j, i_j) \neq (\alpha_{j'}, i_{j'}) \right) \wedge \left(\mathsf{msb}_r(W_{i_1}) = \cdots = \mathsf{msb}_r(W_{i_\mu}) \right)$.

Without loss of generality, assume that an adversary aborts if one of the bad events (including bad_7) occurs. Hence, for $i \in [7]$, $\Pr[\mathsf{bad}_i]$ is the probability that bad_i occurs as long as the other events have not occurred. Then, we have $\Pr[\mathsf{T}_I \in \mathbf{T}_{\mathsf{bad}}] \leq \sum_{i \in [7]} \Pr[\mathsf{bad}_i]$. These bounds are given below, which offer the following bound:

$$\Pr[\mathsf{T}_I \in \mathbf{T}_{\mathsf{bad}}] \leq \frac{2\sigma}{2^k} + \frac{4.5\sigma^2}{2^b} + \frac{4p\sigma}{2^b} + \frac{2\mu p}{2^k} + 2^r \cdot \left(\frac{e\sigma}{\mu 2^r} \right)^\mu . \tag{2}$$

Upper-Bounding $\Pr[\mathsf{bad}_1]$. Regarding the first condition of bad_1, by the randomness of K, we have $\Pr[\exists \alpha \in [p] \text{ s.t. } \mathsf{lsb}_k(X^{(\alpha)}) = K] \leq \frac{p}{2^k}$.

We next evaluate the probability for the second condition of bad_1. For each $\alpha \in [q_{\mathcal{E}}]$ and $i \in [d_\alpha]$, as $V_i^{(\alpha)}$ is chosen from at least $2^b - \sigma - p \geq 2^{b-1}$ elements in $\{0,1\}^b$, we have $\Pr[\mathsf{lsb}_k(V_i^{(\alpha)}) = K] \leq \frac{2^r}{2^{b-1}} \leq \frac{2}{2^k}$. For each $\alpha \in [q_{\mathcal{E}}]$ and $i \in [d_\alpha + 1, \ell_\alpha]$, by the randomness of K, we have $\Pr[\mathsf{lsb}_k(V_i^{(\alpha)}) = K] \leq \frac{1}{2^k}$. These bounds give $\Pr[\exists \alpha \in [q_{\mathcal{E}}], i \in [\ell_\alpha] \text{ s.t. } \mathsf{lsb}_k(V_i^{(\alpha)}) = K] \leq \frac{2\sigma_{\mathcal{E}}}{2^k}$.

Similarly, we have $\Pr[\exists \alpha \in [q_{\mathcal{E}} + 1, q], i \in [d_\alpha] \text{ s.t. } \mathsf{lsb}_k(V_i^{(\alpha)}) = K] \leq \frac{2\sigma_{\mathcal{D}}}{2^k}$.

By using the above bounds, we have $\Pr[\mathsf{bad}_1] \leq \frac{p}{2^k} + \frac{2\sigma_{\mathcal{E}}}{2^k} + \frac{2\sigma_{\mathcal{D}}}{2^k} = \frac{p}{2^k} + \frac{2\sigma}{2^k}$.

Upper-Bounding $\Pr[\mathsf{bad}_2]$. For each $(\alpha, i) \in [q] \times [d_\alpha], (\beta, j) \in [q] \times [d_\beta]$ s.t. $V_{i-1}^{(\alpha)} \neq V_{j-1}^{(\beta)}$, $V_i^{(\alpha)} = W_{i-1}^{(\alpha)} \oplus A_i^{(\alpha)}$ and $V_j^{(\beta)} = W_{j-1}^{(\beta)} \oplus A_j^{(\beta)}$ are satisfied, and $W_{i-1}^{(\alpha)}$ and $W_{j-1}^{(\beta)}$ are respectively chosen from at least 2^{b-1} elements in $\{0,1\}^b$ due to the condition $V_{i-1}^{(\alpha)} \neq V_{j-1}^{(\beta)}$. We thus have $\Pr[V_i^{(\alpha)} = V_j^{(\beta)}] \leq \frac{2}{2^b}$.

Summing the bound for each (α, i), (β, j), we have $\Pr[\mathsf{bad}_2] \leq \binom{\sigma}{2} \cdot \frac{2}{2^b} \leq \frac{\sigma^2}{2^b}$.

Upper-Bounding $\Pr[\mathsf{bad}_3]$. Fix $(\alpha, i) \in [q_{\mathcal{E}}] \times [d_\alpha + 1, \ell_\alpha]$ and $(\beta, j) \in [q] \times [d_\beta]$, and evaluate the probability $\Pr[V_i^{(\alpha)} = V_j^{(\beta)}]$, where $V_j^{(\beta)}$ is defined by using $W_{j-1}^{(\beta)}$. Since bad_1 and bad_5 have not occurred, $W_{j-1}^{(\beta)}$ is defined independently of primitive queries. Since bad_3 has not occurred before, $W_{j-1}^{(\beta)}$ is defined independently of $V_i^{(\alpha)}$. Hence, $W_{i-1}^{(\alpha)}$ is chosen from at least 2^{b-1} elements in $\{0,1\}^b$. We thus have $\Pr[V_i^{(\alpha)} = V_j^{(\beta)}] \leq \frac{2}{2^b}$. Similarly, $\Pr[W_i^{(\alpha)} = W_j^{(\beta)}] \leq \frac{2}{2^b}$.

Summing the bound for each (α, i), (β, j), we have $\Pr[\mathsf{bad}_3] \leq \binom{\sigma}{2} \cdot \frac{4}{2^b} \leq \frac{2\sigma^2}{2^b}$.

Upper-Bounding $\Pr[\mathsf{bad}_4]$. For each $(\alpha, i) \in [q_{\mathcal{E}}] \times [d_\alpha, \ell_\alpha], (\beta, j) \in [q_{\mathcal{E}}] \times [d_\beta, \ell_\beta]$, since $W_i^{(\alpha)}$ and $W_j^{(\beta)}$ are respectively chosen from $\{0,1\}^b$, we have $\Pr[W_i^{(\alpha)} = W_j^{(\beta)}] \leq \frac{1}{2^b}$. By using the bound, we have $\Pr[\mathsf{bad}_4] \leq \binom{\sigma_{\mathcal{E}}}{2} \cdot \frac{1}{2^b} \leq \frac{0.5\sigma_{\mathcal{E}}^2}{2^b}$.

Upper-Bounding $\Pr[\mathsf{bad}_5]$. We first consider a collision between the decryption and offline queries, i.e.,

$$\mathsf{bad}_{5,1} : (\alpha, i) \in [q_\mathcal{D}] \times [\ell_\alpha], \beta \in [p] \text{ s.t. } V_i^{(\alpha)} = X^{(\beta)} \vee W_i^{(\alpha)} = Y^{(\beta)}.$$

Since $W_i^{(\alpha)}$ is chosen from at least 2^{b-1} elements in $\{0,1\}^b$ and $V_i^{(\alpha)}$ is defined by using the previous output $W_{i-1}^{(\alpha)}$, we have $\Pr[\mathsf{bad}_{5,1}] \leq \frac{2p\sigma_\mathcal{D}}{2^b}$.

We next consider a collision between the MAC part of the encryption and offline query-response pairs, i.e.,

$$\mathsf{bad}_{5,2} : (\alpha, i) \in [q_\mathcal{E}] \times [d_\alpha], \beta \in [p] \text{ s.t. } V_i^{(\alpha)} = X^{(\beta)}, \text{ where } V_i^{(\alpha)} = W_{i-1}^{(\alpha)} \oplus A_i^{(\alpha)},$$

$$\mathsf{bad}_{5,3} : (\alpha, i) \in [q_\mathcal{E}] \times [d_\alpha - 1], \beta \in [p] \text{ s.t. } W_i^{(\alpha)} = Y^{(\beta)}.$$

As $W_{i-1}^{(\alpha)}$ is chosen from at least 2^{b-1} elements in $\{0,1\}^b$, we have $\Pr[\mathsf{bad}_{5,2}] \leq \frac{2p\sigma_\mathcal{E}}{2^b}$. Similarly, we have $\Pr[\mathsf{bad}_{5,3}] \leq \frac{2p\sigma_\mathcal{E}}{2^b}$.

We next consider a collision between the PRNG part of the encryption and offline query-response pairs, i.e.,

$$\mathsf{bad}_{5,4} : (\alpha, i) \in [q_\mathcal{E}] \times [d_\alpha, \ell_\alpha], \beta \in [p] \text{ s.t. } X^{(\beta)} = W_i^{(\alpha)} \ (= V_{i+1}^{(\alpha)}) \vee Y^{(\beta)} = W_i^{(\alpha)}.$$

Fix $\beta \in [p]$. For the first condition $X^{(\beta)} = W_i^{(\alpha)}$, by $\neg\mathsf{bad}_7$, the number of inputs $W_i^{(\alpha)}$ such that $\mathsf{msb}_r(W_i^{(\alpha)}) = \mathsf{msb}_r(X^{(\beta)})$ is at most $\mu - 1$. Then, the remaining k-bit parts of the (at most) $\mu - 1$ inputs are defined by using a key K. Since K is chosen from $\{0,1\}^\kappa$, the probability that one of the k-bit parts is equal to $\mathsf{lsb}_k(X^{(\beta)})$ is at most $\frac{\mu-1}{2^k}$. For the second condition, the evaluation is similar to the first condition. Summing the bounds for each β, we have $\Pr[\mathsf{bad}_{5,2}] \leq \frac{2(\mu-1)p}{2^k}$.

We thus have $\Pr[\mathsf{bad}_5] \leq \sum_{i \in [4]} \Pr[\mathsf{bad}_{5,i}] \leq \frac{2p\sigma_\mathcal{D}}{2^b} + \frac{4p\sigma_\mathcal{E}}{2^b} + \frac{2(\mu-1)p}{2^k}$.

Upper-Bounding $\Pr[\mathsf{bad}_6]$. Since an adversary does not make trivial queries and repeated queries, for each $\alpha \in [q_\mathcal{E}]$ and $\beta \in [q_\mathcal{E} + 1, q]$, $(A^{(\alpha)}, M^{(\alpha)}) \neq (A^{(\beta)}, M^{(\beta)})$ is satisfied. By $\neg\mathsf{bad}_2$, the inputs at the last π call in the MAC part are distinct, i.e., $V_{d_\alpha}^{(\alpha)} \neq V_{d_\beta}^{(\beta)}$. Hence, for each $\beta \in [q_\mathcal{E} + 1, q]$, $T^{(\beta)}$ is chosen independently from tags in encryption queries. By $\neg\mathsf{bad}_3$, $T^{(\beta)}$ is chosen independently of ciphertext blocks in encryption queries. By $\neg\mathsf{bad}_5$, $T^{(\beta)}$ is chosen independently of primitive queries. Hence, $W_{d_\alpha}^{(\beta)}$, which is used to define $T^{(\beta)}$, is defined by π in the decision stage, and chosen from at least 2^{b-1} elements. Hence, for each $\beta \in [q_\mathcal{E} + 1, q]$, we have $\Pr[T^{(\beta)} = \hat{T}^{(\beta)}] \leq \frac{2}{2^b}$.

Summing the bound for each $\alpha \in [q_\mathcal{E} + 1, q]$, $\Pr[\mathsf{bad}_6] \leq \frac{2q_\mathcal{D}}{2^b}$.

Upper-Bounding $\Pr[\mathsf{bad}_7]$. Fix μ distinct pairs $(\alpha_1, i_1) \in [q_\mathcal{E}] \times [d_{\alpha_1}, \ell_{\alpha_1}], \ldots, (\alpha_\mu, i_\mu) \in [q_\mathcal{E}] \times [d_{\alpha_\mu}, \ell_{\alpha_\mu}]$, and evaluate the probability $\Pr[\mathsf{msb}_r(W_{i_1}^{(\alpha_1)}) = \cdots = \mathsf{msb}_r(W_{i_\mu}^{(\alpha_\mu)})]$. For each $j \in [\mu]$, $\mathsf{msb}_r(W_{i_j}^{(\alpha_j)})$ is chosen uniformly at random from $\{0,1\}^r$. We thus have $\Pr[\mathsf{msb}_r(W_{i_1}^{(\alpha_1)}) = \cdots = \mathsf{msb}_r(W_{i_\mu}^{(\alpha_\mu)})] \leq \left(\frac{1}{2^r}\right)^{\mu-1}$.

Summing the bound for each $(\alpha_1, i_1), \ldots, (\alpha_\mu, i_\mu)$, we have $\Pr[\mathsf{bad}_7] \leq \binom{\sigma_\varepsilon}{\mu}$.
$\left(\frac{1}{2^r}\right)^{\mu-1} \leq 2^r \cdot \left(\frac{e\sigma_\varepsilon}{\mu 2^r}\right)^\mu$, using Stirling's approximation $(x! \geq \left(\frac{x}{e}\right)^x$ for any x).

4.7   Analysis for Good Transcript

Let $\tau \in \mathbf{T}_{\mathsf{good}}$. Tags and ciphertexts in τ can be obtained from (dummy) input-output tuples in online queries. By $\neg\mathsf{bad}_6$, response of decryption queries in τ are all **reject**. Hence, we have only to consider a (dummy) user's key, (dummy) input-output pairs of π in online queries, and offline query-response pairs. Let τ_K be the subset of τ with a user's key. Let τ_{online} be the set of offline query-response tuples, τ_{enc} the set of input-output tuples defined by encryption query-response tuples that are not in τ_{online}, and τ_{dec} the set of input-output tuples defined by decryption query-response tuples that are not in $\tau_{\mathsf{enc}} \cup \tau_{\mathsf{online}}$. For a subset $\tau' \subseteq \tau$ and $W \in \{R, I\}$, let $\mathsf{T}_W \vdash \tau'$ be an event that the values defined by T_W satisfy those in τ'.

Firstly, we evaluate $\Pr[\mathsf{T}_R \vdash \tau_{\mathsf{offline}}]$ and $\Pr[\mathsf{T}_I \vdash \tau_{\mathsf{offline}}]$, the probabilities for offline queries. In both worlds, the responses to offline queries are defined by an RP π. We thus have $\Pr[\mathsf{T}_R \vdash \tau_{\mathsf{online}}] = \Pr[\mathsf{T}_I \vdash \tau_{\mathsf{online}}]$. Hereafter, we assume that $\mathsf{T}_R \vdash \tau_{\mathsf{online}}$ and $\mathsf{T}_I \vdash \tau_{\mathsf{online}}$ are satisfied.

Secondly, we evaluate $\Pr[\mathsf{T}_R \vdash \tau_K]$ and $\Pr[\mathsf{T}_I \vdash \tau_K]$, the probabilities for a user's key. In both worlds, a user's key is chosen uniformly at random from $\{0,1\}^k$. We thus have $\Pr[\mathsf{T}_R \vdash \tau_K] = \Pr[\mathsf{T}_I \vdash \tau_K]$. Hereafter, we assume that $\mathsf{T}_R \vdash \tau_K$ and $\mathsf{T}_I \vdash \tau_K$ are satisfied.

Thirdly, we evaluate $\Pr[\mathsf{T}_R \vdash \tau_{\mathsf{enc}}]$ and $\Pr[\mathsf{T}_I \vdash \tau_{\mathsf{enc}}]$, the probabilities for encryption queries. By bad_1, bad_2, bad_3, and bad_4, there is no collision among π's inputs in τ_{enc}. By bad_5, there is no collision between τ_{online} and τ_{enc}. Hence, we all inputs in τ_{enc} are new. By bad_3, bad_4, and bad_5, there is no collision among outputs in τ_{enc}. Hence, we have $\Pr[\mathsf{T}_R \vdash \tau_{\mathsf{enc}}] > 0$. In the real world, all internal values in encryption queries are defined by π, and in the ideal world, by Algorithm 2. In this algorithm, all outputs in the MAC part except for the last outputs are defined by π and the remaining ones are chosen uniformly at random from $\{0,1\}^b$, as all ciphetext blocks and tag ones are chosen uniformly at random from $\{0,1\}^b$. Hence, the output spaces in the ideal world are larger than those in the real one, and we have $\Pr[\mathsf{T}_R \vdash \tau_{\mathsf{enc}}] \geq \Pr[\mathsf{T}_I \vdash \tau_{\mathsf{enc}}]$. Hereafter, we assume that $\mathsf{T}_R \vdash \tau_{\mathsf{enc}}$ and $\mathsf{T}_I \vdash \tau_{\mathsf{enc}}$ are satisfied.

Fourthly, we evaluate $\Pr[\mathsf{T}_R \vdash \tau_{\mathsf{dec}}]$ and $\Pr[\mathsf{T}_I \vdash \tau_{\mathsf{dec}}]$, the probabilities for decryption queries. In both worlds, the internal values in decryption queries are defined by π, that is, chosen from the same spaces. Note that the ideal-world values are defined by Algorithm 2. Hence, we have $\Pr[\mathsf{T}_R \vdash \tau_{\mathsf{dec}}] = \Pr[\mathsf{T}_I \vdash \tau_{\mathsf{dec}}]$

Finally, using the above evaluations, we have

$$\frac{\Pr[\mathsf{T}_R = \tau]}{\Pr[\mathsf{T}_I = \tau]} = \frac{\Pr[\mathsf{T}_R \vdash \tau_{\mathsf{offline}}]\Pr[\mathsf{T}_R \vdash \tau_K]\Pr[\mathsf{T}_R \vdash \tau_{\mathsf{enc}}]\Pr[\mathsf{T}_R \vdash \tau_{\mathsf{dec}}]}{\Pr[\mathsf{T}_I \vdash \tau_{\mathsf{offline}}]\Pr[\mathsf{T}_I \vdash \tau_K]\Pr[\mathsf{T}_I \vdash \tau_{\mathsf{enc}}]\Pr[\mathsf{T}_I \vdash \tau_{\mathsf{dec}}]} \geq 1 \ . \quad (3)$$

5   Hardware Performance

We instantiate PALM for 128-bit security using the PHOTON$_{256}$ lightweight permutation [20]. The instantiation satisfies 128-bit security ($s = 128$). PALM can be realized with 384 bits of memory: a 256-bit state for PHOTON$_{256}$ and a 128-bit key. We use the g function with $n = 4$ (see Eq. 1) because nibble is PHOTON$_{256}$'s minimum processing unit. Our PALM implementation follows the previous LM-DAE implementation with a coprocessor interface and serialized datapath prioritizing circuit area over speed [24]. The TBC-based scheme LM-DAE is selected as a comparison target because it achieves the smallest $3s$ memory, as summarized in Table 1. For a comparison with a permutation-based scheme, we also implement Ascon-128 [15].

Figure 2 shows the datapath architecture of PALM including PHOTON$_{256}$ based on the conventional nibble-serial design [1]. The state array is the main component integrating MixColumnsSerial (MCS) and ShiftRows into a shift register. Each row can shift independently, which is used to implement ShiftRows without a wide selector. MCS is realized by applying the A matrix 8 times [20]. A single PHOTON$_{256}$ round is composed of 143 cycles: 7 for ShiftRows, 72 for MCS, and 64 for SubCells. A single PHOTON$_{256}$ permutation takes 1,716 cycles. The following components are added to extend from PHOTON$_{256}$ to PALM: (i) a 128-bit shift register for storing the secret key K, which is the main overhead, (ii) the g function integrated into the state array, and (iii) additional datapath for feeding message and ciphertext blocks to the state.

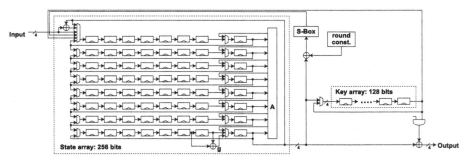

Fig. 2. Datapath architecture of PALM

Figure 3 shows the datapath architecture of our Ascon-128 implementation. By following the design policy for our PALM implementation (and the previous LM-DAE implementation [24]), we implemented Ascon-128 with a serialized architecture and a coprocessor-style interface. The basic architecture follows the conventional serialized implementation of Ascon [19]. The state array comprises five independent 64-bit shift registers that integrate the linear diffusion layer. The implementation processes a single 5-bit S-box calculation for each cycle. A single 320-bit permutation takes 444 cycles in total.

Table 2 compares our PHOTON$_{256}$, PALM, and Ascon-128 implementations with the conventional LM-DAE implementation [24]. The table summarizes the

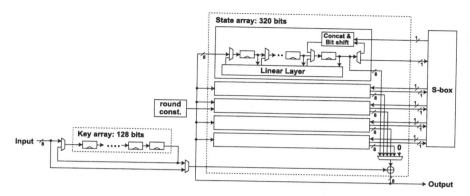

Fig. 3. Datapath architecture of Ascon

circuit area in the number of the NAND gates (GE) and the speed in cycle/byte.[8] The circuit area is obtained by synthesizing the hardware design with the Nan-Gate 45-nm standard cell library [25].

Our PALM implementation achieves 3,585 GE, smaller than the 3,824 GE of LM-DAE. Roughly 30% of the PALM implementation is occupied by the 128-bit key register, which is the main overhead for extending from PHOTON$_{256}$ to PALM. The circuit area is mainly proportional to the memory size because the combinatorial area is small in the serialized architectures. PALM is also faster than LM-DAE; the speed of the PALM and LM-DAE implementations are 107.2 and 127.3 cycles/byte, respectively.

Table 2. Hardware Performance Comparison

Target	Circuit Area (GE)					Enc. Speed (cycles/byte)	Memory (bits)
	Total	State	Key	Tweak	S-box		
LM-DAE[†]	3,717	1,102	1,004	1,012	N/A	127.3	384
Ascon-128	5,707	4,367	953	0	28	55.6	448
PHOTON$_{256}$	2,526	2,187	N/A[‡]	0	28	53.6	256
PALM	3,585	2,222	951	0	28	107.2	384

[†]The hardware performance from [24] evaluated with the same standard cell library. [‡]No key is involved in the PHOTON$_{256}$ hash function.

6 Optimality of Memory Size of PALM

We show that the memory size of PALM, i.e. $3s$ bits, is optimal for a permutation-based SIV-like mode with s-bit security by demonstrating an attack faster than

---

[8] Obtained by dividing the primitive's latency with the message block size.

s bits against a generic construction whose memory size is less than $3s$ bits. The minimum key size is s bits because otherwise the exhaustive key search can be performed with less than 2^s operations. Hence we show an attack against a generic construction only with less than $2s$ bits of state.

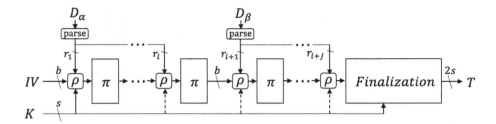

Fig. 4. MAC Part of Generic SIV-like Permutation-Based DAE in Simplified Form.

Generic SIV-Like Permutation-Based DAE. We first specify a generic SIV-like construction, which is depicted in Fig. 4. It first computes a MAC that takes (K, A, M) as input and outputs a $2s$-bit tag. More specifically, a b-bit state S, where $b < 2s$, is first initialized to IV. Then, S is updated by b-bit permutation π in every block. Before each invocation of π, partial bits of K, the whole bits of K, or an empty string is added to S by an updating function ρ, where ρ can be different in each block. A and M can be pre-processed in an injective and invertible way, and does not use additional memory. The generated data is described by a symbol D. Then, a part of bits in D is used to update S in each block, which is iterated until all bits of D are used. Finally, a $2s$-bit tag T is computed from S by some finalization function. Our attack only targets MAC, thus we omit the other part. Moreover, we simplify the construction as follows. We divide D into $D_\alpha \| D_\beta$. Then, the MAC can be described only with two functions; to generate an intermediate S from IV and D_α, and to compute T from S and D_β.

Attack. Attacker's goal is to break the integrity. Namely, the attacker is given an oracle that implements either the encryption of the above generic construction with $b < 2s$ (real) or a random-bit oracle (ideal). The attacker needs to distinguish which oracle is implemented with a complexity less than s bits.

The attacker chooses A, M so that D_α is sufficiently long to generate a collision on S and D_β is very short, say 1 block. Then, the following is processed.

1. The attacker chooses $2^{b/2}$ distinct choices of D_α and a fixed choice of D_β to make $2^{b/2}$ online queries of $D_\alpha \| D_\beta$ to collect the corresponding T.
2. Pick up all the pairs of $D_\alpha \| D_\beta$ and $D'_\alpha \| D_\beta$ that collide on T.
3. For all the picked up pairs, replace D_β with another D'_β and make two more online queries $D_\alpha \| D'_\beta$ and $D'_\alpha \| D'_\beta$ to check if the resulting tags collide.
4. If a tag collision is generated, the oracle is real, otherwise ideal.

Analysis. In step 1, because $2^{b/2}$ distinct D_α are examined, a collision occurs with a high probability at S after processing D_α. Because D_β is fixed, the occurrence of the collision can be observed by checking the tag collision. Note that even if S after processing D_α does not collide, the tag may collide due to the collision generated during the process of D_β. Hence, several tag collisions can be observed. Then in Step 3, we pick up all the colliding pairs. By setting D_β short, the number of additional collisions is negligibly small. For a colliding pair (D_α, D'_α), the tag will collide for any choice of D_β. Hence the tags of $D_\alpha \| D'_\beta$ and $D'_\alpha \| D'_\beta$ will collide. The attack complexity is $2^{b/2}$ online queries.

If the oracle is ideal, i.e. the random-bit oracle, the probability of having colliding tags in Step 1 is smaller than the real construction due to $b < 2s$. Moreover, the probability that the $2s$-bit tags for $D_\alpha \| D'_\beta$ and $D'_\alpha \| D'_\beta$ collide is 2^{-2s}. Since $b < 2s$, the tag collision cannot be generated only with $2^{b/2}$ online queries.

7   Conclusion

In this paper, we proposed a new permutation-based DAE mode PALM that can be implemented with low memory. For a permutation of size b bits and a key of size k bits, we prove $\min\{k, \frac{b}{2}\}$-bit security assuming that the permutation is RP. We then instantiated PALM with PHOTON$_{256}$ and benchmarked its hardware performance to show that the memory size of PALM is in fact competitive with LM-DAE. We also showed that $3s$ bits of memory of PALM is optimal; an attack breaking integrity exists if the memory size is less than $3s$ bits.

References

1. Nalla Anandakumar, N., Peyrin, T., Poschmann, A.: A very compact FPGA implementation of LED and PHOTON. In: Meier, W., Mukhopadhyay, D. (eds.) INDOCRYPT 2014. LNCS, vol. 8885, pp. 304–321. Springer, Cham (2014). https://doi.org/10.1007/978-3-319-13039-2_18
2. Andreeva, E., Daemen, J., Mennink, B., Van Assche, G.: Security of keyed sponge constructions using a modular proof approach. In: Leander, G. (ed.) FSE 2015. LNCS, vol. 9054, pp. 364–384. Springer, Heidelberg (2015). https://doi.org/10.1007/978-3-662-48116-5_18
3. Andreeva, E., Lallemand, V., Purnal, A., Reyhanitabar, R., Roy, A., Vizár, D.: Forkcipher: a new primitive for authenticated encryption of very short messages. In: Galbraith, S.D., Moriai, S. (eds.) ASIACRYPT 2019. LNCS, vol. 11922, pp. 153–182. Springer, Cham (2019). https://doi.org/10.1007/978-3-030-34621-8_6
4. Armknecht, F., Hamann, M., Mikhalev, V.: Lightweight authentication protocols on ultra-constrained RFIDs - myths and facts. In: Saxena, N., Sadeghi, A.-R. (eds.) RFIDSec 2014. LNCS, vol. 8651, pp. 1–18. Springer, Cham (2014). https://doi.org/10.1007/978-3-319-13066-8_1
5. Banik, S., Bogdanov, A., Luykx, A., Tischhauser, E.: SUNDAE: small universal deterministic authenticated encryption for the internet of things. IACR Trans. Symmetric Cryptol. **2018**(3), 1–35 (2018)

6. Bao, Z., Guo, J., Iwata, T., Song, L.: SIV-TEM-PHOTON authenticated encryption and hash family (2019)
7. Bertoni, G., Daemen, J., Hoffert, S., Peeters, M., Assche, G.V., Keer, R.V.: Farfalle: parallel permutation-based cryptography. IACR Trans. Symmetric Cryptol. **2017**(4), 1–38 (2017)
8. Bertoni, G., Daemen, J., Peeters, M., Assche, G.V.: Sponge functions. In: ECRYPT Hash Workshop 2007 (2007)
9. Bertoni, G., Daemen, J., Peeters, M., Van Assche, G.: On the indifferentiability of the sponge construction. In: Smart, N. (ed.) EUROCRYPT 2008. LNCS, vol. 4965, pp. 181–197. Springer, Heidelberg (2008). https://doi.org/10.1007/978-3-540-78967-3_11
10. Bertoni, G., Daemen, J., Peeters, M., Van Assche, G.: Duplexing the sponge: single-pass authenticated encryption and other applications. In: Miri, A., Vaudenay, S. (eds.) SAC 2011. LNCS, vol. 7118, pp. 320–337. Springer, Heidelberg (2012). https://doi.org/10.1007/978-3-642-28496-0_19
11. Bertoni, G., Daemen, J., Peeters, M., Assche, G.V., Keer, R.V.: Using Keccak technology for AE: Ketje, Keyak and more. In: SHA-3 2014 Workshop (2014)
12. Böck, H., Zauner, A., Devlin, S., Somorovsky, J., Jovanovic, P.: Nonce-disrespecting adversaries: practical forgery attacks on GCM in TLS. ePrint 2016, 475 (2016)
13. Chakraborti, A., Datta, N., Jha, A., Mancillas-López, C., Nandi, M., Sasaki, Y.: ESTATE: a lightweight and low energy authenticated encryption mode. IACR Trans. Symmetric Cryptol. **2020**(S1), 350–389 (2020)
14. Chang, D., et al.: Release of unverified plaintext: tight unified model and application to ANYDAE. IACR Trans. Symmetric Cryptol. **2019**(4), 119–146 (2019)
15. Dobraunig, C., Eichlseder, M., Mendel, F., Schläffer, M.: Ascon v1.2: lightweight authenticated encryption and hashing. J. Cryptol. **34**(3), 33 (2021)
16. Dobraunig, C., Mennink, B.: Leakage resilient value comparison with application to message authentication. In: Canteaut, A., Standaert, F.-X. (eds.) EUROCRYPT 2021. LNCS, vol. 12697, pp. 377–407. Springer, Cham (2021). https://doi.org/10.1007/978-3-030-77886-6_13
17. Dworkin, M.: Recommendation for block cipher modes of operation: methods for key wrapping. NIST SP 800-38F (2012)
18. Even, S., Mansour, Y.: A construction of a cipher from a single pseudorandom permutation. J. Cryptol. **10**(3), 151–162 (1997)
19. Groß, H., Wenger, E., Dobraunig, C., Ehrenhöfer, C.: Suit up! - made-to-measure hardware implementations of ASCON. In: DSD 2015, pp. 645–652. IEEE Computer Society (2015)
20. Guo, J., Peyrin, T., Poschmann, A.: The PHOTON family of lightweight hash functions. In: Rogaway, P. (ed.) CRYPTO 2011. LNCS, vol. 6841, pp. 222–239. Springer, Heidelberg (2011). https://doi.org/10.1007/978-3-642-22792-9_13
21. Harkins, D.: RFC5297: synthetic initialization vector (SIV) authenticated encryption using the advanced encryption standard (AES) (2008). https://tools.ietf.org/html/rfc5297
22. Jovanovic, P., Luykx, A., Mennink, B., Sasaki, Y., Yasuda, K.: Beyond conventional security in sponge-based authenticated encryption modes. J. Cryptol. **32**(3), 895–940 (2019)
23. Mouha, N., Mennink, B., Van Herrewege, A., Watanabe, D., Preneel, B., Verbauwhede, I.: Chaskey: An Efficient MAC Algorithm for 32-bit Microcontrollers. In: Joux, A., Youssef, A. (eds.) SAC 2014. LNCS, vol. 8781, pp. 306–323. Springer, Cham (2014). https://doi.org/10.1007/978-3-319-13051-4_19

24. Naito, Y., Sasaki, Y., Sugawara, T.: LM-DAE: low-memory deterministic authenticated encryption for 128-bit security. IACR Trans. Symmetric Cryptol. **2020**(4), 1–38 (2020)
25. NanGate: NanGate FreePDK45 open cell library. http://www.nangate.com
26. NIST: Submission requirements and evaluation criteria for the lightweight cryptography standardization process (2018). https://csrc.nist.gov/Projects/lightweight-cryptography
27. Patarin, J.: The "Coefficients H" technique. In: Avanzi, R.M., Keliher, L., Sica, F. (eds.) SAC 2008. LNCS, vol. 5381, pp. 328–345. Springer, Heidelberg (2009). https://doi.org/10.1007/978-3-642-04159-4_21
28. Rogaway, P., Shrimpton, T.: A provable-security treatment of the key-wrap problem. In: Vaudenay, S. (ed.) EUROCRYPT 2006. LNCS, vol. 4004, pp. 373–390. Springer, Heidelberg (2006). https://doi.org/10.1007/11761679_23

Impossible Differential Cryptanalysis of the FBC Block Cipher

Jiqiang Lu[1,2,3]($\boxtimes$) and Xiao Zhang[1]

[1] School of Cyber Science and Technology, Beihang University, Beijing, China
{lvjiqiang,xiaozhang}@buaa.edu.cn
[2] State Key Laboratory of Cryptology, P. O. Box 5159, Beijing, China
[3] Hangzhou Innovation Institute, Beihang University, Hangzhou, China

Abstract. The FBC block cipher is an award-winning algorithm of the recent Cryptographic Algorithm Design Competition in China. It employs a generalised Feistel structure and has three versions FBC128-128, FBC128-256 and FBC256, which have a 128-bit block size with a 128- or 256-bit user key and a 256-bit block size with a 256-bit user key, respectively. The best previously published cryptanalysis results on FBC are Zhang et al.'s impossible differential attack on 13-round FBC128-128 and Ren et al.'s boomerang attack on 13-round FBC128-256. In this paper, we observe that when conducting impossible differential cryptanalysis of FBC, both inactive and active nibble differences on plaintext and ciphertext as well as a few intermediate states may be exploited for some refined sorting conditions on plaintexts and ciphertexts to filter out preliminary satisfying plaintext/ciphertext pairs efficiently. Taking advantage of this observation, we use Zhang et al.'s 9-round impossible differentials of FBC128 to make key-recovery attacks on 14-round FBC128-128 and 15-round FBC128-256, and similarly we exploit 13-round impossible differentials on FBC256 and make a key-recovery attack on 19-round FBC256. Our results are better than any previously published cryptanalytic results on FBC in terms of the numbers of attacked rounds.

Keywords: Block cipher · FBC · Impossible differential cryptanalysis

1 Introduction

The FBC block cipher was designed by Feng et al. [4] for the Cryptographic Algorithm Design Competition in China, that was organised by the Chinese Association of Cryptologic Research under the guidance of State Cryptography Administration Office, and it became an award-winning algorithm in 2020. FBC employs a generalised Feistel structure, and has three versions FBC128-128, FBC128-256 and FBC256: a 128-bit block size with a 128- or 256-bit user key, and a 256-bit block size with a 256-bit user key, which have a total of 48, 64 and 80 rounds, respectively.

© The Author(s), under exclusive license to Springer Nature Switzerland AG 2023
E. Athanasopoulos and B. Mennink (Eds.): ISC 2023, LNCS 14411, pp. 372–391, 2023.
https://doi.org/10.1007/978-3-031-49187-0_19

Table 1. Main cryptanalytic results on FBC

Cipher	Attack Type	Rounds	Data	Memory	Time	Source
FBC128-128	Linear	11	2^{84} KP	/	$2^{112.54}$	[7]
	Differential	12	2^{122} CP	/	$2^{93.41}$	[7]
	Impossible differential	11	2^{127} CP	/	$2^{94.54}$	[7]
		13	2^{126} CP	2^{52}	$2^{122.96}$	[8]
		14	$2^{125.5}$ CP	$2^{82.5}$	2^{124}	Section 3.1
FBC128-256	Boomerang	13	$2^{117.67}$ CP	/	$2^{247.67}$	[7]
	Impossible differential	15	$2^{126.9}$ CP	$2^{115.9}$	$2^{249.9}$	Section 3.2
FBC256	Impossible differential	19	$2^{255.3}$ CP	$2^{116.3}$	$2^{246.4}$	Section 4

KP/CP: Known/Chosen plaintexts; Memory unit: Bytes; Time unit: Encryptions.

The main published cryptanalytic results on FBC are as follows. In 2019, Ren et al. [7] presented linear [6] and impossible differential [2,5] attacks on 11-round FBC128-128, a differential attack [1] on 12-round FBC128-128, and a boomerang attack on 13-round FBC128-256. In 2022, Zhang et al. [8] gave 9-round impossible differentials and an 13-round impossible differential attack on FBC128-128 using 2^{74} structures of 2^{52} chosen plaintexts; and in particular, they defined a plaintext structure to have a fixed value in the 19 inactive nibble positions on plaintexts and used an usual sorting way by the expected 14 inactive nibble positions on ciphertexts to sieve out preliminary satisfying plaintext/ciphertext pairs efficiently.

In this paper, we observe that when conducting impossible differential cryptanalysis of FBC, both inactive and active nibble differences on plaintext and ciphertext as well as a few intermediate states may be exploited for some sorting conditions on plaintexts and ciphertexts to filter out preliminary satisfying plaintext/ciphertext pairs more efficiently; more specifically, for a structure of plaintexts, except the usual sorting way by the expected inactive nibble positions on ciphertexts (as Zhang et al. have done in [8]), we can exploit some more specific relations among the expected non-zero differences (i.e. at active nibble positions) on both plaintexts and ciphetexts as well as the expected intermediate differences to make a much more refined sorting on plaintexts and ciphertexts, so that preliminary satisfying plaintext/ciphertext pairs can be more efficiently sieved out without additional workload. Taking advantage of this observation, we use Zhang et al.'s 9-round impossible differentials on FBC128 to make key-recovery attacks on 14-round FBC128-128 and 15-round FBC128-256, breaking one or two more rounds than the best previously published attacks on FBC128-128 and FBC128-256, respectively. Similarly, we exploit 13-round impossible differentials on FBC256 to make a key-recovery attack on 19-round FBC256. Table 1 summarises previous and our main cryptanalytic results on FBC.

The remainder of the paper is organised as follows. We briefly describe the notation and the FBC cipher in the next section, present our attacks on FBC128 and FBC256 in Sects. 3 and 4, respectively. Section 5 concludes this paper.

2   Preliminaries

In this section, we give the notation and briefly describe the FBC block cipher.

2.1   Notation

In all descriptions we assume that the bits of an n-bit value are numbered from 0 to $n - 1$ from left to right, a number without a prefix represents a decimal number, a number with prefix $0x$ represents a hexadecimal number, and we use the following notation throughout this paper.

|| bit string concatenation
$\oplus$ bitwise logical exclusive XOR
$\&$ bitwise logical AND
$\neg$ bitwise logical complement
$\lll / \ggg$ left/right rotation of a bit string
$\star$ an arbitrary value of some length, where two values represented by the $\star$ symbol may be different
e the base of the natural logarithm ($\mathsf{e} = 2.71828\cdots$)

2.2   The FBC Block Cipher

FBC [4] has three versions FBC128-128, FBC128-256 and FBC256, which have a 128-bit block size with a 128- or 256-bit user key, and a 256-bit block size with a 256-bit user key, and a total of 48, 64 and 80 rounds, respectively, with Round 0 as the first round.

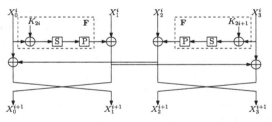

Fig. 1. The FBC round function

The **F** function of FBC, as depicted in Fig. 1, consists of the following three elementary operations:

– Key Addition: Input is XORed with a round key to produce output u.
– Column Transform S: Depending on the block length of the FBC cipher version, representing u as four 32- or 64-bit words $u = (u_0||u_1||u_2||u_3)$, apply the same 4×4-bit bijective S-box S 8 or 16 times in parallel to u to produce output $v = (v_0||v_1||v_2||v_3)$ as $(v_{0,j}||v_{1,j}||v_{2,j}||v_{3,j}) = S(u_{0,j}||u_{1,j}||u_{2,j}||u_{3,j})$, where u_i and v_i are 8-bit for FBC128 and 16-bit for FBC256, and $u_{i,j}$ and $v_{i,j}$ are respectively the j-th bit of u_i and v_i ($i \in [0,3]$, $j \in [0,7]$ for FBC128, and $j \in [0,15]$ for FBC256).

– Row Transform P: Given input v, the output z is defined as $z = v \oplus (v \lll 3) \oplus (v \lll 10)$ for FBC128, and $z = v \oplus (v \lll 17) \oplus (v \lll 58)$ for FBC256.

Table 2. Details of Row Transform of the FBC128 round function

v	0	1	2	3	4	5	6	7
	8	9	10	11	12	13	14	15
	16	17	18	19	20	21	22	23
	24	25	26	27	28	29	30	31
$v \lll 3$	3	4	5	6	7	8	9	10
	11	12	13	14	15	16	17	18
	19	20	21	22	23	24	25	26
	27	28	29	30	31	0	1	2
$v \lll 10$	10	11	12	13	14	15	16	17
	18	19	20	21	22	23	24	25
	26	27	28	29	30	31	0	1
	2	3	4	5	6	7	8	9

Table 3. Details of Row Transform of the FBC256 round function

v	0	1	2	3	4	5	6	7	8	9	10	11	12	13	14	15
	16	17	18	19	20	21	22	23	24	25	26	27	28	29	30	31
	32	33	34	35	36	37	38	39	40	41	42	43	44	45	46	47
	48	49	50	51	52	53	54	55	56	57	58	59	60	61	62	63
$v \lll 17$	17	18	19	20	21	22	23	24	25	26	27	28	29	30	31	32
	33	34	35	36	37	38	39	40	41	42	43	44	45	46	47	48
	49	50	51	52	53	54	55	56	57	58	59	60	61	62	63	0
	1	2	3	4	5	6	7	8	9	10	11	12	13	14	15	16
$v \lll 58$	58	59	60	61	62	63	0	1	2	3	4	5	6	7	8	9
	10	11	12	13	14	15	16	17	18	19	20	21	22	23	24	25
	26	27	28	29	30	31	32	33	34	35	36	37	38	39	40	41
	42	43	44	45	46	47	48	49	50	51	52	53	54	55	56	57

The key schedules of FBC128-128 and FBC256 are as follows. Represent the 128- or 256-bit user key as four 32- or 64-bit words (K_0, K_1, K_2, K_3) respectively, and generate the remaining round keys as $K_{i+4} = (\neg K_i) \oplus (\neg K_{i+1}) \& K_{i+2} \& K_{i+3} \oplus i$ and $K_{i+4} = K_{i+4} \oplus (K_{i+4} \lll 13) \oplus (K_{i+4} \lll 22)$, where $i = 0, 1, \cdots, 2r - 5$, and r is 48 for FBC128-128 and 80 for FBC256.

The key schedule of FBC128-256 is as follows. Represent the 256-bit user key as eight 32-bit words $(K_0, K_1, K_2, K_3, K_4, K_5, K_6, K_7)$, and generate the remaining round keys as $K_{i+8} = (\neg K_i) \oplus (\neg K_{i+1}) \& (K_{i+2}) \& (K_{i+3}) \oplus i$ and $K_{i+8} = (K_{i+8}) \oplus (K_{i+8} \lll 13) \oplus (K_{i+8} \lll 22)$, where $i = 0, 1, \cdots, 119$.

At last, to simplify our subsequent cryptanalysis, we give the details of the Row Transform of FBC128 and FBC256 in Tables 2 and 3, respectively.

3   Impossible Differential Attacks on 14-Round FBC128-128 and 15-Round FBC128-256

In this section, we apply Zhang et al.'s 9-round impossible differentials $(0, 0, e_0, 0)$ $\nrightarrow (e_j, 0, e_j, 0)$ [8] to attack 14-round FBC128-128 and 15-round FBC128-256, by exploiting both inactive and active nibble differences on plaintext and ciphertext as well as a few intermediate states for some more refined sorting conditions on plaintexts and ciphertexts to filter out satisfying plaintext/ciphertext pairs efficiently, where e_m denotes a 32-bit word with zeros in all positions except the 4 bits of the m-th column ($m = 0$ or j) and $j \in \{1, 3, 5, 7\}$. We refer the reader to [8] for more details of Zhang et al.'s 9-round impossible differentials and 13-round FBC128-128 attack.

3.1   Attacking 14-Round FBC128-128

Below we attack Rounds 0–13 of FBC128-128, as illustrated in Fig. 2, by appending two rounds at the beginning and three rounds at the end of Zhang et al.'s 9-round impossible differential.

1. Choose $2^{73.5}$ structures of 2^{52} plaintexts $(P_0^j, P_1^j, P_2^j, P_3^j)$, where in a structure the 19 nibbles $(1, 2, 3, 4, 5, 6, 7, 9, 10, 11, 12, 15, 17, 23, 25, 26, 27, 28, 31)$ of the 2^{52} plaintexts are fixed to certain values and the other 13 nibbles take all the possible values. For each structure, store the 2^{52} plaintexts into a hash table indexed by the following 100 bits:

$$(P_1^j[0] \lll 1) \oplus P_1^j[5], \tag{1}$$

$$(P_1^j[0] \lll 2) \oplus P_1^j[6], \tag{2}$$

$$(P_2^j[2] \lll 1) \oplus P_2^j[3] \oplus (P_2^j[4] \ggg 1), \tag{3}$$

$$(P_0^j[0] \lll 1) \oplus (P_2^j[0] \lll 1) \oplus P_2^j[2] \oplus P_2^j[5], \tag{4}$$

$$(P_0^j[0] \lll 2) \oplus (P_2^j[0] \lll 2) \oplus (P_2^j[4] \ggg 1) \oplus P_2^j[6], \tag{5}$$

$$(P_3^j[0] \lll 1) \oplus P_3^j[5], \tag{6}$$

$$(P_3^j[0] \lll 2) \oplus P_3^j[6], \tag{7}$$

$$C_0^j[0, 2], \tag{8}$$

$$(C_0^j[3] \lll 1) \oplus C_0^j[4] \oplus (C_0^j[5] \ggg 1), \tag{9}$$

$$(C_0^j[3] \lll 1) \oplus (C_0^j[5] \ggg 1) \oplus (C_0^j[6] \lll 1) \oplus C_0^j[7], \tag{10}$$

$$C_2^j[0, 2], \tag{11}$$

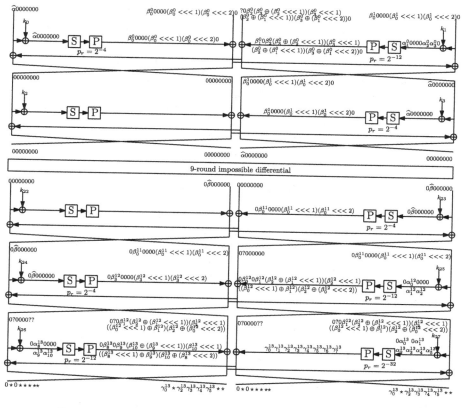

Fig. 2. Impossible differential attack on 14-round FBC128-128

$$C_3^j[0] \oplus C_3^j[3] \oplus C_3^j[6] \oplus ((C_3^j[1] \oplus C_3^j[2] \oplus C_3^j[4] \oplus C_3^j[7]) \lll 1) \oplus$$
$$((C_3^j[0] \oplus C_3^j[4] \oplus C_3^j[6] \oplus C_3^j[7]) \lll 2) \oplus (C_3^j[6] \lll 3), \tag{12}$$

$$C_3^j[2] \oplus (C_3^j[4] \lll 1) \oplus C_3^j[5] \oplus (C_3^j[6] \lll 2) \oplus$$
$$((C_3^j[1] \oplus C_3^j[4] \oplus C_3^j[7]) \lll 3) \oplus ((C_3^j[0] \oplus C_3^j[6]) \lll 4), \tag{13}$$

$$((C_0^j[3] \oplus C_2^j[3]) \lll 1) \oplus C_0^j[4] \oplus C_2^j[4] \oplus ((C_0^j[5] \oplus C_2^j[5]) \ggg 1), \tag{14}$$

$$((C_0^j[1] \oplus C_2^j[1]) \lll 1) \oplus C_0^j[3] \oplus C_2^j[3] \oplus C_0^j[6] \oplus C_2^j[6], \tag{15}$$

$$((C_0^j[1] \oplus C_2^j[1]) \lll 2) \oplus ((C_0^j[5] \oplus C_2^j[5]) \ggg 1) \oplus C_0^j[7] \oplus C_2^j[7], \tag{16}$$

$$C_1^j[0,2,3,4,5] \oplus C_3^j[0,2,3,4,5], \tag{17}$$

$$C_1^j[1] \oplus C_3^j[1] \oplus (C_1^j[6] \ggg 1) \oplus (C_3^j[6] \ggg 1), \tag{18}$$

$$C_1^j[1] \oplus C_3^j[1] \oplus (C_1^j[7] \ggg 2) \oplus (C_3^j[7] \ggg 2). \tag{19}$$

As justified in the appendix, two plaintexts P^{j_0} and P^{j_1} with the same 100-bit index have an input difference $(\Delta X_0^0 = 0x\widehat{\alpha}0000000, \Delta X_1^0 = 0x\gamma_0^0 0000(\gamma_0^0 \lll 1)(\gamma_0^0 \lll 2)0, \Delta X_2^0 = 0x(\widehat{\alpha} \oplus \gamma_1^0)0\gamma_2^0(\gamma_3^0 \oplus (\gamma_2^0 \lll 1))(\gamma_3^0 \lll 1)(\gamma_2^0 \oplus (\gamma_1^0 \lll 1))(\gamma_3^0 \oplus (\gamma_1^0 \lll 2))0, \Delta X_3^0 = 0x\gamma_0^1 0000(\gamma_0^1 \lll 1)(\gamma_0^1 \lll 2)0)$ and an output difference $(\Delta X_0^{14} = 0x0\eta_0 0\eta_1(\eta_2 \oplus (\eta_1 \lll 1))(\eta_2 \lll 1)((\eta_3 \lll 1) \oplus \eta_1)((\eta_3 \lll 2) \oplus \eta_2), \Delta X_1^{14} = \Delta X_3^{14} \oplus 0x0\eta_5 0000(\eta_5 \lll 1)(\eta_5 \lll 2), \Delta X_2^{14} = \Delta X_0^{14} \oplus 0x0\gamma_0^{12}0\gamma_0^{12}(\gamma_2^{12} \oplus (\gamma_1^{12} \lll 1))(\gamma_2^{12} \lll 1)((\gamma_0^{12} \lll 1) \oplus \gamma_1^{12})(\gamma_2^{12} \oplus (\gamma_0^{12} \lll 2)), \Delta X_3^{14} = 0x\gamma_1^{13}(\eta_4 \oplus \gamma_2^{13} \oplus (\gamma_1^{13} \lll 1))(\gamma_3^{13} \oplus (\gamma_2^{13} \lll 1))(\gamma_1^{13} \oplus \gamma_4^{13} \oplus (\gamma_3^{13} \lll 1))(\gamma_2^{13} \oplus \gamma_5^{13} \oplus (\gamma_4^{13} \lll 1))(\gamma_3^{13} \oplus (\gamma_5^{13} \lll 1))(\gamma_4^{13} \oplus (\eta_4 \lll 1))(\gamma_5^{13} \oplus (\eta_4 \lll 2)))$, and by this 100-bit index, we can easily obtain such plaintext pairs, obtain $\widehat{\alpha}$,

$$\widehat{\beta} = \Delta X_2^{14}[1] \oplus ((\Delta X_2^{14}[6] \oplus \Delta X_2^{14}[3]) \ggg 1),$$

$\gamma_0^0, \gamma_1^0, \gamma_2^0, \gamma_3^0, \gamma_0^1, \gamma_0^{12}, \gamma_1^{12}, \gamma_2^{12}, \gamma_1^{13}, \gamma_2^{13}, \gamma_3^{13}, \gamma_4^{13}, \gamma_5^{13}, \eta_0, \eta_1, \eta_2, \eta_3, \eta_4, \eta_5$ from $(\Delta X_0^0, \Delta X_1^0, \Delta X_2^0, \Delta X_3^0, \Delta X_0^{14}, \Delta X_1^{14}, \Delta X_2^{14}, \Delta X_3^{14})$ for a plaintext pair, and keep only the satisfying plaintext pairs with $\widehat{\alpha}, \widehat{\beta}, \gamma_0^0, \gamma_1^0, \gamma_2^0, \gamma_3^0, \gamma_0^1, \gamma_0^{12}, \gamma_1^{12}, \gamma_2^{12}, \gamma_1^{13}, \gamma_2^{13}, \gamma_3^{13}, \gamma_4^{13}, \gamma_5^{13}$ being nonzero. It is expected that the $2^{73.5}$ structures provide a total of $\binom{2^{52}}{2} \times 2^{-100} \times 2^{73.5} = 2^{76.5}$ preliminary satisfying plaintext pairs.

2. Guess $K_0[0]$, partially encrypt every preliminary satisfying plaintext pair (P^{j_0}, P^{j_1}) to check whether there is a difference γ_0^0 at nibble (0) just after the left S function of Round 0, and keep only the qualified plaintext pairs, whose number is expected to be $2^{76.5} \times 2^{-4} = 2^{72.5}$ on average.

3. Guess $K_1[0, 5, 6]$, partially encrypt every remaining plaintext pair (P^{j_0}, P^{j_1}) to check whether there is a difference $(\gamma_1^0, \gamma_2^0, \gamma_3^0)$ at nibbles $(0, 5, 6)$ just after the right S function of Round 0, and keep only the qualified plaintext pairs, whose number is expected to be $2^{72.5} \times 2^{-4 \times 3} = 2^{60.5}$ on average.

4. Guess $K_{26}[1, 6, 7]$, partially decrypt every remaining ciphertext pair (C^{j_0}, C^{j_1}) to check whether there is a difference $(\gamma_6^{13}, \gamma_7^{13}, \gamma_8^{13}) = ((\Delta X_2^{14}[3] \oplus \Delta X_2^{14}[6]) \ggg 1, \Delta X_2^{14}[3], \Delta X_2^{14}[5] \ggg 1)$ at nibbles $(1, 6, 7)$ just after the left S function of Round 13, and keep only the qualified ciphertext pairs, whose number is expected to be $2^{60.5} \times 2^{-4 \times 3} = 2^{48.5}$ on average.

5. Guess $K_{27}[1, 3, 4, 5, 6, 7]$, partially decrypt every remaining ciphertext pair (C^{j_0}, C^{j_1}) to get nibbles $(1, 3, 4, 5, 6, 7)$ of their intermediate values just after the right S function of Round 13, check whether they produce a difference $(\chi_0^{13}, \chi_1^{13}, \cdots, \chi_7^{13}) = 0x(\gamma_1^{13} \star (\gamma_3^{13} \oplus (\gamma_2^{13} \lll 1))(\gamma_1^{13} \oplus \gamma_4^{13} \oplus (\gamma_3^{13} \lll 1))(\gamma_2^{13} \oplus \gamma_5^{13} \oplus (\gamma_4^{13} \lll 1))(\gamma_3^{13} \oplus (\gamma_5^{13} \lll 1)) \star \star)$ just after the right P function of Round 13, and keep only the qualified ciphertext pairs, whose number is expected to be $2^{48.5} \times 2^{-20} = 2^{28.5}$ on average. Now we can obtain $\gamma_3^{12} = \chi_1^{13} \oplus \Delta X_3^{14}[1]$ and $\gamma_0^{11} = \gamma_3^{12} \oplus \eta_5$.

6. Guess $(K_1[2, 3], K_3[0])$, partially decrypt every remaining plaintext pair (P^{j_0}, P^{j_1}) to check whether there is a difference γ_0^1 at nibble (0) just after the right S function of Round 1, and keep only the qualified plaintext pairs, whose number is expected to be $2^{28.5} \times 2^{-4} = 2^{24.5}$ on average.

7. Guess $(K_{26}[3, 4], K_{24}[1])$, partially decrypt every remaining ciphertext pair (C^{j_0}, C^{j_1}) to check whether there is a difference γ_3^{12} at nibble (1) just after

the left S function of Round 12, and keep only the qualified ciphertext pairs, whose number is expected to be $2^{24.5} \times 2^{-4} = 2^{20.5}$ on average.

8. Guess $(K_{27}[0,2], K_{25}[1,6,7])$, partially decrypt every remaining ciphertext pair (C^{j_0}, C^{j_1}) to check whether there is a difference $(\gamma_0^{12}, \gamma_1^{12}, \gamma_2^{12})$ at nibbles $(1,6,7)$ just after the right S function of Round 12, and keep only the qualified ciphertext pairs, whose number is expected to be $2^{20.5} \times 2^{-4 \times 3} = 2^{8.5}$ on average.

9. Guess $K_{25}[3,4]$, compute $K_{23}[1]$ with $(K_{24}[1], K_{25}[1], K_{26}[1], K_{27}[0-7])$ by FBC128-128 key schedule, partially decrypt every remaining ciphertext pair (C^{j_0}, C^{j_1}) to check whether there is a difference γ_0^{11} at nibble (1) just after the right S function of Round 11; if yes, discard the guessed 104-bit subkey and try another one.

10. For every remaining $(K_{24}[1], K_{25}[1,3,4,6,7], K_{26}[1,3,4,6,7], K_{27}[0-7])$ after Step 9, exhaustively search the remaining 52 key bits $(K_{24}[0,2-7], K_{25}[0,2,5], K_{26}[0,2,5])$ to determine the 128-bit user key by the FBC key schedule.

The attack requires $2^{73.5} \times 2^{52} = 2^{125.5}$ chosen plaintexts, and has a memory complexity of about $2^{52} \times 16 \times 2 + 2^{76.5} \times 16 \times 2 \times 2 \approx 2^{82.5}$ bytes if we filter out the $2^{76.5}$ preliminary satisfying plaintext pairs by checking the $2^{73.5}$ structures one by one and reusing the storage for a structure. The attack's time complexity is dominated by Steps 8 and 10. Step 8 has a time complexity of about $2 \times 2^{20.5} \times 2^{96} \approx 2^{117.5}$ 0.5-round FBC128-128 encryptions. It is expected that there are $2^{104} \times (1 - 2^{-4})^{2^{8.5}} \approx 2^{104} \times e^{-2^{4.5}} \approx 2^{72}$ guesses of $(K_0[0], K_1[0,2,3,5,6], K_3[0], K_{24}[1], K_{25}[1,3,4,6,7], K_{26}[1,3,4,6,7], K_{27}[0-7])$ passing Step 9, and thus Step 10 has a time complexity of about $2^{72} \times 2^{52} \approx 2^{124}$ 14-round FBC128-128 encryptions. Therefore, except the $2^{125.5}$ chosen plaintexts, the attack has a total time complexity of approximately $2^{117.5} \times \frac{1}{14} \times \frac{1}{2} + 2^{124} \approx 2^{124}$ 14-round FBC128-128 encryptions.

3.2 Attacking 15-Round FBC128-256

Similarly, we can attack 15-round FBC128-256 by appending three rounds at the beginning and three rounds at the end of Zhang et al.'s 9-round impossible differential, as follows. Figure 3 illustrates the attack.

1. Choose $2^{34.9}$ structures of 2^{92} plaintexts $(P_0^j, P_1^j, P_2^j, P_3^j)$, where in a structure the 9 nibbles $(1,2,3,4,7,9,15,25,31)$ of the 2^{92} plaintexts are fixed to certain values and the other 23 nibbles take all the possible values. For each structure, store the 2^{92} plaintexts into a hash table indexed by the following 108 bits:

$$(P_0^j[0] \lll 1) \oplus P_0^j[5], \tag{20}$$

$$(P_0^j[0] \lll 2) \oplus P_0^j[6], \tag{21}$$

$$(P_1^j[2] \lll 1) \oplus P_1^j[3] \oplus (P_1^j[4] \ggg 1), \tag{22}$$

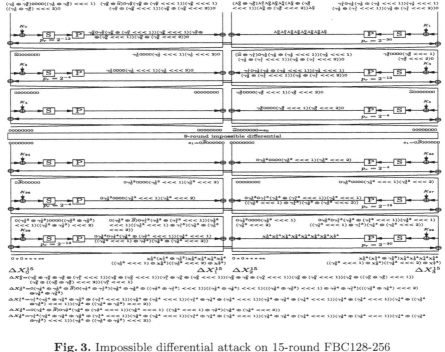

Fig. 3. Impossible differential attack on 15-round FBC128-256

$$(P_1^j[2] \lll 1) \oplus (P_1^j[4] \ggg 1) \oplus (P_1^j[5] \lll 1) \oplus P_1^j[6], \tag{23}$$

$$(P_2^j[0] \lll 1) \oplus (P_2^j[1] \lll 1) \oplus P_2^j[2] \oplus (P_2^j[3] \lll 1) \oplus (P_2^j[3] \lll 2) \oplus$$
$$P_2^j[5] \oplus (P_2^j[5] \lll 2) \oplus (P_2^j[5] \lll 3) \oplus (P_2^j[6] \lll 1) \oplus (P_2^j[6] \lll 2) \oplus$$
$$(P_2^j[7] \lll 1) \oplus (P_2^j[7] \ggg 1), \tag{24}$$

$$(P_2^j[0] \lll 2) \oplus (P_2^j[1] \ggg 1) \oplus P_2^j[3] \oplus (P_2^j[3] \lll 2) \oplus (P_2^j[4] \ggg 1) \oplus$$
$$(P_2^j[5] \lll 1) \oplus (P_2^j[5] \lll 3) \oplus (P_2^j[6] \lll 2) \oplus (P_2^j[7] \lll 2), \tag{25}$$

$$(P_3^j[2] \lll 1) \oplus (P_3^j[4] \ggg 1) \oplus P_3^j[3], \tag{26}$$

$$(P_3^j[0] \lll 1) \oplus P_3^j[2] \oplus P_3^j[5], \tag{27}$$

$$(P_3^j[0] \lll 2) \oplus (P_3^j[4] \ggg 1) \oplus P_3^j[6], \tag{28}$$

Indexes (8)−(19) in Sect. 3.1 with superscripts plus 1.

Likewise, two plaintexts P^{j_0} and P^{j_1} with the same 108-bit index have an input difference ($\Delta X_0^0 = 0x\phi_0 0000(\phi_0 \lll 1)(\phi_0 \lll 2)0, \Delta X_1^0 = 0x(\gamma_6^0 \oplus \widehat{\alpha})0\gamma_7^0(\gamma_8^0 \oplus (\gamma_7^0 \lll 1))(\gamma_8^0 \lll 1)(\gamma_7^0 \oplus (\gamma_6^0 \lll 1))(\gamma_8^0 \oplus (\gamma_6^0 \lll 2))0, \Delta X_2^0 = 0x(\phi_1 \oplus \gamma_2^0 \oplus (\gamma_1^0 \lll 1))(\gamma_3^0 \oplus (\gamma_2^0 \lll 1))(\gamma_1^0 \oplus \gamma_4^0 \oplus (\gamma_3^0 \lll 1))(\gamma_2^0 \oplus \gamma_5^0 \oplus (\gamma_4^0 \lll 1))(\gamma_3^0 \oplus (\gamma_5^0 \lll 1))(\gamma_4^0 \oplus (\phi_1 \lll 1))(\gamma_5^0 \oplus (\phi_1 \lll 2))(\gamma_1^0 \lll 1), \Delta X_3^0 = 0x\gamma_1^1 0\gamma_2^1(\gamma_3^1 \oplus (\gamma_2^1 \lll 1))(\gamma_3^1 \lll 1)(\gamma_2^1 \oplus (\gamma_1^1 \lll 1))(\gamma_3^1 \oplus (\gamma_1^1 \lll 2))0$) and an output difference ($\Delta X_0^{15} = 0x0\eta_0 0\eta_1(\eta_2 \oplus (\eta_1 \lll 1))(\eta_2 \lll 1)((\eta_3 \lll 1) \oplus$

$\eta_1)((\eta_3 \lll 2) \oplus \eta_2), \Delta X_1^{15} = \Delta X_3^{15} \oplus 0x0\eta_5 0000(\eta_5 \lll 1)(\eta_5 \lll 2), \Delta X_2^{15} = \Delta X_0^{15} \oplus 0x0\gamma_0^{13}0\gamma_1^{13}(\gamma_2^{13} \oplus (\gamma_1^{13} \lll 1))(\gamma_2^{13} \lll 1)((\gamma_0^{13} \lll 1) \oplus \gamma_1^{13})(\gamma_2^{13} \oplus (\gamma_0^{13} \lll 2)), \Delta X_3^{15} = 0x\gamma_1^{14}(\eta_4 \oplus \gamma_2^{14} \oplus (\gamma_1^{14} \lll 1))(\gamma_3^{14} \oplus (\gamma_2^{14} \lll 1))(\gamma_1^{14} \oplus \gamma_4^{14} \oplus (\gamma_3^{14} \lll 1))(\gamma_2^{14} \oplus \gamma_5^{14} \oplus (\gamma_4^{14} \lll 1))(\gamma_3^{14} \oplus (\gamma_5^{14} \lll 1))(\gamma_4^{14} \oplus (\eta_4 \lll 1))(\gamma_5^{14} \oplus (\eta_4 \lll 2)))$, and by this 108-bit index, we can easily obtain such plaintext pairs, obtain $\widehat{\alpha}$,

$$\widehat{\beta} = \Delta X_2^{15}[1] \oplus ((\Delta X_2^{15}[6] \oplus \Delta X_2^{15}[3]) \ggg 1),$$

$\gamma_1^0, \gamma_2^0, \cdots, \gamma_8^0, \gamma_1^1, \gamma_2^1, \gamma_3^1, \gamma_0^{13}, \gamma_1^{13}, \gamma_2^{13}, \gamma_1^{14}, \gamma_2^{14}, \gamma_3^{14}, \gamma_4^{14}, \gamma_5^{14}, \phi_0, \phi_1, \eta_0, \eta_1, \eta_2, \eta_3, \eta_4, \eta_5$ from $(\Delta X_0^0, \Delta X_1^0, \Delta X_2^0, \Delta X_3^0, \Delta X_0^{15}, \Delta X_1^{15}, \Delta X_2^{15}, \Delta X_3^{15})$ for a plaintext pair, and keep only the satisfying plaintext pairs with $\widehat{\alpha}, \widehat{\beta}$, $\gamma_1^0, \gamma_2^0, \cdots, \gamma_8^0, \gamma_1^1, \gamma_2^1, \gamma_3^1, \gamma_0^{13}, \gamma_1^{13}, \gamma_2^{13}, \gamma_1^{14}, \gamma_2^{14}, \gamma_3^{14}, \gamma_4^{14}, \gamma_5^{14}$ being nonzero. (A justification is given in the full version of this paper.) It is expected that the $2^{34.9}$ structures provide a total of $\binom{2^{92}}{2} \times 2^{-108} \times 2^{34.9} = 2^{109.9}$ preliminary satisfying plaintext pairs.

2. Guess $K_0[0, 5, 6]$, partially encrypt every preliminary satisfying plaintext pair (P^{j_0}, P^{j_1}) to check whether there is a difference $(\gamma_6^0, \gamma_7^0, \gamma_8^0)$ at nibbles $(0, 5, 6)$ just after the left S function of Round 0, and keep only the qualified plaintext pairs, whose number is expected to be $2^{109.9} \times 2^{-4 \times 3} = 2^{97.9}$ on average.

3. Guess $K_{28}[1, 6, 7]$, partially decrypt every remaining ciphertext pair (C^{j_0}, C^{j_1}) to check whether there is a difference $(\gamma_6^{14}, \gamma_7^{14}, \gamma_8^{14}) = ((\Delta X_2^{15}[3] \oplus \Delta X_2^{15}[6]) \ggg 1, \Delta X_2^{15}[3], \Delta X_2^{15}[5] \ggg 1)$ at nibbles $(1, 6, 7)$ just after the left S function of Round 14, and keep only the qualified ciphertext pairs, whose number is expected to be $2^{97.9} \times 2^{-4 \times 3} = 2^{85.9}$ on average.

4. Guess $K_1[0, 2, 3, 4, 5, 6]$, partially encrypt every remaining plaintext pair (P^{j_0}, P^{j_1}) to get nibbles $(0, 2, 3, 4, 5, 6)$ of their intermediate values just after the right S function of Round 0, check whether they produce a difference $(\lambda_0^0 \lambda_1^0 \lambda_2^0 \lambda_3^0 \lambda_4^0 \lambda_5^0 \lambda_6^0 \lambda_7^0) = 0x \star (\gamma_3^0 \oplus (\gamma_2^0 \lll 1))(\gamma_1^0 \oplus \gamma_4^0 \oplus (\gamma_3^0 \lll 1))(\gamma_2^0 \oplus \gamma_5^0 \oplus (\gamma_4^0 \lll 1))(\gamma_3^0 \oplus (\gamma_5^0 \lll 1)) \star \star (\gamma_1^0 \lll 1)$ just after the right P function of Round 0, and keep only the qualified plaintext pairs, whose number is expected to be $2^{85.9} \times 2^{-4 \times 5} = 2^{65.9}$ on average. Now we can obtain $\gamma_0^2 = \lambda_0^0 \oplus \Delta X_2^0[0]$, $\gamma_0^0 = \gamma_0^2 \oplus \phi_1$ and $\gamma_0^1 = \gamma_0^2 \oplus \phi_0$.

5. Guess $K_{29}[1, 3, 4, 5, 6, 7]$, partially decrypt every remaining ciphertext pair (C^{j_0}, C^{j_1}) to get nibbles $(1, 3, 4, 5, 6, 7)$ of their intermediate values just after the right S function of Round 14, check whether they produce a difference $(\chi_0^{14}, \chi_1^{14}, \cdots, \chi_7^{14}) = 0x(\gamma_1^{14} \star (\gamma_3^{14} \oplus (\gamma_2^{14} \lll 1))(\gamma_1^{14} \oplus \gamma_4^{14} \oplus (\gamma_3^{14} \lll 1))(\gamma_2^{14} \oplus \gamma_5^{14} \oplus (\gamma_4^{14} \lll 1))(\gamma_3^{14} \oplus (\gamma_5^{14} \lll 1)) \star \star)$ just after the right P function of Round 14, and keep only the qualified ciphertext pairs, whose number is expected to be $2^{65.9} \times 2^{-4 \times 5} = 2^{45.9}$ on average. Now we can obtain $\gamma_3^{13} = \chi_1^{14} \oplus \Delta X_3^{15}[1]$ and $\gamma_0^{12} = \gamma_3^{13} \oplus \eta_5$.

6. Guess $(K_0[2, 3], K_2[0])$, partially encrypt every satisfying plaintext pair (P^{j_0}, P^{j_1}) to check whether there is a difference γ_0^1 at nibble (0) just after the left S function of Round 1, and keep only the qualified plaintext pairs, whose number is expected to be $2^{45.9} \times 2^{-4} = 2^{41.9}$ on average.

7. Guess $(K_{28}[3, 4], K_{26}[1])$, partially decrypt every remaining ciphertext pair (C^{j_0}, C^{j_1}) to check whether there is a difference γ_3^{13} at nibble (1) just after

the left S function of Round 13, and keep only the qualified ciphertext pairs, whose number is expected to be $2^{41.9} \times 2^{-4} = 2^{37.9}$ on average.

8. Guess $(K_1[1,7], K_3[0,5,6])$, partially encrypt every remaining plaintext pair (P^{j_0}, P^{j_1}) to check whether there is a difference $(\gamma_1^1, \gamma_2^1, \gamma_3^1)$ at nibbles $(0,5,6)$ just after the right S function of Round 1, and keep only the qualified plaintext pairs, whose number is expected to be $2^{37.9} \times 2^{-4\times3} = 2^{25.9}$ on average.

9. Guess $(K_3[2,3], K_5[0])$, partially decrypt every remaining plaintext pair (P^{j_0}, P^{j_1}) to check whether there is a difference γ_0^2 at nibble (0) just after the right S function of Round 2, and keep only the qualified plaintext pairs, whose number is expected to be $2^{25.9} \times 2^{-4} = 2^{21.9}$ on average.

10. Guess $(K_{29}[0,2], K_{27}[1,6,7])$, partially decrypt every remaining ciphertext pair (C^{j_0}, C^{j_1}) to check whether there is a difference $(\gamma_0^{13}, \gamma_1^{13}, \gamma_2^{13})$ at nibbles $(1,6,7)$ just after the right S function of Round 13, and keep only the qualified ciphertext pairs, whose number is expected to be $2^{21.9} \times 2^{-4\times3} = 2^{9.9}$ on average.

11. Guess $(K_{27}[3,4], K_{25}[1])$, partially decrypt every remaining ciphertext pair (C^{j_0}, C^{j_1}) to check whether there is a difference γ_0^{12} at nibble (1) just after the right S function of Round 12; if yes, discard the guessed 160-bit subkey and try another one.

12. For every remaining $(K_0[0,2,3,5,6], K_1, K_2[0], K_3[0,2,3,5,6], K_5[0])$ after Step 11, exhaustively search the remaining 176 key bits to determine the 256-bit user key by the FBC128-256 key schedule.

The attack requires $2^{34.9} \times 2^{92} = 2^{126.9}$ chosen plaintexts, and has a memory complexity of about $2^{92} \times 16 \times 2 + 2^{109.9} \times 16 \times 2 \times 2 \approx 2^{115.9}$ bytes if we filter out the $2^{109.9}$ qualified plaintext pairs by checking the $2^{34.9}$ structures one by one and reusing the storage for a structure. The attack's time complexity is dominated by Step 12. It is expected that there are $2^{160} \times (1 - 2^{-4})^{2^{9.9}} \approx 2^{160} \times e^{-2^{5.9}} \approx 2^{73.9}$ guessed 160-bit subkeys passing Step 11, and thus Step 12 has a time complexity of about $2^{73.9} \times 2^{176} \approx 2^{249.9}$ 15-round FBC128-256 encryptions.

4   Impossible Differential Attack on 19-Round FBC256

In this section, we give 13-round impossible differentials of FBC256 and present an impossible differential attack on 19-round FBC256. Likewise, an important point for this attack is that we exploit some specific relations among the concerned differences to devise sorting conditions on plaintexts and ciphertexts so as to filter out preliminary satisfying plaintext/ciphertext pairs efficiently.

4.1   13-Round Impossible Differentials of FBC256

Our 13-round impossible differentials on FBC256 are $(0, 0, e_0, 0) \nrightarrow (e_j, 0, e_j, 0)$, constructed in a miss-in-the-middle manner [3], where e_m denotes a 64-bit word with zeros in all positions except the 4 bits of the m-th column ($m = 0$ or j) and $j \in \{1, 15\}$. A proof is given in the full version of this paper.

4.2 Attacking 19-Round FBC256

As illustrated in Fig. 4, we can use a 13-round impossible differential to attack 19-round FBC256, by appending three rounds at the beginning and three rounds at the end of the 13-round impossible differential, as follows.

1. Choose $2^{155.3}$ structures of 2^{100} plaintexts $(P_0^j, P_1^j, P_2^j, P_3^j)$, where in a structure the 39 nibbles $(1-5, 7-14, 1-4, 7-11, 13, 1, 3, 7-10, 1-4, 7-11, 13)$ of the 2^{100} plaintexts are fixed to certain values and the other 25 nibbles take all the possible values. For each structure, store the 2^{100} plaintexts into a hash table indexed by the following 244 bits:

$$P_0^j[0] \oplus P_0^j[6], \tag{29}$$

$$(P_0^j[0] \lll 2) \oplus P_0^j[15], \tag{30}$$

$$P_1^j[5] \oplus (P_1^j[12] \lll 1) \oplus (P_1^j[14] \lll 2), \tag{31}$$

$$(P_1^j[6] \lll 2) \oplus (P_1^j[12] \lll 2) \oplus (P_1^j[14] \ggg 1) \oplus P_1^j[15], \tag{32}$$

$$(P_2^j[2] \ggg 2) \oplus (P_2^j[4] \ggg 1) \oplus P_2^j[5] \oplus (P_2^j[12] \lll 1) \oplus (P_2^j[14] \lll 2), \tag{33}$$

$$P_2^j[0] \oplus (P_2^j[2] \ggg 3) \oplus P_2^j[6] \oplus P_2^j[12], \tag{34}$$

$$(P_2^j[2] \ggg 2) \oplus (P_2^j[4] \ggg 1) \oplus P_2^j[11] \oplus (P_2^j[13] \lll 1), \tag{35}$$

$$(P_2^j[0] \lll 2) \oplus (P_2^j[13] \ggg 2) \oplus (P_2^j[14] \ggg 1) \oplus P_2^j[15], \tag{36}$$

$$P_3^j[5] \oplus (P_3^j[12] \lll 1) \oplus (P_3^j[14] \lll 2), \tag{37}$$

$$P_3^j[0] \oplus P_3^j[6] \oplus P_3^j[12], \tag{38}$$

$$(P_3^j[0] \lll 2) \oplus (P_3^j[14] \ggg 1) \oplus P_3^j[15], \tag{39}$$

$$C_0^j[2, 3, 4, 5, 8, 9, 10, 11, 12, 14], \tag{40}$$

$$C_0^j[0] \oplus (C_0^j[7] \lll 1) \oplus (C_0^j[13] \lll 1) \oplus (C_0^j[15] \ggg 2), \tag{41}$$

$$C_0^j[6] \oplus (C_0^j[13] \lll 1) \oplus (C_0^j[15] \ggg 2), \tag{42}$$

$$C_1^j[2, 4, 8, 9, 10, 11], \tag{43}$$

$$C_2^j[2, 3, 4, 5, 8, 9, 10, 11, 12, 14], \tag{44}$$

$$C_3^j[2, 4, 8, 9, 10, 11], \tag{45}$$

$$C_3^j[0] \oplus (C_3^j[5] \ggg 1) \oplus C_3^j[6] \oplus (C_3^j[7] \lll 1) \oplus (C_3^j[14] \lll 1), \tag{46}$$

$$(C_3^j[3] \ggg 2) \oplus (C_3^j[5] \ggg 1) \oplus C_3^j[12] \oplus (C_3^j[14] \lll 1), \tag{47}$$

$$C_3^j[1] \oplus (C_3^j[3] \ggg 3) \oplus C_3^j[7] \oplus C_3^j[13], \tag{48}$$

$$(C_3^j[0] \lll 2) \oplus (C_3^j[1] \lll 3) \oplus (C_3^j[14] \ggg 1) \oplus C_3^j[15], \tag{49}$$

$$C_1^j[3, 5, 6, 12, 13, 14, 15] \oplus C_3^j[3, 5, 6, 12, 13, 14, 15], \tag{50}$$

$$(C_1^j[0] \ggg 1) \oplus C_1^j[1] \oplus (C_3^j[0] \ggg 1) \oplus C_3^j[1], \tag{51}$$

$$(C_1^j[0] \ggg 1) \oplus C_1^j[7] \oplus (C_3^j[0] \ggg 1) \oplus C_3^j[7], \tag{52}$$

$$C_0^j[0] \oplus (C_0^j[1] \lll 1) \oplus (C_0^j[15] \ggg 2) \oplus C_2^j[0] \oplus (C_2^j[1] \lll 1) \oplus$$

$$(C_2^j[15] \ggg 2), \tag{53}$$

$$C_0^j[6] \oplus (C_0^j[13] \lll 1) \oplus (C_0^j[15] \ggg 2) \oplus C_2^j[6] \oplus (C_2^j[13] \lll 1) \oplus$$
$$(C_2^j[15] \ggg 2), \tag{54}$$

$$C_0^j[1] \oplus C_0^j[7] \oplus C_0^j[13] \oplus C_2^j[1] \oplus C_2^j[7] \oplus C_2^j[13]. \tag{55}$$

Likewise, two plaintexts P^{j_0} and P^{j_1} with the same 244-bit index have an input difference ($\Delta X_0^0 = 0x\phi_0 00000\phi_0 00000000(\phi_0 \lll 2), \Delta X_1^0 = 0x(\gamma_0^0 \oplus \widehat{\alpha})0000((\gamma_1^0 \lll 1) \oplus (\gamma_2^0 \lll 3))(\gamma_1^0 \oplus \gamma_0^0)00000\gamma_1^0 0(\gamma_2^0 \lll 1)(\gamma_2^0 \oplus (\gamma_0^0 \lll 2)), \Delta X_2^0 = 0x\phi_1 0(\gamma_7^0 \lll 3)0((\gamma_4^0 \lll 1) \oplus (\gamma_7^0 \lll 3))(\gamma_4^0 \oplus (\gamma_8^0 \lll 1) \oplus (\gamma_8^0 \lll 3))(\phi_1 \oplus \gamma_5^0)0000((\gamma_6^0 \lll 1) \oplus \gamma_4^0)(\gamma_6^0 \oplus \gamma_5^0)(\gamma_7^0 \lll 1)(\gamma_7^0 \oplus (\gamma_8^0 \lll 1))(\gamma_8^0 \oplus (\phi_1 \lll 2)), \Delta X_3^0 = 0x\gamma_0^1 0000((\gamma_1^1 \lll 1) \oplus (\gamma_2^1 \lll 3))(\gamma_1^1 \oplus \gamma_0^1)00000\gamma_1^1 0(\gamma_2^1 \lll 1)(\gamma_2^1 \oplus (\gamma_0^1 \lll 2)))$ and an output difference ($\Delta X_0^{19} = 0x(\phi_2 \oplus (\phi_3 \lll 1))(\phi_3 \oplus \widehat{\beta})0000(\phi_2 \oplus (\phi_4 \lll 1))(\phi_3 \oplus \phi_4)00000\phi_4 0(\phi_2 \lll 2), \Delta X_1^{19} = \Delta X_3^{19} \oplus 0x(\phi_6 \lll 1)\phi_6 00000\phi_6 00000000, \Delta X_2^{19} = \Delta X_0^{19} \oplus 0x(\gamma_1^{17} \oplus (\gamma_2^{17} \lll 1))\gamma_2^{17}0000((\gamma_3^{17} \lll 1) \oplus \gamma_1^{17})(\gamma_2^{17} \oplus \gamma_3^{17})00000\gamma_3^{17}0(\gamma_1^{17} \lll 2), \Delta X_3^{19} = 0x(\gamma_3^{18} \oplus(\phi_5 \lll 1))\phi_5 0(\gamma_7^{18} \lll 3)0((\gamma_6^{18} \lll 1) \oplus (\gamma_8^{18} \lll 3))(\gamma_6^{18} \oplus (\gamma_8^{18} \lll 1) \oplus \gamma_3^{18})(\gamma_6^{18} \oplus \phi_5)0000((\gamma_7^{18} \lll 1) \oplus \gamma_3^{18})(\gamma_7^{18} \oplus \gamma_6^{18})(\gamma_8^{18} \lll 1)(\gamma_8^{18} \oplus (\gamma_3^{18} \lll 2)))$, and by this 244-bit index, we can efficiently obtain such plaintext pairs, obtain $\widehat{\alpha}, \widehat{\beta}, \gamma_0^0, \gamma_1^0, \gamma_2^0, \gamma_4^0, \gamma_5^0, \cdots, \gamma_8^0, \gamma_0^1, \gamma_1^1, \gamma_2^1, \gamma_1^{17}, \gamma_2^{17}, \gamma_3^{17}, \gamma_3^{18}, \gamma_5^{18}, \gamma_6^{18}, \gamma_7^{18}, \gamma_8^{18}, \phi_0, \phi_1, \cdots, \phi_6$ from the $(\Delta X_0^0, \Delta X_1^0, \Delta X_2^0, \Delta X_3^0, \Delta X_0^{19}, \Delta X_1^{19}, \Delta X_2^{19}, \Delta X_3^{19})$ for a plaintext pair, and keep only the satisfying plaintext pairs with $\widehat{\alpha}, \widehat{\beta}, \gamma_0^0, \gamma_1^0, \gamma_2^0, \gamma_4^0, \gamma_5^0, \cdots, \gamma_8^0, \gamma_0^1, \gamma_1^1, \gamma_2^1, \gamma_1^{17}, \gamma_2^{17}, \gamma_3^{17}, \gamma_3^{18}, \gamma_5^{18}, \gamma_6^{18}, \gamma_7^{18}, \gamma_8^{18}$ being nonzero. (A justification is given in the full version of this paper.) It is expected that the $2^{155.3}$ structures provide a total of $\binom{2^{100}}{2} \times 2^{-244} \times 2^{155.3} = 2^{110.3}$ preliminary satisfying plaintext pairs.

2. Guess $K_0[0, 6, 15]$, partially encrypt every preliminary satisfying plaintext pair (P^{j_0}, P^{j_1}) to check whether there is a difference $(\gamma_0^0, \gamma_1^0, \gamma_2^0)$ at nibbles $(0, 6, 15)$ just after the left S function of Round 0, and keep only the qualified plaintext pairs, whose number is expected to be $2^{110.3} \times 2^{-4 \times 3} = 2^{98.3}$ on average.

3. Guess $K_{36}[0, 1, 7]$, partially decrypt every remaining ciphertext pair (C^{j_0}, C^{j_1}) to check whether there is a difference $(\gamma_0^{18}, \gamma_1^{18}, \gamma_2^{18}) = (\Delta X_2^{19}[15] \ggg 2, \Delta X_2^{19}[7] \oplus \Delta X_2^{19}[13], \Delta X_2^{19}[13])$ at nibbles $(0, 1, 7)$ just after the left S function of Round 18, and keep only the qualified ciphertext pairs, whose number is expected to be $2^{98.3} \times 2^{-4 \times 3} = 2^{86.3}$ on average.

4. Guess $K_1[0, 5, 6, 12, 14, 15]$, partially encrypt every remaining plaintext pair (P^{j_0}, P^{j_1}) to get nibbles $(0, 5, 6, 12, 14, 15)$ of their intermediate values just after the right S function of Round 0, check whether they produce a difference $0x(\eta_0^0 0\eta_1^0 0\eta_2^0\eta_3^0\eta_4^0 0000\eta_5^0\eta_6^0\eta_7^0\eta_8^0\eta_9^0) = 0x(\star 0(\gamma_6^0 \lll 3)0((\gamma_4^0 \lll 1) \oplus (\gamma_7^0 \lll 3))(\gamma_4^0 \oplus (\gamma_5^0 \lll 1) \oplus (\gamma_8^0 \lll 3)) \star 0000((\gamma_6^0 \lll 1) \oplus \gamma_4^0)(\gamma_6^0 \oplus \gamma_5^0)(\gamma_7^0 \lll 1)(\gamma_7^0 \oplus (\gamma_8^0 \lll 1))\star)$ after the right P function of Round 0, and keep only the qualified plaintext pairs, whose number is expected to be $2^{86.3} \times 2^{-4 \times 5} = 2^{66.3}$ on average. Now we can obtain $\gamma_0^2 = \eta_0^0 \oplus \Delta X_2^0[0]$, $\gamma_3^0 = \gamma_0^2 \oplus \phi_1$ and $\gamma_3^1 = \gamma_0^2 \oplus \phi_0$.

Fig. 4. Impossible differential attack on 19-round FBC256

5. Guess $K_{37}[0, 1, 6, 7, 13, 15]$, partially decrypt every remaining ciphertext pair (C^{j_0}, C^{j_1}) to get nibbles $(0, 1, 6, 7, 13, 15)$ of their intermediate values just after the right S function of Round 18, check whether they produce a difference $0x(\chi_0^{18}\chi_1^{18}0\chi_2^{18}0\chi_3^{18}\chi_4^{18}\chi_5^{18}0000\chi_6^{18}\chi_7^{18}\chi_8^{18}\chi_9^{18}) = 0x(\star \star 0(\gamma_7^{18} \lll 3)0((\gamma_5^{18} \lll 1) \oplus (\gamma_8^{18} \lll 3))(\gamma_5^{18} \oplus (\gamma_6^{18} \lll 1) \oplus \gamma_3^{18}) \star 0000((\gamma_7^{18} \lll 1) \oplus \gamma_5^{18})(\gamma_7^{18} \oplus \gamma_6^{18})(\gamma_8^{18} \lll 1)(\gamma_8^{18} \oplus (\gamma_3^{18} \lll 2)))$ just after the right P

function of Round 18, and keep only the qualified ciphertext pairs, whose number is expected to be $2^{66.3} \times 2^{-20} = 2^{46.3}$ on average. Now we can obtain $\gamma_0^{17} = \chi_1^{18} \oplus \Delta X_3^{19}[1]$ and $\gamma_0^{16} = \gamma_0^{17} \oplus \phi_6$.

6. Guess $(K_0[1, 10], K_2[0])$, partially decrypt every remaining plaintext pair (P^{j_0}, P^{j_1}) to check whether there is a difference γ_3^1 at nibble (0) just after the left S function of Round 1, and keep only the qualified plaintext pairs, whose number is expected to be $2^{46.3} \times 2^{-4} = 2^{42.3}$ on average.

7. Guess $(K_{36}[2, 11], K_{34}[1])$, partially decrypt every remaining ciphertext pair (C^{j_0}, C^{j_1}) to check whether there is a difference γ_0^{17} at nibble (1) of their intermediate values just after the left S function of Round 17, and keep only the qualified plaintext pairs, whose number is expected to be $2^{42.3} \times 2^{-4} = 2^{38.3}$ on average.

8. Guess $(K_1[1, 7, 9, 10], K_3[0, 6, 15])$, partially encrypt every remaining plaintext pair (P^{j_0}, P^{j_1}) to check whether there is a difference $(\gamma_0^1, \gamma_1^1, \gamma_2^1)$ at nibbles (0, 6, 15) just after the right S function of Round 1, and keep only the qualified plaintext pairs, whose number is expected to be $2^{38.3} \times 2^{-4 \times 3} = 2^{26.3}$ on average.

9. Guess $(K_{37}[2, 8, 10, 11], K_{35}[0, 1, 7])$, partially decrypt every remaining ciphertext pair (C^{j_0}, C^{j_1}) to check whether there is a difference $(\gamma_1^{17}, \gamma_2^{17}, \gamma_3^{17})$ at nibbles (0, 1, 7) just after the right S function of Round 17, and keep only the qualified plaintext pairs, whose number is expected to be $2^{26.3} \times 2^{-4 \times 3} = 2^{14.3}$ on average.

10. Guess $(K_1[2, 4, 11], K_3[1, 10], K_5[0])$, partially encrypt every remaining plaintext pair (P^{j_0}, P^{j_1}) to check whether there is a difference γ_0^2 at nibble (0) just after the right S function of Round 2, and keep only the qualified plaintext pairs, whose number is expected to be $2^{14.3} \times 2^{-4} = 2^{10.3}$ on average.

11. Guess $(K_{37}[3, 5, 12], K_{35}[2, 11], K_{33}[1])$, partially decrypt every remaining ciphertext pair (C^{j_0}, C^{j_1}) to check whether there is a difference γ_0^{16} at nibble (1) just after the right S function of Round 16; if yes, discard the guessed 200-bit subkey and try another one.

12. For every remaining subkey guess $(K_0[0, 1, 6, 10, 15], K_1[0, 1, 2, 4, 5, 6, 7, 9, 10, 11, 12, 14, 15], K_2[0], K_3[0, 1, 6, 10, 15])$, exhaustively search the remaining 160 key bits $(K_0[2 - 5, 7 - 9, 11 - 14], K_1[3, 8, 13], K_2[1 - 15], K_3[2 - 5, 7 - 9, 11 - 14])$ to determine the 256-bit user key by the FBC256 key schedule.

The attack requires $2^{155.3} \times 2^{100} = 2^{255.3}$ chosen plaintexts, and has a memory complexity of about $2^{100} \times 16 \times 2 + 2^{110.3} \times 16 \times 2 \times 2 \approx 2^{116.3}$ bytes if we filter out the $2^{110.3}$ qualified plaintext pairs by checking the $2^{155.3}$ structures one by one and reusing the storage for a structure. Except the $2^{255.3}$ chosen plaintexts, the attack's time complexity is dominated by Step 12. It is expected that there are $2^{200} \times (1 - 2^{-4})^{2^{10.3}} \approx 2^{200} \times \mathsf{e}^{-2^{6.3}} \approx 2^{86.4}$ subkey guess passing Step 11, and thus Step 12 has a time complexity of about $2^{86.4} \times 2^{160} = 2^{246.4}$ 19-round FBC256 encryptions.

5   Conclusion

The FBC block cipher is an award-winning algorithm of the Cryptographic Algorithm Design Competition in China. In this paper, by exploiting both inactive and active nibble differences on plaintext and ciphertext as well as some intermediate states to sieve out preliminary satisfying plaintext/ciphertext pairs efficiently, we have used Zhang et al.'s 9-round impossible differential on FBC128 to make key-recovery attacks on 14-round FBC128-128 and 15-round FBC128-256, and we have exploited 13-round impossible differentials on FBC256 to make a key-recovery attack on 19-round FBC256. Our attacks are better than any previously published attacks on FBC in terms of the numbers of attacked rounds.

Acknowledgements. This work was supported by State Key Laboratory of Cryptology (No. MMKFKT202114). Jiqiang Lu was Qianjiang Special Expert of Hangzhou.

Appendix: Filtering Details of the 100-Bit Index on FBC128-128

Under a structure, a pair of plaintexts (P^{j_0}, P^{j_1}) with the same 100-bit index (1)–(18) have the following features:

- Indexes (1) and (2) guarantee that $P_1^{j_0} \oplus P_1^{j_1} = \Delta X_1^0 = 0x\gamma_0^0 0000(\gamma_0^0 \lll 1)(\gamma_0^0 \lll 2)0$, where γ_0^0 is an indeterminate nibble difference. This is because

$$\text{Index } (1): (P_1^{j_0}[0] \lll 1) \oplus P_1^{j_0}[5] = (P_1^{j_1}[0] \lll 1) \oplus P_1^{j_1}[5]$$
$$\Rightarrow \quad \Delta P_1[5] = \Delta P_1[0] \lll 1,$$
$$\text{Index } (2): (P_1^{j_0}[0] \lll 2) \oplus P_1^{j_0}[6] = (P_1^{j_1}[0] \lll 2) \oplus P_1^{j_1}[6]$$
$$\Rightarrow \quad \Delta P_1[6] = \Delta P_1[0] \lll 2,$$

so under a plaintext structure we have the above guarantee after letting

$$\gamma_0^0 = P_1^{j_0}[0] \oplus P_1^{j_1}[0] = \Delta P_1[0].$$

- Indexes (3)–(5) guarantee that $P_2^{j_0} \oplus P_2^{j_1} = \Delta X_2^0 = 0x\hat{\alpha}0000000$ and $P_2^{j_0} \oplus P_2^{j_1} = \Delta X_2^0 = 0x(\hat{\alpha} \oplus \gamma_1^0)0\gamma_2^0(\gamma_3^0 \oplus (\gamma_2^0 \lll 1))(\gamma_3^0 \lll 1)(\gamma_2^0 \oplus (\gamma_1^0 \lll 1))(\gamma_3^0 \oplus (\gamma_1^0 \lll 2))0$, where $\hat{\alpha}, \gamma_1^0, \gamma_2^0, \gamma_3^0$ are indeterminate nibble differences. This is because

Index (3) : $(P_2^{j_0}[2] \lll 1) \oplus P_2^{j_0}[3] \oplus (P_2^{j_0}[4] \ggg 1) =$
$\qquad (P_2^{j_1}[2] \lll 1) \oplus P_2^{j_1}[3] \oplus (P_2^{j_1}[4] \ggg 1)$
$\Rightarrow \quad \Delta P_2[3] = (\Delta P_2[4] \ggg 1) \oplus (\Delta P_2[2] \lll 1),$

Index (4) : $(P_0^{j_0}[0] \lll 1) \oplus (P_2^{j_0}[0] \lll 1) \oplus P_2^{j_0}[2] \oplus P_2^{j_0}[5] =$
$\qquad (P_0^{j_1}[0] \lll 1) \oplus (P_2^{j_1}[0] \lll 1) \oplus P_2^{j_1}[2] \oplus P_2^{j_1}[5]$
$\Rightarrow \quad \Delta P_2[5] = \Delta P_2[2] \oplus ((\Delta P_0[0] \oplus \Delta P_2[0]) \lll 1),$

Index (5) : $(P_0^{j_0}[0] \lll 2) \oplus (P_2^{j_0}[0] \lll 2) \oplus (P_2^{j_0}[4] \ggg 1) \oplus P_2^{j_0}[6] =$
$\qquad (P_0^{j_1}[0] \lll 2) \oplus (P_2^{j_1}[0] \lll 2) \oplus (P_2^{j_1}[4] \ggg 1) \oplus P_2^{j_1}[6]$
$\Rightarrow \quad \Delta P_2[6] = (\Delta P_2[4] \ggg 1) \oplus ((\Delta P_0[0] \oplus \Delta P_2[0]) \lll 2),$

so under a plaintext structure we have the above guarantees after letting

$$\widehat{\alpha} = P_0^{j_0}[0] \oplus P_0^{j_1}[0] = \Delta P_0[0],$$
$$\gamma_1^0 = (P_2^{j_0}[0] \oplus P_2^{j_1}[0]) \oplus \widehat{\alpha} = \Delta P_2[0] \oplus \widehat{\alpha},$$
$$\gamma_2^0 = P_2^{j_0}[2] \oplus P_2^{j_1}[2] = \Delta P_2[2],$$
$$\gamma_3^0 = (P_2^{j_0}[4] \oplus P_2^{j_1}[4]) \ggg 1 = \Delta P_2[4] \ggg 1.$$

– Indexes (6) and (7) guarantee that $P_3^{j_0} \oplus P_3^{j_1} = \Delta X_3^0 = 0x\gamma_0^1 0000(\gamma_0^1 \lll 1)(\gamma_0^1 \lll 2)0$, where γ_0^1 is an indeterminate nibble difference. This is because

Index (6) : $(P_3^{j_0}[0] \lll 1) \oplus P_3^{j_0}[5] = (P_3^{j_1}[0] \lll 1) \oplus P_3^{j_1}[5]$
$\Rightarrow \quad \Delta P_3[5] = \Delta P_3[0] \lll 1,$

Index (7) : $(P_3^{j_0}[0] \lll 2) \oplus P_3^{j_0}[6] = (P_3^{j_1}[0] \lll 2) \oplus P_3^{j_1}[6]$
$\Rightarrow \quad \Delta P_3[6] = \Delta P_3[0] \lll 2,$

so under a plaintext structure we have the above guarantee after letting

$$\gamma_0^1 = P_3^{j_0}[0] \oplus P_3^{j_1}[0] = \Delta P_3[0].$$

– Indexes (8)–(10) guarantee that $C_0^{j_0} \oplus C_0^{j_1} = \Delta X_0^{14} = 0x0 \star 0 \star \star \star \star \star = 0x0\eta_0 0\eta_1(\eta_2 \oplus (\eta_1 \lll 1))(\eta_2 \lll 1)((\eta_3 \lll 1) \oplus \eta_1)((\eta_3 \lll 2) \oplus \eta_2)$, where $\eta_0, \eta_1, \eta_2, \eta_3$ are indeterminate nibble differences. This is because

Index (8) : $C_0^{j_0}[0, 2] = C_0^{j_1}[0, 2] \Rightarrow \Delta X_0^{14}[0, 2] = 0,$

Index (9) : $(C_0^{j_0}[3] \lll 1) \oplus C_0^{j_0}[4] \oplus (C_0^{j_0}[5] \ggg 1) =$
$\qquad (C_0^{j_1}[3] \lll 1) \oplus C_0^{j_1}[4] \oplus (C_0^{j_1}[5] \ggg 1)$
$\Rightarrow \quad \Delta C_0[4] = (\Delta C_0[5] \ggg 1) \oplus (\Delta C_0[3] \lll 1),$

Index (10) : $(C_0^{j_0}[3] \lll 1) \oplus (C_0^{j_0}[5] \ggg 1) \oplus (C_0^{j_0}[6] \lll 1) \oplus C_0^{j_0}[7] =$
$\qquad (C_0^{j_1}[3] \lll 1) \oplus (C_0^{j_1}[5] \ggg 1) \oplus (C_0^{j_1}[6] \lll 1) \oplus C_0^{j_1}[7]$

$$\Rightarrow \quad \Delta C_0[7] = (\Delta C_0[3] \lll 1) \oplus (\Delta C_0[5] \ggg 1) \oplus (\Delta C_0[6] \lll 1),$$

so under a plaintext structure we have the above guarantee after letting

$$\eta_0 = C_0^{j_0}[1] \oplus C_0^{j_1}[1] = \Delta C_0[1],$$
$$\eta_1 = C_0^{j_0}[3] \oplus C_0^{j_1}[3] = \Delta C_0[3],$$
$$\eta_2 = (C_0^{j_0}[5] \oplus C_0^{j_1}[5]) \ggg 1 = \Delta C_0[5] \ggg 1,$$
$$\eta_3 = (C_0^{j_0}[6] \oplus C_0^{j_1}[6] \oplus \eta_1) \ggg 1 = (\Delta C_0[6] \oplus \eta_1) \ggg 1.$$

- Index (11) guarantees that $C_2^{j_0}[0,2] \oplus C_2^{j_1}[0,2] = \Delta X_2^{14}[0,2] = 0$, because

$$\text{Index (11)} : C_2^{j_0}[0,2] = C_2^{j_1}[0,2] \Rightarrow \Delta X_2^{14}[0,2] = 0.$$

- Indexes (12)–(13) guarantee that $C_3^{j_0} \oplus C_3^{j_1} = \Delta X_3^{14} = 0x\gamma_1^{13}(\eta_4 \oplus \gamma_2^{13} \oplus (\gamma_1^{13} \lll 1))(\gamma_3^{13} \oplus (\gamma_2^{13} \lll 1))(\gamma_1^{13} \oplus \gamma_4^{13} \oplus (\gamma_3^{13} \lll 1))(\gamma_2^{13} \oplus \gamma_5^{13} \oplus (\gamma_4^{13} \lll 1))(\gamma_3^{13} \oplus (\gamma_5^{13} \lll 1))(\gamma_4^{13} \oplus (\eta_4 \lll 1))(\gamma_5^{13} \oplus (\eta_4 \lll 2))$, where $\eta_4, \gamma_1^{13}, \gamma_2^{13}, \gamma_3^{13}, \gamma_4^{13}, \gamma_5^{13}$ are indeterminate nibble differences. This is because

$$\text{Index (12)} : C_3^{j_0}[0] \oplus C_3^{j_0}[3] \oplus C_3^{j_0}[6] \oplus ((C_3^{j_0}[1] \oplus C_3^{j_0}[2] \oplus C_3^{j_0}[4] \oplus$$
$$C_3^{j_0}[7]) \lll 1) \oplus ((C_3^{j_0}[0] \oplus C_3^{j_0}[4] \oplus C_3^{j_0}[6] \oplus C_3^{j_0}[7]) \lll 2) \oplus$$
$$(C_3^{j_0}[6] \lll 3) = C_3^{j_1}[0] \oplus C_3^{j_1}[3] \oplus C_3^{j_1}[6] \oplus ((C_3^{j_1}[1] \oplus$$
$$C_3^{j_1}[2] \oplus C_3^{j_1}[4] \oplus C_3^{j_1}[7]) \lll 1) \oplus ((C_3^{j_1}[0] \oplus C_3^{j_1}[4] \oplus C_3^{j_1}[6]$$
$$\oplus C_3^{j_1}[7]) \lll 2) \oplus (C_3^{j_1}[6] \lll 3)$$
$$\Rightarrow \quad \Delta C_3[3] = \Delta C_3[0] \oplus \Delta C_3[6] \oplus (\Delta C_3[6] \lll 3) \oplus$$
$$((\Delta C_3[1] \oplus \Delta C_3[2] \oplus \Delta C_3[4] \oplus \Delta C_3[7]) \lll 1) \oplus$$
$$((\Delta C_3[0] \oplus \Delta C_3[4] \oplus \Delta C_3[6] \oplus \Delta C_3[7]) \lll 2),$$
$$\text{Index (13)} : C_3^{j_0}[2] \oplus (C_3^{j_0}[4] \lll 1) \oplus C_3^{j_0}[5] \oplus (C_3^{j_0}[6] \lll 2) \oplus$$
$$((C_3^{j_0}[1] \oplus C_3^{j_0}[4] \oplus C_3^{j_0}[7]) \lll 3) \oplus ((C_3^{j_0}[0] \oplus C_3^{j_0}[6]) \lll 4)$$
$$= C_3^{j_1}[2] \oplus (C_3^{j_1}[4] \lll 1) \oplus C_3^{j_1}[5] \oplus (C_3^{j_1}[6] \lll 2) \oplus$$
$$((C_3^{j_1}[1] \oplus C_3^{j_1}[4] \oplus C_3^{j_1}[7]) \lll 3) \oplus ((C_3^{j_1}[0] \oplus C_3^{j_1}[6]) \lll 4)$$
$$\Rightarrow \quad \Delta C_3[5] = \Delta C_3[2] \oplus (\Delta C_3[4] \lll 1) \oplus (\Delta C_3[6] \lll 2) \oplus ((\Delta C_3[1]$$
$$\oplus \Delta C_3[4] \oplus \Delta C_3[7]) \lll 3) \oplus ((\Delta C_3[0] \oplus \Delta C_3[6]) \lll 4),$$

so under a plaintext structure we have the above guarantee after letting

$$\eta_4 = C_3^{j_0}[1] \oplus C_3^{j_1}[1] \oplus C_3^{j_0}[4] \oplus C_3^{j_1}[4] \oplus C_3^{j_0}[7] \oplus C_3^{j_1}[7] \oplus$$
$$((C_3^{j_0}[0] \oplus C_3^{j_1}[0] \oplus C_3^{j_0}[6] \oplus C_3^{j_1}[6]) \lll 1)$$
$$= \Delta C_3[1] \oplus \Delta C_3[4] \oplus \Delta C_3[7] \oplus ((\Delta C_3[0] \oplus \Delta C_3[6]) \lll 1),$$
$$\gamma_1^{13} = C_3^{j_0}[0] \oplus C_3^{j_1}[0] = \Delta C_3[0],$$

$$\gamma_2^{13} = C_3^{j_0}[4] \oplus C_3^{j_1}[4] \oplus ((C_3^{j_0}[6] \oplus C_3^{j_1}[6]) \lll 1) \oplus C_3^{j_0}[7] \oplus C_3^{j_1}[7]$$
$$= \Delta C_3[4] \oplus (\Delta C_3[6] \lll 1) \oplus \Delta C_3[7],$$
$$\gamma_3^{13} = C_3^{j_0}[2] \oplus C_3^{j_1}[2] \oplus ((C_3^{j_0}[4] \oplus C_3^{j_1}[4] \oplus C_3^{j_0}[7] \oplus C_3^{j_1}[7]) \lll 1) \oplus$$
$$((C_3^{j_0}[6] \oplus C_3^{j_1}[6]) \lll 2)$$
$$= \Delta C_3[2] \oplus ((\Delta C_3[4] \oplus \Delta C_3[7]) \lll 1) \oplus (\Delta C_3[6] \lll 2),$$
$$\gamma_4^{13} = C_3^{j_0}[6] \oplus C_3^{j_1}[6] \oplus ((C_3^{j_0}[0] \oplus C_3^{j_1}[0] \oplus C_3^{j_0}[6] \oplus C_3^{j_1}[6]) \lll 2) \oplus$$
$$((C_3^{j_0}[1] \oplus C_3^{j_1}[1] \oplus C_3^{j_0}[4] \oplus C_3^{j_1}[4] \oplus C_3^{j_0}[7] \oplus C_3^{j_1}[7]) \lll 1)$$
$$= \Delta C_3[6] \oplus ((\Delta C_3[0] \oplus \Delta C_3[6]) \lll 2) \oplus$$
$$((\Delta C_3[1] \oplus \Delta C_3[4] \oplus \Delta C_3[7]) \lll 1),$$
$$\gamma_5^{13} = C_3^{j_0}[7] \oplus C_3^{j_1}[7] \oplus ((C_3^{j_0}[0] \oplus C_3^{j_1}[0] \oplus C_3^{j_0}[6] \oplus C_3^{j_1}[6]) \lll 3) \oplus$$
$$((C_3^{j_0}[1] \oplus C_3^{j_1}[1] \oplus C_3^{j_0}[4] \oplus C_3^{j_1}[4] \oplus C_3^{j_0}[7] \oplus C_3^{j_1}[7]) \lll 2)$$
$$= \Delta C_3[7] \oplus ((\Delta C_3[0] \oplus \Delta C_3[6]) \lll 3) \oplus$$
$$((\Delta C_3[1] \oplus \Delta C_3[4] \oplus \Delta C_3[7]) \lll 2).$$

– Indexes (14)–(16) guarantee that $C_0^{j_0} \oplus C_0^{j_1} \oplus C_2^{j_0} \oplus C_2^{j_1} = \Delta X_3^{13} = 0x0\gamma_0^{12}0\gamma_1^{12}$ $(\gamma_2^{12} \oplus (\gamma_1^{12} \lll 1))(\gamma_2^{12} \lll 1)((\gamma_0^{12} \lll 1) \oplus \gamma_1^{12})(\gamma_2^{12} \oplus (\gamma_0^{12} \lll 2))$, where $\gamma_0^{12}, \gamma_1^{12}, \gamma_2^{12}$ are indeterminate nibble differences. This is because

Index (14) : $((C_0^{j_0}[3] \oplus C_2^{j_0}[3]) \lll 1) \oplus C_0^{j_0}[4] \oplus C_2^{j_0}[4] \oplus$
$$((C_0^{j_0}[5] \oplus C_2^{j_0}[5]) \ggg 1) = ((C_0^{j_1}[3] \oplus C_2^{j_1}[3]) \lll 1) \oplus$$
$$C_0^{j_1}[4] \oplus C_2^{j_1}[4] \oplus ((C_0^{j_1}[5] \oplus C_2^{j_1}[5]) \ggg 1)$$
$$\Rightarrow \quad \Delta C_0[4] \oplus \Delta C_2[4] = ((\Delta C_0[3] \oplus \Delta C_2[3]) \lll 1) \oplus$$
$$((\Delta C_0[5] \oplus \Delta C_2[5]) \ggg 1),$$

Index (15) : $((C_0^{j_0}[1] \oplus C_2^{j_0}[1]) \lll 1) \oplus C_0^{j_0}[3] \oplus C_2^{j_0}[3] \oplus C_0^{j_0}[6] \oplus C_2^{j_0}[6] =$
$$((C_0^{j_1}[1] \oplus C_2^{j_1}[1]) \lll 1) \oplus C_0^{j_1}[3] \oplus C_2^{j_1}[3] \oplus C_0^{j_1}[6] \oplus C_2^{j_1}[6]$$
$$\Rightarrow \quad \Delta C_0[6] \oplus \Delta C_2[6] = ((\Delta C_0[1] \oplus \Delta C_2[1]) \lll 1) \oplus$$
$$\Delta C_0[3] \oplus \Delta C_2[3],$$

Index (16) : $((C_0^{j_0}[1] \oplus C_2^{j_0}[1]) \lll 2) \oplus ((C_0^{j_0}[5] \oplus C_2^{j_0}[5]) \ggg 1) \oplus$
$$C_0^{j_0}[7] \oplus C_2^{j_0}[7] = ((C_0^{j_1}[1] \oplus C_2^{j_1}[1]) \lll 2) \oplus$$
$$((C_0^{j_1}[5] \oplus C_2^{j_1}[5]) \ggg 1) \oplus C_0^{j_1}[7] \oplus C_2^{j_1}[7]$$
$$\Rightarrow \quad \Delta C_0[7] \oplus \Delta C_2[7] = ((\Delta C_0[1] \oplus \Delta C_2[1]) \lll 2) \oplus$$
$$((\Delta C_0[5] \oplus \Delta C_2[5]) \ggg 1),$$

so under a plaintext structure we have the above guarantee after letting

$$\gamma_0^{12} = C_0^{j_0}[1] \oplus C_0^{j_1}[1] \oplus C_2^{j_0}[1] \oplus C_2^{j_1}[1] = \Delta C_0[1] \oplus \Delta C_2[1],$$
$$\gamma_1^{12} = C_0^{j_0}[3] \oplus C_0^{j_1}[3] \oplus C_2^{j_0}[3] \oplus C_2^{j_1}[3] = \Delta C_0[3] \oplus \Delta C_2[3],$$
$$\gamma_2^{12} = (C_0^{j_0}[5] \oplus C_0^{j_1}[5] \oplus C_2^{j_0}[5] \oplus C_2^{j_1}[5]) \ggg 1 = (\Delta C_0[5] \oplus \Delta C_2[5]) \ggg 1.$$

– Index (17) guarantees that $C_1^{j_0}[0,2,3,4,5] \oplus C_1^{j_1}[0,2,3,4,5] = \Delta X_1^{14}[0,2,3,4,5] = \Delta X_3^{14}[0,2,3,4,5] = C_3^{j_0}[0,2,3,4,5] \oplus C_3^{j_1}[0,2,3,4,5]$, because

$$\text{Index } (17) : C_1^{j_0}[0,2,3,4,5] \oplus C_3^{j_0}[0,2,3,4,5] =$$
$$C_1^{j_1}[0,2,3,4,5] \oplus C_3^{j_1}[0,2,3,4,5]$$
$$\Rightarrow \quad \Delta C_1[0,2,3,4,5] = \Delta C_3[0,2,3,4,5].$$

– Indexes (18) and (19) guarantee that $C_1^{j_0} \oplus C_1^{j_1} \oplus C_3^{j_0} \oplus C_3^{j_1} = \Delta X_0^{13} = 0x0\eta_5 0000(\eta_5 \lll 1)(\eta_5 \lll 2)$, where η_5 is an indeterminate nibble difference. This is because

$$\text{Index } (18) : C_1^{j_0}[1] \oplus C_3^{j_0}[1] \oplus (C_1^{j_0}[6] \ggg 1) \oplus (C_3^{j_0}[6] \ggg 1) =$$
$$C_1^{j_1}[1] \oplus C_3^{j_1}[1] \oplus (C_1^{j_1}[6] \ggg 1) \oplus (C_3^{j_1}[6] \ggg 1)$$
$$\Rightarrow \quad \Delta C_1[6] \oplus \Delta C_3[6] = (\Delta C_1[1] \oplus \Delta C_3[1]) \lll 1,$$
$$\text{Index } (19) : C_1^{j_0}[1] \oplus C_3^{j_0}[1] \oplus (C_1^{j_0}[7] \ggg 2) \oplus (C_3^{j_0}[7] \ggg 2) =$$
$$C_1^{j_1}[1] \oplus C_3^{j_1}[1] \oplus (C_1^{j_1}[7] \ggg 2) \oplus (C_3^{j_1}[7] \ggg 2)$$
$$\Rightarrow \quad \Delta C_1[7] \oplus \Delta C_3[7] = (\Delta C_1[1] \oplus \Delta C_3[1]) \lll 2,$$

so under a plaintext structure we have the above guarantee after letting

$$\eta_5 = C_1^{j_0}[1] \oplus C_1^{j_1}[1] \oplus C_3^{j_0}[1] \oplus C_3^{j_1}[1] = \Delta C_1[1] \oplus \Delta C_3[1].$$

References

1. Biham, E., Shamir, A.: Differential Cryptanalysis of the Data Encryption Standard. Springer, New York (1993). https://doi.org/10.1007/978-1-4613-9314-6
2. Biham, E., Biryukov, A., Shamir, A.: Cryptanalysis of skipjack reduced to 31 rounds using impossible differentials. In: Stern, J. (ed.) EUROCRYPT 1999. LNCS, vol. 1592, pp. 12–23. Springer, Heidelberg (1999). https://doi.org/10.1007/3-540-48910-X_2
3. Biham, E., Biryukov, A., Shamir, A.: Miss in the middle attacks on IDEA and Khufu. In: Knudsen, L. (ed.) FSE 1999. LNCS, vol. 1636, pp. 124–138. Springer, Heidelberg (1999). https://doi.org/10.1007/3-540-48519-8_10
4. Feng, X., et al.: On the lightweight block cipher FBC. J. Cryptol. Res. **6**, 768–785 (2019)
5. Knudsen, L.R.: DEAL – a 128-bit block cipher. Technical report, Department of Informatics, University of Bergen, Norway (1998)
6. Matsui, M.: Linear cryptanalysis method for DES cipher. In: Helleseth, T. (ed.) EUROCRYPT 1993. LNCS, vol. 765, pp. 386–397. Springer, Heidelberg (1994). https://doi.org/10.1007/3-540-48285-7_33
7. Ren, B., Chen, J., Zhou, S., Jin, X., Xia, Z., Liang, K.: Cryptanalysis of raindrop and FBC. In: Liu, J.K., Huang, X. (eds.) NSS 2019. LNCS, vol. 11928, pp. 536–551. Springer, Cham (2019). https://doi.org/10.1007/978-3-030-36938-5_33
8. Zhang, Y., Liu, G., Li, C., Shen, X.: Impossible differential cryptanalysis of FBC-128. J. Inf. Secur. Appl. **69**, 103279 (2022)

Fregata: Faster Homomorphic Evaluation of AES via TFHE

Benqiang Wei[1,2], Ruida Wang[1,2], Zhihao Li[1,2], Qinju Liu[1,2], and Xianhui Lu[1,2(✉)]

[1] State Key Laboratory of Information Security, Institute of Information Engineering, Chinese Academy of Sciences, Beijing, China
luxianhui@iie.ac.cn
[2] School of Cyber Security, University of Chinese Academy of Sciences, Beijing, China

Abstract. Gentry et al. [26] first presented a homomorphic evaluation of the AES-128 based on the BGV scheme, however, it suffered from high evaluation latency. Despite considerable efforts have been directed towards designing FHE-friendly symmetric encryption algorithms, the efficient homomorphic evaluation of the well-studied and standardized AES remains an attractive challenge for researchers in the transciphering community.

In this paper, we present a novel homomorphic evaluation framework based on the TFHE scheme, demonstrating the optimal latency for AES-128 evaluation. Specifically, we propose mixed packing to achieve efficient S-box evaluation and an optimized circuit bootstrapping as a bridge to connect the whole evaluation framework. Furthermore, we show the versatility of our evaluation framework by extending it to other ciphers, such as SM4. To validate the effectiveness of our proposed framework, we conduct implementation experiments, which indicate that the evaluation of AES takes 86 s on a single core, a 3× improvement over the state-of-the-art [39]. Moreover, with a 16-thread parallel implementation, it takes about 9 s. For SM4 evaluation, it takes only 78 s on a single core, about 73× improvement compared to publicly available BGV-based solution [40].

Keywords: TFHE · Transciphering · AES · Circuit bootstrapping

1 Introduction

Fully homomorphic encryption (FHE) enables the computation of arbitrary functions to be performed on encrypted data without decryption. Prior to 2009, FHE had been considered an open problem until Gentry proposed the first feasible fully homomorphic encryption based in ideal lattices [25]. This seminal work starts the prelude to the booming development of fully homomorphic encryption. Some representative schemes include BGV [6], BFV [5,24], CKKS [10], FHEW [23], TFHE [11,12], Final [3] and [30].

© The Author(s), under exclusive license to Springer Nature Switzerland AG 2023
E. Athanasopoulos and B. Mennink (Eds.): ISC 2023, LNCS 14411, pp. 392–412, 2023.
https://doi.org/10.1007/978-3-031-49187-0_20

However, the size of homomorphic ciphertext is generally several orders of magnitude larger than the corresponding plaintext, as a result, the data sender would suffer from large ciphertext expansion and communication cost, particularly on the embedded devices with limited bandwidth, memory and computing power. To address this problem, transciphering is firstly proposed by Naehrig et al. [36]. The main idea behind transciphering is that instead of using homomorphic encryption to encrypt data, the client sends the data encrypted by symmetric encryption ($\mathcal{E}$) to the server. Then, the server homomorphically evaluates the symmetric encryption scheme's decryption circuit ($\mathcal{E}^{-1}$) to convert the symmetrically-encrypted data ($\mathcal{E}(m)$) into homomorphic ciphertext. Afterward, the server can proceed to perform the actual function on homomorphic ciphertext. Therefore, the homomorphic evaluation of $\mathcal{E}^{-1}$ becomes a critical problem within the transciphering framework.

The Advanced Encryption Standard (AES) is a widely embraced block encryption standard by the United States federal government, known for its efficiency and prevalent use in securing sensitive information across diverse applications. Therefore, AES stands as one of the top choices for application in the transciphering framework. However, despite its popularity, current research widely acknowledges that AES is not inherently well-suited as an FHE-friendly symmetric encryption scheme. The primary limitation lies in its exceptionally high multiplicative depth, leading to significantly long latency during homomorphic evaluation. To address this issue, some researchers have shifted their focus on designing FHE-friendly symmetric encryption algorithms like LowMC [1], Chaghri [2], Rubato [28], Pasta [20], Elisabeth [16]. However, none of these alternatives have been standardized, and some have been found to be vulnerable to attacks. The efficient homomorphic evaluation of the well-studied and standardized AES remains an attractive challenge for researchers in the transciphering community. Consequently, extensive efforts have been dedicated to improving the homomorphic evaluation latency of AES to make it more amenable to fully homomorphic encryption.

State-of-the-Art. Early in 2012, Gentry et al. [26] presented the first homomorphic evaluation of the AES circuit based on the BGV scheme. The main breakthrough in their work is the homomorphic evaluation of the S-box, which converts the inverse X^{-1} of the finite field $\mathbb{F}_{2^8}$ into the multiplication X^{254}, requiring only three multiplicative depths by leveraging the frobenius automorphism. Overall, the multiplicative depth required to evaluate AES-128 is 40. And they provided two versions of implementation: (1) leveled evaluation version (no bootstrapping): this version demands larger encryption parameter sets but has a relatively shorter latency of about 4 min, resulting in a throughput of 2 s per block. However, it comes with the limitation of not supporting the evaluation of further operations beyond the current computation. (2) bootstrapping version: this version allows for the use of smaller parameters, but the overall evaluation latency increases to up to 18 min due to the use of bootstrapping, resulting in a throughput of 5.8 s per block. Despite the longer delay, this allows further calculations after the homomorphic execution of the AES.

The TFHE scheme supports faster bootstrapping, in particular the introduction of functional bootstrapping [4], which provides a powerful tool to support lookup table calculation for arbitrary functions. Stracovsky et al. [38] reported that they utilized functional bootstrapping technique to evaluate a single block of AES in 4 min. Note that they utilize 16 threads to process 16 bytes in the state matrix in parallel. But they did not provide detailed implementation, only a poster presentation was made at FHE.org in 2022. Recently Trama et al. [39] conducted a comprehensive analysis of a faster AES evaluation implementation based on functional bootstrapping and multi-value bootstrapping techniques. Specifically, instead of directly encrypting a byte, they divide 8-bit into two 4-bit messages to be encrypted, allowing them to use smaller parameters. Thus, for XOR, S-box and multiplication operations on 8-bit message in the encrypted domain, they are transformed into operations between 4-bit messages and evaluated by functional bootstrapping lookup tables. Finally, they evaluated an AES block in 4.5 min using sequential execution on a standard laptop. Indeed, functional bootstrapping is effective for handling S-box lookup table calculation efficiently, but it may be not efficient enough for a substantial number of XOR and multiplication operations. Relying on functional bootstrapping for these operations lead to a reduction in the overall evaluation efficiency. Moreover, the latency for the parallel implementation using 16 cores is about 28 s and still much lower than the amortization time of the BGV-based scheme. An intriguing question arises:

Whether the homomorphic evaluation latency of an AES block based on the TFHE scheme can approach or even reach the same amortization time as that achieved by the BGV-based scheme?

1.1 Contributions

In this paper, we present a novel evaluation framework for faster AES homomorphic evaluation. Specifically, instead of relying on expensive functional bootstrapping, we use inexpensive CMUX gate as the base unit and propose mixed packing technique for efficient S-box evaluation. We also incorporate optimized circuit bootstrapping as a bridge of the framework to speed up the overall evaluation efficiency. We also show that our new evaluation framework can be extended to other Feistel structure ciphers, such as SM4.

Finally, we implemented our proposed framework based on the TFHEpp homomorphic encryption library [34]. Experiment results demonstrate remarkable performance improvements for both AES and SM4 homomorphic evaluation. For AES, the evaluation time of a single block takes only 86 s with a single thread, which is a 3× improvement compared to the state-of-the-art [39]. With 16-thread parallelization, the evaluation time reduces to approximately 9 s, which is very close to the amortization time of the BGV method. For SM4, the evaluation time is about 78 s, a 73× improvement when compared to publicly available BGV-based approach [40].

1.2   Related Works

The homomorphic evaluation of AES has been studied using various homomorphic encryption schemes, in addition to the BGV-based approach presented by Gentry et al. [26]. Cheon et al. [9] evaluated the AES circuit based on vDGHV [18] scheme that supports integer batch processing, and Coron et al. [15] used a variant of vDGHV scheme with the scale-invariant property. Doröz et al. [21] proposed the AES evaluation based on the modified LTV scheme. However, their evaluation efficiency is still unsatisfactory.

Although AES has an algebraic structure that matches well with the plaintext space of some homomorphic encryption schemes, it is not trivial and has great multiplicative depth, resulting very long evaluation time. Therefore, some works attempt to perform the homomorphic evaluation on lightweight block ciphers with low evaluation depth, such as SIMON [31] and Prince [22] algorithm. Moreover, symmetric ciphers with low multiplicative depth are designed for FHE, such as block cipher LowMC [1].

Since stream ciphers only involve XOR operations in the process of encryption and decryption, thus key generation can be done offline in advance, new stream cipher design criteria for FHE is to minimize the multiplicative complexity and depth of the algorithm, such as FLIP [35], Kreyvium [7], Rasta [19] and its variants Dasta [29], Masta [27], Pasta [20], Fasta [14] and Elisabeth [16].

1.3   Organization.

We first review the TFHE scheme and give a brief introduction to different bootstrapping types in Sect. 2. In Sect. 3, we provide a short specification of AES. A novel framework is proposed to evaluate AES in Sect. 4. We demonstrate the scalability of our evaluation framework by giving an efficient evaluation implementation of SM4 in Sect. 5. Implementation results and performance analysis are provided in Sect. 6. Our conclusion is shown in Sect. 7.

2   Preliminaries

2.1   Notations

We denote by λ the security parameter. The set $\{0,1\}$ is written as $\mathbb{B}$. The real torus $\mathbb{T} = \mathbb{R}/\mathbb{Z}$ is the set of real numbers modulo 1. $\mathfrak{R}$ is the ring $\mathbb{Z}[X]/(X^N+1)$ of integer polynomials modulo $X^N + 1$, and $\mathbb{T}_N[X]$ is $\mathbb{R}[X]/(X^N+1)$ mod 1 of torus polynomials, where N is a power of 2. $\mathbb{B}_N[X]$ denotes the polynomials with binary coefficients. Note that $\mathbb{T}$ is a $\mathbb{Z}$-module and $\mathbb{T}_N[X]$ is a $\mathfrak{R}$-module. We use $< \cdot >$ to denote the inner product.

2.2   The TFHE Scheme

In this subsection, we will review the TFHE scheme. TFHE is a fully homomorphic encryption scheme proposed by Chillotti et al. [11], which is based on the (ring) learning with errors [33,37] problem. There are three main forms of ciphertext in TFHE, which are summarized as follows:

– **TLWE ciphertext:** TLWE encrypts a plaintext value $\mu \in \mathbb{T}$ into a ciphertext $(\vec{a}, b) \in \mathbb{T}^{n+1}$, where $b = <\vec{a}, \vec{s}> + \mu + e$, the vector $\vec{a}$ is uniformly sampled from $\mathbb{T}^n$, the secret key $\vec{s}$ is uniformly sampled from $\mathbb{B}^n$, and the error $e \in \mathbb{T}$ is sampled from a Gaussian distribution with mean 0 and standard deviation σ.

– **TRLWE ciphertext:** TRLWE encrypts a plaintext polynomial $\mu(x) \in \mathbb{T}_N[X]$ into a ciphertext $(\vec{a}, b) \in \mathbb{T}_N[X]^{k+1}$, where $b = <\vec{a}, \vec{s}> + \mu + e$, the vector $\vec{a}$ is uniformly sampled from $\mathbb{T}_N[X]^k$, the secret key $\vec{s}$ is uniformly sampled from $\mathbb{B}_N[X]^k$, and the error $e \in \mathbb{T}_N[X]$ is a polynomial with random coefficients $e_i \in \mathbb{T}$ sampled from a Gaussian distribution with mean 0 and standard deviation σ. If omitted, $k = 1$.

– **TRGSW ciphertext:** TRGSW encrypts the message $\mu \in \mathfrak{R}$ into $C = Z + \mu \cdot G \in \mathcal{M}_{(k+1)l,k+1}(\mathbb{T}_N[X])$, where $Z \in \mathcal{M}_{(k+1)l,k+1}(\mathbb{T}_N[X])$ is matrix such that each line is a random **TRLWE** ciphertext of 0 under the same key, and G is gadget matrix which is used to control the noise propagation.

2.3   Homomorphic Arithmetic of TFHE

In this subsection, we briefly revisit some algorithms in the TFHE scheme.

Controlled Mux Gate. There are two kinds of controlled Mux gates as follows, one built by gate bootstrapping, named bootsMUX and the other by external product, called CMUX.

– $bootsMUX(c, d_0, d_1) = c?d_1 : d_0 = (c \wedge d_1) \oplus ((1 - c) \wedge d_0)$
– $CMUX(c, d_1, d_0) = c \boxdot (d_1 - d_0) + d_0$, where $\boxdot$ denotes the external product TRGSW × TRLWE → TRLWE.

Key Switching. In [12], Chillotti et al. proposed two kinds of Key Switching. The first one is *Public Functional KeySwitching*, which allows switching from TLWE to T(R)LWE samples, such as packing TLWE samples into TRLWE sample or switching secret key. It can also evaluate the public linear function f on the input TLWE samples. The second one is *Private Functional KeySwitching*. The private linear function on the input TLWE samples is evaluated by encoding the secret f into the KeySwitch key.

Blind Rotation. Blind rotation is the core operation of TFHE bootstrapping. It rotates the coefficients of test polynomial blindly using encrypted numbers. The blind rotation operation is mainly constructed by the external product, and its complexity comes from the frequent transformations of FFT and IFFT.

2.4   Bootstrapping Types of TFHE

There are several types of bootstrapping involved in the TFHE scheme, we summarize as follows.

Functional Bootstrapping (FBS). The most important feature of TFHE is the so-called gate bootstrapping. The term gate bootstrapping refers to the fact that every gate evaluation is followed by fast bootstrapping. For example, homomorphic NAND gate is $bootsNAND(c_1, c_2) = Bootstrap((\vec{0}, \frac{5}{8}) - c_1 - c_2)$. Functional bootstrapping (or programmable bootstrapping, PBS) was firstly proposed by Boura et al. [4]. The technique is an extension of TFHE gate bootstrapping, which allows to reset the noise to a fixed level and evaluates an arbitrary function on the input at the same time. In more detail, the test polynomial can encode all function values in a discrete manner, then lookup table (LUT) evaluation is performed by using LWE ciphertext as a selector in Blind Rotation.

Multi-Value Bootstrapping (MVBS). Carpov et al. [8] firstly introduced a multi-value bootstrapping technique, which supports the evaluation of multiple functions on the same input ciphertext using only one blind rotation. Firstly, extract a common function v from all functions (TV_{F_i}), then use the input ciphertext to blindly rotate test polynomial v, finally $\frac{TV_{F_i}}{v}$ (with small norm coefficient) is multiplied by accumulator ACC to obtain the functional result respectively.

An alternative multi-value bootstrapping technique, PBSmanyLUT, was proposed by Chillotti et al. [13]. PBSmanyLUT firstly uses modulus switching to set some of the lowest bits of the phase to zero so that all function values can be encoded in a test polynomial. Then only one blind rotation is utilized to obtain all desired function values.

Circuit Bootstrapping (CBS). Circuit bootstrapping, proposed in [12], can convert a TLWE sample with large noise amplitude over binary message space (e.g., amplitude $\frac{1}{4}$ over $\{0, \frac{1}{2}\}$) to a TRGSW sample with a lower noise over the integer message space $\{0, 1\}$, which is 10 times more expensive than the gate bootstrapping, but enables the possibility of fully composable CMUX circuits.

3   Specification of AES

AES-128, being the variant of AES with a 128-bit key, operates on a 128-bit plaintext message (16 bytes), which is represented as a state matrix. The AES encryption process comprises multiple rounds (in this case, 10 rounds for AES-128), each consisting of four main operations: SubBytes, ShiftRows, MixColumns, and AddRoundKey. These operations are applied to the state matrix iteratively to achieve encryption. The state matrix is organized as a 4×4 array of bytes, where each byte represents a single element of the state matrix as follows.

$$\begin{pmatrix} A_0 & A_4 & A_8 & A_{12} \\ A_1 & A_5 & A_9 & A_{13} \\ A_2 & A_6 & A_{10} & A_{14} \\ A_3 & A_7 & A_{11} & A_{15} \end{pmatrix}$$

- **SubBytes:** Also known as S-box, the S-box transforms each element of state matrix non-linearly using a lookup table with special mathematical properties:

$$\begin{pmatrix} B_0 & B_4 & B_8 & B_{12} \\ B_1 & B_5 & B_9 & B_{13} \\ B_2 & B_6 & B_{10} & B_{14} \\ B_3 & B_7 & B_{11} & B_{15} \end{pmatrix} = \begin{pmatrix} S(A_0) & S(A_4) & S(A_8) & S(A_{12}) \\ S(A_1) & S(A_5) & S(A_9) & S(A_{13}) \\ S(A_2) & S(A_6) & S(A_{10}) & S(A_{14}) \\ S(A_3) & S(A_7) & S(A_{11}) & S(A_{15}) \end{pmatrix}$$

- **ShiftRows:** In a 4×4 state matrix, the first row remains unchanged, while the second row undergoes a cyclic shift to the left by one byte. Similarly, the third row is shifted cyclically to the left by two bytes, and the fourth row is shifted cyclically to the left by three bytes.
- **MixColumns:** This is essentially a multiplication operation of the state matrix and fixed scalar matrix:

$$\begin{pmatrix} C_0 & C_4 & C_8 & C_{12} \\ C_1 & C_5 & C_9 & C_{13} \\ C_2 & C_6 & C_{10} & C_{14} \\ C_3 & C_7 & C_{11} & C_{15} \end{pmatrix} = \begin{pmatrix} 02 & 03 & 01 & 01 \\ 01 & 02 & 03 & 01 \\ 01 & 01 & 02 & 03 \\ 03 & 01 & 01 & 02 \end{pmatrix} \begin{pmatrix} B_0 & B_4 & B_8 & B_{12} \\ B_5 & B_9 & B_{13} & B_1 \\ B_{10} & B_{14} & B_2 & B_6 \\ B_{15} & B_3 & B_7 & B_{11} \end{pmatrix}$$

- **AddRoundKey:** Key addition is very simple, it refers to performing bitwise XOR of state matrix C_i with the current round key. All round keys are generated in advance by the key schedule, and each round key is also 16 bytes (128 bits).

Notice that there is one more AddRoundKey operation before the first round starts. And in the last round, no MixColumns operation is performed.

4   Homomorphic Evaluation of AES

In the TFHE scheme, gate bootstrapping or functional bootstrapping implements the computation of the accumulator through the successive CMUX gates, that is to say, assuming that the dimension of TLWE ciphertext is n, then the computation cost of a gate bootstrapping is about n times that of external multiplication. Thus, we consider using a cheaper CMUX as basic gate, constructed by the external multiplication of TRGSW and TRLWE ciphertext, to evaluate the S-box. However, note that the output ciphertext form of external multiplication is TRLWE. When we move to the next round of evaluation of AES, we need TRGSW ciphertext as the selector ciphertext. Thus, in order to address this incompatibility, the circuit bootstrapping must be used to convert TLWE ciphertext to TRGSW ciphertext to maintain the operation of the whole circuit. Meanwhile, in order to efficiently evaluate the XOR operation in AddRoundKey, we choose to encode the message $\{0,1\}$ to $\{0,1/2\}$ over Torus, which makes XOR to be simple addition.

In [12], the authors give three packing techniques to optimize lookup table: horizontal packing, vertical packing and mixed packing. Next, in Sect. 4.1, we analyze the cost of their application to the S-box. Circuit bootstrapping, as a bridge for ciphertext conversion, would be the bottleneck of the whole computation. We combine the recently proposed PBSmanyLUT technique [13] to reduce the internal computational cost in Sect. 4.2. Our full description of the AES evaluation is shown in Sect. 4.3.

4.1 Discussion on S-Box Lookup Table

For an 8-to-8-bit S-box lookup table, its output table size is 256×8. Specifically, in the parameter settings we assume the degree of the ring polynomial $N = 1024$ and give a customized lookup table optimization algorithm for the S-box. Next, we analyze the effect of different packing methods on S-box evaluation optimization. Notice that we now assume that the ciphertext form of all selector bits is TRGSW.

- Horizontal packing: We can pack each line of the output result as a TRLWE ciphertext, each S-box lookup table can get the lookup results at the same time using $128 + 64 + 32 + 16 + 8 + 4 + 2 + 1 = 255$ CMUX gates, located in the first 8 coefficients of the result TRLWE ciphertext, so we can reduce CMUX consumption by 8 times compared with no packing.
- Vertical packing: We can pack each column of the output result as a TRLWE sample, and then use the blind rotation algorithm for each TRLWE ciphertext to obtain the desired value, which is located at the constant term position of each resulting TRLWE ciphertext. Each blind rotation requires 8 CMUX gates, thus, we need $8 \times 8 = 64$ CMUX gates in total in one S-box evaluation, decreasing by a factor of 32 CMUX consumption compared with no packing.
- Mixed packing: here $2^8 \cdot 8 = 2 \cdot N = 2048$, we can combine horizontal and vertical packing to pack all the output results into two TRLWE ciphertexts. Firstly, we use the last one TRGSW ciphertext to pick out the target TRLWE through one CMUX gate, and then use the remaining 7 TRGSW samples to perform the blind rotation on the target TRLWE, the desired value would be located in the first 8 positions of the resulting TRLWE. In this way, we only need to use 8 CMUX gates to implement the evaluation of the S-box.

Based on the above analysis, we choose to use mixed packing to accelerate the evaluation of the S-box further. It is noted that to be compatible with other operations of AES, we just need to use the SampleExtract algorithm to obtain the corresponding TLWE without any cost. And finally, we use KeySwitch algorithm to switch the dimension of TLWE ciphertext. Our S-box lookup table combined with mixed packing is shown in Algorithm 1.

4.2 Optimization of Circuit Bootstrapping

Circuit bootstrapping, as a bridge, can convert TLWE to TRGSW ciphertext, connecting the entire leveled evaluation circuit. The authors of [12] observed that each line of TRGSW is TRLWE ciphertext encrypting the message $\mu \cdot s_i \cdot \frac{1}{\mathcal{B}^j}$ for $1 \leq i \leq k + 1$ and $1 \leq j \leq \ell$. Thus the core idea of circuit bootstrapping

---

Algorithm 1. LUTMixedPacking

Input: Eight TRGSW ciphertexts $C_0, \cdots, C_7$
Input: Two TRLWE ciphertexts used for packing S-box d_0, d_1
Output: Eight TLWE ciphertexts $c_0, \cdots, c_7$
1: ACC $\leftarrow$ CMUX(C_7, d_1, d_0)
2: **for** $i = 0$ to 6 **do**
3:     ACC $\leftarrow$ CMUX($C_i, X^{-8 \cdot 2^i \pmod{2N}} \cdot$ ACC, ACC)
4: **end for**
5: **for** $i = 0$ to 7 **do**
6:     $c_i' \leftarrow$ SampleExtract(ACC, i)
7:     $c_i \leftarrow$ KeySwitch(c_i')
8: **end for**
9: **return** $c_0, \cdots, c_7$

---

is to reconstruct each TRLWE ciphertext in the TRGSW ciphertext using the TLWE ciphertext, which runs about 0.137 s for a 110-bit security parameter. Circuit bootstrapping algorithm is divided into two steps:

- The first step converts the TLWE encryption of μ into the TLWE ciphertexts $\mu \cdot \frac{1}{\mathfrak{B}^j}$ using the ℓ TFHE functional bootstrapping technique, which accounts for about 70% of the total time.
- The second step is to multiply the secret key s_i to the TLWE ciphertext obtained in the previous step using the $(k + 1)\ell$ private key switching algorithm, which accounts for 30% of the total time.

It is worth noting that since the input TLWE ciphertext is the same in the first step, ℓ bootstrapping operations can be optimized by multi-value bootstrapping [8] or PBSmanyLUT technique [13]. In detail, multi-value bootstrapping supports the evaluation of multiple functions on the same input using only one blind rotation. Firstly, extract a common function v_0 from all functions TV_{F_i}, then use the input ciphertext to blindly rotate test polynomial v_0, finally TV_{F_i}/v_0(with small norm coefficient) is multiplied by accumulator ACC to obtain the result respectively. The PBSmanyLUT first uses the modulus switching to set some lowest bits of the phase to zero, and then uses just one blind rotation to obtain all the function values, it must be noted that we need to set the test polynomial accordingly. The resultant ciphertext produced by PBSmanyLUT has less noise compared with multi-value bootstrapping, so we use PBSmanyLUT to accelerate the first step of circuit bootstrapping.

Recall that our message space of TLWE is the entire Torus, however, the LUT evaluation can only compute polynomial functions with negacyclic property due to the fact that $X^{i+N} \equiv -X^i \bmod X^N + 1$. We set a new test polynomial that satisfies this property for PBSmanyLUT as follows:

$$P(X) = \sum_{i=0}^{\frac{N}{2^\rho \cdot 2}-1} \sum_{j=0}^{2^\rho-1} (-1) \cdot \frac{1}{2\mathfrak{B}^j} X^{2^\rho \cdot i + j} + \sum_{i=\frac{N}{2^\rho \cdot 2}}^{\frac{N}{2^\rho}-1} \sum_{j=0}^{2^\rho-1} \frac{1}{2\mathfrak{B}^j} X^{2^\rho \cdot i + j}$$

where $\rho = \lceil \log_2(\ell) \rceil$ and $\mathfrak{B}$ is the basis of gadget. Then, the ℓ independent bootstrappings in circuit bootstrapping could be replaced by:

$$\begin{cases} \{\mathrm{ct}_i\}_{i\in[1,\ell]} \leftarrow \mathbf{PBSmanyLUT}\left(\mathrm{ct}_{\mathrm{in}}, \mathrm{BSK}, P(x) \cdot X^{N/2^{\rho+1}}, 1, 0, \rho\right) \\ \forall i \in [1,\ell], \mathrm{ct}_i + \left(0, \frac{1}{2\mathfrak{B}^i}\right) \end{cases}$$

For more details on $\mathbf{PBSmanyLUT}$ please refer to Algorithm 6 of [13], and the proof is the same as Lemma 4 of [13]. Our circuit bootstrapping combined with the PBSmanyLUT technique is presented in Algorithm 2.

Algorithm 2. CBwithPBSmanyLUT

Input: a test polynomial $P(X)$
Input: a level 0 TLWE ciphertext: ct_{in}
Input: a bootstrapping key from level 0 to level 2: BSK
Input: $k+1$ private keyswitch keys from level 2 to level 1: KS
Output: a level 1 TRGSW ciphertext C
1: $\{\mathrm{ct}_i\}_{i\in[1,\ell]} \leftarrow \mathbf{PBSmanyLUT}\left(\mathrm{ct}_{\mathrm{in}}, \mathrm{BSK}, P(X) \cdot X^{N/2^{\rho+1}}, 1, 0, \rho\right)$
2: **for** $w = 1$ to ℓ **do**
3: $\quad \mathrm{ct}'_w = \mathrm{ct}_w + \left(0, \frac{1}{2\mathfrak{B}^w}\right)$
4: $\quad$ **for** $u = 1$ to $k+1$ **do**
5: $\quad\quad c^{(u,w)} = $ Private KeySwitch(KS, ct'_w)
6: $\quad$ **end for**
7: **end for**
8: **return** $C = (c^{u,w})_{1 \leq u \leq k+1, 1 \leq w \leq \ell}$

4.3 Full Description of the AES Evaluation

In the above two subsections, we have presented an efficient evaluation of Sub-Bytes and an optimization regarding circuit bootstrapping. It is obvious that the ShiftRows operation is free and AddRoundKey is also almost free due to message encoding. The additional operation that needs to be handled is MixColumns. The MixColumns operation is a 4×4 matrix multiplication with constant terms $\{x+1, x, 1\}$ modulo $(x^8+x^4+x^3+x+1)$. Interestingly, this modular multiplication can be computed by simple XOR and shift operation [21], as shown below. Here we represent a byte from the lowest bit to the highest bit as $(b_0 b_1 b_2 b_3 b_4 b_5 b_6 b_7)$.

$$b_0 b_1 b_2 b_3 b_4 b_5 b_6 b_7 \xrightarrow{\times 1} b_0 b_1 b_2 b_3 b_4 b_5 b_6 b_7$$

$$b_0 b_1 b_2 b_3 b_4 b_5 b_6 b_7 \xrightarrow{\times x} b_7 b_0 b_1 b_2 b_3 b_4 b_5 b_6 \oplus 0 b_7 0 b_7 b_7 000$$

$$b_0 b_1 b_2 b_3 b_4 b_5 b_6 b_7 \xrightarrow{\times (x+1)} b_0 b_1 b_2 b_3 b_4 b_5 b_6 b_7 \oplus b_7 b_0 b_1 b_2 b_3 b_4 b_5 b_6 \oplus 0 b_7 0 b_7 b_7 000$$

In this way, we can convert all the multiplication operations in MixColumns into bitwise XOR operation and simple shift, which is exactly what we want.

Thus, ShiftRows, AddRoundKey and MixColumns can be performed at Level 0, while SubBytes would be performed in Level 1. Our evaluation framework[1] is clearly presented in Fig. 1, the details of the corresponding algorithm are given in Appendix A.

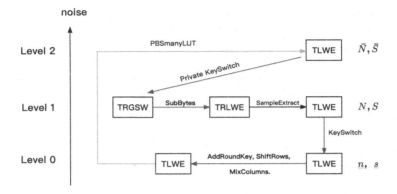

Fig. 1. Fregata: the homomorphic evaluation framework of AES performed at different levels.

Noise Analysis. The circuit bootstrapping algorithm crosses 3 levels, each involving different ciphertext types with their own parameter settings and associated keys. The main difference between the three encryption levels is the amount of noise supported, the higher the level, the lower the noise. Level 0 corresponds to small parameters, large noise, instantaneous computation, but only very limited linear operations can be tolerated.

Indeed, the first step of the circuit bootstrapping, that is, the PBSmanyLUT, plays the role of refreshing noise throughout the evaluation process. Now we analyze the internal noise variance of the ciphertext from the PBSmanyLUT to the end in each round.

The homomorphic evaluation of S-box in Fig. 1 contains five homomorphic operations: PBSmanyLUT, Private KeySwitch, Sbox lookup table, SampleExtract and Public KeySwitch, where the SampleExtract operation does not introduce any noise and Public KeySwitch is utilized to adjust the parameters from (N, S) to $(\underline{n}, \underline{s})$. Thus, we can calculate the error after Public KeySwitch on Level 0 by analyzing the error variance of each step separately. Firstly, according to Theorem 4 in [13], we have

---

[1] We called our framework "Fregata", which cleverly reads like "Free Gate", emphasizing the fact that it eliminates the cost for XOR gate due to message encoding. Its speed reflects our efficient homomorphic evaluation of S-box.

$$Var(PBSmanyLUT) \leq \underline{n\bar{\ell}}(k+1)\bar{N}\frac{\bar{B_g}^2+2}{12}Var(BSK)$$

$$+ \underline{n}\frac{q^2 - \bar{B_g}^{2\bar{\ell}}}{24\bar{B_g}^{2\bar{\ell}}}(1 + \frac{k\bar{N}}{2}) + \frac{nk\bar{N}}{32} + \frac{n}{16}(1 - \frac{k\bar{N}}{2})^2$$

After performing Private KeySwitch, by Theorem 2.7 in [12], we have

$$Var(TRGSW) \leq Var(PBSmanyLUT) + \bar{t}\bar{N}\bar{B_{ks}}^2 Var(privateKS)$$

In order to evaluate the Sbox, we use 8 CMUX gates to lookup table and then perform SampleExtract and KeySwitch in Algorithm 1, we have

$$Var(\text{TLWE}_{\text{Level0}}) \leq 8 \cdot ((k+1)\ell N\beta^2 Var(TRGSW))$$

$$+ Var(TRLWE_{SBox}) + \underline{n}tNB_{ks}^2 Var(KS)$$

where $Var(BSK), Var(privateKS), Var(TRLWE_{Sbox})$ and $Var(KS)$ can be found in [12].

5   Scalability: Homomorphic Evaluation of SM4

In this section, we will show that our evaluation framework can be also extended to the homomorphic evaluation of other ciphers, such as symmetric encryption scheme SM4. SM4 is a Chinese block cipher standard used for protecting wireless networks and was released publicly in 2006 [17]. Now it has become the international standard of ISO/IEC, which effectively promotes the improvement of ISO/IEC symmetric cryptographic algorithms. The structure of SM4 is similar to the AES algorithm, but it uses generalized Feistel structure. And its encryption computation requires up to 32 rounds, where each round contains four parts: key addition, S-box, linear transformation and XOR operation as follows. Let the plaintext inputs be $(X_0, X_1, X_2, X_3) \in (\mathbb{Z}_2^{32})^4$ and round keys be $rk_i \in \mathbb{Z}_2^{32}(i = 0, 1, 2, \cdots, 31)$, which are derived from the initial key through the key expansion.

- Key addition: the 32-bit output word $A = (a_0, a_1, a_2, a_3) \in (\mathbb{Z}_2^8)^4 = (X_{i+1} \oplus X_{i+2} \oplus X_{i+3} \oplus rk_i)$;
- Non-linear substitution(S-box) τ: the 32-bit output word $B = (b_0, b_1, b_2, b_3) \in (\mathbb{Z}_2^8)^4$ is derived by $(S(a_0), S(a_1), S(a_2), S(a_3))$;
- Linear transformation: the 32-bit output word $C = L(B) = B \oplus (B \lll_{32} 2) \oplus (B \lll_{32} 10) \oplus (B \lll_{32} 18) \oplus (B \lll_{32} 24)$;
- XOR operation: $X_{i+4} = C \oplus X_i$.

After 32 rounds the final encryption result is $(X_{35}, X_{34}, X_{33}, X_{32})$. Xue [40] presented the homomorphic evaluation of SM4 based on the BGV scheme using Gentry's method [26]. However, since the number of rounds in SM4 is more than

three times that of AES, the evaluation of SM4 must use large encryption parameters to match the multiplicative depth, resulting extremely long latency. To be
specific, it takes up to 6 h and 1.5 h in leveled and bootstrapped implementation
version.

Next, we give an efficient evaluation of SM4 based on our evaluation framework. Notice that in the homomorphic SM4 evaluation, the results of the previous
few rounds are superimposed on the XOR operation and key addition of next
round. To be precise, during the final XOR operation of each round, the noise
of ciphertext C would be superimposed on the noise of ciphertext X_i from the
previous round in the encrypted domain. As a result, the noise magnitude of the
ciphertext generated by the final XOR operation increases with each round of
evaluation. Moreover, three noisy TLWE ciphertexts and a fresh TLWE ciphertext of round key will participate in key addition of the next round. Therefore,
intuitively, after several rounds of evaluation, the TLWE ciphertexts generated
by the key addition operation will be extremely noisy, leading to decryption
failure.

It is a bit tricky to actually determine at which round the decryption would
fail. We experimentally verify that the TLWE ciphertext generated by key addition after eight rounds of evaluation will fail to decrypt with a high probability
due to excessive noise. Therefore, we fix this issue by introducing the identity
bootstrapping (more details about identity bootstrapping algorithm, please see
Algorithm 3 of [11]) after each round of evaluation. In this way, we can avoid
the problem of excessive noise due to key addition.

Finally, we redesign the homomorphic evaluation flow of SM4 by introducing identity bootstrapping on level 0, all homomorphic operations performed at
different levels are presented in Fig. 2.

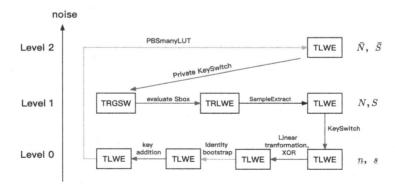

Fig. 2. Diagram of the homomorphic evaluation of SM4 performed at different levels.

6   Implementation and Performance Results

In this section, we implement our proposed framwork to test the accuracy and efficiency of evaluating AES and SM4 based on the TFHE scheme. All the experiments were conducted on a single core of 12th Gen Intel(R) Core(TM) i5-12500 × 12 with 15.3 GB RAM, running the Ubuntu 20.04 operating system.

6.1   Parameters Selection.

Note that the original implementation of circuit bootstrapping[2] is not compatible with the TFHE library[3]. TFHEpp [34] is full Scracthed pure C++ version of TFHE, which supports circuit bootstrapping and private PBSmanyLUT [13]. Therefore, we implement the homomorphic evaluation of SM4 and AES in the TFHEpp library. Circuit bootstrapping crosses 3 levels, each involving different ciphertext types with their own parameter settings and associated keys. Specifically, the relevant parameters of the three levels are shown in Table 1. All of our parameters are estimated to be above $\lambda = 128$ bit security according to the latest iteration of the LWE estimator[4].

Table 1. Parameters for levels 0, 1 and 2 in circuit bootstrapping mode

Level	dimension of the TLWE	noise stdev	decomposition basis	decomposition length
0	$\underline{n} = 635$	$\underline{\alpha} = 2^{-15}$	–	–
1	$N = 1024$	$\alpha = 2^{-25}$	$B_g = 2^6$	$\ell = 3$
2	$\bar{N} = 2048$	$\bar{\alpha} = 2^{-44}$	$\bar{B}_g = 2^9$	$\bar{\ell} = 4$
$1 \rightarrow 0$	–	–	$B_{ks} = 2^2$	$t = 7$
$2 \rightarrow 1$	–	–	$\bar{B}_{ks} = 2^3$	$\bar{t} = 10$

6.2   Performance and Analysis

Our implementation focuses on testing the latency time of the evaluation of a single block. In order to demonstrate the efficiency of our evaluation method as much as possible, we also evaluate the AES based on trivial gate bootstrapping mode, where all computational units of AES are replaced by bootsXOR and bootsMUX gates in TFHE. Meanwhile, for SM4, since the numbers of shift bits are exactly a multiple of 2 in the linear transformation, we choose to use two-bit wise encryption and provide efficient implementation using functional

---

[2] https://github.com/tfhe/experimental-tfhe.
[3] https://github.com/tfhe/tfhe.
[4] https://bitbucket.org/malb/lwe-estimator.

bootstrapping. If we adopt larger-bit (> 2) wise encryption, we would need to extract the ciphertext of the corresponding bit from the ciphertext to perform the shift operation of linear transformation, which is an extremely costly operation [32]. The experiments are run 1000 times on a single core of our machine, and we take the average time as running latency time. The specific implementation results are presented in Table 2.

Table 2. Our execution times compared to the state of the art using just one thread (The data with $*$ refers to 16 threads).

scheme	mode	AES	SM4
BGV	leveled	Gentry et al. [26] 4 mins	Xue [40] 6 h
	bootstrapped	[26] 18 mins	[40] 1.58 h
TFHE	gate bootstrapping	1.43 h	1.68 h
	functional bootstrapping	Stracovsky et al. [38] 4.2 mins*	
		Trama et al. [39] 4.5 mins	6.1 mins
	circuit bootstrapping	**86** s	**78** s

It can be seen that our novel evaluation based on circuit bootstrapping mode achieves the best latency performance. Specifically, the homomorphic AES evaluation based on circuit bootstrapping mode takes 86 s, which is about 3 times faster than the state-of-the-art [39]. The circuit bootstrapping mode takes 78 s to perform SM4 with one CPU thread, which is up to 73× reduction in latency compared with Xue [40] and 4.7 × reduction compared with functional bootstrapping mode. Considering that our implementation uses only one CPU thread, using the OpenMP library can offer more speedups for our implementation since circuit bootstrappings each round are performed in parallel in our evaluation framework. For example, we expect to achieve an evaluation of AES in about 9 s if we use the "i7-server" as described in Trama et al. [39].

Although the number of encryption rounds of AES is only 10, less than SM4, it requires $16 \times 10 = 160$ S-box LUTs. The number of rounds of SM4 is up to 32, with only 4 paralleled LUTs each round, requiring a total of $32 \times 4 = 128$ LUTs. Moreover, the main consumption time of our evaluation mode comes from circuit bootstrapping before the S-box, resulting in the homomorphic evaluation of AES being slower than SM4. Table 3 and Table 4 detail the time portion of each part of the AES and SM4 evaluation based on circuit bootstrapping, respectively. Notice that the circuit bootstrapping becomes the most expensive part of the computation, while the S-box lookup table takes about only 16 ms, which is almost negligible.

Table 3. The time spent for each core operation of AES evaluation and their percentage relative to the total time in circuit bootstrapping mode.

Operation	Circuit Boot	SubBytes	Identity KS	Total time
Time (Ratio)	84.48 s (98.31%)	18.48 ms (0.02%)	1.42 s (1.65%)	**86 s**

Table 4. The time spent for each core operation of SM4 evaluation and their percentage relative to the total time in circuit bootstrapping mode. Identity KS denotes KeySwitch after SampleExtract and Identity Boot represents Identity bootstrapping.

Operation	Circuit Boot	S-box LUT	Identity KS	Identity Boot	Total time
Time (Ratio)	68.11 s (87.66%)	15.59 ms (0.02%)	1.43 s (1.83%)	8.1 s (10.41%)	**78 s**

7 Conclusion

In this paper, we propose a novel evaluation framework to achieve faster AES evaluation based on the circuit bootstrapping of TFHE. We utilize techniques such as hybrid packing and optimized circuit bootstrapping to achieve the optimal latency of current AES homomorphic evaluation, which is about 3 times faster than the state-of-the-art implementation. Meanwhile, our framework can be extended to other Feistel structured ciphers, for example, we achieve efficient evaluation of the block cipher SM4, which is 73× faster than the current best publicly available implementation. Although TFHE-based evaluation is far inferior to BGV-based packing method in terms of amortization rate, our framework combined with multi-thread would hopefully approach the amortization time further.

Improving the efficiency of the circuit bootstrapping would be our next research direction, especially the optimization of private KeySwitching. We hope that our work could provide a guide for designing new FHE-friendly symmetric encryption algorithms.

Acknowledgement. We thank the anonymous ISC2023 reviewers for their helpful comments. This work was supported by the Huawei Technologies Co., Ltd. and CAS Project for Young Scientists in Basic Research Grant No. YSBR-035.

A Detailed Algorithms

Algorithm 3. Homomorphic evaluation of AES via circuit bootstrapping

---

Input: two TRLWE ciphertexts used for packing AES S-box: d_0, d_1
Input: the TLWE ciphertext of the $(16 * i + j)$-th input bit $C_{i,j}^{input\_tlwe}$, where $0 \leq i \leq 15, 0 \leq j \leq 7$;
Input: the TLWE ciphertext of the $(16 * i + j)$-th bit of the r-th round key $C_{r,i,j}^{rk\_tlwe}$, where $0 \leq r \leq 10, 0 \leq i \leq 15, 0 \leq j \leq 7$
Output: C^{output_tlwe}: double-encrypted ciphertext $Enc^{HE}\left(Enc^{AES}\left(m, rk\right)\right)$
1: // AddRoundKey
2: $C^{input\_tlwe} = C^{input\_tlwe} + C_0^{rk\_tlwe}$
3: **for** $r = 1$ to 9 **do**
4:    // Circuit bootstrapping and SubBytes
5:    **for** $i = 0$ to 15 **do**
6:       **for** $j = 0$ to 7 **do**
7:          $C_{i,j}^{trgsw} = CBwithPBSmanyLUT(C_{i,j}^{input\_tlwe})$
8:       **end for**
9:       $C_i^{input\_tlwe} = LUTMixedPacking(C_i^{trgsw}, d_0, d_1)$
10:   **end for**
11:   // ShiftRows
12:   $C^{input\_tlwe} = \text{CipherShiftRows}(C^{input\_tlwe})$
13:   // Mixcolums
14:   $C^{input\_tlwe} = \text{CipherMixcolums}(C^{input\_tlwe})$
15:   // AddRoundKey
16:   $C^{input\_tlwe} = C^{input\_tlwe} + C_r^{rk\_tlwe}$
17: **end for**
18: // Circuit bootstrapping and SubBytes
19: **for** $i = 0$ to 15 **do**
20:   **for** $j = 0$ to 7 **do**
21:      $C_{i,j}^{trgsw} = CBwithPBSmanyLUT(C_{i,j}^{input\_tlwe})$
22:   **end for**
23:   $C_i^{output\_tlwe} = LUTMixedPacking(C_i^{trgsw}, d_0, d_1)$
24: **end for**
25: // ShiftRows
26: $C^{output\_tlwe} = \text{CipherShiftRows}(C^{output\_tlwe})$
27: // AddRoundKey
28: $C^{output\_tlwe} = C^{output\_tlwe} + C_{10}^{rk\_tlwe}$
29: **return** C^{output_tlwe}

Algorithm 4. CipherShiftsRows

Input: $C_{i,j}^{input\_tlwe}$, $0 \leq i \leq 15, 0 \leq j \leq 7$
Output: $C_{i,j}^{output\_tlwe}$, $0 \leq i \leq 15, 0 \leq j \leq 7$
1: **for** $i = 0$ to 15 **do**
2:    $C_i^{output\_tlwe} = C_{5i \pmod{16}}^{input\_tlwe}$
3: **end for**
4: **return** C^{output_tlwe}

Algorithm 5. CipherMixColums

Input: $C_{i,j}^{input\_tlwe}$, $0 \le i \le 15, 0 \le j \le 7$
Output: $C_{i,j}^{output\_tlwe}$, $0 \le i \le 15, 0 \le j \le 7$
1: **for** $i = 0$ to 3 **do**
2:     $Tmp = C_{4i}^{input\_tlwe} + C_{4i+1}^{input\_tlwe} + C_{4i+2}^{input\_tlwe} + C_{4i+3}^{input\_tlwe}$
3:     $Tm = C_{4i}^{input\_tlwe} + C_{4i+1}^{input\_tlwe}$
4:     $Tm = \text{CipherMul2}(Tm)$
5:     $C_{4i}^{output\_tlwe} = C_{4i}^{input\_tlwe} + Tm + Tmp$
6:     $Tm = C_{4i+1}^{input\_tlwe} + C_{4i+2}^{input\_tlwe}$
7:     $Tm = \text{CipherMul2}(Tm)$
8:     $C_{4i+1}^{output\_tlwe} = C_{4i+1}^{input\_tlwe} + Tm + Tmp$
9:     $Tm = C_{4i+2}^{input\_tlwe} + C_{4i+3}^{input\_tlwe}$
10:     $Tm = \text{CipherMul2}(Tm)$
11:     $C_{4i+2}^{output\_tlwe} = C_{4i+2}^{input\_tlwe} + Tm + Tmp$
12:     $Tm = C_{4i+3}^{input\_tlwe} + C_{4i}^{input\_tlwe}$
13:     $Tm = \text{CipherMul2}(Tm)$
14:     $C_{4i+3}^{output\_tlwe} = C_{4i+3}^{input\_tlwe} + Tm + Tmp$
15: **end for**
16: **return** C^{output_tlwe}

Algorithm 6. CipherMul2

Input: $C_i^{input\_tlwe}$, $0 \le i \le 7$
Output: $C_j^{output\_tlwe}$, $0 \le i \le 7$
1: $C_0^{output\_tlwe} = C_7^{input\_tlwe}$
2: $C_1^{output\_tlwe} = C_0^{input\_tlwe} + C_7^{input\_tlwe}$
3: $C_2^{output\_tlwe} = C_1^{input\_tlwe}$
4: $C_3^{output\_tlwe} = C_2^{input\_tlwe} + C_7^{input\_tlwe}$
5: $C_4^{output\_tlwe} = C_3^{input\_tlwe} + C_7^{input\_tlwe}$
6: $C_5^{output\_tlwe} = C_4^{input\_tlwe}$
7: $C_6^{output\_tlwe} = C_5^{input\_tlwe}$
8: $C_7^{output\_tlwe} = C_6^{input\_tlwe}$
9: **return** C^{output_tlwe}

References

1. Albrecht, M.R., Rechberger, C., Schneider, T., Tiessen, T., Zohner, M.: Ciphers for MPC and FHE. In: Oswald, E., Fischlin, M. (eds.) EUROCRYPT 2015. LNCS, vol. 9056, pp. 430–454. Springer, Heidelberg (2015). https://doi.org/10.1007/978-3-662-46800-5_17
2. Ashur, T., Mahzoun, M., Toprakhisar, D.: Chaghri - a FHE-friendly block cipher. In: Proceedings of the 2022 ACM SIGSAC Conference on Computer and Communications Security, CCS 2022, pp. 139–150. ACM (2022)
3. Bonte, C., Iliashenko, I., Park, J., Pereira, H.V.L., Smart, N.P.: FINAL: faster FHE instantiated with NTRU and LWE. In: Agrawal, S., Lin, D. (eds.) ASIACRYPT 2022. LNCS, vol. 13792, pp. 188–215. Springer, Cham (2022). https://doi.org/10.1007/978-3-031-22966-4_7

4. Boura, C., Gama, N., Georgieva, M., Jetchev, D.: Simulating homomorphic evaluation of deep learning predictions. In: Dolev, S., Hendler, D., Lodha, S., Yung, M. (eds.) CSCML 2019. LNCS, vol. 11527, pp. 212–230. Springer, Cham (2019). https://doi.org/10.1007/978-3-030-20951-3_20

5. Brakerski, Z.: Fully homomorphic encryption without modulus switching from classical GapSVP. In: Safavi-Naini, R., Canetti, R. (eds.) CRYPTO 2012. LNCS, vol. 7417, pp. 868–886. Springer, Heidelberg (2012). https://doi.org/10.1007/978-3-642-32009-5_50

6. Brakerski, Z., Gentry, C., Vaikuntanathan, V.: (Leveled) fully homomorphic encryption without bootstrapping. In: Innovations in Theoretical Computer Science 2012, pp. 309–325. ACM, New York (2012)

7. Canteaut, A., et al.: Stream ciphers: a practical solution for efficient homomorphic-ciphertext compression. J. Cryptol. **31**(3), 885–916 (2018). https://doi.org/10.1007/s00145-017-9273-9

8. Carpov, S., Izabachène, M., Mollimard, V.: New techniques for multi-value input homomorphic evaluation and applications. In: Matsui, M. (ed.) CT-RSA 2019. LNCS, vol. 11405, pp. 106–126. Springer, Cham (2019). https://doi.org/10.1007/978-3-030-12612-4_6

9. Cheon, J.H., et al.: Batch fully homomorphic encryption over the integers. In: Johansson, T., Nguyen, P.Q. (eds.) EUROCRYPT 2013. LNCS, vol. 7881, pp. 315–335. Springer, Heidelberg (2013). https://doi.org/10.1007/978-3-642-38348-9_20

10. Cheon, J.H., Kim, A., Kim, M., Song, Y.: Homomorphic encryption for arithmetic of approximate numbers. In: Takagi, T., Peyrin, T. (eds.) ASIACRYPT 2017. LNCS, vol. 10624, pp. 409–437. Springer, Cham (2017). https://doi.org/10.1007/978-3-319-70694-8_15

11. Chillotti, I., Gama, N., Georgieva, M., Izabachène, M.: Faster fully homomorphic encryption: bootstrapping in less than 0.1 seconds. In: Cheon, J.H., Takagi, T. (eds.) ASIACRYPT 2016. LNCS, vol. 10031, pp. 3–33. Springer, Heidelberg (2016). https://doi.org/10.1007/978-3-662-53887-6_1

12. Chillotti, I., Gama, N., Georgieva, M., Izabachène, M.: Faster packed homomorphic operations and efficient circuit bootstrapping for TFHE. In: Takagi, T., Peyrin, T. (eds.) ASIACRYPT 2017. LNCS, vol. 10624, pp. 377–408. Springer, Cham (2017). https://doi.org/10.1007/978-3-319-70694-8_14

13. Chillotti, I., Ligier, D., Orfila, J.-B., Tap, S.: Improved programmable bootstrapping with larger precision and efficient arithmetic circuits for TFHE. In: Tibouchi, M., Wang, H. (eds.) ASIACRYPT 2021. LNCS, vol. 13092, pp. 670–699. Springer, Cham (2021). https://doi.org/10.1007/978-3-030-92078-4_23

14. Cid, C., Indrøy, J.P., Raddum, H.: FASTA – a stream cipher for fast FHE evaluation. In: Galbraith, S.D. (ed.) CT-RSA 2022. LNCS, vol. 13161, pp. 451–483. Springer, Cham (2022). https://doi.org/10.1007/978-3-030-95312-6_19

15. Coron, J.-S., Lepoint, T., Tibouchi, M.: Scale-invariant fully homomorphic encryption over the integers. In: Krawczyk, H. (ed.) PKC 2014. LNCS, vol. 8383, pp. 311–328. Springer, Heidelberg (2014). https://doi.org/10.1007/978-3-642-54631-0_18

16. Cosseron, O., Hoffmann, C., Méaux, P., Standaert, F.: Towards case-optimized hybrid homomorphic encryption - featuring the elisabeth stream cipher. In: Agrawal, S., Lin, D. (eds.) ASIACRYPT 2022. LNCS, vol. 13793, pp. 32–67. Springer, Cham (2022). https://doi.org/10.1007/978-3-031-22969-5_2

17. Diffie, W., Ledin, G.: SMS4 encryption algorithm for wireless networks. Cryptology ePrint Archive, Report 2008/329 (2008). https://eprint.iacr.org/2008/329

18. van Dijk, M., Gentry, C., Halevi, S., Vaikuntanathan, V.: Fully homomorphic encryption over the integers. In: Gilbert, H. (ed.) EUROCRYPT 2010. LNCS, vol. 6110, pp. 24–43. Springer, Heidelberg (2010). https://doi.org/10.1007/978-3-642-13190-5_2
19. Dobraunig, C., et al.: Rasta: a cipher with low ANDdepth and few ANDs per bit. In: Shacham, H., Boldyreva, A. (eds.) CRYPTO 2018. LNCS, vol. 10991, pp. 662–692. Springer, Cham (2018). https://doi.org/10.1007/978-3-319-96884-1_22
20. Dobraunig, C., Grassi, L., Helminger, L., Rechberger, C., Schofnegger, M., Walch, R.: Pasta: a case for hybrid homomorphic encryption. IACR Trans. Cryptogr. Hardw. Embed. Syst. **2023**(3), 30–73 (2023). https://doi.org/10.46586/tches.v2023.i3.30-73
21. Doröz, Y., Hu, Y., Sunar, B.: Homomorphic AES evaluation using the modified LTV scheme. Des. Codes Cryptogr. **80**, 333–358 (2016). https://doi.org/10.1007/s10623-015-0095-1
22. Doröz, Y., Shahverdi, A., Eisenbarth, T., Sunar, B.: Toward practical homomorphic evaluation of block ciphers using prince. In: Böhme, R., Brenner, M., Moore, T., Smith, M. (eds.) FC 2014. LNCS, vol. 8438, pp. 208–220. Springer, Heidelberg (2014). https://doi.org/10.1007/978-3-662-44774-1_17
23. Ducas, L., Micciancio, D.: FHEW: bootstrapping homomorphic encryption in less than a second. In: Oswald, E., Fischlin, M. (eds.) EUROCRYPT 2015. LNCS, vol. 9056, pp. 617–640. Springer, Heidelberg (2015). https://doi.org/10.1007/978-3-662-46800-5_24
24. Fan, J., Vercauteren, F.: Somewhat practical fully homomorphic encryption. Cryptology ePrint Archive, Report 2012/144 (2012). https://eprint.iacr.org/2012/144
25. Gentry, C.: A fully homomorphic encryption scheme (2009)
26. Gentry, C., Halevi, S., Smart, N.P.: Homomorphic evaluation of the AES circuit. In: Safavi-Naini, R., Canetti, R. (eds.) CRYPTO 2012. LNCS, vol. 7417, pp. 850–867. Springer, Heidelberg (2012). https://doi.org/10.1007/978-3-642-32009-5_49
27. Ha, J., et al.: Masta: an HE-friendly cipher using modular arithmetic. IEEE Access **8**, 194741–194751 (2020)
28. Ha, J., Kim, S., Lee, B., Lee, J., Son, M.: Rubato: noisy ciphers for approximate homomorphic encryption. In: Dunkelman, O., Dziembowski, S. (eds.) EUROCRYPT 2022. LNCS, vol. 13275, pp. 581–610. Springer, Cham (2022). https://doi.org/10.1007/978-3-031-06944-4_20
29. Hebborn, P., Leander, G.: Dasta - alternative linear layer for rasta. IACR Trans. Symmetric Cryptol. **2020**(3), 46–86 (2020)
30. Lee, Y., et al.: Efficient FHEW bootstrapping with small evaluation keys, and applications to threshold homomorphic encryption. In: Hazay, C., Stam, M. (eds.) EUROCRYPT 2023. LNCS, vol. 14006, pp. 227–256. Springer, Cham (2023). https://doi.org/10.1007/978-3-031-30620-4_8
31. Lepoint, T., Naehrig, M.: A comparison of the homomorphic encryption schemes FV and YASHE. In: Pointcheval, D., Vergnaud, D. (eds.) AFRICACRYPT 2014. LNCS, vol. 8469, pp. 318–335. Springer, Cham (2014). https://doi.org/10.1007/978-3-319-06734-6_20
32. Liu, Z., Micciancio, D., Polyakov, Y.: Large-precision homomorphic sign evaluation using FHEW/TFHE bootstrapping. IACR Cryptology ePrint Archive, p. 1337 (2021). https://eprint.iacr.org/2021/1337
33. Lyubashevsky, V., Peikert, C., Regev, O.: On ideal lattices and learning with errors over rings. In: Gilbert, H. (ed.) EUROCRYPT 2010. LNCS, vol. 6110, pp. 1–23. Springer, Heidelberg (2010). https://doi.org/10.1007/978-3-642-13190-5_1

34. Matsuoka, K.: TFHEpp: pure C++ implementation of TFHE cryptosystem (2020). https://github.com/virtualsecureplatform/TFHEpp

35. Méaux, P., Journault, A., Standaert, F.-X., Carlet, C.: Towards stream ciphers for efficient FHE with low-noise ciphertexts. In: Fischlin, M., Coron, J.-S. (eds.) EUROCRYPT 2016. LNCS, vol. 9665, pp. 311–343. Springer, Heidelberg (2016). https://doi.org/10.1007/978-3-662-49890-3_13

36. Naehrig, M., Lauter, K.E., Vaikuntanathan, V.: Can homomorphic encryption be practical? In: Proceedings of the 3rd ACM Cloud Computing Security Workshop, CCSW, pp. 113–124. ACM, New York (2011)

37. Regev, O.: On lattices, learning with errors, random linear codes, and cryptography. J. ACM **56**(6), 34:1–34:40 (2009)

38. Stracovsky, R., Mahdavi, R.A., Kerschbaum, F.: Faster evaluation of AES using TFHE. Poster Session, FHE.Org - 2022 (2022). https://rasoulam.github.io/data/poster-aes-tfhe.pdf

39. Trama, D., Clet, P., Boudguiga, A., Sirdey, R.: At last! A homomorphic AES evaluation in less than 30 seconds by means of TFHE. IACR Cryptology ePrint Archive, p. 1020 (2023). https://eprint.iacr.org/2023/1020

40. Xue, Y.: Homomorphic evaluation of the SM4. IACR Cryptology ePrint Archive, p. 1340 (2020). https://eprint.iacr.org/2020/1340

Key Management

Efficient Forward Secrecy for TLS-PSK from Pure Symmetric Cryptography

Li Duan[1,2], Yong Li[2(✉)], and Lijun Liao[2]

[1] Paderborn University, Paderborn, Germany
liduan@mail.upb.de
[2] Huawei Technologies Düsseldorf, Düsseldorf, Germany
{li.duan,yong.li1,lijun.liao}@huawei.com

Abstract. Transport layer security (TLS) is by far the most important protocol on the Internet for establishing secure session keys and providing authentication and secure communications. In various environments, the TLS pre-shared key cipher suite (TLS-PSK) is an attractive option for remote authentication, for example, between servers and constrained clients like smart cards, in mobile phone authentication, EMV-based payment, or authentication via electronic ID cards. However, without (EC)DHE, plain TLS-PSK does not have essential security features such as forward secrecy due to its fully symmetric keys and key schedule. In this work, we propose highly efficient methods for enhancing the security of plain TLS-PSK. First, we extend the key evolving scheme (KES) notion, which enables the construction of pure symmetric key based AKE protocols with perfect forward secrecy (PFS), and our construction of KES does not depend on any asymmetric cryptographic primitives. Moreover, we design mechanisms to re-synchronize PSKs of two communication parties with logarithmic complexity, whereas the existing protocols only tolerate ±1 de-synchronization, or have linear complexity for re-synchronization. In addition, we show that our protocol is highly efficient, both asymptotically and practically, by comparing it with existing TLS-PSK in performance with identical security parameters. Finally, we show that our generic KES construction can be perfectly integrated into all (fully symmetric) TLS-PSK with minimum modification of the original protocol itself.

Keywords: authenticated key exchange · pre-shared key · transport layer security · formal security model · perfect forward secrecy

1 Introduction

TLS is undoubtedly the most prominent key exchange protocol in use today. While the security of most popular applications is built upon the Diffie-Hellman or RSA-based cipher suites of TLS, several important applications use less common cipher suites [17,20,21]. One such application is remote authentication of

© The Author(s), under exclusive license to Springer Nature Switzerland AG 2023
E. Athanasopoulos and B. Mennink (Eds.): ISC 2023, LNCS 14411, pp. 415–434, 2023.
https://doi.org/10.1007/978-3-031-49187-0_21

resource-restricted clients like smart cards. In these scenarios, efficient computation and low power consumption are usually the most demanded system features. Instead of using the asymmetric-key-based cipher suites of TLS, applications can employ a variant that assumes pre-shared symmetric keys (PSK) between client and server. The corresponding cipher suite family is termed TLS with pre-shared keys (TLS-PSK) and is available in many TLS implementations, e.g., Openssl, BouncyCastle, CyaSSL, Cryptlib [7,10,15,16]. However, due to its fully symmetric keys and key schedule, TLS-PSK does not have essential security features such as forward secrecy [14]. If one long-term PSK is compromised, the adversary can obtain all session keys of the past sessions and destroy the security of previously encrypted messages. Therefore, an enhanced version of TLS-PSK with *perfect forward secrecy* (PFS) is, both in theory and in practice, significant and urgent.

Forward secrecy (FS) is a *de facto* security requirement for authenticated key exchange (AKE) protocols. A protocol with FS means that even if a participant's long term secrets are compromised after completing an AKE session, the session keys established previously remain secure. Two typical paradigms to achieve FS are using asymmetric cryptography (e.g., FS for TLS 1.3 from strong RSA and GGM assumptions by Aviram *et al.* [1]) and using key evolving techniques.

Key Evolving Technique for Symmetric-Key AKE. The notion of forward secrecy in symmetric cryptography was first formalized by Bellare and Yee in 2003 [4]. The authors also constructed forward secure encryption and message authentication code from pseudorandom bit generators with FS (FSPRG).

A symmetric key evolving scheme for AKE appeared in the SASI protocol in 2007 [6], and the name key evolving scheme (KES) was given by Dousti *et al.* in [9] in 2015. Although the KES notion was not well formalized then, the intuition is similar to its asymmetric peer. A new key K_i is derived from the previous K_{i-1} as $K_i = F(K_{i-1})$, where $F(\cdot)$ can be a cryptographic hash function, a pseudorandom function (PRF) and other one-way functions. $F(\cdot)$ can also take in auxiliary input, such as identifiers or key versions. Later, various symmetric AKE schemes were proposed from key evolving schemes [2,9]. Boyd *et al.* proposed a symmetric key AKE based on key linear evolution and puncturable PRF in 2021 [5] with synchronization robustness. However, these protocols have to be decomposed carefully before integrating into TLS-PSK.

Distinction from FSPRG and KLE Security. In FSPRG security [4] $\mathcal{A}$ gets exactly $K_1, K_2, K_3, \cdots$ one by one before sending a flag to get the challenged state st_i. The most notable difference in our new KES security notion is that, as shown in $\mathbf{Game}_{KES}^{Real}$ and $\mathbf{Game}_{KES}^{Rand}$ (see Fig. 1), an adversary $\mathcal{A}$ does *not* have to obtain new keys in a fixed order or in a step length of one. KES security game allows $\mathcal{A}$ to jump arbitrarily ahead and get a K_v by querying the challenger with a value v, as long as $i < v \le T_{max}$.

The key linear evolution (KLE) formalized by Boyd *et al.* in 2021 [5] is similar to FSPRG, where a "key derivation key" (KDK) works identically as a state in FSPRG. In the KLE security game in [5], $\mathcal{A}$ selects in advance of any initialization an index ℓ, and outputs a guess bit after obtaining all keys $\{K_i\}_{i=0}^{\ell}$ and the KDK $st_{\ell+1}$. In this paper we do not require that the challenger knows an ℓ in advance, or keys that are always generated in canonical order.

The notion of non-linear evolution, especially its security, was not formalized in [5] but implemented with puncturable PRF. Thus, our KES notion captures KES's functional and security requirement more generically.

1.1 Our Contribution and Organization of the Paper

To meet the challenges of enhancing symmetric key based AKE (SAKE) such as TLS-PSK with PFS, we make the following contribution in this paper.

- We propose a more generic notions of a key evolving scheme (KES) that captures the essential properties needed for forward secrecy.
- We design fast mechanisms to update LTK to any given version, which enables two parties to re-synchronize keys with logarithmic complexity, whereas the existing protocols either only tolerate ± 1 de-synchronization, or have linear complexity for re-synchronization.
- Finally, we integrate KES into TLS-PSK. We show that the resulting TLS-PSK protocols are highly efficient in practice. Compared with other existing solutions, our proposals are more modular, flexible, efficient, and more compatible with TLS-PSK.

The notations, the KES notion and the concrete construction of KES are presented in Sects. 2 and 3. The security model for symmetric key AKE is presented in Sect. 4. The extended TLS-PSK protocols are presented in Sect. 5 and the TLS integration is evaluated in Sect. 6.

2 Notation and Preliminaries

2.1 Notation

We let $n \in \mathbb{N}$ denote the security parameter and 1^n the string that consists of n ones. Let $[n] = \{1, \ldots, n\} \subset \mathbb{N}$ be the set of integers $\{1, 2, \cdots, n\}$. If S is a set, $a \xleftarrow{\$} S$ denotes the action of sampling a uniformly random element from S. If $\mathcal{A}()$ is an algorithm, $m \xleftarrow{\$} \mathcal{A}^{O(\cdot)}()$ denotes that $\mathcal{A}$ (probabilistically) outputs m with the help of another algorithm $O(\cdot)$. $X\|Y$ denote the operation concatenating two binary strings X and Y. We use $\Pr[A : B]$ to denote the probability that B happens if action A is taken. $|E|$ denotes the number of objects in set E.

2.2 Cryptographic Primitives

To construct KES and TLS extension, we use standard cryptographic primitives such as message authentication code (MAC, MAC = (MAC.Gen, MAC.Tag, MAC.Vfy)), collision resistant hash function (H()), pseudorandom function (PRF, $\mathbb{F}$ = (FKGen, PRF)) and authenticated symmetric key encryption with associated data (AEAD, $\Pi = (\mathsf{KGen}, \mathsf{ENC}, \mathsf{DEC})$). The syntax of these schemes can be found in Appendix B.

Due to the page limitation, we refer the reader to [19] and [13] for the semantic security definition of all the cryptographic primitives above.

3 Symmetric Key Evolving Scheme

Two critical components for a pure symmetric key based AKE protocol are the key evolving scheme (KES) and the session key agreement protocol. To discuss a KES formally, we need its syntax first.

Definition 1 (Key evolving scheme, KES). *A key evolving scheme is a pair of algorithm* $\Pi_{\mathsf{KES}} = (\mathsf{Init}, \mathsf{KES})$ *defined as follows.*

- $\mathsf{Init}(1^n) \rightarrow \mathsf{st}_0$. *The non-deterministic algorithm* $\mathsf{Init}(1^n)$ *takes the security parameter* 1^n *as input and outputs the initial state* st_0 *that also defines the key space.*
- $\mathsf{KES}(\mathsf{st}_i, v) \rightarrow (\mathsf{K}_v, \mathsf{st}_v)$ *The deterministic algorithm* $\mathsf{KES}()$ *takes a state and a target phase number* $i < v \leq T_{max}$ *as input, and it outputs the new key* K_v *and new state* st_v, *where* T_{max} *is the maximal possible phases.*

Then, we define the most critical property of a KES called key independence. The security game gives the adversary a real-or-random challenge, as shown in Fig. 1, where $\mathsf{transKey}$ is the set of previously generated keys in each game.

Definition 2 (Key independence). *We say that a key evolving scheme* Π *has* $(t, \epsilon_{\mathsf{KES}})$ *key independence if it holds for any adversary* $\mathcal{A}$ *with running time* $t' \leq t$ *that its advantage*

$$\mathsf{Adv}_{\mathcal{A}, \mathsf{k\text{-}ind}}^{\Pi} := \left| \Pr[\mathbf{Game}_{\mathsf{KES}}^{\mathsf{Real}}(\mathcal{A}) \rightarrow 0] - \Pr[\mathbf{Game}_{\mathsf{KES}}^{\mathsf{Rand}}(\mathcal{A}) \rightarrow 0] \right| \leq \epsilon_{\mathsf{KES}}.$$

3.1 Key Eolving Scheme Construction

We organize LTKs in a (virtual) binary tree structure $\mathcal{T}$, where all LTKs correspond to the leaves of $\mathcal{T}$. Each node n of $\mathcal{T}$ is labelled in the following way.

- If n is the root node, then n has the label "1";
- If n is the left child of a node with label L, then n has the label $L \| $ "0";
- If n is the right child of a node with label L, then n has the label $L \| $ "1",

where "1" and "0" are two distinct encoded characters. We also associate a key to each node using $\mathsf{DERIVE}()$ shown in Fig. 2, where K_L is the key for the left child and K_R for the right one. The key associated with the root node is generated uniformly at random, while all other keys are derived by calling $\mathsf{DERIVE}()$ recursively. It is easy to observe that a label also reflects the *"derivable"* relation. Namely, if node n has label L_n, node m has label L_m and L_m is a prefix of L_n, then the key associated with n can be derived with the key associated

$\mathbf{Game}_{\mathsf{KES}}^{\mathsf{Real}}(\mathcal{A})$	$\mathbf{Game}_{\mathsf{KES}}^{\mathsf{Rand}}(\mathcal{A})$
$1:$ $\mathsf{st}_0 \leftarrow \mathsf{Init}(1^n)$;	$1:$ $\mathsf{st}_0 \leftarrow \mathsf{Init}(1^n)$;
$2:$ $i \leftarrow 0$; flag $\leftarrow$ **false**; transKey $\leftarrow \emptyset$;	$2:$ $i \leftarrow 0$; flag $\leftarrow$ **false**; transKey $\leftarrow \emptyset$;
$3:$ **while** $i < \mathsf{T}_{max} \wedge$ flag $=$ **false**	$3:$ **while** $i < \mathsf{T}_{max} \wedge$ flag $=$ **false**
$4:$ $(v,d) \leftarrow \mathcal{A}(\mathsf{transKey}, 1^n)$;	$4:$ $(v,d) \leftarrow \mathcal{A}(\mathsf{transKey}, 1^n)$;
$5:$ **if** $i < v \leq \mathsf{T}_{max}$	$5:$ **if** $i < v \leq \mathsf{T}_{max}$
$6:$ $(\mathsf{K}_v, \mathsf{st}_v) \leftarrow \mathsf{KES}(\mathsf{st}_i, v)$;	$6:$ $(\mathsf{K}_v, \mathsf{st}_v) \leftarrow \mathsf{KES}(\mathsf{st}_i, v)$; $\mathsf{K}_v \xleftarrow{\$} \mathcal{K}$;
$7:$ $i \leftarrow v$; $\mathsf{st}_i \leftarrow \mathsf{st}_v$;	$7:$ $i \leftarrow v$; $\mathsf{st}_i \leftarrow \mathsf{st}_v$;
$8:$ transKey $\leftarrow$ transKey $\cup \{\mathsf{K}_v\}$;	$8:$ transKey $\leftarrow$ transKey $\cup \{\mathsf{K}_v\}$;
$9:$ **endif**	$9:$ **endif**
$10:$ **if** $d =$ **true**	$10:$ **if** $d =$ **true**
$11:$ flag $\leftarrow$ **true**;	$11:$ flag $\leftarrow$ **true**;
$12:$ **endif**	$12:$ **endif**
$13:$ **endwhile**	$13:$ **endwhile**
$14:$ $b' \in \{0,1\} \xleftarrow{\$} \mathcal{A}(\mathsf{st}_i, \mathsf{transKey})$	$14:$ $b' \in \{0,1\} \xleftarrow{\$} \mathcal{A}(\mathsf{st}_i, \mathsf{transKey})$
$15:$ **return** b'	$15:$ **return** b'

Fig. 1. The security games $\mathbf{Game}_{\mathsf{KES}}^{\mathsf{Real}}$ and $\mathbf{Game}_{\mathsf{KES}}^{\mathsf{Rand}}$ for KES, with difference marked in gray in line 6. The variable d (line 4 in both games) is used by $\mathcal{A}$ to terminate the key derivation loop before reaching T_{max}.

with m via DERIVE(). We do not distinguish i and label L_i for simplicity in the following description.

An LTK evolving can be triggered by a critical event or time change. Here we do not distinguish these two options and use the term *phase* and an index to distinguish the keys.

Working LTK, States and Basic KES. In each phase i, a key user maintains the working LTK K_i and an internal state st_i. Each st_i contains a set of keys. As shown in Fig. 2, our basic KES works as follows.

– **(Initialization)** At phase $T = 0$, there is no working LTK but an initial state st_0.
– **(Derive new LTK)** In each phase $T > 0$, first search for the ancestor[1] of K_{i+1} in st_i. This search can easily be done by searching for the key labels which are prefixes of $i + 1$. Then K_{i+1} is computed from one of its ancestors.
– **(Compute new state)** Once K_{i+1} is located, all key labels on its RIGHT co-path[2] with ancestors in st_i can be determined. These keys are then derived using DERIVE() on their ancestors recursively.

---

[1] We consider a node itself as one of its ancestors. Hence, its label is also a prefix of its own.

[2] From here on, we use co-path to denote the right co-path.

- (**Delete old keys and clean-up**) K_i must be deleted for FS. As future LTKs are either the sibling of K_{i+1} or descendants of nodes on its co-path, other keys are unnecessary and even harmful. Therefore, the nodes on the path from the root to K_{i+1} (excluding K_{i+1}) must also be deleted.
- (**Confirm new LTK and state**) Finally, K_{i+1} is set to be the working LTK and the remaining keys are kept as st_{i+1}.

KES(st_i)

---

1 :   Derive and store K_{i+1} with DERIVE() and st_i;
2 :   Derive all K on the co-path of K_{i+1} with DERIVE() and st_i;
3 :   Delete all K$'$ on the path of K_{i+1} except itself;
4 :   Delete K_i;
5 :   Keep as st_{i+1} all the remaining keys except K_{i+1};
6 :   **return** (st_{i+1}, K_{i+1});

DERIVE(K)

---

1 : $K_L \leftarrow PRF_1(K, "0")$;
2 : $K_R \leftarrow PRF_1(K, "1")$;
3 :   **return** (K_L, K_R);

Fig. 2. Basic tree-based KES with one-by-one, linear evolution.

We illustrate the basic KES with the example in Fig. 3. Let the number of leaves be four. So, there can be four LTKs in the lifespan of the tree.

- In phase $T = 0$, the key K at the root is kept as st_0.
- In phase $T = 1$, K_1 is the new working LTK (marked in red). As the key at the root is an ancestor of K_1, the parent of K_1 can be derived from K. On the other hand, the co-path of K_1 covers K_2 and K_R, which can also be derived from K and kept as st_1 (marked in green). The path of K_1 covers its parent and K, so these two keys are deleted. The deleted keys are marked as dashed circles.
- In phase $T = 2$, K_2 becomes the new working LTK. As K_2 is already in st_1 and K_R is the sole node on K_2's co-path derivable from st_1, so it is only necessary to delete K_1 and keep K_R as st_2.
- In phase $T = 3$, K_3 becomes the new working LTK derived from K_R. The sibling of K_3 is kept as st_3. Key K_2 and K_R are deleted.
- In phase $T = 4$, the only leaf key in st_3 can be used as K_4.

Jumping Forward to an Arbitrary State and Π_{KES}. The basic KES can be used in a canonical way to update from current state st_i step by step to arbitrary future states st_v and keys, which takes steps linear in the gap $v - i$,

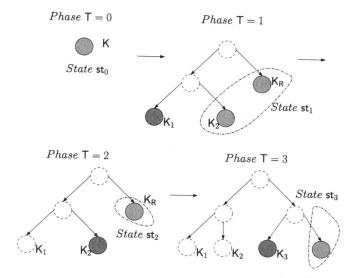

Fig. 3. An example of basic KES execution. (Color figure online)

i.e., a time complexity of $\mathcal{O}(\mathsf{T}_{max})$. This time complexity is also preserved in the PRF-based FSPRG (Construction 2.4 in [4]) and KLE (Fig. 3 in [5]).

We present a more efficient way to reach st_v and K_v as shown in $\Pi_{\mathsf{KES}}.\mathsf{KES}()$ in Fig. 4. In tree $\mathcal{T}$, once the ancestor K_j of the target LTK K_v is found in st_i, it only takes a number logarithmic in T_{max} of $\mathsf{DERIVE}()$ calls to derive the key K_v. Moreover, the ancestor search takes $\mathcal{O}\left(\log\left(\log T_{max}\right)\right)$ steps in a sorted list, so in total it takes $\mathcal{O}(\log T_{max})$ steps to evolve from st_i to the target working LTK K_v and st_v.

Security of Π_{KES}. We summarize the security of Π_{KES} in Theorem 1.

Theorem 1 (Π_{KES} key independence). *If* $\mathsf{PRF}_1()$ *is a* $(t, \epsilon_{\mathsf{PRF}_1})$ *secure PRF, then* Π_{KES} *in Fig. 4 has key independence. More specifically, if the maximal phase is* T_{max}, *then for any* $\mathcal{A}$ *with running time* $t' \approx t$

$$\mathsf{Adv}^{\Pi_{\mathsf{KES}}}_{\mathcal{A},\mathsf{k\text{-}inde}} \leq \mathcal{O}((\log(T_{max}))) \cdot \epsilon_{\mathsf{PRF}_1}, \tag{1}$$

Proof. The proof proceeds in a sequence of games. We use $\Pr[\mathcal{A}, G_j]$ to denote the probability that $\mathcal{A}$ outputs 0 in Game G_j.

Game 0. This game is the real KES oracle game, so we have

$$\Pr[\mathcal{A}, \mathbf{Game}^{\mathsf{Real}}_{\mathsf{KES}}] = \Pr[\mathcal{A}, G_0]$$

Game 1. In this game we change the $\mathsf{PRF}_1()$ for leaf nodes, which output the LTKs, to a random function with the same domain and range. As there are at most $\mathcal{O}(\log(T_{max}))$ such modifications, we have

$$\Pr[\mathcal{A}, G_0] \leq \Pr[\mathcal{A}, G_1] + \mathcal{O}\left(\log(T_{max})\right) \cdot \epsilon_{\mathsf{PRF}_1}$$

KES(st$_i$, v)

---

1 :   IF $i \geq v$: abort;

2 :   Search **in st$_i$ for** a K$_j$ s.t. isPrefix(j, v) = TRUE;

3 :   IF no such j exists : abort;

4 :   Derive K$_v$ with DERIVE() and K$_j$;

5 :   Derive all K on the co-path of K$_v$ with DERIVE() and st$_i$;

6 :   Delete all K' NOT on the co-path of K$_v$ except K$_v$;

7 :   Keep as st$_v$ all the remaining node keys except K$_v$;

8 :   **return** (st$_v$, K$_v$);

---

isPrefix(j, v)

---

1 :   IF len(j) > len(v) : **return** FALSE;

2 : $n \leftarrow$ len(j);

3 :   IF $j = (v)_n$: **return** TRUE;

4 :   **return** FALSE;

DERIVE(K)

---

1 :   K$_L$ ← PRF$_1$(K, "0");

2 :   K$_R$ ← PRF$_1$(K, "1");

3 :   **return** (K$_L$, K$_R$);

Fig. 4. Tree-based KES Π_{KES}, arbitrary jump with $i < v \leq T_{max}$. The term $(v)_n$ means the first n bits of v.

On the other hand, this game is exactly **Game**$_{\mathsf{KES}}^{\mathsf{Rand}}$. So we have

$$\mathsf{Adv}_{\mathcal{A},\mathsf{k\text{-}inde}}^{\Pi_{\mathsf{KES}}} = |\Pr[\mathcal{A}, G_0] - \Pr[\mathcal{A}, G_1]| \leq \mathcal{O}(\log(T_{max})) \cdot \epsilon_{\mathsf{PRF}_1}$$

which is exactly (1).   □

Extending the Lifetime of the Keys. Depending on the setting, the last leaf can either be used as an LTK or as the root for the next tree but not both, if forward secrecy is required. Let $\mathsf{st}_{\tau-1} := \{\mathsf{K}\}$ be the state corresponding to the second right-most leaf of the tree. Let m be the number of leaves of the new tree. Then the LTK K$_\tau$ is derived by calling one-step KES with K as the root and $\log m$ as the depth. The example in Fig. 5 shows the operations needed in $T = 4$ for deriving a new key K$_4$.

4   The Symmetric AKE Security Model

We extend the formal security model for two-party AKE protocols introduced by Bellare and Rogaway [3] and the symmetric key variant [5].

We use matching origin sessions instead of Guaranteed Delivery Matching conversations [5] for defining the partnership of session oracles. We also separate the KES states from LTKs in the Corrupt() query.

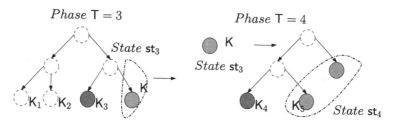

Fig. 5. An example of tree extension. In phase 4, st_3 is used as a root state for the next tree.

4.1 Execution Environment

In the following let $\ell, d \in \mathbb{N}$ be positive integers. In the execution environment, we fix a set of ℓ honest parties $\{P_1, \ldots, P_\ell\}$. Each party holds (symmetric) long term keys with all other parties. We denote with $\mathsf{LTK}^{i,j}$ the symmetric LTK used by P_i to establish secure communication with P_j. Formally, all parties maintain several state variables as described in Table 1.

Table 1. Internal States of Parties

Variable	Description
LTK^i	a vector which contains an entry $\mathsf{LTK}^{i,j}$ per party P_j
st^i	a vector of states maintained by P_i to evolve the corresponding $\mathsf{LTK}^{i,j}$
τ_i	denotes, that LTK^i was corrupted after the τ_i-th query of $\mathcal{A}$
f_i	a vector denoting the freshness of all long term keys. It contains entry $f_{i,j} \in \{\mathsf{exposed}, \mathsf{fresh}\}$ for each $\mathsf{LTK}^{i,j}$ in LTK^i

The variables of each party P_i will be initialized according to the following rules: The state vector st^i are chosen randomly from the root state space of KES and the vector LTK^i is computed accordingly. For all parties P_i, P_j with $i, j \in \{1, \ldots, \ell\}$ and with $i \neq j$, and long-term keys LTK^i, it holds that $\mathsf{LTK}^{i,j} = \mathsf{LTK}^{j,i}$ (synchronized), and $\mathsf{LTK}^{i,i} := \emptyset$. All entries in f_i are set to fresh. τ_i is set to $\tau_i := \infty$, which means that all parties are initially not corrupted.

Each honest party P_i can sequentially and concurrently execute the protocol multiple times, which is characterized by a collection of oracles $\{\pi_i^s : i \in [\ell], s \in [d]\}$. An oracle π_i^s behaves as party P_i carrying out a process to execute the s-th protocol instance with some partner P_j. We assume each oracle π_i^s maintains a list of independent internal state variables as described in Table 2.

The variables of each oracle π_i^s will be initialized with the following rules: The execution-state Φ_i^s is set to `negotiating`. The variable kst_i^s is set to fresh. All other variables are set to only contain the empty string $\emptyset$. At some point, each oracle π_i^s completes the execution with a state $\Phi_i^s \in \{\mathsf{accept}, \mathsf{reject}\}$.

Table 2. Internal States of Oracles

Variable	Description
Φ_i^s	denotes the execution-state $\Phi_i^s \in \{\texttt{negotiating}, \texttt{accept}, \texttt{reject}\}$
Pid_i^s	stores the identity of the intended communication partner
ρ_i^s	denotes the role $\rho_i^s \in \{\mathsf{Client}, \mathsf{Server}\}$
sk_i^s	stores the session application key(s) sk_i^s in $\mathcal{SKS}$, the session key space.
T_i^s	records the transcript of messages sent and received by oracle π_i^s
kst_i^s	denotes the freshness $\mathsf{kst}_i^s \in \{\mathsf{exposed}, \mathsf{fresh}\}$ of the session key

Furthermore, we will always assume (for simplicity) that $\mathsf{sk}_i^s = \emptyset$ if an oracle has not reached accept-state (yet).

Definition 1 (Correctness). *We say that an* AKE *protocol* Π *is correct, if for any two oracles* π_i^s, π_j^t *that are matching origin-sessions with* $\mathsf{Pid}_i^s = j$ *and* $\mathsf{Pid}_j^t = i$ *and* $\Phi_i^s = \mathtt{accept}$ *and* $\Phi_j^t = \mathtt{accept}$ *it always holds that* $\mathsf{sk}_i^s = \mathsf{sk}_j^t$.

Adversarial Model. An adversary $\mathcal{A}$ may interact with $\{\pi_i^s\}$ by issuing the following queries.

- $\mathsf{Send}(\pi_i^s, m)$: This query sends message m to oracle π_i^s. The oracle will respond with the next message m^* (if there is any) that should be sent according to the protocol specification and its internal states.
- $\mathsf{RevealKey}(\pi_i^s)$: Oracle π_i^s responds to a $\mathsf{RevealKey}$-query with the contents of variable sk_i^s, the application keys. At the same time the challenger sets $\mathsf{kst}_i^s = \mathsf{exposed}$. If at the time when $\mathcal{A}$ issues this query there exists another oracle π_j^t that forms matching origin-sessions with π_i^s, then we also set $\mathsf{kst}_j^t = \mathsf{exposed}$ for π_j^t.
- $\mathsf{Corrupt}(P_i, [])$: Depending on the second input parameter, oracle π_i^1 responds with the long-term secrets of party P_i.
  - If $\mathcal{A}$ queries $\mathsf{Corrupt}(P_i, [P_j])$, oracle π_i^1 returns the symmetric long term key $\mathsf{LTK}^{i,j}$ stored in LTK^i and sets $f_{i,j} := \mathsf{exposed}$.
  - If $\mathcal{A}$ queries $\mathsf{Corrupt}(P_i, [\top])$, oracle π_i^1 returns the vector LTK^i and st^i, and sets $f_{i,j} := \mathsf{exposed}$ for all entries $f_{i,*} \in f_i$.
- $\mathsf{Test}(\pi_i^s)$: This query may only be asked once throughout the security experiment. If the oracle has state $\Omega = \mathtt{reject}$ or $\mathsf{sk} = \emptyset$, then it returns a predefined failure symbol $\perp$. Otherwise it flips a fair coin b, samples a random element sk_0 from session key space $\mathcal{SKS}$, sets $\mathsf{sk}_1 = \mathsf{sk}_i^s$ to the real session key, and returns sk_b.

4.2 Security Game

In the game, the following steps are performed: Given the security parameter κ the challenger implements the collection of oracles $\{\pi_i^s : i, j \in [\ell], s \in [d]\}$ with respect to Π. In this process, the challenger also generates a long-term key vector LTK^i for each party P_i, $i \in [\ell]$. Finally, the challenger gives the adversary $\mathcal{A}$ all identifiers $\{P_i\}$ and all public information (if any) as input. Next the adversary may start issuing Send, RevealKey, and Corrupt queries. At the end of the game, the adversary queries the Test oracle, outputs a triple (i, s, b') and terminates.

Definition 2 (Matching Origin-Sessions). *Consider two parties $\mathcal{P}_i$ and $\mathcal{P}_j$ with corresponding oracles π_i^s and π_j^t. π_i^s and π_j^t are said to be matching origin-sessions, if $\mathsf{T}_i^s = \mathsf{T}_j^t$ and $\Phi_i^s = \Phi_j^t = \mathsf{accept}$.*

Definition 3 (Correctness). *We say that an AKE protocol Σ is correct, if for any two oracles π_i^s, π_j^t that are matching origin-sessions with $\mathsf{Pid}_i^s = j$ and $\mathsf{Pid}_j^t = i$ and $\Phi_i^s = \mathsf{accept}$ and $\Phi_j^s = \mathsf{accept}$ it always holds that $\mathsf{sk}_i^s = \mathsf{sk}_j^t$.*

Definition 4 (AKE Security). *We say that an adversary (t, ϵ)-breaks an AKE protocol, if $\mathcal{A}$ runs in time $t' \leq t$, and at least one of the following two conditions holds:*

1. *When $\mathcal{A}$ terminates, then with probability at least ϵ there exists an oracle π_i^s such that*
   - *π_i^s 'accepts' with $\mathsf{Pid}_i^s = j$ when $\mathcal{A}$ issues its τ_0-th query, and*
   - *both P_i and the intended partner P_j are not corrupted throughout the security game, and*
   - *π_i^s has internal state $\mathsf{kst}_i^s = \mathsf{fresh}$, and*
   - *there is no unique oracle π_j^t such that π_i^s and π_j^t are matching origin-sessions.*

   If an oracle π_i^s accepts in the above sense, then we say that π_i^s accepts maliciously and define $\mathcal{A}$'s advantage in this case as

   $$\mathsf{Adv}_{\mathcal{A},\mathsf{AUTH}} = \Pr[\textit{Malicious acceptance happens}]$$

2. *When $\mathcal{A}$ terminates and outputs a triple (i, s, b') such that*
   - *π_i^s 'accepts' – with a unique oracle π_j^t such that π_i^s and π_j^t are matching origin sessions – when $\mathcal{A}$ issues its τ_0-th query, and*
   - *$\mathcal{A}$ did not issue a RevealKey-query to oracle π_i^s nor to π_j^t, i.e. $\mathsf{kst}_i^s = \mathsf{fresh}$, and*
   - *P_i is τ_i-corrupted and P_j is τ_j-corrupted,*

   If an adversary $\mathcal{A}$ outputs (i, s, b') such that $b' = b_i^s$ and the above conditions are met, then we say that $\mathcal{A}$ answers the Test-challenge correctly. We define $\mathcal{A}$'s advantage in this case as the probability that b' equals b_i^s

   $$\mathsf{Adv}_{\mathcal{A},\mathsf{k\text{-}ind}} = \left| \Pr[b_i^s = b'] - \frac{1}{2} \right|.$$

The advantage of $\mathcal{A}$ in the AKE security game is defined

$$\mathsf{Adv}_{\mathcal{A},\mathsf{AKE}} = \mathsf{Adv}_{\mathcal{A},\mathsf{AUTH}} + \mathsf{Adv}_{\mathcal{A},\mathsf{k\text{-}ind}}$$

$\mathcal{A}$ (t, ϵ) breaks an AKE protocol if $\mathsf{Adv}_{\mathcal{A},\mathsf{AKE}} > \epsilon$ with running time $\leq t$. We say that the AKE protocol is (t, ϵ)-secure, if there exists no adversary that (t, ϵ)-breaks it.

Definition 5 (Symmetric-key based AKE Security with Perfect Forward Secrecy). *We say that a symmetric key based AKE protocol is (t, ϵ)-secure with perfect forward secrecy (PFS), if it is (t, ϵ)-secure in the sense of Definition 4 and $\tau_i, \tau_j \geq \tau_0$.*

Remark on the Security Model for TLS 1.2. Authenticated Confidential Channel Establishment (ACCE) [12] is the first formal model to analyze a full version of TLS 1.2 (TLS-(EC)DHE). A symmetric key ACCE model can be derived from our AKE model by replacing the key indistinguishability (Test()-query) with ciphertext indistinguishability (Encrypt()- and Decrypt()- queries) in ACCE. We include the symmetric key ACCE model in the full version of this paper, and we refer the reader to [12] for the complete description of the original ACCE, its motivation and its connection with AKE models.

5   Forward Secrecy for TLS

5.1   New Construction for TLS-PSK 1.2 Protocol with PFS

PRF and Derivation of *pms* and *ms*. For TLS-PSK in TLS 1.2, a client or a server computes from the pre-master secret (pms) the master secret (ms). If the PSK is N bytes long, then the corresponding *pms* is the concatenation of the 2-byte representation (uint16) of the integer value N, N zero bytes, the 2-byte representation of N once again, and finally, the PSK itself. The key derivation function for *ms* is a pseudorandom function named as PRF_TLS, which takes pms, $label_1$, r_C and r_S as input and is implemented with HMAC. More specifically,

$$pms = N||0\cdots0||N||\mathsf{PSK}.$$
$$ms = \mathsf{PRF\_TLS}(pms, r_C||r_S||lable_1)$$

From *ms*, all further secret values are derived as shown in Fig. 6 via the pseudorandom function PRF_TLS().

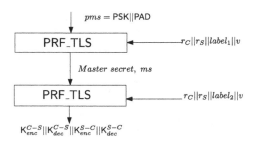

Fig. 6. Overview of TLS 1.2 key schedule. The labels $label_1$, $label_2$ are constants specified in [8].

Construction and Security

Set Up. The client has been provisioned with or evolved into K_v and the corresponding state st_v. The server has been provisioned with or evolved to K_w and the corresponding state st_w, and here the key K_w is used as the current pre-shared key PSK for TLS-PSK. The labels v and w can be different, i.e., not necessarily synchronized. An unsynchronized state may be caused by misconfiguration, unstable network or attacks.

Protocol Execution. The protocol executes once the set-up is completed, as shown in Fig. 7. The ⌐blue⌐ parts are our modifications. Let h be the header of a stateful length-hiding authenticated encryption scheme [12,18]. We use CryptoF() as a short hand notation for the functions [8] that outputs $fin_C || C_C$, where $fin_C := \mathsf{PRF\_TLS}(ms, label_3 || \mathsf{H}(m_1 || \cdots || m_6))$ and $C_C := \mathsf{StE.Enc}(K_{enc}^{Client}, len || h || fin_C || st_e)$ and st_e is the internal state of the encryption scheme. The output of CryptoF() on the server side is $fin_S || C_S$, where $fin_S := \mathsf{PRF\_TLS}(ms, label_4 || \mathsf{H}(m_1 || \cdots || m_8))$ and $C_S := \mathsf{StE.Enc}(K_{enc}^{Server}, len || h || fin_S || st_e)$.

5.2 New Construction for TLS-PSK 1.3 Protocol with PFS

The important gadgets of TLS 1.3 key schedule are illustrated in Fig. 8. Given a constant c, a secret K, two labels ℓ_0, ℓ_1 and a transcript T_0, two PRFs $\mathbb{F}_1$ and $\mathbb{F}_2$ are defined as:

$$\mathbb{F}_1(c, K || \ell_0 || T_0) = \mathsf{HKDF.Extract}(c, \mathsf{DeriveSecret}(K, \ell_0 || T_0)) \qquad (2)$$

$$\mathbb{F}_2(K, \ell_0 || \ell_1 || T_0) = \mathsf{HKDF.Expand}(\mathsf{DeriveSecret}(K, \ell_0 || T_0), \ell_1). \qquad (3)$$

We use $\mathbb{F}_1$ and $\mathbb{F}_2$ in the description of our extension of TLS-PSK 1.3.

Protocol Extension and Security. In the original TLS PSK, the server continues if a PSK with the given identifier can be retrieved and binders can be verified. Otherwise, the server aborts.

Here, we also use the PSK identifier to locate the right key to update. When received, the PSK identifier is parsed as the concatenation of a tree id T_{id} and a phase id. The server searches with T_{id} for this client's KES tree and uses the phase id to evolve the PSK. If the LTK can be derived correctly, i.e., the KES tree exists and the phase is valid, then the process will continue till the end. Otherwise, the server will abort. Therefore, the behaviour of the server is identical to that in the original TLS-PSK, and whole KES can be seamlessly integrated into TLS without affecting the original TLS stack. See Fig. 9 for the remaining details, where the ⌐blue⌐ parts are our modifications.

Security and Re-synchronization for Strong Robustness. The security theorems of both extensions of TLS-PSK can be found in Appendix A, and proofs can be found in the full version.

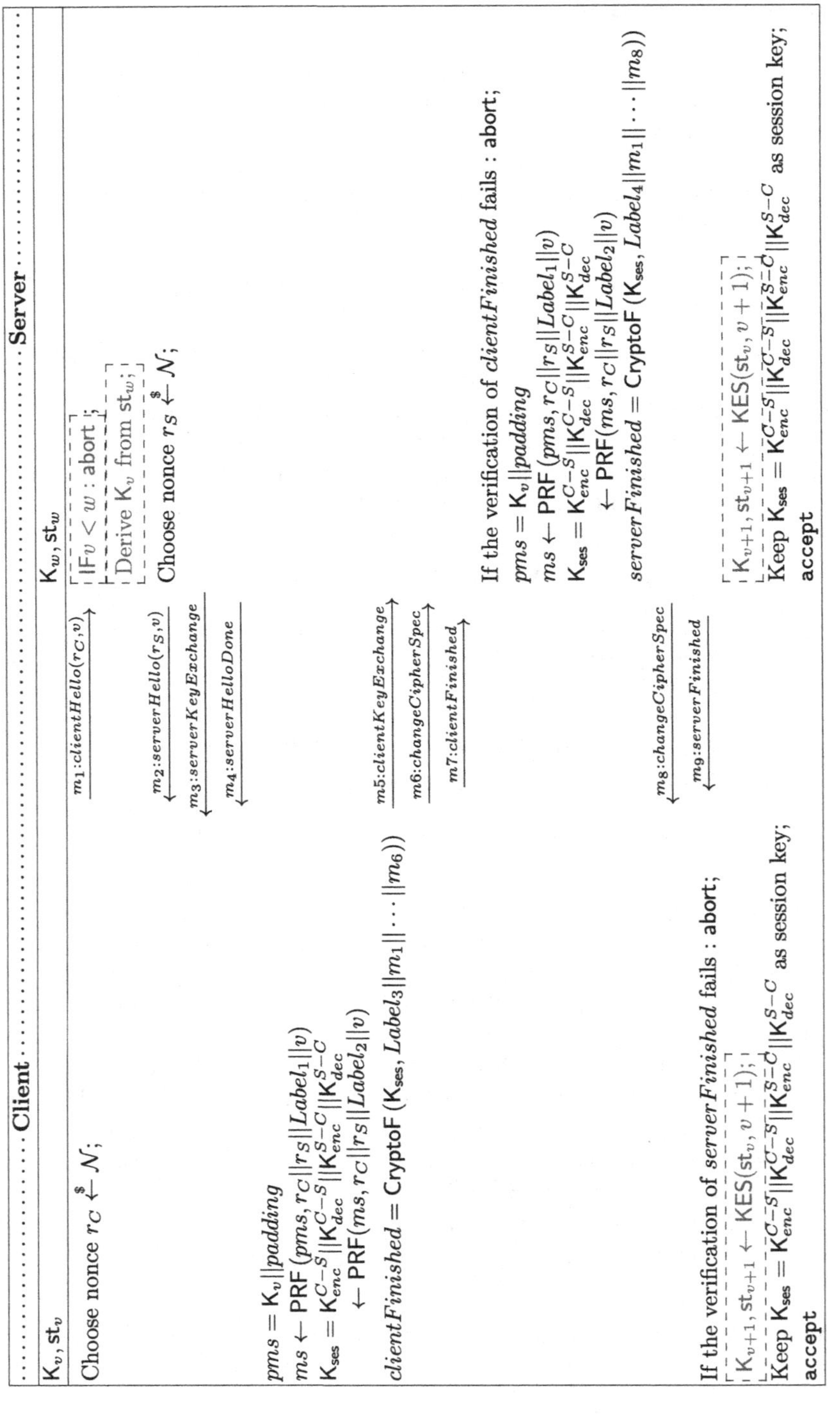

Fig. 7. Extended TLS-PSK(1.2) protocol TLS12$_{\text{KES}}$ with PFS (Color figure online)

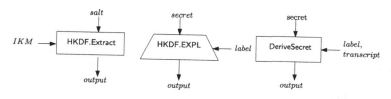

Fig. 8. Gadgets in TLS 1.3 key schedule [11].

```
···················· Client ················································································· Server ···············
Kᵥ, stᵥ
Choose nonce r_C ←$ 𝒩;                          m₁:ClientHello(r_C,v)    IF v < w : abort;
                                                                         Derive Kᵥ from st_w ;
                                                m₂:ServerHello(r_S,v)    Kᵥ, st_w
                                              ←                          Choose nonce r_S ←$ 𝒩;
                                                                         Verify binders with derived binder_entry_key;
                                                                         Derive secrets and compute ServerFinished:
                                                                         ess = HKDF.Extract(Kᵥ, |0|ₕ)
                                                                         hss = 𝔽₁('0', ess||ℓ₁||T₀)
                                                                         K_hs^{S−C} = 𝔽₂(hss, ℓ₃||ℓ₇||T₁)
                                                                         IV_hs^{S−C} = 𝔽₂(hss, ℓ₃||'IV'||T₁)
                                                                         K_fin^{S−C} = 𝔽₂(hss, ℓ₃||ℓ₆||T₁)
                                                                         S_finished = HMAC(K_fin^{S−C}, H(T₁))
                                                                         ServerFinished = Enc(K_hs^{S−C}, IV_hs^{S−C}, S_finished)
                                                m₃:ServerFinished
                                              ←
ess = HKDF.Extract(Kᵥ, |0|ₕ)
hss = 𝔽₁('0', ess||ℓ₁||T₀)
Derive K_hs^{S−C}, IV_hs^{S−C}, K_fin^{S−C} as Server does.
If the verification of ServerFinished fails : abort;

Derive secrets and compute ClientFinished:
K_hs^{C−S} = 𝔽₂(hss, ℓ₂||ℓ₇||T₁)
IV_hs^{C−S} = 𝔽₂(hss, ℓ₂||'IV'||T₁)
K_fin^{C−S} = 𝔽₂(hss, ℓ₂||ℓ₆||T₁)
C_finished = HMAC(K_fin^{C−S}, H(T₂))
ClientFinished = Enc(K_hs^{C−S}, IV_hs^{C−S}, C_finished)
                                                m₄:ClientFinished
                                              →                          Derive K_hs^{C−S}, IV_hs^{C−S}, K_fin^{C−S} as Client does.
                                                                         If the verification of ClientFinished fails : abort;
ms = 𝔽₁('0', hss||ℓ₁||T₀)                                                ms = 𝔽₁('0', hss||ℓ₁||T₀)
K_app^{C−S} = 𝔽₂(ms, ℓ₄||ℓ₇||T₂)                                          K_app^{C−S} = 𝔽₂(ms, ℓ₄||ℓ₇||T₂)
K_app^{S−C} = 𝔽₂(ms, ℓ₅||ℓ₇||T₂)                                          K_app^{S−C} = 𝔽₂(ms, ℓ₅||ℓ₇||T₂)
Kᵥ₊₁, stᵥ₊₁ ← KES(stᵥ, v + 1);                                           K_{w+1}, st_{w+1} ← KES(st_w, v + 1);
accept                                                                   accept
```

$$K_{hs}^{S-C} = \mathbb{F}_2(\mathsf{hss}, \ell_3 \| \ell_7 \| T_1)$$
$$IV_{hs}^{S-C} = \mathbb{F}_2(\mathsf{hss}, \ell_3 \| \text{'IV'} \| T_1)$$
$$K_{fin}^{S-C} = \mathbb{F}_2(\mathsf{hss}, \ell_3 \| \ell_6 \| T_1)$$
$$S_{finished} = \mathrm{HMAC}(K_{fin}^{S-C}, H(T_1))$$

Fig. 9. Extended TLS (1.3)-PSK protocol: TLS13$_{\mathsf{KES}}$ with PFS. The boxed parts are our modifications. (Color figure online)

Both TLS12$_{\mathsf{KES}}$ and TLS13$_{\mathsf{KES}}$ have the weak robustness defined in [5]. If we consider the case where a client has an unsynchronized state (i.e., client's state index is smaller than that of the server), then there are two approaches to achieve strong robustness. The first approach is to let the server response with its own label, adding one more round of communication. The second approach is to let the client re-try with a label double as large. The round complexity of the second approach is upper-bounded by $\mathcal{O}\left(\log(T_{max})^2\right)$.

6   Implementation and Performance Evaluation

We integrate our implementation with Bouncy Castle TLS library v1.70[3] with less than 700 lines of code, without modifying the library. This demonstrates also how simple it is to integrate our protocol in TLS.

Figure 10 shows the benchmark result of three PSK options in different environments. For ECDHE-PSK, TLS_ECDHE_PSK _WITH_AES_128_GCM_SHA256 with Curve25519 for the ECDHE is applied and TLS_PSK_WITH_AES_128_GCM_SHA256 is used for this work and the plain PSK. We run the TLS server on a machine with OS Ubuntu 18.04 LTS, and Intel(R) Xeon(R) CPU E5-2470 v2 @ 2.40GHz. The TLS clients are on the same host as the server for the loopback test. For the LAN tests, the TLS clients are on another machine but with the same settings as the server. We use the tool Wonder Shaper[4] to set the maximum upload and download rate. For the WAN test, the clients are on a typical laptop (Windows 10, Intel Core i7-8565U @1.80 GHz) and are connected to the server via VPN over the Internet.

In all tests, we start the TLS server before activating the TLS clients. The results are taken as an average of 60 s of continuous measurements. As illustrated in Fig. 10, in all settings, our work is only slightly slower than plain PSK, and is obviously much faster than (TLS-)ECDHE-PSK. Further discussion about deployment and implementation is in Appendix C.

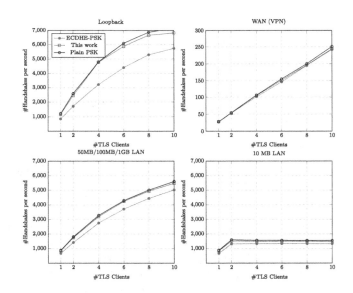

Fig. 10. Speed of handshakes

---

[3] https://www.bouncycastle.org/.

[4] https://github.com/magnific0/wondershaper.

A   Security Theorems for Extended TLS-PSK

Theorem 2 (Extended TLS 1.2, authenticity). *It holds for the advantage of any adversary $\mathcal{A}_1$ running in time $t' \approx t$ trying to break the authenticity of* $\mathsf{TLS12_{KES}}$ *that*

$$\mathsf{Adv}_{\mathcal{A}_1,\mathsf{AUTH}} \leq \frac{(d \cdot l)^2}{|\mathcal{N}|} + (d \cdot l)^2 \cdot \left(\epsilon_{\mathsf{KES}} + 2\epsilon_{\mathsf{PRF\_TLS}} + \epsilon_{\mathsf{MAC}} \right)$$

where d is the maximal number of parties, ℓ the maximal number of sessions each party can have, $\mathcal{N}$ the space of nonces, $\epsilon_{\mathsf{PRF\_TLS}}$ the advantage against the pseudorandom function $\mathsf{PRF\_TLS}$ *for MAC key generation, ϵ_{KES} the advantage against the key evolving scheme* KES *used for PSK update, ϵ_{MAC} the advantage against the message authentication code* MAC *for acknowledgement messages, and the running time of all these adversaries is bound by t.*

Theorem 3 (Extended TLS 1.2, ACCE security). *It holds for the advantage of any adversary $\mathcal{A}_2$ running in time $t' \approx t$ against the symmetric ACCE protocol* $\mathsf{TLS12_{KES}}$ *that*

$$\mathsf{Adv}_{\mathcal{A}_2,\mathsf{ACCE}} \leq \mathsf{Adv}_{\mathcal{A}_1,\mathsf{AUTH}} + \frac{(d \cdot l)^2}{|\mathcal{N}|}$$
$$+ (d \cdot l)^2 \cdot (\epsilon_{\mathsf{KES}} + 2\epsilon_{\mathsf{PRF\_TLS}} + 2\epsilon_{\mathsf{ENC}})$$

where the running time of all these adversaries is bound by t, ϵ_{ENC} the advantage against the encryption scheme[5], and the other variables are as defined in Theorem 2.

Theorem 4 (Extended TLS 1.3, authenticity). *It holds for the advantage of any adversary $\mathcal{A}_1$ running in time $t' \approx t$ trying to break the authenticity of* $\mathsf{TLS13_{KES}}$ *that*

$$\mathsf{Adv}_{\mathcal{A}_1,\mathsf{AUTH}} \leq \frac{(d \cdot l)^2}{|\mathcal{N}|} + (d \cdot l)^2 \cdot \left(\epsilon_{\mathsf{KES}} + \epsilon_{\mathsf{HKDF.Extract}} + \epsilon_{\mathsf{PRF}_1} \right.$$
$$\left. + 2\epsilon_{\mathsf{PRF}_2} + \epsilon_{\mathsf{MAC}} + \epsilon_{\mathsf{ENC}} \right)$$

where d is the maximal number of parties, ℓ the maximal number of sessions each party can have, $\mathcal{N}$ the space of nonces, $\epsilon_{\mathsf{HKDF.Extract}}$ the advantage against the pseudorandom function $\mathsf{HKDF.Extract}()$, $\epsilon_{\mathsf{PRF}_1}$ *the advantage against the pseudo random function* $\mathbb{F}_1()$, ϵ_{KES} *the advantage against the key evolving scheme* KES *used for PSK update, $\epsilon_{\mathsf{PRF}_2}$ the advantage against the pseudorandom function* $\mathbb{F}_2()$, ϵ_{MAC} *the advantage against the MAC scheme* $\mathsf{HMAC}()$ ϵ_{ENC} *the advantage against the AEAD scheme* ENC *for handshake messages, and the running time of all these adversaries is bound by t.*

---

[5] The encryption scheme should be a stateful length-hiding authenticated encryption as defined in [12].

Theorem 5 (Extended TLS 1.3, key indistinguishability). *It holds for the advantage of any adversary $\mathcal{A}_2$ running in time $t' \approx t$ against the key indistinguishability of the symmetric AKE protocol* $\mathsf{TLS13_{KES}}$ *that*

$$\mathsf{Adv}_{\mathcal{A}_2,\mathsf{KI}} \leq \mathsf{Adv}_{\mathcal{A}_1,\mathsf{AUTH}} + \frac{(d \cdot l)^2}{|\mathcal{N}|}$$
$$+ (d \cdot l)^2 \cdot (\epsilon_{\mathsf{KES}} + 2\epsilon_{\mathsf{PRF}_1} + 2\epsilon_{\mathsf{PRF}_2} + \epsilon_{\mathsf{ENC}})$$

where the running time of all these adversaries is bound by t, and the other variables are as defined in Theorem 4.

B   Cryptographic Primitives

Definition 3. *(Message Authentication Code, MAC) A MAC scheme* $\mathsf{MAC} = (\mathsf{MAC.Gen}, \mathsf{MAC.Tag}, \mathsf{MAC.Vfy})$ *consists of three algorithms* $\mathsf{MAC.Gen}, \mathsf{MAC.Tag}$ *and* $\mathsf{MAC.Vfy}$ *described as below.*

- $\mathsf{MAC.Gen}(1^n) \xrightarrow{\$} \mathsf{k}$. *The non-deterministic key generation algorithm* $\mathsf{MAC.Gen}()$ *takes the security parameter 1^n as the input and outputs the secret key* k.
- $\mathsf{MAC.Tag}(\mathsf{k}, m) \xrightarrow{\$} \tau$. *The (non-deterministic) message tagging algorithm* $\mathsf{MAC.Tag}()$ *takes the secret key k and a message m as the input and outputs the authentication tag τ.*
- $\mathsf{MAC.Vfy}(\mathsf{k}, m, \tau) = b$. *The deterministic tag verification algorithm* $\mathsf{MAC.Vfy}()$ *takes the MAC secret key k, a message m and a tag τ as input and outputs a boolean value b. Value b is* TRUE *iff τ is a valid MAC tag on m.*

Definition 4. *(Collision-resistant Hash Function) A hash function $H : \mathcal{M} \to \mathcal{D}$ is collision resistant if there exists a negligible function $\epsilon_{\mathsf{coll}}()$ such that for any algorithm $\mathcal{A}$ with running time bounded by $\mathsf{poly}(n)$, it holds that*

$$\Pr\left[\begin{array}{c}(m_0, m_1) \leftarrow \mathcal{A}(1^n, H) : \\ m_0 \neq m_1 \bigwedge H(m_0) = H(m_1)\end{array}\right] \leq \epsilon_{\mathsf{coll}}(n),$$

where $\mathcal{M}$ is the message space and $\mathcal{D}$ is the hash image space.

Definition 5. *(Pseudorandom function, PRF) A pseudorandom function* $\mathbb{F} = (\mathsf{FKGen}, \mathsf{PRF})$ *consists of two algorithms* FKGen *and* PRF *described as below.*

- $\mathbb{F}.\mathsf{FKGen}(1^n) \xrightarrow{\$} \mathsf{k}$. *The non-deterministic key generation algorithm* $\mathsf{FKGen}()$ *takes the security parameter 1^n as the input and outputs the secret key* k.
- $\mathbb{F}.\mathsf{PRF}(\mathsf{k}, x) = y$. *The PRF evaluation algorithm* $\mathsf{PRF}()$ *takes as the input the secret key k and a value x in the domain and outputs an image y. We also use shorthand notation* $\mathbb{F}()$ *or* $\mathsf{PRF}()$ *for* $\mathbb{F}.\mathsf{PRF}()$.

Definition 6. *(authenticated symmetric key encryption scheme with associated data, AEAD [19]) An AEAD encryption scheme $\Pi = (\mathsf{KGen}, \mathsf{ENC}, \mathsf{DEC})$ consists of three algorithms* $\mathsf{KGen}, \mathsf{ENC}$ *and* DEC *described as below.*

- $\Pi.\mathsf{KGen}(1^n) \xrightarrow{\$} \mathsf{k}$. *The non-deterministic key generation algorithm* $\mathsf{KGen}()$ *takes the security parameter* 1^n *as the input and outputs one encryption-decryption key* k.
- $\Pi.\mathsf{ENC}(\mathsf{k}, m) \xrightarrow{\$} \mathsf{CT}$. *The (non-deterministic) encryption algorithm* $\mathsf{ENC}()$ *takes the key* k *and a message* m *as the input and outputs a ciphertext* CT.
- $\Pi.\mathsf{DEC}(\mathsf{k}, \mathsf{CT}) = m'$. *The deterministic decryption algorithm* $\mathsf{DEC}()$ *takes the key* k, *a ciphertext* CT *as input and outputs a plaintext* m'.

C   Discussion About Deployment and Implementation

Secure Storage of Key Materials and Side Channels. To ensure the functionality of TLS-PSK proposed in this paper, KES trees must be maintained reliably by the server. The persistent storage of KES trees can be realized with non-volatile memory, or relying on hardware security module (HSM) with ciphertexts databases. Depending on the concrete implementation, side channels may exist in the software, the hardware, the time of I/O and network latency. It remains an interesting research topic to mitigate the possible side channel attacks.

Parallel Sessions and Compatibility with Resumption and Session Ticket. As long as the parallel handshakes can be serialized by the server and client, protocols in Fig. 7 and Fig. 9 can work properly. On the other hand, the update can also be periodic instead of session-triggered. In each period, parallel session can use identical PSK as in the original TLS-PSK.

Besides KES, our current TLS-PSK implementation does not modify other TLS extensions, including the resumption and session ticket. Thus, it can work with resumption and session ticket as the original TLS-PSK does, but (EC)DHE must be disabled in resumption if we stick to symmetric-key-based TLS-PSK.

References

1. Aviram, N., Gellert, K., Jager, T.: Session resumption protocols and efficient forward security for TLS 1.3 0-RTT. J. Cryptol. **34**(3), 20 (2021)
2. Avoine, G., Canard, S., Ferreira, L.: Symmetric-key authenticated key exchange (SAKE) with perfect forward secrecy. In: Jarecki, S. (ed.) CT-RSA 2020. LNCS, vol. 12006, pp. 199–224. Springer, Cham (2020). https://doi.org/10.1007/978-3-030-40186-3_10
3. Bellare, M., Rogaway, P.: Entity authentication and key distribution. In: Stinson, D.R. (ed.) CRYPTO 1993. LNCS, vol. 773, pp. 232–249. Springer, Heidelberg (1994). https://doi.org/10.1007/3-540-48329-2_21
4. Bellare, M., Yee, B.: Forward-security in private-key cryptography. In: Joye, M. (ed.) CT-RSA 2003. LNCS, vol. 2612, pp. 1–18. Springer, Heidelberg (2003). https://doi.org/10.1007/3-540-36563-X_1
5. Boyd, C., Davies, G.T., de Kock, B., Gellert, K., Jager, T., Millerjord, L.: Symmetric key exchange with full forward security and robust synchronization. Cryptology ePrint Archive, Report 2021/702 (2021). https://ia.cr/2021/702

6. Chien, H.Y.: SASI: a new ultralightweight RFID authentication protocol providing strong authentication and strong integrity. IEEE Trans. Dependable Secure Comput. 4(4), 337–340 (2007)
7. Developers, B.S.: Bouncy Castle Crypto APIs (2013). http://www.bouncycastle.org
8. Dierks, T., Rescorla, E.: The Transport Layer Security (TLS) Protocol Version 1.2. RFC 5246 (Proposed Standard) (2008). http://www.ietf.org/rfc/rfc5246.txt. Updated by RFCs 5746, 5878
9. Dousti, M.S., Jalili, R.: Forsakes: a forward-secure authenticated key exchange protocol based on symmetric key-evolving schemes. Adv. Math. Commun. 9(4), 471 (2015)
10. Gutmann, P.: Cryptlib (2014). https://www.cs.auckland.ac.nz/~pgut001/cryptlib
11. Rescorla, E.: The transport layer security (TLS) protocol version 1.3. draft-ietf-tls-tls13-26. Internet Engineering Task Force (2018). https://tools.ietf.org/html/draft-ietf-tls-tls13-26
12. Jager, T., Kohlar, F., Schäge, S., Schwenk, J.: On the security of TLS-DHE in the standard model. In: Safavi-Naini, R., Canetti, R. (eds.) CRYPTO 2012. LNCS, vol. 7417, pp. 273–293. Springer, Heidelberg (2012). https://doi.org/10.1007/978-3-642-32009-5_17
13. Katz, J., Lindell, Y.: Introduction to Modern Cryptography. CRC Press, Boca Raton (2014)
14. Li, Y., Schäge, S., Yang, Z., Kohlar, F., Schwenk, J.: On the security of the pre-shared key ciphersuites of TLS. In: Krawczyk, H. (ed.) PKC 2014. LNCS, vol. 8383, pp. 669–684. Springer, Heidelberg (2014). https://doi.org/10.1007/978-3-642-54631-0_38
15. OpenSSL: The OpenSSL project (2013). http://www.openssl.org
16. Ouska, T.: CyaSSL (2013). http://www.wolfssl.com/yaSSL/Home.html
17. Urien, P., Cogneau, L., Martin, P.: EMV support for TLS-PSK. draft-urien-tls-psk-emv-02 (2011). http://tools.ietf.org/html/draft-urien-tls-psk-emv-02
18. Paterson, K.G., Ristenpart, T., Shrimpton, T.: Tag size *Does* matter: attacks and proofs for the TLS record protocol. In: Lee, D.H., Wang, X. (eds.) ASIACRYPT 2011. LNCS, vol. 7073, pp. 372–389. Springer, Heidelberg (2011). https://doi.org/10.1007/978-3-642-25385-0_20
19. Rogaway, P.: Authenticated-encryption with associated-data. In: Atluri, V. (ed.) ACM CCS 02: 9th Conference on Computer and Communications Security, pp. 98–107. ACM Press (2002)
20. Urien, P.: EMV-TLS, a secure payment protocol for NFC enabled mobiles. In: 2014 International Conference on Collaboration Technologies and Systems, CTS 2014, Minneapolis, MN, USA, 19–23 May 2014, pp. 203–210. IEEE (2014). https://doi.org/10.1109/CTS.2014.6867565
21. Urien, P.: Innovative DTLS/TLS security modules embedded in SIM cards for IoT trusted and secure services. In: 13th IEEE Annual Consumer Communications & Networking Conference, CCNC 2016, Las Vegas, NV, USA, 9–12 January 2016, pp. 276–277. IEEE (2016). https://doi.org/10.1109/CCNC.2016.7444778

On the Privacy-Preserving Infrastructure for Authenticated Key Exchange

Li Duan[1,2] and Yong Li[2(✉)]

[1] Paderborn University, Paderborn, Germany
`liduan@mail.upb.de`
[2] Huawei Technologies Düsseldorf, Düsseldorf, Germany
`{li.duan,yong.li1}@huawei.com`

Abstract. Privacy-preserving authenticated key exchange (PPAKE) protocols aim at providing both session key indistinguishability and party identifier hiding. Parties in PPAKEs usually interact with a public key infrastructure (PKI) or similar services for authentication, especially for validating certificates and other identity-binding tokens during the handshake. However, these essential validation messages, which have not been captured in current models, open attack surfaces for adversaries. In this paper, we propose a new refined infrastructure model (RI) for privacy in the infrastructure. As the cryptographic core, we also present a novel certificate validation protocol (CVP) that can be instantiated with anonymous Bloom filter key encapsulation mechanisms (ANO-BFKEM). The new CVP protects user identity in certificate validation, thus enhances the privacy guarantee of PPAKE.

Keywords: privacy · cryptographic protocols · public key infrastructure · formal model · privacy-preserving authenticated key exchange

1 Introduction

Billions of users rely on the Internet in their daily lives, and protecting user privacy, especially user identifiers, has always been a challenge for the research community and industry. As exposing the victim's identifier (ID) can be a stepping stone for more devastating attacks [4,14,19], avoiding ID leakage from the beginning of the communication is ideal.

Various notions have been formalized for authenticated key exchange protocols (AKE) with privacy guarantees. Identity concealed key exchange [21,32] and privacy-preserving authenticated key exchange (PPAKE) [2,25,27] are frequently used for their privacy feature. On the other hand, PPAKE protocols still rely on infrastructures for validating the participants' certificates or ID-binding tokens. Typical infrastructures are key generation center (KGC), key management system (KMS), and public key infrastructure (PKI). PKI provides status information on certificates via interactive protocols.

© The Author(s), under exclusive license to Springer Nature Switzerland AG 2023
E. Athanasopoulos and B. Mennink (Eds.): ISC 2023, LNCS 14411, pp. 435–454, 2023.
https://doi.org/10.1007/978-3-031-49187-0_22

The certificate validation logic has been modeled in previous AKE and PPAKE works with a simple operation usually called *verify certificate* [2, 8, 18, 20, 27]. Theoretically, an AKE session should reach the state of `reject` and set its session key to an invalid value $\perp$, when the certificate status response indicates invalidity. In practice, any participants should terminate the handshake immediately upon seeing an invalid certificate. For instance, in Transport Layer Security (TLS) [15], a client should terminate its connection with the server, if the server's certificate is in the certificate revocation list (CRL) [9] or the response of the Online Certificate Status Protocol (OCSP) [16] is invalid or unknown.

1.1 Certificate Validation Tells ID

However, this oversimplification of certificate validation in AKE/PPAKE models leaves chances for adversaries who look for the ID, as the validation responses are required to be non-malleable but not necessarily confidential in the ideal world [7] in theory. We show a concrete attack against ID privacy here. The messages sent to and received from the certification authority (CA) during the TLS handshake are marked red in Fig. 1.

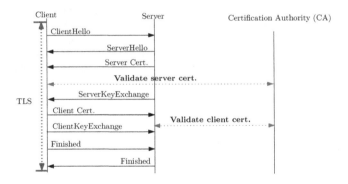

Fig. 1. Certificate status queries in TLS Handshake, marked in dotted red lines. (Color figure online)

Suppose that a client and a server use OCSP for validating certificates. An OCSP request [16] contains the protocol version, the service request, **the target certificate identifier** and optional extensions. The OCSP response for each certificate contains the **target certificate identifier**, certificate status value, response validity interval and optional extensions. Thus, it is straight forward to identify the real communicating parties.

Similar patterns can be observed in PPAKE proposals in [2, 25, 27] as shown in Fig. 2. During the handshake, a party sends its certificate $\mathsf{cert}_V, V \in \{\mathsf{Client}, \mathsf{Server}\}$ encrypted with a handshake key k to its peer, which will trigger a certificate validation implicitly. If the validation is implemented with plain OCSP, then the OCSP messages enable an adversary to break the privacy of the protocol without much effort.

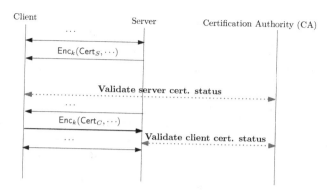

Fig. 2. Privacy leakage from certificate status checking messages in dotted red lines. This pattern can be found in Protocols 1, 2 and 3 in [25]. The IB-CAKE in Figure 2 of [21] also has this pattern, where ID functions as a certificate and must be verified. (Color figure online)

1.2 Problem Statement and Technical Overview

Adversaries. We model the adversary $\mathcal{A}$ as an information thief who aims to know the ID of a legitimate user of CA. Intuitively, $\mathcal{A}$ is an external attacker who can manipulate all the communications over a well-defined part of the network and even obtain secret information held by a CA under certain conditions. But $\mathcal{A}$ **cannot** control any CA or the target client directly. This intuition will be formalized with oracle queries and the CVP freshness in Sect. 3.2.

Avoid Channel Assumptions. The attacks in Sect. 1.1 originate from the fact that current PPAKE notions have not captured any infrastructure protocol messages in the handshake, and an external adversary $\mathcal{A}$ can read the ID-related messages in plaintexts.

To mitigate such attacks, one may be tempted to assume that secure channels exist before a PPAKE handshake, such as active TLS channels between clients and CA. This assumption, however, falls into a circular argument, which can be easily seen by asking the following questions. How can such channels themselves be established initially? Is another protocol Π' needed for establishing such a channel so that ID is not leaked? If so, how can the infrastructure supporting Π' avoid ID leakage? Does it rely on another such channel? One may also argue that a fully manual setup of a private channel can evict the attacks, but that solution does not scale, and it also introduces strong system assumptions.

Challenges and Our Solution. Hence, we tackle the ID-leaking problem in the infrastructure in another way. We aim to construct a self-contained infrastructure which has confidentiality and privacy against any information-stealing adversary $\mathcal{A}$. To systematically construct the cryptographic core of this infrastructure, we first provide an abstraction of any certificate validation mechanism called certificate verification protocol (CVP). Then, we set the constraints for public parameters. As CVP is formalized as a public service which does not assume pre-shared symmetric keys or long-term user key pairs, we leverage public key encryption (PKE) variants and compose them with other tools to meet the following secrecy and privacy (anonymity) challenges.

- *Forward secrecy of Queries.* Client and CA have to exchange messages, but conventional IND-CPA and IND-CCA PKE do not guarantee secrecy after decryption key exposure. On the other hand, as mentioned in our adversary model, $\mathcal{A}$ can corrupt the CA to obtain the decryption key at some time τ. Moreover, forward secrecy, i.e., secrecy of messages sent before τ, is essential for CVP. Thus we use an enhanced PKE primitive called Bloom Filter Encryption [10] for the CVP messages, which can disable the decryption key on received ciphertexts without changing the public key. This disabling operation is called puncturing.
- *Receiver-anonymity of Queries.* Encryption and puncturing do not directly lead to anonymity or privacy, as the ciphertext itself may leak the receiver's ID. An example is any PKE with ciphertexts containing a linkable signature σ. By linkable we mean it is easy to link σ to a public verification key bound to a unique ID. However, CA usually has a unique ID, and a user $\mathcal{C}_0$ may always contact the same CA Server_0. If such a PKE with signatures is used, $\mathcal{C}_0$'s behaviour can be distinguished from another $\mathcal{C}_1$ who does not use this Server_0 by verifying σ against Server_0's public key. Therefore, we also need the encryption scheme to be an anonymous PKE [3] which hides the correct receiver's public key and identity in the ciphertext.
- *Forward Receiver-anonymity.* The previous problems are addressed in this paper with pure algorithmic solutions, but the impact of a leaked decryption key (via $\mathcal{A}$'s corruption) on anonymity must also be considered. The subtlety is that in Bloom Filter Encryption, the decryption key records information about the punctured ciphertext to disable their decryption. If the key is seen in plaintext, it tells whether the key owner has received a given ciphertext, breaking the receiver's **forward** anonymity against $\mathcal{A}$. Therefore, we need extra tools together with another layer of encryption to hide the records against later corruption. We opt for a physical unclonable function (PUF) as it is a well-understood notion and widely deployed in practice [11].

1.3   Our Contribution and Paper Outline

We believe it is essential to have clear assumptions about the privacy guarantee in infrastructures and sound construction of certificate validation protocols, so we made the following contributions in this paper.

- We propose a formal model with set-up assumptions and queries to analyze the privacy threats to PKI-like infrastructure. We call it the Refined Infrastructure Model (RI).
- The cryptographic core of a privacy-preserving infrastructure is a certificate validation protocol (CVP). We formalize CVP and present new CVP

protocols based on anonymous Bloom filter key encapsulation mechanism (ANO-BFKEM) and PUF. Although our results should primarily be considered as an initial exploration of CVP with provable forward secrecy and anonymity, it is also possible to implement the instantiation in Fig. 7.

The related work is surveyed in Sect. 1.4 and the essential cryptographic primitives are introduced in Sect. 2. The refined infrastructure model (RI) is presented in Sect. 3. Our new CVP protocol is presented in Sect. 3.3 with its instantiation from ANO-BFKEM and PUF. Finally, the conclusion and possible future work are covered in Sect. 4.

1.4   Related Work

AKE with Privacy. In 2019, Arfaoui *et al.* [2] defined privacy in AKE protocols with a formal indistinguishability-based (game-based) model to analyze TLS 1.3. This privacy-preserving authenticated key exchange (PPAKE) model constrains an adversary's ability to link sessions to party identifiers. For example, attacks are only allowed for completed sessions and server's ID cannot be a target. The unilateral privacy guarantee of TLS 1.3 [15] is discussed thoroughly under this model [2]. In the sequel, Schäge *et al.* [27] proposed a strong model for privacy preserving authenticated key exchange in 2020, by removing some constraints on the privacy adversary. An alternative model, the ID-concealing AKE, was proposed by Zhao [32] in 2016 and then extended by Lian *et al.* [21] with new constructions in 2021. The construction depends on a key generation center (KGC), an infrastructure frequently used in identity-based encryption schemes. In the same conference, Ramacher *et al.* proposed a model with fine-grained definitions of privacy in PPAKE [25], relaxing even more constraints on privacy adversaries. For example, interrupted sessions can be the target of privacy attacks. Except for the one relying on a pre-shared symmetric key, which is less secure, the constructions in [25] use certificates for the exact identification of the communicating peers. In 2022, Lyu *et al.* [24] present another alternative model and constructions for PPAKE over broadcast channels. All of the models above assume anonymity on the network layer and that the adversary can only see part of the messages on the application layer but does not make any assumption about the cryptographic infrastructure.

Bloom Filter Encryption and Anonymous Public Key Encryption. As a variant of puncturable encryption (PE) [12], Bloom filter key encapsulation mechanism (BFKEM) was first introduced by Derler *et al.* [10] (**DGJSS** henceforth) for constructing efficient 0-RTT AKE with forward secrecy. BFKEM has its public-private key pair associated with a Bloom filter (BF) [5]. As in a PE, the private key sk of BFKEM can be updated (punctured) to disable it on a set of ciphertexts but remain useful for others. Another attractive merit of BFKEM is that its public key remains *unmodified* after puncturing. However, BFKEM alone cannot guarantee forward privacy, as the private key stores the information about which ciphertext is punctured.

Initially formalized by Bellare *et al.* [3] in 2001 and refined in Halevi's note on sufficient condition for key-privacy in 2005 [13], the notion of anonymous public key encryption (ANO-PKE) has been widely used in analyzing anonymous identity-based encryption (IBE/ANO-IBE) [1], designing anonymous hierarchical identity-based encryption [6] and broadcast encryption [22]. ANO-PKE ensures that any adversary $\mathcal{A}$ cannot efficiently decide whether a given ciphertext is encrypted under which public key, even when the plaintext(s) and the candidate public keys are chosen by $\mathcal{A}$. Nevertheless, ANO-PKE alone as a primitive does not guarantee anything after private key exposure. Given all static private keys, it is trivial to find out what the content and who the receiver is by decrypting the ciphertext, i.e., ANO-PKE alone does guarantee forward secrecy.

2   Notation and Preliminaries

The Greek letter $\lambda \in \mathbb{N}$ is used to denote the security parameter and 1^λ for the unary string of length λ. Let $[n] = \{1, \ldots, n\} \subset \mathbb{N}$ be the set of integers from 1 to n. The term $a \xleftarrow{\$} S$ denotes the action of sampling an element a from a set S uniformly at random, and $|S|$ is the number of elements in set S. If $\mathcal{A}()$ is an algorithm, then $m \xleftarrow{\$} \mathcal{A}^{O(\cdot)}()$ means that $\mathcal{A}$ outputs m with the help of another oracle $O(\cdot)$. Let $X||Y$ denote the operation concatenating two binary strings X and Y. $\Pr[A : B]$ denotes the probability that event A happens if B holds or action B has been taken. We use PPT for *polynomial probabilistic time*. We use $\epsilon_{X,Y}^Z$ and $\mathsf{Adv}_{X,Y}^Z$ to denote the advantage of adversary X against scheme Y in security game Z. Other notations will be introduced when necessary.

Bloom filter [5] can offer efficient membership testing.

Definition 1 (Bloom Filter). *A Bloom filter for a given data set $\mathbb{D}$ consists of three algorithms* (BFGen, BFUpdate, BFCheck) *defined as follows.*

- BFGen$(m, k) \xrightarrow{\$} (\mathbb{H}_{\mathsf{BF}}, T)$. *This initialization algorithm generates the set of hash functions* $\mathbb{H}_{\mathsf{BF}} = \{\mathsf{H}_j : \mathbb{D} \to [m]\}_{j \in [k]}$ *and a bit array T of length m on input of positive integer m and the number of hash functions k. T is initialized with all zeros.*
- BFUpdate$(\mathbb{H}_{\mathsf{BF}}, T, c) \to T'$. *This algorithm records a new element c in $\mathbb{D}$ by hashing c with every* $\mathsf{H}_j \in \mathbb{H}_{\mathsf{BF}}$, *sets* $\{T[\mathsf{H}_j(c)]\}_{j \in [k]}$ *to one, and outputs the updated array T'.*
- BFCheck$(\mathbb{H}_{\mathsf{BF}}, T, c) \to b$. *This algorithm outputs one only if every bit in the set* $\{T[\mathsf{H}_\gamma(c)]\}_{j \in [k]}$ *is one. It outputs zero otherwise.*

Definition 2 (BFKEM [10]). *A Bloom filter key encapsulation scheme* BFKEM *consists of the following four PPT algorithms.*

- BFK.KGen$(1^\lambda, m, k) \xrightarrow{\$} (\mathsf{ek}, \mathsf{dk})$. *The non-deterministic key generation algorithm* BFK.KGen *takes the security parameter 1^λ, parameters m and k as the input, and outputs a public-private key pair* $(\mathsf{ek}, \mathsf{dk})$.

- BFK.Enc(ek) $\xrightarrow{\$}$ (c, K). *The encapsulation algorithm* BFK.Enc() *takes* ek *as the input and outputs a ciphertext* CT *and a symmetric key* K.
- BFK.Punc(dk, c) $\rightarrow$ dk′. *The puncture algorithm* BFK.Punc() *takes the private key* dk *as input and outputs an updated private key* dk′.
- BFK.Dec(dk, c) $\rightarrow$ K. *The decapsulation algorithm* BFK.Dec() *takes* dk *and* CT *as input, and outputs a symmetric key* K *or* $\perp$ *if decapsulation fails.*

Similarly to Anonymous Public Key Encryption [1,3], we can formalize anonymous BFKEM (ANO-BFKEM). For better readability, we defer the formal definition of anonymity to Sect. 3 and refer the reader to [10] for IND-CPA and IND-CCA BFKEM definitions.

Definition 3 (Physical unclonable function, PUF, [26,30]). *Let* λ *be the security parameter. Let* $\mathsf{dist}(y, z)$ *be the statistical distance between two random variables* y *and* z. $\mathcal{U}_\kappa$ *the uniform random distribution over* $\{0, 1\}^\kappa$. *We say a function* $\mathbb{F}() : \{0, 1\}^{\kappa_1} \rightarrow \{0, 1\}^{\kappa_2}$ *is a physical unclonable function if it can fulfill all the requirements below, where* κ_1 *and* κ_2 *are polynomial functions of* λ.

1. *(Unclonable) Let* $\hat{\mathbb{F}}()$ *be any data-based clone of* $\mathbb{F}$ *generated in polynomial time. We say that* $\mathbb{F}()$ *is unclonable, if for* $\mathsf{negl}(\lambda)$, *a negligible functions of* λ, *it holds that*

$$\Pr \left[\begin{array}{c} y = z: \\ x \xleftarrow{\$} \mathcal{U}_{\kappa_1}; y \leftarrow \mathbb{F}(x); \\ z \leftarrow \hat{\mathbb{F}}(x); \end{array} \right] \leq \mathsf{negl}(\lambda);$$

2. *(Unpredictable and indistinguishable) For any PPT* $\mathcal{A}_1$ *and* $\mathcal{A}_2$, *it holds that*

$$\mathsf{Adv}^{\mathsf{PRE\text{-}PUF}}_{\mathcal{A}_1, \mathbb{F}}(1^\lambda) \leq \mathsf{negl}_{\mathsf{PRE\text{-}PUF}}(\lambda) \text{ and } \mathsf{Adv}^{\mathsf{IND\text{-}PUF}}_{\mathcal{A}_2, \mathbb{F}}(1^\lambda) \leq \mathsf{negl}_{\mathsf{IND\text{-}PUF}}(\lambda),$$

where $\mathsf{negl}_{\mathsf{PRE\text{-}PUF}}(\lambda)$ *and* $\mathsf{negl}_{\mathsf{IND\text{-}PUF}}(\lambda)$ *are two negligible functions of* λ *and*

$$\mathsf{Adv}^{\mathsf{PRE\text{-}PUF}}_{\mathcal{A}, \mathbb{F}}(1^\lambda) = \left| \Pr \left[\begin{array}{c} y = z: \\ \mathsf{begin\ challenge} \leftarrow \mathcal{A}^{\mathcal{O}_{\mathbb{F}()}}(1^\lambda); \\ x \xleftarrow{\$} \mathcal{U}_{\kappa_1}; y \leftarrow \mathbb{F}(x); z \leftarrow \mathcal{A}(x) \end{array} \right] \right| \quad (1)$$

$$\mathsf{Adv}^{\mathsf{IND\text{-}PUF}}_{\mathcal{A}, \mathbb{F}}(1^\lambda) = \left| \Pr \left[\begin{array}{c} b = b' = z: \\ b \xleftarrow{\$} \{0, 1\}; \\ x \xleftarrow{\$} \mathcal{U}_{\kappa_1}; z_0 \leftarrow \mathbb{F}(x); z_1 \xleftarrow{\$} \mathcal{U}_{\kappa_2} \\ b' \leftarrow \mathcal{A}^{\mathcal{O}_{\mathbb{F}()}}(z_b) \end{array} \right] - \frac{1}{2} \right|. \quad (2)$$

We also use an EUF-CMA signature scheme SIG = (SIG.Gen SIG.Sign, SIG.Vfy) and a symmetric encryption scheme Π = (KGen, ENC, DEC) with IND-CCA security.

3   Refined Infrastructure Model and CVP Construction

Execution Environment Intuition. When analyzing cryptographic infrastructures, we assume that the adversary cannot effectively utilize the leakage from the carrier protocol below the application layer, such as TCP/IP and LTE, as there are other ways to obfuscate low-level messages, such as anonymous routing [28]. Therefore, we adopt a network setting that is similar to the one in [25,27] as shown in Fig. 3, where trusted gateway, router or proxy can be used to permute message origins/destinations in the low level and $\mathcal{A}$ cannot see this permutation.

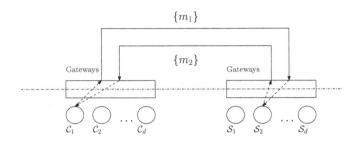

Fig. 3. Intuition of network setting in Refined Infrastructure Model and PPAKE. $\mathcal{C}_1$ communicates with $\mathcal{S}_2$ and dashed parts cannot be seen by $\mathcal{A}$ directly.

3.1   CVP Syntax and Setup Assumptions

In the Refined Infrastructure model (RI), we consider the infrastructure as a set of servers $\{\mathcal{S}_i\}$ that provide certificate validation services via a certificate validation protocol (CVP). Each server has its own public parameters PP and public-private key pairs.

Definition 4 (Parameter Generation). *A (public) parameter generation algorithm* $\mathsf{PPGen}(\cdot)$ *for an infrastructure works as follows. For a given server identifier* $\mathcal{S}_i$*, compute* $\left(\mathsf{PP}_{\mathcal{S}_i}, (\mathsf{pk}_{\mathcal{S}_i}, \mathsf{sk}_{\mathcal{S}_i})\right) \xleftarrow{\$} \mathsf{PPGen}(1^\lambda, \mathcal{S}_i)$*, where* 1^λ *is the security parameter,* $\mathsf{PP}_{\mathcal{S}_i}$ *is the public parameter published by* $\mathcal{S}_i$*, and* $(\mathsf{pk}_{\mathcal{S}_i}, \mathsf{sk}_{\mathcal{S}_i})$ *the public-private key pair(s) of* $\mathcal{S}_i$*.*

We allow $\mathsf{pk}_{\mathcal{S}_i}$ to be an empty string to keep our definition compatible with KGC and KMS, which use symmetric cryptography only. We also allow $(\mathsf{pk}_{\mathcal{S}_i}, \mathsf{sk}_{\mathcal{S}_i})$ to be a list of keys for different purposes. For example, $\mathsf{pk}_{\mathcal{S}_i}$ may contain an encryption key $\mathsf{ek}_{\mathcal{S}_i}$ and a signature verification key $\mathsf{pk}_{\mathcal{S}_i}$, so is the corresponding $\mathsf{sk}_{\mathcal{S}_i}$[1]. With the outputs of $\mathsf{PPGen}()$, we now model the CVP.

Definition 5 (Abstract Certificate). *We define an abstract certificate* cert *as* cert = $(\mathsf{cID}, \mathsf{ID}, \mathsf{pk}_{\mathsf{cID}}, \sigma_{\mathsf{CA}})$*, where* cID *is the identifier of* cert*,* ID *the identifier of the certificate owner (subject),* $\mathsf{pk}_{\mathsf{cID}}$ *the public key of the subject if it exists, and* σ_{CA} *the authentication token generated on the certificate by the certification authority.*

---

[1] We abuse the notation a little here for conciseness. Please see our concrete construction for the instantiation of $(\mathsf{pk}_{\mathcal{S}_i}, \mathsf{sk}_{\mathcal{S}_i})$.

Definition 6 (Two-message CVP). *A two-message certificate validation protocol (CVP) is a tuple of algorithms* $\Pi_{cvp} = (CVP_1, CVP_2, CVP_3)$ *that work as follows. Let* $PP_{\mathcal{S}_i}$ *and* $(pk_{\mathcal{S}_i}, sk_{\mathcal{S}_i})$ *be as defined in Definition 4.*

- *The client computes* $(m_1, st_1) \xleftarrow{\$} CVP_1(PP_{\mathcal{S}_i}, pk_{\mathcal{S}_i}, cert)$, *sends* m_1 *to the server* $\mathcal{S}_i$ *and keeps the state* st_1.
- $\mathcal{S}_i$ *responds with* $m_2 \leftarrow CVP_2(PP_{\mathcal{S}_i}, sk_{\mathcal{S}_i}, m_1)$ *and then enters state* $\lrcorner$, *where* $\lrcorner$ *is the state of "finished".*
- *The client recovers the validation result as* $v \leftarrow CVP_3(st_1, m_2)$. *In any case, the client session will enter the state* $\lrcorner$ *after receiving* m_2 *and stop reacting.*

We also need set-up assumptions in Fig. 4 to eliminate trivial attacks. First, it is trivial to distinguish different ciphersuites and lengths of certificate chains, both of which are determined by PP. Therefore we restrict our modeling to the case where Assumptions 1 and 2 hold. Although Assumptions 3 and 4 eliminate timing attacks in the current model, we believe that timing attacks must be considered but can be mitigated in the real world [31].

---

1. All system members (clients and CAs) share the same PP.
2. All cipher suites, channels, CVP message format and the number of CVP executions for validating each certificate are determined by PP.
3. All operations happen instantly.
4. Certificate status change happens, and the information propagates instantly to all CAs.

Fig. 4. List of set-up assumptions for privacy-preserving infrastructures.

3.2 The Refined Infrastructure Model

Execution Environment. The numbers $d, \ell \in \mathbb{N}$ are positive integers. A set of d honest parties $\{P_1, \ldots, P_d\}$ is fixed in the execution environment. We use an index $i \in [d]$ to identify a party in the security experiment. We use $\{\mathcal{PK}\}$ and $\{\mathcal{SK}\}$ to denote spaces for long-term public or private keys, respectively. Furthermore, all parties maintain state variables listed in Table 1.

Table 1. Internal states of parties

Variable	Description
sk_i	the secret key of a public key pair (pk_i, sk_i)
c_i	the corruption status $c_i \in \{\text{exposed}, \text{fresh}\}$ of sk_i
τ_i	the index of the query (τ_i-th) made by the adversary, which causes sk_i to be exposed

Each party P_i can execute the protocol for arbitrary times sequentially and concurrently, which is modelled by a collection of oracles $\{\pi_i^s : i \in [d], s \in [\ell]\}$. Oracle π_i^s behaves as party P_i executing the s-th protocol instance with some intended partner P_j.

Adversarial Model. An adversary $\mathcal{A}$ in our model is a probabilistic algorithm with polynomial running time (PPT), which takes as input the security parameter 1^λ and the public information. $\mathcal{A}$ may interact with these oracles by issuing the following queries.

The additional functions and lists are as in Table 2.

Table 2. Additional variables, functions and lists in RI model

Term	Description
vid	is a virtual identifier of a party P_i, emulating what a real-world proxy or a gate way does to hide a real party (See Fig. 3 for the intuition.)
$\mathcal{L}_{\text{vid}}$	stores active vids
d_{vid}	indicates the bit choice in the DrawOracle() and TestID()
real(vid)	denotes the party ID that is chosen for vid, if that vid is defined
$\mathcal{L}_{\text{inst}}$	stores all vid that have been used. Each element has the form $\{(\text{vid}, d_{\text{vid}}, P_i, P_j)\}$
$\mathcal{L}_{\text{act}}$	stores party indices that bound with <u>active</u> vids

- DrawOracle(P_i, P_j): This query takes as input two party indices and binds them to a vid. If $P_i \in \mathcal{L}_{\text{act}}$ or $P_j \in \mathcal{L}_{\text{act}}$, this query aborts and outputs $\perp$. A new vid will be chosen at random. The challenger will flip a random coin $d_{\text{vid}} \xleftarrow{\$} \{0,1\}$. Then real(vid) will be set to i if $e_{\text{vid}} = 0$, and real(vid) $= j$ if $e_{\text{vid}} = 1$. The list $\mathcal{L}_{\text{act}}$ will be updated to $\mathcal{L}_{\text{act}} \cup \{P_i, P_j\}$. Finally, if no aborts happens, vid and additional information will be recorded in $\mathcal{L}_{\text{vid}}$ and $\mathcal{L}_{\text{inst}}$, and vid will be output to $\mathcal{A}$.
- NewSession(vid, vid$'$): If vid $\in \mathcal{L}_{\text{vid}}$ and vid$' \in \mathcal{L}_{\text{vid}}$, this query will initiate a new oracle π_i^s with real(vid) $= P_i$ and Pid$_i^s = $ real(vid$'$), and output the handle π_{vid}^s to $\mathcal{A}$. Otherwise it will output $\perp$.
- Send(π_{vid}^s, m): If vid $\notin \mathcal{L}_{\text{vid}}$, this query will output $\perp$. Otherwise, this query sends message m to oracle $\pi_{\text{real(vid)}}^s$. The oracle will respond with the next message m^* (if there is any) that should be sent according to the protocol specification and its internal states.
- RevealID(vid): If vid $\in \mathcal{L}_{\text{inst}}$, return real($vid$).
- Corrupt(P_i): Oracle π_i responds with the long-term secret key sk_i (if any defined) of party P_i. Once a party has responded to any Corrupt()$-$ query, it stops responding to any other queries.

- Free(vid): this query will not output anything but do the following. If vid $\in$ $\mathcal{L}_{\text{vid}}$, look for the parties in $\mathcal{L}_{\text{inst}}$, remove vid from $\mathcal{L}_{\text{vid}}$ and parties from $\mathcal{L}_{\text{act}}$. End all negotiating sessions that are associated with party $P_{\text{real(vid)}}$.

Each (session) process oracle π_{vid}^s have extra state variables defined in Table 3. Initially, $\text{cst}_{\text{cID}} = \text{unknown}$.

Table 3. (Extra) State variables of oracle π_{vid}^s

ρ	the role of in π_{vid}^s in CVP, $\rho \in \{\text{Client}, \text{Server}\}$
cID	the certificate identity π_{vid}^s is querying
cst_{cID}	the certificate state, $\text{cst}_{\text{cID}} \in \{\text{good}, \text{revoked}, \text{unknown}\}$
Server	the vid of the CA server that the client π_{vid}^s contacts
st	the state of an oracle, $\text{st} \in \{\lrcorner, \text{negotiating}\}$

Let $\mathcal{L}_{\text{cID}}$ be the list of certificate identities involved, and $\mathcal{L}_S$ the list of all CAs. We have the following Test-oracles to assess the impact of $\mathcal{A}$'s behaviors.

- TestCert(π_{vid}^s): This oracle first tosses a fair coin $b \xleftarrow{\$} \{0,1\}$. If $|\mathcal{L}_{\text{cID}}| \leq 1$, return $\perp$. If π_{vid}^s or $\pi_{\text{vid}}^s.\text{cID}$ is undefined, return $\perp$. Otherwise, TestCert() sets $\text{cID}_0 \leftarrow \pi_{\text{vid}}^s.\text{cID}$ and $\text{cID}_1 \xleftarrow{\$} \mathcal{L}_{\text{cID}} \backslash \{\pi_{\text{vid}}^s.\text{cID}\}$, and finally responses to $\mathcal{A}$ with cID_b.
- TestCA$(\mathcal{C}_{\text{vid}}^s)$: If $\mathcal{C}_{\text{vid}}^s$ or $\mathcal{C}_{\text{vid}}^s.\text{Server}$ is undefined, or $|\mathcal{L}_S| \leq 1$, set $e \xleftarrow{\$} \{0,1\}$ and return $\perp$. Otherwise, this oracle set $e = e_{\pi_{\text{vid}}^s.\text{Server}}$.

Intuitively, TestCert() checks if the certificate ID is leaked, and TestCA() checks if the CA's ID is leaked. To eliminate trivial attacks, we need a freshness definition for the oracles.

Definition 7 (Matching conversation [17]). *Let $T_{x,y}$ be all the messages sent and received by π_x^y, and $T'_{x,y}$ be $T_{x,y}$ truncated by the last message. We say that π_i^s and π_j^t have matching conversations, if*

- *π_i^s sends the last message of the CVP and it holds that $T_{j,t} = T_{i,s}$, or*
- *π_j^t sends the last message of the CVP and it holds that $T'_{j,t} = T'_{i,s}$.*

Definition 8 (Two-message CVP freshness). *Let $\text{Send}(m)$ be the τ-th query that make π_{vid}^s enter state $\lrcorner$. We say that an oracle π_{vid}^s is CVP-fresh, if all the following conditions hold.*

- *If $\pi_{\text{vid}}^s.\rho = \text{Server}$, then there must exist a $\mathcal{C}_{\text{vid}'}^t$ to which π_{vid}^s has matching conversations and the first Corrupt(real(vid)) must be a τ_i-th query, $\tau_i > \tau$.*
- *If $\pi_{\text{vid}}^s.\rho = \text{Client}$ with $\pi_{\text{vid}}^s.\text{Server} = \text{vid}'$, then there must exist a $\mathcal{S}_{\text{vid}'}^t$ to which π_{vid}^s has matching conversations, and the first Corrupt(real(vid')) must be a τ_j-th query with $\tau_j > \tau$.*

– RevealID(vid) *has never been made. If* π_{vid}^s *has matching conversations with* $\pi_{\text{vid}'}^t$, *then* RevealID(vid') *has never been made.*

Intuitively, one oracle's freshness implies its talking partner's freshness.

To model privacy threats against CVP we need more fine-grained definitions that depend on the number of CAs and whether they can be corrupted. An overview of the privacy notions can be found in Fig. 5. In a notion RI-XY, $X \in \{S, M\}$ means whether there is only a single (S) CA, or multiple (M) CAs, while $Y \in \{S, W\}$ denotes whether strong corruption (S) of CA is allowed, or only weak corruption (W) is allowed.

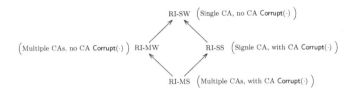

Fig. 5. The hierarchy of RI privacy notions, where $A \rightarrow B$ means A implies B.

There is no need to consider TestCA() for RI-SW and RI-SS, where all clients contact the same CA with a publicly known identity. For conciseness, we present only the strongest privacy definition in the multi-CA settings. We define $\mathcal{O}_{\text{RI-MS}} = \{$DrawOracle(), NewSession(), Send(), Corrupt(), RevealID(), Free()$\}$.

Definition 9 (CVP strong privacy in multi-CA setting, RI-MS). *We define the advantage for* RI-MS *privacy as*

$$\text{Adv}_{\mathcal{A},\Pi_{\text{cvp}}}^{\text{RI-MS}} = \text{Adv}_{\mathcal{A},\Pi_{\text{cvp}}}^{\text{RI-MS-cert}} + \text{Adv}_{\mathcal{A},\Pi_{\text{cvp}}}^{\text{RI-MS-CA}} \quad with \tag{3}$$

$$\text{Adv}_{\mathcal{A},\Pi_{\text{cvp}}}^{\text{RI-MS-cert}} = \left| \Pr \left[\begin{array}{c} b = b' : \\ \{(\text{PP}_i, \text{pk}_i)\} \xleftarrow{\$} \text{PPGen}(1^\lambda); \\ \pi_{\text{vid}}^s \xleftarrow{\$} \mathcal{A}^{\mathcal{O}_{\text{RI-MS}}}(1^\lambda, \{(\text{PP}_i, \text{pk}_i)\}) \\ b \xleftarrow{\$} \text{TestCert}(\pi_{\text{vid}}^s); \\ b' \leftarrow \mathcal{A}^{\mathcal{O}_{\text{RI-MS}}}(1^\lambda, \{(\text{PP}_i, \text{pk}_i)\}); \end{array} \right] - \frac{1}{2} \right|, \tag{4}$$

$$\text{Adv}_{\mathcal{A},\Pi_{\text{cvp}}}^{\text{RI-MS-CA}} = \left| \Pr \left[\begin{array}{c} e' = e : \\ \{(\text{PP}_i, \text{pk}_i)\} \xleftarrow{\$} \text{PPGen}(1^\lambda); \\ \mathcal{C}_{\text{vid}}^s \xleftarrow{\$} \mathcal{A}^{\mathcal{O}_{\text{RI-MS}}}(1^\lambda, \{(\text{PP}_i, \text{pk}_i)\}) \\ e \xleftarrow{\$} \text{TestCA}(\mathcal{C}_{\text{vid}}^s); \\ e' \leftarrow \mathcal{A}^{\mathcal{O}_{\text{RI-MS}}}(1^\lambda, \{(\text{PP}_i, \text{pk}_i)\}); \end{array} \right] - \frac{1}{2} \right|, \tag{5}$$

where π_{vid}^s *and* $\mathcal{C}_{\text{vid}}^s$ *are fresh in the sense of Definition 8.*

3.3   CVP Construction

We finally present our CVP construction from **DGJSS** Bloom Filter Key Encapsulation Mechanism [10] which fulfills the following definition of anonymity. The shaded parts are where this notion does not support full corruption and where we need PUFs for a complete CVP.

Definition 10 (Weak ANO-BFKEM**).** *An* IND-CCA BFKEM *is also (weakly) anonymous if for every PPT adversary* $\mathcal{A}$, *there exists a negligible function* $\mathrm{negl}_{\mathrm{ANO}}$, *such that*

$$
\mathsf{Adv}^{\mathrm{wANO\text{-}BFKEM}}_{\mathcal{A},\mathrm{BFKEM}} = \left| \Pr \left[\begin{array}{c} e = e' : \\ \{\mathsf{ek}\} \leftarrow \mathsf{BFK.KGen}(1^\lambda); \mathcal{C} \leftarrow \emptyset; \\ (\mathsf{ek}_i, \mathsf{ek}_j) \leftarrow \mathcal{A}^{\mathcal{O}(\cdot)}(1^\lambda, \{\mathsf{ek}\}) \\ \text{with } \mathsf{ek}_i, \mathsf{ek}_j \in \{\mathsf{ek}\}, i, j \notin \mathcal{C}; \\ e \xleftarrow{\$} \{0, 1\}; \\ \textbf{if } e = 0 \\ \textbf{then } (\mathsf{ek}_0, \mathsf{dk}_0) \leftarrow (\mathsf{ek}_i, \mathsf{dk}_i); \\ \textbf{else } (\mathsf{ek}_0, \mathsf{dk}_0) \leftarrow (\mathsf{ek}_j, \mathsf{dk}_j); \\ (c, \mathsf{K}) \xleftarrow{\$} \mathsf{BFK.Enc}(\mathsf{ek}_0); \\ \mathsf{BFK.Punc}(\mathsf{dk}_0, c); \\ e' \leftarrow \mathcal{A}^{\mathcal{O}_w(i,j,\cdot)}(c) ; \end{array} \right] - \frac{1}{2} \right| \leq \mathrm{negl}_{\mathrm{ANO}}(\lambda),
$$

$$(6)$$

where $\mathcal{O}(\cdot) := \{\mathsf{BFK.Enc}(i, \cdot), \mathsf{BFK.Punc}(i, \cdot), \mathsf{BFK.Dec}(i, \cdot), \mathsf{Corrupt}(i, \cdot)\}^d_{i=1}$, $\mathcal{O}_w(i, j, \cdot) := \{\mathsf{BFK.Enc}(i, \cdot), \mathsf{BFK.Punc}(i, \cdot), \mathsf{BFK.Dec}(i, \cdot), \mathsf{Corrupt}_{i' \notin \{i,j\}}(i', \cdot)$ $\}^d_{i,i'=1}$, *the oracle* $\mathsf{BFK.Enc}(i, m)$ *calls* $\mathsf{BFK.Enc}(\mathsf{ek}_i, m)$ *and returns the ciphertext,* $\mathsf{BFK.Punc}(i, \cdot)$ *has no output but takes a ciphertext* c *as input and calls* $\mathsf{BFK.Punc}(\mathsf{dk}_i, c)$, $\mathsf{BFK.Dec}(i, \cdot)$ *takes a ciphertext* c *as input and returns* $\mathsf{BFK.Dec}$ (dk_i, c), *and* $\mathsf{Corrupt}(i)$ *returns* dk_i *and sets* $\mathcal{C} \leftarrow \mathcal{C} \cup \{i\}$.

In Fig. 6 we review the IND-CPA **DGJSS**. IND-CPA **DGJSS** can be transformed into an IND-CCA secure BFKEM via a variant of Fujisaki-Okamoto transformation as proved by the authors [10].

To prove its anonymity, we need the following bilinear computational Diffie-Hellman problem to be hard.

Definition 11 (BCDH). *Let* **param** $= (q, e, \mathbb{G}_1, \mathbb{G}_2, \mathbb{G}_T, g_1, g_2) \xleftarrow{\$} \mathbf{BilGen}$ (1^λ), $\mathbf{BilGen}()$ *be a bilinear group generation algorithm, and* $(g_1^r, g_1^\alpha, g_2^\alpha, h_2)$ *with* $(r, \alpha) \xleftarrow{\$} \mathbb{Z}_q$ *and* $h_2 \xleftarrow{\$} \mathbb{G}_2$. *We define the advantage of an adversary* $\mathcal{A}$ *in the bilinear computational Diffie-Hellman (***BCDH***) problem w.r.t.* **BilGen** *as*

$$
\mathsf{Adv}^{\mathbf{BCDH}}_{\mathcal{A},\mathbf{BilGen}} = \Pr[h_a = e(g_1, h_2)^{r\alpha} : h_a \leftarrow \mathcal{A}(\mathbf{param}, g_1^r, g_1^\alpha, g_2^\alpha, h_2)]
$$

Let $\mathbf{param} := (q, e, \mathbb{G}_1, \mathbb{G}_2, \mathbb{G}_T, g_1, g_2) \overset{\$}{\leftarrow} \mathbf{BilGen}(1^\lambda)$ and q be the order of $\mathbb{G}_1$.
Let the key space $\mathcal{K}$ be $\{0,1\}^\lambda$. Let $G : \mathcal{IDS} \to \mathbb{G}_2$ and $E : \mathbb{G}_T \to \{0,1\}^\lambda$ be two
hash functions, where $\mathcal{IDS}$ is the identity space (binary strings).

- BFK.KGen$(1^\lambda, m, k) \overset{\$}{\to} (\mathsf{ek}, \mathsf{dk})$. This algorithm calls BFGen$(m, k) \overset{\$}{\to} (\mathbb{H}_{\mathsf{BF}}, T)$
  to generate a Bloom filter instance $(\mathbb{H}_{\mathsf{BF}}, T)$ with $\mathbb{H}_{\mathsf{BF}} = \{\mathsf{H}_j\}_{j \in [k]}$. It then
  chooses a random $\alpha \overset{\$}{\leftarrow} \mathbb{Z}_q$ and returns

$$\left(\mathsf{ek} := (g_1^\alpha, \mathbb{H}_{\mathsf{BF}}), \mathsf{dk} := (T, \{\mathsf{dk}[i] := G(i)^\alpha\}_{i \in [m]})\right).$$

- BFK.Enc$(\mathsf{ek}) \overset{\$}{\to} (c, \mathsf{K})$. This algorithm BFK.Enc() takes ek as the input and
  parse it as $(g_1^\alpha, \mathbb{H}_{\mathsf{BF}})$. It samples a symmetric key $\mathsf{K} \overset{\$}{\leftarrow} \mathcal{K}$ and $r \overset{\$}{\leftarrow} \mathbb{Z}_q$. Then
  for all $j \in [k]$, it computes

$$i_j = \mathsf{H}_j(g_1^r), \mathsf{H}_j \in \mathbb{H}_{\mathsf{BF}},$$
$$y_j = e\left(g_1^\alpha, G(i_j)\right)^r,$$

  and $c := \left(g_1^r, \{E(y_j) \oplus \mathsf{K}\}_{j \in [k]}\right) \in \left(\mathbb{G}_1 \times (\{0,1\}^\lambda)^k\right)$. Finally it returns (c, K).
- BFK.Punc$(\mathsf{dk}, c) \to \mathsf{dk}'$. The puncture algorithm BFK.Punc() takes the private
  key $\mathsf{dk} = (T, \{\mathsf{dk}[i]\}_{i \in [m]})$ and a ciphertext $c = \left(g_1^r, \{E(y_j) \oplus \mathsf{K}\}_{j \in [k]}\right)$ as input. It
  first calls $T' = \mathsf{BFUpdate}(\mathbb{H}_{\mathsf{BF}}, T, g_1^r)$ to compute T'. Then for all $i \in [m]$, it
  sets

$$\mathsf{dk}'[i] := \begin{cases} \mathsf{dk}[i] & \text{if } T'[i] = 0, \text{ and} \\ \bot & \text{if } T'[i] = 1 \end{cases},$$

  where $T'[i]$ is the i-th bit of T'.
  Finally it outputs an updated private key $\mathsf{dk}' = (T', \{\mathsf{dk}'[i]\}_{i \in [m]})$.
- BFK.Dec(dk, c) :   This   algorithm   BFK.Dec()   takes $\mathsf{dk} =$
  $(T, \{\mathsf{dk}[i] := G(i)^\alpha\}_{i \in [m]})$ and $c = (c[0], \{c[i_1], \cdots, c[i_k]\})$ as input. It
  first runs BFCheck$(\mathbb{H}_{\mathsf{BF}}, T, c[0])$. If the result is 1, then this algorithm outputs
  $\bot$. If the result is 0, it picks the smallest i^* such that $\mathsf{dk}[i^*] \neq \bot$, then
  computes

$$y_{i^*} := e(c[0]^r, \mathsf{dk}[i^*]) = e(g_1^r, (G(i^*))^\alpha)$$

  and finally outputs $\mathsf{K} := E(y_{i^*}) \oplus c[i^*]$.

Fig. 6. DGJSS, an IND-CPA BFKEM from hashed **BF-IBE**.

Theorem 1 (Anonymity of DGJSS). *If the public parameters are indistinguishable, and* **BCDH** *is hard w.r.t.* **BilGen***, then the* ***Fujisaki-Okamoto-transformed*** **DGJSS** *is a weak ANO-BFKEM in the sense of Definition 10.*

Note that FO-transformed **DGJSS** has exactly the same form of ciphertexts.
See Appendix A for the proof.

Adding PUF Against Full Corruption. As we cannot let the adversary see dk in plaintext via $\mathsf{Corrupt}()$, we take the controlled PUF defined in [30] as a building block. The merits of PUF include that (1) it cannot be cloned by repeated sampling by any $\mathcal{A}$ in polynomial time, and (2) its output is pseudo-random. Thus, $\mathcal{A}$ cannot compute the output of a PUF unless it has physical access to it. See Definition 3 for the syntax and security of PUF.

Let $\mathbb{F}() : \{0,1\}^{\lambda} \to \{0,1\}^{L(\lambda)}$ be a PUF. Let $\mathsf{H}() : \{0,1\}^{L(\lambda)} \to \mathcal{K}$, where $\mathcal{K}$ is a key space of Π' and $\Pi' = (\mathsf{KGen}', \mathsf{Enc}', \mathsf{Dec}')$ is an IND-CCA symmetric key encryption scheme. Let $s \xleftarrow{\$} \{0,1\}^{\lambda}$ and $\mathsf{CT}_{\mathsf{dk}_j} \xleftarrow{\$} \mathsf{Enc}'(\mathsf{H}(\mathbb{F}(s)), \mathsf{dk}_j)$. We construct $\Pi^{\mathsf{hw}}_{\mathsf{cvp}}$ shown in Fig. 7, where $\mathcal{N}$ is the nonce space.

Client_i		$\mathsf{CA\ Server}_j$
$\{\mathsf{PP}_j\}, \{(\mathsf{ek}_j, \mathsf{pk}_j)\}$		$\mathsf{PP}_j, (\mathsf{sk}_j, \mathsf{pk}_j), \left(\mathsf{ek}_j, s, \mathsf{CT}_{\mathsf{dk}_j}\right),$ $\mathbb{F}(), \mathsf{DB} = \{(\mathsf{cID}, \mathsf{cst}_{\mathsf{cID}})\}$
// CVP_1: Choose nonce $x \xleftarrow{\$} \mathcal{N}$; Pick $(\mathsf{ek}_j, \mathsf{pk}_j)$ $(c_1, \mathsf{K}) \xleftarrow{\$} \mathsf{BFK.Enc}(\mathsf{ek}_j)$; $c_2 \xleftarrow{\$} \mathsf{Enc}(\mathsf{K}, \mathsf{cID}\|\|x)$	$\xrightarrow{m_1:(c_1,c_2)}$	// CVP_2: $\mathsf{dk}_j \leftarrow \mathsf{Dec}'(\mathsf{H}(\mathbb{F}(s)), \mathsf{CT}_{\mathsf{dk}_j})$ **if** $\bot = \mathsf{BFK.Dec}(\mathsf{dk}_j, c_1)$: Choose random $\mathsf{K} \xleftarrow{\$} \mathcal{K}, y \xleftarrow{\$} \mathcal{N}$; $\mathsf{cID} \xleftarrow{\$} \mathcal{IDS}; \mathsf{cst}_{\mathsf{cID}} \leftarrow \mathsf{unknown}$; **else** : $\mathsf{K} \leftarrow \mathsf{BFK.Dec}(\mathsf{dk}_i, c_1)$; $\mathsf{cID}\|\|x \leftarrow \mathsf{DEC}(\mathsf{K}, c_2), y \leftarrow x + 1$; $\mathsf{cst}_{\mathsf{cID}} \leftarrow \mathsf{SearchDB}(\mathsf{DB}, \mathsf{cID})$; // puncture dk_j : $\mathsf{dk}_j \leftarrow \mathsf{BFK.Punc}(\mathsf{dk}_j, c_1)$; $\mathsf{CT}_{\mathsf{dk}_j} \xleftarrow{\$} \mathsf{Enc}'(\mathsf{H}(\mathbb{F}(s)), \mathsf{dk}_j)$ $\sigma \xleftarrow{\$} \mathsf{SIG.Sign}(\mathsf{sk}_j, \mathsf{cID}\|\|\mathsf{cst}_{\mathsf{cID}}\|\|y)$; $c_3 \xleftarrow{\$} \mathsf{ENC}(\mathsf{K}, \mathsf{cID}\|\|\mathsf{cst}_{\mathsf{cID}}\|\|y\|\|\sigma)$; $\dashv$;
// CVP_3: **if** $\bot = \mathsf{DEC}(\mathsf{K}, c_3)$: $\dashv$; Parse $m \leftarrow \mathsf{DEC}(\mathsf{K}, c_3)$ as $\mathsf{cID}'\|\|\mathsf{cst}\|\|y\|\|\sigma$; **if** $y \neq x + 1$ OR $\mathsf{cID}' \neq \mathsf{cID}$: $\dashv$; **if** $\mathsf{SIG.Vfy}(\mathsf{pk}_j, \mathsf{cID}'\|\|\mathsf{cst}\|\|y\|\|\sigma) \neq$ **true** : $\dashv$; **else** Store $(\mathsf{cID}, \mathsf{cst}_{\mathsf{cID}})$ and $\dashv$;	$\xleftarrow{m_2:c_3}$	

Fig. 7. $\Pi^{\mathsf{hw}}_{\mathsf{cvp}}$: two-message CVP based on PUF $\mathbb{F}()$ and BFKEM instantiated with **DGJSS**. The shaded parts rely on PUF and the encryption Π'.

We can argue the security and anonymity of $\Pi^{\mathsf{hw}}_{\mathsf{cvp}}$ as follows. The indistinguishability of cert is guaranteed by the IND-CCA security and puncturability of **DGJSS**. On the other hand, $\mathcal{A}$ only learns s and $\mathsf{CT}_{\mathsf{dk}_j}$ via $\mathsf{Corrupt}()$, as $\mathbb{F}()$ cannot be taken away or cloned by $\mathcal{A}$. Due to the pseudo-randomness and unpredictability of $\mathbb{F}()$'s outputs, and the indistinguishability of $\mathsf{CT}_{\mathsf{dk}_j}$, $\mathcal{A}$ learns nothing about the "real" decryption key dk_j. Therefore, CA's anonymity is also preserved. We refer the reader to Appendix B for the proof.

Theorem 2. *If* BFKEM *is* **DGJSS**, H() *a cryptographic hash function modelled as a random oracle,* $\mathbb{F}()$ *a controlled PUF,* $\Pi = $ (KGen, ENC, DEC) *and* Π' $= $ (KGen', ENC', DEC') *are* IND-CCA *secure symmetric length-hiding encryption schemes, and* SIG $= ($ SIG.Gen SIG.Sign, SIG.Vfy) *is an* EUF-CMA *secure signature scheme, then the protocol* Π_{cvp} *has* RI-MS *privacy (Definition 9) in the multi-CA setting in the random oracle model. More specifically, for any PPT* $\mathcal{A}$ *against* Π_{cvp}, *there exist adversaries* $\mathcal{B}_1$ *against* SIG, $\mathcal{B}_2$ *and* $\mathcal{B}_3$ *against* $\mathbb{F}()$, $\mathcal{B}_4$ *against* Π', $\mathcal{B}_5$ *against* BFKEM, *and* $\mathcal{B}_6$ *against* Π *such that*

$$\mathsf{Adv}^{\text{RI-MS}}_{\mathcal{A},\Pi_{\text{cvp}}} \leq 2 \cdot \left(\frac{(d\ell)^2}{|\mathcal{N}|} + (d\ell)^2 \cdot \left(\epsilon^{\text{EUF-CMA}}_{\mathcal{B}_1,\text{SIG}} + \epsilon^{\text{PRE-PUF}}_{\mathcal{B}_2,\mathbb{F}} + \epsilon^{\text{IND-PUF}}_{\mathcal{B}_3,\mathbb{F}} \right. \right.$$
$$\left. \left. + \epsilon^{\text{IND-CCA}}_{\mathcal{B}_4,\Pi'} + \epsilon^{\text{wANO-BFKEM}}_{\mathcal{B}_5,\text{BFKEM}} + \epsilon^{\text{IND-CCA}}_{\mathcal{B}_6,\Pi} \right) \right), \quad (7)$$

where $\mathcal{N}$ *is the nonce space,* d *the maximal number of parties,* ℓ *the maximal number of sessions owned by one party.*

4   Conclusion and Future Work

In this paper, we propose a refined infrastructure model (RI) and construct a concrete CVP with provable security and near-optimal anonymity for an infrastructure that supports PPAKE. It is interesting to investigate how we can use obfuscations to replace PUF in the construction. Direct application of indistinguishability obfuscation [23] does not seem to work, as hard-coded $\mathsf{Dec}(\mathsf{dk}_i, \cdot)$ and $\mathsf{Dec}(\mathsf{dk}_j, \cdot)$ are two distinct circuits with different functionalities.

A   Proof of Theorem 1

Proof. The forward IND-CCA security of **DGJSS** after Fujisaki-Okamoto transformation (FO) can be obtained directly from the original Theorem 1, 2 and 3 in [10]. Moreover, FO-transformed **DGJSS** has exactly the same form of ciphertexts, although the changes lies in encryption and decryption.

Hence, we only have to prove the anonymity.

Anonymity Against Weak Corruptions. After receiving the challenge c, $\mathcal{A}$ cannot use Corrupt() on i and j (See Definition 10), so whether dk_i or dk_j has been punctured on c is hidden from $\mathcal{A}$. Any other party's keys, thanks to the IND-CCA security, will output $\perp$ when used for decrypting c, except when collision of nonces happens. Moreover, the probability that a nonce collision happens is negligible. Thus, the anonymity against weak corruption can be reduced to ciphertext anonymity.

Ciphertext Anonymity. The transformation does not change the form of the encapsulation (ciphertext), which is $c = (g_1^r, \{E(y_j) \oplus \mathsf{K}\}_{j \in [k]})$. The first term is uniformly random in $\mathbb{G}_1$. If K is uniformly random in $\{0,1\}^\lambda$, then the distribution of any $E(y_j) \oplus \mathsf{K}$, is uniformly random in $\{0,1\}^\lambda$ when observed alone. So for any α_0, α_1, it is hard to distinguish $(g_1^r, E(e(g_1^{\alpha_0}, G(i_j))^r) \oplus \mathsf{K})$ from $(g_1^r, E(e(g_1^{\alpha_1}, G(i_j))^r) \oplus \mathsf{K})$.

Furthermore, note that the adversary $\mathcal{A}$ cannot corrupt party 0 or party 1 for the corresponding ek_0 or ek_1 before receiving the challenge c. So if **BCDH** is hard, then it is also hard for $\mathcal{A}$ to distinguish the following two ensembles for any $\alpha_0, \alpha_1, i_j, j$ in the random oracle model.

$$(g_1^r, E(e(g_1^{\alpha_0}, G(i_j))^r) \oplus \mathsf{K}, E(e(g_1^{\alpha_0}, G(i_{j+1}))^r) \oplus \mathsf{K})$$
$$(g_1^r, E(e(g_1^{\alpha_0}, G(i_j))^r) \oplus \mathsf{K}, E(e(g_1^{\alpha_1}, G(i_{j+1}))^r) \oplus \mathsf{K})$$

This is because $\mathcal{A}$ has zero advantage if it has not made a correct $E(y_j)$ query to the random oracle $E(\cdot)$ with $y_j = e(g_1^{\alpha_0}, G(i_j))^r$ or $y_j = e(g_1^{\alpha_1}, G(i_j))^r$. With a hybrid argument for $j = 1$ to k, we can conclude that $\mathcal{A}$ has negligible advantage in distinguishing $(g_1^r, \{E(e(g_1^{\alpha_0}, G(i_j))^r\}_{j \in [k]})$ from $(g_1^r, \{E(e(g_1^{\alpha_1}, G(i_j))^r\}_{j \in [k]})$.

Therefore, the FO-transformed **DGJSS** is a weak ANO-BFKEM. $\qquad\square$

B   Proof Sketch of Theorem 2

Proof. (sketch) We use a sequence of games [29]. Let $\mathsf{Adv}[\mathsf{S}_{A,i}]$ be the advantage of $\mathcal{A}$'s advantage in Game i.

Game 0. This game is identical to the RI-MS security experiment described in Definition 9. Thus, we have

$$\mathsf{Adv}[\mathsf{S}_{\mathcal{A},0}] = \mathsf{Adv}_{\mathcal{A},\Pi_{\mathsf{cvp}}^{\mathsf{hw}}}^{\mathsf{RI\text{-}MS}}$$

Game 1. In this game we add an abort rule. The challenger aborts, if there exists any oracle π_i^s that chooses a random nonce r_i or r_j which is not unique.

$$\mathsf{Adv}[\mathsf{S}_{\mathcal{A},0}] \leq \mathsf{Adv}[\mathsf{S}_{\mathcal{A},1}] + \frac{(d \cdot \ell)^2}{|\mathcal{N}|}$$

Game 2. We add another abort rule in this game. The challenger try to guess which oracle will be the oracle received $\mathsf{TestCert}()$ and TestCA, and its partner oracle. If the guess is incorrect, then we abort this game. Thus

$$\mathsf{Adv}[\mathsf{S}_{\mathcal{A},1}] \leq (d \cdot \ell)^2 \cdot \mathsf{Adv}[\mathsf{S}_{\mathcal{A},2}]$$

Game 3. This game is identical to the previous one except for one abort rule. If the adversary succeeds in making any client accept a forged signature, abort. Then we have

$$\mathsf{Adv}[\mathsf{S}_{\mathcal{A},2}] \leq \mathsf{Adv}[\mathsf{S}_{\mathcal{A},3}] + \epsilon_{\mathcal{B}_1,\mathsf{SIG}}^{\mathsf{EUF\text{-}CMA}}.$$

Game 4. We modify the game such that on receiving Corrupt(), the challenger return a randomly encrypted CT instead of CT_{dk_j}. Thanks to the IND-PUF, PRE-PUF properties of the PUF $\mathbb{F}$, and IND-CCA security of Π', we have

$$\mathsf{Adv}[S_{\mathcal{A},3}] \leq \mathsf{Adv}[S_{\mathcal{A},4}] + \epsilon_{\mathcal{B}_2,\mathbb{F}}^{\mathsf{PRE\text{-}PUF}} + \epsilon_{\mathcal{B}_3,\mathbb{F}}^{\mathsf{IND\text{-}PUF}} + \epsilon_{\mathcal{B}_4,\Pi'}^{\mathsf{IND\text{-}CCA}}.$$

Note that $\mathcal{A}$ can only steal information but cannot physically control any party or access the PUF $\mathbb{F}()$. Moreover, even the honest owner (CA) cannot duplicate $\mathbb{F}()$ or efficiently predict the output of $\mathbb{F}()$ with probability greater than $\epsilon_{\mathcal{B}_2,\mathbb{F}}^{\mathsf{PRE\text{-}PUF}}$. So $\mathcal{A}$ cannot generate a good enough $\mathbb{F}'$, which can produce the decryption key with probability greater than $\epsilon_{\mathcal{B}_2,\mathbb{F}}^{\mathsf{PRE\text{-}PUF}}$, or distinguish a random key from the output of $\mathbb{F}$ with probability greater than $\epsilon_{\mathcal{B}_3,\mathbb{F}}^{\mathsf{IND\text{-}PUF}}$.

Game 5. Now we modify the game such that m_1 is encrypted with the public key of another candidate of vid. Due to the fact that **DGJSS** is a weak ANO-BFKEM and the IND-CCA of Π, we have

$$\mathsf{Adv}[S_{\mathcal{A},4}] \leq \mathsf{Adv}[S_{\mathcal{A},5}] + \epsilon_{\mathcal{B}_5,\mathsf{BFKEM}}^{\mathsf{ANO,IND\text{-}CCA}} + \epsilon_{\mathcal{B}_6,\Pi}^{\mathsf{IND\text{-}CCA}}.$$

By collecting all the relations above, we proved Theorem 2.

References

1. Abdalla, M., et al.: Searchable encryption revisited: consistency properties, relation to anonymous IBE, and extensions. In: Shoup, V. (ed.) CRYPTO 2005. LNCS, vol. 3621, pp. 205–222. Springer, Heidelberg (2005). https://doi.org/10.1007/11535218_13
2. Arfaoui, G., Bultel, X., Fouque, P.A., Nedelcu, A., Onete, C.: The privacy of the TLS 1.3 protocol. In: Proceedings on Privacy Enhancing Technologies 2019, pp. 190–210 (2019)
3. Bellare, M., Boldyreva, A., Desai, A., Pointcheval, D.: Key-privacy in public-key encryption. In: Boyd, C. (ed.) ASIACRYPT 2001. LNCS, vol. 2248, pp. 566–582. Springer, Heidelberg (2001). https://doi.org/10.1007/3-540-45682-1_33
4. Bilge, L., Strufe, T., Balzarotti, D., Kirda, E.: All your contacts are belong to us: automated identity theft attacks on social networks. In: Proceedings of the 18th International Conference on World Wide Web, pp. 551–560 (2009)
5. Bloom, B.H.: Space/time trade-offs in hash coding with allowable errors. Commun. ACM **13**(7), 422–426 (1970)
6. Boyen, X., Waters, B.: Anonymous hierarchical identity-based encryption (without random oracles). In: Dwork, C. (ed.) CRYPTO 2006. LNCS, vol. 4117, pp. 290–307. Springer, Heidelberg (2006). https://doi.org/10.1007/11818175_17
7. Canetti, R.: Universally composable security: a new paradigm for cryptographic protocols. In: Proceedings 42nd IEEE Symposium on Foundations of Computer Science, pp. 136–145. IEEE (2001)
8. Canetti, R., Krawczyk, H.: Analysis of key-exchange protocols and their use for building secure channels. In: Pfitzmann, B. (ed.) EUROCRYPT 2001. LNCS, vol. 2045, pp. 453–474. Springer, Heidelberg (2001). https://doi.org/10.1007/3-540-44987-6_28

9. Cooper, D., Santesson, S., Farrell, S., Boeyen, S., Housley, R., Polk, W.: Internet X.509 public key infrastructure certificate and certificate revocation list (CRL) profile. RFC 5280 (proposed standard) (2008). http://www.ietf.org/rfc/rfc5280.txt

10. Derler, D., Gellert, K., Jager, T., Slamanig, D., Striecks, C.: Bloom filter encryption and applications to efficient forward-secret 0-RTT key exchange. J. Cryptol. **34**(2), 1–59 (2021). https://doi.org/10.1007/s00145-021-09374-3

11. Gao, Y., Al-Sarawi, S.F., Abbott, D.: Physical unclonable functions. Nature Electron. **3**(2), 81–91 (2020)

12. Green, M.D., Miers, I.: Forward secure asynchronous messaging from puncturable encryption. In: 2015 IEEE Symposium on Security and Privacy, pp. 305–320. IEEE (2015)

13. Halevi, S.: A sufficient condition for key-privacy. Cryptology ePrint Archive (2005)

14. Heinrich, A., Stute, M., Kornhuber, T., Hollick, M.: Who can find my devices? Security and privacy of apple's crowd-sourced Bluetooth location tracking system. arXiv preprint arXiv:2103.02282 (2021)

15. Internet Engineering Task Force, Rescorla, E.: The transport layer security (TLS) protocol version 1.3. RFC 8446 (2018). http://datatracker.ietf.org/doc/html/rfc8446

16. Internet Engineering Task Force, Santesson, S., Myers, M., Ankney, R., Malpani, A., Galperin, S., Adams, C.: X.509 internet public key infrastructure online certificate status protocol - OCSP. RFC 6960 (2013). http://datatracker.ietf.org/doc/html/rfc6960

17. Jager, T., Kohlar, F., Schäge, S., Schwenk, J.: Generic compilers for authenticated key exchange. In: Abe, M. (ed.) ASIACRYPT 2010. LNCS, vol. 6477, pp. 232–249. Springer, Heidelberg (2010). https://doi.org/10.1007/978-3-642-17373-8_14

18. Krawczyk, H.: HMQV: a high-performance secure Diffie-Hellman protocol. In: Shoup, V. (ed.) CRYPTO 2005. LNCS, vol. 3621, pp. 546–566. Springer, Heidelberg (2005). https://doi.org/10.1007/11535218_33

19. Krombholz, K., Hobel, H., Huber, M., Weippl, E.: Advanced social engineering attacks. J. Inf. Secur. Appl. **22**, 113–122 (2015)

20. Li, Y., Schäge, S.: No-match attacks and robust partnering definitions: defining trivial attacks for security protocols is not trivial. In: Thuraisingham, B.M., Evans, D., Malkin, T., Xu, D. (eds.) Proceedings of the 2017 ACM SIGSAC Conference on Computer and Communications Security, CCS 2017, Dallas, TX, USA, 30 October–03 November 2017, pp. 1343–1360. ACM (2017). https://doi.org/10.1145/3133956.3134006

21. Lian, H., Pan, T., Wang, H., Zhao, Y.: Identity-based identity-concealed authenticated key exchange. In: Bertino, E., Shulman, H., Waidner, M. (eds.) ESORICS 2021. LNCS, vol. 12973, pp. 651–675. Springer, Cham (2021). https://doi.org/10.1007/978-3-030-88428-4_32

22. Libert, B., Paterson, K.G., Quaglia, E.A.: Anonymous broadcast encryption: adaptive security and efficient constructions in the standard model. In: Fischlin, M., Buchmann, J., Manulis, M. (eds.) PKC 2012. LNCS, vol. 7293, pp. 206–224. Springer, Heidelberg (2012). https://doi.org/10.1007/978-3-642-30057-8_13

23. Lin, H.: Indistinguishability obfuscation from SXDH on 5-linear maps and locality-5 PRGs. In: Katz, J., Shacham, H. (eds.) CRYPTO 2017. LNCS, vol. 10401, pp. 599–629. Springer, Cham (2017). https://doi.org/10.1007/978-3-319-63688-7_20

24. Lyu, Y., Liu, S., Han, S., Gu, D.: Privacy-preserving authenticated key exchange in the standard model. Cryptology ePrint Archive (2022)

25. Ramacher, S., Slamanig, D., Weninger, A.: Privacy-preserving authenticated key exchange: stronger privacy and generic constructions. In: Bertino, E., Shulman, H., Waidner, M. (eds.) ESORICS 2021. LNCS, vol. 12973, pp. 676–696. Springer, Cham (2021). https://doi.org/10.1007/978-3-030-88428-4_33

26. Rührmair, U., Sölter, J., Sehnke, F.: On the foundations of physical unclonable functions. Cryptology ePrint Archive (2009)

27. Schäge, S., Schwenk, J., Lauer, S.: Privacy-preserving authenticated key exchange and the case of IKEv2. In: Kiayias, A., Kohlweiss, M., Wallden, P., Zikas, V. (eds.) PKC 2020. LNCS, vol. 12111, pp. 567–596. Springer, Cham (2020). https://doi.org/10.1007/978-3-030-45388-6_20

28. Shi, E., Wu, K.: Non-interactive anonymous router. In: Canteaut, A., Standaert, F.-X. (eds.) EUROCRYPT 2021. LNCS, vol. 12698, pp. 489–520. Springer, Cham (2021). https://doi.org/10.1007/978-3-030-77883-5_17

29. Shoup, V.: Sequences of games: a tool for taming complexity in security proofs. Cryptology ePrint Archive, Report 2004/332 (2004). http://eprint.iacr.org/

30. Wallrabenstein, J.R.: Practical and secure IoT device authentication using physical unclonable functions. In: 2016 IEEE 4th International Conference on Future Internet of Things and Cloud (FiCloud), pp. 99–106. IEEE (2016)

31. Wang, Y., Paccagnella, R., He, E.T., Shacham, H., Fletcher, C.W., Kohlbrenner, D.: Hertzbleed: turning power {Side-Channel} attacks into remote timing attacks on x86. In: 31st USENIX Security Symposium (USENIX Security 2022), pp. 679–697 (2022)

32. Zhao, Y.: Identity-concealed authenticated encryption and key exchange. In: Proceedings of the 2016 ACM SIGSAC Conference on Computer and Communications Security, pp. 1464–1479 (2016)

Hybrid Group Key Exchange
with Application to Constrained Networks

Colin Boyd[1], Elsie Mestl Fondevik[1,2(✉)], Kristian Gjøsteen[1],
and Lise Millerjord[1]

[1] Norwegian University of Science and Technology, Trodheim, Norway
{colin.boyd,elsie.mestl,kristian.gjosteen,lise.millerjord}@ntnu.no
[2] Kongsberg Defence & Aerospace, Asker, Norway

Abstract. We expand the security model for group key exchange of Poettering et al. (CT-RSA 2021) to allow for more fine-tuned reveal of both state and keying material. The expanded model is used to analyse the security of hybrid group key exchange schemes, compositions of distinct group key exchange schemes where either subprotocol may be separately compromised. We then construct a hybrid group key exchange protocol that we show to be as secure as its sub-protocols. Furthermore, we use the notion of a secure element to develop a lightweight, low transmission group key exchange protocol. This protocol is used to develop a hybrid scheme that offers dynamic group membership and is suitable for use in constrained networks.

Keywords: hybrid scheme · group key exchange · mobile ad hoc networks · secure element

1 Introduction

When developing a cryptographic protocol for a specific use case the intended environment, the application and the expected adversarial threat, should be taken into consideration. However, sometimes the stakeholder requirements are contradictory, e.g. a lightweight system with limited key storage will have trouble running a key exchange protocol which needs to use post-quantum cryptography (PQC). There are then three approaches; one is to relax the requirements sufficiently until a protocol can be found; a second is to develop an entirely new protocol that fulfills all the requirements; a third is to partition the stakeholder requirements into distinct requirement sets such that a suitable protocol can be found for each set of requirements, and then somehow combine these protocols.

Initially, the first approach is a good place to start. Often in an initial phase requirements are set as desired and not as needed. A second evaluation could resolve any conflicting requirements. If this, however, does not resolve the conflicts then relaxing/removing requirements is not an ideal approach.

© The Author(s), under exclusive license to Springer Nature Switzerland AG 2023
E. Athanasopoulos and B. Mennink (Eds.): ISC 2023, LNCS 14411, pp. 455–472, 2023.
https://doi.org/10.1007/978-3-031-49187-0_23

The second approach, developing a new protocol, is a favorite of all cryptographers, but not a good solution for systems that are likely to be deployed in the near future. If a completely new scheme is to be developed, it is likely that it has not had enough time to mature nor for extensive testing.

In this paper we explore the third approach. We consider the combination of multiple group key exchange protocols to generate a new hybrid protocol that can achieve a set of properties that neither of the initial protocols achieve independently. These properties may range from security notions to network and architectural features.

1.1 Use Case

The use case that inspired this work is group key exchange for search and rescue operations over emergency networks. They are mobile ad hoc networks meant to function even when general telecommunication infrastructure is compromised due to natural or man-made disasters [8]. Semi-permanent mobile infrastructure can be flown in and supplement remaining infrastructure or be used standalone. Handheld and vehicle mounted devices can also be used in a transmission mode to function as nodes in the network [9,10,19]. Naturally, these networks are sub-optimal compared to the permanent networks.

Law enforcement and rescue organizations use such emergency networks when participating in rescue missions. It is used by the participants to communicate during the mission, both in and out of field, to enable cooperation. One of the main forms of communication is voice messages with short life expectancy; such as voice commands that only need to remain secure until the action is performed. After that the command will be known by everyone independent of whether security was broken or not (e.g. the message «*A go to B*» is leaked once it is evident that A is moving towards B). Yet, the ability to inform the team where medical personnel is needed or when a situation has become so unstable that the team needs to retreat, is life critical information that needs to be reliably communicated. Therefore, due to the short message lifespan, reliability and availability have traditionally had a higher priority than confidentiality, integrity and forward secrecy in these settings [12].

Current real-world solutions for key management in these scenarios load pre-shared keys prior to mission start [23]. As a result, emergency networks are vulnerable to loss of keying material since no dynamic key agreement is in place. A more robust solution is therefore desirable.

1.2 Our Contributions

Our main contributions in this paper are threefold.

HYBRID PROTOCOL. First, we build upon the security model of Poettering et al. [18] to allow a more fine-grained reveal suitable when running multiple group key exchange algorithms as one. We use this model to develop and prove a *hybrid* group key exchange protocol at least as secure as its subprotocols. Furthermore, we show that depending on how session windows (epochs) are computed the security notions inherited by the resulting hybrid protocol vary.

SECURE ELEMENT. As our second contribution, we consider how to model *secure elements* used for group key exchange. The secure element is tamper-proof and user-specific, and hence it is reasonable to prevent adversarial access to internally stored secret information and states. As a result, an adversary may only access the element (if at all) the same way specific users would access it.

We design a group key exchange protocol using secure elements. We show that this protocol offers forward secrecy (FS), a limited form of post-compromise security (PCS) as well as exclusion-style based dynamic group membership.

PROTOCOL PROPERTIES. Finally, we combine the secure element protocol with a group key exchange protocol that offers dynamic group membership to get a stronger, novel protocol with full dynamic group membership.

The secure element protocol will be used as the main contributor for FS and weak PCS and as a result the hybrid construction will have minimal overhead. Only when group members are added or removed is the second protocol utilized. As such we achieve a group key exchange protocol with minimal transmission overhead while at the same time offering full dynamic group membership.

1.3 Related Work

Hybrid constructions are known constructions in the cryptographic community, either by combining symmetric and asymmetric schemes [3,11,13], or more recently combining PQC schemes with classical schemes [7,21]. In this paper we introduce a model for hybrid construction that only requires that the subprotocols are group key exchange protocols.

Secure elements have been used in the literature before. A session key distribution scheme using secure elements was proposed by Shoup [20]. It focuses on extending the key exchange model [4] and introducing a two-party key distribution scheme. It does not perform a full key exchange, nor does it take group communication into account; two of the main focus areas of this paper.

The continuous group key exchange protocol MLS [2] also offers the use of pre-shared keys to lower the update cost and potentially increase security. The reduced cost is, however, only computational and does not lower the size of transmitted packets. In order for a session to maintain forward secrecy, updates for all end users in the session still need to be performed regularly. In comparison, the pre-shared keys used in our secure element protocol will reduce computational costs, as well as greatly reduce transmission size. The greatest benefit, however, is that key generation failure due to missing packets can be easily rectified with minimal overhead, both computational as well as transmission-wise.

2 Prerequisites

We build upon the generic group key exchange model presented by Poettering et al. [17], and use the syntax presented in Definition 1 in our work.

Definition 1 (Group Key Agreement (adapted from [18])). *A group key exchange protocol, Π, is a tuple of PPT algorithms* (**gen, init, exec, proc**), *defined as follows:*

- **gen** *generates a pair of public and private authentication keys,* (sk, pk), *per user when applicable.*
- **init** *takes an instance identifier, iid, and generates an initial state, σ.*
- **exec** *takes as input a secret key,* sk *(when applicable), a state σ, and a command, cmd, and returns a new state σ'.*
- **proc** *takes as input a secret key,* sk *(when applicable), a state, σ, and a ciphertext, c, and returns either a new state, σ' or $\bot$ (failure).*

In addition to these four algorithms, two procedures are used to distribute and store information. Their detail is part of the environment running the protocol.

- snd_{iid} is an instance-specific procedure that takes a ciphertext, c, as input and distributes it to the desired recipients as well as the adversary.
- key_{iid} is an instance-specific key-processing procedure. It takes a group key, k, with corresponding id, kid, as input and delivers it to the application layer. The identifier is passed to the adversary.

Another three functions are utilized to extract encoded information. The specifics are defined by the concrete protocol being analyzed.

- **mem** takes a key identifier, kid, as input and returns the set of instances with access to the key.
- **rec** takes a ciphertext, c, as input and returns the set of instances that should receive the data.
- **getEpoch** takes either a state, σ, or key identifier, kid, as input and returns the current epoch, t.

Additionally, we consider there to be an implicit mapping between instance ids and public keys, and let pk_{iid} denote a public key associated with instance iid. Furthermore, two instances iid_1 and iid_2, with key ids kid_1 and kid_2, respectively, are considered partners if $kid_1 = kid_2$.

Epochs are used to capture the notion of PCS as well as *forward secrecy (FS)* by compartmentalising the generated session keys into smaller time frames or windows. Conceptually, a protocol offers FS when all session keys from previous epochs are secure when a state of the current epoch is exposed. Equivalently, a protocol offers PCS when all session keys in future epochs are secure if a state of the current epoch is exposed.

The security of the model is game-based. Authentication is optional and marked with gray boxes in the experiment (Fig. 1). The experiment has been adapted to include a toggle, $X \in \{\{FS\}, \{FS, PCS\}\}$, to prove only FS or also include PCS. The non-shaded boxed parts in Fig. 1 are only included when $PCS \in X$. The goal of the adversary is *key indistinguishability (KIND)*.

Definition 2 (X-KIND Secure (adapted from [18])). *Let Π be a group key exchange protocol and let $\mathcal{A}$ be an X-KIND-adversary against Π playing the black parts of the security game in Fig. 1. The advantage of $\mathcal{A}$ is*

$$\mathsf{Adv}_{\Pi}^{X\text{-}KIND}(\mathcal{A}) = |\Pr\left[X\text{-}KIND_{\Pi}(\mathcal{A}) = 0\right] - \Pr\left[X\text{-}KIND_{\Pi}(\mathcal{A}) = 1\right]|.$$

The protocol, Π, is X-KIND ϵ-secure if $\mathsf{Adv}_{\Pi}^{X\text{-}KIND}(\mathcal{A}) < \epsilon$.

A group key exchange protocol is *dynamic* if group members can be added or removed during run time, otherwise the protocol is *static*.

3 Hybrid Group Key Exchange

Sometimes we want to combine two group key exchange protocols, either to combine properties of each subprotocol into one protocol, or because we do not fully trust either one. Specifically, we desire that the combined protocol gains the best properties and security goals from either of its subprotocols. Furthermore, we want the combined protocol to remain secure unless both protocols are broken.

3.1 Hybrid Security Model

Our hybrid scheme runs the two protocols independently as subprotocols. The two group keys produced by the sub-protocols will be combined using a key derivation function in order to generate a group key for the hybrid scheme.

Definition 3. *Let $\Pi_i = (\mathbf{gen}_i, \mathbf{init}_i, \mathbf{exec}_i, \mathbf{proc}_i)$, $i \in \{1, 2\}$, be two group key exchange protocols. We define a hybrid group key exchange protocol, Π, to be a group key exchange protocol with the following additional algorithmic properties.*

- **gen** *generates public and private authentication keys* $(\mathsf{sk}, \mathsf{pk})$, *where* $\mathsf{sk} = (\mathsf{sk}_0, \mathsf{sk}_1, \mathsf{sk}_2)$ *and* $\mathsf{pk} = (\mathsf{pk}_0, \mathsf{pk}_1, \mathsf{pk}_2)$ *and* $(\mathsf{sk}_i, \mathsf{pk}_i), i \in \{1, 2\}$ *is a long term key pair for protocol* Π_i, *and* $(\mathsf{sk}_0, \mathsf{pk}_0)$ *is a long term key pair for the hybrid protocol when applicable. If subprotocol* Π_i *does not have authentication, the long term key pair is set to* ϵ.
- **init** *takes an instance identifier, iid, as input. Returns a three tuple state* $\sigma = (\sigma_0, \sigma_1, \sigma_2)$ *where* σ_1 *and* σ_2 *are independent initial states for instance iid in protocols* Π_1 *and* Π_2, *respectively.*
- **exec** *takes a secret key* $\mathsf{sk} = (\mathsf{sk}_0, \mathsf{sk}_1, \mathsf{sk}_2)$ *(when applicable), state* $\sigma = (\sigma_0, \sigma_1, \sigma_2)$, *and command cmd as input, and outputs state* $\sigma' = (\sigma_0', \sigma_1', \sigma_2')$. *The states* σ_1' *and* σ_2' *are generated by* $\mathbf{exec}_1$ *and* $\mathbf{exec}_2$ *on the inputs* $(\mathsf{sk}_1, cmd_1, \sigma_1)$ *and* $(\mathsf{sk}_2, cmd_2, \sigma_2)$, *respectively, when* $cmd_i, i \in \{1, 2\}$ *is a valid command in the specific subprotocol extracted from cmd.*
- **proc** *takes a secret key,* $\mathsf{sk} = (\mathsf{sk}_0, \mathsf{sk}_1, \mathsf{sk}_2)$ *(when applicable), state,* $\sigma = (\sigma_0, \sigma_1, \sigma_2)$, *and ciphertext, c, as input, and outputs state* $\sigma' = (\sigma_0', \sigma_1', \sigma_2')$. *The states* σ_1' *and* σ_2' *are generated by* $\mathbf{proc}_1$ *and* $\mathbf{proc}_2$ *on inputs* $(\mathsf{sk}_1, c_1, \sigma_1)$ *and* $(\mathsf{sk}_2, c_2, \sigma_2)$, *respectively, when* $c_i, i \in \{1, 2\}$ *is a valid ciphertext in the specific subprotocol derived from c.*

The group key $\mathsf{k} = kdf(\mathsf{k_0}, \mathsf{k_1}, \mathsf{k_2})$ *is created by combining keys* $\mathsf{k_1}$ *and* $\mathsf{k_2}$ *as generated by protocols* Π_1 *and* Π_2*, respectively, together with any additional secret information* $\mathsf{k_0}$*. Let* k_i*,* $i \in \{0, 1, 2\}$ *have session key id* kid_i*. The session key id of* k *is then a combination of the sub key ids,* $kid = (kid_0, kid_1, kid_2)$*.*

Together with the helper functions and procedures defined and available in the group key exchange model we add two information extraction algorithms.

- **isHybrid** Takes a group key exchange protocol, Π, as input and returns true if Π is a hybrid group key exchange protocol, or false otherwise.
- **subProt** Takes a group session key id, kid, as input and returns either a value 0, 1, or 2 as output depending on whether the key id belongs to a key generated by the entire protocol, i.e. return 0; or to the first or second subprotocol, i.e. return 1 or 2, respectively.

It is clear that a hybrid scheme is a group key exchange protocol as in accordance to Definition 1, and we can use the security model to prove the hybrid protocol is secure. However, the reveal oracle does not capture the full complexity of the hybrid protocol. Since the subprotocols used in a hybrid protocol can run and store information on separate hardware it should be possible to expose the subprotocol states separately. The experiment as it originally stands (black part of Fig. 1), does not allow for such distinctions. An additional reveal oracle is added to the protocol to allow this more fine-grained reveal. Additionally, we allow corruption of an instance as well as the corruption of its separate subprotocols. Lastly, we allow session keys of the subprotocols to be revealed and add bookkeeping to ensure that the revealed information is appropriately tracked. The new information is displayed in blue in Fig. 1.

Definition 4. *Let* Π *be a hybrid group key exchange protocol and let* $\mathcal{A}$ *be a KIND-adversary against* Π *playing the security game presented in Fig. 1. The advantage of* $\mathcal{A}$ *is*

$$\mathsf{Adv}_{\Pi}^{X\text{-}KIND}(\mathcal{A}) = |\Pr\left[X\text{-}KIND_{\Pi}(\mathcal{A}) = 0\right] - \Pr\left[X\text{-}KIND_{\Pi}(\mathcal{A}) = 1\right]|.$$

The protocol, Π *is X-KIND* ϵ*-secure if* $\mathsf{Adv}_{\Pi}^{X\text{-}KIND}(\mathcal{A}) < \epsilon.$

There are two natural ways of registering epochs that will yield different security guarantees. The first version is to represent the epoch as a two tuple $t = (t_1, t_2)$ consisting of the epochs t_1 and t_2 from the two subprotocols Π_1 and Π_2, respectively. The second possibility is to use the epoch of only one of the subprotocols directly. We call an epoch generated as in the first style for *combined*. If the epoch is generated according to the second style, then the epoch is *inherited*. Depending on the style of epoch the hybrid protocol may achieve drastically different security notions.

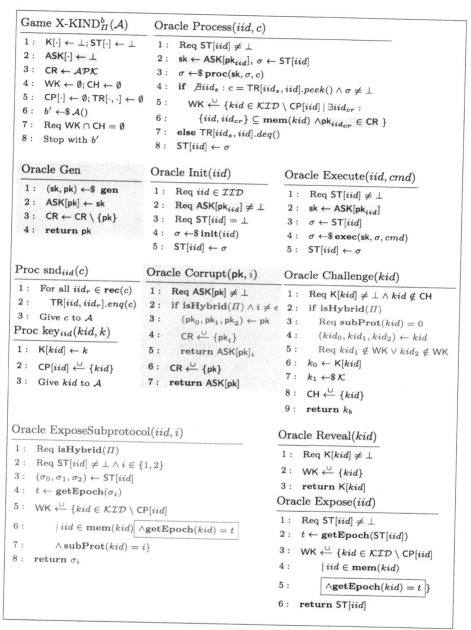

Fig. 1. The security experiment for group key exchange. Information in black is according to the original model [17] while the blue has been added to allow for hybrid construction. K is the set of group keys, ST is the state set, ASK, $\mathcal{APK}$ are the secret and public authentication key set, respectively, CR is the set of corrupted long term keys, WK are the weak group keys, CH is the set of challenged group keys, CP is the set of computed group keys and TR is the set of messages to be transmitted.

3.2   Hybrid Protocol Construction

The natural construction of a hybrid group key exchange protocol combines the resulting session keys from two independently running subprotocols. No additional operations are performed by the scheme itself.

In order to incorporate this construction into our model we make two minor alteration to the subprotocols. First, the hybrid scheme needs access to the generated session keys. Second, the subprotocols are blocked from sending ciphertexts. Sending will only be performed by the hybrid scheme. In both cases additional information needs to be available to the hybrid construction. As such, we slightly augment what parameters are returned: the subprotocol algorithms $\mathbf{exec}_i$ and $\mathbf{proc}_i$ return the state σ_1, generated key k_i, key id kid_i and generated ciphertext c_i. Figure 2 formally defines a canonical hybrid scheme.

$\mathbf{gen}()$	$\mathbf{init}(iid)$
1 : $\mathsf{sk}_1, \mathsf{sk}_2, \mathsf{pk}_1, \mathsf{pk}_2 \leftarrow \epsilon$	1 : $\sigma_1 \leftarrow \mathbf{init}_1(iid)$
2 : $(\mathsf{sk}_1, \mathsf{pk}_1) \leftarrow \mathbf{gen}_1()$	2 : $\sigma_2 \leftarrow \mathbf{init}_2(iid)$
3 : $(\mathsf{sk}_2, \mathsf{pk}_2) \leftarrow \mathbf{gen}_2()$	3 : **return** $(\epsilon, \sigma_1, \sigma_2)$
4 : **return** $(\mathsf{sk}_1, \mathsf{sk}_2, \mathsf{pk}_1, \mathsf{pk}_2)$	

$\mathbf{exec}(\mathsf{sk}, \sigma, cmd)$	$\mathbf{proc}(\mathsf{sk}, \sigma, c)$
1 : $(\epsilon, \mathsf{sk}_1, \mathsf{sk}_2) \leftarrow \mathsf{sk}$	1 : $(\epsilon, \mathsf{sk}_1, \mathsf{sk}_2) \leftarrow \mathsf{sk}$
2 : $(\epsilon, \sigma_1, \sigma_2) \leftarrow \sigma$	2 : $(\epsilon, \sigma_1, \sigma_2) \leftarrow \sigma$
3 : $(\epsilon, cmd_1, cmd_2) \leftarrow cmd$	3 : $(\epsilon, c_1, c_2) \leftarrow c$
4 : $(\sigma_1, k_1, kid_1, c_1) \leftarrow \mathbf{exec}_1(\mathsf{sk}_1, \sigma_1, cmd_1)$	4 : $(\sigma_1, k_1, kid_1) \leftarrow \mathbf{proc}_1(\mathsf{sk}_1, \sigma_1, c_1)$
5 : $(\sigma_2, k_2, kid_2, c_2) \leftarrow \mathbf{exec}_2(\mathsf{sk}_2, \sigma_2, cmd_2)$	5 : $(\sigma_2, k_2, kid_2) \leftarrow \mathbf{proc}_2(\mathsf{sk}_2, \sigma_2, c_2)$
6 : $\mathbf{snd}_{\mathsf{sk}.iid}(c_1, c_2)$	6 : $k \leftarrow kdf(k_1, k_2)$
7 : $k \leftarrow kdf(k_1, k_2)$	7 : $kid \leftarrow (kid_1, kid_2)$
8 : $kid \leftarrow (kid_1, kid_2)$	8 : $\mathbf{key}_{\mathsf{sk}.iid}(kid, k)$
9 : $\mathbf{key}_{\mathsf{sk}.iid}(kid, k)$	9 : **return** $(\epsilon, \sigma_1, \sigma_2)$
10 : **return** $(\epsilon, \sigma_1, \sigma_2)$	

Fig. 2. Formal protocol definition of a hybrid protocol $\Pi = (\mathbf{gen}, \mathbf{init}, \mathbf{exec}, \mathbf{proc})$ generated from group key exchange protocols $\Pi_1 = (\mathbf{gen}_1, \mathbf{init}_1, \mathbf{exec}_1, \mathbf{proc}_1)$ and $\Pi_2 = (\mathbf{gen}_2, \mathbf{init}_2, \mathbf{exec}_2, \mathbf{proc}_2)$.

Theorem 1. *Let Π be the hybrid protocol from Fig. 2 with subprotocols Π_1 and Π_2. Let $\mathcal{A}$ be a PPT-adversary against Π, then there exists a PPT-adversary $\mathcal{B}_1$ against Π_1 and a PPT-adversary $\mathcal{B}_2$ against Π_2, such that*

$$\mathsf{Adv}_{\Pi}^{Y\text{-}KIND}(\mathcal{A}) \leq \min\left[\mathsf{Adv}_{\Pi}^{X1\text{-}KIND}(\mathcal{B}_1), \mathsf{Adv}_{\Pi}^{X2\text{-}KIND}(\mathcal{B}_2)\right],$$

and $X1, X2 \in \{\{FS\}, \{FS, PCS\}\}$.

If epoch is inherited from subprotocol Π_i *then* $Y = Xi$. *On the other hand, if epoch is combined then* $Y = X1 \cap X2$.

Proof (sketch). We construct the adversaries $\mathcal{B}_i$, $i \in \{1, 2\}$. They interact with a security experiment for the subprotocol Π_i that has challenge bit b_i. The security experiment is modified so that $\mathcal{B}_i$ uses its own security experiment for Π_i with (unknown) challenge bit b_i while it executes Π_{3-i} and the combined protocol, Π, itself. The hybrid protocol Π uses epoch style inherited from Π_i.

The simulation of Π by $\mathcal{B}_i$ is further modified so that the session key is never computed until the adversary either reveals the session key or a challenge query is made. If the session key is revealed, then $\mathcal{B}_i$ makes a reveal query to its security experiment to get k_{i,b_i}. If the instance is challenged, then $\mathcal{B}_i$ makes a challenge query to its security experiment.

If $\mathcal{A}$ queries *ExposeSubprotocol(iid, i)* for a challenged instance *iid* the adversary $\mathcal{B}_i$ returns challenge key k_{i,b_i}. If $\mathcal{A}$ terminates with $\perp$ that means it discovers that the output from *ExposeSubprotocol(iid, i)* was fabricated and we let $\mathcal{B}_i$ output 0 and stops, if $\mathcal{A}$ returns b then $\mathcal{B}$ stops and returns b.

If *ExposeSubprotocol(iid, i)* was not queried at a challenged instance, then $\mathcal{B}_i$ terminates with output b when $\mathcal{A}$ stops with output b.

As a result we get that

$$\mathsf{Adv}_\Pi^{Xi\text{-}KIND}(\mathcal{A}) \le \mathsf{Adv}_\Pi^{Xi\text{-}KIND}(\mathcal{B}_i),$$

meaning that

$$\mathsf{Adv}_\Pi^{Y\text{-}KIND}(\mathcal{A}) \le \min\left[\mathsf{Adv}_\Pi^{X1\text{-}KIND}(\mathcal{B}_1), \mathsf{Adv}_\Pi^{X2\text{-}KIND}(\mathcal{B}_2)\right]$$

where Y is either $X1$ or $X2$ depending on who it inherited its epoch from.

In the case of a combined epoch, recall that the only difference between a protocol that is FS secure and one that also provides PCS, is the amount and combination of queries it is legally allowed to make, where queries against an FS protocol is a subset of valid queries made against the same protocol but for FS and PCS. Keeping the argument form above but setting the security notion to the lower bound of the two subprotocols we get the second theorem statement where Y is the intersection of both $X1$ and $X2$.   □

As a result, we discover that a hybrid protocol consisting of two subprotocols with identical security notions will obtain that security notion as well, independent of how epochs are computed. If, however, the two protocols have distinct security achievements, the level of security the hybrid scheme achieves relies solely on the choice of epoch computation. What this intuitively means is that the hybrid scheme achieves a form of reduced PCS, where certain types of updates will result in a healed state while others will only ensure FS.

4   Secure Element

A secure element is a tamper-resistant chip that contains storage, computing power and memory [14–16,22,24]. It is designed to deliberately hinder both leakage and side-channel attacks. It is tamper-resistant to prevent an adversary from physically opening the hardware device to extract keying information [16]. Any such attempt should result in a physical reaction that automatically destroys any keys stored on the device. Similarly, trying to load new software will result in key-removal, where new keys would have to be reloaded.

Due to the tamper-resistant nature of the secure element, the interface of the device can be carefully chosen to limit information flow out of the secured environment. Only specific queries can be made available and will not be processed if the input arguments do not comply with internally stored access restrictions. In such cases no output will be returned.

We consider key generation and distribution as well as software loading to be performed in accordance to current security and cryptographic standards, but essentially consider it to be out of scope for this paper. (Any discussion of these issues will largely be orthogonal to what we do discuss.) We will instead focus on the interface and functional requirements needed of the secure element.

4.1   Representation

Secure elements are real-world hardware devices that act like an interactive black box and can as such be modeled as an oracle, $\mathcal{O}_{SE}$.

The secure element is user-specific and loaded with a pre-shared symmetric secret key mk_τ called *master key*, along with a corresponding timestamp τ. The secure element might not have access to a clock, but will evolve the master key based on received timestamps τ'. The new timestamp will then be stored in place of the old value. The master key can only be ratcheted forward and the secure element will not process any input if the received timestamp τ' is less than the internally stored value τ.

The holder of a secure element does not have knowledge or access to the master key mk_τ directly. It can only access mk_τ indirectly by querying the secure element with a group $\mathcal{G}$, timestamp τ' and session transcript Γ. The secure element will then return a *session master key* $sm_{\tau',0}$ created by hashing the received group together with the master key evolved to timestamp τ' and the received transcript. If either the timestamp τ' is less than the internally stored value, or the owner of the secure element is not a member of the group $\mathcal{G}$, then $sm_{\tau',0} = \bot$. Formally we define the secure element oracle as follows:

Definition 5. *Let $\mathcal{G}$ be a group, Γ a transcript, τ' the timestamp input by the user, and τ the current timestamp of the master key. Then an instance iid may query the secure element oracle, $\mathcal{O}_{SE}^{(iid)}$, for a session master key according to*

$$\mathcal{O}_{SE}^{(iid)}(\mathcal{G}, \Gamma, \tau')$$

1: **if** $iid \notin \mathcal{G}$ **or** $\tau > \tau'$:

2:      **return** $\perp$

3: $mk_{\tau'} \leftarrow \mathsf{Evolve}(mk_\tau, \tau' - \tau)$

4: $sm_{\tau',0} \leftarrow H(\mathcal{G}, mk_{\tau'}, \Gamma)$

5: **return** $sm_{\tau',0}$

where H is a hash function, and $\mathsf{Evolve}(\cdot, \cdot)$ is an algorithm that takes two arguments. The second argument specifies the number of times the first argument is to be ratcheted using a key derivation function.

4.2   A Basic Group Key Exchange Protocol

The secure element oracle described in the previous section can be viewed as a very simple group key exchange protocol as seen in Fig. 3. The oracle provides FS and PCS but as we will see in this section the group key exchange protocol provides forward secrecy but only a limited version of post compromise security.

The protocol has two commands, $\mathsf{Cmd}_\Pi = \{(\mathbf{newSMK}, \mathcal{G}, \Gamma, \tau), (\mathbf{ratchet})\}$, that either generates a new session master key using the oracle from Definition 5 (**newSMK**) or ratchets the existing session master key (**ratchet**). Since **newSMK** takes the group as input, the secure element ratchet protocol offers dynamic group membership although the exclusion of members relies on the fact that the secure element is secure and acts as desired.

The secure element ratchet protocol offers implicit authentication through the use of a pre-shared master key, and does not use an asymmetric key pair to sign and authenticate messages.

The epoch is defined as a tuple (τ, t) where the first variable refers to the timestamp of the secure element and the second to the number of ratchets of the session master key generated from mk_τ. The epochs are compared using lexicographic ordering.

Theorem 2. *Let $\mathcal{A}$ be an adversary against Π, the secure element ratchet protocol described in Fig. 3. Then the advantage of $\mathcal{A}$ is*

$$\mathsf{Adv}_\Pi^{FS\text{-}KIND}(\mathcal{A}) \leq (l_{h_1} + l_{h_2})/n + \mathsf{Adv}_{\mathcal{O}_{SE}}^{ROR}(\mathcal{B}),$$

where n is the number of possible key values, and l_{h_1} is the number of Expose *queries and l_{h_2} is the number of* Reveal *queries.*

Proof. We model $\mathsf{Evolve}(\cdot, \cdot)$ and G as hash functions in the random oracle model. The proof will be executed as a series of game hops (Fig. 4).

Game 0: Original secure element ratchet protocol.

$$\Pr[\mathrm{G0}] = \mathsf{Adv}_\Pi^{FS\text{-}KIND}(\mathcal{A})$$

Game 1: The protocol execution of the **ratchet** command is exchanged with a random value.

gen()	init(iid)
1 : **return** ϵ	1 : $\sigma \leftarrow (iid, 0, 0, 0, 0, 0)$
	2 : **return** σ

exec(σ, cmd)	proc(σ, c)
1 : **Req** ($cmd \in \mathsf{Cmd}_\sqcap$)	1 : $(cmd, c') \leftarrow c$
2 : $(iid, \mathcal{G}', \Gamma', \tau', t', sm_{\tau',t'}) \leftarrow \sigma$	2 : **Req** ($cmd \in \mathsf{Cmd}_\sqcap$)
3 : **if** cmd is **newSMK**	3 : $(iid, \mathcal{G}', \Gamma', \tau', t', sm_{\tau',t}) \leftarrow \sigma$
4 : $(cmd', \mathcal{G}, \Gamma, \tau) \leftarrow cmd$	4 : **if** cmd is **newSMK**
5 : $sm_{\tau,0} \leftarrow \mathcal{O}_{SE}^{(iid)}(\mathcal{G}, \Gamma, \tau)$	5 : $(cmd', \mathcal{G}, \Gamma, \tau) \leftarrow cmd$
6 : $\sigma \leftarrow (iid, \mathcal{G}, \Gamma, \tau, 0, sm_{\tau,0})$	6 : $sm_{\tau,0} \leftarrow \mathcal{O}_{SE}^{(iid)}(\mathcal{G}, \Gamma, \tau)$
7 : **if** cmd is **ratchet**	7 : $\sigma \leftarrow (iid, \mathcal{G}, \Gamma, \tau, 0, sm_{\tau,0})$
8 : $sm_{\tau',t'+1} \leftarrow \mathsf{Evolve}(sm_{\tau',t'}, 1)$	8 : **if** cmd is **ratchet** $\wedge\, c' \geq t'$
9 : $\sigma \leftarrow (iid, \mathcal{G}', \Gamma', \tau', t'+1, sm_{\tau',t'+1})$	9 : $sm_{\tau',c'} \leftarrow \mathsf{Evolve}(sm_{\tau',t'}, t' - c')$
10 : $cmd \leftarrow (cmd, t'+1)$	10 : $\sigma \leftarrow (iid, \mathcal{G}', \Gamma', \tau', c', sm_{\tau',c'})$
11 : $\mathsf{k} \leftarrow G(sm_{\tau,t})$	11 : $\mathsf{k} \leftarrow G(sm_{\tau,t})$
12 : $kid \leftarrow G(\mathcal{G}, \Gamma, \tau, t)$	12 : $kid \leftarrow G(\mathcal{G}, \Gamma, \tau, t)$
13 : **snd**$_{iid}(cmd)$	13 : **key**$_{iid}(kid, \mathsf{k})$
14 : **key**$_{iid}(kid, \mathsf{k})$	
15 : **return** σ	

Fig. 3. Secure Element ratchet protocol description consisting of two commands to either generate a new session master key or to ratchet the existing key forward. The function $\mathsf{Evolve}(\cdot, \cdot)$ is a function as described in Definition 5 and G is a hash function.

An adversary that can differentiate between Game 0 and Game 1 can differentiate between a random value and a value generated by a hash function from an unknown random value. Since we are in the random oracle model, in order to differentiate the adversary must have queried the random oracle at the existing pre-image, so

$$|\Pr[G0] - \Pr[G1]| \leq \frac{l_{h_1}}{n}.$$

Game 2: The protocol execution of the secure element oracle is exchanged for a random value.

An adversary that can differentiate between Game 1 and Game 2 can differentiate between a random value and a secure element oracle, so

$$|\Pr[G1] - \Pr[G2]| \leq \mathsf{Adv}_{\mathcal{O}_{SE}}^{ROR}(\mathcal{B}).$$

Game 3: The session key is exchanged for a random value.

gen()	init(iid)
1: **return** ϵ	1: $\sigma \leftarrow (iid, 0, 0, 0, 0, 0)$
	2: **return** σ

exec(σ, cmd)		proc(σ, c)	
1: **Req** ($cmd \in \mathsf{Cmd_\sqcap}$)		1: $(cmd, c') \leftarrow c$	
2: $(iid, \mathcal{G}', \Gamma', \tau', t', sm_{\tau',t'}) \leftarrow \sigma$		2: **Req** ($cmd \in \mathsf{Cmd_\sqcap}$)	
3: **if** cmd is **newSMK**		3: $(iid, \mathcal{G}', \Gamma', \tau', t', sm_{\tau',t}) \leftarrow \sigma$	
4: $(cmd', \mathcal{G}, \Gamma, \tau) \leftarrow cmd$		4: **if** cmd is **newSMK**	
5: $sm_{\tau,0} \leftarrow \mathcal{O}_{SE}^{(iid)}(\mathcal{G}, \Gamma, \tau)$	**G0 – G1**	5: $(cmd', \mathcal{G}, \Gamma, \tau) \leftarrow cmd$	
6: $sm_{\tau,0} \leftarrow\!\!\$\ \mathfrak{R}$	**G2 – G3**	6: $sm_{\tau,0} \leftarrow \mathcal{O}_{SE}^{(iid)}(\mathcal{G}, \Gamma, \tau)$	**G0 – G1**
7: $\sigma \leftarrow (iid, \mathcal{G}, \Gamma, \tau, 0, sm_{\tau,0})$		7: $sm_{\tau,0} \leftarrow\!\!\$\ \mathfrak{R}$	**G2 – G3**
8: **if** cmd is **ratchet**		8: $\sigma \leftarrow (iid, \mathcal{G}, \Gamma, \tau, 0, sm_{\tau,0})$	
9: $sm_{\tau',t'+1} \leftarrow \mathsf{Evolve}(sm_{\tau',t'}, 1)$	**G0**	9: **if** cmd is **ratchet** $\wedge\ c' \geq t'$	
10: $sm_{\tau',t'+1} \leftarrow\!\!\$\ \mathfrak{R}$	**G1 – G3**	10: $sm_{\tau',c'} \leftarrow \mathsf{Evolve}(sm_{\tau',t'}, t' - c')$	**G0**
11: $\sigma \leftarrow (iid, \mathcal{G}', \Gamma', \tau', t'+1, sm_{\tau',t'+1})$		11: $sm_{\tau',c'} \leftarrow\!\!\$\ \mathfrak{R}$	**G1 – G3**
12: $cmd \leftarrow (cmd, t'+1)$		12: $\sigma \leftarrow (iid, \mathcal{G}', \Gamma', \tau', c', sm_{\tau',c'})$	
13: $k \leftarrow G(sm_{\tau,t})$	**G0 – G2**	13: $k \leftarrow G(sm_{\tau,t})$	**G0 – G2**
14: $k \leftarrow\!\!\$\ \mathfrak{R}$	**G3**	14: $k \leftarrow\!\!\$\ \mathfrak{R}$	**G3**
15: $kid \leftarrow G(\mathcal{G}, \Gamma, \tau, t)$		15: $kid \leftarrow G(\mathcal{G}, \Gamma, \tau, t)$	
16: $\mathbf{snd}_{iid}(cmd)$		16: $\mathbf{key}_{iid}(kid, k)$	
17: $\mathbf{key}_{iid}(kid, k)$			
18: **return** σ			

Fig. 4. Gamehops of protocol Fig. 3 for protocol Theorem 2.

An adversary that differentiates between Game 2 and Game 3 can differentiate between a hash value and a random value, so

$$| \Pr[G2] - \Pr[G3]| \leq \frac{l_{h_2}}{n}.$$

Finally, an adversary can only win in Game 3 with probability $\frac{1}{2}$ since either value that could be returned by the challenge oracle would be sampled from the same, uniform distribution, so it has advantage 0. The claim follows.   □

Note that if the epoch window was only changed when the secure element oracle is queried, the protocol would be PCS. However, this would potentially mean larger session windows.

5 Protocol

Finally, we developed a group key exchange protocol with dynamic group membership that functions over mobile ad hoc networks. The developed protocol provides forward secrecy as well as post compromise security.

Situational Requirements. For group communication over emergency networks, we should distinguish between *required* and *desired* properties.

Availability is a requirement. Some transmissions may be dropped but even when some key updates are lost the group members should be able to reconnect without major overhead.

The ability to *add users* is a requirement. In rescue missions new personnel may join after the operation has started. However, they need to be able to do so without having reliable access to all group members, as we do not want to recall everyone to redistribute key material. It is important that existing members are not in danger of being ejected from a group when new members are added.

The ability to *remove users* from the group is a desired property. The same restrictions apply for removing as for adding users, but it is of lower priority due to the emphasis on availability. The ability to remove users also gives rise to a desire for *post-compromise security*; we want future communication to recover after a corruption has been detected.

Forward secrecy allows for earlier keys to remain secure after a session key of a device has been compromised. Since loss of equipment is not an unreasonable assumption, and since personal information such as medical history might be sent over these networks, we consider this a highly desirable property and should be a priority when developing the protocol. That said, due to availability concerns, it is not a strict requirement.

Situational Restrictions. Communication over emergency networks comes with a number of restrictions. In particular there will be varying connectivity, restricted bandwidth, high bit error rate and a high probability of packet loss due to the lack of reliable infrastructure. There will also be dead-spots where group members will be temporarily out of reach, and at times users may intentionally not answer while still being able to receive, e.g. due to radio silence.

Thus, our communication protocol must tolerate that some group member does not receive some messages or packets. If a key update message is lost, the affected user should be able to catch up later with minimal overhead [12].

Furthermore, there should be no response requirement or need to acknowledge that a message has been received. Since users may be in silent mode, or the response message is lost in transit, the instance that initiates an update should therefore not rely on other group members being able to respond.

The setup phase does not face the same network restrictions and difficulties that are present later during use. During setup, information can be shared using a more stable network or through a wired connection. We therefore allow for larger transmissions without errors or packet loss to occur during this stage.

Discussion. Existing continuous group key agreement schemes such as MLS [2] have the desired properties that we would like to achieve for our protocol where it obtains both dynamic group membership as well as post compromise security and forward secrecy. It does, however, not take the situational restrictions applicable to a mobile ad hoc network into consideration since it requires all members to be active in order to achieve its security goal [2]. In fact, it specifically states that the protocol should «*mandate key updates from clients that are not otherwise sending messages and evict clients which are idle for too long.*» [5, Section 7.2.2].

Furthermore, if packets are dropped such that existing group members miss out on updates, then a reintroduction to the group needs to be issued to every member that did not receive the update. This operation is essentially a new group member addition and has substantial transmission overhead when multiple members need to be reintroduced. It is thus not an ideal solution for unreliable networks as it may substantially lower availability.

5.1 Protocol Description

The hybrid scheme presented in this section combines the secure element ratchet protocol from Fig. 3 with a group key exchange protocol that provides dynamic group membership, e.g. TreeKEM [1,6].

The desired result follows almost directly from Theorem 1, only epoch style and command set needs to be specified. In the remainder of the paper we let subprotocol one, Π_1, be the secure element ratchet protocol from Fig. 3 and let subprotocol two, Π_2, be a PCS,FS-KIND ϵ-secure group key exchange protocol with dynamic group membership. The hybrid protocol will be denoted Π.

To specify the command set we need to make some requirements of the second protocol. Let $\mathsf{Cmd}_{\Pi 2}$ be the command set of subprotocol Π_2. We require that $\mathsf{Cmd}_{\Pi 2}$ contains two commands, here denoted Add_Π and $\mathsf{Remove}_{\Pi n}$, where the former includes a specified instance into the group while the second algorithm excludes. The command set Cmd_Π can be viewed as a subset of the space $\mathsf{Cmd}_{\Pi 1} \times \mathsf{Cmd}_{\Pi 2}$ defined as follows:

$$\mathsf{Cmd}_\Pi = \{(\mathbf{newSMK}, cmd_2) : cmd_2 \in (\mathsf{Cmd}_{\Pi 2} \cup \{\epsilon\})\} \cup \{(\mathbf{ratchet}, \epsilon)\}$$

It should be noted that the second subprotocol is the main contributor for dynamic group membership in order to reduce some of the trust placed on the secure element component. We do, however, allow addition and removal of group members without communication with Π_2, as seen in the command $cmd = (\mathbf{newSMK}, \epsilon)$. This is to ensure that the protocol offers dynamic group membership even when the bandwidth is limited.

Using a combined epoch or an epoch inherited from Π_1 the protocol achieves forward secrecy. If the epoch is inherited from Π_2 the hybrid construction achieves PCS as well. In practice this means that any time a user is added or removed to the group all previous or future session keys are secured.

From the discussion above and Theorem 1 the following statement follows.

Lemma 1. *Let Π be the hybrid protocol described above. Let $\mathcal{A}$ be a PPT-adversary against Π, then there exists a PPT-adversary $\mathcal{B}_1$ against Π_1 and a PPT-adversary $\mathcal{B}_2$ against Π_2, such that*

$$\mathsf{Adv}_\Pi^{Y\text{-}KIND}(\mathcal{A}) \leq \min\left[(l_{h_1} + l_{h_2})/n + \mathsf{Adv}_{\mathcal{O}_{SE}}^{ROR}(\mathcal{B}), \mathsf{Adv}_{\Pi_2}^{FS,PCS\text{-}KIND}(\mathcal{B}_2)\right].$$

If epoch is inherited from the secure element ratchet protocol then $Y = FS$. On the other hand, if epoch is inherited from Π_2 then $Y = FS, PCS$.

5.2   Discussion on Credibility of the Secure Element Assumptions

Is the assumption of a secure element as presented above too strong for real world applications? Also, assuming a secure element, do we need anything else?

The answer to the first question is *almost*. As with any technology, a secure element cannot be guaranteed to be safe against future attacks. We therefore considered secure elements as hardware devices more secure than regular technology products, but not impenetrable.

The applications described for this use case are mobile ad hoc networks and more specifically emergency networks. These are circumstances that generally require special equipment to function. Hence requiring this equipment to be fitted with special hardware is not an unrealistic assumption. This can be specially constructed equipment for the environment or physical add-ons that are plugged into an already existing device such as a phone. It is important to note that information generated by a secure element, but processed and used by a non-secure CPU, does not have the security guarantee of secure elements, since an adversary can access the information while it is being processed. Hence, any information that needs the highest degree of protection, such as the master key, should only be indirectly available through the secure element oracle.

It should be required that the master key is evolved on a regular basis since a total attack prevention can never be guaranteed. If the secure element were to be compromised at any point in time the current master key and any future derivations of said key will be compromised. However, all messages sent using previous master key will remain secure.

The second question, is a secure element sufficient on its own, is largely answered by the above discussion. By relying only on the secure element, we leave ourselves vulnerable to a singular point of failure that would completely remove any future security if a successful attack was launched. Furthermore, without adding any additional protection to the construction we rely on the trustworthiness of any secure-element manufacturer to not add any back-doors, either intentionally or unintentionally. Both of these concerns can be alleviated by using the secure element as part of a hybrid scheme.

Acknowledgements. Boyd and Millerjord are supported by the Research Council of Norway under Project No. 288545.

References

1. Alwen, J., et al.: Keep the dirt: tainted TreeKEM, adaptively and actively secure continuous group key agreement. Cryptology ePrint Archive, Report 2019/1489 (2019). https://ia.cr/2019/1489
2. Barnes, R., Beurdouche, B., Robert, R., Millican, J., Omara, E., Cohn-Gordon, K.: The Messaging Layer Security (MLS) Architecture, chap. Pre-Shared Keys. Network Working Group (2022). https://messaginglayersecurity.rocks/mls-protocol/draft-ietf-mls-protocol.html#name-pre-shared-keys

3. Barnes, R., Bhargavan, K., Lipp, B., Wood, C.A.: Hybrid Public Key Encryption. RFC 9180 (2022). https://doi.org/10.17487/RFC9180, https://www.rfc-editor.org/info/rfc9180

4. Bellare, M., Rogaway, P.: Entity authentication and key distribution. In: Stinson, D.R. (ed.) CRYPTO 1993. LNCS, vol. 773, pp. 232–249. Springer, Heidelberg (1994). https://doi.org/10.1007/3-540-48329-2_21

5. Beurdouche, B., Rescorla, E., Omara, E., Inguva, S., Duric, A.: The Messaging Layer Security (MLS) Architecture, chap. Forward and Post-Compromise Security. Network Working Group (2022). https://messaginglayersecurity.rocks/mls-architecture/draft-ietf-mls-architecture.html#name-forward-and-post-compromise

6. Bhargavan, K., Barnes, R., Rescorla, E.: TreeKEM: asynchronous decentralized key management for large dynamic groups. Research Report, Inria Paris (2018). https://hal.inria.fr/hal-02425247

7. Crockett, E., Paquin, C., Stebila, D.: Prototyping post-quantum and hybrid key exchange and authentication in TLS and SSH. https://csrc.nist.gov/CSRC/media/Events/Second-PQC-Standardization-Conference/documents/accepted-papers/stebila-prototyping-post-quantum.pdf

8. ETSI: Tetra (2021). https://www.etsi.org/technologies/tetra

9. Fazeldehkordi, E., Amiri, I.S., Akanbi, O.A.: Chapter 2 - literature review. In: Fazeldehkordi, E., Amiri, I.S., Akanbi, O.A. (eds.) A Study of Black Hole Attack Solutions, pp. 7–57. Syngress (2016). https://doi.org/10.1016/B978-0-12-805367-6.00002-8, https://www.sciencedirect.com/science/article/pii/B9780128053676000028

10. Gutiérrez-Reina, D., Marín, S.L.T., Barrero, F., Bessis, N., Asimakopoulou, E.: Evaluation of ad hoc networks in disaster scenarios. In: 2011 Third International Conference on Intelligent Networking and Collaborative Systems, pp. 759–764 (2011)

11. Kurosawa, K., Desmedt, Y.: A new paradigm of hybrid encryption scheme. In: Franklin, M. (ed.) CRYPTO 2004. LNCS, vol. 3152, pp. 426–442. Springer, Heidelberg (2004). https://doi.org/10.1007/978-3-540-28628-8_26

12. Lien, Y.N., Jang, H.C., Tsai, T.C.: A MANET based emergency communication and information system for catastrophic natural disasters. In: 2009 29th IEEE International Conference on Distributed Computing Systems Workshops, pp. 412–417 (2009)

13. Linn, J.: Privacy enhancement for internet electronic mail: part I: message encryption and authentication procedures. RFC 1421 (1993). https://doi.org/10.17487/RFC1421, https://www.rfc-editor.org/info/rfc1421

14. Microchip: Atecc608a. https://www.microchip.com/en-us/product/atecc608a

15. NXP: Edgelock SE050: Plug and trust secure element family - enhanced IoT security with high flexibility. https://www.nxp.com/products/security-and-authentication/authentication/edgelock-se050-plug-and-trust-secure-element-family-enhanced-iot-security-with-high-flexibility:SE050

16. Platform, G.: Introduction to secure element (2018). https://globalplatform.org/wp-content/uploads/2018/05/Introduction-to-Secure-Element-15May2018.pdf

17. Poettering, B., Rösler, P., Schwenk, J., Stebila, D.: SoK: game-based security models for group key exchange. In: Paterson, K.G. (ed.) CT-RSA 2021. LNCS, vol. 12704, pp. 148–176. Springer, Cham (2021). https://doi.org/10.1007/978-3-030-75539-3_7

18. Poettering, B., Röler, P., Schwenk, J., Stebila, D.: SoK: Game-based security models for group key exchange. Cryptology ePrint Archive, Report 2021/305 (2021). https://ia.cr/2021/305
19. Quispe, L.E., Mengual, L.: Behavior of ad hoc routing protocols, analyzed for emergency and rescue scenarios, on a real urban area. Expert Syst. Appl. **41**, 2565–2573 (2014)
20. Shoup, V., Rubin, A.: Session key distribution using smart cards. In: Maurer, U. (ed.) EUROCRYPT 1996. LNCS, vol. 1070, pp. 321–331. Springer, Heidelberg (1996). https://doi.org/10.1007/3-540-68339-9_28
21. Stebila, D., Fluhrer, S., Gueron, S.: Hybrid key exchange in TLS 1.3. Internet-Draft draft-ietf-tls-hybrid-design-06, Internet Engineering Task Force (2023). https://datatracker.ietf.org/doc/draft-ietf-tls-hybrid-design/06/, work in Progress
22. STMicroelectronics: Stsafe-a100. https://www.st.com/en/secure-mcus/stsafe-a100.html
23. TCCA: Voice & data. https://tcca.info/tetra/tetra-your-service/voice-data/
24. Thales: SIM, eSIM and secure elements. https://www.thalesgroup.com/en/markets/digital-identity-and-security/mobile/secure-elements

Functional and Updatable Encryption

Dynamic Multi-server Updatable Encryption

Jodie Knapp[1,2(✉)] and Elizabeth A. Quaglia[2]

[1] University of Surrey, Guildford, England
j.knapp@surrey.ac.uk
[2] Information Security Group, Royal Holloway, University of London, London, England
elizabeth.quaglia@rhul.ac.uk

Abstract. In this paper, we propose the *Dynamic Multi-Server* Updatable Encryption (DMUE) primitive as an extension of standard public-key updatable encryption. Traditional UE aims to have efficient ciphertext updates performed by an untrusted server such that the compromise of several cryptographic keys and update tokens does not reduce the standard security of encryption. The update token supports outsourced ciphertext updates without requiring the server to decrypt and re-encrypt the ciphertext and it is typically derived from old and new keys. To mitigate the risk of a single point of failure in single-server UE and thus improve the resilience of the scheme, we formalise a multi-server variant of UE to treat the issue of token leakage. We can achieve a distributed update process by providing each server with an update token and requiring a *threshold* of servers to engage honestly. However, servers may act dishonestly or need to be replaced over time, so our primitive must cater to dynamic committee changes in the servers participating across epochs. Inspired by the work of Benhamouda et al. (TCC'20) on dynamic proactive secret sharing, we propose a *generic* DMUE scheme built from public-key UE and dynamic proactive secret sharing primitives and prove the ciphertext unlinkability of freshly encrypted versus updated ciphertexts.

Keywords: Public-Key Updatable Encryption · Dynamic Committees · Threshold Secret Sharing · Trust Management · and Security

1 Introduction

Outsourcing encrypted data is a common practice for individuals and organisations wanting to store their information in a secure manner over long periods. Yet the server storing the information cannot always be trusted and there is greater opportunity for an adversary to corrupt the cryptographic key used for encryption. One solution to managing security in this setting is the updatable encryption (UE) primitive [6,14,22], which is utilised for privacy preservation

© The Author(s), under exclusive license to Springer Nature Switzerland AG 2023
E. Athanasopoulos and B. Mennink (Eds.): ISC 2023, LNCS 14411, pp. 475–495, 2023.
https://doi.org/10.1007/978-3-031-49187-0_24

in multiple applications such as cloud storage; online medical information and blockchain technology. Informally, UE allows a data owner to outsource the storage and key rotation of ciphertexts, from one epoch to the next, to an untrusted server. The server updates the ciphertext using an update token derived from old and new cryptographic keys, which *evolve* with every *epoch*, such that they do not learn anything about the underlying information in the update process. Updatable encryption is traditionally viewed as a symmetric primitive, however, more recently it has been defined in the *public-key* setting (PKUE) [20] which has allowed research to explore outsourced ciphertext updates whereby the users can receive messages from multiple senders directly in the cloud environment [1,16,26]. We focus on the PKUE primitive in this work.[1]

The core purpose of (PK)UE is to reduce the impact of key exposure and, in turn, token exposure, preserving standard encryption security such as confidentiality and the updatable notion of *unlinkability* [19]. Despite efforts to increase security in any UE setting, there remain risks with respect to security and resilience. The most prevalent risk is a *single point of failure* if the server is corrupted by an external adversary. In this scenario, a data owner's encrypted data will remain encrypted under the same key, defeating the purpose of UE as an adversary has more time in which to corrupt the cryptographic key and learn the underlying message. A second possible scenario occurs when the server acts dishonestly in the sense of failure to update ciphertexts correctly, if at all. If the ciphertext is updated incorrectly then the data owner may be misled upon decrypting the ciphertext. To illustrate, if the encrypted data is regarding a personal financial account and the update is incorrect then the data owner may be misinformed about the amount of money in their account.

A natural solution to this issue is to *distribute* the token, used to update ciphertexts, across *multiple servers* such that some pre-defined *threshold* of servers can ensure the ciphertext is updated in each epoch. This solution works, but a *static* set of servers does not reflect the real world because servers often change over long periods or possibly need to be removed from a scheme due to dishonest behaviour. To illustrate, suppose we wish to store a secret on a public-key blockchain such that nodes of the blockchain structure are considered to be the servers in a multi-server UE scheme. The authors of [3] demonstrated that *node churning* needs to be taken into consideration when designing a scheme for this application. This led us to propose a multi-server PKUE primitive supporting a *dynamic committee* of servers from one epoch to the next. We call this primitive dynamic multi-server updatable encryption (DMUE) such that the ciphertext update process is designed to be *deterministic* and *ciphertext-independent*. We note that the approach of having an evolving committee of servers is similar to previous works such as [2,21,23,28].

---

[1] The authors of [11,12] established definitions for updatable *public-key* encryption (UPKE) using an alternative update procedure. One can view UPKE as a distinct primitive to PKUE [20] since the token mechanism used in a UPKE scheme only updates the public key. By contrast, PKUE updates public and secret key pairs as well as the ciphertext.

More concretely, DMUE captures servers in specific epochs each possessing an update token, whereby their tokens are utilised in the process of updating a ciphertext. Moreover, the committee of servers in consecutive epochs may differ and so a *redistribution protocol* is required to provide new servers with their corresponding tokens. Defining the security of a DMUE primitive proves to be challenging and nuanced due to the bi-directional nature of key updates [18,24] in the design of a PKUE scheme. Moreover, the inference of keys from tokens is further complicated in the multi-server setting since an adversary can only succeed in their attack if they corrupt a *threshold* of server tokens in any given time period, with the servers and threshold potentially evolving with each epoch. Note, the adversary modelled is assumed to be *mobile* [28], which means they can dynamically and actively corrupt servers at any given time in a DMUE scheme, provided their corruption capabilities are bounded.

Contributions. Our contributions are threefold: we formalise a dynamic multi-server updatable primitive called DMUE in Sect. 2, used to mitigate the problem of a single point of failure in standard PKUE schemes. In Sect. 3 we present a new notion of security against update unlinkable chosen ciphertext attacks (MUE-IND-CCA), which captures a mobile adversary attempting to corrupt a threshold or more of secret update tokens. It is crucial to maintain confidentiality through the ciphertext update unlinkability notion as it guarantees a ciphertext generated by the update algorithm is unlinkable from a ciphertext generated by fresh encryption, even when the adversary sees many updated ciphertexts of chosen messages. We highlight that the focus of our paper is to capture a notion of *confidentiality* in the threshold multi-server PKUE setting. However, we also note that extending the security framework to capture ciphertext integrity is possible, thus preventing adversarial ciphertext forgeries, and is included in a full version of this work for completeness. In Sect. 4 we present a generic construction of DMUE built from a single-server public-key UE primitive and a dynamic threshold secret sharing scheme. The crux of our generic construction is that the data owner acts as the dealer and distributes a vector of n update tokens shares per epoch to the corresponding servers. Then at least a threshold of t servers can reconstruct the complete (*master*) token and proceed to update the ciphertext to encryption in epoch $(e + 1)$. This is achieved using standard PKUE and secret-sharing techniques. We then consider the practicalities of applying DMUE by providing an overview of a concrete scheme built from dynamic proactive secret sharing, in which an old server committee participates in a redistribution process to refresh and securely distribute update tokens to the new epoch server committee. We conclude our work by proving that our generic DMUE scheme satisfies the ciphertext unlinkability security notion we propose.

Related Work To the best of our knowledge, there has been no discussion within the UE literature that considers the insecurity of a UE scheme following a single-point-of-failure (SPOF) with respect to the server performing cipher-text updates. We believe it is a natural step to explore the resilience of a UE scheme to further support the strong security guarantees desired in this area of research. Not only is our solution of a multi-server UE primitive a novel design, but it also enables us to consider dynamic changes in servers over time which is essential if a server becomes corrupt or can no longer provide a service. The most closely aligned primitive to DMUE is threshold proxy re-encryption (PRE) [7,31] whereby schemes distribute the process of ciphertext re-encryption and decryption delegation using secret sharing and standard PRE as building blocks. More recently, the authors of [27] proposed the first *proactive* threshold PRE primitive, labelled PB-TPRE, which extends the work of [7,31] by addressing the issue of long-term secret shares as well a change in the proxies possessing shares. Consequently, the authors of [27] propose similar techniques to our generic DMUE construction. However, it is notable that the work on PB-TPRE demonstrates provable security of a concrete scheme that achieves the weaker confidentiality notion of chosen plaintext security as opposed to our work which is proven to satisfy security against chosen ciphertext attacks. Furthermore, we highlight that the fundamental differences between DMUE and PB-TPRE primitives stem from the distinctions between the standard PKUE and PRE primitives. In particular, proxy re-encryption (PRE) was first introduced by [5] as a primitive in which a proxy server re-encrypts a ciphertext under a sender's secret key and *delegates* decryption under a recipient's secret key. In contrast, UE uses the technique of key rotation for *time* updates from one epoch to the next. Further differences between the two primitives have been explored extensively in [10,19,22]. Besides the PRE primitive, the recent work of [15] uses a similar approach to our own ideas. The authors propose the first policy-based single-sign-on (SSO) system to prevent service providers from tracking users' behaviour. To achieve this, their primitive distributes tokens, conditioned on users' attributes, to multiple service providers in order to shield attributes and access patterns from individual entities. Whilst access control is not a focus of UE research, we observe that the methods used in [15] to mitigate SPOF are akin to our own core ideas.

2   Dynamic Multi-server Updatable Encryption

In this Section, we introduce the notation used in this paper, followed by a formal definition of a DMUE scheme and the corresponding definition of correctness.

Notation. A traditional updatable encryption scheme is defined by epochs of time e_i from the range of time $i = \{0, \ldots, \mathsf{max}\}$. We denote the current epoch e or use the subscript notation e_i for $i \in \mathbb{N}$ if we define multiple epochs at once. Further, (e_i, e_{i+1}) are two consecutive epochs for any $i \in \mathbb{N}$, the token is denoted $\Delta_{e_{i+1}}$ to update a ciphertext to epoch e_{i+1}, and $\tilde{e}$ represents the challenge epoch in security games. In the *dynamic multi-server* setting, we define for epoch e_i a set of servers $S_{e_i} = \{S^j\}_{j \in [n]}$ where $S_{e_{i+1}}$ may not be the same set, and update token $\Delta_{e_{i+1}}^j$ pertains to the token server S^j possesses. We use $(\mathcal{MSP}, \mathcal{CSP})$ to respectively denote the message space and ciphertext space of our scheme.

Extending the PKUE primitive to the dynamic multi-server setting (DMUE), a data owner must distribute tokens to every qualified server in the committee for that epoch, who respectively work together to update the ciphertext.

The dynamic aspect of this primitive enables different sets of servers, chosen by the data owner at the time of token creation, to perform the ciphertext update in successive epochs. Formally, a DMUE primitive is defined as $\Pi_{\mathsf{DMUE}} = (\mathsf{Setup}, \mathsf{KG}, \mathsf{TG}, \mathsf{Enc}, \mathsf{Dec}, \mathsf{Upd})$ whereby algorithms $(\mathsf{KG}, \mathsf{Enc}, \mathsf{Dec})$ are formalised as in standard PKUE [20] and the data owner runs all algorithms asides from Upd, the latter of which is run by the servers in a given epoch.[2]

Definition 1 (DMUE). *Given a set of servers S of size $n \in \mathbb{N}$ and a threshold $t \leq n$, a dynamic multi-server updatable encryption scheme is defined by a tuple of six PPT algorithms $\Pi_{\mathsf{DMUE}} = (\mathsf{Setup}, \mathsf{KG}, \mathsf{TG}, \mathsf{Enc}, \mathsf{Dec}, \mathsf{Upd})$ as follows.*

1. $\mathsf{Setup}(1^\lambda) \xrightarrow{\$} pp$: the setup algorithm is run by the data owner, who uses security parameter 1^λ as input and randomly outputs the public parameters pp.

2. $\mathsf{KG}(pp, e_i) \xrightarrow{\$} k_{e_i} := (pk_{e_i}, sk_{e_i})$: given public parameters, the data owner runs the probabilistic key generation algorithm and outputs the public and private key pair (pk_{e_i}, sk_{e_i}) for epoch $\{e_i\}_{i \in [0,\mathsf{max}]}$.

3. $\mathsf{TG}(pp, sk_{e_i}, k_{e_{i+1}}, S_{e_{i+1}}) \rightarrow \{\Delta^j_{e_{i+1}}\}_{j \in [n]}$: the token generation algorithm is run by the data owner, who uses the following inputs: public parameters, the old epoch secret key sk_{e_i}, the new epoch public and private key-pair $k_{e_{i+1}} := (pk_{e_{i+1}}, sk_{e_{i+1}})$ generated by the key generation algorithm, and the new set of servers $S_{e_{i+1}} = \{S^j\}_{j \in [n]}$. The deterministically computed output is n update tokens $\{\Delta^j_{e_{i+1}}\}_{j \in [n]}$, which are securely sent to the *chosen* servers $S^j \in S_{e_{i+1}}$.[3]

4. $\mathsf{Enc}(pp, pk_{e_i}, m) \xrightarrow{\$} C_{e_i}$: given public parameters and the epoch public key pk_{e_i}, the data owner runs the probabilistic encryption algorithm on message $m \in \mathcal{MSP}$ and outputs the ciphertext C_{e_i}.

5. $\mathsf{Dec}(pp, sk_{e_i}, C_{e_i}) \rightarrow \{m, \perp\}$: given public parameters and the epoch secret key, the data owner is able to run the deterministic decryption algorithm in order to output message m or abort $(\perp)$.

6. $\mathsf{Upd}(pp, \{\Delta^k_{e_{i+1}}\}_{k \in \mathbb{N}}, C_{e_i}) \rightarrow C_{e_{i+1}}$: for some $k \geq t$, the subset $S' \in S_{e_{i+1}}$ of servers, such that $|S'| = k$, can deterministically update ciphertext C_{e_i} using their tokens $\Delta^k_{e_{i+1}}$ to output an updated ciphertext $C_{e_{i+1}}$.

Correctness. Intuitively, defining the correctness of the DMUE primitive follows from the definition of correctness for the single server PKUE primitive. Specifically, the correctness property ensures that fresh encryptions and updated ciphertexts should decrypt to the underlying plaintext, given the appropriate epoch key. However, the multi-server setting additionally has to encapsulate the

---

[2] We note that in the multi-server setting, the update process is interactive and is therefore a protocol. However, we chose to use the term algorithm to stay in keeping with the single-server PKUE terminology as Π_{DMUE} can reduce to the single-server setting when $n = t = 1$.

[3] Note in the definition of DMUE that the data owner chooses the committee of servers $\{S_{e_{i+1}}\}_{\forall i \in \mathbb{N}}$.

concept of ciphertext updates from a *threshold* number of tokens. The formal definition of correctness follows.

Definition 2 (Correctness). *Given security parameter λ and threshold $t \leq k \leq n$, dynamic multi-server updatable encryption scheme (Π_{DMUE}) for n servers, as formalised in Definition 1, is correct if for any message $m \in \mathcal{MSP}$, for any $l \in \{0, \ldots, \mathsf{max} - 1\}$ such that max denotes the final epoch of the scheme, and $i = (l + 1)$, there exists a negligible function negl such that the following holds with overwhelming probability.*

$$\Pr \begin{bmatrix} pp \xleftarrow{\$} \mathsf{Setup}(1^\lambda); \\ k_{e_i} = (pk_{e_i}, sk_{e_i}) \xleftarrow{\$} \mathsf{KG}(pp, e_i); \\ \{\Delta^j_{e_i}\}_{j \in [n]} \leftarrow \mathsf{TG}(pp, sk_{e_{i-1}}, k_{e_i}, S_{e_i}); \\ C_{e_l} \xleftarrow{\$} \mathsf{Enc}(pp, pk_{e_l}, m); \\ \{C_{e_i} \leftarrow \mathsf{Upd}(pp, \{\Delta^k_{e_i}\}_{k \in \mathbb{N}}, C_{e_{i-1}}) : \\ i \in \{l + 1, \cdots, \mathsf{max}\} \wedge |k| \geq t\}; \\ \mathsf{Dec}(pp, sk_{e_{\mathsf{max}}}, C_{e_{\mathsf{max}}}) = m \end{bmatrix} \geq 1 - \mathsf{negl}(1^\lambda).$$

Remark 1. The *multi-server* aspect of Definition 1 affects the TG and Upd algorithm definitions compared to standard PKUE algorithms. Note, we have omitted the formal definition of traditional PKUE [20] due to lack of space, however, we emphasise that Definition 1 satisfies the PKUE definition when $t = n = 1$.

3   Security Modelling

In this Section, we define a notion of security satisfying the highest level of *confidentiality* achievable in *deterministic* PKUE schemes. More specifically, the experiment models dynamic multi-server PKUE security against *update unlinkable chosen ciphertext* attacks (MUE-IND-CCA security). Crucially, unlinkability needs modelling to ensure that a ciphertext generated by the update algorithm is indistinguishable from a ciphertext generated by fresh encryption. Note, capturing the full capabilities of an adversary attacking a DMUE scheme is inherently challenging due to the *bi-directional* nature of ciphertext updates [18,24,30]. Consequently, it is necessary to record inferable information obtained from corrupted keys, tokens, and ciphertexts.

We start by detailing the lists recorded and oracles necessary to model the security of a DMUE scheme. For clarity, we will separate descriptions of oracles specific to the DMUE setting versus standard PKUE oracles, that is, the remaining oracles required in security modelling that are unchanged from the security framework of single-server PKUE [20]. The lists and oracles play a vital role in preventing trivial wins and guaranteeing security by capturing, in the lists a challenger maintains, the information an adversary can infer. Further, lists are checked after oracle queries as well and they're incorporated into the winning conditions of the security experiment.

We observe that our security model defines an adversary $\mathcal{A} := \{\mathcal{A}_I, \mathcal{A}_{II}\}$, representing a malicious outside adversary ($\mathcal{A}_I$) and dishonest server ($\mathcal{A}_{II}$). Typically, only adversary $\mathcal{A}_I$ is considered in single server PKUE, as the literature assumes the lone server is honest. Conversely, the main motivation in our work is tackling the issue of a single point of failure regarding server updates. Thus, we have to consider adversary $\mathcal{A}_{II}$ to capture the threat of dishonesty or collusion of a *threshold* or more servers. To be succinct, our security experiment and definition uses the notation $\mathcal{A}$, however, we capture both types simultaneously. That is, an outside adversary is modelled in the usual manner of UE, through lists recording corrupted and inferable information. Specific to a corrupt server, the token corruption oracle is crucial in recording any epoch in which a threshold or more tokens have been corrupted.

- $\mathcal{L} = \{(e', C_{e'})_{e' \in [e]}\}$: the list containing the epoch and corresponding ciphertext in which the adversary learns (through queries to the update oracle $\mathcal{O}_{\mathsf{Upd}}$) an updated version of an *honestly generated* ciphertext.
- $\mathcal{K} = \{e' \in [e]\}$: the list of epoch(s) in which the adversary has obtained an epoch secret key through calls to $\mathcal{O}_{\mathsf{Corrupt\text{-}Key}}(e')$.
- $\mathcal{T} = \{e' \in [e]\}$: the list of epoch(s) in which the adversary has obtained at least a *threshold* number of update tokens through calls to $\mathcal{O}_{\mathsf{Corrupt\text{-}Token}}(e')$.
- $\mathcal{C} = \{(e', C_{e'})_{e' \in [e]}\}$: the list containing the epoch and corresponding ciphertext in which the adversary learns (through queries to the update oracle $\mathcal{O}_{\mathsf{Upd}}$) an *updated version* of the challenge ciphertext.
- $\mathcal{C}^* \leftarrow \{e' \in \{0, \ldots, e_{\max}\} | \mathsf{challenge\text{-}equal}(e') = \mathsf{true}\}$: the list of challenge-equal ciphertexts, defined by a recursive predicate $\mathsf{challenge\text{-}equal}$, such that $\mathsf{true} \leftarrow \mathsf{challenge\text{-}equal}(e')$ iff : $(e' \in \mathcal{C}) \vee (\mathsf{challenge\text{-}equal}(e' - 1) \wedge e' \in \mathcal{T}) \vee (\mathsf{challenge\text{-}equal}(e' + 1) \wedge (e' + 1) \in \mathcal{T})$.

Fig. 1. The set of lists $\mathbf{L} := \{\mathcal{L}, \mathcal{K}, \mathcal{T}, \mathcal{C}^*\}$ the challenger maintains in the global state (GS) as a record of during security games.

Lists. We provide Fig. 1 as a descriptive summary of the lists maintained by the challenger (as part of the global state GS) in the ensuing security experiment. We note that the main deviation in the list description compared to the single server PKUE setting [20] is found in list $\mathcal{T}$. Here, the challenger maintains a count of how many server tokens have been corrupted per epoch (see Fig. 2), and only records the epochs in which a *threshold* number token have been corrupted. List $\mathcal{C}^*$, which is an extension of list $\mathcal{C}$, is also modified to the multi-server setting.

This list contains the epoch and corresponding ciphertext in which the adversary learns (through queries to the update oracle $\mathcal{O}_{\mathsf{Upd}}$) an *updated version* of the challenge ciphertext. In greater detail, a CCA-secure DMUE scheme with deterministic re-encryption requires a challenger to record all updates of honestly generated ciphertexts and maintain a list of challenge-equal epochs ($\mathcal{C}^*$) in which a version of the challenge ciphertext can be inferred. That is, list $\mathcal{C}^*$ incorporates a *challenge-equal predicate* presented in Fig. 1 which encapsulate all of the *challenge-equal epochs* in which the adversary knows a *version* of the challenge ciphertext, either from calls to the update oracle or through computation. To illustrate, if $\{e, e+1\} \in \mathcal{C}^*$, it is possible for an adversary to perform the update computation of the ciphertext since the adversary can infer information using corrupted ciphertexts and tokens from epochs $\{e, e+1\} \in (\mathcal{C}, \mathcal{T})$. Thus, if an adversary knows a ciphertext $\tilde{C}_e$ from challenge epoch e and the update token Δ_{e+1}, then the adversary can compute the updated ciphertext to the epoch $(e+1)$ and realise challenge ciphertext $\tilde{C}_{e+1}$.

3.1   Oracles

First, we present an important predicate in updatable encryption security modelling as it will be utilised in the running of decryption and update oracles in our security experiment.[4] Crucially, the isChallenge predicate defined by [19] is used to prevent the decryption of an updated challenge ciphertext, irrespective of whether the updatable encryption scheme is designed for probabilistic or deterministic ciphertext updates. Informally, the isChallenge(k_{e_i}, C) predicate detects any queries to the decryption and update oracles on challenge ciphertexts ($\tilde{C}$), or versions (i.e., updates) of the challenge ciphertext.

Definition 3 (isChallenge Predicate). *Given challenge epoch $\tilde{e}$ and challenge ciphertext $\tilde{C}$, the isChallenge predicate, on inputs of the current epoch key k_{e_i} and queried ciphertext C_{e_i}, responds in one of three ways:*

1. If $(e_i = \tilde{e}) \wedge (C_{e_i} = \tilde{C})$, return true;
2. If $(e_i > \tilde{e}) \wedge (\tilde{C} \neq \bot)$, return true if $\tilde{C}_{e_i} = C_{e_i}$ in which $\tilde{C}_{e_i}$ is computed iteratively by running $\mathsf{Upd}(pp, \Delta_{e_{l+1}}, \tilde{C}_{e_l})$ for $e_l = \{\tilde{e}, \ldots, e_i\}$;
3. Otherwise, return false.

Now we describe the five oracles $\mathcal{O} = \{\mathcal{O}_{\mathsf{Dec}}, \mathcal{O}_{\mathsf{Next}}, \mathcal{O}_{\mathsf{Upd}}, \mathcal{O}_{\mathsf{Corrupt\text{-}Token}}, \mathcal{O}_{\mathsf{Corrupt\text{-}Key}}\}$ at a high level before providing detail of how they run.

- $\mathcal{O}_{\mathsf{Dec}}$: to prevent an adversary from trivially winning by querying the decryption of a queried challenge ciphertext, the following condition must be satisfied. The predicate isChallenge (Definition 3) must return false. In this case, the decryption of a valid ciphertext under the current epoch secret key is returned. Else, the failure symbol $\bot$ is returned.

---

[4] A predicate is a statement or mathematical assertion that contains variables. The outcome of the predicate may be true or false depending on the input values.

- $\mathcal{O}_{\text{Upd}}$: the update oracle only accepts and responds to calls regarding *honestly generated* ciphertexts or derivations of the challenge ciphertext, by checking lists $\{\mathcal{L}, \mathcal{C}^*\}$ respectively. If this is the case, the output is an update of the queried ciphertext to the current epoch. Next, the updated ciphertext and current epoch are added to the list $\mathcal{L}$. Moreover, if the isChallenge predicate returns *true* on the input of the *queried* key and ciphertext, then the current epoch is added to the *challenge-equal* epoch list $\mathcal{C}^*$.

- $\mathcal{O}_{\text{Next}}$: queries to the next oracle in challenge epoch e result in an update of the global state to the epoch $(e+1)$. This is achieved by running key and token generation algorithms to output the epoch key pair $k_{e+1} = (pk_{e+1}, sk_{e+1})$ and tokens $\Delta^j_{e+1}, \forall j \in [n]$, respectively. If the query is in an epoch such that the adversary has corrupted the epoch key *or* the epoch belongs to list $\mathcal{L}$, then the current challenge ciphertext must be updated to the next epoch using a threshold or more of the generated update tokens and the new ciphertext is added to the list of honestly updated ciphertexts ($\mathcal{L}$).

- $\mathcal{O}_{\text{Corrupt-Token}}, \mathcal{O}_{\text{Corrupt-Key}}$: queries to these oracles allow the corruption of a threshold number of tokens and epoch secret key respectively. The restriction for both oracles is that the adversary's query must be from an epoch preceding the challenge-epoch e. Additionally, if an adversary queries the corrupt-token oracle for server S^j, not in the queried epoch server committee $S_{e'}$ then the corrupt-token oracle returns a failure symbol $\perp$.

Security Experiment. After the initialisation which outputs a global state (Fig. 3) and with a challenge public key pk_e, the adversary proceeds to query the oracles in Figs. 2 and 3. They output a challenge message m' and ciphertext C' in the queried epoch e. Before proceeding, the challenger must check that the given message and ciphertext are valid (belongs to $\mathcal{MSP}, \mathcal{CSP}$ respectively). Otherwise, the challenger aborts the game and returns $\perp$. Moving forward, the challenger randomly chooses bit $b \in \{0, 1\}$ which dictates whether the DMUE encryption algorithm or a version of the update algorithm is run on the respective challenge inputs $\{m', C'\}$. The resulting output is a challenge ciphertext $C^{(b)}$ such that for $b = 0$ the ciphertext is from fresh encryption and for $b = 1$ the ciphertext is generated by the update algorithm UpdateCh.[5] The global state must be updated by the challenger, especially the set of lists $\mathbf{L}$. Equipped with a challenge output $C^{(b)}$ and public parameters, the adversary can query the oracles again before outputting a guess bit $b' \in \{0, 1\}$. The adversary succeeds in the security experiment if they satisfy certain winning conditions and successfully guess the correct bit ($b' = b$).

Definition 4 (MUE-IND-CCA-Security). *Definition 1 of a dynamic multi-server updatable encryption scheme (Π_{DMUE}) is MUE-IND-CCA secure against update unlinkable chosen ciphertext attacks following Fig. 4 if for any PPT adversary $\mathcal{A}$ the following advantage is negligible over security parameter λ:*

---

[5] Algorithm UpdateCh is used as compact notation, following the notation of [8], to denote the process of repeated application of the update algorithm from epoch $\{e + 1, \ldots, \tilde{e}\}$.

$\mathcal{O}_{\mathsf{Upd}}(C_{e_i})$
    if $((e_i, C_{e_i}) \notin \mathcal{L}) \vee (e_i \notin \mathcal{C}^*)$ **then**
        return $\perp$
    else
        for $e_l = \{e_{i+1}, \ldots, e\}$ **do**
            $C_{e_l} \leftarrow \mathsf{Upd}(pp, \{\Delta_{e_l}^k\}_{t \leq k \leq n}, C_{e_i})$
    $C_e \leftarrow C_{e_l}$
    return C_e
    $\mathcal{L} \leftarrow \mathcal{L} \cup \{(e, C_e)\}$
    if $\mathsf{isChallenge}(k_{e_i}, C_{e_i}) = \text{true}$ **then**
        $\mathcal{C}^* \leftarrow \mathcal{C}^* \cup \{e\}$

$\mathcal{O}_{\mathsf{Next}}(e)$

    $k_{e+1} := (pk_{e+1}, sk_{e+1}) \overset{\$}{\leftarrow} \mathsf{KG}(pp, e+1)$
    $\{\Delta_{e+1}^j\}_{j \in [n]} \leftarrow \mathsf{TG}(pp, sk_e, k_{e+1}, S_{e+1})$
    Update GS
    $(pp, k_{e+1}, T_{e+1}, \mathbf{L}, e+1)$
    if $(e \in \mathcal{K}) \vee (C, e) \in \mathcal{L}$ **then**
        $(C', e+1) \leftarrow \mathsf{Upd}(pp, \{\Delta_{e+1}^k\}_{|k| \geq t}, C)$
    $\mathcal{L} \leftarrow \mathcal{L} \cup \{(C', e+1)\}$

$\mathcal{O}_{\mathsf{Corrupt\text{-}Token}}(e', j)$

    if $(e' \geq e) \vee (S^j \notin S_{e'})$ **then**
        return $\perp$
    else
        return $\Delta_{e'}^j$, some $j \in [n]$
        Store tokens in a list $T_{e'}$
    if $|T_{e'}| \geq t$ tokens have been corrupted in epoch e' **then**
        $\mathcal{T} \leftarrow \mathcal{T} \cup \{e'\}$

Fig. 2. Details of oracles an adversary $\mathcal{A}$ has access to during the security experiment of Definition 4 that is specific to the multi-server setting.

$$\mathsf{Adv}_{\Pi_{\mathsf{DMUE}}, \mathcal{A}}^{\mathsf{MUE\text{-}IND\text{-}CCA}, b}(1^\lambda) := | \Pr[\mathsf{Exp}_{\Pi_{\mathsf{DMUE}}, \mathcal{A}}^{\mathsf{MUE\text{-}IND\text{-}CCA}, 0}(1^\lambda) = 1] -$$
$$\Pr[\mathsf{Exp}_{\Pi_{\mathsf{DMUE}}, \mathcal{A}}^{\mathsf{MUE\text{-}IND\text{-}CCA}, 1}(1^\lambda) = 1]| \leq \mathsf{negl}(1^\lambda),$$

for some polynomial time function $\mathsf{negl}(\cdot)$.

Preventing Trivial Wins and Ciphertext Updates. We demonstrate the importance of the challenger recording lists $\mathcal{T}$ in the corrupt-token oracle, and list $\mathcal{C}^*$ in the update oracle. Without the restrictions imposed on the corrupt-token oracle, the following can occur. If an adversary $\mathcal{A}$ corrupts t or more tokens $\{\Delta_{e+1}^k\}_{k \geq t}$ from the corresponding server committee S_{e+1}, in an epoch proceeding the challenge epoch $\tilde{e}$, then $\mathcal{A}$ is capable of trivially updating the ciphertext into the next epoch $(e+1)$, using a computed token, following Definition 1. Consequently, we place restrictions on calls to $\mathcal{O}_{\mathsf{Corrupt\text{-}Token}}$ and impose the win-

---

$\mathsf{Init}(1^\lambda)$

$pp \xleftarrow{\$} \mathsf{Setup}(1^\lambda)$

$k_0 := (pk_0, sk_0) \xleftarrow{\$} \mathsf{KG}(pp, 0);$

$\Delta_0 \leftarrow \perp$

$T_0 \leftarrow \mathsf{TG}(pp, k_0, S_0)$ such that

$T_0 := \{\Delta_0^1, \ldots, \Delta_0^n\}$

$e \leftarrow 0$

$\mathbf{L} \in \emptyset$

return GS

GS $:= (pp, k_0, T_0, \mathbf{L}, 0)$

$\mathcal{O}_{\mathsf{Dec}}(C_e)$

    if $\mathsf{isChallenge}(k_{e_i}, C_{e_i}) = $ true **then**

        return $\perp$

    else

        $m \leftarrow \mathsf{Dec}(pp, sk_e, C)$

        return m

$\mathcal{O}_{\mathsf{Corrupt\text{-}Key}}(e')$

    if $(e' \geq e)$ **then**

        return $\perp$

    else

        return $sk_{e'}$

    $\mathcal{K} \leftarrow \mathcal{K} \cup \{e'\}$

Fig. 3. The oracles an adversary has access to for the experiment capturing Definition 4 that remain unchanged from the single-server setting of a PKUE scheme.

ning condition in Fig. 4. This condition states that the intersection of lists $\mathcal{K}$ and $\mathcal{C}^*$ must be empty. Thus, the challenge epoch cannot belong to the set of epochs in which a threshold of update tokens have been obtained/inferred, and there doesn't exist a single epoch where the adversary knows both the epoch key (public and secret key components) and the (updated) challenge-ciphertext [22]. The distinction of DMUE security modelling from single-server PKUE is that list $\mathcal{T} \in \mathcal{C}^*$ does not record epochs in which token corruption occurred when the number of tokens corrupted is less than some threshold. That is, DMUE security modelling tolerates a certain level (below the threshold) of token corruption in any given epoch as less than the threshold of corrupted tokens does not provide the adversary with meaningful information.

4 Our Construction

In this Section, we use Definition 1 as a basis for formalising a *generic* DMUE construction. We achieve this using *dynamic proactive secret sharing* (DPSS) [2,21,23] and single server PKUE primitives as building blocks. Before going into detail about our construction, we present the formal definition of a DPSS protocol, as well as defining DPSS correctness and secrecy properties.

4.1 Construction Preliminaries

Dynamic proactive secret sharing (DPSS) [23] is an extension of traditional secret sharing [4,29] such that shares belonging to a committee of parties are refreshed after some time has passed. A standard threshold secret sharing scheme (SS) [4,29] has a dealer D distribute some secret s among a set of shareholders $\mathcal{P} =$

$$\mathsf{Exp}_{\Pi_{\mathsf{DMUE}},\mathcal{A}}^{\mathsf{MUE\text{-}IND\text{-}CCA},b}(1^\lambda)$$

GS $\overset{\$}{\leftarrow}$ Init(1^λ); GS $:= (pp, k_0, T_0, \mathbf{L}, 0)$ such that $\mathbf{L} := \{\mathcal{L}, \mathcal{K}, \mathcal{T}, \mathcal{C}^*\}$

$k_{e-1} \overset{\$}{\leftarrow}$ KG$(pp, e-1)$; $k_e \overset{\$}{\leftarrow}$ KG(pp, e) such that

$k_{e-1} := (pk_{e-1}, sk_{e-1})$, $k_e := (pk_e, sk_e)$

$\{\Delta_e^j\}_{j \in [n]} \leftarrow$ TG(pp, sk_{e-1}, k_e, S_e)

$(m', C') \overset{\$}{\leftarrow} \mathcal{A}^{\mathcal{O}}(pp, pk_e)$

if $(m' \notin \mathcal{MSP}) \vee (C' \notin \mathcal{CSP})$ then

    return $\bot$

else

    $b \overset{\$}{\leftarrow} \{0,1\}$

    $C^{(0)} \overset{\$}{\leftarrow}$ Enc(pp, pk_e, m') and

    $C^{(1)} \leftarrow$ UpdCh$(pp, \{\Delta_e^k\}_{|k| \geq t}, C')$

    $\mathcal{C}^* \leftarrow \mathcal{C}^* \cup \{e\}$; $\tilde{e} \leftarrow \{e\}$

$b' \overset{\$}{\leftarrow} \mathcal{A}^{\mathcal{O}}(pp, C^{(b)})$

if $(\mathcal{K} \cap \mathcal{C}^* = \emptyset)$ then

    return b'

Else abort.

Fig. 4. The security experiment for MUE-IND-CCA-security of a DMUE scheme. Let $\mathcal{O} = \{\mathcal{O}_{\mathsf{Dec}}, \mathcal{O}_{\mathsf{Corrupt\text{-}Key}}, \mathcal{O}_{\mathsf{Next}}, \mathcal{O}_{\mathsf{Upd}}, \mathcal{O}_{\mathsf{Corrupt\text{-}Token}}\}$ denote the set of oracles that adversary $\mathcal{A}$ calls during the experiment, where the latter three oracles capture the multi-server aspect of a DMUE scheme.

$\{P^1, P^2, \ldots, P^n\}$ of n parties, according to an efficiently samplable distribution of the set of secrets labelled $\mathcal{S} = \{\mathcal{S}_\lambda\}_{\lambda \in \mathbb{N}}$, with security parameter λ. The aim of threshold SS is that no subset $t' < t$ of parties in P can learn the secret s, including an adversary controlling t' parties. Conversely, every subset $t' \geq t$ of parties in P is capable of reconstructing s. *Proactive* secret sharing schemes [17, 25] (PSS) are designed for applications in which the long-term confidentiality of a secret matter, is achieved by a *refresh* of shares and consequently enable a reset of corrupted parties to uncorrupted. Observe that the secret itself remains constant, it is only the shares that are refreshed. *Dynamic* PSS (DPSS) [2, 21, 23] is a primitive with the same benefits as PSS plus an additional feature allowing the group of parties participating to change periodically. The following is a formal definition of DPSS protocol Π_{DPSS}=(Share, Redistribute, Recon) [2].

Definition 5 (DPSS Protocol). *Given a dealer $\mathcal{D}$, a secret $s \in \mathcal{S}_\lambda$ for security parameter λ, $L \in \mathbb{N}$ periods, and a set of $\{n^{(i)}\}_{i \in [L]}$ authorised parties $P^i = \{P_1^i, \ldots, P_n^i\}$, a (t, n) dynamic proactive secret sharing scheme is a tuple of four PPT algorithms $\Pi_{\mathsf{DPSS}} = (\mathsf{Setup}, \mathsf{Share}, \mathsf{Redistribute}, \mathsf{Recon})$ defined as follows:*

- **Share Phase:** $\mathcal{D}$ takes as input the secret s and performs the following steps non-interactively:

1. $\mathsf{Setup}(1^\lambda) \overset{\$}{\to} pp$: a probabilistic algorithm that takes as input security parameter 1^λ and outputs public parameters pp, which are broadcast to all parties in P.

2. $\mathsf{Share}(pp, s, i) \overset{\$}{\to} \{s_1^i, \dots, s_n^i\}$: a probabilistic algorithm that takes as input the secret $s \in \mathcal{S}_\lambda$ and period i, outputting n secret shares $\{s_j^i\}_{j\in[n]}$, one for each party in P.

3. Distribute s_j^i to party $P_j^i \in P^i$ for every $i \in [L]$ over a secret, authenticated channel.

- **Redistribution Phase**: the algorithm $\mathsf{Redistribute}$ takes as input consecutive periods $(i, i+1) \leq L$, the set of parties (P^i, P^{i+1}) and the vector of secrets $\{s_j^i\}_{j\in[n]}$ belonging to P^i, such that P^i need to refresh and communicate their vector of secret shares to the potentially different set of parties P^{i+1}. The output is a vector of secrets $\{s_{j'}^{i+1}\}_{j'\in[n]}$.

- **Reconstruction Phase**: In period i, any party in $P^i = \{P_1^i, \dots, P_n^i\}_{i\in[L]}$ can participate in the following steps.
   1. Communication:
      (a) Each party $P_j^i, j \in [n]$ sends their share s_j^i over a secure broadcast channel to all other parties in P^i.
      (b) P^i parties independently check that they have received $(t-1)$ or more shares. If so, they proceed to the processing phase.
   2. Processing: Once P_j^i has a set of t' shares labelled S', they independently do the following:
      (a) $\mathsf{Recon}(pp, S', i) \to \{s, \bot\}$: a deterministic algorithm that takes as input the set S' of t' shares and outputs the secret s for period $i \in [L]$ if $t' \geq t$ or outputs abort $\bot$ otherwise.

The following two definitions are regarding the correctness and secrecy of a dynamic proactive secret sharing scheme Π_{DPSS}. We assume these properties hold when proving the correctness and security of a proposed construction presented in Chapter 5.

Definition 6 (DPSS Correctness). *Π_{DPSS} is correct if $\forall \lambda \in \mathbb{N}$ and for all possible sets of $\{n^{(i)}\}_{i\in[L]}$ authorised parties P^i, given $\mathsf{Setup}(1^\lambda) \overset{\$}{\to} pp$; for all secrets $s \in \mathcal{S}_\lambda$ and any subset of $t' \geq t$ shares S' from $\mathsf{Share}(pp, s, i) \overset{\$}{\to} \{s_1^i, \dots, s_n^i\}$ communicated by parties in P^i, there exists a negligible function $\mathsf{negl}(\cdot)$ such that*

$$\Pr[\mathsf{Recon}(pp, S', i) \neq s] \leq \mathsf{negl}(1^\lambda).$$

Definition 7 (DPSS Secrecy). *Π_{DPSS} is secret if $\forall \lambda \in \mathbb{N}$ and for all possible sets of $\{n^{(i)}\}_{i\in[L]}$ authorised parties P^i, given $\mathsf{Setup}(1^\lambda) \overset{\$}{\to} pp$; for all secrets $s \in \mathcal{S}_\lambda$ and any subset of $t' < t$ shares S' from $\mathsf{Share}(pp, s, i) \overset{\$}{\to} \{s_1^i, \dots, s_n^i\}$ communicated by parties in P, there exists a negligible function $\mathsf{negl}(\cdot)$ such that*

$$\Pr[\mathsf{Recon}(pp, S', i) \neq \bot] \leq \mathsf{negl}(1^\lambda).$$

Remark 2. In this work we focus on building our DMUE scheme from dynamic threshold secret sharing, however, observe that we can easily extend the construction of DMUE to be built from an alternative multi-party functionality, namely, a version of multi-party computation (MPC) [9,13].

4.2   Building DMUE

Recall, a DMUE primitive is designed for the distribution of tokens, to multiple untrusted servers, which are used in the ciphertext update process. A threshold of servers can reconstruct the whole update token (Δ_e) for a given epoch (e), using the corresponding server tokens. By design, the threshold is necessary to correctly update the ciphertext into a new epoch. Moreover, the set of servers in any given epoch is fluid to allow for the removal of corrupted servers and support the realistic nature of long-term secret storage in which servers may need to change. Intuitively, DPSS is an ideal building block candidate since the techniques used cater to changes in the shareholders, achieved via a redistribution process from one epoch to the next. Additionally, it is required in a DPSS scheme (see Definition 5) that the secret is re-shared in every period in such a way that the shares from different windows of time cannot be combined to recover the secret. The only way to recover the secret is to obtain enough shares from the *same* period, a task which the literature [17] assumes is beyond the adversary's grasp and the redundancy of sharing allows robustness in the periods of the scheme. We incorporate the aforementioned techniques into the design of our DMUE construction.

High-Level Idea. The key idea of our construction is that we leverage a single-server PKUE scheme and share the update token using a threshold secret sharing protocol. Intuitively, the update token in our construction will be formed from the current and preceding epoch keys, such that the data owner $(\mathcal{D})$, taking the position of the dealer in the DPSS scheme, distributes a vector of *token shares* $\{\Delta_{e_i}^j\}_{j \in [n]}$ to the set of n servers $S_{e_i} := \{S_{e_i}^1, \ldots, S_{e_i}^n\}$ for current epoch $e_i, \forall i \in \mathbb{N}$. Token share generation will take place after TG is run by $\mathcal{D}$ and this will occur for every epoch up to the final epoch $(e_{\max})$. The algorithm Upd will also be adapted to the multi-server setting in line with Definition 1, such that a threshold of t or more servers in set $S_{e_{i+1}}$ are required to reconstruct the update token $\Delta_{e_{i+1}}$ and then independently perform the update process in the classical PKUE sense. Observe a key point clarified after the construction (Remark 3) is that the set of servers in consecutive epochs may overlap, and so they should not be able to learn the shares of the old or new epochs even though they participate in the redistribution process.

For ease of defining a generic construction, we design the scheme such that the *dynamic* feature is achieved in a trivial way, and does not use the DPSS techniques to evolve server committees. In other words, we do not trust the servers and assume the server committees for each epoch are selected by data owner $\mathcal{D}$ in some way. However, after presenting our construction in Definition 8 we will make practical considerations which allow for the servers in a given epoch to participate in the redistribution process of token shares in order to reduce the data owners' computational cost. More formally, we construct a DMUE scheme as follows.

Definition 8 (DMUE Generic Construction). *Given a (t,n) dynamic secret sharing scheme $\Pi_{SS} = ($ SS.Setup, Share, Redistribute, Recon $)$ from Definition 5 (Definition 5) and a standard public-key UE scheme $\Pi_{PKUE} = ($ UE.Setup, UE.KG, UE.TG, UE.Enc, UE.Dec, UE.Upd $)$, a DMUE scheme is defined by a tuple of six PPT algorithms $\Pi_{DMUE} = ($ Setup, KG, TG, Enc, Dec, Upd $)$ as follows.*

1. Setup$(1^\lambda) \xrightarrow{\$} pp$: run SS.Setup and UE.Setup on input security parameter 1^λ to randomly output the public parameters $pp := (pp_{SS}, pp_{UE})$ respectively.

2. KG$(pp, e_i) \xrightarrow{\$} k_{e_i} := (pk_{e_i}, sk_{e_i})$: given public parameters pp, run the probabilistic key generation algorithm UE.KG to output the public and private key pair $k_{e_i} = (pk_{e_i}, sk_{e_i})$ for epoch $e_i, i \in \mathbb{N}, i \leq (\text{max} - 1)$.

3. TG$(pp, sk_{e_i}, k_{e_{i+1}}, S_{e_{i+1}}) \rightarrow \{\Delta_{e_{i+1}}^j\}_{j \in [n]}$: the data owner runs UE.TG to compute token $\Delta_{e_{i+1}}$, followed by Share$(pp_{SS}, S_{e_{i+1}}, \Delta_{e_{i+1}}) \rightarrow \{\Delta_{e_{i+1}}^j\}_{j \in [n]}$. Next, the data owner securely distributes $\Delta_{e_{i+1}}^j$ to server $S^j \in S_{e_{i+1}}$, where $S_{e_{i+1}}$ is the committee of servers for new epoch e_{i+1}.

4. Enc$(pp, pk_{e_i}, m) \xrightarrow{\$} C_{e_i}$: given public parameters and the epoch public key pk_{e_i}, the data owner runs the probabilistic encryption algorithm UE.Enc on message $m \in \mathcal{MSP}$ and outputs the ciphertext C_{e_i}.

5. Dec$(pp, sk_{e_i}, C_{e_i}) \rightarrow \{m, \perp\}$: given public parameters and the epoch secret key, the owner is able to run the deterministic decryption algorithm UE.Dec in order to output message m or abort $(\perp)$.

6. Upd$(pp, \{\Delta_{e_{i+1}}^k\}_{k \in \mathbb{N}, |k| \geq t}, C_{e_i}) \rightarrow C_{e_{i+1}}$: given any valid subset $S' \subseteq S_{e_{i+1}}$ of the epoch e_{i+1} committee of servers, such that $|S'| \geq t$, shareholders in S' can reconstruct the update token by running Recon$(pp_{SS}, \{\Delta_{e_{i+1}}^k\}_{k \geq t}) \rightarrow \Delta_{e_{i+1}}$: Individually they can then update the ciphertext using the update algorithm UE.Upd$(pp_{UE}, \Delta_{e_{i+1}}, C_{e_i}) \rightarrow C_{e_{i+1}}$.

Correctness. We show below our construction Π_{DMUE}, presented in Definition 8, satisfies correctness (Definition 2). Observe that by definition, the secret reconstruction algorithm Recon from Π_{DPSS}, used in step 6 of the update process, satisfies correctness following Definition 6 formalised at the start of this Section.

Theorem 1 (Correctness of Construction). *Π_{DMUE} is correct assuming the underlying public-key UE scheme Π_{PKUE} and the underlying secret sharing scheme Π_{SS} satisfy their respective definitions of correctness.*

Proof. Following Definition 2, Π_{DMUE} is correct if Dec$(pp, sk_{e_{max}}, C_{e_{max}})$ outputs m with overwhelming probability, whereby $C_{e_{max}}$ has been generated iteratively by the update algorithm Upd. In fact, this means the decryption algorithm UE.Dec is run and outputs m on the same honestly generated inputs. Note, one of the inputs is an update of the ciphertext to the final epoch $(C_{e_{max}})$. Therefore, we assume this ciphertext has been generated correctly by entering a reconstruction phase of the SS scheme, that is, $\mathsf{Recon}(pp_{SS}, \{\Delta^k_{e_i+1}\}_{k \geq t})$ is run to output token Δ_{e_i+1}. In turn, the resulting token is input into $\mathsf{UE.Upd}(pp_{UE}, \Delta_{e_i+1}, C_{e_i})$ such that $C_{e_{max}}$ is output. Let us assume instead that Recon and/or $\mathsf{UE.Upd}$ output $\perp$, contradicting both correctness assumptions, resulting in $\mathsf{UE.Dec}$ outputting $\perp$. In turn, the DMUE decryption algorithm Dec will also output $\perp$ instead of m, which violates correctness in Definition 2. However, the assumptions that the failure symbol $\perp$ is output by the reconstruction phase or PKUE update algorithm contradict our assumption that the SS and PKUE schemes satisfy correctness. Thus, using proof by contradiction we can conclude that the DMUE scheme Π_{DMUE} also satisfies correctness. $\square$

Practical Considerations: In Definition 8 of a generic DMUE scheme, the selection of epoch committees and generation of their respective update tokens arise from the data owner $(\mathcal{D})$. The advent of every epoch calls for $\mathcal{D}$ to generate token shares for the newly selected server committee. However, in Definition 8 we can also consider the involvement of the epoch server committee as a more elegant and *practical* solution to sharing the computational cost of token generation. That is, we can introduce a *redistribution phase* (following Definition 5) amongst the server committee during the running of token generation (TG) to exchange secret shares from one server committee to the next. Importantly, the redistribution techniques from DPSS literature support the refresh of the shares as an additional layer of security, such that these new shares still reconstruct the same secret. In the following, we redefine the running of token generation (Step 3 of Definition 8) to support server committee involvement in the redistribution phase.

$$\mathsf{TG}(pp, sk_{e_i}, k_{e_i+1}, S_{e_i+1}) \rightarrow \{\Delta^j_{e_i+1}\}_{j \in [n]} :$$

1. $\mathsf{TG}(pp, sk_{e_0}, k_{e_1}, S_{e_1}) \rightarrow \{\Delta^j_{e_1}\}_{j \in [n]}$: the DMUE token generation algorithm is run in epoch e_0, as detailed in step 3 of Definition 8.
2. *Redistribution Phase:* To proactively redistribute token shares to a new epoch, the redistribution phase is run by data owner $\mathcal{D}$ and the committee of servers (S_{e_i}) in epoch $e_i, \forall i \in [1, \mathsf{max} - 1]$. Using information provided by the data owner (this could be, for instance, a masking polynomial if Shamir's secret sharing [29] is being used), the servers in S_{e_i} proceed to refresh their individual secret token shares $\{\Delta^j_{e_i}\}_{j \in [n]}$. The new vector of token shares is labelled $\{\Delta^{j'}_{e_i+1}\}_{j' \in [n]}$, and they are securely distributed to the corresponding server $S^{j'} \in S_{e_i+1}$.

To explain the second step in more detail, the *refresh* of token shares can be achieved during the running of token share generation described above, using the underlying redistribution phase of the chosen concrete DPSS scheme (Π_{DPSS}). For instance, secret shares are refreshed in the Shamir-based [29] DPSS scheme of [2] in such a way that shareholders from the current committee *mask* their polynomial P with some polynomial Q, such that no party in this committee learns shares for new polynomial $P' := P + Q$ given to the next shareholder committee, and vice versa. Thus, care needs to be taken in the choice of DPSS scheme so as to preserve security, especially if there is a crossover between the old and new server committees. In line with the proposed DPSS scheme from the authors of [2], an overlap of *one* server possessing the same share in both committees is not a security issue, since the threshold of the scheme is not violated. However, we must make the following stipulation if the crossover of servers is above the threshold to ensure the security (Definition 4, Sect. 3) holds in Definition 8.

Remark 3. If a threshold t or more servers, $S^j = S^{j'}$ for $S^j \in S_{e_i}$ and $S^{j'} \in S_{e_{i+1}}$ respectively, overlap in two consecutive server committees then we necessitate distinct token shares ($\Delta_{e_i}^j \neq \Delta_{e_{i+1}}^{j'}$).

5 Security Analysis

In this Section, we present and prove the formal statements of security for our DMUE generic construction Π_{DMUE} from Definition 8. The following statement of security is for our ciphertext unlinkability notion defined in Sect. 3. At a high level, we will separate our proof into two cases: when an adversary corrupts less than the threshold number of token shares, versus an adversary that corrupts a threshold or more token shares. In each case, we can rely on the security of the underlying building blocks. Specifically, we assume the secrecy of the DPSS scheme and the satisfaction of the corresponding single-server PKUE security notion.

Theorem 2. *Assume that Π_{DPSS} satisfies secrecy and suppose that Π_{PKUE} is a public-key updatable encryption scheme satisfying MUE-IND-CCA security for $t = n = 1$. Then Π_{DMUE} is a MUE-IND-CCA secure scheme.*

Proof. Following Definition 4, we want to show that there exists some negligible function negl under security parameter λ such that

$$\mathrm{Adv}_{\Pi_{\mathsf{DMUE}}, \mathcal{A}}^{\mathsf{MUE\text{-}IND\text{-}CCA}, b}(1^\lambda) \leq \mathsf{negl}(1^\lambda). \tag{1}$$

given the security experiment detailed in Sect. 3, Fig. 4. To prove Eq. 1, we must focus on two separate cases: first when an adversary $\mathcal{A}$ has corrupted $l < t$ token shares in the corresponding security game epoch $\tilde{e}$ and second when $\mathcal{A}$ has corrupted $l \geq t$ token shares. Following the assumptions in Theorem 2, we note that for either scenario we also assume the adversary's challenge message and ciphertext (m', C') were created in some epoch $e < \tilde{e}$ before the current epoch $\tilde{e}$, otherwise, the security experiment will output $\perp$.

Case ($l < t$) : Recall that *secrecy* is satisfied in the DPSS scheme Π_{DPSS}, the formal definition of which is detailed in Sect. 4. Consequently, an adversary has too few token shares from epoch $\tilde{e}$ to reconstruct the secret update token $\Delta_{\tilde{e}}$.

In the case that the challenger randomly chose bit $b = 1$ (for $b = \{0,1\}$) $\mathcal{A}$ cannot manually update their challenge ciphertext C' to ciphertext $C'_{\tilde{e}} := C^{(1)}$ due to the secrecy property. Moreover, if $\mathcal{A}$ queries oracle $\mathcal{O}_{\mathsf{Upd}}(C')$ to update the challenge ciphertext iteratively via epochs $\{e+1, \ldots, \tilde{e}\}$, as detailed in Fig. 2, $\mathcal{A}$ is still incapable of winning the experiment as the update oracle will add $\tilde{e}$ to the list of challenge-equal epochs $\mathcal{C}^*$ and winning conditions $(\mathcal{K} \cap \mathcal{C}^*) = \emptyset$ mean that $\bot$ is output. Therefore, $\mathcal{A}$ is reduced to guessing bit b (in this case $b = 1$) which results in the advantage

$$\mathrm{Adv}_{\Pi_{\mathsf{DMUE}},\mathcal{A}}^{\mathsf{MUE\text{-}IND\text{-}CCA},1}(1^\lambda) = |\Pr[\mathsf{Exp}_{\Pi_{\mathsf{DMUE}},\mathcal{A}}^{\mathsf{MUE\text{-}IND\text{-}CCA},1}(1^\lambda) = 1] - \frac{1}{2}| \le \mathsf{negl}(1^\lambda).$$

If the challenger randomly chose bit $b = 0$, $\mathcal{A}$ would either have to query the epoch secret key corruption oracle to obtain $sk_{\tilde{e}}$ to manually decrypt the ciphertext $C^{(0)}$, or make calls to the decryption oracle. The assumed security of Π_{PKUE} is essential in this instance to prevent trivial wins. We note that both of the named oracles are detailed in Fig. 3. The former scenario requires $\mathcal{A}$ query oracle $\mathcal{O}_{\mathsf{Corrupt\text{-}Key}}(\tilde{e})$ which results in output $\bot$ to prevent trivial wins. The latter scenario means $\mathcal{A}$ calls oracle $\mathcal{O}_{\mathsf{Dec}}(C^{(0)})$ which will result in output $\bot$ due to the decryption oracle conditions. Specifically, the first condition of the isChallenge predicate (Definition 3, Sect. 3.1) is satisfied since $C^{(0)}$ is a challenge ciphertext and $\bot$ is output. Note that the output $(\bot)$ does not inform the adversary whether or not the ciphertext is derived from fresh encryption in epoch $\tilde{e}$ or an update from a prior epoch. Therefore, $\mathcal{A}$ is reduced to guessing bit b (in this case $b = 0$) which results in the advantage

$$\mathrm{Adv}_{\Pi_{\mathsf{DMUE}},\mathcal{A}}^{\mathsf{MUE\text{-}IND\text{-}CCA},0}(1^\lambda) = |\Pr[\mathsf{Exp}_{\Pi_{\mathsf{DMUE}},\mathcal{A}}^{\mathsf{MUE\text{-}IND\text{-}CCA},0}(1^\lambda) = 1] - \frac{1}{2}| \le \mathsf{negl}(1^\lambda).$$

Consequently, Eq. 1 holds when $l < r$.

Case $(l \ge t)$: oracle $\mathcal{O}_{\mathsf{Corrupt\text{-}Token}}$ stipulates that the challenger needs to add the challenge epoch $\tilde{e}$ to list $\mathcal{T}$ (Fig. 1). Crucially, epochs in $\mathcal{T}$ are incorporated into list $\mathcal{C}^*$ which captures all *challenge-equal* epochs. Thus, epoch $\tilde{e}$ belongs to $\mathcal{C}^*$ and winning conditions in our security experiment prevent trivial wins. That is, the intersection of sets $(\mathcal{K} \cap \mathcal{C}^*)$ must be empty to prevent a trivial win from occurring. See the end of Sect. 3 for more depth on trivial wins.

If $t = n = 1$ we can rely on the assumed security of Π_{PKUE}, namely, Definition 4 is satisfied. Therefore, in the case of $(l \ge r)$ and for either choice of $b = \{0,1\}$, $\mathcal{A}$ is reduced to guessing bit b which results in the advantage

$$\mathrm{Adv}_{\Pi_{\mathsf{DMUE}},\mathcal{A}}^{\mathsf{MUE\text{-}IND\text{-}CCA},b}(1^\lambda) = |\Pr[\mathsf{Exp}_{\Pi_{\mathsf{DMUE}},\mathcal{A}}^{\mathsf{MUE\text{-}IND\text{-}CCA},b}(1^\lambda) = 1] - \frac{1}{2}| \le \mathsf{negl}(1^\lambda).$$

Given the above, we can conclude that the Eq. 1 is satisfied for any number (l) of corrupted tokens. $\qquad\square$

Closing Discussion. In this paper, we formalised a DMUE primitive and defined a generic construction, the latter of which was built from single-server PKUE and dynamic threshold secret sharing (DPSS) primitives. As such, the performance of our proposed DMUE scheme (from Definition 8) is directly reflected by the cost of adding a DPSS scheme to PKUE. In the future, we believe it is of interest to develop concrete DMUE schemes to formally analyse the efficiency, costs and security levels attained in the multi-server versus single-server setting of PKUE.

References

1. Alamati, N., Montgomery, H., Patranabis, S.: Symmetric primitives with structured secrets. In: Boldyreva, A., Micciancio, D. (eds.) CRYPTO 2019. LNCS, vol. 11692, pp. 650–679. Springer, Cham (2019). https://doi.org/10.1007/978-3-030-26948-7_23

2. Baron, J., Defrawy, K.E., Lampkins, J., Ostrovsky, R.: Communication-optimal proactive secret sharing for dynamic groups. In: Malkin, T., Kolesnikov, V., Lewko, A.B., Polychronakis, M. (eds.) ACNS 2015. LNCS, vol. 9092, pp. 23–41. Springer, Cham (2015). https://doi.org/10.1007/978-3-319-28166-7_2

3. Benhamouda, F., et al.: Can a blockchain keep a secret? IACR Cryptology ePrint Archive **2020**, 464 (2020)

4. Blakley, G.R.: Safeguarding cryptographic keys. In: Proceedings of the AFIPS National Computer Conference, NCC 1979, vol. 48, pp. 313–318. International Workshop on Managing Requirements Knowledge (MARK), IEEE (1979)

5. Blaze, M., Bleumer, M., Strauss, G.: Divertible protocols and atomic proxy cryptography. In: Nyberg, K. (ed.) EUROCRYPT 1998. LNCS, vol. 1403, pp. 127–144. Springer, Cham (1998). https://doi.org/10.1007/bfb0054122

6. Boneh, D., Lewi, K., Montgomery, H., Raghunathan, A.: Key homomorphic PRFs and their applications. In: Canetti, R., Garay, J.A. (eds.) CRYPTO 2013. LNCS, vol. 8042, pp. 410–428. Springer, Heidelberg (2013). https://doi.org/10.1007/978-3-642-40041-4_23

7. Chen, X., Liu, Y., Li, Y., Lin, C.: Threshold proxy re-encryption and its application in blockchain. In: Sun, X., Pan, Z., Bertino, E. (eds.) ICCCS 2018. LNCS, vol. 11066, pp. 16–25. Springer, Cham (2018). https://doi.org/10.1007/978-3-030-00015-8_2

8. Cini, V., Ramacher, S., Slamanig, D., Striecks, C., Tairi, E.: Updatable signatures and message authentication codes. In: Garay, J.A. (ed.) PKC 2021. LNCS, vol. 12710, pp. 691–723. Springer, Cham (2021). https://doi.org/10.1007/978-3-030-75245-3_25

9. Cramer, R., Damgård, I., Maurer, U.: General secure multi-party computation from any linear secret-sharing scheme. In: Preneel, B. (ed.) EUROCRYPT 2000. LNCS, vol. 1807, pp. 316–334. Springer, Heidelberg (2000). https://doi.org/10.1007/3-540-45539-6_22

10. Davidson, A., Deo, A., Lee, E., Martin, K.: Strong post-compromise secure proxy re-encryption. In: Jang-Jaccard, J., Guo, F. (eds.) ACISP 2019. LNCS, vol. 11547, pp. 58–77. Springer, Cham (2019). https://doi.org/10.1007/978-3-030-21548-4_4

11. Dodis, Y., Karthikeyan, H., Wichs, D.: Updatable public key encryption in the standard model. In: Nissim, K., Waters, B. (eds.) TCC 2021. LNCS, vol. 13044, pp. 254–285. Springer, Cham (2021). https://doi.org/10.1007/978-3-030-90456-2_9

12. Eaton, E., Jao, D., Komlo, C., Mokrani, Y.: Towards post-quantum key-updatable public-key encryption via supersingular isogenies. In: AlTawy, R., Hülsing, A. (eds.) SAC 2021. LNCS, vol. 13203, pp. 461–482. Springer, Cham (2022). https://doi.org/10.1007/978-3-030-99277-4_22

13. Evans, D., et al.: A pragmatic introduction to secure multi-party computation. Found. Trends® Priv. Secur. 2(2–3), 70–246 (2018)

14. Everspaugh, A., Paterson, K., Ristenpart, T., Scott, S.: Key rotation for authenticated encryption. In: Katz, J., Shacham, H. (eds.) CRYPTO 2017. LNCS, vol. 10403, pp. 98–129. Springer, Cham (2017). https://doi.org/10.1007/978-3-319-63697-9_4

15. Frederiksen, T.K., Hesse, J., Poettering, B., Towa, P.: Attribute-based single sign-on: Secure, private, and efficient. Cryptology ePrint Archive, Paper 2023/915 (2023). https://eprint.iacr.org/2023/915

16. Galteland, Y.J., Pan, J.: Backward-leak UNI-directional updatable encryption from (homomorphic) public key encryption. In: Boldyreva, A., Kolesnikov, V. (eds.) PKC 2023. LNCS, vol. 13941, pp. 399–428. Springer, Cham (2023). https://doi.org/10.1007/978-3-031-31371-4_14

17. Herzberg, A., Jarecki, S., Krawczyk, H., Yung, M.: Proactive secret sharing or: how to cope with perpetual leakage. In: Coppersmith, D. (ed.) CRYPTO 1995. LNCS, vol. 963, pp. 339–352. Springer, Heidelberg (1995). https://doi.org/10.1007/3-540-44750-4_27

18. Jiang, Y.: The direction of updatable encryption does not matter much. In: Moriai, S., Wang, H. (eds.) ASIACRYPT 2020. LNCS, vol. 12493, pp. 529–558. Springer, Cham (2020). https://doi.org/10.1007/978-3-030-64840-4_18

19. Klooß, M., Lehmann, A., Rupp, A.: (R)CCA secure updatable encryption with integrity protection. In: Ishai, Y., Rijmen, V. (eds.) EUROCRYPT 2019. LNCS, vol. 11476, pp. 68–99. Springer, Cham (2019). https://doi.org/10.1007/978-3-030-17653-2_3

20. Knapp, J., Quaglia, E.A.: Epoch confidentiality in updatable encryption. In: Ge, C., Guo, F. (eds.) ProvSec 2022. LNCS, vol. 13600, pp. 60–67. Springer, Cham (2022). https://doi.org/10.1007/978-3-031-20917-8_5

21. Komargodski, I., Paskin-Cherniavsky, A.: Evolving secret sharing: dynamic thresholds and robustness. In: Kalai, Y., Reyzin, L. (eds.) TCC 2017. LNCS, vol. 10678, pp. 379–393. Springer, Cham (2017). https://doi.org/10.1007/978-3-319-70503-3_12

22. Lehmann, A., Tackmann, B.: Updatable encryption with post-compromise security. In: Nielsen, J.B., Rijmen, V. (eds.) EUROCRYPT 2018. LNCS, vol. 10822, pp. 685–716. Springer, Cham (2018). https://doi.org/10.1007/978-3-319-78372-7_22

23. S. K. D. Maram, F. Zhang, L. Wang, A. Low, Y. Zhang, A. Juels, and D. Song. CHURP: dynamic-committee proactive secret sharing. In: Proceedings of the 2019 ACM SIGSAC Conference on Computer and Communications Security, pp. 2369–2386. CCS 2019, Association for Computing Machinery (2019)

24. Nishimaki, R.: The direction of updatable encryption does matter. Cryptology ePrint Archive (2021)

25. Ostrovsky, R., Yung, M.: How to withstand mobile virus attacks. In: Proceedings of the Tenth Annual ACM Symposium on Principles of Distributed Computing, pp. 51–59. ACM, Association for Computing Machinery (1991)

26. Qian, C., Galteland, Y. J., Davies, G.T.: Extending updatable encryption: public key, tighter security and signed ciphertexts. Cryptology ePrint Archive (2023)

27. Raghav, Andola, N., Verma, K., Venkatesan, S., Verma, S.: Proactive threshold-proxy re-encryption scheme for secure data sharing on cloud. J. Supercomput. 1–29 (2023)
28. Schultz, D., Liskov, B., Liskov, M.: MPSS: mobile proactive secret sharing. ACM Trans. Inf. Syst. Secur. 13 (2010)
29. Shamir, A.: How to share a secret. Commun. ACM 22(11), 612–613 (1979)
30. Slamanig, D., Striecks, C.: Puncture'em all: updatable encryption with no-directional key updates and expiring ciphertexts. Cryptology ePrint Archive (2021)
31. Yang, P., Cao, Z., Dong, X.: Threshold proxy re-signature. J. Syst. Sci. Complex. 24(4), 816–824 (2011)

Trace-and-Revoke Quadratic Functional Encryption

Qiuwei Zheng(ID) and Jun Zhao$^{(\boxtimes)}$(ID)

East China Normal University, Shanghai 200062, China
junzhao9412@gmail.com

Abstract. This work investigates trace-and-revoke system in the context of functional encryption (FE) for quadratic functions. Trace-and-revoke system allows a content distributor to identify malicious users who distribute their secret keys to build a pirate decryption box, and revoke their decryption capabilities. FE scheme for quadratic functions restricts the decryption of an encrypted message x, such that the use of secret key associated with a quadratic function (or degree-2 polynomial) f recovers only $f(x)$ and nothing else. Our construction achieves semi-adaptive simulation-based security with private black-box traceability under (bilateral) k-Lin assumptions. This is the first traceable FE scheme for quadratic functions. Prior to our work, all known the traceable FE schemes only deal with inner-product evaluation [CT-RSA'20, ESORICS'22]. Technically, we employ Wee's FE scheme for quadratic functions [TCC'20], with tracing technique from the trace-and-revoke systems of Agrawal *et al.* [CCS'17] and Luo *et al.* [ESORICS'22] to achieve our goal.

Keywords: Trace-and-revoke · Functional encryption for quadratic function · Black-box traceability

1 Introduction

Traitor tracing scheme [9] studied the problem of identifying the users that contributed to building a malicious decoder. In a traitor tracing scheme, ciphertexts are associated with encrypted data and public key pk; each legitimate user $i \in [N]$ of the system is provided a secret key sk_i that allows him to decrypt the content, where N denotes the total number of users in the scheme. In the face of some malicious users (traitors) colluding to build a pirate decoder with a non-negligible probability of decrypting the ciphertext, there is an efficient tracing algorithm that outputs at least one malicious user by interacting with any such (black-box) pirate decoder. Notice that, this is the demand for the tracing security of traitor tracing scheme.

The traitor tracing schemes have been studied extensively [6,8,18,21], and many primitives become more practical when they have the property of tracing, such as *broadcast encryption*(BE) [7,14], *attribute-based encryption*(ABE) [19], *identity-based encryption*(IBE) [15] and so on. Traitor tracing schemes are mainly

© The Author(s), under exclusive license to Springer Nature Switzerland AG 2023
E. Athanasopoulos and B. Mennink (Eds.): ISC 2023, LNCS 14411, pp. 496–515, 2023.
https://doi.org/10.1007/978-3-031-49187-0_25

explored in the context of traditional *public key encryption* (PKE), without considering the primitives beyond the all-or-nothing property of PKE.

Recently, Do *et al.* [10] introduce tracing feature into *functional encryption* (FE), namely the notion of *traceable functional encryption* (TFE). They employ the FE scheme for inner product functionality of Abdalla *et al.* [1], with tracing technique of Boneh-Franklin scheme [6], and give the first concrete construction of *traceable inner product functional encryption* (TIPFE). In their scheme, the ciphertext is associated with message vector $\mathbf{x}$, and the secret key is generated for a tuple $(i, \mathbf{y})$ representing user identity and functional vector; the decryption reveals nothing about message $\mathbf{x}$ except the inner product $\langle \mathbf{x}, \mathbf{y} \rangle$. Their scheme supports one-target security and *private* traceability which means that the tracing algorithm requires the master secret key of system, and only the central authority can find out the traitors' identities.

Luo *et al.* [20] propose an adaptively (indistinguishability-based) secure TIPFE construction that supports *public* traceability [8,21], which means the tracing algorithm only needs the public key and no additional secrets. Furthermore, there is a revocation set $\mathcal{R}$ in their scheme. A user can decrypt the ciphertext if and only if the user's identity does not belong to this revocation set $\mathcal{R}$ [2]. If any traitors are identified, the authority can add their identities into $\mathcal{R}$, so that these traitors can no longer decrypt future generated ciphertexts.

Traceable functional encryption offers unique capabilities for digital rights management and secure data sharing in real-world scenarios. Content providers can encrypt their content using TFE, allowing authorized users to perform specific operations on the content while preserving privacy to a certain extent and providing the ability to trace any unauthorized sharing or misuse.

Besides the inner product functionality, functional encryption for quadratic functions (or *quadratic functional encryption*, QFE) is desirable from the viewpoint of both theory and practice. For a function class $\mathcal{F}_{n,m}$, each function $f \in \mathcal{F}_{n,m}$ is represented by a vector $\mathbf{y} \in \mathbb{Z}_p^{nm}$. The ciphertext is associated with message vectors $(\mathbf{x}_1, \mathbf{x}_2) \in \mathbb{Z}_p^n \times \mathbb{Z}_p^m$, and a secret key is generated for the functional vector $\mathbf{y}$; the decryption reveals nothing about message $(\mathbf{x}_1, \mathbf{x}_2)$ except the result of $\mathbf{y}^\top(\mathbf{x}_1 \otimes \mathbf{x}_2)$, where $\otimes$ denotes the Kronecker product.

At this point, given recent progress in the quadratic functional encryptions [4,5,12,22,23], a natural question is: *Can we construct TFE for quadratic functions?*

1.1 Result

In this paper, we initiate the study of *trace-and-revoke quadratic functional encryption* (TRQFE, or more formally *trace-and-revoke functional encryption for quadratic functions*). We investigate traitor tracing system in the context of QFE, and obtain the first traceable QFE scheme that achieves semi-adaptive simulation-based security under k-Lin and bilateral k-Lin assumptions. Our scheme considers a strong notion of *black-box distinguisher* [10,14]. Given an oracle access to a black-box pirate decoder D, this tracing notion requires D to distinguish the ciphertexts from two messages of its choice, instead of requiring its ability of decryption. Our scheme satisfies *private* traceability, and tracing algorithm can only be performed by the central authority who owns the master secret key. Moreover, our scheme supports the functionality of user revocation as in [20].

1.2   Technical Overview

In this overview, we explain our construction of TRQFE scheme with private traceability. The top-level strategy of our TRQFE construction is to combine the tracing technique of [2,20] with Wee's QFE scheme [23], which can be proven the semi-adaptive secure under k-Lin assumption and bilateral k-Lin assumption in prime-order bilinear groups. Before the details, we begin with some preliminaries.

Notation. We will work with asymmetric bilinear group $(\mathbb{G}_1, \mathbb{G}_2, \mathbb{G}_T, e)$ of prime order p and use implicit representation $[\mathbf{M}]_s = g_s^{\mathbf{M}}$ for matrix $\mathbf{M}$ over $\mathbb{Z}_p$, where $s \in \{1, 2, T\}$ and g_s is the respective generator of $\mathbb{G}_s$. Besides, we use $\otimes$ to denote the Kronecker product of matrices and $\langle \cdot \rangle$ to denote the inner product of vectors. The mixed-product property of Kronecker product tells us that $(\mathbf{A} \otimes \mathbf{B})(\mathbf{C} \otimes \mathbf{D}) = \mathbf{AC} \otimes \mathbf{BD}$ for any matrices $\mathbf{A}, \mathbf{B}, \mathbf{C}, \mathbf{D}$ of proper sizes. We use $[N]$ to denote the set of natural numbers $\{1, 2, \ldots, N\}$. Then, we review the following concrete FE scheme which will be used in our TRQFE.

Tools. A *two-slot Functional encryption for inner products* (two-slot IPFE) [13,16,17] scheme IPFE consists of four algorithms (iSetup, iKeyGen, iEnc, iDec): algorithm iSetup generates the master public key impk and master secret key imsk; algorithm iEnc encrypts the vector $\mathbf{x}_1, \mathbf{x}_2$ which are the input of the public slot and private slot respectively; algorithm iKeyGen generates the secret key for vector $\mathbf{y}_1$ and $\mathbf{y}_2$; and algorithm iDec gives $\langle \mathbf{x}_1, \mathbf{y}_1 \rangle + \langle \mathbf{x}_2, \mathbf{y}_2 \rangle$. We require the simulation-based security with following simulator: $\widetilde{\mathsf{iEnc}}$ does not take $\mathbf{x}_1, \mathbf{x}_2$ as input and $\widetilde{\mathsf{iKeyGen}}$ has an extra input $\langle \mathbf{x}_1, \mathbf{y}_1 \rangle + \langle \mathbf{x}_2, \mathbf{y}_2 \rangle$. Notice that, in a real two-slot IPFE scheme, the private slot encrypts $\mathbf{0}$.

Recap. Let us review the trace-and-revoke IPFE scheme of Luo *et al.* [20]. iSetup is used to generate public-private key pair (impk, imsk) and publish a public directory pd. For the sake of brevity, we denote

$$\mathsf{iEnc}(\cdot) = \mathsf{iEnc}(\mathsf{impk}, \cdot) \quad \text{and} \quad \mathsf{iKeyGen}(\cdot) = \mathsf{iKeyGen}(\mathsf{imsk}, \cdot).$$

A ciphertext of vector $\mathbf{x} \in \mathbb{Z}_p^n$, and a secret key for user i with inner product function $\mathbf{y}' \in \mathbb{Z}_p^n$ are as follows:

$$\mathsf{ct}_\mathbf{x} : \mathsf{iEnc}(\mathbf{x} \otimes \mathbf{v}_\mathcal{R})$$
$$\mathsf{sk}_{\mathbf{y}',i} : \mathsf{iKeyGen}(\mathbf{y}' \otimes \mathbf{u}_i) \quad \mathbf{u}_i \leftarrow \mathbb{Z}_p^t$$

where $\mathbf{v}_\mathcal{R} \in \mathbb{Z}_p^t \setminus \{\mathbf{0}\}$ is generated deterministically from the revocation set $\mathcal{R}$ such that $\mathbf{u}_i^\top \mathbf{v}_\mathcal{R} = 0$ for all $i \in \mathcal{R}$; each $(i, \mathbf{u}_i)$ pair should be appended to pd.

For $\mathsf{sk}_{\mathbf{y}',i}$ where $i \notin \mathcal{R}$, decryption uses the mixed-product property of Kronecker product and works as follows:

$$\frac{\mathsf{iDec}(\mathsf{ct}_{\mathbf{x}}, \mathsf{sk}_{\mathbf{y}',i})}{\langle \mathbf{v}_{\mathcal{R}}, \mathbf{u}_i \rangle} = \frac{\langle \mathbf{x} \otimes \mathbf{v}_{\mathcal{R}}, \mathbf{y}' \otimes \mathbf{u}_i \rangle}{\langle \mathbf{v}_{\mathcal{R}}, \mathbf{u}_i \rangle} = \frac{\langle \mathbf{x}, \mathbf{y}' \rangle \cdot \langle \mathbf{v}_{\mathcal{R}}, \mathbf{u}_i \rangle}{\langle \mathbf{v}_{\mathcal{R}}, \mathbf{u}_i \rangle} = \langle \mathbf{x}, \mathbf{y}' \rangle. \quad (1)$$

Our Strategy. We want to apply the above tracing technique into QFE. This is based on the observation that we can rewrite the equality (1) as follows:

$$\begin{aligned} \mathbf{y}^\top(\mathbf{x}_1 \otimes \mathbf{x}_2) &= \frac{\mathbf{y}^\top(\mathbf{x}_1 \otimes \mathbf{x}_2) \cdot \mathbf{u}_i^\top \mathbf{v}_{\mathcal{R}}}{\mathbf{u}_i^\top \mathbf{v}_{\mathcal{R}}} = \frac{(\mathbf{y} \otimes \mathbf{u}_i)^\top((\mathbf{x}_1 \otimes \mathbf{x}_2) \otimes \mathbf{v}_{\mathcal{R}})}{\mathbf{u}_i^\top \mathbf{v}_{\mathcal{R}}} \\ &= \frac{(\mathbf{y} \otimes \mathbf{u}_i)^\top(\mathbf{x}_1 \otimes \mathbf{x}_2 \otimes \mathbf{v}_{\mathcal{R},1} \otimes \mathbf{v}_{\mathcal{R},2})}{\mathbf{u}_i^\top \mathbf{v}_{\mathcal{R}}} \end{aligned} \quad (2)$$

where $\mathbf{x}_1, \mathbf{x}_2 \in \mathbb{Z}_p^n$, quadratic function $\mathbf{y} \in \mathbb{Z}_p^{n^2}$ and $\mathbf{v}_{\mathcal{R}}, \mathbf{u}_i \in \mathbb{Z}_p^t$. Here,

- the first row follows the idea from previous TIPFE that we reviewed above;
- the second row decomposes $\mathbf{v}_{\mathcal{R}}$ into two smaller vectors $\mathbf{v}_{\mathcal{R},1}, \mathbf{v}_{\mathcal{R},2} \in \mathbb{Z}_p^{\sqrt{t}}$ such that $\mathbf{v}_{\mathcal{R}} = \mathbf{v}_{\mathcal{R},1} \otimes \mathbf{v}_{\mathcal{R},2}$.

There exists a permutation matrix $\mathbf{T} \in \mathbb{Z}_p^{n^2 t \times n^2 t}$, which is uniquely determined by n and t (see Sect. 2.1), such that

$$\mathbf{x}_1 \otimes \mathbf{x}_2 \otimes \mathbf{v}_{\mathcal{R},1} \otimes \mathbf{v}_{\mathcal{R},2} = \mathbf{T}(\mathbf{x}_1 \otimes \mathbf{v}_{\mathcal{R},1} \otimes \mathbf{x}_2 \otimes \mathbf{v}_{\mathcal{R},2}).$$

We further rewrite the equality (2) as

$$\mathbf{y}^\top(\mathbf{x}_1 \otimes \mathbf{x}_2) = \frac{(\mathbf{y} \otimes \mathbf{u}_i)^\top \mathbf{T}(\mathbf{x}_1 \otimes \mathbf{v}_{\mathcal{R},1} \otimes \mathbf{x}_2 \otimes \mathbf{v}_{\mathcal{R},2})}{\mathbf{u}_i^\top \mathbf{v}_{\mathcal{R}}} \quad (3)$$

We obtain the form of $(\mathbf{x}_1 \otimes \mathbf{v}_{\mathcal{R},1}) \otimes (\mathbf{x}_2 \otimes \mathbf{v}_{\mathcal{R},2})$ that fits the quadratic functions. With this, we can simply employ Wee's QFE scheme [23] to achieve our goal: The ciphertext for vectors $\mathbf{x}_1, \mathbf{x}_2 \in \mathbb{Z}_p^n$, and a secret key for user i with quadratic function $\mathbf{y} \in \mathbb{Z}_p^{n^2}$ are as follows:

$$\mathsf{ct}_{\mathbf{x}_1, \mathbf{x}_2} : \begin{cases} \underbrace{[\mathbf{A}_1\mathbf{s}_1 + \mathbf{x}_1 \otimes \mathbf{v}_{\mathcal{R},1}]_1}_{\mathbf{c}_1}, \quad \underbrace{[\mathbf{A}_2\mathbf{s}_2 + \mathbf{x}_2 \otimes \mathbf{v}_{\mathcal{R},2}]_2}_{\mathbf{c}_2}, \\ \underbrace{\mathsf{iEnc}\Big([\mathbf{s}_1 \otimes (\mathbf{x}_2 \otimes \mathbf{v}_{\mathcal{R},2}), \mathbf{c}_1 \otimes \mathbf{s}_2]_1\Big)}_{\mathsf{ict}} \end{cases} \quad (4)$$

$$\mathsf{sk}_{\mathbf{y},i} : \mathsf{iKeyGen}\Big([(\mathbf{y} \otimes \mathbf{u}_i)^\top \mathbf{T}(\mathbf{A}_1 \otimes \mathbf{I}_{n\sqrt{t}}), (\mathbf{y} \otimes \mathbf{u}_i)^\top \mathbf{T}(\mathbf{I}_{n\sqrt{t}} \otimes \mathbf{A}_2)]_2\Big)$$

where $\mathbf{A}_1, \mathbf{A}_2 \leftarrow \mathbb{Z}_p^{n\sqrt{t} \times k}, \mathbf{s}_1, \mathbf{s}_2 \leftarrow \mathbb{Z}_p^k, \mathbf{u}_i \leftarrow \mathbb{Z}_p^t, \mathbf{I}_{n\sqrt{t}}$ is the identity matrix of size $n\sqrt{t}$. Here we slightly abuse the notation $[\mathbf{a}, \mathbf{b}]_s$ to denote the input of concatenated vectors $[\mathbf{a}\|\mathbf{b}]_s$ (or $[(\mathbf{a}\|\mathbf{b})^\top]_s$) in the context of iKeyGen and iEnc, where $s \in \{1, 2\}$.

The decryption follows the equality (3). More specifically, we first assemble ict and $\mathsf{sk}_{\mathbf{y},i}$ together by the decryption procedure of underlying IPFE as follows:

$$
\begin{aligned}
&\mathsf{iDec}(\mathsf{ict}, \mathsf{sk}_{\mathbf{y},i})\\
&= (\mathbf{y} \otimes \mathbf{u}_i)^{\top} \mathbf{T}\Big((\mathbf{A}_1 \otimes \mathbf{I}_{n\sqrt{t}})\big(\mathbf{s}_1 \otimes (\mathbf{x}_2 \otimes \mathbf{v}_{\mathcal{R},2})\big) + (\mathbf{I}_{n\sqrt{t}} \otimes \mathbf{A}_2)(\mathbf{c}_1 \otimes \mathbf{s}_2)\Big)\\
&= (\mathbf{y} \otimes \mathbf{u}_i)^{\top} \mathbf{T}\Big(\mathbf{A}_1 \mathbf{s}_1 \otimes (\mathbf{x}_2 \otimes \mathbf{v}_{\mathcal{R},2}) + \mathbf{c}_1 \otimes \mathbf{A}_2 \mathbf{s}_2\Big).
\end{aligned}
$$

The decryption result is constructed in such a way that it exactly satisfies the following equation:

$$
\mathbf{c}_1 \otimes \mathbf{c}_2 = \overbrace{\mathbf{x}_1 \otimes \mathbf{v}_{\mathcal{R},1} \otimes \mathbf{x}_2 \otimes \mathbf{v}_{\mathcal{R},2}}^{\text{the part we need}} + \overbrace{\mathbf{A}_1 \mathbf{s}_1 \otimes (\mathbf{x}_2 \otimes \mathbf{v}_{\mathcal{R},2}) + \mathbf{c}_1 \otimes \mathbf{A}_2 \mathbf{s}_2}^{\text{cross terms}}. \tag{5}
$$

Observe that, given $\mathsf{ct}_{\mathbf{x}_1,\mathbf{x}_2}$ and $\mathsf{sk}_{\mathbf{y},i}$, one can recover

$$
(\mathbf{y} \otimes \mathbf{u}_i)^{\top} \mathbf{T}(\mathbf{x}_1 \otimes \mathbf{v}_{\mathcal{R},1} \otimes \mathbf{x}_2 \otimes \mathbf{v}_{\mathcal{R},2}) = (\mathbf{y} \otimes \mathbf{u}_i)^{\top} \mathbf{T}(\mathbf{c}_1 \otimes \mathbf{c}_2) - \mathsf{iDec}(\mathsf{ict}, \mathsf{sk}_{\mathbf{y},i})
$$

and even obtain $\mathbf{y}^{\top}(\mathbf{x}_1 \otimes \mathbf{x}_2)$ according to the equality (3).

The semi-adaptive security inherits from Wee's QFE and we will focus on the tracing algorithm.

Traceability. We use the notion of *black-box distinguisher* from [10,14], which requires the pirate distinguisher D to be able to distinguish the encryption of two adversarially-chosen message tuples $(\mathbf{x}_{0,1}^*, \mathbf{x}_{0,2}^*), (\mathbf{x}_{1,1}^*, \mathbf{x}_{1,2}^*)$. Let N be the number of users and each user is assigned with a unique index $i \in [N]$. We adapt the construction idea of probe ciphertexts as [2,20]. Considering a subset of suspect traitors $S_i = \{i, i+1, \ldots, N+1\} \setminus \mathcal{R}$ for $i = 1, \ldots, N+1$. The tracing algorithm will generate a series of probe ciphertexts c^{S_i} associated to S_i with following properties:

- The distribution of c^{S_1} corresponds to the normal encryption of $(\mathbf{x}_{0,1}^*, \mathbf{x}_{0,2}^*)$.
- The distribution of $c^{S_{N+1}}$ corresponds to the normal encryption of $(\mathbf{x}_{1,1}^*, \mathbf{x}_{1,2}^*)$.
- The probe ciphertexts c^{S_i} and $c^{S_{i+1}}$ are indistinguishable without the secret key for index i.

To achieve these properties, we first set $\mathbf{v}_{S_i} \in \mathbb{Z}_p^t$ as follows: If $i = 1$, set $\mathbf{v}_{S_i} = \mathbf{0}$; If $i = N+1$, set $\mathbf{v}_{S_i} = \mathbf{v}_{\mathcal{R}}$; Otherwise, compute $\mathbf{v}_{S_i}$ such that:

$$
\mathbf{u}_j^{\top} \mathbf{v}_{S_i} = 0 \text{ or all } j \in S_i \cup \mathcal{R}; \qquad \mathbf{u}_j^{\top} \mathbf{v}_{S_i} = \mathbf{u}_j^{\top} \mathbf{v}_{\mathcal{R}} \text{ for all } j \in S_1 \setminus S_i.
$$

Then find $\mathbf{v}_{S_i,1}, \mathbf{v}_{S_i,2} \in \mathbb{Z}_p^{\sqrt{t}}$ such that $\mathbf{v}_{S_i,1} \otimes \mathbf{v}_{S_i,2} = \mathbf{v}_{S_i}$. Given imsk and $([\mathbf{A}_1]_1, [\mathbf{A}_1]_2, [\mathbf{A}_2]_2)$ within pk, we complete the structure of $\mathsf{sk}_{\mathbf{y},i}$ in (4) and construct the probe ciphertext associated to S_i as follows:

$$c^{S_i} : \begin{cases} \underbrace{[\mathbf{A}_1 \mathbf{s}_1 + \tilde{\mathbf{x}}_{i,1}^*]_1}_{\mathbf{c}_{i,1}}, \quad [\mathbf{A}_2 \mathbf{s}_2 + \tilde{\mathbf{x}}_{i,2}^*]_2, \\ \mathsf{iEnc}\left([\mathbf{s}_1 \otimes \tilde{\mathbf{x}}_{i,2}^*, \mathbf{c}_{i,1} \otimes \mathbf{s}_2]_1, [\mathbf{c}_{i,3}, 0]_1\right) \end{cases}$$

$$\mathsf{sk}_{\mathbf{y},i} : \mathsf{iKeyGen}\left([(\mathbf{y} \otimes \mathbf{u}_i)^\top \mathbf{T}(\mathbf{A}_1 \otimes \mathbf{I}_{n\sqrt{t}}), (\mathbf{y} \otimes \mathbf{u}_i)^\top \mathbf{T}(\mathbf{I}_{n\sqrt{t}} \otimes \mathbf{A}_2)]_2, \underbrace{[(\mathbf{y} \otimes \mathbf{u}_i)^\top, 0]_2}_{\text{private slot of IPFE}}\right)$$

(6)

where $\mathbf{s}_1, \mathbf{s}_2 \leftarrow \mathbb{Z}_p^k, \mathbf{u}_i \leftarrow \mathbb{Z}_p^t$ and

$$\tilde{\mathbf{x}}_{i,1}^* = \mathbf{x}_{0,1}^* \otimes \mathbf{v}_{S_i,1} + \mathbf{x}_{1,1}^* \otimes \mathbf{v}_{S_i,1}, \quad \tilde{\mathbf{x}}_{i,2}^* = -\mathbf{x}_{0,2}^* \otimes \mathbf{v}_{S_i,2} + \mathbf{x}_{1,2}^* \otimes \mathbf{v}_{S_i,2},$$

$$\mathbf{c}_{i,3} = \mathbf{x}_{0,1}^* \otimes \mathbf{x}_{1,2}^* \otimes \mathbf{v}_{S_i} - \mathbf{x}_{1,1}^* \otimes \mathbf{x}_{0,2}^* \otimes \mathbf{v}_{S_i} - \mathbf{x}_{0,1}^* \otimes \mathbf{x}_{0,2}^* \otimes \mathbf{v}_\mathcal{R}.$$

We remark that $(\tilde{\mathbf{x}}_{i,1}^*, \tilde{\mathbf{x}}_{i,2}^*)$ comes from the combination of $(\mathbf{x}_{0,1}^*, \mathbf{x}_{0,2}^*)$, $(\mathbf{x}_{1,1}^*, \mathbf{x}_{1,2}^*)$. Taking advantage of the private slot of IPFE, we use $\mathbf{c}_{i,3}$ to cancel the cross terms, which come from the expansion of Kronecker product $\tilde{\mathbf{x}}_{i,1}^* \otimes \tilde{\mathbf{x}}_{i,2}^*$, and keep only the parts we need. The construction of $\mathbf{c}_{i,3}$ is similar to the cross terms in equality (5). By this construction, the decryption of probe ciphertext c^{S_i}, under functional secret key $\mathsf{sk}_{\mathbf{y},j}$ of user $j \in [N]$, reveals the result $\hat{z}$ where

$$\hat{z} = \mathbf{y}^\top(\mathbf{x}_{0,1}^* \otimes \mathbf{x}_{0,2}^*) \cdot (\mathbf{u}_j^\top \mathbf{v}_\mathcal{R} - \mathbf{u}_j^\top \mathbf{v}_{S_i}) + \mathbf{y}^\top(\mathbf{x}_{1,1}^* \otimes \mathbf{x}_{1,2}^*) \cdot \mathbf{u}_j^\top \mathbf{v}_{S_i}.$$

Considering the assignment of $\mathbf{v}_{S_i}$, we have

$$\hat{z} = \begin{cases} \mathbf{y}^\top(\mathbf{x}_{0,1}^* \otimes \mathbf{x}_{0,2}^*) \cdot \mathbf{u}_j^\top \mathbf{v}_\mathcal{R} \impliedby \text{if } \mathbf{u}_j^\top \mathbf{v}_{S_i} = 0 \qquad \impliedby \text{if } j \in S_i \cup \mathcal{R}, \\ \mathbf{y}^\top(\mathbf{x}_{1,1}^* \otimes \mathbf{x}_{1,2}^*) \cdot \mathbf{u}_j^\top \mathbf{v}_\mathcal{R} \impliedby \text{if } \mathbf{u}_j^\top \mathbf{v}_{S_i} = \mathbf{u}_j^\top \mathbf{v}_\mathcal{R} \impliedby \text{if } j \in S_1 \setminus S_i. \end{cases}$$

Therefore, the three properties mentioned above are satisfied readily. See Sect. 4 for more details. We finally mention that the last position of IPFE private slot will only be used in the security proof. In our real TRQFE scheme, this position of private slot only encrypts 0, as shown in (6).

Organization. In Sect. 2, we provide some definitions and recall some assumptions required for our work. In Sect. 3, we present the detailed construction of our TRQFE scheme, and prove its security. In Sect. 4, we will demonstrate the core properties of probe ciphertexts, which is derived from their construction in tracing algorithm, and then prove the black-box traceability. In Sect. 5, we provide a brief summary of the entire paper.

2   Preliminaries

Notation. For a finite set S, we write $s \leftarrow S$ to denote that s is picked uniformly from finite set S. Then, we use $|S|$ to denote the size of the set S. Let $\approx_s$ stand for two distributions being statistically indistinguishable, and $\approx_c$ denote two distributions being computationally indistinguishable. We use lower-case boldface to denote vectors (e.g., $\mathbf{s}$) and upper-case boldface to denote matrices (e.g. $\mathbf{S}$). We use $\mathbf{I}_n$ to denote the identity matrix of size n. For any positive integer N, we use $[N]$ to denote the set $\{1, 2, \ldots, N\}$.

Lemma 1 (Two-tailed Chernoff Bound). *Let $X_1, X_2, \ldots, X_n$ be independent Poisson trials with success probabilities $p_1, p_2, \ldots, p_n$. Let $X = \sum_{i=1}^{n} X_i$ and $\mu = \sum_{i=1}^{n} p_i$. For $0 < \delta < 1$, we have*

$$\Pr\left[|X - \mu| \geq \delta\mu\right] \leq 2e^{-\mu\delta^2/3}.$$

2.1 Kronecker Product

The Kronecker product for matrices $\mathbf{A} = (a_{i,j}) \in \mathbb{Z}_p^{m \times n}$, $\mathbf{B} \in \mathbb{Z}_p^{s \times t}$ is defined as

$$\mathbf{A} \otimes \mathbf{B} = \begin{pmatrix} a_{1,1}\mathbf{B} & \cdots & a_{1,n}\mathbf{B} \\ \vdots & \ddots & \vdots \\ a_{m,1}\mathbf{B} & \cdots & a_{m,n}\mathbf{B} \end{pmatrix} \in \mathbb{Z}_p^{ms \times nt}$$

and for matrices $\mathbf{A}, \mathbf{B}, \mathbf{C}, \mathbf{D}$ of proper sizes, we will use the following facts:

$$(\mathbf{A} \otimes \mathbf{B})(\mathbf{C} \otimes \mathbf{D}) = \mathbf{A}\mathbf{C} \otimes \mathbf{B}\mathbf{D}, \qquad (\mathbf{A} \otimes \mathbf{B})^\top = \mathbf{A}^\top \otimes \mathbf{B}^\top.$$

For column vectors $(\mathbf{a}, \mathbf{b}, \mathbf{c}, \mathbf{d}) \in \mathbb{Z}_p^s \times \mathbb{Z}_p^m \times \mathbb{Z}_p^n \times \mathbb{Z}_p^t$, there exists permutation matrices $\mathbf{T}_1 \in \mathbb{Z}_p^{mn \times mn}$ and $\mathbf{T}_2 \in \mathbb{Z}_p^{mnst \times mnst}$ such that

$$\mathbf{a} \otimes \mathbf{c} \otimes \mathbf{b} \otimes \mathbf{d} = \mathbf{a} \otimes \mathbf{T}_1(\mathbf{b} \otimes \mathbf{c}) \otimes \mathbf{d} = \mathbf{T}_2(\mathbf{a} \otimes \mathbf{b} \otimes \mathbf{c} \otimes \mathbf{d})$$

where $\mathbf{T}_1$ is uniquely determined by m and n, $\mathbf{T}_2 = \mathbf{I}_s \otimes \mathbf{T}_1 \otimes \mathbf{I}_t$. Formally, $\mathbf{T}_1$ is a square binary matrix that has exactly one entry of 1 in each row and each column and 0s elsewhere, which can permute the rows of $\mathbf{b} \otimes \mathbf{c}$ to make $\mathbf{c} \otimes \mathbf{b}$.

2.2 Bilinear Groups

A generator $\mathcal{G}$ takes as input a security parameter 1^λ and outputs a description $\mathbb{G} := (p, \mathbb{G}_1, \mathbb{G}_2, \mathbb{G}_T, e)$, where p is a prime, $\mathbb{G}_1$, $\mathbb{G}_2$ and $\mathbb{G}_T$ are cyclic groups of order p, and $e : \mathbb{G}_1 \times \mathbb{G}_2 \to \mathbb{G}_T$ is a non-degenerate bilinear map. Group operations in $\mathbb{G}_1$, $\mathbb{G}_2$, $\mathbb{G}_T$ and bilinear map e are computable in deterministic polynomial time in λ. Let $g_1 \in \mathbb{G}_1$, $g_2 \in \mathbb{G}_2$ and $g_T = e(g_1, g_2) \in \mathbb{G}_T$ be the respective generators, we employ *implicit representation* of group elements: for a matrix $\mathbf{M}$ over $\mathbb{Z}_p$, we define $[\mathbf{M}]_s = g_s^{\mathbf{M}}$ for all $s \in \{1, 2, T\}$, where exponentiation is carried out component-wise. Given $[\mathbf{A}]_1, [\mathbf{B}]_2$ where $\mathbf{A}$ and $\mathbf{B}$ have proper sizes, we let $e([\mathbf{A}]_1, [\mathbf{B}]_2) = [\mathbf{A}\mathbf{B}]_T$. This computation can be performed via element-wise bilinear mapping over matrix multiplication. Furthermore, we can even compute $[\mathbf{A} \otimes \mathbf{B}]_T$ from $[\mathbf{A}]_1, [\mathbf{B}]_2$, by applying e into the definition of Kronecker product.

For $s \in \{1, 2\}$, we recall *matrix Diffie-Hellman (MDDH) assumption* on $\mathbb{G}_s$ [11]:

Assumption 1 (MDDH$_{k,\ell}^m$ Assumption on $\mathbb{G}_s$, $s \in \{1,2\}$) *Let $k, \ell, m \in \mathbb{N}$. We say that the MDDH$_{k,\ell}^m$ assumption holds in $\mathbb{G}_s$ if for all PPT adversaries $\mathcal{A}$, the following advantage function is negligible in λ.*

$$\mathsf{Adv}_{\mathcal{A},\mathbb{G}_s}^{\mathrm{MDDH}_{k,\ell}^m}(\lambda) = \big| \Pr[\mathcal{A}(\mathbb{G}, [\mathbf{M}]_s, [\mathbf{MS}]_s) = 1] - \Pr[\mathcal{A}(\mathbb{G}, [\mathbf{M}]_s, [\mathbf{U}]_s) = 1] \big|$$

where $\mathbb{G} := (p, \mathbb{G}_1, \mathbb{G}_2, \mathbb{G}_T, e) \leftarrow \mathcal{G}(1^\lambda)$, $\mathbf{M} \leftarrow \mathbb{Z}_p^{\ell \times k}$, $\mathbf{S} \leftarrow \mathbb{Z}_p^{k \times m}$ and $\mathbf{U} \leftarrow \mathbb{Z}_p^{\ell \times m}$.

Escala *et al.* [11] showed that

$$k\text{-Lin} \Rightarrow \mathrm{MDDH}_{k,\ell}^1 \Rightarrow \mathrm{MDDH}_{k,\ell}^m$$

with a tight security reduction. The MDDH$_{k,\ell}^m$ assumption holds *unconditionally* when $\ell \leq k$ and is implied by k-Lin assumption when $\ell > k$. When $k = 1$, we call it *symmetric external Diffie-Hellman (SXDH) assumption*; when $k = 2$, we call it *decisional linear (DLIN) assumption*.

Assumption 2 (Bilateral MDDH$_{k,\ell}^m$ Assumption on $\mathbb{G}_s$, $s \in \{1,2\}$) *Let $k, \ell, m \in \mathbb{N}$. We say that the BI-MDDH$_{k,\ell}^m$ assumption holds in $\mathbb{G}_s$ if for all PPT adversaries $\mathcal{A}$, the following advantage function is negligible in λ.*

$$\mathsf{Adv}_{\mathcal{A},\mathbb{G}_s}^{\mathrm{BI\text{-}MDDH}_{k,\ell}^m}(\lambda) = \big| \Pr[\mathcal{A}(\mathbb{G}, \{[\mathbf{M}]_s, [\mathbf{MS}]_s\}_{s \in \{1,2\}}) = 1] - \Pr[\mathcal{A}(\mathbb{G}, \{[\mathbf{M}]_s, [\mathbf{U}]_s\}_{s \in \{1,2\}}) = 1] \big|$$

where $\mathbb{G} := (p, \mathbb{G}_1, \mathbb{G}_2, \mathbb{G}_T, e) \leftarrow \mathcal{G}(1^\lambda)$, $\mathbf{M} \leftarrow \mathbb{Z}_p^{\ell \times k}$, $\mathbf{S} \leftarrow \mathbb{Z}_p^{k \times m}$ and $\mathbf{U} \leftarrow \mathbb{Z}_p^{\ell \times m}$.

The BI-MDDH$_{k,\ell}^m$ assumption does not hold with parameter $k = 1$. For parameter $k > 1$, we have BI-MDDH$_{k,\ell}^m \Rightarrow$ MDDH$_{k,\ell}^m$. When $k = 2$, we call it *bilateral decisional linear (Bi-DLIN) assumption*.

2.3 Two-Slot IPFE over Bilinear Groups

We adapt Gong's two-slot IPFE over cyclic groups [13]. Let n, m represent two independent parameters. Here, we will focus on the following functionality:

$$\mathcal{X} = \mathbb{G}_1^n \times \mathbb{G}_1^m, \mathcal{Y} = \mathbb{G}_2^n \times \mathbb{G}_2^m, \mathcal{Z} = \mathbb{G}_T$$
$$\mathcal{F} : [\mathbf{x}_1, \mathbf{x}_2]_1 \times [\mathbf{y}_1, \mathbf{y}_2]_2 \mapsto [\mathbf{x}_1^\top \mathbf{y}_1 + \mathbf{x}_2^\top \mathbf{y}_2]_T$$

and equipped with two-slot IPFE simulator $(\widetilde{\mathsf{iSetup}}, \widetilde{\mathsf{iEnc}}, \widetilde{\mathsf{iKeyGen}})$ which takes a value from $\mathbb{G}_2$ as the last input for the SIM-security.

2.4 Trace-and-Revoke Functional Encryption

For set $\mathcal{X}, \mathcal{Y}, \mathcal{Z}$, we call $\mathcal{F} : \mathcal{X} \times \mathcal{Y} \to \mathcal{Z}$ an functionality which induces a family of functions mapping from $\mathcal{X}$ to $\mathcal{Z}$ indexed by $\mathcal{Y}$. Let p be a prime and $\mathcal{X} = \mathbb{Z}_p^n \times \mathbb{Z}_p^m, \mathcal{Y} = \mathbb{Z}_p^{nm}, \mathcal{Z} = \mathbb{Z}_p$ with some $n, m \in \mathbb{N}$. For $(\mathbf{x}_1, \mathbf{x}_2) \in \mathcal{X}, \mathbf{y} \in \mathcal{Y}$, we define the quadratic function (QF):

$$\mathcal{F}_{\mathsf{QF}} : ((\mathbf{x}_1, \mathbf{x}_2), \mathbf{y}) \mapsto \mathbf{y}^\top (\mathbf{x}_1 \otimes \mathbf{x}_2).$$

We follow the definition in [2] and a trace-and-revoke functional encryption scheme for functionality $\mathcal{F} : \mathcal{X} \times \mathcal{Y} \to \mathcal{Z}$ consists of the following five PPT algorithms:

- Setup$(1^\lambda, 1^N) \rightarrow (\mathsf{pk}, \mathsf{msk}, \mathsf{pd})$: The Setup algorithm takes security parameter 1^λ and the number of users 1^N as input, outputs master public/secret key pair $(\mathsf{pk}, \mathsf{msk})$ and an initially empty public directory pd.
- KeyGen$(\mathsf{msk}, y, i) \rightarrow (\mathsf{sk}_{y,i}, \mathsf{pd}_i)$: The KeyGen algorithm takes master secret key msk, function $y \in \mathcal{Y}$ and the index of user $i \in [N]$ as input, outputs a functional secret key sk_y and some public information pd_i for i.
- Enc$(\mathsf{pk}, x, \mathcal{R}) \rightarrow \mathsf{ct}_x$: The Enc algorithm takes public key pk, message $x \in \mathcal{X}$ and a revocation set $\mathcal{R}$ as input, outputs a ciphertext ct_x.
- Dec$(\mathsf{pd}, \mathsf{ct}_x, \mathsf{sk}_{y,i}) \rightarrow z$: The decryption algorithm takes public directory pd, a ciphertext ct_x and a functional secret key $\mathsf{sk}_{y,i}$ for user i as input, outputs $z \in \mathcal{Z}$.
- Trace$^D(\mathsf{msk}, \mathsf{pd}, \mathcal{R}, \mu(\cdot), x_0^*, x_1^*) \rightarrow \mathcal{T}$: The tracing algorithm takes $\mathsf{msk}, \mathsf{pd}$, $\mathcal{R} \subseteq [N]$, two messages $x_0^*, x_1^* \in \mathcal{X}$ which can be got from decoder D and $\mu(\cdot)$ denoting the probability that the decoder D can distinguish between the ciphertexts of x_0^* and x_1^* as input. It has oracle access to black-box decoder D and outputs a set $\mathcal{T}$ of traitor(s) which contains at least one identity $i^* \in [N]$ or $\perp$.

Correctness. We require that for all $\lambda \in \mathbb{N}$, $x \in \mathcal{X}$ and $y \in \mathcal{Y}$, $\mathcal{R} \subseteq [N]$, $i \in [N] \setminus \mathcal{R}$, it holds that

$$\Pr\left[\mathsf{Dec}(\mathsf{pd}, \mathsf{ct}_x, \mathsf{sk}_{y,i}) = \mathcal{F}(x, y) : \begin{array}{l} (\mathsf{pk}, \mathsf{msk}, \mathsf{pd}) \leftarrow \mathsf{Setup}(1^\lambda, 1^N) \\ (\mathsf{sk}_{y,i}, \mathsf{pd}_i) \leftarrow \mathsf{KeyGen}(\mathsf{msk}, y, i) \\ \mathsf{ct}_x \leftarrow \mathsf{Enc}(\mathsf{pk}, x, \mathcal{R}) \end{array} \right] = 1.$$

For quadratic function $\mathcal{F}_{\mathsf{QF}}$, as a relaxation, we require the correctness described above holds when $\mathcal{F}_{\mathsf{QF}}(x, y) \in B$ where $B \subseteq \mathbb{Z}_p$ has polynomial size [13,23].

Semi-adaptive Simulation-Based Security (SIM-security) [3]. There exists a simulator $(\widetilde{\mathsf{Setup}}, \widetilde{\mathsf{Enc}}, \widetilde{\mathsf{KeyGen}})$ such that: for every efficient stateful adversary $\mathcal{A}$, the advantage $\mathsf{Adv}_{\mathcal{A}}^{\mathsf{TFE}}$ in distinguishing the following two distributions are negligible in λ.

$$\left[\begin{array}{l} (\mathsf{mpk}, \mathsf{msk}) \leftarrow \mathsf{Setup}(1^\lambda, 1^N) \\ x^* \leftarrow \mathcal{A}(\mathsf{mpk}) \\ \mathsf{ct}^* \leftarrow \mathsf{Enc}(\mathsf{mpk}, x^*) \\ \textbf{output } \alpha \leftarrow \mathcal{A}^{\mathsf{KeyGen}(\mathsf{msk}, \cdot)}(\mathsf{mpk}, \mathsf{ct}^*) \end{array} \right] \quad \text{and} \quad \left[\begin{array}{l} (\mathsf{mpk}, \widetilde{\mathsf{msk}}) \leftarrow \widetilde{\mathsf{Setup}}(1^\lambda, 1^N) \\ x^* \leftarrow \mathcal{A}(\mathsf{mpk}) \\ \widetilde{\mathsf{ct}}^* \leftarrow \widetilde{\mathsf{Enc}}(\widetilde{\mathsf{msk}}) \\ \textbf{output } \alpha \leftarrow \mathcal{A}^{\widetilde{\mathsf{KeyGen}}(\widetilde{\mathsf{msk}}, \cdot, \cdot)}(\mathsf{mpk}, \widetilde{\mathsf{ct}}^*) \end{array} \right]$$

where $\widetilde{\mathsf{KeyGen}}(\widetilde{\mathsf{msk}}, \cdot, \cdot)$ gets y along with $\mathcal{F}(x^*, y)$ whenever $\mathcal{A}$ makes a query $y \in \mathcal{Y}$ to $\mathsf{KeyGen}(\mathsf{msk}, \cdot)$.

μ-useful Black-box Distinguisher D [10]. For all $\lambda \in \mathbb{N}, x \in \mathcal{X}$, set $\mathcal{R} \subseteq [N]$, $i \in [N]$, a non-negligible function $\mu(\cdot)$ in λ and every efficient stateful adversary $\mathcal{A}$, we define the advantage $\mathsf{Adv}_{\mathcal{A}}^D$ of black-box distinguisher D that $\mathcal{A}$ wins the following game $\mathsf{Exp}_b^D(1^\lambda, \mathcal{A})$ where

$$\mathsf{Adv}_{\mathcal{A}}^D = |1 - 2\Pr[\mathsf{Exp}_b^D(1^\lambda, \mathcal{A}) = 1]| \geq 2\mu(\lambda).$$

$$\begin{array}{|l|}
\hline
\mathsf{Exp}_b^D(1^\lambda, \mathcal{A}) \\
\hline
(\mathsf{pk}, \mathsf{msk}, \mathsf{pd}) \leftarrow \mathsf{Setup}(1^\lambda, 1^N) \\
(D, \mathcal{R}, x_0^*, x_1^*) \leftarrow \mathcal{A}^{\mathsf{KeyGen}(\mathsf{msk}, \cdot, \cdot)}(\mathsf{pk}) \\
b \leftarrow \{0,1\}, \mathsf{ct}_{x_b^*} \leftarrow \mathsf{Enc}(\mathsf{pk}, x_b^*, \mathcal{R}) \\
b' \leftarrow \mathcal{A}^D(\mathsf{ct}_{x_b^*}) \\
\textbf{output}\quad 1\quad \textit{if } b' = b, \quad 0 \quad \textit{otherwise} \\
\hline
\end{array}$$

where $\mathcal{A}$ makes secret key query with $y \in \mathcal{Y}$ and $i \in [N]$ to $\mathsf{KeyGen}(\mathsf{msk}, \cdot, \cdot)$ satisfying $\mathcal{F}(x_0^*, y) \neq \mathcal{F}(x_1^*, y)$.

In this paper, we call black-box distinguisher D is indeed μ-useful (μ-useful black-box distinguisher D) when $\mathsf{Adv}_{\mathcal{A}}^D \geq 2\mu(\lambda)$, i.e., it can distinguish between the encryption of two messages x_0^*, x_1^* (of the adversary's choice) with a non-negligible probability.

Traceability. Here, we show the definition of private black-box traceability. For every efficient stateful adversary $\mathcal{A}$, we define the advantage $\mathsf{Adv}_{\mathcal{A}}^{\mathsf{TFE,Tracing}}$ that $\mathcal{A}$ wins the following game:

- Setup : Challenger runs $(\mathsf{pk}, \mathsf{msk}, \mathsf{pd}) \leftarrow \mathsf{Setup}(1^\lambda, 1^N)$ and give pk to $\mathcal{A}$. In addition, challenger maintains the public directory pd.
- Key Query : $\mathcal{A}$ submit key query $(y, i) \in \mathcal{Y} \times [N]$, the challenger stores all these pairs and replies with the functional secret keys $\mathsf{sk}_{\mathbf{y}, i}$ for those queried pairs. Let $\mathcal{I}$ be the set of key queries performed by $\mathcal{A}$.
- Black-Box Distinguisher Generation : $\mathcal{A}$ outputs a revocation set $\mathcal{R} \subseteq [N]$, two messages $x_0^*, x_1^* \in \mathcal{X}$ such that $\mathcal{F}(x_0^*, y_i) \neq \mathcal{F}(x_1^*, y_i)$ for all $y_i \in \mathcal{Y}$ and $i \in \mathcal{I}$, and a μ-useful black-box distinguisher D.
- Output : The challenger runs $\mathsf{Trace}(\mathsf{pd}, \mathsf{msk}, \mathcal{R}, \mu(\cdot), x_0^*, x_1^*)$ and outputs an index set $\mathcal{T} \subseteq [N]$ of malicious users.

We say that the adversary $\mathcal{A}$ wins the game if the provided black-box distinguisher D is μ-useful; and $\mathcal{T} = \emptyset$ or $\mathcal{T} \not\subseteq I$.

Definition 1 (Black-box Traceability). *A traceable quadratic functional encryption scheme satisfies black-box traceability if for all PPT $\mathcal{A}$, the advantage $\mathsf{Adv}_{\mathcal{A}}^{\mathsf{TFE, Tracing}}$ is negligible for any μ-useful distinguisher D, where μ is non-negligible.*

3 Trace-and-Revoke Functional Encryption for Quadratic Functions

In this section, we present our trace-and-revoke quadratic function encryption (TRQFE) scheme, which achieves semi-adaptive simulation-based security under MDDH and Bı-MDDH assumption.

3.1 Scheme

Let the tuple $\mathsf{IPFE} = (\mathsf{iSetup}, \mathsf{iKeyGen}, \mathsf{iEnc}, \mathsf{iDec})$ be a two-slot IPFE scheme, as defined in Sect. 2.3. Our trace-and-revoke functional encryption scheme for quadratic functions works as follows.

- $\mathsf{Setup}(1^\lambda, 1^N) \rightarrow (\mathsf{pk}, \mathsf{msk}, \mathsf{pd})$: Algorithm runs $\mathbb{G} = (\mathbb{G}_1, \mathbb{G}_2, \mathbb{G}_T, e) \leftarrow \mathcal{G}(p)$ to generate bilinear group parameters and $(\mathsf{impk}, \mathsf{imsk}) \leftarrow \mathsf{iSetup}(1^\lambda, 1^{2nk\sqrt{t}})$. Sample $\mathbf{A}_1, \mathbf{A}_2 \leftarrow \mathbb{Z}_p^{n\sqrt{t} \times k}$ and outputs $\mathsf{pk} = (\mathbb{G}, [\mathbf{A}_1]_1, [\mathbf{A}_1]_2, [\mathbf{A}_2]_2, \mathsf{impk})$, a master secret key $\mathsf{msk} = \mathsf{imsk}$ and an initially empty public directory pd.
- $\mathsf{KeyGen}(\mathsf{msk}, \mathbf{y}, i) \rightarrow (\mathsf{sk}_{\mathbf{y},i}, \mathsf{pd}_i)$: Given the msk, a quadratic function $\mathbf{y} \in \mathbb{Z}_p^{n^2}$, and an index $i \in [N]$, it samples a vector $\mathbf{u}_i \leftarrow \mathbb{Z}_p^t$. The pair $\mathsf{pd}_i = (i, \mathbf{u}_i)$ is appended to the public directory pd. Then, output

$$\mathsf{sk}_{\mathbf{y},i} \leftarrow \mathsf{iKeyGen}\Big(\mathsf{msk}, [(\mathbf{y} \otimes \mathbf{u}_i)^\top \mathbf{T}(\mathbf{A}_1 \otimes \mathbf{I}_{n\sqrt{t}}), (\mathbf{y} \otimes \mathbf{u}_i)^\top \mathbf{T}(\mathbf{I}_{n\sqrt{t}} \otimes \mathbf{A}_2)]_2,$$

$$\underbrace{[(\mathbf{y} \otimes \mathbf{u}_i)^\top, 0]_2}_{\text{private slot of IPFE}}\Big)$$

  where the permutation matrix $\mathbf{T} \in \mathbb{Z}_p^{n^2 t \times n^2 t}$ is uniquely determined by n and $\sqrt{t}$.
- $\mathsf{Enc}(\mathsf{pk}, (\mathbf{x}_1, \mathbf{x}_2), \mathcal{R}) \rightarrow \mathsf{ct}$: Given the pk, vectors $(\mathbf{x}_1, \mathbf{x}_2) \in \mathbb{Z}_p^n \times \mathbb{Z}_p^n$, and a revocation set $\mathcal{R}$ where $|\mathcal{R}| \leq N$, it computes $\mathbf{v}_\mathcal{R} \in \mathbb{Z}_p^t \setminus \{\mathbf{0}\}$ such that $\mathbf{u}_j^\top \mathbf{v}_\mathcal{R} = 0$ for all $j \in \mathcal{R}$. Then, sample $\mathbf{s}_1, \mathbf{s}_2 \leftarrow \mathbb{Z}_p^k$ and compute

$$\mathbf{c}_1 = \mathbf{A}_1 \mathbf{s}_1 + \mathbf{x}_1 \otimes \mathbf{v}_{\mathcal{R},1}, \quad \mathbf{c}_2 = \mathbf{A}_2 \mathbf{s}_2 + \mathbf{x}_2 \otimes \mathbf{v}_{\mathcal{R},2},$$

$$\mathsf{ict} \leftarrow \mathsf{iEnc}(\mathsf{impk}, [\mathbf{s}_1 \otimes (\mathbf{x}_2 \otimes \mathbf{v}_{\mathcal{R},2}), \mathbf{c}_1 \otimes \mathbf{s}_2]_1, [\mathbf{0}]_1)$$

  where $\mathbf{v}_{\mathcal{R},1} \otimes \mathbf{v}_{\mathcal{R},2} = \mathbf{v}_\mathcal{R}$ and $\mathbf{v}_{\mathcal{R},1}, \mathbf{v}_{\mathcal{R},2} \in \mathbb{Z}_p^{\sqrt{t}}, \mathbf{0} \in \mathbb{Z}_p^{n^2 t + 1}$. Output the ciphertext as $\mathsf{ct} = ([\mathbf{c}_1]_1, [\mathbf{c}_2]_2, \mathsf{ict}, \mathcal{R})$.
- $\mathsf{Dec}(\mathsf{pd}, \mathsf{ct}, \mathsf{sk}_{\mathbf{y},i}) \rightarrow z$: Given the public directory pd, ciphertext ct, and functional secret key $\mathsf{sk}_{\mathbf{y},i}$, proceed as follows:
  1. Parse ct as $([\mathbf{c}_1]_1, [\mathbf{c}_2]_2, \mathsf{ict}, \mathcal{R})$. If $i \in \mathcal{R}$, then abort.
  2. Compute $\mathbf{v}_\mathcal{R} \in \mathbb{Z}_p^t \setminus \{\mathbf{0}\}$ such that $\mathbf{u}_j^\top \mathbf{v}_\mathcal{R} = 0$ for all $j \in \mathcal{R}$.
  3. Compute

$$[\hat{z}]_T = [(\mathbf{y} \otimes \mathbf{u}_i)^\top \mathbf{T} \cdot (\mathbf{c}_1 \otimes \mathbf{c}_2)]_T \cdot (\mathsf{iDec}(\mathsf{ict}, \mathsf{sk}_{\mathbf{y},i}))^{-1}$$

  and recover $\hat{z} \in \mathbb{Z}_p$ via discrete logarithm in basis $\mathbb{G}_T$. Finally, output

$$z = \frac{\hat{z}}{\mathbf{u}_i^\top \mathbf{v}_\mathcal{R}}.$$

- $\mathsf{Trace}^D(\mathsf{msk}, \mathsf{pd}, \mathcal{R}, \mu(\cdot), (\mathbf{x}_{0,1}^*, \mathbf{x}_{0,2}^*), (\mathbf{x}_{1,1}^*, \mathbf{x}_{1,2}^*)) \rightarrow \mathcal{T}$: The algorithm takes the master secret key msk, public directory pd, a revocation set $\mathcal{R} \subseteq [N]$, a non-negligible function $\mu(\cdot)$ in λ and two different tuples of vectors $(\mathbf{x}_{0,1}^*, \mathbf{x}_{0,2}^*) \in \mathbb{Z}_p^n \times \mathbb{Z}_p^n$, $(\mathbf{x}_{1,1}^*, \mathbf{x}_{1,2}^*) \in \mathbb{Z}_p^n \times \mathbb{Z}_p^n$ as input, and proceed as follows:
  1. Denote $S_i = \{i, i+1, \dots, N+1\} \setminus \mathcal{R}$ for each $i \in [N+1]$.

2. Compute $\mathbf{v}_{\mathcal{R}} \in \mathbb{Z}_p^t \setminus \{\mathbf{0}\}$ such that $\mathbf{u}_j^\top \mathbf{v}_{\mathcal{R}} = 0$ for all $j \in \mathcal{R}$. Find $\mathbf{v}_{\mathcal{R},1}, \mathbf{v}_{\mathcal{R},2} \in \mathbb{Z}_p^{\sqrt{t}}$ such that $\mathbf{v}_{\mathcal{R},1} \otimes \mathbf{v}_{\mathcal{R},2} = \mathbf{v}_{\mathcal{R}}$.

3. For $i = 1, 2, \ldots, N+1$, do:

   (a) Compute $\mathbf{v}_{S_i} \in \mathbb{Z}_p^t$ as follows:

   If $i = 1$, set $\mathbf{v}_{S_i} = \mathbf{0}$. If $i = N+1$, set $\mathbf{v}_{S_i} = \mathbf{v}_{\mathcal{R}}$. Otherwise, compute $\mathbf{v}_{S_i}$ such that:

   i. $\mathbf{u}_j^\top \mathbf{v}_{S_i} = 0$ for all $j \in S_i \cup \mathcal{R}$,

   ii. $\mathbf{u}_j^\top \mathbf{v}_{S_i} = \mathbf{u}_j^\top \mathbf{v}_{\mathcal{R}}$ for all $j \in S_1 \setminus S_i$.

   Then find $\mathbf{v}_{S_i,1}, \mathbf{v}_{S_i,2} \in \mathbb{Z}_p^{\sqrt{t}}$ such that $\mathbf{v}_{S_i,1} \otimes \mathbf{v}_{S_i,2} = \mathbf{v}_{S_i}$.

   (b) Let $\mathbf{count}_i = 0$.

   (c) Prepare and compute parts of the probe ciphertext as follows:

$$\tilde{\mathbf{x}}_{i,1}^* = \mathbf{x}_{0,1}^* \otimes \mathbf{v}_{S_i,1} + \mathbf{x}_{1,1}^* \otimes \mathbf{v}_{S_i,1}, \tilde{\mathbf{x}}_{i,2}^* = -\mathbf{x}_{0,2}^* \otimes \mathbf{v}_{S_i,2} + \mathbf{x}_{1,2}^* \otimes \mathbf{v}_{S_i,2},$$
$$\mathbf{c}_{i,3} = \mathbf{x}_{0,1}^* \otimes \mathbf{x}_{1,2}^* \otimes \mathbf{v}_{S_i} - \mathbf{x}_{1,1}^* \otimes \mathbf{x}_{0,2}^* \otimes \mathbf{v}_{S_i} - \mathbf{x}_{0,1}^* \otimes \mathbf{x}_{0,2}^* \otimes \mathbf{v}_{\mathcal{R}}.$$

$$(7)$$

   (d) For $l = 1, 2, \ldots, L = \lambda N^2/\mu(\lambda)$, do:

   i. Sample $\mathbf{s}_1, \mathbf{s}_2 \leftarrow \mathbb{Z}_p^k$, compute

$$\mathbf{c}_{i,1} = \mathbf{A}_1 \mathbf{s}_1 + \tilde{\mathbf{x}}_{i,1}^*, \quad \mathbf{c}_{i,2} = \mathbf{A}_2 \mathbf{s}_2 + \tilde{\mathbf{x}}_{i,2}^*,$$
$$\mathsf{ict}_i \leftarrow \mathsf{iEnc}\left(\mathsf{impk}, \mathsf{imsk}, [\mathbf{s}_1 \otimes \tilde{\mathbf{x}}_{i,2}^*, \mathbf{c}_{i,1} \otimes \mathbf{s}_2]_1, [\mathbf{c}_{i,3}, 0]_1\right)$$

$$(8)$$

   and compose the probe ciphertext $c_l^{S_i} = ([\mathbf{c}_{i,1}]_1, [\mathbf{c}_{i,2}]_2, \mathsf{ict}_i, \mathcal{R})$.

   ii. Feed D with $c_l^{S_i}$ and obtain a binary value b_l^i. If $b_l^i = 0$, then set $\mathbf{count}_i = \mathbf{count}_i + 1$.

   (e) Output $\tilde{P}_i = \mathbf{count}_i/N$.

4. Let $\mathcal{T}$ be the set of all $i \in [N]$ for which $|\tilde{P}_i - \tilde{P}_{i+1}| \geq \mu(\lambda)/N$. If there is no such i, assign $\mathcal{T} = \emptyset$. Finally, output the set $\mathcal{T}$ as malicious user(s).

For the correctness and the security proof, we require that $t > N$, and the vector $\mathbf{v}_{\mathcal{R}}$ should be uniquely determined by $\mathcal{R}$ and pd, in the same unique way across all algorithms (i.e., in algorithm Enc, step 2 of algorithm Dec, and step 2 of algorithm Trace) in the scheme. A trivial method is that sorting the vectors $\mathbf{u}_j (j \in \mathcal{R})$ based on numerical order or lexicographic order, and running a deterministic linear system solver. We remark that vector $\mathbf{v}_{S_i}$ in step 3.(a) of algorithm Trace should be computed in the same way.

As for splitting the vector $\mathbf{v}_{\mathcal{R}}$ (or $\mathbf{v}_{S_i}$) into the Kronecker product of two smaller vectors such that $\mathbf{v}_{\mathcal{R},1} \otimes \mathbf{v}_{\mathcal{R},2} = \mathbf{v}_{\mathcal{R}}$ (or $\mathbf{v}_{S_i,1} \otimes \mathbf{v}_{S_i,2} = \mathbf{v}_{S_i}$), this problem is well-known as *nearest Kronecker product* (or *Kronecker product approximation*), and can be solved by applying the *singular value decomposition* (SVD).

Remark 1. When we construct probe ciphertext c^{S_i}, encryption for ict_i requires imsk and the input of $\mathbf{c}_{i,3}$ in private slot of IPFE, so it follows that our scheme supports only *private* black-box traceability. It leaves as an open problem to construct a traceable QFE scheme which supports *public* black-box traceability.

Correctness. For all $\mathbf{x}_1, \mathbf{x}_2 \in \mathbb{Z}_p^n$ and $\mathbf{y} \in \mathbb{Z}_p^{n^2}$, we have

$$[z_1]_T := [(\mathbf{y} \otimes \mathbf{u}_i)^\top \mathbf{T}(\mathbf{c}_1 \otimes \mathbf{c}_2)]_T,$$

$$z_1 = \underbrace{(\mathbf{y} \otimes \mathbf{u}_i)^\top \mathbf{T}(\hat{\mathbf{x}}_1 \otimes \hat{\mathbf{x}}_2)}_{a_1} + \underbrace{(\mathbf{y} \otimes \mathbf{u}_i)^\top \mathbf{T}(\mathbf{A}_1 \mathbf{s}_1 \otimes \hat{\mathbf{x}}_2)}_{a_2} + \underbrace{(\mathbf{y} \otimes \mathbf{u}_i)^\top \mathbf{T}(\mathbf{c}_1 \otimes \mathbf{A}_2 \mathbf{s}_2)}_{a_3}$$

$$(9)$$

where $\hat{\mathbf{x}}_1 = \mathbf{x}_1 \otimes \mathbf{v}_{\mathcal{R},1}, \hat{\mathbf{x}}_2 = \mathbf{x}_2 \otimes \mathbf{v}_{\mathcal{R},2}$. By the correctness of underlying IPFE scheme, we have

$$
\begin{aligned}
[z_2]_T &:= \mathsf{iDec}(\mathsf{ict}, \mathsf{sk}_{\mathbf{y},i}) \\
&= \left[(\mathbf{y} \otimes \mathbf{u}_i)^\top \mathbf{T}(\mathbf{A}_1 \otimes \mathbf{I}_{n\sqrt{t}})(\mathbf{s}_1 \otimes \hat{\mathbf{x}}_2) + (\mathbf{y} \otimes \mathbf{u}_i)^\top \mathbf{T}(\mathbf{I}_{n\sqrt{t}} \otimes \mathbf{A}_2)(\mathbf{c}_1 \otimes \mathbf{s}_2) \right]_T \\
&= \left[\underbrace{(\mathbf{y} \otimes \mathbf{u}_i)^\top \mathbf{T}(\mathbf{A}_1 \mathbf{s}_1 \otimes \hat{\mathbf{x}}_2)}_{a_2} + \underbrace{(\mathbf{y} \otimes \mathbf{u}_i)^\top \mathbf{T}(\mathbf{c}_1 \otimes \mathbf{A}_2 \mathbf{s}_2)}_{a_3} \right]_T
\end{aligned}
$$

$$(10)$$

where the equality uses the mixed-product property of the Kronecker product. According to equality (9) and (10), we have $[\hat{z}]_T = [z_1]_T \cdot [z_2]_T^{-1} = [z_1 - z_2]_T$ where

$$
\begin{aligned}
\hat{z} = z_1 - z_2 &= \underbrace{(\mathbf{y} \otimes \mathbf{u}_i)^\top \mathbf{T}(\hat{\mathbf{x}}_1 \otimes \hat{\mathbf{x}}_2)}_{a_1} \\
&= (\mathbf{y} \otimes \mathbf{u}_i)^\top \mathbf{T}(\mathbf{x}_1 \otimes \mathbf{v}_{\mathcal{R},1} \otimes \mathbf{x}_2 \otimes \mathbf{v}_{\mathcal{R},2}) \\
&= (\mathbf{y} \otimes \mathbf{u}_i)^\top (\mathbf{x}_1 \otimes \mathbf{x}_2 \otimes \mathbf{v}_{\mathcal{R},1} \otimes \mathbf{v}_{\mathcal{R},2}) = (\mathbf{y}^\top \otimes \mathbf{u}_i^\top)((\mathbf{x}_1 \otimes \mathbf{x}_2) \otimes \mathbf{v}_{\mathcal{R}}) \\
&= \mathbf{y}^\top (\mathbf{x}_1 \otimes \mathbf{x}_2) \otimes \mathbf{u}_i^\top \mathbf{v}_{\mathcal{R}} = \mathbf{y}^\top (\mathbf{x}_1 \otimes \mathbf{x}_2) \cdot \mathbf{u}_i^\top \mathbf{v}_{\mathcal{R}}
\end{aligned}
$$

$$(11)$$

Correctness then follows readily.

3.2 Simulator

Before proceeding the security proof, we first describe the simulator. Let $(\widetilde{\mathsf{iSetup}},$ $\widetilde{\mathsf{iKeyGen}}, \widetilde{\mathsf{iEnc}})$ be the simulator of underlying IPFE scheme, the simulator of our scheme works as follows.

- $\widetilde{\mathsf{Setup}}(1^\lambda, 1^N)$: Run $\mathbb{G} = (\mathbb{G}_1, \mathbb{G}_2, \mathbb{G}_T, e) \leftarrow \mathcal{G}(p)$. Sample

$$\mathbf{A}_1, \mathbf{A}_2 \leftarrow \mathbb{Z}_p^{n\sqrt{t} \times k}, \quad \mathbf{u}_i \leftarrow \mathbb{Z}_p^t \text{ for all } i \in [N], \quad (\mathsf{impk}, \widetilde{\mathsf{imsk}}) \leftarrow \widetilde{\mathsf{iSetup}}(1^\lambda, 1^{2nk\sqrt{t}})$$

and set $\mathsf{pd} := \{(i, \mathbf{u}_i)\}$. Then output

$$\mathsf{pk} = (\mathbb{G}, [\mathbf{A}_1]_1, [\mathbf{A}_1]_2, [\mathbf{A}_2]_2, \widetilde{\mathsf{impk}}) \quad \text{and} \quad \widetilde{\mathsf{msk}} = (\widetilde{\mathsf{imsk}}, \mathbf{A}_1, \mathbf{A}_2, \mathsf{pd}).$$

- $\widetilde{\mathsf{KeyGen}}(\widetilde{\mathsf{msk}}, \mathbf{y}, i)$: Sample $\mathbf{c}_1, \mathbf{c}_2 \leftarrow \mathbb{Z}_p^{n\sqrt{t}}$ and output

$$\mathsf{sk}_{\mathbf{y},i} \leftarrow \widetilde{\mathsf{iKeyGen}}\Big(\widetilde{\mathsf{imsk}}, \big[(\mathbf{y} \otimes \mathbf{u}_i)^\top \mathbf{T}(\mathbf{A}_1 \otimes \mathbf{I}_{n\sqrt{t}}), (\mathbf{y} \otimes \mathbf{u}_i)^\top \mathbf{T}(\mathbf{I}_{n\sqrt{t}} \otimes \mathbf{A}_2)\big]_2,$$

$$\big[(\mathbf{y} \otimes \mathbf{u}_i)^\top, (\mathbf{y} \otimes \mathbf{u}_i)^\top \mathbf{T}(\mathbf{c}_1 \otimes \mathbf{c}_2) - \mu\big]_2\Big).$$

- $\widetilde{\mathsf{Enc}}(\widetilde{\mathsf{imsk}}, \mathcal{R})$: Output $\widetilde{\mathsf{ct}} = \Big([\mathbf{c}_1]_1, [\mathbf{c}_2]_2, \widetilde{\mathsf{iEnc}}(\widetilde{\mathsf{imsk}}), \mathcal{R}\Big)$.

3.3 Security

Theorem 1. *Under the* MDDH *and* BI-MDDH *assumption on* $\mathbb{G}_1, \mathbb{G}_2$, *if the underlying* IPFE *satisfies semi-adaptive SIM-security as defined in Sect. 2.4, our TRQFE scheme achieves semi-adaptive SIM-security.*

Proof. We proceed via a series of games. Let $\mathbf{y}, (\mathbf{x}_1, \mathbf{x}_2)$ be the semi-adaptive challenge. Considering a fixed revocation set $\mathcal{R}$ and its derived vectors $\mathbf{v}_{\mathcal{R}} = \mathbf{v}_{\mathcal{R},1} \otimes \mathbf{v}_{\mathcal{R},2} \in \mathbb{Z}_p^t$ (where $\mathbf{v}_{\mathcal{R},1}, \mathbf{v}_{\mathcal{R},2} \in \mathbb{Z}_p^{\sqrt{t}}$) as described in algorithm Enc, across all the games.

Game 0. Real Game.

Game 1. Identical to Game_0 except we replace $(\mathsf{iSetup}, \mathsf{iKeyGen}, \mathsf{iEnc})$ with $(\widetilde{\mathsf{iSetup}}, \widetilde{\mathsf{iKeyGen}}, \widetilde{\mathsf{iEnc}})$. The challenge ciphertext and secret key for $(\mathbf{y}, i)$ are as follows:

$$\widetilde{\mathsf{ct}} = \left([\mathbf{c}_1]_1, [\mathbf{c}_2]_2, \widetilde{\mathsf{iEnc}}(\widetilde{\mathsf{imsk}}), \mathcal{R} \right)$$

$$\mathsf{sk}_{\mathbf{y},i} \leftarrow \widetilde{\mathsf{iKeyGen}}\left(\widetilde{\mathsf{imsk}}, \left[(\mathbf{y} \otimes \mathbf{u}_i)^\top \mathbf{T}(\mathbf{A}_1 \otimes \mathbf{I}_{n\sqrt{t}}), (\mathbf{y} \otimes \mathbf{u}_i)^\top \mathbf{T}(\mathbf{I}_{n\sqrt{t}} \otimes \mathbf{A}_2) \right]_2, \right.$$
$$\left. \left[(\mathbf{y} \otimes \mathbf{u}_i)^\top, \boxed{(\mathbf{y} \otimes \mathbf{u}_i)^\top \mathbf{T}\left(\mathbf{A}_1 \mathbf{s}_1 \otimes (\mathbf{x}_2 \otimes \mathbf{v}_{\mathcal{R},2}) + \mathbf{c}_1 \otimes \mathbf{A}_2 \mathbf{s}_2 \right)} \right]_2 \right)$$

where $\mathbf{c}_1 = \mathbf{A}_1 \mathbf{s}_1 + \mathbf{x}_1 \otimes \mathbf{v}_{\mathcal{R},1}, \mathbf{c}_2 = \mathbf{A}_2 \mathbf{s}_2 + \mathbf{x}_2 \otimes \mathbf{v}_{\mathcal{R},2}$. We have $\mathsf{Game}_0 \approx_c \mathsf{Game}_1$ by the security of underlying IPFE scheme. The reduction samples

$$\mathbf{A}_1, \mathbf{A}_2 \leftarrow \mathbb{Z}_p^{n\sqrt{t} \times k}, \quad \mathbf{s}_1, \mathbf{s}_2 \leftarrow \mathbb{Z}_p^k$$

and upon receiving $\mathbf{y}, (\mathbf{x}_1, \mathbf{x}_2)$ from $\mathcal{A}$, submits $[\mathbf{s}_1 \otimes (\mathbf{x}_2 \otimes \mathbf{v}_{\mathcal{R},2}), \mathbf{c}_1 \otimes \mathbf{s}_2]_1$ as the semi-adaptive challenge of IPFE.

Game 2. Identical to Game_1 except we replace $\mathsf{sk}_{\mathbf{y},i}$ with

$$\mathsf{sk}_{\mathbf{y},i} \leftarrow \widetilde{\mathsf{iKeyGen}}\left(\widetilde{\mathsf{imsk}}, \left[(\mathbf{y} \otimes \mathbf{u}_i)^\top \mathbf{T}(\mathbf{A}_1 \otimes \mathbf{I}_{n\sqrt{t}}), (\mathbf{y} \otimes \mathbf{u}_i)^\top \mathbf{T}(\mathbf{I}_{n\sqrt{t}} \otimes \mathbf{A}_2) \right]_2, \right.$$
$$\left. \left[(\mathbf{y} \otimes \mathbf{u}_i)^\top, \boxed{(\mathbf{y} \otimes \mathbf{u}_i)^\top \mathbf{T}(\mathbf{c}_1 \otimes \mathbf{c}_2) - \mathbf{y}^\top (\mathbf{x}_1 \otimes \mathbf{x}_2) \cdot \mathbf{u}_i^\top \mathbf{v}_{\mathcal{R}}} \right]_2 \right).$$

We have $\mathsf{Game}_2 \equiv \mathsf{Game}_1$ according to the correctness (11), which tells us that

$$(\mathbf{y} \otimes \mathbf{u}_i)^\top \mathbf{T}(\mathbf{c}_1 \otimes \mathbf{c}_2) - \mathbf{y}^\top (\mathbf{x}_1 \otimes \mathbf{x}_2) \cdot \mathbf{u}_i^\top \mathbf{v}_{\mathcal{R}} = (\mathbf{y} \otimes \mathbf{u}_i)^\top \mathbf{T}\left(\mathbf{A}_1 \mathbf{s}_1 \otimes (\mathbf{x}_2 \otimes \mathbf{v}_{\mathcal{R},2}) + \mathbf{c}_1 \otimes \mathbf{A}_2 \mathbf{s}_2 \right).$$

Game 3. Identical to Game_2 except we replace $\boxed{[\mathbf{A}_1 \mathbf{s}_1 + \mathbf{x}_1 \otimes \mathbf{v}_{\mathcal{R},1}]_1}$ in $\widetilde{\mathsf{ct}}$ with $\boxed{[\mathbf{c}_1]_1}$ where $\mathbf{c}_1 \leftarrow \mathbb{Z}_p^{n\sqrt{t}}$. Then we have $\mathsf{Game}_3 \approx_c \mathsf{Game}_2$ via BI-MDDH$^1_{k, n\sqrt{t}}$ assumption, which tells us that for all $\mathbf{x}_1$,

$$([\mathbf{A}_1]_1, [\mathbf{A}_1]_2, [\mathbf{A}_1 \mathbf{s} + \mathbf{x}_1 \otimes \mathbf{v}_{\mathcal{R},1}]_1, [\mathbf{A}_1 \mathbf{s} + \mathbf{x}_1 \otimes \mathbf{v}_{\mathcal{R},1}]_2) \approx_c ([\mathbf{A}_1]_1, [\mathbf{A}_1]_2, [\mathbf{c}_1]_1, [\mathbf{c}_1]_2)$$

where $\mathbf{s} \leftarrow \mathbb{Z}_p^k, \mathbf{c}_1 \leftarrow \mathbb{Z}_p^{n\sqrt{t}}$. The reduction then samples

$$\mathbf{A}_2 \leftarrow \mathbb{Z}_p^{n\sqrt{t} \times k}, \quad \mathbf{s}_2 \leftarrow \mathbb{Z}_p^k, \quad (\mathsf{impk}, \widetilde{\mathsf{imsk}}) \leftarrow \widetilde{\mathsf{iSetup}}(1^\lambda, 1^{2nk\sqrt{t}})$$

and sets $\mathbf{c}_2 := \mathbf{A}_2\mathbf{s}_2 + \mathbf{x}_2 \otimes \mathbf{v}_{\mathcal{R},2}$. Note that we can compute pk and $\widetilde{\mathsf{ct}}$ given $[\mathbf{A}_1]_1, [\mathbf{A}_1]_2, [\mathbf{c}_1]_1$. And we can sample $\mathsf{sk}_{\mathbf{y},i}$ by computing $[\mathbf{c}_1 \otimes \mathbf{c}_2]_2$ given $[\mathbf{c}_1]_2, \mathbf{c}_2$.

Game 4. Identical to Game_3 except we replace $\boxed{[\mathbf{A}_2\mathbf{s}_2 + \mathbf{x}_2 \otimes \mathbf{v}_{\mathcal{R},2}]_2}$ in $\widetilde{\mathsf{ct}}$ with $\boxed{[\mathbf{c}_2]_2}$ where $\mathbf{c}_2 \leftarrow \mathbb{Z}_p^{n\sqrt{t}}$. Then we have $\mathsf{Game}_4 \approx_c \mathsf{Game}_3$ via $\mathrm{MDDH}_{k,n\sqrt{t}}^1$ assumption, which tells us that for all $\mathbf{x}_2$,

$$([\mathbf{A}_2]_2, [\mathbf{A}_2\mathbf{s} + \mathbf{x}_2 \otimes \mathbf{v}_{\mathcal{R},2}]_2) \approx_c ([\mathbf{A}_2]_2, [\mathbf{c}_2]_2),$$

where $\mathbf{s} \leftarrow \mathbb{Z}_p^k, \mathbf{c}_2 \leftarrow \mathbb{Z}_p^{n\sqrt{t}}$.

Finally, the Game_4 is exactly the output of the simulator described in Sect. 3.2 by setting $\mu = \mathbf{y}^\top(\mathbf{x}_1 \otimes \mathbf{x}_2) \cdot \mathbf{u}_i^\top \mathbf{v}_{\mathcal{R}}$.

4   Traceability

In this section, we prove the traceability of our TRQFE scheme. We start with the following lemma.

Lemma 2. *Given a μ-useful black-box distinguisher D, two different tuples of vectors $(\mathbf{x}_{0,1}^*, \mathbf{x}_{0,2}^*), (\mathbf{x}_{1,1}^*, \mathbf{x}_{1,2}^*)$, and a revocation set $\mathcal{R}^*$ of up to N revoked users, then the algorithm Trace interacting with D does not return $\emptyset$ with overwhelming probability. Furthermore, for $\mathcal{T} \neq \emptyset$, D contains the secret keys for all $i \in \mathcal{T}$.*

Proof. We first demonstrate the core properties of probe ciphertext c^{S_i}, which is defined in the algorithm Trace of Sect. 3.1. Follow the correctness (11), we know that the decryption of probe ciphertext $c^{S_i} = ([\mathbf{c}_{i,1}]_1, [\mathbf{c}_{i,2}]_2, \mathsf{ict}_i, \mathcal{R}^*)$, by functional secret key $\mathsf{sk}_{\mathbf{y},j}$ of user $j \in [N]$, reveals $[\hat{z}_{ij}]_T = [z_{ij,1} - z_{ij,2}]_T$. Recalling the variables assignment in (7) and (8) of algorithm Trace, we have

$$
\begin{aligned}
z_{ij,1} &:= (\mathbf{y} \otimes \mathbf{u}_j)^\top \mathbf{T}(\mathbf{c}_{i,1} \otimes \mathbf{c}_{i,2}) \\
&= \underbrace{(\mathbf{y} \otimes \mathbf{u}_j)^\top \mathbf{T}(\tilde{\mathbf{x}}_{i,1}^* \otimes \tilde{\mathbf{x}}_{i,2}^*)}_{b_1} + \underbrace{(\mathbf{y} \otimes \mathbf{u}_j)^\top \mathbf{T}(\mathbf{A}_1\mathbf{s}_1 \otimes \tilde{\mathbf{x}}_{i,2}^*)}_{b_2} + \underbrace{(\mathbf{y} \otimes \mathbf{u}_j)^\top \mathbf{T}(\mathbf{c}_{i,1} \otimes \mathbf{A}_2\mathbf{s}_2)}_{b_3}
\end{aligned}
$$

$$
\begin{aligned}
z_{ij,2} &:= \mathsf{iDec}(\mathsf{ict}_i, \mathsf{sk}_{\mathbf{y},j}) \\
&= \underbrace{(\mathbf{y} \otimes \mathbf{u}_j)^\top \mathbf{T}(\mathbf{A}_1\mathbf{s}_1 \otimes \tilde{\mathbf{x}}_{i,2}^*)}_{b_2} + \underbrace{(\mathbf{y} \otimes \mathbf{u}_j)^\top \mathbf{T}(\mathbf{c}_{i,1} \otimes \mathbf{A}_2\mathbf{s}_2)}_{b_3} + \underbrace{(\mathbf{y} \otimes \mathbf{u}_j)^\top \mathbf{c}_{i,3}}_{b_4}
\end{aligned}
$$

$$
\hat{z}_{ij} = z_{ij,1} - z_{ij,2} = \underbrace{(\mathbf{y} \otimes \mathbf{u}_j)^\top \mathbf{T}(\tilde{\mathbf{x}}_{i,1}^* \otimes \tilde{\mathbf{x}}_{i,2}^*)}_{b_1} - \underbrace{(\mathbf{y} \otimes \mathbf{u}_j)^\top \mathbf{c}_{i,3}}_{b_4}
$$

where $\mathbf{T}(\tilde{\mathbf{x}}_{i,1}^* \otimes \tilde{\mathbf{x}}_{i,2}^*) - \mathbf{c}_{i,3} = -\mathbf{x}_{0,1}^* \otimes \mathbf{x}_{0,2}^* \otimes \mathbf{v}_{S_i} + \mathbf{x}_{1,1}^* \otimes \mathbf{x}_{1,2}^* \otimes \mathbf{v}_{S_i} + \mathbf{x}_{0,1}^* \otimes \mathbf{x}_{0,2}^* \otimes \mathbf{v}_{\mathcal{R}^*}$.
The construction of $\mathbf{c}_{i,3}$ exactly cancels the cross terms that come from $\tilde{\mathbf{x}}_{i,1}^* \otimes \tilde{\mathbf{x}}_{i,2}^*$.
Hence we know that

$$
\begin{aligned}
\hat{z}_{ij} &= (\mathbf{y} \otimes \mathbf{u}_j)^\top (-\mathbf{x}_{0,1}^* \otimes \mathbf{x}_{0,2}^* \otimes \mathbf{v}_{S_i} + \mathbf{x}_{1,1}^* \otimes \mathbf{x}_{1,2}^* \otimes \mathbf{v}_{S_i} + \mathbf{x}_{0,1}^* \otimes \mathbf{x}_{0,2}^* \otimes \mathbf{v}_{\mathcal{R}^*}) \\
&= -\mathbf{y}^\top (\mathbf{x}_{0,1}^* \otimes \mathbf{x}_{0,2}^*) \cdot \mathbf{u}_j^\top \mathbf{v}_{S_i} + \mathbf{y}^\top (\mathbf{x}_{1,1}^* \otimes \mathbf{x}_{1,2}^*) \cdot \mathbf{u}_j^\top \mathbf{v}_{S_i} + \mathbf{y}^\top (\mathbf{x}_{0,1}^* \otimes \mathbf{x}_{0,2}^*) \cdot \mathbf{u}_j^\top \mathbf{v}_{\mathcal{R}^*} \\
&= \mathbf{y}^\top (\mathbf{x}_{0,1}^* \otimes \mathbf{x}_{0,2}^*) \cdot (\mathbf{u}_j^\top \mathbf{v}_{\mathcal{R}} - \mathbf{u}_j^\top \mathbf{v}_{S_i}) + \mathbf{y}^\top (\mathbf{x}_{1,1}^* \otimes \mathbf{x}_{1,2}^*) \cdot \mathbf{u}_j^\top \mathbf{v}_{S_i}.
\end{aligned}
$$

Further, considering the properties of $\mathbf{v}_{S_i}$ and $\mathbf{v}_{S_{i+1}}$, we have

$$
\begin{aligned}
\hat{z}_{ij} &= \begin{cases} \mathbf{y}^\top (\mathbf{x}_{0,1}^* \otimes \mathbf{x}_{0,2}^*) \cdot \mathbf{u}_j^\top \mathbf{v}_{\mathcal{R}^*}, & \text{if } j \in S_i \cup \mathcal{R}^*, \\ \mathbf{y}^\top (\mathbf{x}_{1,1}^* \otimes \mathbf{x}_{1,2}^*) \cdot \mathbf{u}_j^\top \mathbf{v}_{\mathcal{R}^*}, & \text{if } j \in S_1 \setminus S_i, \end{cases} \\
\hat{z}_{(i+1)j} &= \begin{cases} \mathbf{y}^\top (\mathbf{x}_{0,1}^* \otimes \mathbf{x}_{0,2}^*) \cdot \mathbf{u}_j^\top \mathbf{v}_{\mathcal{R}^*}, & \text{if } j \in S_{i+1} \cup \mathcal{R}^*, \\ \mathbf{y}^\top (\mathbf{x}_{1,1}^* \otimes \mathbf{x}_{1,2}^*) \cdot \mathbf{u}_j^\top \mathbf{v}_{\mathcal{R}^*}, & \text{if } j \in S_1 \setminus S_{i+1}. \end{cases}
\end{aligned}
\tag{12}
$$

Therefore, $\hat{z}_{ij} = \hat{z}_{(i+1)j}$ holds for any $j \in [N] \setminus \{i\}$. That is, the decryption results of the probe ciphertexts $c^{S_i}, c^{S_{i+1}}$ are the same under all secret keys, except for $\mathsf{sk}_{\mathbf{y},i}$. It implies that no adversary can distinguish between the probe ciphertexts c^{S_i} and $c^{S_{i+1}}$ without having the functional secret key for the user of index i.

We now show that the algorithm Trace will output at least one index $i \in [N]$ of malicious user(s). Let $P_i = \Pr[D(c^{S_i}) = 0 : c^{S_i}]$ for $i \in [N+1]$, where $c^{S_i} = ([\mathbf{c}_{i,1}]_1, [\mathbf{c}_{i,2}]_2, \mathsf{ict}_i, \mathcal{R}^*)$ is the probe ciphertext as described in algorithm Trace. We already know that the decryption of c^{S_i}, by secret key $\mathsf{sk}_{\mathbf{y},j}$ of user $j \in [N]$, gives

$$
\hat{z}_{ij} = \mathbf{y}^\top (\mathbf{x}_{0,1}^* \otimes \mathbf{x}_{0,2}^*) \cdot (\mathbf{u}_j^\top \mathbf{v}_{\mathcal{R}} - \mathbf{u}_j^\top \mathbf{v}_{S_i}) + \mathbf{y}^\top (\mathbf{x}_{1,1}^* \otimes \mathbf{x}_{1,2}^*) \cdot \mathbf{u}_j^\top \mathbf{v}_{S_i}.
$$

Since $\mathbf{v}_{S_1} = \mathbf{0}$ and $\mathbf{v}_{S_{N+1}} = \mathbf{v}_{\mathcal{R}^*}$, it implies that c^{S_1} and $c^{S_{N+1}}$ are the genuine encryption of the message vectors $(\mathbf{x}_{0,1}^*, \mathbf{x}_{0,2}^*)$ and $(\mathbf{x}_{1,1}^*, \mathbf{x}_{1,2}^*)$, respectively. According the definition of μ-useful black-box distinguisher, we have $|P_1 - P_{N+1}| \geq 2\mu(\lambda)$. Hence there exists at least one index $i \in [N]$ such that $|P_i - P_{i+1}| \geq 2\mu(\lambda)/N$ by the triangle inequality. Applying Lemma 1 about Chernoff bound, since the number of times $L = \lambda N^2/\mu(\lambda)$, we have $|\tilde{P}_i - P_i| \leq \mu(\lambda)/2N$ for all $i \in [N]$ with overwhelming probability. Therefore, $|\tilde{P}_i - \tilde{P}_{i+1}| \geq 2\mu(\lambda)/N - 2(\mu(\lambda)/2N) = \mu(\lambda)/N$, which implies that the algorithm Trace will output at least one such index $i \in [N]$.

We conclude that $|\tilde{P}_i - \tilde{P}_{i+1}| \geq \mu(\lambda)/N$ holds for all $i \in \mathcal{T}$. We already show that D cannot distinguish between c^{S_i} and $c^{S_{i+1}}$ without having the secret key for the index $i \in \mathcal{T}$ by the security of our TRQFE scheme. On the contrary, if D does not hold the secret key $\mathsf{sk}_{\mathbf{y},i}$ for $i \in \mathcal{T}$, we cannot observe that $|\tilde{P}_i - \tilde{P}_{i+1}| \geq \mu(\lambda)/N$.

Then, we prove the black-box traceability of our scheme.

Theorem 2. *Under the* MDDH *and* BI-MDDH *assumption on* $\mathbb{G}_1, \mathbb{G}_2$, *if the underlying* IPFE *satisfies semi-adaptive SIM-security, our TRQFE scheme satisfies private black-box traceability as defined in Definition 1.*

Proof. Suppose that an adversary $\mathcal{A}$ can break the black-box traceability with non-negligible probability. We will build a probabilistic polynomial-time adversary $\mathcal{B}$ that breaks the semi-adaptive SIM-security of our TRQFE scheme. We adapt the security game from [20] into the context of QFE. $\mathcal{A}$, $\mathcal{B}$ and the TRQFE challenger proceed as follows:

- **Setup:** The challenger runs $(\mathsf{pk}, \mathsf{msk}, \mathsf{pd}) \leftarrow \mathsf{Setup}(1^\lambda, 1^N)$. $\mathcal{B}$ obtains the public key $\mathsf{pk} = (\mathbb{G}, [\mathbf{A}_1]_1, [\mathbf{A}_1]_2, [\mathbf{A}_2]_2, \mathsf{impk})$ and relays it to $\mathcal{A}$. Note that pd is an initially empty public directory.
- **Query:**
  - **Public Information Query.** When $\mathcal{A}$ asks an index $i \in [N]$, $\mathcal{B}$ sample a vector $u_i \leftarrow \mathbb{Z}_p^t$ and sends it to $\mathcal{A}$. And $\mathcal{B}$ set $\mathsf{pd}_i = (i, u_i)$ and updates the public directory $\mathsf{pd} = \mathsf{pd} \cup \{\mathsf{pd}_i\}$.
  - **Revoked User's Key Query.** This query can be made only once. $\mathcal{A}$ submit a set $\mathcal{R}^*$ of up to N revoked users, and the corresponding function vectors $\mathbf{y}_j^* \in \mathcal{Y}$ for all $j \in \mathcal{R}^*$. For any index $j \in \mathcal{R}^*$ such that $\mathsf{pd}_j \notin \mathsf{pd}$, $\mathcal{B}$ generates pd_j and updates the public directory $\mathsf{pd} = \mathsf{pd} \cup \{\mathsf{pd}_j\}$. Then $\mathcal{B}$ forwards to the challenger who runs $(\mathsf{sk}_{\mathbf{y}_j^*, j}, \mathsf{pd}_j) \leftarrow \mathsf{KeyGen}(\mathsf{msk}, \mathbf{y}_j^*, j)$, and returns all the secret keys $\mathsf{sk}_{\mathbf{y}_j^*, j}$ for all $j \in \mathcal{R}^*$.
  - **Non-Revoked User's Key Query.** When $\mathcal{A}$ makes a secret key query for a pair $(i, y) \in [N] \times \mathcal{Y}$, $\mathcal{B}$ updates the set of queried pairs $\mathcal{Q} = \mathcal{Q} \cup \{(i, y)\}$ and the set of queried indices $\mathcal{I} = \mathcal{I} \cup \{i\}$. If $\mathsf{pd}_i \notin \mathsf{pd}$, $\mathcal{B}$ generates pd_i and updates the public directory $\mathsf{pd} = \mathsf{pd} \cup \{\mathsf{pd}_i\}$. Then $\mathcal{B}$ forwards to the challenger who runs $(\mathsf{sk}_{\mathbf{y}, i}, \mathsf{pd}_i) \leftarrow \mathsf{KeyGen}(\mathsf{msk}, \mathbf{y}, j)$, and returns the secret keys $\mathsf{sk}_{\mathbf{y}, i}$.
- **Black-box Distinguisher Generation:** $\mathcal{A}$ outputs a μ-useful black-box distinguisher D and two different tuples of vectors $(\mathbf{x}_{0,1}^*, \mathbf{x}_{0,2}^*) \in \mathbb{Z}_p^n \times \mathbb{Z}_p^n$, $(\mathbf{x}_{1,1}^*, \mathbf{x}_{1,2}^*) \in \mathbb{Z}_p^n \times \mathbb{Z}_p^n$ such that $\mathbf{y}^\top(\mathbf{x}_{0,1}^* \otimes \mathbf{x}_{0,2}^*) \neq \mathbf{y}^\top(\mathbf{x}_{1,1}^* \otimes \mathbf{x}_{1,2}^*)$ for all functions $\mathbf{y} \in \mathcal{Q}$. $\mathcal{B}$ forwards to the challenger who runs Trace^D, and generates $\tilde{\mathbf{x}}_{i,1}^*, \tilde{\mathbf{x}}_{i,2}^*, \mathbf{c}_{i,3}$ for all $i \in [N]$, as described in (7) of algorithm Trace. Then the challenger outputs a set $\mathcal{T}$.
- **Output:** Suppose that $\mathcal{A}$ breaks the private black-box traceability, that is, D is indeed μ-useful and $\mathcal{T} = \emptyset$ or $\mathcal{T} \not\subseteq \mathcal{I}$. If $\mathcal{T} = \emptyset$, $\mathcal{B}$ aborts. Otherwise, $\mathcal{B}$ chooses a random index r such that $r \in \mathcal{T}$ but $r \notin \mathcal{I}$, and sends r to the challenger. Then challenger generates two probe ciphertexts $c^{S_r}, c^{S_{r+1}}$ as described in (8) of algorithm Trace. Take c^{S_r} for example, that is,

$$\mathbf{s}_1, \mathbf{s}_2 \leftarrow \mathbb{Z}_p^k, \quad \mathbf{c}_{r,1} = \mathbf{A}_1 \mathbf{s}_1 + \tilde{\mathbf{x}}_{r,1}^*, \quad \mathbf{c}_{r,2} = \mathbf{A}_2 \mathbf{s}_2 + \tilde{\mathbf{x}}_{r,2}^*,$$

$$\mathsf{ict}_r \leftarrow \mathsf{iEnc}\left(\mathsf{impk}, \mathsf{imsk}, [\mathbf{s}_1 \otimes \tilde{\mathbf{x}}_{r,2}^*, \mathbf{c}_{r,1} \otimes \mathbf{s}_2]_1, [\mathbf{c}_{r,3}, 0]_1\right),$$

$$c^{S_r} = ([\mathbf{c}_{r,1}]_1, [\mathbf{c}_{r,2}]_2, \mathsf{ict}_r, \mathcal{R}^*).$$

The challenger sample a random bit $b \leftarrow \{0, 1\}$ to decide which ciphertext to return to $\mathcal{B}$. If $b = 0$, let $c_b^* = c^{S_r}$. Otherwise, let $c_b^* = c^{S_{r+1}}$. Upon receiving the challenge ciphertext c_b^* from the challenger, $\mathcal{B}$ runs D on c_b^* which outputs a bit $b' \in \{0, 1\}$. If $b' = b$ we say that $\mathcal{B}$ succeeds.

Based on Lemma 2, we already know that the set $\mathcal{T}$, which is output by running algorithm Trace on D, contains at least one user index $i \in [N]$ with overwhelming probability, and D contains the secret keys for all $i \in \mathcal{T}$. Besides, equations (12) tell us that D can only distinguish between $c_0^* = c^{S_r}$ and $c_1^* = c^{S_{r+1}}$ when it holds the secret key for the index $r \in \mathcal{T}$. We conclude that D holds the secret key for index r since $r \in \mathcal{T}$, and so that D is able to distinguish between c_0^* and c_1^*. Formally, the decryption of $c_0^* = c^{S_r}$ under secret key $\mathsf{sk}_{\mathbf{y},r}$ gives $\mathbf{y}^\top (\mathbf{x}_{0,1}^* \otimes \mathbf{x}_{0,2}^*)$, while the decryption of $c_1^* = c^{S_{r+1}}$ under secret key $\mathsf{sk}_{\mathbf{y},r}$ gives $\mathbf{y}^\top (\mathbf{x}_{1,1}^* \otimes \mathbf{x}_{1,2}^*)$. Therefore, $(b' = b, b' \leftarrow D(c_b^*))$ holds with a non-negligible probability.

In summary, the advantage of $\mathcal{A}$ that breaks the private black-box traceability is exactly the the same as the advantage of $\mathcal{B}$ that breaks the security of our TRQFE scheme with overwhelming probability.

5 Conclusion

In this paper, we proposed the first trace-and-revoke functional encryption for quadratic functions, which achieves semi-adaptive simulation-based security under k-Lin and bilateral k-Lin assumptions. Our scheme supports the functionality of traitor tracing and user revocation. More specifically, the scheme was proven to satisfy private black-box traceability under the same assumptions mentioned earlier. The reason it is limited to private traceability is due to the necessity of the master secret key for constructing probe ciphertext during the traitor tracing process. The construction of a traceable quadratic functional encryption scheme with improved efficiency, while also supporting public black-box traceability, remains an open problem.

References

1. Abdalla, M., Bourse, F., De Caro, A., Pointcheval, D.: Simple functional encryption schemes for inner products. In: Katz, J. (ed.) PKC 2015. LNCS, vol. 9020, pp. 733–751. Springer, Heidelberg (2015). https://doi.org/10.1007/978-3-662-46447-2_33
2. Agrawal, S., Bhattacherjee, S., Phan, D.H., Stehlé, D., Yamada, S.: Efficient public trace and revoke from standard assumptions: extended abstract. In: Thuraisingham, B.M., Evans, D., Malkin, T., Xu, D. (eds.) ACM CCS 2017, pp. 2277–2293. ACM Press (2017). https://doi.org/10.1145/3133956.3134041
3. Agrawal, S., Gorbunov, S., Vaikuntanathan, V., Wee, H.: Functional encryption: new perspectives and lower bounds. In: Canetti, R., Garay, J.A. (eds.) CRYPTO 2013, Part II. LNCS, vol. 8043, pp. 500–518. Springer, Heidelberg (2013). https://doi.org/10.1007/978-3-642-40084-1_28
4. Agrawal, S., Goyal, R., Tomida, J.: Multi-input quadratic functional encryption from pairings. In: Malkin, T., Peikert, C. (eds.) CRYPTO 2021, Part IV. LNCS, vol. 12828, pp. 208–238. Springer, Heidelberg, Virtual Event (2021). https://doi.org/10.1007/978-3-030-84259-8_8

5. Baltico, C.E.Z., Catalano, D., Fiore, D., Gay, R.: Practical functional encryption for quadratic functions with applications to predicate encryption. In: Katz, J., Shacham, H. (eds.) CRYPTO 2017, Part I. LNCS, vol. 10401, pp. 67–98. Springer, Heidelberg (2017). https://doi.org/10.1007/978-3-319-63688-7_3

6. Boneh, D., Franklin, M.K.: An efficient public key traitor tracing scheme. In: Wiener, M.J. (ed.) CRYPTO 1999. LNCS, vol. 1666, pp. 338–353. Springer, Heidelberg (1999). https://doi.org/10.1007/3-540-48405-1_22

7. Boneh, D., Sahai, A., Waters, B.: Fully collusion resistant traitor tracing with short ciphertexts and private keys. In: Vaudenay, S. (ed.) EUROCRYPT 2006. LNCS, vol. 4004, pp. 573–592. Springer, Heidelberg (2006). https://doi.org/10.1007/11761679_34

8. Boneh, D., Waters, B.: A fully collusion resistant broadcast, trace, and revoke system. In: Juels, A., Wright, R.N., De Capitani di Vimercati, S. (eds.) ACM CCS 2006, pp. 211–220. ACM Press (2006). https://doi.org/10.1145/1180405.1180432

9. Chor, B., Fiat, A., Naor, M.: Tracing traitors. In: Desmedt, Y. (ed.) CRYPTO'94. LNCS, vol. 839, pp. 257–270. Springer, Heidelberg (1994). https://doi.org/10.1007/3-540-48658-5_25

10. Do, X.T., Phan, D.H., Pointcheval, D.: Traceable inner product functional encryption. In: Jarecki, S. (ed.) CT-RSA 2020. LNCS, vol. 12006, pp. 564–585. Springer, Heidelberg (2020). https://doi.org/10.1007/978-3-030-40186-3_24

11. Escala, A., Herold, G., Kiltz, E., Ràfols, C., Villar, J.: An algebraic framework for Diffie-Hellman assumptions. In: Canetti, R., Garay, J.A. (eds.) CRYPTO 2013, Part II. LNCS, vol. 8043, pp. 129–147. Springer, Heidelberg (2013). https://doi.org/10.1007/978-3-642-40084-1_8

12. Gay, R.: A new paradigm for public-key functional encryption for degree-2 polynomials. In: Kiayias, A., Kohlweiss, M., Wallden, P., Zikas, V. (eds.) PKC 2020, Part I. LNCS, vol. 12110, pp. 95–120. Springer, Heidelberg (2020). https://doi.org/10.1007/978-3-030-45374-9_4

13. Gong, J., Qian, H.: Simple and efficient FE for quadratic functions. Des. Codes Crypt. 89(8), 1757–1786 (2021). https://doi.org/10.1007/s10623-021-00871-x

14. Goyal, R., Koppula, V., Waters, B.: Collusion resistant traitor tracing from learning with errors. In: Diakonikolas, I., Kempe, D., Henzinger, M. (eds.) 50th ACM STOC, pp. 660–670. ACM Press (2018). https://doi.org/10.1145/3188745.3188844

15. Goyal, V.: Reducing trust in the PKG in identity based cryptosystems. In: Menezes, A. (ed.) CRYPTO 2007. LNCS, vol. 4622, pp. 430–447. Springer, Heidelberg (2007). https://doi.org/10.1007/978-3-540-74143-5_24

16. Lin, H., Luo, J.: Compact adaptively secure ABE from k-Lin: Beyond NC^1 and towards NL. In: Canteaut, A., Ishai, Y. (eds.) EUROCRYPT 2020, Part III. LNCS, vol. 12107, pp. 247–277. Springer, Heidelberg (2020). https://doi.org/10.1007/978-3-030-45727-3_9

17. Lin, H., Vaikuntanathan, V.: Indistinguishability obfuscation from DDH-like assumptions on constant-degree graded encodings. In: Dinur, I. (ed.) 57th FOCS, pp. 11–20. IEEE Computer Society Press (2016). https://doi.org/10.1109/FOCS.2016.11

18. Ling, S., Phan, D.H., Stehlé, D., Steinfeld, R.: Hardness of k-LWE and applications in traitor tracing. In: Garay, J.A., Gennaro, R. (eds.) CRYPTO 2014, Part I. LNCS, vol. 8616, pp. 315–334. Springer, Heidelberg (2014). https://doi.org/10.1007/978-3-662-44371-2_18

19. Liu, Z., Cao, Z., Wong, D.S.: Blackbox traceable CP-ABE: How to catch people leaking their keys by selling decryption devices on eBay. In: Sadeghi, A.R., Gligor,

V.D., Yung, M. (eds.) ACM CCS 2013, pp. 475–486. ACM Press (2013). https://doi.org/10.1145/2508859.2516683

20. Luo, F., Al-Kuwari, S., Wang, H., Han, W.: Generic construction of trace-and-revoke inner product functional encryption. In: Atluri, V., Di Pietro, R., Jensen, C.D., Meng, W. (eds.) ESORICS 2022, Part I. LNCS, vol. 13554, pp. 259–282. Springer, Heidelberg (2022). https://doi.org/10.1007/978-3-031-17140-6_13

21. Nishimaki, R., Wichs, D., Zhandry, M.: Anonymous traitor tracing: how to embed arbitrary information in a key. In: Fischlin, M., Coron, J.S. (eds.) EUROCRYPT 2016, Part II. LNCS, vol. 9666, pp. 388–419. Springer, Heidelberg (2016). https://doi.org/10.1007/978-3-662-49896-5_14

22. Tomida, J.: Unbounded quadratic functional encryption and more from pairings. In: Hazay, C., Stam, M. (eds.) EUROCRYPT 2023, Part III. LNCS, vol. 14006, pp. 543–572. Springer, Heidelberg (2023). https://doi.org/10.1007/978-3-031-30620-4_18

23. Wee, H.: Functional encryption for quadratic functions from k-lin, revisited. In: Pass, R., Pietrzak, K. (eds.) TCC 2020, Part I. LNCS, vol. 12550, pp. 210–228. Springer, Heidelberg (2020). https://doi.org/10.1007/978-3-030-64375-1_8

Function-Hiding Zero Predicate Inner Product Functional Encryption from Pairings

Ming Wan, Geng Wang[✉], Shi-Feng Sun, and Dawu Gu

School of Electronic Information and Electrical Engineering, Shanghai Jiao Tong University, 200240 Shanghai, People's Republic of China
{wanming,wanggxx,shifeng.sun,dwgu}@sjtu.edu.cn

Abstract. In this work, we investigate the possibility of constructing function-hiding predicate functional encryption (FH-P-FE), which provides full attribute-hiding and function-hiding securities. Concretely, the security of FH-P-FE guarantees that (1), the functional secret keys hide the underlying functions and (2), the decryption works with an access control as in predicate encryption (PE). Our results show that the new paradigm is achievable. To achieve this goal, we first give a formal definition of FH-P-FE and its security model under an indistinguishability-based notion. Then we construct a secret-key function-hiding zero predicate inner product functional encryption (FH-ZP-IPFE) from pairings. In a FH-ZP-IPFE, both secret keys and ciphertexts are associated with vectors. Given a secret key for a policy $x \in \mathbb{Z}_q^n$ and a function $u \in \mathbb{Z}_q^m$, and a ciphertext for an attribute $y \in \mathbb{Z}_q^n$ and a message $v \in \mathbb{Z}_q^m$, a decryptor learns the inner product value $\langle u, v \rangle$ if and only if $\langle x, y \rangle = 0$ mod q. Our construction is efficient, where the functional secret key and ciphertext both contain $(n+m+1)$ group elements. We prove the security in the generic group model of bilinear groups.

Keywords: Predicate Encryption · Function Privacy · Inner Product Functional Encryption · Generic Group Model

1 Introduction

In the last two decades, various advanced encryption primitives such as identity-based encryption (IBE) [2,3,13,18], attribute-based encryption (ABE) [10,14,21,32] and predicate encryption (PE) [4,22,24] have been introduced to provide more fine-grained control over encrypted data. Later, these works were unified under the general notion of functional encryption (FE) [5,17,25,28]. In a FE scheme, the holder of the master secret key is able to delegate arbitrary decryption keys that allow users to learn specific functions of the data, and nothing else. Specifically, given an encryption of a message x and a functional secret key for a function f in some function class $\mathcal{F}$, a decryptor only learns the value $f(x)$ and no additional information about x.

© The Author(s), under exclusive license to Springer Nature Switzerland AG 2023
E. Athanasopoulos and B. Mennink (Eds.): ISC 2023, LNCS 14411, pp. 516–534, 2023.
https://doi.org/10.1007/978-3-031-49187-0_26

FH-FE and FH-IPFE. Function-hiding functional encryption (FH-FE) [8, 15,16] is a strengthened notion of FE. It has the additional property that the functional secret keys themselves also hide the underlying functions. In normal FE schemes, the functional secret keys may reveal the associated functions and leak sensitive information. To address this problem, the security notion of FH-FE is defined by the property that no additional information about both message x and function f will be leaked to decryptors. Particularly, function-hiding inner product functional encryption (FH-IPFE) [11,19,25,35] is a special case of FH-FE supporting inner product functionality. Specifically, in a FH-IPFE scheme, both secret keys and ciphertexts are associated with vectors $x \in \mathbb{Z}_q^n$ and $y \in \mathbb{Z}_q^n$. Given a secret key sk_x for x and a ciphertext ct_y for y, the decryption algorithm outputs the inner product value $\langle x, y \rangle$. Moreover, the security notion of FH-IPFE guarantees that the decryptor learns no additional information about both x and y. Interestingly, FH-IPFE has been shown to be expressive and efficient enough to support many practical applications [25].

FE with Fine-Grained Access Control. Recently, the notion of FE with a more fine-grained syntax [1,26,29] (also known as attribute-based functional encryption (AB-FE)), has been studied in the literature to capture various settings of FE. They consider the setting that each plaintext m consists of two parts, namely $m := (x, u)$, where x is an attribute and u is a message. Furthermore, each function f also consists of two parts, namely, $f := (P, g) \in \mathcal{P} \times \mathcal{G}$, where P is a predicate over the attributes, and g is a function over the messages. Then, given a secret key for f and a ciphertext for m, a decryptor acts as: $f(m) = \begin{cases} g(u) & P(x) = 1 \\ \perp & P(x) = 0 \end{cases}$. If x is also hidden, then it is called predicate functional encryption (P-FE). This notion is also somewhat stronger than the original FE since the value $g(u)$ is extracted if and only if $P(x) = 1$. As it was pointed out in [20], for inner product functional encryption (IPFE), releasing a set of n secret keys corresponding to a basis of $\mathbb{Z}_q^n$ entirely breaks the security of the IPFE system. If allowed to embed access policies, the IPFE system may be more resilient from such information leakage even when many secret keys are issued. They considered the cases where the attribute x is public [1,26,29] or private [20] and gave various constructions of attribute-based inner product functional encryption (AB-IPFE) or predicate inner product functional encryption (P-IPFE) depending on group-based and lattice-based assumptions.

FH-P-FE. However, all previous FE schemes with fine-grained access control did not consider the function-hiding property. In some specific application scenarios such as biometric authentication and statistical analysis on encrypted data, the associated functions may contain sensitive information. This motivates us to ask the following question:

Question 1. *Is it possible to design a function-hiding predicate functional encryption (FH-P-FE) scheme that achieves the function-hiding property and* *fine-grained access control, without revealing any additional information about* $m := (x, u)$ *and* $f := (\mathrm{P}, g)$ *apart from whether they are satisfied or not by the embedded policy?*

In this paper, we answer the above question by constructing a (secret-key) function-hiding zero predicate inner product encryption (FH-ZP-IPFE) scheme, where the attribute is set to be private. Roughly speaking, in a FH-ZP-IPFE, both secret keys and ciphertexts are associated with vectors. Given a secret key for a policy $x \in \mathbb{Z}_q^n$ and a function $u \in \mathbb{Z}_q^m$, and a ciphertext for an attribute $y \in \mathbb{Z}_q^n$ and a message $v \in \mathbb{Z}_q^m$, a decryptor learns the inner product value $\langle u, v \rangle$ if and only if $\langle x, y \rangle = 0 \mod q$. The syntax of FH-ZP-IPFE corresponds to the notion of FH-P-FE by defining the predicate P and the function g as $\mathrm{P}_y(x) = 1$ if $\langle x, y \rangle = 0 \mod q$ (called zero predicate), and $g_u(v) = \langle u, v \rangle \mod q$, respectively. Additionally, the function-hiding property guarantees that (1) with a successful decryption, the decryptor only learns the inner product value and no additional information about (x, u) and (y, v) and (2) otherwise, the decryptor gains no information about both (x, u) and (y, v). In other words, the proposed scheme simultaneously achieves data privacy (with respect to y and v) and function privacy (with respect to x and u) [8,16,30].

1.1 Our Contribution

In this work, we focus on the construction of (secret-key) FH-P-FE scheme, specifically, the FH-ZP-IPFE scheme. This is the first work that considers P-FE with function-hiding property. Our results show that FH-P-FE is achievable and our main contributions include:

- We formally define the notion of (secret-key) FH-P-FE and its security model. We generalize the notion of FH-FE and predicate functional encryption (P-FE) to FH-P-FE. We also define a notion of indistinguishability-based security for FH-P-FE, where an adversary may request any polynomial-size functional secret keys and ciphertexts but can not decide which random bit b is chosen in the challenge phase.
- We then give a construction of (secret-key) FH-ZP-IPFE scheme, where functional secret key and ciphertext both contain $n + m + 1$ group elements. Here, n is the dimension of policy x and attribute y, m is the dimension of function u and message v. Note that it is almost optimal sized since in the state-of-the-art construction of plain FH-IPFE [25] without fine-grained access control, their functional secret key and ciphertext both contain $m + 1$ group elements. We consider the fine-grained access control supporting zero inner product predicate, so parameters (specifically for functional secret key and ciphertext) in our scheme grow with n group elements. At last, we prove the indistinguishability-based security of the proposed scheme in the generic group model.
- To assess the practicality of our FH-ZP-IPFE scheme, we provide a complete implementation of our scheme in C++. We also perform a series of micro-benchmarks on our FH-ZP-IPFE scheme for a wide range of dimension set-

tings. Our results show that our scheme is efficient and practical enough to deploy for real-world scenarios.

In Table 1, we provide a comparison of existing AB-FE, P-FE and FH-FE schemes with our proposed FH-ZP-IPFE with respect to the functionality and security model.

Table 1. Comparison of our results with existing schemes

Scheme	Access Policy	Functionality	Attribute-Hiding	Function-Hiding
[11, 19, 25, 35]	✗	Inner Product	✗	✓
[1]	NC1	Inner Product	✗	✗
[26]	GC	Inner Product	✗	✗
[29]	ABP	Inner Product	Partially	✗
[20]	Inner Product	Inner Product	✓	✗
This work	Inner Product	Inner Product	✓	✓

GC: general circuits and ABP: arithmetic branching programs.

1.2 Technical Overview

The main idea of our construction is to use a random matrix $\mathbf{R} \in \mathbb{Z}_q^{(n+m) \times (n+m)}$ to hide the information of $\boldsymbol{x}, \boldsymbol{u}$ and $\boldsymbol{y}, \boldsymbol{v}$. In more detail, in our construction, the master secret key is $\mathbf{R}$ and $\mathbf{R}^{-1}$. The ciphertext $\mathrm{ct}_{\boldsymbol{y},\boldsymbol{v}} = (C_1, C_2)$ for $\boldsymbol{y}, \boldsymbol{v}$ contains two parts $C_1 = g_2^{\gamma}$ and $C_2 = g_2^{\mathbf{R}\begin{pmatrix} \gamma \boldsymbol{v} \\ \beta \boldsymbol{y} \end{pmatrix}}$ and the decryption key $\mathrm{sk}_{\boldsymbol{x},\boldsymbol{u}} = (K_1, K_2)$ for $\boldsymbol{x}, \boldsymbol{u}$ also contains two parts $K_1 = g_1^{\omega}$ and $K_2 = g_1^{(\omega \boldsymbol{u}^{\top}, \alpha \boldsymbol{x}^{\top}) \mathbf{R}^{-1}}$. Note that α, β, ω and γ are random values, generated while running the corresponding algorithms. The decryption algorithm works as, first computing $D_1 = e(K_1, C_1)$ and $D_2 = e(K_2, C_2)$, then finding z such that $(D_1)^z = D_2$. The correctness follows by the fact if $\langle \boldsymbol{x}, \boldsymbol{y} \rangle = 0 \mod q$, then $z = \langle \boldsymbol{u}, \boldsymbol{v} \rangle$ and otherwise, z is a random value.

The security of our FH-ZP-IPFE scheme guarantees two aspects:

- First, if $\langle \boldsymbol{x}, \boldsymbol{y} \rangle = 0 \mod q$, except for the predicate $\mathrm{P}_{\boldsymbol{x}}(\boldsymbol{y})$ and inner product value $\langle \boldsymbol{u}, \boldsymbol{v} \rangle$, no additional information about $\boldsymbol{x}, \boldsymbol{u}, \boldsymbol{y}, \boldsymbol{v}$ is leaked.
- Second, if $\langle \boldsymbol{x}, \boldsymbol{y} \rangle \neq 0 \mod q$, except for the predicate $\mathrm{P}_{\boldsymbol{x}}(\boldsymbol{y})$, no additional information about $\boldsymbol{x}, \boldsymbol{u}, \boldsymbol{y}, \boldsymbol{v}$ is leaked.

Note that $D_1 = [\omega \gamma]_T$ and $D_2 = [\omega \gamma \langle \boldsymbol{u}, \boldsymbol{v} \rangle + \alpha \beta \langle \boldsymbol{x}, \boldsymbol{y} \rangle]_T$ and $\alpha, \beta, \gamma, \omega$ are all random elements. In this case, if $\langle \boldsymbol{x}, \boldsymbol{y} \rangle = 0 \mod q$, $\langle \boldsymbol{u}, \boldsymbol{v} \rangle$ is extracted and $\boldsymbol{x}, \boldsymbol{u}, \boldsymbol{y}, \boldsymbol{v}$ is hidden by uniformly random $\mathbf{R}$ in addition to α, ω, β and γ, respectively. This is due to the fact that in the generic model, those random elements are all replaced by formal variables and can not be canceled else where. On the other hand, $\langle \boldsymbol{x}, \boldsymbol{y} \rangle \neq 0 \mod q$, then $\langle \boldsymbol{u}, \boldsymbol{v} \rangle$ is also hidden by $\omega \gamma$, see Sect. 4 for more details.

1.3   Related Work

AB-IPFE was first considered in [1,26,29], where they viewed the attributes as public. A very recent work [20] also gave a construction of P-IPFE, where the attributes are private. However, they all did not achieve the function-hiding property. In fact, in their constructions, they even need the function as a part of input for decryption algorithms. Another line of researching for FH-IPFE was by [11,19,25,35], they all only considered the plain FH-IPFE without any access control. In other words, the functional secret key always decrypts the ciphertext to get the inner product value as long as the value is located in a limited range.

1.4   Organization

The rest of this paper is organized as follows. In Sect. 2, we define notation and provide background definitions. In Sect. 3, we formally define the syntax of FH-P-FE and its security model. In Sect. 4, we present our construction for (secret-key) FH-ZP-IPFE and prove it secure in the generic group model. In Sect. 5, we implement our scheme and show the experiment results. Finally, we conclude the paper in Sect. 6.

2   Preliminaries

Notation. In this work, we use λ to denote the security parameter. We say a function $\epsilon(\lambda)$ is negligible in λ if $\epsilon(\lambda) = o\left(\frac{1}{\lambda^c}\right)$ for all positive integers c. For a positive integer n, we write $[n]$ to denote the set $\{1, 2, \cdots, n\}$. For a finite set S, we denote by $x \leftarrow S$ the operation of sampling a uniformly random element x from S. Similarly, for a distribution D, we denote by $x \leftarrow D$ the operation of sampling a random x according to the distribution D.

We use lowercase unbolded letters (e.g., α or a) to denote scalars. We write column vectors as lowercase bold letters (e.g., v) and matrices as uppercase bold letters (e.g., $\mathbf{M}$). We recall that $\mathbb{GL}_n(\mathbb{Z}_q)$ is the general linear group of $(n \times n)$ matrices over $\mathbb{Z}_q$ (i.e., invertible matrices over $\mathbb{Z}_q$). For a matrix $\mathbf{R}$, we use $\mathbf{R}^\top$ to denote the transpose of $\mathbf{R}$ and $\det(\mathbf{R})$ to denote its determinant. We use the shorthand g^v where $v = (v_1, \cdots, v_n)^\top$ to denote the vector of group elements $(g^{v_1}, \cdots, g^{v_n})^\top$ and naturally extend this notation to matrices $\mathbf{M}$.

2.1   Bilinear Groups

We briefly recall the basic definition of an asymmetric bilinear group [13,23]. Let $\mathbb{G}_1$, $\mathbb{G}_2$ and $\mathbb{G}_T$ be three distinct groups of prime order q, and let $e : \mathbb{G}_1 \times \mathbb{G}_2 \mapsto \mathbb{G}_T$ be a function mapping two elements from $\mathbb{G}_1$ and $\mathbb{G}_2$ onto the target group $\mathbb{G}_T$. Let g_1, g_2 and g_T be generators of $\mathbb{G}_1$, $\mathbb{G}_2$ and $\mathbb{G}_T$, respectively. We write the group operation in groups multiplicatively and write 1 to denote their multiplicative identity. We say that the tuple $(\mathbb{G}_1, \mathbb{G}_2, \mathbb{G}_T, q, e)$ is an asymmetric bilinear group if the following properties hold:

- **Efficiency**: The group operations in $\mathbb{G}_1, \mathbb{G}_2, \mathbb{G}_T$ as well the map $e(\cdot, \cdot)$ are all efficiently computable.
- **Non-degeneracy**: $e(g_1, g_2) = g_T \neq 1$.
- **Bilinearity**: $e(g_1^a, g_2^b) = g_T^{ab}$ for all $a, b \in \mathbb{Z}_q$.

In this work, we additionally let $[a]_1$, $[b]_2$ and $[c]_T$ denote encodings of a, b, c in $\mathbb{G}_1, \mathbb{G}_2, \mathbb{G}_T$, i.e. g_1^a, g_2^b and g_T^c respectively. For a vector $\boldsymbol{v}$ or matrix $\mathbf{M}$, we use the shorthand $[\boldsymbol{v}]$ or $[\mathbf{M}]$ (for any of the three groups) to denote the group elements obtained by encoding each entry of $\boldsymbol{v}$ and $\mathbf{M}$ respectively. Furthermore, for any scalar $k \in \mathbb{Z}_q$ and vectors $\boldsymbol{v}, \boldsymbol{w} \in \mathbb{Z}_q^n$, we write $[\boldsymbol{v}]^k = [k\boldsymbol{v}]$ and $[\boldsymbol{v}][\boldsymbol{w}] = [\boldsymbol{v} + \boldsymbol{w}]$. The pairing operation over groups is also extended to vectors and matrices as follows, $e([\boldsymbol{v}^\top]_1, [\boldsymbol{w}]_2) = [\langle \boldsymbol{v}, \boldsymbol{w} \rangle]_T$ and $e([\boldsymbol{v}^\top]_1, [\mathbf{M}]_2) = [\boldsymbol{v}^\top \mathbf{M}]_T$. It is not hard to see that the above operations are all efficiently computable.

2.2 Generic Bilinear Group Model

We prove the security of our constructions in a generic model of bilinear groups [12], which is an extension of generic group model [27,34] adapted to bilinear groups. In the generic group model, access to the group elements is replaced by "handles." In this case, an adversary in the generic group model is also only given access to a stateful oracle which carries out the group operations, and in the bilinear group setting, the pairing operation. The generic group oracle maintains internally a list mapping from handles to group elements, which is used to answer the oracle queries. Thus, when a cryptographic scheme is shown to satisfy some security property in the generic group model, it means that no efficient adversary can break that security property applying the group operations as a black-box oracle. The following definition is taken verbatim from [8] and originally appeared in [25].

Definition 2 (Generic Bilinear Group Oracle). *A generic bilinear group oracle is a stateful oracle BG that responds to queries as follows:*

- *On a query BG.Setup (1^λ), the oracle generates two fresh handles $\mathrm{pp}, \mathrm{sp} \leftarrow \{0,1\}^\lambda$ and a prime q. It outputs $(\mathrm{pp}, \mathrm{sp}, q)$. It stores the generated values, initializes an empty table $\mathrm{T} \leftarrow \{\}$, and sets the internal state so subsequent invocations of BG.Setup fail.*
- *On a query BG.Encode (k, x, i), where $k \in \{0,1\}^\lambda$, $x \in \mathbb{Z}_q$ and $i \in \{1, 2, T\}$, the oracle checks that $k = \mathrm{sp}$ (return $\perp$ otherwise). The oracle then generates a fresh handle $h \leftarrow \{0,1\}^\lambda$, adds the entry $h \mapsto (x, i)$ to table T, and outputs h.*
- *On a query BG.Add (k, h_1, h_2), where $k, h_1, h_2 \in \{0,1\}^\lambda$, the oracle checks that $k = \mathrm{pp}$, that the handles h_1, h_2 are present in its internal table T and are mapped to the values (x_1, i_1) and (x_2, i_2), respectively, with $i_1 = i_2$ (return $\perp$ otherwise). The oracle then generates a fresh handle $h \leftarrow \{0,1\}^\lambda$, computes $x = x_1 + x_2 \in \mathbb{Z}_q$, adds the entry $h \mapsto (x, i_1)$ to T, and outputs h.*

- *On a query* BG.Pair (k, h_1, h_2), *where* k, h_1, h_2 , *the oracle checks that* $k = pp$, *that the handles* h_1, h_2 *are present in* T *and are mapped to values* $(x_1, 1)$ *and* $(x_2, 2)$, *respectively (returning* $\perp$ *otherwise). The oracle then generates a fresh handle* $h \leftarrow \{0, 1\}^\lambda$, *computes* $x = x_1 x_2 \in \mathbb{Z}_q$, *adds the entry* $h \mapsto (x, T)$ *to* T, *and outputs* h.
- *On a query* BG.ZeroTest (k, h) *where* $k, h \in \{0, 1\}^\lambda$, *the oracle checks that* $k = pp$, *that the handle* h *is present in* T *and it maps to some value* (x, i) *(returning* $\perp$ *otherwise). The oracle then outputs "zero" if* $x = 0 \in \mathbb{Z}_q$ *and "non-zero" otherwise.*

We notice that in the generic group model, the random elements will often be substituted to formal variables when analyzing the security of constructed schemes. In order to distinguish between a specific value and a formal variable, we will explicitly write x if it is a specific value and $\hat{x}$ if it is a formal variable. This notation will also naturally extend to vectors $\hat{v}$ and matrices $\hat{\mathbf{M}}$ where their each entry is a formal variable.

We also use the Schwartz-Zippel lemma [33,37] in the security proof, stated below.

Lemma 3 (Schwartz-Zippel [33,37], **adapted).** *Fix a prime* q *and let* $f \in \mathbb{F}_q[\hat{x}_1, \cdots, \hat{x}_n]$ *be an* n-variate polynomial with degree at most d and which is not identically zero. Then,*

$$\Pr[x_1, \cdots, x_n \leftarrow \mathbb{F}_q : f(x_1, \cdots, x_n) = 0] \leq \frac{d}{q}.$$

2.3   Function-Hiding Functional Encryption

We recall the definition of FH-FE and its security model [19,25,35].

Definition 4. *A (secret-key) FH-FE is a tuple of algorithms* $\Pi =$ (Setup, KeyGen, Enc, Dec) *defined over a message space* $\mathcal{M}$ *and a function class* $\mathcal{F}$ *with the following properties:*

- Setup $(1^\lambda) \mapsto (pp, msk)$: *On input a security parameter* λ, *the setup algorithm* Setup *outputs the public parameters* pp *and the master secret key* msk.
- KeyGen $(pp, msk, f) \mapsto sk_f$: *On input the public parameters* pp, *the maser secret key* msk *and a function* $f \in \mathcal{F}$, *the key generation algorithm* KeyGen *outputs a functional secret key* sk_f.
- Enc $(pp, msk, m) \mapsto ct_m$: *On input the public parameters* pp, *the master secret key* msk *and a message* $m \in \mathcal{M}$, *the encryption algorithm* Enc *outputs a ciphertext* ct_m.
- Dec $(pp, sk_f, ct_m) \mapsto z$: *On input the public parameters* pp, *a functional secret key* sk_f, *and a ciphertext* ct_m, *the decryption algorithm* Dec *outputs a value* z.

Correctness. An FH-FE scheme $\Pi = (\text{Setup}, \text{KeyGen}, \text{Enc}, \text{Dec})$ defined above is correct if for all messages $m \in \mathcal{M}$ and all functions $f \in \mathcal{F}$, the following condition holds: Letting $(\text{pp}, \text{msk}) \leftarrow \text{Setup}(1^\lambda)$, $\text{sk}_f \leftarrow \text{KeyGen}(\text{pp}, \text{msk}, f)$, and $\text{ct}_m \leftarrow \text{Enc}(\text{pp}, \text{msk}, m)$, then

$$\Pr[\text{Dec}(\text{pp}, \text{sk}_f, \text{ct}_m) = f(m)] = 1 - \epsilon(\lambda),$$

where the probability is taken over the internal randomness of the Setup, Enc and KeyGen algorithms, and $\epsilon(\lambda)$ is a negligible function.

IND Security. We review the indistinguishability-based security for FH-FE. Let $\Pi = (\text{Setup}, \text{KeyGen}, \text{Enc}, \text{Dec})$ be a FH-FE scheme. We define the following experiment between a challenger $\mathcal{C}$ and an adversary $\mathcal{A}$ that can make key generation and encryption oracle queries. In the following, we let $\mathcal{M}$ be our attribute space and $\mathcal{F}$ be our function class.

Definition 5 $\left(\text{Experiment } \text{Exp}_\Pi^b\right)$. *Let* $b \in \{0, 1\}$. *The challenger* $\mathcal{C}$ *computes* $(\text{pp}, \text{msk}) \leftarrow \text{Setup}(1^\lambda)$, *gives* pp *to the adversary* $\mathcal{A}$, *and then responds to each oracle query type made by* $\mathcal{A}$ *in the following manner.*

- *__Key generation oracle.__ on input a pair of* (f_0, f_1), *the challenger computes and returns* $\text{sk}_{f_b} \leftarrow \text{KeyGen}(\text{pp}, \text{msk}, f_b)$.
- *__Encryption oracle.__ On input a pair of* (m_0, m_1), *the challenger computes and returns* $\text{ct}_{m_b} \leftarrow \text{Enc}(\text{pp}, \text{msk}, m_b)$.

Eventually, $\mathcal{A}$ outputs a bit b', which is also the output of the experiment, denoted by $\text{Exp}_\Pi^b(\mathcal{A})$.

Definition 6 (Admissibility). *For an adversary* $\mathcal{A}$, *let* Q_1 *and* Q_2 *be the total number of key generation and encryption oracle queries made by* $\mathcal{A}$, *respectively. For* $b \in \{0, 1\}$, *let* $f_b^{(1)}, \cdots, f_b^{(Q_1)} \in \mathcal{F}$ *and* $m_b^{(1)}, \cdots, m_b^{(Q_2)} \in \mathcal{M}$ *be the corresponding functions and messages that* $\mathcal{A}$ *submits to the key generation and encryption oracles, respectively. We say that* $\mathcal{A}$ *is admissible if for all* $i \in [Q_1]$ *and* $j \in [Q_2]$, *we have that*

$$f_0^{(i)}(m_0^{(j)}) = f_1^{(i)}(m_1^{(j)}).$$

Definition 7 (IND Security for FH-FE). *We define a FH-FE scheme denoted as* $\Pi = (\text{Setup}, \text{KeyGen}, \text{Enc}, \text{Dec})$ *as fully-secure if for all efficient and admissible adversaries* $\mathcal{A}$,

$$\left|\Pr\left[\text{Exp}_\Pi^0(\mathcal{A}) = 1\right] - \Pr\left[\text{Exp}_\Pi^1(\mathcal{A}) = 1\right]\right| = \epsilon(\lambda),$$

where $\epsilon(\lambda)$ *is a negligible function.*

3 Function-Hiding Predicate Functional Encryption

In this section, we formally give the definition of FH-P-FE, which is inspired by combining FHFE [11,19,25,35] with P-FE [1,20,26,29]. Generally, in a (secret-key) FH-P-FE scheme, the secret key is associated with a predicate P and a function g, and the ciphertext is associated with an attribute x and a message u. Given a secret key for $f := (P, g)$, and a ciphertext for $m := (x, u)$, a decryptor learns the functional value $g(u)$ if and only if $P(x) = 1$.

Definition 8. *A (secret-key) FH-P-FE is a tuple of algorithms $\Pi = $ (Setup, KeyGen, Enc, Dec) defined over an attribute space $\mathcal{X}$ and a message space $\mathcal{U}$ as well as a predicate class $\mathcal{P}$ and a function class $\mathcal{G}$ with the following properties:*

- *Setup $(1^\lambda) \mapsto (\text{pp}, \text{msk})$: On input a security parameter λ, the setup algorithm Setup outputs the public parameters pp and the master secret key msk.*
- *KeyGen $(\text{pp}, \text{msk}, P, g) \mapsto \text{sk}_{P,g}$: On input the public parameters pp, the maser secret key msk, a predicate $P \in \mathcal{P}$ and a function $g \in \mathcal{G}$, the key generation algorithm KeyGen outputs a functional secret key $\text{sk}_{P,g}$.*
- *Enc $(\text{pp}, \text{msk}, x, u) \mapsto \text{ct}_{x,u}$: On input the public parameters pp, the maser secret key msk, an attribute $x \in \mathcal{X}$ and a message $u \in \mathcal{U}$, the encryption algorithm Enc outputs a ciphertext $\text{ct}_{x,u}$.*
- *Dec $(\text{pp}, \text{sk}_{P,g}, \text{ct}_{x,u}) \mapsto z/\bot$: On input the public parameters pp, a functional secret key $\text{sk}_{P,g}$, and a ciphertext $\text{ct}_{x,u}$, the decryption algorithm Dec outputs a value z or $\bot$.*

Correctness. An FH-P-FE scheme $\Pi = $ (Setup, KeyGen, Enc, Dec) defined above is correct if for all attributes $x \in \mathcal{X}$, messages $u \in \mathcal{U}$ and all predicates $P \in \mathcal{P}$, functions $g \in \mathcal{G}$, the following condition holds: Letting $(\text{pp}, \text{msk}) \leftarrow$ Setup (1^λ), $\text{sk}_{P,g} \leftarrow$ KeyGen (msk, P, g), and $\text{ct}_{x,u} \leftarrow$ Enc $(\text{pp}, \text{msk}, x, u)$, then

- If $P(x) = 1$, $\Pr[\text{Dec}(\text{pp}, \text{sk}_{P,g}, \text{ct}_{x,u}) = g(u)] = 1 - \epsilon(\lambda)$,
- If $P(x) = 0$, $\Pr[\text{Dec}(\text{pp}, \text{sk}_{P,g}, \text{ct}_{x,u}) = \bot] = 1 - \epsilon(\lambda)$,

where the probability is taken over the internal randomness of the Setup, Enc and KeyGen algorithms, and $\epsilon(\lambda)$ is a negligible function.

Indistinguishability-Based Security. Let $\Pi = $ (Setup, KeyGen, Enc, Dec) be a FH-P-FE scheme. We now define the following experiment between a challenger $\mathcal{C}$ and an adversary $\mathcal{A}$ that can make key generation and encryption oracle queries. In the following, we let $\mathcal{X}$ be our attribute space, $\mathcal{U}$ be our message space, $\mathcal{P}$ be our predicate class and $\mathcal{G}$ be our function class.

Definition 9 $\left(\text{Experiment } \text{Exp}_\Pi^b\right)$. *Let $b \in \{0, 1\}$. The challenger $\mathcal{C}$ computes $(\text{pp}, \text{msk}) \leftarrow$ Setup (1^λ), gives pp to the adversary $\mathcal{A}$, and then responds to each oracle query type made by $\mathcal{A}$ in the following manner.*

- **Key generation oracle.** *on input a pair of* $(P_0, g_0), (P_1, g_1)$, *the challenger computes and returns* $\mathrm{sk}_{P_b, g_b} \leftarrow \mathrm{KeyGen}\,(\mathrm{pp}, \mathrm{msk}, P_b, g_b)$.
- **Encryption oracle.** *On input a pair of* $(x_0, u_0), (x_1, u_1)$, *the challenger computes and returns* $\mathrm{ct}_{x_b, u_b} \leftarrow \mathrm{Enc}\,(\mathrm{pp}, \mathrm{msk}, x_b, u_b)$.

Eventually, $\mathcal{A}$ outputs a bit b', which is also the output of the experiment, denoted by $\mathrm{Exp}_{\Pi}^{b}\,(\mathcal{A})$.

Definition 10 (Admissibility). *For an adversary* $\mathcal{A}$, *let* Q_1 *and* Q_2 *be the total number of key generation and encryption oracle queries made by* $\mathcal{A}$, *respectively. For* $b \in \{0,1\}$, *let* $(P_b^{(1)}, g_b^{(1)}), \cdots, (P_b^{(Q_1)}, g_b^{(Q_1)}) \in \mathcal{P} \times \mathcal{G}$ *and* $(x_b^{(1)}, u_b^{(1)}), \cdots, (x_b^{(Q_2)}, u_b^{(Q_2)}) \in \mathcal{X} \times \mathcal{U}$ *be the corresponding predicates (functions) and attributes (messages) that* $\mathcal{A}$ *submits to the key generation and encryption oracles, respectively. We say that* $\mathcal{A}$ *is admissible if for all* $i \in [Q_1]$ *and* $j \in [Q_2]$, *we have that*

- *if* $P_0^{(i)}(x_0^{(j)}) = 0$, *then* $P_1^{(i)}(x_1^{(j)}) = 0$,
- *and if* $P_0^{(i)}(x_0^{(j)}) = 1$, *then* $P_1^{(i)}(x_1^{(j)}) = 1$ *and* $g_0^{(i)}(u_0^{(j)}) = g_1^{(i)}(u_1^{(j)})$.

Definition 11 (IND Security for FH-P-FE). *We define a FH-P-FE scheme denoted as* $\Pi = (\mathrm{Setup}, \mathrm{KeyGen}, \mathrm{Enc}, \mathrm{Dec})$ *as fully-secure if for all efficient and admissible adversaries* $\mathcal{A}$,

$$\left| \Pr\left[\mathrm{Exp}_{\Pi}^{0}\,(\mathcal{A}) = 1\right] - \Pr\left[\mathrm{Exp}_{\Pi}^{1}\,(\mathcal{A}) = 1\right] \right| = \epsilon(\lambda),$$

where $\epsilon\,(\lambda)$ *is a negligible function.*

4 Our FH-ZP-IPFE Scheme

In this section, we give our construction of function-hiding zero predicate inner product functional encryption (FH-ZP-IPFE). FH-ZP-IPFE is a special case of FH-P-FE that supports inner product functionality. Additionally, the predicate is represented by a vector x as P_x such that for an attribute y, $P_x(y) = 1$ if and only if $\langle x, y \rangle = 0 \mod q$. The function is represented by a vector u as g_u such that for a message v, $g_u(v) = \langle u, v \rangle$. In more details, in a FH-ZP-IPFE, each secret key $\mathrm{sk}_{x,u}$ is associated with vectors $x \in \mathbb{Z}_q^n, u \in \mathbb{Z}_q^m$ and each ciphertext $\mathrm{ct}_{y,v}$ is also associated with vectors $y \in \mathbb{Z}_q^n, v \in \mathbb{Z}_q^m$. Given a secret key $\mathrm{sk}_{x,u}$ and a ciphertext $\mathrm{ct}_{y,v}$, a decryptor learns the inner product value $\langle u, v \rangle$ if and only if $P_x(y) = 1$. Then we show that the proposed scheme is indistinguishability-based secure (Definition 11) in the generic group model.

4.1 Construction

Fix a security parameter $\lambda \in \mathbb{N}$ and let n, m be a positive integer. Let S be a polynomial-sized subset of $\mathbb{Z}_q$. We construct a FH-ZP-IPFE scheme $\Pi = (\mathrm{Setup}, \mathrm{KeyGen}, \mathrm{Enc}, \mathrm{Dec})$ as follows.

- Setup $(1^\lambda, S) \mapsto (\mathrm{pp}, \mathrm{msk})$: On input a security parameter λ and a set $S \subseteq \mathbb{Z}_q$, the setup algorithm Setup samples an asymmetric bilinear group $(\mathbb{G}_1, \mathbb{G}_2, \mathbb{G}_T, q, e)$ and chooses generators $g_1 \in \mathbb{G}_1$ and $g_2 \in \mathbb{G}_2$. Then it samples $\mathbf{R} \leftarrow \mathbb{GL}_{n+m}(\mathbb{Z}_q)$ and computes $\mathbf{R}^{-1}$. Finally, the setup algorithm outputs the public parameters $\mathrm{pp} = (\mathbb{G}_1, \mathbb{G}_2, \mathbb{G}_T, q, e, S)$ and the master secret key $\mathrm{msk} = (\mathrm{pp}, g_1, g_2, \mathbf{R}, \mathbf{R}^{-1})$.
- KeyGen $(\mathrm{pp}, \mathrm{msk}, \boldsymbol{x}, \boldsymbol{u}) \mapsto \mathrm{sk}_{\boldsymbol{x}, \boldsymbol{u}}$: On input the public parameters pp, the maser secret key msk, a policy $\boldsymbol{x} \in \mathbb{Z}_q^n$ and a function $\boldsymbol{u} \in \mathbb{Z}_q^m$, the key generation algorithm KeyGen chooses random elements $\omega, \alpha \leftarrow \mathbb{Z}_q$ and outputs the pair

$$\mathrm{sk} = (K_1, K_2) = \left([\omega]_1, \left[\left(\omega \boldsymbol{u}^\top, \alpha \boldsymbol{x}^\top \right) \mathbf{R}^{-1} \right]_1 \right).$$

- Enc $(\mathrm{pp}, \mathrm{msk}, \boldsymbol{y}, \boldsymbol{v}) \mapsto \mathrm{ct}_{\boldsymbol{y}, \boldsymbol{v}}$: On input the public parameters pp, the maser secret key msk, an attribute $\boldsymbol{y} \in \mathbb{Z}_q^n$ and a message $\boldsymbol{v} \in \mathbb{Z}_q^m$, the encryption algorithm Enc chooses random elements $\beta, \gamma \leftarrow \mathbb{Z}_q$ and outputs the pair

$$\mathrm{ct}_{\boldsymbol{y}, \boldsymbol{v}} = (\mathrm{ct}_1, \mathrm{ct}_2) = \left([\gamma]_2, \left[\mathbf{R} \begin{pmatrix} \gamma \boldsymbol{v} \\ \beta \boldsymbol{y} \end{pmatrix} \right]_2 \right).$$

- Dec $(\mathrm{pp}, \mathrm{sk}_{\boldsymbol{x}, \boldsymbol{u}}, \mathrm{ct}_{\boldsymbol{y}, \boldsymbol{v}}) \mapsto z$: On input the public parameters pp, a functional secret key $\mathrm{sk}_{\boldsymbol{x}, \boldsymbol{u}}$ and a ciphertext $\mathrm{ct}_{\boldsymbol{y}, \boldsymbol{v}}$, the decryption algorithm Dec computes

$$D_1 = e(K_1, C_1) \text{ and } D_2 = e(K_2, C_2).$$

Then it checks whether there exists $z \in S$ such that $(D_1)^z = D_2$, If so, the decryption algorithm outputs z. Otherwise, it outputs $\perp$. Note that this algorithm is efficient[1] since $|S| = poly(\lambda)$.

Correctness. The correctness of Π follows from the fact that for any secret key $\mathrm{sk}_{\boldsymbol{x}, \boldsymbol{u}} = (K_1, K_2)$ corresponding to a policy $\boldsymbol{x}$ and a function $\boldsymbol{u}$ and any ciphertext $\mathrm{ct}_{\boldsymbol{y}, \boldsymbol{v}} = (C_1, C_2)$ corresponding to an attribute $\boldsymbol{y}$ and a message $\boldsymbol{v}$, we have that

$$D_1 = e(k_1, C_1) = [\omega \gamma]_T \text{ and } D_2 = e(K_2, C_2) = [\omega \gamma \langle \boldsymbol{u}, \boldsymbol{v} \rangle + \alpha \beta \langle \boldsymbol{x}, \boldsymbol{y} \rangle]_T.$$

In this case, if $\mathrm{P}_{\boldsymbol{x}}(\boldsymbol{y}) = 1$, namely, $\langle \boldsymbol{x}, \boldsymbol{y} \rangle = 0 \mod q$, then $D_2 = [\omega \gamma \langle \boldsymbol{u}, \boldsymbol{v} \rangle]_T$ and the decryption algorithm outputs $z = \langle \boldsymbol{u}, \boldsymbol{v} \rangle$ as long as $z \in S$. The correctness follows.

4.2   IND Security

We first state a lemma that plays an important role in our proof. Specifically, we use a variant of lemma due to [9] that originally appeared in [7]. The following is taken verbatim from [8].

---

[1] Usually, S is set to $[-B, B]$ for polynomial bounded B, the discrete log can be efficiently computed by Pollard-Lambda algorithms.

Lemma 12 ([7–9]). *Let $\hat{\mathbf{R}}$ be an $n \times n$ matrix of distinct formal variables $\hat{r}_{i,j}$, and $\boldsymbol{u}, \boldsymbol{v} \in \mathbb{F}_q^n$ be two arbitrary non-zero vectors. Let $\hat{\boldsymbol{u}}^\top = \boldsymbol{u}^\top \hat{\mathbf{R}}^{-1}$ and $\hat{\boldsymbol{v}} = \hat{\mathbf{R}}\boldsymbol{v}$ be two vectors of rational functions over the $\hat{r}_{i,j}$ formal variables. Let P be a polynomial over the entries of $\hat{\boldsymbol{u}}$ and $\hat{\boldsymbol{v}}$ such that each monomial contains exactly one entry from $\hat{\boldsymbol{u}}$ and one from $\hat{\boldsymbol{v}}$. Then if P is identically a constant over the $\hat{r}_{i,j}$ variables, it must be a constant multiple of the inner product of $\hat{\boldsymbol{u}}$ and $\hat{\boldsymbol{v}}$.*

Theorem 13. *The FH-ZP-IPFE scheme Π constructed above is IND secure in the generic group model.*

Proof. Let Q_1 and Q_2 be the total number of key generation and encryption oracle queries made by $\mathcal{A}$, respectively. We present two hybrid experiments, beginning with the original IND experiment defined in Definition 11.

- $\mathrm{Exp}_0^{(b)}$ is the original experiment. The adversary $\mathcal{A}$ receives the public parameters, the secret keys for $\left(\boldsymbol{x}_b^{(1)}, \boldsymbol{u}_b^{(1)}\right), \cdots, \left(\boldsymbol{x}_b^{(Q_1)}, \boldsymbol{u}_b^{(Q_1)}\right) \in \mathbb{Z}_q^{n+m}$ and the ciphertexts for $\left(\boldsymbol{y}_b^{(1)}, \boldsymbol{v}_b^{(1)}\right), \cdots, \left(\boldsymbol{y}_b^{(Q_2)}, \boldsymbol{v}_b^{(Q_2)}\right) \in \mathbb{Z}_q^{n+m}$. Thus, in the generic group model, the adversary $\mathcal{A}$ has access to the handles of elements $\{[\omega_i]_1\}_i$, $\left\{\left[\left(\omega_i(\boldsymbol{u}_b^{(i)})^\top, \alpha_i(\boldsymbol{x}_b^{(i)})^\top\right)\mathbf{R}^{-1}\right]_1\right\}_i$, $\{[\gamma_j]_2\}_j$ and $\left\{\left[\mathbf{R}\begin{pmatrix}\gamma_j \boldsymbol{v}_b^{(j)}\\ \beta_j \boldsymbol{y}_b^{(j)}\end{pmatrix}\right]_2\right\}_j$.

- $\mathrm{Exp}_1^{(b)}$ is obtained from $\mathrm{Exp}_0^{(b)}$ by modifying the random elements chosen by challenger $\mathcal{C}$ to formal variables. Recall that the only distinguishing information the adversary can obtain in the generic group model is the responses to zero-test queries in the target group. We can imagine replacing $\{\omega_i\}_i$, $\{\alpha_i\}_i$, $\{\beta_j\}_j$, $\{\gamma_j\}_j$ and the entries of $\mathbf{R}$ with formal variables. So we let $\hat{\mathbf{R}}$ be a $(n+m) \times (n+m)$ matrix of formal variables $\hat{r}_{i,j}$ for $i, j \in [n+m]$. In this case, for every zero-test query submitted by $\mathcal{A}$, the resulting zero-test expressions are substituted by rational functions of above variables. For simplicity, when taking each zero-test query, we multiply the expressions by $|\det(\hat{\mathbf{R}})|$, which does not change whether the final result is zero or not. By construction, this results in a polynomial of degree at most $(n+m+4)$ over the formal variables. Hence, for each zero-test, the difference between Exp_0 and Exp_1 is $\frac{n+m+4}{q}$, due to the Schwartz-Zippel lemma (Lemma 3). Assuming that $\mathcal{A}$ makes zero-tests for p (which is a polynomial-size) times, by union bound, the difference between Exp_0 and Exp_1 can be bounded by $\frac{p(n+m+4)}{q}$, which is negligible. In other words, $\mathcal{A}$ can not distinguish this switch except with negligible probability.

For simplicity, we define $(\hat{\boldsymbol{c}}^{(i)})^\top := \left[\left(\hat{\alpha}_i^{-1}\hat{\omega}_i(\boldsymbol{u}_b^{(i)})^\top, (\boldsymbol{x}_b^{(i)})^\top\right)\hat{\mathbf{R}}^{-1}\right]_1$ and $\hat{\boldsymbol{w}}^{(j)} = \left[\hat{\mathbf{R}}\begin{pmatrix}\hat{\beta}_j^{-1}\hat{\gamma}_j\boldsymbol{v}_b^{(j)}\\ \boldsymbol{y}_b^{(j)}\end{pmatrix}\right]_2$. Now in Exp_1, we rewrite the handles of the elements given to

$\mathcal{A}$, $\{[\hat{\omega}_i]_1\}_i$, $\left\{\left[\left(\hat{\omega}_i(\boldsymbol{u}_b^{(i)})^\top, \hat{\alpha}_i(\boldsymbol{x}_b^{(i)})^\top\right)\mathbf{R}^{-1}\right]_1\right\}_i$, $\{[\hat{\gamma}_j]_2\}_j$ and $\left\{\left[\hat{\mathbf{R}}\begin{pmatrix}\hat{\gamma}_j\boldsymbol{v}_b^{(j)}\\ \hat{\beta}_j\boldsymbol{y}_b^{(j)}\end{pmatrix}\right]_2\right\}_j$.

Using this notation, we will write down a general expression for any zero-test query submitted by the adversary. We consider all the possible ways that $\mathcal{A}$ can produce elements in the target group, (1) pairing its ciphertext or functional secret key elements with a constant in the other group, or (2) pairing its ciphertext elements with functional secret key elements, where δ_i, $\zeta_{i,j}$, $\eta_{i,j,l}$, $\theta_{i,k}$, $\kappa_{i,j,k}$, $\mu_{i,j,k,l}$, ν_j and $\rho_{j,l}$ represent coefficients submitted by $\mathcal{A}$.

- Pairing $K_1^{(i)}$ with constants in $\mathbb{G}_2$: $\delta_i \hat{\omega}_i$.
- Pairing $K_1^{(i)}$ with $C_1^{(j)}$: $\zeta_{i,j} \hat{\omega}_i \hat{\gamma}_j$.
- Pairing $K_1^{(i)}$ with $C_2^{(j)}$: $\sum_l \eta_{i,j,l} \hat{\omega}_i \hat{\beta}_j (\hat{\boldsymbol{w}}^{(j)})^{(l)}$.
- Pairing $K_2^{(i)}$ with constants in $\mathbb{G}_2$: $\sum_k \theta_{i,k} \hat{\alpha}_i (\hat{\boldsymbol{c}}^{(i)})^{(k)}$.
- Pairing $K_2^{(i)}$ with $C_1^{(j)}$: $\sum_k \kappa_{i,j,k} \hat{\alpha}_i (\hat{\boldsymbol{c}}^{(i)})^{(k)} \hat{\gamma}_j$.
- Pairing $K_2^{(i)}$ with $C_2^{(j)}$: $\sum_{k,l} \mu_{i,j,k,l} \hat{\alpha}_i (\hat{\boldsymbol{c}}^{(i)})^{(k)} \hat{\beta}_j (\hat{\boldsymbol{w}}^{(j)})^{(l)}$.
- Pairing $C_1^{(j)}$ with constants in $\mathbb{G}_1$: $\nu_j \hat{\gamma}_j$.
- Pairing $C_2^{(j)}$ with constants in $\mathbb{G}_1$: $\sum_l \rho_{j,l} \hat{\beta}_j (\hat{\boldsymbol{w}}^{(j)})^{(l)}$.

Then we write a general linear combination of such elements, and this results in the following expression.

$$
\sum_i \delta_i \hat{\omega}_i + \sum_{i,j} \zeta_{i,j} \hat{\omega}_i \hat{\gamma}_j + \sum_{i,j,l} \eta_{i,j,l} \hat{\omega}_i \hat{\beta}_j (\hat{\boldsymbol{w}}^{(j)})^{(l)} + \sum_{i,k} \theta_{i,k} \hat{\alpha}_i (\hat{\boldsymbol{c}}^{(i)})^{(k)}
$$
$$
+ \sum_{i,j,k} \kappa_{i,j,k} \hat{\alpha}_i (\hat{\boldsymbol{c}}^{(i)})^{(k)} \hat{\gamma}_j + \sum_{i,j,k,l} \mu_{i,j,k,l} \hat{\alpha}_i (\hat{\boldsymbol{c}}^{(i)})^{(k)} \hat{\beta}_j (\hat{\boldsymbol{w}}^{(j)})^{(l)}
$$
$$
+ \sum_j \nu_j \hat{\gamma}_j + \sum_{j,l} \rho_{j,l} \hat{\beta}_j (\hat{\boldsymbol{w}}^{(j)})^{(l)}
$$
$$
= \sum_j \hat{\beta}_j \left(\sum_{i,l} \eta_{i,j,l} \hat{\omega}_i (\hat{\boldsymbol{w}}^{(j)})^{(l)} + \sum_{i,k,l} \mu_{i,j,k,l} \hat{\alpha}_i (\hat{\boldsymbol{c}}^{(i)})^{(k)} (\hat{\boldsymbol{w}}^{(j)})^{(l)} + \sum_l \rho_{j,l} (\hat{\boldsymbol{w}}^{(j)})^{(l)} \right)
$$
$$
+ \sum_i \delta_i \hat{\omega}_i + \sum_{i,j} \zeta_{i,j} \hat{\omega}_i \hat{\gamma}_j + \sum_{i,k} \theta_{i,k} \hat{\alpha}_i (\hat{\boldsymbol{c}}^{(i)})^{(k)} + \sum_{i,j,k} \kappa_{i,j,k} \hat{\alpha}_i (\hat{\boldsymbol{c}}^{(i)})^{(k)} \hat{\gamma}_j + \sum_j \nu_j \hat{\gamma}_j
$$

Now any potentially distinguishing zero-test query must result in an identically zero rational function for at least one setting of $b \in \{0, 1\}$ and thus must set the coefficient on $\hat{\beta}_j$ to some scaling of $\hat{\beta}_j^{-1}$ for one of these settings since $\hat{\beta}_j$ does not appear in the other terms. This implies a few things about the adversary's coefficients.

- **Condition 1.** For each j, l, $\rho_{j,l} = 0$, since each entry of $\hat{\boldsymbol{w}}^{(j)}$ is a sum over distinct formal variables from $\hat{\mathbf{R}}$ which cannot be canceled out elsewhere in the coefficient on $\hat{\beta}_j$. Then we can rewrite the above expression as,

$$
\sum_j \hat{\beta}_j \left(\sum_{i,l} \eta_{i,j,l} \hat{\omega}_i (\hat{\boldsymbol{w}}^{(j)})^{(l)} + \sum_{i,k,l} \mu_{i,j,k,l} \hat{\alpha}_i (\hat{\boldsymbol{c}}^{(i)})^{(k)} (\hat{\boldsymbol{w}}^{(j)})^{(l)} \right) + \sum_i \delta_i \hat{\omega}_i
$$
$$
+ \sum_{i,j} \zeta_{i,j} \hat{\omega}_i \hat{\gamma}_j + \sum_{i,k} \theta_{i,k} \hat{\alpha}_i (\hat{\boldsymbol{c}}^{(i)})^{(k)} + \sum_{i,j,k} \kappa_{i,j,k} \hat{\alpha}_i (\hat{\boldsymbol{c}}^{(i)})^{(k)} \hat{\gamma}_j + \sum_j \nu_j \hat{\gamma}_j
$$

- **Condition 2.** By a similar argument, for each i, j, l, $\eta_{i,j,l} = 0$, since each entry of $\hat{\boldsymbol{w}}^{(j)}$ cannot be canceled out elsewhere in the coefficient on $\hat{\omega}_i \hat{\beta}_j$. Then we can rewrite the above expression as,

$$
\sum_j \hat{\beta}_j \left(\sum_i \hat{\alpha}_i \left(\sum_{k,l} \mu_{i,j,k,l} (\hat{\boldsymbol{c}}^{(i)})^{(k)} (\hat{\boldsymbol{w}}^{(j)})^{(l)} \right) \right) + \sum_i \delta_i \hat{\omega}_i + \sum_{i,j} \zeta_{i,j} \hat{\omega}_i \hat{\gamma}_j
$$
$$
+ \sum_{i,k} \theta_{i,k} \hat{\alpha}_i (\hat{\boldsymbol{c}}^{(i)})^{(k)} + \sum_{i,j,k} \kappa_{i,j,k} \hat{\alpha}_i (\hat{\boldsymbol{c}}^{(i)})^{(k)} \hat{\gamma}_j + \sum_j \nu_j \hat{\gamma}_j.
$$

- **Condition 3.** For each i, j, the coefficient on $\hat{\alpha}_i$ within each $\hat{\beta}_j$ coefficient must be some scaling of $\hat{\alpha}_i^{-1}$. Then by Lemma 12, for each i, j, the coefficients $\{\mu_{i,j,k,l}\}_{k,l}$ must be set to induce a scaling of the inner product of $\hat{\boldsymbol{c}}^{(i)}$ and $\hat{\boldsymbol{w}}^{(j)}$. Let $k_{i,j}$ denote this scaling. We can rewrite the above expression as follows.

$$
\sum_{i,j} \hat{\alpha}_i \hat{\beta}_j k_{i,j} \left(\hat{\alpha}_i^{-1} \hat{\beta}_j^{-1} \hat{\omega}_i \hat{\gamma}_j \langle \boldsymbol{u}_b^{(i)}, \boldsymbol{v}_b^{(j)} \rangle + \langle \boldsymbol{x}_b^{(i)}, \boldsymbol{y}_b^{(j)} \rangle \right) + \sum_i \delta_i \hat{\omega}_i + \sum_{i,j} \zeta_{i,j} \hat{\omega}_i \hat{\gamma}_j
$$
$$
+ \sum_{i,k} \theta_{i,k} \hat{\alpha}_i (\hat{\boldsymbol{c}}^{(i)})^{(k)} + \sum_{i,j,k} \kappa_{i,j,k} \hat{\alpha}_i (\hat{\boldsymbol{c}}^{(i)})^{(k)} \hat{\gamma}_j + \sum_j \nu_j \hat{\gamma}_j
$$
$$
= \sum_{i,j} k_{i,j} \hat{\omega}_i \hat{\gamma}_j \langle \boldsymbol{u}_b^{(i)}, \boldsymbol{v}_b^{(j)} \rangle + \sum_{i,j} \hat{\alpha}_i \hat{\beta}_j k_{i,j} \langle \boldsymbol{x}_b^{(i)}, \boldsymbol{y}_b^{(j)} \rangle + \sum_i \delta_i \hat{\omega}_i + \sum_{i,j} \zeta_{i,j} \hat{\omega}_i \hat{\gamma}_j
$$
$$
+ \sum_{i,k} \theta_{i,k} \hat{\alpha}_i (\hat{\boldsymbol{c}}^{(i)})^{(k)} + \sum_{i,j,k} \kappa_{i,j,k} \hat{\alpha}_i (\hat{\boldsymbol{c}}^{(i)})^{(k)} \hat{\gamma}_j + \sum_j \nu_j \hat{\gamma}_j.
$$

- **Condition 4.** For each i, k, $\theta_{i,k} = 0$, by a similar argument as in **Condition 1**, since each entry of $\hat{\boldsymbol{c}}^{(i)}$ is a sum over distinct formal variables from $\hat{\mathbf{R}}$ which cannot be canceled out elsewhere in the coefficient on $\hat{\alpha}_i$. We can rewrite the above expression as follows.

$$
= \sum_{i,j} k_{i,j} \hat{\omega}_i \hat{\gamma}_j \langle \boldsymbol{u}_b^{(i)}, \boldsymbol{v}_b^{(j)} \rangle + \sum_{i,j} \hat{\alpha}_i \hat{\beta}_j k_{i,j} \langle \boldsymbol{x}_b^{(i)}, \boldsymbol{y}_b^{(j)} \rangle + \sum_i \delta_i \hat{\omega}_i
$$
$$
+ \sum_{i,j} \zeta_{i,j} \hat{\omega}_i \hat{\gamma}_j + \sum_{i,j,k} \kappa_{i,j,k} \hat{\alpha}_i (\hat{\boldsymbol{c}}^{(i)})^{(k)} \hat{\gamma}_j + \sum_j \nu_j \hat{\gamma}_j.
$$

- **Condition 5.** for each i, j, k, $\kappa_{i,j,k} = 0$, since each entry of $\hat{\boldsymbol{c}}^{(i)}$ cannot be canceled out elsewhere in the coefficient on $\hat{\alpha}_i \hat{\gamma}_j$. Then we can rewrite the above expression as,

$$
\sum_{i,j} k_{i,j} \hat{\omega}_i \hat{\gamma}_j \langle \boldsymbol{u}_b^{(i)}, \boldsymbol{v}_b^{(j)} \rangle + \sum_{i,j} \hat{\alpha}_i \hat{\beta}_j k_{i,j} \langle \boldsymbol{x}_b^{(i)}, \boldsymbol{y}_b^{(j)} \rangle
$$
$$
+ \sum_i \delta_i \hat{\omega}_i + \sum_{i,j} \zeta_{i,j} \hat{\omega}_i \hat{\gamma}_j + \sum_j \nu_j \hat{\gamma}_j.
$$

Now observe that we need the coefficient on $\hat{\alpha}_i \hat{\beta}_j$ to be zero in order to obtain a successful zero-test. We consider two cases.

- For each i, j, $k_{i,j} = 0$, then the remaining term is

$$\sum_i \delta_i \hat{\omega}_i + \sum_{i,j} \zeta_{i,j} \hat{\omega}_i \hat{\gamma}_j + \sum_j \nu_j \hat{\gamma}_j,$$

which is independent of the bit b. Thus, such a zero-test cannot be used to distinguish.
- Otherwise, let Q be the sets of pair (i, j) such that $k_{i,j} \neq 0$. If the coefficients on $\hat{\alpha}_i \hat{\beta}_j$ is zero for some b, this implies that $\langle \boldsymbol{x}_b^{(i)}, \boldsymbol{y}_b^{(j)} \rangle = 0 \mod q$ for each pair $(i, j) \in Q$. Then by admissibility, this implies that $\langle \boldsymbol{u}_0^{(i)}, \boldsymbol{v}_0^{(j)} \rangle = \langle \boldsymbol{u}_1^{(i)}, \boldsymbol{v}_1^{(j)} \rangle$. Then it is clear that the remaining expression

$$\sum_i \delta_i \hat{\omega}_i + \sum_{i,j} \zeta_{i,j} \hat{\omega}_i \hat{\gamma}_j + \sum_j \nu_j \hat{\gamma}_j,$$

is also independent of the bit b. This completes the proof.

5   Implementation and Evaluation

To evaluate the practicality of our main construction, we implemented our FH-ZP-IPFE scheme. Our implementation uses the RELIC [6] library to implement the pairing group operations and the finite field arithmetic in $\mathbb{Z}_q$. In our benchmarks, we measure the time needed to encrypt, issue functional secret keys for, and decrypt the inner product for $(n+m)$-dimensional binary vectors for several different values of $(n + m)$. Following by the suggestion in [25], we measure the performance with respect to matrices $\mathbf{R}$ and $\mathbf{R}^*$ that are sampled uniformly at random. Using simulated rather than real matrices has no effect on the benchmarks of the underlying FH-ZP-IPFE operations.

We run all of our benchmarks on a Linux desktop with a 6-core Intel Core i5-10500H 2.50 GHz processor and 16 GB of RAM. We run benchmarks over the curve MNT224 and assume the bound of inner products as 3×10^9 when solving discrete logarithm. The concrete performance numbers of FH-ZP-IPFE scheme are summarized in Table 2.

Table 2. Micro-benchmarks for our FH-ZP-IPFE scheme over the MNT224 curve

Dimension $(n + m)$	Encryption	KeyGen	Dec
$(n + m) = 1024$	1.01 s	5.058 s	4.446 s
$(n + m) = 2048$	2.694 s	10.772 s	8.104 s
$(n + m) = 4096$	8.556 s	24.604 s	16.138 s

6 Conclusion and Future Work

In this paper, we give the first formal definition of function-hiding predicate functional encryption (FH-P-FE) and its security model. We then show that this paradigm is achievable by giving a direct construction of secret-key function-hiding zero predicate inner product functional encryption (FH-ZP-IPFE) from pairings and prove it secure in the generic bilinear group model. This is the first construction of FE with fine-grained access control in the function-hiding setting. There are also several work desired to be further considered.

- Construction of FH-ZP-IPFE with smaller master secret key size. Note in our construction, the size of master secret key is $O(n^2)$ and the run-time complexity of setup algorithm is $O(n^3)$ since we need to compute $\mathbf{R}^{-1}$.
- Construction of quadratic functional encryption (QFE) [31, 36] with fine-grained access control (such as inner product predicates). QFE is the only one FE schemes that has proven to be achievable beyond linear function without trivial expansions. So it is interesting to give such a construction, although it may not be in the function-hiding setting.

Acknowledgment. This work is supported by the National Natural Science Foundation of China (No. 62202294) and the National Key R&D Program of China (No. 2020YFA0712300).

References

1. Abdalla, M., Catalano, D., Gay, R., Ursu, B.: Inner-product functional encryption with fine-grained access control. In: Moriai, S., Wang, H. (eds.) ASIACRYPT 2020. LNCS, vol. 12493, pp. 467–497. Springer, Cham (2020). https://doi.org/10.1007/978-3-030-64840-4_16
2. Agrawal, S., Boneh, D., Boyen, X.: Efficient lattice (H)IBE in the standard model. In: Gilbert, H. (ed.) EUROCRYPT 2010. LNCS, vol. 6110, pp. 553–572. Springer, Heidelberg (2010). https://doi.org/10.1007/978-3-642-13190-5_28
3. Agrawal, S., Boneh, D., Boyen, X.: Lattice basis delegation in fixed dimension and shorter-ciphertext hierarchical IBE. In: Rabin, T. (ed.) CRYPTO 2010. LNCS, vol. 6223, pp. 98–115. Springer, Heidelberg (2010). https://doi.org/10.1007/978-3-642-14623-7_6
4. Agrawal, S., Freeman, D.M., Vaikuntanathan, V.: Functional encryption for inner product predicates from learning with errors. In: Lee, D.H., Wang, X. (eds.) ASIACRYPT 2011. LNCS, vol. 7073, pp. 21–40. Springer, Heidelberg (2011). https://doi.org/10.1007/978-3-642-25385-0_2
5. Agrawal, S., Libert, B., Stehlé, D.: Fully secure functional encryption for inner products, from standard assumptions. In: Robshaw, M., Katz, J. (eds.) CRYPTO 2016. LNCS, vol. 9816, pp. 333–362. Springer, Heidelberg (2016). https://doi.org/10.1007/978-3-662-53015-3_12
6. Aranha, D.F., Gouvêa, C.P.L., Markmann, T., Wahby, R.S., Liao, K.: RELIC is an Efficient LIbrary for Cryptography. https://github.com/relic-toolkit/relic

7. Badrinarayanan, S., Miles, E., Sahai, A., Zhandry, M.: Post-zeroizing obfuscation: new mathematical tools, and the case of evasive circuits. In: Fischlin, M., Coron, J.-S. (eds.) EUROCRYPT 2016. LNCS, vol. 9666, pp. 764–791. Springer, Heidelberg (2016). https://doi.org/10.1007/978-3-662-49896-5_27

8. Bartusek, J., et al.: Public-key function-private hidden vector encryption (and more). In: Galbraith, S.D., Moriai, S. (eds.) ASIACRYPT 2019. LNCS, vol. 11923, pp. 489–519. Springer, Cham (2019). https://doi.org/10.1007/978-3-030-34618-8_17

9. Bartusek, J., Guan, J., Ma, F., Zhandry, M.: Return of GGH15: provable security against zeroizing attacks. In: Beimel, A., Dziembowski, S. (eds.) TCC 2018. LNCS, vol. 11240, pp. 544–574. Springer, Cham (2018). https://doi.org/10.1007/978-3-030-03810-6_20

10. Bethencourt, J., Sahai, A., Waters, B.: Ciphertext-policy attribute-based encryption. In: 2007 IEEE Symposium on Security and Privacy (SP 2007), pp. 321–334 (2007). https://doi.org/10.1109/SP.2007.11

11. Bishop, A., Jain, A., Kowalczyk, L.: Function-hiding inner product encryption. In: Iwata, T., Cheon, J.H. (eds.) ASIACRYPT 2015. LNCS, vol. 9452, pp. 470–491. Springer, Heidelberg (2015). https://doi.org/10.1007/978-3-662-48797-6_20

12. Boneh, D., Boyen, X., Goh, E.-J.: Hierarchical identity based encryption with constant size ciphertext. In: Cramer, R. (ed.) EUROCRYPT 2005. LNCS, vol. 3494, pp. 440–456. Springer, Heidelberg (2005). https://doi.org/10.1007/11426639_26

13. Boneh, D., Franklin, M.: Identity-based encryption from the weil pairing. In: Kilian, J. (ed.) CRYPTO 2001. LNCS, vol. 2139, pp. 213–229. Springer, Heidelberg (2001). https://doi.org/10.1007/3-540-44647-8_13

14. Boneh, D., et al.: Fully key-homomorphic encryption, arithmetic circuit ABE and compact garbled circuits. In: Nguyen, P.Q., Oswald, E. (eds.) EUROCRYPT 2014. LNCS, vol. 8441, pp. 533–556. Springer, Heidelberg (2014). https://doi.org/10.1007/978-3-642-55220-5_30

15. Boneh, D., Raghunathan, A., Segev, G.: Function-private identity-based encryption: hiding the function in functional encryption. In: Canetti, R., Garay, J.A. (eds.) CRYPTO 2013. LNCS, vol. 8043, pp. 461–478. Springer, Heidelberg (2013). https://doi.org/10.1007/978-3-642-40084-1_26

16. Boneh, D., Raghunathan, A., Segev, G.: Function-private subspace-membership encryption and its applications. In: Sako, K., Sarkar, P. (eds.) ASIACRYPT 2013. LNCS, vol. 8269, pp. 255–275. Springer, Heidelberg (2013). https://doi.org/10.1007/978-3-642-42033-7_14

17. Boneh, D., Sahai, A., Waters, B.: Functional encryption: definitions and challenges. In: Ishai, Y. (ed.) TCC 2011. LNCS, vol. 6597, pp. 253–273. Springer, Heidelberg (2011). https://doi.org/10.1007/978-3-642-19571-6_16

18. Cash, D., Hofheinz, D., Kiltz, E., Peikert, C.: Bonsai trees, or how to delegate a lattice basis. In: Gilbert, H. (ed.) EUROCRYPT 2010. LNCS, vol. 6110, pp. 523–552. Springer, Heidelberg (2010). https://doi.org/10.1007/978-3-642-13190-5_27

19. Datta, P., Dutta, R., Mukhopadhyay, S.: Functional encryption for inner product with full function privacy. In: Cheng, C.-M., Chung, K.-M., Persiano, G., Yang, B.-Y. (eds.) PKC 2016. LNCS, vol. 9614, pp. 164–195. Springer, Heidelberg (2016). https://doi.org/10.1007/978-3-662-49384-7_7

20. Dowerah, U., Dutta, S., Mitrokotsa, A., Mukherjee, S., Pal, T.: Unbounded predicate inner product functional encryption from pairings. Cryptology ePrint Archive, Paper 2023/483 (2023). https://eprint.iacr.org/2023/483, https://eprint.iacr.org/2023/483

21. Gorbunov, S., Vaikuntanathan, V., Wee, H.: Attribute-based encryption for circuits. In: Proceedings of the Forty-Fifth Annual ACM Symposium on Theory of Computing. p. 545–554. STOC '13, Association for Computing Machinery, New York, NY, USA (2013). https://doi.org/10.1145/2488608.2488677

22. Gorbunov, S., Vaikuntanathan, V., Wee, H.: Predicate encryption for circuits from LWE. In: Gennaro, R., Robshaw, M. (eds.) CRYPTO 2015. LNCS, vol. 9216, pp. 503–523. Springer, Heidelberg (2015). https://doi.org/10.1007/978-3-662-48000-7_25

23. Joux, A.: A one round protocol for tripartite Diffie–Hellman. In: Bosma, W. (ed.) ANTS 2000. LNCS, vol. 1838, pp. 385–393. Springer, Heidelberg (2000). https://doi.org/10.1007/10722028_23

24. Katz, J., Sahai, A., Waters, B.: Predicate encryption supporting disjunctions, polynomial equations, and inner products. In: Smart, N. (ed.) EUROCRYPT 2008. LNCS, vol. 4965, pp. 146–162. Springer, Heidelberg (2008). https://doi.org/10.1007/978-3-540-78967-3_9

25. Kim, S., Lewi, K., Mandal, A., Montgomery, H., Roy, A., Wu, D.J.: Function-hiding inner product encryption is practical. In: Catalano, D., De Prisco, R. (eds.) SCN 2018. LNCS, vol. 11035, pp. 544–562. Springer, Cham (2018). https://doi.org/10.1007/978-3-319-98113-0_29

26. Lai, Q., Liu, F.-H., Wang, Z.: New lattice two-stage sampling technique and its applications to functional encryption – stronger security and smaller ciphertexts. In: Canteaut, A., Standaert, F.-X. (eds.) EUROCRYPT 2021. LNCS, vol. 12696, pp. 498–527. Springer, Cham (2021). https://doi.org/10.1007/978-3-030-77870-5_18

27. Nechaev, V.I.: Complexity of a determinate algorithm for the discrete logarithm. Math. Notes 55(2), 165–172 (1994)

28. O'Neill, A.: Definitional issues in functional encryption. Cryptology ePrint Archive, Paper 2010/556 (2010). https://eprint.iacr.org/2010/556

29. Pal, T., Dutta, R.: CCA secure attribute-hiding inner product encryption from minimal assumption. In: Baek, J., Ruj, S. (eds.) ACISP 2021. LNCS, vol. 13083, pp. 254–274. Springer, Cham (2021). https://doi.org/10.1007/978-3-030-90567-5_13

30. Patranabis, S., Mukhopadhyay, D., Ramanna, S.C.: function private predicate encryption for low min-entropy predicates. In: Lin, D., Sako, K. (eds.) PKC 2019. LNCS, vol. 11443, pp. 189–219. Springer, Cham (2019). https://doi.org/10.1007/978-3-030-17259-6_7

31. Ryffel, T., Pointcheval, D., Bach, F., Dufour-Sans, E., Gay, R.: Partially encrypted deep learning using functional encryption. In: Wallach, H., Larochelle, H., Beygelzimer, A., d'Alché Buc, F., Fox, E., Garnett, R. (eds.) Advances in Neural Information Processing Systems. vol. 32. Curran Associates, Inc. (2019). https://proceedings.neurips.cc/paper/2019/file/9d28de8ff9bb6a3fa41fddfdc28f3bc1-Paper.pdf

32. Sahai, A., Waters, B.: Fuzzy identity-based encryption. In: Cramer, R. (ed.) EUROCRYPT 2005. LNCS, vol. 3494, pp. 457–473. Springer, Heidelberg (2005). https://doi.org/10.1007/11426639_27

33. Schwartz, J.T.: Fast probabilistic algorithms for verification of polynomial identities. J. ACM 27(4), 701–717 (1980)

34. Shoup, V.: Lower bounds for discrete logarithms and related problems. In: Fumy, W. (ed.) EUROCRYPT 1997. LNCS, vol. 1233, pp. 256–266. Springer, Heidelberg (1997). https://doi.org/10.1007/3-540-69053-0_18

35. Tomida, J., Abe, M., Okamoto, T.: Efficient functional encryption for inner-product values with full-hiding security. In: Bishop, M., Nascimento, A.C.A. (eds.) ISC 2016. LNCS, vol. 9866, pp. 408–425. Springer, Cham (2016). https://doi.org/10.1007/978-3-319-45871-7_24

36. Wee, H.: Functional encryption for quadratic functions from k-lin, revisited. In: Pass, R., Pietrzak, K. (eds.) TCC 2020. LNCS, vol. 12550, pp. 210–228. Springer, Cham (2020). https://doi.org/10.1007/978-3-030-64375-1_8

37. Zippel, R.: Probabilistic algorithms for sparse polynomials. In: Ng, E.W. (ed.) Symbolic and Algebraic Computation. LNCS, vol. 72, pp. 216–226. Springer, Heidelberg (1979). https://doi.org/10.1007/3-540-09519-5_73

Signatures, Hashes, and Cryptanalysis

Robust Property-Preserving Hash Meets Homomorphism

Keyang Liu$^{(\boxtimes)}$ [ID], Xingxin Li [ID], and Tsuyoshi Takagi

Department of Mathematical Informatics, The University of Tokyo, Tokyo, Japan
`stephenkobylky2022@g.ecc.u-tokyo.ac.jp`, `lixingxin@g.ecc.u-tokyo.ac.jp`,
`takagi@mist.i.u-tokyo.ac.jp`

Abstract. Boyle et al. introduced the Property-Preserving Hash (PPH) concept in 2019, spawning a series of subsequent research endeavors over the following two years. A PPH function compresses an input x into a short hash value while revealing a pre-defined one-bit property of the input from that hash value. A PPH is robust (RPPH) if no probabilistic polynomial-time adversary can find an input whose hash value cannot correctly reveal the property of inputs.

This research studies a homomorphic variant of RPPH, denoted as Homomorphic Robust Property-Preserving Hash (HRPPH). This variant is particularly beneficial in privacy computing scenarios, where certain computations of private data are required, but access to the original data is intentionally restricted. The contributions of our study are twofold:

1. We define HRPPH and demonstrate two previously explored properties: Hamming weight and Gap-k Greater-Than, which lack an HRPPH.
2. We prove that two types of properties, the perfectly compressive and enumerable properties, may construct corresponding HRPPH.

Keywords: Homomorphism · Property-Preserving Hash · Privacy Computing · Collision Resistance

1 Introduction

The ability to compress data into a short hash value while preserving specific properties of the inputs is of considerable importance nowadays. A well-known example is the Collision-Resistant Hash Function (CRHF), which can determine the equality of different inputs through their fixed-length outputs. In 2019, Boyle et al. introduced a novel concept, the Property-Preserving Hash (PPH), which preserves one pre-defined property other than equlity [7]. A PPH enables the evaluation of a predetermined property predicate P using an evaluation function $Eval$ predicated on the hash values of the inputs. With overwhelming probability, the results of the property predicates (i.e., $P(x, y)$ for two inputs x and y) will coincide with the output of the evaluation function utilizing the hash values (i.e., $Eval(h(x), h(y))$ for the PPH function h).

© The Author(s), under exclusive license to Springer Nature Switzerland AG 2023
E. Athanasopoulos and B. Mennink (Eds.): ISC 2023, LNCS 14411, pp. 537–556, 2023.
https://doi.org/10.1007/978-3-031-49187-0_27

To address the security concern, Boyle et al. introduced the concept of (direct-access) robustness. A PPH is robust if any Probabilistic Polynomial-Time (PPT) adversary, given access to the scheme's description (i.e., h), can only find incorrect inputs that violate the correctness (i.e., finding x, y such that $P(x, y) \neq Eval(h(x), h(y))$) with a negligible probability. The following studies [13–15] have focused on constructing (R)PPH for testifying if the Hamming distance between two bit-strings is less than a pre-defined threshold t.

We notice the utility of RPPH is limited, as it can only reveal the properties of inputs. This limitation is particularly evident in its inability to handle complex data preprocessing, such as scaling or computing the mean of inputs, which are helpful in numerous applications. This work introduces the concept of homomorphism into RPPH to overcome this limitation. We denote this new primitive as the Homomorphic Robust Property-Preserving Hash (HRPPH).

1.1 Motivation

We propose HRPPH for the scenario where the server needs to process private data from clients for its goodness (e.g., training a generative AI model with data of users). In such a scenario, access to plaintext data easily triggers privacy concerns, interaction with clients is impossible, and computation over raw data is necessary. HRPPH facilitates the server's computation of $P(f(x_1, x_2, ...)) = Eval(f(h(x_1), h(x_2), ...))$ for a certain function f that is supported by the homomorphism. HRPPH can be a novel tool for constructing privacy-preserving applications in this context.

One concrete example is evaluating a linear regression model $f(x) = ax + b$. The server wants to check whether the predicted result $f(x)$ is adequately close to the actual data y. If both x and y are private, complex protocols such as multi-party computation would be required to yield the result $|f(x) - y| < t$. However, these solutions are usually costly, typically when frequent computations and comparisons are necessary for model tuning. With an HRPPH h of property $P(x, y) = |x - y| < t$, we only need to compute $Eval(ah(x) + h(b), h(y))$ to testify P. We provide a candidate HRPPH for this use case in Sect. 4.3.

1.2 Related Works

Prior Works of PPH. Boyle et al. pioneered the study of PPH in [7]. They proposed the definition of PPH and introduced the term 'robust' for evaluating the correctness of compression techniques. Additionally, they proposed certain gap property predicates that effectively disregard the inputs' properties within a pre-defined interval in Robust Property Preserving Hash (RPPH) constructions. This gap serves as a mechanism to cover errors introduced through compression, thereby ensuring the correctness of the property. The plausible construction of RPPH for the newly introduced gap-Hamming weight property was both elegant and precise, subsequently inciting other researchers' interest in this field.

In 2021, Fleischhacker and Simkin [14] studied the property of the exact Hamming attribute and offered a refined construction of RPPH based on a bilinear group. In the following work [13], Fleischhacker et al. use Bloom look-up tables and standard Short Integer Solution (SIS) assumptions to propose a new quantum-resistant RPPH. The most recent result in RPPH is attributed to Holmgren et al. [15]. They harnessed the power of error-correcting code technology alongside certain collision-resistant hash functions for constructing RPPHs.

In summary, current research primarily concentrates on the properties of Hamming distances, approaching the compactness to the possible lower bound. While most constructions employ some form of homomorphism, they are not consistently homomorphic beyond certain operations, leading to additional overhead for output length, as demonstrated in [15].

HRPPH Compared to Other Primitives. To delineate the distinction of HRPPH, it is helpful to briefly review some similar cryptographic primitives and their comparison with HRPPH.

Homomorphic encryption(HE), as in [8,10], is a cryptographic protocol that allows for outsourcing complex computations to a server. The server can manipulate the ciphertext to perform these computations, yet the plaintext results are accessible exclusively to the user possessing the secret key. HE requires additional interaction with the data owner for decryption, while HRPPH doesn't need that with the cost of a one-bit-only result. Therefore, HRPPH is more suitable for privacy-preserving protocols where interaction is limited, and the result is simple.

Homomorphic hash functions, another cryptographic primitive, are pivotal in protocols devised to authenticate dynamic content. LtHash [3] is an excellent example widely used for validating incremental data updates. HRPPH extends the utility of homomorphic hash functions beyond revealing equality to disclosing an additional one-bit property. This extra property makes HRPPH more usable in secure computation protocols [18].

Functional Encryption (FE) [6] is similar to HRPPH in terms of functionality. In FE, a data owner may encrypt data into ciphertext, while the data consumer can obtain a result of a pre-defined computation using a derived key. For instance, [9] offers a practical construction to compute the inner product of inputs with another public vector. The distinction between functional encryption and HRPPH lies in two aspects: 1. HRPPH reduces the data owner's workload since there is no key in HRPPH, and anyone can reveal the property freely. 2. HRPPH is more flexible with homomorphic operations than the fixed operation supported by FE.

1.3 Our Contributions and Techniques

In this paper, we introduce the definition of HRPPH. We discuss the impossible results of the Exact Hamming weight property and the integer Gap-k Greater-Than property. We propose two methodologies for building HRPPH for two distinct property types and provide practical examples for each. The main contributions are summarized as follows:

K. Liu et al.

HRPPH Definition and Theoretical Outcomes. In Sect. 3, we define HRPPH and examine whether the previously studied property predicates of RPPH can have an HRPPH. We present two negative findings indicating that robustness, homomorphism, and property preservation may conflict.

No HRPPH for Hamming Weight. Our first result demonstrates that it is not feasible to construct an HRPPH for the Hamming weight property, defined as $Hamming_t(x) := |x| < t; x \in \{0,1\}^n$. We first show that any HRPPH for $Hamming_t(x)$ must be collision resistant. Next, we prove no homomorphism on $(\{0,1\}^n, \bigoplus)$ that is collision-resistant. Consequently, there is no HRPPH for $Hamming_t(x)$.

No HRPPH for Gap-k Greater-Than. We further illustrate that the Gap-k Greater-Than property proposed by [7] cannot possess an HRPPH for any k. The reason is that the property partitions the group in a way that contradicts the homomorphism structure.

Our Proposed HRPPH Constructions. Section 4 proposes two methodologies for constructing an HRPPH, accompanied by applicable instances.

HRPPH for Perfectly Compressive Property. Initially, we define perfectly compressive properties and demonstrate that they consistently possess an HRPPH. A perfectly compressive property needs a non-trivial normal subgroup of the domain group, wherein cosets consistently share identical properties. The term "perfectly" indicates that the compression from the domain group to the quotient group will not introduce errors when evaluating the property. We show that these properties result in a perfectly compressive HRPPH that remains invulnerable to robustness compromise by any adversary.

HRPPH for Enumerable Property. Secondly, inspired by existing works [15], we proposed a general HRPPH construction for enumerable properties. This construction is suitable for properties that segregate the input domain X into two sets X_1 and X_0 where $|X_0| \gg |X_1|$. This construction requires X_1 to be enumerable under specific constraints. We use these constraints with a generalized homomorphic collision-resistant hash function (HCRHF) to reveal the property robustly. As an example, we propose an HRPPH of integer-close-to property $ICT_t(x) := |x| < t$, given an integer $t > 0$ and $x \in (\mathbb{Z}, +)$. Our HRPPH supports integer addition and constant scaling, which allows our construction to be applied to linear systems.

2 Preliminary

This section provides the basic notations and definitions used throughout the paper.

We use the notation $x \leftarrow_r X$ to denote sampling x uniformly at random from a set X and $|X|$ to represent the cardinality of X. The symbol $\leftarrow$ denotes the assignment of a variable. A group defined over set X with a binary operation $\odot$ is denoted as $(X, \odot)$. We will also use X to represent the group if the operation is clear from the context. $\mathbb{Z}$ denotes integer ring. For any positive integer n, $\mathbb{Z}_n$ represents the additive group of integers modulo n. $\mathbb{N}$ represents the additive group of natural numbers. A column vector is denoted by the bold character $\boldsymbol{x}$. $\lambda \in \mathbb{N}$ represents the security parameter. $poly(\lambda)$ denotes any function bounded by a polynomial in λ. We use $negl(\lambda)$ to denote any negligible function f that for any $c \in \mathbb{N}$, there exists an $l \in \mathbb{N}$ such that for all $\lambda > l$, $f(\lambda) < 1/\lambda^c$.

2.1   Boolean Group

Here, we recall the definition of the boolean group.

Definition 1 (Boolean Group [17]). *A boolean group* $(X, \odot)$ *is a group that satisfies the property that for every element* $x \in X$, $x \odot x = 0$, *where* 0 *is the identity element of* X.

Since every element in a boolean group is self-inversive, a boolean group is abelian. Therefore, a boolean group is an elementary abelian group of order 2, which leads to the following property:

Property 1 (Basis Theorem for Finite Abelian Groups). Every finite boolean group is isomorphic to a finite direct product of a 2-elements group.

Above property implies that any boolean group $(X, \odot)$ is isomorphic to $(\mathbb{Z}_2^{log|X|}, +)$. Hence, we can always find a primary decomposition that maps X into a binary vector space $\mathbb{Z}_2^{log|X|}$.

2.2   Cryptographic Assumption

We recall the strong RSA assumption for general groups of unknown order as introduced in [5].

Definition 2 (Strong RSA for General Groups of Unknown Order [5]).
Given a security parameter λ, *let* $GGen(\lambda)$ *be a randomized function that returns a group* $\mathbb{G}$ *of unknown order. For any generator* $g \in \mathbb{G}$ *and for all probabilistic polynomial time (PPT) adversaries* $\mathcal{A}$, *we have:*

$$\Pr\left[\begin{array}{l} (x, e) \in \mathbb{G} \times \mathbb{Z} \leftarrow \mathcal{A}(\mathbb{G}, g) \\ \quad s.t.\ e\ is\ an\ odd\ prime \end{array} : x^e \equiv g \right] \leq negl(\lambda).$$

This assumption extends the traditional strong RSA assumption [1] to groups such as ideal class groups or hyperelliptic Jacobians [11]. By using ideal class groups in the function $GGen$, we can reduce the size of the group elements and remove the trusted setup process required by RSA modulo.

3   Homomorphic Robust Property-Preserving Hash (HRPPH)

We now define HRPPH as an extension of RPPH [7].

Definition 3 (HRPPH). *Given a security parameter* λ, *an HRPPH family* $\mathcal{H} = \{h : X \to Y\}$ *for 2 groups* $(X, \odot)$ *and* $(Y, \otimes)$ *and a predicate* $P : X \to \{0, 1\}$ *has the following three algorithms:*

- *$Samp(\lambda) \to h$ is a randomized PPT algorithm that samples $h \leftarrow_r \mathcal{H}$.*
- *$Hash(h, x) \to y$ is an efficient deterministic PPT algorithm that computes the hash of the input x.*
- *$Eval(h, y) \to \{0, 1\}$ is an efficient deterministic PPT algorithm that takes the input of a hash value and outputs a single bit.*

The HRPPH scheme requires the following properties:

- *Homomorphism: $\forall x_0, x_1 \in X$ and $h \in \mathcal{H}$,*

$$h(x_0 \odot x_1) = h(x_0) \otimes h(x_1).$$

- *Compression: $\forall h \in \mathcal{H}$, the kernel K_h satisfies $|K_h| > 1$. If $|X|$ is finite, the compression rate is defined as $\eta = \frac{log|Y|}{log|X|}$.*
- *Robustness: For any PPT adversary $\mathcal{A}$,*

$$\Pr\left[\begin{matrix} h \leftarrow Samp(\lambda) \\ x \leftarrow \mathcal{A}(h) \end{matrix} : Eval(h, h(x)) \neq P(x) \right] \leq negl(\lambda).$$

Compared to the original definition of RPPH, HRPPH changes:

1. The evaluation function $Eval$ only takes one input because the users can compute functions of hash values through homomorphic operations.
2. We rewrite the compression requirement to allow inputs from infinity groups. An HRPPH scheme is compressive if its kernel has more than one element.
3. The Robustness of RPPH in the original paper [7] can have different oracles that the adversary could access to distinguish various types of robustness. In this paper, we only discuss the most challenging case where the adversary has direct access to the description of the RPPH (i.e., h).

3.1   No HRPPH for Hamming Weight

Given the definition of HRPPH, our first interest is to examine the possibility of constructing an HRPPH from existing RPPHs. We define a single-input predicate accepting inputs from $(\{0, 1\}^n, \bigoplus)$ for measuring hamming weights.

Definition 4 (Hamming weight predicates). *Let $n \in \mathbb{N}$, $0 < t < n$, and $x \in \{0, 1\}^n$. The Hamming weight predicate, $Ham_{n,t}(x)$, is defined as follows:*

$$Ham_{n,t}(x) := \begin{cases} 1 & |x| \leq t \\ 0 & |x| > t \end{cases}.$$

It is straightforward to deduce that the Hamming weight predicate implies an exact Hamming predicate when the second input corresponds to an all-zero string. By integrating the concept of homomorphism, we can compute $P(x_1 \oplus \cdots \oplus x_n)$ derived from $h(x_1), \cdots, h(x_n)$ for any $(x_1, \cdots, x_n) \in \mathbb{Z}_2^n$. Consequently, an HRPPH of hamming weight predicate leads to an RPPH for the Exact Hamming Predicate. However, existing constructions of RPPH for the exact Hamming predicate, as described in [13–15], are not holomorphic according to our standard definition. Thus, they cannot construct an HRPPH for our Hamming weight predicate. We will demonstrate that no HRPPH construction exists for the Hamming weight predicate and the exact Hamming predicate.

We start with the definition of collision resistance. Given a security parameter λ, a function h is collision-resistant if it satisfies the following criteria for all Probabilistic Polynomial-Time (PPT) adversaries $\mathcal{A}$:

$$\Pr \left[\begin{matrix} h \leftarrow Samp(\lambda) \\ (x_0, x_1) \leftarrow \mathcal{A}(h) \\ s.t.\ x_0, x_1 \in X \end{matrix} : \begin{matrix} x_0 \neq x_1 \\ h(x_0) = h(x_1) \end{matrix} \right] \leq negl(\lambda).$$

Our first result shows no HRPPH exists for the Hamming weight predicate:

Theorem 1. *Given a security parameter λ and arbitrary integer $0 < t < n$, there is no HRPPH for $(\{0,1\}^n, \oplus)$ and predicate $Ham_{n,t}$.*

Proof. We first show that the HRPPH for $Ham_{n,t}$ must be collision-resistant. Denote the identity element of $(\{0,1\}^n, \oplus)$ as 0^n. Let us assume the existence of an HRPPH for $Ham_{n,t}$ that is not collision-resistant. Under this assumption, there exists an adversary $\mathcal{A}$ such that

$$\Pr \left[\begin{matrix} h \leftarrow Samp(\lambda) \\ (x_0, x_1) \leftarrow \mathcal{A}(h) \\ s.t.\ x_0, x_1 \in X \end{matrix} : \begin{matrix} x_0 \neq x_1 \\ h(x_0) = h(x_1) \end{matrix} \right] > negl(\lambda).$$

Let $y \leftarrow x_0 \oplus x_1 \in K_h$ and $y \neq 0^n$.

If $|y| > t$, we have $h(y) = h(0^n)$ and $Ham_{n,t}(y) \neq Ham_{n,t}(0^n)$.

If $|y| \leq t$, let's define y' by randomly flipping $t - |y| + 1$ zeros of y, and $y'' \leftarrow y' \oplus y$. It is straightforward that $|y''| = t - |y| + 1$ and $|y'| = t + 1$, which implies $Ham_{n,t}(y') \neq Ham_{n,t}(y'')$ even though $h(y') = h(y'')$. Therefore

$$\Pr \left[\begin{matrix} x \leftarrow \mathcal{A}(h) \\ Eval(h, h(x)) \neq Ham_{n,t}(x) \end{matrix} \middle| \begin{matrix} x_0, x_1 \leftarrow \mathcal{A}(h) \\ s.t.\ x_0 \neq x_1,\ h(x_0) = h(x_1) \end{matrix} \right] = 1.$$

$$\Pr \left[\begin{matrix} x \leftarrow \mathcal{A}(h) \\ s.t.\ Eval(h, h(x)) \neq Ham_{n,t}(x) \end{matrix} \right] \geq \Pr \left[\begin{matrix} (x_0, x_1) \leftarrow \mathcal{A}(h) \\ s.t.\ x_0 \neq x_1 \\ h(x_0) = h(x_1) \end{matrix} \right]$$
$$> negl(\lambda).$$

Hence, h is not robust, contradicting the definition of HRPPH. Therefore, any HRPPH for $Ham_{n,t}$ must be collision-resistant.

The next step is to prove there does not exist a Collision-Resistant Hash Function (CRHF) for $(\{0,1\}^n, \bigoplus)$.

Assume there is a CRHF $h : (\{0,1\}^n, \bigoplus) \to (Y, \bigotimes)$. As h is a homomorphic function and $(\{0,1\}^n, \bigoplus)$ constitutes a Boolean group, it follows that Y must also be a Boolean group. By Property 1, Y is isomorphic to $(\mathbb{Z}_2^m, +)$ for a $0 < m < n$. By encoding $(\{0,1\}^n, \bigoplus)$ in $(\mathbb{Z}_2^n, +)$, we can derive an isomorphic homomorphic function $h' : \mathbb{Z}_2^n \to \mathbb{Z}_2^m$.

We define $a_i \ \forall \ 0 < i \le n$ as the bit string in $\{0,1\}^n$, wherein only the i_{th} bit is 1, and the remaining bits are all 0. We extend this notation to represent the corresponding vector $\boldsymbol{a_i} \in \mathbb{Z}_2^n$. An adversary $\mathcal{A}$ can query $h(a_1), \cdots, h(a_n)$ to acquire n elements in Y. Utilizing the isomorphism, $\mathcal{A}$ obtains $h'(\boldsymbol{a_i})$ for every $0 < i \le n$ and subsequently constructs a matrix $A \in \mathbb{Z}_2^{m \times n}$ by positioning each component $h'(\boldsymbol{a_i})$ as a column. It is straightforward to infer that $h'(\boldsymbol{x}) = A\boldsymbol{x}$.

Since the equation $A\boldsymbol{x} = \boldsymbol{0}$ can be solved in polynomial time, $\mathcal{A}$ can output a $\boldsymbol{y} \in \mathbb{Z}_2^n$ such that $A\boldsymbol{y} = 0$. For any arbitrary $\boldsymbol{x} \in \mathbb{Z}_2^n$, it holds that $h'(\boldsymbol{x} + \boldsymbol{y}) = A\boldsymbol{x} + A\boldsymbol{y} = h'(\boldsymbol{x})$. Leveraging the isomorphism, we deduce that the corresponding bit strings x and y satisfy $h(x \bigoplus y) = h(x)$. Consequently, $(x, x \bigoplus y)$ constitutes a collision pair for h, which can be computed by $n = poly(\lambda)$ queries and a PPT algorithm. Therefore, h is not collision-resistant.

By synthesizing the results above, we can claim that it is impossible to construct a collision-resistant hash for $(\{0,1\}^n, \bigoplus)$, and by extension, to construct an HRPPH for $Ham_{n,t}$.

$\square$

The above result shows that the Hamming weight property prevents HRPPH construction.

3.2   No HRPPH for Gap-k Greater-Than

Boyle et al. studied another property known as the Gap-k Greater-Than [7] and gave an RPPH construction. We also explore whether this property could yield a corresponding HRPPH. We reformulate it into a single-input property:

Definition 5 (Gap-k Greater-Than predicates). *Let $k > 0$ be an arbitrary integer and $*$ be an arbitrary symbol (indicating it can be either 0 or 1). Given an input $x \in \mathbb{Z}$, the Gap-k Greater-Than property is defined as follows:*

$$Gap_k(x) = \begin{cases} 1 & x > k \\ 0 & x < -k \\ * & otherwise \end{cases}.$$

We now present our second negative claim: it is not possible to construct an HRPPH for the Gap-k Greater-Than property over $(\mathbb{Z}, +)$.

Theorem 2. *For arbitrary integer $k > 0$, there is no HRPPH for $(\mathbb{Z}, +)$ and predicates Gap_k.*

Intuitively, the Gap-k Greater-Than property roughly divides the integer group into two symmetrical infinite sets (i.e., $(-\infty, -k)$ and (k, ∞), while the interval $[-k, k]$ is negligible in comparison to $\mathbb{Z}$). Because all quotient groups of $(\mathbb{Z}, +)$ must follow the form of $\mathbb{Z}_l$ for some $l > 0$, any evaluation function will incorrectly evaluate approximately half of the elements within the input group. An adversary can always find inputs that breach the robustness requirement by employing an appropriate sampling algorithm. Appendix A presents the formal proof of Theorem 2.

The Theorem 2 and Theorem 1 signify that there can be a conflict between the distribution of a property over the input group and the structure of the group itself. We cannot reveal arbitrary property from a homomorphic hash even if an RPPH can be constructed over one operation. However, it is still possible to create many HRPPHs for other properties. In the subsequent section, we will present two properties with generic methods for constructing an HRPPH.

4   Our Constructions of HRPPH

The main idea of our constructions is to define property from the view of homomorphism rather than vice versa. An HRPPH, denoted as h, is a homomorphic surjection that segregates the definition domain into discrete cosets of the kernel K_h. These cosets collectively constitute a partition of the domain group. On the other hand, the property P divide the underlying set of domain group X into two sets, X_0 and X_1, where $X_i = \{x | x \in X, i \in \{0, 1\}, P(x) = i\}$. If any pair of elements originating from the same cosets defined by h are located in distinct sets X_0 and X_1, one of these elements must be evaluated incorrectly. Thus, our goal is to prevent any adversary from finding these pairs.

The first approach is to prevent such bad inputs. This requires identifying a non-trivial kernel in which each coset of the kernel falls entirely within either X_0 or X_1. Therefore, any property defined over a non-trivial kernel's cosets can effectively create an HRPPH construction.

The second approach deals with situations where bad inputs are unavoidable due to the structure of the domain group. In this case, the strategy is to: 1. make the bad inputs relatively less than the input domain; 2. hide these bad inputs through computational hard problems. For the first requirement, our input domain should be considerably larger than the kernel (i.e., it has a big enough group order). Since a bad input can form a collision pair from its coset, we can leverage collision resistance to hide the kernel (i.e., the group order) for our second requirement. This solution leads to our second HRPPH construction.

4.1   HRPPH for Perfectly Compressive Property

First, we introduce the Perfectly Compressive Property:

Definition 6 (Perfectly Compressive Property). *A property predicate P : $X \rightarrow \{0, 1\}$ is a Perfectly Compressive Property for a group $(X, \odot)$ if there exists a normal subgroup $G \lhd X$ such that $|G| > 1$ and $P(x \odot y) = P(x)$ holds for all $y \in G$.*

This definition requires the property to be a partition of all cosets by a non-trivial normal subgroup. The term perfect illustrates the compression caused by the homomorphism will not affect the evaluation of the property. A property demonstrating such perfect compression attributes implies the existence of a construction for the HRPPH:

Theorem 3 (Perfectly Compressive HRPPH). *For any perfectly compressive property P defined on $(X, \odot)$ with a normal subgroup G, there exists an HRPPH $h : X \to X/G$ where $Eval(h, h(x)) := P(h(x))$.*

Proof. Given that $G \lhd X$, we can define a homomorphism h according to the homomorphism axiom. As $h(x) \in X/G \subset X$, both $P(h(x))$ and $Eval(h, h(x))$ are computable.

Since $|G| > 1$, h demonstrates compressive characteristics.

For an arbitrary input x, if $x \in X/G$, $Eval(h, h(x)) = Eval(h, x) = P(x)$ holds trivially. For $x \notin X/G$, there exists $y \in G$ such that $x = h(x) \odot y$. Consequently, $Eval(h, h(x)) = P(h(x)) = P(h(x) \odot y) = P(x)$. Therefore, for all $x \in X, \Pr[Eval(h, h(x) = P(x))] = 1$, implying h is robust.

Thus, h qualifies as an HRPPH.

□

This construction derives from the definition of HRPPH and its inherent compression behavior. Its robustness, with a probability of one, qualifies it as perfectly compressive.

This solution is difficult to apply for a given predicate like hamming weight. However, it is not difficult to define such a property when the input domain group is clear. Therefore, this property can be used to reveal if a specific computation flow over inputs can yield an output satisfying some properties. We present an example of HRPPH for set operation in Appendix B.

4.2   HRPPH for Enumerable Property

For properties that do not have perfect compressibility, an alternative solution is to make finding the kernel a difficult problem. Therefore, we must hide the bad inputs with a homomorphic collision-resistant hash function. Without loss of generality, we assume $|X_0| \gg |X_1|$ (recall $X_i := \{x | x \in X; P(x) = i\}$). We define the enumerable property as follows:

Definition 7. *A property P is termed an enumerable property if a normal subgroup $G \lhd X$ and a subset X_1 exist, such that a deterministic polynomial-time algorithm is capable of enumerating all elements from $aG \cap X_1, \forall a \in X$.*

The enumerable property needs a polynomial-time algorithm capable of enumerating all possible input candidates x satisfying $P(x) = 1$ for the given hash value. Later, we can verify the correctness of the guess through the collision-resistant function. We will demonstrate that this enumeration algorithm is crucial for revealing the property. Holmgren et al. have demonstrated that the exact

Hamming property is enumerable [15], employing a parity check matrix P of an efficient syndrome list decodable code against t errors. It is crucial to note that since the input candidate could expose the pre-image of the hash value in X_1, the real domain of this HRPPH should be within X_0 to prevent leakage. This HRPPH will only reveal if the function of multiple inputs belongs to X_1.

Before constructing an HRPPH, we present a generalized definition of the homomorphic collision-resistant hash function (HCRHF):

Definition 8. *Given a security parameter λ, a family of HCRHF $\mathcal{H} = \{h : X \to Y\}$ for two groups $(X, \odot)$ and $(Y, \otimes)$ requires the following two algorithms:*

- *$Samp(\lambda) \to h$ is a randomized PPT algorithm that samples $h \leftarrow_r \mathcal{H}$.*
- *$Hash(h, x) \to y$ is an efficient deterministic PPT algorithm that computes the hash $h(x) \in Y$.*

The HCRHF scheme requires the following properties:

- *$Homomorphism$: $\forall x_0, x_1 \in X$ and $h \in \mathcal{H}$, $h(x_0 \odot x_1) = h(x_0) \otimes h(x_1)$.*
- *$Compression$: $\forall h \in \mathcal{H}$, the kernel K_h satisfying $|K_h| > 1$. If $|X|$ is finite, the compression rate is defined as $\eta = \frac{\log|Y|}{\log|X|}$.*
- *$Collision\text{-}Resistance$: For all PPT adversary $\mathcal{A}$, satisfying*

$$\Pr \begin{bmatrix} h \leftarrow Samp(\lambda) \\ x_0, x_1 \leftarrow \mathcal{A}(h) & : & x_0 \neq x_1 \\ s.t.\ x_0, x_1 \in X & & h(x_0) = h(x_1) \end{bmatrix} \leq negl(\lambda).$$

Our definition extends the one proposed by [15] by using the standard homomorphism definition where the homomorphic operations exist for the whole input domain. This allows our HCRHF to support homomorphism with arbitrary times, unlike its predecessor, which only supports a single homomorphic operation. We give a general construction of HRPPH for enumerable properties based on HCRHF:

Theorem 4 (Enumerable HRPPH). *Given a security parameter λ, a group $(X, \odot)$ of size $\log|X| > poly(\lambda)$, and an enumerable property P with the corresponding normal subgroup G, if there exists a HCRHF D for $(X, \odot)$ with kernel K_D satisfying $|K_D| * |G| > |X|$, then there exists an HRPPH for P on $(X, \odot)$.*

Proof. We can construct a homomorphism $E : X \to X/G$, and define the following HRPPH:

- Samp: Randomly sample $D \leftarrow Samp_{HCRHF}(\lambda)$, and return the description of $h \leftarrow (E, D)$.
- Hash: For an arbitrary input $x \in X$, return $h(x) \leftarrow (E(x), D(x))$.
- Eval: For a hash value $h(x) = (y_1, y_2)$, enumerate $Z \leftarrow \{z | D(z) = y_2, z \in y_1 G \cap X_1\}$. If $|Z| > 0$, then return 1; otherwise, return 0.

$E(z)G \cap X_1$ is the intersection of a coset $E(z)G$ and X_1. Since we can enumerate it in a deterministic polynomial-time algorithm, $Eval$ can be executed in polynomial time.

It is trivial to show that h is compressive ($\eta = \frac{log(|x|^2/(|K_D|*|G|))}{log(|X|)} = 2 - \frac{log(|K_D|*|G|)}{log(|X|)} < 1$) and homomorphic (both D and E are homomorphisms for the same domain group). We only prove it is robust:

If $P(x) = 1$, then $x \in Z$. Since $x \in E(x)G \cap X_1$, we have

$$\Pr\left[\begin{array}{c} x \leftarrow \mathcal{A}(h) \\ s.t.P(x) = 1, Eval(h, h(x)) = 0 \end{array}\right] = 0.$$

If $P(x) = 0$, suppose a PPT adversary $\mathcal{A}$ can break the robustness with probability ρ:

$$\Pr\left[\begin{array}{c} x \leftarrow \mathcal{A}(h) \\ s.t.P(x) = 0, Eval(h, h(x)) = 1 \end{array}\right] = \rho.$$

By computing $Eval(h, h(x)) = 1$, the adversary can obtain y such that $y \in E(x)G \cap X_1$ and $D(x) = D(y)$ in polynomial time. Hence,

$$\Pr\left[\begin{array}{c} x, y \leftarrow \mathcal{A}(h) \\ s.t.D(x) = D(y) \end{array}\right] \geq \rho.$$

Since D is collision-resistant, we have

$$\Pr\left[\begin{array}{c} x \leftarrow \mathcal{A}(h) \\ s.t.P(x) = 0, \\ Eval(h, h(x)) = 1 \end{array}\right] \leq \Pr\left[\begin{array}{c} x, y \leftarrow \mathcal{A}(h) \\ s.t.D(x) = D(y) \end{array}\right] \leq negl(\lambda).$$

Ultimately, h is robust:

$$\Pr\left[\begin{array}{c} x \leftarrow \mathcal{A}(h) \\ s.t.P(x) \neq Eval(h, h(x)) \end{array}\right] \leq negl(\lambda).$$

$\square$

The above construction generalizes the construction of RPPH in [15] with homomorphism. If an HCRHF exists, this construction can be used for any enumerable property defined over the domain groups. We now provide an example of HRPPH for property over $(\mathbb{Z}, +)$.

4.3   HRPPH for Integer-Close-To Property

Following the idea of Hamming weight property, we propose an Integer-Close-To (ICT) predicate for the integer addition group $(\mathbb{Z}, +)$ as follows:

Definition 9. *Given a positive integer t and an arbitrary input x from $\mathbb{Z}$. The ICT property is defined as:*

$$ICT_t(x) = \begin{cases} 1 & |x| < t \\ 0 & otherwise \end{cases} ; x \in \mathbb{Z}.$$

The ICT property provides a measure of proximity between two integers. This measure is a fundamental operation in classification tasks or regression computations. This property can be evaluated privately using techniques such as zero-knowledge range proofs. However, homomorphism in our HRPPH allows the ICT property to be evaluated for the computational result of input data without leaking the computation flow and input data.

For instance, consider a machine learning model $f(x_1, x_2, \cdots, x_n)$, where different participants hold each x_i. We can compare if the predicted results of this model are sufficiently close to the actual result y through homomorphism.

Since small integers are countable, we can map each integer to an appropriate subgroup $E : \mathbb{Z} \rightarrow \mathbb{Z}_d$, ensuring that $|\frac{t}{d}| < poly(\lambda)$. This mapping allows us to recover candidate inputs directly from their encoded values.

Next, we need to identify an HCRHF for the integer addition group. We propose the unknown-order-based homomorphic hash and demonstrate that it is an HCRHF for the integer group $\mathbb{Z}$.

Definition 10 (Unknown-Order-based Homomorphic Hash). *For a given security parameter λ and a randomized function GGen that can return a group of unknown order, we define the following hash function:*

- ***Samp$_{UO}$**(λ) $\rightarrow h$: Sample $\mathbb{G} \leftarrow GGen(\lambda)$ and $g \leftarrow_r \mathbb{G}$ and return $h \leftarrow (\mathbb{G}, g)$.*
- ***Hash**$(h, x) \rightarrow y$: For an input $x \in \mathbb{Z}$, output $h(x) = g^x$.*

The above scheme supports homomorphic operations : $h(x_1)h(x_2) = h(x_1 + x_2)$.

Lemma 1. *The homomorphic hash defined in Definition 10 is an HCRHF for inputs from $(\mathbb{Z}, +)$.*

Proof. Compression and homomorphism are trivial. We only prove the collision resistance by extending the proof in [1].

We assume that the existing PPT adversary $\mathcal{A}$ can find a collision for the above scheme such that $g^{x_0} \equiv g^{x_1}$ for $x_0, x_1 \in \mathbb{Z}$ with probability ρ. Without loss of generality, assume $x_0 < x_1$. Randomly pick an odd prime integer $l < x_0$ and $gcd(l, x_1 - x_0) = 1$, and let $x_1' = x_1 - x_0 + l$. We will have $g^l \equiv g^{x_1'}$ where $l \neq x_1'$ and $gcd(l, x_1') = 1$.

Since l is co-prime to x_1', we can get $rl + bx_1' = 1$ for $r, b \in \mathbb{Z}$ by the extended Euclidean function. Assuming $m = g^{r+b}$ and $e = l$, we get $m^e = g^{lr}g^{lb} = g^{lr+bx_1'} \equiv g$.

If the Strong RSA for general groups of unknown order holds

$$negl(\lambda) \geq \Pr \left[\begin{array}{c} (x, e) \in \mathbb{G} \times \mathbb{Z} \leftarrow \mathcal{A}(\mathbb{G}, g) \\ s.t. \text{ e is an odd prime} \end{array} : x^e \equiv g \right] \geq \rho.$$

Hence,

$$\Pr \left[\begin{array}{c} (\mathbb{G}, g) \leftarrow Samp_{UO}(\lambda) \\ x_0, x_1 \leftarrow \mathcal{A}(\mathbb{G}, g) \\ s.t. \ x_0 \neq x_1 \end{array} : g^{x_0} \equiv g^{x_1} \right] \leq negl(\lambda).$$

$\square$

- Inputs: Given a security parameter λ and an integer t, we define the property predicate as ICT_t.
- Samp: Randomly samples $(\mathbb{G}, g) \leftarrow Samp_{UO}(\lambda)$ and selects a proper integer $d = t/poly(\lambda) \in \mathbb{Z}, d > 1$, and the description of h is $(d, \mathbb{G}, g)$.
- Hash: For input x, returns $(x \bmod d, g^x)$.
- Eval: For input $y = (y_1, y_2)$, computes $Z \leftarrow \{z | z = y_1 + kd, \forall |z| < t; \ k \in \mathbb{Z}\}$. Returns 1 if and only if
$$\exists z \in Z \ s.t. g^z \equiv y_2.$$

Fig. 1. HRPPH for ICT_t

Using this HCRHF, we can have the HRPPH as Fig. 1. The above scheme is an HRPPH following Theorem 4. We offer three remarks about the construction:

1. According to our HCRHF from Definition 10, x is defined over the integer group $(\mathbb{Z}, +)$.
2. Our scheme also supports linear scaling. Given that $h(x) = (y_1, y_2)$, we can state $h(ax) = (ay_1, y_2^a)$ for all $a \in \mathbb{Z}$. This property supports applications like integer linear regression.
3. The output is a fixed length $log(d) + log(n) = poly(\lambda)$.

Our construction supports linear computation over the inputs. Hence, one could employ this HRPPH in a privacy-preserving computing scheme like a linear regression model f, such that $y = f(h(x_1), h(x_2), \ldots, h(x_n))$ where $x_i \in X_0$, and subsequently evaluate $Eval(y - h(c))$ to ascertain whether $f(x_1, x_2, \ldots, x_n)$ is proximate to c or not.

5   Conclusion and Future Works

In this study, we introduced the definitions for Homomorphic Robust Property-Preserving Hash (HRPPH) (Definition 3). We demonstrated the impracticality of constructing an HRPPH for the Hamming weight property (Theorem 1) and the Gap-k Greater-Than property (Theorem 2). This limitation arises because the property's input partitioning is incompatible with its inherent homomorphism. Subsequently, we presented two methods for constructing HRPPHs: one for perfectly compressive properties (Theorem 3) and another for enumerable properties (Theorem 4). We also provided an example of HRPPH construction for the Integer-Close-To property (Subsect. 4.3).

Despite these developments, several questions remain open for further exploration. First, we are interested in establishing a general connection between property predicates, the structure of the input group (or ring), and the potential existence of an HRPPH. Secondly, our interest is in whether we can construct a ring homomorphic collision-resistant hash function and thereby ring HRPPH.

Finally, considering the potential of HRPPH as a building block for privacy-preserving computational protocols, we aim to find applications that can fully harness the capabilities of HRPPH.

Acknowledgements. This work was done when all authors belonged to The University of Tokyo and was supported by: JST CREST, Grant Number JPMJCR2113; JST SPRING, Grant Number JPMJSP2108; JSPS KAKENHI Grant Number, JP23KJ0385; JSPS Postdoctoral Fellowships for Research in Japan (No. P21073).

A   Proof of Theorem 2

Theorem 2. *For arbitrary integer $k > 0$, there is no HRPPH for $(\mathbb{Z}, +)$ and predicates Gap_k.*

Proof. Assume we have h as an HRPPH for Gap-k Greater-Than. As the kernel K_h satisfies $|K_h| > 1$, there exists $l \in K_h$ such that $h(x) \cong \mathbb{Z}_l$, which is finite. Suppose h encodes the outputs into a finite group Y, represented by $log(n)$ bits. We will check set $S_- = [-2n, -n]$ and $S_+ = [n, 2n]$. It's easy to see that for all $x \in S_+$, $P(x) = 1$ and for all $x \in S_-$, $P(x) = 0$. Since $n \geq l$, we can suppose $n = al + b$, where $0 \leq b < l$. We denote L_x as the pre-image of $h(x)$ such that $L_x := [\cdots, x - 2l, x - l, x, x + l, x + 2l, \cdots]$. If $b \leq \frac{l}{3}$, we examine below five cases:

1. If $0 < x \leq b$, $|L_x \cap S_-| = |L_x \cap S_+| = a$. Hence, $Eval(h, x)$ is wrong with probability $P_1 = \frac{1}{2}$.
2. If $b < x \leq l - 2b$, $|L_x \cap S_-| = a$, while $|L_x \cap S_+| = a + 1$. Hence, $Eval(h, x)$ is wrong with probability $P_2 > \frac{a}{2a+1} \geq \frac{1}{3}$.
3. If $l - 2b < x \leq 2b$, $|L_x \cap S_-| = |L_x \cap S_+| = a + 1$. Hence, $Eval(h, x)$ is wrong with probability $P_3 = \frac{1}{2}$.
4. If $2b < x \leq l - b$, $|L_x \cap S_-| = a + 1$ and $|L_x \cap S_+| = a$. Hence, $Eval(h, x)$ is wrong with probability $P_4 > \frac{a}{2a+1} \geq \frac{1}{3}$.
5. If $l - b < x \leq l$, $|L_x \cap S_-| = |L_x \cap S_+| = a$. Hence, $Eval(h, x)$ is wrong with probability $P_5 = \frac{1}{2}$.

By adding them all, we obtain

$$\Pr\left[Eval(h, h(x)) \neq P(x) \middle| \begin{array}{l} x \in S_+ \cup S_- \\ b \leq \frac{l}{3} \end{array}\right] = P_1 \times \Pr[0 < x \bmod l \leq b]$$

$$+ P_2 \times \Pr[b < x \bmod l \leq l - 2b]$$

$$\cdots$$

$$+ P_5 \times \Pr[l - b < x \bmod l \leq l]$$

$$\geq \frac{1}{3}.$$

We obtain the same result for $\frac{l}{3} < b \leq \frac{l}{2}$ by switching $(b, l - 2b)$ to $(2b, l - b)$ and similar result for $\frac{2l}{3} < b \leq l$ by switching $(2b - l, l - b)$ to $(b, 2l - 2b)$.

Adding up all the cases for b, we have:

$$\Pr[Eval(h, h(x)) \neq P(x) | x \in S_+ \cup S_-] \geq \frac{1}{3}.$$

By randomly picking elements from $S_+ \cup S_-$, the adversary can find a wrong result with a probability of at least $\frac{1}{3}$, which contradicts the robustness requirements. Hence, no HRPPH exists for Gap_k with an arbitrary k.

□

B   Computing Private Set Intersection Subset by HRPPH

In this section, we propose a new variant of Private Set Intersection (PSI) and resolve it with an HRPPH:

Problem 1 (Private Set Intersection Subset (PSIS)). Given a universal set $\mathcal{U}$ and $n > 2$ participants $A_1, A_2, \cdots, A_n$ each with their corresponding sets $S_1, S_2, \cdots, S_n$, where $S_i \subset \mathcal{U}, 0 < i \leq n$. Let $S_0 \subset \mathcal{U}$ be a small query set such that $|S_i| \gg |S_0|, \forall 0 < i \leq n$. All participants must return $S_0 \cap S_1 \cap \cdots \cap S_n$ without disclosing any information about other elements in each private set S_i.

The scenario outlined above can arise when multiple participants possess large amounts of data (e.g., database sharding), and auditors need to verify the consistency of specific data across all participants. Several protocols can be used to resolve this problem, and we provide a method that utilizes HRPPH to highlight its features. For the sake of this discussion, we will not compare our approach with existing PSI protocols.

We assume all participants to be honest but curious, meaning they will adhere to the protocol but are interested in learning more about the others' sets. We begin by defining a property of the PSI predicate:

$$PSI_t(S) := \begin{cases} 1 & t \in S \\ 0 & otherwise \end{cases}, S \subset \mathcal{U}.$$

Previous works [14, 16] have demonstrated that if a global pseudo-random function (PRF) $f : \mathbb{Z} \times \mathcal{U} \to \mathbb{Z}_q$ exists to encode a universal set $\mathcal{U}$ into $\mathbb{Z}_q$ for some large prime q with $poly(\lambda)$ bits, any set $S \subset \mathcal{U}$ can be encoded as a deterministic polynomial $Q_S = \prod_i (x - s_i) \in \mathbb{Z}_q[x], \forall s_i \in S$. The polynomial ring $\mathbb{Z}_q[x]$ can define the following zero point property:

$$ZeroPoint_t(Q_S) := \begin{cases} 1 & Q_S(t) = 0 \\ 0 & otherwise \end{cases}.$$

Below, we prove a lemma for applying our property to the $PSIS$ problem.

Lemma 2. *For two random sets S_1 and S_2 drawn from a universal set $\mathcal{U}$ encoded into $\mathbb{Z}_q$ through a PRF, and the corresponding polynomials Q_{S_1}, Q_{S_2} defined as $Q_S = \prod_{s_i \in S}(x - s_i) \in \mathbb{Z}_q[x], \forall s_i \in S$, it holds that $\Pr[PSI_t(S_1 \cap S_2) \neq ZeroPoint_t(Q_{S_1} + Q_{S_2})] \leq negl(\lambda).$*

Proof. 1. If $PSI_t(S_1 \cap S_2) = 1$, then $PSI_t(S_1) = 1$ and $PSI_t(S_2) = 1$, which implies $Q_{S_1}(t) = Q_{S_2}(t) = 0$. Therefore,

$$\Pr\left[ZeroPoint_t(Q_{S_1} + Q_{S_2}) = 1 | PSI_t(S_1 \cap S_2) = 1\right] = 1.$$

2. If $PSI_t(S_1 \cap S_2) = 0$, then both $Q_{S_1}(t)$ and $Q_{S_2}(t)$ are non-zero. We have

$$\Pr[ZeroPoint_t(Q_{S_1} + Q_{S_2}) = 1 | PSI_t(S_1 \cap S_2) = 0]$$
$$= \Pr[Q_{S_1}(t) + Q_{S_2}(t) = 0 | Q_{S_1}(t), Q_{S_2}(t) \neq 0].$$

Given that $Q_{S_1}(t) = \prod_i(t - s_i)$ for all $s_i \in S_1$, and S_1 is independent to S_2 encoded through a pseudo-random hash, $Q_{S_1}(t)$ and $Q_{S_2}(t)$ are random in $\mathbb{Z}_q$. Therefore, the above equation is equivalent to randomly selecting two values from $\mathbb{Z}_q$ that sum to zero, which has a probability of $\frac{1}{q} = negl(\lambda)$. Hence,

$$\Pr[PSI_t(S_1 \cap S_2) \neq ZeroPoint_t(Q_{S_1} + Q_{S_2})]$$
$$= \frac{1}{q} \Pr[PSI_t(S_1 \cap S_2) = 0] \leq negl(\lambda).$$

$\square$

Assuming we have an HRPPH $h : \mathbb{Z}_q[x] \to Y$ for the property $ZeroPoint_t$, for all $t \in S_0$, we can use a secure aggregation to construct a probabilistic algorithm to solve the Private Set Intersection with Subsets (PSIS) problem.

Inspired by the one-time pad protocol of [4], we present a simple construction using our HRPPH for PSIS in Fig. 2. Our model assumes access to a global random coin c, which can be distributed.

- Given a query set S_0, a globally generated random coin $c \in \mathbb{Z}$, a pseudo-random function (PRF) f, and n participants A_i:
1. Compute $Q_{S_i} = \prod_{s \in S_i}(x - f(c, s))$ and $Q_{S_0} = \prod_{s \in S_0}(x - f(c, s))$.
2. Sample an instance of $h_{Q_{S_0}}$ and compute $R_i = r_i * h_{Q_{S_0}}(Q_{S_i}) \in Y$ for a random non-zero $r_i \in \mathbb{Z}_q$.
3. Randomly pick U_{ij} from Y and send U_{ij} to corresponding A_j for $j \neq i$.
4. Compute $F_i = \sum_j U_{ji} + R_i - \sum_k U_{ik}$ and $F_i(t)$ for $t \in S_0$.
5. Broadcast $F_i(t)$ and aggregate the result for all i to get the final outputs $I = \{t | \sum_i F_i(t) = 0\}$.

Fig. 2. Protocol for PSIS

Since $F = \sum_i F_i = \sum_i R_i$, it holds that $Eval_t(h, \sum_i R_i) = ZeroPoint_t(\sum_i Q_{S_i})$ by Lemma 2. Therefore, with overwhelming probability, $I = S_0 \cap S_1 \cap \cdots \cap S_n$ in our protocol. The protocol is entirely randomized by U_{ij}. The only message containing information about the private sets is $F_i(t)$, obscured by random values from all participants. The hash is also randomized by r_i without compromising the correctness of $Eval$ ($ZeroPoint_t(Q_S) = ZeroPoint_t(r * Q_S)$ for all $r \in \mathbb{Z}_q$, $r \neq 0$). Thus, the protocol preserves privacy and protects against collusion among $n - 2$ participants.

We now construct an HRPPH for the property $ZeroPoint_t$, $\forall t \in S_0$. It is evident that $G \leftarrow \{kQ_{S_0}, \forall k \in \mathbb{Z}_q[x]\}$ is a free group generated by $Q_{S_0} \in \mathbb{Z}_q[x]$ which is non-trivial and normal. Therefore, it defines a quotient group, specifically $\mathbb{Z}_q[x]/Q_{S_0}$, and we get an surjective homomorphism $\mathbb{Z}_q[x] \to \mathbb{Z}_q[x]/Q_{S_0}$. Moreover, due to $Q_S + Q_{S_0}(t) = Q_S(t)$ for all $t \in S_0$, we establish that

$$\forall k \in \mathbb{Z}_q[x], \ ZeroPoint_t(Q_S + k * Q_{S_0}) = ZeroPoint_t(Q_S).$$

According to Definition 6, $ZeroPoint_t(Q)$ is a perfectly compressive property. By Theorem 3, we have an HRPPH construction we depict in Fig. 3 for all properties $ZeroPoint_t$, $\forall t \in S_0$.

- Inputs: Given a security parameter λ, and a polynomial $Q_{S_0} \in \mathbb{Z}_q[x]$ with t as a zero point.
- Sample: The description of $h_{Q_{S_0}}$ is (Q_{S_0}).
- Hash: For arbitrary inputs $Q_S \in \mathbb{Z}_q[x]$, return $h_{Q_{S_0}}(Q_S) = Q_S \ mod \ Q_{S_0}$.
- Eval:

$$Eval_t(h_{Q_{S_0}}, h_{Q_{S_0}}(Q_S)) = \begin{cases} 1 & h_{Q_{S_0}}(Q_S)(t) = 0 \\ 0 & otherwise. \end{cases}$$

Fig. 3. HRPPH for $ZeroPoint_t$

We can use this HRPPH in our protocol. In our PSIS protocol, we can use the query set S_0 to generate the description of the hash $h_{Q_{S_0}}$. Since $\mathcal{U}$ is finite, the compression rate equals $\frac{|S_0|}{|S_i|}$ with lower bound $\frac{|S_0|}{q}$.

The above HRPPH scheme shares some ideas with the multi-input intersection RPPH proposed by [14]. We show three distinct features of our construction:

1. Our HRPPH is perfectly compressive and does not rely on any difficult assumptions for its robustness.
2. Our HRPPH is indeed a ring homomorphism, i.e., it supports polynomial multiplication. Since $ZeroPoint_t(Q_{S_1} * Q_{S_2}) = PSI_t(Q_{S_1 \cup S_2})$, our construction can compute a mix of PSI and PSU over the subset in a more complicated scenario.
3. For multiple query cases, each participant A_i can compute Q_{S_i} in the offline phase and only quickly compute the polynomial division for $h_{Q_{S_0}}(Q_{S_i})$ for each query.

In the case of n parties, where $|S_0| = w$ and $|S_i| = m$ and each element has l bits. Our scheme requires a total message size of $2wnl$ bits for secure aggregation. Each party must perform $O(m \log m + w \log w)$ operations for hash computation and results evaluation [12]. Regarding communication cost, our scheme is comparable to the state-of-the-art $O(wnl)$ bits [2]. However, our scheme is more costly regarding computation overhead, which should be $O(m)$ in [2]. This is primarily due to the need to perform modulation operations for all private polynomials, which are more costly than the set intersection over plaintext. In addition, Our scheme is more powerful than the work [2] since our scheme supports PSU operations.

References

1. Barić, N., Pfitzmann, B.: Collision-free accumulators and fail-stop signature schemes without trees. In: Fumy, W. (ed.) EUROCRYPT 1997. LNCS, vol. 1233, pp. 480–494. Springer, Heidelberg (1997). https://doi.org/10.1007/3-540-69053-0_33

2. Bay, A., Erkin, Z., Hoepman, J.H., Samardjiska, S., Vos, J.: Practical multi-party private set intersection protocols. IEEE Trans. Inf. Forensics Secur. **17**, 1–15 (2022). https://doi.org/10.1109/TIFS.2021.3118879

3. Bellare, M., Micciancio, D.: A new paradigm for collision-free hashing: incrementality at reduced cost. In: Fumy, W. (ed.) EUROCRYPT 1997. LNCS, vol. 1233, pp. 163–192. Springer, Heidelberg (1997). https://doi.org/10.1007/3-540-69053-0_13

4. Bonawitz, K., et al.: Practical secure aggregation for privacy-preserving machine learning. In: Proceedings of the 2017 ACM SIGSAC Conference on Computer and Communications Security - CCS '17, pp. 1175–1191 (2017). https://doi.org/10.1145/3133956.3133982

5. Boneh, D., Bünz, B., Fisch, B.: Batching techniques for accumulators with applications to IOPs and stateless blockchains. In: Boldyreva, A., Micciancio, D. (eds.) CRYPTO 2019. LNCS, vol. 11692, pp. 561–586. Springer, Cham (2019). https://doi.org/10.1007/978-3-030-26948-7_20

6. Boneh, D., Sahai, A., Waters, B.: Functional encryption: definitions and challenges. In: Ishai, Y. (ed.) TCC 2011. LNCS, vol. 6597, pp. 253–273. Springer, Heidelberg (2011). https://doi.org/10.1007/978-3-642-19571-6_16

7. Boyle, E., LaVigne, R., Vaikuntanathan, V.: Adversarially robust property-preserving hash functions. In: 10th Innovations in Theoretical Computer Science Conference (ITCS 2019). Leibniz International Proceedings in Informatics (LIPIcs), vol. 124, pp. 16:1–16:20 (2019). https://doi.org/10.4230/LIPIcs.ITCS.2019.16

8. Brakerski, Z., Vaikuntanathan, V.: Fully homomorphic encryption from Ring-LWE and security for key dependent messages. In: Rogaway, P. (ed.) CRYPTO 2011. LNCS, vol. 6841, pp. 505–524. Springer, Heidelberg (2011). https://doi.org/10.1007/978-3-642-22792-9_29

9. Castagnos, G., Laguillaumie, F., Tucker, I.: Practical fully secure unrestricted inner product functional encryption modulo p. In: Peyrin, T., Galbraith, S. (eds.) ASIACRYPT 2018. LNCS, vol. 11273, pp. 733–764. Springer, Cham (2018). https://doi.org/10.1007/978-3-030-03329-3_25

10. Chillotti, I., Gama, N., Georgieva, M., Izabachène, M.: Faster fully homomorphic encryption: bootstrapping in less than 0.1 seconds. In: Cheon, J.H., Takagi, T. (eds.) ASIACRYPT 2016. LNCS, vol. 10031, pp. 3–33. Springer, Heidelberg (2016). https://doi.org/10.1007/978-3-662-53887-6_1

11. Dobson, S., Galbraith, S., Smith, B.: Trustless unknown-order groups. Math. Cryptol. **1**(22), 25–39 (2021)

12. Feist, D., Khovratovich, D.: Fast amortized KZG proofs. Cryptology ePrint Archive, Paper 2023/033 (2023). https://eprint.iacr.org/2023/033

13. Fleischhacker, N., Larsen, K.G., Simkin, M.: Property-preserving hash functions for hamming distance from standard assumptions. In: Dunkelman, O., Dziembowski, S. (eds.) Advances in Cryptology – EUROCRYPT 2022. EUROCRYPT 2022. LNCS, vol. 13276, pp. 764–781. Springer, Cham (2022). https://doi.org/10.1007/978-3-031-07085-3_26

14. Fleischhacker, N., Simkin, M.: Robust property-preserving hash functions for hamming distance and more. In: Canteaut, A., Standaert, F.-X. (eds.) EUROCRYPT 2021. LNCS, vol. 12698, pp. 311–337. Springer, Cham (2021). https://doi.org/10.1007/978-3-030-77883-5_11

15. Holmgren, J., Liu, M., Tyner, L., Wichs, D.: Nearly optimal property preserving hashing. In: Advances in Cryptology - CRYPTO 2022 (2022). https://eprint.iacr.org/2022/842

16. Ruan, O., Mao, H.: Efficient private set intersection using point-value polynomial representation. Secur. Commun. Netw. **2020** (2020). https://doi.org/10.1155/2020/8890677

17. Smithson, R.: A note on finite Boolean rings. Math. Mag. **37**(5), 325–327 (1964). https://doi.org/10.1080/0025570X.1964.11975554

18. Zhu, R., Huang, Y.: JIMU: faster LEGO-based secure computation using additive homomorphic hashes. In: Takagi, T., Peyrin, T. (eds.) ASIACRYPT 2017. LNCS, vol. 10625, pp. 529–572. Springer, Cham (2017). https://doi.org/10.1007/978-3-319-70697-9_19

Withdrawable Signature: How to Call Off a Signature

Xin Liu$^{(\boxtimes)}$ [ID], Joonsang Baek [ID], and Willy Susilo [ID]

Institute of Cybersecurity and Cryptology, School of Computing and Information Technology, University of Wollongong, Wollongong, Australia
xl879@uowmail.edu.au, {baek,wsusilo}@uow.edu.au

Abstract. Digital signatures are a cornerstone of security and trust in cryptography, providing authenticity, integrity, and non-repudiation. Despite their benefits, traditional digital signature schemes suffer from inherent immutability, offering no provision for a signer to retract a previously issued signature. This paper introduces the concept of a withdrawable signature scheme, which allows for the retraction of a signature without revealing the signer's private key or compromising the security of other signatures the signer created before. This property, defined as "withdrawability", is particularly relevant in decentralized systems, such as e-voting, blockchain-based smart contracts, and escrow services, where signers may wish to revoke or alter their commitment.

The core idea of our construction of a withdrawable signature scheme is to ensure that the parties with a withdrawable signature are not convinced whether the signer signed a specific message. This ability to generate a signature while preventing validity from being verified is a fundamental requirement of our scheme, epitomizing the property of *withdrawability*. After formally defining security notions for withdrawable signatures, we present two constructions of the scheme based on the pairing and the discrete logarithm. We provide proofs that both constructions are unforgeable under insider corruption and satisfy the criteria of withdrawability. We anticipate our new type of signature will significantly enhance flexibility and security in digital transactions and communications.

Keywords: Digital signatures · Withdrawable signature scheme · Withdrawability

1 Introduction

Digital signatures are instrumental in constructing trust and security, acting as the essential mechanism for authentication, data integrity, and non-repudiation

This work is partly supported by the Australian Research Council (ARC) Discovery Project DP200100144. W. Susilo is supported by the ARC Laureate Fellowship FL230100033.

© The Author(s), under exclusive license to Springer Nature Switzerland AG 2023

E. Athanasopoulos and B. Mennink (Eds.): ISC 2023, LNCS 14411, pp. 557–577, 2023.
https://doi.org/10.1007/978-3-031-49187-0_28

in contemporary digital communications and transactions. In specific applications of digital signature schemes, such as decentralized e-voting systems, there may arise a natural need for the signer to possess the capability to "undo" a digital signature. Undoing a digital signature implies that the signer may desire to *retract* the signature they created, as seen in e-voting systems where a voter might wish to change or withdraw their vote before the final vote tally.

However, in traditional digital signature schemes, undoing a digital signature is impossible, as it persists indefinitely once a signature is created. Furthermore, digital signatures provide authenticity, integrity, and non-repudiation for signed messages. As a result, when a message is signed, the non-repudiation of its content is guaranteed, meaning that once the signature is generated, the signer cannot rescind it. In light of this limitation, one might ask whether it is possible for a signer to efficiently revoke or withdraw a previously issued digital signature without revealing their private key or compromising the security of other signatures created by the signer. We answer this question by presenting a *withdrawable signature* scheme that provides a practical and secure solution for revocating or withdrawing a signature in a desirable situation.

We note that a traditional signature scheme can achieve "withdrawability" by employing a trusted third party (TTP) to establish signature revocation lists. In cases where a signer desires to invalidate a signature, they notify the TTP, which subsequently adds the revoked signature to the revocation list. This enables future verifiers to consult the revocation list via the TTP, allowing them to determine if the signature has been previously revoked before acknowledging its validity. As all participants fully trust the TTP, including the revoked signature in the revocation list ensures its validity and enables the withdrawal of the signature. However, this approach has a centralized nature as it depends on the TTP's involvement, which may not be desirable in decentralized systems. As in decentralized systems, signers may prefer to manage their signatures without relying on centralized authorities. Therefore, constructing a withdrawable signature scheme that does not rely on a TTP turns out to be a non-trivial problem to solve.

Withdrawable signatures can have various applications in different scenarios where the ability to revoke a signature without compromising the signer's private key is demanded. Here are some potential applications:

Smart Contracts [19]. In the context of blockchain-based smart contracts, withdrawable signatures can enable users to sign off on contract conditions while retaining the ability to revoke their commitment. This can be particularly useful in situations where the fulfillment of the contract depends on the actions of multiple parties or external events.

E-Voting Systems [9]. In a decentralized e-voting system, withdrawable signatures enable voters to securely sign their votes while retaining the option to modify or retract their choices before the final votes count. This additional flexibility improves the voting procedure by allowing voters to respond to fresh insights or unfolding events before the voting period concludes.

Escrow Services [6]. Withdrawable signatures could be employed in decentralized escrow services where multiple parties must sign off on a transaction. If one party decides not to proceed with the transaction due to disputes or changes in conditions, they can revoke their signature without affecting the security of other parties' signatures.

In light of the above discussion, we require the following three properties from the withdrawable signature:

1. A withdrawable signature should be verifiable, especially, it should be verified through the signer's valid public key.
2. Only the signer can generate a valid withdrawable signature.
3. A withdrawable signature, once withdrawn, cannot become valid again without the original signer's involvement.

In the forthcoming subsection, we provide a technical outline of the withdrawable signature scheme, focusing on the technical challenges we had to face.

1.1 Technical Overview

The most important feature of our withdrawable signature scheme is *withdrawability*. The idea behind this is that a signer, Alice, should not only be able to sign a message m with her private key to obtain the signature σ but also have the option to revoke the signature if she changes her mind. This means the signature σ will no longer be verifiable with Alice's valid public key. In what follows, we describe the challenges to realizing the withdrawable signature at a technical level.

First Attempt: A Simple Withdrawable Signature Scheme with TTP. As mentioned earlier, one straightforward solution to achieve withdrawability is to have a trusted third party (TTP) maintain a signature revocation list. However, if we want to attain withdrawability without relying on a revocation list, an alternative approach can be explored as follows: In this approach, the signer, Alice, "hides" a signature ω by encrypting it using her public key and the TTP's public key, resulting in a hidden signature σ. For example, the BLS signature [4] on a message m, computed as $\omega = H(m)^{\mathsf{sk}_s}$ with the signer's secret key $\mathsf{sk}_s \in \mathbb{Z}_p$ and the hash function $H : \{0,1\}^* \to \mathbb{Z}_p$, can be encrypted into $\sigma = (g^{\mathsf{sk}_t a} \cdot H(m)^{\mathsf{sk}_s}, g^a)$, where g^{sk_t} is the TTP's public key, with sk_t as the corresponding secret key, and $a \in \mathbb{Z}_p^*$ is a uniform random value chosen by the signer.

The hidden signature σ preserves the verifiability of the signature as the verification works by checking whether the following equality holds: $e(g^{\mathsf{sk}_t a} \cdot H(m)^{\mathsf{sk}_s}, g) \overset{?}{=} e(g^{\mathsf{sk}_t}, g^a)e(H(m), g^{\mathsf{sk}_s})$, where g^{sk_s} is the signer's public key.

In the above scheme, everyone can ensure that the signer has generated a valid signature for the message m under her public key $\mathsf{pk}_s (= g^{\mathsf{sk}_s})$, but they cannot extract the original signature $\omega (= H(m)^{\mathsf{sk}_s})$ from σ. (No party except for the TTP can obtain ω.) The signer then has the option to withdraw σ merely by taking no action. Later, the signer can request the TTP to "decrypt" the signature σ into the original signature ω using the TTP's secret key sk_t.

Towards a Withdrawable Signature Scheme Without TTP. Implementing a withdrawable signature scheme using a TTP presents a significant drawback, as signers, particularly in decentralized and trustless systems, may wish to achieve withdrawability without reliance on the TTP. How can we achieve withdrawability without the help of the TTP? One possible method involves directly removing the TTP and allowing the signer to create σ using a secret random value $r \in \mathbb{Z}_p^*$ chosen by her, which can be regarded as equivalent to the TTP's secret key $\mathsf{sk_t}$. Subsequently, the signer publishes the corresponding "public key", represented as g^r, and selects another random value $a \in \mathbb{Z}_p^*$.

The withdrawable signature σ is then computed as $\sigma = (g^{ra} \cdot H(m)^{\mathsf{sk}_s}, g^a)$, where the verification of σ can be easily performed using the public keys g^{sk_s} and g^r (with the value g^a) with the following verification algorithm: $e(g^{ra} \cdot H(m)^{\mathsf{sk}_s}, g) \stackrel{?}{=} e(g^r, g^a)e(H(m), g^{\mathsf{sk}_s})$.

However, without the TTP, the signature σ immediately becomes a valid signature that can be verified using the signer's public keys $(g^{\mathsf{sk_t}}, g^r)$; thus, the withdrawability is lost.

Because of this issue, we still need to introduce an additional entity that, while not a TTP, will act as a specific verifier chosen by the signer. More specifically, the signer can produce a signature that cannot be authenticated solely by the signer's public key but also requires the verifier's secret key. This ensures the signature appears unverifiable to everyone except for the chosen verifier, as everyone can only be convinced that the signature was created either by the signer or the verifier. If the verifier cannot transform back this signature into a signature that can be verified using the signer's public key only, this scheme will achieve the withdrawability. In particular, only the signer has the option to transform this signature into a verifiable one. To optimize the length of the withdrawable signature, we limit the number of specific verifiers to one.

Another technical issue then surfaces: How can a signer transform the withdrawable signature into a signature that can be directly verifiable using the signer's public key (and possibly with additional public parameters)? A straightforward solution might be having the signer re-sign the message with her secret key. However, this newly generated signature will have no connection to the original withdrawable signature.

Our Response to the Challenges. To overcome the aforementioned limitations, we introduce a designated-verifier signature scheme to generate a withdrawable signature for a message m, denoted as σ, rather than directly generating a regular signature. For a signer Alice, she can create a withdrawable signature for a certain verifier, Bob. Later, if Alice wants to withdraw the signature σ, she just takes no action. If Alice wants to transform the withdrawable signature, she executes an algorithm, "Confirm", to lift the limitation on verifying σ and yield a signature $\tilde{\sigma}$, which we call "confirmed signature", verifiable using both Alice's and Bob's public keys. Note that the confirmed signature $\tilde{\sigma}$ can then be deterministically traced back to the original σ.

Generally, there is a withdrawable signature scheme involving two parties, denoted by user_1 and user_2. Without loss of generality, assume that user_1 is the signing user, while user_2 is the certain verifier. Let a set of their public keys be $\gamma = \{\mathsf{pk}_{\mathsf{user}_1}, \mathsf{pk}_{\mathsf{user}_2}\}$. At a high level, we leverage the structure of the underlying regular signature to construct a withdrawable signature σ designated to the verifier user_2. Later with the signer's secret key $\mathsf{sk}_{\mathsf{user}_1}$ and σ, user_1 can generate a verifiable signature for m of the public key set γ. This signature is the confirmed signature $\widetilde{\sigma}$ and can easily be linked with the withdrawable signature σ through the public key set γ.

If we still take the BLS-like signature scheme as a concrete instantiation with $\mathsf{pk}_{\mathsf{user}_1} = g^{\mathsf{sk}_{\mathsf{user}_1}}$, $\mathsf{pk}_{\mathsf{user}_2} = g^{\mathsf{sk}_{\mathsf{user}_2}}$, and two hash functions $H_1 : \{0,1\}^* \to \mathbb{G}$ and $H_2 : \{0,1\}^* \to \mathbb{Z}_p^*$. The signer user_1 can generate the withdrawable signature σ of message m for user_2 as follows:

$$y \xleftarrow{\$} \mathbb{Z}_p^*, r = H_2(m, g^y \cdot H_1(m)^{\mathsf{sk}_{\mathsf{user}_1}}), u = H_1(m)^r$$
$$\sigma = \left(e(u^y \cdot H_1(m)^{\mathsf{sk}_{\mathsf{user}_1}}, g^{\mathsf{sk}_{\mathsf{user}_2}}), g^y, u \right).$$

The verification algorithm of σ can be performed using the secret key of user_2 and the public key of user_1 as follows:

$$e(H_1(m)^{r \cdot y} \cdot H_1(m)^{\mathsf{sk}_{\mathsf{user}_1}}, g^{\mathsf{sk}_{\mathsf{user}_2}}) \stackrel{?}{=} e(u^{\mathsf{sk}_{\mathsf{user}_2}}, g^y)e(H_1(m)^{\mathsf{sk}_{\mathsf{user}_2}}, g^{\mathsf{sk}_{\mathsf{user}_1}}).$$

Now, assume that user_1 needs to transform σ into a confirmed signature that is associated with γ. Since user_1 has the secret key $\mathsf{sk}_{\mathsf{user}_1}$, user_1 can easily reconstruct randomness $r = H_2(m, g^y \cdot H_1(m)^{\mathsf{sk}_{\mathsf{user}_1}})$ and transform σ into a confirmed signature $\widetilde{\sigma}$ for m of public key set γ with r as follows.

$$\widetilde{\sigma} = \left(g^{\mathsf{sk}_{\mathsf{user}_2} \cdot \mathsf{sk}_{\mathsf{user}_1} \cdot r} H_1(m)^{\mathsf{sk}_{\mathsf{user}_1}}, g^r, u, (g^{\mathsf{sk}_{\mathsf{user}_2}})^r \right).$$

This withdrawable signature scheme achieves withdrawability in such a way that even if user_2 reveals its secret key $\mathsf{sk}_{\mathsf{user}_2}$, other users won't be convinced that σ was generated from user_1. This is due to the potential for user_2 to compute the same σ using $\mathsf{sk}_{\mathsf{user}_2}$, as described below:

$$\sigma = \left(e(u^y \cdot H_1(m)^{\mathsf{sk}_{\mathsf{user}_2}}, g^{\mathsf{sk}_{\mathsf{user}_1}}), g^y, u \right)$$
$$= \left(e(u^y \cdot H_1(m)^{\mathsf{sk}_{\mathsf{user}_1}}, g^{\mathsf{sk}_{\mathsf{user}_2}}), g^y, u \right).$$

Later in this paper, we show that a withdrawable signature scheme can be constructed using the Schnorr [16]-like signature scheme.

1.2   Our Contributions

Motivated by the absence of the type of signature scheme we want for various aforementioned applications, we present the concept withdrawable signature scheme. Our contributions in this regard can be summarized as follows:

1. We provide a formal definition of a *withdrawable signature* scheme that reflects all the characteristics we discussed previously.

2. We formulate security notions of withdrawable signature, reflecting the *withdrawability* and *unforgeability*, two essential security properties.
3. We propose two constructions of withdrawable signature schemes based on discrete logarithm (DL) and pairing.

This paper is organized as follows: We first review the related work in Sect. 2. In Sect. 3, we provide a comprehensive definition of withdrawable signatures, including their syntax and security notion. Section 4 begins with a detailed overview of the preliminaries we used to build our withdrawable signature schemes, then we give the full description of our two proposed constructions. Following that, Sect. 5 focuses on the security analysis of these two withdrawable signature constructions.

2   Related Work

In this section, we review the previous work relevant to our withdrawable signature scheme and highlight differences between our scheme and existing ones.

Designated-Verifier Signature Scheme. The concept of designated-verifier signature (or proof) (DVS) was introduced by Jakobsson et al. [8], and independently by Chaum [5]. Since then, the field has been studied for several decades and admitted instantiations from a variety of assumptions [11, 21–24].

Revocable Group Signature Scheme. Group signature [1,3,5] allows any member within a group to authenticate a message on behalf of the collective. In the context of revocable group signature schemes [2,12,15], revocation refers to the capability of the group manager to revoke a member's signing privilege.

Revocable Ring Signature Scheme. The notion of revocable ring signatures [13] was first introduced in 2007. This concept added new functionality where a specified group of revocation authorities could remove the signer's anonymity. In [27], Zhang *et al.* presented a revocable and linkable ring signature (RLRS) scheme. This innovative framework empowers a revocation authority to reveal the real signer's identity in a linkable ring signature scheme [14].

Universal Designated Verifier Signature Scheme. Designated-verifier signature schemes have multiple variations, including Universal Designated Verifier Signature (UDVS) schemes. Steinfeld et al. proposed the first UDVS scheme based on the bilinear group [17]. They developed two other UDVS schemes, which expanded the conventional Schnorr/RSA signature schemes [18]. Following the work by Steinfeld et al., several UDVS schemes have been proposed in literature [7,20,25,26]. Additionally, the first lattice-based UDVS was proposed in [10], this approach was subsequently further developed in other studies, one of which is referenced here.

Discussion on Differences. Our withdrawable signature constructions presented above comprise two primary parts: withdrawable signature generation and transformation of a withdrawable signature into a confirmed one. When viewed through the "withdrawability" requirements of the first part, our withdrawable signature scheme is relevant to existing group and ring signatures, wherein the signer retains anonymity within a two-party setup. What distinguishes our approach is the second transformation stage, which offers a unique feature not found in the aforementioned revocable group and ring signatures. Our scheme empowers signers to retract their signatures independently, without relying on a certain group manager or a set of revocation authorities. Additionally, the right to remove its "anonymity" rests solely with the signer.

Readers might also discern similarities between our withdrawable signature scheme and the designated-verifier signature (DVS) scheme. In the withdrawable signature generation phase of our scheme, the generated signature can only convince a specific verifier (the designated verifier) that the signer has generated a signature, the same as the core concept of DVS. Note that a DVS holds 'non-transferability", which means that a DVS cannot be transferred by either the signer or the verifier to convince a third party. Although this non-transferability aligns with our concept of withdrawability, our scheme diverges by permitting the signer to transform the withdrawable signature into one that's verifiable using both the signer's and verifier's public keys, challenging the foundational property of DVS.

To achieve this additional property at the transformation stage, we consider leveraging the structural properties of existing regular signatures. Provided that our withdrawable signature scheme was derived from a particular signature, which has been generated with the signer's secret key, only the signer can access this underlying regular signature during the transformation stage. Then one might have also noticed that the construction of our withdrawable signature scheme is related to the UDVS scheme. In a UDVS scheme, once the signer produces a signature on a message, any party possessing this message-signature pair can designate a third party as the certain verifier by producing a DVS with this message-signature pair for this verifier. Much like DVS, UDVS is bound by non-transferability as well. Meanwhile, our withdrawable signature scheme takes another different approach than UDVS's as our scheme does not require the signer to reveal the underlying regular signature at the withdrawable signature generation stage.

In our withdrawable signature scheme construction, the underlying regular signature is treated as a secret held by the signer. This secret ensures the signer creates a corresponding withdrawable signature specific to a certain (designated) verifier. Later at the transformation stage, we require the additional input as the public key set of signer and verifier and the signer's secret key to reconstruct the underlying additional regular signature. With these inputs, we can finalize our transformation algorithm.

3   Definitions

In this section, we provide a comprehensive overview of the syntax and security notion of withdrawable signature.

3.1   Notation and Terminology

Throughout this paper, we use λ as the security parameter. By $a \xleftarrow{\$} \mathcal{S}$, we denote an element a is chosen uniformly at random from a set $\mathcal{S}$. Let $\mathcal{S} = \{\mathsf{pk}_1, \cdots, \mathsf{pk}_\mu\}$ be a set of public keys, where each public key pk_i is generated by the same key generation algorithm $\mathsf{KeyGen}(1^k)$ and $\mu = |\mathcal{S}|$. The corresponding secret key of pk_i is denoted by sk_i. Given two distinct public keys $\mathsf{pk}_s, \mathsf{pk}_j \xleftarrow{\$} \mathcal{S}$ where $j \neq s$, the signer's public key is denoted by pk_s.

3.2   Withdrawable Signature: A Formal Definition

Naturally, our withdrawable signature scheme involves two parties: signers and verifiers. At a high level, the scheme consists of two stages, i.e., generating a withdrawable signature and transforming it into a confirmed signature. These two stages are all completed by the signer.

More precisely, a withdrawable signature scheme $\mathcal{WS}$ consists of five polynomial time algorithms, $(\mathsf{KeyGen}, \mathsf{WSign}, \mathsf{WSVerify}, \mathsf{Confirm}, \mathsf{CVerify})$, each of which is described below:

- $(\mathsf{pk}, \mathsf{sk}) \leftarrow \mathsf{KeyGen}(1^k)$: The key generation algorithm takes the security parameters 1^k as input, to return a public/secret key pair $(\mathsf{pk}, \mathsf{sk})$.
- $\sigma \leftarrow \mathsf{WSign}(m, \mathsf{sk}_s, \gamma)$: The "withdrawable signing" algorithm takes as input a message m, signer's secret key sk_s and $\gamma = \{\mathsf{pk}_s, \mathsf{pk}_j\}$ where $\mathsf{pk}_s, \mathsf{pk}_j \in \mathcal{S}$, to return a new withdrawable signature σ of m respect to pk_s, which is designated to verifier pk_j.
- $1/0 \leftarrow \mathsf{WSVerify}(m, \mathsf{sk}_j, \mathsf{pk}_s, \sigma)$: The "withdrawable signature verification" algorithm takes as input a withdrawable signature σ of m with respect to pk_s, the designated verifier's secret key sk_j, to return either 1 or 0.
- $\widetilde{\sigma} \leftarrow \mathsf{Confirm}(m, \mathsf{sk}_s, \gamma, \sigma)$: The "confirm" algorithm takes as input a withdrawable signature σ of m with respect to pk_s, signer's secret key sk_s, the public key set γ, to return a confirmed signature $\widetilde{\sigma}$ of m, $\widetilde{\sigma}$ is a verifiable signature with respect to γ.
- $1/0 \leftarrow \mathsf{CVerify}(m, \gamma, \sigma, \widetilde{\sigma})$: The "confirmed signature verification" algorithm takes as input a confirmed signature $\widetilde{\sigma}$ of m with respect to γ, and the corresponding withdrawable signature σ, to return either 1 or 0.

3.3   Security Notions of Withdrawable Signature

The security notion of a withdrawable signature scheme $\mathcal{WS}$ covers the properties of correctness, unforgeability under insider corruption, and withdrawability three aspects.

Correctness. As long as the withdrawable signature σ is verifiable through the withdrawable signature verification algorithm $\mathsf{WSVerify}$, it can be concluded that the corresponding confirmed signature $\widetilde{\sigma}$ will also be verifiable through the confirm verification algorithm $\mathsf{CVerify}$.

Unforgeability under insider corruption. Nobody except the signer can transform a verifiable withdrawable signature σ generated from sk_s for pk_j into corresponding confirmed signature $\widetilde{\sigma}$, even the adversary can always obtain the secret key sk_j of the verifier.

Withdrawability. The withdrawability means that, given a verifiable withdrawable signature σ, it must be intractable for any PPT adversary $\mathcal{A}$ to distinguish whether σ was generated by the signer or the verifier.

Below, we provide formal security definitions. The formal definitions of correctness, unforgeability under insider corruption, and withdrawability.

We call a withdrawable signature scheme $\mathcal{WS}$ secure if it is *correct, unforgeable under insider corruption, withdrawable.*

Definition 1 (Correctness). *A withdrawable signature scheme $\mathcal{WS}$ is considered correct for any security parameter k, any public key set γ, and any message $m \in \{0,1\}^*$, if with following algorithms:*

- $(\mathsf{pk}_s, \mathsf{sk}_s), (\mathsf{pk}_j, \mathsf{sk}_j) \leftarrow \mathsf{KeyGen}(1^k)$
- $\gamma \leftarrow \{\mathsf{pk}_s, \mathsf{pk}_j\}$
- $\sigma \leftarrow \mathsf{WSign}(m, \mathsf{sk}_s, \gamma)$
- $\widetilde{\sigma} \leftarrow \mathsf{Confirm}(m, \mathsf{sk}_s, \gamma, \sigma)$

it holds with an overwhelming probability (in k) that the corresponding verification algorithms:

$$\mathsf{WSVerify}(m, \mathsf{sk}_j, \mathsf{pk}_s, \sigma) = 1 \ and \ \mathsf{CVerify}(m, \gamma, \sigma, \widetilde{\sigma}) = 1.$$

Definition 2 (Unforgeability under insider corruption). *Considering an unforgeability under insider corruption experiment $\mathsf{Exp}_{\mathcal{WS},\mathcal{A}}^{\mathrm{EUF\text{-}CMA}}(1^k)$ for a PPT adversary $\mathcal{A}$ and security parameter k.*

The three oracles we use to build the $\mathsf{Exp}_{\mathcal{WS},\mathcal{A}}^{\mathrm{EUF\text{-}CMA}}(1^k)$ are shown as follows.

Oracle $\mathcal{O}_i^{\mathsf{Corrupt}}(\cdot)$	Oracle $\mathcal{O}_{\mathsf{sk}_s,\gamma}^{\mathsf{WSign}}(\cdot)$	Oracle $\mathcal{O}_{\mathsf{sk}_s,\sigma,\gamma}^{\mathsf{Confirm}}(\cdot)$
if $i \neq s$,	if $\mathsf{pk}_s \in \gamma \wedge s \notin \mathcal{CO}$,	if $\sigma \in \mathcal{W}$
$\quad \mathcal{CO} \leftarrow \mathcal{CO} \cup \mathsf{sk}_i$	$\quad \sigma \leftarrow \mathsf{WSign}(m, \mathsf{sk}_s, \gamma)$	$\quad \mathcal{M} \leftarrow \mathcal{M} \cup \{m\}$
$\quad$ **return** sk_i	$\quad \mathcal{W} \leftarrow \mathcal{W} \cup \{\sigma\}$	$\quad \widetilde{\sigma} \leftarrow \mathsf{Confirm}(m, \mathsf{sk}_s, \gamma, \sigma)$
else return $\perp$	$\quad$ **return** σ	$\quad$ **return** $\widetilde{\sigma}$
	else return $\perp$	**else return** $\perp$

With these three oracles, we have the following experiment $\mathsf{Exp}_{\mathcal{WS},\mathcal{A}}^{\mathrm{EUF\text{-}CMA}}(1^k)$:

$$\mathsf{Exp}_{\mathcal{WS},\mathcal{A}}^{\mathrm{EUF\text{-}CMA}}(1^k)$$

---

for $i = 1$ **to** μ **do**

   $(\mathsf{pk}_i, \mathsf{sk}_i) \leftarrow \mathsf{KeyGen}(1^k), s, j \in [1, \mu], j \neq s;$

   $\mathcal{CO}, \mathcal{W}, \mathcal{M} \leftarrow \emptyset;$

   $(m^*, \widetilde{\sigma}^*) \leftarrow \mathcal{A}^{\mathcal{O}_i^{\mathsf{Corrupt}}(\cdot), \mathcal{O}_{\mathsf{sk}_s, \gamma}^{\mathsf{WSign}}(\cdot), \mathcal{O}_{\mathsf{sk}_s, \sigma, \gamma}^{\mathsf{Confirm}}(\cdot)}(1^k, \gamma^*, \sigma^*)$

if $\gamma^* = \{\mathsf{pk}_s, \mathsf{pk}_j\}, j \in \mathcal{CO} \wedge m^* \notin \mathcal{M}$

   $\wedge \mathsf{WSVerify}(m^*, \mathsf{sk}_j, \mathsf{pk}_s, \sigma^*) = 1 \wedge \mathsf{CVerify}(m^*, \gamma^*, \sigma^*, \widetilde{\sigma}^*) = 1$

   return 1

else return 0

A withdrawable signature scheme $\mathcal{WS}$ is unforgeable under insider corruption of EUF-CMA security if for all PPT adversary $\mathcal{A}$, there exists a negligible function negl *such that:*

$$\Pr[\mathsf{Exp}_{\mathcal{WS},\mathcal{A}}^{\mathrm{EUF\text{-}CMA}}(1^k) = 1] \leq \mathsf{negl}(1^k).$$

Definition 3 (Withdrawability). *Assume two public/secret key pairs are generated as* $(\mathsf{pk}_0, \mathsf{sk}_0), (\mathsf{pk}_1, \mathsf{sk}_1) \leftarrow \mathsf{KeyGen}(1^k)$. *Let* $\gamma = \{\mathsf{pk}_0, \mathsf{pk}_1\}$ *and* $b \xleftarrow{\$} \{0, 1\}$, *considering a withdrawability experiment* $\mathsf{Exp}_{\mathcal{WS},\mathcal{A}}^{\mathsf{Withdraw}}(1^k)$ *for a PPT adversary $\mathcal{A}$ and security parameter k.*

The oracle we use to build our withdrawability experiment $\mathsf{Exp}_{\mathcal{WS}}^{\mathsf{Withdraw}}(1^k)$ *is shown as follows.*

Oracle $\mathcal{O}_{\mathsf{sk}_s, \gamma}^{\mathsf{WSign}}(\cdot)$

---

if $\gamma = \{\mathsf{pk}_0, \mathsf{pk}_1\}, b \xleftarrow{\$} \{0, 1\}$

   $\sigma_b \leftarrow \mathsf{WSign}(m, \mathsf{sk}_b, \gamma)$

   $\mathcal{M} \leftarrow \mathcal{M} \cup \{m\}$

   return σ_b

else return $\perp$

With this signing oracle, we have the following experiment $\mathsf{Exp}_{\mathcal{WS}}^{\mathsf{Withdraw}}(1^k)$:

$$\mathsf{Exp}_{\mathcal{WS},\mathcal{A}}^{\mathsf{Withdraw}}(1^k)$$

---

for $i = 0$ **to** 1 **do**

   $(\mathsf{pk}_i, \mathsf{sk}_i) \leftarrow \mathsf{KeyGen}(1^k), \gamma = \{\mathsf{pk}_0, \mathsf{pk}_1\}$

   $b \xleftarrow{\$} \{0, 1\}, \mathcal{M} \leftarrow \emptyset;$

if $\gamma = \{\mathsf{pk}_0, \mathsf{pk}_1\} \wedge m^* \notin \mathcal{M}$

   $\sigma_b \leftarrow \mathsf{WSign}(m^*, \mathsf{sk}_b, \gamma)$

   $b' \leftarrow \mathcal{A}^{\mathcal{O}_{\mathsf{sk}_b, \gamma}^{\mathsf{WSign}}(\cdot)}(1^k, m^*, \sigma_b^*)$

if $b = b'$

   return 1

else return 0

A withdrawable signature $\mathcal{WS}$ *achieves withdrawability if, for any PPT adversary* $\mathcal{A}$, *as long as the* Confirm *algorithm hasn't been executed, there exists a negligible function* negl *such that:*

$$\Pr[\mathsf{Exp}_{\mathcal{WS},\mathcal{A}}^{\mathsf{Withdraw}}(1^k) = 1] \leq \frac{1}{2} + \mathsf{negl}(1^k).$$

4 Our Withdrawable Signature Schemes

In this section, we present two specific constructions of withdrawable signatures. We start by introducing the necessary preliminaries that form the basis of our constructions.

4.1 Preliminaries

Digital Signatures. A signature scheme DS consists of three PPT algorithms, described as follows:

$$\mathsf{DS} = \begin{cases} (\mathsf{pk}, \mathsf{sk}) & \leftarrow \mathsf{KeyGen}(1^k) \\ \sigma & \leftarrow \mathsf{Sign}(m, \mathsf{sk}) \\ 0/1 & \leftarrow \mathsf{Verify}(m, \mathsf{pk}, \sigma) \end{cases}$$

The relevant security model of existential unforgeability against chosen-message attacks (EUF-CMA) for digital signature schemes is given in Appendix A.

Bilinear Groups. Let $\mathbb{G}_1$, $\mathbb{G}_2$ and $\mathbb{G}_T$ be three (multiplicative) cyclic groups of prime order p. Let g_1 be a generator of $\mathbb{G}_1$ and g_2 be a generator of $\mathbb{G}_2$. A bilinear map is a map $e : \mathbb{G}_1 \times \mathbb{G}_2 \to \mathbb{G}_T$ with the following properties:

- **Bilinearity:** For all $u \in \mathbb{G}_1$, $v \in \mathbb{G}_2$ and $a, b \in \mathbb{Z}_p$, we have $e(u^a, v^b) = e(u, v)^{ab}$.
- **Non-degeneracy:** $e(g_1, g_2) \neq 1$ (i.e. $e(g_1, g_2)$ generates $\mathbb{G}_T$).
- **Computability:** For all $u \in \mathbb{G}_1$, $v \in \mathbb{G}_2$, there exists an efficient algorithm to compute $e(u, v)$.

If $\mathbb{G}_1 = \mathbb{G}_2$, then e is *symmetric* (Type-1) and *asymmetric* (Type-2 or 3) otherwise. For Type-2 pairings, there is an efficiently computable homomorphism $\phi : \mathbb{G}_2 \to \mathbb{G}_1$. For Type-3 pairings no such homomorphism is known.

4.2 A Construction Based on BLS

Suppose $\mathbb{G}$ is a generic group of prime order p, and g is a generator, with two hash functions $H_1 : \{0, 1\}^* \to \mathbb{G}$ and $H_2 : \{0, 1\}^* \to \mathbb{Z}_p^*$. $\mathbb{PG} : \mathbb{G} \times \mathbb{G} = \mathbb{G}_T$ is a Type-1 bilinear pairing as defined in Sect. 4.1.

Let BLS.DS denotes the BLS signature scheme [4], which contains three algorithms: BLS.DS = (KeyGen, BLS.Sign, BLS.Verify). Comprehensive details of these three algorithms are outlined in [4]. The output of the signing algorithm is denoted as $\omega \leftarrow \mathsf{BLS.Sign}(m, \mathsf{sk}_s)$ where ω is derived as follows: $\omega = H_1(m)^{\mathsf{sk}_s}$.

Following this, we have a construction of a withdrawable signature based on the original BLS signature (Fig. 1):

$$
\begin{array}{ll}
\underline{\textsf{Setup}(\cdot)} & \underline{\textsf{KeyGen}(1^k)} \\[4pt]
\quad \text{define } H_1 : \{0,1\}^* \to \mathbb{G} & \quad \mathsf{sk}_s \xleftarrow{\$} \mathbb{Z}_p, \ \mathsf{pk}_s = g^{\mathsf{sk}_s} \\[4pt]
\quad \text{define } H_2 : \{0,1\}^* \to \mathbb{Z}_p^* & \quad \textbf{return } (\mathsf{pk}_s, \mathsf{sk}_s) \\[4pt]
\textbf{return } H_1, H_2 &
\end{array}
$$

$\underline{\textsf{WSign}(m, \mathsf{sk}_s, \gamma)}$

$\text{parse } \gamma = \{\mathsf{pk}_s, \mathsf{pk}_j\}$

$\boxed{\omega = H_1(m)^{\mathsf{sk}_s}}$

$y \xleftarrow{\$} \mathbb{Z}_p^*, \ r = H_2(m, g^y \cdot \omega)$

$\sigma_1 \leftarrow e(H_1(m)^{r \cdot y} \cdot \omega, \mathsf{pk}_j)$

$\sigma_2 \leftarrow g^y, \ \sigma_3 \leftarrow H_1(m)^r$

$\sigma = (\sigma_1, \sigma_2, \sigma_3)$

$\textbf{return } \sigma$

$\underline{\textsf{WSVerify}(m, \mathsf{sk}_j, \mathsf{pk}_s, \sigma)}$

$\text{parse } \sigma = (\sigma_1, \sigma_2, \sigma_3)$

$\textbf{if } \sigma_1 = e(\sigma_3, \sigma_2^{\mathsf{sk}_j}) e(H_1(m)^{\mathsf{sk}_j}, \mathsf{pk}_s)$

$\quad = e(\sigma_3^{\mathsf{sk}_j}, \sigma_2) e(H_1(m)^{\mathsf{sk}_j}, \mathsf{pk}_s)$

$\quad \textbf{return } 1$

$\textbf{else return } 0$

$\underline{\textsf{Confirm}(m, \mathsf{sk}_s, \gamma, \sigma)}$

$\text{parse } \sigma = (\sigma_1, \sigma_2, \sigma_3)$

$\boxed{\omega = H_1(m)^{\mathsf{sk}_s}}$

$r' = H_2(m, \sigma_2 \cdot \omega)$

$\delta_1 \leftarrow \mathsf{pk}_j^{\mathsf{sk}_s \cdot r'} \cdot \omega$

$\delta_2 \leftarrow \mathsf{pk}_j^{r'}, \ \delta_3 \leftarrow g^{r'}, \ \delta_4 \leftarrow \sigma_3$

$\widetilde{\sigma} = (\delta_1, \delta_2, \delta_3, \delta_4)$

$\textbf{return } \widetilde{\sigma}$

$\underline{\textsf{CVerify}(m, \gamma, \sigma, \widetilde{\sigma})}$

$\text{parse } \widetilde{\sigma} = (\delta_1, \delta_2, \delta_3, \delta_4)$

$\text{parse } \sigma = (\sigma_1, \sigma_2, \sigma_3)$

$\quad \textbf{if } \delta_4 = \sigma_3,$

$\quad\quad e(\delta_1, g) = e(\mathsf{pk}_s, \delta_2) e(H_1(m), \mathsf{pk}_s),$

$\quad\quad e(\delta_4, g) = e(H_1(m), \delta_3),$

$\quad\quad e(\delta_2, g) = e(\delta_3, \mathsf{pk}_j)$

$\quad \textbf{return } 1$

$\textbf{else return } 0$

Fig. 1. A Construction Based on BLS

4.3   A Construction Based on Schnorr

Recall that $\mathbb{G}$ is a generic group of prime order p, and g is a generator, with hash function $H : \{0,1\}^* \to \mathbb{Z}_p$.

Let Sch.DS denote the Schnorr signature scheme [16], which contains three algorithms: Sch.DS = (KeyGen, Sch.Sign, Sch.Verify). Details of these three algorithms are outlined in [16]. The output of the signing algorithm is also denoted as $\omega \leftarrow \textsf{Sch.Sign}(m, \mathsf{sk}_s)$ where $\omega = (t, z)$ is derived as follows:

A randomness e is randomly selected from $\mathbb{Z}_p$, then u is calculated as $u = g^e$. The value t is computed using the hash function $t = H(m, u)$. Finally, z is calculated as $z = (e - x \cdot t) \mod p$.

Following this, we have a construction of a withdrawable signature based on the Schnorr signature (Fig. 2):

Setup($\cdot$)

   define $H : \{0,1\}^* \to \mathbb{Z}_p$

return H

KeyGen(1^k)

   $\mathsf{sk}_s \xleftarrow{\$} \mathbb{Z}_p$, $\mathsf{pk}_s = g^{\mathsf{sk}_s}$

return $(\mathsf{pk}_s, \mathsf{sk}_s)$

WSign(m, sk_s, γ)

parse $\gamma = \{\mathsf{pk}_s, \mathsf{pk}_j\}$

$e \xleftarrow{\$} \mathbb{Z}_p^*$, $t = H(m, g^e)$

$z = e - \mathsf{sk}_s \cdot t$

$\boxed{\omega = (t, z)}$

$r = H(m, g^{\mathsf{sk}_s \cdot e})$

$\sigma_1 \leftarrow g^e$, $\sigma_2 \leftarrow \mathsf{pk}_j^{z - r \cdot t}$, $\sigma_3 \leftarrow g^r$

$\sigma = (\sigma_1, \sigma_2, \sigma_3)$

return σ

WSVerify($m, \mathsf{sk}_j, \mathsf{pk}_s, \sigma$)

parse $\sigma = (\sigma_1, \sigma_2, \sigma_3)$

$t' = H(m, \sigma_1)$

if $\sigma_2 = (\sigma_1 \cdot (\mathsf{pk}_s \cdot \sigma_3)^{-t'})^{\mathsf{sk}_j}$

   return 1

else return 0

Confirm($m, \mathsf{sk}_s, \gamma, \sigma$)

  parse $\sigma = (\sigma_1, \sigma_2, \sigma_3)$

  $e_s \xleftarrow{\$} \mathbb{Z}_p^*$, $r' = H(m, \sigma_1^{\mathsf{sk}_s})$

  $t_s = H(m, g^{e_s})$

  $z_s = e_s - \mathsf{sk}_s \cdot t_s$

  $\boxed{\omega_s = (t_s, z_s)}$

  $e_j \xleftarrow{\$} \mathbb{Z}_p^*$, $t_j = H(\mathsf{pk}_j, e_j)$

  $z_j = e_j - r' \cdot t_j$

  $\delta_1 \leftarrow t_s$, $\delta_2 \leftarrow z_s - r' \cdot t_s$

  $\delta_3 \leftarrow \sigma_3$, $\delta_4 \leftarrow t_j$, $\delta_5 \leftarrow z_j$

  $\widetilde{\sigma} = (\delta_1, \delta_2, \delta_3, \delta_4, \delta_5)$

return $\widetilde{\sigma}$

CVerify($m, \gamma, \sigma, \widetilde{\sigma}$)

  parse $\widetilde{\sigma} = (\delta_1, \delta_2, \delta_3, \delta_4, \delta_5)$

  parse $\sigma = (\sigma_1, \sigma_2, \sigma_3)$

  if $\delta_3 = \sigma_3$,

     $\delta_1 = H(m, g^{\delta_2} \cdot \mathsf{pk}_s^{\delta_1} \cdot \delta_3^{\delta_1})$,

     $\delta_4 = H(\mathsf{pk}_j, g^{\delta_5} \cdot \delta_3^{\delta_4})$

  return 1

  else return 0

Fig. 2. A Construction Based on Schnorr

5   Security Analysis

In this section, we provide the security analysis of our two constructed withdrawable signature schemes.

5.1   Security of Our Withdrawable Signature Scheme Based on BLS

Theorem 1. *If the underlying BLS signature scheme* BLS.DS *is unforgeable against chosen-message attacks (EUF-CMA) as defined in Appendix A, our withdrawable signature scheme based on BLS presented in Sect. 4.2 is unforgeable* *under insider corruption (Definition 2) in the random oracle model with reduction loss* $L = q_{H_1}$ *where* q_{H_1} *denotes the number of hash queries to the random oracle* H_1.

Proof. We show how to build a simulator $\mathcal{B}$ to provide unforgeability under insider corruption for our withdrawable signature scheme based on BLS in the random oracle model.

Setup. $\mathcal{B}$ has access to the algorithm $\mathcal{C}$, which provides unforgeability in the random oracle for our underlying signature scheme BLS.DS. $\mathcal{C}$ executes the EUF-CMA game of BLS.DS, denoted as $\mathsf{Exp}_{\mathcal{A}}^{\mathrm{EUF\text{-}CMA}}$ which includes a signing oracle denoted as $\mathcal{O}_{\mathsf{sk}_s}^{\mathsf{BLS.DS}}(\cdot)$, where $\mathcal{O}_{\mathsf{sk}_s}^{\mathsf{BLS.DS}}(\cdot) : \omega \leftarrow \mathsf{BLS.Sign}(m, \mathsf{sk}_s)$.

For $s \in [1, q_\mu]$, $\mathcal{C}$ first generates $(\mathsf{pk}_s, \mathsf{sk}_s) \leftarrow \mathsf{KeyGen}(1^k)$. $\mathcal{B}$ then generates $\mathcal{S} = \{\mathsf{pk}_1, \cdots, \mathsf{pk}_{s-1}, \mathsf{pk}_{s+1}, \cdots, \mathsf{pk}_\mu\}$ and gains pk_s from $\mathcal{C}$.

$\mathcal{B}$ now can set the public key set of the signer and a specific (designated) verifier as $\gamma = \{\mathsf{pk}_s, \mathsf{pk}_j\}$ where $j \neq s$ and provide γ to $\mathcal{A}$.

Oracle Simulation. $\mathcal{B}$ answers the oracle queries as follows.

Corruption Query. The adversary $\mathcal{A}$ makes secret key queries of $\mathsf{pk}_i, i \in [1, \mu]$ in this phase. If $\mathcal{A}$ queries for the secret key of pk_s, abort. Otherwise, $\mathcal{B}$ returns the corresponding sk_i to $\mathcal{A}$, and adds sk_i to the corrupted secret key list $\mathcal{CO}$.

H-Query. The adversary $\mathcal{A}$ makes hash queries in this phase. $\mathcal{C}$ simulates H_1 as a random oracle, $\mathcal{B}$ then answers the hash queries of H_1 through $\mathcal{C}$.

Signature Query. $\mathcal{A}$ outputs a message m_i and queries for withdrawable signature with signer pk_s and the specific (designated) verifier pk_j. If the signer isn't pk_s, $\mathcal{B}$ abort. Otherwise, $\mathcal{B}$ sets m_i as the input of $\mathcal{C}$. $\mathcal{B}$ then asks for the signing output of $\mathcal{C}$ as $\omega_i \leftarrow \mathsf{BLS.Sign}(m_i, \mathsf{sk}_s)$. With $\omega_i = H_1(m_i)^{\mathsf{sk}_s}$ from $\mathcal{C}$, $\mathcal{B}$ could respond to the signature query of $\mathcal{A}$ with the specific verifier pk_j as follows:

- $\mathcal{O}_{\mathsf{sk}_s,\gamma}^{\mathsf{WSign}}(\cdot)$: Given the output ω_i of $\mathcal{C}$, $\mathcal{B}$ can compute the withdrawable signature $\sigma_i \leftarrow \mathcal{O}_{\mathsf{sk}_s,\gamma}^{\mathsf{WSign}}(\cdot)$ for $\mathcal{A}$ as:
  1. $r_i, y_i \xleftarrow{\$} \mathbb{Z}_p^*$, $\sigma_i = \left(e(H_1(m_i)^{y_i \cdot r_i} \cdot \omega_i, \mathsf{pk}_j), H_1(m_i)^{r_i}, g^{y_i} \right)$
- $\mathcal{O}_{\mathsf{sk}_s,\sigma,\gamma}^{\mathsf{Confirm}}(\cdot)$: With ω_i and σ_i, $\mathcal{B}$ can compute the corresponding confirmed signature $\widetilde{\sigma}_i \leftarrow \mathcal{O}_{\mathsf{sk}_s,\sigma,\gamma}^{\mathsf{Confirm}}(\cdot)$ for $\mathcal{A}$ with underlying signature $\omega_i = H_1(m_i)^{\mathsf{sk}_s}$ and r_i as:
  1. Compute $\delta_{1,i} = \mathsf{pk}_s^{\mathsf{sk}_j \cdot r_i} \cdot \sigma_i$.
  2. Compute $\delta_{2,i} = \mathsf{pk}_j^{r_i}$, $\delta_{3,i} = g^{r_i}$, $\delta_{4,i} = H_1(m_i)^{r_i}$
  3. $\widetilde{\sigma}_i = (\delta_{1,i}, \delta_{2,i}, \delta_{3,i}, \delta_{4,i})$

Meanwhile, $\mathcal{B}$ sets $\mathcal{M} \leftarrow \mathcal{M} \cup m_i$ and $\mathcal{W} \leftarrow \mathcal{W} \cup \sigma_i$.

Forgery. On the forgery phase, the simulator $\mathcal{B}$ returns a withdrawable signature σ^* for signer pk_s that designated to verifier pk_j, and $\gamma^* = \{\mathsf{pk}_s, \mathsf{pk}_j\}$ on some m^* that has not been queried before. σ^* is generated by $\mathcal{B}$ as follows:

$$\sigma^* = \left(e(H_1(m^*)^{r^* \cdot y^*} H_1(m^*)^{\mathsf{sk}_j}, \mathsf{pk}_s), g^{y^*}, H_1(m^*)^{r^*} \right)$$

Then σ^* could be transformed into $\widetilde{\sigma}^*$ under γ^* correctly. After $\mathcal{A}$ transforms σ^* into $\widetilde{\sigma}^*$, if $\widetilde{\sigma}^*$ could not be verified through $\mathsf{CVerify}(m^*, \gamma^*, \sigma^*, \widetilde{\sigma}^*)$, abort.

Otherwise, if $\widetilde{\sigma}^* = (\delta_1^*, \delta_2^*, \delta_3^*, \delta_4^*)$ is valid, $\mathcal{B}$ then could obtain a forged signature ω^* for pk_s on m^*. Since $\mathcal{B}$ is capable of directly computing $\mathsf{pk}_s^{\mathsf{sk}_j \cdot r}$, the forged signature ω^* can be determined as: $\omega^* = \delta_1^* / \mathsf{pk}_s^{\mathsf{sk}_j \cdot r}$.

Therefore, we can use $\mathcal{A}$ to break the unforgeability in the EUF-CMA model of our underlying signature scheme BLS.DS, which contradicts the property of our underlying signature scheme.

Probability of Successful Simulation. All queried signatures ω_i are simulatable, and the forged signature is reducible because the message m^* cannot be chosen for a signature query as it will be used for the signature forgery. Therefore, the probability of successful simulation is $\frac{1}{q_{H_1}}$ for q_{H_1} queries. $\qquad\square$

Theorem 2. *Our withdrawable signature scheme based on BLS presented in Sect. 4.2 is withdrawable (Definition 3) in the random oracle model.*

Proof. In our proof of Theorem 2, $\mathcal{B}$ sets the challenge signer/verifier public key set as $\gamma = \{\mathsf{pk}_0, \mathsf{pk}_1\}$ and associated secret key set as $\delta = \{\mathsf{sk}_0, \mathsf{sk}_1\}$. The signer is denoted as pk_b where $b \xleftarrow{\$} \{0,1\}$, and the specific verifier is denoted as pk_{1-b}.

Oracle Simulation. $\mathcal{B}$ answers the oracle queries as follows.

<u>H-Query.</u> The adversary $\mathcal{A}$ makes hash queries in this phase, where $\mathcal{B}$ simulates H_1 as a random oracle.

<u>Signature Query.</u> $\mathcal{A}$ outputs a message m_i and queries for withdrawable signature with corresponding signer pk_s and the specific verifier pk_j, $\mathcal{B}$ responses the signature query of $\mathcal{A}$ as follows:

- $\mathcal{O}_{\mathsf{sk}_b, \gamma}^{\mathsf{WSign}}(\cdot)$:

$$r_i, y_i \xleftarrow{\$} \mathbb{Z}_p^*, \sigma_{b,i} = \left(e(H_1(m_i)^{r_i \cdot y_i} \cdot H_1(m_i)^{\mathsf{sk}_b}, \mathsf{pk}_{1-b}), H_1(m_i)^{r_i}, g^{y_i} \right).$$

Meanwhile, $\mathcal{B}$ sets $\mathcal{M} \leftarrow \mathcal{M} \cup m_i$.

Challenge. On the challenge phrase, $\mathcal{A}$ gives $\mathcal{B}$ a message $m^* \notin \mathcal{M}$, where $m^* \notin \mathcal{M}$. $\mathcal{B}$ now executes the challenge phrase and computes the challenge withdrawable signature σ_b^* for $\mathcal{A}$ where $b \xleftarrow{\$} [0, 1]$ as follows:

$$\sigma_0^* = \left(e(H_1(m^*)^{r^* \cdot y^*} \cdot H_1(m^*)^{\mathsf{sk}_0}, \mathsf{pk}_1), H_1(m^*)^{r^*}, g^{y^*} \right)$$

$$\sigma_1^* = \left(e(H_1(m^*)^{r^* \cdot y^*} \cdot H_1(m)^{\mathsf{sk}_1}, \mathsf{pk}_0), H_1(m^*)^{r^*}, g^{y^*} \right)$$

$$= \left(e(H_1(m^*)^{r^* \cdot y^*} \cdot H_1(m^*)^{\mathsf{sk}_0}, \mathsf{pk}_1), H_1(m^*)^{r^*}, g^{y^*} \right) = \sigma_0^*.$$

Guess. $\mathcal{A}$ outputs a guess b' of b. The simulator outputs true if $b' = b$. Otherwise, false.

Probability of Breaking the Withdrawability Property. It's easy to see that σ_0^* and σ_1^* have the same distributions, hence they are indistinguishable.

Therefore, the adversary $\mathcal{A}$ only has a probability $1/2$ of guessing the signer's identity correctly.

Probability of Successful Simulation. There is no abort in our simulation, the probability of successful simulation is 1. $\square$

5.2   Security of the Withdrawable Signature Scheme Based on Schnorr

Theorem 3. *If the underlying Schnorr signature scheme* Sch.DS *is unforgeable against chosen-message attacks (*EUF-CMA*) as defined in Appendix A, our withdrawable signature scheme based on Schnorr presented in Sect. 4.3 is unforgeable under insider corruption (Definition 2) in the random oracle model with reduction loss $L = 2q_H - 1$ where q_H denotes the number of hash queries to the random oracle H.*

The proof of Theorem 3 follows the same proof structure shown in Proof 5.1, which also contains three algorithms, $\mathcal{A}$, $\mathcal{B}$, and $\mathcal{C}$. The completed proof of Theorem 3 is given in Appendix B.

Theorem 4. *Our withdrawable signature scheme based on Schnorr presented in Sect. 4.3 is withdrawable (Definition 3) in the random oracle model.*

The complete detailed proof of Theorem 4 is available in Appendix B.

6   Conclusion

In this paper, we discussed the challenges associated with traditional signature schemes and the need for a mechanism to revoke or replace signatures. We introduced a unique withdrawability feature for signature schemes, allowing signers to have the ability to call off their signatures as withdrawable signatures, and later, the signature could be transformed into a confirmed signature that could be verified through their public keys.

Furthermore, we proposed cryptographic primitives and two constructions of the withdrawable signature based on the BLS/Schnorr signature. We formally proved that the two proposed constructions are unforgeable under insider corruption and satisfy withdrawability.

There are several directions for future work: one is improving the efficiency of our withdrawable signature scheme. Exploring further to discover practical applications and use cases of withdrawable signature schemes can also be an interesting avenue for future work.

A   Security Definitions of Existing Cryptographic Primitives

Definition 4 (EUF-CMA). *Given a signature scheme* DS $=$ (KeyGen, Sign, Verify), *and a ppt adversary $\mathcal{A}$, considering the following game* $\mathrm{Exp}_{\mathcal{A}}^{\mathrm{EUF\text{-}CMA}}$:

- *Let SP be the system parameters. The challenger $\mathcal{B}$ runs the key generation algorithm to generate a key pair $(\mathsf{pk}, \mathsf{sk})$ and sends pk to the adversary $\mathcal{A}$. The challenger keeps sk to respond to signature queries from the adversary.*
- *$\mathcal{A}$ is given access to an oracle $\mathcal{O}_{\mathsf{sk}}^{\mathsf{Sign}}(\cdot)$ such that $\mathcal{O}_{\mathsf{sk}}^{\mathsf{Sign}}(\cdot) : \sigma \leftarrow \mathsf{Sign}(m, \mathsf{sk})$.*
- *$\mathcal{A}$ outputs a message m^*, and returns a forged signature σ_{m^*} on m^*.*
- *$\mathcal{A}$ succeeds if σ_{m^*} is a valid signature of the message m^* and the signature of m^* has not been queried in the query phase.*

A signature scheme is (t, q_s, ε)-secure in the EUF-CMA security model if there exists no adversary who can win the above game in time t with advantage ε after it has made q_s signature queries.

B   Security Proofs of Our Withdrawable Signature

We give the detailed proof of Theorem 3 as follows.

Proof. We show how to build a simulator $\mathcal{B}$ to provide unforgeability under insider corruption for our withdrawable signature scheme based on Schnorr in the random oracle model.

Setup. Simulator $\mathcal{B}$ has access to algorithm $\mathcal{C}$, which provides unforgeability in the random oracle for our underlying Schnorr signature scheme Sch.DS.

$\mathcal{C}$ executes the EUF-CMA game of Sch.DS, denoted as $\mathsf{Exp}_{\mathcal{A}}^{\mathsf{EUF\text{-}CMA}}$ which includes a signing oracle $\mathcal{O}_{\mathsf{sk}_s}^{\mathsf{Sch.Sign}}(\cdot)$, where $\mathcal{O}_{\mathsf{sk}_s}^{\mathsf{Sch.Sign}}(\cdot) : \omega \leftarrow \mathsf{Sch.Sign}(m, \mathsf{sk}_s)$. $\mathcal{B}$ first generates $\mathcal{S} = \{\mathsf{pk}_1, \cdots, \mathsf{pk}_{s-1}, \mathsf{pk}_{s+1}, \cdots, \mathsf{pk}_\mu\}$, $\mathcal{C}$ generates $(\mathsf{pk}_s, \mathsf{sk}_s) \leftarrow$ KeyGen(1^k), $\mathcal{B}$ then gains pk_s from $\mathcal{C}$ and sets $s \in [1, q_\mu]$.

$\mathcal{B}$ now can set the public key set of the signer with a specific (designated) verifier as $\gamma = \{\mathsf{pk}_s, \mathsf{pk}_j\}$ where $j \neq s$ and provide γ to $\mathcal{A}$.

Oracle Simulation. $\mathcal{B}$ answers the oracle queries as follows.

Corruption Query. The adversary $\mathcal{A}$ makes secret key queries of public key $\mathsf{pk}_i, i \in [1, \mu]$ in this phase. If $\mathcal{A}$ queries for the secret key of pk_s, abort. Otherwise, $\mathcal{B}$ returns the corresponding sk_i to $\mathcal{A}$, and add sk_i to the corrupted secret key list $\mathcal{CO}$.

H-Query. $\mathcal{C}$ simulates H as a random oracle, $\mathcal{B}$ then answers the hash queries of H through $\mathcal{C}$.

Signature Query. $\mathcal{A}$ outputs a message m_i and queries for withdrawable signature with corresponding signer pk_s and specific verifier pk_j. If the signer isn't pk_s, abort. Otherwise, $\mathcal{B}$ sets m_i as the input of $\mathcal{C}$. $\mathcal{B}$ then asks the signing output of $\mathcal{C}$ as $\omega_i = \mathsf{Sch.Sign}(m_i, \mathsf{sk}_s)$. With ω_i, $\mathcal{B}$ could response the signature query for the specific verifier pk_j chosen by $\mathcal{A}$ as follows:

- $\mathcal{O}_{\mathsf{sk}_s, \gamma}^{\mathsf{WSign}}(\cdot)$: With the output of $\mathcal{C}$, $\mathcal{B}$ can compute the withdrawable signature $\sigma_i \leftarrow \mathcal{O}_{\mathsf{sk}_s, \gamma}^{\mathsf{WSign}}(\cdot)$ for $\mathcal{A}$ with $\omega_i = (t_i, z_i) = (H(m_i, u_i), z_i)$ as:
  1. Randomly choose $r_i \xleftarrow{\$} \mathbb{Z}_p^*$

2. Compute $\sigma_{1,i} = g^{z_i} \mathsf{pk}_s^{t_i}$, $\sigma_{2,i} = \mathsf{pk}_j^{z_i - r_i \cdot t_i}$, $\sigma_{3,i} = g^{r_i}$
3. $\sigma_i = (\sigma_{1,i}, \sigma_{2,i}, \sigma_{3,i})$

- $\mathcal{O}_{\mathsf{sk}_s,\sigma,\gamma}^{\mathsf{Confirm}}(\cdot)$: $\mathcal{B}$ then queries for the Schnorr signature of m_i again to $\mathcal{C}$ and returns a corresponding $\omega_{s,i} = (t_{s,i}, z_{s,i})$ instead. With ω_i, $\omega_{s,i}$ and σ_i, $\mathcal{B}$ can compute the confirmed signature $\widetilde{\sigma}_i \leftarrow \mathcal{O}_{\mathsf{sk}_s,\sigma,\gamma}^{\mathsf{Confirm}}(\cdot)$ for $\mathcal{A}$ as follows:

1. Compute $\delta_{1,i} = g^{z_{s,i}} \mathsf{pk}_s^{t_{s,i}}$, $\delta_{2,i} = z_{s,i} - r_i \cdot t_{s,i}$.
2. Randomly choose $e_{j,i}, t_{j,i} \xleftarrow{\$} \mathbb{Z}_p^*$, $\delta_{4,i} = t_{j,i}$
3. Compute $\delta_{5,i} = e_{j,i} - r_i \cdot t_{j,i}$
4. $\widetilde{\sigma}_i = (\delta_{1,i}, \delta_{2,i}, \delta_{3,i}, \delta_{4,i}, \delta_{5,i})$

Meanwhile, $\mathcal{B}$ sets the queried message set as $\mathcal{M} \leftarrow \mathcal{M} \cup m$ and queried withdrawable signature set as $\mathcal{W} \leftarrow \mathcal{W} \cup \sigma$.

Forgery. On the forgery phase, $\mathcal{B}$ returns a withdrawable signature σ^* for $\gamma^* = \{\mathsf{pk}_s, \mathsf{pk}_j\}$ on some m^* that has not been queried before. Then σ^* could be transformed into $\widetilde{\sigma}^*$ under γ^* correctly. After $\mathcal{A}$ transforms σ^* into $\widetilde{\sigma}^*$, if $\widetilde{\sigma}^*$ could not be verified through $\mathsf{CVerify}(m^*, \gamma^*, \sigma^*, \widetilde{\sigma}^*)$, abort.

Otherwise, if $\widetilde{\sigma}^* = (\delta_1^*, \delta_2^*, \delta_3^*, \delta_4^*, \delta_5^*)$ is valid, $\mathcal{B}$ then could obtain a forged signature ω^* for pk_s on m^*. Since $\mathcal{B}$ is capable of directly computing $r^* \cdot t_s^*$, the forged signature ω^* can be determined as: $\omega^* = \delta_2^* + r^* \cdot t_s^*$.

Therefore, we can use $\mathcal{A}$ to break the unforgeability in the EUF-CMA model of our underlying signature scheme Sch.DS, which contradicts the property of our underlying signature scheme.

Probability of Successful Simulation. All queried signatures ω_i are simulatable, and the forged signature is reducible because the message m^* cannot be chosen for a signature query as it will be used for the signature forgery. Therefore, the probability of successful simulation is $\frac{1}{2q_H - 1}$. $\qquad \square$

We give the proof of Theorem 4 as follows.

Proof. In our proof of Theorem 4, $\mathcal{B}$ sets the challenge public key set as $\gamma = \{\mathsf{pk}_0, \mathsf{pk}_1\}$ and associated secret key set $\delta = \{\mathsf{sk}_0, \mathsf{sk}_1\}$. The signer is denoted as pk_b where $b \xleftarrow{\$} \{0,1\}$, and the specific verifier is denoted as pk_{1-b}.

Oracle Simulation. $\mathcal{B}$ answers the oracle queries as follows.

H-Query. The adversary $\mathcal{A}$ makes hash queries in this phase where $\mathcal{B}$ simulates H as a random oracle.

Signature Query. $\mathcal{A}$ outputs a message m_i and queries the withdrawable signature for corresponding signer pk_s and specific verifier pk_j, $\mathcal{B}$ responses the signature queries of $\mathcal{A}$ as follows:

- $\mathcal{O}_{\mathsf{sk}_b,\gamma}^{\mathsf{WSign}}(\cdot)$: $e_i \xleftarrow{\$} \mathbb{Z}_p^*$, $t_i = H(m_i, g^{e_i})$, $\sigma_{b,i} = \left(g^{e_i}, \mathsf{pk}_{1-b}^{z_{b,i}}\right) = \left(g^{e_i}, \mathsf{pk}_{1-b}^{e_i - \mathsf{sk}_b \cdot t_i}\right)$

Meanwhile, $\mathcal{B}$ sets $\mathcal{M} \leftarrow \mathcal{M} \cup m_i$.

Challenge. In the challenge phase, $\mathcal{A}$ gives $\mathcal{B}$ a message m^*, where $m^* \notin \mathcal{M}$. $\mathcal{B}$ now computes the challenge withdrawable signature of m^* as σ_b^* for $\mathcal{A}$ where $b \xleftarrow{\$} \{0,1\}$ and $r^* \xleftarrow{\$} \mathbb{Z}_p^*$ as follows:

$$\sigma_0^* = \left(g^{e^*}, \mathsf{pk}_1^{z_0^* - r^* \cdot t^*} \right) = \left(g^{e^*}, g^{\mathsf{sk}_1(e^* - \mathsf{sk}_0 \cdot t^* - r^* \cdot t^*)} \right)$$

$$\sigma_1^* = \left(g^{e^*}, \mathsf{pk}_s^{z_1^* - r^* \cdot t^*} \right) = \left(g^{e^*}, (g^{e^*})^{\mathsf{sk}_1} \mathsf{pk}_0^{-\mathsf{sk}_1 \cdot t^*} g^{-\mathsf{sk}_1 \cdot r^* \cdot t^*} \right)$$

$$= \left(g^{e^*}, g^{\mathsf{sk}_1(e^* - \mathsf{sk}_0 \cdot t^* - r^* \cdot t^*)} \right) = \sigma_0^*.$$

Guess. $\mathcal{A}$ outputs a guess b' of b. The simulator outputs true if $b' = b$. Otherwise, false.

Probability of Breaking the Withdrawability Property. It's easy to see that σ_0^* and σ_1^* have the same distributions, hence they are indistinguishable. Therefore, the adversary $\mathcal{A}$ only has a probability $1/2$ of guessing the signer's identity correctly.

Probability of Successful Simulation. There is no abort in our simulation, therefore, the probability of successful simulation is 1. □

References

1. Abhilash, M., Amberker, B.: Efficient group signature scheme using lattices. Int. J. Inf. Technol. **14**(4), 1845–1854 (2022). https://doi.org/10.1007/s41870-022-00891-3
2. Attrapadung, N., Emura, K., Hanaoka, G., Sakai, Y.: Revocable group signature with constant-size revocation list. Comput. J. **58**(10), 2698–2715 (2015)
3. Beullens, W., Dobson, S., Katsumata, S., Lai, Y.F., Pintore, F.: Group signatures and more from isogenies and lattices: generic, simple, and efficient. Des. Codes Cryptogr. **91**, 2141–2200 (2023). https://doi.org/10.1007/s10623-023-01192-x
4. Boneh, D., Lynn, B., Shacham, H.: Short signatures from the Weil pairing. In: Boyd, C. (ed.) ASIACRYPT 2001. LNCS, vol. 2248, pp. 514–532. Springer, Heidelberg (2001). https://doi.org/10.1007/3-540-45682-1_30
5. Chaum, D., van Heyst, E.: Group signatures. In: Davies, D.W. (ed.) EUROCRYPT 1991. LNCS, vol. 547, pp. 257–265. Springer, Heidelberg (1991). https://doi.org/10.1007/3-540-46416-6_22
6. Horne, B., Pinkas, B., Sander, T.: Escrow services and incentives in peer-to-peer networks. In: Proceedings of the 3rd ACM Conference on Electronic Commerce, pp. 85–94 (2001)
7. Huang, X., Susilo, W., Mu, Y., Wu, W.: Secure universal designated verifier signature without random oracles. Int. J. Inf. Secur. **7**, 171–183 (2008). https://doi.org/10.1007/s10207-007-0021-2
8. Jakobsson, M., Sako, K., Impagliazzo, R.: Designated verifier proofs and their applications. In: Maurer, U. (ed.) EUROCRYPT 1996. LNCS, vol. 1070, pp. 143–154. Springer, Heidelberg (1996). https://doi.org/10.1007/3-540-68339-9_13

9. Kurbatov, O., Kravchenko, P., Poluyanenko, N., Shapoval, O., Kuznetsova, T.: Using ring signatures for an anonymous e-voting system. In: 2019 IEEE International Conference on Advanced Trends in Information Theory (ATIT), pp. 187–190. IEEE (2019)

10. Li, B., Liu, Y., Yang, S.: Lattice-based universal designated verifier signatures. In: 2018 IEEE 15th International Conference on e-Business Engineering (ICEBE), pp. 329–334. IEEE (2018)

11. Li, Y., Susilo, W., Mu, Y., Pei, D.: Designated verifier signature: definition, framework and new constructions. In: Indulska, J., Ma, J., Yang, L.T., Ungerer, T., Cao, J. (eds.) UIC 2007. LNCS, vol. 4611, pp. 1191–1200. Springer, Heidelberg (2007). https://doi.org/10.1007/978-3-540-73549-6_116

12. Libert, B., Vergnaud, D.: Group signatures with verifier-local revocation and backward unlinkability in the standard model. In: Garay, J.A., Miyaji, A., Otsuka, A. (eds.) CANS 2009. LNCS, vol. 5888, pp. 498–517. Springer, Heidelberg (2009). https://doi.org/10.1007/978-3-642-10433-6_34

13. Liu, D.Y., Liu, J.K., Mu, Y., Susilo, W., Wong, D.S.: Revocable ring signature. J. Comput. Sci. Technol. **22**, 785–794 (2007). https://doi.org/10.1007/s11390-007-9096-5

14. Liu, J.K., Wong, D.S.: Linkable ring signatures: security models and new schemes. In: Gervasi, O., et al. (eds.) ICCSA 2005. LNCS, vol. 3481, pp. 614–623. Springer, Heidelberg (2005). https://doi.org/10.1007/11424826_65

15. Nakanishi, T., Fujii, H., Hira, Y., Funabiki, N.: Revocable group signature schemes with constant costs for signing and verifying. IEICE Trans. Fundam. Electron. Commun. Comput. Sci. **93**(1), 50–62 (2010)

16. Schnorr, C.P.: Efficient identification and signatures for smart cards. In: Brassard, G. (ed.) CRYPTO 1989. LNCS, vol. 435, pp. 239–252. Springer, New York (1990). https://doi.org/10.1007/0-387-34805-0_22

17. Steinfeld, R., Bull, L., Wang, H., Pieprzyk, J.: Universal designated-verifier signatures. In: Laih, C.-S. (ed.) ASIACRYPT 2003. LNCS, vol. 2894, pp. 523–542. Springer, Heidelberg (2003). https://doi.org/10.1007/978-3-540-40061-5_33

18. Steinfeld, R., Wang, H., Pieprzyk, J.: Efficient extension of standard Schnorr/RSA signatures into universal designated-verifier signatures. In: Bao, F., Deng, R., Zhou, J. (eds.) PKC 2004. LNCS, vol. 2947, pp. 86–100. Springer, Heidelberg (2004). https://doi.org/10.1007/978-3-540-24632-9_7

19. Szabo, N.: The idea of smart contracts. Nick Szabo's Papers and Concise Tutorials **6**(1), 199 (1997)

20. Thanalakshmi, P., Anbazhagan, N., Joshi, G.P., Yang, E.: A quantum resistant universal designated verifier signature proof. AIMS Math. **8**(8), 18234–18250 (2023)

21. Thorncharoensri, P., Susilo, W., Baek, J.: Aggregatable certificateless designated verifier signature. IEEE Access **8**, 95019–95031 (2020)

22. Tian, H., Chen, X., Li, J.: A short non-delegatable strong designated verifier signature. In: Susilo, W., Mu, Y., Seberry, J. (eds.) ACISP 2012. LNCS, vol. 7372, pp. 261–279. Springer, Heidelberg (2012). https://doi.org/10.1007/978-3-642-31448-3_20

23. Xin, X., Ding, L., Li, C., Sang, Y., Yang, Q., Li, F.: Quantum public-key designated verifier signature. Quantum Inf. Process. **21**(1), 33 (2022). https://doi.org/10.1007/s11128-021-03387-4

24. Yamashita, K., Hara, K., Watanabe, Y., Yanai, N., Shikata, J.: Designated verifier signature with claimability. In: Proceedings of the 10th ACM Asia Public-Key Cryptography Workshop, pp. 21–32 (2023)

25. Yang, M., Shen, X.Q., Wang, Y.M.: Certificateless universal designated verifier signature schemes. J. China Univ. Posts Telecommun. **14**(3), 85–94 (2007)
26. Zhang, R., Furukawa, J., Imai, H.: Short signature and universal designated verifier signature without random oracles. In: Ioannidis, J., Keromytis, A., Yung, M. (eds.) ACNS 2005. LNCS, vol. 3531, pp. 483–498. Springer, Heidelberg (2005). https://doi.org/10.1007/11496137_33
27. Zhang, X., Liu, J.K., Steinfeld, R., Kuchta, V., Yu, J.: Revocable and linkable ring signature. In: Liu, Z., Yung, M. (eds.) Inscrypt 2019. LNCS, vol. 12020, pp. 3–27. Springer, Cham (2020). https://doi.org/10.1007/978-3-030-42921-8_1

An Improved BKW Algorithm for Solving LWE with Small Secrets

Yu Wei[1,2], Lei Bi[1,2(✉)], Kunpeng Wang[1,2], and Xianhui Lu[1,2]

[1] State Key Laboratory of Information Security, Institute of Information Engineering, Chinese Academy of Sciences, Beijing, China
{weiyu,bilei,wangkunpeng,luxianhui}@iie.ac.cn
[2] School of Cyber Security, University of Chinese Academy of Sciences, Beijing, China

Abstract. The Blum–Kalai–Wasserman (BKW) algorithm is an important combinatorial algorithm for solving the Learning With Errors (LWE) problem. In this paper, we focus on the LWE problem with small secrets and present an improved BKW algorithm. BKW algorithm has two phases, the reduction phase and the solving phase and our new algorithm uses new techniques to optimize both of them. For the first phase, we combine the modulus switching technique with coding theory and for the second one, we use a new pruning guessing strategy for the small secrets. To the best of our knowledge, our algorithm is currently the fastest BKW-style algorithm for solving LWE with small secrets. The bit-security of our new algorithm reduces by 6–19 bits compared with the most efficient and commonly used BKW algorithm introduced in [CRYPTO'15].

Keywords: Lattice-based cryptography · Concrete security · Learning with Errors · BKW

1 Introduction

With the development of quantum computers, post-quantum cryptography has become a major topic in recent years. Since cryptosystems based on lattice hard problems can resist attacks from quantum computers, they are being studied extensively by cryptologists.

The LWE problem, introduced by Regev [36] in 2005, has become one of the most promising cryptographic problems in lattice-based cryptography. It is a crucial component for designing advanced cryptographic primitives. It has a wide range of cryptographic applications and the schemes based their security on LWE are believed quantum-safe.

Informally, a set of LWE instances can be presented as

$$(\mathbf{A}, \mathbf{z} = \mathbf{s}\mathbf{A} + \mathbf{e} \bmod q) \in \mathbb{Z}_q^{n \times m} \times \mathbb{Z}_q^m,$$

where $\mathbf{s}$ is a fixed secret vector sampled from a given distribution over $\mathbb{Z}_q$ and $\mathbf{e} \in \mathbb{Z}_q^m$ is a short error vector. The Search-LWE problem aims to recover $\mathbf{s}$ given

© The Author(s), under exclusive license to Springer Nature Switzerland AG 2023
E. Athanasopoulos and B. Mennink (Eds.): ISC 2023, LNCS 14411, pp. 578–595, 2023.
https://doi.org/10.1007/978-3-031-49187-0_29

a set of LWE instances. The Decision-LWE problem is to distinguish a set of LWE instances from uniform ones over $\mathbb{Z}_q^{n \times m} \times \mathbb{Z}_q^m$.

In practical cryptographic constructions, the entries of $\mathbf{s}$ are usually taken from a bounded alphabet of size B. For example, $B = 3$ means that the secret is ternary, which is usually used in Fully Homomorphic Encryption (FHE) schemes [12,21]. What's more, there are also some cryptographic schemes in the NIST's PQC standardization process selecting secret vectors from small distributions, such as Kyber [11] and Saber [19].

The existing attacks on LWE can be categorized into three groups: the algebraic attacks, the lattice reduction attacks, and the combinatorial attacks. The algebraic attacks [4,7] transform solving LWE into solving non-linear equations in a sub-exponential time when the error is sufficiently small. The lattice reduction attacks [5,15,29,30,32,37] usually reduce the LWE problem to a Short Integer Solution (SIS) problem or a Bounded Distance Decoding (BDD) problem and then settle it with lattice reduction algorithms. The combinatorial attacks generally include the well-known BKW algorithm [2] and the Meet-In-The-Middle (MITM) attack [16].

We focus on the BKW algorithm in this paper. BKW has two phases, the reduction phase and the solving phase. The reduction phase, a type of Gaussian elimination, reduces some positions to zero in each step. The solving phase refers to the hypothesis testing stage. Specifically, in the reduction phase, the BKW algorithm utilizes a sort-and-match technique on the columns of matrix $\mathbf{A}$ to reduce a fixed number of b positions to zero in each reduction step. After the reduction, it deals with a new LWE problem with reduced dimensions and increased noise. In the solving phase, it performs hypothesis testing on some candidate sub-solutions to recover some entries of $\mathbf{s}$. Figure 1 provides a brief framework of the BKW algorithm.

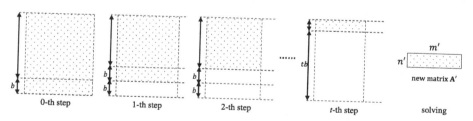

Fig. 1. The brief framework of the BKW algorithm. After t reduction steps, there are $t \cdot b$ positions that are reduced to zero. A new matrix $\mathbf{A}' \in \mathbb{Z}_q^{n' \times m'}$ are obtained. The values of n', m' will be described in detail in Sect. 3.

In this paper, we present a new BKW algorithm for solving LWE with small secrets, both the reduction phase and the solving phase are improved. For the first phase, we combine the modulus switching technique with coding theory and for the second one, we use a new pruning guessing strategy for the small secrets.

1.1   Contributions

Our main contributions are as follows.

The Reduction Phase. In the previous work, the most efficient and commonly used BKW-style algorithm is the coded-BKW algorithm [25], which realizes the sort-and-match technique by using coding theory. However, we have discovered that using this method can become costly in terms of decoding and reduction if the value of q is large. This is due to the fact that the time complexity of coded-BKW is essentially dependent on q^b with b being independent of q.

Intuitively, decreasing q can reduce the time complexity of the reduction phase and we accomplish this by using the modulus switching technique. Therefore, we consider applying the modulus switching to map the LWE instance mod q to a scaled LWE instance mod p, where $p < q$ is a positive integer, to reduce the time complexity. However, the usage of the modulus switching technique results in an additional rounding noise, the size of which is related to that of $\mathbf{s}$. It means that the modulus switching technique in this context only works well when the secret is small.

Specifically, we perform modulus switching to the subvectors of the column vectors in $\mathbf{A}$ to make sure that the sort-and-match is applied in the sense of mod p, where $p < q$ is a positive integer. After the modulus switching, we map the subvectors into the nearest codeword in a linear lattice code over $\mathbb{Z}_p$. Then the subvectors mapped to the same codeword are matched (added or subtracted) to generate new columns of $\mathbf{A}$.

Our new reduction method decreases the time complexity of the decoding procedure and reduction procedure while ensuring that more positions can be reduced. This process may result in an additional rounding noise except for the coding noise, but by selecting the entries of $\mathbf{s}$ small enough, this effect is negligible. With appropriate parameter selection in our algorithm, the final noise can be controlled to a small level that does not affect the whole procedure.

The Solving Phase. In the solving phase, we guess some candidates of the sub-secret and then distinguish the correct one. The coded-BKW utilizes exhaustive searching and the FFT distinguisher which is questioned by Ducas [18] whether it can really effectively distinguish two known distributions. For the fact that the entries of the secret vector in our cases are relatively small, we use a new pruning guessing strategy [14] and utilize the optimal distinguisher instead of the FFT distinguisher for the hypothesis testing.

Our new pruning guessing strategy inspired by [14] is to guess a certain number of candidates of $\mathbf{s}$ in decreasing order of probability until find the correct one instead of exhaustive searching. Although the impact on the overall cost is minimal, it makes our guessing step simpler and more efficient. Then for the hypothesis testing of the candidates of the secret, we distinguish the distributions by using the optimal distinguished [26], which computes the log-likelihood ratio based on the Neyman-Pearson lemma [34].

Applications and Comparisons. We estimate the bit-security by using our new BKW algorithm on some LWE instances with small secrets, under the assumption that the number of samples is unlimited. We also compare the estimation results of our new algorithm with the most efficient and commonly used BKW-style algorithm, i.e., the coded-BKW in the lattice-estimator [1]. We use the parameters of the schemes Kyber [11], Saber [19] and FHE [12,21] to show the comparison. The results are given in Tables 1 and 2. It can be seen that our new BKW algorithm outperforms coded-BKW, with an improvement of 6–19 bits.

We note that we do not compare our BKW algorithm with lattice attacks because BKW-style algorithms are less efficient in practical security estimation. We focus on improving the BKW-style algorithm to close the gap between it and the lattice attacks. It turns out that our new BKW algorithm does narrow down the gap between the BKW-style algorithm and the lattice reduction attacks.

Table 1. Comparison of the bit-security by using BKW-style algorithms on Kyber and Saber

Schemes	n	q	Secret Dist	coded-BKW [1]	OURS	Improvements
Kyber512	512	3329	B_3	178.8	167.4	**11.4**
Kyber768	768	3329	B_2	238.3	225.3	**13.0**
Kyber1024	1024	3329	B_2	315.0	308.5	**6.5**
LightSaber	512	8192	B_5	171.7	158.7	**13.0**
Saber	768	8192	B_4	237.3	224.5	**12.8**
FireSaber	1024	8192	B_3	302.7	290.0	**12.7**

* B_η is a central Binomial distribution which draws entries in $[-\eta, \eta]$.

1.2 Related Work

The BKW algorithm, which is similar to Wagner's [38] generalized birthday algorithm, was originally proposed to solve the Learning Parity with Noise (LPN) problem with sub-exponential complexity [8]. Later, a lot of improvements for BKW on solving the LPN problem appeared [9,10,20,22,28,41].

Subsequently, the BKW algorithm was extended to solve the LWE problem. The first BKW algorithm (plain BKW) was proposed for solving LWE by Albrecht [2] in 2013. Then in the past ten years, the BKW algorithm has had many developments in the reduction phase and the solving phase [3,13,17,23–27,33,35].

All the developments in the reduction phase can be summarized into two main categories, one combining modulus switching technique and one combining coding theory, both of which reduce the entries of column vectors in $\mathbf{A}$ to small values but not to zero, allowing to reduce more entries per step.

Table 2. Comparison of the bit-security by using BKW-style algorithms on FHE

$\log n$	$\log q$	coded-BKW [1]	OURS	Improvements
10	25	255.1	237.0	**18.1**
10	27	288.6	271.1	**17.5**
10	29	271.1	259.7	**11.4**
10	31	298.4	281.1	**16.9**
11	27	532.8	524.1	**8.7**
11	29	542.4	531.4	**11.0**
11	48	500.5	490.5	**10.0**
11	50	520.1	514.6	**5.5**
11	51	530.0	510.3	**19.7**
9	200	619.7	604.7	**15.0**
9	250	770.2	755.2	**15.0**
10	270	563.6	553.7	**9.9**
10	300	619.7	610.8	**8.9**
10	320	657.8	648.4	**9.4**
11	200	625.8	610.2	**15.6**
11	250	773.9	760.5	**13.4**

* The standard deviation of the error is $\sigma = 3.2$ and $\mathbf{s} \in \{-1, 0, 1\}^n$.

The LMS-BKW algorithm [3], which combines lazy modulus switching with plain BKW, searches for collisions by considering the top $\log_2 p$ bits of each element in $\mathbb{Z}_q$. It looks for collisions in the sense of mod p but still performs reduction in the sense of mod q. This kind of reduction method was improved in [13], which was called Smooth-LMS. It partially reduces one additional position after reducing a given number of positions of column vectors in $\mathbf{A}$. The coded-BKW algorithm [25] maps the considered subvectors of matrix $\mathbf{A}$ into the nearest codeword in a linear lattice code over $\mathbb{Z}_q$. If the subvectors are mapped to the same codeword, they are matched (added or subtracted) to form a new subvector for the subsequent reduction step. It was improved in [23, 24, 33] with a combination of lattice sieving.

There are other improvements of the BKW algorithm except those in the reduction phase. In 2015, the solving phase was improved by using the FFT technique [17]. The research of sample complexity of the BKW algorithm can be checked in [26, 27]. In 2020, Qian et al. [35] introduced a new BKW algorithm for binary uniform errors.

1.3 Organization

The rest of this paper is arranged as follows. In Sect. 2 we state some necessary background. In Sect. 3 we discuss the framework of the previous BKW algorithm on LWE briefly. Then, in Sect. 4 we introduce our new BKW algorithm in terms of both the reduction phase and the solving phase. Next, in Sect. 5 we analyze the time complexity of our new algorithm in detail and show some results of solving specific LWE instances in Sect. 6. Finally, we conclude this paper in Sect. 7.

2 Preliminaries

2.1 Notations

We denote matrices by bold uppercase letters, e.g. $\mathbf{A}$, and vectors by bold lowercase letters, e.g. $\mathbf{v}$. The L_2-norm of a vector $\mathbf{v} = (v_1, v_2, \cdots, v_n)$ in Euclidean space $\mathbb{R}^n$ with n dimensions is defined as the square root of the sum of the squares of its components: $||\mathbf{v}|| = \sqrt{v_1^2 + \cdots + v_n^2}$. We denote $||\mathbf{v} - \mathbf{w}||$ as the Euclidean distance between two vectors $\mathbf{v}$ and $\mathbf{w}$ in $\mathbb{R}^n$. Select $x \in \mathbb{R}$, let $[x]$ denote the closest integer to x and $\{x\} = x - [x]$. We let $\log(\cdot)$ denote the 2-logarithm. The set of integers in $\left[-\frac{q-1}{2}, \frac{q-1}{2}\right]$ represents elements in $\mathbb{Z}_q$.

2.2 Discrete Gaussian Distribution

Denote the discrete Gaussian distribution over $\mathbb{Z}$ with mean 0 and variance σ^2 as $D_{\mathbb{Z},\sigma}$. The distribution $\chi_{\sigma,q}$ with variance σ^2 over $\mathbb{Z}_q$ (often be written as χ_σ) is obtained by folding $D_{\mathbb{Z},\sigma}$ and accumulating the probability mass function over all integers in each residue class mod q. Even while the discrete Gaussian distribution often does not precisely take the typical features of the continuous one, we will still be able to use the continuous features since they will be close enough. If two independent distributions X is taken from χ_{σ_1} and Y is taken from χ_{σ_2}, then their sum $X + Y$ is taken from $\chi_{\sqrt{\sigma_1^2+\sigma_2^2}}$.

2.3 The LWE Problem

Definition 1 ([36]). *Let n, q, m be positive integers. $\mathcal{S}$ is the secret distribution over $\mathbb{Z}_q^n$ and χ is an error distribution over $\mathbb{Z}$. For $\mathbf{s} \leftarrow \mathcal{S}$, denote $LWE_{\mathbf{s},\chi}$ the probability distribution on $\mathbb{Z}_q^n \times \mathbb{Z}_q$ obtained by sampling $\mathbf{a} \in \mathbb{Z}_q^n$ uniformly random, sampling $e \leftarrow \chi$ and returning*

$$(\mathbf{a}, z) = (\mathbf{a}, \langle \mathbf{a}, \mathbf{s} \rangle + e) \in \mathbb{Z}_q^n \times \mathbb{Z}_q.$$

We define two kinds of LWE problems:

- *Decision-LWE: Given m samples, distinguish the uniform distribution over $\mathbb{Z}_q^n \times \mathbb{Z}_q$ from $LWE_{\mathbf{s},\chi}$.*
- *Search-LWE: Given m samples from $LWE_{n,q,\mathbf{s},\chi}$, recover $\mathbf{s}$.*

The LWE problem can be reformulated as a decoding problem. Here are m samples

$$(\mathbf{a}_1, z_1), (\mathbf{a}_2, z_2), \cdots, (\mathbf{a}_m, z_m),$$

selected from $L_{\mathbf{s},\chi}$, where $\mathbf{a}_i \in \mathbb{Z}_q^n$, $z_i \in \mathbb{Z}_q$. Write $\mathbf{y} = (y_1, y_2, \cdots, y_m) = \mathbf{s}\mathbf{A}$ and $\mathbf{z} = (z_1, z_2, \cdots, z_m) \in \mathbb{Z}_q^m$. Therefore,

$$\mathbf{z} = \mathbf{s}\mathbf{A} + \mathbf{e},$$

where $\mathbf{A} = \begin{bmatrix} \mathbf{a}_1^T \mathbf{a}_2^T \cdots \mathbf{a}_m^T \end{bmatrix} \in \mathbb{Z}_q^{n \times m}$, $z_i = y_i + e_i = \langle \mathbf{s}, \mathbf{a}_i \rangle + e_i$ and $e_i \leftarrow \chi$. The matrix $\mathbf{A}$ is responsible for generating a linear code in the field of $\mathbb{Z}_q$ and $\mathbf{z}$ represents the received message. The task of discovering $\mathbf{s}$ is equivalent to finding the codeword $\mathbf{y} = \mathbf{s}\mathbf{A}$, where the distance between $\mathbf{z}$ and $\mathbf{y}$ is smallest.

2.4   The Transformation of Secret Distribution

A simple transformation [6, 28] can be used to guarantee that $\mathbf{s}$ follows the error distribution χ_σ.

Through Gaussian elimination, we first transform $\mathbf{A}_{n \times m}$ into systematic form. Suppose that the first n columns of $\mathbf{A}$ are linearly independent and denoted by the matrix $\mathbf{A}_0$. Write $\mathbf{D} = \mathbf{A}_0^{-1}$ and $\hat{\mathbf{s}} = \mathbf{s}\mathbf{D}^{-1} - (z_1, z_2 \cdots, z_n)$. Thus, we can get a similar problem that $\hat{\mathbf{A}} = (\mathbf{I}, \hat{\mathbf{a}}_{n+1}^T, \hat{\mathbf{a}}_{n+2}^T, \cdots, \hat{\mathbf{a}}_m^T)$, where $\hat{\mathbf{A}} = \mathbf{D}\mathbf{A}$. And then calculate

$$\hat{\mathbf{z}} = \mathbf{z} - (z_1, z_2, \cdots, z_n) \hat{\mathbf{A}} = (\mathbf{0}, \hat{z}_{n+1}, \hat{z}_{n+2}, \cdots, \hat{z}_m).$$

By this transformation, each component in $\mathbf{s}$ is distributed according to χ_σ, which makes sense to some famous attack algorithms for solving LWE.

2.5   Sample Amplification

Since many LWE-based schemes only supply a finite number of samples, the BKW attack, which requires an exponential number of samples, is not practical. As a result, sample amplification is frequently required to increase the number of available samples. Assume that here are m samples $(\mathbf{a}_1, z_1), (\mathbf{a}_2, z_2), \cdots, (\mathbf{a}_m, z_m)$, selected from $L_{\mathbf{s},\chi}$, where $\mathbf{a}_i \in \mathbb{Z}_q^n$, $z_i \in \mathbb{Z}_q$. In order to create more samples, we can calculate

$$\left(\sum_{j \in I} \pm \mathbf{a}_j, \sum_{j \in I} \pm z_j \right),$$

where I is an index set of size k.

We can generate up to $C_m^k 2^{k-1}$ samples from an initial set of m samples. The standard deviation of the noise rises to $\sqrt{k} \cdot \sigma$. Additionally, The sample dependency also rises.

2.6   The Coding Theory

Definition 2 (Construction A). *Let q be a prime and $\mathscr{C} \in \mathbb{Z}_q$ be a linear code of length n and dimension k. Applying construction A to $\mathscr{C}$ we can get the lattice $\mathcal{L}$ denoted by*

$$\mathcal{L}(\mathscr{C}) = \{\mathbf{x} \in \mathbb{R}^n : \mathbf{x} = \mathbf{c} \mod q, \mathbf{c} \in \mathscr{C}\}.$$

Thus, the task to find the nearest vector to $\mathbf{y} \in \mathbb{Z}_q^n$ in $\mathscr{C}$ is equivalent to finding the nearest lattice vector in $\mathcal{L}(\mathscr{C})$ of $\mathbf{y}$. We usually take a mean-squared-error quantizer to perform this task. Let $V(\mathcal{L})$ be the fundamental Voronoi region of $\mathcal{L}$, that is $V = \{\mathbf{v} \in \mathbb{R}^n : ||\mathbf{v}|| \leq ||\mathbf{v} - \mathbf{x}||, \forall \mathbf{x} \in \mathcal{L}\}$. The distance obtained by the mean-squared quantizer can be represented by the normalized second moment

$$G = \frac{1}{Vol(\mathcal{V})^{\frac{2}{n}} \cdot n} \int_V \frac{||\mathbf{v}||^2}{Vol(V)} d\mathbf{v}, \tag{1}$$

where $Vol(V) = q^{n-k}$. It is known that

$$\frac{1}{2\pi e} < G < \frac{1}{12}, \tag{2}$$

where when the lattice is generated by $\mathbb{Z}_n$ we can get the upper bound and when the lattice is generated by construction A from q-ary random linear codes we can get the lower bound asymptotically [31,40].

3   The BKW Algorithm

In this section, we introduce the framework of BKW, specifically focusing on its reduction phase and solving phase.

3.1   The Reduction Phase

The BKW algorithm utilizes a sort-and-match technique on the columns of matrix $\mathbf{A}$ to reduce a fixed number of b positions to zero. Thus the row dimension of matrix $\mathbf{A}$ will be reduced step by step and we will get a new LWE instance with a smaller dimension and larger error norm. The main procedure of the reduction step is as follows.

In the first iteration, we sort the columns of $\mathbf{A}$ into different groups based on the last b entries and search for collisions. If the b positions of some columns are matched, such columns are in the same group. By using two columns $\mathbf{a}_{i_1}^{\mathrm{T}}, \mathbf{a}_{i_2}^{\mathrm{T}}$ satisfying

$$\mathbf{a}_{i_1}^{\mathrm{T}} \pm \mathbf{a}_{i_2}^{\mathrm{T}} = (* \cdots * \underbrace{0 \cdots 0}_{b}),$$

we create a new column vector $\mathbf{a}^{(1)} = \mathbf{a}_{i_1} \pm \mathbf{a}_{i_2}$ for the new matrix $\mathbf{A}^{(1)}$ (original matrix $\mathbf{A} = \mathbf{A}^{(0)}$). For the new column, the corresponding error term is calculated as $z^{(1)} = z_{i_1} \pm z_{i_2}$. So we get a new equation

$$z^{(1)} = \mathbf{s} \cdot \mathbf{a}^{(1)} + e^{(1)} \bmod q,$$

where $e^{(1)} = e_{i_1} \pm e_{i_2}$ follows the discrete Gaussian distribution with standard deviation $\sqrt{2}\sigma$.

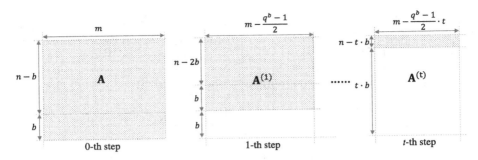

Fig. 2. A high-level description of the variation of matrix $\mathbf{A}$ in the reduction step. The red color refers to positions that have not been reduced yet and the white color refers to reduced positions. (Color figure online)

There are two approaches to match vectors in the reduction phase:

- **LF1** Select a fixed column in each group and then add or subtract others with it to generate new samples. This method ensures the independence of the samples in the solving stage, but it gradually reduces the sample size by $\frac{q^b-1}{2}$ in each iteration, and therefore a large initial sample size is required.
- **LF2** Add or subtract any pairs of columns in each group to generate new samples. This method can create a huge number of new columns but lead to an increase in the sample correlation.

We use LF1 to create new columns for the next reduction step. After the first iteration, the last b positions of column vectors in $\mathbf{A}^{(1)}$ is zero, and the number of columns in $\mathbf{A}^{(1)}$ is $m - \frac{q^b-1}{2}$. Corresponding to $\mathbf{A}^{(1)}$, we have

$$\mathbf{z}^{(1)} = \left(z_1^{(1)}, z_2^{(1)}, \cdots, z_{m-\frac{q^b-1}{2}}^{(1)} \right),$$

and the error follows the discrete Gaussian distribution with standard deviation $\sqrt{2}\sigma$. The variation of matrix $\mathbf{A}$ can be seen in Fig. 2.

Repeat the reduction step for t times, we will reduce the last $n - t \cdot b$ entries of columns in $\mathbf{A}$ to zero. The noise is increased, following the discrete Gaussian distribution with standard deviation $\sqrt{2^t}\sigma$.

3.2   The Solving Phase

After the reduction phase, we have a new LWE instance where the dimension of the secret is $n' = n - t \cdot b$ and the error has standard deviation $\sqrt{2^t}\sigma$. The column vectors in $\mathbf{A}$ are all zero except for the n' positions. Then we have new samples like

$$z_i = \bar{\mathbf{s}} \cdot \bar{\mathbf{a}} + \bar{e}_i \bmod q, \tag{3}$$

where $\bar{\mathbf{s}}, \bar{\mathbf{a}}$ denote the first n' positions of the original $\mathbf{s}, \mathbf{a}$ respectively, the error $\bar{e}_i$ follow the Gaussian distribution $\chi_{\sqrt{2^t}\sigma}$ and $i = 1, 2, \cdots, m', m' = m - \frac{(q^b-1)t}{2}$.

Now the problem is to find the correct $\bar{\mathbf{s}} \in \mathbb{Z}_q^{n'}$ among all candidates. For each candidate $\tilde{\mathbf{s}}$, we compute

$$\tilde{e}_i = z_i - \tilde{\mathbf{s}} \cdot \bar{\mathbf{a}} \bmod q \tag{4}$$

and determine the accuracy by checking the distribution of $\tilde{e}_i$. If $\tilde{e}_i$ follows a discrete Gaussian distribution, we determine the corresponding candidate $\tilde{\mathbf{s}}$ is correct.

4   Our Improved BKW Algorithm

In this section, we introduce our new BKW algorithm on LWE with small secrets. The improvements of the reduction phase and the solving phase are in Subsect. 4.1 and Subsect. 4.2, respectively.

4.1   A New Reduction Method

We present a new reduction step that combines coding theory from previous work and the idea of modulus switching, based on the sort-and-match.

The time complexity of the BKW algorithm is primarily based on the size of its collision set, which is $(q^b - 1)/2$ and b does not depend on q. Therefore, reducing the value of q by modulus switching can potentially lower the time complexity. So we first apply the modulus switching, instead of directly mapping some subvectors into the nearest codewords. This involves mapping the LWE instance mod q to a scaled LWE instance mod p before searching for collisions, where $p < q$ is a positive integer.

After performing modulus switching to the considered subvectors of the columns in $\mathbf{A}$, we can map them into the nearest codewords in a linear lattice code over $\mathbb{Z}_p$. Then, each of them will be sorted according to which codeword it was mapped into. Then the subvectors mapped to the same codeword are added or subtracted to create new columns of $\mathbf{A}$. The main framework of the reduction method of our new BKW algorithm is shown in Fig. 3.

This method can significantly reduce the time complexity of the decoding procedure and the reduction procedure while ensuring that more positions are reduced per step, at the expense of adding some additional rounding noise and coding noise. But with suitable parameter selection in our algorithm, these noises can be controlled small enough that does not affect the whole BKW algorithm.

Begin with $z_i = \langle \mathbf{a}_i, \mathbf{s} \rangle + e_i \bmod q$, where e_i follows the discrete Gaussian distribution with the standard deviation σ. For simplicity, we write it as $z = \langle \mathbf{a}, \mathbf{s} \rangle + e \bmod q$ and then rewrite it slightly as an equality

$$z = \langle \mathbf{a}, \mathbf{s} \rangle + e + kq \tag{5}$$

over integers, for some $k \in \mathbb{Z}$. Select another modulo $p < q$ and multiply both sides of the above equation by p/q, we get

$$\frac{p}{q}z = \frac{p}{q}\langle \mathbf{a}, \mathbf{s} \rangle + \frac{p}{q}e + kp = \left\langle \frac{p}{q}\mathbf{a}, \mathbf{s} \right\rangle + \frac{p}{q}e + kp. \tag{6}$$

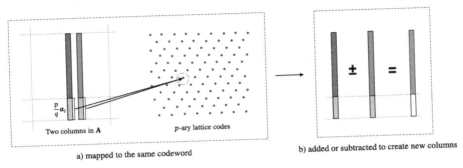

a) mapped to the same codeword

b) added or subtracted to create new columns

Fig. 3. The main framework of the reduction method of our new BKW algorithm.

By writing $\frac{p}{q}\mathbf{a} = \left[\frac{p}{q}\mathbf{a}\right] + \left\{\frac{p}{q}\mathbf{a}\right\}$, we get

$$\frac{p}{q}z = \left\langle \left[\frac{p}{q}\mathbf{a}\right], \mathbf{s}\right\rangle + \left\langle \left\{\frac{p}{q}\mathbf{a}\right\}, \mathbf{s}\right\rangle + \frac{p}{q}e + kp. \tag{7}$$

Take a collision index set I with size $\frac{p^b-1}{2}$ and denote $\left[\frac{p}{q}\mathbf{a}_I\right]$ as the subvector corresponding to this collision index set. We obtain

$$\frac{p}{q}z' = \left\langle \left[\frac{p}{q}\mathbf{a}_I\right], \mathbf{s}_I\right\rangle + \left\langle \left\{\frac{p}{q}\mathbf{a}_I\right\}, \mathbf{s}_I\right\rangle + \frac{p}{q}e' \mod p, \tag{8}$$

where z' and e' are parts of the real z and e since we only consider the collision parts of vectors here.

We denote the rounding term $\left\langle \left\{\frac{p}{q}\mathbf{a}_I\right\}, \mathbf{s}_I\right\rangle$ as the new noise e''. The term $\left\{\frac{p}{q}\mathbf{a}_I\right\}$ will take values in a narrow small interval $[-1/2, 1/2]$. So we find that in order to keep the rounding noise e'' as small as possible, the entries of the secret should be selected from a small distribution.

Here we get a new LWE instance

$$\bar{z} = \langle \bar{\mathbf{a}}, \mathbf{s}_I\rangle + \bar{e} \mod p, \tag{9}$$

where $\bar{z} = \frac{p}{q}z'$, $\bar{\mathbf{a}} = \left[\frac{p}{q}\mathbf{a}_I\right]$, $\bar{e} = e'' + \frac{p}{q}e'$.

Now, we can improve the reduction step by employing coding theory in the sense of modulo p. In the i-th iteration step, find a p-ary linear code

$$\mathscr{C}_i = \{\mathbf{G}\mathbf{u} : \mathbf{u} \in \mathbb{Z}_p^b\}$$

with dimension b, length $l_i \geq b$, and a generating matrix $\mathbf{G} \in \mathbb{Z}_p^{l_i \times b}$. It can generate a linear lattice code by construction A. Then we can map the considered subvectors after modulus switching into the closest codeword in the lattice code.

If decoding efficiently, we can find $\mathbf{u}_I \in \mathbb{Z}_p^b$ satisfying that $\mathbf{G}\mathbf{u}_I$ is very near to $\left[\frac{p}{q}\mathbf{a}_I\right] \in \mathbb{Z}_p^{l_i}$. The Euclidean distance between $\mathbf{G}\mathbf{u}_I$ and $\left[\frac{p}{q}\mathbf{a}_I\right]$ is as small as possible. Thus we have

$$\left[\frac{p}{q}\mathbf{a}_I\right] = \mathbf{G}\mathbf{u}_I + \mathbf{t}_I \quad \text{mod } p, \tag{10}$$

where the norm of error part $\mathbf{t}_I \in \mathbb{Z}_p^{l_i}$ is small enough. So we get a new LWE problem

$$\bar{\bar{z}} = \langle \bar{\bar{\mathbf{a}}}, \mathbf{s}_I \rangle + \bar{\bar{e}} \quad \text{mod } p, \tag{11}$$

where $\bar{\bar{z}}$ is the same as $\bar{z} = \frac{p}{q}z'$, $\bar{\bar{\mathbf{a}}} = \mathbf{G}\mathbf{u}_I$, and the new error consists of three parts $\bar{\bar{e}} = \langle \mathbf{s}_I, \mathbf{t}_I \rangle + \bar{e} = \langle \mathbf{s}_I, \mathbf{t}_I \rangle + e'' + \frac{p}{q}e' = \langle \mathbf{s}_I, \mathbf{t}_I \rangle + \left\langle \mathbf{s}_I, \left\{\frac{p}{q}\mathbf{a}_I\right\}\right\rangle + \frac{p}{q}e'$.

According to which codeword $\left[\frac{p}{q}\mathbf{a}_I\right]$ was mapped to, we can sort them into different groups. Then we can create new vectors for the next iteration step by adding or subtracting vectors in the same group. Assume that two subvectors $\bar{\bar{\mathbf{a}}}_1$ and $\bar{\bar{\mathbf{a}}}_2$ are mapped to the same codeword, we can cancel out the first term of Eq. (11) by calculating

$$\langle \bar{\bar{\mathbf{a}}}_1, \mathbf{s}_I \rangle \pm \langle \bar{\bar{\mathbf{a}}}_2, \mathbf{s}_I \rangle \tag{12}$$

and leave behind an accumulated error term $\bar{\bar{e}}^{(1)} = \bar{\bar{e}}_1 \pm \bar{\bar{e}}_2$. The accumulated error is introduced by the coding, modulus switching, and the original error.

After t reduction steps like this, we will reduce $n_{\text{red}} = \sum_{i=1}^{t} l_i$ positions of column vectors in $\mathbf{A}$. The error corresponding to each column is

$$\hat{e} = \sum_{j=1}^{2^t} \bar{\bar{e}}_{i_j}. \tag{13}$$

Assume that the coding noise remains discrete Gaussian. From some known results in Subsect. 2.6, the variance of noise introduced by code $[l_i, b]$ in the i-th step is

$$\sigma_c^2 = \frac{2^i p^{2(1-b/l_i)}}{12}. \tag{14}$$

In order to keep the coding noise equal in every dimension, we will employ a list of codes with decreasing rate as the coding noise in the initial steps will increase exponentially. To summarize, the variance of the total noise is upper bounded by $\sigma_f^2 = \frac{5}{4} \cdot 2^t \cdot \sigma^2 + n_{\text{red}} \cdot \sigma^2 \cdot \sigma_c^2$. With suitable parameter selection, these noises can be controlled small enough that does not affect the next phase.

4.2   A New Solving Method

In this subsection, we present a new pruning guessing strategy to guess some possible $\mathbf{s}$ in decreasing order of probability. And then we utilize the most powerful distinguishing method to test whether the guesses are correct or not.

Assume that after reduction, we have a new LWE problem where the dimension of the new secret is n_{guess}. Then the reduced equations are in the form of

$$e = z - \sum_{j=1}^{n_{\text{guess}}} a_j \cdot s_j. \tag{15}$$

The next task in the solving phase is to guess some possible values of $\mathbf{s} = (s_1, s_2, \cdots, s_{n_{\text{guess}}})$ and then distinguish whether the guess is correct or not. For the right guess, the observed error will follow a discrete Gaussian distribution. Otherwise, it will be uniform.

A Pruning Guessing Strategy. We use a pruning guessing strategy that limits the number of candidates to guess the secret in decreasing order of probability until finding the right guess.

More precisely, we sort the candidates of the secret vector $\mathbf{s}$ in decreasing order of probability. Then start guessing from the candidate with the highest probability until finding the right solution. When the probability of the candidate is very small, we have no need to guess. Therefore, we use a pruning guessing strategy to limit the number of candidates. Although the impact on the overall cost is minimal, it can make our guessing step simpler and more efficient. Then we use a polynomial-time method inspired by [14] to calculate the expected number of guesses until we find the correct secret.

Suppose that each s_i has r possible values, there are $r^{n_{\text{guess}}}$ possible values if using exhaustive search. We find that it is very costly to calculate all the probabilities of every single outcome, sort them in decreasing order of probability, and then calculate the expected number of guesses.

To deal with this problem, we take advantage of the fact that the frequency of each possible secret follows a multinomial distribution [39]. Assume that there are n_0 entries are 0 with probability p_0, n_1 entries are 1 with probability p_1, $\cdots$, and n_{r-1} entries are $r - 1$ with probability p_{r-1}, where $\sum_{i=0}^{r-1} n_i = n_{\text{guess}}$. Thus this kind of secret has the same probability

$$\prod_{k=0}^{r-1} p_k{}^{n_k} = \frac{n!}{n_0! n_1! \cdots n_{r-1}!} \tag{16}$$

The total number of different probabilities is just $C_{n_{\text{guess}}+r-1}^{n_{\text{guess}}}$, roughly about $\mathcal{O}(n_{\text{guess}}^{r-1})$ for a fixed small r. Therefore, the number of unique probabilities is limited so that it is efficient to sort them and then calculate the expected number of guesses.

Now we can use a polynomial-time approach to evaluate the expected number of guesses. Let $\bar{p}_1, \bar{p}_2, \cdots, \bar{p}_t$ denote the unique probabilities satisfying that $\bar{p}_1 \leq \bar{p}_2 \leq \cdots \leq \bar{p}_t$. The number of $\bar{p}_i$ occurs is denoted by f_i. And we let $F_i = \sum_{j=1}^{i} f_{t-i+j}$. So the expected number of guesses is

$$N_{\text{guess}} = \sum_{i=1}^{t} \bar{p}_{t-i+1}(F_i + \sum_{j=1}^{f_{t-i+1}} j) = \sum_{i=1}^{t} \bar{p}_{t-i+1}(F_i + \frac{\bar{p}_{t-i+1}(\bar{p}_{t-i+1} + 1)}{2}) \tag{17}$$

Optimal Distinguisher. To distinguish whether the guess is correct or not, we use the optimal distinguisher based on the Neyman-Pearson lemma to perform hypothesis testing. The main idea is to calculate the log-likelihood ratio, which is the optimal test to distinguish two known distributions.

Let χ_{σ_f} denote the discrete Gaussian distribution under the right guess. Let $\mathcal{U}$ denote the uniform distribution under the wrong guess. We compute the log-likelihood ratio

$$\sum_{i=-(q-1)/2}^{(q-1)/2} F(e) \log \frac{\Pr[e \leftarrow \chi_{\sigma_f} : e = i]}{\Pr[e \leftarrow \mathcal{U} : e = i]}, \tag{18}$$

where $F(e)$ denotes the frequency of e corresponding to the guess of $\mathbf{s}$. We select the guess of $\mathbf{s}$ that optimizes the Eq. (18) by maximizing its value.

4.3   Algorithm Summary

The detailed description of our improved BKW algorithm is presented in Algorithm 1, which consists of four main steps. Performing t_1 plain BKW steps aims to balance the merging noise and the additional noise. If not, directly performing new BKW reduction steps will cause a huge accumulation of coding noise and rounding noise at the beginning of the iteration. This new BKW algorithm significantly outperforms the previous best BKW-style variants for some specific LWE parameters, which will be demonstrated in Sect. 6.

Algorithm 1: Improved BKW algorithm (framework)

Input: Matrix $A \in \mathbb{Z}_q^{n \times m}$, received vector $\mathbf{z} \in \mathbb{Z}_q^m$, parameters $t_1, t_2, b, n_{\text{guess}}, n_{\text{fft}}$.

begin

  Gaussian elimination to transform the secret distribution into error distribution;

  Perform t_1 plain BKW steps to eliminate $t_1 \cdot b$ positions;

  Perform t_2 new BKW reduction steps to eliminate n_{red} positions;

  for *each guess of n_{guess} positions* **do**

  | distinguish it with the optimal distinguisher;

  return correct guess

---

5   Complexity Analysis

In this section, we analyze the time complexity of the presented BKW algorithm in Algorithm 1.

Theorem 1. *Let (n, q, σ) be LWE parameters. Let $t_1, t_2, b, n_{\text{guess}}, p, m$ be the parameters in our BKW algorithm. Let M be the required number of samples in the solving phase and N_{guess} is the value of Eq. (17). The time complexity*

required for a successful run of our BKW algorithm can be estimated as $\frac{C_{\mathrm{BKW}}}{P_0}$,
where P_0 is the successful probability and

$$C_{\mathrm{BKW}} = C_{\mathrm{reduce}} + C_{\mathrm{solve}},$$

where $C_{\mathrm{reduce}} = C_{\mathrm{trans}} + C_{\mathrm{plain}} + C_{\mathrm{red}}$, $C_{\mathrm{solve}} = N_{\mathrm{guess}} \cdot M$.

- *$C_{\mathrm{trans}} = (m-n-t_1 \cdot b) \cdot (n+1) \cdot \left\lceil \frac{n-t_1 \cdot b}{b-1} \right\rceil$ is the complexity of the transformation from secret distribution to noise distribution by Gaussian elimination.*
- *$C_{\mathrm{plain}} = \sum_{i=1}^{t_1} (m - \frac{(q^b-1)\cdot i}{2})(n+1-i \cdot b)$ is the cost of t_1 plain BKW steps, where $\frac{(q^b-1)}{2}$ is the collision index size and the sample size gradually decrease by $\frac{(q^b-1)}{2}$ because we use LF1 to merge.*
- *$C_{\mathrm{red}} = \sum_{i=1}^{t_2} 4 \cdot l_i \cdot (M + \frac{i\cdot(p^b-1)}{2}) + \sum_{i=1}^{t_2} (M + \frac{(p^b-1)\cdot(i-1)}{2})(n_{\mathrm{guess}} + \sum_{j=1}^{i} l_j)$ is the cost of t_2 new BKW steps, where*

$$M = c_0 \cdot e^{2\pi (\frac{\sigma_{\mathrm{final}}\sqrt{2\pi}}{p})^2}$$

is the required number of samples in the solving phase, c_0 is a small positive constant and $\sigma_{\mathrm{final}}^2 = n_{\mathrm{red}}\sigma_c^2\sigma^2 + 2^{t_1+t_2}\sigma^2 + \frac{1}{4} \cdot 2^{t_2}\sigma^2$, where n_{red} and σ_c^2 can be checked in Subsect. 4.1. The first term $\sum_{i=1}^{t_2} 4 \cdot l_i \cdot (M + \frac{i\cdot(p^b-1)}{2})$ is the upper bound of the decoding cost, where $M + \frac{i\cdot(p^b-1)}{2}$ is the sample size in the $(t_2 - i + 1)$-th step.

6   Bit-Security Estimation and Comparison

In this section, we apply our new BKW algorithm and coded-BKW algorithm for solving various LWE with small secrets. The bit-security estimation results are shown in Tables 1 and 2. To simplify the calculation, we make some assumptions.

- The number of required samples is unlimited.
- The complexity of operations over $\mathbb{C}$ and $\mathbb{Z}_q$ is equal in our estimation.
- The successful probability is $P_0 = 0.99$.

We consider Kyber [11] and Saber [19] schemes, whose secrets are usually taken from a central Binomial distribution $\mathbf{B}_\eta$ (draws entries in $[-\eta, \eta]$). We also consider some FHE-type parameters with the entries of the secret vector chosen from $\{-1, 0, 1\}$.

We estimate the bit-security of the schemes by using our new BKW algorithm and compare the results with coded-BKW. The comparison is shown in Tables 1 and 2. As can be seen, our new BKW algorithm outperforms the former best coded-BKW in the lattice-estimator [1] and the improvement is 6–19 bits.

7   Conclusion

In this paper, we introduce a new BKW algorithm for LWE with small secrets. For the two phases of BKW, we improve them by combining the modulus switching technique with coding theory and using a new pruning guessing strategy respectively. We compare our algorithm with previous coded-BKW on LWE with different type parameters. The result shows that our algorithm outperforms coded-BKW in all cases and the improvement is up to 19 bits. However, the BKW-style algorithms require a large memory consumption that limits their practical application and it is interesting to find time-sample trade-offs for these algorithms in the future.

Acknowledgements. We thank the anonymous ISC2023 reviewers for their helpful comments. This work was supported by the National Key Research and Development Program of China (Grant No. 2022YFB2702701) and the Key Research Program of the Chinese Academy of Sciences (Grant No. ZDRW-XX-2022-1).

References

1. Lattice-estimator. https://github.com/malb/lattice-estimator. Accessed 4 Oct 2023
2. Albrecht, M.R., Cid, C., Faugère, J.C., et al.: On the complexity of the BKW algorithm on LWE. Des. Codes Cryptogr. **74**, 325–354 (2015). https://doi.org/10.1007/s10623-013-9864-x
3. Albrecht, M.R., Faugère, J.-C., Fitzpatrick, R., Perret, L.: Lazy modulus switching for the BKW algorithm on LWE. In: Krawczyk, H. (ed.) PKC 2014. LNCS, vol. 8383, pp. 429–445. Springer, Heidelberg (2014). https://doi.org/10.1007/978-3-642-54631-0_25
4. Albrecht, M.R., Cid, C., Faugère, J.C., et al.: On the complexity of the Arora-Ge algorithm against LWE. In: SCC 2012 – Third International Conference on Symbolic Computation and Cryptography, pp. 93–99. Urdiales C., Spain (2012)
5. Albrecht, M.R., Fitzpatrick, R., Göpfert, F.: On the efficacy of solving LWE by reduction to Unique-SVP. In: Lee, H.-S., Han, D.-G. (eds.) ICISC 2013. LNCS, vol. 8565, pp. 293–310. Springer, Cham (2014). https://doi.org/10.1007/978-3-319-12160-4_18
6. Applebaum, B., Cash, D., Peikert, C., Sahai, A.: Fast cryptographic primitives and circular-secure encryption based on hard learning problems. In: Halevi, S. (ed.) CRYPTO 2009. LNCS, vol. 5677, pp. 595–618. Springer, Heidelberg (2009). https://doi.org/10.1007/978-3-642-03356-8_35
7. Arora, S., Ge, R.: New algorithms for learning in presence of errors. In: Aceto, L., Henzinger, M., Sgall, J. (eds.) ICALP 2011. LNCS, vol. 6755, pp. 403–415. Springer, Heidelberg (2011). https://doi.org/10.1007/978-3-642-22006-7_34
8. Blum, A., Kalai, A.T., Wasserman, H.: Noise-tolerant learning, the parity problem, and the statistical query model. J. ACM **50**, 506–519 (2003). https://doi.org/10.1145/792538.792543
9. Bogos, S., Tramèr, F., Vaudenay, S.: On solving LPN using BKW and variants. Cryptogr. Commun. **8**, 331–369 (2016). https://doi.org/10.1007/s12095-015-0149-2

10. Bogos, S., Vaudenay, S.: Optimization of LPN solving algorithms. In: Cheon, J.H., Takagi, T. (eds.) ASIACRYPT 2016. LNCS, vol. 10031, pp. 703–728. Springer, Heidelberg (2016). https://doi.org/10.1007/978-3-662-53887-6_26

11. Bos, J.W., Ducas, L., Kiltz, E., et al.: CRYSTALS-Kyber: a CCA-secure module-lattice-based KEM. In: 2018 IEEE European Symposium on Security and Privacy, pp. 353–367 (2018)

12. Brakerski, Z., Vaikuntanathan, V.: Efficient fully homomorphic encryption from (standard) LWE. In: 2011 IEEE 52nd Annual Symposium on Foundations of Computer Science, pp. 97–106. Palm Springs, CA, USA (2014). https://doi.org/10.1109/FOCS.2011.12

13. Budroni, A., Guo, Q., Johansson, T., Mårtensson, E., Wagner, P.S.: Making the BKW algorithm practical for LWE. In: Bhargavan, K., Oswald, E., Prabhakaran, M. (eds.) INDOCRYPT 2020. LNCS, vol. 12578, pp. 417–439. Springer, Cham (2020). https://doi.org/10.1007/978-3-030-65277-7_19

14. Budroni, A., Mårtensson, E.: Improved estimation of key enumeration with applications to solving LWE. In: 2023 IEEE International Symposium on Information Theory, pp. 495–500. Taipei, Taiwan (2023)

15. Chen, Y., Nguyen, P.Q.: BKZ 2.0: better lattice security estimates. In: Lee, D.H., Wang, X. (eds.) ASIACRYPT 2011. LNCS, vol. 7073, pp. 1–20. Springer, Heidelberg (2011). https://doi.org/10.1007/978-3-642-25385-0_1

16. Dong, X., Hua, J., Sun, S., Li, Z., Wang, X., Hu, L.: Meet-in-the-middle attacks revisited: key-recovery, collision, and preimage attacks. In: Malkin, T., Peikert, C. (eds.) CRYPTO 2021. LNCS, vol. 12827, pp. 278–308. Springer, Cham (2021). https://doi.org/10.1007/978-3-030-84252-9_10

17. Duc, A., Tramèr, F., Vaudenay, S.: Better algorithms for LWE and LWR. In: Oswald, E., Fischlin, M. (eds.) EUROCRYPT 2015. LNCS, vol. 9056, pp. 173–202. Springer, Heidelberg (2015). https://doi.org/10.1007/978-3-662-46800-5_8

18. Ducas, L., Pulles, L.N.: Does the dual-sieve attack on learning with errors even work? In: Handschuh, H., Lysyanskaya, A. (eds.) Advances in Cryptology – CRYPTO 2023. CRYPTO 2023. LNCS, vol. 14083, pp. 37–69. Springer, Cham (2023). https://doi.org/10.1007/978-3-031-38548-3_2

19. D'Anvers, J.-P., Karmakar, A., Sinha Roy, S., Vercauteren, F.: Saber: module-LWR based key exchange, CPA-secure encryption and CCA-secure KEM. In: Joux, A., Nitaj, A., Rachidi, T. (eds.) AFRICACRYPT 2018. LNCS, vol. 10831, pp. 282–305. Springer, Cham (2018). https://doi.org/10.1007/978-3-319-89339-6_16

20. Levieil, É., Fouque, P.-A.: An improved LPN algorithm. In: De Prisco, R., Yung, M. (eds.) SCN 2006. LNCS, vol. 4116, pp. 348–359. Springer, Heidelberg (2006). https://doi.org/10.1007/11832072_24

21. Gentry, C.: A fully homomorphic encryption scheme. Ph.D. thesis, Stanford University (2009). https://dl.acm.org/doi/book/10.5555/1834954

22. Guo, Q., Johansson, T., Löndahl, C.: Solving LPN using covering codes. In: Sarkar, P., Iwata, T. (eds.) ASIACRYPT 2014. LNCS, vol. 8873, pp. 1–20. Springer, Heidelberg (2014). https://doi.org/10.1007/978-3-662-45611-8_1

23. Guo, Q., Johansson, T., Mårtensson, E., Stankovski, P.: Coded-BKW with sieving. In: Takagi, T., Peyrin, T. (eds.) ASIACRYPT 2017. LNCS, vol. 10624, pp. 323–346. Springer, Cham (2017). https://doi.org/10.1007/978-3-319-70694-8_12

24. Guo, Q., Johansson, T., Mårtensson, E., et al.: On the asymptotics of solving the LWE problem using coded-BKW with sieving. IEEE Trans. Inf. Theory **65**(8), 5243–5259 (2019). https://doi.org/10.1109/TIT.2019.2906233

25. Guo, Q., Johansson, T., Stankovski, P.: Coded-BKW: solving LWE using lattice codes. In: Gennaro, R., Robshaw, M. (eds.) CRYPTO 2015. LNCS, vol. 9215, pp. 23–42. Springer, Heidelberg (2015). https://doi.org/10.1007/978-3-662-47989-6_2
26. Guo, Q., Mårtensson, E., Stankovski Wagner, P.: On the sample complexity of solving LWE using BKW-style algorithms. In: 2021 IEEE International Symposium on Information Theory, pp. 2405–2410. IEEE Press (2021). https://doi.org/10.1109/ISIT45174.2021.9518190
27. Guo, Q., Mårtensson, E., Stankovski Wagner, P.: Modeling and simulating the sample complexity of solving LWE using BKW-style algorithms. Cryptogr. Commun. **15**(2), 331–350 (2023). https://doi.org/10.1007/s12095-022-00597-0
28. Kirchner, P.: Improved generalized birthday attack. IACR Cryptol. ePrint Arch. 2011, 377 (2011). https://api.semanticscholar.org/CorpusID:15196823
29. Lindner, R., Peikert, C.: Better key sizes (and attacks) for LWE-based encryption. In: Kiayias, A. (ed.) CT-RSA 2011. LNCS, vol. 6558, pp. 319–339. Springer, Heidelberg (2011). https://doi.org/10.1007/978-3-642-19074-2_21
30. Liu, M., Nguyen, P.Q.: Solving BDD by enumeration: an update. In: Dawson, E. (ed.) CT-RSA 2013. LNCS, vol. 7779, pp. 293–309. Springer, Heidelberg (2013). https://doi.org/10.1007/978-3-642-36095-4_19
31. Loeliger, H.A.: Averaging bounds for lattices and linear codes. IEEE Trans. Inf. Theory **43**(6), 1767–1773 (1991). https://doi.org/10.1109/18.641543
32. Micciancio, D., Regev, O.: Lattice-based cryptography. In: Bernstein, D.J., Buchmann, J., Dahmen, E. (eds.) Post-Quantum Cryptography, pp. 147–191. Springer, Berlin, Heidelberg (2009). https://doi.org/10.1007/978-3-540-88702-7_5
33. Mårtensson, E.: The asymptotic complexity of coded-BKW with sieving using increasing reduction factors. In: 2019 IEEE International Symposium on Information Theory, pp. 2579–2583. IEEE Press (2019). https://doi.org/10.1109/ISIT.2019.8849218
34. Neyman, J., Pearson, E.S.: On the problem of the most efficient tests of statistical hypotheses. In: Kotz, S., Johnson, N.L. (eds.) Breakthroughs in Statistics. Springer Series in Statistics. Springer, New York, NY (1933). https://doi.org/10.1007/978-1-4612-0919-5_6
35. Qian, X., Liu, J., Gu, C., et al.: An improved BKW algorithm for LWE with binary uniform errors. In: 5th International Conference on Computer and Communication Systems, pp. 87–92. Shanghai, China (2020). https://doi.org/10.1109/ICCCS49078.2020.9118492
36. Regev, O.: On lattices, learning with errors, random linear codes, and cryptography. J. ACM **56**(6), 1–40 (2005). https://doi.org/10.1145/1568318.1568324
37. Schnorr, C.P., Euchner, M.: Lattice basis reduction: improved practical algorithms and solving subset sum problems. Math. Program. **66**, 181–199 (1994). https://doi.org/10.1007/BF01581144
38. Wagner, D.: A generalized birthday problem. In: Yung, M. (ed.) CRYPTO 2002. LNCS, vol. 2442, pp. 288–304. Springer, Heidelberg (2002). https://doi.org/10.1007/3-540-45708-9_19
39. Multinomial distribution. https://www.britannica.com/science/multinomial-distribution. Accessed 26 July 2023
40. Zamir, R., Feder, M.: On lattice quantization noise. In: 1994 Proceedings of IEEE Data Compression Conference, pp. 380–389. Snowbird, UT, USA (1994). https://doi.org/10.1109/DCC.1994.305946
41. Zhang, B., Jiao, L., Wang, M.: Faster algorithms for solving LPN. In: Fischlin, M., Coron, J.-S. (eds.) EUROCRYPT 2016. LNCS, vol. 9665, pp. 168–195. Springer, Heidelberg (2016). https://doi.org/10.1007/978-3-662-49890-3_7

Author Index

© The Editor(s) (if applicable) and The Author(s), under exclusive license
to Springer Nature Switzerland AG 2023
E. Athanasopoulos and B. Mennink (Eds.): ISC 2023, LNCS 14411, pp. 597–598, 2023.
https://doi.org/10.1007/978-3-031-49187-0

Printed in the United States
by Baker & Taylor Publisher Services